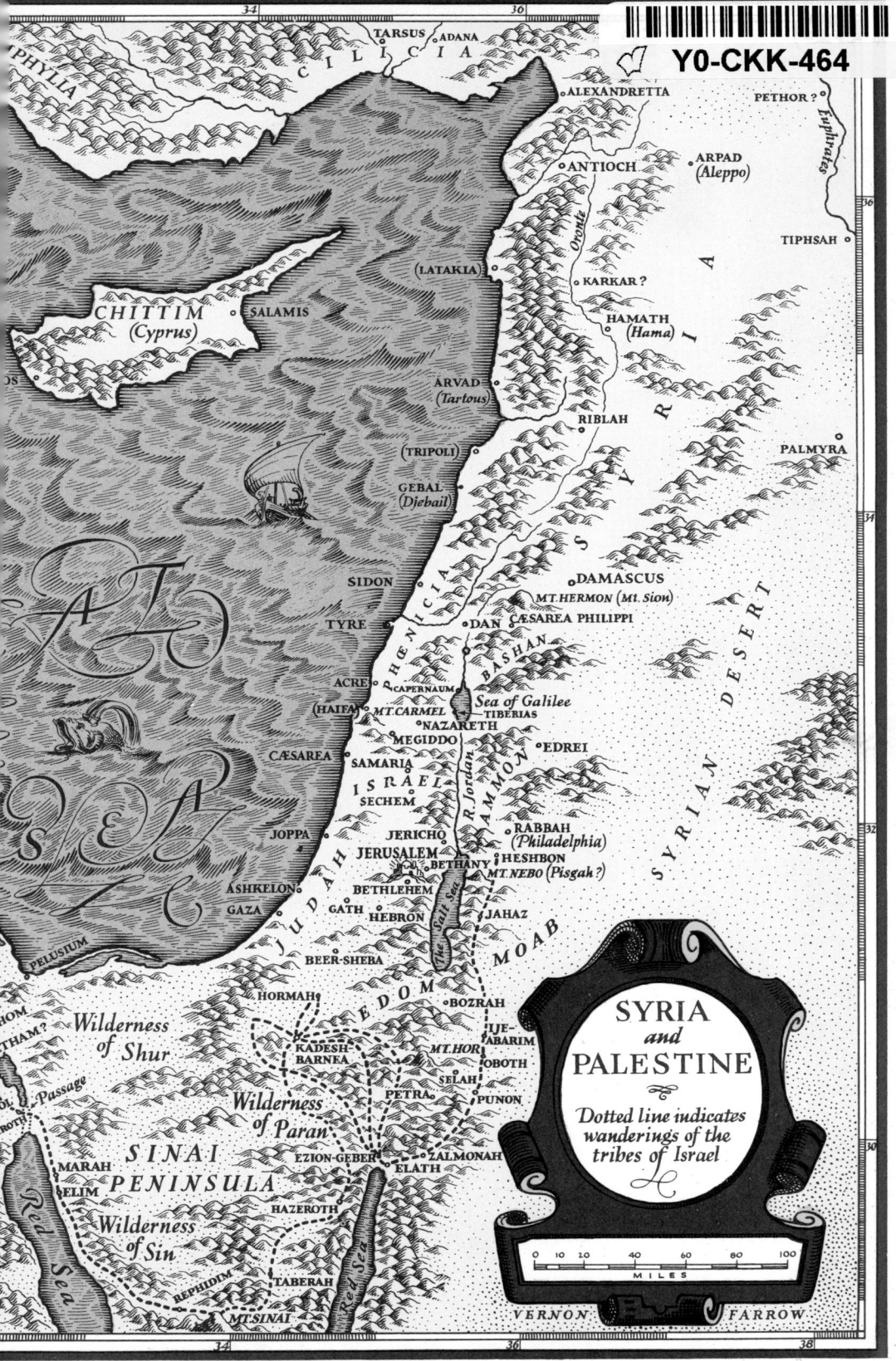

THE BIBLE

First set down in Hebrew, Aramaic, and Greek in the regions adjoining the eastern part of the Mediterranean Sea within the period from 750 B.C. to 150 A.D. by various prophets, teachers, story tellers, poets, philosophers, dramatists, and historians, many of them unknown.

THIS TRANSLATION,

known as THE AUTHORIZED VERSION, was made at the instigation of King James the First during the years 1604 to 1611 by four and fifty learned men of the Church of England who took account of the earlier labors of St. Jerome, John Wycliffe, Martin Luther, William Tyndale, Miles Coverdale, William Whittingham, and others.

In this edition the text of the King James Version is followed, except in the case of Proverbs, Job, Ecclesiastes, and the Song of Songs, where that of the Revised Version is used; the arrangement of the books is by time and subject matter; prose passages are printed as prose, verse as verse, drama as drama, letters as letters; the spelling and punctuation are modernized; genealogies and repetitions are omitted, as well as the whole of Chronicles, the minor Epistles, and similar unimportant passages throughout, to the end that the Bible may be read as living literature.

THE BIBLE

DESIGNED TO BE READ
AS LIVING LITERATURE
THE OLD AND THE NEW
TESTAMENTS IN THE
KING JAMES VERSION

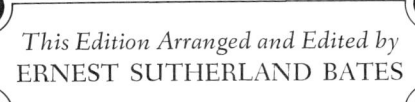

This Edition Arranged and Edited by
ERNEST SUTHERLAND BATES

SIMON AND SCHUSTER · NEW YORK

Copyright 1936 by Simon & Schuster, Inc.,
630 Fifth Avenue, New York, New York 10020.
Copyright renewed © 1965 by Simon & Schuster, Inc.

All rights reserved, including the rights to the introduction, the preface to each book, and the special selection, arrangement, and presentation of the text of this volume, and other new and supplementary material.

Manufactured in the United States of America.

THIRTY-FIRST PRINTING

The Bible as LITERATURE

The Longevity of Literature

APART FROM SENTIMENT, quite as a matter of simple realistic fact, art outlasts all other forms of human endeavor. Kingdoms, empires, and civilizations rise and fall; their laws, their political organizations, their religions vanish; their customs and all their ways of life disappear from the face of the earth; but the art that they have managed to create remains. So true is this, that it is usually from the artistic records that have come down to us, that historians and archeologists reconstruct the story of the past, more or less complete according as it was embodied at the time in pottery, painting, and sculpture, works of architecture, or works of literature.

And of all forms of art, literature, recorded on the frailest of materials, has had the strongest lien on immortality. More than a millennium of ruin has destroyed the Theatre of Dionysus, most famous in the world, but the greatest of the plays produced there are still enacted today. The Pyramid Texts will probably outlast the Pyramids. True even of the centuries of parchment and papyrus, the superior longevity of the written word was established beyond the possibility of rivalry when through the invention of movable type it attained the perpetuity of printing. Shakespeare was uttering no futile boast when he declared—

"Not marble, nor the gilded monuments
Of princes, shall outlast this powerful rhyme";

the very name of the noble youth to whom he dedicated it is uncertain, the personality of the author himself is so shadowy that not a few men, otherwise intelligent, have attributed his work to strangers, but the powerful rhyme is, if anything, more powerful than when it was first uttered.

THE BIBLE AS LITERATURE

Barring some strange degradation of human nature which should cause it to lose entirely its sense of values, literature is the safest of our possessions. No minor reversion to barbarism or contemporary burning of the books need worry us. Harried as we have been by fortune, slaves of mechanical necessity, poor enough in spiritual qualities in all conscience, we human beings nevertheless have in the past chosen to preserve our literature as our one priceless treasure, and so long as we remain human in any sense that the word now conveys, this happy condition will continue.

It would be, however, the grossest of pretenses to maintain that this treasure has ever been universally enjoyed or to deny that during considerable periods it has been almost entirely neglected. For various reasons, large sections of world literature have at one time or another temporarily lost their power of inspiration, for all but a few scholars.

Decline in Knowledge of the Bible

Now the Bible, containing the best of a great people's literature during nearly ten centuries, is regarded throughout the Western World as the most important of the world's books. But though esteemed as highly as ever, perhaps as pure literature esteemed more highly than ever, it is not read as formerly.

This work, which through the King James translation became a part of the very body of our language, which was often the one book in the possession of our pioneering ancestors, its teachings intertwined in the warp and woof of the American tradition, not always for good but unquestionably making us what we have been and are, this food of their fathers is neglected by the children. When it became no longer possible to regard the Bible as the literal word of God, or to turn superstitiously after the manner of the Virgilian lots to any chance text for immediate guidance in one's particular affairs, with the loss of authority came also, unfortunately, a loss of interest. Through having been made too exclusively sacred, the Bible forfeited momentarily its enormous secular power. With its study in the schools limited or even proscribed by sectarian jealousy, after having been virtually the whole of education, the Bible seemed to drop out of education altogether. In the long run, this will not matter, since one may safely prophesy that the Bible will outlive every sect fashioned upon it

THE BIBLE AS LITERATURE

as Homer has outlived every pagan cult of Greece, but the loss to the immediate contemporary generation is incalculable.

Few things could be culturally more deplorable than that to-day the average college graduate, who fancies himself educated, should never have read the Book of Job, should be unfamiliar with Isaiah, and should hardly be able to identify those mighty men of valor, Joshua the son of Nun, Gideon, and Jephthah, or those most famous of scarlet women, Rahab, Delilah, Bath-sheba—and should not only be thus abysmally ignorant but should feel no incentive to be otherwise. For this is nothing less than a loss of racial memory, a forgetfulness of our cultural heritage that is as serious in the life of nations as is for the individual the loss of personality attendant upon certain forms of neurotic disease.

Not only deplorable but unnecessary—because the outstanding qualities of Biblical literature are precisely those that have more and more come into favor in recent years. In striking contrast to Greek literature, that of the Bible is marked by three great characteristics: it is collective rather than individual in inspiration and workmanship; it is realistic rather than idealistic in manner; it is free and flexible rather than constrained in form.

With the exception of the Prophetical Books, all those of the Old Testament are anonymous, and the Prophets belonged to a definite school with a common style; though in the New Testament, where the individualistic note is, of course, introduced with Christianity, authors' names have been affixed to all but one of the books; yet Mark, Luke, and Paul are the only ones of whom we have any certainty. The Bible as a whole is essentially folk literature in which the speakers and writers are at one with their audience, expressing the interests and collective wisdom of their group—at first, the larger group of the whole Jewish nation, later the smaller group of Christian disciples.

Like that of folk literature everywhere, the language is vividly realistic. Doubtless, among other reasons for the long continuance of the belief in the literal truth of the Scriptural narratives is the fact that they were composed with an imaginative realization of small details which makes the account of every incident seem like the report of an eye-witness. The same realistic habit of mind appears in the thought and the emotions; Jehovah was to the Jews no poetic myth or philosophic theory but the

THE BIBLE AS LITERATURE

most tremendous of concrete realities to which their behavior was the appropriate response. When they ventured at all beyond the realm of orthodoxy, they went far; the Prophets actually remade the Jewish religion, while the determined skepticism of Job and the thorough-going pessimism of Ecclesiastes have few rivals in other literatures. And the one entirely secular work that strayed into the sacred canon, the Song of Songs, is the most impassioned and voluptuous of all love poetry.

Finally, though the Hebrews may have used an elementary metre in their verse, their main principle of versification was a parallelism of word, phrase, or strophe, which, though distinct from the structure of prose, was very close to it, supplying through the King James translation the ultimate basis for the free verse of Walt Whitman and the polyphonic prose of Amy Lowell. So, in these various ways, the Bible might be said to be almost contemporary.

Defects of the Traditional Presentation

Yet, little can be done to revive the reading of the Bible so long as it is presented in the traditional manner. Certainly, no literary format was ever less conducive to pleasure or understanding than is the curious and complicated panoply in which the Scriptures have come down to us. None but a work of transcendent literary genius could have survived such a handicap at all. The absurdities of the accepted arrangement and presentation, so great that only the sanctity of century-old tradition and the conservatism of ecclesiastical habit could have blinded men to their existence, are well summarized by Sir Arthur Quiller-Couch in a striking passage of his excellent essay, "On Reading the Bible":

"Let me, amplifying a hint from Dr. Moulton, ask you to imagine a volume including the great books of our literature all bound together in some such order as this: "Paradise Lost," Darwin's "Descent of Man," "The Anglo-Saxon Chronicle," Walter Map, Mill "On Liberty," Hooker's "Ecclesiastical Polity," "The Annual Register," Froissart, Adam Smith's "Wealth of Nations," "Domesday Book," "La Morte d'Arthur," Campbell's "Lives of the Lord Chancellors," Boswell's "Johnson," Barbour's "The Bruce," Hakluyt's "Voyages," Clarendon, Macaulay, the plays of Shakespeare, Shelley's "Prometheus Unbound," "The Faerie Queene," Palgrave's "Golden Treasury," Bacon's "Essays,"

THE BIBLE AS LITERATURE

Swinburne's "Poems and Ballads," Fitzgerald's "Omar Khayyam," Wordsworth, Browning, "Sartor Resartus," Burton's "Anatomy of Melancholy," Burke's "Letters on a Regicide Peace," "Ossian," "Piers Plowman," Burke's "Thoughts on the Present Discontents," Quarles, Newman's "Apologia," Donne's "Sermons," Ruskin, Blake, "The Deserted Village," "Manfred," Blair's "Grave," "The Complaint of Deor," Bailey's "Festus," Thompson's "Hound of Heaven."

"Will you next imagine that in this volume most of the authors' names are lost; that, of the few that survive a number have found their way into wrong places; that Ruskin, for example, is credited with "Sartor Resartus"; that "Laus Veneris" and "Dolores" are ascribed to Queen Elizabeth, "The Anatomy of Melancholy" to Charles II; and that, as for the titles, these were never invented by the authors, but by a Committee?

"Will you still go on to imagine that all the poetry is printed as prose; while all the long paragraphs of prose are broken up into short verses, so that they resemble the little passages set out for parsing or analysis in an examination paper?

"Have we done? By no means. Having effected all this, let us pepper the result over with italics and numerals, print it in double columns, with a marginal gutter on either side, each gutter pouring down an inky flow of references and cross references. Then, and not till then, is the outward disguise complete—so far as you are concerned. It remains only then to appoint it to be read in Churches, and oblige the child to get selected portions of it by heart on Sundays. But you are yet to imagine that the authors themselves have taken a hand in the game: that the later ones suppose all the earlier ones to have been predicting all the time in a nebulous fashion what they themselves have to tell, and indeed to have written mainly with that object: so that Macaulay and Adam Smith, for example, constantly interrupt the thread of their discourse to affirm that what they tell us must be right because Walter Map or the author of "Piers Plowman" foretold it ages before."

Sir Arthur went on to dream of an edition which, in contrast to this ugliness and confusion, "should clothe the Bible in a dress through which its beauty might best shine." Several attempts to fulfil such an ideal have already been made in the past, probably the most successful of them being also the earliest, "The Modern Readers' Bible," edited by Professor

THE BIBLE AS LITERATURE

Richard G. Moulton in 1895, and published by Macmillan. To Professor Moulton as first in the field belongs undying credit, and no subsequent editor but has been and will continue to be under the deepest obligation to his labors. Yet neither he nor any of his successors quite accomplished their aim, which rather obviously remains still in the realm of things desirable rather than in that of things achieved.

A certain timidity has seemed to haunt the counsels of the boldest, a reluctance to make any changes not absolutely necessary: thus, while the longer poems have been printed as poetry, the numerous fragments of verse interspersed in the narrative have been left in prose form, or, while modern paragraphing has been adopted, the cumbersome punctuation of the King James version has been retained—as if the matchless beauty of that translation lay, not in the diction and the phrasing, but in the profuse use of colons and semicolons; as for quotation marks, nearly all editors have apparently felt, for some reason not entirely clear, that there was something intrinsically irreverent in their employment. All this conservatism was, however, natural enough until recently; one remembers that the first publication of even the Revised Version was greeted in many quarters as an almost blasphemous undertaking.

But the time has surely come when a purely literary edition of the Bible is called for: one in which the sole care shall be to present the text in as enjoyable and understandable a form as possible. This simple aim involves, nevertheless, much more than merely taking fuller advantage of the helpful devices of modern typography; it involves, as Sir Arthur Quiller-Couch pointed out, a problem of arrangement.

The finest aesthetic qualities may be ruined by redundancy and irrelevance, and from the literary point of view the Bible is full of both. To the later Jewish compilers, of course, every word in it was sacred, and when they yielded to the temptation to emphasize, their stresses were different from ours. Rightly enough, the legal codes of Leviticus and Deuteronomy were as important in their eyes as the historical narrative surrounding them, but, though this may still be true for the special scholar to-day, it most decidedly is not true for the general reader.

In following the epic history of the Jews through the first sixteen books of the Old Testament, the reader is hopelessly thrown off his course by the legal codes, the census reports and genealogies, the beautiful

THE BIBLE AS LITERATURE

but totally out-of-place fiction of Ruth, the double narrative of the same events in Kings and Chronicles. He then comes upon another piece of prose fiction in Esther, the poetic drama of Job, the lyrical anthology of the Psalms, the collection of folk Proverbs, the philosophical treatise of Ecclesiastes, and the secular love poetry of the Song of Songs—nearly all of this section being the product of a late highly self-conscious period; after which, without warning, he is whirled back four hundred years to the early group of the Prophets who made their appearance once before in the Book of Kings. Then, if he can indeed recognize without difficulty the greatness and appreciate the special quality of the pre-exilic Amos, Hosea, and Isaiah, and could even, if he had a fair chance, detect the poignant difference in the post-exilic work of the mighty Unknown Poet at the end of Isaiah, as he goes on from these, Jeremiah, and Ezekiel to the later imitative school of minor prophets, his ears are dinned with endless ever weaker repetitions (always excepting Micah, who belongs among the earlier writers). Also, misplaced amid the Prophetical Books, he encounters the prose fiction of Daniel and Jonah, similar in type to Ruth and Esther—propagandist fiction all of it, four antithetical works, Ruth and Jonah generous appeals for international tolerance, Esther and Daniel impassioned pleas for patriotism.

So in the New Testament, which is generally admitted to be on a considerably lower literary level than the Old Testament, the reader finds his sense of the events in the life of Jesus confused both by the repetitions and the divergences of the four Gospels, while the thunderous utterances of Paul, that burst into lightning in Corinthians and Romans, are dulled, to our ears, by his constant iteration and are further weakened by echoes in the other epistolary writers.

Thus, one is emboldened to proclaim the final heresy—that the part is greater than the whole, and that, for literary appreciation, one wants not all the Bible but the best of it. Such at any rate is the point of view of this edition.

Purpose of the Present Edition

To afford a consecutive narrative from the creation to the exile, supplementing this by a selection from the Apocryphal I Maccabees (taken like the rest from the King James version) in order to complete the

THE BIBLE AS LITERATURE

story down to the time of Jesus; to emphasize the greatest of the Prophets and minimize the others; to rearrange the drama, poetry, and fiction, adding to the latter the world-famous tales of Judith, Tobit, and Susanna and the Elders together with selections from Ecclesiasticus and the Wisdom of Solomon (all in the King James translation of the Apocrypha); to give the basic biography of Jesus found in the Gospel according to Mark, the earliest and most authoritative, supplemented by those incidents and teachings not found in Mark but in the other Gospels; to restrict the utterances of Paul to those only that have immortal value and to omit entirely the unimportant pseudonymous epistles; and, so far as sequence of contents permits, to print all the works in the order of their composition: these liberties are necessary if one seeks to put out primarily the most readable Bible.

The same singleness of purpose dictates the use of the King James translation except in the few instances of Job, Ecclesiastes, Proverbs, and the Song of Songs where the Revised Version is admittedly far superior. It also necessitates the elimination of confusing scholia and irrelevant repetitions, as well as the reduction of explanatory notes and back matter to a minimum. An edition for scholars is one thing; an edition for readers quite another. The latter should make use of the results of the former, but surely should not parade them.

If the present edition attains in any degree its high and humble aim of fostering appreciation and love of the Bible as literature, or if, even, it merely inspires others to perform the same task more adequately, in either case, it will have been well worth while.

—Ernest Sutherland Bates

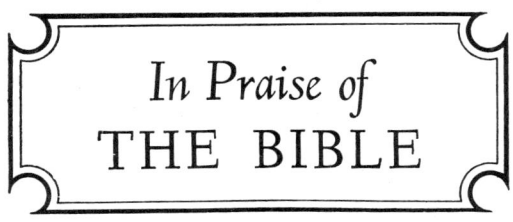

In Praise of THE BIBLE

The greater the intellectual progress of the ages, the more fully will it be possible to employ the Bible not only as the Foundation, but as the instrument of education.
—Johann Wolfgang von Goethe

I believe it would startle and move anyone if they could make a certain effort of imagination and read it freshly like a Book, not droningly and chillily like a portion of the Bible.
—Robert Louis Stevenson

The period of the Reformation was a judgment day for Europe, when all the nations were presented with an open Bible and all the emancipation of heart and intellect which an open Bible involves.
—Thomas Carlyle

Peruse the books of philosophers with all their pomp of diction. How meager, how contemptible are they when compared with the Scriptures!
—Jean Jacques Rousseau

How many ages and generations have brooded and wept and agonized over this book! What untellable joys and ecstasies, what support to martyrs at the stake, from it! To what myriads has it been the shore and rock of safety—the refuge from driving tempest and wreck! Translated in all languages, how it has united this diverse world! Of its thousands there is not a verse, not a word, but is thick-studded with human emotion.
—Walt Whitman

IN PRAISE OF THE BIBLE

Everything that I have written, every greatness that has been in any thought of mine, whatever I have done in my life has been simply due to the fact that when I was a child my mother daily read with me a part of the Bible and daily made me learn a part of it by heart.

—John Ruskin

Apart from all questions of religious and historical import, the Bible is the epic of the world. It unrolls a vast panorama in which the ages move before us in a long train of solemn imagery from the creation of the world onward. Against this gorgeous background we see mankind strutting, playing their little part on the stage of history. We see them taken from the dust and returning to the dust. We see the rise and fall of empires, we see great cities, now the hive of busy industry, now silent and desolate—a den of wild beasts. All life's fever is there, its hopes and joys, its suffering and sin and sorrow.

—J. G. Frazer

The Bible, what a book! Large and wise as the world based on the abysses of creation, and towering aloft into the blue secrets of heaven. Sunrise and sunset, promise and fulfilment, birth and death—the whole drama of humanity—are contained in this one book. It is the Book of Books. The Jews may readily be consoled at the loss of Jerusalem, and the Temple, and Ark of the Covenant, and all the crown jewels of King Solomon. Such forfeiture is as naught when weighed against the Bible, the imperishable treasure that they have saved. If I do not err, it was Mahomet who named the Jews the "People of the Book," a name which in Eastern countries has remained theirs to the present day, and is deeply significant. That one book is to the Jews their country. Within the well-fenced boundaries of that book they live and have their being; they enjoy their inalienable citizenship, are strong to admiration; thence none can dislodge them. Absorbed in the perusal of their sacred book, they little heeded the changes that were wrought in the real world around them. Nations rose and vanished, states flourished and decayed, revolutions raged throughout the earth—but they, the Jews, sat poring over this book, unconscious of the wild chase of time that rushed on above their heads.

—Heinrich Heine

THE OLD TESTAMENT
Part I
HISTORICAL BOOKS

THE BOOK OF GENESIS
    The Creation of the World 3
    The Fall of Man 5
    The First Murder 9
    The Flood 10
    The Tower of Babel 15
    The Story of Abraham 16
    The Story of Isaac and Rebekah 31
    The Story of Jacob 36
    The Story of Joseph and His Brethren 57

THE BOOK OF EXODUS
    The Escape from Egypt 79
    The Song of Moses 98
    The Journey to Sinai 100
    The Giving of the Law 105
    The Calf of Gold 111

THE BOOK OF LEVITICUS
    The Holiness Code 117

THE BOOK OF NUMBERS
    Wanderings in the Wilderness 121
    The Story of Balaam 136
    The War with the Midianites 144

THE BOOK OF DEUTERONOMY
    The Death of Moses 148

CONTENTS

THE BOOK OF JOSHUA
- The Destruction of Jericho 159
- The Destruction of Ai 165
- The Craft of the Gibeonites 169
- The Long Day's Battle 171

THE BOOK OF JUDGES
- The Story of Ehud 175
- The Story of Deborah 177
- The Song of Deborah 179
- The Story of Gideon 182
- The Story of Abimelech 190
- The Story of Jephthah's Daughter 195
- The Story of Samson 196
- The Benjamite War 205

THE FIRST BOOK OF SAMUEL
- The Birth of Samuel 214
- Hannah's Thanksgiving 216
- The Call of Samuel 217
- The Loss of the Ark 219
- The Anointing of Saul 221
- The Beginning of the Reign of Saul 227
- David and Goliath 237
- The Friendship of David and Jonathan 242
- The Flight of David 248
- The Witch of Endor 261
- The Death of Saul 263

THE SECOND BOOK OF SAMUEL
- The Lament of David 267
- The Triumph of David 269
- David and Bath-sheba 277
- The Rebellion of Absalom 281

THE FIRST BOOK OF THE KINGS
- The Death of David 297
- The Reign of Solomon 301
- The Division of the Kingdom 315
- Elijah the Tishbite 316

THE SECOND BOOK OF THE KINGS
- The Miracle of Elisha 328

CONTENTS

    The Conspiracy of Jehu 341
    The Death of Elisha 344
    The Fall of Israel 345
    The Reign of Hezekiah 346
    The Reforms of Josiah 353
    The Fall of Judah 357
THE FIRST BOOK OF ESDRAS
    The Return from Captivity 361
THE BOOK OF NEHEMIAH
    The Rebuilding of the Walls 369
    The Prohibition of Mixed Marriages 371
THE FIRST BOOK OF THE MACCABEES
    The Greek Tyranny 374
    The Rebellion of the Maccabees 378

Part II

PROPHETICAL BOOKS

THE WORDS OF AMOS
    "The Lord Will Roar from Zion" 385
    "Hear This Word That the Lord Hath Spoken" . . . 389
    "Hear This Word, Ye Kine of Bashan" 390
    "Hear Ye This Word Which I Take Up Against You" . . 392
    "Seek Ye Me, and Ye Shall Live" 392
    "Wailing Shall Be in All Streets" 393
    "Woe to Them That Are at Ease in Zion" 393
    Symbolism of the Grasshoppers, the Fire, and the Plumbline . . 395
    "Amos Hath Conspired Against Thee" 395
    Symbolism of the Fruit 396
    "Smite the Lintel" 397
THE WORD OF THE LORD THAT CAME UNTO HOSEA
    Symbolism of Gomer 400
    "When Israel Was a Child" 402
    "O Israel, Return unto the Lord" 403
THE WORD OF THE LORD
    THAT CAME UNTO MICAH THE MORASTHITE
    "Hear, All Ye People" 406
    "Hear, I Pray You, O Heads of Jacob" 407

[xvii]

CONTENTS

"But in the Last Days" 409
"Now Gather Thyself in Troops" 410
"Hear Ye Now What the Lord Saith" 411

THE VISION OF ISAIAH
The Call of the Prophet 414
"Hear, O Heavens" 415
"And It Shall Come to Pass" 417
"Therefore Thou Hast Forsaken Thy People" 417
"Enter into the Rock" 418
"Because the Daughters of Zion Are Haughty" . . . 419
"Now Will I Sing to My Wellbeloved" 420
"The People That Walked in Darkness" 421
"The Lord Sent a Word" 421
"O Assyrian, the Rod of Mine Anger" 423
"And There Shall Come Forth a Rod" 426
"Behold, I Will Stir Up the Medes" 427
"Rejoice Not Thou, Whole Palestina" 429
"Because in the Night Ar of Moab" 430
"Behold, Damascus Is Taken Away" 431
"Woe to the Land Shadowing with Wings" 433
The Burden of Egypt 434
"As Whirlwinds in the South Pass Through" 435
"He Calleth to Me out of Seir" 436
"In the Forest in Arabia" 437
"Howl, Ye Ships of Tarshish" 437
"Behold, the Lord Maketh the Earth Empty" 439
"O Lord, Thou Art My God" 441
"In That Day Shall This Song Be Sung" 442
"Lord, Thou Wilt Ordain Peace" 443
"In That Day the Lord" 444
The Covenant with Death 444
"Woe to Them That Go Down to Egypt" 446
The Character of the Liberal 447
The Women That Are at Ease 448
"Come Near, Ye Nations, to Hear" 448
"Seek Ye Out of the Book of the Lord" 450
The Song of Hezekiah 451

[xviii]

CONTENTS

THE WORD OF THE LORD WHICH CAME UNTO ZEPHANIAH
   "I Will Utterly Consume All Things" 454
   "Gather Yourselves Together" 456

THE VISION OF NAHUM THE ELKOHITE
   "He That Dasheth in Pieces" 460

THE BURDEN OF HABAKKUK
   "O Lord, How Long?" 465

THE WORDS OF JEREMIAH
   The Call of Jeremiah 470
   Jeremiah's Manifesto 471
   "Declare Ye in Judah" 474
   "O Ye Children of Benjamin" 477
   The Judgment Because of Tophet 480
   "The Way of the Heathen" 481
   "Wherefore Doth the Way of the Wicked Prosper?" . . . 483
   Symbolism of the Girdle 483
   Speech to the King and Queen 484
   "Judah Mourneth" 485
   Sentences 485
   Sermon on the Sabbath 486
   Parable of the Potter 487
   Jeremiah's Discourse in Tophet 488
   Jeremiah in the Stocks 489
   "O Lord, Thou Hast Deceived Me" 490
   Parable of the Figs 491
   The Cup of the Lord's Fury 492
   Jeremiah's Sermon in the Temple 493
   Jeremiah's Letter to the Captives in Babylon 495
   Prophecy of the Return 497
   The New Covenant 500
   The Writing of Jeremiah's Prophecies 500
   The Imprisonment of Jeremiah 503
   Jeremiah Taken to Egypt 509
   Jeremiah's Book on Babylon 512

LAMENTATIONS 514

THE BOOK OF THE PROPHET EZEKIEL
   The Vision of God 528
   The Symbolic Siege of Jerusalem 532

CONTENTS

Jerusalem the Harlot. 534
The Parable of the Two Eagles. 537
The Principle of Personal Responsibility. 539
Aholah and Aholibah. 542
The Lamentation for Tyre 544
The Dragon of the Sea 546
"Wail for the Multitude of Egypt". 547
The Shepherds of Israel 549
The Valley of Dry Bones. 551
Symbolism of the Two Sticks 553
The Invasion of Gog 554

THE RHAPSODIES OF THE UNKNOWN PROPHET
"Comfort Ye, Comfort Ye My People". 560
"Behold My Servant" 563
"Remember These, O Jacob and Israel". 563
"Come Down, and Sit in the Dust". 566
"Listen, O Isles, unto Me" 566
"Awake! Awake! Put on Strength!". 567
"Behold, My Servant Shall Deal Prudently" 568
"Sing, O Barren". 570
"Ho, Every One That Thirsteth" 572
"Arise, Shine!" 573
"The Spirit of the Lord God Is upon Me" 576
"For Zion's Sake" 577
"Who Is This That Cometh from Edom?" 579
"I Will Mention the Lovingkindness of the Lord" 579

THE VISION OF OBADIAH
"We Have Heard a Rumour from the Lord" 583

THE MESSAGE OF HAGGAI
The Rebuilding of the Temple. 586

THE VISION OF ZECHARIAH
The Angel in the Myrtle Trees. 589

THE WORD OF THE LORD THAT CAME TO JOEL
"Alas for the Day!" 592

MALACHI, MY MESSENGER
The Messenger of the Covenant. 596

[xx]

CONTENTS

Part III

POETRY, DRAMA, FICTION, AND PHILOSOPHY

THE BOOK OF PSALMS: *An Anthology of Sacred Poetry*

I.	"Blessed Is the Man"	601
II.	"Why Do the Heathen Rage?"	601
IV.	"Hear Me When I Call"	602
VI.	"O Lord, Rebuke Me Not"	603
VIII.	"O Lord Our Lord, How Excellent Is Thy Name"	603
IX.	"I Will Praise Thee, O Lord"	604
XIV.	"The Fool Hath Said in His Heart"	605
XV.	"Lord, Who Shall Abide in Thy Tabernacle?"	606
XVI.	"Preserve Me, O God"	606
XIX.	"The Heavens Declare the Glory of God"	607
XX.	"The Lord Hear Thee in the Day of Trouble"	608
XXI.	"The King Shall Joy in Thy Strength"	608
XXII.	"My God, My God, Why Hast Thou Forsaken Me?"	609
XXIII.	"The Lord Is My Shepherd"	611
XXIV.	"The Earth Is the Lord's"	612
XXVII.	"The Lord Is My Light"	612
XXIX.	"Give Unto the Lord"	613
XXX.	"I Will Extol Thee, O Lord"	614
XXXVII.	"Fret Not Thyself Because of Evildoers"	615
XXXIX.	"I Said, 'I Will Take Heed to My Ways' "	618
XLII.	"As the Hart Panteth After the Water Brooks"	619
XLIII.	"Judge Me, O God"	620
XLV.	"My Heart Is Inditing a Good Matter"	620
XLVI.	"God Is Our Refuge and Strength"	621
XLVII.	"O Clap Your Hands, All Ye People"	622
XLVIII.	"Great Is the Lord"	623
XLIX.	"Hear This, All Ye People"	624
LI.	"Have Mercy Upon Me, O God"	625
LXII.	"Truly My Soul Waiteth upon God"	626
LXIII.	"O God, Thou Art My God"	627
LXV.	"Praise Waiteth for Thee, O God"	628
LXVII.	"God Be Merciful unto Us"	629
LXVIII.	"Let God Arise"	629
LXXII.	"Give the King Thy Judgments"	632

[xxi]

CONTENTS

LXXXIV.	"How Amiable Are Thy Tabernacles"	633
LXXXV.	"Lord, Thou Hast Been Favorable unto Thy Land"	634
LXXXVII.	"His Foundation Is in the Holy Mountains"	635
LXXXVIII.	"O Lord God of My Salvation"	635
XC.	"Lord, Thou Hast Been Our Dwelling Place"	636
XCI.	"He That Dwelleth in the Secret Place of the Most High"	637
XCII.	"It Is a Good Thing to Give Thanks unto the Lord"	638
XCIII.	"The Lord Reigneth"	639
XCV.	"O Come, Let Us Sing unto the Lord"	640
XCVIII.	"O Sing unto the Lord a New Song"	641
C.	"Make a Joyful Noise unto the Lord"	641
CII.	"Hear My Prayer, O Lord"	642
CIII.	"Bless the Lord, O My Soul"	643
CIV.	"Bless the Lord, O My Soul"	645
CVIII.	"O God, My Heart Is Fixed"	647
CX.	"The Lord Said unto My Lord"	648
CXIV.	"When Israel Went out of Egypt"	648
CXV.	"Not unto Us, O Lord"	649
CXVI.	"I Love the Lord"	650
CXX.	"In My Distress I Cried unto the Lord"	651
CXXI.	"I Will Lift Up Mine Eyes unto the Hills"	652
CXXII.	"I Was Glad When They Said unto Me"	652
CXXIII.	"Unto Thee Lift I Up Mine Eyes"	653
CXXIV.	" 'If It Had Not Been the Lord' "	653
CXXV.	"They That Trust in the Lord"	654
CXXVI.	"When the Lord Turned Again the Captivity of Zion"	654
CXXVII.	"Except the Lord Build the House"	654
CXXVIII.	"Blessed Is Every One That Feareth the Lord"	655
CXXIX.	" 'Many a Time Have They Afflicted Me' "	655
CXXX.	"Out of the Depths Have I Cried"	656
CXXXI.	"Lord, My Heart Is Not Haughty"	656
CXXXIII.	"Behold, How Good and How Pleasant"	657
CXXXVI.	"O Give Thanks unto the Lord"	657
CXXXVII.	"By the Rivers of Babylon"	659
CXXXIX.	"O Lord, Thou Hast Searched Me"	659
CXLV.	"I Will Extol Thee, My God"	660
CXLVII.	"Praise Ye the Lord"	662
CXLVIII.	"Praise Ye the Lord"	663

CONTENTS

CXLIX. "Praise Ye the Lord"	664
CL. "Praise Ye the Lord"	664
THE BOOK OF PROVERBS: *An Anthology of Gnomic Poetry*	
"Hear, My Sons, the Instruction of a Father"	667
"The Lips of a Strange Woman Drop Honey"	668
"Go to the Ant, Thou Sluggard"	669
"There Be Six Things Which the Lord Hateth"	669
"My Son, Keep the Commandment of Thy Father"	670
"At the Window of My House"	671
"Doth Not Wisdom Cry?"	672
"Wisdom Hath Builded Her House"	674
"He That Correcteth a Scorner"	675
"The Fear of the Lord Is the Beginning of Wisdom"	675
"The Foolish Woman Is Clamorous"	675
The Proverbs of Solomon	676
"Who Hath Woe?"	686
The Hezekiah Collection	687
The Words of Agur	693
The Words of King Lemuel	695
"A Virtuous Woman Who Can Find?"	696
THE BOOK OF JOB: *A Philosophical Drama*	699
ECCLESIASTES; OR, THE PREACHER	755
THE SONG OF SONGS: *A Fragmentary Wedding Idyll*	772
RUTH: *A Tale*	787
JONAH: *A Tale*	795
DANIEL: *A Tale*	800
ESTHER: *A Tale*	826
JUDITH: *A Tale*	842
SUSANNA AND THE ELDERS: *A Tale*	858
TOBIT: *A Tale*	864
THE WISDOM OF JESUS THE SON OF SIRACH; OR, ECCLESIASTICUS	
A Prologue	881
"All Wisdom Cometh from the Lord"	881
"Honour a Physician"	883
"The Pride of the Height"	884
"Let Us Now Praise Famous Men"	886
"Simon, the High Priest"	891

CONTENTS

THE WISDOM OF SOLOMON
    The Immortality of the Righteous 895
    The Reward of the Righteous 895
    In Praise of Wisdom 896
    The God of Love 897

THE NEW TESTAMENT

THE GOSPEL ACCORDING TO MARK:
    A Biography of Jesus of Nazareth
    Part I: Ministry in Galilee 901
    Part II: Ministry in Judea 922
    Appendix 932

THE GOSPEL ACCORDING TO MATTHEW: *Selections*
    The Birth of Jesus 935
    The Temptation 937
    The Sermon on the Mount 938
    Jesus and John the Baptist 945
    Parables of the Kingdom 947
    On the Priests, Scribes, and Pharisees 954
    The Last Judgment 960
    The Trial of Jesus 965
    The Crucifixion of Jesus 966
    The Resurrection of Jesus 969

THE GOSPEL ACCORDING TO LUKE: *Selections*
    Preface 972
    The Birth of John the Baptist 972
    The Birth and Youth of Jesus 976
    Jesus and John the Baptist 979
    Incidents of the Ministry of Jesus 981
    The Trial of Jesus 999
    The Crucifixion of Jesus 1000
    The Resurrection of Jesus 1002

THE GOSPEL ACCORDING TO JOHN: *Selections*
    Prologue 1007
    John the Baptist and Jesus 1007
    The Gathering of the Disciples 1009
    The Marriage in Cana 1010
    The Visit of Nicodemus by Night 1010

CONTENTS

    The Woman of Samaria 1012
    The Pool of Bethesda 1014
    The Woman Taken in Adultery 1015
    The Pool of Siloam 1016
    In Solomon's Porch 1019
    The Raising of Lazarus 1020
    The Last Supper 1024
    The Betrayal of Jesus 1032
    The Trial of Jesus 1034
    The Crucifixion of Jesus 1035
    The Resurrection of Jesus 1038
THE ACTS OF THE APOSTLES: *A History of the Early Church*
    The Ascension 1044
    Pentecost 1046
    The Ministry of Peter and John 1049
    The Martyrdom of Stephen 1054
    The Ministry of Philip 1057
    The Conversion of Saul 1059
    The Spread of the Gospel 1061
    Paul's First Missionary Journey 1067
    Paul's Second Missionary Journey 1073
    Paul's Third Missionary Journey 1080
    Paul Seized and Imprisoned 1086
    Paul's Defence Before Agrippa 1095
    Paul Taken to Rome 1098
THE LETTERS OF PAUL
    To the Thessalonians. I 1104
    To the Thessalonians. II 1110
    To the Galatians 1114
    To the Corinthians. I 1122
    To the Corinthians. II 1138
    To the Romans 1147
    To the Philippians 1162
    To the Colossians 1168
    To Philemon 1172
A LETTER TO THE HEBREWS 1176
A LETTER OF JAMES 1185
A LETTER OF JOHN 1193

CONTENTS

THE REVELATION OF JESUS CHRIST

   Prologue 1199
      I. *The Book Sealed with Seven Seals* 1204
      II. *The Opening of the Seals* 1206
      III. *The Seven Trumpets* 1209
      IV. *The Woman Clothed with the Sun* 1213
      V. *The Seven Vials* 1218
      VI. *The Last Judgment* 1224
      VII. *The New Jerusalem* 1226
   Epilogue 1229

A NOTE ON TRANSLATIONS 1233
DATES OF THE BOOKS: A REFERENCE TABLE 1237
A GLOSSARY OF BIBLICAL TERMS 1241
A CHAPTER KEY 1282

THE OLD TESTAMENT

PART ONE

HISTORICAL BOOKS

THE BOOK OF GENESIS

The book that for over two thousand years has meant to millions of readers the beginning of the Bible was in time of composition very far from the beginning. In its final form it was two hundred and fifty years later than Jeremiah, three hundred and fifty years later than Isaiah, four hundred years later than Amos. It was later than Judges, Samuel, and Kings. Nor is it properly a separate book at all but part of the great compilation of the Hexateuch (including Genesis, Exodus, Leviticus, Numbers, Deuteronomy, and Joshua), of which the first five sections, constituting the Jewish "Law," were translated into Greek about the middle of the third century B.C. and only then received the names by which we know them: Genesis (Beginning), Exodus (Going Out), Leviticus (the Book of the Levites), Numbers (the Census), Deuteronomy (the Second Giving of the Law).

The magnificent compilation of the Hexateuch, covering the period from the Creation through the conquest of Canaan, was put together about the middle of the fourth century B.C. out of materials from various sources. The central narrative was supplied by welding together two much earlier accounts, one written in the ninth century in the Southern Kingdom, the other a century later in the Northern Kingdom, the former called in textual criticism the J Document from its use of the name "Jahveh" for God, the latter the E Document from its employment of the name "Elohim." The J Document, from which come the stories of Adam and Eve, Abraham, Isaac, and Jacob, is thoroughly primitive, naive, and anthropomorphic in its conceptions but is incomparably vivid as sheer narrative. The E Document, whose crowning contribution is the story of Joseph, is somewhat subtler in characterization and breathes a higher moral and religious spirit. To these must be added the P Document, an Exilic work of the priests, concerned primarily in bringing out the symbolic significance of events with relation to the numerous Jewish rites and ceremonies; it is seen at its best in the sublime account of the Creation in the first chapter where the main purpose was achieved on a stupendous scale by the division into seven days, turning the very origin of the universe into a glorification of the Jewish Sabbath.

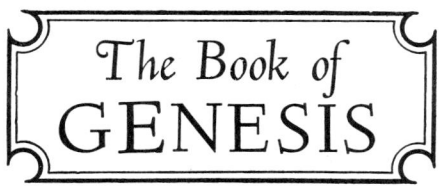

The Creation of the World

IN THE BEGINNING God created the heaven and the earth. And the earth was without form, and void; and darkness was upon the face of the deep. And the Spirit of God moved upon the face of the waters. And God said, "Let there be light": and there was light. And God saw the light, that it was good: and God divided the light from the darkness. And God called the light Day, and the darkness he called Night. And the evening and the morning were the first day.

And God said, "Let there be a firmament in the midst of the waters, and let it divide the waters from the waters." And God made the firmament, and divided the waters which were under the firmament from the waters which were above the firmament: and it was so. And God called the firmament Heaven. And the evening and the morning were the second day.

And God said, "Let the waters under the heaven be gathered together unto one place, and let the dry land appear": and it was so. And God called the dry land Earth; and the gathering together of the waters called he Seas: and God saw that it was good. And God said, "Let the earth bring forth grass, the herb yielding seed, and the fruit tree yielding fruit after his kind, whose seed is in itself, upon the earth": and it was so. And the earth brought forth grass, and herb yielding seed after his kind, and the tree yielding fruit, whose seed was in itself, after his kind: and God saw that it was good. And the evening and the morning were the third day.

And God said, "Let there be lights in the firmament of the

THE BOOK OF GENESIS

heaven to divide the day from the night; and let them be for signs, and for seasons, and for days, and years; and let them be for lights in the firmament of the heaven to give light upon the earth."

And it was so. And God made two great lights; the greater light to rule the day, and the lesser light to rule the night: he made the stars also. And God set them in the firmament of the heaven to give light upon the earth. And to rule over the day and over the night, and to divide the light from the darkness: and God saw that it was good. And the evening and the morning were the fourth day.

And God said, "Let the waters bring forth abundantly the moving creature that hath life, and fowl that may fly above the earth in the open firmament of heaven." And God created great whales, and every living creature that moveth, which the waters brought forth abundantly, after their kind, and every winged fowl after his kind: and God saw that it was good. And God blessed them, saying, "Be fruitful, and multiply, and fill the waters in the seas, and let fowl multiply in the earth." And the evening and the morning were the fifth day.

And God said, "Let the earth bring forth the living creature after his kind, cattle, and creeping thing, and beast of the earth after his kind": and it was so. And God made the beast of the earth after his kind, and cattle after their kind, and every thing that creepeth upon the earth after his kind: and God saw that it was good.

And God said, "Let us make man in our image, after our likeness: and let them have dominion over the fish of the sea, and over the fowl of the air, and over the cattle, and over all the earth, and over every creeping thing that creepeth upon the earth." So God created man in his own image, in the image of God created he him; male and female created he them. And God blessed them, and God said unto them, "Be fruitful, and multiply, and replenish the earth, and subdue it: and have dominion over the fish of the sea, and over the fowl of the air, and over every living thing that moveth upon the earth." And God said,

THE BOOK OF GENESIS

"Behold, I have given you every herb bearing seed, which is upon the face of all the earth, and every tree, in the which is the fruit of a tree yielding seed; to you it shall be for meat. And to every beast of the earth, and to every fowl of the air, and to every thing that creepeth upon the earth, wherein there is life, I have given every green herb for meat." And it was so. And God saw every thing that he had made, and, behold, it was very good. And the evening and the morning were the sixth day.

Thus the heavens and the earth were finished, and all the host of them. And on the seventh day God ended his work which he had made; and he rested on the seventh day from all his work which he had made. And God blessed the seventh day, and sanctified it: because that in it he had rested from all his work which God created and made.

The Fall of Man

In the day that the Lord God made the earth and the heavens, and every plant of the field before it was in the earth, and every herb of the field before it grew (for the Lord God had not caused it to rain upon the earth, and there was not a man to till the ground) there went up a mist from the earth, and watered the whole face of the ground. And the Lord God formed man of the dust of the ground, and breathed into his nostrils the breath of life; and man became a living soul.

And the Lord God planted a garden eastward in Eden; and there he put the man whom he had formed. And out of the ground made the Lord God to grow every tree that is pleasant to the sight, and good for food; the tree of life also in the midst of the garden, and the tree of knowledge of good and evil. And a river went out of Eden to water the garden; and from thence it was parted, and became into four heads. The name of the first is Pison: that is it which compasseth the whole land of Havilah, where there is gold; and the gold of that land is good: there is bdellium and the onyx stone. And the name of the second river is Gihon: the same is it that compasseth the whole land of Ethiopia. And the name of the third river is Hiddekel: that is it

THE BOOK OF GENESIS

which goeth toward the east of Assyria. And the fourth river is Euphrates.

And the Lord God took the man, and put him into the garden of Eden to dress it and to keep it. And the Lord God commanded the man, saying, "Of every tree of the garden thou mayest freely eat: but of the tree of the knowledge of good and evil, thou shalt not eat of it: for in the day that thou eatest thereof thou shalt surely die."

And the Lord God said,

"It is not good that the man should be alone; I will make him a help meet for him." And out of the ground the Lord God formed every beast of the field, and every fowl of the air; and brought them unto Adam to see what he would call them: and whatsoever Adam called every living creature, that was the name thereof. And Adam gave names to all cattle, and to the fowl of the air, and to every beast of the field; but for Adam there was not found a help meet for him.

And the Lord God caused a deep sleep to fall upon Adam, and he slept: and he took one of his ribs, and closed up the flesh instead thereof; and the rib, which the Lord God had taken from man, made he a woman, and brought her unto the man.

And Adam said,

> "This is now bone of my bones,
> And flesh of my flesh:
> She shall be called Woman,
> Because she was taken out of Man."

Therefore shall a man leave his father and his mother, and shall cleave unto his wife: and they shall be one flesh. And they were both naked, the man and his wife, and were not ashamed.

Now the serpent was more subtil than any beast of the field which the Lord God had made.

And he said unto the woman,

"Yea, hath God said, 'Ye shall not eat of every tree of the garden'?"

And the woman said unto the serpent,

THE BOOK OF GENESIS

"We may eat of the fruit of the trees of the garden: but of the fruit of the tree which is in the midst of the garden, God hath said, 'Ye shall not eat of it, neither shall ye touch it, lest ye die.'"

And the serpent said unto the woman,

"Ye shall not surely die: for God doth know that in the day ye eat thereof, then your eyes shall be opened, and ye shall be as gods, knowing good and evil."

And when the woman saw that the tree was good for food, and that it was pleasant to the eyes, and a tree to be desired to make one wise, she took of the fruit thereof, and did eat, and gave also unto her husband with her; and he did eat. And the eyes of them both were opened, and they knew that they were naked; and they sewed fig leaves together, and made themselves aprons.

And they heard the voice of the Lord God walking in the garden in the cool of the day: and Adam and his wife hid themselves from the presence of the Lord God amongst the trees of the garden.

And the Lord God called unto Adam, and said unto him,

"Where art thou?"

And he said,

"I heard thy voice in the garden, and I was afraid, because I was naked; and I hid myself."

And he said,

"Who told thee that thou wast naked? Hast thou eaten of the tree, whereof I commanded thee that thou shouldest not eat?"

And the man said,

"The woman whom thou gavest to be with me, she gave me of the tree, and I did eat."

And the Lord God said unto the woman,

"What is this that thou hast done?"

And the woman said, "The serpent beguiled me, and I did eat."

And the Lord God said unto the serpent,

> "Because thou hast done this,
> Thou art cursed above all cattle,

THE BOOK OF GENESIS

> And above every beast of the field;
> Upon thy belly shalt thou go,
> And dust shalt thou eat
> All the days of thy life:
> And I will put enmity between thee and the woman,
> And between thy seed and her seed;
> It shall bruise thy head,
> And thou shalt bruise his heel."

Unto the woman he said,
> "I will greatly multiply thy sorrow and thy conception;
> In sorrow thou shalt bring forth children;
> And thy desire shall be to thy husband,
> And he shall rule over thee."

And unto Adam he said,
"Because thou hast hearkened unto the voice of thy wife, and hast eaten of the tree, of which I commanded thee, saying, 'Thou shalt not eat of it':

> "Cursed is the ground for thy sake;
> In sorrow shalt thou eat of it all the days of thy life.
> Thorns also and thistles shall it bring forth to thee;
> And thou shalt eat the herb of the field;
> In the sweat of thy face shalt thou eat bread,
> Till thou return unto the ground;
> For out of it wast thou taken:
> For dust thou art,
> And unto dust shalt thou return."

And Adam called his wife's name Eve; because she was the mother of all living. Unto Adam also and to his wife did the Lord God make coats of skins, and clothed them.

And the Lord God said, "Behold, the man is become as one of us, to know good and evil: and now, lest he put forth his hand, and take also of the tree of life, and eat, and live for ever—" therefore the Lord God sent him forth from the garden of Eden, to till the ground from whence he was taken. So he drove out the man; and he placed at the east of the garden of Eden Cherubims, and a flaming sword which turned every way, to keep the way of the tree of life.

The First Murder

And Adam knew Eve his wife; and she conceived, and bore Cain, and said, "I have gotten a man from the Lord." And she again bore his brother Abel. And Abel was a keeper of sheep, but Cain was a tiller of the ground. And in process of time it came to pass that Cain brought of the fruit of the ground an offering unto the Lord. And Abel, he also brought of the firstlings of his flock and of the fat thereof. And the Lord had respect unto Abel and to his offering: but unto Cain and to his offering he had not respect. And Cain was very wroth, and his countenance fell.

And the Lord said unto Cain,

"Why art thou wroth? and why is thy countenance fallen? If thou doest well, shalt thou not be accepted? and if thou doest not well, sin lieth at the door. And unto thee shall be his desire, and thou shalt rule over him."

And Cain talked with Abel his brother: and it came to pass, when they were in the field, that Cain rose up against Abel his brother, and slew him.

And the Lord said unto Cain, "Where is Abel thy brother?" And he said, "I know not: am I my brother's keeper?"

And he said,

"What hast thou done? the voice of thy brother's blood crieth unto me from the ground. And now art thou cursed from the earth, which hath opened her mouth to receive thy brother's blood from thy hand. When thou tillest the ground, it shall not henceforth yield unto thee her strength; a fugitive and a vagabond shalt thou be in the earth."

And Cain said unto the Lord,

"My punishment is greater than I can bear. Behold, thou hast driven me out this day from the face of the earth; and from thy face shall I be hid; and I shall be a fugitive and a vagabond in the earth; and it shall come to pass that every one that findeth me shall slay me."

And the Lord said unto him,

"Therefore whosoever slayeth Cain, vengeance shall be taken on him sevenfold." And the Lord set a mark upon Cain, lest any finding him should kill him.

And Cain went out from the presence of the Lord, and dwelt in the land of Nod, on the east of Eden.

And Adam knew his wife again; and she bore a son, and called his name Seth: "For God," said she, "hath appointed me another seed instead of Abel, whom Cain slew." And to Seth, to him also there was born a son; and he called his name Enos: then began men to call upon the name of the Lord.

And the days of Adam after he had begotten Seth were eight hundred years: and he begot sons and daughters. And all the days that Adam lived were nine hundred and thirty years: and he died.

The Flood

And it came to pass, when men began to multiply on the face of the earth, and daughters were born unto them, that the sons of God saw the daughters of men that they were fair; and they took them wives of all which they chose.

And the Lord said, "My spirit shall not always strive with man, for that he also is flesh: yet his days shall be a hundred and twenty years."

There were giants in the earth in those days; and also after that, when the sons of God came in unto the daughters of men, and they bore children to them, the same became mighty men which were of old, men of renown. And God saw that the wickedness of man was great in the earth, and that every imagination of the thoughts of his heart was only evil continually. And it repented the Lord that he had made man on the earth, and it grieved him at his heart.

And the Lord said, "I will destroy man whom I have created

THE BOOK OF GENESIS

from the face of the earth; both man, and beast, and the creeping thing, and the fowls of the air; for it repenteth me that I have made them."

But Noah found grace in the eyes of the Lord.

Noah was a just man and perfect in his generations, and Noah walked with God. And Noah begot three sons, Shem, Ham, and Japheth.

And God said unto Noah, "The end of all flesh is come before me; for the earth is filled with violence through them; and, behold, I will destroy them with the earth. Make thee an ark of gopher wood; rooms shalt thou make in the ark, and shalt pitch it within and without with pitch. And this is the fashion which thou shalt make it of: the length of the ark shall be three hundred cubits, the breadth of it fifty cubits, and the height of it thirty cubits. A window shalt thou make to the ark, and in a cubit shalt thou finish it above; and the door of the ark shalt thou set in the side thereof; with lower, second, and third stories shalt thou make it. And, behold, I, even I, do bring a flood of waters upon the earth, to destroy all flesh, wherein is the breath of life, from under heaven; and every thing that is in the earth shall die. But with thee will I establish my covenant; and thou shalt come into the ark, thou, and thy sons, and thy wife, and thy sons' wives with thee. And of every living thing of all flesh, two of every sort shalt thou bring into the ark, to keep them alive with thee; they shall be male and female. Of fowls after their kind, and of cattle after their kind, of every creeping thing of the earth after his kind, two of every sort shall come unto thee, to keep them alive. And take thou unto thee of all food that is eaten, and thou shalt gather it to thee; and it shall be for food for thee, and for them."

Thus did Noah; according to all that God commanded him, so did he. And the Lord said unto Noah, "Come thou and all thy house into the ark; for thee have I seen righteous before me in this generation. Of every clean beast thou shalt take to thee by sevens, the male and his female: and of beasts that are not clean by two, the male and his female. Of fowls also of the air by sev-

THE BOOK OF GENESIS

ens, the male and the female; to keep seed alive upon the face of all the earth. For yet seven days, and I will cause it to rain upon the earth forty days and forty nights; and every living substance that I have made will I destroy from off the face of the earth."

And Noah did according unto all that the Lord commanded him. And Noah went in, and his sons, and his wife, and his sons' wives with him, into the ark, because of the waters of the flood. Of clean beasts, and of beasts that are not clean, and of fowls, and of every thing that creepeth upon the earth, there went in two and two unto Noah into the ark, the male and the female, as God had commanded Noah. And it came to pass after seven days that the waters of the flood were upon the earth. In the six hundredth year of Noah's life, in the second month, the seventeenth day of the month, the same day were all the fountains of the great deep broken up, and the windows of heaven were opened. And the waters prevailed, and were increased greatly upon the earth; and the ark went upon the face of the waters. And the waters prevailed exceedingly upon the earth; and all the high hills, that were under the whole heaven, were covered. Fifteen cubits upward did the waters prevail; and the mountains were covered. And all flesh died that moved upon the earth, both of fowl, and of cattle, and of beast, and of every creeping thing that creepeth upon the earth, and every man. All in whose nostrils was the breath of life, of all that was in the dry land, died. And every living substance was destroyed which was upon the face of the ground, both man, and cattle, and the creeping things, and the fowl of the heaven; and they were destroyed from the earth: and Noah only remained alive, and they that were with him in the ark. And the waters prevailed upon the earth a hundred and fifty days.

And God remembered Noah, and every living thing, and all the cattle that was with him in the ark: and God made a wind to pass over the earth, and the waters assuaged. The fountains also of the deep and the windows of heaven were stopped, and the rain from heaven was restrained; and the waters returned from off the earth continually: and after the end of the hundred

THE BOOK OF GENESIS

and fifty days the waters were abated. And the ark rested in the seventh month, on the seventeenth day of the month, upon the mountains of Ararat. And the waters decreased continually until the tenth month: in the tenth month, on the first day of the month, were the tops of the mountains seen.

And it came to pass at the end of forty days that Noah opened the window of the ark which he had made: and he sent forth a raven, which went forth to and fro, until the waters were dried up from off the earth. Also he sent forth a dove from him, to see if the waters were abated from off the face of the ground; but the dove found no rest for the sole of her foot, and she returned unto him into the ark, for the waters were on the face of the whole earth: then he put forth his hand, and took her, and pulled her in unto him into the ark. And he stayed yet other seven days; and again he sent forth the dove out of the ark; and the dove came in to him in the evening; and, lo, in her mouth was an olive leaf plucked off: so Noah knew that the waters were abated from off the earth. And he stayed yet other seven days; and sent forth the dove; which returned not again unto him any more. And it came to pass in the six hundredth and first year, in the first month, the first day of the month, the waters were dried up from off the earth: and Noah removed the covering of the ark, and looked, and, behold, the face of the ground was dry. And in the second month, on the seven and twentieth day of the month, was the earth dried.

And God spoke unto Noah, saying, "Go forth of the ark, thou, and thy wife, and thy sons, and thy sons' wives with thee. Bring forth with thee every living thing that is with thee, of all flesh, both of fowl, and of cattle, and of every creeping thing that creepeth upon the earth; that they may breed abundantly in the earth, and be fruitful, and multiply upon the earth."

And Noah went forth, and his sons, and his wife, and his sons' wives with him. Every beast, every creeping thing, and every fowl, and whatsoever creepeth upon the earth, after their kinds, went forth out of the ark.

And Noah built an altar unto the Lord; and took of every

THE BOOK OF GENESIS

clean beast, and of every clean fowl, and offered burnt offerings on the altar. And the Lord smelled a sweet savour; and the Lord said in his heart,

"I will not again curse the ground any more for man's sake; for the imagination of man's heart is evil from his youth; neither will I again smite any more every thing living, as I have done. While the earth remaineth, seedtime and harvest, and cold and heat, and summer and winter, and day and night shall not cease."

And God blessed Noah and his sons, and said unto them, "Be fruitful, and multiply, and replenish the earth. And the fear of you and the dread of you shall be upon every beast of the earth, and upon every fowl of the air, upon all that moveth upon the earth, and upon all the fishes of the sea; into your hand are they delivered. Every moving thing that liveth shall be meat for you; even as the green herb have I given you all things. But flesh with the life thereof, which is the blood thereof, shall ye not eat. And surely your blood of your lives will I require; at the hand of every beast will I require it, and at the hand of man; at the hand of every man's brother will I require the life of man. Whoso sheddeth man's blood, by man shall his blood be shed: for in the image of God made he man."

And God spoke unto Noah, and to his sons with him, saying, "And I, behold, I establish my covenant with you, and with your seed after you; and with every living creature that is with you, of the fowl, of the cattle, and of every beast of the earth with you; from all that go out of the ark, to every beast of the earth. And I will establish my covenant with you; neither shall all flesh be cut off any more by the waters of a flood; neither shall there any more be a flood to destroy the earth."

And God said,

"This is the token of the covenant which I make between me and you and every living creature that is with you, for perpetual generations: I do set my bow in the cloud, and it shall be for a token of a covenant between me and the earth. And it shall come to pass, when I bring a cloud over the earth, that the bow shall be seen in the cloud: and I will remember my covenant, which is between me and you and every living creature of all flesh; and the waters shall no more become a flood to destroy all flesh. And the bow shall be in the cloud; and I will look upon it, that I may remember the everlasting covenant between God and every living creature of all flesh that is upon the earth."

And God said unto Noah, "This is the token of the covenant, which I have established between me and all flesh that is upon the earth."

And Noah began to be a husbandman, and he planted a vineyard: and he drank of the wine, and was drunken; and he was uncovered within his tent. And Ham, the father of Canaan, saw the nakedness of his father, and told his two brethren without. And Shem and Japheth took a garment, and laid it upon both their shoulders, and went backward, and covered the nakedness of their father; and their faces were backward, and they saw not their father's nakedness.

And Noah awoke from his wine, and knew what his younger son had done unto him. And he said,

"Cursed be Canaan; a servant of servants shall he be unto his brethren." And he said, "Blessed be the Lord God of Shem; and Canaan shall be his servant. God shall enlarge Japheth, and he shall dwell in the tents of Shem; and Canaan shall be his servant."

And Noah lived after the flood three hundred and fifty years. And all the days of Noah were nine hundred and fifty years: and he died.

The Tower of Babel

And the whole earth was of one language, and of one speech. And it came to pass, as they journeyed from the east, that they found a plain in the land of Shinar; and they dwelt there. And they said one to another,

"Go to, let us make brick, and burn them thoroughly." And they had brick for stone, and slime had they for mortar. And they said, "Go to, let us build us a city and a tower, whose top may reach unto heaven; and let us make us a name, lest we be scattered abroad upon the face of the whole earth."

And the Lord came down to see the city and the tower, which the children of men builded. And the Lord said, "Behold, the people is one, and they have all one language; and this they begin to do: and now nothing will be restrained from them, which they have imagined to do. Go to, let us go down, and there confound their language, that they may not understand one another's speech."

So the Lord scattered them abroad from thence upon the face of all the earth: and they left off to build the city. Therefore is the name of it called Babel; because the Lord did there confound the language of all the earth: and from thence did the Lord scatter them abroad upon the face of all the earth.

The Story of Abraham

Now these are the generations of Terah: Terah begot Abram, Nahor, and Haran; and Haran begot Lot. And Haran died before his father Terah in the land of his nativity, in Ur of the Chaldees. And Abram and Nahor took them wives: the name of Abram's wife was Sarai; and the name of Nahor's wife, Milcah, the daughter of Haran, the father of Milcah, and the father of Iscah. But Sarai was barren; she had no child.

And Terah took Abram his son, and Lot the son of Haran his son's son, and Sarai his daughter-in-law, his son Abram's wife; and they went forth with them from Ur of the Chaldees, to go into the land of Canaan; and they came unto Haran, and dwelt there. And the days of Terah were two hundred and five years: and Terah died in Haran.

Now the Lord had said unto Abram, "Get thee out of thy country, and from thy kindred, and from thy father's house, unto a land that I will show thee: and I will make of thee a great nation, and I will bless thee, and make thy name great; and thou shalt be a blessing. And I will bless them that bless thee, and curse him that curseth thee: and in thee shall all families of the earth be blessed."

THE BOOK OF GENESIS

So Abram departed, as the Lord had spoken unto him; and Lot went with him: and Abram was seventy and five years old when he departed out of Haran. And Abram took Sarai his wife, and Lot his brother's son, and all their substance that they had gathered, and the souls that they had gotten in Haran; and they went forth to go into the land of Canaan; and into the land of Canaan they came. And Abram passed through the land unto the place of Sichem, unto the plain of Moreh. And the Canaanite was then in the land.

And the Lord appeared unto Abram, and said, "Unto thy seed will I give this land."

And there builded he an altar unto the Lord, who appeared unto him. And he removed from thence unto a mountain on the east of Beth-el, and pitched his tent, having Beth-el on the west, and Hai on the east: and there he builded an altar unto the Lord, and called upon the name of the Lord. And Abram journeyed, going on still toward the south. And there was a famine in the land: and Abram went down into Egypt to sojourn there; for the famine was grievous in the land. And it came to pass, when he was come near to enter into Egypt, that he said unto Sarai his wife, "Behold now, I know that thou art a fair woman to look upon: therefore it shall come to pass, when the Egyptians shall see thee, that they shall say, 'This is his wife': and they will kill me, but they will save thee alive. Say, I pray thee, thou art my sister: that it may be well with me for thy sake; and my soul shall live because of thee."

And it came to pass that, when Abram was come into Egypt, the Egyptians beheld the woman that she was very fair. The princes also of Pharaoh saw her, and commended her before Pharaoh: and the woman was taken into Pharaoh's house. And he entreated Abram well for her sake: and he had sheep, and oxen, and he-asses, and menservants, and maidservants, and she-asses, and camels. And the Lord plagued Pharaoh and his house with great plagues because of Sarai Abram's wife.

And Pharaoh called Abram, and said, "What is this that thou hast done unto me? why didst thou not tell me that she was thy

THE BOOK OF GENESIS

wife? Why saidst thou, 'She is my sister'? so I might have taken her to me to wife: now therefore behold thy wife, take her, and go thy way."

And Pharaoh commanded his men concerning him: and they sent him away, and his wife, and all that he had. And Abram went up out of Egypt, he, and his wife, and all that he had, and Lot with him, into the south. And Abram was very rich in cattle, in silver, and in gold. And he went on his journeys from the south even to Beth-el, unto the place where his tent had been at the beginning, between Beth-el and Hai; unto the place of the altar, which he had made there at the first: and there Abram called on the name of the Lord. And Lot also, which went with Abram, had flocks, and herds, and tents. And the land was not able to bear them, that they might dwell together: for their substance was great, so that they could not dwell together. And there was a strife between the herdsmen of Abram's cattle and the herdsmen of Lot's cattle: and the Canaanite and the Perizzite dwelled then in the land.

And Abram said unto Lot, "Let there be no strife, I pray thee, between me and thee, and between my herdsmen and thy herdsmen; for we be brethren. Is not the whole land before thee? separate thyself, I pray thee, from me: if thou wilt take the left hand, then I will go to the right; or if thou depart to the right hand, then I will go to the left."

And Lot lifted up his eyes, and beheld all the plain of Jordan, that it was well watered every where, before the Lord destroyed Sodom and Gomorrah, even as the garden of the Lord, like the land of Egypt, as thou comest unto Zoar. Then Lot chose him all the plain of Jordan; and Lot journeyed east: and they separated themselves the one from the other. Abram dwelled in the land of Canaan, and Lot dwelled in the cities of the plain, and pitched his tent toward Sodom. But the men of Sodom were wicked and sinners before the Lord exceedingly. And the Lord said unto Abram, after that Lot was separated from him, "Lift up now thine eyes, and look from the place where thou art northward, and southward, and eastward, and westward: for all the

THE BOOK OF GENESIS

land which thou seest, to thee will I give it, and to thy seed for ever. And I will make thy seed as the dust of the earth: so that if a man can number the dust of the earth, then shall thy seed also be numbered. Arise, walk through the land in the length of it and in the breadth of it; for I will give it unto thee."

Then Abram removed his tent, and came and dwelt in the plain of Mamre, which is in Hebron, and built there an altar unto the Lord.

And it came to pass in the days of Amraphel king of Shinar, Arioch king of Ellasar, Chedorlaomer king of Elam, and Tidal king of nations; that these made war with Bera king of Sodom, and with Birsha king of Gomorrah, Shinab king of Admah, and Shemeber king of Zeboiim, and the king of Bela, which is Zoar. All these were joined together in the vale of Siddim, which is the Salt Sea. Twelve years they served Chedorlaomer, and in the thirteenth year they rebelled. And in the fourteenth year came Chedorlaomer, and the kings that were with him, and smote the Rephaims in Ashteroth Karnaim, and the Zuzims in Ham, and the Emims in Shaveh Kiriathaim, and the Horites in their Mount Seir, unto El-paran, which is by the wilderness. And they returned, and came to En-mishpat, which is Kadesh, and smote all the country of the Amalekites, and also the Amorites, that dwelt in Hazezon-tamar. And there went out the king of Sodom, and the king of Gomorrah, and the king of Admah, and the king of Zeboiim, and the king of Bela (the same is Zoar); and they joined battle with them in the vale of Siddim; with Chedorlaomer the king of Elam, and with Tidal king of nations, and Amraphel king of Shinar, and Arioch king of Ellasar; four kings with five. And the vale of Siddim was full of slimepits; and the kings of Sodom and Gomorrah fled, and fell there; and they that remained fled to the mountain. And they took all the goods of Sodom and Gomorrah, and all their victuals, and went their way. And they took Lot, Abram's brother's son, who dwelt in Sodom, and his goods, and departed.

And there came one that had escaped, and told Abram the Hebrew: for he dwelt in the plain of Mamre the Amorite, brother

THE BOOK OF GENESIS

of Eshcol, and brother of Aner; and these were confederate with Abram. And when Abram heard that his brother was taken captive, he armed his trained servants, born in his own house, three hundred and eighteen, and pursued them unto Dan. And he divided himself against them, he and his servants, by night, and smote them, and pursued them unto Hobah, which is on the left hand of Damascus. And he brought back all the goods, and also brought again his brother Lot, and his goods, and the women also, and the people.

Now Sarai Abram's wife bore him no children: and she had a handmaid, an Egyptian, whose name was Hagar. And Sarai said unto Abram, "Behold now, the Lord hath restrained me from bearing: I pray thee, go in unto my maid; it may be that I may obtain children by her."

And Abram hearkened to the voice of Sarai. And Sarai Abram's wife took Hagar her maid the Egyptian, after Abram had dwelt ten years in the land of Canaan, and gave her to her husband Abram to be his wife. And he went in unto Hagar, and she conceived: and when she saw that she had conceived, her mistress was despised in her eyes.

And Sarai said unto Abram, "My wrong be upon thee: I have given my maid into thy bosom; and when she saw that she had conceived, I was despised in her eyes: the Lord judge between me and thee."

But Abram said unto Sarai, "Behold, thy maid is in thy hand; do to her as it pleaseth thee."

And when Sarai dealt hardly with her, she fled from her face. And the angel of the Lord found her by a fountain of water in the wilderness, by the fountain in the way to Shur.

And he said, "Hagar, Sarai's maid, whence camest thou? and whither wilt thou go?"

And she said, "I flee from the face of my mistress Sarai."

And the angel of the Lord said unto her, "Return to thy mistress, and submit thyself under her hands." And the angel of the Lord said unto her, "I will multiply thy seed exceedingly, that it shall not be numbered for multitude." And the angel of the

THE BOOK OF GENESIS

Lord said unto her, "Behold, thou art with child, and shalt bear a son, and shalt call his name Ishmael; because the Lord hath heard thy affliction. And he will be a wild man; his hand will be against every man, and every man's hand against him; and he shall dwell in the presence of all his brethren."

And she called the name of the Lord that spoke unto her, "Thou God seest me": for she said, "Have I also here looked after him that seeth me?" Wherefore the well was called Beer-lahai-roi; behold, it is between Kadesh and Bered. And Hagar bore Abram a son: and Abram called his son's name, which Hagar bore, Ishmael. And Abram was fourscore and six years old, when Hagar bore Ishmael to Abram.

And when Abram was ninety years old and nine, the Lord appeared to Abram, and said unto him, "I am the Almighty God; walk before me, and be thou perfect. And I will make my covenant between me and thee, and will multiply thee exceedingly."

And Abram fell on his face: and God talked with him, saying, "As for me, behold, my covenant is with thee, and thou shalt be a father of many nations. Neither shall thy name any more be called Abram, but thy name shall be Abraham; for a father of many nations have I made thee. This is my covenant, which ye shall keep, between me and you and thy seed after thee; every man child among you shall be circumcised. And ye shall circumcise the flesh of your foreskin; and it shall be a token of the covenant betwixt me and you. And he that is eight days old shall be circumcised among you, every man child in your generations, he that is born in the house, or bought with money of any stranger, which is not of thy seed. He that is born in thy house, and he that is bought with thy money, must needs be circumcised: and my covenant shall be in your flesh for an everlasting covenant. And the uncircumcised man child whose flesh of his foreskin is not circumcised, that soul shall be cut off from his people; he hath broken my covenant."

And God said unto Abraham, "As for Sarai thy wife, thou shalt not call her name Sarai, but Sarah shall her name be."

And Abraham took Ishmael his son, and all that were born in

THE BOOK OF GENESIS

his house, and all that were bought with his money, every male among the men of Abraham's house; and circumcised the flesh of their foreskin in the selfsame day, as God had said unto him. And Abraham was ninety years old and nine, when he was circumcised in the flesh of his foreskin. And Ishmael his son was thirteen years old, when he was circumcised in the flesh of his foreskin. In the selfsame day was Abraham circumcised, and Ishmael his son. And all the men of his house, born in the house, and bought with money of the stranger, were circumcised with him.

And the Lord appeared unto him in the plains of Mamre: and he sat in the tent door in the heat of the day; and he lifted up his eyes and looked, and, lo, three men stood by him: and when he saw them, he ran to meet them from the tent door, and bowed himself toward the ground, and said, "My Lord, if now I have found favour in thy sight, pass not away, I pray thee, from thy servant: let a little water, I pray you, be fetched, and wash your feet, and rest yourselves under the tree: and I will fetch a morsel of bread, and comfort ye your hearts; after that ye shall pass on: for therefore are ye come to your servant."

And they said, "So do, as thou hast said."

And Abraham hastened into the tent unto Sarah, and said, "Make ready quickly three measures of fine meal, knead it, and make cakes upon the hearth."

And Abraham ran unto the herd, and fetched a calf tender and good, and gave it unto a young man; and he hastened to dress it. And he took butter, and milk, and the calf which he had dressed, and set it before them; and he stood by them under the tree, and they did eat.

And they said unto him, "Where is Sarah thy wife?"

And he said, "Behold, in the tent."

And he said, "I will certainly return unto thee according to the time of life; and, lo, Sarah thy wife shall have a son."

And Sarah heard it in the tent door, which was behind him. Now Abraham and Sarah were old and well stricken in age; and it ceased to be with Sarah after the manner of women. Therefore

THE BOOK OF GENESIS

Sarah laughed within herself, saying, "After I am waxed old shall I have pleasure, my lord being old also?"

And the Lord said unto Abraham, "Wherefore did Sarah laugh, saying, 'Shall I of a surety bear a child, which am old?' Is any thing too hard for the Lord? At the time appointed I will return unto thee, according to the time of life, and Sarah shall have a son."

Then Sarah denied, saying, "I laughed not": for she was afraid. And he said, "Nay; but thou didst laugh."

And the men rose up from thence, and looked toward Sodom: and Abraham went with them to bring them on the way.

And the Lord said, "Shall I hide from Abraham that thing which I do; seeing that Abraham shall surely become a great and mighty nation, and all the nations of the earth shall be blessed in him? For I know him, that he will command his children and his household after him, and they shall keep the way of the Lord, to do justice and judgment; that the Lord may bring upon Abraham that which he hath spoken of him."

And the Lord said, "Because the cry of Sodom and Gomorrah is great, and because their sin is very grievous; I will go down now, and see whether they have done altogether according to the cry of it, which is come unto me; and if not, I will know."

And the men turned their faces from thence, and went toward Sodom: but Abraham stood yet before the Lord.

And Abraham drew near, and said, "Wilt thou also destroy the righteous with the wicked? Peradventure there be fifty righteous within the city: wilt thou also destroy and not spare the place for the fifty righteous that are therein? That be far from thee to do after this manner, to slay the righteous with the wicked: and that the righteous should be as the wicked, that be far from thee: shall not the Judge of all the earth do right?" And the Lord said, "If I find in Sodom fifty righteous within the city, then I will spare all the place for their sakes."

And Abraham answered and said, "Behold now, I have taken upon me to speak unto the Lord, which am but dust and ashes. Peradventure there shall lack five of the fifty righteous: wilt thou destroy all the city for lack of five?" And he said, "If I find there forty and five, I will not destroy it."

And he spoke unto him yet again, and said, "Peradventure there shall be forty found there." And he said, "I will not do it for forty's sake."

And he said unto him, "Oh let not the Lord be angry, and I will speak: peradventure there shall thirty be found there." And he said, "I will not do it, if I find thirty there."

And he said, "Behold now, I have taken upon me to speak unto the Lord: peradventure there shall be twenty found there." And he said, "I will not destroy it for twenty's sake."

And he said, "Oh let not the Lord be angry, and I will speak yet but this once: peradventure ten shall be found there." And he said, "I will not destroy it for ten's sake."

And the Lord went his way, as soon as he had left communing with Abraham; and Abraham returned unto his place.

And there came two angels to Sodom at even; and Lot sat in the gate of Sodom: and Lot seeing them rose up to meet them; and he bowed himself with his face toward the ground. And he said, "Behold now, my lords, turn in, I pray you, into your servant's house, and tarry all night, and wash your feet, and ye shall rise up early, and go on your ways."

And they said, "Nay; but we will abide in the street all night."

And he pressed upon them greatly; and they turned in unto him, and entered into his house; and he made them a feast, and did bake unleavened bread, and they did eat. But before they lay down, the men of the city, even the men of Sodom, compassed the house round, both old and young, all the people from every quarter: and they called unto Lot, and said unto him, "Where are the men which came in to thee this night? bring them out unto us, that we may know them."

And Lot went out at the door unto them, and shut the door after him, and said, "I pray you, brethren, do not so wickedly. Behold now, I have two daughters which have not known man; let me, I pray you, bring them out unto you, and do ye to them

THE BOOK OF GENESIS

as is good in your eyes: only unto these men do nothing; for therefore came they under the shadow of my roof."

And they said, "Stand back!" And they said again, "This one fellow came in to sojourn, and he will needs be a judge: now will we deal worse with thee than with them."

And they pressed sore upon the man, even Lot, and came near to break the door. But the men put forth their hand, and pulled Lot into the house to them, and shut to the door. And they smote the men that were at the door of the house with blindness, both small and great: so that they wearied themselves to find the door. And the men said unto Lot, "Hast thou here any besides? sons-in-law, and thy sons, and thy daughters, and whatsoever thou hast in the city, bring them out of this place: for we will destroy this place, because the cry of them is waxen great before the face of the Lord; and the Lord hath sent us to destroy it."

And Lot went out, and spoke unto his sons-in-law, which married his daughters, and said, "Up, get you out of this place; for the Lord will destroy this city." But he seemed as one that mocked unto his sons-in-law.

And when the morning arose, then the angels hastened Lot, saying, "Arise, take thy wife, and thy two daughters, which are here; lest thou be consumed in the iniquity of the city."

And while he lingered, the men laid hold upon his hand, and upon the hand of his wife, and upon the hand of his two daughters; the Lord being merciful unto him: and they brought him forth, and set him without the city. And it came to pass, when they had brought them forth abroad, that he said, "Escape for thy life; look not behind thee, neither stay thou in all the plain; escape to the mountain, lest thou be consumed."

And Lot said unto them, "Oh, not so, my Lord: behold now, thy servant hath found grace in thy sight, and thou hast magnified thy mercy, which thou hast showed unto me in saving my life; and I cannot escape to the mountain, lest some evil take me, and I die. Behold now, this city is near to flee unto, and it is a little one. Oh, let me escape thither (is it not a little one?), and my soul shall live."

THE BOOK OF GENESIS

And he said unto him, "See, I have accepted thee concerning this thing also, that I will not overthrow this city, for the which thou hast spoken. Haste thee, escape thither; for I cannot do any thing till thou be come thither." (Therefore the name of the city was called Zoar.)

The sun was risen upon the earth when Lot entered into Zoar. Then the Lord rained upon Sodom and upon Gomorrah brimstone and fire from the Lord out of heaven; and he overthrew those cities, and all the plain, and all the inhabitants of the cities, and that which grew upon the ground.

But his wife looked back from behind him, and she became a pillar of salt.

And Abraham got up early in the morning to the place where he stood before the Lord. And he looked toward Sodom and Gomorrah, and toward all the land of the plain, and beheld, and, lo, the smoke of the country went up as the smoke of a furnace. And it came to pass, when God destroyed the cities of the plain, that God remembered Abraham, and sent Lot out of the midst of the overthrow, when he overthrew the cities in the which Lot dwelt. And Lot went up out of Zoar, and dwelt in the mountain, and his two daughters with him; for he feared to dwell in Zoar: and he dwelt in a cave, he and his two daughters.

And the firstborn said unto the younger, "Our father is old, and there is not a man in the earth to come in unto us after the manner of all the earth. Come, let us make our father drink wine, and we will lie with him, that we may preserve seed of our father."

And they made their father drink wine that night: and the firstborn went in, and lay with her father; and he perceived not when she lay down, nor when she arose. And it came to pass on the morrow that the firstborn said unto the younger, "Behold, I lay yesternight with my father: let us make him drink wine this night also; and go thou in, and lie with him, that we may preserve seed of our father."

And they made their father drink wine that night also: and

THE BOOK OF GENESIS

the younger arose, and lay with him; and he perceived not when she lay down, nor when she arose. Thus were both the daughters of Lot with child by their father. And the firstborn bore a son, and called his name Moab: the same is the father of the Moabites unto this day. And the younger, she also bore a son, and called his name Ben-ammi: the same is the father of the children of Ammon unto this day.

And the Lord visited Sarah as he had said, and the Lord did unto Sarah as he had spoken. For Sarah conceived, and bore Abraham a son in his old age, at the set time of which God had spoken to him. And Abraham called the name of his son that was born unto him, whom Sarah bore to him, Isaac. And Abraham circumcised his son Isaac being eight days old, as God had commanded him. And Abraham was a hundred years old, when his son Isaac was born unto him.

And Sarah said, "God hath made me to laugh, so that all that hear will laugh with me." And she said, "Who would have said unto Abraham that Sarah should have given children suck? for I have borne him a son in his old age."

And the child grew, and was weaned: and Abraham made a great feast the same day that Isaac was weaned. And Sarah saw the son of Hagar the Egyptian, which she had borne unto Abraham, mocking. Wherefore she said unto Abraham, "Cast out this bondwoman and her son: for the son of this bondwoman shall not be heir with my son, even with Isaac."

And the thing was very grievous in Abraham's sight because of his son. And God said unto Abraham, "Let it not be grievous in thy sight because of the lad, and because of thy bondwoman; in all that Sarah hath said unto thee, hearken unto her voice; for in Isaac shall thy seed be called. And also of the son of the bondwoman will I make a nation, because he is thy seed."

And Abraham rose up early in the morning, and took bread, and a bottle of water, and gave it unto Hagar, putting it on her shoulder, and the child, and sent her away: and she departed, and wandered in the wilderness of Beer-sheba. And the water was spent in the bottle, and she cast the child under one of the shrubs. And she went, and sat her down over against him a good way off, as it were a bowshot: for she said, "Let me not see the death of the child." And she sat over against him, and lifted up her voice, and wept.

And God heard the voice of the lad; and the angel of God called to Hagar out of heaven, and said unto her, "What aileth thee, Hagar? fear not; for God hath heard the voice of the lad where he is. Arise, lift up the lad, and hold him in thine hand; for I will make him a great nation."

And God opened her eyes, and she saw a well of water; and she went, and filled the bottle with water, and gave the lad drink. And God was with the lad; and he grew, and dwelt in the wilderness, and became an archer. And he dwelt in the wilderness of Paran: and his mother took him a wife out of the land of Egypt.

And it came to pass after these things that God did tempt Abraham, and said unto him, "Abraham": and he said, "Behold, here I am."

And he said, "Take now thy son, thine only son Isaac, whom thou lovest, and get thee into the land of Moriah; and offer him there for a burnt offering upon one of the mountains which I will tell thee of."

And Abraham rose up early in the morning, and saddled his ass, and took two of his young men with him, and Isaac his son, and cleft the wood for the burnt offering, and rose up, and went unto the place of which God had told him. Then on the third day Abraham lifted up his eyes, and saw the place afar off. And Abraham said unto his young men, "Abide ye here with the ass; and I and the lad will go yonder and worship, and come again to you."

And Abraham took the wood of the burnt offering, and laid it upon Isaac his son; and he took the fire in his hand, and a knife; and they went both of them together. And Isaac spoke unto Abraham his father, and said, "My father": and he said,

THE BOOK OF GENESIS

"Here am I, my son." And he said, "Behold the fire and the wood: but where is the lamb for a burnt offering?" And Abraham said, "My son, God will provide himself a lamb for a burnt offering": so they went both of them together.

And they came to the place which God had told him of; and Abraham built an altar there, and laid the wood in order, and bound Isaac his son, and laid him on the altar upon the wood. And Abraham stretched forth his hand, and took the knife to slay his son.

And the angel of the Lord called unto him out of heaven, and said, "Abraham, Abraham": and he said, "Here am I."

And he said, "Lay not thine hand upon the lad, neither do thou any thing unto him: for now I know that thou fearest God, seeing thou hast not withheld thy son, thine only son from me."

And Abraham lifted up his eyes, and looked, and beheld behind him a ram caught in a thicket by his horns: and Abraham went and took the ram, and offered him up for a burnt offering in the stead of his son. And Abraham called the name of that place Jehovah-jireh: as it is said to this day, "In the mount of the Lord it shall be seen."

So Abraham returned unto his young men, and they rose up and went together to Beer-sheba; and Abraham dwelt at Beer-sheba.

And Sarah was a hundred and seven and twenty years old: these were the years of the life of Sarah. And Sarah died in Kirjath-arba; the same is Hebron in the land of Canaan: and Abraham came to mourn for Sarah, and to weep for her. And Abraham stood up from before his dead, and spoke unto the sons of Heth, saying,

"I am a stranger and a sojourner with you: give me a possession of a burying place with you, that I may bury my dead out of my sight."

And the children of Heth answered Abraham, saying unto him,

"Hear us, my lord: thou art a mighty prince among us: in the choice of our sepulchres bury thy dead; none of us shall withhold from thee his sepulchre, but that thou mayest bury thy dead."

And Abraham stood up, and bowed himself to the people of the land, even to the children of Heth. And he communed with them, saying,

"If it be your mind that I should bury my dead out of my sight; hear me, and intreat for me to Ephron the son of Zohar, that he may give me the cave of Machpelah, which he hath, which is in the end of his field; for as much money as it is worth he shall give it me for a possession of a burying place amongst you."

And Ephron dwelt among the children of Heth: and Ephron the Hittite answered Abraham in the audience of the children of Heth, even of all that went in at the gate of his city, saying,

"Nay, my lord, hear me: the field give I thee, and the cave that is therein, I give it thee; in the presence of the sons of my people give I it thee: bury thy dead."

And Abraham bowed down himself before the people of the land. And he spake unto Ephron in the audience of the people of the land, saying,

"But if thou wilt give it, I pray thee, hear me: I will give thee money for the field; take it of me, and I will bury my dead there."

And Ephron answered Abraham, saying unto him,

"My lord, hearken unto me: the land is worth four hundred shekels of silver; what is that betwixt me and thee? bury therefore thy dead."

And Abraham hearkened unto Ephron; and Abraham weighed to Ephron the silver, which he had named in the audience of the sons of Heth, four hundred shekels of silver, current money with the merchant. And the field of Ephron, which was in Machpelah, which was before Mamre, the field, and the cave which was therein, and all the trees that were in the field, that were in all the borders round about, were made sure unto Abraham for a possession in the presence of the children of Heth, before all that went in at the gate of his city. And after this, Abraham buried Sarah his wife in the cave of the field of Machpelah before Mamre: the same is Hebron in the land of Canaan. And the field, and the cave that is therein, were made sure unto Abraham for a possession of a burying place by the sons of Heth.

The Story of Isaac and Rebekah

And Abraham was old, and well stricken in age: and the Lord had blessed Abraham in all things. And Abraham said unto his eldest servant of his house, that ruled over all that he had, "Put, I pray thee, thy hand under my thigh: and I will make thee swear by the Lord, the God of heaven, and the God of the earth, that thou shalt not take a wife unto my son of the daughters of the Canaanites, among whom I dwell: but thou shalt go unto my country, and to my kindred, and take a wife unto my son Isaac."

And the servant said unto him, "Peradventure the woman will not be willing to follow me unto this land: must I needs bring thy son again unto the land from whence thou camest?"

And Abraham said unto him, "Beware thou that thou bring not my son thither again. The Lord God of heaven, which took me from my father's house, and from the land of my kindred, and which spoke unto me, and that swore unto me, saying, 'Unto thy seed will I give this land'; he shall send his angel before thee, and thou shalt take a wife unto my son from thence. And if the woman will not be willing to follow thee, then thou shalt be clear from this my oath: only bring not my son thither again."

And the servant put his hand under the thigh of Abraham his master, and swore to him concerning that matter. And the servant took ten camels of the camels of his master, and departed; for all the goods of his master were in his hand: and he arose, and went to Mesopotamia, unto the city of Nahor. And he made his camels to kneel down without the city by a well of water at the time of the evening, even the time that women go out to draw water.

And he said, "O Lord God of my master Abraham, I pray thee, send me good speed this day, and show kindness unto my master Abraham. Behold, I stand here by the well of water; and the daughters of the men of the city come out to draw water.

THE BOOK OF GENESIS

Let it come to pass that the damsel to whom I shall say, 'Let down thy pitcher, I pray thee, that I may drink'; and she shall say, 'Drink, and I will give thy camels drink also': let the same be she that thou hast appointed for thy servant Isaac; and thereby shall I know that thou hast showed kindness unto my master."

And it came to pass, before he had done speaking, that, behold, Rebekah came out, who was born to Bethuel, son of Milcah, the wife of Nahor, Abraham's brother, with her pitcher upon her shoulder. And the damsel was very fair to look upon, a virgin, neither had any man known her: and she went down to the well, and filled her pitcher, and came up.

And the servant ran to meet her, and said, "Let me, I pray thee, drink a little water of thy pitcher." And she said, "Drink, my lord"; and she hastened, and let down her pitcher upon her hand, and gave him drink. And when she had done giving him drink, she said, "I will draw water for thy camels also, until they have done drinking." And she hastened, and emptied her pitcher into the trough, and ran again unto the well to draw water, and drew for all his camels. And the man wondering at her held his peace, to wit whether the Lord had made his journey prosperous or not.

And it came to pass, as the camels had done drinking, that the man took a golden earring of half a shekel weight, and two bracelets for her hands of ten shekels' weight of gold; and said, "Whose daughter art thou? tell me, I pray thee: is there room in thy father's house for us to lodge in?"

And she said unto him, "I am the daughter of Bethuel the son of Milcah, which she bore unto Nahor." She said moreover unto him, "We have both straw and provender enough, and room to lodge in."

And the man bowed down his head, and worshipped the Lord. And he said, "Blessed be the Lord God of my master Abraham, who hath not left destitute my master of his mercy and his truth: I being in the way, the Lord led me to the house of my master's brethren."

And the damsel ran, and told them of her mother's house

THE BOOK OF GENESIS

these things. And Rebekah had a brother, and his name was Laban: and Laban ran out unto the man, unto the well. And it came to pass, when he saw the earring and bracelets upon his sister's hands, and when he heard the words of Rebekah his sister, saying, "Thus spoke the man unto me"; that he came unto the man; and, behold, he stood by the camels at the well.

And he said, "Come in, thou blessed of the Lord; wherefore standest thou without? for I have prepared the house, and room for the camels."

And the man came into the house; and he ungirded his camels, and gave straw and provender for the camels, and water to wash his feet, and the men's feet that were with him. And there was set meat before him to eat: but he said, "I will not eat until I have told mine errand." And he said, "Speak on."

And he said, "I am Abraham's servant. And the Lord hath blessed my master greatly; and he is become great: and he hath given him flocks, and herds, and silver, and gold, and menservants, and maidservants, and camels, and asses. And Sarah my master's wife bore a son to my master when she was old: and unto him hath he given all that he hath. And my master made me swear, saying, 'Thou shalt not take a wife to my son of the daughters of the Canaanites, in whose land I dwell: but thou shalt go unto my father's house, and to my kindred, and take a wife unto my son.' And I said unto my master, 'Peradventure the woman will not follow me.' And he said unto me, 'The Lord, before whom I walk, will send his angel with thee, and prosper thy way; and thou shalt take a wife for my son of my kindred, and of my father's house: then shalt thou be clear from this my oath, when thou comest to my kindred; and if they give not thee one, thou shalt be clear from my oath.' And I came this day unto the well, and said, 'O Lord God of my master Abraham, if now thou do prosper my way which I go, behold, I stand by the well of water; and it shall come to pass that when the virgin cometh forth to draw water, and I say to her, "Give me, I pray thee, a little water of thy pitcher to drink"; and she say to me, "Both drink thou, and I will also draw for thy camels": let the same be the woman whom the Lord hath appointed out for my master's son.' And before I had done speaking in mine heart, behold, Rebekah came forth with her pitcher on her shoulder; and she went down unto the well, and drew water: and I said unto her, 'Let me drink, I pray thee.' And she made haste, and let down her pitcher from her shoulder, and said, 'Drink, and I will give thy camels drink also': so I drank, and she made the camels drink also. And I asked her, and said, 'Whose daughter art thou?' And she said, 'The daughter of Bethuel, Nahor's son, whom Milcah bore unto him': and I put the earring upon her face, and the bracelets upon her hands. And I bowed down my head, and worshipped the Lord, and blessed the Lord God of my master Abraham, which had led me in the right way to take my master's brother's daughter unto his son. And now if ye will deal kindly and truly with my master, tell me: and if not, tell me; that I may turn to the right hand, or to the left."

Then Laban and Bethuel answered and said, "The thing proceedeth from the Lord: we cannot speak unto thee bad or good. Behold, Rebekah is before thee, take her, and go, and let her be thy master's son's wife, as the Lord hath spoken."

And it came to pass that, when Abraham's servant heard their words, he worshipped the Lord, bowing himself to the earth. And the servant brought forth jewels of silver, and jewels of gold, and raiment, and gave them to Rebekah: he gave also to her brother and to her mother precious things. And they did eat and drink, he and the men that were with him, and tarried all night; and they rose up in the morning, and he said, "Send me away unto my master."

And her brother and her mother said, "Let the damsel abide with us a few days, at the least ten; after that she shall go."

And he said unto them, "Hinder me not, seeing the Lord hath prospered my way; send me away that I may go to my master."

And they said, "We will call the damsel, and enquire at her mouth."

And they called Rebekah, and said unto her, "Wilt thou go with this man?"

THE BOOK OF GENESIS

And she said, "I will go."

And they sent away Rebekah their sister, and her nurse, and Abraham's servant, and his men. And they blessed Rebekah, and said unto her, "Thou art our sister, be thou the mother of thousands of millions, and let thy seed possess the gate of those which hate them."

And Rebekah arose, and her damsels, and they rode upon the camels, and followed the man: and the servant took Rebekah, and went his way.

And Isaac came from the way of the well Lahai-roi; for he dwelt in the south country. And Isaac went out to meditate in the field at the eventide: and he lifted up his eyes, and saw, and, behold, the camels were coming.

And Rebekah lifted up her eyes, and when she saw Isaac, she lighted off the camel. For she had said unto the servant, "What man is this that walketh in the field to meet us?" And the servant had said, "It is my master": therefore she took a veil, and covered herself.

And the servant told Isaac all things that he had done. And Isaac brought her into his mother Sarah's tent, and took Rebekah, and she became his wife; and he loved her: and Isaac was comforted after his mother's death.

And these are the days of the years of Abraham's life which he lived, a hundred threescore and fifteen years. Then Abraham gave up the ghost, and died in a good old age, an old man, and full of years; and was gathered to his people. And his sons Isaac and Ishmael buried him in the cave of Machpelah, in the field of Ephron the son of Zohar the Hittite, which is before Mamre: the field which Abraham purchased of the sons of Heth: there was Abraham buried, and Sarah his wife.

And Isaac was forty years old when he took Rebekah to wife, the daughter of Bethuel the Syrian of Padan-aram, the sister to Laban the Syrian. And Isaac intreated the Lord for his wife, because she was barren: and the Lord was intreated of him, and

THE BOOK OF GENESIS

Rebekah his wife conceived. And the children struggled together within her; and she said, "If it be so, why am I thus?"

And she went to enquire of the Lord.

And the Lord said unto her,

> "*Two nations are in thy womb,*
> *And two manner of people shall be separated from thy bowels;*
> *And the one people shall be stronger than the other people;*
> *And the elder shall serve the younger.*"

And when her days to be delivered were fulfilled, behold, there were twins in her womb. And the first came out red, all over like a hairy garment; and they called his name Esau. And after that came his brother out, and his hand took hold on Esau's heel; and his name was called Jacob: and Isaac was threescore years old when she bore them. And the boys grew: and Esau was a cunning hunter, a man of the field; and Jacob was a plain man, dwelling in tents.

And Isaac loved Esau, because he did eat of his venison: but Rebekah loved Jacob.

The Story of Jacob

And Jacob sod pottage: and Esau came from the field, and he was faint: and Esau said to Jacob, "Feed me, I pray thee, with that same red pottage; for I am faint" (therefore was his name called Edom).

And Jacob said, "Sell me this day thy birthright."

And Esau said, "Behold, I am at the point to die: and what profit shall this birthright do to me?"

And Jacob said, "Swear to me this day!"

And he swore unto him: and he sold his birthright unto Jacob. Then Jacob gave Esau bread and pottage of lentils; and he did eat and drink, and rose up, and went his way: thus Esau despised his birthright.

And Esau was forty years old when he took to wife Judith the daughter of Beeri the Hittite, and Bashemath the daughter

THE BOOK OF GENESIS

of Elon the Hittite: which were a grief of mind unto Isaac and to Rebekah.

And it came to pass that when Isaac was old, and his eyes were dim, so that he could not see, he called Esau his eldest son, and said unto him, "My son": and he said unto him, "Behold, here am I."

And he said, "Behold now, I am old, I know not the day of my death. Now therefore take, I pray thee, thy weapons, thy quiver and thy bow, and go out to the field, and take me some venison; and make me savoury meat, such as I love, and bring it to me, that I may eat; that my soul may bless thee before I die."

And Rebekah heard when Isaac spoke to Esau his son. And Esau went to the field to hunt for venison, and to bring it. And Rebekah spoke unto Jacob her son, saying,

"Behold, I heard thy father speak unto Esau thy brother, saying, 'Bring me venison, and make me savoury meat, that I may eat, and bless thee before the Lord before my death.' Now therefore, my son, obey my voice according to that which I command thee. Go now to the flock, and fetch me from thence two good kids of the goats; and I will make them savoury meat for thy father, such as he loveth: and thou shalt bring it to thy father, that he may eat, and that he may bless thee before his death."

And Jacob said to Rebekah his mother, "Behold, Esau my brother is a hairy man, and I am a smooth man. My father peradventure will feel me, and I shall seem to him as a deceiver; and I shall bring a curse upon me, and not a blessing."

And his mother said unto him, "Upon me be thy curse, my son: only obey my voice, and go fetch me them."

And he went, and fetched, and brought them to his mother; and his mother made savoury meat, such as his father loved. And Rebekah took goodly raiment of her eldest son Esau, which were with her in the house, and put them upon Jacob her younger son; and she put the skins of the kids of the goats upon his hands, and upon the smooth of his neck; and she gave the savoury meat and the bread, which she had prepared, into the hand of her son Jacob.

THE BOOK OF GENESIS

And he came unto his father, and said, "My father": and he said, "Here am I; who art thou, my son?"

And Jacob said unto his father, "I am Esau thy firstborn; I have done according as thou badest me: arise, I pray thee, sit and eat of my venison, that thy soul may bless me."

And Isaac said unto his son, "How is it that thou hast found it so quickly, my son?"

And he said, "Because the Lord thy God brought it to me."

And Isaac said unto Jacob, "Come near, I pray thee, that I may feel thee, my son, whether thou be my very son Esau or not."

And Jacob went near unto Isaac his father; and he felt him, and said, "The voice is Jacob's voice, but the hands are the hands of Esau."

And he discerned him not, because his hands were hairy, as his brother Esau's hands: so he blessed him. And he said, "Art thou my very son Esau?"

And he said, "I am."

And he said, "Bring it near to me, and I will eat of my son's venison, that my soul may bless thee."

And he brought it near to him, and he did eat: and he brought him wine, and he drank. And his father Isaac said unto him, "Come near now, and kiss me, my son."

And he came near, and kissed him: and he smelled the smell of his raiment, and blessed him, and said,

> "*See, the smell of my son*
> *Is as the smell of a field which the Lord hath blessed:*
> *Therefore God give thee of the dew of heaven,*
> *And the fatness of the earth,*
> *And plenty of corn and wine:*
> *Let people serve thee,*
> *And nations bow down to thee:*
> *Be lord over thy brethren,*
> *And let thy mother's sons bow down to thee:*
> *Cursed be every one that curseth thee,*
> *And blessed be he that blesseth thee.*"

THE BOOK OF GENESIS

And it came to pass, as soon as Isaac had made an end of blessing Jacob, and Jacob was yet scarce gone out from the presence of Isaac his father, that Esau his brother came in from his hunting. And he also had made savoury meat, and brought it unto his father, and said unto his father, "Let my father arise, and eat of his son's venison, that thy soul may bless me."

And Isaac his father said unto him, "Who art thou?"

And he said, "I am thy son, thy firstborn Esau."

And Isaac trembled very exceedingly, and said, "Who? where is he that hath taken venison, and brought it me, and I have eaten of all before thou camest, and have blessed him? yea, and he shall be blessed."

And when Esau heard the words of his father, he cried with a great and exceeding bitter cry, and said unto his father, "Bless me, even me also, O my father."

And he said, "Thy brother came with subtilty, and hath taken away thy blessing."

And he said, "Is not he rightly named Jacob? for he hath supplanted me these two times: he took away my birthright; and, behold, now he hath taken away my blessing." And he said, "Hast thou not reserved a blessing for me?"

And Isaac answered and said unto Esau,

"Behold, I have made him thy lord, and all his brethren have I given to him for servants; and with corn and wine have I sustained him: and what shall I do now unto thee, my son?"

And Esau said unto his father, "Hast thou but one blessing. my father? bless me, even me also, O my father."

And Esau lifted up his voice, and wept.

And Isaac his father answered and said unto him,

> *"Behold, thy dwelling shall be the fatness of the earth,*
> *And of the dew of heaven from above;*
> *And by thy sword shalt thou live,*
> *And shalt serve thy brother;*
> *And it shall come to pass when thou shalt have the dominion,*
> *That thou shalt break his yoke from off thy neck."*

THE BOOK OF GENESIS

And Esau hated Jacob because of the blessing wherewith his father blessed him: and Esau said in his heart, "The days of mourning for my father are at hand; then will I slay my brother Jacob."

And these words of Esau her elder son were told to Rebekah: and she sent and called Jacob her younger son, and said unto him, "Behold, thy brother Esau, as touching thee, doth comfort himself, purposing to kill thee. Now therefore, my son, obey my voice; and arise, flee thou to Laban my brother to Haran. And tarry with him a few days, until thy brother's fury turn away; until thy brother's anger turn away from thee, and he forget that which thou hast done to him. Then I will send, and fetch thee from thence: why should I be deprived also of you both in one day?"

And Rebekah said to Isaac, "I am weary of my life because of the daughters of Heth: If Jacob take a wife of the daughters of Heth, such as these which are of the daughters of the land, what good shall my life do me?"

And Isaac called Jacob, and blessed him, and charged him, and said unto him, "Thou shalt not take a wife of the daughters of Canaan. Arise, go to Padan-aram, to the house of Bethuel thy mother's father; and take thee a wife from thence of the daughters of Laban thy mother's brother. And God Almighty bless thee, and make thee fruitful, and multiply thee, that thou mayest be a multitude of people; and give thee the blessing of Abraham, to thee, and to thy seed with thee; that thou mayest inherit the land wherein thou art a stranger, which God gave unto Abraham."

And Jacob went out from Beer-sheba, and went toward Haran. And he lighted upon a certain place, and tarried there all night, because the sun was set; and he took of the stones of that place, and put them for his pillows, and lay down in that place to sleep. And he dreamed, and, behold, a ladder set up on the earth, and the top of it reached to heaven: and, behold, the angels of God ascending and descending on it. And, behold, the Lord stood above it, and said,

THE BOOK OF GENESIS

"I am the Lord God of Abraham thy father, and the God of Isaac: the land whereon thou liest, to thee will I give it, and to thy seed; and thy seed shall be as the dust of the earth, and thou shalt spread abroad to the west, and to the east, and to the north, and to the south: and in thee and in thy seed shall all the families of the earth be blessed. And, behold, I am with thee, and will keep thee in all places whither thou goest, and will bring thee again into this land; for I will not leave thee until I have done that which I have spoken to thee of."

And Jacob awaked out of his sleep, and he said, "Surely the Lord is in this place; and I knew it not."

And he was afraid, and said, "How dreadful is this place! this is none other but the house of God, and this is the gate of heaven."

And Jacob rose up early in the morning, and took the stone that he had put for his pillows, and set it up for a pillar, and poured oil upon the top of it. And he called the name of that place Beth-el: but the name of that city was called Luz at the first. And Jacob vowed a vow, saying, "If God will be with me, and will keep me in this way that I go, and will give me bread to eat, and raiment to put on, so that I come again to my father's house in peace; then shall the Lord be my God: and this stone, which I have set for a pillar, shall be God's house: and of all that thou shalt give me I will surely give the tenth unto thee."

Then Jacob went on his journey, and came into the land of the people of the east. And he looked, and beheld a well in the field, and, lo, there were three flocks of sheep lying by it; for out of that well they watered the flocks: and a great stone was upon the well's mouth. And thither were all the flocks gathered: and they rolled the stone from the well's mouth, and watered the sheep, and put the stone again upon the well's mouth in his place.

And Jacob said unto them, "My brethren, whence be ye?" And they said, "Of Haran are we."

And he said unto them, "Know ye Laban the son of Nahor?" And they said, "We know him."

THE BOOK OF GENESIS

And he said unto them, "Is he well?" And they said, "He is well: and, behold, Rachel his daughter cometh with the sheep."

And he said, "Lo, it is yet high day, neither is it time that the cattle should be gathered together: water ye the sheep, and go and feed them." And they said, "We cannot, until all the flocks be gathered together, and till they roll the stone from the well's mouth; then we water the sheep."

And while he yet spoke with them, Rachel came with her father's sheep: for she kept them. And it came to pass, when Jacob saw Rachel the daughter of Laban his mother's brother, and the sheep of Laban his mother's brother, that Jacob went near, and rolled the stone from the well's mouth, and watered the flock of Laban his mother's brother. And Jacob kissed Rachel, and lifted up his voice, and wept. And Jacob told Rachel that he was her father's brother, and that he was Rebekah's son: and she ran and told her father. And it came to pass, when Laban heard the tidings of Jacob his sister's son, that he ran to meet him, and embraced him, and kissed him, and brought him to his house. And he told Laban all these things. And Laban said to him, "Surely thou art my bone and my flesh." And he abode with him the space of a month.

And Laban said unto Jacob, "Because thou art my brother, shouldest thou therefore serve me for nought? tell me, what shall thy wages be?"

And Laban had two daughters: the name of the elder was Leah, and the name of the younger was Rachel. Leah was tender-eyed; but Rachel was beautiful and well favoured. And Jacob loved Rachel; and said, "I will serve thee seven years for Rachel thy younger daughter."

And Laban said, "It is better that I give her to thee than that I should give her to another man. Abide with me."

And Jacob served seven years for Rachel; and they seemed unto him but a few days, for the love he had to her. And Jacob said unto Laban, "Give me my wife, for my days are fulfilled, that I may go in unto her."

And Laban gathered together all the men of the place, and

THE BOOK OF GENESIS

made a feast. And it came to pass in the evening that he took Leah his daughter, and brought her to him; and he went in unto her. And Laban gave unto his daughter Leah Zilpah his maid for a handmaid.

And it came to pass that in the morning, behold, it was Leah: and he said to Laban, "What is this thou hast done unto me? did not I serve with thee for Rachel? wherefore then hast thou beguiled me?"

And Laban said, "It must not be so done in our country, to give the younger before the firstborn. Fulfil her week, and we will give thee this also for the service which thou shalt serve with me yet seven other years."

And Jacob did so, and fulfilled her week: and he gave him Rachel his daughter to wife also. And Laban gave to Rachel his daughter Bilhah his handmaid to be her maid. And he went in also unto Rachel, and he loved also Rachel more than Leah, and served with him yet seven other years.

And when the Lord saw that Leah was hated, he opened her womb: but Rachel was barren. And Leah conceived, and bore a son, and she called his name Reuben: for she said, "Surely the Lord hath looked upon my affliction; now therefore my husband will love me." And she conceived again, and bore a son; and said, "Because the Lord hath heard that I was hated, he hath therefore given me this son also": and she called his name Simeon. And she conceived again, and bore a son; and said, "Now this time will my husband be joined unto me, because I have borne him three sons": therefore was his name called Levi. And she conceived again, and bore a son: and she said, "Now will I praise the Lord": therefore she called his name Judah; and left bearing.

And when Rachel saw that she bore Jacob no children, Rachel envied her sister; and said unto Jacob, "Give me children, or else I die."

And Jacob's anger was kindled against Rachel: and he said, "Am I in God's stead, who hath withheld from thee the fruit of the womb?"

THE BOOK OF GENESIS

And she said, "Behold my maid Bilhah, go in unto her; and she shall bear upon my knees, that I may also have children by her."

And she gave him Bilhah her handmaid to wife: and Jacob went in unto her. And Bilhah conceived, and bore Jacob a son. And Rachel said, "God hath judged me, and hath also heard my voice, and hath given me a son": therefore called she his name Dan. And Bilhah Rachel's maid conceived again, and bore Jacob a second son. And Rachel said, "With great wrestlings have I wrestled with my sister, and I have prevailed": and she called his name Naphtali.

When Leah saw that she had left bearing, she took Zilpah her maid, and gave her Jacob to wife. And Zilpah Leah's maid bore Jacob a son. And Leah said, "A troop cometh": and she called his name Gad. And Zilpah Leah's maid bore Jacob a second son. And Leah said, "Happy am I, for the daughters will call me blessed": and she called his name Asher.

And Reuben went in the days of wheat harvest, and found mandrakes in the field, and brought them unto his mother Leah. Then Rachel said to Leah, "Give me, I pray thee, of thy son's mandrakes."

And she said unto her, "Is it a small matter that thou hast taken my husband? and wouldest thou take away my son's mandrakes also?"

And Rachel said, "Therefore he shall lie with thee to-night for thy son's mandrakes."

And Jacob came out of the field in the evening, and Leah went out to meet him, and said, "Thou must come in unto me; for surely I have hired thee with my son's mandrakes." And he lay with her that night.

And God hearkened unto Leah, and she conceived, and bore Jacob a fifth son. And Leah said, "God hath given me my hire, because I have given my maiden to my husband": and she called his name Issachar. And Leah conceived again, and bore Jacob the sixth son. And Leah said, "God hath endued me with a good dowry; now will my husband dwell with me, because I have

THE BOOK OF GENESIS

borne him six sons": and she called his name Zebulun. And afterwards she bore a daughter, and called her name Dinah.

And God remembered Rachel, and God hearkened to her, and opened her womb. And she conceived, and bore a son; and said, "God hath taken away my reproach": and she called his name Joseph; and said, "The Lord shall add to me another son."

And it came to pass, when Rachel had borne Joseph, that Jacob said unto Laban, "Send me away, that I may go unto mine own place, and to my country. Give me my wives and my children, for whom I have served thee, and let me go: for thou knowest my service which I have done thee."

And Laban said unto him, "I pray thee, if I have found favour in thine eyes, tarry: for I have learned by experience that the Lord hath blessed me for thy sake." And he said, "Appoint me thy wages, and I will give it."

And he said unto him, "Thou knowest how I have served thee, and how thy cattle was with me. For it was little which thou hadst before I came, and it is now increased unto a multitude; and the Lord hath blessed thee since my coming: and now when shall I provide for mine own house also?"

And he said, "What shall I give thee?"

And Jacob said, "Thou shalt not give me any thing: if thou wilt do this thing for me, I will again feed and keep thy flock. I will pass through all thy flock to-day, removing from thence all the speckled and spotted cattle, and all the brown cattle among the sheep, and the spotted and speckled among the goats: and of such shall be my hire. So shall my righteousness answer for me in time to come, when it shall come for my hire before thy face: every one that is not speckled and spotted among the goats, and brown among the sheep, that shall be counted stolen with me."

And Laban said, "Behold, I would it might be according to thy word."

And he removed that day the he-goats that were ringstreaked and spotted, and all the she-goats that were speckled and spotted, and every one that had some white in it, and all the brown

THE BOOK OF GENESIS

among the sheep, and gave them into the hand of his sons. And he set three days' journey betwixt himself and Jacob: and Jacob fed the rest of Laban's flocks.

And Jacob took him rods of green poplar, and of the hazel and chestnut tree; and peeled white strakes in them, and made the white appear which was in the rods. And he set the rods which he had peeled before the flocks in the gutters in the watering troughs when the flocks came to drink, that they should conceive when they came to drink. And the flocks conceived before the rods, and brought forth cattle ringstreaked, speckled, and spotted. And Jacob did separate the lambs, and set the faces of the flocks toward the ringstreaked, and all the brown in the flock of Laban; and he put his own flocks by themselves, and put them not unto Laban's cattle. And it came to pass, whensoever the stronger cattle did conceive, that Jacob laid the rods before the eyes of the cattle in the gutters, that they might conceive among the rods. But when the cattle were feeble, he put them not in: so the feebler were Laban's, and the stronger Jacob's. And the man increased exceedingly, and had much cattle, and maidservants, and menservants, and camels, and asses.

And he heard the words of Laban's sons, saying,

"Jacob hath taken away all that was our father's; and of that which was our father's hath he gotten all this glory."

And Jacob beheld the countenance of Laban and, behold, it was not toward him as before. And the Lord said unto Jacob,

"Return unto the land of thy fathers, and to thy kindred; and I will be with thee."

And Jacob sent and called Rachel and Leah to the field unto his flock and said unto them,

"I see your father's countenance, that it is not toward me as before; but the God of my father hath been with me. And ye know that with all my power I have served your father. And your father hath deceived me, and changed my wages ten times; but God suffered him not to hurt me. If he said thus, 'The speckled shall be thy wages'; then all the cattle bore speckled: and if he said thus, 'The ringstreaked shall be thy hire'; then bore all the

THE BOOK OF GENESIS

cattle ringstreaked. Thus God hath taken away the cattle of your father, and given them to me. And it came to pass at the time that the cattle conceived, that I lifted up mine eyes, and saw in a dream, and, behold, the rams which leaped upon the cattle were ringstreaked, speckled, and grisled. And the angel of God spoke unto me in a dream, saying, 'Jacob.' And I said, 'Here am I.' And he said, 'Lift up now thine eyes, and see, all the rams which leap upon the cattle are ringstreaked, speckled, and grisled: for I have seen all that Laban doeth unto thee. I am the God of Beth-el, where thou anointedst the pillar, and where thou vowedst a vow unto me: now arise, get thee out from this land, and return unto the land of thy kindred.'"

And Rachel and Leah answered and said unto him, "Is there yet any portion or inheritance for us in our father's house? Are we not counted of him strangers? for he hath sold us, and hath quite devoured also our money. For all the riches which God hath taken from our father, that is ours, and our children's: now then, whatsoever God hath said unto thee, do."

Then Jacob rose up, and set his sons and his wives upon camels; and he carried away all his cattle, and all his goods which he had gotten, the cattle of his getting, which he had gotten in Padan-aram, for to go to Isaac his father in the land of Canaan. And Laban went to shear his sheep: and Rachel had stolen the images that were her father's. And Jacob stole away unawares to Laban the Syrian, in that he told him not that he fled. So he fled with all that he had; and he rose up, and passed over the river, and set his face toward the mount Gilead.

And it was told Laban on the third day that Jacob was fled. And he took his brethren with him, and pursued after him seven days' journey; and they overtook him in the mount Gilead. And God came to Laban the Syrian in a dream by night, and said unto him, "Take heed that thou speak not to Jacob either good or bad."

Then Laban overtook Jacob. Now Jacob had pitched his tent in the mount: and Laban with his brethren pitched in the Mount of Gilead. And Laban said to Jacob,

THE BOOK OF GENESIS

"What hast thou done, that thou hast stolen away unawares to me, and carried away my daughters, as captives taken with the sword? Wherefore didst thou flee away secretly, and steal away from me; and didst not tell me, that I might have sent thee away with mirth, and with songs, with tabret, and with harp? And hast not suffered me to kiss my sons and my daughters? thou hast now done foolishly in so doing. It is in the power of my hand to do you hurt: but the God of your father spoke unto me yesternight, saying, 'Take thou heed that thou speak not to Jacob either good or bad.' And now, though thou wouldest needs be gone, because thou sore longedst after thy father's house, yet wherefore hast thou stolen my gods?"

And Jacob answered and said to Laban, "Because I was afraid: for I said, 'Peradventure thou wouldest take by force thy daughters from me.' With whomsoever thou findest thy gods, let him not live: before our brethren discern thou what is thine with me, and take it to thee." For Jacob knew not that Rachel had stolen them.

And Laban went into Jacob's tent, and into Leah's tent, and into the two maidservants' tents; but he found them not. Then went he out of Leah's tent, and entered into Rachel's tent. Now Rachel had taken the images, and put them in the camel's furniture, and sat upon them. And Laban searched all the tent, but found them not. And she said to her father, "Let it not displease my lord that I cannot rise up before thee; for the custom of women is upon me." And he searched, but found not the images.

And Jacob was wroth, and chid with Laban: and Jacob answered and said to Laban, "What is my trespass? what is my sin, that thou hast so hotly pursued after me? Whereas thou hast searched all my stuff, what hast thou found of all thy household stuff? set it here before my brethren and thy brethren, that they may judge betwixt us both. This twenty years have I been with thee; thy ewes and thy she-goats have not cast their young, and the rams of thy flock have I not eaten. That which was torn of beasts I brought not unto thee; I bore the loss of it; of my hand

THE BOOK OF GENESIS

didst thou require it, whether stolen by day, or stolen by night. Thus I was; in the day the drought consumed me, and the frost by night; and my sleep departed from mine eyes. Thus have I been twenty years in thy house; I served thee fourteen years for thy two daughters, and six years for thy cattle: and thou hast changed my wages ten times. Except the God of my father, the God of Abraham, and the fear of Isaac, had been with me, surely thou hadst sent me away now empty. God hath seen mine affliction and the labour of my hands, and rebuked thee yesternight."

And Laban answered and said unto Jacob, "These daughters are my daughters, and these children are my children, and these cattle are my cattle, and all that thou seest is mine: and what can I do this day unto these my daughters, or unto their children which they have borne? Now therefore come thou, let us make a covenant, I and thou; and let it be for a witness between me and thee."

And Jacob took a stone, and set it up for a pillar. And Jacob said unto his brethren, "Gather stones"; and they took stones, and made a heap: and they did eat there upon the heap. And Laban called it Jegar-sahadutha: but Jacob called it Galeed. And Laban said,

"This heap is a witness between me and thee this day." Therefore was the name of it called Galeed and Mizpah; for he said, "The Lord watch between me and thee, when we are absent one from another. If thou shalt afflict my daughters, or if thou shalt take other wives beside my daughters, no man is with us; see, God is witness betwixt me and thee."

And Laban said to Jacob,

"Behold this heap, and behold this pillar, which I have cast betwixt me and thee! This heap be witness, and this pillar be witness, that I will not pass over this heap to thee, and that thou shalt not pass over this heap and this pillar unto me, for harm. The God of Abraham, and the God of Nahor, the God of their father, judge betwixt us."

Then Jacob offered sacrifice upon the mount, and called his

brethren to eat bread: and they did eat bread, and tarried all night in the mount. And early in the morning Laban rose up, and kissed his sons and his daughters, and blessed them: and Laban departed, and returned unto his place.

And Jacob went on his way, and the angels of God met him. And when Jacob saw them, he said, "This is God's host": and he called the name of that place Mahanaim. And Jacob sent messengers before him to Esau his brother unto the land of Seir, the country of Edom. And he commanded them, saying, "Thus shall ye speak unto my lord Esau: 'Thy servant Jacob saith thus, "I have sojourned with Laban, and stayed there until now; and I have oxen, and asses, flocks, and menservants, and womenservants; and I have sent to tell my lord, that I may find grace in thy sight." ' "

And the messengers returned to Jacob, saying, "We came to thy brother Esau, and also he cometh to meet thee, and four hundred men with him."

Then Jacob was greatly afraid and distressed; and he divided the people that was with him, and the flocks, and herds, and the camels, into two bands; and said, "If Esau come to the one company, and smite it, then the other company which is left shall escape."

And Jacob said, "O God of my father Abraham, and God of my father Isaac, the Lord which saidst unto me, 'Return unto thy country, and to thy kindred, and I will deal well with thee!' I am not worthy of the least of all the mercies, and of all the truth, which thou hast showed unto thy servant; for with my staff I passed over this Jordan; and now I am become two bands. Deliver me, I pray thee, from the hand of my brother, from the hand of Esau: for I fear him, lest he will come and smite me, and the mother with the children. And thou saidst, 'I will surely do thee good, and make thy seed as the sand of the sea, which cannot be numbered for multitude.' "

And he lodged there that same night; and took of that which came to his hand a present for Esau his brother: two hundred she-goats, and twenty he-goats, two hundred ewes, and twenty rams, thirty milch camels with their colts, forty kine, and ten bulls, twenty she-asses, and ten foals. And he delivered them into the hand of his servants, every drove by themselves; and said unto his servants, "Pass over before me, and put a space betwixt drove and drove."

And he commanded the foremost, saying, "When Esau my brother meeteth thee, and asketh thee, saying, 'Whose art thou? and whither goest thou? and whose are these before thee?' then thou shalt say, 'They be thy servant Jacob's; it is a present sent unto my lord Esau: and, behold, also he is behind us.'"

And so commanded he the second, and the third, and all that followed the droves, saying, "On this manner shall ye speak unto Esau, when ye find him. And say ye moreover, 'Behold, thy servant Jacob is behind us.'" For he said, "I will appease him with the present that goeth before me, and afterward I will see his face; peradventure he will accept of me."

So went the present over before him: and himself lodged that night in the company. And he rose up that night, and took his two wives, and his two womenservants, and his eleven sons, and passed over the ford Jabbok. And he took them, and sent them over the brook, and sent over that he had.

And Jacob was left alone; and there wrestled a man with him until the breaking of the day. And when he saw that he prevailed not against him, he touched the hollow of his thigh; and the hollow of Jacob's thigh was out of joint, as he wrestled with him. And he said, "Let me go, for the day breaketh." And he said, "I will not let thee go, except thou bless me."

And he said unto him, "What is thy name?" And he said "Jacob." And he said, "Thy name shall be called no more Jacob, but Israel: for as a prince hast thou power with God and with men, and hast prevailed."

And Jacob asked him, and said, "Tell me, I pray thee, thy name." And he said, "Wherefore is it that thou dost ask after my name?" And he blessed him there.

And Jacob called the name of the place Peniel: "For I have seen God face to face, and my life is preserved." And as he passed over Penuel the sun rose upon him, and he halted upon his thigh. Therefore the children of Israel eat not of the sinew which shrank, which is upon the hollow of the thigh, unto this day: because he touched the hollow of Jacob's thigh in the sinew that shrank.

And Jacob lifted up his eyes, and looked, and, behold, Esau came, and with him four hundred men. And he divided the children unto Leah, and unto Rachel, and unto the two handmaids. And he put the handmaids and their children foremost, and Leah and her children after, and Rachel and Joseph hindermost. And he passed over before them, and bowed himself to the ground seven times, until he came near to his brother. And Esau ran to meet him, and embraced him, and fell on his neck, and kissed him: and they wept. And he lifted up his eyes, and saw the women and the children; and said, "Who are those with thee?" And he said, "The children which God hath graciously given thy servant."

Then the handmaidens came near, they and their children and they bowed themselves. And Leah also with her children came near, and bowed themselves: and after came Joseph near and Rachel, and they bowed themselves.

And he said, "What meanest thou by all this drove which I met?" And he said, "These are to find grace in the sight of my lord."

And Esau said, "I have enough, my brother; keep that thou hast unto thyself." And Jacob said, "Nay, I pray thee, if now I have found grace in thy sight, then receive my present at my hand: for therefore I have seen thy face, as though I had seen the face of God, and thou wast pleased with me. Take, I pray thee, my blessing that is brought to thee; because God hath dealt graciously with me, and because I have enough."

And he said, "Let us take our journey, and let us go, and I will go before thee."

And he said unto him, "My lord knoweth that the children are tender, and the flocks and herds with young are with me: and if men should overdrive them one day, all the flock will die. Let my lord, I pray thee, pass over before his servant: and I will

THE BOOK OF GENESIS

lead on softly, according as the cattle that goeth before me and the children be able to endure, until I come unto my lord unto Seir."

And Esau said, "Let me now leave with thee some of the folk that are with me." And he said, "What needeth it? let me find grace in the sight of my lord."

So Esau returned that day on his way unto Seir. And Jacob journeyed to Succoth, and built him a house, and made booths for his cattle: therefore the name of the place is called Succoth. And Jacob came to Shalem, a city of Shechem, which is in the land of Canaan, when he came from Padan-aram; and pitched his tent before the city. And he bought a parcel of a field, where he had spread his tent, at the hand of the children of Hamor, Shechem's father, for a hundred pieces of money. And he erected there an altar, and called it El-elohe-Israel.

And Dinah the daughter of Leah, which she bore unto Jacob, went out to see the daughters of the land. And when Shechem the son of Hamor the Hivite, prince of the country, saw her, he took her, and lay with her, and defiled her. And his soul cleaved unto Dinah the daughter of Jacob, and he loved the damsel, and spoke kindly unto the damsel. And Shechem spoke unto his father Hamor, saying, "Get me this damsel to wife."

And Jacob heard that he had defiled Dinah his daughter: now his sons were with his cattle in the field: and Jacob held his peace until they were come. And Hamor the father of Shechem went out unto Jacob to commune with him. And the sons of Jacob came out of the field when they heard it: and the men were grieved, and they were very wroth, because he had wrought folly in Israel in lying with Jacob's daughter; which thing ought not to be done. And Hamor communed with them, saying,

"The soul of my son Shechem longeth for your daughter: I pray you give her him to wife. And make ye marriages with us, and give your daughters unto us, and take our daughters unto you. And ye shall dwell with us: and the land shall be before you; dwell and trade ye therein, and get you possessions therein."

THE BOOK OF GENESIS

And Shechem said unto her father and unto her brethren, "Let me find grace in your eyes, and what ye shall say unto me I will give. Ask me never so much dowry and gift, and I will give according as ye shall say unto me: but give me the damsel to wife."

And the sons of Jacob answered Shechem and Hamor his father deceitfully, and said, because he had defiled Dinah their sister, "We cannot do this thing, to give our sister to one that is uncircumcised; for that were a reproach unto us. But in this will we consent unto you: if ye will be as we be, that every male of you be circumcised; then will we give our daughters unto you, and we will take your daughters to us, and we will dwell with you, and we will become one people. But if ye will not hearken unto us, to be circumcised; then will we take our daughter, and we will be gone."

And their words pleased Hamor, and Shechem Hamor's son. And the young man deferred not to do the thing, because he had delight in Jacob's daughter: and he was more honourable than all the house of his father.

And Hamor and Shechem his son came unto the gate of their city, and communed with the men of their city, saying,

"These men are peaceable with us; therefore let them dwell in the land, and trade therein; for the land, behold, it is large enough for them; let us take their daughters to us for wives, and let us give them our daughters. Only herein will the men consent unto us for to dwell with us, to be one people, if every male among us be circumcised, as they are circumcised. Shall not their cattle and their substance and every beast of theirs be ours? only let us consent unto them, and they will dwell with us."

And unto Hamor and unto Shechem his son hearkened all that went out of the gate of his city; and every male was circumcised, all that went out of the gate of his city. And it came to pass on the third day, when they were sore, that two of the sons of Jacob, Simeon and Levi, Dinah's brethren, took each man his sword, and came upon the city boldly, and slew all the males.

THE BOOK OF GENESIS

And they slew Hamor and Shechem his son with the edge of the sword, and took Dinah out of Shechem's house, and went out. The sons of Jacob came upon the slain, and spoiled the city, because they had defiled their sister. They took their sheep, and their oxen, and their asses, and that which was in the city, and that which was in the field, and all their wealth, and all their little ones, and their wives took they captive, and spoiled even all that was in the house.

And Jacob said to Simeon and Levi, "Ye have troubled me to make me to stink among the inhabitants of the land, among the Canaanites and the Perizzites: and I being few in number, they shall gather themselves together against me, and slay me; and I shall be destroyed, I and my house."

And they said, "Should he deal with our sister as with a harlot?"

And God said unto Jacob, "Arise, go up to Beth-el, and dwell there: and make there an altar unto God, that appeared unto thee when thou fleddest from the face of Esau thy brother."

Then Jacob said unto his household, and to all that were with him, "Put away the strange gods that are among you, and be clean, and change your garments: and let us arise, and go up to Beth-el; and I will make there an altar unto God, who answered me in the day of my distress, and was with me in the way which I went."

And they gave unto Jacob all the strange gods which were in their hand, and all their earrings which were in their ears; and Jacob hid them under the oak which was by Shechem. And they journeyed: and the terror of God was upon the cities that were round about them, and they did not pursue after the sons of Jacob.

So Jacob came to Luz, which is in the land of Canaan, that is, Beth-el, he and all the people that were with him. And he built there an altar, and called the place El-beth-el: because there God appeared unto him, when he fled from the face of his brother. But Deborah Rebekah's nurse died, and she was buried beneath

Beth-el under an oak: and the name of it was called Allon-bachuth.

And God appeared unto Jacob again, when he came out of Padan-aram, and blessed him. And God said unto him, "Thy name is Jacob: thy name shall not be called any more Jacob, but Israel shall be thy name": and he called his name Israel.

And God said unto him, "I am God Almighty: be fruitful and multiply; a nation and a company of nations shall be of thee, and kings shall come out of thy loins; and the land which I gave Abraham and Isaac, to thee I will give it, and to thy seed after thee will I give the land."

And God went up from him in the place where he talked with him. And Jacob set up a pillar in the place where he talked with him, even a pillar of stone: and he poured a drink offering thereon, and he poured oil thereon. And Jacob called the name of the place where God spoke with him, Beth-el.

And they journeyed from Beth-el; and there was but a little way to come to Ephrath: and Rachel travailed, and she had hard labour. And it came to pass, when she was in hard labour, that the midwife said unto her, "Fear not; thou shalt have this son also." And it came to pass, as her soul was in departing (for she died), that she called his name Ben-oni: but his father called him Benjamin. And Rachel died, and was buried in the way to Ephrath, which is Beth-lehem. And Jacob set a pillar upon her grave: that is the pillar of Rachel's grave unto this day.

And Israel journeyed, and spread his tent beyond the tower of Edar. And it came to pass, when Israel dwelt in that land, that Reuben went and lay with Bilhah his father's concubine: and Israel heard it.

And Jacob came unto Isaac his father unto Mamre, unto the city of Arbah, which is Hebron, where Abraham and Isaac sojourned. And the days of Isaac were a hundred and fourscore years. And Isaac gave up the ghost, and died, and was gathered unto his people, being old and full of days: and his sons Esau and Jacob buried him.

THE BOOK OF GENESIS

The Story of Joseph and His Brethren

Joseph, being seventeen years old, was feeding the flock with his brethren; and the lad was with the sons of Bilhah, and with the sons of Zilpah, his father's wives: and Joseph brought unto his father their evil report. Now Israel loved Joseph more than all his children, because he was the son of his old age: and he made him a coat of many colours. And when his brethren saw that their father loved him more than all his brethren, they hated him, and could not speak peaceably unto him. And Joseph dreamed a dream, and he told it his brethren: and they hated him yet the more. And he said unto them,

"Hear, I pray you, this dream which I have dreamed: for, behold, we were binding sheaves in the field, and, lo, my sheaf arose, and also stood upright; and, behold, your sheaves stood round about, and made obeisance to my sheaf."

And his brethren said to him, "Shalt thou indeed reign over us? or shalt thou indeed have dominion over us?"

And they hated him yet the more for his dreams, and for his words. And he dreamed yet another dream, and told it his brethren, and said,

"Behold, I have dreamed a dream more; and, behold, the sun and the moon and the eleven stars made obeisance to me."

And he told it to his father, and to his brethren: and his father rebuked him, and said unto him, "What is this dream that thou hast dreamed? Shall I and thy mother and thy brethren indeed come to bow down ourselves to thee to the earth?"

And his brethren envied him; but his father observed the saying. And his brethren went to feed their father's flock in Shechem.

And Israel said unto Joseph, "Do not thy brethren feed the flock in Shechem? come, and I will send thee unto them." And he said to him, "Here am I."

And he said to him, "Go, I pray thee, see whether it be well with thy brethren, and well with the flocks; and bring me word again."

So he sent him out of the vale of Hebron, and he came to

THE BOOK OF GENESIS

Shechem. And a certain man found him, and, behold, he was wandering in the field: and the man asked him, saying, "What seekest thou?" And he said, "I seek my brethren: tell me, I pray thee, where they feed their flocks." And the man said, "They are departed hence; for I heard them say, 'Let us go to Dothan.'"

And Joseph went after his brethren, and found them in Dothan. And when they saw him afar off, even before he came near unto them, they conspired against him to slay him. And they said one to another, "Behold, this dreamer cometh. Come now therefore, and let us slay him, and cast him into some pit, and we will say, 'Some evil beast hath devoured him': and we shall see what will become of his dreams."

And Reuben heard it, and he delivered him out of their hands; and said, "Let us not kill him." And Reuben said unto them, "Shed no blood, but cast him into this pit that is in the wilderness, and lay no hand upon him"; that he might rid him out of their hands, to deliver him to his father again.

And it came to pass, when Joseph was come unto his brethren, that they stripped Joseph out of his coat, his coat of many colours that was on him; and they took him, and cast him into a pit; and the pit was empty, there was no water in it. And they sat down to eat bread: and they lifted up their eyes and looked, and, behold, a company of Ishmaelites came from Gilead with their camels bearing spicery and balm and myrrh, going to carry it down to Egypt. And Judah said unto his brethren,

"What profit is it if we slay our brother, and conceal his blood? Come and let us sell him to the Ishmaelites, and let not our hand be upon him; for he is our brother and our flesh."

And his brethren were content. Then there passed by Midianites merchantmen; and they drew and lifted up Joseph out of the pit, and sold Joseph to the Ishmaelites for twenty pieces of silver: and they brought Joseph into Egypt.

And Reuben returned unto the pit; and, behold, Joseph was not in the pit; and he rent his clothes. And he returned unto his brethren, and said, "The child is not; and I, whither shall I go?"

THE BOOK OF GENESIS

And they took Joseph's coat, and killed a kid of the goats, and dipped the coat in the blood; and they sent the coat of many colours, and they brought it to their father; and said, "This have we found: know now whether it be thy son's coat or no."

And he knew it, and said, "It is my son's coat; an evil beast hath devoured him; Joseph is without doubt rent in pieces."

And Jacob rent his clothes, and put sackcloth upon his loins, and mourned for his son many days. And all his sons and all his daughters rose up to comfort him; but he refused to be comforted; and he said, "For I will go down into the grave unto my son mourning." Thus his father wept for him.

And Joseph was brought down to Egypt; and Potiphar, an officer of Pharaoh, captain of the guard, an Egyptian, bought him of the hands of the Ishmaelites, which had brought him down thither. And the Lord was with Joseph, and he was a prosperous man; and he was in the house of his master the Egyptian. And his master saw that the Lord was with him, and that the Lord made all that he did to prosper in his hand. And Joseph found grace in his sight, and he served him: and he made him overseer over his house, and all that he had he put into his hand. And it came to pass from the time that he had made him overseer in his house, and over all that he had, that the Lord blessed the Egyptian's house for Joseph's sake; and the blessing of the Lord was upon all that he had in the house, and in the field. And he left all that he had in Joseph's hand; and he knew not ought he had, save the bread which he did eat. And Joseph was a goodly person, and well favoured.

And it came to pass after these things, that his master's wife cast her eyes upon Joseph; and she said, "Lie with me." But he refused, and said unto his master's wife, "Behold, my master wotteth not what is with me in the house, and he hath committed all that he hath to my hand! There is none greater in this house than I; neither hath he kept back any thing from me but thee, because thou art his wife: how then can I do this great wickedness, and sin against God?"

THE BOOK OF GENESIS

And it came to pass, as she spoke to Joseph day by day, that he hearkened not unto her, to lie by her, or to be with her.

And it came to pass about this time, that Joseph went into the house to do his business; and there was none of the men of the house there within. And she caught him by his garment, saying, "Lie with me": and he left his garment in her hand, and fled, and got him out.

And it came to pass, when she saw that he had left his garment in her hand, and was fled forth, that she called unto the men of her house, and spoke unto them, saying, "See, he hath brought in a Hebrew unto us to mock us; he came in unto me to lie with me, and I cried with a loud voice; and it came to pass, when he heard that I lifted up my voice and cried, that he left his garment with me, and fled, and got him out."

And she laid up his garment by her, until his lord came home. And she spoke unto him according to these words, saying, "The Hebrew servant, which thou hast brought unto us, came in unto me to mock me; and it came to pass, as I lifted up my voice and cried, that he left his garment with me, and fled out."

And it came to pass, when his master heard the words of his wife, which she spoke unto him, saying, "After this manner did thy servant to me"; that his wrath was kindled. And Joseph's master took him, and put him into the prison, a place where the king's prisoners were bound: and he was there in the prison.

But the Lord was with Joseph, and showed him mercy, and gave him favour in the sight of the keeper of the prison. And the keeper of the prison committed to Joseph's hand all the prisoners that were in the prison; and whatsoever they did there, he was the doer of it. The keeper of the prison looked not to any thing that was under his hand; because the Lord was with him, and that which he did, the Lord made it to prosper.

And it came to pass after these things that the butler of the king of Egypt and his baker had offended their lord the king of Egypt. And Pharaoh was wroth against two of his officers, against the chief of the butlers, and against the chief of the bakers. And he put them in ward in the house of the captain of the

THE BOOK OF GENESIS

guard, into the prison, the place where Joseph was bound. And the captain of the guard charged Joseph with them, and he served them: and they continued a season in ward.

And they dreamed a dream both of them, each man his dream in one night, each man according to the interpretation of his dream, the butler and the baker of the king of Egypt, which were bound in the prison. And Joseph came in unto them in the morning, and looked upon them, and, behold, they were sad. And he asked Pharaoh's officers that were with him in the ward of his lord's house, saying, "Wherefore look ye so sadly to-day?"

And they said unto him, "We have dreamed a dream, and there is no interpreter of it."

And Joseph said unto them, "Do not interpretations belong to God? tell me them, I pray you."

And the chief butler told his dream to Joseph, and said to him, "In my dream, behold, a vine was before me; and in the vine were three branches: and it was as though it budded, and her blossoms shot forth; and the clusters thereof brought forth ripe grapes; and Pharaoh's cup was in my hand: and I took the grapes, and pressed them into Pharaoh's cup, and I gave the cup into Pharaoh's hand."

And Joseph said unto him, "This is the interpretation of it. The three branches are three days. Yet within three days shall Pharaoh lift up thine head, and restore thee unto thy place: and thou shalt deliver Pharaoh's cup into his hand, after the former manner when thou wast his butler. But think on me when it shall be well with thee, and show kindness, I pray thee, unto me, and make mention of me unto Pharaoh, and bring me out of this house: for indeed I was stolen away out of the land of the Hebrews: and here also have I done nothing that they should put me into the dungeon."

When the chief baker saw that the interpretation was good, he said unto Joseph, "I also was in my dream, and, behold, I had three white baskets on my head: and in the uppermost basket there was of all manner of bakemeats for Pharaoh; and the birds did eat them out of the basket upon my head."

THE BOOK OF GENESIS

And Joseph answered and said, "This is the interpretation thereof. The three baskets are three days. Yet within three days shall Pharaoh lift up thy head from off thee, and shall hang thee on a tree; and the birds shall eat thy flesh from off thee."

And it came to pass the third day, which was Pharaoh's birthday, that he made a feast unto all his servants: and he lifted up the head of the chief butler and of the chief baker among his servants. And he restored the chief butler unto his butlership again; and he gave the cup into Pharaoh's hand. But he hanged the chief baker: as Joseph had interpreted to them. Yet did not the chief butler remember Joseph, but forgot him.

And it came to pass at the end of two full years that Pharaoh dreamed: and, behold, he stood by the river. And, behold, there came up out of the river seven well favoured kine and fatfleshed; and they fed in a meadow. And, behold, seven other kine came up after them out of the river, ill favoured and leanfleshed; and stood by the other kine upon the brink of the river. And the ill favoured and leanfleshed kine did eat up the seven well favoured and fat kine. So Pharaoh awoke.

And he slept and dreamed the second time: and, behold, seven ears of corn came up upon one stalk, rank and good. And, behold, seven thin ears and blasted with the east wind sprung up after them. And the seven thin ears devoured the seven rank and full ears. And Pharaoh awoke, and, behold, it was a dream.

And it came to pass in the morning that his spirit was troubled; and he sent and called for all the magicians of Egypt, and all the wise men thereof: and Pharaoh told them his dream; but there was none that could interpret them unto Pharaoh. Then spoke the chief butler unto Pharaoh, saying,

"I do remember my faults this day. Pharaoh was wroth with his servants, and put me in ward in the captain of the guard's house, both me and the chief baker: and we dreamed a dream in one night, I and he; we dreamed each man according to the interpretation of his dream. And there was there with us a young man, a Hebrew, servant to the captain of the guard; and we told him, and he interpreted to us our dreams; to each man ac-

THE BOOK OF GENESIS

cording to his dream he did interpret. And it came to pass, as he interpreted to us, so it was; me he restored unto mine office, and him he hanged."

Then Pharaoh sent and called Joseph, and they brought him hastily out of the dungeon: and he shaved himself, and changed his raiment, and came in unto Pharaoh. And Pharaoh said unto Joseph, "I have dreamed a dream, and there is none that can interpret it: and I have heard say of thee that thou canst understand a dream to interpret it."

And Joseph answered Pharaoh, saying, "It is not in me: God shall give Pharaoh an answer of peace."

And Pharaoh said unto Joseph, "In my dream, behold, I stood upon the bank of the river. And, behold, there came up out of the river seven kine, fatfleshed and well favoured; and they fed in a meadow. And, behold, seven other kine came up after them, poor and very ill favoured and leanfleshed, such as I never saw in all the land of Egypt for badness. And the lean and the ill favoured kine did eat up the first seven fat kine; and when they had eaten them up, it could not be known that they had eaten them; but they were still ill favoured, as at the beginning. So I awoke. And I saw in my dream, and, behold, seven ears came up in one stalk, full and good. And, behold, seven ears withered, thin, and blasted with the east wind, sprung up after them. And the thin ears devoured the seven good ears: and I told this unto the magicians; but there was none that could declare it to me."

And Joseph said unto Pharaoh,

"The dream of Pharaoh is one. God hath showed Pharaoh what he is about to do. The seven good kine are seven years; and the seven good ears are seven years: the dream is one. And the seven thin and ill favoured kine that came up after them are seven years; and the seven empty ears blasted with the east wind shall be seven years of famine. This is the thing which I have spoken unto Pharaoh. What God is about to do he showeth unto Pharaoh. Behold, there come seven years of great plenty throughout all the land of Egypt, and there shall arise after them seven

THE BOOK OF GENESIS

years of famine; and all the plenty shall be forgotten in the land of Egypt; and the famine shall consume the land. And the plenty shall not be known in the land by reason of that famine following; for it shall be very grievous. And for that the dream was doubled unto Pharaoh twice; it is because the thing is established by God, and God will shortly bring it to pass. Now therefore let Pharaoh look out a man discreet and wise, and set him over the land of Egypt. Let Pharaoh do this, and let him appoint officers over the land, and take up the fifth part of the land of Egypt in the seven plenteous years. And let them gather all the food of those good years that come, and lay up corn under the hand of Pharaoh, and let them keep food in the cities. And that food shall be for store to the land against the seven years of famine, which shall be in the land of Egypt; that the land perish not through the famine."

And the thing was good in the eyes of Pharaoh, and in the eyes of all his servants. And Pharaoh said unto his servants, "Can we find such a one as this is, a man in whom the Spirit of God is?"

And Pharaoh said unto Joseph, "Forasmuch as God hath showed thee all this, there is none so discreet and wise as thou art. Thou shalt be over my house, and according unto thy word shall all my people be ruled: only in the throne will I be greater than thou." And Pharaoh said unto Joseph, "See, I have set thee over all the land of Egypt."

And Pharaoh took off his ring from his hand, and put it upon Joseph's hand, and arrayed him in vestures of fine linen, and put a gold chain about his neck; and he made him to ride in the second chariot which he had; and they cried before him, "Bow the knee": and he made him ruler over all the land of Egypt.

And Pharaoh said unto Joseph, "I am Pharaoh, and without thee shall no man lift his hand or foot in all the land of Egypt." And Pharaoh called Joseph's name Zaphnath-paaneah; and he gave him to wife Asenath the daughter of Poti-pherah priest of On. And Joseph went out over all the land of Egypt.

And Joseph was thirty years old when he stood before Pharaoh king of Egypt. And Joseph went out from the presence of Pharaoh, and went throughout all the land of Egypt. And in the seven plenteous years the earth brought forth by handfuls. And he gathered up all the food of the seven years, which were in the land of Egypt, and laid up the food in the cities: the food of the field, which was round about every city, laid he up in the same. And Joseph gathered corn as the sand of the sea, very much, until he left numbering; for it was without number. And unto Joseph were born two sons before the years of famine came, which Asenath the daughter of Poti-pherah priest of On bore unto him. And Joseph called the name of the firstborn Manasseh. "For God," said he, "hath made me forget all my toil, and all my father's house." And the name of the second called he Ephraim. "For God hath caused me to be fruitful in the land of my affliction."

And the seven years of plenteousness, that was in the land of Egypt, were ended. And the seven years of dearth began to come, according as Joseph had said: and the dearth was in all lands; but in all the land of Egypt there was bread. And when all the land of Egypt was famished, the people cried to Pharaoh for bread: and Pharaoh said unto all the Egyptians, "Go unto Joseph; what he saith to you, do." And the famine was over all the face of the earth. And Joseph opened all the storehouses, and sold unto the Egyptians; and the famine waxed sore in the land of Egypt. And all countries came into Egypt to Joseph for to buy corn; because that the famine was so sore in all lands.

Now when Jacob saw that there was corn in Egypt, Jacob said unto his sons, "Why do ye look one upon another?" And he said, "Behold, I have heard that there is corn in Egypt: get you down thither, and buy for us from thence; that we may live, and not die."

And Joseph's ten brethren went down to buy corn in Egypt. But Benjamin, Joseph's brother, Jacob sent not with his brethren; for he said, "Lest peradventure mischief befall him." And the sons of Israel came to buy corn among those that came: for the famine was in the land of Canaan. And Joseph was the governor over the land, and he it was that sold to all the people of the

THE BOOK OF GENESIS

land: and Joseph's brethren came, and bowed down themselves before him with their faces to the earth.

And Joseph saw his brethren, and he knew them, but made himself strange unto them, and spoke roughly unto them; and he said unto them, "Whence come ye?" And they said, "From the land of Canaan to buy food."

And Joseph knew his brethren, but they knew not him. And Joseph remembered the dreams which he dreamed of them, and said unto them, "Ye are spies; to see the nakedness of the land ye are come."

And they said unto him, "Nay, my lord, but to buy food are thy servants come. Thy servants are twelve brethren, the sons of one man in the land of Canaan; and, behold, the youngest is this day with our father, and one is not."

And Joseph said unto them, "That is it that I spoke unto you, saying, 'Ye are spies.' Hereby ye shall be proved: by the life of Pharaoh ye shall not go forth hence, except your youngest brother come hither. Send one of you, and let him fetch your brother, and ye shall be kept in prison, that your words may be proved, whether there be any truth in you: or else by the life of Pharaoh surely ye are spies." And he put them all together into ward three days.

And Joseph said unto them the third day, "This do, and live; for I fear God. If ye be true men, let one of your brethren be bound in the house of your prison: go ye, carry corn for the famine of your houses: but bring your youngest brother unto me; so shall your words be verified, and ye shall not die."

And he turned himself about from them, and wept; and returned to them again, and communed with them, and took from them Simeon, and bound him before their eyes.

Then Joseph commanded to fill their sacks with corn, and to restore every man's money into his sack, and to give them provision for the way: and thus did he unto them. And they laded their asses with the corn, and departed thence. And as one of them opened his sack to give his ass provender in the inn, he espied his money; for, behold, it was in his sack's mouth. And he said unto his brethren, "My money is restored; and, lo, it is even in my sack": and their heart failed them, and they were afraid, saying one to another, "What is this that God hath done unto us?"

And they came unto Jacob their father unto the land of Canaan, and told him all that befell unto them.

And Jacob their father said unto them, "Me have ye bereaved of my children: Joseph is not, and Simeon is not, and ye will take Benjamin away: all these things are against me."

And Reuben spoke unto his father, saying, "Slay my two sons, if I bring him not to thee: deliver him into my hand, and I will bring him to thee again."

And he said, "My son shall not go down with you; for his brother is dead, and he is left alone: if mischief befall him by the way in the which ye go, then shall ye bring down my gray hairs with sorrow to the grave."

And the famine was sore in the land. And it came to pass, when they had eaten up the corn which they had brought out of Egypt, their father said unto them, "Go again, buy us a little food."

And Judah spoke unto him, saying, "The man did solemnly protest unto us, saying, 'Ye shall not see my face, except your brother be with you.' If thou wilt send our brother with us, we will go down and buy thee food. But if thou wilt not send him, we will not go down: for the man said unto us, 'Ye shall not see my face, except your brother be with you.'"

And Israel said, "Wherefore dealt ye so ill with me, as to tell the man whether ye had yet a brother?"

And they said, "The man asked us straitly of our state, and of our kindred, saying, 'Is your father yet alive? have ye another brother?' and we told him according to the tenor of these words: could we certainly know that he would say, 'Bring your brother down'?"

And Judah said unto Israel his father, "Send the lad with me, and we will arise and go; that we may live, and not die, both we, and thou, and also our little ones. I will be surety for him; of my hand shalt thou require him: if I bring him not unto thee, and set him before thee, then let me bear the blame for ever: for except we had lingered, surely now we had returned this second time."

And their father Israel said unto them, "If it must be so now, do this; take of the best fruits in the land in your vessels, and carry down the man a present, a little balm, and a little honey, spices, and myrrh, nuts, and almonds. And take double money in your hand; and the money that was brought again in the mouth of your sacks, carry it again in your hand; peradventure it was an oversight. Take also your brother, and arise, go again unto the man. And God Almighty give you mercy before the man, that he may send away your other brother, and Benjamin. If I be bereaved of my children, I am bereaved."

And the men took that present, and they took double money in their hand, and Benjamin; and rose up, and went down to Egypt, and stood before Joseph. And when Joseph saw Benjamin with them, he said to the ruler of his house,

"Bring these men home, and slay, and make ready; for these men shall dine with me at noon."

And the man did as Joseph bade; and the man brought the men into Joseph's house. And the men were afraid, because they were brought into Joseph's house; and they said,

"Because of the money that was returned in our sacks at the first time are we brought in; that he may seek occasion against us, and fall upon us, and take us for bondmen, and our asses."

And they came near to the steward of Joseph's house, and they communed with him at the door of the house, and said,

"O sir, we came indeed down at the first time to buy food; and it came to pass, when we came to the inn, that we opened our sacks, and, behold, every man's money was in the mouth of his sack, our money in full weight: and we have brought it again in our hand. And other money have we brought down in our hands to buy food: we cannot tell who put our money in our sacks."

And he said, "Peace be to you, fear not: your God, and the

God of your father, hath given you treasure in your sacks: I had your money."

And he brought Simeon out unto them. And the man brought the men into Joseph's house, and gave them water, and they washed their feet; and he gave their asses provender. And they made ready the present against Joseph came at noon: for they heard that they should eat bread there. And when Joseph came home, they brought him the present which was in their hand into the house, and bowed themselves to him to the earth.

And he asked them of their welfare, and said, "Is your father well, the old man of whom ye spoke? Is he yet alive?"

And they answered, "Thy servant our father is in good health, he is yet alive." And they bowed down their heads, and made obeisance.

And he lifted up his eyes, and saw his brother Benjamin, his mother's son, and said, "Is this your younger brother, of whom ye spoke unto me?" And he said, "God be gracious unto thee, my son."

And Joseph made haste; for his bowels did yearn upon his brother: and he sought where to weep; and he entered into his chamber, and wept there. And he washed his face, and went out, and refrained himself and said, "Set on bread." And they set on for him by himself, and for them by themselves, and for the Egyptians, which did eat with him, by themselves: because the Egyptians might not eat bread with the Hebrews; for that is an abomination unto the Egyptians. And they sat before him, the firstborn according to his birthright, and the youngest according to his youth: and the men marvelled one at another. And he took and sent messes unto them from before him: but Benjamin's mess was five times so much as any of theirs. And they drank, and were merry with him.

And he commanded the steward of his house, saying, "Fill the men's sacks with food, as much as they can carry, and put every man's money in his sack's mouth. And put my cup, the silver cup, in the sack's mouth of the youngest, and his corn money." And he did according to the word that Joseph had spoken.

THE BOOK OF GENESIS

As soon as the morning was light, the men were sent away, they and their asses. And when they were gone out of the city, and not yet far off, Joseph said unto his steward, "Up, follow after the men; and when thou dost overtake them, say unto them, 'Wherefore have ye rewarded evil for good? Is not this it in which my lord drinketh, and whereby indeed he divineth? ye have done evil in so doing.'"

And he overtook them, and he spoke unto them these same words. And they said unto him, "Wherefore saith my lord these words? God forbid that thy servants should do according to this thing. Behold, the money, which we found in our sacks' mouths, we brought again unto thee out of the land of Canaan: how then should we steal out of thy lord's house silver or gold? With whomsoever of thy servants it be found, both let him die, and we also will be my lord's bondmen."

And he said, "Now also let it be according unto your words: he with whom it is found shall be my servant; and ye shall be blameless."

Then they speedily took down every man his sack to the ground, and opened every man his sack. And he searched, and began at the eldest, and left at the youngest: and the cup was found in Benjamin's sack. Then they rent their clothes, and laded every man his ass, and returned to the city. And Judah and his brethren came to Joseph's house; for he was yet there: and they fell before him on the ground.

And Joseph said unto them, "What deed is this that ye have done? wot ye not that such a man as I can certainly divine?"

And Judah said, "What shall we say unto my lord? what shall we speak? or how shall we clear ourselves? God hath found out the iniquity of thy servants: behold, we are my lord's servants, both we, and he also with whom the cup is found."

And he said, "God forbid that I should do so: but the man in whose hand the cup is found, he shall be my servant; and as for you, get you up in peace unto your father."

Then Judah came near unto him, and said, "Oh my lord, let thy servant, I pray thee, speak a word in my lord's ears, and let not thine anger burn against thy servant: for thou art even as Pharaoh. My lord asked his servants, saying, 'Have ye a father, or a brother?' And we said unto my lord, 'We have a father, an old man, and a child of his old age, a little one; and his brother is dead, and he alone is left of his mother, and his father loveth him.' And thou saidst unto thy servants, 'Bring him down unto me, that I may set mine eyes upon him.' And we said unto my lord, 'The lad cannot leave his father: for if he should leave his father, his father would die.' And thou saidst unto thy servants, 'Except your youngest brother come down with you, ye shall see my face no more.' And it came to pass when we came up unto thy servant my father, we told him the words of my lord. And our father said, 'Go again, and buy us a little food.' And we said, 'We cannot go down: if our youngest brother be with us, then will we go down: for we may not see the man's face, except our youngest brother be with us.' And thy servant my father said unto us, 'Ye know that my wife bore me two sons; and the one went out from me, and I said, "Surely he is torn in pieces"; and I saw him not since: and if ye take this also from me, and mischief befall him, ye shall bring down my gray hairs with sorrow to the grave.' Now therefore when I come to thy servant my father, and the lad be not with us; seeing that his life is bound up in the lad's life; it shall come to pass, when he seeth that the lad is not with us, that he will die: and thy servants shall bring down the gray hairs of thy servant our father with sorrow to the grave. For thy servant became surety for the lad unto my father, saying, 'If I bring him not unto thee, then I shall bear the blame to my father for ever.' Now therefore, I pray thee, let thy servant abide instead of the lad a bondman to my lord; and let the lad go up with his brethren. For how shall I go up to my father, and the lad be not with me? lest peradventure I see the evil that shall come on my father."

Then Joseph could not refrain himself before all them that stood by him; and he cried, "Cause every man to go out from me." And there stood no man with him, while Joseph made himself known unto his brethren. And he wept aloud: and the Egyptians

THE BOOK OF GENESIS

and the house of Pharaoh heard. And Joseph said unto his brethren,

"I am Joseph; doth my father yet live?"

And his brethren could not answer him; for they were troubled at his presence. And Joseph said unto his brethren,

"Come near to me, I pray you." And they came near. And he said,

"I am Joseph your brother, whom ye sold into Egypt. Now therefore be not grieved, nor angry with yourselves, that ye sold me hither: for God did send me before you to preserve life. For these two years hath the famine been in the land: and yet there are five years, in the which there shall neither be earing nor harvest. And God sent me before you to preserve you a posterity in the earth, and to save your lives by a great deliverance. So now it was not you that sent me hither, but God: and he hath made me a father to Pharaoh, and lord of all his house, and a ruler throughout all the land of Egypt. Haste ye, and go up to my father, and say unto him, 'Thus saith thy son Joseph, "God hath made me lord of all Egypt: come down unto me, tarry not: and thou shalt dwell in the land of Goshen, and thou shalt be near unto me, thou, and thy children, and thy children's children, and thy flocks, and thy herds, and all thou hast: and there will I nourish thee; for yet there are five years of famine; lest thou, and thy household, and all that thou hast, come to poverty."' And, behold, your eyes see, and the eyes of my brother Benjamin, that it is my mouth that speaketh unto you. And ye shall tell my father of all my glory in Egypt, and of all that ye have seen; and ye shall haste and bring down my father hither."

And he fell upon his brother Benjamin's neck, and wept; and Benjamin wept upon his neck. Moreover he kissed all his brethren, and wept upon them: and after that his brethren talked with him. To all of them he gave each man changes of raiment; but to Benjamin he gave three hundred pieces of silver, and five changes of raiment. And to his father he sent after this manner; ten asses laden with the good things of Egypt, and ten she-asses laden with corn and bread and meat for his father by the way.

THE BOOK OF GENESIS

So he sent his brethren away, and they departed: and he said unto them,

"See that ye fall not out by the way."

And they went up out of Egypt, and came into the land of Canaan unto Jacob their father, and told him, saying,

"Joseph is yet alive, and he is governor over all the land of Egypt."

And Jacob's heart fainted, for he believed them not. And they told him all the words of Joseph, which he had said unto them: and when he saw the wagons which Joseph had sent to carry him, the spirit of Jacob their father revived. And Israel said,

"It is enough; Joseph my son is yet alive: I will go and see him before I die."

And they took their cattle, and their goods, which they had gotten in the land of Canaan, and came into Egypt, Jacob, and all his seed with him: his sons, and his sons' sons with him, his daughters, and his sons' daughters, and all his seed brought he with him into Egypt.

And he sent Judah before him unto Joseph, to direct his face unto Goshen; and they came into the land of Goshen. And Joseph made ready his chariot, and went up to meet Israel his father, to Goshen, and presented himself unto him; and he fell on his neck, and wept on his neck a good while. And Israel said unto Joseph, "Now let me die, since I have seen thy face, because thou art yet alive."

And Israel dwelt in the land of Egypt, in the country of Goshen; and they had possessions therein, and grew, and multiplied exceedingly. And Jacob lived in the land of Egypt seventeen years: so the whole age of Jacob was a hundred forty and seven years. And the time drew nigh that Israel must die: and he called his son Joseph, and said unto him, "If now I have found grace in thy sight, put, I pray thee, thy hand under my thigh, and deal kindly and truly with me; bury me not, I pray thee, in Egypt. But I will lie with my fathers, and thou shalt carry me out of Egypt, and bury me in their burying place."

THE BOOK OF GENESIS

And he said, "I will do as thou hast said." And he said, "Swear unto me." And he swore unto him.

And Jacob called unto his sons, and said, "Gather yourselves together, that I may tell you that which shall befall you in the last days.

"Gather yourselves together, and hear, ye sons of Jacob;
And hearken unto Israel your father.

Reuben, thou art my firstborn,
My might, and the beginning of my strength,
The excellency of dignity, and the excellency of power:
Unstable as water, thou shalt not excel;
Because thou wentest up to thy father's bed;
Then defiledst thou it: he went up to my couch.

Simeon and Levi are brethren;
Instruments of cruelty are in their habitations.
O my soul, come not thou into their secret;
Unto their assembly, mine honour, be not thou united:
For in their anger they slew a man,
And in their selfwill they digged down a wall.
Cursed be their anger, for it was fierce;
And their wrath, for it was cruel:
I will divide them in Jacob,
And scatter them in Israel.

Judah, thou art he whom thy brethren shall praise:
Thy hand shall be in the neck of thine enemies;
Thy father's children shall bow down before thee.
Judah is a lion's whelp:
From the prey, my son, thou art gone up:
He stooped down, he couched as a lion,
And as an old lion; who shall rouse him up?
The sceptre shall not depart from Judah,
Nor a lawgiver from between his feet,
Until Shiloh come; and unto him shall the gathering of the
    people be.

THE BOOK OF GENESIS

Binding his foal unto the vine,
And his ass's colt unto the choice vine;
He washed his garments in wine,
And his clothes in the blood of grapes:
His eyes shall be red with wine,
And his teeth white with milk.

Zebulun shall dwell at the haven of the sea;
And he shall be for a haven of ships;
And his border shall be unto Zidon.

Issachar is a strong ass
Couching down between two burdens:
And he saw that rest was good,
And the land that it was pleasant;
And bowed his shoulder to bear,
And became a servant unto tribute.

Dan shall judge his people,
As one of the tribes of Israel.
Dan shall be a serpent by the way,
An adder in the path,
That biteth the horse's heels,
So that his rider shall fall backward.

Gad, a troop shall overcome him:
But he shall overcome at the last.

Out of Asher his bread shall be fat,
And he shall yield royal dainties.

Naphtali is a hind let loose:
He giveth goodly words.

Joseph is a fruitful bough,
Even a fruitful bough by a well;
Whose branches run over the wall:
The archers have sorely grieved him,
And shot at him, and hated him:
But his bow abode in strength,

THE BOOK OF GENESIS

And the arms of his hands were made strong
By the hands of the mighty God of Jacob
(From thence is the shepherd, the stone of Israel):
Even by the God of thy father, who shall help thee;
And by the Almighty, who shall bless thee
With blessings of heaven above,
Blessings of the deep that lieth under,
Blessings of the breasts, and of the womb:
The blessings of thy father have prevailed
Above the blessings of my progenitors
Unto the utmost bound of the everlasting hills:
They shall be on the head of Joseph,
And on the crown of the head of him that was separate
    from his brethren.

Benjamin shall ravin as a wolf:
In the morning he shall devour the prey,
And at night he shall divide the spoil."

All these are the twelve tribes of Israel: and this is it that their father spoke unto them, and blessed them; every one according to his blessing he blessed them. And he charged them, and said unto them,

"I am to be gathered unto my people: bury me with my fathers in the cave that is in the field of Ephron the Hittite, in the cave that is in the field of Machpelah, which is before Mamre, in the land of Canaan, which Abraham bought with the field of Ephron the Hittite for a possession of a burying place. There they buried Abraham and Sarah his wife; there they buried Isaac and Rebekah his wife; and there I buried Leah. The purchase of the field and of the cave that is therein was from the children of Heth."

And when Jacob had made an end of commanding his sons, he gathered up his feet into the bed, and yielded up the ghost, and was gathered unto his people.

And Joseph fell upon his father's face, and wept upon him, and kissed him. And Joseph commanded his servants the physi-

THE BOOK OF GENESIS

cians to embalm his father: and the physicians embalmed Israel. And forty days were fulfilled for him; for so are fulfilled the days of those which are embalmed: and the Egyptians mourned for him threescore and ten days.

And Joseph went up to bury his father: and with him went up all the servants of Pharaoh, the elders of his house, and all the elders of the land of Egypt, and all the house of Joseph, and his brethren, and his father's house: only their little ones, and their flocks, and their herds, they left in the land of Goshen. And his sons did unto him according as he commanded them: for his sons carried him into the land of Canaan, and buried him in the cave of the field of Machpelah, which Abraham bought with the field for a possession of a burying place of Ephron the Hittite, before Mamre. And Joseph returned into Egypt, he, and his brethren, and all that went up with him to bury his father, after he had buried his father.

And Joseph dwelt in Egypt, he, and his father's house: and Joseph lived a hundred and ten years. And Joseph saw Ephraim's children of the third generation: the children also of Machir the son of Manasseh were brought up upon Joseph's knees. And Joseph said unto his brethren, "I die: and God will surely visit you, and bring you out of this land unto the land which he swore to Abraham, to Isaac, and to Jacob." And Joseph took an oath of the children of Israel, saying, "God will surely visit you, and ye shall carry up my bones from hence." So Joseph died, being a hundred and ten years old: and they embalmed him, and he was put in a coffin in Egypt.

THE BOOK OF EXODUS

Throughout the Hexateuch and indeed all the historical books of the Old Testament, the enclosed snatches of poetry are much older than the surrounding narrative. Frequently they are fragments of poems now otherwise totally lost, but occasionally also they are complete in themselves, such as the heroic "Song of Moses" which certainly goes back as far as the twelfth century. For us to-day the main interest in Exodus lies in the personality of Moses and in the narrative of the escape from Egypt; for the Jews, however, even more important was the elaborate system of legislation attributed to their great lawgiver. Much of this was probably derived from Egyptian and Babylonian codes, in which earlier analogues for the Ten Commandments and many other items have been found; much of it was also unquestionably later than the time of Moses. While retaining abundant savage elements, Jewish legislation was on the whole remarkably enlightened and humane. The treatment of slaves, euphemistically rendered "servants" in the King James translation, was actually better than that accorded them in the United States in the first half of the nineteenth century. There were many attempts to regulate trade so as to secure fair dealing, and "usury"—by which was meant the taking of any interest on loans—was strictly forbidden. The divorce laws were more liberal than in modern England, and in specified cases women as well as men were permitted to take advantage of them. Hospitality to aliens was enjoined, and charity to widows and orphans; there were also numerous laws that aimed to safeguard the rights of the poor and to prevent the rise of a landed aristocracy.

The Escape from Egypt

NOW THERE AROSE up a new king over Egypt, which knew not Joseph. And he said unto his people, "Behold, the people of the children of Israel are more and mightier than we. Come on, let us deal wisely with them; lest they multiply, and it come to pass that, when there falleth out any war, they join also unto our enemies, and fight against us, and so get them up out of the land."

Therefore they did set over them taskmasters to afflict them with their burdens. And they built for Pharaoh treasure cities, Pithom and Rameses. But the more they afflicted them, the more they multiplied and grew. And they were grieved because of the children of Israel. And the Egyptians made the children of Israel to serve with rigour: and they made their lives bitter with hard bondage, in mortar, and in brick, and in all manner of service in the field: all their service, wherein they made them serve, was with rigour.

And the king of Egypt spoke to the Hebrew midwives, of which the name of the one was Shiphrah, and the name of the other Puah: and he said, "When ye do the office of a midwife to the Hebrew women, and see them upon the stools; if it be a son, then ye shall kill him: but if it be a daughter, then she shall live."

But the midwives feared God, and did not as the king of Egypt commanded them, but saved the men children alive.

And the king of Egypt called for the midwives, and said unto them, "Why have ye done this thing, and have saved the men children alive?"

THE BOOK OF EXODUS

And the midwives said unto Pharaoh, "Because the Hebrew women are not as the Egyptian women; for they are lively, and are delivered ere the midwives come in unto them."

Therefore God dealt well with the midwives: and the people multiplied, and waxed very mighty. And it came to pass, because the midwives feared God, that he made them houses.

And Pharaoh charged all his people, saying, "Every son that is born ye shall cast into the river, and every daughter ye shall save alive."

And there went a man of the house of Levi, and took to wife a daughter of Levi. And the woman conceived, and bore a son; and when she saw him that he was a goodly child, she hid him three months. And when she could not longer hide him, she took for him an ark of bulrushes, and daubed it with slime and with pitch, and put the child therein; and she laid it in the flags by the river's brink. And his sister stood afar off, to wit what would be done to him.

And the daughter of Pharaoh came down to wash herself at the river; and her maidens walked along by the river's side; and when she saw the ark among the flags, she sent her maid to fetch it. And when she had opened it, she saw the child: and, behold, the babe wept. And she had compassion on him, and said, "This is one of the Hebrews' children."

Then said his sister to Pharaoh's daughter, "Shall I go and call to thee a nurse of the Hebrew women, that she may nurse the child for thee?"

And Pharaoh's daughter said to her, "Go!"

And the maid went and called the child's mother.

And Pharaoh's daughter said unto her, "Take this child away, and nurse it for me, and I will give thee thy wages."

And the woman took the child, and nursed it. And the child grew, and she brought him unto Pharaoh's daughter, and he became her son. And she called his name Moses; and she said, "Because I drew him out of the water."

And it came to pass in those days, when Moses was grown, that he went out unto his brethren, and looked on their burdens;

THE BOOK OF EXODUS

and he spied an Egyptian smiting an Hebrew, one of his brethren. And he looked this way and that way, and when he saw that there was no man, he slew the Egyptian, and hid him in the sand. And when he went out the second day, behold, two men of the Hebrews strove together: and he said to him that did the wrong, "Wherefore smitest thou thy fellow?" And he said, "Who made thee a prince and a judge over us? intendest thou to kill me, as thou killedst the Egyptian?" And Moses feared, and said, "Surely this thing is known."

Now when Pharaoh heard this thing, he sought to slay Moses. But Moses fled from the face of Pharaoh, and dwelt in the land of Midian: and he sat down by a well.

Now the priest of Midian had seven daughters: and they came and drew water, and filled the troughs to water their father's flock. And the shepherds came and drove them away: but Moses stood up and helped them, and watered their flock. And when they came to Reuel their father, he said, "How is it that ye are come so soon to-day?"

And they said, "An Egyptian delivered us out of the hand of the shepherds, and also drew water enough for us, and watered the flock."

And he said unto his daughters, "And where is he? why is it that ye have left the man? call him, that he may eat bread."

And Moses was content to dwell with the man: and he gave Moses Zipporah his daughter. And she bore him a son, and he called his name Gershom: for he said, "I have been a stranger in a strange land."

And it came to pass in process of time that the king of Egypt died: and the children of Israel sighed by reason of the bondage, and they cried, and their cry came up unto God by reason of the bondage. And God heard their groaning, and God remembered his covenant with Abraham, with Isaac, and with Jacob. And God looked upon the children of Israel, and God had respect unto them.

Now Moses kept the flock of Jethro his father-in-law, the priest of Midian: and he led the flock to the backside of the desert, and

THE BOOK OF EXODUS

came to the mountain of God, even to Horeb. And the angel of the Lord appeared unto him in a flame of fire out of the midst of a bush: and he looked, and, behold, the bush burned with fire, and the bush was not consumed. And Moses said,

"I will now turn aside, and see this great sight, why the bush is not burnt."

And when the Lord saw that he turned aside to see, God called unto him out of the midst of the bush, and said,

"Moses, Moses."

And he said, "Here am I."

And he said, "Draw not nigh hither: put off thy shoes from off thy feet, for the place whereon thou standest is holy ground." Moreover he said, "I am the God of thy father, the God of Abraham, the God of Isaac, and the God of Jacob." And Moses hid his face; for he was afraid to look upon God. And the Lord said,

"I have surely seen the affliction of my people which are in Egypt, and have heard their cry by reason of their taskmasters; for I know their sorrows. And I am come down to deliver them out of the hand of the Egyptians, and to bring them up out of that land unto a good land and a large, unto a land flowing with milk and honey; unto the place of the Canaanites, and the Hittites, and the Amorites, and the Perizzites, and the Hivites, and the Jebusites. Now therefore, behold, the cry of the children of Israel is come unto me: and I have also seen the oppression wherewith the Egyptians oppress them. Come now therefore, and I will send thee unto Pharaoh, that thou mayest bring forth my people the children of Israel out of Egypt."

And Moses said unto God, "Who am I, that I should go unto Pharaoh, and that I should bring forth the children of Israel out of Egypt?"

And he said, "Certainly I will be with thee; and this shall be a token unto thee, that I have sent thee. When thou hast brought forth the people out of Egypt, ye shall serve God upon this mountain."

And Moses said unto God, "Behold, when I come unto the children of Israel, and shall say unto them, 'The God of your

THE BOOK OF EXODUS

fathers hath sent me unto you'; and they shall say to me, 'What is his name?' what shall I say unto them?"

And God said unto Moses, "I AM THAT I AM": and he said, "Thus shalt thou say unto the children of Israel, I AM hath sent me unto you." And God said moreover unto Moses, "Thus shalt thou say unto the children of Israel, 'The Lord God of your fathers, the God of Abraham, the God of Isaac, and the God of Jacob, hath sent me unto you.' And they shall hearken to thy voice: and thou shalt come, thou and the elders of Israel, unto the king of Egypt, and ye shall say unto him, 'The Lord God of the Hebrews hath met with us: and now let us go, we beseech thee, three days' journey into the wilderness, that we may sacrifice to the Lord our God.' And I am sure that the king of Egypt will not let you go, no, not by a mighty hand. And I will stretch out my hand, and smite Egypt with all my wonders which I will do in the midst thereof: and after that he will let you go. And I will give this people favour in the sight of the Egyptians: and it shall come to pass that, when ye go, ye shall not go empty: but every woman shall borrow of her neighbour, and of her that sojourneth in her house, jewels of silver, and jewels of gold, and raiment: and ye shall put them upon your sons, and upon your daughters; and ye shall spoil the Egyptians."

And Moses answered and said, "But, behold, they will not believe me, nor hearken unto my voice: for they will say, 'The Lord hath not appeared unto thee.'"

And the Lord said unto him, "What is that in thine hand?"

And he said, "A rod."

And he said, "Cast it on the ground." And he cast it on the ground, and it became a serpent; and Moses fled from before it.

And the Lord said unto Moses, "Put forth thine hand, and take it by the tail." And he put forth his hand, and caught it, and it became a rod in his hand.

And the Lord said furthermore unto him, "Put now thine hand into thy bosom." And he put his hand into his bosom: and when he took it out, behold, his hand was leprous as snow.

And he said, "Put thine hand into thy bosom again." And he

THE BOOK OF EXODUS

put his hand into his bosom again; and plucked it out of his bosom, and, behold, it was turned again as his other flesh.

"And it shall come to pass, if they will not believe thee, neither hearken to the voice of the first sign, that they will believe the voice of the latter sign. And it shall come to pass, if they will not believe also these two signs, neither hearken unto thy voice, that thou shalt take of the water of the river, and pour it upon the dry land: and the water which thou takest out of the river shall become blood upon the dry land."

And Moses said unto the Lord, "O my Lord, I am not eloquent, neither heretofore, nor since thou hast spoken unto thy servant: but I am slow of speech, and of a slow tongue."

And the Lord said unto him, "Who hath made man's mouth? or who maketh the dumb, or deaf, or the seeing, or the blind? have not I the Lord? Now therefore go, and I will be with thy mouth, and teach thee what thou shalt say."

And he said, "O my Lord, send, I pray thee, by the hand of him whom thou wilt send."

And the anger of the Lord was kindled against Moses, and he said, "Is not Aaron the Levite thy brother? I know that he can speak well. And also, behold, he cometh forth to meet thee: and when he seeth thee, he will be glad in his heart. And thou shalt speak unto him, and put words in his mouth: and I will be with thy mouth, and with his mouth, and will teach you what ye shall do. And he shall be thy spokesman unto the people: and he shall be, even he shall be to thee instead of a mouth, and thou shalt be to him instead of God. And thou shalt take this rod in thine hand, wherewith thou shalt do signs."

And Moses went and returned to Jethro his father-in-law, and said unto him, "Let me go, I pray thee, and return unto my brethren which are in Egypt, and see whether they be yet alive."

And Jethro said to Moses, "Go in peace."

And the Lord said unto Moses in Midian, "Go, return into Egypt: for all the men are dead which sought thy life."

And Moses took his wife and his sons, and set them upon an

THE BOOK OF EXODUS

ass, and he returned to the land of Egypt: and Moses took the rod of God in his hand. And Moses and Aaron went and gathered together all the elders of the children of Israel; and Aaron spoke all the words which the Lord had spoken unto Moses, and did the signs in the sight of the people. And the people believed; and when they heard that the Lord had visited the children of Israel, and that he had looked upon their affliction, then they bowed their heads and worshipped.

And afterward Moses and Aaron went in, and told Pharaoh, "Thus saith the Lord God of Israel, 'Let my people go, that they may hold a feast unto me in the wilderness.'"

And Pharaoh said, "Who is the Lord, that I should obey his voice to let Israel go? I know not the Lord, neither will I let Israel go."

And they said, "The God of the Hebrews hath met with us: let us go, we pray thee, three days' journey into the desert, and sacrifice unto the Lord our God; lest he fall upon us with pestilence, or with the sword."

And the king of Egypt said unto them, "Wherefore do ye, Moses and Aaron, let the people from their works? get you unto your burdens."

And Pharaoh commanded the same day the taskmasters of the people, and their officers, saying, "Ye shall no more give the people straw to make brick, as heretofore: let them go and gather straw for themselves. And the tale of the bricks, which they did make heretofore, ye shall lay upon them; ye shall not diminish ought thereof: for they be idle; therefore they cry, saying, 'Let us go and sacrifice to our God.' Let there more work be laid upon the men, that they may labour therein; and let them not regard vain words."

And the taskmasters of the people went out, and their officers, and they spoke to the people, saying, "Thus saith Pharaoh, 'I will not give you straw. Go ye, get you straw where ye can find it: yet not ought of your work shall be diminished.'"

So the people were scattered abroad throughout all the land

THE BOOK OF EXODUS

of Egypt to gather stubble instead of straw. And the taskmasters hastened them, saying, "Fulfil your works, your daily tasks, as when there was straw."

And the officers of the children of Israel, which Pharaoh's taskmasters had set over them, were beaten, and demanded, "Wherefore have ye not fulfilled your task in making brick both yesterday and to-day, as heretofore?"

Then the officers of the children of Israel came and cried unto Pharaoh, saying, "Wherefore dealest thou thus with thy servants? There is no straw given unto thy servants, and they say to us, 'Make brick': and, behold, thy servants are beaten; but the fault is in thine own people."

But he said, "Ye are idle, ye are idle: therefore ye say, 'Let us go and do sacrifice to the Lord.' Go therefore now, and work; for there shall no straw be given you, yet shall ye deliver the tale of bricks."

And the officers of the children of Israel did see that they were in evil case, after it was said, "Ye shall not minish ought from your bricks of your daily task."

And they met Moses and Aaron, who stood in the way, as they came forth from Pharaoh; and they said unto them, "The Lord look upon you, and judge; because ye have made our savour to be abhorred in the eyes of Pharaoh, and in the eyes of his servants, to put a sword in their hand to slay us."

And Moses returned unto the Lord, and said, "Lord, wherefore hast thou so evil entreated this people? why is it that thou hast sent me? For since I came to Pharaoh to speak in thy name, he hath done evil to this people; neither hast thou delivered thy people at all."

And God spoke unto Moses, and said unto him, "I am the Lord; and I appeared unto Abraham, unto Isaac, and unto Jacob, by the name of God Almighty, but by my name JEHOVAH was I not known to them. And I have also established my covenant with them, to give them the land of Canaan, the land of their pilgrimage, wherein they were strangers. And I have also heard the groaning of the children of Israel, whom the Egyptians keep

THE BOOK OF EXODUS

in bondage; and I have remembered my covenant. Wherefore say unto the children of Israel, 'I am the Lord, and I will bring you out from under the burdens of the Egyptians, and I will rid you out of their bondage, and I will redeem you with a stretched out arm, and with great judgments; and I will take you to me for a people, and I will be to you a God; and ye shall know that I am the Lord your God, which bringeth you out from under the burdens of the Egyptians. And I will bring you in unto the land, concerning the which I did swear to give it to Abraham, to Isaac, and to Jacob; and I will give it you for an heritage: I am the Lord.'"

And Moses spoke so unto the children of Israel: but they hearkened not unto Moses for anguish of spirit, and for cruel bondage.

And the Lord said unto Moses, "See, I have made thee a god to Pharaoh: and Aaron thy brother shall be thy prophet. Thou shalt speak all that I command thee: and Aaron thy brother shall speak unto Pharaoh, that he send the children of Israel out of his land. And I will harden Pharaoh's heart, and multiply my signs and my wonders in the land of Egypt. But Pharaoh shall not hearken unto you, that I may lay my hand upon Egypt, and bring forth mine armies, and my people the children of Israel, out of the land of Egypt by great judgments. And the Egyptians shall know that I am the Lord, when I stretch forth mine hand upon Egypt, and bring out the children of Israel from among them."

(And Moses was fourscore years old, and Aaron fourscore and three years old, when they spoke unto Pharaoh.)

And the Lord spoke unto Moses and unto Aaron, saying, "When Pharaoh shall speak unto you, saying, 'Show a miracle for you'; then thou shalt say unto Aaron, 'Take thy rod, and cast it before Pharaoh,' and it shall become a serpent."

And Moses and Aaron went in unto Pharaoh, and they did so as the Lord had commanded: and Aaron cast down his rod before Pharaoh, and before his servants, and it became a serpent. Then Pharaoh also called the wise men and the sorcerers: now the magicians of Egypt, they also did in like manner with their enchantments. For they cast down every man his rod, and they

THE BOOK OF EXODUS

became serpents: but Aaron's rod swallowed up their rods. And he hardened Pharaoh's heart, that he hearkened not unto them; as the Lord had said.

And the Lord spoke unto Moses, "Say unto Aaron, 'Take thy rod, and stretch out thine hand upon the waters of Egypt, upon their streams, upon their rivers, and upon their ponds, and upon all their pools of water, that they may become blood; and that there may be blood throughout all the land of Egypt, both in vessels of wood, and in vessels of stone.'"

And Moses and Aaron did so, as the Lord commanded; and he lifted up the rod, and smote the waters that were in the river, in the sight of Pharaoh, and in the sight of his servants; and all the waters that were in the river were turned to blood. And the fish that was in the river died; and the river stank, and the Egyptians could not drink of the water of the river; and there was blood throughout all the land of Egypt. And the magicians of Egypt did so with their enchantments: and Pharaoh's heart was hardened, neither did he hearken unto them; as the Lord had said. And Pharaoh turned and went into his house, neither did he set his heart to this also. And all the Egyptians digged round about the river for water to drink; for they could not drink of the water of the river. And seven days were fulfilled, after that the Lord had smitten the river.

And the Lord spoke unto Moses, "Say unto Aaron, 'Stretch forth thine hand with thy rod over the streams, over the rivers, and over the ponds, and cause frogs to come up upon the land of Egypt.'"

And Aaron stretched out his hand over the waters of Egypt; and the frogs came up, and covered the land of Egypt. And the magicians did so with their enchantments, and brought up frogs upon the land of Egypt.

Then Pharaoh called for Moses and Aaron, and said, "Intreat the Lord, that he may take away the frogs from me, and from my people; and I will let the people go, that they may do sacrifice unto the Lord."

And Moses said unto Pharaoh, "Glory over me: when shall I

THE BOOK OF EXODUS

intreat for thee, and for thy servants, and for thy people, to destroy the frogs from thee and thy houses, that they may remain in the river only?"

And he said, "To-morrow."

And he said, "Be it according to thy word: that thou mayest know that there is none like unto the Lord our God. And the frogs shall depart from thee, and from thy houses, and from thy servants, and from thy people; they shall remain in the river only."

And Moses and Aaron went out from Pharaoh: and Moses cried unto the Lord because of the frogs which he had brought against Pharaoh. And the Lord did according to the word of Moses; and the frogs died out of the houses, out of the villages, and out of the fields. And they gathered them together upon heaps: and the land stank. But when Pharaoh saw that there was respite, he hardened his heart, and hearkened not unto them; as the Lord had said.

And the Lord said unto Moses, "Say unto Aaron, 'Stretch out thy rod, and smite the dust of the land, that it may become lice throughout all the land of Egypt.'"

And they did so; for Aaron stretched out his hand with his rod, and smote the dust of the earth, and it became lice in man, and in beast; all the dust of the land became lice throughout all the land of Egypt. And the magicians did so with their enchantments to bring forth lice, but they could not: so there were lice upon man, and upon beast. Then the magicians said unto Pharaoh, "This is the finger of God": and Pharaoh's heart was hardened, and he hearkened not unto them; as the Lord had said.

And the Lord said unto Moses,

"Rise up early in the morning, and stand before Pharaoh; lo, he cometh forth to the water; and say unto him, 'Thus saith the Lord, "Let my people go, that they may serve me. Else, if thou wilt not let my people go, behold, I will send swarms of flies upon thee, and upon thy servants, and upon thy people, and into thy houses: and the houses of the Egyptians shall be full of swarms of flies, and also the ground whereon they are. And I will sever in that day the land of Goshen, in which my people dwell, that no swarms of flies shall be there; to the end thou mayest know that I am the Lord in the midst of the earth. And I will put a division between my people and thy people: to-morrow shall this sign be.'"

And the Lord did so; and there came a grievous swarm of flies into the house of Pharaoh, and into his servants' houses, and into all the land of Egypt: the land was corrupted by reason of the swarm of flies.

And Pharaoh called for Moses and for Aaron, and said, "Go ye, sacrifice to your God in the land."

And Moses said, "It is not meet so to do; for we shall sacrifice the abomination of the Egyptians to the Lord our God: lo, shall we sacrifice the abomination of the Egyptians before their eyes, and will they not stone us? We will go three days' journey into the wilderness, and sacrifice to the Lord our God, as he shall command us."

And Pharaoh said, "I will let you go, that ye may sacrifice to the Lord your God in the wilderness; only ye shall not go very far away: intreat for me."

And Moses said, "Behold, I go out from thee, and I will intreat the Lord that the swarms of flies may depart from Pharaoh, from his servants, and from his people, to-morrow: but let not Pharaoh deal deceitfully any more in not letting the people go to sacrifice to the Lord."

And Moses went out from Pharaoh, and intreated the Lord. And the Lord did according to the word of Moses; and he removed the swarms of flies from Pharaoh, from his servants, and from his people; there remained not one. And Pharaoh hardened his heart at this time also, neither would he let the people go.

Then the Lord said unto Moses, "Go in unto Pharaoh, and tell him, 'Thus saith the Lord God of the Hebrews, "Let my people go, that they may serve me." For if thou refuse to let them go, and wilt hold them still, behold, the hand of the Lord is upon thy cattle which is in the field, upon the horses, upon the asses, upon the camels, upon the oxen, and upon the sheep: there shall be a very grievous murrain. And the Lord shall sever between

THE BOOK OF EXODUS

the cattle of Israel and the cattle of Egypt: and there shall nothing die of all that is the children's of Israel.'"

And the Lord appointed a set time, saying, "To-morrow the Lord shall do this thing in the land."

And the Lord did that thing on the morrow, and all the cattle of Egypt died: but of the cattle of the children of Israel died not one. And Pharaoh sent, and, behold, there was not one of the cattle of the Israelites dead. And the heart of Pharaoh was hardened, and he did not let the people go.

And the Lord said unto Moses and unto Aaron, "Take to you handfuls of ashes of the furnace and let Moses sprinkle it toward the heaven in the sight of Pharaoh. And it shall become small dust in all the land of Egypt, and shall be a boil breaking forth with blains upon man, and upon beast, throughout all the land of Egypt."

And they took ashes of the furnace, and stood before Pharaoh; and Moses sprinkled it up toward heaven; and it became a boil breaking forth with blains upon man, and upon beast. And the magicians could not stand before Moses because of the boils; for the boil was upon the magicians, and upon all the Egyptians. And the Lord hardened the heart of Pharaoh, and he hearkened not unto them; as the Lord had spoken unto Moses.

And the Lord said unto Moses, "Stretch forth thine hand toward heaven, that there may be hail in all the land of Egypt, upon man, and upon beast, and upon every herb of the field, throughout the land of Egypt."

And Moses stretched forth his rod toward heaven: and the Lord sent thunder and hail, and the fire ran along upon the ground; and the Lord rained hail upon the land of Egypt. So there was hail, and fire mingled with the hail, very grievous, such as there was none like it in all the land of Egypt since it became a nation. And the hail smote throughout all the land of Egypt all that was in the field, both man and beast; and the hail smote every herb of the field, and broke every tree of the field. Only in the land of Goshen, where the children of Israel were, was there no hail.

THE BOOK OF EXODUS

And Pharaoh sent, and called for Moses and Aaron, and said unto them, "I have sinned this time: the Lord is righteous, and I and my people are wicked. Intreat the Lord (for it is enough) that there be no more mighty thunderings and hail; and I will let you go, and ye shall stay no longer."

And Moses went out of the city from Pharaoh, and spread abroad his hands unto the Lord: and the thunders and hail ceased, and the rain was not poured upon the earth. And when Pharaoh saw that the rain and the hail and the thunders were ceased, he sinned yet more, and hardened his heart, he and his servants. And the heart of Pharaoh was hardened, neither would he let the children of Israel go; as the Lord had spoken by Moses.

And the Lord said unto Moses, "Stretch out thine hand over the land of Egypt for the locusts, that they may come up upon the land of Egypt, and eat every herb of the land, even all that the hail hath left."

And Moses stretched forth his rod over the land of Egypt, and the Lord brought an east wind upon the land all that day, and all that night; and when it was morning, the east wind brought the locusts. And the locusts went up over all the land of Egypt, and rested in all the coasts of Egypt: very grievous were they; before them there were no such locusts as they, neither after them shall be such. For they covered the face of the whole earth, so that the land was darkened; and they did eat every herb of the land, and all the fruit of the trees which the hail had left: and there remained not any green thing in the trees, or in the herbs of the field, through all the land of Egypt.

Then Pharaoh called for Moses and Aaron in haste; and he said, "I have sinned against the Lord your God, and against you. Now therefore forgive, I pray thee, my sin only this once, and intreat the Lord your God, that he may take away from me this death only."

And he went out from Pharaoh, and intreated the Lord. And the Lord turned a mighty strong west wind, which took away the locusts, and cast them into the Red sea; there remained not one locust in all the coasts of Egypt. But the Lord hardened

THE BOOK OF EXODUS

Pharaoh's heart, so that he would not let the children of Israel go.

And the Lord said unto Moses, "Stretch out thine hand toward heaven, that there may be darkness over the land of Egypt, even darkness which may be felt."

And Moses stretched forth his hand toward heaven; and there was a thick darkness in all the land of Egypt three days. They saw not one another, neither rose any from his place for three days: but all the children of Israel had light in their dwellings.

And Pharaoh called unto Moses, and said, "Go ye, serve the Lord; only let your flocks and your herds be stayed: let your little ones also go with you."

And Moses said, "Thou must give us also sacrifices and burnt offerings, that we may sacrifice unto the Lord our God. Our cattle also shall go with us; there shall not a hoof be left behind; for thereof must we take to serve the Lord our God; and we know not with what we must serve the Lord, until we come thither." But the Lord hardened Pharaoh's heart, and he would not let them go.

And the Lord said unto Moses, "Yet will I bring one plague more upon Pharaoh, and upon Egypt; afterwards he will let you go hence: when he shall let you go, he shall surely thrust you out hence altogether. Speak now in the ears of the people, and let every man borrow of his neighbor, and every woman of her neighbor, jewels of silver, and jewels of gold."

And the Lord gave the people favour in the sight of the Egyptians. Moreover the man Moses was very great in the land of Egypt, in the sight of Pharaoh's servants, and in the sight of the people.

And Moses said, "Thus saith the Lord, 'About midnight will I go out into the midst of Egypt. And all the firstborn in the land of Egypt shall die, from the firstborn of Pharaoh that sitteth upon his throne, even unto the firstborn of the maidservant that is behind the mill; and all the firstborn of beasts. And there shall be a great cry throughout all the land of Egypt, such as there was none like it, nor shall be like it any more.' But against

THE BOOK OF EXODUS

any of the children of Israel shall not a dog move his tongue, against man or beast: that ye may know how that the Lord doth put a difference between the Egyptians and Israel. And all these thy servants shall come down unto me, and bow down themselves unto me, saying, 'Get thee out, and all the people that follow thee': and after that I will go out." And he went out from Pharaoh in a great anger.

And the Lord said unto Moses, "Pharaoh shall not hearken unto you; that my wonders may be multiplied in the land of Egypt."

And Moses and Aaron did all these wonders before Pharaoh: and the Lord hardened Pharaoh's heart, so that he would not let the children of Israel go out of his land.

Then Moses called for all the elders of Israel, and said unto them, "Draw out and take you a lamb according to your families, and kill the passover. And ye shall take a bunch of hyssop, and dip it in the blood that is in the basin, and strike the lintel and the two side posts with the blood that is in the basin; and none of you shall go out at the door of his house until the morning. For the Lord will pass through to smite the Egyptians; and when he seeth the blood upon the lintel, and on the two side posts, the Lord will pass over the door, and will not suffer the destroyer to come in unto your houses to smite you. And ye shall observe this thing for an ordinance to thee and to thy sons for ever. And it shall come to pass, when ye be come to the land which the Lord will give you, according as he hath promised, that ye shall keep this service. And it shall come to pass, when your children shall say unto you, 'What mean ye by this service?' that ye shall say, 'It is the sacrifice of the Lord's passover, who passed over the houses of the children of Israel in Egypt, when he smote the Egyptians, and delivered our houses.'"

And the people bowed the head and worshipped. And the children of Israel went away, and did as the Lord had commanded Moses and Aaron, so did they.

And it came to pass that at midnight the Lord smote all the firstborn in the land of Egypt, from the firstborn of Pharaoh that

THE BOOK OF EXODUS

sat on his throne unto the firstborn of the captive that was in the dungeon; and all the firstborn of cattle. And Pharaoh rose up in the night, he, and all his servants, and all the Egyptians; and there was a great cry in Egypt; for there was not a house where there was not one dead.

And he called for Moses and Aaron by night, and said, "Rise up, and get you forth from among my people, both ye and the children of Israel; and go, serve the Lord, as ye have said. Also take your flocks and your herds, as ye have said, and be gone; and bless me also."

And the Egyptians were urgent upon the people, that they might send them out of the land in haste; for they said, "We be all dead men."

And the people took their dough before it was leavened, their kneadingtroughs being bound up in their clothes upon their shoulders. And the children of Israel did according to the word of Moses; and they borrowed of the Egyptians jewels of silver, and jewels of gold, and raiment: and the Lord gave the people favour in the sight of the Egyptians, so that they lent unto them such things as they required. And they spoiled the Egyptians.

And the children of Israel journeyed from Rameses to Succoth, about six hundred thousand on foot that were men, beside children. And a mixed multitude went up also with them; and flocks, and herds, even very much cattle. And they baked unleavened cakes of the dough which they brought forth out of Egypt, for it was not leavened; because they were thrust out of Egypt, and could not tarry, neither had they prepared for themselves any victual.

(Now the sojourning of the children of Israel, who dwelt in Egypt, was four hundred and thirty years. And it came to pass at the end of the four hundred and thirty years, even the selfsame day it came to pass, that all the hosts of the Lord went out from the land of Egypt. It is a night to be much observed unto the Lord for bringing them out from the land of Egypt: this is that night of the Lord to be observed of all the children of Israel in their generations.)

THE BOOK OF EXODUS

And it came to pass, when Pharaoh had let the people go, that God led them not through the way of the land of the Philistines, although that was near; for God said, "Lest peradventure the people repent when they see war, and they return to Egypt": but God led the people about, through the way of the wilderness of the Red Sea. And the children of Israel went up harnessed out of the land of Egypt. And Moses took the bones of Joseph with him: for he had straitly sworn the children of Israel, saying, "God will surely visit you; and ye shall carry up my bones away hence with you."

And the Lord went before them by day in a pillar of a cloud, to lead them the way; and by night in a pillar of fire, to give them light; to go by day and night: he took not away the pillar of the cloud by day, nor the pillar of fire by night, from before the people.

And it was told the king of Egypt that the people fled: and the heart of Pharaoh and of his servants was turned against the people, and they said, "Why have we done this, that we have let Israel go from serving us?"

And he made ready his chariot, and took his people with him: and he took six hundred chosen chariots, and all the chariots of Egypt, and captains over every one of them. And the Lord hardened the heart of Pharaoh king of Egypt, and he pursued after the children of Israel: and the children of Israel went out with a high hand. But the Egyptians pursued after them, all the horses and chariots of Pharaoh, and his horsemen, and his army, and overtook them encamping by the sea, beside Pi-hahiroth, before Baal-zephon.

And when Pharaoh drew nigh, the children of Israel lifted up their eyes, and, behold, the Egyptians marched after them; and they were sore afraid: and the children of Israel cried out unto the Lord. And they said unto Moses, "Because there were no graves in Egypt, hast thou taken us away to die in the wilderness? wherefore hast thou dealt thus with us, to carry us forth out of Egypt? Is not this the word that we did tell thee in Egypt,

THE BOOK OF EXODUS

saying, 'Let us alone, that we may serve the Egyptians'? For it had been better for us to serve the Egyptians, than that we should die in the wilderness."

And Moses said unto the people, "Fear ye not, stand still, and see the salvation of the Lord, which he will show to you to-day: for the Egyptians whom ye have seen to-day, ye shall see them again no more for ever. The Lord shall fight for you, and ye shall hold your peace."

And the angel of God, which went before the camp of Israel, removed and went behind them; and the pillar of the cloud went from before their face, and stood behind them: and it came between the camp of the Egyptians and the camp of Israel; and it was a cloud and darkness to them, but it gave light by night to these: so that the one came not near the other all the night. And Moses stretched out his hand over the sea; and the Lord caused the sea to go back by a strong east wind all that night, and made the sea dry land, and the waters were divided. And the children of Israel went into the midst of the sea upon the dry ground: and the waters were a wall unto them on their right hand, and on their left.

And the Egyptians pursued, and went in after them to the midst of the sea, even all Pharaoh's horses, his chariots, and his horsemen. And it came to pass that in the morning watch the Lord looked unto the host of the Egyptians through the pillar of fire and of the cloud, and troubled the host of the Egyptians, and took off their chariot wheels, that they drove them heavily: so that the Egyptians said, "Let us flee from the face of Israel; for the Lord fighteth for them against the Egyptians."

And the Lord said unto Moses, "Stretch out thine hand over the sea, that the waters may come again upon the Egyptians, upon their chariots, and upon their horsemen."

And Moses stretched forth his hand over the sea, and the sea returned to his strength when the morning appeared; and the Egyptians fled against it; and the Lord overthrew the Egyptians in the midst of the sea. And the waters returned, and cov-

THE BOOK OF EXODUS

ered the chariots, and the horsemen, and all the host of Pharaoh that came into the sea after them; there remained not so much as one of them.

But the children of Israel walked upon dry land in the midst of the sea; and the waters were a wall unto them on their right hand, and on their left. Thus the Lord saved Israel that day out of the hand of the Egyptians; and Israel saw the Egyptians dead upon the sea shore. And Israel saw that great work which the Lord did upon the Egyptians: and the people feared the Lord, and believed the Lord, and his servant Moses.

The Song of Moses

Then sang Moses and the children of Israel this song unto the Lord, and spoke, saying,

"I will sing unto the Lord, for he hath triumphed gloriously:
The horse and his rider hath he thrown into the sea.
The Lord is my strength and song,
And he is become my salvation:
He is my God, and I will prepare him a habitation;
My father's God, and I will exalt him.

The Lord is a man of war:
The Lord is his name.
Pharaoh's chariots and his host hath he cast into the sea:
His chosen captains also are drowned in the Red Sea.
The depths have covered them:
They sank into the bottom as a stone.

Thy right hand, O Lord, is become glorious in power:
Thy right hand, O Lord, hath dashed in pieces the enemy.
And in the greatness of thine excellency thou hast overthrown
  them that rose up against thee:
Thou sentest forth thy wrath, which consumed them as
  stubble.
And with the blast of thy nostrils the waters were gathered
  together,
The floods stood upright as a heap,

THE BOOK OF EXODUS

And the depths were congealed in the heart of the sea.
The enemy said, 'I will pursue, I will overtake, I will divide
    the spoil;
My lust shall be satisfied upon them;
I will draw my sword, my hand shall destroy them.'
Thou didst blow with thy wind, the sea covered them:
They sank as lead in the mighty waters.

Who is like unto thee, O Lord, among the gods?
Who is like thee, glorious in holiness,
Fearful in praises, doing wonders?
Thou stretchedst out thy right hand,
The earth swallowed them.
Thou in thy mercy hast led forth the people which thou hast
    redeemed:
Thou hast guided them in thy strength unto thy holy habita-
    tion.
The people shall hear, and be afraid:
Sorrow shall take hold on the inhabitants of Palestina.
Then the dukes of Edom shall be amazed;
The mighty men of Moab, trembling shall take hold upon
    them;
All the inhabitants of Canaan shall melt away.
Fear and dread shall fall upon them;
By the greatness of thine arm they shall be as still as a stone;
Till thy people pass over, O Lord,
Till the people pass over, which thou hast purchased.
Thou shalt bring them in, and plant them in the mountain
    of thine inheritance,
In the place, O Lord, which thou hast made for thee to
    dwell in,
In the Sanctuary, O Lord, which thy hands have established.
The Lord shall reign for ever and ever."

And Miriam the prophetess, the sister of Aaron, took a timbrel in her hand; and all the women went out after her with timbrels and with dances. And Miriam answered them,

THE BOOK OF EXODUS

*"Sing ye to the Lord, for he hath triumphed gloriously;
The horse and his rider hath he thrown into the sea."*

The Journey to Sinai

So Moses brought Israel from the Red Sea, and they went out into the wilderness of Shur; and they went three days in the wilderness, and found no water. And when they came to Marah, they could not drink of the waters of Marah, for they were bitter: therefore the name of it was called Marah. And the people murmured against Moses, saying, "What shall we drink?"

And he cried unto the Lord; and the Lord showed him a tree, which when he had cast into the waters, the waters were made sweet: there he made for them a statute and an ordinance, and there he proved them, and said, "If thou wilt diligently hearken to the voice of the Lord thy God, and wilt do that which is right in his sight, and wilt give ear to his commandments, and keep all his statutes, I will put none of these diseases upon thee, which I have brought upon the Egyptians: for I am the Lord that healeth thee."

And they came to Elim, where were twelve wells of water, and threescore and ten palm trees: and they encamped there by the waters.

And they took their journey from Elim, and all the congregation of the children of Israel came unto the wilderness of Sin, which is between Elim and Sinai, on the fifteenth day of the second month after their departing out of the land of Egypt.

And the whole congregation of the children of Israel murmured against Moses and Aaron in the wilderness; and the children of Israel said unto them, "Would to God we had died by the hand of the Lord in the land of Egypt, when we sat by the flesh pots, and when we did eat bread to the full; for ye have brought us forth into this wilderness, to kill this whole assembly with hunger."

Then said the Lord unto Moses, "Behold, I will rain bread from heaven for you; and the people shall go out and gather a

THE BOOK OF EXODUS

certain rate every day, that I may prove them, whether they will walk in my law, or no. And it shall come to pass that on the sixth day they shall prepare that which they bring in; and it shall be twice as much as they gather daily."

And Moses and Aaron said unto all the children of Israel, "At even, then ye shall know that the Lord hath brought you out from the land of Egypt; and in the morning, then ye shall see the glory of the Lord; for that he heareth your murmurings against the Lord: and what are we, that ye murmur against us?"

And it came to pass, that at even the quails came up, and covered the camp: and in the morning the dew lay round about the host. And when the dew that lay was gone up, behold, upon the face of the wilderness there lay a small round thing, as small as the hoar frost on the ground. And when the children of Israel saw it, they said one to another, "It is manna": for they wist not what it was.

And Moses said unto them, "This is the bread which the Lord hath given you to eat. This is the thing which the Lord hath commanded, 'Gather of it every man according to his eating, an omer for every man, according to the number of your persons; take ye every man for them which are in his tents.'"

And the children of Israel did so, and gathered, some more, some less. And when they did mete it with an omer, he that gathered much had nothing over, and he that gathered little had no lack; they gathered every man according to his eating.

And Moses said, "Let no man leave of it till the morning."

Notwithstanding they hearkened not unto Moses; but some of them left of it until the morning, and it bred worms, and stank: and Moses was wroth with them. And they gathered it every morning, every man according to his eating: and when the sun waxed hot, it melted.

And it came to pass that on the sixth day they gathered twice as much bread, two omers for one man: and all the rulers of the congregation came and told Moses. And he said unto them, "This is that which the Lord hath said, 'To-morrow is the rest of the

THE BOOK OF EXODUS

holy sabbath unto the Lord: bake that which ye will bake to-day, and seethe that ye will seethe; and that which remaineth over lay up for you to be kept until the morning.'"

And they laid it up till the morning, as Moses bade: and it did not stink, neither was there any worm therein. And Moses said, "Eat that to-day; for to-day is a sabbath unto the Lord: to-day ye shall not find it in the field. Six days ye shall gather it; but on the seventh day, which is the sabbath, in it there shall be none."

And it came to pass that there went out some of the people on the seventh day for to gather, and they found none.

And the house of Israel called the name thereof Manna: and it was like coriander seed, white; and the taste of it was like wafers made with honey.

And Moses said, "This is the thing which the Lord commandeth, 'Fill an omer of it to be kept for your generations; that they may see the bread wherewith I have fed you in the wilderness, when I brought you forth from the land of Egypt.'"

And Moses said unto Aaron, "Take a pot, and put an omer full of manna therein, and lay it up before the Lord, to be kept for your generations."

As the Lord commanded Moses, so Aaron laid it up before the Testimony, to be kept. And the children of Israel did eat manna forty years, until they came to a land inhabited; they did eat manna until they came unto the borders of the land of Canaan.

And all the congregation of the children of Israel journeyed from the wilderness of Sin, after their journeys, according to the commandment of the Lord, and pitched in Rephidim: and there was no water for the people to drink. Wherefore the people did chide with Moses, and said, "Give us water that we may drink."

And Moses said unto them, "Why chide ye with me? wherefore do ye tempt the Lord?"

And the people thirsted there for water; and the people murmured against Moses, and said, "Wherefore is this that thou

THE BOOK OF EXODUS

hast brought us up out of Egypt, to kill us and our children and our cattle with thirst?"

And Moses cried unto the Lord, saying, "What shall I do unto this people? they be almost ready to stone me."

And the Lord said unto Moses, "Go on before the people, and take with thee of the elders of Israel; and thy rod, wherewith thou smotest the river, take in thine hand, and go. Behold, I will stand before thee there upon the rock in Horeb; and thou shalt smite the rock, and there shall come water out of it, that the people may drink."

And Moses did so in the sight of the elders of Israel. And he called the name of the place Massah, and Meribah, because of the chiding of the children of Israel, and because they tempted the Lord, saying, "Is the Lord among us, or not?"

Then came Amalek, and fought with Israel in Rephidim. And Moses said unto Joshua, "Choose us out men, and go out, fight with Amalek: to-morrow I will stand on the top of the hill with the rod of God in mine hand."

So Joshua did as Moses had said to him, and fought with Amalek: and Moses, Aaron, and Hur went up to the top of the hill. And it came to pass, when Moses held up his hand, that Israel prevailed: and when he let down his hand, Amalek prevailed. But Moses' hands were heavy; and they took a stone, and put it under him, and he sat thereon; and Aaron and Hur stayed up his hands, the one on the one side, and the other on the other side; and his hands were steady until the going down of the sun. And Joshua discomfited Amalek and his people with the edge of the sword.

Jethro, the priest of Midian, Moses' father-in-law, heard of all that God had done for Moses, and for Israel his people, and that the Lord had brought Israel out of Egypt. Then Jethro, Moses' father-in-law, took Zipporah, Moses' wife, after he had sent her back, and her two sons; of which the name of the one was Gershom: for he said, "I have been an alien in a strange land," and the name of the other was Eliezer: "For the God of my father," said he, "was mine help, and delivered me from the sword of Pharaoh."

And Jethro, Moses' father-in-law, came with his sons and his wife unto Moses into the wilderness, where he encamped at the mount of God: and he said unto Moses, "I thy father-in-law Jethro am come unto thee, and thy wife, and her two sons with her."

And Moses went out to meet his father-in-law, and did obeisance, and kissed him; and they asked each other of their welfare; and they came into the tent. And Moses told his father-in-law all that the Lord had done unto Pharaoh and to the Egyptians for Israel's sake, and all the travail that had come upon them by the way, and how the Lord delivered them. And Jethro rejoiced for all the goodness which the Lord had done to Israel, whom he had delivered out of the hand of the Egyptians. And Jethro said, "Blessed be the Lord, who hath delivered you out of the hand of the Egyptians, and out of the hand of Pharaoh, who hath delivered the people from under the hand of the Egyptians. Now I know that the Lord is greater than all gods: for in the thing wherein they dealt proudly he was above them."

And Jethro, Moses' father-in-law, took a burnt offering and sacrifices for God: and Aaron came, and all the elders of Israel, to eat bread with Moses' father-in-law before God. And it came to pass on the morrow that Moses sat to judge the people: and the people stood by Moses from the morning unto the evening.

And when Moses' father-in-law saw all that he did to the people, he said, "What is this thing that thou doest to the people? why sittest thou thyself alone, and all the people stand by thee from morning unto even?"

And Moses said unto his father-in-law, "Because the people come unto me to enquire of God. When they have a matter, they come unto me; and I judge between one and another, and I do make them know the statutes of God, and his laws."

And Moses' father-in-law said unto him, "The thing that thou doest is not good. Thou wilt surely wear away, both thou, and

THE BOOK OF EXODUS

this people that is with thee: for this thing is too heavy for thee; thou art not able to perform it thyself alone. Hearken now unto my voice, I will give thee counsel, and God shall be with thee: Be thou for the people to God-ward, that thou mayest bring the causes unto God: and thou shalt teach them ordinances and laws, and shalt show them the way wherein they must walk, and the work that they must do. Moreover thou shalt provide out of all the people able men, such as fear God, men of truth, hating covetousness; and place such over them, to be rulers of thousands, and rulers of hundreds, rulers of fifties, and rulers of tens: and let them judge the people at all seasons: and it shall be that every great matter they shall bring unto thee, but every small matter they shall judge: so shall it be easier for thyself, and they shall bear the burden with thee. If thou shalt do this thing, and God command thee so, then thou shalt be able to endure, and all this people shall also go to their place in peace."

So Moses hearkened to the voice of his father-in-law, and did all that he had said. And Moses chose able men out of all Israel, and made them heads over the people, rulers of thousands, rulers of hundreds, rulers of fifties, and rulers of tens. And they judged the people at all seasons: the hard causes they brought unto Moses, but every small matter they judged themselves.

And Moses let his father-in-law depart; and he went his way into his own land.

The Giving of the Law

In the third month, when the children of Israel were gone forth out of the land of Egypt, the same day came they into the wilderness of Sinai. For they were departed from Rephidim, and were come to the desert of Sinai, and had pitched in the wilderness; and there Israel camped before the mount.

And Moses went up unto God, and the Lord called unto him out of the mountain, saying, "Thus shalt thou say to the house of Jacob, and tell the children of Israel: 'Ye have seen what I did unto the Egyptians, and how I bore you on eagles' wings, and

THE BOOK OF EXODUS

brought you unto myself. Now therefore, if ye will obey my voice indeed, and keep my covenant, then ye shall be a peculiar treasure unto me above all people: for all the earth is mine.'"

And the Lord said unto Moses, "Go unto the people, and sanctify them to-day and to-morrow, and let them wash their clothes, and be ready against the third day: for the third day the Lord will come down in the sight of all the people upon Mount Sinai. And thou shalt set bounds unto the people round about, saying, 'Take heed to yourselves, that ye go not up into the mount, or touch the border of it: whosoever toucheth the mount shall be surely put to death.' There shall not a hand touch it, but he shall surely be stoned, or shot through; whether it be beast or man, it shall not live: when the trumpet soundeth long, they shall come up to the mount."

And Moses went down from the mount unto the people, and sanctified the people; and they washed their clothes. And he said unto the people, "Be ready against the third day: come not at your wives."

And it came to pass on the third day in the morning, that there were thunders and lightnings, and a thick cloud upon the mount, and the voice of the trumpet exceedingly loud; so that all the people that was in the camp trembled. And Moses brought forth the people out of the camp to meet with God; and they stood at the nether part of the mount. And Mount Sinai was altogether on a smoke, because the Lord descended upon it in fire; and the smoke thereof ascended as the smoke of a furnace, and the whole mount quaked greatly. And when the voice of the trumpet sounded long, and waxed louder and louder, Moses spoke, and God answered him by a voice. And the Lord came down upon Mount Sinai, on the top of the mount: and the Lord called Moses up to the top of the mount; and Moses went up.

And God spoke all these words, saying, "I am the Lord thy God, which have brought thee out of the land of Egypt, out of the house of bondage.

"Thou shalt have no other gods before me.

"Thou shalt not make unto thee any graven image, or any like-

THE BOOK OF EXODUS

ness of any thing that is in heaven above, or that is in the earth beneath, or that is in the water under the earth: thou shalt not bow down thyself to them, nor serve them: for I the Lord thy God am a jealous God, visiting the iniquity of the fathers upon the children unto the third and fourth generation of them that hate me; and showing mercy unto thousands of them that love me, and keep my commandments.

"Thou shalt not take the name of the Lord thy God in vain; for the Lord will not hold him guiltless that taketh his name in vain.

"Remember the sabbath day, to keep it holy. Six days shalt thou labour, and do all thy work: but the seventh day is the sabbath of the Lord thy God: in it thou shalt not do any work, thou, nor thy son, nor thy daughter, thy manservant, nor thy maidservant, nor thy cattle, nor thy stranger that is within thy gates: for in six days the Lord made heaven and earth, the sea, and all that in them is, and rested the seventh day: wherefore the Lord blessed the sabbath day, and hallowed it.

"Honour thy father and thy mother: that thy days may be long upon the land which the Lord thy God giveth thee.

"Thou shalt not kill.

"Thou shalt not commit adultery.

"Thou shalt not steal.

"Thou shalt not bear false witness against thy neighbor.

"Thou shalt not covet thy neighbor's house, thou shalt not covet thy neighbor's wife, nor his manservant, nor his maidservant, nor his ox, nor his ass, nor any thing that is thy neighbour's.

"Now these are the judgments which thou shalt set before them:

"If thou buy a Hebrew servant, six years he shall serve: and in the seventh he shall go out free for nothing. If he came in by himself, he shall go out by himself: if he were married, then his wife shall go out with him. If his master have given him a wife, and she have borne him sons or daughters; the wife and her children shall be her master's, and he shall go out by himself. And if the servant shall plainly say, 'I love my master, my wife, and my children; I will not go out free': then his master shall bring

THE BOOK OF EXODUS

him unto the judges; he shall also bring him to the door, or unto the door post; and his master shall bore his ear through with an awl; and he shall serve him for ever.

"And if a man sell his daughter to be a maidservant, she shall not go out as the menservants do. If she please not her master, who hath betrothed her to himself, then shall he let her be redeemed: to sell her unto a strange nation he shall have no power, seeing he hath dealt deceitfully with her. And if he have betrothed her unto his son, he shall deal with her after the manner of daughters. If he take him another wife; her food, her raiment, and her duty of marriage, shall he not diminish. And if he do not these three unto her, then shall she go out free without money.

"He that smiteth a man, so that he die, shall be surely put to death. And if a man lie not in wait, but God deliver him into his hand; then I will appoint thee a place whither he shall flee. But if a man come presumptuously upon his neighbor, to slay him with guile; thou shalt take him from mine altar, that he may die. And he that smiteth his father, or his mother, shall be surely put to death.

"And he that stealeth a man, and selleth him, or if he be found in his hand, he shall surely be put to death.

"And he that curseth his father, or his mother, shall surely be put to death.

"And if men strive together, and one smite another with a stone, or with his fist, and he die not, but keepeth his bed: if he rise again, and walk abroad upon his staff, then shall he that smote him be quit: only he shall pay for the loss of his time, and shall cause him to be thoroughly healed.

"And if a man smite his servant, or his maid, with a rod, and he die under his hand; he shall be surely punished. Notwithstanding, if he continue a day or two, he shall not be punished: for he is his money.

"If men strive, and hurt a woman with child, so that her fruit depart from her, and yet no mischief follow: he shall be surely punished, according as the woman's husband will lay upon him;

THE BOOK OF EXODUS

and he shall pay as the judges determine. And if any mischief follow, then thou shalt give life for life, eye for eye, tooth for tooth, hand for hand, foot for foot, burning for burning, wound for wound, stripe for stripe.

"And if a man smite the eye of his servant, or the eye of his maid, that it perish; he shall let him go free for his eye's sake. And if he smite out his manservant's tooth, or his maidservant's tooth; he shall let him go free for his tooth's sake.

"If an ox gore a man or a woman, that they die: then the ox shall be surely stoned, and his flesh shall not be eaten; but the owner of the ox shall be quit. But if the ox were wont to push with his horn in time past, and it hath been testified to his owner, and he hath not kept him in, but that he hath killed a man or a woman; the ox shall be stoned, and his owner also shall be put to death. If there be laid on him a sum of money, then he shall give for the ransom of his life whatsoever is laid upon him. Whether he have gored a son, or have gored a daughter, according to this judgment shall it be done unto him. If the ox shall push a manservant or a maidservant; he shall give unto their master thirty shekels of silver, and the ox shall be stoned.

"And if a man shall open a pit, or if a man shall dig a pit, and not cover it, and an ox or an ass fall therein; the owner of the pit shall make it good, and give money unto the owner of them; and the dead beast shall be his.

"And if one man's ox hurt another's, that he die; then they shall sell the live ox, and divide the money of it; and the dead ox also they shall divide. Or if it be known that the ox hath used to push in time past, and his owner hath not kept him in; he shall surely pay ox for ox; and the dead shall be his own.

"If a man shall steal an ox, or a sheep, and kill it, or sell it; he shall restore five oxen for an ox, and four sheep for a sheep. If a thief be found breaking up, and be smitten that he die, there shall no blood be shed for him. If the sun be risen upon him, there shall be blood shed for him: for he should make full restitution; if he have nothing, then he shall be sold for his theft. If

THE BOOK OF EXODUS

the theft be certainly found in his hand alive, whether it be ox, or ass, or sheep; he shall restore double.

"If a man deliver unto his neighbour an ass, or an ox, or a sheep, or any beast, to keep; and it die, or be hurt, or driven away, no man seeing it: then shall an oath of the Lord be between them both, that he hath not put his hand unto his neighbour's goods; and the owner of it shall accept thereof, and he shall not make it good. And if it be stolen from him, he shall make restitution unto the owner thereof. If it be torn in pieces, then let him bring it for witness, and he shall not make good that which was torn. And if a man borrow ought of his neighbour, and it be hurt, or die, the owner thereof being not with it, he shall surely make it good. But if the owner thereof be with it, he shall not make it good: if it be an hired thing, it came for his hire.

"And if a man entice a maid that is not betrothed, and lie with her, he shall surely endow her to be his wife. If her father utterly refuse to give her unto him, he shall pay money according to the dowry of virgins.

"Thou shalt not suffer a witch to live.

"Whosoever lieth with a beast shall surely be put to death.

"He that sacrificeth unto any god, save unto the Lord only, he shall be utterly destroyed.

"Thou shalt neither vex a stranger, nor oppress him: for ye were strangers in the land of Egypt.

"Ye shall not afflict any widow, or fatherless child. If thou afflict them in any wise, and they cry at all unto me, I will surely hear their cry; and my wrath shall wax hot, and I will kill you with the sword; and your wives shall be widows, and your children fatherless.

"If thou lend money to any of my people that is poor by thee, thou shalt not be to him as a usurer, neither shalt thou lay upon him usury. If thou at all take thy neighbour's raiment to pledge, thou shalt deliver it unto him by that the sun goeth down: for that is his covering only, it is his raiment for his skin: wherein shall he sleep? and it shall come to pass, when he crieth unto me, that I will hear; for I am gracious.

THE BOOK OF EXODUS

"Thou shalt not revile the gods, nor curse the ruler of thy people."

And he gave unto Moses, when he had made an end of communing with him upon Mount Sinai, two tables of testimony, tables of stone, written with the finger of God.

The Calf of Gold

And when the people saw that Moses delayed to come down out of the mount, the people gathered themselves together unto Aaron, and said unto him, "Up, make us gods, which shall go before us; for as for this Moses, the man that brought us up out of the land of Egypt, we wot not what is become of him."

And Aaron said unto them, "Break off the golden earrings, which are in the ears of your wives, of your sons, and of your daughters, and bring them unto me."

And all the people broke off the golden earrings which were in their ears, and brought them unto Aaron. And he received them at their hand, and fashioned it with a graving tool, after he had made it a molten calf: and they said, "These be thy gods, O Israel, which brought thee up out of the land of Egypt."

And when Aaron saw it, he built an altar before it; and Aaron made proclamation, and said, "To-morrow is a feast to the Lord."

And they rose up early on the morrow, and offered burnt offerings, and brought peace offerings; and the people sat down to eat and to drink, and rose up to play.

And the Lord said unto Moses, "Go, get thee down, for thy people, which thou broughtest out of the land of Egypt, have corrupted themselves. They have turned aside quickly out of the way which I commanded them: they have made them a molten calf, and have worshipped it, and have sacrificed thereunto, and said, 'These be thy gods, O Israel, which have brought thee up out of the land of Egypt.'"

And the Lord said unto Moses, "I have seen this people, and, behold, it is a stiffnecked people. Now therefore let me alone, that my wrath may wax hot against them, and that I may consume them: and I will make of thee a great nation."

THE BOOK OF EXODUS

And Moses besought the Lord his God, and said, "Lord, why doth thy wrath wax hot against thy people, which thou hast brought forth out of the land of Egypt with great power, and with a mighty hand? Wherefore should the Egyptians speak, and say, 'For mischief did he bring them out, to slay them in the mountains, and to consume them from the face of the earth'? Turn from thy fierce wrath, and repent of this evil against thy people. Remember Abraham, Isaac, and Israel, thy servants, to whom thou sworest by thine own self, and saidst unto them, 'I will multiply your seed as the stars of heaven, and all this land that I have spoken of will I give unto your seed, and they shall inherit it for ever.'"

And the Lord repented of the evil which he thought to do unto his people. And Moses turned, and went down from the mount, and the two tables of the testimony were in his hand: the tables were written on both their sides; on the one side and on the other were they written. And the tables were the work of God, and the writing was the writing of God, graven upon the tables. And when Joshua heard the noise of the people as they shouted, he said unto Moses, "There is a noise of war in the camp."

And he said, "It is not the voice of them that shout for mastery, neither is it the voice of them that cry for being overcome: but the noise of them that sing do I hear."

And it came to pass, as soon as he came nigh unto the camp, that he saw the calf, and the dancing: and Moses' anger waxed hot, and he cast the tables out of his hands, and broke them beneath the mount. And he took the calf which they had made, and burnt it in the fire, and ground it to powder, and strewed it upon the water, and made the children of Israel drink of it.

And Moses said unto Aaron, "What did this people unto thee, that thou hast brought so great a sin upon them?"

And Aaron said, "Let not the anger of my lord wax hot: thou knowest the people, that they are set on mischief. For they said unto me, 'Make us gods, which shall go before us: for as for this Moses, the man that brought us up out of the land of Egypt, we

THE BOOK OF EXODUS

wot not what is become of him.' And I said unto them, 'Whosoever hath any gold, let them break it off.' So they gave it me: then I cast it into the fire, and there came out this calf."

And when Moses saw that the people were naked (for Aaron had made them naked unto their shame among their enemies), then Moses stood in the gate of the camp, and said, "Who is on the Lord's side? let him come unto me." And all the sons of Levi gathered themselves together unto him.

And he said unto them, "Thus saith the Lord God of Israel, 'Put every man his sword by his side, and go in and out from gate to gate throughout the camp, and slay every man his brother, and every man his companion, and every man his neighbour.'" And the children of Levi did according to the word of Moses: and there fell of the people that day about three thousand men.

And it came to pass on the morrow that Moses said unto the people, "Ye have sinned a great sin: and now I will go up unto the Lord; peradventure I shall make an atonement for your sin."

And Moses returned unto the Lord, and said, "Oh, this people have sinned a great sin, and have made them gods of gold. Yet now, if thou wilt forgive their sin——; and if not, blot me, I pray thee, out of thy book which thou hast written."

And the Lord said unto Moses, "Whosoever hath sinned against me, him will I blot out of my book. Therefore now go, lead the people unto the place of which I have spoken unto thee: behold, mine Angel shall go before thee: nevertheless in the day when I visit I will visit their sin upon them."

And the Lord plagued the people, because they made the calf, which Aaron made.

And the Lord said unto Moses, "Depart, and go up hence, thou and the people which thou hast brought up out of the land of Egypt, unto the land which I swore unto Abraham, to Isaac, and to Jacob, saying, 'Unto thy seed will I give it': unto a land flowing with milk and honey: for I will not go up in the midst of thee; for thou art a stiffnecked people: lest I consume thee in the way."

And when the people heard these evil tidings, they mourned:

THE BOOK OF EXODUS

and no man did put on him his ornaments. And the children of Israel stripped themselves of their ornaments by the mount Horeb. And Moses took the tabernacle, and pitched it without the camp, afar off from the camp, and called it the tabernacle of the congregation. And it came to pass that every one which sought the Lord went out unto the tabernacle of the congregation, which was without the camp. And it came to pass, when Moses went out unto the tabernacle, that all the people rose up, and stood every man at his tent door, and looked after Moses, until he was gone into the tabernacle. And it came to pass, as Moses entered into the tabernacle, the cloudy pillar descended, and stood at the door of the tabernacle, and the Lord talked with Moses. And all the people saw the cloudy pillar stand at the tabernacle door: and all the people rose up and worshipped, every man in his tent door. And the Lord spoke unto Moses face to face, as a man speaketh unto his friend.

And Moses said unto the Lord, "See, thou sayest unto me, 'Bring up this people': and thou hast not let me know whom thou wilt send with me. Yet thou hast said, 'I know thee by name, and thou hast also found grace in my sight.' Now therefore, I pray thee, if I have found grace in thy sight, show me now thy way, that I may know thee, that I may find grace in thy sight: and consider that this nation is thy people."

And he said, "My presence shall go with thee, and I will give thee rest."

And he said unto him, "If thy presence go not with me, carry us not up hence. For wherein shall it be known here that I and thy people have found grace in thy sight? is it not in that thou goest with us? so shall we be separated, I and thy people, from all the people that are upon the face of the earth."

And the Lord said unto Moses, "I will do this thing also that thou hast spoken: for thou hast found grace in my sight, and I know thee by name."

And he said, "I beseech thee, show me thy glory."

And he said, "I will make all my goodness pass before thee, and I will proclaim the name of the Lord before thee; and will

THE BOOK OF EXODUS

be gracious to whom I will be gracious, and will show mercy on whom I will show mercy." And he said, "Thou canst not see my face: for there shall no man see me, and live." And the Lord said, "Behold, there is a place by me, and thou shalt stand upon a rock: and it shall come to pass, while my glory passeth by, that I will put thee in a cleft of the rock, and will cover thee with my hand while I pass by: and I will take away mine hand, and thou shalt see my back parts: but my face shall not be seen."

And the Lord said unto Moses, "Hew thee two tables of stone like unto the first: and I will write upon these tables the words that were in the first tables, which thou brokest. And be ready in the morning, and come up in the morning unto Mount Sinai, and present thyself there to me in the top of the mount. And no man shall come up with thee, neither let any man be seen throughout all the mount; neither let the flocks nor herds feed before that mount."

And he hewed two tables of stone like unto the first; and Moses rose up early in the morning, and went up unto Mount Sinai, as the Lord had commanded him, and took in his hand the two tables of stone.

And it came to pass, when Moses came down from Mount Sinai with the two tables of testimony in Moses' hand, when he came down from the mount, that Moses wist not that the skin of his face shone while he talked with him. And when Aaron and all the children of Israel saw Moses, behold, the skin of his face shone; and they were afraid to come nigh him. And Moses called unto them; and Aaron and all the rulers of the congregation returned unto him: and Moses talked with them. And afterward all the children of Israel came nigh: and he gave them in commandment all that the Lord had spoken with him in Mount Sinai.

THE BOOK OF LEVITICUS

THE BOOK OF LEVITICUS, *with the exception of the Holiness Code and minor passages, embodies a legal system not only half a millennium later than parts of that in Exodus but also two centuries later than the one that follows it in Deuteronomy. The Deuteronomic legislation had been a product of the great prophetic revival of the seventh century with its mighty endeavor to moralize and spiritualize the entire life of the people. The Holiness Code in Leviticus belongs rather with Deuteronomy than where it is found. It was a last expiring effort, composed under the influence of Ezekiel during the Exile, to retain the prophetic spirit that emphasized inner righteousness of motive behind observance of the outward law. Its forecast of the teaching of Jesus in the admonition, "Thou shalt love thy neighbor as thyself," expresses the guiding principle of the noblest phase of Jewish legislation. But as this appears in Leviticus it is enmeshed in such trivialities as the injunctions regarding the proper cut of hair and beard. And the bulk of the book is of the latter character, made up of the minute regulations concerning matters of ritual which constituted the code promulgated by the priest Ezra in 397 B.C. None the less, it is to be remembered that we owe to writers of this priestly school the compilation of the Hexateuch and the preservation of the work of the greater men who had preceded them. In formalizing Judaism, the priests stabilized it and made it able to endure through centuries to come.*

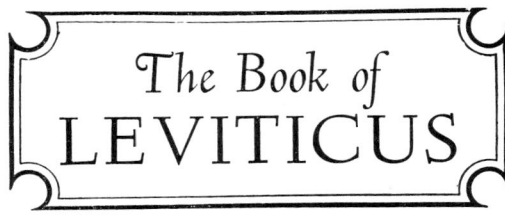

The Holiness Code

AND THE LORD SPOKE unto Moses, saying, "Speak unto all the congregation of the children of Israel, and say unto them, 'Ye shall be holy: for I the Lord your God am holy.

"'Ye shall fear every man his mother, and his father, and keep my sabbaths: I am the Lord your God.

"'Turn ye not unto idols, nor make to yourselves molten gods: I am the Lord your God.

"'And if ye offer a sacrifice of peace offerings unto the Lord, ye shall offer it at your own will. It shall be eaten the same day ye offer it, and on the morrow: and if ought remain until the third day, it shall be burnt in the fire. And if it be eaten at all on the third day, it is abominable; it shall not be accepted. Therefore every one that eateth it shall bear his iniquity, because he hath profaned the hallowed thing of the Lord: and that soul shall be cut off from among his people.

"'And when ye reap the harvest of your land, thou shalt not wholly reap the corners of thy field, neither shalt thou gather the gleanings of thy harvest. And thou shalt not glean thy vineyard, neither shalt thou gather every grape of thy vineyard; thou shalt leave them for the poor and stranger: I am the Lord your God.

"'Ye shall not steal, neither deal falsely, neither lie one to another.

"'And ye shall not swear by my name falsely, neither shalt thou profane the name of thy God: I am the Lord.

"'Thou shalt not defraud thy neighbour, neither rob him: the

THE BOOK OF LEVITICUS

wages of him that is hired shall not abide with thee all night until the morning.

" 'Thou shalt not curse the deaf, nor put a stumblingblock before the blind, but shalt fear thy God: I am the Lord.

" 'Ye shall do no unrighteousness in judgment: thou shalt not respect the person of the poor, nor honour the person of the mighty: but in righteousness shalt thou judge thy neighbour.

" 'Thou shalt not go up and down as a talebearer among thy people: neither shalt thou stand against the blood of thy neighbour: I am the Lord.

" 'Thou shalt not hate thy brother in thine heart: thou shalt in any wise rebuke thy neighbour, and not suffer sin upon him. Thou shalt not avenge, nor bear any grudge against the children of thy people, but thou shalt love thy neighbour as thyself: I am the Lord.

" 'Ye shall keep my statutes. Thou shalt not let thy cattle gender with a diverse kind: thou shalt not sow thy field with mingled seed: neither shall a garment mingled of linen and woollen come upon thee.

" 'And whosoever lieth carnally with a woman, that is a bondmaid, betrothed to a husband, and not at all redeemed, nor freedom given her; she shall be scourged; they shall not be put to death, because she was not free. And he shall bring his trespass offering unto the Lord, unto the door of the tabernacle of the congregation, even a ram for a trespass offering. And the priest shall make an atonement for him with the ram of the trespass offering before the Lord for his sin which he hath done: and the sin which he hath done shall be forgiven him.

" 'And when ye shall come into the land, and shall have planted all manner of trees for food, then ye shall count the fruit thereof as uncircumcised: three years shall it be as uncircumcised unto you: it shall not be eaten of. But in the fourth year all the fruit thereof shall be holy to praise the Lord withal. And in the fifth year shall ye eat of the fruit thereof, that it may yield unto you the increase thereof: I am the Lord your God.

THE BOOK OF LEVITICUS

"'Ye shall not eat any thing with the blood: neither shall ye use enchantment, nor observe times.

"'Ye shall not round the corners of your heads, neither shalt thou mar the corners of thy beard.

"'Ye shall not make any cuttings in your flesh for the dead, nor print any marks upon you: I am the Lord.

"'Do not prostitute thy daughter, to cause her to be a whore; lest the land fall to whoredom, and the land become full of wickedness.

"'Ye shall keep my sabbaths, and reverence my sanctuary: I am the Lord.

"'Regard not them that have familiar spirits, neither seek after wizards, to be defiled by them: I am the Lord your God.

"'Thou shalt rise up before the hoary head, and honour the face of the old man, and fear thy God: I am the Lord.

"'And if a stranger sojourn with thee in your land, ye shall not vex him. But the stranger that dwelleth with you shall be unto you as one born among you, and thou shalt love him as thyself; for ye were strangers in the land of Egypt: I am the Lord your God.

"'Ye shall do no unrighteousness in judgment, in meteyard, in weight, or in measure. Just balances, just weights, a just ephah, and a just hin, shall ye have: I am the Lord your God, which brought you out of the land of Egypt.

"'Sanctify yourselves therefore, and be ye holy: for I am the Lord your God.'"

THE BOOK OF NUMBERS

The highly apocryphal census attributed to Moses with which the Book of Numbers opens and from which it derives its name is of little importance to anyone to-day. On the other hand, the narrative portions of the book possess the same drive and swift dramatic appeal that are found elsewhere throughout the historical sections of the Old Testament.

Of special interest is the story of Balaam in whom we meet a transitional figure between the primitive soothsayer and the type of moral prophet, unique among the Hebrews, into whom the soothsayer developed, both supposed to possess special knowledge of the will of God, the soothsayer crudely through a reading of outward omens, the prophet subtly through consulting his inner intuitions. To judge from the figure of Calchas in the Iliad, the possibilities of a similar development existed among the Greeks, but with them the prophetic spirit was early canalized into the oracles or formalized in the Mysteries.

The Book of NUMBERS

Wanderings in the Wilderness

AND ON THE DAY that the tabernacle was reared up the cloud covered the tabernacle, namely, the tent of the testimony: and at even there was upon the tabernacle as it were the appearance of fire, until the morning. So it was always: the cloud covered it by day, and the appearance of fire by night. And when the cloud was taken up from the tabernacle, then after that the children of Israel journeyed: and in the place where the cloud abode, there the children of Israel pitched their tents. At the commandment of the Lord the children of Israel journeyed, and at the commandment of the Lord they pitched: as long as the cloud abode upon the tabernacle they rested in their tents. And when the cloud tarried long upon the tabernacle many days, then the children of Israel kept the charge of the Lord, and journeyed not. And so it was, when the cloud was a few days upon the tabernacle; according to the commandment of the Lord they abode in their tents, and according to the commandment of the Lord they journeyed. And so it was, when the cloud abode from even unto the morning, and that the cloud was taken up in the morning, then they journeyed: whether it was by day or by night that the cloud was taken up, they journeyed. Or whether it were two days, or a month, or a year, that the cloud tarried upon the tabernacle, remaining thereon, the children of Israel abode in their tents, and journeyed not: but when it was taken up, they journeyed. At the commandment of the Lord they rested in the tents, and at the commandment of the Lord they jour-

THE BOOK OF NUMBERS

neyed: they kept the charge of the Lord, at the commandment of the Lord by the hand of Moses.

And they departed from the mount of the Lord three days' journey: and the ark of the covenant of the Lord went before them in the three days' journey, to search out a resting place for them. And the cloud of the Lord was upon them by day, when they went out of the camp. And it came to pass, when the ark set forward, that Moses said,

> "Rise up, Lord,
> And let thine enemies be scattered;
> And let them that hate thee flee before thee."

And when it rested, he said,

> "Return, O Lord,
> Unto the many thousands of Israel."

And the mixt multitude that was among them fell a-lusting: and the children of Israel also wept again, and said, "Who shall give us flesh to eat? We remember the fish, which we did eat in Egypt freely; the cucumbers, and the melons, and the leeks, and the onions, and the garlic. But now our soul is dried away: there is nothing at all, beside this manna, before our eyes."

And the manna was as coriander seed, and the colour thereof as the colour of bdellium. And the people went about, and gathered it, and ground it in mills, or beat it in a mortar, and baked it in pans, and made cakes of it: and the taste of it was as the taste of fresh oil. And when the dew fell upon the camp in the night, the manna fell upon it.

Then Moses heard the people weep throughout their families, every man in the door of his tent: and the anger of the Lord was kindled greatly; Moses also was displeased. And Moses said unto the Lord, "Wherefore hast thou afflicted thy servant? and wherefore have I not found favour in thy sight, that thou layest the burden of all this people upon me? Have I conceived all this people? have I begotten them, that thou shouldest say unto me, 'Carry them in thy bosom, as a nursing father beareth the sucking child, unto the land which thou sworest unto their fathers'? Whence

THE BOOK OF NUMBERS

should I have flesh to give unto all this people? for they weep unto me, saying, 'Give us flesh, that we may eat.' I am not able to bear all this people alone, because it is too heavy for me. And if thou deal thus with me, kill me, I pray thee, out of hand, if I have found favour in thy sight; and let me not see my wretchedness."

And the Lord said unto Moses, "Gather unto me seventy men of the elders of Israel, whom thou knowest to be the elders of the people, and officers over them; and bring them unto the tabernacle of the congregation, that they may stand there with thee. And I will come down and talk with thee there: and I will take of the spirit which is upon thee, and will put it upon them; and they shall bear the burden of the people with thee, that thou bear it not thyself alone. And say thou unto the people, 'Sanctify yourselves against to-morrow, and ye shall eat flesh: for ye have wept in the ears of the Lord, saying, "Who shall give us flesh to eat? for it was well with us in Egypt": therefore the Lord will give you flesh, and ye shall eat. Ye shall not eat one day, nor two days, nor five days, neither ten days, nor twenty days; but even a whole month, until it come out at your nostrils, and it be loathsome unto you: because that ye have despised the Lord which is among you, and have wept before him, saying, "Why came we forth out of Egypt?"'"

And Moses said, "The people, among whom I am, are six hundred thousand footmen; and thou hast said, 'I will give them flesh, that they may eat a whole month.' Shall the flocks and the herds be slain for them, to suffice them? or shall all the fish of the sea be gathered together for them, to suffice them?"

And the Lord said unto Moses, "Is the Lord's hand waxed short? thou shalt see now whether my word shall come to pass unto thee or not."

And Moses went out, and told the people the words of the Lord, and gathered the seventy men of the elders of the people, and set them round about the tabernacle. And the Lord came down in a cloud, and spoke unto him, and took of the spirit that was upon him, and gave it unto the seventy elders: and it came to pass that, when the spirit rested upon them, they prophesied,

THE BOOK OF NUMBERS

and did not cease. But there remained two of the men in the camp, the name of the one was Eldad, and the name of the other Medad: and the spirit rested upon them; and they were of them that were written, but went not out unto the tabernacle: and they prophesied in the camp. And there ran a young man, and told Moses, and said,

"Eldad and Medad do prophesy in the camp."

And Joshua the son of Nun, the servant of Moses, one of his young men, answered and said, "My lord Moses, forbid them!"

And Moses said unto him, "Enviest thou for my sake? would God that all the Lord's people were prophets, and that the Lord would put his spirit upon them!"

And Moses got him into the camp, he and the elders of Israel. And there went forth a wind from the Lord, and brought quails from the sea, and let them fall by the camp, as it were a day's journey on this side, and as it were a day's journey on the other side, round about the camp, and as it were two cubits high upon the face of the earth. And the people stood up all that day, and all that night, and all the next day, and they gathered the quails: he that gathered least gathered ten homers: and they spread them all abroad for themselves round about the camp. And while the flesh was yet between their teeth, ere it was chewed, the wrath of the Lord was kindled against the people, and the Lord smote the people with a very great plague. And he called the name of that place Kibroth-hattaavah: because there they buried the people that lusted. And the people journeyed from Kibroth-hattaavah unto Hazeroth; and abode at Hazeroth.

And Miriam and Aaron spoke against Moses because of the Ethiopian woman whom he had married (for he had married an Ethiopian woman). And they said, "Hath the Lord indeed spoken only by Moses? hath he not spoken also by us?"

And the Lord heard it. (Now the man Moses was very meek, above all the men which were upon the face of the earth.) And the Lord spoke suddenly unto Moses, and unto Aaron, and unto

THE BOOK OF NUMBERS

Miriam, "Come out ye three unto the tabernacle of the congregation."

And they three came out. And the Lord came down in the pillar of the cloud, and stood in the door of the tabernacle, and called Aaron and Miriam: and they both came forth. And he said, "Hear now my words: if there be a prophet among you, I the Lord will make myself known unto him in a vision, and will speak unto him in a dream. My servant Moses is not so, who is faithful in all mine house. With him will I speak mouth to mouth, even apparently, and not in dark speeches; and the similitude of the Lord shall he behold: wherefore then were ye not afraid to speak against my servant Moses?"

And the anger of the Lord was kindled against them; and he departed. And the cloud departed from off the tabernacle; and, behold, Miriam became leprous, white as snow: and Aaron looked upon Miriam, and, behold, she was leprous. And Aaron said unto Moses,

"Alas, my lord, I beseech thee, lay not the sin upon us, wherein we have done foolishly, and wherein we have sinned. Let her not be as one dead, of whom the flesh is half consumed when he cometh out of his mother's womb."

And Moses cried unto the Lord, saying, "Heal her now, O God, I beseech thee."

And the Lord said unto Moses, "If her father had but spit in her face, should she not be ashamed seven days? let her be shut out from the camp seven days, and after that let her be received in again." And Miriam was shut out from the camp seven days: and the people journeyed not till Miriam was brought in again. And afterward the people removed from Hazeroth, and pitched in the wilderness of Paran.

And the Lord spoke unto Moses, saying, "Send thou men, that they may search the land of Canaan, which I give unto the children of Israel: of every tribe of their fathers shall ye send a man, every one a ruler among them."

THE BOOK OF NUMBERS

And Moses by the commandment of the Lord sent them from the wilderness of Paran: all those men were heads of the children of Israel. And Moses sent them to spy out the land of Canaan, and said unto them,

"Get you up this way southward, and go out into the mountain: and see the land, what it is; and the people that dwelleth therein, whether they be strong or weak, few or many; and what the land is that they dwell in, whether it be good or bad; and what cities they be that they dwell in, whether in tents, or in strong holds; and what the land is, whether it be fat or lean, whether there be wood therein, or not. And be ye of good courage, and bring of the fruit of the land."

Now the time was the time of the firstripe grapes. So they went up, and searched the land from the wilderness of Zin unto Rehob, as men come to Hamath. And they ascended by the south, and came unto Hebron; where Ahiman, Sheshai, and Talmai, the children of Anak, were. (Now Hebron was built seven years before Zoan in Egypt.) And they came unto the brook of Eshcol, and cut down from thence a branch with one cluster of grapes, and they bore it between two upon a staff; and they brought of the pomegranates, and of the figs. The place was called the brook Eshcol, because of the cluster of grapes which the children of Israel cut down from thence. And they returned from searching of the land after forty days.

And they went and came to Moses, and to Aaron, and to all the congregation of the children of Israel, unto the wilderness of Paran, to Kadesh; and brought back word unto them, and unto all the congregation, and showed them the fruit of the land. And they told him, and said, "We came unto the land whither thou sentest us, and surely it floweth with milk and honey; and this is the fruit of it. Nevertheless the people be strong that dwell in the land, and the cities are walled, and very great: and moreover we saw the children of Anak there. The Amalekites dwell in the land of the south: and the Hittites, and the Jebusites, and the Amorites, dwell in the mountains: and the Canaanites dwell by the sea, and by the coast of Jordan."

THE BOOK OF NUMBERS

And Caleb stilled the people before Moses, and said, "Let us go up at once, and possess it; for we are well able to overcome it."

But the men that went up with him said, "We be not able to go up against the people; for they are stronger than we."

And they brought up an evil report of the land which they had searched unto the children of Israel, saying, "The land, through which we have gone to search it, is a land that eateth up the inhabitants thereof; and all the people that we saw in it are men of a great stature. And there we saw the giants, the sons of Anak, which come of the giants: and we were in our own sight as grasshoppers, and so we were in their sight."

And all the congregation lifted up their voice, and cried; and the people wept that night. And all the children of Israel murmured against Moses and against Aaron: and the whole congregation said unto them, "Would God that we had died in the land of Egypt! or would God we had died in this wilderness! And wherefore hath the Lord brought us unto this land, to fall by the sword, that our wives and our children should be a prey? were it not better for us to return into Egypt?"

And they said one to another, "Let us make a captain, and let us return into Egypt."

Then Moses and Aaron fell on their faces before all the assembly of the congregation of the children of Israel. And Joshua the son of Nun, and Caleb the son of Jephunneh, which were of them that searched the land, rent their clothes: and they spoke unto all the company of the children of Israel, saying, "The land, which we passed through to search it, is an exceeding good land. If the Lord delight in us, then he will bring us into this land, and give it us; a land which floweth with milk and honey. Only rebel not ye against the Lord, neither fear ye the people of the land; for they are bread for us: their defence is departed from them, and the Lord is with us: fear them not."

But all the congregation bade stone them with stones. And the glory of the Lord appeared in the tabernacle of the congregation before all the children of Israel.

THE BOOK OF NUMBERS

And the Lord said unto Moses, "How long will this people provoke me? and how long will it be ere they believe me, for all the signs which I have showed among them? I will smite them with the pestilence, and disinherit them, and will make of thee a greater nation and mightier than they."

And Moses said unto the Lord, "Then the Egyptians shall hear it (for thou broughtest up this people in thy might from among them); and they will tell it to the inhabitants of this land: for they have heard that thou Lord art among this people, that thou Lord art seen face to face, and that thy cloud standeth over them, and that thou goest before them, by day time in a pillar of a cloud, and in a pillar of fire by night. Now if thou shalt kill all this people as one man, then the nations which have heard the fame of thee will speak, saying, 'Because the Lord was not able to bring this people into the land which he swore unto them, therefore he hath slain them in the wilderness.' And now, I beseech thee, let the power of my Lord be great, according as thou hast spoken, saying, 'The Lord is longsuffering, and of great mercy, forgiving iniquity and transgression, and by no means clearing the guilty, visiting the iniquity of the fathers upon the children unto the third and fourth generation.' Pardon, I beseech thee, the iniquity of this people according unto the greatness of thy mercy, and as thou hast forgiven this people, from Egypt even until now."

And the Lord said, "I have pardoned according to thy word: but as truly as I live, all the earth shall be filled with the glory of the Lord. Because all those men which have seen my glory, and my miracles, which I did in Egypt and in the wilderness, and have tempted me now these ten times, and have not hearkened to my voice; surely they shall not see the land which I swore unto their fathers, neither shall any of them that provoked me see it. How long shall I bear with this evil congregation, which murmur against me? I have heard the murmurings of the children of Israel, which they murmur against me. Say unto them, 'As truly as I live,' saith the Lord, 'as ye have spoken in mine ears, so will I do to you: your carcases shall fall in this

THE BOOK OF NUMBERS

wilderness; and all that were numbered of you, according to your whole number, from twenty years old and upward, which have murmured against me, doubtless ye shall not come into the land, concerning which I swore to make you dwell therein, save Caleb the son of Jephunneh, and Joshua the son of Nun. But your little ones, which ye said should be a prey, them will I bring in, and they shall know the land which ye have despised. But as for you, your carcases, they shall fall in this wilderness. And your children shall wander in the wilderness forty years, and bear your whoredoms, until your carcases be wasted in the wilderness. After the number of the days in which ye searched the land, even forty days, each day for a year, shall ye bear your iniquities, even forty years, and ye shall know my breach of promise. I the Lord have said, "I will surely do it unto all this evil congregation, that are gathered together against me: in this wilderness they shall be consumed, and there they shall die." ' "

And the men, which Moses sent to search the land, who returned, and made all the congregation to murmur against him, by bringing up a slander upon the land, even those men that did bring up the evil report upon the land, died by the plague before the Lord. But Joshua the son of Nun, and Caleb the son of Jephunneh, which were of the men that went to search the land, lived still. And Moses told these sayings unto all the children of Israel: and the people mourned greatly.

And they rose up early in the morning, and got them up into the top of the mountain, saying, "Lo, we be here, and will go up unto the place which the Lord hath promised: for we have sinned."

And Moses said, "Wherefore now do ye transgress the commandment of the Lord? but it shall not prosper. Go not up, for the Lord is not among you; that ye be not smitten before your enemies. For the Amalekites and the Canaanites are there before you, and ye shall fall by the sword: because ye are turned away from the Lord, therefore the Lord will not be with you."

But they presumed to go up unto the hill top: nevertheless the ark of the covenant of the Lord, and Moses, departed not out of the camp. Then the Amalekites came down, and the Canaanites which dwelt in that hill, and smote them, and discomfited them, even unto Hormah.

And while the children of Israel were in the wilderness, they found a man that gathered sticks upon the sabbath day. And they that found him gathering sticks brought him unto Moses and Aaron, and unto all the congregation. And they put him in ward, because it was not declared what should be done to him.

And the Lord said unto Moses, "The man shall be surely put to death: all the congregation shall stone him with stones without the camp." And all the congregation brought him without the camp, and stoned him with stones, and he died; as the Lord commanded Moses.

Now Korah, the son of Izhar, the son of Kohath, the son of Levi, and Dathan and Abiram, the sons of Eliab, and On, the son of Peleth, sons of Reuben, took men; and they rose up before Moses, with certain of the children of Israel, two hundred and fifty princes of the assembly, famous in the congregation, men of renown; and they gathered themselves together against Moses and against Aaron, and said unto them, "Ye take too much upon you, seeing all the congregation are holy, every one of them, and the Lord is among them: wherefore then lift ye up yourselves above the congregation of the Lord?"

And when Moses heard it, he fell upon his face: and he spoke unto Korah and unto all his company, saying, "Even to-morrow the Lord will show who are his, and who is holy; and will cause him to come near unto him: even him whom he hath chosen will he cause to come near unto him. This do: take you censers, Korah, and all his company; and put fire therein, and put incense in them before the Lord to-morrow: and it shall be that the man whom the Lord doth choose, he shall be holy: ye take too much upon you, ye sons of Levi."

And Moses sent to call Dathan and Abiram, the sons of Eliab: which said. "We will not come up. Is it a small thing that thou

THE BOOK OF NUMBERS

hast brought us up out of a land that floweth with milk and honey, to kill us in the wilderness, except thou make thyself altogether a prince over us? Moreover thou hast not brought us into a land that floweth with milk and honey, or given us inheritance of fields and vineyards: wilt thou put out the eyes of these men? we will not come up."

And Moses was very wroth, and said unto the Lord, "Respect not thou their offering: I have not taken one ass from them, neither have I hurt one of them."

And the Lord spoke unto Moses, saying, "Speak unto the congregation, saying, 'Get you up from about the tabernacle of Korah, Dathan, and Abiram.'"

And Moses rose up and went unto Dathan and Abiram; and the elders of Israel followed him. And he spoke unto the congregation, saying, "Depart, I pray you, from the tents of these wicked men, and touch nothing of theirs, lest ye be consumed in all their sins."

So they got up from the tabernacle of Korah, Dathan, and Abiram, on every side: and Dathan and Abiram came out, and stood in the door of their tents, and their wives, and their sons, and their little children. And Moses said, "Hereby ye shall know that the Lord hath sent me to do all these works; for I have not done them of mine own mind. If these men die the common death of all men, or if they be visited after the visitation of all men; then the Lord hath not sent me. But if the Lord make a new thing, and the earth open her mouth, and swallow them up, with all that appertain unto them, and they go down quick into the pit; then ye shall understand that these men have provoked the Lord."

And it came to pass, as he had made an end of speaking all these words, that the ground clove asunder that was under them: and the earth opened her mouth, and swallowed them up, and their houses, and all the men that appertained unto Korah, and all their goods. They, and all that appertained to them, went down alive into the pit, and the earth closed upon them: and they perished from among the congregation. And all Israel that

THE BOOK OF NUMBERS

were round about them fled at the cry of them: for they said, "Lest the earth swallow us up also." And there came out a fire from the Lord, and consumed the two hundred and fifty men that offered incense.

Then came the children of Israel, even the whole congregation, into the desert of Zin in the first month: and the people abode in Kadesh; and Miriam died there, and was buried there. And there was no water for the congregation: and they gathered themselves together against Moses and against Aaron. And the people chid with Moses, and spoke, saying, "Would God that we had died when our brethren died before the Lord! And why have ye brought up the congregation of the Lord into this wilderness, that we and our cattle should die there? And wherefore have ye made us to come up out of Egypt, to bring us in unto this evil place? it is no place of seed, or of figs, or of vines, or of pomegranates; neither is there any water to drink."

And Moses and Aaron went from the presence of the assembly unto the door of the tabernacle of the congregation, and they fell upon their faces: and the glory of the Lord appeared unto them. And the Lord spoke unto Moses, saying, "Take the rod, and gather thou the assembly together, thou, and Aaron thy brother, and speak ye unto the rock before their eyes; and it shall give forth his water, and thou shalt bring forth to them water out of the rock: so thou shalt give the congregation and their beasts drink."

And Moses took the rod from before the Lord, as he commanded him. And Moses and Aaron gathered the congregation together before the rock, and he said unto them,

"Hear now, ye rebels; must we fetch you water out of this rock?"

And Moses lifted up his hand, and with his rod he smote the rock twice: and the water came out abundantly, and the congregation drank, and their beasts also.

And the Lord spoke unto Moses and Aaron, "Because ye believed me not, to sanctify me in the eyes of the children of Israel,

THE BOOK OF NUMBERS

therefore ye shall not bring this congregation into the land which I have given them. This is the water of Meribah; because the children of Israel strove with the Lord, and he was sanctified in them."

And Moses sent messengers from Kadesh unto the king of Edom, "Thus saith thy brother Israel, 'Thou knowest all the travail that hath befallen us: how our fathers went down into Egypt, and we have dwelt in Egypt a long time; and the Egyptians vexed us, and our fathers: and when we cried unto the Lord, he heard our voice, and sent an angel, and hath brought us forth out of Egypt: and, behold, we are in Kadesh, a city in the uttermost of thy border. Let us pass, I pray thee, through thy country: we will not pass through the fields, or through the vineyards, neither will we drink of the water of the wells: we will go by the king's high way, we will not turn to the right hand nor to the left, until we have passed thy borders.'"

And Edom said unto him, "Thou shalt not pass by me, lest I come out against thee with the sword."

And the children of Israel said unto him, "We will go by the high way: and if I and my cattle drink of thy water, then I will pay for it: I will only, without doing any thing else, go through on my feet."

And he said, "Thou shalt not go through." And Edom came out against him with much people, and with a strong hand. Thus Edom refused to give Israel passage through his border: wherefore Israel turned away from him.

And the children of Israel, even the whole congregation, journeyed from Kadesh, and came unto Mount Hor. And the Lord spoke unto Moses and Aaron in Mount Hor, by the coast of the land of Edom, saying,

"Aaron shall be gathered unto his people: for he shall not enter into the land which I have given unto the children of Israel, because ye rebelled against my word at the water of Meribah. Take Aaron and Eleazar his son, and bring them up unto Mount

THE BOOK OF NUMBERS

Hor: and strip Aaron of his garments, and put them upon Eleazar his son: and Aaron shall be gathered unto his people, and shall die there."

And Moses did as the Lord commanded: and they went up into Mount Hor in the sight of all the congregation. And Moses stripped Aaron of his garments, and put them upon Eleazar his son; and Aaron died there in the top of the mount: and Moses and Eleazar came down from the mount. And when all the congregation saw that Aaron was dead, they mourned for Aaron thirty days, even all the house of Israel.

And they journeyed from Mount Hor by the way of the Red Sea, to compass the land of Edom: and the soul of the people was much discouraged because of the way. And the people spoke against God, and against Moses, "Wherefore have ye brought us up out of Egypt to die in the wilderness? for there is no bread, neither is there any water; and our soul loatheth this light bread."

And the Lord sent fiery serpents among the people, and they bit the people; and much people of Israel died. Therefore the people came to Moses, and said, "We have sinned, for we have spoken against the Lord, and against thee; pray unto the Lord, that he take away the serpents from us." And Moses prayed for the people. And the Lord said unto Moses, "Make thee a fiery serpent, and set it upon a pole: and it shall come to pass that every one that is bitten, when he looketh upon it, shall live."

And Moses made a serpent of brass, and put it upon a pole, and it came to pass that if a serpent had bitten any man, when he beheld the serpent of brass, he lived.

And the children of Israel set forward, and pitched in Oboth. And they journeyed from Oboth, and pitched at Ije-abarim, in the wilderness which is before Moab, toward the sunrising. From thence they removed, and pitched in the valley of Zared. From thence they removed, and pitched on the other side of Arnon, which is in the wilderness that cometh out of the coasts of the Amorites: for Arnon is the border of Moab, between Moab and

THE BOOK OF NUMBERS

the Amorites. Wherefore it is said in the Book of the Wars of the Lord,

> "What he did in the Red Sea,
> And in the brooks of Arnon,
> And at the stream of the brooks
> That goeth down to the dwelling of Ar,
> And lieth upon the border of Moab."

And from thence they went to Beer: that is the well whereof the Lord spoke unto Moses, "Gather the people together, and I will give them water." Then Israel sang this song,

> "Spring up, O well; sing ye unto it:
> The princes digged the well,
> The nobles of the people digged it,
> By the direction of the lawgiver,
> With their staves."

And from the wilderness they went to Mattanah: and from Mattanah to Nahaliel: and from Nahaliel to Bamoth: and from Bamoth in the valley, that is in the country of Moab, to the top of Pisgah, which looketh toward Jeshimon. And Israel sent messengers unto Sihon king of the Amorites, saying,

"Let me pass through thy land: we will not turn into the fields, or into the vineyards; we will not drink of the waters of the well: but we will go along by the king's high way, until we be past thy borders."

And Sihon would not suffer Israel to pass through his border: but Sihon gathered all his people together, and went out against Israel into the wilderness: and he came to Jahaz, and fought against Israel. And Israel smote him with the edge of the sword, and possessed his land from Arnon unto Jabbok, even unto the children of Ammon: for the border of the children of Ammon was strong. And Israel took all these cities: and Israel dwelt in all the cities of the Amorites, in Heshbon, and in all the villages thereof. For Heshbon was the city of Sihon the king of the Amorites, who had fought against the former king of Moab, and

THE BOOK OF NUMBERS

taken all his land out of his hand, even unto Arnon. Wherefore they that speak in proverbs say,

> "Come into Heshbon,
> Let the city of Sihon be built and prepared:
> For there is a fire gone out of Heshbon,
> A flame from the city of Sihon:
> It hath consumed Ar of Moab,
> The lords of the high places of Arnon.
> Woe to thee, Moab!
> Thou art undone, O people of Chemosh:
> He hath given his sons that escaped,
> And his daughters, into captivity unto Sihon king of the
>   Amorites.
> We have shot at them; Heshbon is perished even unto Dibon,
> And we have laid them waste even unto Nophah, which
>   reacheth unto Medeba."

And they turned and went up by the way of Bashan: and Og the king of Bashan went out against them, he, and all his people, to the battle of Edrei. And the Lord said unto Moses, "Fear him not: for I have delivered him into thy hand, and all his people, and his land; and thou shalt do to him as thou didst unto Sihon king of the Amorites, which dwelt at Heshbon."

So they smote him, and his sons, and all his people, until there was none left him alive: and they possessed his land.

The Story of Balaam

And the children of Israel set forward, and pitched in the plains of Moab on this side Jordan by Jericho. And Moab was sore afraid of the people, because they were many: and Moab was distressed because of the children of Israel. And Moab said unto the elders of Midian,

"Now shall this company lick up all that are round about us, as the ox licketh up the grass of the field."

And Balak the son of Zippor was king of the Moabites at that time. He sent messengers therefore unto Balaam the son of Beor

THE BOOK OF NUMBERS

to Pethor, which is by the river of the land of the children of his people, to call him, saying,

"Behold, there is a people come out from Egypt: behold, they cover the face of the earth, and they abide over against me. Come now therefore, I pray thee, curse me this people; for they are too mighty for me: peradventure I shall prevail, that we may smite them, and that I may drive them out of the land: for I wot that he whom thou blessest is blessed, and he whom thou cursest is cursed."

And the elders of Moab and the elders of Midian departed with the rewards of divination in their hand; and they came unto Balaam, and spoke unto him the words of Balak. And he said unto them, "Lodge here this night, and I will bring you word again, as the Lord shall speak unto me": and the princes of Moab abode with Balaam.

And God came unto Balaam, and said, "What men are these with thee?"

And Balaam said unto God, "Balak the son of Zippor, king of Moab, hath sent unto me, saying, 'Behold, there is a people come out of Egypt, which covereth the face of the earth: come now, curse me them; peradventure I shall be able to overcome them, and drive them out.'"

And God said unto Balaam, "Thou shalt not go with them; thou shalt not curse the people: for they are blessed."

And Balaam rose up in the morning, and said unto the princes of Balak, "Get you into your land: for the Lord refuseth to give me leave to go with you."

And the princes of Moab rose up, and they went unto Balak, and said, "Balaam refuseth to come with us."

And Balak sent yet again princes, more, and more honourable than they. And they came to Balaam, and said to him, "Thus saith Balak the son of Zippor, 'Let nothing, I pray thee, hinder thee from coming unto me: for I will promote thee unto very great honour, and I will do whatsoever thou sayest unto me: come therefore, I pray thee, curse me this people.'"

And Balaam answered and said unto the servants of Balak,

THE BOOK OF NUMBERS

"If Balak would give me his house full of silver and gold, I cannot go beyond the word of the Lord my God, to do less or more. Now therefore, I pray you, tarry ye also here this night, that I may know what the Lord will say unto me more."

And God came unto Balaam at night, and said unto him, "If the men come to call thee, rise up, and go with them; but yet the word which I shall say unto thee, that shalt thou do."

And Balaam rose up in the morning, and saddled his ass, and went with the princes of Moab. And God's anger was kindled because he went: and the angel of the Lord stood in the way for an adversary against him. Now he was riding upon his ass, and his two servants were with him. And the ass saw the angel of the Lord standing in the way, and his sword drawn in his hand: and the ass turned aside out of the way, and went into the field: and Balaam smote the ass, to turn her into the way. But the angel of the Lord stood in a path of the vineyards, a wall being on this side, and a wall on that side. And when the ass saw the angel of the Lord, she thrust herself unto the wall, and crushed Balaam's foot against the wall: and he smote her again. And the angel of the Lord went further, and stood in a narrow place, where was no way to turn either to the right hand or to the left. And when the ass saw the angel of the Lord, she fell down under Balaam: and Balaam's anger was kindled, and he smote the ass with a staff.

And the Lord opened the mouth of the ass, and she said unto Balaam, "What have I done unto thee, that thou hast smitten me these three times?"

And Balaam said unto the ass, "Because thou hast mocked me: I would there were a sword in mine hand, for now would I kill thee."

And the ass said unto Balaam, "Am not I thine ass, upon which thou hast ridden ever since I was thine unto this day? was I ever wont to do so unto thee?" And he said, "Nay."

Then the Lord opened the eyes of Balaam, and he saw the angel of the Lord standing in the way, and his sword drawn in his hand: and he bowed down his head, and fell flat on his face.

THE BOOK OF NUMBERS

And the angel of the Lord said unto him, "Wherefore hast thou smitten thine ass these three times? behold, I went out to withstand thee, because thy way is perverse before me: and the ass saw me, and turned from me these three times: unless she had turned from me, surely now also I had slain thee, and saved her alive."

And Balaam said unto the angel of the Lord, "I have sinned; for I knew not that thou stoodest in the way against me: now therefore, if it displease thee, I will get me back again."

And the angel of the Lord said unto Balaam, "Go with the men: but only the word that I shall speak unto thee, that thou shalt speak."

So Balaam went with the princes of Balak. And when Balak heard that Balaam was come, he went out to meet him unto a city of Moab, which is in the border of Arnon, which is in the utmost coast.

And Balak said unto Balaam, "Did I not earnestly send unto thee to call thee? wherefore camest thou not unto me? am I not able indeed to promote thee to honour?"

And Balaam said unto Balak, "Lo, I am come unto thee: have I now any power at all to say any thing? the word that God putteth in my mouth, that shall I speak."

And Balaam went with Balak, and they came unto Kirjath-huzoth. And Balak offered oxen and sheep, and sent to Balaam, and to the princes that were with him. And it came to pass on the morrow, that Balak took Balaam, and brought him up into the high places of Baal, that thence he might see the utmost part of the people.

And Balaam said unto Balak, "Build me here seven altars, and prepare me here seven oxen and seven rams."

And Balak did as Balaam had spoken; and Balak and Balaam offered on every altar a bullock and a ram. And Balaam said unto Balak, "Stand by thy burnt offering, and I will go: peradventure the Lord will come to meet me: and whatsoever he showeth me I will tell thee." And he went to a high place.

And God met Balaam: and he said unto him, "I have prepared

THE BOOK OF NUMBERS

seven altars, and I have offered upon every altar a bullock and a ram." And the Lord put a word in Balaam's mouth, and said, "Return unto Balak, and thus thou shalt speak."

And he returned unto him, and, lo, he stood by his burnt sacrifice, he, and all the princes of Moab. And he took up his parable, and said,

> "Balak the king of Moab hath brought me from Aram,
> Out of the mountains of the east.
> 'Come, curse me Jacob,
> And come, defy Israel,'
> How shall I curse, whom God hath not cursed?
> Or how shall I defy, whom the Lord hath not defied?
> For from the top of the rocks I see him,
> And from the hills I behold him:
> Lo, the people shall dwell alone,
> And shall not be reckoned among the nations.
> Who can count the dust of Jacob,
> And the number of the fourth part of Israel?
> Let me die the death of the righteous,
> And let my last end be like his!"

And Balak said unto Balaam, "What hast thou done unto me? I took thee to curse mine enemies, and, behold, thou hast blessed them altogether."

And he answered and said, "Must I not take heed to speak that which the Lord hath put in my mouth?"

And Balak said unto him, "Come, I pray thee, with me unto another place, from whence thou mayest see them: thou shalt see but the utmost part of them, and shalt not see them all: and curse me them from thence."

And he brought him into the field of Zophim, to the top of Pisgah, and built seven altars, and offered a bullock and a ram on every altar. And he said unto Balak, "Stand here by thy burnt offering, while I meet the Lord yonder."

And the Lord met Balaam, and put a word in his mouth, and said, "Go again unto Balak, and say thus."

THE BOOK OF NUMBERS

And when he came to him, behold, he stood by his burnt offering, and the princes of Moab with him. And Balak said unto him, "What hath the Lord spoken?"

And he took up his parable, and said,

> "Rise up, Balak, and hear;
> Hearken unto me, thou son of Zippor:
> God is not a man, that he should lie;
> Neither the son of man, that he should repent:
> Hath he said, and shall he not do it?
> Or hath he spoken, and shall he not make it good?
> Behold, I have received commandment to bless:
> And he hath blessed; and I cannot reverse it.
> He hath not beheld iniquity in Jacob,
> Neither hath he seen perverseness in Israel:
> The Lord his God is with him,
> And the shout of a king is among them.
> God brought them out of Egypt;
> He hath as it were the strength of a unicorn.
> Surely there is no enchantment against Jacob,
> Neither is there any divination against Israel:
> According to this time it shall be said of Jacob and of Israel,
>   'What hath God wrought!'
> Behold, the people shall rise up as a great lion,
> And lift up himself as a young lion:
> He shall not lie down until he eat of the prey,
> And drink the blood of the slain."

And Balak said unto Balaam, "Neither curse them at all, nor bless them at all."

But Balaam answered and said unto Balak, "Told not I thee, saying, 'All that the Lord speaketh, that I must do'?"

And Balak said unto Balaam, "Come, I pray thee, I will bring thee unto another place; peradventure it will please God that thou mayest curse me them from thence."

And Balak brought Balaam unto the top of Peor, that looketh toward Jeshimon. And Balaam said unto Balak, "Build me here

THE BOOK OF NUMBERS

seven altars, and prepare me here seven bullocks and seven rams." And Balak did as Balaam had said, and offered a bullock and a ram on every altar.

And when Balaam saw that it pleased the Lord to bless Israel, he went not, as at other times, to seek for enchantments, but he set his face toward the wilderness. And Balaam lifted up his eyes, and he saw Israel abiding in his tents according to their tribes; and the spirit of God came upon him. And he took up his parable, and said,

> "Balaam the son of Beor hath said,
> And the man whose eyes are open hath said:
> He hath said, which heard the words of God,
> Which saw the vision of the Almighty,
> Falling into a trance, but having his eyes open:
>
> 'How goodly are thy tents, O Jacob,
> Thy tabernacles, O Israel!
> As the valleys are they spread forth,
> As gardens by the river's side,
> As the trees of lignaloes which the Lord hath planted,
> As cedar trees beside the waters.
> He shall pour the water out of his buckets,
> And his seed shall be in many waters,
> And his king shall be higher than Agag,
> And his kingdom shall be exalted.
> God brought him forth out of Egypt;
> He hath as it were the strength of a unicorn:
> He shall eat up the nations his enemies,
> And shall break their bones,
> And pierce them through with his arrows.
> He couched, he lay down as a lion,
> And as a great lion: who shall stir him up?
> Blessed is he that blesseth thee,
> And cursed is he that curseth thee.'"

And Balak's anger was kindled against Balaam, and he smote

THE BOOK OF NUMBERS

his hands together: and Balak said unto Balaam, "I called thee to curse mine enemies, and, behold, thou hast altogether blessed them these three times. Therefore now flee thou to thy place: I thought to promote thee unto great honour; but, lo, the Lord hath kept thee back from honour."

And Balaam said unto Balak, "Spoke I not also to thy messengers which thou sentest unto me, saying, 'If Balak would give me his house full of silver and gold, I cannot go beyond the commandment of the Lord, to do either good or bad of mine own mind; but what the Lord saith, that will I speak'? And now, behold, I go unto my people: come therefore, and I will advertise thee what this people shall do to thy people in the latter days."

And he took up his parable, and said,

> "Balaam the son of Beor hath said,
> And the man whose eyes are open hath said:
> He hath said, which heard the words of God,
> And knew the knowledge of the most High,
> Which saw the vision of the Almighty,
> Falling into a trance, but having his eyes open:
>
> 'I shall see him, but not now:
> I shall behold him, but not nigh:
> There shall come a Star out of Jacob,
> And a Sceptre shall rise out of Israel,
> And shall smite the corners of Moab,
> And destroy all the children of Seth.
> And Edom shall be a possession,
> Seir also shall be a possession for his enemies;
> And Israel shall do valiantly.
> Out of Jacob shall come he that shall have dominion,
> And shall destroy him that remaineth of the city.'"

And when he looked on Amalek, he took up his parable, and said,

> "Amalek was the first of the nations;
> But his latter end shall be that he perish for ever."

THE BOOK OF NUMBERS

And he looked on the Kenites, and took up his parable, and said,

> "Strong is thy dwellingplace,
> And thou puttest thy nest in a rock.
> Nevertheless the Kenite shall be wasted,
> Until Asshur shall carry thee away captive."

And he took up his parable, and said,

> "Alas, who shall live when God doeth this!
> And ships shall come from the coast of Chittim,
> And shall afflict Asshur, and shall afflict Eber,
> And he also shall perish for ever."

And Balaam rose up, and went and returned to his place: and Balak also went his way.

The War with the Midianites

And, behold, one of the children of Israel came and brought unto his brethren a Midianitish woman in the sight of Moses, and in the sight of all the congregation of the children of Israel, who were weeping before the door of the tabernacle of the congregation. And when Phinehas, the son of Eleazar, the son of Aaron the priest, saw it, he rose up from among the congregation, and took a javelin in his hand; and he went after the man of Israel into the tent, and thrust both of them through, the man of Israel, and the woman through her belly. So the plague was stayed from the children of Israel. And those that died in the plague were twenty and four thousand.

And the Lord spoke unto Moses, saying, "Phinehas, the son of Eleazar, the son of Aaron the priest, hath turned my wrath away from the children of Israel, while he was zealous for my sake among them, that I consumed not the children of Israel in my jealousy. Wherefore say, 'Behold, I give unto him my covenant of peace: and he shall have it, and his seed after him, even the covenant of an everlasting priesthood; because he was zeal-

THE BOOK OF NUMBERS

ous for his God, and made an atonement for the children of Israel.'"

(Now the name of the Israelite that was slain, even that was slain with the Midianitish woman, was Zimri, the son of Salu, a prince of a chief house among the Simeonites. And the name of the Midianitish woman that was slain was Cozbi, the daughter of Zur; he was head over a people, and of a chief house in Midian.)

And the Lord spoke unto Moses, saying, "Vex the Midianites, and smite them: for they vex you with their wiles, wherewith they have beguiled you in the matter of Peor, and in the matter of Cozbi, the daughter of a prince of Midian, their sister, which was slain in the day of the plague for Peor's sake."

And they warred against the Midianites, as the Lord commanded Moses; and they slew all the males. And they slew the kings of Midian, beside the rest of them that were slain; namely, Evi, and Rekem, and Zur, and Hur, and Reba, five kings of Midian: Balaam also the son of Beor they slew with the sword. And the children of Israel took all the women of Midian captives, and their little ones, and took the spoil of all their cattle, and all their flocks, and all their goods. And they burnt all their cities wherein they dwelt, and all their goodly castles, with fire. And they took all the spoil, and all the prey, both of men and of beasts. And they brought the captives, and the prey, and the spoil, unto Moses, and Eleazar the priest, and unto the congregation of the children of Israel, unto the camp at the plains of Moab, which are by Jordan near Jericho.

And Moses, and Eleazar the priest, and all the princes of the congregation, went forth to meet them without the camp. And Moses was wroth with the officers of the host, with the captains over thousands, and captains over hundreds, which came from the battle. And Moses said unto them,

"Have ye saved all the women alive? Behold, these caused the children of Israel, through the counsel of Balaam, to commit trespass against the Lord in the matter of Peor, and there was a plague among the congregation of the Lord. Now therefore kill

THE BOOK OF NUMBERS

every male among the little ones, and kill every woman that hath known man by lying with him. But all the women children, that have not known a man by lying with him, keep alive for yourselves. And do ye abide without the camp seven days: whosoever hath killed any person, and whosoever hath touched any slain, purify both yourselves and your captives on the third day, and on the seventh day. And purify all your raiment, and all that is made of skins, and all work of goats' hair, and all things made of wood."

And the officers which were over thousands of the host, the captains of thousands, and captains of hundreds, came near unto Moses: and they said unto Moses, "Thy servants have taken the sum of the men of war which are under our charge, and there lacketh not one man of us. We have therefore brought an oblation for the Lord, what every man hath gotten, of jewels of gold, chains, and bracelets, rings, earrings, and tablets, to make an atonement for our souls before the Lord."

And Moses and Eleazar the priest took the gold of them, even all wrought jewels. And all the gold of the offering that they offered up to the Lord, of the captains of thousands, and of the captains of hundreds, was sixteen thousand seven hundred and fifty shekels. (For the men of war had taken spoil, every man for himself.) And Moses and Eleazar the priest took the gold of the captains of thousands and of hundreds, and brought it into the tabernacle of the congregation, for a memorial for the children of Israel before the Lord.

THE BOOK OF DEUTERONOMY

The book of deuteronomy *has been a kind of Rosetta Stone for modern Biblical criticism, the discovery of its meaning offering a central clue for unraveling the tangled problem of the Hexateuch and for the proper orientation of the whole work of the prophetical school. For Deuteronomy is none other than the mysterious "book of the law" found in the temple in 621 B.C. during the reign of Josiah and made the basis of that monarch's reforms, as recounted in the Second Book of Kings. It was a recodification of Jewish law secretly prepared, in all probability, during the suppression of the prophets in the tyrannical reign of Manasseh, 693-639 B.C. The ascription of its authorship to Moses was as natural as it is to-day for the Supreme Court of the United States to find the essence of its latest decisions hidden somewhere in the Constitution. Nor with the magical powers traditionally attributed to Moses did it seem at all improbable that he should have included an account of his own death. Our contemporary ideas of historical evidence, copyright, plagiarism, and forgery must, of course, all be dismissed in approaching the problem. In spite of their emphasis upon inner motivation, the prophets were fully in accord with the social-mindedness especially characteristic of the Jews. Literature was regarded as a communal possession instead of as a piece of private property. The writer was not concerned with the personal prestige of authorship but simply strove to give his work the widest influence possible, which naturally led to his seeking the support of such great names as those of Moses, David, or Solomon. The Deuteronomic laws, the prophetical writers believed, were such as Moses intended and desired; hence there was no dishonesty in ascribing them to him. It was merely an example of the more open ancient way of obtaining the same sanction of tradition that moderns are wont to secure by more indirect methods.*

The Book of DEUTERONOMY

The Death of Moses

AND THE LORD SAID UNTO MOSES, "Behold, thy days approach that thou must die: call Joshua, and present yourselves in the tabernacle of the congregation, that I may give him a charge."

And Moses and Joshua went, and presented themselves in the tabernacle of the congregation. And the Lord appeared in the tabernacle in a pillar of a cloud: and the pillar of the cloud stood over the door of the tabernacle.

And the Lord said unto Moses, "Behold, thou shalt sleep with thy fathers; and this people will rise up, and go a-whoring after the gods of the strangers of the land, whither they go to be among them, and will forsake me, and break my covenant which I have made with them. Then my anger shall be kindled against them in that day, and I will forsake them, and I will hide my face from them, and they shall be devoured, and many evils and troubles shall befall them; so that they will say in that day, 'Are not these evils come upon us, because our God is not among us?' And I will surely hide my face in that day for all the evils which they shall have wrought, in that they are turned unto other gods. Now therefore write ye this song for you, and teach it the children of Israel: put it in their mouths, that this song may be a witness for me against the children of Israel. For when I shall have brought them into the land which I swore unto their fathers, that floweth with milk and honey; and they shall have eaten and filled themselves, and waxen fat; then will they turn unto other gods, and serve them, and provoke me, and break my covenant. And it shall come to pass, when many evils and troubles

THE BOOK OF DEUTERONOMY

are befallen them, that this song shall testify against them as a witness; for it shall not be forgotten out of the mouths of their seed: for I know their imagination which they go about, even now, before I have brought them into the land which I swore."

Moses therefore wrote this song the same day, and taught it the children of Israel.

"Give ear, O ye heavens, and I will speak;
And hear, O earth, the words of my mouth.
My doctrine shall drop as the rain,
My speech shall distil as the dew,
As the small rain upon the tender herb,
And as the showers upon the grass:
Because I will publish the name of the Lord:
Ascribe ye greatness unto our God.
He is the Rock, his work is perfect:
For all his ways are judgment:
A God of truth and without iniquity,
Just and right is he.
They have corrupted themselves, their spot is not the spot of
    his children:
They are a perverse and crooked generation.
Do ye thus requite the Lord,
O foolish people and unwise?
Is not he thy father that hath bought thee?
Hath he not made thee, and established thee?

Remember the days of old,
Consider the years of many generations:
Ask thy father, and he will show thee;
Thy elders, and they will tell thee.
When the Most High divided to the nations their inheritance,
When he separated the sons of Adam,
He set the bounds of the people
According to the number of the children of Israel.
For the Lord's portion is his people;
Jacob is the lot of his inheritance.

THE BOOK OF DEUTERONOMY

He found him in a desert land,
And in the waste howling winderness;
He led him about, he instructed him,
He kept him as the apple of his eye.
As an eagle stirreth up her nest,
Fluttereth over her young,
Spreadeth abroad her wings, taketh them,
Beareth them on her wings:
So the Lord alone did lead him,
And there was no strange god with him.
He made him ride on the high places of the earth,
That he might eat the increase of the fields;
And he made him to suck honey out of the rock,
And oil out of the flinty rock;
Butter of kine, and milk of sheep, with fat of lambs,
And rams of the breed of Bashan, and goats,
With the fat of kidneys of wheat;
And thou didst drink the pure blood of the grape.

But Jeshurun waxed fat, and kicked:
Thou art waxen fat, thou art grown thick, thou art covered with fatness;
Then he forsook God which made him,
And lightly esteemed the Rock of his salvation.
They provoked him to jealousy with strange gods,
With abominations provoked they him to anger.
They sacrificed unto devils, not to God;
To Gods whom they knew not,
To new gods that came newly up,
Whom your fathers feared not.
Of the Rock that begot thee thou art unmindful,
And hast forgotten God that formed thee.

And when the Lord saw it, he abhorred them,
Because of the provoking of his sons, and of his daughters.
And he said, 'I will hide my face from them,
I will see what their end shall be:

THE BOOK OF DEUTERONOMY

For they are a very froward generation,
Children in whom is no faith.
They have moved me to jealousy with that which is not God;
They have provoked me to anger with their vanities;
And I will move them to jealousy with those which are not a
    people;
I will provoke them to anger with a foolish nation.
For a fire is kindled in mine anger,
And shall burn unto the lowest hell,
And shall consume the earth with her increase,
And set on fire the foundations of the mountains.
I will heap mischiefs upon them;
I will spend mine arrows upon them.
They shall be burnt with hunger, and devoured with burning
    heat,
And with bitter destruction;
I will also send the teeth of beasts upon them,
With the poison of serpents of the dust.
The sword without, and terror within,
Shall destroy both the young man and the virgin,
The suckling also with the man of gray hairs.
I said, "I would scatter them into corners,
I would make the remembrance of them to cease from among men":
Were it not that I feared the wrath of the enemy,
Lest their adversaries should behave themselves strangely,
And lest they should say, "Our hand is high,
And the Lord hath not done all this."

For they are a nation void of counsel,
Neither is there any understanding in them.
O that they were wise, that they understood this,
That they would consider their latter end!'
How should one chase a thousand,
And two put ten thousand to flight,
Except their Rock had sold them,
And the Lord had shut them up?

THE BOOK OF DEUTERONOMY

For their rock is not as our Rock,
Even our enemies themselves being judges.
For their vine is of the vine of Sodom,
And of the fields of Gomorrah:
Their grapes are grapes of gall,
Their clusters are bitter:
Their wine is the poison of dragons,
And the cruel venom of asps.

'Is not this laid up in store with me,
Sealed up among my treasures?
To me belongeth vengeance, and recompense;
Their foot shall slide in due time:
For the day of their calamity is at hand,
And the things that shall come upon them make haste.'
For the Lord shall judge his people,
And repent himself for his servants,
When he seeth that their power is gone,
And there is none shut up, or left.
And he shall say, 'Where are their gods,
Their rock in whom they trusted,
Which did eat the fat of their sacrifices,
And drank the wine of their drink offerings?
Let them rise up and help you,
And be your protection.'
'See now that I, even I, am he,
And there is no god with me:
I kill, and I make alive;
I wound, and I heal:
Neither is there any that can deliver out of my hand.
For I lift up my hand to heaven,
And say, "I live for ever.
If I whet my glittering sword,
And mine hand take hold on judgment;
I will render vengeance to mine enemies,
And will reward them that hate me.

THE BOOK OF DEUTERONOMY

I will make mine arrows drunk with blood,
And my sword shall devour flesh;
With the blood of the slain and of the captives,
From the beginning of revenges upon the enemy."

Rejoice, O ye nations, with his people:
For he will avenge the blood of his servants,
And will render vengeance to his adversaries,
And will be merciful unto his land, and to his people."

And Moses came and spoke all the words of this song in the ears of the people, he, and Hoshea the son of Nun.

And this is the blessing, wherewith Moses the man of God blessed the children of Israel before his death.

And he said,

"The Lord came from Sinai,
And rose up from Seir unto them;
He shined forth from Mount Paran,
And he came with ten thousands of saints:
From his right hand went a fiery law for them.
Yea, he loved the people;
All his saints are in thy hand:
And they sat down at thy feet;
Every one shall receive of thy words.

Let Reuben live, and not die;
And let not his men be few."

And this is the blessing of Judah:

"Hear, Lord, the voice of Judah,
And bring him unto his people:
Let his hands be sufficient for him;
And be thou a help to him from his enemies."

And of Levi:

"Let thy Thummim and thy Urim be with thy holy one,
Whom thou didst prove at Massah,
With whom thou didst strive at the waters of Meribah;

THE BOOK OF DEUTERONOMY

 Who said unto his father and to his mother, 'I have not seen
   him';
 Neither did he acknowledge his brethren,
 Nor knew his own children:
 For they have observed thy word,
 And kept thy covenant.
 They shall teach Jacob thy judgments,
 And Israel thy law:
 They shall put incense before thee,
 And whole burnt sacrifice upon thine altar.
 Bless, Lord, his substance,
 And accept the work of his hands:
 Smite through the loins of them that rise against him,
 And of them that hate him, that they rise not again."

And of Benjamin:

 "The beloved of the Lord shall dwell in safety by him;
 The Lord shall cover him all the day long,
 And he shall dwell between his shoulders."

And of Joseph:

 "Blessed of the Lord be his land,
 For the precious things of heaven, for the dew,
 And for the deep that coucheth beneath,
 And for the precious fruits brought forth by the sun,
 And for the precious things put forth by the moon,
 And for the chief things of the ancient mountains,
 And for the precious things of the lasting hills,
 And for the precious things of the earth and fulness thereof,
 And for the good will of him that dwelt in the bush:
 Let the blessing come upon the head of Joseph,
 And upon the top of the head of him that was separated from
   his brethren.
 His glory is like the firstling of his bullock,
 And his horns are like the horns of unicorns:
 With them he shall push the people together

THE BOOK OF DEUTERONOMY

To the ends of the earth: and they are the ten thousands of
  Ephraim,
And they are the thousands of Manasseh."

And of Zebulun:

"Rejoice, Zebulun, in thy going out;
And, Issachar, in thy tents.
They shall call the people unto the mountain;
There they shall offer sacrifices of righteousness:
For they shall suck of the abundance of the seas,
And of treasures hid in the sand."

And of Gad:

"Blessed be he that enlargeth Gad:
He dwelleth as a lion,
And teareth the arm with the crown of the head.
And he provided the first part for himself,
Because there, in a portion of the lawgiver, was he seated;
And he came with the heads of the people,
He executed the justice of the Lord,
And his judgments with Israel."

And of Dan:

"Dan is a lion's whelp:
He shall leap from Bashan."

And of Naphtali:

"O Naphtali, satisfied with favour,
And full with the blessing of the Lord:
Possess thou the west and the south."

And of Asher:

"Let Asher be blessed with children;
Let him be acceptable to his brethren,
And let him dip his foot in oil.
Thy shoes shall be iron and brass;
And as thy days, so shall thy strength be.

THE BOOK OF DEUTERONOMY

There is none like unto the God of Jeshurun,
Who rideth upon the heaven in thy help,
And in his excellency on the sky.
The eternal God is thy refuge,
And underneath are the everlasting arms:
And he shall thrust out the enemy from before thee;
And shall say, 'Destroy them.'
Israel then shall dwell in safety alone:
The fountain of Jacob
Upon a land of corn and wine;
Also his heavens shall drop down dew.
Happy art thou, O Israel:
Who is like unto thee,
O people saved by the Lord,
The shield of thy help,
And who is the sword of thy excellency!
And thine enemies shall be found liars unto thee;
And thou shalt tread upon their high places."

And Moses went up from the plains of Moab unto the mountain of Nebo, to the top of Pisgah, that is over against Jericho. And the Lord showed him all the land of Gilead, unto Dan, and all Naphtali, and the land of Ephraim, and Manasseh, and all the land of Judah, unto the utmost sea, and the south, and the plain of the valley of Jericho, the city of palm trees, unto Zoar. And the Lord said unto him,

"This is the land which I swore unto Abraham, unto Isaac, and unto Jacob, saying, 'I will give it unto thy seed': I have caused thee to see it with thine eyes, but thou shalt not go over thither."

So Moses the servant of the Lord died there in the land of Moab, according to the word of the Lord. And he buried him in a valley in the land of Moab, over against Beth-peor: but no man knoweth of his sepulchre unto this day. And Moses was a hundred and twenty years old when he died: his eye was not dim, nor his natural force abated. And the children of Israel wept for

THE BOOK OF DEUTERONOMY

Moses in the plains of Moab thirty days: so the days of weeping and mourning for Moses were ended. And Joshua the son of Nun was full of the spirit of wisdom; for Moses had laid his hands upon him: and the children of Israel hearkened unto him, and did as the Lord commanded Moses. And there arose not a prophet since in Israel like unto Moses, whom the Lord knew face to face, in all the signs and the wonders, which the Lord sent him to do in the land of Egypt to Pharaoh, and to all his servants, and to all his land, and in all that mighty hand, and in all the great terror which Moses showed in the sight of all Israel.

THE BOOK OF JOSHUA

THE ABSENCE of heroes in Jewish literature has often been remarked. The pages of Jewish history are thronged with great personalities from Abraham to Judas Maccabeus, but they are rarely presented in a continuously favorable light. It was as if the Jews so concentrated all their idealizing tendencies on the conception of the deity that they were left free to observe human nature with washed eyes. The one notable exception is the Book of Joshua which represents a deliberate attempt to create a military hero as a companion piece to the portrait of Moses the legislator. It was made up out of almost whole cloth by a Deuteronomic writer's very free editing of a few legends so turned as to contradict the earlier accounts in Judges and First Samuel, which show the conquest of Canaan to have been a very slow and laborious affair of centuries, and to present it instead as the achievement of a single mighty soldier. It was a magnificent attempt but a failure. The Jewish genius was at its best only in works of peace, not war. Where Moses seems a very definite human being, Joshua remains a lay figure; the interest is centered not in him but in the adventures of the spies, the collapse of the walls of Jericho, the wiles of the Gibeonites, the staying of the sun—special incidents where the picturesqueness of the legendary material dominates the larger editorial purpose.

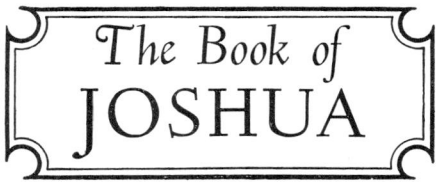

The Book of JOSHUA

The Destruction of Jericho

Now after the death of Moses the servant of the Lord it came to pass that the Lord spoke unto Joshua the son of Nun, Moses' minister, saying,

"Moses my servant is dead; now therefore arise, go over this Jordan, thou, and all this people, unto the land which I do give to them, even to the children of Israel. Every place that the sole of your foot shall tread upon, that have I given unto you, as I said unto Moses. From the wilderness and this Lebanon even unto the great river, the river Euphrates, all the land of the Hittites, and unto the great sea toward the going down of the sun, shall be your coast. There shall not any man be able to stand before thee all the days of thy life: as I was with Moses, so I will be with thee: I will not fail thee, nor forsake thee. Be strong and of a good courage: for unto this people shalt thou divide for an inheritance the land, which I swore unto their fathers to give them. Only be thou strong and very courageous, that thou mayest observe to do according to all the law, which Moses my servant commanded thee: turn not from it to the right hand or to the left, that thou mayest prosper whithersoever thou goest. This book of the law shall not depart out of thy mouth; but thou shalt meditate therein day and night, that thou mayest observe to do according to all that is written therein: for then thou shalt make thy way prosperous, and then thou shalt have good success. Have not I commanded thee? Be strong and of a good courage; be not afraid, neither be thou dismayed: for the Lord thy God is with thee whithersoever thou goest."

THE BOOK OF JOSHUA

Then Joshua commanded the officers of the people, saying,

"Pass through the host, and command the people, saying, 'Prepare you victuals; for within three days ye shall pass over this Jordan, to go in to possess the land, which the Lord your God giveth you to possess it.'"

And Joshua the son of Nun sent out of Shittim two men to spy secretly, saying, "Go view the land, even Jericho."

And they went, and came into a harlot's house, named Rahab, and lodged there. And it was told the king of Jericho, saying,

"Behold, there came men in hither to-night of the children of Israel to search out the country."

And the king of Jericho sent unto Rahab, saying,

"Bring forth the men that are come to thee, which are entered into thine house: for they be come to search out all the country."

And the woman took the two men and hid them, and said thus,

"There came men unto me, but I wist not whence they were: and it came to pass about the time of shutting of the gate, when it was dark, that the men went out: whither the men went I wot not: pursue after them quickly; for ye shall overtake them."

But she had brought them up to the roof of the house, and hid them with the stalks of flax, which she had laid in order upon the roof. And the men pursued after them the way to Jordan unto the fords: and as soon as they which pursued after them were gone out, they shut the gate. And before they were laid down, she came up unto them upon the roof; and she said unto the men,

"I know that the Lord hath given you the land, and that your terror is fallen upon us, and that all the inhabitants of the land faint because of you. For we have heard how the Lord dried up the water of the Red Sea for you, when ye came out of Egypt; and what ye did unto the two kings of the Amorites, that were on the other side Jordan, Sihon and Og, whom ye utterly destroyed. And as soon as we had heard these things, our hearts did melt, neither did there remain any more courage in any man,

THE BOOK OF JOSHUA

because of you: for the Lord your God, he is God in heaven above, and in earth beneath. Now therefore, I pray you, swear unto me by the Lord, since I have showed you kindness, that ye will also show kindness unto my father's house, and give me a true token: and that ye will save alive my father, and my mother, and my brethren, and my sisters, and all that they have, and deliver our lives from death."

And the men answered her,

"Our life for yours, if ye utter not this our business. And it shall be, when the Lord hath given us the land, that we will deal kindly and truly with thee."

Then she let them down by a cord through the window: for her house was upon the town wall, and she dwelt upon the wall. And she said unto them,

"Get you to the mountain, lest the pursuers meet you; and hide yourselves there three days, until the pursuers be returned: and afterward may ye go your way."

And the men said unto her,

"We will be blameless of this thine oath which thou hast made us swear. Behold, when we come into the land, thou shalt bind this line of scarlet thread in the window which thou didst let us down by: and thou shalt bring thy father, and thy mother, and thy brethren, and all thy father's household, home unto thee. And it shall be, that whosoever shall go out of the doors of thy house into the street, his blood shall be upon his head, and we will be guiltless: and whosoever shall be with thee in the house, his blood shall be on our head, if any hand be upon him. And if thou utter this our business, then we will be quit of thine oath which thou hast made us to swear."

And she said, "According unto your words, so be it."

And she sent them away, and they departed: and she bound the scarlet line in the window.

And they went, and came unto the mountain, and abode there three days, until the pursuers were returned: and the pursuers sought them throughout all the way, but found them not. So the two men returned, and descended from the mountain, and passed

THE BOOK OF JOSHUA

over, and came to Joshua the son of Nun, and told him all things that befell them: and they said unto Joshua, "Truly the Lord hath delivered into our hands all the land; for even all the inhabitants of the country do faint because of us."

And Joshua rose early in the morning; and they removed from Shittim, and came to Jordan, he and all the children of Israel, and lodged there before they passed over. And it came to pass after three days that the officers went through the host; and they commanded the people, saying, "When ye see the ark of the covenant of the Lord your God, and the priests the Levites bearing it, then ye shall remove from your place, and go after it. Yet there shall be a space between you and it, about two thousand cubits by measure: come not near unto it, that ye may know the way by which ye must go: for ye have not passed this way heretofore."

And Joshua said unto the people, "Sanctify yourselves: for tomorrow the Lord will do wonders among you."

And Joshua spoke unto the priests, saying, "Take up the ark of the covenant, and pass over before the people."

And they took up the ark of the covenant, and went before the people.

And the Lord said unto Joshua, "This day will I begin to magnify thee in the sight of all Israel, that they may know that, as I was with Moses, so I will be with thee. And thou shalt command the priests that bear the ark of the covenant, saying, 'When ye are come to the brink of the water of Jordan, ye shall stand still in Jordan.'"

And Joshua said unto the children of Israel, "Come hither, and hear the words of the Lord your God." And Joshua said, "Hereby ye shall know that the living God is among you, and that he will without fail drive out from before you the Canaanites, and the Hittites, and the Hivites, and the Perizzites, and the Girgashites, and the Amorites, and the Jebusites. Behold, the ark of the covenant of the Lord of all the earth passeth over before you into Jordan. Now therefore take you twelve men out of the tribes of Israel, out of every tribe a man. And it

THE BOOK OF JOSHUA

shall come to pass, as soon as the soles of the feet of the priests that bear the ark of the Lord, the Lord of all the earth, shall rest in the waters of Jordan, that the waters of Jordan shall be cut off from the waters that come down from above; and they shall stand upon a heap."

And it came to pass, as they that bore the ark were come unto Jordan, and the feet of the priests that bore the ark were dipped in the brim of the water (for Jordan overfloweth all his banks all the time of harvest), that the waters which came down from above stood and rose up upon a heap very far from the city Adam, that is beside Zaretan: and those that came down toward the sea of the plain, even the Salt Sea, failed, and were cut off: and the people passed over right against Jericho. And the priests that bore the ark of the covenant of the Lord stood firm on dry ground in the midst of Jordan, and all the Israelites passed over on dry ground, until all the people were passed clean over Jordan.

Now Jericho was straitly shut up because of the children of Israel: none went out, and none came in. And the Lord said unto Joshua,

"See, I have given into thine hand Jericho, and the king thereof, and the mighty men of valour. And ye shall compass the city, all ye men of war, and go round about the city once. Thus shalt thou do six days. And seven priests shall bear before the ark seven trumpets of rams' horns: and the seventh day ye shall compass the city seven times, and the priests shall blow with the trumpets. And it shall come to pass, that when they make a long blast with the ram's horn, and when ye hear the sound of the trumpet, all the people shall shout with a great shout; and the wall of the city shall fall down flat, and the people shall ascend up every man straight before him."

And Joshua rose early in the morning, and the priests took up the ark of the Lord. And seven priests bearing seven trumpets of rams' horns before the ark of the Lord went on continually, and blew with the trumpets: and the armed men went before them; but the rearward came after the ark of the Lord, the priests

THE BOOK OF JOSHUA

going on, and blowing with the trumpets. And the second day they compassed the city once, and returned into the camp: so they did six days. And it came to pass on the seventh day that they rose early about the dawning of the day, and compassed the city after the same manner seven times: only on that day they compassed the city seven times. And it came to pass at the seventh time, when the priests blew with the trumpets, Joshua said unto the people,

"Shout; for the Lord hath given you the city. And the city shall be accursed, even it, and all that are therein, to the Lord: only Rahab the harlot shall live, she and all that are with her in the house, because she hid the messengers that we sent. And ye, in any wise keep yourselves from the accursed thing, lest ye make yourselves accursed, when ye take of the accursed thing, and make the camp of Israel a curse, and trouble it. But all the silver, and gold, and vessels of brass and iron, are consecrated unto the Lord: they shall come into the treasury of the Lord."

So the people shouted when the priests blew with the trumpets: and it came to pass, when the people heard the sound of the trumpet, and the people shouted with a great shout, that the wall fell down flat, so that the people went up into the city, every man straight before him, and they took the city. And they utterly destroyed all that was in the city, both man and woman, young and old, and ox, and sheep, and ass, with the edge of the sword.

But Joshua had said unto the two men that had spied out the country, "Go into the harlot's house, and bring out thence the woman, and all that she hath, as ye swore unto her."

And the young men that were spies went in, and brought out Rahab, and her father, and her mother, and her brethren, and all that she had; and they brought out all her kindred, and left them without the camp of Israel. And they burnt the city with fire, and all that was therein: only the silver, and the gold, and the vessels of brass and of iron, they put into the treasury of the house of the Lord. And Joshua saved Rahab the harlot alive, and her father's household, and all that she had; and she dwelleth

THE BOOK OF JOSHUA

in Israel even unto this day; because she hid the messengers, which Joshua sent to spy out Jericho.

And Joshua adjured them at that time, saying, "Cursed be the man before the Lord, that riseth up and buildeth this city Jericho: he shall lay the foundation thereof in his firstborn, and in his youngest son shall he set up the gates of it."

So the Lord was with Joshua; and his fame was noised throughout all the country.

The Destruction of Ai

But the children of Israel committed a trespass in the accursed thing: for Achan, the son of Carmi, the son of Zabdi, the son of Zerah, of the tribe of Judah, took of the accursed thing: and the anger of the Lord was kindled against the children of Israel. And Joshua sent men from Jericho to Ai, which is beside Beth-aven, on the east side of Beth-el, and spoke unto them, saying, "Go up and view the country."

And the men went up and viewed Ai. And they returned to Joshua, and said unto him, "Let not all the people go up; but let about two or three thousand men go up and smite Ai; and make not all the people to labour thither; for they are but few."

So there went up thither of the people about three thousand men: and they fled before the men of Ai. And the men of Ai smote of them about thirty and six men: for they chased them from before the gate even unto Shebarim, and smote them in the going down: wherefore the hearts of the people melted, and became as water.

And Joshua rent his clothes, and fell to the earth upon his face before the ark of the Lord until the eventide, he and the elders of Israel, and put dust upon their heads. And Joshua said, "Alas, O Lord God, wherefore hast thou at all brought this people over Jordan, to deliver us into the hand of the Amorites, to destroy us? would to God we had been content, and dwelt on the other side Jordan! O Lord, what shall I say, when Israel turneth their backs before their enemies! For the Canaanites and all the inhabitants of the land shall hear of it, and shall en-

THE BOOK OF JOSHUA

viron us round, and cut off our name from the earth: and what wilt thou do unto thy great name?"

And the Lord said unto Joshua, "Get thee up; wherefore liest thou thus upon thy face? Israel hath sinned, and they have also transgressed my covenant which I commanded them: for they have even taken of the accursed thing, and have also stolen and dissembled also, and they have put it even among their own stuff. Therefore the children of Israel could not stand before their enemies, but turned their backs before their enemies, because they were accursed: neither will I be with you any more, except ye destroy the accursed from among you. Up, sanctify the people, and say, 'Sanctify yourselves against to-morrow: for thus saith the Lord God of Israel, "There is an accursed thing in the midst of thee, O Israel: thou canst not stand before thine enemies, until ye take away the accursed thing from among you." In the morning therefore ye shall be brought according to your tribes: and it shall be, that the tribe which the Lord taketh shall come according to the families thereof; and the family which the Lord shall take shall come by households; and the household which the Lord shall take shall come man by man. And it shall be that he that is taken with the accursed thing, shall be burnt with fire, he and all that he hath: because he hath transgressed the covenant of the Lord, and because he hath wrought folly in Israel.'"

So Joshua rose up early in the morning, and brought Israel by their tribes; and the tribe of Judah was taken: and he brought the family of Judah; and he took the family of the Zarhites: and he brought the family of the Zarhites man by man; and Zabdi was taken: and he brought his household man by man; and Achan, the son of Carmi, the son of Zabdi, the son of Zerah, of the tribe of Judah, was taken. And Joshua said unto Achan,

"My son, give, I pray thee, glory to the Lord God of Israel, and make confession unto him; and tell me now what thou hast done; hide it not from me."

And Achan answered Joshua, and said, "Indeed I have sinned against the Lord God of Israel, and thus and thus have I done:

THE BOOK OF JOSHUA

when I saw among the spoils a goodly Babylonish garment, and two hundred shekels of silver, and a wedge of gold of fifty shekels' weight, then I coveted them, and took them; and, behold, they are hid in the earth in the midst of my tent, and the silver under it."

So Joshua sent messengers, and they ran unto the tent; and, behold, it was hid in his tent, and the silver under it. And they took them out of the midst of the tent, and brought them unto Joshua, and unto all the children of Israel, and laid them out before the Lord. And Joshua, and all Israel with him, took Achan the son of Zerah, and the silver, and the garment, and the wedge of gold, and his sons, and his daughters, and his oxen, and his asses, and his sheep, and his tent, and all that he had: and they brought them unto the valley of Achor. And Joshua said,

"Why hast thou troubled us? the Lord shall trouble thee this day."

And all Israel stoned him with stones, and burned them with fire, after they had stoned them with stones. And they raised over him a great heap of stones unto this day. So the Lord turned from the fierceness of his anger. Wherefore the name of that place was called the valley of Achor, unto this day.

And the Lord said unto Joshua, "Fear not, neither be thou dismayed: take all the people of war with thee, and arise, go up to Ai: see, I have given into thy hand the king of Ai, and his people, and his city, and his land: and thou shalt do to Ai and her king as thou didst unto Jericho and her king: only the spoil thereof, and the cattle thereof, shall ye take for a prey unto yourselves: lay thee an ambush for the city behind it."

So Joshua arose, and all the people of war, to go up against Ai: and Joshua chose out thirty thousand mighty men of valour, and sent them away by night. And he commanded them, saying,

"Behold, ye shall lie in wait against the city, even behind the city: go not very far from the city, but be ye all ready: and I, and all the people that are with me, will approach unto the city: and it shall come to pass, when they come out against us, as at the first, that we will flee before them (for they will come out

THE BOOK OF JOSHUA

after us), till we have drawn them from the city; for they will say, 'They flee before us, as at the first': therefore we will flee before them. Then ye shall rise up from the ambush, and seize upon the city: for the Lord your God will deliver it into your hand. And it shall be, when ye have taken the city, that ye shall set the city on fire: according to the commandment of the Lord shall ye do. See, I have commanded you."

Joshua therefore sent them forth: and they went to lie in ambush, and abode between Beth-el and Ai, on the west side of Ai: but Joshua lodged that night among the people. And Joshua rose up early in the morning, and numbered the people, and went up, he and the elders of Israel, before the people to Ai. And all the people, even the people of war that were with him, went up, and drew nigh, and came before the city, and pitched on the north side of Ai: now there was a valley between them and Ai. And he took about five thousand men, and set them to lie in ambush between Beth-el and Ai, on the west side of the city. And when they had set the people, even all the host that was on the north of the city, and their liers in wait on the west of the city, Joshua went that night into the midst of the valley.

And it came to pass, when the king of Ai saw it, that they hastened and rose up early, and the men of the city went out against Israel to battle, he and all his people, at a time appointed, before the plain; but he wist not that there were liers in ambush against him behind the city. And Joshua and all Israel made as if they were beaten before them, and fled by the way of the wilderness. And all the people that were in Ai were called together to pursue after them: and they pursued after Joshua, and were drawn away from the city. And there was not a man left in Ai or Beth-el, that went not out after Israel: and they left the city open, and pursued after Israel. And the Lord said unto Joshua,

"Stretch out the spear that is in thy hand toward Ai; for I will give it into thine hand."

And Joshua stretched out the spear that he had in his hand toward the city. And the ambush arose quickly out of their

THE BOOK OF JOSHUA

place, and they ran as soon as he had stretched out his hand: and they entered into the city, and took it, and hastened and set the city on fire. And when the men of Ai looked behind them, they saw, and, behold, the smoke of the city ascended up to heaven, and they had no power to flee this way or that way: and the people that fled to the wilderness turned back upon the pursuers. And when Joshua and all Israel saw that the ambush had taken the city, and that the smoke of the city ascended, then they turned again, and slew the men of Ai. And the other issued out of the city against them; so they were in the midst of Israel, some on this side, and some on that side: and they smote them, so that they let none of them remain or escape. And the king of Ai they took alive, and brought him to Joshua.

And it came to pass, when Israel had made an end of slaying all the inhabitants of Ai in the field, in the wilderness wherein they chased them, and when they were all fallen on the edge of the sword, until they were consumed, that all the Israelites returned unto Ai, and smote it with the edge of the sword. And so it was, that all that fell that day, both of men and women, were twelve thousand, even all the men of Ai. For Joshua drew not his hand back, wherewith he stretched out the spear, until he had utterly destroyed all the inhabitants of Ai. Only the cattle and the spoil of that city Israel took for a prey unto themselves, according unto the word of the Lord which he commanded Joshua. And Joshua burnt Ai, and made it a heap for ever, even a desolation unto this day. And the king of Ai he hanged on a tree until eventide: and as soon as the sun was down, Joshua commanded that they should take his carcase down from the tree, and cast it at the entering of the gate of the city, and raise thereon a great heap of stones, that remaineth unto this day.

The Craft of the Gibeonites

And when the inhabitants of Gibeon heard what Joshua had done unto Jericho and to Ai, they did work wilily, and went and made as if they had been ambassadors, and took old sacks

THE BOOK OF JOSHUA

upon their asses, and wine bottles, old, and rent, and bound up; and old shoes and clouted upon their feet, and old garments upon them; and all the bread of their provision was dry and mouldy. And they went to Joshua unto the camp at Gilgal, and said unto him, and to the men of Israel, "We be come from a far country: now therefore make ye a league with us."

And the men of Israel said unto the Hivites, "Peradventure ye dwell among us; and how shall we make a league with you?"

And they said unto Joshua, "We are thy servants."

And Joshua said unto them,

"Who are ye? and from whence come ye?"

And they said unto him, "From a very far country thy servants are come because of the name of the Lord thy God: for we have heard the fame of him, and all that he did in Egypt, and all that he did to the two kings of the Amorites, that were beyond Jordan, to Sihon king of Heshbon, and to Og king of Bashan, which was at Ashtaroth. Wherefore our elders and all the inhabitants of our country spoke to us, saying, 'Take victuals with you for the journey, and go to meet them, and say unto them, "We are your servants: therefore now make ye a league with us."' This our bread we took hot for our provision out of our houses on the day we came forth to go unto you; but now, behold, it is dry, and it is mouldy: and these bottles of wine, which we filled, were new; and, behold, they be rent: and these our garments and our shoes are become old by reason of the very long journey."

And Joshua made peace with them, and made a league with them, to let them live: and the princes of the congregation swore unto them. And it came to pass at the end of three days after they had made a league with them, that they heard that they were their neighbours, and that they dwelt among them. And the children of Israel journeyed, and came unto their cities on the third day. Now their cities were Gibeon, and Chephirah, and Beeroth, and Kirjath-jearim. And the children of Israel smote them not, because the princes of the congregation had sworn unto them by the Lord God of Israel.

THE BOOK OF JOSHUA

And Joshua called for them, and he spoke unto them, saying, "Wherefore have ye beguiled us, saying, 'We are very far from you'; when ye dwell among us? Now therefore ye are cursed, and there shall none of you be freed from being bondmen, and hewers of wood and drawers of water for the house of my God."

And they answered Joshua, and said, "Because it was certainly told thy servants, how that the Lord thy God commanded his servant Moses to give you all the land, and to destroy all the inhabitants of the land from before you, therefore we were sore afraid of our lives because of you, and have done this thing. And now, behold, we are in thine hand: as it seemeth good and right unto thee to do unto us, do."

And so did he unto them, and delivered them out of the hand of the children of Israel, that they slew them not. And Joshua made them that day hewers of wood and drawers of water for the congregation, and for the altar of the Lord, even unto this day, in the place which he should choose.

The Long Day's Battle

Now it came to pass, when Adoni-zedec king of Jerusalem had heard how Joshua had taken Ai, and had utterly destroyed it, and how the inhabitants of Gibeon had made peace with Israel, and were among them, they feared greatly, because Gibeon was a great city, as one of the royal cities, and because it was greater than Ai, and all the men thereof were mighty. Wherefore Adoni-zedec king of Jerusalem sent unto Hoham king of Hebron, and unto Piram king of Jarmuth, and unto Japhia king of Lachish, and unto Debir king of Eglon, saying, "Come up unto me, and help me, that we may smite Gibeon: for it hath made peace with Joshua and with the children of Israel."

Therefore the five kings of the Amorites, the king of Jerusalem, the king of Hebron, the king of Jarmuth, the king of Lachish, the king of Eglon, gathered themselves together, and went up, they and all their hosts, and encamped before Gibeon, and made war against it.

And the men of Gibeon sent unto Joshua to the camp to Gil-

THE BOOK OF JOSHUA

gal, saying, "Slack not thy hand from thy servants; come up to us quickly, and save us, and help us: for all the kings of the Amorites that dwell in the mountains are gathered together against us."

So Joshua ascended from Gilgal, he, and all the people of war with him, and all the mighty men of valour. And the Lord said unto Joshua,

"Fear them not: for I have delivered them into thine hand; there shall not a man of them stand before thee."

Joshua therefore came unto them suddenly, and went up from Gilgal all night. And the Lord discomfited them before Israel, and slew them with a great slaughter at Gibeon, and chased them along the way that goeth up to Beth-horon, and smote them to Azekah, and unto Makkedah. And it came to pass, as they fled from before Israel, and were in the going down to Beth-horon, that the Lord cast down great stones from heaven upon them unto Azekah, and they died: they were more which died with hailstones than they whom the children of Israel slew with the sword.

Then spoke Joshua to the Lord in the day when the Lord delivered up the Amorites before the children of Israel, and he said in the sight of Israel,

> "Sun, stand thou still upon Gibeon;
> And thou, Moon, in the valley of Ajalon."
> And the sun stood still,
> And the moon stayed,
> Until the people had avenged themselves upon their enemies.

Is not this written in the book of Jasher? So the sun stood still in the midst of heaven, and hastened not to go down about a whole day. And there was no day like that before it or after it, that the Lord hearkened unto the voice of a man: for the Lord fought for Israel.

And Joshua returned, and all Israel with him, unto the camp to Gilgal. But these five kings fled, and hid themselves in a cave

THE BOOK OF JOSHUA

at Makkedah. And it was told Joshua, saying, "The five kings are found hid in a cave at Makkedah."

And Joshua said, "Roll great stones upon the mouth of the cave, and set men by it for to keep them. And stay ye not, but pursue after your enemies, and smite the hindmost of them; suffer them not to enter into their cities: for the Lord your God hath delivered them into your hand."

And it came to pass, when Joshua and the children of Israel had made an end of slaying them with a very great slaughter, till they were consumed, that the rest which remained of them entered into fenced cities. And all the people returned to the camp to Joshua at Makkedah in peace: none moved his tongue against any of the children of Israel. Then said Joshua,

"Open the mouth of the cave, and bring out those five kings unto me out of the cave."

And they did so, and brought forth those five kings unto him out of the cave, the king of Jerusalem, the king of Hebron, the king of Jarmuth, the king of Lachish, and the king of Eglon. And it came to pass, when they brought out those kings unto Joshua, that Joshua called for all the men of Israel, and said unto the captains of the men of war which went with him,

"Come near, put your feet upon the necks of these kings."

And they came near, and put their feet upon the necks of them. And Joshua said unto them,

"Fear not, nor be dismayed, be strong and of good courage: for thus shall the Lord do to all your enemies against whom ye fight."

And afterward Joshua smote them, and slew them, and hanged them on five trees: and they were hanging upon the trees until the evening. And it came to pass at the time of the going down of the sun, that Joshua commanded, and they took them down off the trees, and cast them into the cave wherein they had been hid, and laid great stones in the cave's mouth, which remain until this very day.

THE BOOK OF JUDGES

Like good wine *that needs no bush, the Book of Judges needs no introduction. Its stories and characters are self-revealing and self-validating. In its original form it is one of the oldest books in the Bible, put together in the ninth century from still earlier material, with the Song of Deborah and the Fable of Jotham in the story of Abimelech going back to the twelfth century; though reworked under Deuteronomic influence in the sixth century, it still retains the bold and striking style of saga literature.*

The Book of JUDGES

The Story of Ehud

AND THE CHILDREN OF ISRAEL did evil in the sight of the Lord, and served Baalim. And they forsook the Lord God of their fathers, which brought them out of the land of Egypt, and followed other gods, of the gods of the people that were round about them, and bowed themselves unto them, and provoked the Lord to anger. And they forsook the Lord, and served Baal and Ashtaroth. And the anger of the Lord was hot against Israel, and he delivered them into the hands of spoilers that spoiled them, and he sold them into the hands of their enemies round about, so that they could not any longer stand before their enemies. Whithersoever they went out, the hand of the Lord was against them for evil, as the Lord had said, and as the Lord had sworn unto them, and they were greatly distressed.

Nevertheless the Lord raised up judges, which delivered them out of the hand of those that spoiled them. And yet they would not hearken unto their judges, but they went a-whoring after other gods, and bowed themselves unto them; they turned quickly out of the way which their fathers walked in, obeying the commandments of the Lord; but they did not so. And when the Lord raised them up judges, then the Lord was with the judge, and delivered them out of the hand of their enemies all the days of the judge: for it repented the Lord because of their groanings by reason of them that oppressed them and vexed them. And it came to pass, when the judge was dead, that they returned, and corrupted themselves more than their fathers, in following other gods to serve them, and to bow down unto

[175]

THE BOOK OF JUDGES

them; they ceased not from their own doings, nor from their stubborn way.

And the children of Israel did evil again in the sight of the Lord: and the Lord strengthened Eglon the king of Moab against Israel, because they had done evil in the sight of the Lord. And he gathered unto him the children of Ammon and Amalek, and went and smote Israel, and possessed the city of palm trees. So the children of Israel served Eglon the king of Moab eighteen years.

But when the children of Israel cried unto the Lord, the Lord raised them up a deliverer, Ehud the son of Gera, a Benjamite, a man lefthanded; and by him the children of Israel sent a present unto Eglon the king of Moab. But Ehud made him a dagger which had two edges, of a cubit length; and he did gird it under his raiment upon his right thigh.

And he brought the present unto Eglon king of Moab: and Eglon was a very fat man. And when he had made an end to offer the present, he sent away the people that bore the present. But he himself turned again from the quarries that were by Gilgal, and said, "I have a secret errand unto thee, O king": who said, "Keep silence."

And all that stood by him went out from him. And Ehud came unto him; and he was sitting in a summer parlour, which he had for himself alone. And Ehud said,

"I have a message from God unto thee."

And he arose out of his seat. And Ehud put forth his left hand, and took the dagger from his right thigh, and thrust it into his belly; and the haft also went in after the blade; and the fat closed upon the blade, so that he could not draw the dagger out of his belly; and the dirt came out. Then Ehud went forth through the porch, and shut the doors of the parlour upon him, and locked them. When he was gone out, his servants came; and when they saw that, behold, the doors of the parlour were locked, they said,

"Surely he covereth his feet in his summer chamber."

And they tarried till they were ashamed: and, behold, he

THE BOOK OF JUDGES

opened not the doors of the parlour; therefore they took a key, and opened them: and, behold, their lord was fallen down dead on the earth.

And Ehud escaped while they tarried, and passed beyond the quarries, and escaped unto Seirath. And it came to pass, when he was come, that he blew a trumpet in the mountain of Ephraim, and the children of Israel went down with him from the mount, and he before them. And he said unto them,

"Follow after me: for the Lord hath delivered your enemies the Moabites into your hand."

And they went down after him, and took the fords of Jordan toward Moab, and suffered not a man to pass over. And they slew of Moab at that time about ten thousand men, all lusty, and all men of valour; and there escaped not a man. So Moab was subdued that day under the hand of Israel. And the land had rest fourscore years.

The Story of Deborah

And the children of Israel did evil in the sight of the Lord, when Ehud was dead. And the Lord sold them into the hand of Jabin king of Canaan, that reigned in Hazor; the captain of whose host was Sisera, which dwelt in Harosheth of the Gentiles. And the children of Israel cried unto the Lord: for he had nine hundred chariots of iron; and twenty years he mightily oppressed the children of Israel.

And Deborah, a prophetess, the wife of Lapidoth, she judged Israel at that time. And she dwelt under the palm tree of Deborah between Ramah and Beth-el in Mount Ephraim; and the children of Israel came up to her for judgment. And she sent and called Barak the son of Abinoam out of Kedesh-naphtali, and said unto him,

"Hath not the Lord God of Israel commanded, saying, 'Go and draw toward Mount Tabor, and take with thee ten thousand men of the children of Naphtali and of the children of Zebulun? And I will draw unto thee to the river Kishon Sisera, the captain of Jabin's army, with his chariots and his multitude;

THE BOOK OF JUDGES

and I will deliver him into thine hand.'" And Barak said unto her,

"If thou wilt go with me, then I will go: but if thou wilt not go with me, then I will not go."

And she said, "I will surely go with thee: notwithstanding the journey that thou takest shall not be for thine honour; for the Lord shall sell Sisera into the hand of a woman."

And Deborah arose, and went with Barak to Kedesh. And Barak called Zebulun and Naphtali to Kedesh; and he went up with ten thousand men at his feet: and Deborah went up with him.

Now Heber the Kenite, which was of the children of Hobab the father-in-law of Moses, had severed himself from the Kenites, and pitched his tent unto the plain of Zaanaim, which is by Kedesh.

And they showed Sisera that Barak the son of Abinoam was gone up to Mount Tabor. And Sisera gathered together all his chariots, even nine hundred chariots of iron, and all the people that were with him, from Harosheth of the Gentiles unto the river of Kishon.

And Deborah said unto Barak, "Up; for this is the day in which the Lord hath delivered Sisera into thine hand: is not the Lord gone out before thee?"

So Barak went down from Mount Tabor, and ten thousand men after him. And the Lord discomfited Sisera, and all his chariots, and all his host, with the edge of the sword before Barak; so that Sisera lighted down off his chariot, and fled away on his feet. But Barak pursued after the chariots, and after the host, unto Harosheth of the Gentiles: and all the host of Sisera fell upon the edge of the sword; and there was not a man left. Howbeit Sisera fled away on his feet to the tent of Jael the wife of Heber the Kenite: for there was peace between Jabin the king of Hazor and the house of Heber the Kenite. And Jael went out to meet Sisera, and said unto him,

"Turn in, my lord, turn in to me; fear not."

THE BOOK OF JUDGES

And when he had turned in unto her into the tent, she covered him with a mantle. And he said unto her,

"Give me, I pray thee, a little water to drink; for I am thirsty."

And she opened a bottle of milk, and gave him drink, and covered him. Again he said unto her,

"Stand in the door of the tent, and it shall be, when any man doth come and enquire of thee, and say, 'Is there any man here?' that thou shalt say, 'No.'"

Then Jael Heber's wife took a nail of the tent, and took a hammer in her hand, and went softly unto him, and smote the nail into his temples, and fastened it into the ground; for he was fast asleep and weary. So he died.

And, behold, as Barak pursued Sisera, Jael came out to meet him, and said unto him,

"Come, and I will show thee the man whom thou seekest."

And when he came into her tent, behold, Sisera lay dead, and the nail was in his temples.

So God subdued on that day Jabin the king of Canaan before the children of Israel. And the hand of the children of Israel prospered, and prevailed against Jabin the king of Canaan, until they had destroyed Jabin king of Canaan.

The Song of Deborah

Then sang Deborah and Barak the son of Abinoam on that day, saying,

> *"Praise ye the Lord for the avenging of Israel,*
> *When the people willingly offered themselves.*
> *Hear, O ye kings; give ear, O ye princes;*
> *I, even I, will sing unto the Lord;*
> *I will sing praise to the Lord God of Israel.*
>
> *Lord, when thou wentest out of Seir,*
> *When thou marchedst out of the field of Edom,*
> *The earth trembled, and the heavens dropped,*
> *The clouds also dropped water.*

THE BOOK OF JUDGES
The mountains melted from before the Lord,
Even that Sinai from before the Lord God of Israel.

In the days of Shamgar the son of Anath,
In the days of Jael, the highways were unoccupied,
And the travellers walked through byways.
The inhabitants of the villages ceased, they ceased in Israel,
Until that I Deborah arose,
That I arose a mother in Israel. They chose new gods;
Then was war in the gates:
Was there a shield or spear seen
Among forty thousand in Israel?
My heart is toward the governors of Israel,
That offered themselves willingly among the people.
Bless ye the Lord.
Speak, ye that ride on white asses,
Ye that sit in judgment, and walk by the way.
They that are delivered from the noise of archers
In the places of drawing water,
There shall they rehearse the righteous acts of the Lord,
Even the righteous acts toward the inhabitants of his villages
    in Israel:
Then shall the people of the Lord go down to the gates.

Awake, awake, Deborah:
Awake, awake, utter a song:
Arise, Barak, and lead thy captivity captive, thou son of
    Abinoam.
Out of Ephraim was there a root of them against Amalek;
After thee, Benjamin, among thy people;
Out of Machir came down governors,
And out of Zebulun they that handle the pen of the writer.
And the princes of Issachar were with Deborah;
Even Issachar, and also Barak;
He was sent on foot into the valley.
For the divisions of Reuben
There were great thoughts of heart.

THE BOOK OF JUDGES

Why abodest thou among the sheepfolds,
To hear the bleatings of the flocks?
For the divisions of Reuben
There were great searchings of heart.
Gilead abode beyond Jordan:
And why did Dan remain in ships?
Asher continued on the sea shore,
And abode in his breaches.
Zebulun and Naphtali were a people that jeoparded their
    lives unto the death
In the high places of the field.

The kings came and fought,
Then fought the kings of Canaan
In Taanach by the waters of Megiddo;
They took no gain of money.
They fought from heaven;
The stars in their courses fought against Sisera.
The river of Kishon swept them away,
That ancient river, the river Kishon.
O my soul, thou hast trodden down strength.
Then were the horsehoofs broken
By the means of the prancings, the prancings of their mighty ones.

'Curse ye Meroz,' said the angel of the Lord,
'Curse ye bitterly the inhabitants thereof;
Because they came not to the help of the Lord,
To the help of the Lord against the mighty.'

Blessed above women shall Jael be,
The wife of Heber the Kenite,
Blessed shall she be above women in the tent.
He asked water, and she gave him milk;
She brought forth butter in a lordly dish.
She put her hand to the nail,
And her right hand to the workmen's hammer:

THE BOOK OF JUDGES

And with the hammer she smote Sisera, she smote off his
    head,
When she had pierced and stricken through his temples.
At her feet he bowed, he fell, he lay down:
At her feet he bowed, he fell:
Where he bowed, there he fell down dead.

The mother of Sisera looked out at a window,
And cried through the lattice,
'Why is his chariot so long in coming?
Why tarry the wheels of his chariots?'
Her wise ladies answered her,
Yea, she returned answer to herself,
'Have they not sped? have they not divided the prey;
To every man a damsel or two;
To Sisera a prey of divers colours,
A prey of divers colours of needlework,
Of divers colours of needlework on both sides, meet for the
    necks of them that take the spoil?'

So let all thine enemies perish, O Lord:
But let them that love him be as the sun when he goeth forth
    in his might."

The Story of Gideon

And the children of Israel did evil in the sight of the Lord: and the Lord delivered them into the hand of Midian seven years. And the hand of Midian prevailed against Israel: and because of the Midianites the children of Israel made them the dens which are in the mountains, and caves, and strong holds. And so it was, when Israel had sown, that the Midianites came up, and the Amalekites, and the children of the east, even they came up against them; and they encamped against them, and destroyed the increase of the earth, till thou come unto Gaza, and left no sustenance for Israel, neither sheep, nor ox, nor ass. For they came up with their cattle and their tents, and they came as grass-

THE BOOK OF JUDGES

hoppers for multitude; for both they and their camels were without number. And they entered into the land to destroy it.

And there came an angel of the Lord, and sat under an oak which was in Ophrah, that pertained unto Joash the Abi-ezrite: and his son Gideon threshed wheat by the winepress, to hide it from the Midianites. And the angel of the Lord appeared unto him, and said unto him, "The Lord is with thee, thou mighty man of valour."

And Gideon said unto him, "Oh my Lord, if the Lord be with us, why then is all this befallen us? and where be all his miracles which our fathers told us of, saying, 'Did not the Lord bring us up from Egypt?' but now the Lord hath forsaken us, and delivered us into the hands of the Midianites."

And the Lord looked upon him, and said, "Go in this thy might, and thou shalt save Israel from the hand of the Midianites: have not I sent thee?"

And he said unto him, "Oh my Lord, wherewith shall I save Israel? behold, my family is poor in Manasseh, and I am the least in my father's house."

And the Lord said unto him, "Surely I will be with thee, and thou shalt smite the Midianites as one man."

And he said unto him, "If now I have found grace in thy sight, then show me a sign that thou talkest with me. Depart not hence, I pray thee, until I come unto thee, and bring forth my present, and set it before thee."

And he said, "I will tarry until thou come again."

And Gideon went in, and made ready a kid, and unleavened cakes of an ephah of flour: the flesh he put in a basket, and he put the broth in a pot, and brought it out unto him under the oak, and presented it. And the angel of God said unto him,

"Take the flesh and the unleavened cakes, and lay them upon this rock, and pour out the broth." And he did so.

Then the angel of the Lord put forth the end of the staff that was in his hand, and touched the flesh and the unleavened cakes; and there rose up fire out of the rock, and consumed the flesh and the unleavened cakes. Then the angel of the Lord departed out of his sight. And when Gideon perceived that he was an angel of the Lord, Gideon said, "Alas, O Lord God! for because I have seen an angel of the Lord face to face."

And the Lord said unto him, "Peace be unto thee; fear not: thou shalt not die."

Then Gideon built an altar there unto the Lord, and called it Jehovah-shalom: unto this day it is yet in Ophrah of the Abi-ezrites. And it came to pass the same night that the Lord said unto him,

"Take thy father's young bullock, even the second bullock of seven years old, and throw down the altar of Baal that thy father hath, and cut down the grove that is by it: and build an altar unto the Lord thy God upon the top of this rock, in the ordered place, and take the second bullock, and offer a burnt sacrifice with the wood of the grove which thou shalt cut down."

Then Gideon took ten men of his servants, and did as the Lord had said unto him: and so it was, because he feared his father's household, and the men of the city, that he could not do it by day, that he did it by night. And when the men of the city arose early in the morning, behold, the altar of Baal was cast down, and the grove was cut down that was by it, and the second bullock was offered upon the altar that was built. And they said one to another, "Who hath done this thing?"

And when they enquired and asked, they said, "Gideon the son of Joash hath done this thing."

Then the men of the city said unto Joash, "Bring out thy son, that he may die: because he hath cast down the altar of Baal, and because he hath cut down the grove that was by it."

And Joash said unto all that stood against him, "Will ye plead for Baal? will ye save him? he that will plead for him, let him be put to death whilst it is yet morning: if he be a god, let him plead for himself, because one hath cast down his altar."

Therefore on that day he called him Jerubbaal, saying, "Let Baal plead against him, because he hath thrown down his altar."

Then all the Midianites and the Amalekites and the children of the east were gathered together, and went over, and pitched

THE BOOK OF JUDGES

in the valley of Jezreel. But the Spirit of the Lord came upon Gideon, and he blew a trumpet; and Abi-ezer was gathered after him. And he sent messengers throughout all Manasseh; who also was gathered after him: and he sent messengers unto Asher, and unto Zebulun, and unto Naphtali; and they came up to meet them. And Gideon said unto God,

"If thou wilt save Israel by mine hand, as thou hast said, behold, I will put a fleece of wool in the floor; and if the dew be on the fleece only, and it be dry upon all the earth beside, then shall I know that thou wilt save Israel by mine hand, as thou hast said." And it was so: for he rose up early on the morrow, and thrust the fleece together, and wrung the dew out of the fleece, a bowl full of water.

And Gideon said unto God, "Let not thine anger be hot against me, and I will speak but this once: let me prove, I pray thee, but this once with the fleece; let it now be dry only upon the fleece, and upon all the ground let there be dew."

And God did so that night: for it was dry upon the fleece only, and there was dew on all the ground.

Then Jerubbaal, who is Gideon, and all the people that were with him, rose up early, and pitched beside the well of Harod; so that the host of the Midianites were on the north side of them, by the hill of Moreh, in the valley. And the Lord said unto Gideon,

"The people that are with thee are too many for me to give the Midianites into their hands, lest Israel vaunt themselves against me, saying, 'Mine own hand hath saved me.' Now therefore go to, proclaim in the ears of the people, saying, 'Whosoever is fearful and afraid, let him return and depart early from Mount Gilead.'"

And there returned of the people twenty and two thousand; and there remained ten thousand. And the Lord said unto Gideon,

"The people are yet too many; bring them down unto the water, and I will try them for thee there: and it shall be, that of whom I say unto thee, 'This shall go with thee,' the same shall

THE BOOK OF JUDGES

go with thee; and of whomsoever I say unto thee, 'This shall not go with thee,' the same shall not go."

So he brought down the people unto the water: and the Lord said unto Gideon, "Every one that lappeth of the water with his tongue, as a dog lappeth, him shalt thou set by himself; likewise every one that boweth down upon his knees to drink."

And the number of them that lapped, putting their hand to their mouth, were three hundred men: but all the rest of the people bowed down upon their knees to drink water. And the Lord said unto Gideon,

"By the three hundred men that lapped will I save you, and deliver the Midianites into thine hand: and let all the other people go every man unto his place."

So the people took victuals in their hand, and their trumpets: and he sent all the rest of Israel every man unto his tent, and retained those three hundred men: and the host of Midian was beneath him in the valley.

And it came to pass the same night, that the Lord said unto him, "Arise, get thee down unto the host; for I have delivered it into thine hand. But if thou fear to go down, go thou with Phurah thy servant down to the host: and thou shalt hear what they say; and afterward shall thine hands be strengthened to go down unto the host."

Then went he down with Phurah his servant unto the outside of the armed men that were in the host. And the Midianites and the Amalekites and all the children of the east lay along in the valley like grasshoppers for multitude; and their camels were without number, as the sand by the sea side for multitude. And when Gideon was come, behold, there was a man that told a dream unto his fellow, and said,

"Behold, I dreamed a dream, and, lo, a cake of barley bread tumbled into the host of Midian, and came unto a tent, and smote it that it fell, and overturned it, that the tent lay along."

And his fellow answered and said,

"This is nothing else save the sword of Gideon the son of

THE BOOK OF JUDGES

Joash, a man of Israel: for into his hand hath God delivered Midian, and all the host."

And it was so, when Gideon heard the telling of the dream, and the interpretation thereof, that he worshipped, and returned into the host of Israel, and said, "Arise; for the Lord hath delivered into your hand the host of Midian."

And he divided the three hundred men into three companies, and he put a trumpet in every man's hand, with empty pitchers, and lamps within the pitchers. And he said unto them, "Look on me, and do likewise: and, behold, when I come to the outside of the camp, it shall be that, as I do, so shall ye do. When I blow with a trumpet, I and all that are with me, then blow ye the trumpets also on every side of all the camp, and say, 'The sword of the Lord, and of Gideon.'"

So Gideon, and the hundred men that were with him, came unto the outside of the camp in the beginning of the middle watch; and they had but newly set the watch: and they blew the trumpets, and broke the pitchers that were in their hands. And the three companies blew the trumpets, and broke the pitchers, and held the lamps in their left hands, and the trumpets in their right hands to blow withal: and they cried, "The sword of the Lord, and of Gideon."

And they stood every man in his place round about the camp and all the host ran, and cried, and fled. And the three hundred blew the trumpets, and the Lord set every man's sword against his fellow, even throughout all the host: and the host fled to Beth-shittah in Zererath, and to the border of Abel-meholah unto Tabbath. And the men of Israel gathered themselves together out of Naphtali, and out of Asher, and out of all Manasseh, and pursued after the Midianites.

And Gideon sent messengers throughout all Mount Ephraim, saying, "Come down against the Midianites, and take before them the waters unto Beth-barah and Jordan."

Then all the men of Ephraim gathered themselves together, and took the waters unto Beth-barah and Jordan. And they took

THE BOOK OF JUDGES

two princes of the Midianites, Oreb and Zeeb; and they slew Oreb upon the rock Oreb, and Zeeb they slew at the winepress of Zeeb, and pursued Midian, and brought the heads of Oreb and Zeeb to Gideon on the other side Jordan.

And the men of Ephraim said unto him, "Why hast thou served us thus, that thou calledst us not, when thou wentest to fight with the Midianites?" And they did chide with him sharply.

And he said unto them, "What have I done now in comparison of you? Is not the gleaning of the grapes of Ephraim better than the vintage of Abi-ezer? God hath delivered into your hands the princes of Midian, Oreb and Zeeb: and what was I able to do in comparison of you?" Then their anger was abated toward him, when he had said that. And Gideon came to Jordan, and passed over, he, and the three hundred men that were with him, faint, yet pursuing them. And he said unto the men of Succoth, "Give, I pray you, loaves of bread unto the people that follow me; for they be faint, and I am pursuing after Zebah and Zalmunna, kings of Midian."

And the princes of Succoth said, "Are the hands of Zebah and Zalmunna now in thine hand, that we should give bread unto thine army?"

And Gideon said, "Therefore when the Lord hath delivered Zebah and Zalmunna into mine hand, then I will tear your flesh with the thorns of the wilderness and with briers."

And he went up thence to Penuel, and spoke unto them likewise and the men of Penuel answered him as the men of Succoth had answered him. And he spoke also unto the men of Penuel, saying, "When I come again in peace, I will break down this tower."

Now Zebah and Zalmunna were in Karkor, and their hosts with them, about fifteen thousand men, all that were left of all the hosts of the children of the east: for there fell a hundred and twenty thousand men that drew sword. And Gideon went up by the way of them that dwelt in tents on the east of Nobah and Jogbehah, and smote the host: for the host was secure. And when Zebah and Zalmunna fled, he pursued after them, and took

THE BOOK OF JUDGES

the two kings of Midian, Zebah and Zalmunna, and discomfited all the host.

And Gideon the son of Joash returned from battle before the sun was up, and caught a young man of the men of Succoth, and enquired of him: and he described unto him the princes of Succoth, and the elders thereof, even threescore and seventeen men. And he came unto the men of Succoth, and said, "Behold, Zebah and Zalmunna, with whom ye did upbraid me, saying, 'Are the hands of Zebah and Zalmunna now in thine hand, that we should give bread unto thy men that are weary?'"

And he took the elders of the city, and thorns of the wilderness and briers, and with them he taught the men of Succoth. And he beat down the tower of Penuel, and slew the men of the city. Then said he unto Zebah and Zalmunna, "What manner of men were they whom ye slew at Tabor?"

And they answered, "As thou art, so were they; each one resembled the children of a king."

And he said, "They were my brethren, even the sons of my mother: as the Lord liveth, if ye had saved them alive, I would not slay you."

And he said unto Jether his firstborn, "Up, and slay them!" But the youth drew not his sword: for he feared, because he was yet a youth.

Then Zebah and Zalmunna said, "Rise thou, and fall upon us: for as the man is, so is his strength."

And Gideon arose, and slew Zebah and Zalmunna, and took away the ornaments that were on their camels' necks.

Then the men of Israel said unto Gideon, "Rule thou over us, both thou, and thy son, and thy son's son also: for thou hast delivered us from the hand of Midian." And Gideon said unto them, "I will not rule over you, neither shall my son rule over you: the Lord shall rule over you."

And Gideon said unto them, "I would desire a request of you, that ye would give me every man the earrings of his prey." (For they had golden earrings, because they were Ishmaelites.) And they answered, "We will willingly give them."

THE BOOK OF JUDGES

And they spread a garment, and did cast therein every man the earrings of his prey. And the weight of the golden earrings that he requested was a thousand and seven hundred shekels of gold; beside ornaments, and collars, and purple raiment that was on the kings of Midian, and beside the chains that were about their camels' necks. And Gideon made an ephod thereof, and put it in his city, even in Ophrah, and all Israel went thither a-whoring after it: which thing became a snare unto Gideon, and to his house.

Thus was Midian subdued before the children of Israel, so that they lifted up their heads no more. And the country was in quietness forty years in the days of Gideon.

And Gideon had threescore and ten sons of his body begotten: for he had many wives. And his concubine that was in Shechem, she also bore him a son, whose name he called Abimelech. And Gideon the son of Joash died in a good old age, and was buried in the sepulchre of Joash his father, in Ophrah of the Abi-ezrites.

And it came to pass, as soon as Gideon was dead, that the children of Israel turned again, and went a-whoring after Baalim, and made Baal-berith their god. And the children of Israel remembered not the Lord their God, who had delivered them out of the hands of all their enemies on every side: neither showed they kindness to the house of Jerubbaal, namely, Gideon, according to all the goodness which he had showed unto Israel.

The Story of Abimelech

And Abimelech the son of Jerubbaal went to Shechem unto his mother's brethren, and communed with them, and with all the family of the house of his mother's father, saying,

"Speak, I pray you, in the ears of all the men of Shechem, 'Whether is better for you, either that all the sons of Jerubbaal, which are threescore and ten persons, reign over you, or that one reign over you?' remember also that I am your bone and your flesh."

And his mother's brethren spoke of him in the ears of all the

THE BOOK OF JUDGES

men of Shechem all these words: and their hearts inclined to follow Abimelech; for they said, "He is our brother." And they gave him threescore and ten pieces of silver out of the house of Baal-berith, wherewith Abimelech hired vain and light persons, which followed him. And he went unto his father's house at Ophrah, and slew his brethren the sons of Jerubbaal, being threescore and ten persons, upon one stone: notwithstanding yet Jotham the youngest son of Jerubbaal was left; for he hid himself. And all the men of Shechem gathered together, and all the house of Millo, and went, and made Abimelech king, by the plain of the pillar that was in Shechem.

And when they told it to Jotham, he went and stood in the top of Mount Gerizim, and lifted up his voice, and cried, and said unto them,

"Hearken unto me, ye men of Shechem, that God may hearken unto you.

>"The trees went forth on a time
>To anoint a king over them;
>And they said unto the olive tree,
>'Reign thou over us.'
>But the olive tree said unto them,
>'Should I leave my fatness,
>Wherewith by me they honour God and man,
>And go to be promoted over the trees?'
>
>And the trees said to the fig tree,
>'Come thou, and reign over us.'
>But the fig tree said unto them,
>'Should I forsake my sweetness,
>And my good fruit,
>And go to be promoted over the trees?'
>
>Then said the trees unto the vine,
>'Come thou, and reign over us.'
>And the vine said unto them,
>'Should I leave my wine,

THE BOOK OF JUDGES

Which cheereth God and man,
And go to be promoted over the trees?'

Then said all the trees unto the bramble,
'Come thou, and reign over us.'
And the bramble said unto the trees,
'If in truth ye anoint
Me king over you,
Come and put your trust in my shadow:
And if not, let fire come out of the bramble,
And devour the cedars of Lebanon.'

"Now therefore, if ye have done truly and sincerely, in that ye have made Abimelech king, and if ye have dealt well with Jerubbaal and his house, and have done unto him according to the deserving of his hands (for my father fought for you, and adventured his life far, and delivered you out of the hand of Midian: and ye are risen up against my father's house this day, and have slain his sons, threescore and ten persons, upon one stone, and have made Abimelech, the son of his maidservant, king over the men of Shechem, because he is your brother); if ye then have dealt truly and sincerely with Jerubbaal and with his house this day, then rejoice ye in Abimelech, and let him also rejoice in you: but if not, let fire come out from Abimelech, and devour the men of Shechem, and the house of Millo; and let fire come out from the men of Shechem, and from the house of Millo, and devour Abimelech."

And Jotham ran away, and fled, and went to Beer, and dwelt there, for fear of Abimelech his brother.

When Abimelech had reigned three years over Israel, then God sent an evil spirit between Abimelech and the men of Shechem; and the men of Shechem dealt treacherously with Abimelech: that the cruelty done to the threescore and ten sons of Jerubbaal might come, and their blood be laid upon Abimelech their brother, which slew them; and upon the men of Shechem, which aided him in the killing of his brethren. And the

THE BOOK OF JUDGES

men of Shechem set liers in wait for him in the top of the mountains, and they robbed all that came along that way by them.

And Gaal the son of Ebed came with his brethren, and went over to Shechem: and the men of Shechem put their confidence in him. And Gaal the son of Ebed said,

"Who is Abimelech, and who is Shechem, that we should serve him? is not he the son of Jerubbaal? and Zebul his officer? serve the men of Hamor the father of Shechem: for why should we serve him? And would to God this people were under my hand! then would I remove Abimelech."

And when Zebul the ruler of the city heard the words of Gaal the son of Ebed, his anger was kindled. And he sent messengers unto Abimelech privily, saying,

"Behold, Gaal the son of Ebed and his brethren be come to Shechem; and, behold, they fortify the city against thee. Now therefore up by night, thou and the people that is with thee, and lie in wait in the field: and it shall be that in the morning, as soon as the sun is up, thou shalt rise early, and set upon the city: and, behold, when he and the people that is with him come out against thee, then mayest thou do to them as thou shalt find occasion."

And Abimelech rose up, and all the people that were with him, by night, and they laid wait against Shechem in four companies. And Gaal the son of Ebed went out, and stood in the entering of the gate of the city: and Abimelech rose up, and the people that were with him, from lying in wait.

And when Gaal saw the people, he said to Zebul, "Behold, there come people down from the top of the mountains."

And Zebul said unto him, "Thou seest the shadow of the mountains as if they were men."

And Gaal spoke again and said, "See there come people down by the middle of the land, and another company come along by the plain of Meonenim."

Then said Zebul unto him, "Where is now thy mouth, wherewith thou saidst, 'Who is Abimelech, that we should serve him?'

THE BOOK OF JUDGES

is not this the people that thou hast despised? go out, I pray now, and fight with them."

And Gaal went out before the men of Shechem, and fought with Abimelech. And Abimelech chased him, and he fled before him, and many were overthrown and wounded, even unto the entering of the gate.

And it came to pass on the morrow that the people went out into the field; and they told Abimelech. And he took the people, and divided them into three companies, and laid wait in the field, and looked, and, behold, the people were come forth out of the city; and he rose up against them, and smote them. And Abimelech, and the company that was with him, rushed forward, and stood in the entering of the gate of the city: and the two other companies ran upon all the people that were in the fields, and slew them. And Abimelech fought against the city all that day; and he took the city, and slew the people that was therein, and beat down the city, and sowed it with salt.

Then went Abimelech to Thebez, and encamped against Thebez, and took it. But there was a strong tower within the city, and thither fled all the men and women, and all they of the city, and shut it to them, and got them up to the top of the tower. And Abimelech came unto the tower, and fought against it, and went hard unto the door of the tower to burn it with fire. And a certain woman cast a piece of a millstone upon Abimelech's head, and all to break his skull. Then he called hastily unto the young man his armourbearer, and said unto him,

"Draw thy sword, and slay me, that men say not of me, 'A woman slew him.'"

And his young man thrust him through, and he died. And when the men of Israel saw that Abimelech was dead, they departed every man unto his place.

Thus God rendered the wickedness of Abimelech, which he did unto his father, in slaying his seventy brethren: and all the evil of the men of Shechem did God render upon their heads: and upon them came the curse of Jotham the son of Jerubbaal.

THE BOOK OF JUDGES

The Story of Jephthah's Daughter

Now Jephthah the Gileadite was a mighty man of valour, and he was the son of a harlot: and Gilead begot Jephthah. And Gilead's wife bore him sons; and his wife's sons grew up, and they thrust out Jephthah, and said unto him, "Thou shalt not inherit in our father's house; for thou art the son of a strange woman."

Then Jephthah fled from his brethren, and dwelt in the land of Tob: and there were gathered vain men to Jephthah, and went out with him.

And it came to pass in process of time that the children of Ammon made war against Israel.

Then the Spirit of the Lord came upon Jephthah, and he passed over Gilead, and Manasseh, and passed over Mizpeh of Gilead, and from Mizpeh of Gilead he passed over unto the children of Ammon. And Jephthah vowed a vow unto the Lord, and said,

"If thou shalt without fail deliver the children of Ammon into mine hands, then it shall be that whatsoever cometh forth of the doors of my house to meet me, when I return in peace from the children of Ammon, shall surely be the Lord's, and I will offer it up for a burnt offering."

So Jephthah passed over unto the children of Ammon to fight against them; and the Lord delivered them into his hands. And he smote them from Aroer, even till thou come to Minnith, even twenty cities, and unto the plain of the vineyards, with a very great slaughter. Thus the children of Ammon were subdued before the children of Israel.

And Jephthah came to Mizpeh unto his house, and, behold, his daughter came out to meet him with timbrels and with dances: and she was his only child; beside her he had neither son nor daughter. And it came to pass, when he saw her, that he rent his clothes, and said,

"Alas, my daughter! thou hast brought me very low, and thou

THE BOOK OF JUDGES

art one of them that trouble me: for I have opened my mouth unto the Lord, and I cannot go back."

And she said unto him,

"My father, if thou hast opened thy mouth unto the Lord, do to me according to that which hath proceeded out of thy mouth; forasmuch as the Lord hath taken vengeance for thee of thine enemies, even of the children of Ammon."

And she said unto her father,

"Let this thing be done for me: let me alone two months, that I may go up and down upon the mountains, and bewail my virginity, I and my fellows."

And he said, "Go!" And he sent her away for two months: and she went with her companions, and bewailed her virginity upon the mountains. And it came to pass at the end of two months that she returned unto her father, who did with her according to his vow which he had vowed: and she knew no man. And it was a custom in Israel that the daughters of Israel went yearly to lament the daughter of Jephthah the Gileadite four days in a year.

The Story of Samson

And the children of Israel did evil again in the sight of the Lord; and the Lord delivered them into the hand of the Philistines forty years.

And there was a certain man of Zorah, of the family of the Danites, whose name was Manoah; and his wife was barren, and bore not. And the angel of the Lord appeared unto the woman, and said unto her,

"Behold now, thou art barren, and bearest not: but thou shalt conceive, and bear a son. Now therefore beware, I pray thee, and drink not wine nor strong drink, and eat not any unclean thing: for, lo, thou shalt conceive, and bear a son; and no razor shall come on his head: for the child shall be a Nazarite unto God from the womb: and he shall begin to deliver Israel out of the hand of the Philistines."

Then the woman came and told her husband, saying,

THE BOOK OF JUDGES

"A man of God came unto me, and his countenance was like the countenance of an angel of God, very terrible: but I asked him not whence he was, neither told he me his name: but he said unto me, 'Behold, thou shalt conceive, and bear a son; and now drink no wine nor strong drink, neither eat any unclean thing: for the child shall be a Nazarite to God from the womb to the day of his death.'"

Then Manoah intreated the Lord, and said, "O my Lord, let the man of God which thou didst send come again unto us, and teach us what we shall do unto the child that shall be born."

And God hearkened to the voice of Manoah; and the angel of God came again unto the woman as she sat in the field: but Manoah her husband was not with her. And the woman made haste, and ran, and showed her husband, and said unto him, "Behold, the man hath appeared unto me, that came unto me the other day."

And Manoah arose, and went after his wife, and came to the man, and said unto him, "Art thou the man that spokest unto the woman?" And he said, "I am."

And Manoah said, "Now let thy words come to pass. How shall we order the child, and how shall we do unto him?"

And the angel of the Lord said unto Manoah, "Of all that I said unto the woman let her beware. She may not eat of any thing that cometh of the vine, neither let her drink wine or strong drink, nor eat any unclean thing: all that I commanded her let her observe."

And Manoah said unto the angel of the Lord, "I pray thee, let us detain thee, until we shall have made ready a kid for thee."

And the angel of the Lord said unto Manoah, "Though thou detain me, I will not eat of thy bread: and if thou wilt offer a burnt offering, thou must offer it unto the Lord." For Manoah knew not that he was an angel of the Lord. And Manoah said unto the angel of the Lord, "What is thy name, that when thy sayings come to pass we may do thee honour?"

And the angel of the Lord said unto him, "Why askest thou thus after my name, seeing it is secret?"

THE BOOK OF JUDGES

So Manoah took a kid with a meat offering, and offered it upon a rock unto the Lord: and the angel did wonderously; and Manoah and his wife looked on. For it came to pass, when the flame went up toward heaven from off the altar, that the angel of the Lord ascended in the flame of the altar. And Manoah and his wife looked on it, and fell on their faces to the ground. But the angel of the Lord did no more appear to Manoah and to his wife. Then Manoah knew that he was an angel of the Lord.

And Manoah said unto his wife, "We shall surely die, because we have seen God."

But his wife said unto him, "If the Lord were pleased to kill us, he would not have received a burnt offering and a meat offering at our hands, neither would he have showed us all these things, nor would as at this time have told us such things as these."

And the woman bore a son, and called his name Samson: and the child grew, and the Lord blessed him. And the Spirit of the Lord began to move him at times in the camp of Dan between Zorah and Eshtaol.

And Samson went down to Timnath, and saw a woman in Timnath of the daughters of the Philistines. And he came up, and told his father and his mother, and said,

"I have seen a woman in Timnath of the daughters of the Philistines: now therefore get her for me to wife."

Then his father and his mother said unto him,

"Is there never a woman among the daughters of thy brethren, or among all my people, that thou goest to take a wife of the uncircumcised Philistines?"

And Samson said unto his father, "Get her for me; for she pleaseth me well."

But his father and his mother knew not that it was of the Lord, that he sought an occasion against the Philistines: for at that time the Philistines had dominion over Israel.

Then went Samson down, and his father and his mother, to Timnath, and came to the vineyards of Timnath: and, behold, a young lion roared against him. And the Spirit of the Lord came

THE BOOK OF JUDGES

mightily upon him, and he rent him as he would have rent a kid, and he had nothing in his hand: but he told not his father or his mother what he had done. And he went down, and talked with the woman; and she pleased Samson well.

And after a time he returned to take her, and he turned aside to see the carcase of the lion: and behold, there was a swarm of bees and honey in the carcase of the lion. And he took thereof in his hands, and went on eating, and came to his father and mother, and he gave them, and they did eat: but he told not them that he had taken the honey out of the carcase of the lion.

So his father went down unto the woman: and Samson made there a feast; for so used the young men to do. And it came to pass, when they saw him, that they brought thirty companions to be with him. And Samson said unto them,

"I will now put forth a riddle unto you: if ye can certainly declare it me within the seven days of the feast, and find it out, then I will give you thirty sheets and thirty changes of garments: but if ye cannot declare it me, then shall ye give me thirty sheets and thirty changes of garments."

And they said unto him, "Put forth thy riddle, that we may hear it."

And he said unto them,

> "Out of the eater came forth meat,
> And out of the strong came forth sweetness."

And they could not in three days expound the riddle. And it came to pass on the seventh day that they said unto Samson's wife, "Entice thy husband, that he may declare unto us the riddle, lest we burn thee and thy father's house with fire: have ye called us to take that we have? is it not so?"

And Samson's wife wept before him, and said, "Thou dost but hate me, and lovest me not: thou hast put forth a riddle unto the children of my people, and hast not told it me."

And he said unto her, "Behold, I have not told it my father nor my mother, and shall I tell it thee?"

And she wept before him the seven days, while their feast

lasted: and it came to pass on the seventh day that he told her, because she lay sore upon him: and she told the riddle to the children of her people. And the men of the city said unto him on the seventh day before the sun went down,

> *"What is sweeter than honey?*
> *And what is stronger than a lion?"*

And he said unto them,

> *"If ye had not plowed with my heifer,*
> *Ye had not found my riddle."*

And the Spirit of the Lord came upon him, and he went down to Ashkelon, and slew thirty men of them, and took their spoil, and gave change of garments unto them which expounded the riddle. And his anger was kindled, and he went up to his father's house. But Samson's wife was given to his companion, whom he had used as his friend. But it came to pass within a while after, in the time of wheat harvest, that Samson visited his wife with a kid; and he said, "I will go in to my wife into the chamber." But her father would not suffer him to go in. And her father said,
"I verily thought that thou hadst utterly hated her; therefore I gave her to thy companion: is not her younger sister fairer than she? take her, I pray thee, instead of her."
And Samson said concerning them, "Now shall I be more blameless than the Philistines, though I do them a displeasure?"
And Samson went and caught three hundred foxes, and took firebrands, and turned tail to tail, and put a firebrand in the midst between two tails. And when he had set the brands on fire, he let them go into the standing corn of the Philistines, and burnt up both the shocks, and also the standing corn, with the vineyards and olives.
Then the Philistines said, "Who hath done this?"
And they answered, "Samson, the son-in-law of the Timnite, because he had taken his wife, and given her to his companion."
And the Philistines came up, and burnt her and her father with fire.

THE BOOK OF JUDGES

And Samson said unto them, "Though ye have done this, yet will I be avenged of you, and after that I will cease."

And he smote them hip and thigh with a great slaughter: and he went down and dwelt in the top of the rock Etam.

Then the Philistines went up, and pitched in Judah, and spread themselves in Lehi. And the men of Judah said, "Why are ye come up against us?"

And they answered, "To bind Samson are we come up, to do to him as he hath done to us."

Then three thousand men of Judah went to the top of the rock Etam, and said to Samson, "Knowest thou not that the Philistines are rulers over us? what is this that thou hast done unto us?"

And he said unto them, "As they did unto me, so have I done unto them."

And they said unto him, "We are come down to bind thee, that we may deliver thee into the hand of the Philistines."

And Samson said unto them, "Swear unto me that ye will not fall upon me yourselves."

And they spoke unto him, saying, "No; but we will bind thee fast, and deliver thee into their hand: but surely we will not kill thee."

And they bound him with two new cords, and brought him up from the rock. And when he came unto Lehi, the Philistines shouted against him: and the Spirit of the Lord came mightily upon him, and the cords that were upon his arms became as flax that was burnt with fire, and his bands loosed from off his hands. And he found a new jawbone of an ass, and put forth his hand, and took it, and slew a thousand men therewith. And Samson said,

"With the jawbone of an ass, heaps upon heaps,
With the jaw of an ass have I slain a thousand men."

And it came to pass, when he had made an end of speaking, that he cast away the jawbone out of his hand, and called that

THE BOOK OF JUDGES

place Ramath-lehi. And he was sore athirst, and called on the Lord, and said,

"Thou hast given this great deliverance into the hand of thy servant: and now shall I die for thirst, and fall into the hand of the uncircumcised?"

But God clove a hollow place that was in the jaw, and there came water thereout; and when he had drunk, his spirit came again, and he revived: wherefore he called the name thereof En-hakkore, which is in Lehi unto this day. And he judged Israel in the days of the Philistines twenty years.

Then went Samson to Gaza, and saw there a harlot, and went in unto her. And it was told the Gazites, saying, "Samson is come hither." And they compassed him in, and laid wait for him all night in the gate of the city, and were quiet all the night, saying, "In the morning, when it is day, we shall kill him."

And Samson lay till midnight, and arose at midnight, and took the doors of the gate of the city, and the two posts, and went away with them, bar and all, and put them upon his shoulders, and carried them up to the top of a hill that is before Hebron.

And it came to pass afterward that he loved a woman in the valley of Sorek, whose name was Delilah. And the lords of the Philistines came up unto her, and said unto her,

"Entice him, and see wherein his great strength lieth, and by what means we may prevail against him, that we may bind him to afflict him: and we will give thee every one of us eleven hundred pieces of silver."

And Delilah said to Samson, "Tell me, I pray thee, wherein thy great strength lieth, and wherewith thou mightest be bound to afflict thee."

And Samson said unto her, "If they bind me with seven green withes that were never dried, then shall I be weak, and be as another man."

Then the lords of the Philistines brought up to her seven green withes which had not been dried, and she bound him with them. Now there were men lying in wait, abiding with her in the chamber. And she said unto him,

"The Philistines be upon thee, Samson." And he broke the withes, as a thread of tow is broken when it toucheth the fire. So his strength was not known. And Delilah said unto Samson, "Behold, thou hast mocked me, and told me lies: now tell me, I pray thee, wherewith thou mightest be bound."

And he said unto her, "If they bind me fast with new ropes that never were occupied, then shall I be weak, and be as another man."

Delilah therefore took new ropes, and bound him therewith, and said unto him, "The Philistines be upon thee, Samson." And there were liers in wait abiding in the chamber. And he broke them from off his arms like a thread.

And Delilah said unto Samson, "Hitherto thou hast mocked me, and told me lies: tell me wherewith thou mightest be bound."

And he said unto her, "If thou weavest the seven locks of my head with the web."

And she fastened it with the pin, and said unto him, "The Philistines be upon thee, Samson."

And he awaked out of his sleep, and went away with the pin of the beam, and with the web. And she said unto him,

"How canst thou say, 'I love thee,' when thine heart is not with me? thou hast mocked me these three times, and hast not told me wherein thy great strength lieth."

And it came to pass, when she pressed him daily with her words, and urged him, so that his soul was vexed unto death, that he told her all his heart, and said unto her, "There hath not come a razor upon mine head; for I have been a Nazarite unto God from my mother's womb: if I be shaven, then my strength will go from me, and I shall become weak, and be like any other man."

And when Delilah saw that he had told her all his heart, she sent and called for the lords of the Philistines, saying, "Come up this once, for he hath showed me all his heart."

THE BOOK OF JUDGES

Then the lords of the Philistines came up unto her, and brought money in their hand. And she made him sleep upon her knees; and she called for a man, and she caused him to shave off the seven locks of his head; and she began to afflict him, and his strength went from him. And she said,

"The Philistines be upon thee, Samson." And he awoke out of his sleep, and said, "I will go out as at other times before, and shake myself." And he wist not that the Lord was departed from him.

But the Philistines took him, and put out his eyes, and brought him down to Gaza, and bound him with fetters of brass; and he did grind in the prison house. Howbeit the hair of his head began to grow again after he was shaven.

Then the lords of the Philistines gathered them together for to offer a great sacrifice unto Dagon their god, and to rejoice: for they said, "Our god hath delivered Samson our enemy into our hand."

And when the people saw him, they praised their god: for they said, "Our god hath delivered into our hands our enemy, and the destroyer of our country, which slew many of us."

And it came to pass, when their hearts were merry, that they said, "Call for Samson, that he may make us sport."

And they called for Samson out of the prison house; and he made them sport: and they set him between the pillars. And Samson said unto the lad that held him by the hand, "Suffer me that I may feel the pillars whereupon the house standeth, that I may lean upon them."

Now the house was full of men and women; and all the lords of the Philistines were there; and there were upon the roof about three thousand men and women that beheld while Samson made sport. And Samson called unto the Lord, and said, "O Lord God, remember me, I pray thee, and strengthen me, I pray thee, only this once, O God, that I may be at once avenged of the Philistines for my two eyes."

And Samson took hold of the two middle pillars upon which the house stood, and on which it was borne up, of the one with

THE BOOK OF JUDGES

his right hand, and of the other with his left. And Samson said, "Let me die with the Philistines."

And he bowed himself with all his might; and the house fell upon the lords, and upon all the people that were therein. So the dead which he slew at his death were more than they which he slew in his life. Then his brethren and all the house of his father came down, and took him, and brought him up, and buried him between Zorah and Eshtaol in the burying place of Manoah his father. And he judged Israel twenty years.

The Benjamite War

And it came to pass in those days, when there was no king in Israel, that there was a certain Levite sojourning on the side of Mount Ephraim, who took to him a concubine out of Bethlehem-judah. And his concubine played the whore against him, and went away from him unto her father's house to Beth-lehem-judah, and was there four whole months. And her husband arose, and went after her, to speak friendly unto her, and to bring her again, having his servant with him, and a couple of asses: and she brought him into her father's house: and when the father of the damsel saw him, he rejoiced to meet him. And his father-in-law, the damsel's father, retained him; and he abode with him three days: so they did eat and drink, and lodged there. And it came to pass on the fourth day, when they arose early in the morning, that he rose up to depart: and the damsel's father said unto his son-in-law, "Comfort thine heart with a morsel of bread, and afterward go your way."

And they sat down, and did eat and drink both of them together: for the damsel's father had said unto the man, "Be content, I pray thee, and tarry all night, and let thine heart be merry."

And when the man rose up to depart, his father-in-law urged him: therefore he lodged there again. And he arose early in the morning on the fifth day to depart: and the damsel's father said, "Comfort thine heart, I pray thee."

And they tarried until afternoon, and they did eat both of

THE BOOK OF JUDGES

them. And when the man rose up to depart, he, and his concubine, and his servant, his father-in-law, the damsel's father, said unto him, Behold, now the day draweth toward evening, I pray you tarry all night: behold, the day groweth to an end, lodge here, that thine heart may be merry; and to-morrow get you early on your way, that thou mayest go home."

But the man would not tarry that night, but he rose up and departed, and came over against Jebus, which is Jerusalem; and there were with him two asses saddled, his concubine also was with him. And when they were by Jebus, the day was far spent; and the servant said unto his master,

"Come, I pray thee, and let us turn in into this city of the Jebusites, and lodge in it."

And his master said unto him, "We will not turn aside hither into the city of a stranger, that is not of the children of Israel; we will pass over to Gibeah."

And he said unto his servant, "Come, and let us draw near to one of these places to lodge all night, in Gibeah, or in Ramah."

And they passed on and went their way; and the sun went down upon them when they were by Gibeah, which belongeth to Benjamin. And they turned aside thither, to go in and to lodge in Gibeah: and when he went in he sat him down in a street of the city: for there was no man that took them into his house to lodging. And, behold, there came an old man from his work out of the field at even, which was also of Mount Ephraim; and he sojourned in Gibeah: but the men of the place were Benjamites. And when he had lifted up his eyes, he saw a wayfaring man in the street of the city: and the old man said,

"Whither goest thou? and whence comest thou?"

And he said unto him,

"We are passing from Beth-lehem-judah toward the side of Mount Ephraim; from thence am I: and I went to Beth-lehem-judah, but I am now going to the house of the Lord; and there is no man that receiveth me to house. Yet there is both straw and provender for our asses; and there is bread and wine also for me,

[206]

THE BOOK OF JUDGES

and for thy handmaid, and for the young man which is with thy servants: there is no want of any thing."

And the old man said,

"Peace be with thee; howsoever let all thy wants lie upon me; only lodge not in the street."

So he brought him into his house, and gave provender unto the asses: and they washed their feet, and did eat and drink. Now as they were making their hearts merry, behold, the men of the city, certain sons of Belial, beset the house round about, and beat at the door, and spoke to the master of the house, the old man, saying, "Bring forth the man that came into thine house, that we may know him."

And the man, the master of the house, went out unto them, and said unto them, "Nay, my brethren, nay, I pray you, do not so wickedly; seeing that this man is come into mine house, do not this folly. Behold, here is my daughter a maiden, and his concubine; them I will bring out now, and humble ye them, and do with them what seemeth good unto you: but unto this man do not so vile a thing."

But the men would not hearken to him: so the man took his concubine, and brought her forth unto them; and they knew her, and abused her all the night until the morning: and when the day began to spring, they let her go. Then came the woman in the dawning of the day, and fell down at the door of the man's house where her lord was, till it was light. And her lord rose up in the morning, and opened the doors of the house, and went out to go his way: and, behold, the woman his concubine was fallen down at the door of the house, and her hands were upon the threshold. And he said unto her,

"Up, and let us be going." But none answered.

Then the man took her up upon an ass, and the man rose up, and got him unto his place. And when he was come into his house, he took a knife, and laid hold on his concubine, and divided her, together with her bones, into twelve pieces, and sent her into all the coasts of Israel. And it was so that all that saw it said,

THE BOOK OF JUDGES

"There was no such deed done nor seen from the day that the children of Israel came up out of the land of Egypt unto this day: consider of it, take advice, and speak your minds."

Then all the children of Israel went out, and the congregation was gathered together as one man, from Dan even to Beer-sheba, with the land of Gilead, unto the Lord in Mizpeh. And the chief of all the people, even of all the tribes of Israel, presented themselves in the assembly of the people of God, four hundred thousand footmen that drew sword. (Now the children of Benjamin heard that the children of Israel were gone up to Mizpeh.) Then said the children of Israel,

"Tell us, how was this wickedness?"

And the Levite, the husband of the woman that was slain, answered and said,

"I came into Gibeah that belongeth to Benjamin, I and my concubine, to lodge. And the men of Gibeah rose against me, and beset the house round about upon me by night, and thought to have slain me: and my concubine have they forced, that she is dead. And I took my concubine, and cut her in pieces, and sent her throughout all the country of the inheritance of Israel: for they have committed lewdness and folly in Israel. Behold, ye are all children of Israel; give here your advice and counsel."

And all the people arose as one man, saying,

"We will not any of us go to his tent, neither will we any of us turn into his house. But now this shall be the thing which we will do to Gibeah; we will go up by lot against it; and we will take ten men of a hundred thoughout all the tribes of Israel, and a hundred of a thousand, and a thousand out of ten thousand, to fetch victual for the people, that they may do, when they come to Gibeah of Benjamin, according to all the folly that they have wrought in Israel."

So all the men of Israel were gathered against the city, knit together as one man. And the tribes of Israel sent men through all the tribe of Benjamin, saying,

"What wickedness is this that is done among you? Now

THE BOOK OF JUDGES

therefore deliver us the men, the children of Belial, which are in Gibeah, that we may put them to death, and put away evil from Israel."

But the children of Benjamin would not hearken to the voice of their brethren the children of Israel: but the children of Benjamin gathered themselves together out of the cities unto Gibeah, to go out to battle against the children of Israel. And the children of Benjamin were numbered at that time out of the cities twenty and six thousand men that drew sword, beside the inhabitants of Gibeah, which were numbered seven hundred chosen men. Among all this people there were seven hundred chosen men lefthanded; every one could sling stones at a hairbreadth, and not miss. And the men of Israel, beside Benjamin, were numbered four hundred thousand men that drew sword: all these were men of war.

And the children of Israel arose, and went up to the house of God, and asked counsel of God, and said, "Which of us shall go up first to the battle against the children of Benjamin?"

And the Lord said, "Judah shall go up first."

And the children of Israel rose up in the morning, and encamped against Gibeah. And the men of Israel went out to battle against Benjamin; and the men of Israel put themselves in array to fight against them at Gibeah. And the children of Benjamin came forth out of Gibeah, and destroyed down to the ground of the Israelites that day twenty and two thousand men. And the people the men of Israel encouraged themselves, and set their battle again in array in the place where they put themselves in array the first day. And the children of Israel went up and wept before the Lord until even, and asked counsel of the Lord, saying,

"Shall I go up again to battle against the children of Benjamin my brother?"

And the Lord said, "Go up against him."

And the children of Israel came near against the children of Benjamin the second day. And Benjamin went forth against them out of Gibeah the second day, and destroyed down to the ground of the children of Israel again eighteen thousand men; all these drew the sword.

Then all the children of Israel, and all the people, went up, and came unto the house of God, and wept, and sat there before the Lord, and fasted that day until even, and offered burnt offerings and peace offerings before the Lord. And the children of Israel enquired of the Lord (for the ark of the covenant of God was there in those days, and Phinehas, the son of Eleazar, the son of Aaron, stood before it in those days), saying,

"Shall I yet again go out to battle against the children of Benjamin my brother, or shall I cease?"

And the Lord said, "Go up; for to-morrow I will deliver them into thine hand."

And Israel set liers in wait round about Gibeah. And the children of Israel went up against the children of Benjamin on the third day, and put themselves in array against Gibeah, as at other times. And the children of Benjamin went out against the people, and were drawn away from the city; and they began to smite of the people, and kill, as at other times, in the highways, of which one goeth up to the house of God, and the other to Gibeah in the field, about thirty men of Israel. So the children of Benjamin saw that they were smitten: for the men of Israel gave place to the Benjamites, because they trusted unto the liers in wait which they had set beside Gibeah. And the liers in wait hastened, and rushed upon Gibeah; and the liers in wait drew themselves along, and smote all the city with the edge of the sword.

Now there was an appointed sign between the men of Israel and the liers in wait, that they should make a great flame with smoke rise up out of the city.

But when the flame began to arise up out of the city with a pillar of smoke, the Benjamites looked behind them, and, behold, the flame of the city ascended up to heaven. And when the men of Israel turned again, the men of Benjamin were amazed: for they saw that evil was come upon them. Therefore they turned

THE BOOK OF JUDGES

their backs before the men of Israel unto the way of the wilderness; but the battle overtook them; and them which came out of the cities they destroyed in the midst of them. Thus they inclosed the Benjamites round about, and chased them, and trod them down with ease over against Gibeah toward the sunrising. And there fell of Benjamin eighteen thousand men; all these were men of valour. And they turned and fled toward the wilderness unto the rock of Rimmon; and they gleaned of them in the highways five thousand men; and pursued hard after them unto Gidom, and slew two thousand men of them. So that all which fell that day of Benjamin were twenty and five thousand men that drew the sword; all these were men of valour. But six hundred men turned and fled to the wilderness unto the rock Rimmon, and abode in the rock Rimmon four months. And the men of Israel turned again upon the children of Benjamin, and smote them with the edge of the sword, as well the men of every city, as the beast, and all that came to hand: also they set on fire all the cities that they came to.

Now the men of Israel had sworn in Mizpeh, saying, "There shall not any of us give his daughter unto Benjamin to wife."

And the people came to the house of God, and abode there till even before God, and lifted up their voices, and wept sore; and said, "O Lord God of Israel, why is this come to pass in Israel, that there should be to-day one tribe lacking in Israel?"

And the people repented them for Benjamin, because that the Lord had made a breach in the tribes of Israel.

Then the elders of the congregation said, "How shall we do for wives for them that remain, seeing the women are destroyed out of Benjamin?"

And they said, "There must be an inheritance for them that be escaped of Benjamin, that a tribe be not destroyed out of Israel. Howbeit we may not give them wives of our daughters: for the children of Israel have sworn, saying, 'Cursed be he that giveth a wife to Benjamin.'"

Then they said, "Behold, there is a feast of the Lord in Shiloh yearly in a place which is on the north side of Beth-el, on the

THE BOOK OF JUDGES

east side of the highway that goeth up from Beth-el to Shechem, and on the south of Lebonah."

Therefore they commanded the children of Benjamin, saying,

"Go and lie in wait in the vineyards; and see, and, behold, if the daughters of Shiloh come out to dance in dances, then come ye out of the vineyards, and catch you every man his wife of the daughters of Shiloh, and go to the land of Benjamin. And it shall be, when their fathers or their brethren come unto us to complain, that we will say unto them, 'Be favourable unto them for our sakes: because we reserved not to each man his wife in the war: for ye did not give unto them at this time, that ye should be guilty.'"

And the children of Benjamin did so, and took them wives, according to their number, of them that danced, whom they caught: and they went and returned unto their inheritance, and repaired the cities, and dwelt in them. And the children of Israel departed thence at that time, every man to his tribe and to his family, and they went out from thence every man to his inheritance. In those days there was no king in Israel: every man did that which was right in his own eyes.

THE FIRST BOOK OF SAMUEL

WHAT WAS SAID of the Book of Judges is also largely true of the First Book of Samuel, save that the narratives of which it is composed —probably originally put together even a little earlier than the Book of Judges—dealt with events nearer to the writers' own time so that their imagination was a trifle more limited by actuality. The theme of the work is twofold: first, the conflict between the older semirepublican government of the Judges represented by Samuel and the rising monarchical party led by Saul, and second, after the monarchy is established, the successful rebellion of David against it. Looking back upon these struggles from the point of view of the later kingdom, when David was accepted as the national hero and when there was at the same time a tendency to glorify the older past, the writers' attitude was, on the whole, decidedly unfavorable to the transitional figure of Saul, although stories emanating from his followers and contradictory of the Samuel-David version were also incorporated in the record. The work was subjected to Deuteronomic revision during the Exile, but as the editors were interested in historical facts, not for their own sake, but as illustrations of religious principles, they did not trouble to iron out these minor discrepancies.

The First Book of SAMUEL

The Birth of Samuel

NOW THERE WAS A CERTAIN MAN of Ramathaim-zophim, of Mount Ephraim, and his name was Elkanah, the son of Jeroham, the son of Elihu, the son of Tohu, the son of Zuph, an Ephrathite: and he had two wives; the name of the one was Hannah, and the name of the other Peninnah: and Peninnah had children, but Hannah had no children. And this man went up out of his city yearly to worship and to sacrifice unto the Lord of hosts in Shiloh. And the two sons of Eli, Hophni and Phinehas, the priests of the Lord, were there.

And when the time was that Elkanah offered, he gave to Peninnah his wife, and to all her sons and her daughters, portions: but unto Hannah he gave a worthy portion; for he loved Hannah: but the Lord had shut up her womb. And her adversary also provoked her sore, for to make her fret, because the Lord had shut up her womb. And as he did so year by year, when she went up to the house of the Lord, so she provoked her; therefore she wept, and did not eat. Then said Elkanah her husband to her,

"Hannah, why weepest thou? and why eatest thou not? and why is thy heart grieved? am not I better to thee than ten sons?"

So Hannah rose up after they had eaten in Shiloh, and after they had drunk. Now Eli the priest sat upon a seat by a post of the temple of the Lord. And she was in bitterness of soul, and prayed unto the Lord, and wept sore. And she vowed a vow, and said,

"O Lord of hosts, if thou wilt indeed look on the affliction of

THE FIRST BOOK OF SAMUEL

thine handmaid, and remember me, and not forget thine handmaid, but wilt give unto thine handmaid a man child, then I will give him unto the Lord all the days of his life, and there shall no razor come upon his head."

And it came to pass, as she continued praying before the Lord, that Eli marked her mouth. Now Hannah, she spoke in her heart; only her lips moved, but her voice was not heard: therefore Eli thought she had been drunken.

And Eli said unto her, "How long wilt thou be drunken? put away thy wine from thee."

And Hannah answered and said, "No, my lord, I am a woman of a sorrowful spirit: I have drunk neither wine nor strong drink, but have poured out my soul before the Lord. Count not thine handmaid for a daughter of Belial: for out of the abundance of my complaint and grief have I spoken hitherto."

Then Eli answered and said, "Go in peace: and the God of Israel grant thee thy petition that thou hast asked of him."

And she said, "Let thine handmaid find grace in thy sight."

So the woman went her way, and did eat, and her countenance was no more sad. And they rose up in the morning early, and worshipped before the Lord, and returned, and came to their house to Ramah: and Elkanah knew Hannah his wife; and the Lord remembered her. Wherefore it came to pass, when the time was come about after Hannah had conceived, that she bore a son, and called his name Samuel, saying, "Because I have asked him of the Lord."

And the man Elkanah, and all his house, went up to offer unto the Lord the yearly sacrifice, and his vow. But Hannah went not up; for she said unto her husband,

"I will not go up until the child be weaned, and then I will bring him, that he may appear before the Lord, and there abide for ever."

And Elkanah her husband said unto her, "Do what seemeth thee good; tarry until thou have weaned him; only the Lord establish his word."

So the woman abode, and gave her son suck until she weaned

THE FIRST BOOK OF SAMUEL

him. And when she had weaned him, she took him up with her, with three bullocks, and one ephah of flour, and a bottle of wine, and brought him unto the house of the Lord in Shiloh: and the child was young. And they slew a bullock, and brought the child to Eli. And she said,

"Oh my lord, as thy soul liveth, my lord, I am the woman that stood by thee here, praying unto the Lord. For this child I prayed; and the Lord hath given me my petition which I asked of him: therefore also I have lent him to the Lord; as long as he liveth he shall be lent to the Lord."

And he worshipped the Lord there.

Hannah's Thanksgiving

And Hannah prayed, and said,

> "My heart rejoiceth in the Lord,
> Mine horn is exalted in the Lord:
> My mouth is enlarged over mine enemies;
> Because I rejoice in thy salvation.
> There is none holy as the Lord:
> For there is none beside thee:
> Neither is there any rock like our God.
> Talk no more so exceeding proudly;
> Let not arrogancy come out of your mouth:
> For the Lord is a God of knowledge,
> And by him actions are weighed.
> The bows of the mighty men are broken,
> And they that stumbled are girded with strength.
> They that were full have hired out themselves for bread;
> And they that were hungry ceased:
> So that the barren hath borne seven;
> And she that hath many children is waxed feeble.
> The Lord killeth, and maketh alive:
> He bringeth down to the grave, and bringeth up.
> The Lord maketh poor, and maketh rich:
> He bringeth low, and lifteth up.

THE FIRST BOOK OF SAMUEL

He raiseth up the poor out of the dust,
And lifteth up the beggar from the dunghill,
To set them among princes,
And to make them inherit the throne of glory:
For the pillars of the earth are the Lord's,
And he hath set the world upon them.
He will keep the feet of his saints,
And the wicked shall be silent in darkness;
For by strength shall no man prevail.
The adversaries of the Lord shall be broken to pieces;
Out of heaven shall he thunder upon them:
The Lord shall judge the ends of the earth;
And he shall give strength unto his king,
And exalt the horn of his anointed."

The Call of Samuel

Now the sons of Eli were sons of Belial; they knew not the Lord. And the priest's custom with the people was that, when any man offered sacrifice, the priest's servant came, while the flesh was in seething, with a fleshhook of three teeth in his hand; and he struck it into the pan, or kettle, or caldron, or pot; all that the fleshhook brought up the priest took for himself. So they did in Shiloh unto all the Israelites that came thither. Also before they burnt the fat, the priest's servant came, and said to the man that sacrificed, "Give flesh to roast for the priest; for he will not have sodden flesh of thee, but raw."

And if any man said unto him, "Let them not fail to burn the fat presently, and then take as much as thy soul desireth"; then he would answer him, "Nay; but thou shalt give it me now: and if not, I will take it by force." Wherefore the sin of the young men was very great before the Lord: for men abhorred the offering of the Lord.

But Samuel ministered before the Lord, being a child, girded with a linen ephod. Moreover his mother made him a little coat, and brought it to him from year to year, when she came up with her husband to offer the yearly sacrifice.

THE FIRST BOOK OF SAMUEL

And Eli blessed Elkanah and his wife, and said, "The Lord give thee seed of this woman for the loan which is lent to the Lord."

And they went unto their own home. And the Lord visited Hannah, so that she conceived, and bore three sons and two daughters. And the child Samuel grew before the Lord.

Now Eli was very old, and heard all that his sons did unto all Israel; and how they lay with the women that assembled at the door of the tabernacle of the congregation. And he said unto them,

"Why do ye such things? for I hear of your evil dealings by all this people. Nay, my sons; for it is no good report that I hear: ye make the Lord's people to transgress. If one man sin against another, the judge shall judge him: but if a man sin against the Lord, who shall intreat for him?"

Notwithstanding they hearkened not unto the voice of their father, because the Lord would slay them. And the child Samuel grew on, and was in favour both with the Lord, and also with men.

And the child Samuel ministered unto the Lord before Eli. And the word of the Lord was precious in those days; there was no open vision.

And it came to pass at that time, when Eli was laid down in his place, and his eyes began to wax dim, that he could not see (and ere the lamp of God went out in the temple of the Lord, where the ark of God was, and Samuel was laid down to sleep), that the Lord called Samuel: and he answered, "Here am I." And he ran unto Eli, and said, "Here am I; for thou calledst me." And he said, "I called not; lie down again." And he went and lay down.

And the Lord called yet again, "Samuel." And Samuel arose and went to Eli, and said, "Here am I; for thou didst call me." And he answered, "I called not, my son; lie down again."

And the Lord called Samuel again the third time. And he arose and went to Eli, and said, "Here am I; for thou didst call me."

THE FIRST BOOK OF SAMUEL

And Eli perceived that the Lord had called the child. Therefore Eli said unto Samuel, "Go, lie down: and it shall be, if he call thee, that thou shalt say, 'Speak, Lord; for thy servant heareth.'" So Samuel went and lay down in his place.

And the Lord came, and stood, and called as at other times, "Samuel, Samuel." Then Samuel answered, "Speak: for thy servant heareth."

And the Lord said to Samuel, "Behold, I will do a thing in Israel, at which both the ears of every one that heareth it shall tingle. In that day I will perform against Eli all things which I have spoken concerning his house: when I begin, I will also make an end. For I have told him that I will judge his house for ever for the iniquity which he knoweth; because his sons made themselves vile, and he restrained them not. And therefore I have sworn unto the house of Eli that the iniquity of Eli's house shall not be purged with sacrifice nor offering for ever."

And Samuel lay until the morning, and opened the doors of the house of the Lord. And Samuel feared to show Eli the vision.

Then Eli called Samuel, and said, "Samuel, my son." And he answered, "Here am I."

And he said, "What is the thing that the Lord hath said unto thee? I pray thee hide it not from me: God do so to thee, and more also, if thou hide any thing from me of all the things that he said unto thee."

And Samuel told him every whit, and hid nothing from him. And he said, "It is the Lord: let him do what seemeth him good."

And Samuel grew, and the Lord was with him, and did let none of his words fall to the ground. And all Israel from Dan even to Beer-sheba knew that Samuel was established to be a prophet of the Lord.

The Loss of the Ark

Now Israel went out against the Philistines to battle, and pitched beside Eben-ezer: and the Philistines pitched in Aphek. And the Philistines put themselves in array against Israel: and when they joined battle, Israel was smitten before the Philis-

THE FIRST BOOK OF SAMUEL

tines: and they slew of the army in the field about four thousand men.

And when the people were come into the camp, the elders of Israel said, "Wherefore hath the Lord smitten us to-day before the Philistines? Let us fetch the ark of the covenant of the Lord out of Shiloh unto us, that, when it cometh among us, it may save us out of the hand of our enemies."

So the people sent to Shiloh, that they might bring from thence the ark of the covenant of the Lord of hosts, which dwelleth between the cherubims: and the two sons of Eli, Hophni and Phinehas, were there with the ark of the covenant of God. And when the ark of the covenant of the Lord came into the camp, all Israel shouted with a great shout, so that the earth rang again.

And when the Philistines heard the noise of the shout, they said, "What meaneth the noise of this great shout in the camp of the Hebrews?"

And they understood that the ark of the Lord was come into the camp. And the Philistines were afraid, for they said, "God is come into the camp."

And they said, "Woe unto us! for there hath not been such a thing heretofore. Woe unto us! who shall deliver us out of the hand of these mighty Gods? these are the Gods that smote the Egyptians with all the plagues in the wilderness. Be strong, and quit yourselves like men, O ye Philistines, that ye be not servants unto the Hebrews, as they have been to you: quit yourselves like men, and fight."

And the Philistines fought, and Israel was smitten, and they fled every man into his tent: and there was a very great slaughter; for there fell of Israel thirty thousand footmen. And the ark of God was taken; and the two sons of Eli, Hophni and Phinehas, were slain.

And there ran a man of Benjamin out of the army, and came to Shiloh the same day with his clothes rent, and with earth upon his head. And when he came, lo, Eli sat upon a seat by the

THE FIRST BOOK OF SAMUEL

wayside watching: for his heart trembled for the ark of God. And when the man came into the city, and told it, all the city cried out.

And when Eli heard the noise of the crying, he said, "What meaneth the noise of this tumult?"

Now Eli was ninety and eight years old; and his eyes were dim, that he could not see. And the man said unto Eli, "I am he that came out of the army, and I fled to-day out of the army." And he said, "What is there done, my son?"

And the messenger answered and said, "Israel is fled before the Philistines, and there hath been also a great slaughter among the people, and thy two sons also, Hophni and Phinehas, are dead, and the ark of God is taken."

And it came to pass, when he made mention of the ark of God, that he fell from off the seat backward by the side of the gate, and his neck broke, and he died: for he was an old man, and heavy. And he had judged Israel forty years.

And his daughter-in-law, Phinehas' wife, was with child, near to be delivered: and when she heard the tidings that the ark of God was taken, and that her father-in-law and her husband were dead, she bowed herself and travailed; for her pains came upon her. And about the time of her death the women that stood by her said unto her, "Fear not: for thou hast borne a son."

But she answered not, neither did she regard it. And she named the child I-chabod, saying, "The glory is departed from Israel": because the ark of God was taken, and because of her father-in-law and her husband. And she said,

> "*The glory is departed from Israel:*
> *For the ark of God is taken.*"

The Anointing of Saul

And Samuel judged Israel all the days of his life. And he went from year to year in circuit to Beth-el, and Gilgal, and

THE FIRST BOOK OF SAMUEL

Mizpeh, and judged Israel in all those places. And his return was to Ramah; for there was his house; and there he judged Israel; and there he built an altar unto the Lord.

And it came to pass, when Samuel was old, that he made his sons judges over Israel. Now the name of his firstborn was Joel; and the name of his second, Abiah: they were judges in Beer-sheba. And his sons walked not in his ways, but turned aside after lucre, and took bribes, and perverted judgment. Then all the elders of Israel gathered themselves together, and came to Samuel unto Ramah, and said unto him,

"Behold, thou art old, and thy sons walk not in thy ways: now make us a king to judge us like all the nations."

But the thing displeased Samuel, when they said, "Give us a king to judge us." And Samuel prayed unto the Lord. And the Lord said unto Samuel,

"Hearken unto the voice of the people in all that they say unto thee: for they have not rejected thee, but they have rejected me, that I should not reign over them. According to all the works which they have done since the day that I brought them up out of Egypt even unto this day, wherewith they have forsaken me, and served other gods, so do they also unto thee. Now therefore hearken unto their voice: howbeit yet protest solemnly unto them, and show them the manner of the king that shall reign over them."

And Samuel told all the words of the Lord unto the people that asked of him a king. And he said,

"This will be the manner of the king that shall reign over you: he will take your sons, and appoint them for himself, for his chariots, and to be his horsemen; and some shall run before his chariots.

"And he will appoint him captains over thousands, and captains over fifties; and will set them to ear his ground, and to reap his harvest, and to make his instruments of war, and instruments of his chariots.

"And he will take your daughters to be confectioners, and to be cooks, and to be bakers.

THE FIRST BOOK OF SAMUEL

"And he will take your fields, and your vineyards, and your oliveyards, even the best of them, and give them to his servants.

"And he will take the tenth of your seed, and of your vineyards, and give to his officers, and to his servants.

"And he will take your menservants, and your maidservants, and your goodliest young men, and your asses, and put them to his work.

"He will take the tenth of your sheep: and ye shall be his servants. And ye shall cry out in that day because of your king which ye shall have chosen you; and the Lord will not hear you in that day."

Nevertheless the people refused to obey the voice of Samuel; and they said,

"Nay; but we will have a king over us; that we also may be like all the nations; and that our king may judge us, and go out before us, and fight our battles."

And Samuel heard all the words of the people, and he rehearsed them in the ears of the Lord. And the Lord said to Samuel, "Hearken unto their voice, and make them a king." And Samuel said unto the men of Israel, "Go ye every man unto his city."

Now there was a man of Benjamin, whose name was Kish, the son of Abiel, the son of Zeror, the son of Bechorath, the son of Aphiah, a Benjamite, a mighty man of power. And he had a son, whose name was Saul, a choice young man, and a goodly: and there was not among the children of Israel a goodlier person than he: from his shoulders and upward he was higher than any of the people.

And the asses of Kish Saul's father were lost. And Kish said to Saul his son, "Take now one of the servants with thee, and arise, go seek the asses."

And he passed through Mount Ephraim, and passed through the land of Shalisha, but they found them not: then they passed through the land of Shalim, and there they were not: and he passed through the land of the Benjamites, but they found them not. And when they were come to the land of Zuph, Saul said

THE FIRST BOOK OF SAMUEL

to his servant that was with him, "Come, and let us return; lest my father leave caring for the asses, and take thought for us."

And he said unto him, "Behold now, there is in this city a man of God, and he is an honourable man; all that he saith cometh surely to pass: now let us go thither; peradventure he can show us our way that we should go."

Then said Saul to his servant, "But, behold, if we go, what shall we bring the man? for the bread is spent in our vessels, and there is not a present to bring to the man of God: what have we?"

And the servant answered Saul again, and said, "Behold, I have here at hand the fourth part of a shekel of silver: that will I give to the man of God, to tell us our way."

(Beforetime in Israel, when a man went to enquire of God, thus he spoke, "Come, and let us go to the seer: for he that is now called a prophet was beforetime called a seer.")

Then said Saul to his servant, "Well said; come, let us go."

So they went unto the city where the man of God was. And as they went up the hill to the city, they found young maidens going out to draw water, and said unto them, "Is the seer here?"

And they answered them, and said,

"He is; behold, he is before you: make haste now, for he came to-day to the city; for there is a sacrifice of the people to-day in the high place: as soon as ye be come into the city, ye shall straightway find him, before he go up to the high place to eat: for the people will not eat until he come, because he doth bless the sacrifice; and afterwards they eat that be bidden. Now therefore get you up; for about this time ye shall find him."

And they went up into the city: and when they were come into the city, behold, Samuel came out against them, for to go up to the high place.

Now the Lord had told Samuel in his ear a day before Saul came, saying,

"To-morrow about this time I will send thee a man out of the land of Benjamin, and thou shalt anoint him to be captain over my people Israel, that he may save my people out of the hand of

THE FIRST BOOK OF SAMUEL

the Philistines: for I have looked upon my people, because their cry is come unto me."

And when Samuel saw Saul, the Lord said unto him, "Behold the man whom I spoke to thee of! this same shall reign over my people."

Then Saul drew near to Samuel in the gate, and said, "Tell me, I pray thee, where the seer's house is."

And Samuel answered Saul, and said, "I am the seer: go up before me unto the high place; for ye shall eat with me to-day, and to-morrow I will let thee go, and will tell thee all that is in thine heart. And as for thine asses that were lost three days ago, set not thy mind on them; for they are found. And on whom is all the desire of Israel? Is it not on thee, and on all thy father's house?"

And Saul answered and said, "Am not I a Benjamite, of the smallest of the tribes of Israel? and my family the least of all the families of the tribe of Benjamin? wherefore then speakest thou so to me?"

And Samuel took Saul and his servant, and brought them into the parlour, and made them sit in the chiefest place among them that were bidden, which were about thirty persons. And Samuel said unto the cook, "Bring the portion which I gave thee, of which I said unto thee, 'Set it by thee.'"

And the cook took up the shoulder, and that which was upon it, and set it before Saul. And Samuel said, "Behold that which is left! set it before thee, and eat: for unto this time hath it been kept for thee since I said, 'I have invited the people.'"

So Saul did eat with Samuel that day. And when they were come down from the high place into the city, Samuel communed with Saul upon the top of the house. And they arose early: and it came to pass, about the spring of the day, that Samuel called Saul to the top of the house, saying,

"Up, that I may send thee away."

And Saul arose, and they went out both of them, he and Samuel, abroad. And as they were going down to the end of the city, Samuel said to Saul,

THE FIRST BOOK OF SAMUEL

"Bid the servant pass on before us—" and he passed on—"but stand thou still a while, that I may show thee the word of God."

Then Samuel took a vial of oil, and poured it upon his head, and kissed him, and said,

"Is it not because the Lord hath anointed thee to be captain over his inheritance? When thou art departed from me to-day, then thou shalt find two men by Rachel's sepulchre in the border of Benjamin at Zelzah; and they will say unto thee, 'The asses which thou wentest to seek are found: and, lo, thy father hath left the care of the asses, and sorroweth for you, saying, "What shall I do for my son?"' Then shalt thou go on forward from thence, and thou shalt come to the plain of Tabor, and there shall meet thee three men going up to God to Beth-el, one carrying three kids, and another carrying three loaves of bread, and another carrying a bottle of wine: and they will salute thee, and give thee two loaves of bread; which thou shalt receive of their hands. After that thou shalt come to the hill of God, where is the garrison of the Philistines: and it shall come to pass, when thou art come thither to the city, that thou shalt meet a company of prophets coming down from the high place with a psaltery, and a tabret, and a pipe, and a harp, before them; and they shall prophesy: and the Spirit of the Lord will come upon thee, and thou shalt prophesy with them, and shalt be turned into another man. And let it be, when these signs are come unto thee, that thou do as occasion serve thee; for God is with thee. And thou shalt go down before me to Gilgal; and, behold, I will come down unto thee, to offer burnt offerings, and to sacrifice sacrifices of peace offerings: seven days shalt thou tarry, till I come to thee, and show thee what thou shalt do."

And Samuel called the people together unto the Lord to Mizpeh, and said unto the children of Israel,

"Thus saith the Lord God of Israel, 'I brought up Israel out of Egypt, and delivered you out of the hand of the Egyptians, and out of the hand of all kingdoms, and of them that oppressed you': and ye have this day rejected your God, who himself saved you out of all your adversities and your tribulations; and ye

THE FIRST BOOK OF SAMUEL

have said unto him, 'Nay, but set a king over us.' Now therefore present yourselves before the Lord by your tribes, and by your thousands."

And when Samuel had caused all the tribes of Israel to come near, the tribe of Benjamin was taken. When he had caused the tribe of Benjamin to come near by their families, the family of Matri was taken, and Saul the son of Kish was taken: and when they sought him, he could not be found. Therefore they enquired of the Lord further, if the man should yet come thither. And the Lord answered,

"Behold, he hath hid himself among the stuff."

And they ran and fetched him thence: and when he stood among the people, he was higher than any of the people from his shoulders and upward. And Samuel said to all the people,

"See ye him whom the Lord hath chosen, that there is none like him among all the people?"

And all the people shouted, and said,

"God save the king."

Then Samuel told the people the manner of the kingdom, and wrote it in a book, and laid it up before the Lord. And Samuel sent all the people away, every man to his house. And Saul also went home to Gibeah; and there went with him a band of men, whose hearts God had touched.

The Beginning of the Reign of Saul

Then Nahash the Ammonite came up, and encamped against Jabesh-gilead: and all the men of Jabesh said unto Nahash, "Make a covenant with us, and we will serve thee."

And Nahash the Ammonite answered them, "On this condition will I make a covenant with you, that I may thrust out all your right eyes, and lay it for a reproach upon all Israel."

And the elders of Jabesh said unto him, "Give us seven days' respite, that we may send messengers unto all the coasts of Israel: and then, if there be no man to save us, we will come out to thee."

Then came the messengers to Gibeah of Saul, and told the

THE FIRST BOOK OF SAMUEL

tidings in the ears of the people: and all the people lifted up their voices, and wept. And, behold, Saul came after the herd out of the field; and Saul said, "What aileth the people that they weep?" And they told him the tidings of the men of Jabesh.

And the Spirit of God came upon Saul when he heard those tidings, and his anger was kindled greatly. And he took a yoke of oxen, and hewed them in pieces, and sent them throughout all the coasts of Israel by the hands of messengers, saying,

"Whosoever cometh not forth after Saul and after Samuel, so shall it be done unto his oxen."

And the fear of the Lord fell on the people, and they came out with one consent. And when he numbered them in Bezek, the children of Israel were three hundred thousand, and the men of Judah thirty thousand. And they said unto the messengers that came,

"Thus shall ye say unto the men of Jabesh-gilead, 'To-morrow, by that time the sun be hot, ye shall have help.'"

And the messengers came and showed it to the men of Jabesh; and they were glad. Therefore the men of Jabesh said,

"To-morrow we will come out unto you, and ye shall do with us all that seemeth good unto you."

And it was so on the morrow, that Saul put the people in three companies; and they came into the midst of the host in the morning watch, and slew the Ammonites until the heat of the day: and it came to pass that they which remained were scattered, so that two of them were not left together.

And all the people went to Gilgal; and there they made Saul king before the Lord in Gilgal; and there they sacrificed sacrifices of peace offerings before the Lord; and there Saul and all the men of Israel rejoiced greatly.

Saul reigned one year; and when he had reigned two years over Israel, Saul chose him three thousand men of Israel; whereof two thousand were with Saul in Michmash and in Mount Beth-el, and a thousand were with Jonathan in Gibeah of Benjamin: and the rest of the people he sent every man to his tent. And

THE FIRST BOOK OF SAMUEL

Jonathan smote the garrison of the Philistines that was in Geba, and the Philistines heard of it. And Saul blew the trumpet throughout all the land, saying, "Let the Hebrews hear." And all Israel heard say that Saul had smitten a garrison of the Philistines, and that Israel also was had in abomination with the Philistines. And the people were called together after Saul to Gilgal.

And the Philistines gathered themselves together to fight with Israel, thirty thousand chariots, and six thousand horsemen, and people as the sand which is on the sea shore in multitude: and they came up, and pitched in Michmash, eastward from Beth-aven. When the men of Israel saw that they were in a strait (for the people were distressed), then the people did hide themselves in caves, and in thickets, and in rocks, and in high places, and in pits. And some of the Hebrews went over Jordan to the land of Gad and Gilead. As for Saul, he was yet in Gilgal, and all the people followed him trembling. And the garrison of the Philistines went out to the passage of Michmash.

Now it came to pass upon a day, that Jonathan the son of Saul said unto the young man that bore his armour, "Come, and let us go over to the Philistines' garrison, that is on the other side." But he told not his father.

And Jonathan said to the young man that bore his armour, "Come, and let us go over unto the garrison of these uncircumcised: it may be that the Lord will work for us: for there is no restraint to the Lord to save by many or by few."

And his armourbearer said unto him, "Do all that is in thine heart: turn thee; behold, I am with thee according to thy heart."

Then said Jonathan, "Behold, we will pass over unto these men, and we will discover ourselves unto them. If they say thus unto us, 'Tarry until we come to you,' then we will stand still in our place, and will not go up unto them. But if they say thus, 'Come up unto us'; then we will go up: for the Lord hath delivered them into our hand: and this shall be a sign unto us."

And both of them discovered themselves unto the garrison of

THE FIRST BOOK OF SAMUEL

the Philistines: and the Philistines said, "Behold, the Hebrews come forth out of the holes where they had hid themselves."

And the men of the garrison answered Jonathan and his armourbearer, and said, "Come up to us, and we will show you a thing."

And Jonathan said unto his armourbearer, "Come up after me: for the Lord hath delivered them into the hand of Israel."

And Jonathan climbed up upon his hands and upon his feet, and his armourbearer after him: and they fell before Jonathan; and his armourbearer slew after him. And that first slaughter, which Jonathan and his armourbearer made, was about twenty men, within as it were a half acre of land, which a yoke of oxen might plow. And there was trembling in the host, in the field, and among all the people: the garrison, and the spoilers, they also trembled, and the earth quaked: so it was a very great trembling.

And the watchmen of Saul in Gibeah of Benjamin looked; and, behold, the multitude melted away, and they went on beating down one another.

Then said Saul unto the people that were with him, "Number now, and see who is gone from us."

And when they had numbered, behold, Jonathan and his armourbearer were not there.

And Saul and all the people that were with him assembled themselves, and they came to the battle: and, behold, every man's sword was against his fellow, and there was a very great discomfiture. Moreover the Hebrews that were with the Philistines before that time, which went up with them into the camp from the country round about, even they also turned to be with the Israelites that were with Saul and Jonathan. Likewise all the men of Israel which had hid themselves in Mount Ephraim, when they heard that the Philistines fled, even they also followed hard after them in the battle. So the Lord saved Israel that day: and the battle passed over unto Beth-aven.

And the men of Israel were distressed that day: for Saul had

THE FIRST BOOK OF SAMUEL

adjured the people, saying, "Cursed be the man that eateth any food until evening, that I may be avenged on mine enemies." So none of the people tasted any food. And all they of the land came to a wood; and there was honey upon the ground. And when the people were come into the wood, behold, the honey dropped; but no man put his hand to his mouth: for the people feared the oath.

But Jonathan heard not when his father charged the people with the oath: wherefore he put forth the end of the rod that was in his hand, and dipped it in an honeycomb, and put his hand to his mouth; and his eyes were enlightened.

Then answered one of the people, and said, "Thy father straitly charged the people with an oath, saying, 'Cursed be the man that eateth any food this day.'"

And the people were faint. Then said Jonathan,

"My father hath troubled the land: see, I pray you, how mine eyes have been enlightened, because I tasted a little of this honey. How much more, if haply the people had eaten freely to-day of the spoil of their enemies which they found? for had there not been now a much greater slaughter among the Philistines?"

And they smote the Philistines that day from Michmash to Aijalon: and the people were very faint. And the people flew upon the spoil, and took sheep, and oxen, and calves, and slew them on the ground: and the people did eat them with the blood.

Then they told Saul, saying, "Behold, the people sin against the Lord, in that they eat with the blood." And he said, "Ye have transgressed: roll a great stone unto me this day."

And Saul said, "Disperse yourselves among the people, and say unto them, 'Bring me hither every man his ox, and every man his sheep,' and slay them here, and eat; and sin not against the Lord in eating with the blood."

And all the people brought every man his ox with him that night, and slew them there. And Saul built an altar unto the Lord: the same was the first altar that he built unto the Lord.

And Saul said, "Let us go down after the Philistines by night,

THE FIRST BOOK OF SAMUEL

and spoil them until the morning light, and let us not leave a man of them."

And they said, "Do whatsoever seemeth good unto thee."

Then said the priest, "Let us draw near hither unto God."

And Saul asked counsel of God, "Shall I go down after the Philistines? wilt thou deliver them into the hand of Israel?"

But he answered him not that day.

And Saul said, "Draw ye near hither, all the chief of the people: and know and see wherein this sin hath been this day. For, as the Lord liveth, which saveth Israel, though it be in Jonathan my son, he shall surely die."

But there was not a man among all the people that answered him.

Then said he unto all Israel, "Be ye on one side, and I and Jonathan my son will be on the other side."

And the people said unto Saul, "Do what seemeth good unto thee."

Therefore Saul said unto the Lord God of Israel, "Give a perfect lot." And Saul and Jonathan were taken: but the people escaped.

And Saul said, "Cast lots between me and Jonathan my son." And Jonathan was taken.

Then Saul said to Jonathan, "Tell me what thou hast done." And Jonathan told him, and said, "I did but taste a little honey with the end of the rod that was in mine hand, and, lo, I must die."

And Saul answered, "God do so and more also: for thou shalt surely die, Jonathan."

And the people said unto Saul, "Shall Jonathan die, who hath wrought this great salvation in Israel? God forbid: as the Lord liveth, there shall not one hair of his head fall to the ground; for he hath wrought with God this day."

So the people rescued Jonathan, that he died not.

Then Saul went up from following the Philistines: and the Philistines went to their own place. So Saul took the kingdom

THE FIRST BOOK OF SAMUEL

over Israel, and fought against all his enemies on every side, against Moab, and against the children of Ammon, and against Edom, and against the kings of Zobah, and against the Philistines: and whithersoever he turned himself, he vexed them. And he gathered a host, and smote the Amalekites, and delivered Israel out of the hands of them that spoiled them.

Now the sons of Saul were Jonathan, and Ishui, and Melchishua: and the names of his two daughters were these; the name of the firstborn Merab, and the name of the younger Michal: and the name of Saul's wife was Ahinoam, the daughter of Ahimaaz: and the name of the captain of his host was Abner, the son of Ner, Saul's uncle. And Kish was the father of Saul; and Ner the father of Abner was the son of Abiel. And there was sore war against the Philistines all the days of Saul: and when Saul saw any strong man, or any valiant man, he took him unto him.

Samuel also said unto Saul, "The Lord sent me to anoint thee to be king over his people, over Israel: now therefore hearken thou unto the voice of the words of the Lord. Thus saith the Lord of hosts, 'I remember that which Amalek did to Israel, how he laid wait for him in the way, when he came up from Egypt. Now go and smite Amalek, and utterly destroy all that they have, and spare them not; but slay both man and woman, infant and suckling, ox and sheep, camel and ass.'"

And Saul gathered the people together, and numbered them in Telaim, two hundred thousand footmen, and ten thousand men of Judah. And Saul came to a city of Amalek, and laid wait in the valley.

And Saul said unto the Kenites, "Go, depart, get you down from among the Amalekites, lest I destroy you with them: for ye showed kindness to all the children of Israel, when they came up out of Egypt."

So the Kenites departed from among the Amalekites. And Saul smote the Amalekites from Havilah until thou comest to Shur, that is over against Egypt. And he took Agag the king of the Amalekites alive, and utterly destroyed all the people with

THE FIRST BOOK OF SAMUEL

the edge of the sword. But Saul and the people spared Agag, and the best of the sheep, and of the oxen, and of the fatlings, and the lambs, and all that was good, and would not utterly destroy them: but every thing that was vile and refuse, that they destroyed utterly.

Then came the word of the Lord unto Samuel, saying,

"It repenteth me that I have set up Saul to be king: for he is turned back from following me, and hath not performed my commandments."

And it grieved Samuel; and he cried unto the Lord all night. And when Samuel rose early to meet Saul in the morning, it was told Samuel, saying, "Saul came to Carmel, and, behold, he set him up a place, and is gone about, and passed on, and gone down to Gilgal."

And Samuel came to Saul: and Saul said unto him, "Blessed be thou of the Lord: I have performed the commandment of the Lord."

And Samuel said, "What meaneth then this bleating of the sheep in mine ears, and the lowing of the oxen which I hear?"

And Saul said, "They have brought them from the Amalekites: for the people spared the best of the sheep and of the oxen, to sacrifice unto the Lord thy God; and the rest we have utterly destroyed."

Then Samuel said unto Saul, "Stay, and I will tell thee what the Lord hath said to me this night."

And he said unto him, "Say on."

And Samuel said, "When thou wast little in thine own sight, wast thou not made the head of the tribes of Israel, and the Lord anointed thee king over Israel? And the Lord sent thee on a journey, and said, 'Go and utterly destroy the sinners the Amalekites, and fight against them until they be consumed.' Wherefore then didst thou not obey the voice of the Lord, but didst fly upon the spoil, and didst evil in the sight of the Lord?"

And Saul said unto Samuel, "Yea, I have obeyed the voice of the Lord, and have gone the way which the Lord sent me, and have brought Agag the king of Amalek, and have utterly destroyed the Amalekites. But the people took of the spoil, sheep

THE FIRST BOOK OF SAMUEL

and oxen, the chief of the things which should have been utterly destroyed, to sacrifice unto the Lord thy God in Gilgal."

And Samuel said, "Hath the Lord as great delight in burnt offerings and sacrifices as in obeying the voice of the Lord? Behold, to obey is better than sacrifice, and to hearken than the fat of rams. For rebellion is as the sin of witchcraft, and stubbornness is as iniquity and idolatry. Because thou hast rejected the word of the Lord, he hath also rejected thee from being king."

And Saul said unto Samuel, "I have sinned: for I have transgressed the commandment of the Lord, and thy words: because I feared the people, and obeyed their voice. Now therefore, I pray thee, pardon my sin, and turn again with me, that I may worship the Lord."

And Samuel said unto Saul, "I will not return with thee: for thou hast rejected the word of the Lord, and the Lord hath rejected thee from being king over Israel."

And as Samuel turned about to go away, he laid hold upon the skirt of his mantle, and it rent. And Samuel said unto him, "The Lord hath rent the kingdom of Israel from thee this day, and hath given it to a neighbour of thine, that is better than thou. And also the Strength of Israel will not lie nor repent: for he is not a man, that he should repent."

Then he said, "I have sinned: yet honour me now, I pray thee, before the elders of my people, and before Israel, and turn again with me, that I may worship the Lord thy God."

So Samuel turned again after Saul; and Saul worshipped the Lord.

Then said Samuel, "Bring ye hither to me Agag the king of the Amalekites."

And Agag came unto him delicately. And Agag said, "Surely the bitterness of death is past."

And Samuel said, "As thy sword hath made women childless, so shall thy mother be childless among women."

And Samuel hewed Agag in pieces before the Lord in Gilgal.

Then Samuel went to Ramah; and Saul went up to his house to Gibeah of Saul. And Samuel came no more to see Saul until

THE FIRST BOOK OF SAMUEL

the day of his death: nevertheless Samuel mourned for Saul: and the Lord repented that he had made Saul king over Israel. And the Lord said unto Samuel,

"How long wilt thou mourn for Saul, seeing I have rejected him from reigning over Israel? fill thine horn with oil, and go, I will send thee to Jesse the Beth-lehemite: for I have provided me a king among his sons."

And Samuel said, "How can I go? if Saul hear it, he will kill me."

And the Lord said, "Take a heifer with thee, and say, 'I am come to sacrifice to the Lord.' And call Jesse to the sacrifice, and I will show thee what thou shalt do: and thou shalt anoint unto me him whom I name unto thee."

And Samuel did that which the Lord spoke, and came to Beth-lehem. And the elders of the town trembled at his coming, and said, "Comest thou peaceably?"

And he said, "Peaceably: I am come to sacrifice unto the Lord: sanctify yourselves, and come with me to the sacrifice."

And he sanctified Jesse and his sons, and called them to the sacrifice. And it came to pass, when they were come, that he looked on Eliab, and said, "Surely the Lord's anointed is before him."

But the Lord said unto Samuel, "Look not on his countenance, or on the height of his stature; because I have refused him: for the Lord seeth not as man seeth; for man looketh on the outward appearance, but the Lord looketh on the heart."

Then Jesse called Abinadab, and made him pass before Samuel. And he said, "Neither hath the Lord chosen this."

Then Jesse made Shammah to pass by. And he said, "Neither hath the Lord chosen this."

Again, Jesse made seven of his sons to pass before Samuel. And Samuel said unto Jesse, "The Lord hath not chosen these."

And Samuel said unto Jesse, "Are here all thy children?"

And he said, "There remaineth yet the youngest, and, behold, he keepeth the sheep."

And Samuel said unto Jesse, "Send and fetch him: for we will not sit down till he come hither."

THE FIRST BOOK OF SAMUEL

And he sent, and brought him in. Now he was ruddy, and withal of a beautiful countenance, and goodly to look to. And the Lord said, "Arise, anoint him: for this is he."

Then Samuel took the horn of oil, and anointed him in the midst of his brethren: and the Spirit of the Lord came upon David from that day forward. So Samuel rose up, and went to Ramah.

But the Spirit of the Lord departed from Saul, and an evil spirit from the Lord troubled him. And Saul's servants said unto him, "Behold now, an evil spirit from God troubleth thee. Let our lord now command thy servants, which are before thee, to seek out a man, who is a cunning player on a harp: and it shall come to pass, when the evil spirit from God is upon thee, that he shall play with his hand, and thou shalt be well."

And Saul said unto his servants, "Provide me now a man that can play well, and bring him to me."

Then answered one of the servants, and said, "Behold, I have seen a son of Jesse the Beth-lehemite, that is cunning in playing, and a mighty valiant man, and a man of war, and prudent in matters, and a comely person, and the Lord is with him."

Wherefore Saul sent messengers unto Jesse, and said, "Send me David thy son, which is with the sheep."

And Jesse took an ass laden with bread, and a bottle of wine, and a kid, and sent them by David his son unto Saul. And David came to Saul, and stood before him: and he loved him greatly; and he became his armourbearer. And Saul sent to Jesse, saying, "Let David, I pray thee, stand before me; for he hath found favour in my sight."

And it came to pass, when the evil spirit from God was upon Saul, that David took a harp, and played with his hand: so Saul was refreshed, and was well, and the evil spirit departed from him.

David and Goliath

Now the Philistines gathered together their armies to battle, and were gathered together at Shochoh, which belongeth to

THE FIRST BOOK OF SAMUEL

Judah, and pitched between Shochoh and Azekah, in Ephes-dammim. And Saul and the men of Israel were gathered together, and pitched by the valley of Elah, and set the battle in array against the Philistines. And the Philistines stood on a mountain on the one side, and Israel stood on a mountain on the other side: and there was a valley between them.

And there went out a champion out of the camp of the Philistines, named Goliath, of Gath, whose height was six cubits and a span. And he had a helmet of brass upon his head, and he was armed with a coat of mail; and the weight of the coat was five thousand shekels of brass. And he had greaves of brass upon his legs, and a target of brass between his shoulders. And the staff of his spear was like a weaver's beam; and his spear's head weighed six hundred shekels of iron: and one bearing a shield went before him. And he stood and cried unto the armies of Israel, and said unto them,

"Why are ye come out to set your battle in array? am not I a Philistine, and ye servants to Saul? choose you a man for you, and let him come down to me. If he be able to fight with me, and to kill me, then will we be your servants: but if I prevail against him, and kill him, then shall ye be our servants, and serve us."

And the Philistine said, "I defy the armies of Israel this day; give me a man, that we may fight together."

When Saul and all Israel heard those words of the Philistine, they were dismayed, and greatly afraid.

Now David was the son of that Ephrathite of Beth-lehem-judah, whose name was Jesse; and he had eight sons: and the man went among men for an old man in the days of Saul. And the three eldest sons of Jesse went and followed Saul to the battle: and the names of his three sons that went to the battle were Eliab the firstborn, and next unto him Abinadab, and the third Shammah. And David was the youngest: and the three eldest followed Saul. But David went and returned from Saul to feed his father's sheep at Beth-lehem.

THE FIRST BOOK OF SAMUEL

(And the Philistine drew near morning and evening, and presented himself forty days.)

And Jesse said unto David his son, "Take now for thy brethren an ephah of this parched corn, and these ten loaves, and run to the camp to thy brethren; and carry these ten cheeses unto the captain of their thousand, and look how thy brethren fare, and take their pledge."

(Now Saul, and they, and all the men of Israel, were in the valley of Elah, fighting with the Philistines.)

And David rose up early in the morning, and left the sheep with a keeper, and took, and went, as Jesse had commanded him; and he came to the trench, as the host was going forth to the fight, and shouted for the battle. For Israel and the Philistines had put the battle in array, army against army. And David left his carriage in the hand of the keeper of the carriage, and ran into the army, and came and saluted his brethren. And as he talked with them, behold, there came up the champion, the Philistine of Gath, Goliath by name, out of the armies of the Philistines, and spoke according to the same words: and David heard them. And all the men of Israel, when they saw the man, fled from him, and were sore afraid.

And the men of Israel said, "Have ye seen this man that is come up? surely to defy Israel is he come up: and it shall be that the man who killeth him, the king will enrich him with great riches, and will give him his daughter, and make his father's house free in Israel."

And David spoke to the men that stood by him, saying, "What shall be done to the man that killeth this Philistine, and taketh away the reproach from Israel? for who is this uncircumcised Philistine, that he should defy the armies of the living God?"

And the people answered him after this manner, saying, "So shall it be done to the man that killeth him."

And Eliab his eldest brother heard when he spoke unto the men; and Eliab's anger was kindled against David, and he said, "Why camest thou down hither? and with whom hast thou left

THE FIRST BOOK OF SAMUEL

those few sheep in the wilderness? I know thy pride, and the naughtiness of thine heart; for thou art come down that thou mightest see the battle."

And David said, "What have I now done? Is there not a cause?"

And he turned from him toward another, and spoke after the same manner: and the people answered him again after the former manner. And when the words were heard which David spoke, they rehearsed them before Saul: and he sent for him.

And David said to Saul, "Let no man's heart fail because of him; thy servant will go and fight with this Philistine."

And Saul said to David, "Thou art not able to go against this Philistine to fight with him: for thou art but a youth, and he a man of war from his youth."

And David said unto Saul, "Thy servant kept his father's sheep, and there came a lion, and a bear, and took a lamb out of the flock: and I went out after him, and smote him, and delivered it out of his mouth: and when he arose against me, I caught him by his beard, and smote him, and slew him. Thy servant slew both the lion and the bear: and this uncircumcised Philistine shall be as one of them, seeing he hath defied the armies of the living God."

David said moreover, "The Lord that delivered me out of the paw of the lion, and out of the paw of the bear, he will deliver me out of the hand of this Philistine."

And Saul said unto David, "Go, and the Lord be with thee."

And Saul armed David with his armour, and he put a helmet of brass upon his head; also he armed him with a coat of mail. And David girded his sword upon his armour, and he essayed to go; for he had not proved it. And David said unto Saul, "I cannot go with these; for I have not proved them."

And David put them off him. And he took his staff in his hand, and chose him five smooth stones out of the brook, and put them in a shepherd's bag which he had, even in a scrip; and his sling was in his hand: and he drew near to the Philistine. And the Philistine came on and drew near unto David; and the man

THE FIRST BOOK OF SAMUEL

that bore the shield went before him. And when the Philistine looked about, and saw David, he disdained him: for he was but a youth, and ruddy, and of a fair countenance. And the Philistine said unto David, "Am I a dog, that thou comest to me with staves?"

And the Philistine cursed David by his gods. And the Philistine said to David, "Come to me, and I will give thy flesh unto the fowls of the air, and to the beasts of the field."

Then said David to the Philistine, "Thou comest to me with a sword, and with a spear, and with a shield: but I come to thee in the name of the Lord of hosts, the God of the armies of Israel, whom thou hast defied. This day will the Lord deliver thee into mine hand; and I will smite thee, and take thine head from thee; and I will give the carcases of the host of the Philistines this day unto the fowls of the air, and to the wild beasts of the earth; that all the earth may know that there is a God in Israel. And all this assembly shall know that the Lord saveth not with sword and spear: for the battle is the Lord's, and he will give you into our hands."

And it came to pass, when the Philistine arose, and came and drew nigh to meet David, that David hastened, and ran toward the army to meet the Philistine. And David put his hand in his bag, and took thence a stone, and slung it, and smote the Philistine in his forehead, that the stone sunk into his forehead; and he fell upon his face to the earth. So David prevailed over the Philistine with a sling and with a stone, and smote the Philistine, and slew him; but there was no sword in the hand of David. Therefore David ran, and stood upon the Philistine, and took his sword, and drew it out of the sheath thereof, and slew him, and cut off his head therewith. And when the Philistines saw their champion was dead, they fled.

And the men of Israel and of Judah arose, and shouted, and pursued the Philistines, until thou come to the valley, and to the gates of Ekron. And the wounded of the Philistines fell down by the way to Shaaraim, even unto Gath, and unto Ekron. And the children of Israel returned from chasing after the Philistines, and they spoiled their tents. And David took the head of the Philistine, and brought it to Jerusalem; but he put his armour in his tent.

The Friendship of David and Jonathan

And it came to pass that the soul of Jonathan was knit with the soul of David, and Jonathan loved him as his own soul. And Saul took him that day, and would let him go no more home to his father's house. Then Jonathan and David made a covenant, because he loved him as his own soul. And Jonathan stripped himself of the robe that was upon him, and gave it to David, and his garments, even to his sword, and to his bow, and to his girdle.

And David went out whithersoever Saul sent him, and behaved himself wisely: and Saul set him over the men of war, and he was accepted in the sight of all the people, and also in the sight of Saul's servants. And it came to pass as they came, when David was returned from the slaughter of the Philistine, that the women came out of all cities of Israel, singing and dancing, to meet king Saul, with tabrets, with joy, and with instruments of music. And the women answered one another as they played, and said,

> "Saul hath slain his thousands,
> And David his ten thousands."

And Saul was very wroth, and the saying displeased him; and he said, "They have ascribed unto David ten thousands, and to me they have ascribed but thousands: and what can he have more but the kingdom?"

And Saul was afraid of David, because the Lord was with him, and was departed from Saul. Therefore Saul removed him from him, and made him his captain over a thousand; and he went out and came in before the people. And David behaved himself wisely in all his ways; and the Lord was with him. Wherefore when Saul saw that he behaved himself very wisely, he was afraid of him. But all Israel and Judah loved David, because he went out and came in before them.

THE FIRST BOOK OF SAMUEL

And Saul said to David,

"Behold my elder daughter Merab, her will I give thee to wife: only be thou valiant for me, and fight the Lord's battles." (For Saul said, "Let not mine hand be upon him, but let the hand of the Philistines be upon him.")

And David said unto Saul, "Who am I? and what is my life, or my father's family in Israel, that I should be son-in-law to the king?"

But it came to pass at the time when Merab Saul's daughter should have been given to David, that she was given unto Adriel the Meholathite to wife. And Michal Saul's daughter loved David: and they told Saul, and the thing pleased him. And Saul said, "I will give him her, that she may be a snare to him, and that the hand of the Philistines may be against him."

Wherefore Saul said to David, "Thou shalt this day be my son-in-law in the one of the twain."

And Saul commanded his servants, saying, "Commune with David secretly, and say, 'Behold, the king hath delight in thee, and all his servants love thee: now therefore be the king's son-in-law.'"

And Saul's servants spoke those words in the ears of David. And David said, "Seemeth it to you a light thing to be a king's son-in-law, seeing that I am a poor man, and lightly esteemed?"

And the servants of Saul told him, saying, "On this manner spoke David."

And Saul said, "Thus shall ye say to David, 'The king desireth not any dowry, but a hundred foreskins of the Philistines, to be avenged of the king's enemies.'"

But Saul thought to make David fall by the hand of the Philistines. And when his servants told David these words, it pleased David well to be the king's son-in-law: and the days were not expired. Wherefore David arose and went, he and his men, and slew of the Philistines two hundred men; and David brought their foreskins, and they gave them in full tale to the king, that he might be the king's son-in-law. And Saul gave him Michal his daughter to wife.

THE FIRST BOOK OF SAMUEL

And Saul saw and knew that the Lord was with David, and that Michal Saul's daughter loved him. And Saul was yet the more afraid of David; and Saul became David's enemy continually.

And Saul spoke to Jonathan his son, and to all his servants, that they should kill David. But Jonathan Saul's son delighted much in David: and Jonathan told David, saying, "Saul my father seeketh to kill thee: now therefore, I pray thee, take heed to thyself until the morning, and abide in a secret place, and hide thyself: and I will go out and stand beside my father in the field where thou art, and I will commune with my father of thee; and what I see, that I will tell thee."

And Jonathan spoke good of David unto Saul his father, and said unto him, "Let not the king sin against his servant, against David; because he hath not sinned against thee, and because his works have been to thee-ward very good: for he did put his life in his hand, and slew the Philistine, and the Lord wrought a great salvation for all Israel: thou sawest it, and didst rejoice: wherefore then wilt thou sin against innocent blood, to slay David without a cause?"

And Saul hearkened unto the voice of Jonathan: and Saul swore, "As the Lord liveth, he shall not be slain."

And Jonathan called David, and Jonathan showed him all those things. And Jonathan brought David to Saul, and he was in his presence, as in times past.

And there was war again: and David went out, and fought with the Philistines, and slew them with a great slaughter; and they fled from him. And the evil spirit from the Lord was upon Saul, as he sat in his house with his javelin in his hand: and David played with his hand. And Saul sought to smite David even to the wall with the javelin; but he slipped away out of Saul's presence, and he smote the javelin into the wall: and David fled, and escaped that night.

Saul also sent messengers unto David's house, to watch him, and to slay him in the morning: and Michal David's wife told him, saying,

THE FIRST BOOK OF SAMUEL

"If thou save not thy life to-night, to-morrow thou shalt be slain."

So Michal let David down through a window: and he went, and fled, and escaped. And Michal took an image, and laid it in the bed, and put a pillow of goats' hair for his bolster, and covered it with a cloth. And when Saul sent messengers to take David, she said,

"He is sick."

And Saul sent the messengers again to see David, saying, "Bring him up to me in the bed, that I may slay him."

And when the messengers were come in, behold, there was an image in the bed, with a pillow of goats' hair for his bolster.

And Saul said unto Michal, "Why hast thou deceived me so, and sent away mine enemy, that he is escaped?"

And Michal answered Saul, "He said unto me, 'Let me go; why should I kill thee?'"

So David fled, and escaped, and came to Samuel to Ramah, and told him all that Saul had done to him. And he and Samuel went and dwelt in Naioth.

And it was told Saul, saying, "Behold, David is at Naioth in Ramah."

And Saul sent messengers to take David: and when they saw the company of the prophets prophesying, and Samuel standing as appointed over them, the Spirit of God was upon the messengers of Saul, and they also prophesied. And when it was told Saul, he sent other messengers, and they prophesied likewise. And Saul sent messengers again the third time, and they prophesied also. Then went he also to Ramah, and came to a great well that is in Sechu: and he asked and said, "Where are Samuel and David?"

And one said, "Behold, they be at Naioth in Ramah."

And he went thither to Naioth in Ramah: and the Spirit of God was upon him also, and he went on, and prophesied, until he came to Naioth in Ramah. And he stripped off his clothes also, and prophesied before Samuel in like manner, and lay down naked all that day and all that night. Wherefore they say,

THE FIRST BOOK OF SAMUEL

"Is Saul also among the prophets?"

And David fled from Naioth in Ramah, and came and said before Jonathan, "What have I done? what is mine iniquity? and what is my sin before thy father, that he seeketh my life?"

And he said unto him, "God forbid; thou shalt not die: behold, my father will do nothing either great or small, but that he will show it me: and why should my father hide this thing from me? it is not so."

And David swore moreover, and said, "Thy father certainly knoweth that I have found grace in thine eyes; and he saith, 'Let not Jonathan know this, lest he be grieved': but truly as the Lord liveth, and as thy soul liveth, there is but a step between me and death."

And Jonathan said unto David, "Come, and let us go out into the field."

And they went out both of them into the field. And Jonathan said unto David, "O Lord God of Israel, when I have sounded my father about to-morrow any time, or the third day, and, behold, if there be good toward David, and I then send not unto thee, and show it thee; the Lord do so and much more to Jonathan: but if it please my father to do thee evil, then I will show it thee, and send thee away, that thou mayest go in peace: and the Lord be with thee, as he hath been with my father. Thou shalt go down quickly, and come to the place where thou didst hide thyself when the business was in hand, and shalt remain by the stone Ezel. And I will shoot three arrows on the side thereof, as though I shot at a mark. And, behold, I will send a lad, saying, 'Go, find out the arrows.' If I expressly say unto the lad, 'Behold, the arrows are on this side of thee, take them'; then come thou: for there is peace to thee, and no hurt; as the Lord liveth. But if I say thus unto the young man, 'Behold, the arrows are beyond thee'; go thy way: for the Lord hath sent thee away. And as touching the matter which thou and I have spoken of, behold, the Lord be between thee and me for ever."

So David hid himself in the field: and when the new moon was come, the king sat him down to eat meat. And the king sat

THE FIRST BOOK OF SAMUEL

upon his seat, as at other times, even upon a seat by the wall: and Jonathan arose, and Abner sat by Saul's side, and David's place was empty. Then Saul's anger was kindled against Jonathan, and he said unto him,

"Thou son of the perverse rebellious woman, do not I know that thou hast chosen the son of Jesse to thine own confusion, and unto the confusion of thy mother's nakedness? For as long as the son of Jesse liveth upon the ground, thou shalt not be established, nor thy kingdom. Wherefore now send and fetch him unto me, for he shall surely die."

And Jonathan answered Saul his father, and said unto him, "Wherefore shall he be slain? what hath he done?"

And Saul cast a javelin at him to smite him: whereby Jonathan knew that it was determined of his father to slay David. So Jonathan arose from the table in fierce anger, and did eat no meat the second day of the month: for he was grieved for David, because his father had done him shame.

And it came to pass in the morning that Jonathan went out into the field at the time appointed with David, and a little lad with him. And he said unto his lad, "Run, find out now the arrows which I shoot."

And as the lad ran, he shot an arrow beyond him. And when the lad was come to the place of the arrow which Jonathan had shot, Jonathan cried after the lad, and said, "Is not the arrow beyond thee?"

And Jonathan cried after the lad, "Make speed, haste, stay not."

And Jonathan's lad gathered up the arrows, and came to his master. But the lad knew not any thing: only Jonathan and David knew the matter. And Jonathan gave his artillery unto his lad, and said unto him, "Go, carry them to the city."

And as soon as the lad was gone, David arose out of a place toward the south, and fell on his face to the ground, and bowed himself three times: and they kissed one another, and wept one with another, until David exceeded. And Jonathan said to David, "Go in peace, forasmuch as we have sworn both of us in the

THE FIRST BOOK OF SAMUEL

name of the Lord, saying, 'The Lord be between me and thee, and between my seed and thy seed for ever.'"

And he arose and departed: and Jonathan went into the city.

The Flight of David

Then came David to Nob to Ahimelech the priest: and Ahimelech was afraid at the meeting of David, and said unto him, "Why art thou alone, and no man with thee?"

And David said unto Ahimelech the priest, "The king hath commanded me a business, and hath said unto me, 'Let no man know any thing of the business whereabout I send thee, and what I have commanded thee: and I have appointed my servants to such and such a place.' Now therefore what is under thine hand? give me five loaves of bread in mine hand, or what there is present."

And the priest answered David, and said, "There is no common bread under mine hand, but there is hallowed bread; if the young men have kept themselves at least from women."

And David answered the priest, and said unto him, "Of a truth women have been kept from us about these three days, since I came out, and the vessels of the young men are holy, and the bread is in a manner common, yea, though it were sanctified this day in the vessel."

So the priest gave him hallowed bread: for there was no bread there but the showbread, that was taken from before the Lord, to put hot bread in the day when it was taken away.

Now a certain man of the servants of Saul was there that day, detained before the Lord; and his name was Doeg, an Edomite, the chiefest of the herdsmen that belonged to Saul.

And David said unto Ahimelech, "And is there not here under thine hand spear or sword? for I have neither brought my sword nor my weapons with me, because the king's business required haste."

And the priest said, "The sword of Goliath the Philistine, whom thou slewest in the valley of Elah, behold, it is here

THE FIRST BOOK OF SAMUEL

wrapped in a cloth behind the ephod: if thou wilt take that, take it: for there is no other save that here."

And David said, "There is none like that; give it me."

And David arose, and fled that day for fear of Saul, and went to Achish the king of Gath. And the servants of Achish said unto him, "Is not this David the king of the land? did they not sing one to another of him in dances, saying,

> "'Saul hath slain his thousands,
> And David his ten thousands'?"

And David laid up these words in his heart, and was sore afraid of Achish the king of Gath. And he changed his behaviour before them, and feigned himself mad in their hands, and scrabbled on the doors of the gate, and let his spittle fall down upon his beard. Then said Achish unto his servants,

"Lo, ye see the man is mad: wherefore then have ye brought him to me? Have I need of mad men, that ye have brought this fellow to play the mad man in my presence? shall this fellow come into my house?"

David therefore departed thence, and escaped to the cave Adullam: and when his brethren and all his father's house heard it, they went down thither to him. And every one that was in distress, and every one that was in debt, and every one that was discontented, gathered themselves unto him; and he became a captain over them: and there were with him about four hundred men.

When Saul heard that David was discovered, and the men that were with him (now Saul abode in Gibeah under a tree in Ramah, having his spear in his hand, and all his servants were standing about him), then Saul said unto his servants that stood about him,

"Hear now, ye Benjamites; will the son of Jesse give every one of you fields and vineyards, and make you all captains of thousands, and captains of hundreds; that all of you have conspired against me, and there is none that showeth me that my

THE FIRST BOOK OF SAMUEL

son hath made a league with the son of Jesse, and there is none of you that is sorry for me, or showeth unto me that my son hath stirred up my servant against me, to lie in wait, as at this day?"

Then answered Doeg the Edomite, which was set over the servants of Saul, and said,

"I saw the son of Jesse coming to Nob, to Ahimelech the son of Ahitub. And he enquired of the Lord for him, and gave him victuals, and gave him the sword of Goliath the Philistine."

Then the king sent to call Ahimelech the priest, the son of Ahitub, and all his father's house, the priests that were in Nob: and they came all of them to the king.

And Saul said, "Hear now, thou son of Ahitub."

And he answered, "Here I am, my lord."

And Saul said unto him, "Why have ye conspired against me, thou and the son of Jesse, in that thou hast given him bread, and a sword, and hast enquired of God for him, that he should rise against me, to lie in wait, as at this day?"

Then Ahimelech answered the king, and said, "And who is so faithful among all thy servants as David, which is the king's son-in-law, and goeth at thy bidding, and is honourable in thine house? Did I then begin to enquire of God for him? be it far from me: let not the king impute any thing unto his servant, nor to all the house of my father: for thy servant knew nothing of all this, less or more."

And the king said, "Thou shalt surely die, Ahimelech, thou, and all thy father's house."

And the king said unto the footmen that stood about him, "Turn, and slay the priests of the Lord; because their hand also is with David, and because they knew when he fled, and did not show it to me."

But the servants of the king would not put forth their hand to fall upon the priests of the Lord. And the king said to Doeg, "Turn thou, and fall upon the priests."

And Doeg the Edomite turned, and he fell upon the priests, and slew on that day fourscore and five persons that did wear a linen ephod. And Nob, the city of the priests, smote he with the

THE FIRST BOOK OF SAMUEL

edge of the sword, both men and women, children and sucklings, and oxen, and asses, and sheep, with the edge of the sword.

And one of the sons of Ahimelech the son of Ahitub, named Abiathar, escaped, and fled after David. And Abiathar showed David that Saul had slain the Lord's priests. And David said unto Abiathar,

"I knew it that day, when Doeg the Edomite was there, that he would surely tell Saul: I have occasioned the death of all the persons of thy father's house. Abide thou with me, fear not: for he that seeketh my life seeketh thy life: but with me thou shalt be in safeguard."

Then they told David, saying, "Behold, the Philistines fight against Keilah, and they rob the threshingfloors."

Therefore David enquired of the Lord, saying, "Shall I go and smite these Philistines?" And the Lord said unto David, "Go, and smite the Philistines, and save Keilah."

And David's men said unto him, "Behold, we be afraid here in Judah: how much more then if we come to Keilah against the armies of the Philistines?"

Then David enquired of the Lord yet again. And the Lord answered him and said, "Arise, go down to Keilah; for I will deliver the Philistines into thine hand."

So David and his men went to Keilah, and fought with the Philistines, and brought away their cattle, and smote them with a great slaughter. So David saved the inhabitants of Keilah.

And it was told Saul that David was come to Keilah. And Saul said, "God hath delivered him into mine hand; for he is shut in, by entering into a town that hath gates and bars."

And Saul called all the people together to war, to go down to Keilah, to besiege David and his men.

Then said David, "O Lord God of Israel, thy servant hath certainly heard that Saul seeketh to come to Keilah, to destroy the city for my sake. Will the men of Keilah deliver me up into his hand? will Saul come down, as thy servant hath heard? O Lord God of Israel, I beseech thee, tell thy servant." And the Lord said, "He will come down."

THE FIRST BOOK OF SAMUEL

Then said David, "Will the men of Keilah deliver me and my men into the hand of Saul?" And the Lord said, "They will deliver thee up."

Then David and his men, which were about six hundred, arose and departed out of Keilah, and went whithersoever they could go. And David abode in the wilderness in strong holds, and remained in a mountain in the wilderness of Ziph. And Saul sought him every day, but God delivered him not into his hand.

Then came up the Ziphites to Saul to Gibeah, saying, "Doth not David hide himself with us in strong holds in the wood, in the hill of Hachilah, which is on the south of Jeshimon? Now therefore, O king, come down according to all the desire of thy soul to come down; and our part shall be to deliver him into the king's hand."

And Saul said, "Blessed be ye of the Lord; for ye have compassion on me. Go, I pray you, prepare yet, and know and see his place where his haunt is, and who hath seen him there: for it is told me that he dealeth very subtly. See therefore, and take knowledge of all the lurking places where he hideth himself, and come ye again to me with the certainty, and I will go with you: and it shall come to pass, if he be in the land, that I will search him out throughout all the thousands of Judah."

And they arose, and went to Ziph before Saul: but David and his men were in the wilderness of Maon, in the plain on the south of Jeshimon. Saul also and his men went to seek him. And they told David: wherefore he came down into a rock, and abode in the wilderness of Maon. And when Saul heard that, he pursued after David in the wilderness of Maon. And Saul went on this side of the mountain, and David and his men on that side of the mountain: and David made haste to get away for fear of Saul; for Saul and his men compassed David and his men round about to take them.

But there came a messenger unto Saul, saying, "Haste thee, and come; for the Philistines have invaded the land."

Wherefore Saul returned from pursuing after David, and

THE FIRST BOOK OF SAMUEL

went against the Philistines: therefore they called that place Sela-hammahlekoth. And David went up from thence, and dwelt in strong holds at En-gedi.

And it came to pass, when Saul was returned from following the Philistines, that it was told him, saying, "Behold, David is in the wilderness of En-gedi."

Then Saul took three thousand chosen men out of all Israel, and went to seek David and his men upon the rocks of the wild goats. And he came to the sheepcotes by the way, where was a cave; and Saul went in to cover his feet: and David and his men remained in the sides of the cave.

And the men of David said unto him, "Behold the day of which the Lord said unto thee, 'Behold, I will deliver thine enemy into thine hand, that thou mayest do to him as it shall seem good unto thee.'"

Then David arose, and cut off the skirt of Saul's robe privily. And it came to pass afterward, that David's heart smote him, because he had cut off Saul's skirt. And he said unto his men, "The Lord forbid that I should do this thing unto my master, the Lord's anointed, to stretch forth mine hand against him, seeing he is the anointed of the Lord."

So David stayed his servants with these words, and suffered them not to rise against Saul. But Saul rose up out of the cave, and went on his way. David also arose afterward, and went out of the cave, and cried after Saul, saying, "My lord the king."

And when Saul looked behind him, David stooped with his face to the earth, and bowed himself.

And David said to Saul, "Wherefore hearest thou men's words, saying, 'Behold, David seeketh thy hurt'? Behold, this day thine eyes have seen how that the Lord had delivered thee to-day into mine hand in the cave: and some bade me kill thee: but mine eye spared thee; and I said, 'I will not put forth mine hand against my lord; for he is the Lord's anointed.' Moreover, my father, see, yea, see the skirt of thy robe in my hand: for in that I cut off the skirt of thy robe, and killed thee not, know thou and see that there is neither evil nor transgression in mine hand, and

THE FIRST BOOK OF SAMUEL

I have not sinned against thee; yet thou huntest my soul to take it. The Lord judge between me and thee, and the Lord avenge me of thee: but mine hand shall not be upon thee. As saith the proverb of the ancients,

" 'Wickedness proceedeth from the wicked:
But mine hand shall not be upon thee.'

"After whom is the king of Israel come out? after whom dost thou pursue? after a dead dog, after a flea. The Lord therefore be judge, and judge between me and thee, and see, and plead my cause, and deliver me out of thine hand."

And it came to pass, when David had made an end of speaking these words unto Saul, that Saul said, "Is this thy voice, my son David?"

And Saul lifted up his voice, and wept. And he said to David, "Thou art more righteous than I: for thou hast rewarded me good, whereas I have rewarded thee evil."

And Saul went home; but David and his men got them up unto the hold.

And Samuel died; and all the Israelites were gathered together, and lamented him, and buried him in his house at Ramah. And David arose, and went down to the wilderness of Paran. And there was a man in Maon, whose possessions were in Carmel; and the man was very great, and he had three thousand sheep, and a thousand goats: and he was shearing his sheep in Carmel. Now the name of the man was Nabal; and the name of his wife Abigail: and she was a woman of good understanding, and of a beautiful countenance: but the man was churlish and evil in his doings; and he was of the house of Caleb.

And David heard in the wilderness that Nabal did shear his sheep. And David sent out ten young men, and David said unto the young men,

"Get you up to Carmel, and go to Nabal, and greet him in my name: and thus shall ye say to him that liveth in prosperity, 'Peace be both to thee, and peace be to thine house, and peace be unto all that thou hast. And now I have heard that thou hast

THE FIRST BOOK OF SAMUEL

shearers: now thy shepherds which were with us, we hurt them not, neither was there ought missing unto them, all the while they were in Carmel. Ask thy young men, and they will show thee. Wherefore let the young men find favour in thine eyes: for we come in a good day: give, I pray thee, whatsoever cometh to thine hand unto thy servants, and to thy son David.'"

And when David's young men came, they spoke to Nabal according to all those words in the name of David, and ceased. And Nabal answered David's servants, and said,

"Who is David? and who is the son of Jesse? there be many servants nowadays that break away every man from his master. Shall I then take my bread, and my water, and my flesh, that I have killed for my shearers, and give it unto men, whom I know not whence they be?"

So David's young men turned their way, and went again, and came and told him all those sayings. And David said unto his men,

"Gird ye on every man his sword."

And they girded on every man his sword; and David also girded on his sword: and there went up after David about four hundred men; and two hundred abode by the stuff. But one of the young men told Abigail, Nabal's wife, saying,

"Behold, David sent messengers out of the wilderness to salute our master; and he railed on them. But the men were very good unto us, and we were not hurt, neither missed we any thing, as long as we were conversant with them, when we were in the fields: they were a wall unto us both by night and day, all the while we were with them keeping the sheep. Now therefore know and consider what thou wilt do; for evil is determined against our master, and against all his household: for he is such a son of Belial that a man cannot speak to him."

Then Abigail made haste, and took two hundred loaves, and two bottles of wine, and five sheep ready dressed, and five measures of parched corn, and a hundred clusters of raisins, and two hundred cakes of figs, and laid them on asses. And she said unto her servants,

THE FIRST BOOK OF SAMUEL

"Go on before me; behold, I come after you." But she told not her husband Nabal.

And it was so, as she rode on the ass, that she came down by the covert of the hill, and, behold, David and his men came down against her; and she met them.

Now David had said, "Surely in vain have I kept all that this fellow hath in the wilderness, so that nothing was missed of all that pertained unto him: and he hath requited me evil for good. So and more also do God unto the enemies of David, if I leave of all that pertain to him by the morning light any that pisseth against the wall."

And when Abigail saw David, she hastened, and lighted off the ass, and fell before David on her face, and bowed herself to the ground, and fell at his feet, and said,

"Upon me, my lord, upon me let this iniquity be: and let thine handmaid, I pray thee, speak in thine audience, and hear the words of thine handmaid. Let not my lord, I pray thee, regard this man of Belial, even Nabal: for as his name is, so is he; Nabal is his name, and folly is with him: but I thine handmaid saw not the young men of my lord, whom thou didst send. Now therefore, my lord, as the Lord liveth, and as thy soul liveth, seeing the Lord hath withheld thee from coming to shed blood, and from avenging thyself with thine own hand, now let thine enemies, and they that seek evil to my lord, be as Nabal. And now this blessing which thine handmaid hath brought unto my lord, let it even be given unto the young men that follow my lord. I pray thee, forgive the trespass of thine handmaid: for the Lord will certainly make my lord a sure house; because my lord fighteth the battles of the Lord, and evil hath not been found in thee all thy days. Yet a man is risen to pursue thee, and to seek thy soul: but the soul of my lord shall be bound in the bundle of life with the Lord thy God; and the souls of thine enemies, them shall he sling out, as out of the middle of a sling. And it shall come to pass, when the Lord shall have done to my lord according to all the good that he hath spoken concerning thee, and

THE FIRST BOOK OF SAMUEL

shall have appointed thee ruler over Israel; that this shall be no grief unto thee, nor offence of heart unto my lord, either that thou hast shed blood causeless, or that my lord hath avenged himself: but when the Lord shall have dealt well with my lord, then remember thine handmaid."

And David said to Abigail,

"Blessed be the Lord God of Israel, which sent thee this day to meet me: and blessed be thy advice, and blessed be thou, which hast kept me this day from coming to shed blood, and from avenging myself with mine own hand. For in very deed, as the Lord God of Israel liveth, which hath kept me back from hurting thee, except thou hadst hastened and come to meet me, surely there had not been left unto Nabal by the morning light any that pisseth against the wall."

So David received of her hand that which she had brought him, and said unto her,

"Go up in peace to thine house; see, I have hearkened to thy voice, and have accepted thy person."

And Abigail came to Nabal; and, behold, he held a feast in his house, like the feast of a king; and Nabal's heart was merry within him, for he was very drunken: wherefore she told him nothing, less or more, until the morning light. But it came to pass in the morning, when the wine was gone out of Nabal, and his wife had told him these things, that his heart died within him, and he became as a stone. And it came to pass, about ten days after, that the Lord smote Nabal, that he died.

And when David heard that Nabal was dead, he said, "Blessed be the Lord, that hath pleaded the cause of my reproach from the hand of Nabal, and hath kept his servant from evil: for the Lord hath returned the wickedness of Nabal upon his own head."

And David sent and communed with Abigail, to take her to him to wife. And when the servants of David were come to Abigail to Carmel, they spoke unto her, saying, "David sent us unto thee, to take thee to him to wife."

THE FIRST BOOK OF SAMUEL

And she arose, and bowed herself on her face to the earth, and said, "Behold, let thine handmaid be a servant to wash the feet of the servants of my lord."

And Abigail hastened, and arose, and rode upon an ass, with five damsels of hers that went after her; and she went after the messengers of David, and became his wife. David also took Ahinoam of Jezreel; and they were also both of them his wives. But Saul had given Michal his daughter, David's wife, to Phalti the son of Laish, which was of Gallim.

And the Ziphites came unto Saul to Gibeah, saying, "Doth not David hide himself in the hill of Hachilah, which is before Jeshimon?"

Then Saul arose, and went down to the wilderness of Ziph, having three thousand chosen men of Israel with him, to seek David in the wilderness of Ziph. And Saul pitched in the hill of Hachilah, which is before Jeshimon, by the way. But David abode in the wilderness, and he saw that Saul came after him into the wilderness. David therefore sent out spies, and understood that Saul was come in very deed. And David arose, and came to the place where Saul had pitched: and David beheld the place where Saul lay, and Abner the son of Ner, the captain of his host: and Saul lay in the trench, and the people pitched round about him.

Then answered David and said to Ahimelech the Hittite, and to Abishai the son of Zeruiah, brother to Joab, saying, "Who will go down with me to Saul to the camp?"

And Abishai said, "I will go down with thee."

So David and Abishai came to the people by night: and, behold, Saul lay sleeping within the trench, and his spear stuck in the ground at his bolster: but Abner and the people lay round about him.

Then said Abishai to David, "God hath delivered thine enemy into thine hand this day: now therefore let me smite him, I pray thee, with the spear even to the earth at once, and I will not smite him the second time."

THE FIRST BOOK OF SAMUEL

And David said to Abishai, "Destroy him not: for who can stretch forth his hand against the Lord's anointed, and be guiltless?"

David said furthermore, "As the Lord liveth, the Lord shall smite him; or his day shall come to die; or he shall descend into battle, and perish. The Lord forbid that I should stretch forth mine hand against the Lord's anointed: but, I pray thee, take thou now the spear that is at his bolster, and the cruse of water, and let us go."

So David took the spear and the cruse of water from Saul's bolster; and they got them away, and no man saw it, nor knew it, neither awaked: for they were all asleep; because a deep sleep from the Lord was fallen upon them. Then David went over to the other side, and stood on the top of a hill afar off; a great space being between them: and David cried to the people, and to Abner the son of Ner, saying, "Answerest thou not, Abner?"

Then Abner answered and said, "Who art thou that criest to the king?"

And David said to Abner, "Art not thou a valiant man? and who is like to thee in Israel? wherefore then hast thou not kept thy lord the king? for there came one of the people in to destroy the king thy lord. This thing is not good that thou hast done. As the Lord liveth, ye are worthy to die, because ye have not kept your master, the Lord's anointed. And now see where the king's spear is, and the cruse of water that was at his bolster."

And Saul knew David's voice, and said, "Is this thy voice, my son David?"

And David said, "It is my voice, my lord, O king."

And he said, "Wherefore doth my lord thus pursue after his servant? for what have I done? or what evil is in mine hand? Now therefore, I pray thee, let my lord the king hear the words of his servant. If the Lord have stirred thee up against me, let him accept an offering: but if they be the children of men, cursed be they before the Lord; for they have driven me out this day from

THE FIRST BOOK OF SAMUEL

abiding in the inheritance of the Lord, saying, 'Go, serve other gods.' Now therefore, let not my blood fall to the earth before the face of the Lord: for the king of Israel is come out to seek a flea, as when one doth hunt a partridge in the mountains."

Then said Saul, "I have sinned: return, my son David: for I will no more do thee harm, because my soul was precious in thine eyes this day: behold, I have played the fool, and have erred exceedingly."

And David answered and said, "Behold the king's spear! and let one of the young men come over and fetch it. The Lord render to every man his righteousness and his faithfulness: for the Lord delivered thee into my hand to-day, but I would not stretch forth mine hand against the Lord's anointed. And, behold, as thy life was much set by this day in mine eyes, so let my life be much set by in the eyes of the Lord, and let him deliver me out of all tribulation."

Then Saul said to David, "Blessed be thou, my son David: thou shalt both do great things, and also shalt still prevail."

So David went on his way, and Saul returned to his place.

And David said in his heart, "I shall now perish one day by the hand of Saul: there is nothing better for me than that I should speedily escape into the land of the Philistines; and Saul shall despair of me, to seek me any more in any coast of Israel: so shall I escape out of his hand." And David arose, and he passed over with the six hundred men that were with him unto Achish, the son of Maoch, king of Gath. And David dwelt with Achish at Gath, he and his men, every man with his household, even David with his two wives, Ahinoam the Jezreelitess, and Abigail the Carmelitess, Nabal's wife. And it was told Saul that David was fled to Gath: and he sought no more again for him.

And David said unto Achish, "If I have now found grace in thine eyes, let them give me a place in some town in the country, that I may dwell there: for why should thy servant dwell in the royal city with thee?"

Then Achish gave him Ziklag that day: wherefore Ziklag pertaineth unto the kings of Judah unto this day. And the time

THE FIRST BOOK OF SAMUEL

that David dwelt in the country of the Philistines was a full year and four months.

The Witch of En-dor

Now Samuel was dead, and all Israel had lamented him, and buried him in Ramah, even in his own city. And Saul had put away those that had familiar spirits, and the wizards, out of the land. And the Philistines gathered themselves together, and came and pitched in Shunem: and Saul gathered all Israel together, and they pitched in Gilboa. And when Saul saw the host of the Philistines, he was afraid, and his heart greatly trembled. And when Saul enquired of the Lord, the Lord answered him not, neither by dreams, nor by Urim, nor by prophets.

Then said Saul unto his servants, "Seek me a woman that hath a familiar spirit, that I may go to her, and enquire of her."

And his servants said to him, "Behold, there is a woman that hath a familiar spirit at En-dor."

And Saul disguised himself, and put on other raiment, and he went, and two men with him, and they came to the woman by night: and he said, "I pray thee, divine unto me by the familiar spirit, and bring me him up, whom I shall name unto thee."

And the woman said unto him, "Behold, thou knowest what Saul hath done, how he hath cut off those that have familiar spirits, and the wizards, out of the land: wherefore then layest thou a snare for my life, to cause me to die?"

And Saul swore to her by the Lord, saying, "As the Lord liveth, there shall no punishment happen to thee for this thing."

Then said the woman, "Whom shall I bring up unto thee?"

And he said, "Bring me up Samuel."

And when the woman saw Samuel, she cried with a loud voice: and the woman spoke to Saul, saying, "Why hast thou deceived me? for thou art Saul."

And the king said unto her, "Be not afraid: for what sawest thou?"

And the woman said unto Saul, "I saw gods ascending out of the earth."

THE FIRST BOOK OF SAMUEL

And he said unto her, "What form is he of?"

And she said, "An old man cometh up; and he is covered with a mantle."

And Saul perceived that it was Samuel, and he stooped with his face to the ground, and bowed himself.

And Samuel said to Saul, "Why hast thou disquieted me, to bring me up?"

And Saul answered, "I am sore distressed; for the Philistines make war against me, and God is departed from me, and answereth me no more, neither by prophets, nor by dreams: therefore I have called thee, that thou mayest make known unto me what I shall do."

Then said Samuel, "Wherefore then dost thou ask of me, seeing the Lord is departed from thee, and is become thine enemy? And the Lord hath done to him, as he spoke by me: for the Lord hath rent the kingdom out of thine hand, and given it to thy neighbour, even to David: because thou obeyedst not the voice of the Lord, nor executedst his fierce wrath upon Amalek, therefore hath the Lord done this thing unto thee this day. Moreover the Lord will also deliver Israel with thee into the hand of the Philistines: and to-morrow shalt thou and thy sons be with me: the Lord also shall deliver the host of Israel into the hand of the Philistines."

Then Saul fell straightway all along on the earth, and was sore afraid, because of the words of Samuel: and there was no strength in him; for he had eaten no bread all the day, nor all the night.

And the woman came unto Saul, and saw that he was sore troubled, and said unto him, "Behold, thine handmaid hath obeyed thy voice, and I have put my life in my hand, and have hearkened unto thy words which thou spokest unto me. Now therefore, I pray thee, hearken thou also unto the voice of thine handmaid, and let me set a morsel of bread before thee; and eat, that thou mayest have strength, when thou goest on thy way."

But he refused, and said, "I will not eat."

THE FIRST BOOK OF SAMUEL

But his servants, together with the woman, compelled him; and he hearkened unto their voice. So he arose from the earth, and sat upon the bed. And the woman had a fat calf in the house; and she hastened, and killed it, and took flour, and kneaded it, and did bake unleavened bread thereof: and she brought it before Saul, and before his servants; and they did eat. Then they rose up, and went away that night.

The Death of Saul

Now the Philistines gathered together all their armies to Aphek: and the Israelites pitched by a fountain which is in Jezreel. And the lords of the Philistines passed on by hundreds, and by thousands: but David and his men passed on in the rearward with Achish.

Then said the princes of the Philistines, "What do these Hebrews here?"

And Achish said unto the princes of the Philistines, "Is not this David, the servant of Saul the king of Israel, which hath been with me these days, or these years, and I have found no fault in him since he fell unto me unto this day?"

And the princes of the Philistines were wroth with him; and the princes of the Philistines said unto him, "Make this fellow return, that he may go again to his place which thou hast appointed him, and let him not go down with us to battle, lest in the battle he be an adversary to us: for wherewith should he reconcile himself unto his master? should it not be with the heads of these men? Is not this David, of whom they sang one to another in dances, saying,

" 'Saul slew his thousands,
And David his ten thousands'?"

Then Achish called David, and said unto him, "Surely, as the Lord liveth, thou hast been upright, and thy going out and thy coming in with me in the host is good in my sight: for I have not found evil in thee since the day of thy coming unto me unto this day: nevertheless the lords favour thee not. Wherefore now return, and go in peace, that thou displease not the lords of the Philistines."

And David said unto Achish, "But what have I done? and what hast thou found in thy servant so long as I have been with thee unto this day, that I may not go fight against the enemies of my lord the king?"

And Achish answered and said to David, "I know that thou art good in my sight, as an angel of God: notwithstanding the princes of the Philistines have said, 'He shall not go up with us to the battle.' Wherefore now rise up early in the morning with thy master's servants that are come with thee: and as soon as ye be up early in the morning, and have light, depart."

So David and his men rose up early to depart in the morning, to return into the land of the Philistines. And the Philistines went up to Jezreel.

Now the Philistines fought against Israel: and the men of Israel fled from before the Philistines, and fell down slain in Mount Gilboa. And the Philistines followed hard upon Saul and upon his sons; and the Philistines slew Jonathan, and Abinadab, and Melchi-shua, Saul's sons. And the battle went sore against Saul, and the archers hit him; and he was sore wounded of the archers. Then said Saul unto his armourbearer,

"Draw thy sword, and thrust me through therewith; lest these uncircumcised come and thrust me through, and abuse me."

But his armourbearer would not; for he was sore afraid. Therefore Saul took a sword, and fell upon it. And when his armourbearer saw that Saul was dead, he fell likewise upon his sword, and died with him. So Saul died, and his three sons, and his armourbearer, and all his men, that same day together.

And when the men of Israel that were on the other side of the valley, and they that were on the other side Jordan, saw that the men of Israel fled, and that Saul and his sons were dead, they forsook the cities, and fled; and the Philistines came and dwelt in them. And it came to pass on the morrow, when the Philistines came to strip the slain, that they found Saul and his three sons

THE FIRST BOOK OF SAMUEL

fallen in Mount Gilboa. And they cut off his head, and stripped off his armour, and sent into the land of the Philistines round about, to publish it in the house of their idols, and among the people. And they put his armour in the house of Ashtaroth: and they fastened his body to the wall of Beth-shan.

And when the inhabitants of Jabesh-gilead heard of that which the Philistines had done to Saul, all the valiant men arose, and went all night, and took the body of Saul and the bodies of his sons from the wall of Beth-shan, and came to Jabesh, and burnt them there. And they took their bones, and buried them under a tree at Jabesh, and fasted seven days.

THE SECOND BOOK OF SAMUEL

There is a plausible and pleasant theory, though one not universally accepted, that the nucleus of the Second Book of Samuel is a court history of David, written by some nobleman immediately conversant with the events of David's reign. In any event, Second Samuel would seem to have been the first of the Biblical books written in anything like its present form and to have started the school of historical writing that continued until the first century B.C. It was the natural mode of procedure, if one stops to think of it, for historians to begin with the period that they knew most about and work gradually backward through the ever-dimming past until they should reach the Creation as their final terminus.

The treatment of the central figure, David, is obviously somewhat apologetic, yet without any such idealization as moderns, living in a so-called scientific age, are wont to bestow upon their national heroes. The unknown Jewish writers of the tenth century B.C. were better historians than the popular Parson Weems of the nineteenth century A.D. It should be remembered, however, that like all the rest of these books Second Samuel was extensively revised in later centuries. For example, in the account of the Bath-sheba incident and the rebuke of David by the prophet Nathan one can clearly see the hand of the Deuteronomist at work. Nevertheless, out of the whole narrative King David, with his most human inconsistencies, emerges as one of the essentially real figures in ancient history.

The Second Book of SAMUEL

The Lament of David

Now it came to pass after the death of Saul, when David had abode two days in Ziklag, it came even to pass on the third day that, behold, a man came out of the camp from Saul with his clothes rent, and earth upon his head: and so it was, when he came to David, that he fell to the earth, and did obeisance.

And David said unto him, "From whence comest thou?" And he said unto him, "Out of the camp of Israel am I escaped."

And David said unto him, "How went the matter? I pray thee, tell me." And he answered that "the people are fled from the battle, and many of the people also are fallen and dead; and Saul and Jonathan his son are dead also."

And David said unto the young man that told him, "How knowest thou that Saul and Jonathan his son be dead?"

And the young man that told him said, "As I happened by chance upon Mount Gilboa, behold, Saul leaned upon his spear; and, lo, the chariots and horsemen followed hard after him. And when he looked behind him, he saw me, and called unto me. And I answered, 'Here am I.' And he said unto me, 'Who art thou?' And I answered him, 'I am an Amalekite.' He said unto me again, 'Stand, I pray thee, upon me, and slay me: for anguish is come upon me, because my life is yet whole in me.' So I stood upon him, and slew him, because I was sure that he could not live after that he was fallen: and I took the crown that was upon his head, and the bracelet that was on his arm, and have brought them hither unto my lord."

THE SECOND BOOK OF SAMUEL

Then David took hold on his clothes, and rent them; and likewise all the men that were with him: and they mourned, and wept, and fasted until even, for Saul, and for Jonathan his son, and for the people of the Lord, and for the house of Israel; because they were fallen by the sword.

And David said unto the young man that told him, "Whence art thou?"

And he answered, "I am the son of a stranger, an Amalekite."

And David said unto him, "How wast thou not afraid to stretch forth thine hand to destroy the Lord's anointed?"

And David called one of the young men, and said, "Go near, and fall upon him." And he smote him that he died.

And David said unto him, "Thy blood be upon thy head; for thy mouth hath testified against thee, saying, 'I have slain the Lord's anointed.'"

And David lamented with this lamentation over Saul and over Jonathan his son (also he bade them teach the children of Judah the use of the bow: behold, it is written in the Book of Jasher):

"The beauty of Israel is slain upon thy high places:
How are the mighty fallen!
Tell it not in Gath,
Publish it not in the streets of Askelon;
Lest the daughters of the Philistines rejoice,
Lest the daughters of the uncircumcised triumph.

Ye mountains of Gilboa,
Let there be no dew, neither let there be rain, upon you, nor
    fields of offerings:
For there the shield of the mighty is vilely cast away,
The shield of Saul, as though he had not been anointed with
    oil.
From the blood of the slain, from the fat of the mighty,
The bow of Jonathan turned not back,
And the sword of Saul returned not empty.

THE SECOND BOOK OF SAMUEL

*Saul and Jonathan were lovely and pleasant in their lives,
And in their death they were not divided:
They were swifter than eagles,
They were stronger than lions.
Ye daughters of Israel, weep over Saul,
Who clothed you in scarlet, with other delights,
Who put ornaments of gold upon your apparel.
How are the mighty fallen in the midst of the battle!
O Jonathan, thou wast slain in thine high places.
I am distressed for thee, my brother Jonathan:
Very pleasant hast thou been unto me:
Thy love to me was wonderful,
Passing the love of women.
How are the mighty fallen,
And the weapons of war perished!"*

The Triumph of David

And it came to pass after this that David enquired of the Lord, saying, "Shall I go up into any of the cities of Judah?" And the Lord said unto him, "Go up." And David said, "Whither shall I go up?" And he said, "Unto Hebron."

So David went up thither, and his two wives also, Ahinoam the Jezreelitess, and Abigail Nabal's wife the Carmelite. And his men that were with him did David bring up, every man with his household: and they dwelt in the cities of Hebron. And the men of Judah came, and there they anointed David king over the house of Judah. And they told David that the men of Jabesh-gilead were they that buried Saul.

And David sent messengers unto the men of Jabesh-gilead, and said unto them, "Blessed be ye of the Lord, that ye have showed this kindness unto your lord, even unto Saul, and have buried him. And now the Lord show kindness and truth unto you: and I also will requite you this kindness, because ye have done this thing. Therefore now let your hands be strengthened, and be ye valiant: for your master Saul is dead, and also the house of Judah have anointed me king over them."

THE SECOND BOOK OF SAMUEL

But Abner the son of Ner, captain of Saul's host, took Ish-bosheth the son of Saul, and brought him over to Mahanaim; and made him king over Gilead, and over the Ashurites, and over Jezreel, and over Ephraim, and over Benjamin, and over all Israel. Ish-bosheth Saul's son was forty years old when he began to reign over Israel, and reigned two years. But the house of Judah followed David. And the time that David was king in Hebron over the house of Judah was seven years and six months.

And Abner the son of Ner, and the servants of Ish-bosheth the son of Saul, went out from Mahanaim to Gibeon. And Joab the son of Zeruiah, and the servants of David, went out, and met together by the pool of Gibeon: and they sat down, the one on the one side of the pool, and the other on the other side of the pool.

And Abner said to Joab, "Let the young men now arise, and play before us." And Joab said, "Let them arise."

Then there arose and went over by number twelve of Benjamin, which pertained to Ish-bosheth the son of Saul, and twelve of the servants of David. And they caught every one his fellow by the head, and thrust his sword in his fellow's side; so they fell down together: wherefore that place was called Helkath-hazzurim, which is in Gibeon. And there was a very sore battle that day; and Abner was beaten, and the men of Israel, before the servants of David.

And there were three sons of Zeruiah there, Joab, and Abishai, and Asahel: and Asahel was as light of foot as a wild roe. And Asahel pursued after Abner; and in going he turned not to the right hand nor to the left from following Abner.

Then Abner looked behind him, and said, "Art thou Asahel?" And he answered, "I am."

And Abner said to him, "Turn thee aside to thy right hand or to thy left, and lay thee hold on one of the young men, and take thee his armour." But Asahel would not turn aside from following of him.

And Abner said again to Asahel, "Turn thee aside from fol-

THE SECOND BOOK OF SAMUEL

lowing me: wherefore should I smite thee to the ground? how then should I hold up my face to Joab thy brother?"

Howbeit he refused to turn aside: wherefore Abner with the hinder end of the spear smote him under the fifth rib, that the spear came out behind him; and he fell down there, and died in the same place: and it came to pass that as many as came to the place where Asahel fell down and died stood still. Joab also and Abishai pursued after Abner: and the sun went down when they were come to the hill of Ammah, that lieth before Giah by the way of the wilderness of Gibeon. And the children of Benjamin gathered themselves together after Abner, and became one troop, and stood on the top of a hill.

Then Abner called to Joab, and said, "Shall the sword devour for ever? knowest thou not that it will be bitterness in the latter end? how long shall it be then, ere thou bid the people return from following their brethren?"

And Joab said, "As God liveth, unless thou hadst spoken, surely then in the morning the people had gone up every one from following his brother."

So Joab blew a trumpet, and all the people stood still, and pursued after Israel no more, neither fought they any more. And Abner and his men walked all that night through the plain, and passed over Jordan, and went through all Bithron, and they came to Mahanaim. And Joab returned from following Abner: and when he had gathered all the people together, there lacked of David's servants nineteen men and Asahel. But the servants of David had smitten of Benjamin, and of Abner's men, so that three hundred and threescore men died. And they took up Asahel, and buried him in the sepulchre of his father, which was in Bethlehem. And Joab and his men went all night, and they came to Hebron at break of day.

Now there was long war between the house of Saul and the house of David: but David waxed stronger and stronger, and the house of Saul waxed weaker and weaker. And it came to pass, while there was war between the house of Saul and the

THE SECOND BOOK OF SAMUEL

house of David, that Abner made himself strong for the house of Saul. And Saul had a concubine, whose name was Rizpah, the daughter of Aiah: and Ish-bosheth said to Abner, "Wherefore hast thou gone in unto my father's concubine?"

Then was Abner very wroth for the words of Ish-bosheth, and said, "Am I a dog's head, which against Judah do show kindness this day unto the house of Saul thy father, to his brethren, and to his friends, and have not delivered thee into the hand of David, that thou chargest me to-day with a fault concerning this woman? So do God to Abner, and more also, except, as the Lord hath sworn to David, even so I do to him; to translate the kingdom from the house of Saul, and to set up the throne of David over Israel and over Judah, from Dan even to Beer-sheba."

And he could not answer Abner a word again, because he feared him.

And Abner sent messages to David on his behalf, saying, "Whose is the land?" saying also, "Make thy league with me, and, behold, my hand shall be with thee, to bring about all Israel unto thee."

And he said, "Well: I will make a league with thee: but one thing I require of thee, that is: thou shalt not see my face, except thou first bring Michal Saul's daughter, when thou comest to see my face."

And David sent messengers to Ish-bosheth Saul's son, saying, "Deliver me my wife Michal, which I espoused to me for a hundred foreskins of the Philistines."

And Ish-bosheth sent, and took her from her husband, even from Phaltiel the son of Laish. And her husband went with her along weeping behind her to Bahurim. Then said Abner unto him, "Go, return." And he returned.

And Abner had communication with the elders of Israel, saying, "Ye sought for David in times past to be king over you: now then do it: for the Lord hath spoken of David, saying, 'By the hand of my servant David I will save my people Israel out of the hand of the Philistines, and out of the hand of all their enemies.'"

THE SECOND BOOK OF SAMUEL

And Abner also spoke in the ears of Benjamin: and Abner went also to speak in the ears of David in Hebron all that seemed good to Israel, and that seemed good to the whole house of Benjamin. So Abner came to David to Hebron, and twenty men with him. And David made Abner and the men that were with him a feast.

And Abner said unto David, "I will arise and go, and will gather all Israel unto my lord the king, that they may make a league with thee, and that thou mayest reign over all that thine heart desireth." And David sent Abner away; and he went in peace.

And, behold, the servants of David and Joab came from pursuing a troop, and brought in a great spoil with them: but Abner was not with David in Hebron; for he had sent him away, and he was gone in peace. When Joab and all the host that was with him were come, they told Joab, saying, "Abner the son of Ner came to the king, and he hath sent him away: and he is gone in peace." Then Joab came to the king, and said, "What hast thou done? behold, Abner came unto thee; why is it that thou hast sent him away, and he is quite gone? Thou knowest Abner the son of Ner, that he came to deceive thee, and to know thy going out and thy coming in, and to know all that thou doest."

And when Joab was come out from David, he sent messengers after Abner, which brought him again from the well of Sirah: but David knew it not. And when Abner was returned to Hebron, Joab took him aside in the gate to speak with him quietly, and smote him there under the fifth rib, that he died, for the blood of Asahel his brother.

And afterward when David heard it, he said, "I and my kingdom are guiltless before the Lord for ever from the blood of Abner the son of Ner. Let it rest on the head of Joab, and on all his father's house; and let there not fail from the house of Joab one that hath an issue, or that is a leper, or that leaneth on a staff, or that falleth on the sword, or that lacketh bread."

So Joab and Abishai his brother slew Abner, because he had slain their brother Asahel at Gibeon in the battle. And David

THE SECOND BOOK OF SAMUEL

said to Joab, and to all the people that were with him, "Rend your clothes, and gird you with sackcloth, and mourn before Abner."

And King David himself followed the bier. And they buried Abner in Hebron: and the king lifted up his voice, and wept at the grave of Abner; and all the people wept. And the king lamented over Abner, and said,

> *"Died Abner as a fool dieth?*
> *Thy hands were not bound,*
> *Nor thy feet put into fetters:*
> *As a man falleth before wicked men, so fellest thou."*

And the sons of Rimmon the Beerothite, Rechab and Baanah, went, and came about the heat of the day to the house of Ishbosheth, who lay on a bed at noon. And they came thither into the midst of the house, as though they would have fetched wheat; and they smote him under the fifth rib: and Rechab and Baanah his brother escaped. For when they came into the house, he lay on his bed in his bedchamber, and they smote him, and slew him, and beheaded him, and took his head, and got them away through the plain all night. And they brought the head of Ishbosheth unto David to Hebron, and said to the king, "Behold the head of Ish-bosheth the son of Saul thine enemy, which sought thy life; and the Lord hath avenged my lord the king this day of Saul, and of his seed."

And David answered Rechab and Baanah his brother, the sons of Rimmon the Beerothite, and said unto them, "As the Lord liveth, who hath redeemed my soul out of all adversity, when one told me, saying, 'Behold, Saul is dead,' thinking to have brought good tidings, I took hold of him, and slew him in Ziklag, who thought that I would have given him a reward for his tidings: how much more, when wicked men have slain a righteous person in his own house upon his bed? shall I not therefore now require his blood of your hand, and take you away from the earth?"

And David commanded his young men, and they slew them,

THE SECOND BOOK OF SAMUEL

and cut off their hands and their feet, and hanged them up over the pool in Hebron. But they took the head of Ish-bosheth, and buried it in the sepulchre of Abner in Hebron.

And the Philistines came up yet again, and spread themselves in the valley of Rephaim. And when David enquired of the Lord, he said,

"Thou shalt not go up; but fetch a compass behind them, and come upon them over against the mulberry trees. And let it be, when thou hearest the sound of a going in the tops of the mulberry trees, that then thou shalt bestir thyself: for then shall the Lord go out before thee, to smite the host of the Philistines."

And David did so, as the Lord had commanded him; and smote the Philistines from Geba until thou come to Gazer.

Again, David gathered together all the chosen men of Israel, thirty thousand. And David arose, and went with all the people that were with him from Baale of Judah, to bring up from thence the ark of God, whose name is called by the name of the Lord of hosts that dwelleth between the cherubims. And they set the ark of God upon a new cart, and brought it out of the house of Abinadab that was in Gibeah: and Uzzah and Ahio, the sons of Abinadab, drove the new cart. And they brought it out of the house of Abinadab which was at Gibeah, accompanying the ark of God: and Ahio went before the ark. And David and all the house of Israel played before the Lord on all manner of instruments made of fir wood, even on harps, and on psalteries, and on timbrels, and on cornets, and on cymbals. And David danced before the Lord with all his might; and David was girded with a linen ephod. So David and all the house of Israel brought up the ark of the Lord with shouting, and with the sound of the trumpet. And as the ark of the Lord came into the city of David, Michal Saul's daughter looked through a window, and saw King David leaping and dancing before the Lord; and she despised him in her heart.

And they brought in the ark of the Lord, and set it in his place, in the midst of the tabernacle that David had pitched for it: and David offered burnt offerings and peace offerings before the Lord. And as soon as David had made an end of offering burnt offerings and peace offerings, he blessed the people in the name of the Lord of hosts. And he dealt among all the people, even among the whole multitude of Israel, as well to the women as men, to every one a cake of bread, and a good piece of flesh, and a flagon of wine. So all the people departed every one to his house.

Then David returned to bless his household. And Michal the daughter of Saul came out to meet David, and said, "How glorious was the king of Israel to-day, who uncovered himself to-day in the eyes of the handmaids of his servants, as one of the vain fellows shamelessly uncovereth himself!"

And David said unto Michal, "It was before the Lord, which chose me before thy father, and before all his house, to appoint me ruler over the people of the Lord, over Israel: therefore will I play before the Lord. And I will yet be more vile than thus, and will be base in mine own sight: and of the maidservants which thou hast spoken of, of them shall I be had in honour."

Therefore Michal the daughter of Saul had no child unto the day of her death.

And David said, "Is there yet any that is left of the house of Saul, that I may show him kindness for Jonathan's sake?"

And there was of the house of Saul a servant whose name was Ziba. And when they had called him unto David, the king said unto him, "Art thou Ziba?" And he said, "Thy servant is he." And the king said, "Is there not yet any of the house of Saul, that I may show the kindness of God unto him?" And Ziba said unto the king, "Jonathan hath yet a son, which is lame on his feet." And the king said unto him, "Where is he?" And Ziba said unto the king, "Behold, he is in the house of Machir, the son of Ammiel, in Lo-debar."

Then King David sent, and fetched him out of the house of Machir, the son of Ammiel, from Lo-debar. Now when Mephibosheth, the son of Jonathan, the son of Saul, was come unto David, he fell on his face, and did reverence. And David said, "Mephibosheth." And he answered, "Behold thy servant!"

THE SECOND BOOK OF SAMUEL

And David said unto him, "Fear not: for I will surely show thee kindness for Jonathan thy father's sake, and will restore thee all the land of Saul thy father; and thou shalt eat bread at my table continually."

And he bowed himself, and said, "What is thy servant, that thou shouldest look upon such a dead dog as I am?"

Then the king called to Ziba, Saul's servant, and said unto him, "I have given unto thy master's son all that pertained to Saul and to all his house. Thou therefore, and thy sons, and thy servants, shall till the land for him, and thou shalt bring in the fruits, that thy master's son may have food to eat: but Mephibosheth thy master's son shall eat bread always at my table." Now Ziba had fifteen sons and twenty servants.

Then said Ziba unto the king, "According to all that my lord the king hath commanded his servant, so shall thy servant do."

"As for Mephibosheth," said the king, "he shall eat at my table, as one of the king's sons."

And Mephibosheth had a young son, whose name was Micha. And all that dwelt in the house of Ziba were servants unto Mephibosheth. So Mephibosheth dwelt in Jerusalem: for he did eat continually at the king's table; and was lame on both his feet.

David and Bath-sheba

And it came to pass in an eveningtide that David arose from off his bed, and walked upon the roof of the king's house: and from the roof he saw a woman washing herself; and the woman was very beautiful to look upon. And David sent and enquired after the woman. And one said, "Is not this Bath-sheba, the daughter of Eliam, the wife of Uriah the Hittite?"

And David sent messengers, and took her; and she came in unto him, and he lay with her; for she was purified from her uncleanness: and she returned unto her house. And the woman conceived, and sent and told David, and said, "I am with child."

And David sent to Joab, saying, "Send me Uriah the Hittite." And Joab sent Uriah to David.

THE SECOND BOOK OF SAMUEL

And when Uriah was come unto him, David demanded of him how Joab did, and how the people did, and how the war prospered. And David said to Uriah, "Go down to thy house, and wash thy feet." And Uriah departed out of the king's house, and there followed him a mess of meat from the king. But Uriah slept at the door of the king's house with all the servants of his lord, and went not down to his house.

And when they had told David, saying, "Uriah went not down unto his house," David said unto Uriah, "Camest thou not from thy journey? why then didst thou not go down unto thine house?"

And Uriah said unto David, "The ark, and Israel, and Judah, abide in tents; and my lord Joab, and the servants of my lord, are encamped in the open fields; shall I then go into mine house, to eat and to drink, and to lie with my wife? as thou livest, and as thy soul liveth, I will not do this thing."

And David said to Uriah, "Tarry here to-day also, and to-morrow I will let thee depart."

So Uriah abode in Jerusalem that day, and the morrow. And when David had called him, he did eat and drink before him; and he made him drunk: and at even he went out to lie on his bed with the servants of his lord, but went not down to his house.

And it came to pass in the morning that David wrote a letter to Joab, and sent it by the hand of Uriah. And he wrote in the letter, saying, "Set ye Uriah in the forefront of the hottest battle, and retire ye from him, that he may be smitten, and die."

And it came to pass, when Joab observed the city, that he assigned Uriah unto a place where he knew that valiant men were. And the men of the city went out, and fought with Joab: and there fell some of the people of the servants of David; and Uriah the Hittite died also.

Then Joab sent and told David all the things concerning the war; and charged the messenger, saying, "When thou hast made an end of telling the matters of the war unto the king, and if so be that the king's wrath arise, and he say unto thee, 'Wherefore

THE SECOND BOOK OF SAMUEL

approached ye so nigh unto the city when ye did fight? knew ye not that they would shoot from the wall? Who smote Abimelech the son of Jerubbesheth? did not a woman cast a piece of a millstone upon him from the wall, that he died in Thebez? why went ye nigh the wall?' then say thou, 'Thy servant Uriah the Hittite is dead also.'"

So the messenger went, and came and showed David all that Joab had sent him for. And the messenger said unto David, "Surely the men prevailed against us, and came out unto us into the field, and we were upon them even unto the entering of the gate. And the shooters shot from off the wall upon thy servants; and some of the king's servants be dead, and thy servant Uriah the Hittite is dead also."

Then David said unto the messenger, "Thus shalt thou say unto Joab, 'Let not this thing displease thee, for the sword devoureth one as well as another: make thy battle more strong against the city, and overthrow it': and encourage thou him."

And when the wife of Uriah heard that Uriah her husband was dead, she mourned for her husband. And when the mourning was past, David sent and fetched her to his house, and she became his wife, and bore him a son. But the thing that David had done displeased the Lord. And the Lord sent Nathan unto David. And he came unto him, and said unto him,

"There were two men in one city; the one rich, and the other poor. The rich man had exceeding many flocks and herds: but the poor man had nothing, save one little ewe lamb, which he had bought and nourished up: and it grew up together with him, and with his children; it did eat of his own meat, and drank of his own cup, and lay in his bosom, and was unto him as a daughter.

"And there came a traveller unto the rich man, and he spared to take of his own flock and of his own herd, to dress for the wayfaring man that was come unto him; but took the poor man's lamb, and dressed it for the man that was come to him."

And David's anger was greatly kindled against the man; and

THE SECOND BOOK OF SAMUEL

he said to Nathan, "As the Lord liveth, the man that hath done this thing shall surely die: and he shall restore the lamb fourfold, because he did this thing, and because he had no pity."

And Nathan said to David, "Thou art the man. Thus saith the Lord God of Israel, 'I anointed thee king over Israel, and I delivered thee out of the hand of Saul; and I gave thee thy master's house, and thy master's wives into thy bosom, and gave thee the house of Israel and of Judah; and if that had been too little, I would moreover have given unto thee such and such things. Wherefore hast thou despised the commandment of the Lord, to do evil in his sight? thou hast killed Uriah the Hittite with the sword, and hast taken his wife to be thy wife, and hast slain him with the sword of the children of Ammon. Now therefore the sword shall never depart from thine house; because thou hast despised me, and hast taken the wife of Uriah the Hittite to be thy wife.' Thus saith the Lord, 'Behold, I will raise up evil against thee out of thine own house, and I will take thy wives before thine eyes, and give them unto thy neighbour, and he shall lie with thy wives in the sight of this sun. For thou didst it secretly: but I will do this thing before all Israel, and before the sun.'"

And David said unto Nathan, "I have sinned against the Lord."

And Nathan said unto David, "The Lord also hath put away thy sin; thou shalt not die. Howbeit, because by this deed thou hast given great occasion to the enemies of the Lord to blaspheme, the child also that is born unto thee shall surely die."

And Nathan departed unto his house. And the Lord struck the child that Uriah's wife bore unto David, and it was very sick. David therefore besought God for the child; and David fasted, and went in, and lay all night upon the earth. And the elders of his house arose, and went to him, to raise him up from the earth: but he would not, neither did he eat bread with them. And it came to pass on the seventh day that the child died. And the servants of David feared to tell him that the child was dead: for they said, "Behold, while the child was yet alive, we spoke

THE SECOND BOOK OF SAMUEL

unto him, and he would not hearken unto our voice: how will he then vex himself, if we tell him that the child is dead?"

But when David saw that his servants whispered, David perceived that the child was dead: therefore David said unto his servants, "Is the child dead?" And they said, "He is dead."

Then David arose from the earth, and washed, and anointed himself, and changed his apparel, and came into the house of the Lord, and worshipped: then he came to his own house; and when he required, they set bread before him, and he did eat. Then said his servants unto him, "What thing is this that thou hast done? thou didst fast and weep for the child, while it was alive; but when the child was dead, thou didst rise and eat bread."

And he said, "While the child was yet alive, I fasted and wept: for I said, 'Who can tell whether God will be gracious to me, that the child may live?' But now he is dead, wherefore should I fast? can I bring him back again? I shall go to him, but he shall not return to me."

And David comforted Bath-sheba his wife, and went in unto her, and lay with her: and she bore a son, and he called his name Solomon: and the Lord loved him. And he sent by the hand of Nathan the prophet; and he called his name Jedidiah, because of the Lord.

The Rebellion of Absalom

And it came to pass after this, that Absalom the son of David had a fair sister, whose name was Tamar; and Amnon the son of David loved her. And Amnon was so vexed, that he fell sick for his sister Tamar; for she was a virgin and Amnon thought it hard for him to do any thing to her.

But Amnon had a friend, whose name was Jonadab, the son of Shimeah David's brother: and Jonadab was a very subtile man. And he said unto him, "Why art thou, being a king's son, lean from day to day? wilt thou not tell me?"

And Amnon said unto him, "I love Tamar, my brother Absalom's sister."

THE SECOND BOOK OF SAMUEL

And Jonadab said unto him, "Lay thee down on thy bed, and make thyself sick: and when thy father cometh to see thee, say unto him, 'I pray thee, let my sister Tamar come, and give me meat, and dress the meat in my sight, that I may see it, and eat it at her hand.'"

So Amnon lay down, and made himself sick: and when the king was come to see him, Amnon said unto the king, "I pray thee, let Tamar my sister come, and make me a couple of cakes in my sight, that I may eat at her hand."

Then David sent home to Tamar, saying, "Go now to thy brother Amnon's house, and dress him meat."

So Tamar went to her brother Amnon's house; and he was laid down. And she took flour, and kneaded it, and made cakes in his sight, and did bake the cakes. And she took a pan, and poured them out before him; but he refused to eat. And Amnon said, "Have out all men from me." And they went out every man from him.

And Amnon said unto Tamar, "Bring the meat into the chamber, that I may eat of thine hand." And Tamar took the cakes which she had made, and brought them into the chamber to Amnon her brother. And when she had brought them unto him to eat, he took hold of her, and said unto her, "Come lie with me, my sister."

And she answered him, "Nay, my brother, do not force me; for no such thing ought to be done in Israel: do not thou this folly. And I, whither shall I cause my shame to go? and as for thee, thou shalt be as one of the fools in Israel. Now therefore, I pray thee, speak unto the king; for he will not withhold me from thee." Howbeit he would not hearken unto her voice; but, being stronger than she, forced her, and lay with her

Then Amnon hated her exceedingly; so that the hatred wherewith he hated her was greater than the love wherewith he had loved her. And Amnon said unto her, "Arise, be gone."

And she said unto him, "There is no cause: this evil in sending me away is greater than the other that thou didst unto me."

THE SECOND BOOK OF SAMUEL

But he would not hearken unto her. Then he called his servant that ministered unto him, and said, "Put now this woman out from me, and bolt the door after her." And she had a garment of divers colours upon her: for with such robes were the king's daughters that were virgins apparelled. Then his servant brought her out, and bolted the door after her.

And Tamar put ashes on her head; and rent her garment of divers colours that was on her, and laid her hand on her head, and went on crying. And Absalom her brother said unto her, "Hath Amnon thy brother been with thee? but hold now thy peace, my sister: he is thy brother; regard not this thing." So Tamar remained desolate in her brother Absalom's house.

But when King David heard of all these things, he was very wroth. And Absalom spoke unto his brother Amnon neither good nor bad: for Absalom hated Amnon, because he had forced his sister Tamar.

And it came to pass after two full years that Absalom had sheepshearers in Baal-hazor, which is beside Ephraim: and Absalom invited all the king's sons. And Absalom came to the king, and said, "Behold now, thy servant hath sheepshearers; let the king, I beseech thee, and his servants go with thy servant."

And the king said to Absalom, "Nay, my son, let us not all now go, lest we be chargeable unto thee." And he pressed him: howbeit he would not go, but blessed him.

Then said Absalom, "If not, I pray thee, let my brother Amnon go with us."

And the king said unto him, "Why should he go with thee?"

But Absalom pressed him, that he let Amnon and all the king's sons go with him.

Now Absalom had commanded his servants, saying, "Mark ye now when Amnon's heart is merry with wine, and when I say unto you, 'Smite Amnon'; then kill him, fear not: have not I commanded you? Be courageous, and be valiant."

And the servants of Absalom did unto Amnon as Absalom had commanded. Then all the king's sons arose, and every man

THE SECOND BOOK OF SAMUEL

got him up upon his mule, and fled. And it came to pass, while they were in the way, that tidings came to David, saying, "Absalom hath slain all the king's sons, and there is not one of them left."

Then the king arose, and tore his garments, and lay on the earth; and all his servants stood by with their clothes rent. And Jonadab, the son of Shimeah David's brother, answered and said, "Let not my lord suppose that they have slain all the young men the king's sons; for Amnon only is dead: for by the appointment of Absalom this hath been determined from the day that he forced his sister Tamar. Now therefore let not my lord the king take the thing to his heart, to think that all the king's sons are dead: for Amnon only is dead."

But Absalom fled, and went to Geshur, and was there three years. And the soul of King David longed to go forth unto Absalom: for he was comforted concerning Amnon, seeing he was dead.

Now Joab the son of Zeruiah perceived that the king's heart was toward Absalom. And Joab sent to Tekoah, and fetched thence a wise woman, and said unto her, "I pray thee, feign thyself to be a mourner, and put on now mourning apparel, and anoint not thyself with oil, but be as a woman that had a long time mourned for the dead: and come to the king, and speak on this manner unto him." So Joab put the words in her mouth.

And when the woman of Tekoah spoke to the king, she fell on her face to the ground, and did obeisance, and said, "Help, O king."

And the king said unto her, "What aileth thee?"

And she answered, "I am indeed a widow woman, and mine husband is dead. And thy handmaid had two sons, and they two strove together in the field, and there was none to part them, but the one smote the other, and slew him. And, behold, the whole family is risen against thine handmaid, and they said, 'Deliver him that smote his brother, that we may kill him, for the life of his brother whom he slew; and we will destroy the

THE SECOND BOOK OF SAMUEL

heir also': and so they shall quench my coal which is left, and shall not leave to my husband neither name nor remainder upon the earth."

And the king said unto the woman, "Go to thine house, and I will give charge concerning thee."

And the woman of Tekoah said unto the king, "My lord, O king, the iniquity be on me, and on my father's house: and the king and his throne be guiltless." And the king said, "Whosoever saith ought unto thee, bring him to me, and he shall not touch thee any more." Then the woman said, "Let thine handmaid, I pray thee, speak one word unto my lord the king."

And he said, "Say on."

And the woman said, "Wherefore then hast thou thought such a thing against the people of God? for the king doth speak this thing as one which is faulty, in that the king doth not fetch home again his banished. For we must needs die, and are as water spilt on the ground, which cannot be gathered up again; neither doth God respect any person: yet doth he devise means, that his banished be not expelled from him. Now therefore that I am come to speak of this thing unto my lord the king, it is because the people have made me afraid: and thy handmaid said, 'I will now speak unto the king; it may be that the king will perform the request of his handmaid. For the king will hear, to deliver his handmaid out of the hand of the man that would destroy me and my son together out of the inheritance of God.' Then thine handmaid said, 'The word of my lord the king shall now be comfortable': for as an angel of God, so is my lord the king to discern good and bad: therefore the Lord thy God will be with thee."

Then the king answered and said unto the woman, "Hide not from me, I pray thee, the thing that I shall ask thee."

And the woman said, "Let my lord the king now speak."

And the king said, "Is not the hand of Joab with thee in all this?" And the woman answered and said, "As thy soul liveth, my lord the king, none can turn to the right hand or to the left from

THE SECOND BOOK OF SAMUEL

ought that my lord the king hath spoken: for thy servant Joab, he bade me, and he put all these words in the mouth of thine handmaid. To fetch about this form of speech hath thy servant Joab done this thing: and my lord is wise, according to the wisdom of an angel of God, to know all things that are in the earth."

And the king said unto Joab, "Behold now, I have done this thing: go therefore, bring the young man Absalom again."

And Joab fell to the ground on his face, and bowed himself, and thanked the king: and Joab said, "To-day thy servant knoweth that I have found grace in thy sight, my lord, O king, in that the king hath fulfilled the request of his servant."

So Joab arose and went to Geshur, and brought Absalom to Jerusalem. And the king said, "Let him turn to his own house, and let him not see my face." So Absalom returned to his own house, and saw not the king's face.

But in all Israel there was none to be so much praised as Absalom for his beauty: from the sole of his foot even to the crown of his head there was no blemish in him. And when he polled his head (for it was at every year's end that he polled it: because the hair was heavy on him, therefore he polled it), he weighed the hair of his head at two hundred shekels after the king's weight. And unto Absalom there were born three sons, and one daughter, whose name was Tamar: she was a woman of a fair countenance.

So Absalom dwelt two full years in Jerusalem, and saw not the king's face. Therefore Absalom sent for Joab, to have sent him to the king; but he would not come to him: and when he sent again the second time, he would not come. Therefore he said unto his servants, "See, Joab's field is near mine, and he hath barley there; go and set it on fire." And Absalom's servants set the field on fire.

Then Joab arose, and came to Absalom unto his house, and said unto him, "Wherefore have thy servants set my field on fire?"

And Absalom answered Joab, "Behold, I sent unto thee, saying, 'Come hither, that I may send thee to the king, to say, "Wherefore am I come from Geshur? it had been good for me to

THE SECOND BOOK OF SAMUEL

have been there still": now therefore let me see the king's face; and if there be any iniquity in me, let him kill me.'"

So Joab came to the king, and told him: and when he had called for Absalom, he came to the king, and bowed himself on his face to the ground before the king: and the king kissed Absalom.

And it came to pass after this that Absalom prepared him chariots and horses, and fifty men to run before him. And Absalom rose up early, and stood beside the way of the gate: and it was so, that when any man that had a controversy came to the king for judgment, then Absalom called unto him, and said, "Of what city art thou?"

And he said, "Thy servant is of one of the tribes of Israel."

And Absalom said unto him, "See, thy matters are good and right; but there is no man deputed of the king to hear thee." Absalom said moreover, "Oh that I were made judge in the land, that every man which hath any suit or cause might come unto me, and I would do him justice!"

And it was so, that when any man came nigh to him to do him obeisance, he put forth his hand, and took him, and kissed him. And on this manner did Absalom to all Israel that came to the king for judgment: so Absalom stole the hearts of the men of Israel.

And it came to pass after forty years that Absalom said unto the king, "I pray thee, let me go and pay my vow, which I have vowed unto the Lord, in Hebron. For thy servant vowed a vow while I abode at Geshur in Syria, saying, 'If the Lord shall bring me again indeed to Jerusalem, then I will serve the Lord.'"

And the king said unto him, "Go in peace." So he arose, and went to Hebron.

But Absalom sent spies throughout all the tribes of Israel, saying, "As soon as ye hear the sound of the trumpet, then ye shall say, 'Absalom reigneth in Hebron.'"

And with Absalom went two hundred men out of Jerusalem, that were called; and they went in their simplicity, and they knew not any thing. And Absalom sent for Ahithophel the Gil-

THE SECOND BOOK OF SAMUEL

onite, David's counsellor, from his city, even from Giloh, while he offered sacrifices. And the conspiracy was strong; for the people increased continually with Absalom.

And there came a messenger to David, saying, "The hearts of the men of Israel are after Absalom."

And David said unto all his servants that were with him at Jerusalem, "Arise, and let us flee; for we shall not else escape from Absalom: make speed to depart, lest he overtake us suddenly, and bring evil upon us, and smite the city with the edge of the sword."

And the king's servants said unto the king, "Behold, thy servants are ready to do whatsoever my lord the king shall appoint."

And the king went forth, and all his household after him. And the king left ten women, which were concubines, to keep the house. And the king went forth, and all the people after him, and tarried in a place that was far off. And all his servants passed on beside him; and all the Cherethites, and all the Pelethites, and all the Gittites, six hundred men which came after him from Gath, passed on before the king.

Then said the king to Ittai the Gittite, "Wherefore goest thou also with us? return to thy place, and abide with the king: for thou art a stranger, and also an exile. Whereas thou camest but yesterday, should I this day make thee go up and down with us? seeing I go whither I may, return thou, and take back thy brethren: mercy and truth be with thee."

And Ittai answered the king, and said, "As the Lord liveth, and as my lord the king liveth, surely in what place my lord the king shall be, whether in death or life, even there also will thy servant be."

And David said to Ittai, "Go and pass over." And Ittai the Gittite passed over, and all his men, and all the little ones that were with him. And all the country wept with a loud voice, and all the people passed over: the king also himself passed over the brook Kidron, and all the people passed over, toward the way of the wilderness.

And one told David, saying, "Ahithophel is among the con-

THE SECOND BOOK OF SAMUEL

spirators with Absalom." And David said, "O Lord, I pray thee, turn the counsel of Ahithophel into foolishness."

And it came to pass that when David was come to the top of the mount, where he worshipped God, behold, Hushai the Archite came to meet him with his coat rent, and earth upon his head: unto whom David said, "If thou passest on with me, then thou shalt be a burden unto me: but if thou return to the city, and say unto Absalom, 'I will be thy servant, O king; as I have been thy father's servant hitherto, so will I now also be thy servant': then mayest thou for me defeat the counsel of Ahithophel. And hast thou not there with thee Zadok and Abiathar the priests? therefore it shall be, that what thing soever thou shalt hear out of the king's house, thou shalt tell it to Zadok and Abiathar the priests. Behold, they have there with them their two sons, Ahimaaz Zadok's son, and Jonathan Abiathar's son; and by them ye shall send unto me every thing that ye can hear."

So Hushai David's friend came into the city, and Absalom came into Jerusalem.

And when David was a little past the top of the hill, behold, Ziba the servant of Mephibosheth met him, with a couple of asses saddled, and upon them two hundred loaves of bread, and a hundred bunches of raisins, and a hundred of summer fruits, and a bottle of wine.

And the king said unto Ziba, "What meanest thou by these?" And Ziba said, "The asses be for the king's household to ride on; and the bread and summer fruit for the young men to eat; and the wine, that such as be faint in the wilderness may drink."

And the king said, "And where is thy master's son?" And Ziba said unto the king, "Behold, he abideth at Jerusalem: for he said, 'To-day shall the house of Israel restore me the kingdom of my father.'"

Then said the king to Ziba, "Behold, thine are all that pertained unto Mephibosheth." And Ziba said, "I humbly beseech thee that I may find grace in thy sight, my lord, O king."

And when King David came to Bahurim, behold, thence came

THE SECOND BOOK OF SAMUEL

out a man of the family of the house of Saul, whose name was Shimei, the son of Gera: he came forth, and cursed still as he came. And he cast stones at David, and at all the servants of King David: and all the people and all the mighty men were on his right hand and on his left. And thus said Shimei when he cursed, "Come out, come out, thou bloody man, and thou man of Belial. The Lord hath returned upon thee all the blood of the house of Saul, in whose stead thou hast reigned; and the Lord hath delivered the kingdom into the hand of Absalom thy son: and, behold, thou art taken in thy mischief, because thou art a bloody man."

Then said Abishai the son of Zeruiah unto the king, "Why should this dead dog curse my lord the king? let me go over, I pray thee, and take off his head."

And the king said, "What have I to do with you, ye sons of Zeruiah? so let him curse, because the Lord hath said unto him, 'Curse David.' Who shall then say, 'Wherefore hast thou done so?'" And David said to Abishai, and to all his servants, "Behold, my son, which came forth of my bowels, seeketh my life: how much more now may this Benjamite do it? let him alone, and let him curse; for the Lord hath bidden him. It may be that the Lord will look on mine affliction, and that the Lord will requite me good for his cursing this day."

And as David and his men went by the way, Shimei went along on the hill's side over against him, and cursed as he went, and threw stones at him, and cast dust. And the king, and all the people that were with him, came weary, and refreshed themselves there.

And Absalom, and all the people the men of Israel, came to Jerusalem, and Ahithophel with him. And it came to pass, when Hushai the Archite, David's friend, was come unto Absalom, that Hushai said unto Absalom, "God save the king, God save the king." And Absalom said to Hushai, "Is this thy kindness to thy friend? why wentest thou not with thy friend?"

And Hushai said unto Absalom, "Nay; but whom the Lord, and this people, and all the men of Israel, choose, his will I be,

THE SECOND BOOK OF SAMUEL

and with him will I abide. And again, whom should I serve? should I not serve in the presence of his son? as I have served in thy father's presence, so will I be in thy presence."

Then said Absalom to Ahithophel, "Give counsel among you what we shall do."

And Ahithophel said unto Absalom, "Go in unto thy father's concubines, which he hath left to keep the house; and all Israel shall hear that thou art abhorred of thy father: then shall the hands of all that are with thee be strong."

So they spread Absalom a tent upon the top of the house; and Absalom went in unto his father's concubines in the sight of all Israel. And the counsel of Ahithophel, which he counselled in those days, was as if a man had enquired at the oracle of God: so was all the counsel of Ahithophel both with David and with Absalom. Moreover Ahithophel said unto Absalom, "Let me now choose out twelve thousand men, and I will arise and pursue after David this night: and I will come upon him while he is weary and weak handed, and will make him afraid: and all the people that are with him shall flee; and I will smite the king only: and I will bring back all the people unto thee: the man whom thou seekest is as if all returned: so all the people shall be in peace." And the saying pleased Absalom well, and all the elders of Israel.

Then said Absalom, "Call now Hushai the Archite also, and let us hear likewise what he saith."

And when Hushai was come to Absalom, Absalom spoke unto him, saying, "Ahithophel hath spoken after this manner: shall we do after his saying? if not; speak thou."

And Hushai said unto Absalom, "The counsel that Ahithophel hath given is not good at this time. For," said Hushai, "thou knowest thy father and his men, that they be mighty men, and they be chafed in their minds, as a bear robbed of her whelps in the field: and thy father is a man of war, and will not lodge with the people. Behold, he is hid now in some pit, or in some other place: and it will come to pass, when some of them be overthrown at the first, that whosoever heareth it will say, 'There is a slaughter among the people that follow Absalom.' And he also that is valiant, whose heart is as the heart of a lion, shall utterly melt: for all Israel knoweth that thy father is a mighty man, and they which be with him are valiant men. Therefore I counsel that all Israel be generally gathered unto thee, from Dan even to Beer-sheba, as the sand that is by the sea for multitude; and that thou go to battle in thine own person. So shall we come upon him in some place where he shall be found, and we will light upon him as the dew falleth on the ground: and of him and of all the men that are with him there shall not be left so much as one. Moreover, if he be gotten into a city, then shall all Israel bring ropes to that city, and we will draw it into the river, until there be not one small stone found there."

And Absalom and all the men of Israel said, "The counsel of Hushai the Archite is better than the counsel of Ahithophel." For the Lord had appointed to defeat the good counsel of Ahithophel, to the intent that the Lord might bring evil upon Absalom.

Then said Hushai unto Zadok and to Abiathar the priests, "Thus and thus did Ahithophel counsel Absalom and the elders of Israel; and thus and thus have I counselled. Now therefore send quickly, and tell David, saying, 'Lodge not this night in the plains of the wilderness, but speedily pass over; lest the king be swallowed up, and all the people that are with him.'"

Now Jonathan and Ahimaaz stayed by En-rogel; for they might not be seen to come into the city: and a wench went and told them; and they went and told King David. Nevertheless a lad saw them, and told Absalom: but they went both of them away quickly, and came to a man's house in Bahurim, which had a well in his court; whither they went down. And the woman took and spread a covering over the well's mouth, and spread ground corn thereon; and the thing was not known. And when Absalom's servants came to the woman to the house, they said, "Where is Ahimaaz and Jonathan?" And the woman said unto them, "They be gone over the brook of water." And when they had sought and could not find them, they returned to Jerusalem.

THE SECOND BOOK OF SAMUEL

And it came to pass, after they were departed, that they came up out of the well, and went and told King David, and said unto David, "Arise, and pass quickly over the water: for thus hath Ahithophel counselled against you."

Then David arose, and all the people that were with him and they passed over Jordan: by the morning light there lacked not one of them that was not gone over Jordan.

And when Ahithophel saw that his counsel was not followed, he saddled his ass, and arose, and got him home to his house, to his city, and put his household in order, and hanged himself, and died, and was buried in the sepulchre of his father.

And David numbered the people that were with him, and set captains of thousands and captains of hundreds over them. And David sent forth a third part of the people under the hand of Joab, and a third part under the hand of Abishai the son of Zeruiah, Joab's brother, and a third part under the hand of Ittai the Gittite. And the king said unto the people, "I will surely go forth with you myself also."

But the people answered, "Thou shalt not go forth: for if we flee away, they will not care for us; neither if half of us die, will they care for us: but now thou art worth ten thousand of us: therefore now it is better that thou succour us out of the city."

And the king said unto them, "What seemeth you best I will do." And the king stood by the gate side, and all the people came out by hundreds and by thousands.

And the king commanded Joab and Abishai and Ittai, saying, "Deal gently for my sake with the young man, even with Absalom." And all the people heard when the king gave all the captains charge concerning Absalom.

So the people went out into the field against Israel: and the battle was in the wood of Ephraim, where the people of Israel were slain before the servants of David, and there was there a great slaughter that day of twenty thousand men. For the battle was there scattered over the face of all the country: and the wood devoured more people that day than the sword devoured.

And Absalom met the servants of David. And Absalom rode

THE SECOND BOOK OF SAMUEL

upon a mule, and the mule went under the thick boughs of a great oak, and his head caught hold of the oak, and he was taken up between heaven and the earth; and the mule that was under him went away. And a certain man saw it, and told Joab, and said, "Behold, I saw Absalom hanged in an oak."

And Joab said unto the man that told him, "And, behold, thou sawest him, and why didst thou not smite him there to the ground? and I would have given thee ten shekels of silver, and a girdle."

And the man said unto Joab, "Though I should receive a thousand shekels of silver in mine hand, yet would I not put forth mine hand against the king's son: for in our hearing the king charged thee and Abishai and Ittai, saying, 'Beware that none touch the young man Absalom.' Otherwise I should have wrought falsehood against mine own life: for there is no matter hid from the king, and thou thyself wouldest have set thyself against me."

Then said Joab, "I may not tarry thus with thee."

And he took three darts in his hand, and thrust them through the heart of Absalom, while he was yet alive in the midst of the oak. And ten young men that bore Joab's armour compassed about and smote Absalom, and slew him. And Joab blew the trumpet, and the people returned from pursuing after Israel: for Joab held back the people. And they took Absalom, and cast him into a great pit in the wood, and laid a very great heap of stones upon him: and all Israel fled every one to his tent.

Then said Ahimaaz the son of Zadok, "Let me now run, and bear the king tidings, how that the Lord hath avenged him of his enemies." And Joab said unto him, "Thou shalt not bear tidings this day, but thou shalt bear tidings another day: but this day thou shalt bear no tidings, because the king's son is dead."

Then said Joab to Cushi, "Go tell the king what thou hast seen." And Cushi bowed himself unto Joab, and ran.

Then said Ahimaaz the son of Zadok yet again to Joab, "But howsoever, let me, I pray thee, also run after Cushi." And Joab said, "Wherefore wilt thou run, my son, seeing that thou hast no tidings ready?"

THE SECOND BOOK OF SAMUEL

"But howsoever," said he, "let me run." And he said unto him, "Run." Then Ahimaaz ran by the way of the plain, and overran Cushi.

And David sat between the two gates: and the watchman went up to the roof over the gate unto the wall, and lifted up his eyes, and looked, and behold a man running alone. And the watchman cried, and told the king. And the king said, "If he be alone, there is tidings in his mouth." And he came apace, and drew near.

And the watchman saw another man running: and the watchman called unto the porter, and said, "Behold another man running alone." And the king said, "He also bringeth tidings."

And the watchman said, "Me thinketh the running of the foremost is like the running of Ahimaaz the son of Zadok." And the king said, "He is a good man, and cometh with good tidings."

And Ahimaaz called, and said unto the king, "All is well." And he fell down to the earth upon his face before the king, and said, "Blessed be the Lord thy God, which hath delivered up the men that lifted up their hand against my lord the king."

And the king said, "Is the young man Absalom safe?"

And Ahimaaz answered, "When Joab sent the king's servant, and me thy servant, I saw a great tumult, but I knew not what it was."

And the king said unto him, "Turn aside, and stand here." And he turned aside, and stood still.

And, behold, Cushi came; and Cushi said, "Tidings, my lord the king: for the Lord hath avenged thee this day of all them that rose up against thee."

And the king said unto Cushi, "Is the young man Absalom safe?"

And Cushi answered, "The enemies of my lord the king, and all that rise against thee to do thee hurt, be as that young man is."

And the king was much moved, and went up to the chamber over the gate, and wept: and as he went, thus he said,

"O my son Absalom, my son, my son Absalom! would God I had died for thee, O Absalom, my son, my son!"

THE FIRST BOOK OF THE KINGS

From the time of King Solomon actual records were kept both by the priests and by lay writers. Shortly before the fall of Judah, these were compiled into a consecutive history of the monarchy, interpreted from the point of view of the prophets. Convinced that righteousness is rewarded by prosperity and sin by misery, the authors explained the political failures of the Jewish monarchs by their and their people's apostasy from the strict worship of Jehovah, and minimized the successes of such great apostates as Kings Omri and Ahab. To the writers, the figures of the prophets Elijah and Elisha were far more important than those of any of the rulers. In the Books of the Kings we are reading what is primarily a religious philosophy of history rather than history proper, yet as always with the Jewish writers the ideas are conveyed through such vivid pictures of concrete personalities that the latter have for us a value in themselves over and above the principles they are designed to illustrate.

The First Book of THE KINGS

The Death of David

NOW KING DAVID WAS OLD and stricken in years; and they covered him with clothes, but he got no heat. Wherefore his servants said unto him,

"Let there be sought for my lord the king a young virgin: and let her stand before the king, and let her cherish him, and let her lie in thy bosom, that my lord the king may get heat."

So they sought for a fair damsel throughout all the coasts of Israel, and found Abishag a Shunammite, and brought her to the king. And the damsel was very fair, and cherished the king, and ministered to him: but the king knew her not.

Then Adonijah the son of Haggith exalted himself, saying, "I will be king": and he prepared him chariots and horsemen, and fifty men to run before him. And his father had not displeased him at any time in saying, "Why hast thou done so?" and he also was a very goodly man; and his mother bore him after Absalom. And he conferred with Joab the son of Zeruiah, and with Abiathar the priest: and they following Adonijah helped him. But Zadok the priest, and Benaiah the son of Jehoiada and Nathan, the prophet, and Shimei, and Rei, and the mighty men which belonged to David, were not with Adonijah. Wherefore Nathan spoke unto Bath-sheba the mother of Solomon, saying,

"Hast thou not heard that Adonijah the son of Haggith doth reign, and David our lord knoweth it not? Now therefore come, let me, I pray thee, give thee counsel, that thou mayest save thine own life, and the life of thy son Solomon. Go and get thee in unto King David, and say unto him, 'Didst not thou, my lord,

THE FIRST BOOK OF THE KINGS

O king, swear unto thine handmaid, saying, "Assuredly Solomon thy son shall reign after me, and he shall sit upon my throne"? why then doth Adonijah reign?' Behold, while thou yet talkest there with the king, I also will come in after thee, and confirm thy words."

And Bath-sheba went in unto the king into the chamber: and the king was very old; and Abishag the Shunammite ministered unto the king. And Bath-sheba bowed, and did obeisance unto the king. And the king said, "What wouldest thou?"

And she said unto him,

"My lord, thou sworest by the Lord thy God unto thine handmaid, saying, 'Assuredly Solomon thy son shall reign after me, and he shall sit upon my throne.' And now, behold, Adonijah reigneth; and now, my lord the king, thou knowest it not. And he hath slain oxen and fat cattle and sheep in abundance, and hath called all the sons of the king, and Abiathar the priest, and Joab the captain of the host: but Solomon thy servant hath he not called. And thou, my lord, O king, the eyes of all Israel are upon thee, that thou shouldest tell them who shall sit on the throne of my lord the king after him. Otherwise it shall come to pass, when my lord the king shall sleep with his fathers, that I and my son Solomon shall be counted offenders."

And, lo, while she yet talked with the king, Nathan the prophet also came in. And they told the king, saying,

"Behold Nathan the prophet!"

And when he was come in before the king, he bowed himself before the king with his face to the ground. And Nathan said,

"My lord, O king, hast thou said, 'Adonijah shall reign after me, and he shall sit upon my throne'? For he is gone down this day, and hath slain oxen and fat cattle and sheep in abundance, and hath called all the king's sons, and the captains of the host, and Abiathar the priest; and, behold, they eat and drink before him, and say, 'God save King Adonijah.' But me, even me thy servant, and Zadok the priest, and Benaiah the son of Jehoiada, and thy servant Solomon, hath he not called. Is this thing done

THE FIRST BOOK OF THE KINGS

by my lord the king, and thou hast not showed it unto thy servant, who should sit on the throne of my lord the king after him?"

Then King David answered and said, "Call me Bath-sheba."

And she came into the king's presence, and stood before the king. And the king swore, and said,

"As the Lord liveth, that hath redeemed my soul out of all distress, even as I swore unto thee by the Lord God of Israel, saying, 'Assuredly Solomon thy son shall reign after me, and he shall sit upon my throne in my stead': even so will I certainly do this day."

Then Bath-sheba bowed with her face to the earth, and did reverence to the king, and said, "Let my lord King David live for ever."

And King David said, "Call me Zadok the priest, and Nathan the prophet, and Benaiah the son of Jehoiada." And they came before the king.

The king also said unto them, "Take with you the servants of your lord, and cause Solomon my son to ride upon mine own mule, and bring him down to Gihon: and let Zadok the priest and Nathan the prophet anoint him there king over Israel: and blow ye with the trumpet, and say, 'God save King Solomon.' Then ye shall come up after him, that he may come and sit upon my throne; for he shall be king in my stead: and I have appointed him to be ruler over Israel and over Judah."

So Zadok the priest, and Nathan the prophet, and Benaiah the son of Jehoiada, and the Cherethites, and the Pelethites, went down, and caused Solomon to ride upon King David's mule, and brought him to Gihon. And Zadok the priest took a horn of oil out of the tabernacle, and anointed Solomon. And they blew the trumpet; and all the people said, "God save King Solomon!" And all the people came up after him, and the people piped with pipes, and rejoiced with great joy, so that the earth rent with the sound of them.

And Adonijah and all the guests that were with him heard it as they had made an end of eating. And all the guests that were

THE FIRST BOOK OF THE KINGS

with Adonijah were afraid, and rose up, and went every man his way. And Adonijah feared because of Solomon, and arose, and went, and caught hold on the horns of the altar.

And it was told Solomon, saying, "Behold, Adonijah feareth King Solomon: for, lo, he hath caught hold on the horns of the altar, saying, 'Let King Solomon swear unto me to-day that he will not slay his servant with the sword.'"

And Solomon said, "If he will show himself a worthy man, there shall not a hair of him fall to the earth: but if wickedness shall be found in him, he shall die."

So King Solomon sent, and they brought him down from the altar. And he came and bowed himself to King Solomon: and Solomon said unto him, "Go to thine house."

Now the days of David drew nigh that he should die; and he charged Solomon his son, saying,

"I go the way of all the earth: be thou strong therefore, and show thyself a man; and keep the charge of the Lord thy God, to walk in his ways, to keep his statutes, and his commandments, and his judgments, and his testimonies, as it is written in the law of Moses, that thou mayest prosper in all that thou doest, and whithersoever thou turnest thyself: that the Lord may continue his word which he spoke concerning me, saying, 'If thy children take heed to their way, to walk before me in truth with all their heart and with all their soul, there shall not fail thee' (said he) 'a man on the throne of Israel.' Moreover thou knowest also what Joab the son of Zeruiah did to me, and what he did to the two captains of the hosts of Israel, unto Abner the son of Ner, and unto Amasa the son of Jether, whom he slew, and shed the blood of war in peace, and put the blood of war upon his girdle that was about his loins, and in his shoes that were on his feet. Do therefore according to thy wisdom, and let not his hoar head go down to the grave in peace. But show kindness unto the sons of Barzillai the Gileadite, and let them be of those that eat at thy table: for so they came to me when I fled because of Absalom thy brother. And, behold, thou hast with thee Shimei the son of Gera, a Benjamite of Bahurim,

THE FIRST BOOK OF THE KINGS

which cursed me with a grievous curse in the day when I went to Mahanaim: but he came down to meet me at Jordan, and I swore to him by the Lord, saying, 'I will not put thee to death with the sword.' Now therefore hold him not guiltless: for thou art a wise man, and knowest what thou oughtest to do unto him; but his hoar head bring thou down to the grave with blood."

So David slept with his fathers, and was buried in the city of David. And the days that David reigned over Israel were forty years: seven years reigned he in Hebron, and thirty and three years reigned he in Jerusalem.

The Reign of Solomon

Then sat Solomon upon the throne of David his father; and his kingdom was established greatly.

And Adonijah the son of Haggith came to Bath-sheba the mother of Solomon. And she said, "Comest thou peaceably?" And he said, "Peaceably." He said moreover, "I have somewhat to say unto thee." And she said, "Say on." And he said, "Thou knowest that the kingdom was mine, and that all Israel set their faces on me, that I should reign: howbeit the kingdom is turned about, and is become my brother's: for it was his from the Lord. And now I ask one petition of thee, deny me not." And she said unto him, "Say on." And he said, "Speak, I pray thee, unto Solomon the king (for he will not say thee nay), that he give me Abishag the Shunammite to wife." And Bath-sheba said, "Well; I will speak for thee unto the king." Bath-sheba therefore went unto King Solomon, to speak unto him for Adonijah. And the king rose up to meet her, and bowed himself unto her, and sat down on his throne, and caused a seat to be set for the king's mother; and she sat on his right hand. Then she said, "I desire one small petition of thee; I pray thee, say me not nay." And the king said unto her, "Ask on, my mother: for I will not say thee nay." And she said, "Let Abishag the Shunammite be given to Adonijah thy brother to wife." And King Solomon answered and said unto his mother, "And why dost thou ask Abishag the Shunammite for Adonijah? ask for him the kingdom also; for he

THE FIRST BOOK OF THE KINGS

is mine elder brother; even for him, and for Abiathar the priest, and for Joab the son of Zeruiah." Then King Solomon swore by the Lord, saying, "God do so to me, and more also, if Adonijah have not spoken this word against his own life. Now therefore, as the Lord liveth, which hath established me, and set me on the throne of David my father, and who hath made me a house, as he promised, Adonijah shall be put to death this day." And King Solomon sent by the hand of Benaiah the son of Jehoiada; and he fell upon him that he died.

And unto Abiathar the priest said the king, "Get thee to Anathoth, unto thine own fields; for thou art worthy of death: but I will not at this time put thee to death, because thou borest the ark of the Lord God before David my father, and because thou hast been afflicted in all wherein my father was afflicted." So Solomon thrust out Abiathar from being priest unto the Lord; that he might fulfil the word of the Lord, which he spoke concerning the house of Eli in Shiloh.

Then tidings came to Joab: for Joab had turned after Adonijah, though he turned not after Absalom. And Joab fled unto the tabernacle of the Lord, and caught hold on the horns of the altar. And it was told King Solomon that Joab was fled unto the tabernacle of the Lord; and, behold, he is by the altar. Then Solomon sent Benaiah the son of Jehoiada, saying, "Go, fall upon him." And Benaiah came to the tabernacle of the Lord, and said unto him, "Thus saith the king, 'Come forth.'" And he said, "Nay; but I will die here." And Benaiah brought the king word again, saying, "Thus said Joab, and thus he answered me." And the king said unto him, "Do as he hath said, and fall upon him, and bury him; that thou mayest take away the innocent blood, which Joab shed, from me, and from the house of my father. And the Lord shall return his blood upon his own head, who fell upon two men more righteous and better than he, and slew them with the sword, my father David not knowing thereof, to wit, Abner the son of Ner, captain of the host of Israel, and Amasa the son of Jether, captain of the host of Judah. Their blood shall therefore return upon the head of Joab, and upon the head of his

THE FIRST BOOK OF THE KINGS

seed for ever: but upon David, and upon his seed, and upon his house, and upon his throne, shall there be peace for ever from the Lord." So Benaiah the son of Jehoiada went up, and fell upon him, and slew him: and he was buried in his own house in the wilderness.

And the king sent and called for Shimei, and said unto him, "Build thee a house in Jerusalem, and dwell there, and go not forth thence any whither. For it shall be, that on the day thou goest out, and passest over the brook Kidron, thou shalt know for certain that thou shalt surely die: thy blood shall be upon thine own head." And Shimei said unto the king, "The saying is good: as my lord the king hath said, so will thy servant do." And Shimei dwelt in Jerusalem many days. And it came to pass, at the end of three years, that two of the servants of Shimei ran away unto Achish son of Maachah king of Gath. And they told Shimei, saying, "Behold, thy servants be in Gath." And Shimei arose, and saddled his ass, and went to Gath to Achish to seek his servants: and Shimei went, and brought his servants from Gath. And it was told Solomon that Shimei had gone from Jerusalem to Gath, and was come again. And the king sent and called for Shimei, and said unto him, "Did I not make thee to swear by the Lord, and protested unto thee, saying, 'Know for a certain, on the day thou goest out, and walkest abroad any whither, that thou shalt surely die'? and thou saidst unto me, 'The word that I have heard is good.' Why then hast thou not kept the oath of the Lord, and the commandment that I have charged thee with?" The king said moreover to Shimei, "Thou knowest all the wickedness which thine heart is privy to, that thou didst to David my father: therefore the Lord shall return thy wickedness upon thine own head; and King Solomon shall be blessed, and the throne of David shall be established before the Lord for ever." So the king commanded Benaiah the son of Jehoiada; which went out, and fell upon him, that he died. And the kingdom was established in the hand of Solomon.

And Solomon made affinity with Pharaoh king of Egypt, and took Pharaoh's daughter, and brought her into the city of David,

THE FIRST BOOK OF THE KINGS

until he had made an end of building his own house, and the house of the Lord, and the wall of Jerusalem round about. Only the people sacrificed in high places, because there was no house built unto the name of the Lord, until those days. And Solomon loved the Lord, walking in the statutes of David his father: only he sacrificed and burnt incense in high places. And the king went to Gibeon to sacrifice there; for that was the great high place: a thousand burnt offerings did Solomon offer upon that altar.

In Gibeon the Lord appeared to Solomon in a dream by night: and God said, "Ask what I shall give thee." And Solomon said, "Thou hast showed unto thy servant David my father great mercy, according as he walked before thee in truth, and in righteousness, and in uprightness of heart with thee; and thou hast kept for him this great kindness, that thou hast given him a son to sit on his throne, as it is this day. And now, O Lord my God, thou hast made thy servant king instead of David my father: and I am but a little child: I know not how to go out or come in. And thy servant is in the midst of thy people which thou hast chosen, a great people, that cannot be numbered nor counted for multitude. Give therefore thy servant an understanding heart to judge thy people, that I may discern between good and bad: for who is able to judge this thy so great a people?" And the speech pleased the Lord, that Solomon had asked this thing. And God said unto him, "Because thou hast asked this thing, and hast not asked for thyself long life; neither hast asked riches for thyself, nor hast asked the life of thine enemies; but hast asked for thyself understanding to discern judgment; behold, I have done according to thy words: lo, I have given thee a wise and an understanding heart; so that there was none like thee before thee, neither after thee shall any arise like unto thee. And I have also given thee that which thou hast not asked, both riches, and honour; so that there shall not be any among the kings like unto thee all thy days. And if thou wilt walk in my ways, to keep my statutes and my commandments, as thy father David did walk, then I will lengthen thy days."

THE FIRST BOOK OF THE KINGS

And Solomon awoke; and, behold, it was a dream. And he came to Jerusalem, and stood before the ark of the covenant of the Lord, and offered up burnt offerings, and offered peace offerings, and made a feast to all his servants.

Then came there two women, that were harlots, unto the king, and stood before him. And the one woman said, "O my lord, I and this woman dwell in one house; and I was delivered of a child with her in the house. And it came to pass the third day after that I was delivered, that this woman was delivered also: and we were together; there was no stranger with us in the house, save we two in the house. And this woman's child died in the night; because she overlaid it. And she arose at midnight, and took my son from beside me, while thine handmaid slept, and laid it in her bosom, and laid her dead child in my bosom. And when I rose in the morning to give my child suck, behold, it was dead: but when I had considered it in the morning, behold, it was not my son, which I did bear." And the other woman said, "Nay; but the living is my son, and the dead is thy son." And this said, "No; but the dead is thy son, and the living is my son." Thus they spoke before the king. Then said the king, "The one saith, 'This is my son that liveth, and thy son is the dead': and the other saith, 'Nay; but thy son is the dead, and my son is the living.'" And the king said, "Bring me a sword." And they brought a sword before the king. And the king said, "Divide the living child in two, and give half to the one, and half to the other." Then spoke the woman whose the living child was unto the king, for her bowels yearned upon her son, and she said, "O my lord, give her the living child, and in no wise slay it." But the other said, "Let it be neither mine nor thine, but divide it." Then the king answered and said, "Give her the living child, and in no wise slay it: she is the mother thereof." And all Israel heard of the judgment which the king had judged; and they feared the king: for they saw that the wisdom of God was in him, to do judgment.

And Solomon reigned over all kingdoms from the river unto the land of the Philistines, and unto the border of Egypt: they

THE FIRST BOOK OF THE KINGS

brought presents, and served Solomon all the days of his life. And Solomon's provision for one day was thirty measures of fine flour, and threescore measures of meal, ten fat oxen, and twenty oxen out of the pastures, and a hundred sheep, beside harts, and roebucks, and fallowdeer, and fatted fowl. For he had dominion over all the region on this side the river, from Tiphsah even to Azzah, over all the kings on this side the river: and he had peace on all sides round about him. And Judah and Israel dwelt safely, every man under his vine and under his fig tree, from Dan even to Beer-sheba, all the days of Solomon.

And Solomon had forty thousand stalls of horses for his chariots, and twelve thousand horsemen. And those officers provided victual for King Solomon, and for all that came unto King Solomon's table, every man in his month: they lacked nothing. Barley also and straw for the horses and dromedaries brought they unto the place where the officers were, every man according to his charge.

And God gave Solomon wisdom and understanding exceeding much, and largeness of heart, even as the sand that is on the sea shore. And Solomon's wisdom excelled the wisdom of all the children of the east country, and all the wisdom of Egypt. For he was wiser than all men; than Ethan the Ezrahite, and Heman, and Chalcol, and Darda, the sons of Mahol: and his fame was in all nations round about. And he spoke three thousand proverbs: and his songs were a thousand and five. And he spoke of trees, from the cedar tree that is in Lebanon even unto the hyssop that springeth out of the wall: he spoke also of beasts, and of fowl, and of creeping things, and of fishes. And there came of all people to hear the wisdom of Solomon, from all kings of the earth, which had heard of his wisdom.

And Hiram king of Tyre sent his servants unto Solomon; for he had heard that they had anointed him king in the room of his father: for Hiram was ever a lover of David. And Solomon sent to Hiram, saying, "Thou knowest how that David my father could not build a house unto the name of the Lord his God for the wars which were about him on every side, until the Lord

THE FIRST BOOK OF THE KINGS

put them under the soles of his feet. But now the Lord my God hath given me rest on every side, so that there is neither adversary nor evil occurrent. And, behold, I purpose to build a house unto the name of the Lord my God, as the Lord spoke unto David my father, saying, 'Thy son, whom I will set upon thy throne in thy room, he shall build a house unto my name.' Now therefore command thou that they hew me cedar trees out of Lebanon; and my servants shall be with thy servants: and unto thee will I give hire for thy servants according to all that thou shalt appoint: for thou knowest that there is not among us any that can skill to hew timber like unto the Sidonians."

And it came to pass, when Hiram heard the words of Solomon, that he rejoiced greatly, and said, "Blessed be the Lord this day, which hath given unto David a wise son over this great people." And Hiram sent to Solomon, saying, "I have considered the things which thou sentest to me for: and I will do all thy desire concerning timber of cedar, and concerning timber of fir. My servants shall bring them down from Lebanon unto the sea: and I will convey them by sea in floats unto the place that thou shalt appoint me, and will cause them to be discharged there, and thou shalt receive them; and thou shalt accomplish my desire, in giving food for my household."

So Hiram gave Solomon cedar trees and fir trees according to all his desire. And Solomon gave Hiram twenty thousand measures of wheat for food to his household, and twenty measures of pure oil: thus gave Solomon to Hiram year by year. And the Lord gave Solomon wisdom, as he promised him: and there was peace between Hiram and Solomon; and they two made a league together.

And King Solomon raised a levy out of all Israel; and the levy was thirty thousand men. And he sent them to Lebanon, ten thousand a month by courses: a month they were in Lebanon, and two months at home: and Adoniram was over the levy. And Solomon had threescore and ten thousand that bore burdens, and fourscore thousand hewers in the mountains; beside the chief of Solomon's officers which were over the work, three

THE FIRST BOOK OF THE KINGS

thousand and three hundred, which ruled over the people that wrought in the work. And the king commanded, and they brought great stones, costly stones, and hewed stones, to lay the foundation of the house. And Solomon's builders and Hiram's builders did hew them, and the stonesquarers: so they prepared timber and stones to build the house.

And it came to pass in the four hundred and eightieth year after the children of Israel were come out of the land of Egypt, in the fourth year of Solomon's reign over Israel, in the month Zif, which is the second month, that he began to build the house of the Lord. And the house which King Solomon built for the Lord, the length thereof was threescore cubits, and the breadth thereof twenty cubits, and the height thereof thirty cubits. And the porch before the temple of the house, twenty cubits was the length thereof, according to the breadth of the house; and ten cubits was the breadth thereof before the house. And for the house he made windows of narrow lights.

And against the wall of the house he built chambers round about, against the walls of the house round about, both of the temple and of the oracle: and he made chambers round about. The nethermost chamber was five cubits broad, and the middle was six cubits broad, and the third was seven cubits broad: for without in the wall of the house he made narrowed rests round about, that the beams should not be fastened in the walls of the house. And the house, when it was in building, was built of stone made ready before it was brought thither: so that there was neither hammer nor ax nor any tool of iron heard in the house, while it was in building. The door for the middle chamber was in the right side of the house: and they went up with winding stairs into the middle chamber, and out of the middle into the third. So he built the house, and finished it; and covered the house with beams and boards of cedar. And then he built chambers against all the house, five cubits high: and they rested on the house with timber of cedar. And he built the walls of the house within with boards of cedar, both the floor of the house, and the walls of the ceiling: and he covered them on the inside

THE FIRST BOOK OF THE KINGS

with wood, and covered the floor of the house with planks of fir. And he built twenty cubits on the sides of the house, both the floor and the walls with boards of cedar: he even built them for it within, even for the oracle, even for the most holy place. And the house, that is, the temple before it, was forty cubits long. And the cedar of the house within was carved with knops and open flowers: all was cedar; there was no stone seen. And the oracle he prepared in the house within, to set there the ark of the covenant of the Lord. And the oracle in the forepart was twenty cubits in length, and twenty cubits in breadth, and twenty cubits in the height thereof: and he overlaid it with pure gold; and so covered the altar which was of cedar. So Solomon overlaid the house within with pure gold: and he made a partition by the chains of gold before the oracle; and he overlaid it with gold. And the whole house he overlaid with gold, until he had finished all the house: also the whole altar that was by the oracle he overlaid with gold.

And within the oracle he made two cherubims of olive tree, each ten cubits high. And five cubits was the one wing of the cherub, and five cubits the other wing of the cherub: from the uttermost part of the one wing unto the uttermost part of the other were ten cubits. And the other cherub was ten cubits: both the cherubims were of one measure and one size. The height of the one cherub was ten cubits, and so was it of the other cherub. And he set the cherubims within the inner house: and they stretched forth the wings of the cherubims, so that the wing of the one touched the one wall, and the wing of the other cherub touched the other wall; and their wings touched one another in the midst of the house. And he overlaid the cherubims with gold. And he carved all the walls of the house round about with carved figures of cherubims, and palm trees and open flowers, within and without. And the floor of the house he overlaid with gold, within and without.

And for the entering of the oracle he made doors of olive tree: the lintel and side posts were a fifth part of the wall. The two doors also were of olive tree; and he carved upon them carvings

THE FIRST BOOK OF THE KINGS

of cherubims and palm trees and open flowers, and overlaid them with gold, and spread gold upon the cherubims, and upon the palm trees. So also made he for the door of the temple posts of olive tree, a fourth part of the wall. And the two doors were of fir tree: the two leaves of the one door were folding, and the two leaves of the other door were folding. And he carved thereon cherubims and palm trees and open flowers: and covered them with gold fitted upon the carved work. And he built the inner court with three rows of hewed stone, and a row of cedar beams.

In the fourth year was the foundation of the house of the Lord laid, in the month Zif: and in the eleventh year, in the month Bul, which is the eighth month, was the house finished throughout all the parts thereof, and according to all the fashion of it. So was he seven years in building it.

But Solomon was building his own house thirteen years, and he finished all his house. He built also the house of the forest of Lebanon; the length thereof was a hundred cubits, and the breadth thereof fifty cubits, and the height thereof thirty cubits, upon four rows of cedar pillars, with cedar beams upon the pillars. And it was covered with cedar above upon the beams, that lay on forty-five pillars, fifteen in a row. And there were windows in three rows, and light was against light in three ranks. And all the doors and posts were square, with the windows: and light was against light in three ranks. And he made a porch of pillars; the length thereof was fifty cubits, and the breadth thereof thirty cubits: and the porch was before them: and the other pillars and the thick beam were before them. Then he made a porch for the throne where he might judge, even the porch of judgment: and it was covered with cedar from one side of the floor to the other. And his house where he dwelt had another court within the porch, which was of the like work. Solomon made also a house for Pharaoh's daughter, whom he had taken to wife, like unto this porch. All these were of costly stones, according to the measures of hewed stones, sawed with saws, within and without, even from the foundation unto the coping, and so on the outside toward the great court. And the

THE FIRST BOOK OF THE KINGS

foundation was of costly stones, even great stones, stones of ten cubits, and stones of eight cubits. And above were costly stones, after the measures of hewed stones, and cedars. And the great court round about was with three rows of hewed stones, and a row of cedar beams, both for the inner court of the house of the Lord, and for the porch of the house.

And King Solomon made a navy of ships in Ezion-geber, which is beside Eloth, on the shore of the Red Sea, in the land of Edom. And Hiram sent in the navy his servants, shipmen that had knowledge of the sea, with the servants of Solomon. And they came to Ophir, and fetched from thence gold, four hundred and twenty talents, and brought it to King Solomon.

And when the queen of Sheba heard of the fame of Solomon concerning the name of the Lord, she came to prove him with hard questions. And she came to Jerusalem with a very great train, with camels that bore spices, and very much gold, and precious stones: and when she was come to Solomon, she communed with him of all that was in her heart. And Solomon told her all her questions: there was not any thing hid from the king, which he told her not. And when the queen of Sheba had seen all Solomon's wisdom, and the house that he had built, and the meat of his table, and the sitting of his servants, and the attendance of his ministers, and their apparel, and his cupbearers, and his ascent by which he went up unto the house of the Lord; there was no more spirit in her. And she said to the king, "It was a true report that I heard in mine own land of thy acts and of thy wisdom. Howbeit I believed not the words, until I came, and mine eyes had seen it: and, behold, the half was not told me: thy wisdom and prosperity exceedeth the fame which I heard. Happy are thy men, happy are these thy servants, which stand continually before thee, and that hear thy wisdom. Blessed be the Lord thy God, which delighted in thee, to set thee on the throne of Israel: because the Lord loved Israel for ever, therefore made he thee king, to do judgment and justice."

And she gave the king a hundred and twenty talents of gold, and of spices very great store, and precious stones: there came

THE FIRST BOOK OF THE KINGS

no more such abundance of spices as these which the queen of Sheba gave to King Solomon. And the navy also of Hiram, that brought gold from Ophir, brought in from Ophir great plenty of almug trees, and precious stones. And the king made of the almug trees pillars for the house of the Lord, and for the king's house, harps also and psalteries for singers: there came no such almug trees, nor were seen unto this day. And King Solomon gave unto the queen of Sheba all her desire, whatsoever she asked, beside that which Solomon gave her of his royal bounty. So she turned and went to her own country, she and her servants.

Now the weight of gold that came to Solomon in one year was six hundred threescore and six talents of gold, beside that he had of the merchantmen, and of the traffic of the spice merchants, and of all the kings of Arabia, and of the governors of the country. And King Solomon made two hundred targets of beaten gold: six hundred shekels of gold went to one target.

And he made three hundred shields of beaten gold; three pounds of gold went to one shield: and the king put them in the house of the forest of Lebanon. Moreover the king made a great throne of ivory, and overlaid it with the best gold. The throne had six steps, and the top of the throne was round behind: and there were stays on either side on the place of the seat, and two lions stood beside the stays. And twelve lions stood there on the one side and on the other upon the six steps: there was not the like made in any kingdom. And all King Solomon's drinking vessels were of gold, and all the vessels of the house of the forest of Lebanon were of pure gold; none were of silver: it was nothing accounted of in the days of Solomon. For the king had at sea a navy of Tharshish with the navy of Hiram: once in three years came the navy of Tharshish, bringing gold, and silver, ivory, and apes, and peacocks. So King Solomon exceeded all the kings of the earth for riches and for wisdom.

But King Solomon loved many strange women, together with the daughter of Pharaoh, women of the Moabites, Ammonites, Edomites, Sidonians, and Hittites; of the nations concerning which the Lord said unto the children of Israel, "Ye shall not go

THE FIRST BOOK OF THE KINGS

in to them, neither shall they come in unto you: for surely they will turn away your heart after their gods": Solomon cleaved unto these in love. And he had seven hundred wives, princesses, and three hundred concubines: and his wives turned away his heart. For it came to pass, when Solomon was old, that his wives turned away his heart after other gods: and his heart was not perfect with the Lord his God, as was the heart of David his father. For Solomon went after Ashtoreth the goddess of the Sidonians, and after Milcom the abomination of the Ammonites. And Solomon did evil in the sight of the Lord, and went not fully after the Lord, as did David his father. Then did Solomon build a high place for Chemosh, the abomination of Moab, in the hill that is before Jerusalem, and for Molech, the abomination of the children of Ammon. And likewise did he for all his strange wives, which burnt incense and sacrificed unto their gods.

And the Lord was angry with Solomon, because his heart was turned from the Lord God of Israel, which had appeared unto him twice, and had commanded him concerning this thing, that he should not go after other gods: but he kept not that which the Lord commanded. Wherefore the Lord said unto Solomon,

"Forasmuch as this is done of thee, and thou hast not kept my covenant and my statutes, which I have commanded thee, I will surely rend the kingdom from thee, and will give it to thy servant. Notwithstanding in thy days I will not do it for David thy father's sake: but I will rend it out of the hand of thy son. Howbeit I will not rend away all the kingdom; but will give one tribe to thy son for David my servant's sake, and for Jerusalem's sake which I have chosen."

And Jeroboam the son of Nebat, an Ephrathite of Zereda, Solomon's servant, whose mother's name was Zeruah, a widow woman, even he lifted up his hand against the king. And this was the cause that he lifted up his hand against the king: Solomon built Millo, and repaired the breaches of the city of David his father. And the man Jeroboam was a mighty man of valour:

THE FIRST BOOK OF THE KINGS

and Solomon seeing the young man that he was industrious, he made him ruler over all the charge of the house of Joseph. And it came to pass at that time, when Jeroboam went out of Jerusalem, that the prophet Ahijah the Shilonite found him in the way; and he had clad himself with a new garment; and they two were alone in the field: and Ahijah caught the new garment that was on him, and rent it in twelve pieces: and he said to Jeroboam,

"Take thee ten pieces: for thus saith the Lord, the God of Israel, 'Behold, I will rend the kingdom out of the hand of Solomon, and will give ten tribes to thee: because that they have forsaken me, and have worshipped Ashtoreth the goddess of the Sidonians, Chemosh the god of the Moabites, and Milcom the god of the children of Ammon, and have not walked in my ways, to do that which is right in mine eyes, and to keep my statutes and my judgments, as did David his father. Howbeit I will not take the whole kingdom out of his hand: but I will make him prince all the days of his life for David my servant's sake, whom I chose, because he kept my commandments and my statutes: but I will take the kingdom out of his son's hand, and will give it unto thee, even ten tribes. And unto his son will I give one tribe, that David my servant may have a light alway before me in Jerusalem, the city which I have chosen me to put my name there. And I will take thee, and thou shalt reign according to all that thy soul desireth, and shalt be king over Israel. And it shall be, if thou wilt hearken unto all that I command thee, and wilt walk in my ways, and do that is right in my sight, to keep my statutes and my commandments, as David my servant did; that I will be with thee, and build thee a sure house, as I built for David, and will give Israel unto thee. And I will for this afflict the seed of David, but not for ever.'"

Solomon sought therefore to kill Jeroboam. And Jeroboam arose, and fled into Egypt, unto Shishak king of Egypt, and was in Egypt until the death of Solomon. And the rest of the acts of Solomon, and all that he did, and his wisdom, are they not written in the Book of the Acts of Solomon? And the time that Solo-

THE FIRST BOOK OF THE KINGS

mon reigned in Jerusalem over all Israel was forty years. And Solomon slept with his fathers, and was buried in the city of David his father: and Rehoboam his son reigned in his stead.

The Division of the Kingdom

And Rehoboam went to Shechem: for all Israel were come to Shechem to make him king. And it came to pass, when Jeroboam the son of Nebat, who was yet in Egypt, heard of it (for he was fled from the presence of King Solomon, and Jeroboam dwelt in Egypt); that they sent and called him. And Jeroboam and all the congregation of Israel came, and spoke unto Rehoboam, saying,

"Thy father made our yoke grievous: now therefore make thou the grievous service of thy father, and his heavy yoke which he put upon us, lighter, and we will serve thee."

And he said unto them, "Depart yet for three days, then come again to me." And the people departed.

And King Rehoboam consulted with the old men, that stood before Solomon his father while he yet lived, and said, "How do ye advise that I may answer this people?"

And they spoke unto him, saying, "If thou wilt be a servant unto this people this day, and wilt serve them, and answer them, and speak good words to them, then they will be thy servants for ever."

But he forsook the counsel of the old men, which they had given him, and consulted with the young men that were grown up with him, and which stood before him: and he said unto them, "What counsel give ye that we may answer this people, who have spoken to me, saying, 'Make the yoke which thy father did put upon us lighter'?"

And the young men that were grown up with him spoke unto him, saying, "Thus shalt thou speak unto this people that spoke unto thee, saying, 'Thy father made our yoke heavy, but make thou it lighter unto us'; thus shalt thou say unto them, 'My little finger shall be thicker than my father's loins. And now whereas my father did lade you with a heavy yoke, I will add to your yoke: my father hath chastised you with whips, but I will chastise you with scorpions.'"

So Jeroboam and all the people came to Rehoboam the third day, as the king had appointed, saying, "Come to me again the third day."

And the king answered the people roughly, and forsook the old men's counsel that they gave him, and spoke to them after the counsel of the young men, saying, "My father made your yoke heavy, and I will add to your yoke: my father also chastised you with whips, but I will chastise you with scorpions."

Wherefore the king hearkened not unto the people; for the cause was from the Lord, that he might perform his saying, which the Lord spoke by Ahijah the Shilonite unto Jeroboam the son of Nebat.

So when all Israel saw that the king hearkened not unto them, the people answered the king, saying, "What portion have we in David? neither have we inheritance in the son of Jesse: to your tents, O Israel: now see to thine own house, David." So Israel departed unto their tents.

But as for the children of Israel which dwelt in the cities of Judah, Rehoboam reigned over them. Then King Rehoboam sent Adoram, who was over the tribute; and all Israel stoned him with stones, that he died. Therefore King Rehoboam made speed to get him up to his chariot, to flee to Jerusalem. So Israel rebelled against the house of David unto this day. And it came to pass, when all Israel heard that Jeroboam was come again, that they sent and called him unto the congregation, and made him king over all Israel: there was none that followed the house of David, but the tribe of Judah only.

Elijah the Tishbite

And in the thirty and eighth year of Asa king of Judah began Ahab the son of Omri to reign over Israel: and Ahab the son of Omri reigned over Israel in Samaria twenty and two years. And

THE FIRST BOOK OF THE KINGS

Ahab the son of Omri did evil in the sight of the Lord above all that were before him. And it came to pass, as if it had been a light thing for him to walk in the sins of Jeroboam the son of Nebat, that he took to wife Jezebel the daughter of Ethbaal King of the Sidonians, and went and served Baal, and worshipped him. And he reared up an altar for Baal in the house of Baal, which he had built in Samaria. And Ahab made a grove; and Ahab did more to provoke the Lord God of Israel to anger than all the kings of Israel that were before him.

And Elijah the Tishbite, who was of the inhabitants of Gilead, said unto Ahab, "As the Lord God of Israel liveth, before whom I stand, there shall not be dew nor rain these years, but according to my word."

And the word of the Lord came unto him, saying, "Get thee hence, and turn thee eastward, and hide thyself by the brook Cherith, that is before Jordan. And it shall be that thou shalt drink of the brook; and I have commanded the ravens to feed thee there."

So he went and did according unto the word of the Lord: for he went and dwelt by the brook Cherith, that is before Jordan. And the ravens brought him bread and flesh in the morning, and bread and flesh in the evening; and he drank of the brook. And it came to pass after a while, that the brook dried up, because there had been no rain in the land.

And the word of the Lord came unto him, saying, "Arise, get thee to Zarephath, which belongeth to Sidon, and dwell there: behold, I have commanded a widow woman there to sustain thee."

So he arose and went to Zarephath. And when he came to the gate of the city, behold, the widow woman was there gathering of sticks: and he called to her, and said, "Fetch me, I pray thee, a little water in a vessel, that I may drink." And as she was going to fetch it, he called to her, and said, "Bring me, I pray thee, a morsel of bread in thine hand."

And she said, "As the Lord thy God liveth, I have not a cake, but a handful of meal in a barrel, and a little oil in a cruse: and,

THE FIRST BOOK OF THE KINGS

behold, I am gathering two sticks, that I may go in and dress it for me and my son, that we may eat it, and die."

And Elijah said unto her, "Fear not; go and do as thou hast said: but make me thereof a little cake first, and bring it unto me, and after make for thee and for thy son. For thus saith the Lord God of Israel, 'The barrel of meal shall not waste, neither shall the cruse of oil fail, until the day that the Lord sendeth rain upon the earth.'"

And she went and did according to the saying of Elijah: and she, and he, and her house, did eat many days. And the barrel of meal wasted not, neither did the cruse of oil fail, according to the word of the Lord, which he spoke by Elijah.

And it came to pass after these things, that the son of the woman, the mistress of the house, fell sick; and his sickness was so sore that there was no breath left in him. And she said unto Elijah, "What have I to do with thee, O thou man of God? art thou come unto me to call my sin to remembrance, and to slay my son?"

And he said unto her, "Give me thy son."

And he took him out of her bosom, and carried him up into a loft, where he abode, and laid him upon his own bed. And he cried unto the Lord, and said, "O Lord my God, hast thou also brought evil upon the widow with whom I sojourn, by slaying her son?"

And he stretched himself upon the child three times, and cried unto the Lord, and said, "O Lord my God, I pray thee, let this child's soul come into him again."

And the Lord heard the voice of Elijah; and the soul of the child came into him again, and he revived. And Elijah took the child, and brought him down out of the chamber into the house, and delivered him unto his mother: and Elijah said, "See, thy son liveth."

And the woman said to Elijah, "Now by this I know that thou art a man of God, and that the word of the Lord in thy mouth is truth."

And it came to pass after many days, that the word of the

THE FIRST BOOK OF THE KINGS

Lord came to Elijah in the third year, saying, "Go, show thyself unto Ahab; and I will send rain upon the earth." And Elijah went to show himself unto Ahab.

And there was a sore famine in Samaria. And Ahab called Obadiah, which was the governor of his house. (Now Obadiah feared the Lord greatly: for it was so, when Jezebel cut off the prophets of the Lord, that Obadiah took a hundred prophets, and hid them by fifty in a cave, and fed them with bread and water.) And Ahab said unto Obadiah, "Go into the land, unto all fountains of water, and unto all brooks: peradventure we may find grass to save the horses and mules alive, that we lose not all the beasts."

So they divided the land between them to pass throughout it: Ahab went one way by himself, and Obadiah went another way by himself. And as Obadiah was in the way, behold, Elijah met him: and he knew him, and fell on his face, and said, "Art thou that my lord Elijah?"

And he answered him, "I am: go, tell thy lord, 'Behold, Elijah is here.'"

And he said, "What have I sinned, that thou wouldest deliver thy servant into the hand of Ahab, to slay me? As the Lord thy God liveth, there is no nation or kingdom, whither my lord hath not sent to seek thee: and when they said, 'He is not there'; he took an oath of the kingdom and nation, that they found thee not. And now thou sayest, 'Go, tell thy lord, "Behold, Elijah is here."' And it shall come to pass, as soon as I am gone from thee, that the Spirit of the Lord shall carry thee whither I know not; and so when I come and tell Ahab, and he cannot find thee, he shall slay me: but I thy servant fear the Lord from my youth. Was it not told my lord what I did when Jezebel slew the prophets of the Lord, how I hid a hundred men of the Lord's prophets by fifty in a cave, and fed them with bread and water? And now thou sayest, 'Go, tell thy lord, "Behold, Elijah is here"': and he shall slay me."

And Elijah said, "As the Lord of hosts liveth, before whom I stand, I will surely show myself unto him to-day."

THE FIRST BOOK OF THE KINGS

So Obadiah went to meet Ahab, and told him: and Ahab went to meet Elijah.

And it came to pass, when Ahab saw Elijah, that Ahab said unto him, "Art thou he that troubleth Israel?"

And he answered, "I have not troubled Israel; but thou, and thy father's house, in that ye have forsaken the commandments of the Lord, and thou hast followed Baalim. Now therefore send, and gather to me all Israel unto Mount Carmel, and the prophets of Baal four hundred and fifty, and the prophets of the groves four hundred, which eat at Jezebel's table."

So Ahab sent unto all the children of Israel, and gathered the prophets together unto Mount Carmel. And Elijah came unto all the people, and said, "How long halt ye between two opinions? if the Lord be God, follow him: but if Baal, then follow him." And the people answered him not a word.

Then said Elijah unto the people, "I, even I only, remain a prophet of the Lord; but Baal's prophets are four hundred and fifty men. Let them therefore give us two bullocks; and let them choose one bullock for themselves, and cut it in pieces, and lay it on wood, and put no fire under: and I will dress the other bullock, and lay it on wood, and put no fire under: and call ye on the name of your gods, and I will call on the name of the Lord: and the God that answereth by fire, let him be God." And all the people answered and said, "It is well spoken."

And Elijah said unto the prophets of Baal, "Choose you one bullock for yourselves, and dress it first; for ye are many; and call on the name of your gods, but put no fire under."

And they took the bullock which was given them, and they dressed it, and called on the name of Baal from morning even until noon, saying, "O Baal, hear us." But there was no voice, nor any that answered. And they leaped upon the altar which was made.

And it came to pass at noon, that Elijah mocked them, and said, "Cry aloud: for he is a god; either he is talking, or he is pursuing, or he is in a journey, or peradventure he sleepeth, and must be awaked."

THE FIRST BOOK OF THE KINGS

And they cried aloud, and cut themselves after their manner with knives and lancets, till the blood gushed out upon them. And it came to pass, when midday was past, and they prophesied until the time of the offering of the evening sacrifice, that there was neither voice, nor any to answer, nor any that regarded.

And Elijah said unto all the people, "Come near unto me." And all the people came near unto him. And he repaired the altar of the Lord that was broken down. And Elijah took twelve stones, according to the number of the tribes of the sons of Jacob, unto whom the word of the Lord came, saying, "Israel shall be thy name": and with the stones he built an altar in the name of the Lord: and he made a trench about the altar, as great as would contain two measures of seed. And he put the wood in order, and cut the bullock in pieces, and laid him on the wood, and said, "Fill four barrels with water, and pour it on the burnt sacrifice, and on the wood." And he said, "Do it the second time." And they did it the second time. And he said, "Do it the third time." And they did it the third time. And the water ran round about the altar; and he filled the trench also with water.

And it came to pass at the time of the offering of the evening sacrifice, that Elijah the prophet came near, and said, "Lord God of Abraham, Isaac, and of Israel, let it be known this day that thou art God in Israel, and that I am thy servant, and that I have done all these things at thy word. Hear me, O Lord, hear me, that this people may know that thou art the Lord God, and that thou hast turned their heart back again."

Then the fire of the Lord fell, and consumed the burnt sacrifice, and the wood, and the stones, and the dust, and licked up the water that was in the trench. And when all the people saw it, they fell on their faces: and they said, "The Lord, he is the God; the Lord, he is the God."

And Elijah said unto them, "Take the prophets of Baal; let not one of them escape." And they took them: and Elijah brought them down to the brook Kishon, and slew them there.

THE FIRST BOOK OF THE KINGS

And Elijah said unto Ahab, "Get thee up, eat and drink; for there is a sound of abundance of rain."

So Ahab went up to eat and to drink. And Elijah went up to the top of Carmel; and he cast himself down upon the earth, and put his face between his knees, and said to his servant, "Go up now, look toward the sea." And he went up, and looked, and said, "There is nothing." And he said, "Go again seven times."

And it came to pass at the seventh time, that he said, "Behold, there ariseth a little cloud out of the sea, like a man's hand." And he said, "Go up, say unto Ahab, 'Prepare thy chariot, and get thee down, that the rain stop thee not.'"

And it came to pass in the mean while, that the heaven was black with clouds and wind, and there was a great rain. And Ahab rode, and went to Jezreel. And the hand of the Lord was on Elijah; and he girded up his loins, and ran before Ahab to the entrance of Jezreel.

And Ahab told Jezebel all that Elijah had done, and withal how he had slain all the prophets with the sword. Then Jezebel sent a messenger unto Elijah, saying, "So let the gods do to me, and more also, if I make not thy life as the life of one of them by to-morrow about this time."

And when he saw that, he arose, and went for his life, and came to Beer-sheba, which belongeth to Judah, and left his servant there. But he himself went a day's journey into the wilderness, and came and sat down under a juniper tree: and he requested for himself that he might die; and said, "It is enough; now, O Lord, take away my life; for I am not better than my fathers."

And as he lay and slept under a juniper tree, behold, then an angel touched him, and said unto him, "Arise and eat."

And he looked, and, behold, there was a cake baked on the coals, and a cruse of water at his head. And he did eat and drink, and laid him down again. And the angel of the Lord came again the second time, and touched him, and said, "Arise and eat; because the journey is too great for thee."

THE FIRST BOOK OF THE KINGS

And he arose, and did eat and drink, and went in the strength of that meat forty days and forty nights unto Horeb the mount of God. And he came thither unto a cave, and lodged there. And, behold, the Lord passed by, and a great and strong wind rent the mountains, and broke in pieces the rocks before the Lord; but the Lord was not in the wind: and after the wind an earthquake; but the Lord was not in the earthquake: and after the earthquake a fire; but the Lord was not in the fire: and after the fire a still small voice. And it was so, when Elijah heard it, that he wrapped his face in his mantle, and went out, and stood in the entering in of the cave. And, behold, there came a voice unto him, and said,

"What doest thou here, Elijah?"

And he said, "I have been very jealous for the Lord God of hosts: because the children of Israel have forsaken thy covenant, thrown down thine altars, and slain thy prophets with the sword; and I, even I only, am left; and they seek my life, to take it away."

And the Lord said unto him, "Go, return on thy way to the wilderness of Damascus: and when thou comest, anoint Hazael to be king over Syria; and Jehu the son of Nimshi shalt thou anoint to be king over Israel; and Elisha the son of Shaphat of Abel-meholah shalt thou anoint to be prophet in thy room. And it shall come to pass that him that escapeth the sword of Hazael shall Jehu slay: and him that escapeth from the sword of Jehu shall Elisha slay. Yet I have left me seven thousand in Israel, all the knees which have not bowed unto Baal, and every mouth which hath not kissed him."

So he departed thence, and found Elisha the son of Shaphat, who was plowing with twelve yoke of oxen before him, and he with the twelfth: and Elijah passed by him, and cast his mantle upon him. And he left the oxen, and ran after Elijah, and said, "Let me, I pray thee, kiss my father and my mother, and then I will follow thee." And he said unto him, "Go back again: for what have I done to thee?"

And he returned back from him, and took a yoke of oxen, and

slew them, and boiled their flesh with the instruments of the oxen, and gave unto the people, and they did eat. Then he arose, and went after Elijah, and ministered unto him.

And it came to pass after these things, that Naboth the Jezreelite had a vineyard, which was in Jezreel, hard by the palace of Ahab king of Samaria. And Ahab spoke unto Naboth, saying, "Give me thy vineyard, that I may have it for a garden of herbs, because it is near unto my house: and I will give thee for it a better vineyard than it; or, if it seem good to thee, I will give thee the worth of it in money."

And Naboth said to Ahab, "The Lord forbid it me, that I should give the inheritance of my fathers unto thee."

And Ahab came into his house heavy and displeased because of the word which Naboth the Jezreelite had spoken to him: for he had said, "I will not give thee the inheritance of my fathers." And he laid him down upon his bed, and turned away his face, and would eat no bread.

But Jezebel his wife came to him, and said unto him, "Why is thy spirit so sad, that thou eatest no bread?"

And he said unto her, "Because I spoke unto Naboth the Jezreelite, and said unto him, 'Give me thy vineyard for money; or else, if it please thee, I will give thee another vineyard for it': and he answered, 'I will not give thee my vineyard.'"

And Jezebel his wife said unto him, "Dost thou now govern the kingdom of Israel? arise, and eat bread, and let thine heart be merry: I will give thee the vineyard of Naboth the Jezreelite."

So she wrote letters in Ahab's name, and sealed them with his seal, and sent the letters unto the elders and to the nobles that were in his city, dwelling with Naboth. And she wrote in the letters, saying, "Proclaim a fast, and set Naboth on high among the people: and set two men, sons of Belial, before him, to bear witness against him, saying, 'Thou didst blaspheme God and the king.' And then carry him out, and stone him, that he may die."

And the men of his city, even the elders and the nobles who were the inhabitants in his city, did as Jezebel had sent unto

THE FIRST BOOK OF THE KINGS

them, and as it was written in the letters which she had sent unto them. They proclaimed a fast, and set Naboth on high among the people. And there came in two men, children of Belial, and sat before him: and the men of Belial witnessed against him, even against Naboth, in the presence of the people, saying, "Naboth did blaspheme God and the king." Then they carried him forth out of the city, and stoned him with stones, that he died.

Then they sent to Jezebel, saying, "Naboth is stoned, and is dead." And it came to pass, when Jezebel heard that Naboth was stoned, and was dead, that Jezebel said to Ahab, "Arise, take possession of the vineyard of Naboth the Jezreelite, which he refused to give thee for money: for Naboth is not alive, but dead."

And it came to pass, when Ahab heard that Naboth was dead, that Ahab rose up to go down to the vineyard of Naboth the Jezreelite, to take possession of it.

And the word of the Lord came to Elijah the Tishbite, saying, "Arise, go down to meet Ahab king of Israel, which is in Samaria: behold, he is in the vineyard of Naboth, whither he is gone down to possess it. And thou shalt speak unto him, saying, 'Thus saith the Lord, "Hast thou killed, and also taken possession?"' And thou shalt speak unto him, saying, 'Thus saith the Lord, "In the place where dogs licked the blood of Naboth shall dogs lick thy blood, even thine."'"

And Ahab said to Elijah, "Hast thou found me, O mine enemy?"

And he answered, "I have found thee: because thou hast sold thyself to work evil in the sight of the Lord. Behold, I will bring evil upon thee, and will take away thy posterity, and will cut off from Ahab him that pisseth against the wall, and him that is shut up and left in Israel, and will make thine house like the house of Jeroboam the son of Nebat, and like the house of Baasha the son of Ahijah, for the provocation wherewith thou hast provoked me to anger, and made Israel to sin. And of Jezebel also spoke the Lord, saying, 'The dogs shall eat Jezebel by the wall

THE FIRST BOOK OF THE KINGS

of Jezreel.' Him that dieth of Ahab in the city the dogs shall eat; and him that dieth in the field shall the fowls of the air eat."

And it came to pass, when Ahab heard those words, that he rent his clothes, and put sackcloth upon his flesh, and fasted, and lay in sackcloth, and went softly. And the word of the Lord came to Elijah the Tishbite, saying, "Seest thou how Ahab humbleth himself before me? because he humbleth himself before me, I will not bring evil in his days: but in his son's days will I bring the evil upon his house."

THE SECOND BOOK OF THE KINGS

THE DIVISION between the First and Second Books of the Kings is purely artificial, as there is no break in the narrative or alteration of point of view, except that the account of the actual fall of Jerusalem was written later than the rest during the Exile. There is, however, a striking contrast of character between the protagonists of the two works. The stern and solitary Elijah, coming out of the wilderness and retiring into it, dramatic and mysterious, irreconcilable in his hostility to the reigning powers of his day, was of the type later seen in Amos and John the Baptist. The milder figure of his disciple Elisha, on the other hand, is that of one who belongs to a movement instead of initiating it. His is emphatically the world of men; the "sons of the prophets" in whose company he is found is a semiprofessional association; in fomenting the rebellion of Jehu he enters directly into political life, and, as regards statesmanship, unwisely so, since however beneficial Jehu's fidelity to the religion of Jehovah may have been his ruthless slaughter of the opposing faction further weakened the strength of the kingdom. The hope of exercising direct influence upon the monarchy was often present to the prophets and in the case of Isaiah was superbly realized, but it was very dangerous to their independence and integrity, as the attainment of political influence brought with it great temptations to corruption. In the years following Elisha the order fell into such disrepute that Amos, who was to inaugurate the prophetic revival of the seventh century, stoutly declared that he was "neither a prophet nor the son of a prophet."

Of special interest in the Second Book of the Kings are the accounts of the reigns of Hezekiah and Josiah: the former for its references to Isaiah and its story of Sennacherib's strange defeat, also mentioned by Herodotus but attributed by him to an incursion of field mice which gnawed away the bowstrings of the Assyrian warriors—from which some modern critics have inferred that the Assyrian army succumbed to an attack of the bubonic plague frequently carried by rodents; the narrative of the reign of Josiah still more significant for its precious account of the discovery of the all-important Book of Deuteronomy.

The Second Book of THE KINGS

The Miracles of Elisha

AND IT CAME TO PASS, when the Lord would take up Elijah into heaven by a whirlwind, that Elijah went with Elisha from Gilgal. And Elijah said unto Elisha, "Tarry here, I pray thee; for the Lord hath sent me to Beth-el." And Elisha said unto him, "As the Lord liveth, and as thy soul liveth, I will not leave thee."

So they went down to Beth-el. And the sons of the prophets that were at Beth-el came forth to Elisha, and said unto him, "Knowest thou that the Lord will take away thy master from thy head to-day?" And he said, "Yea, I know it; hold ye your peace."

And Elijah said unto him, "Elisha, tarry here, I pray thee; for the Lord hath sent me to Jericho." And he said, "As the Lord liveth, and as thy soul liveth, I will not leave thee."

So they came to Jericho. And the sons of the prophets that were at Jericho came to Elisha, and said unto him, "Knowest thou that the Lord will take away thy master from thy head to-day?" And he answered, "Yea, I know it; hold ye your peace."

And Elijah said unto him, "Tarry, I pray thee, here; for the Lord hath sent me to Jordan." And he said, "As the Lord liveth, and as thy soul liveth, I will not leave thee."

And they two went on. And fifty men of the sons of the prophets went, and stood to view afar off: and they two stood by Jordan. And Elijah took his mantle, and wrapped it together, and smote the waters, and they were divided hither and thither,

THE SECOND BOOK OF THE KINGS

so that they two went over on dry ground. And it came to pass, when they were gone over, that Elijah said unto Elisha,

"Ask what I shall do for thee, before I be taken away from thee."

And Elisha said, "I pray thee, let a double portion of thy spirit be upon me."

And he said, "Thou hast asked a hard thing: nevertheless, if thou see me when I am taken from thee, it shall be so unto thee; but if not, it shall not be so."

And it came to pass, as they still went on, and talked, that, behold, there appeared a chariot of fire, and horses of fire, and parted them both asunder; and Elijah went up by a whirlwind into heaven. And Elisha saw it, and he cried,

"My father, my father, the chariot of Israel, and the horsemen thereof!"

And he saw him no more: and he took hold of his own clothes, and rent them in two pieces. He took up also the mantle of Elijah that fell from him, and went back, and stood by the bank of Jordan. And he took the mantle of Elijah that fell from him, and smote the waters, and said,

"Where is the Lord God of Elijah?"

And when he also had smitten the waters, they parted hither and thither: and Elisha went over. And when the sons of the prophets which were to view at Jericho saw him, they said,

"The spirit of Elijah doth rest on Elisha."

And they came to meet him, and bowed themselves to the ground before him. And they said unto him, "Behold now, there be with thy servants fifty strong men; let them go, we pray thee, and seek thy master: lest peradventure the Spirit of the Lord hath taken him up, and cast him upon some mountain, or into some valley."

And he said, "Ye shall not send." And when they urged him till he was ashamed, he said, "Send!" They sent therefore fifty men; and they sought three days, but found him not. And when they came again to him (for he tarried at Jericho), he said unto them, "Did I not say unto you, 'Go not'?"

THE SECOND BOOK OF THE KINGS

And the men of the city said unto Elisha, "Behold, I pray thee, the situation of this city is pleasant, as my lord seeth: but the water is naught, and the ground barren."

And he said, "Bring me a new cruse, and put salt therein."

And they brought it to him. And he went forth unto the spring of the waters, and cast the salt in there, and said, "Thus saith the Lord, 'I have healed these waters; there shall not be from thence any more death or barren land.'"

So the waters were healed unto this day, according to the saying of Elisha which he spoke.

And he went up from thence unto Beth-el; and as he was going up by the way, there came forth little children out of the city, and mocked him, and said unto him, "Go up, thou bald head; go up, thou bald head."

And he turned back, and looked on them, and cursed them in the name of the Lord. And there came forth two she-bears out of the wood, and tore forty and two children of them.

And he went from thence to Mount Carmel, and from thence he returned to Samaria.

And Mesha king of Moab was a sheepmaster, and rendered unto the king of Israel a hundred thousand lambs, and a hundred thousand rams, with the wool. But it came to pass, when Ahab was dead, that the king of Moab rebelled against the king of Israel.

And King Jehoram went out of Samaria the same time, and numbered all Israel. And he went and sent to Jehoshaphat the king of Judah, saying, "The king of Moab hath rebelled against me: wilt thou go with me against Moab to battle?"

And he said, "I will go up: I am as thou art, my people as thy people, and my horses as thy horses."

And he said, "Which way shall we go up?"

And he answered, "The way through the wilderness of Edom."

So the king of Israel went, and the king of Judah, and the king

THE SECOND BOOK OF THE KINGS

of Edom: and they fetched a compass of seven days' journey: and there was no water for the host, and for the cattle that followed them. And the king of Israel said, "Alas! that the Lord hath called these three kings together, to deliver them into the hand of Moab!"

But Jehoshaphat said, "Is there not here a prophet of the Lord, that we may enquire of the Lord by him?"

And one of the king of Israel's servants answered and said, "Here is Elisha the son of Shaphat, which poured water on the hands of Elijah."

And Jehoshaphat said, "The word of the Lord is with him."

So the king of Israel and Jehoshaphat and the king of Edom went down to him. And Elisha said unto the king of Israel, "What have I to do with thee? get thee to the prophets of thy father, and to the prophets of thy mother."

And the king of Israel said unto him, "Nay: for the Lord hath called these three kings together, to deliver them into the hand of Moab."

And Elisha said, "As the Lord of hosts liveth, before whom I stand, surely, were it not that I regard the presence of Jehoshaphat the king of Judah, I would not look toward thee, nor to see thee. But now bring me a minstrel."

And it came to pass, when the minstrel played, that the hand of the Lord came upon him. And he said, "Thus saith the Lord, 'Make this valley full of ditches.' For thus saith the Lord, 'Ye shall not see wind, neither shall ye see rain; yet that valley shall be filled with water, that ye may drink, both ye, and your cattle, and your beasts.' And this is but a light thing in the sight of the Lord: he will deliver the Moabites also into your hand. And ye shall smite every fenced city, and every choice city, and shall fell every good tree, and stop all wells of water, and mar every good piece of land with stones."

And it came to pass in the morning, when the meat offering was offered, that, behold, there came water by the way of Edom, and the country was filled with water.

THE SECOND BOOK OF THE KINGS

And when all the Moabites heard that the kings were come up to fight against them, they gathered all that were able to put on armour, and upward, and stood in the border. And they rose up early in the morning, and the sun shone upon the water, and the Moabites saw the water on the other side as red as blood; and they said, "This is blood: the kings are surely slain, and they have smitten one another: now therefore, Moab, to the spoil."

And when they came to the camp of Israel, the Israelites rose up and smote the Moabites, so that they fled before them: but they went forward smiting the Moabites, even in their country. And they beat down the cities, and on every good piece of land cast every man his stone, and filled it; and they stopped all the wells of water, and felled all the good trees: only in Kir-haraseth left they the stones thereof; howbeit the slingers went about it, and smote it.

Now there cried a certain woman of the wives of the sons of the prophets unto Elisha, saying, "Thy servant my husband is dead; and thou knowest that thy servant did fear the Lord: and the creditor is come to take unto him my two sons to be bondmen."

And Elisha said unto her, "What shall I do for thee? tell me, what hast thou in the house?"

And she said, "Thine handmaid hath not any thing in the house, save a pot of oil."

Then he said, "Go, borrow thee vessels abroad of all thy neighbours, even empty vessels; borrow not a few. And when thou art come in, thou shalt shut the door upon thee and upon thy sons, and shalt pour out into all those vessels, and thou shalt set aside that which is full."

So she went from him, and shut the door upon her and upon her sons, who brought the vessels to her; and she poured out. And it came to pass, when the vessels were full, that she said unto her son, "Bring me yet a vessel." And he said unto her, "There is not a vessel more." And the oil stayed.

Then she came and told the man of God. And he said, "Go,

THE SECOND BOOK OF THE KINGS

sell the oil, and pay thy debt, and live thou and thy children of the rest."

And it fell on a day, that Elisha passed to Shunem, where was a great woman; and she constrained him to eat bread. And so it was that as oft as he passed by, he turned in thither to eat bread. And she said unto her husband, "Behold now, I perceive that this is a holy man of God, which passeth by us continually. Let us make a little chamber, I pray thee, on the wall; and let us set for him there a bed, and a table, and a stool, and a candlestick: and it shall be, when he cometh to us, that he shall turn in thither."

And it fell on a day, that he came thither, and he turned into the chamber, and lay there. And he said to Gehazi his servant, "Call this Shunammite."

And when he had called her, she stood before him. And he said unto him, "Say now unto her, 'Behold, thou hast been careful for us with all this care; what is to be done for thee? wouldest thou be spoken for to the king, or to the captain of the host?'"

And she answered, "I dwell among mine own people."

And he said, "What then is to be done for her?" And Gehazi answered, "Verily she hath no child, and her husband is old."

And he said, "Call her." And when he had called her, she stood in the door. And he said, "About this season, according to the time of life, thou shalt embrace a son." And she said, "Nay, my lord, thou man of God, do not lie unto thine handmaid."

And the woman conceived, and bore a son at that season that Elisha had said unto her, according to the time of life. And when the child was grown, it fell on a day, that he went out to his father to the reapers.

And he said unto his father, "My head, my head."

And he said to a lad, "Carry him to his mother."

And when he had taken him, and brought him to his mother, he sat on her knees till noon, and then died. And she went up, and laid him on the bed of the man of God, and shut the door upon him, and went out.

THE SECOND BOOK OF THE KINGS

And she called unto her husband, and said, "Send me, I pray thee, one of the young men, and one of the asses, that I may run to the man of God, and come again." And he said, "Wherefore wilt thou go to him to-day? it is neither new moon, nor sabbath." And she said, "It shall be well."

Then she saddled an ass, and said to her servant, "Drive, and go forward; slack not thy riding for me, except I bid thee."

So she went and came unto the man of God to Mount Carmel. And it came to pass, when the man of God saw her afar off, that he said to Gehazi his servant, "Behold, yonder is that Shunammite. Run now, I pray thee, to meet her, and say unto her, 'Is it well with thee? is it well with thy husband? is it well with the child?'" And she answered, "It is well."

And when she came to the man of God to the hill, she caught him by the feet: but Gehazi came near to thrust her away. And the man of God said, "Let her alone; for her soul is vexed within her: and the Lord hath hid it from me, and hath not told me."

Then she said, "Did I desire a son of my lord? did I not say, 'Do not deceive me'?"

Then he said to Gehazi, "Gird up thy loins, and take my staff in thine hand, and go thy way: if thou meet any man, salute him not; and if any salute thee, answer him not again: and lay my staff upon the face of the child."

And the mother of the child said, "As the Lord liveth, and as thy soul liveth, I will not leave thee." And he arose, and followed her.

And Gehazi passed on before them, and laid the staff upon the face of the child; but there was neither voice, nor hearing. Wherefore he went again to meet him, and told him, saying, "The child is not awaked."

And when Elisha was come into the house, behold, the child was dead, and laid upon his bed. He went in therefore, and shut the door upon them twain, and prayed unto the Lord. And he went up, and lay upon the child, and put his mouth upon his mouth, and his eyes upon his eyes, and his hands upon his hands:

THE SECOND BOOK OF THE KINGS

and he stretched himself upon the child; and the flesh of the child waxed warm. Then he returned, and walked in the house to and fro; and went up, and stretched himself upon him: and the child sneezed seven times, and the child opened his eyes.

And he called Gehazi, and said, "Call this Shunammite." So he called her. And when she was come in unto him, he said, "Take up thy son." Then she went in, and fell at his feet, and bowed herself to the ground, and took up her son, and went out.

And Elisha came again to Gilgal: and there was a dearth in the land; and the sons of the prophets were sitting before him: and he said unto his servant, "Set on the great pot, and seethe pottage for the sons of the prophets."

And one went out into the field to gather herbs, and found a wild vine, and gathered thereof wild gourds his lap full, and came and shred them into the pot of pottage: for they knew them not. So they poured out for the men to eat. And it came to pass, as they were eating of the pottage, that they cried out, and said,

"O thou man of God, there is death in the pot."

And they could not eat thereof. But he said, "Then bring meal." And he cast it into the pot; and he said, "Pour out for the people, that they may eat."

And there was no harm in the pot.

Now Naaman, captain of the host of the king of Syria, was a great man with his master, and honourable, because by him the Lord had given deliverance unto Syria: he was also a mighty man in valour, but he was a leper. And the Syrians had gone out by companies, and had brought away captive out of the land of Israel a little maid; and she waited on Naaman's wife. And she said unto his mistress, "Would God my lord were with the prophet that is in Samaria! for he would recover him of his leprosy."

THE SECOND BOOK OF THE KINGS

And one went in, and told his lord, saying, "Thus and thus said the maid that is of the land of Israel."

And the king of Syria said, "Go to, go, and I will send a letter unto the king of Israel."

And he departed, and took with him ten talents of silver, and six thousand pieces of gold, and ten changes of raiment. And he brought the letter to the king of Israel, saying, "Now when this letter is come unto thee, behold, I have therewith sent Naaman my servant to thee, that thou mayest recover him of his leprosy."

And it came to pass, when the king of Israel had read the letter, that he rent his clothes, and said, "Am I God, to kill and to make alive, that this man doth send unto me to recover a man of his leprosy? wherefore consider, I pray you, and see how he seeketh a quarrel against me."

And it was so, when Elisha the man of God had heard that the king of Israel had rent his clothes, that he sent to the king, saying, "Wherefore hast thou rent thy clothes? let him come now to me, and he shall know that there is a prophet in Israel."

So Naaman came with his horses and with his chariot, and stood at the door of the house of Elisha. And Elisha sent a messenger unto him, saying, "Go and wash in Jordan seven times, and thy flesh shall come again to thee, and thou shalt be clean."

But Naaman was wroth, and went away, and said, "Behold, I thought, 'He will surely come out to me, and stand, and call on the name of the Lord his God, and strike his hand over the place, and recover the leper.' Are not Abana and Pharpar, rivers of Damascus, better than all the waters of Israel? may I not wash in them, and be clean?" So he turned and went away in a rage.

And his servants came near, and spoke unto him, and said, "My father, if the prophet had bid thee do some great thing, wouldest thou not have done it? how much rather then, when he saith to thee, 'Wash, and be clean'?"

Then went he down, and dipped himself seven times in Jordan, according to the saying of the man of God: and his flesh

THE SECOND BOOK OF THE KINGS

came again like unto the flesh of a little child, and he was clean. And he returned to the man of God, he and all his company, and came, and stood before him: and he said, "Behold, now I know that there is no God in all the earth, but in Israel: now therefore, I pray thee, take a blessing of thy servant."

But he said, "As the Lord liveth, before whom I stand, I will receive none." And he urged him to take it; but he refused.

And Naaman said, "Shall there not then, I pray thee, be given to thy servant two mules' burden of earth? for thy servant will henceforth offer neither burnt offering nor sacrifice unto other gods, but unto the Lord. In this thing the Lord pardon thy servant, that when my master goeth into the house of Rimmon to worship there, and he leaneth on my hand, and I bow myself in the house of Rimmon: when I bow down myself in the house of Rimmon, the Lord pardon thy servant in this thing."

And he said unto him, "Go in peace." So he departed from him a little way.

But Gehazi, the servant of Elisha the man of God, said, "Behold, my master hath spared Naaman this Syrian, in not receiving at his hands that which he brought: but, as the Lord liveth, I will run after him, and take somewhat of him."

So Gehazi followed after Naaman. And when Naaman saw him running after him, he lighted down from the chariot to meet him, and said, "Is all well?"

And he said, "All is well. My master hath sent me, saying, 'Behold, even now there be come to me from Mount Ephraim two young men of the sons of the prophets: give them, I pray thee, a talent of silver, and two changes of garments.'"

And Naaman said, "Be content, take two talents." And he urged him, and bound two talents of silver in two bags, with two changes of garments, and laid them upon two of his servants; and they bore them before him. And when he came to the tower, he took them from their hand, and bestowed them in the house: and he let the men go, and they departed.

But he went in, and stood before his master. And Elisha said

THE SECOND BOOK OF THE KINGS

unto him, "Whence comest thou, Gehazi?" And he said, "Thy servant went no whither." And he said unto him, "Went not mine heart with thee, when the man turned again from his chariot to meet thee? Is it a time to receive money, and to receive garments, and oliveyards, and vineyards, and sheep, and oxen, and menservants, and maidservants? The leprosy therefore of Naaman shall cleave unto thee, and unto thy seed for ever." And he went out from his presence a leper as white as snow.

And the sons of the prophets said unto Elisha, "Behold now, the place where we dwell with thee is too strait for us. Let us go, we pray thee, unto Jordan, and take thence every man a beam, and let us make us a place there, where we may dwell."
And he answered, "Go ye."
And one said, "Be content, I pray thee, and go with thy servants."
And he answered, "I will go."
So he went with them. And when they came to Jordan, they cut down wood. But as one was felling a beam, the ax head fell into the water; and he cried, and said, "Alas, master!" for it was borrowed.
And the man of God said, "Where fell it?" And he showed him the place. And he cut down a stick, and cast it in thither; and the iron did swim. Therefore said he, "Take it up to thee." And he put out his hand, and took it.

Then the king of Syria warred against Israel, and took counsel with his servants, saying, "In such and such a place shall be my camp."
And the man of God sent unto the king of Israel, saying, "Beware that thou pass not such a place; for thither the Syrians are come down."
And the king of Israel sent to the place which the man of God told him and warned him of, and saved himself there, not once nor twice.
Therefore the heart of the king of Syria was sore troubled for

THE SECOND BOOK OF THE KINGS

this thing; and he called his servants, and said unto them, "Will ye not show me which of us is for the king of Israel?"

And one of his servants said, "None, my lord, O king: but Elisha, the prophet that is in Israel, telleth the king of Israel the words that thou speakest in thy bedchamber."

And he said, "Go and spy where he is, that I may send and fetch him." And it was told him, saying, "Behold, he is in Dothan." Therefore sent he thither horses, and chariots, and a great host: and they came by night, and compassed the city about.

And when the servant of the man of God was risen early, and gone forth, behold, a host compassed the city both with horses and chariots. And his servant said unto him, "Alas, my master! how shall we do?"

And he answered, "Fear not: for they that be with us are more than they that be with them."

And Elisha prayed, and said, "Lord, I pray thee, open his eyes, that he may see." And the Lord opened the eyes of the young man; and he saw: and, behold, the mountain was full of horses and chariots of fire round about Elisha.

And when they came down to him, Elisha prayed unto the Lord, and said, "Smite this people, I pray thee, with blindness." And he smote them with blindness according to the word of Elisha.

And Elisha said unto them, "This is not the way, neither is this the city: follow me, and I will bring you to the man whom ye seek." But he led them to Samaria.

And it came to pass, when they were come into Samaria, that Elisha said, "Lord, open the eyes of these men, that they may see." And the Lord opened their eyes, and they saw; and, behold, they were in the midst of Samaria.

And the king of Israel said unto Elisha, when he saw them, "My father, shall I smite them? shall I smite them?"

And he answered, "Thou shalt not smite them: wouldest thou smite those whom thou hast taken captive with thy sword and with thy bow? set bread and water before them, that they may eat and drink, and go to their master."

THE SECOND BOOK OF THE KINGS

And he prepared great provision for them: and when they had eaten and drunk, he sent them away, and they went to their master. So the bands of Syria came no more into the land of Israel.

And Elisha came to Damascus; and Ben-hadad the king of Syria was sick; and it was told him, saying, "The man of God is come hither."

And the king said unto Hazael, "Take a present in thine hand, and go, meet the man of God, and enquire of the Lord by him, saying, 'Shall I recover of this disease?'"

So Hazael went to meet him, and took a present with him, even of every good thing of Damascus, forty camels' burden, and came and stood before him, and said, "Thy son Ben-hadad king of Syria hath sent me to thee, saying, 'Shall I recover of this disease?'"

And Elisha said unto him, "Go, say unto him, 'Thou mayest certainly recover': howbeit the Lord hath showed me that he shall surely die." And he settled his countenance steadfastly, until he was ashamed: and the man of God wept.

And Hazael said, "Why weepeth my lord?"

And he answered, "Because I know the evil that thou wilt do unto the children of Israel: their strong holds wilt thou set on fire, and their young men wilt thou slay with the sword, and wilt dash their children, and rip up their women with child."

And Hazael said, "But what, is thy servant a dog, that he should do this great thing?"

And Elisha answered, "The Lord hath showed me that thou shalt be king over Syria."

So he departed from Elisha, and came to his master, who said to him, "What said Elisha to thee?" And he answered, "He told me that thou shouldest surely recover."

And it came to pass on the morrow, that he took a thick cloth, and dipped it in water, and spread it on his face, so that he died: and Hazael reigned in his stead.

THE SECOND BOOK OF THE KINGS

The Conspiracy of Jehu

And Elisha the prophet called one of the children of the prophets, and said unto him, "Gird up thy loins, and take this box of oil in thine hand, and go to Ramoth-gilead: and when thou comest thither, look out there Jehu the son of Jehoshaphat the son of Nimshi, and go in, and make him arise up from among his brethren, and carry him to an inner chamber. Then take the box of oil, and pour it on his head, and say, 'Thus saith the Lord, "I have anointed thee king over Israel."' Then open the door, and flee, and tarry not."

So the young man, even the young man the prophet, went to Ramoth-gilead. And when he came, behold, the captains of the host were sitting; and he said, "I have an errand to thee, O captain."

And Jehu said, "Unto which of all us?"

And he said, "To thee, O captain."

And he arose, and went into the house; and he poured the oil on his head, and said unto him, "Thus saith the Lord God of Israel, 'I have anointed thee king over the people of the Lord, even over Israel. And thou shalt smite the house of Ahab thy master, that I may avenge the blood of my servants the prophets, and the blood of all the servants of the Lord, at the hand of Jezebel. For the whole house of Ahab shall perish: and I will cut off from Ahab him that pisseth against the wall, and him that is shut up and left in Israel: and I will make the house of Ahab like the house of Jeroboam the son of Nebat, and like the house of Baasha the son of Ahijah: and the dogs shall eat Jezebel in the portion of Jezreel, and there shall be none to bury her.'"

And he opened the door, and fled.

Then Jehu came forth to the servants of his lord: and one said unto him, "Is all well? wherefore came this mad fellow to thee?"

And he said unto them, "Ye know the man, and his communication."

And they said, "It is false; tell us now."

THE SECOND BOOK OF THE KINGS

And he said, "Thus and thus spoke he to me, saying, 'Thus saith the Lord, "I have anointed thee king over Israel."'"

Then they hastened, and took every man his garment, and put it under him on the top of the stairs, and blew with trumpets, saying, "Jehu is king."

So Jehu the son of Jehoshaphat the son of Nimshi conspired against Joram. (Now Joram had kept Ramoth-gilead, he and all Israel, because of Hazael king of Syria. But King Joram was returned to be healed in Jezreel of the wounds which the Syrians had given him, when he fought with Hazael king of Syria.) And Jehu said, "If it be your minds, then let none go forth nor escape out of the city to go to tell it in Jezreel."

So Jehu rode in a chariot, and went to Jezreel; for Joram lay there. And Ahaziah king of Judah was come down to see Joram. And there stood a watchman on the tower in Jezreel, and he spied the company of Jehu as he came, and said, "I see a company." And Joram said, "Take a horseman, and send to meet them, and let him say, 'Is it peace?'"

So there went one on horseback to meet him, and said, "Thus saith the king, 'Is it peace?'" And Jehu said, "What hast thou to do with peace? turn thee behind me." And the watchman told, saying, "The messenger came to them, but he cometh not again."

Then he sent out a second on horseback, which came to them, and said, "Thus saith the king, 'Is it peace?'" And Jehu answered, "What hast thou to do with peace? turn thee behind me." And the watchman told, saying, "He came even unto them, and cometh not again: and the driving is like the driving of Jehu the son of Nimshi; for he driveth furiously."

And Joram said, "Make ready." And his chariot was made ready. And Joram king of Israel and Ahaziah king of Judah went out, each in his chariot, and they went out against Jehu, and met him in the portion of Naboth the Jezreelite.

And it came to pass, when Joram saw Jehu, that he said, "Is it peace, Jehu?"

And he answered, "What peace, so long as the whoredoms of thy mother Jezebel and her witchcrafts are so many?"

THE SECOND BOOK OF THE KINGS

And Joram turned his hands, and fled, and said to Ahaziah, "There is treachery, O Ahaziah."

And Jehu drew a bow with his full strength, and smote Jehoram between his arms, and the arrow went out at his heart, and he sunk down in his chariot. Then said Jehu to Bidkar his captain, "Take up, and cast him in the portion of the field of Naboth the Jezreelite: for remember how that, when I and thou rode together after Ahab his father, the Lord laid his burden upon him. 'Surely I have seen yesterday the blood of Naboth, and the blood of his sons,' saith the Lord; 'and I will requite thee in this plot,' saith the Lord. Now therefore take and cast him into the plot of ground, according to the word of the Lord."

But when Ahaziah the king of Judah saw this, he fled by the way of the garden house. And Jehu followed after him, and said, "Smite him also in the chariot." And they did so at the going up to Gur, which is by Ibleam. And he fled to Megiddo, and died there.

And when Jehu was come to Jezreel, Jezebel heard of it; and she painted her face, and tired her head, and looked out at a window. And as Jehu entered in at the gate, she said, "Had Zimri peace, who slew his master?"

And he lifted up his face to the window, and said, "Who is on my side? who?" And there looked out to him two or three eunuchs.

And he said, "Throw her down." So they threw her down: and some of her blood was sprinkled on the wall, and on the horses: and he trod her under foot. And when he was come in, he did eat and drink, and said, "Go, see now this cursed woman, and bury her: for she is a king's daughter."

And they went to bury her: but they found no more of her than the skull, and the feet, and the palms of her hands.

Wherefore they came again, and told him. And he said, "This is the word of the Lord, which he spoke by his servant Elijah the Tishbite, saying, 'In the portion of Jezreel shall dogs eat the flesh of Jezebel: and the carcase of Jezebel shall be as dung upon the face of the field in the portion of Jezreel; so that they shall not say, "This is Jezebel."'"

THE SECOND BOOK OF THE KINGS

Now the rest of the acts of Jehu, and all that he did, and all his might, are they not written in the Book of the Chronicles of the Kings of Israel? And Jehu slept with his fathers: and they buried him in Samaria. And Jehoahaz his son reigned in his stead. And the time that Jehu reigned over Israel in Samaria was twenty and eight years.

The Death of Elisha

In the three and twentieth year of Joash, the son of Ahaziah king of Judah, Jehoahaz the son of Jehu began to reign over Israel in Samaria, and reigned seventeen years. And Jehoahaz slept with his fathers; and they buried him in Samaria: and Joash his son reigned in his stead.

Now Elisha was fallen sick of his sickness whereof he died. And Joash the king of Israel came down unto him, and wept over his face, and said, "O my father, my father, the chariot of Israel, and the horsemen thereof."

And Elisha said unto him, "Take bow and arrows." And he took unto him bow and arrows.

And he said to the king of Israel, "Put thine hand upon the bow." And he put his hand upon it: and Elisha put his hands upon the king's hands.

And he said, "Open the window eastward." And he opened it. Then Elisha said, "Shoot." And he shot.

And he said, "The arrow of the Lord's deliverance, and the arrow of deliverance from Syria: for thou shalt smite the Syrians in Aphek, till thou have consumed them."

And he said, "Take the arrows." And he took them.

And he said unto the king of Israel, "Smite upon the ground." And he smote thrice, and stayed.

And the man of God was wroth with him, and said, "Thou shouldest have smitten five or six times; then hadst thou smitten Syria till thou hadst consumed it: whereas now thou shalt smite Syria but thrice."

And Elisha died, and they buried him. And the bands of the Moabites invaded the land at the coming in of the year. And it

THE SECOND BOOK OF THE KINGS

came to pass, as they were burying a man, that, behold, they spied a band of men; and they cast the man into the sepulchre of Elisha: and when the man was let down, and touched the bones of Elisha, he revived, and stood up on his feet.

The Fall of Israel

In the twelfth year of Ahaz king of Judah began Hoshea the son of Elah to reign in Samaria over Israel nine years. And he did that which was evil in the sight of the Lord, but not as the kings of Israel that were before him. Against him came up Shalmaneser king of Assyria; and Hoshea became his servant, and gave him presents. And the king of Assyria found conspiracy in Hoshea: for he had sent messengers to So king of Egypt, and brought no present to the king of Assyria, as he had done year by year: therefore the king of Assyria shut him up, and bound him in prison. Then the king of Assyria came up throughout all the land, and went up to Samaria, and besieged it three years. In the ninth year of Hoshea the king of Assyria took Samaria, and carried Israel away into Assyria, and placed them in Halah and in Habor by the river of Gozan, and in the cities of the Medes.

For so it was that the children of Israel had sinned against the Lord their God, which had brought them up out of the land of Egypt, from under the hand of Pharaoh king of Egypt, and had feared other gods, and walked in the statutes of the heathen, whom the Lord cast out from before the children of Israel, and of the kings of Israel, which they had made. And the children of Israel did secretly those things that were not right against the Lord their God, and they built them high places in all their cities, from the tower of the watchmen to the fenced city. And they set them up images and groves in every high hill, and under every green tree: and there they burnt incense in all the high places, as did the heathen whom the Lord carried away before them; and wrought wicked things to provoke the Lord to anger. For they served idols, whereof the Lord had said unto them, "Ye shall not do this thing." Yet the Lord testified against Is-

THE SECOND BOOK OF THE KINGS

rael, and against Judah, by all the prophets, and by all the seers, saying, "Turn ye from your evil ways, and keep my commandments and my statutes, according to all the law which I commanded your fathers, and which I sent to you by my servants the prophets."

Notwithstanding they would not hear, but hardened their necks, like to the neck of their fathers, that did not believe in the Lord their God. And they rejected his statutes, and his covenant that he made with their fathers, and his testimonies which he testified against them; and they followed vanity, and became vain, and went after the heathen that were round about them, concerning whom the Lord had charged them, that they should not do like them. And they left all the commandments of the Lord their God, and made them molten images, even two calves, and made a grove, and worshipped all the host of heaven, and served Baal. And they caused their sons and their daughters to pass through the fire, and used divination and enchantments, and sold themselves to do evil in the sight of the Lord, to provoke him to anger. Therefore the Lord was very angry with Israel, and removed them out of his sight: there was none left but the tribe of Judah only.

And the king of Assyria brought men from Babylon, and from Cuthah, and from Ava, and from Hamath, and from Sepharvaim, and placed them in the cities of Samaria instead of the children of Israel: and they possessed Samaria, and dwelt in the cities thereof.

The Reign of Hezekiah

Now it came to pass in the third year of Hoshea son of Elah king of Israel, that Hezekiah the son of Ahaz king of Judah began to reign. Twenty and five years old was he when he began to reign; and he reigned twenty and nine years in Jerusalem. His mother's name also was Abi, the daughter of Zachariah. And he did that which was right in the sight of the Lord, according to all that David his father did. He removed the high places, and broke the images, and cut down the groves, and

[346]

THE SECOND BOOK OF THE KINGS

broke in pieces the brazen serpent that Moses had made: for unto those days the children of Israel did burn incense to it: and he called it Nehushtan. He trusted in the Lord God of Israel; so that after him was none like him among all the kings of Judah, nor any that were before him. For he cleaved to the Lord, and departed not from following him, but kept his commandments, which the Lord commanded Moses. And the Lord was with him; and he prospered whithersoever he went forth: and he rebelled against the king of Assyria, and served him not. He smote the Philistines, even unto Gaza, and the borders thereof, from the tower of the watchmen to the fenced city.

And it came to pass in the fourth year of King Hezekiah, which was the seventh year of Hoshea son of Elah king of Israel, that Shalmaneser king of Assyria came up against Samaria, and besieged it. And at the end of three years they took it: even in the sixth year of Hezekiah, that is the ninth year of Hoshea king of Israel, Samaria was taken. And the king of Assyria did carry away Israel unto Assyria, and put them in Halah and in Habor by the river of Gozan, and in the cities of the Medes.

Now in the fourteenth year of King Hezekiah did Sennacherib king of Assyria come up against all the fenced cities of Judah, and took them. And Hezekiah king of Judah sent to the king of Assyria to Lachish, saying, "I have offended; return from me: that which thou puttest on me will I bear."

And the king of Assyria appointed unto Hezekiah king of Judah three hundred talents of silver and thirty talents of gold. And Hezekiah gave him all the silver that was found in the house of the Lord, and in the treasures of the king's house. At that time did Hezekiah cut off the gold from the doors of the temple of the Lord, and from the pillars which Hezekiah king of Judah had overlaid, and gave it to the king of Assyria.

And the king of Assyria sent Tartan and Rabsaris and Rabshakeh from Lachish to King Hezekiah with a great host against Jerusalem. And they went up and came to Jerusalem. And when they were come up, they came and stood by the conduit of the upper pool, which is in the highway of the fuller's field. And

THE SECOND BOOK OF THE KINGS

when they had called to the king, there came out to them Eliakim the son of Hilkiah, which was over the household, and Shebna the scribe, and Joah the son of Asaph the recorder. And Rab-shakeh said unto them,

"Speak ye now to Hezekiah, 'Thus saith the great king, the king of Assyria, "What confidence is this wherein thou trustest? Thou sayest (but they are but vain words) I have counsel and strength for the war. Now on whom dost thou trust, that thou rebellest against me? Now, behold, thou trustest upon the staff of this bruised reed, even upon Egypt, on which if a man lean, it will go into his hand, and pierce it: so is Pharaoh king of Egypt unto all that trust on him. But if ye say unto me, 'We trust in the Lord our God': is not that he, whose high places and whose altars Hezekiah hath taken away, and hath said to Judah and Jerusalem, 'Ye shall worship before this altar in Jerusalem'? Now therefore, I pray thee, give pledges to my lord the king of Assyria, and I will deliver thee two thousand horses, if thou be able on thy part to set riders upon them. How then wilt thou turn away the face of one captain of the least of my master's servants, and put thy trust on Egypt for chariots and for horsemen? Am I now come up without the Lord against this place to destroy it? The Lord said to me, 'Go up against this land, and destroy it.'"'"

Then said Eliakim the son of Hilkiah, and Shebna, and Joah, unto Rab-shakeh,

"Speak, I pray thee, to thy servants in the Syrian language; for we understand it: and talk not with us in the Jews' language in the ears of the people that are on the wall."

But Rab-shakeh said unto them,

"Hath my master sent me to thy master, and to thee, to speak these words? hath he not sent me to the men which sit on the wall, that they may eat their own dung, and drink their own piss with you?"

Then Rab-shakeh stood and cried with a loud voice in the Jews' language, and spoke, saying,

THE SECOND BOOK OF THE KINGS

"Hear the word of the great king, the king of Assyria: thus saith the king, 'Let not Hezekiah deceive you: for he shall not be able to deliver you out of his hand; neither let Hezekiah make you trust in the Lord, saying, "The Lord will surely deliver us, and this city shall not be delivered into the hand of the king of Assyria."' Hearken not to Hezekiah: for thus saith the king of Assyria, 'Make an agreement with me by a present, and come out to me, and then eat ye every man of his own vine, and every one of his fig tree, and drink ye every one the waters of his cistern: until I come and take you away to a land like your own land, a land of corn and wine, a land of bread and vineyards, a land of oil olive and of honey, that ye may live, and not die: and hearken not unto Hezekiah, when he persuadeth you, saying, "The Lord will deliver us." Hath any of the gods of the nations delivered at all his land out of the hand of the king of Assyria? Where are the gods of Hamath, and of Arpad? where are the gods of Sepharvaim, Hena, and Ivah? have they delivered Samaria out of mine hand? Who are they among all the gods of the countries, that have delivered their country out of mine hand, that the Lord should deliver Jerusalem out of mine hand?'"

But the people held their peace, and answered him not a word: for the king's commandment was, saying, "Answer him not."

Then came Eliakim the son of Hilkiah, which was over the household, and Shebna the scribe, and Joah the son of Asaph the recorder, to Hezekiah with their clothes rent, and told him the words of Rab-shakeh. And it came to pass, when King Hezekiah heard it, that he rent his clothes, and covered himself with sackcloth, and went into the house of the Lord. And he sent Eliakim, which was over the household, and Shebna the scribe, and the elders of the priests, covered with sackcloth, to Isaiah the prophet the son of Amoz. And they said unto him,

"Thus saith Hezekiah, 'This day is a day of trouble, and of rebuke, and blasphemy: for the children are come to the birth, and there is not strength to bring forth. It may be the Lord thy God will hear all the words of Rab-shakeh, whom the king of

THE SECOND BOOK OF THE KINGS

Assyria his master hath sent to reproach the living God; and will reprove the words which the Lord thy God hath heard: wherefore lift up thy prayer for the remnant that are left.' "

So the servants of King Hezekiah came to Isaiah. And Isaiah said unto them,

"Thus shall ye say to your master, 'Thus saith the Lord, "Be not afraid of the words which thou hast heard, with which the servants of the king of Assyria have blasphemed me. Behold, I will send a blast upon him, and he shall hear a rumour, and shall return to his own land; and I will cause him to fall by the sword in his own land." ' "

And Hezekiah prayed before the Lord, and said,

"O Lord God of Israel, which dwellest between the cherubims, thou art the God, even thou alone, of all the kingdoms of the earth; thou hast made heaven and earth. Lord, bow down thine ear, and hear: open, Lord, thine eyes, and see: and hear the words of Sennacherib, which hath sent him to reproach the living God. Of a truth, Lord, the kings of Assyria have destroyed the nations and their lands, and have cast their gods into the fire: for they were no gods, but the work of men's hands, wood and stone: therefore they have destroyed them. Now therefore, O Lord our God, I beseech thee, save thou us out of his hand, that all the kingdoms of the earth may know that thou art the Lord God, even thou only."

Then Isaiah the son of Amoz sent to Hezekiah, saying,

"Thus saith the Lord God of Israel, 'That which thou hast prayed to me against Sennacherib king of Assyria I have heard.' This is the word that the Lord hath spoken concerning him: 'The virgin the daughter of Zion hath despised thee, and laughed thee to scorn; the daughter of Jerusalem hath shaken her head at thee. Whom hast thou reproached and blasphemed? and against whom hast thou exalted thy voice, and lifted up thine eyes on high? even against the Holy One of Israel. By thy messengers thou hast reproached the Lord, and hast said, "With the multitude of my chariots I am come up to the height of the mountains, to the sides of Lebanon, and will cut down the tall cedar trees

THE SECOND BOOK OF THE KINGS

thereof, and the choice fir trees thereof: and I will enter into the lodgings of his borders, and into the forest of his Carmel." Because thy rage against me and thy tumult is come up into mine ears, therefore I will put my hook in thy nose, and my bridle in thy lips, and I will turn thee back by the way by which thou camest.'

"Therefore thus saith the Lord concerning the king of Assyria, 'He shall not come into this city, nor shoot an arrow there, nor come before it with shield, nor cast a bank against it. By the way that he came, by the same shall he return, and shall not come into this city,' saith the Lord. 'For I will defend this city, to save it, for mine own sake, and for my servant David's sake.'"

And it came to pass that night, that the angel of the Lord went out, and smote in the camp of the Assyrians a hundred fourscore and five thousand: and when they arose early in the morning, behold, they were all dead corpses. So Sennacherib king of Assyria departed, and went and returned, and dwelt at Nineveh. And it came to pass, as he was worshipping in the house of Nisroch his god, that Adrammelech and Sharezer his sons smote him with the sword: and they escaped into the land of Armenia. And Esarhaddon his son reigned in his stead.

In those days was Hezekiah sick unto death. And the prophet Isaiah the son of Amoz came to him, and said unto him, "Thus saith the Lord, 'Set thine house in order; for thou shalt die, and not live.'"

Then he turned his face to the wall, and prayed unto the Lord, saying, "I beseech thee, O Lord, remember now how I have walked before thee in truth and with a perfect heart, and have done that which is good in thy sight." And Hezekiah wept sore.

And it came to pass, afore Isaiah was gone out into the middle court, that the word of the Lord came to him, saying, "Turn again, and tell Hezekiah the captain of my people, 'Thus saith the Lord, the God of David thy father, "I have heard thy prayer, I have seen thy tears: behold, I will heal thee: on the third day

THE SECOND BOOK OF THE KINGS

thou shalt go up unto the house of the Lord. And I will add unto thy days fifteen years; and I will deliver thee and this city out of the hand of the king of Assyria; and I will defend this city for mine own sake, and for my servant David's sake." ' "

And Isaiah said, "Take a lump of figs." And they took and laid it on the boil, and he recovered.

And Hezekiah said unto Isaiah, "What shall be the sign that the Lord will heal me, and that I shall go up into the house of the Lord the third day?"

And Isaiah said, "This sign shalt thou have of the Lord, that the Lord will do the thing that he hath spoken: shall the shadow go forward ten degrees, or go back ten degrees?" And Hezekiah answered,

"It is a light thing for the shadow to go down ten degrees: nay, but let the shadow return backward ten degrees."

And Isaiah the prophet cried unto the Lord: and he brought the shadow ten degrees backward, by which it had gone down in the dial of Ahaz.

At that time Berodach-baladan, the son of Baladan, king of Babylon, sent letters and a present unto Hezekiah: for he had heard that Hezekiah had been sick. And Hezekiah hearkened unto them, and showed them all the house of his precious things, the silver, and the gold, and the spices, and the precious ointment, and all the house of his armour, and all that was found in his treasures: there was nothing in his house, nor in all his dominion, that Hezekiah showed them not.

Then came Isaiah the prophet unto King Hezekiah, and said unto him, "What said these men? and from whence came they unto thee?"

And Hezekiah said, "They are come from a far country, even from Babylon."

And he said, "What have they seen in thine house?"

And Hezekiah answered, "All the things that are in mine house have they seen: there is nothing among my treasures that I have not showed them."

And Isaiah said unto Hezekiah, "Hear the word of the Lord.

THE SECOND BOOK OF THE KINGS

'Behold, the days come, that all that is in thine house, and that which thy fathers have laid up in store unto this day, shall be carried into Babylon: nothing shall be left,' saith the Lord. 'And of thy sons that shall issue from thee, which thou shalt beget, shall they take away; and they shall be eunuchs in the palace of the king of Babylon.'"

Then said Hezekiah unto Isaiah, "Good is the word of the Lord which thou hast spoken." And he said, "Is it not good, if peace and truth be in my days?"

And the rest of the acts of Hezekiah, and all his might, and how he made a pool, and a conduit, and brought water into the city, are they not written in the Book of the Chronicles of the Kings of Judah? And Hezekiah slept with his fathers: and Manasseh his son reigned in his stead.

The Reforms of Josiah

Manasseh was twelve years old when he began to reign, and reigned fifty and five years in Jerusalem. And his mother's name was Hephzi-bah. And he did that which was evil in the sight of the Lord, after the abominations of the heathen, whom the Lord cast out before the children of Israel. For he built up again the high places which Hezekiah his father had destroyed; and he reared up altars for Baal, and made a grove, as did Ahab king of Israel; and worshipped all the host of heaven, and served them.

And Manasseh slept with his fathers, and was buried in the garden of his own house, in the garden of Uzza: and Amon his son reigned in his stead. And he did that which was evil in the sight of the Lord, as his father Manasseh did. And he walked in all the way that his father walked in, and served the idols that his father served, and worshipped them. And the servants of Amon conspired against him, and slew the king in his own house. And the people of the land slew all them that had conspired against King Amon; and the people of the land made Josiah his son king in his stead.

Josiah was eight years old when he began to reign, and he reigned thirty and one years in Jerusalem. And his mother's name

THE SECOND BOOK OF THE KINGS

was Jedidah, the daughter of Adaiah of Boscath. And he did that which was right in the sight of the Lord, and walked in all the way of David his father, and turned not aside to the right hand or to the left.

And it came to pass in the eighteenth year of King Josiah, that the king sent Shaphan the son of Azaliah, the son of Meshullam, the scribe, to the house of the Lord, saying, "Go up to Hilkiah the high priest, that he may sum the silver which is brought into the house of the Lord, which the keepers of the door have gathered of the people: and let them deliver it into the hand of the doers of the work, that have the oversight of the house of the Lord: and let them give it to the doers of the work which is in the house of the Lord, to repair the breaches of the house—unto carpenters, and builders, and masons, and to buy timber and hewn stone to repair the house." Howbeit there was no reckoning made with them of the money that was delivered into their hand, because they dealt faithfully.

And Hilkiah the high priest said unto Shaphan the scribe, "I have found the book of the law in the house of the Lord." And Hilkiah gave the book to Shaphan, and he read it.

And Shaphan the scribe came to the king, and brought the king word again, and said, "Thy servants have gathered the money that was found in the house, and have delivered it into the hand of them that do the work, that have the oversight of the house of the Lord." And Shaphan the scribe showed the king, saying, "Hilkiah the priest hath delivered me a book." And Shaphan read it before the king.

And it came to pass, when the king had heard the words of the book of the law, that he rent his clothes. And the king commanded Hilkiah the priest, and Ahikam the son of Shaphan, and Achbor the son of Michaiah, and Shaphan the scribe, and Asahiah a servant of the king's, saying, "Go ye, enquire of the Lord for me, and for the people, and for all Judah, concerning the words of this book that is found: for great is the wrath of the Lord that is kindled against us, because our fathers have not hearkened

THE SECOND BOOK OF THE KINGS

unto the words of this book, to do according unto all that which is written concerning us."

So Hilkiah the priest, and Ahikam, and Achbor, and Shaphan, and Asahiah, went unto Huldah the prophetess, the wife of Shallum the son of Tikvah, the son of Harhas, keeper of the wardrobe (now she dwelt in Jerusalem in the college); and they communed with her. And she said unto them, "Thus saith the Lord God of Israel, 'Tell the man that sent you to me, "Thus saith the Lord, 'Behold, I will bring evil upon this place, and upon the inhabitants thereof, even all the words of the book which the king of Judah hath read: because they have forsaken me, and have burned incense unto other gods, that they might provoke me to anger with all the works of their hands; therefore my wrath shall be kindled against this place, and shall not be quenched.'"' But to the king of Judah which sent you to enquire of the Lord, thus shall ye say to him, 'Thus saith the Lord God of Israel, "As touching the words which thou hast heard: because thine heart was tender, and thou hast humbled thyself before the Lord, when thou heardest what I spoke against this place, and against the inhabitants thereof, that they should become a desolation and a curse, and hast rent thy clothes, and wept before me; I also have heard thee," saith the Lord. "Behold therefore, I will gather thee unto thy fathers, and thou shalt be gathered into thy grave in peace; and thine eyes shall not see all the evil which I will bring upon this place."'" And they brought the king word again.

And the king sent, and they gathered unto him all the elders of Judah and of Jerusalem. And the king went up into the house of the Lord, and all the men of Judah and all the inhabitants of Jerusalem with him, and the priests, and the prophets, and all the people, both small and great: and he read in their ears all the words of the book of the covenant which was found in the house of the Lord.

And the king stood by a pillar, and made a covenant before the Lord, to walk after the Lord, and to keep his commandments

THE SECOND BOOK OF THE KINGS

and his testimonies and his statutes with all their heart and all their soul, to perform the words of this covenant that were written in this book. And all the people stood to the covenant. And the king commanded Hilkiah the high priest, and the priests of the second order, and the keepers of the door, to bring forth out of the temple of the Lord all the vessels that were made for Baal, and for the grove, and for all the host of heaven: and he burned them without Jerusalem in the fields of Kidron, and carried the ashes of them unto Beth-el. And he put down the idolatrous priests, whom the kings of Judah had ordained to burn incense in the high places in the cities of Judah, and in the places round about Jerusalem; them also that burned incense unto Baal, to the sun, and to the moon, and to the planets, and to all the host of heaven. And he brought out the grove from the house of the Lord, without Jerusalem, unto the brook Kidron, and burned it at the brook Kidron, and stamped it small to powder, and cast the powder thereof upon the graves of the children of the people. And he broke down the houses of the sodomites, that were by the house of the Lord, where the women wove hangings for the grove. And he brought all the priests out of the cities of Judah, and defiled the high places where the priests had burned incense, from Geba to Beer-sheba, and broke down the high places of the gates that were in the entering in of the gate of Joshua the governor of the city, which were on a man's left hand at the gate of the city. (Nevertheless the priests of the high places came not up to the altar of the Lord in Jerusalem, but they did eat of the unleavened bread among their brethren.) And he defiled Topheth, which is in the valley of the children of Hinnom, that no man might make his son or his daughter to pass through the fire to Molech. And he took away the horses that the kings of Judah had given to the sun, at the entering in of the house of the Lord, by the chamber of Nathan-melech the chamberlain, which was in the suburbs, and burned the chariots of the sun with fire. And the altars that were on the top of the upper chamber of Ahaz, which the kings of Judah had made, and

THE SECOND BOOK OF THE KINGS

the altars which Manasseh had made in the two courts of the house of the Lord, did the king beat down, and broke them down from thence, and cast the dust of them into the brook Kidron. And the high places that were before Jerusalem, which were on the right hand of the mount of corruption, which Solomon the king of Israel had builded for Ashtoreth the abomination of the Sidonians, and for Chemosh the abomination of the Moabites, and for Milcom the abomination of the children of Ammon, did the king defile. And he broke in pieces the images, and cut down the groves, and filled their places with the bones of men.

And like unto him was there no king before him that turned to the Lord with all his heart, and with all his soul, and with all his might, according to all the law of Moses; neither after him arose there any like him.

Now the rest of the acts of Josiah, and all that he did, are they not written in the Book of the Chronicles of the Kings of Judah? In his days Pharaoh-nechoh king of Egypt went up against the king of Assyria to the river Euphrates: and King Josiah went against him; and he slew him at Megiddo, when he had seen him. And his servants carried him in a chariot dead from Megiddo, and brought him to Jerusalem, and buried him in his own sepulchre. And the people of the land took Jehoahaz the son of Josiah, and anointed him, and made him king in his father's stead.

The Fall of Judah

And Pharaoh-nechoh made Eliakim the son of Josiah king in the room of Josiah his father, and turned his name to Jehoiakim, and took Jehoahaz away: and he came to Egypt, and died there. Jehoiakim was twenty and five years old when he began to reign; and he reigned eleven years in Jerusalem. In his days Nebuchadnezzar king of Babylon came up, and Jehoiakim became his servant three years: then he turned and rebelled against him. Now the rest of the acts of Jehoiakim, and all that he did, are they not written in the Book of the Chronicles of the Kings of Judah? So

THE SECOND BOOK OF THE KINGS

Jehoiakim slept with his fathers: and Jehoiachin his son reigned in his stead. Jehoiachin was eighteen years old when he began to reign, and he reigned in Jerusalem three months.

At that time the servants of Nebuchadnezzar king of Babylon came up against Jerusalem, and the city was besieged. And Nebuchadnezzar king of Babylon came against the city, and his servants did besiege it. And Jehoiachin the king of Judah went out to the king of Babylon, he, and his mother, and his servants, and his princes, and his officers: and the king of Babylon took him in the eighth year of his reign. And he carried out thence all the treasures of the house of the Lord, and the treasures of the king's house, and cut in pieces all the vessels of gold which Solomon king of Israel had made in the temple of the Lord, as the Lord had said. And he carried away all Jerusalem, and all the princes, and all the mighty men of valour, even ten thousand captives, and all the craftsmen and smiths: none remained, save the poorest sort of the people of the land. And he carried away Jehoiachin to Babylon, and the king's mother, and the king's wives, and his officers, and the mighty of the land, those carried he into captivity from Jerusalem to Babylon. And all the men of might, even seven thousand, and craftsmen and smiths a thousand, all that were strong and apt for war, even them the king of Babylon brought captive to Babylon.

And the king of Babylon made Mattaniah his father's brother king in his stead, and changed his name to Zedekiah. Zedekiah was twenty and one years old when he began to reign, and he reigned eleven years in Jerusalem. And his mother's name was Hamutal, the daughter of Jeremiah of Libnah. And he did that which was evil in the sight of the Lord, according to all that Jehoiakim had done. For through the anger of the Lord it came to pass in Jerusalem and Judah, until he had cast them out from his presence, that Zedekiah rebelled against the king of Babylon.

And it came to pass in the ninth year of his reign, in the tenth month, in the tenth day of the month, that Nebuchadnezzar king of Babylon came, he, and all his host, against Jerusalem, and pitched against it; and they built forts against it round about.

THE SECOND BOOK OF THE KINGS

And the city was besieged unto the eleventh year of King Zedekiah. And on the ninth day of the fourth month the famine prevailed in the city, and there was no bread for the people of the land.

And the city was broken up, and all the men of war fled by night by the way of the gate between two walls, which is by the king's garden (now the Chaldees were against the city round about): and the king went the way toward the plain. And the army of the Chaldees pursued after the king, and overtook him in the plains of Jericho: and all his army were scattered from him. So they took the king, and brought him up to the king of Babylon to Riblah; and they gave judgment upon him. And they slew the sons of Zedekiah before his eyes, and put out the eyes of Zedekiah, and bound him with fetters of brass, and carried him to Babylon.

And in the fifth month, on the seventh day of the month, which is the nineteenth year of King Nebuchadnezzar king of Babylon, came Nebuzar-adan, captain of the guard, a servant of the king of Babylon, unto Jerusalem: and he burnt the house of the Lord, and the king's house, and all the houses of Jerusalem, and every great man's house burnt he with fire. And all the army of the Chaldees, that were with the captain of the guard, broke down the walls of Jerusalem round about. Now the rest of the people that were left in the city, and the fugitives that fell away to the king of Babylon, with the remnant of the multitude, did Nebuzar-adan the captain of the guard carry away. But the captain of the guard left of the poor of the land to be vinedressers and husbandmen.

THE FIRST BOOK OF ESDRAS

During the period of the Exile (586–538 B.C.) a surprising amount of literary work was done, mainly by the priesthood who, as already mentioned, absorbed but at the same time formalized the prophetic spirit in their successful effort to keep alive the religious life of the community. With the return from captivity but still in the ignominious position of a subject people, the Jews passed the next century in a discouragingly slow effort to revive their national consciousness. Much assistance was rendered by the enthusiasm of Nehemiah in rebuilding the walls of Jerusalem in 444 B.C. and still more by the promulgation of the code of Ezra in 397 B.C. By the beginning of the fourth century, a genuine revival of national culture and literature was under way.

What was to be a great literary century opened with its weakest work—the arid Books of the Chronicles, a hopelessly unhistorical rewriting of Jewish history from the standpoint of the priesthood. At the end of his account, the feeble Chronicler was aided by the vigorous personal memoirs of Nehemiah and Ezra which he wove into his narrative in the wrong order. The delightful, though probably quite mythical, story of Zorobabel included in our text is not found in the authorized version of Ezra but is taken from the much expanded Greek Books of Esdras, a part of the Biblical Apocrypha which developed among the Jews of Alexandria.

The First Book of ESDRAS

The Return from Captivity

IN THE FIRST YEAR of Cyrus king of the Persians, that the word of the Lord might be accomplished, that he had promised by the mouth of Jeremy; the Lord raised up the spirit of Cyrus the king of the Persians, and he made proclamation through all his kingdom, and also by writing, saying,

"Thus saith Cyrus king of the Persians: 'The Lord of Israel, the most high Lord, hath made me king of the whole world, and commanded me to build him a house at Jerusalem in Jewry. If therefore there be any of you that are of his people, let the Lord, even his Lord, be with him, and let him go up to Jerusalem that is in Judea, and build the house of the Lord of Israel: for he is the Lord that dwelleth in Jerusalem.'"

Then the chief of the families of Judea and of the tribe of Benjamin stood up; the priests also, and the Levites, and all they whose mind the Lord had moved to go up, and to build a house for the Lord at Jerusalem. And they that dwelt round about them, and helped them in all things with silver and gold, with horses and cattle, and with very many free gifts of a great number whose minds were stirred up thereto. King Cyrus also brought forth the holy vessels, which Nabuchodonosor had carried away from Jerusalem, and had set up in his temple of idols. Now when Cyrus king of the Persians had brought them forth, he delivered them to Mithridates his treasurer: and by him they were delivered to Sanabassar the governor of Judea. And this was the number of them; a thousand golden cups, and a thousand of silver, censers of silver twenty-nine, vials of gold thirty,

THE FIRST BOOK OF ESDRAS

and of silver two thousand four hundred and ten, and a thousand other vessels. So all the vessels of gold and of silver, which were carried away, were five thousand four hundred threescore and nine.

But in the time of Artaxerxes king of the Persians Belemus, and Mithridates, and Tabellius, and Rathumus, and Beeltethmus, and Semellius the secretary, with others that were in commission with them, dwelling in Samaria and other places, wrote unto him against them that dwelt in Judea and Jerusalem these letters following:

"To King Artaxerxes our lord: thy servants, Rathumus the storywriter, and Semellius the scribe, and the rest of their council, and the judges that are in Celosyria and Phenice:

"Be it now known to the lord the king that the Jews that are come up from you to us, being come into Jerusalem, that rebellious and wicked city, do build the marketplaces, and repair the walls of it, and do lay the foundation of the temple. Now if this city and the walls thereof be made up again, they will not only refuse to give tribute, but also rebel against kings."

Then the king wrote back again to Rathumus the storywriter, to Beeltethmus, to Semellius the scribe, and to the rest that were in commission, and dwellers in Samaria and Syria and Phenice, after this manner:

"I have read the epistle which ye have sent unto me: therefore I commanded to make diligent search, and it hath been found that that city was from the beginning practising against kings; and the men therein were given to rebellion and war: and that mighty kings and fierce were in Jerusalem, who reigned and exacted tributes in Celosyria and Phenice. Now therefore I have commanded to hinder those men from building the city, and heed to be taken that there be no more done in it; and that those wicked workers proceed no further to the annoyance of kings."

Then King Artaxerxes his letters being read, Rathumus, and Semellius the scribe, and the rest that were in commission with

THE FIRST BOOK OF ESDRAS

them, removing in haste toward Jerusalem with a troop of horsemen and a multitude of people in battle array, began to hinder the builders; and the building of the temple in Jerusalem ceased until the second year of the reign of Darius king of the Persians.

Now when Darius reigned, he made a great feast unto all his subjects, and unto all his household, and unto all the princes of Media and Persia, and to all the governors and captains and lieutenants that were under him, from India unto Ethiopia, of a hundred twenty and seven provinces. And when they had eaten and drunken, and being satisfied were gone home, then Darius the king went into his bedchamber, and slept, and soon after awaked.

Then three young men, that were of the guard that kept the king's body, spoke one to another:

"Let every one of us speak a sentence: he that shall overcome, and whose sentence shall seem wiser than the others, unto him shall the King Darius give great gifts, and great things in token of victory: as, to be clothed in purple, to drink in gold, and to sleep upon gold, and a chariot with bridles of gold, and a headtire of fine linen, and a chain about his neck; and he shall sit next to Darius because of his wisdom, and shall be called Darius his cousin."

And then every one wrote his sentence, sealed it, and laid it under King Darius his pillow, and said that, when the king is risen, some will give him the writings; and of whose side the king and the three princes of Persia shall judge that his sentence is the wisest, to him shall the victory be given, as was appointed.

The first wrote, "Wine is the strongest."

The second wrote, "The king is strongest."

The third wrote, "Women are strongest: but above all things Truth beareth away the victory."

Now when the king was risen up, they took their writings, and delivered them unto him, and so he read them. And sending forth he called all the princes of Persia and Media, and the governors, and the captains, and the lieutenants, and the chief of-

THE FIRST BOOK OF ESDRAS

ficers, and sat him down in the royal seat of judgment; and the writings were read before them. And he said, "Call the young men, and they shall declare their own sentences." So they were called, and came in. And he said unto them, "Declare unto us your mind concerning the writings."

Then began the first, who had spoken of the strength of wine, and he said thus,

"O ye men, how exceeding strong is wine! it causeth all men to err that drink it. It maketh the mind of the king and of the fatherless child to be all one; of the bondman and of the freeman, and of the poor man and of the rich. It turneth also every thought into jollity and mirth, so that a man remembereth neither sorrow nor debt. And it maketh every heart rich, so that a man remembereth neither king nor governor; and it maketh to speak all things by talents. And when they are in their cups, they forget their love both to friends and brethren, and a little after draw out swords: but when they are from the wine, they remember not what they have done. O ye men, is not wine the strongest, that enforceth to do thus?"

Then the second, that had spoken of the strength of the king, began to say,

"O ye men, do not men excel in strength, that bear rule over sea and land, and all things in them? But yet the king is more mighty: for he is lord of all these things, and hath dominion over them; and whatsoever he commandeth them they do. If he bid them make war the one against the other, they do it: if he send them out against the enemies, they go, and break down mountains, walls, and towers. They slay and are slain, and transgress not the king's commandment: if they get the victory, they bring all to the king, as well the spoil, as all things else. Likewise for those that are no soldiers, and have not to do with wars, but use husbandry, when they have reaped again that which they had sown, they bring it to the king, and compel one another to pay tribute unto the king. O ye men, how should not the king be mightiest, when in such sort he is obeyed?"

THE FIRST BOOK OF ESDRAS

Then the third, who had spoken of women, and of the truth (this was Zorobabel), began to speak.

"O ye men, it is not the great king, nor the multitude of men, neither is it wine, that excelleth; who is it then that ruleth them, or hath the lordship over them? are they not women? Women have borne the king and all the people that bear rule by sea and land. Even of them came they: and they nourished them up that planted the vineyards, from whence the wine cometh. These also make garments for men; these bring glory unto men; and without women cannot men be. Yea, and if men have gathered together gold and silver, or any other goodly thing, do they not love a woman which is comely in favour and beauty? And letting all those things go, do they not gape, and even with open mouth fix their eyes fast on her; and have not all men more desire unto her than unto silver or gold, or any goodly thing whatsoever? A man leaveth his own father that brought him up, and his own country, and cleaveth unto his wife. He sticketh not to spend his life with his wife, and remembereth neither father, nor mother, nor country. By this also ye must know that women have dominion over you: do ye not labour and toil, and give and bring all to the woman? Yea, a man taketh his sword, and goeth his way to rob and to steal, to sail upon the sea and upon rivers; and looketh upon a lion, and goeth in the darkness; and when he hath stolen, spoiled, and robbed, he bringeth it to his love. Yea, many there be that have run out of their wits for women, and become servants for their sakes. Many also have perished, have erred, and sinned, for women. And now do ye not believe me? is not the king great in his power? do not all regions fear to touch him? Yet did I see him and Apame the king's concubine, the daughter of the admirable Bartacus, sitting at the right hand of the king, and taking the crown from the king's head, and setting it upon her own head; she also struck the king with her left hand. And yet for all this the king gaped and gazed upon her with open mouth: if she laughed upon him, he laughed also; but if she took any displeasure at him, the

THE FIRST BOOK OF ESDRAS

king was fain to flatter, that she might be reconciled to him again. O ye men, how can it be but women should be strong, seeing they do thus?"

Then the king and the princes looked one upon another: so he began to speak of the truth.

"O ye men, are not women strong? great is the earth, high is the heaven, swift is the sun in his course, for he compasseth the heavens round about, and fetcheth his course again to his own place in one day. Is he not great that maketh these things? therefore great is the truth, and stronger than all things. All the earth calleth upon the truth, and the heaven blesseth it: All works shake and tremble at it, and with it is no unrighteous thing. Wine is wicked, the king is wicked, women are wicked, all the children of men are wicked, and such are all their wicked works; and there is no truth in them; in their unrighteousness also they shall perish. As for the truth, it endureth, and is always strong; it liveth and conquereth for evermore. With her there is no accepting of persons or rewards; but she doeth the things that are just, and refraineth from all unjust and wicked things; and all men do well like of her works. Neither in her judgment is any unrighteousness; and she is the strength, kingdom, power, and majesty, of all ages. Blessed be the God of truth." And with that he held his peace. And all the people then shouted, and said, "Great is Truth, and mighty above all things."

Then said the king unto him, "Ask what thou wilt more than is appointed in the writing, and we will give it thee, because thou art found wisest; and thou shalt sit next me, and shalt be called my cousin."

Then said he unto the king, "Remember thy vow, which thou hast vowed to build Jerusalem, in the day when thou camest to thy kingdom, and to send away all the vessels that were taken away out of Jerusalem, which Cyrus set apart, when he vowed to destroy Babylon, and to send them again thither. Thou also hast vowed to build up the temple, which the Edomites burned when Judea was made desolate by the Chaldees. And now, O lord the king, this is that which I require, and which I desire of

THE FIRST BOOK OF ESDRAS

thee, and this is the princely liberality proceeding from thyself: I desire therefore that thou make good the vow, the performance whereof with thine own mouth thou hast vowed to the King of heaven."

Then Darius the king stood up, and kissed him, and wrote letters for him unto all the treasurers and lieutenants and captains and governors, that they should safely convey on their way both him, and all those that go up with him to build Jerusalem.

Now when this young man was gone forth, he lifted up his face to heaven toward Jerusalem, and praised the King of heaven, and said, "From thee cometh victory, from thee cometh wisdom, and thine is the glory, and I am thy servant. Blessed art thou, who hast given me wisdom: for to thee I give thanks, O Lord of our fathers." And so he took the letters, and went out, and came unto Babylon, and told it all his brethren. And they praised the God of their fathers, because he had given them freedom and liberty to go up, and to build Jerusalem, and the temple which is called by his name: and they feasted with instruments of music and gladness seven days.

THE BOOK OF NEHEMIAH

OF THE TWO memoir writers, whose work in its original form was an exception to the general anonymity of the nonprophetical books of the Old Testament, Nehemiah the courtier-cupbearer was much more gifted as an author than Ezra the priest. He succeeded in stamping his personality upon his writing so that his figure stands out as that of a surprisingly modern type of character in his energy, his will to action, his benevolent intentions, and his self-complacency. The movement that he and Ezra inaugurated was on the whole undoubtedly beneficial, but their harsh abolition of mixed marriages produced much hardship at the time and led to the noble protest in the Book of Ruth.

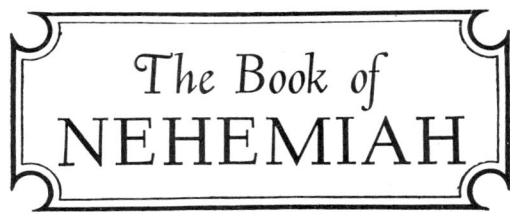

The Book of NEHEMIAH

The Rebuilding of the Walls

THE WORDS OF NEHEMIAH the son of Hachaliah. And it came to pass in the month Chisleu, in the twentieth year, as I was in Shushan the palace, that Hanani, one of my brethren, came, he and certain men of Judah; and I asked them concerning the Jews that had escaped, which were left of the captivity, and concerning Jerusalem. And they said unto me,

"The remnant that are left of the captivity there in the province are in great affliction and reproach: the wall of Jerusalem also is broken down, and the gates thereof are burned with fire."

And it came to pass, when I heard these words, that I sat down and wept, and mourned certain days, and fasted, and prayed before the God of heaven, and said,

"I beseech thee, O Lord God of heaven, the great and terrible God, that keepeth covenant and mercy for them that love him and observe his commandments: O Lord, I beseech thee, let now thine ear be attentive to the prayer of thy servant, and to the prayer of thy servants, who desire to fear thy name: and prosper, I pray thee, thy servant this day, and grant him mercy in the sight of this man."

For I was the king's cupbearer. And it came to pass in the month Nisan, in the twentieth year of Artaxerxes the king, that wine was before him: and I took up the wine, and gave it unto the king. Now I had not been beforetime sad in his presence. Wherefore the king said unto me,

"Why is thy countenance sad, seeing thou art not sick? this is nothing else but sorrow of heart."

THE BOOK OF NEHEMIAH

Then I was very sore afraid, and said unto the king,

"Let the king live for ever: why should not my countenance be sad, when the city, the place of my fathers' sepulchres, lieth waste, and the gates thereof are consumed with fire?"

Then the king said unto me, "For what dost thou make request?"

So I prayed to the God of heaven. And I said unto the king, "If it please the king, and if thy servant have found favour in thy sight, that thou wouldest send me unto Judah, unto the city of my fathers' sepulchres, that I may build it."

And the king said unto me (the queen also sitting by him), "For how long shall thy journey be? and when wilt thou return?"

So it pleased the king to send me; and I set him a time. Moreover I said unto the king,

"If it please the king, let letters be given me to the governors beyond the river, that they may convey me over till I come into Judah; and a letter unto Asaph the keeper of the king's forest, that he may give me timber to make beams for the gates of the palace which appertained to the house, and for the wall of the city, and for the house that I shall enter into."

And the king granted me, according to the good hand of my God upon me. So I came to Jerusalem, and was there three days.

And I arose in the night, I and some few men with me; neither told I any man what my God had put in my heart to do at Jerusalem: neither was there any beast with me, save the beast that I rode upon. And I went out by night by the gate of the valley even before the dragon well, and to the dung port, and viewed the walls of Jerusalem, which were broken down, and the gates thereof were consumed with fire. Then I went on to the gate of the fountain, and to the king's pool: but there was no place for the beast that was under me to pass. Then I went up in the night by the brook, and viewed the wall, and turned back, and entered by the gate of the valley, and so returned. And the rulers knew not whither I went, or what I did; neither had I as yet told it to

THE BOOK OF NEHEMIAH

the Jews, nor to the priests, nor to the nobles, nor to the rulers, nor to the rest that did the work. Then said I unto them,

"Ye see the distress that we are in, how Jerusalem lieth waste, and the gates thereof are burned with fire: come, and let us build up the wall of Jerusalem, that we be no more a reproach."

Then Eliashib the high priest rose up with his brethren the priests, and they builded the sheep gate; they sanctified it, and set up the doors of it; even unto the tower of Meah they sanctified it, unto the tower of Hananeel. And next unto him builded the men of Jericho. And next to them builded Zaccur the son of Imri. But the fish gate did the sons of Hassenaah build, who also laid the beams thereof, and set up the doors thereof, the locks thereof, and the bars thereof. And next unto them repaired Meremoth the son of Urijah, the son of Koz. And next unto them repaired Meshullam the son of Berechiah, the son of Meshezabeel. And next unto them repaired Zadok the son of Baana. And next unto them the Tekoites repaired; but their nobles put not their necks to the work of their Lord. Moreover the old gate repaired Jehoiada the son of Paseah, and Meshullam the son of Besodeiah; they laid the beams thereof, and set up the doors thereof, and the locks thereof, and the bars thereof. And next unto them repaired Melatiah the Gibeonite, and Jadon the Meronothite, the men of Gibeon, and of Mizpah, unto the throne of the governor on this side the river. Next unto him repaired Uzziel the son of Harhaiah, of the goldsmiths. Next unto him also repaired Hananiah the son of one of the apothecaries, and they fortified Jerusalem unto the broad wall.

The Prohibition of Mixed Marriages

In those days also saw I Jews that had married wives of Ashdod, of Ammon, and of Moab: and their children spoke half in the speech of Ashdod, and could not speak the Jews' language, but according to the language of each people. And I contended with them, and cursed them, and smote certain of them, and plucked off their hair, and made them swear by God, saying,

THE BOOK OF NEHEMIAH

"Ye shall not give your daughters unto their sons, nor take their daughters unto your sons, or for yourselves. Did not Solomon king of Israel sin by these things? yet among many nations was there no king like him, who was beloved of his God, and God made him king over all Israel: nevertheless even him did outlandish women cause to sin. Shall we then hearken unto you to do all this great evil, to transgress against our God in marrying strange wives?"

And one of the sons of Joiada, the son of Eliashib the high priest, was son-in-law to Sanballat the Horonite: therefore I chased him from me. Remember them, O my God, because they have defied the priesthood, and the covenant of the priesthood, and of the Levites. Thus cleansed I them from all strangers, and appointed the wards of the priests and the Levites, every one in his business. Remember me, O my God, for good.

THE FIRST BOOK OF THE MACCABEES

THE CONQUESTS of Alexander the Great brought the Jews under Greek sovereignty. Aside from the gradual infiltration of Hellenic culture, this made little difference in their status until in the middle of the second century B.C. Antiochus Epiphanes, strangely intolerant for a Greek, attempted to suppress the Jewish religion. His deliberate outraging of all that the Jews held sacred caused the heroic and successful rebellion of Simon and Judas Maccabeus who secured religious freedom for their people until the destruction of Jerusalem in A.D. 70. The almost contemporary account of the rebellion in the Apocryphal Books of the First and Second Maccabees thus forms a fitting close to the long series of Biblical histories in its triumphant reassertion of that worship of Jehovah which is the central theme of all of them.

The First Book of the MACCABEES

The Greek Tyranny

AND IT HAPPENED, after that Alexander son of Philip, the Macedonian, who came out of the land of Chettiim, had smitten Darius king of the Persians and Medes, that he reigned in his stead, the first over Greece, and made many wars, and won many strong holds, and slew the kings of the earth, and went through to the ends of the earth, and took spoils of many nations, insomuch that the earth was quiet before him; whereupon he was exalted, and his heart was lifted up. And he gathered a mighty strong host, and ruled over countries, and nations, and kings, who became tributaries unto him. And after these things he fell sick, and perceived that he should die. Wherefore he called his servants, such as were honourable, and had been brought up with him from his youth, and parted his kingdom among them, while he was yet alive. So Alexander reigned twelve years, and then died. And his servants bore rule every one in his place.

And after his death they all put crowns upon themselves; so did their sons after them many years; and evils were multiplied in the earth. And there came out of them a wicked root, Antiochus surnamed Epiphanes, son of Antiochus the king, who had been a hostage at Rome, and he reigned in the hundred and thirty and seventh year of the kingdom of the Greeks. In those days went there out of Israel wicked men, who persuaded many, saying,

"Let us go and make a covenant with the heathen that are

THE FIRST BOOK OF THE MACCABEES

round about us: for since we departed from them we have had much sorrow."

So this device pleased them well. Then certain of the people were so forward herein, that they went to the king, who gave them licence to do after the ordinances of the heathen: whereupon they built a place of exercise at Jerusalem according to the customs of the heathen, and made themselves uncircumcised, and forsook the holy covenant, and joined themselves to the heathen, and were sold to do mischief.

Now when the kingdom was established before Antiochus, he thought to reign over Egypt, that he might have the dominion of two realms. Wherefore he entered into Egypt with a great multitude, with chariots, and elephants, and horsemen, and a great navy, and made war against Ptolemee king of Egypt: but Ptolemee was afraid of him, and fled; and many were wounded to death. Thus they got the strong cities in the land of Egypt, and he took the spoils thereof.

And after that Antiochus had smitten Egypt, he returned again in the hundred forty and third year, and went up against Israel and Jerusalem with a great multitude, and entered proudly into the sanctuary, and took away the golden altar, and the candlestick of light, and all the vessels thereof, and the table of the showbread, and the pouring vessels, and the vials, and the censers of gold, and the veil, and the crowns, and the golden ornaments that were before the temple, all which he pulled off. He took also the silver and the gold, and the precious vessels: also he took the hidden treasures which he found. And when he had taken all away, he went into his own land, having made a great massacre, and spoken very proudly. Therefore there was great mourning in Israel, in every place where they were, so that the princes and elders mourned, the virgins and young men were made feeble, and the beauty of women was changed. Every bridegroom took up lamentation, and she that sat in the marriage chamber was in heaviness. The land also was moved for the inhabitants thereof, and all the house of Jacob

THE FIRST BOOK OF THE MACCABEES

was covered with confusion. And after two years fully expired the king sent his chief collector of tribute unto the cities of Juda, who came unto Jerusalem with a great multitude, and spoke peaceable words unto them, but all was deceit: for when they had given him credence, he fell suddenly upon the city, and smote it very sore, and destroyed much people of Israel. And when he had taken the spoils of the city, he set it on fire, and pulled down the houses and walls thereof on every side. But the women and children took they captive, and possessed the cattle.

Then builded they the city of David with a great and strong wall, and with mighty towers, and made it a strong hold for them. And they put therein a sinful nation, wicked men, and fortified themselves therein. They stored it also with armour and victuals, and when they had gathered together the spoils of Jerusalem, they laid them up there, and so they became a sore snare: for it was a place to lie in wait against the sanctuary, and an evil adversary to Israel. Thus they shed innocent blood on every side of the sanctuary, and defiled it: insomuch that the inhabitants of Jerusalem fled because of them: whereupon the city was made a habitation of strangers, and became strange to those that were born in her, and her own children left her. Her sanctuary was laid waste like a wilderness, her feasts were turned into mourning, her sabbaths into reproach, her honour into contempt. As had been her glory, so was her dishonour increased, and her excellency was turned into mourning.

Moreover King Antiochus wrote to his whole kingdom that all should be one people, and every one should leave his laws: so all the heathen agreed according to the commandment of the king. Yea, many also of the Israelites consented to his religion, and sacrificed unto idols, and profaned the sabbath. For the king had sent letters by messengers unto Jerusalem and the cities of Juda, that they should follow the strange laws of the land, and forbid burnt offerings, and sacrifice, and drink offerings, in the temple; and that they should profane the sabbaths and

THE FIRST BOOK OF THE MACCABEES

festival days, and pollute the sanctuary and holy people, set up altars, and groves, and chapels of idols, and sacrifice swine's flesh, and unclean beasts; that they should also leave their children uncircumcised, and make their souls abominable with all manner of uncleanness and profanation: to the end they might forget the law, and change all the ordinances. And whosoever would not do according to the commandment of the king, he said, he should die. In the selfsame manner wrote he to his whole kingdom, and appointed overseers over all the people, commanding the cities of Juda to sacrifice, city by city. Then many of the people were gathered unto them, to wit, every one that forsook the law; and so they committed evils in the land, and drove the Israelites into secret places, even wheresoever they could flee for succour.

Now the fifteenth day of the month Casleu, in the hundred forty and fifth year, they set up the abomination of desolation upon the altar, and builded idol altars throughout the cities of Juda on every side, and burnt incense at the doors of their houses, and in the streets. And when they had rent in pieces the books of the law which they found, they burnt them with fire. And wheresoever was found with any the book of the testament, or if any consented to the law, the king's commandment was that they should put him to death. Thus did they by their authority unto the Israelites every month, to as many as were found in the cities. Now the five and twentieth day of the month they did sacrifice upon the idol altar, which was upon the altar of God. At which time according to the commandment they put to death certain women that had caused their children to be circumcised. And they hanged the infants about their necks, and rifled their houses, and slew them that had circumcised them.

Howbeit many in Israel were fully resolved and confirmed in themselves not to eat any unclean thing. Wherefore they chose rather to die, that they might not be defiled with meats, and that they might not profane the holy covenant: so then they died. And there was very great wrath upon Israel.

THE FIRST BOOK OF THE MACCABEES

The Rebellion of the Maccabees

In those days arose Mattathias the son of John, the son of Simeon, a priest of the sons of Joarib, from Jerusalem, and dwelt in Modin. And he had five sons, Joannan, called Caddis; Simon, called Thassi; Judas, who was called Maccabeus; Eleazar, called Avaran; and Jonathan, whose surname was Apphus. And when he saw the blasphemies that were committed in Juda and Jerusalem, he said,

"Woe is me! wherefore was I born to see this misery of my people, and of the holy city, and to dwell there, when it was delivered into the hand of the enemy, and the sanctuary into the hand of strangers? Her temple is become as a man without glory. Her glorious vessels are carried away into captivity, her infants are slain in the streets, her young men with the sword of the enemy. What nation hath not had a part in her kingdom, and gotten of her spoils? All her ornaments are taken away; of a free woman she is become a bondslave. And, behold, our sanctuary, even our beauty and our glory, is laid waste, and the Gentiles have profaned it. To what end therefore shall we live any longer?"

Then Mattathias and his sons rent their clothes, and put on sackcloth, and mourned very sore. In the mean while the king's officers, such as compelled the people to revolt, came into the city Modin, to make them sacrifice. And when many of Israel came unto them, Mattathias also and his sons came together. Then answered the king's officers, and said to Mattathias on this wise,

"Thou art a ruler, and an honourable and great man in this city, and strengthened with sons and brethren. Now therefore come thou first, and fulfil the king's commandment, like as all the heathen have done, yea, and the men of Juda also, and such as remain at Jerusalem: so shalt thou and thy house be in the number of the king's friends, and thou and thy children shall be honoured with silver and gold, and many rewards."

Then Mattathias answered and spoke with a loud voice,

THE FIRST BOOK OF THE MACCABEES

"Though all the nations that are under the king's dominion obey him, and fall away every one from the religion of their fathers, and give consent to his commandments: yet will I and my sons and my brethren walk in the covenant of our fathers. God forbid that we should forsake the law and the ordinances. We will not hearken to the king's words, to go from our religion, either on the right hand, or the left."

Now when he had left speaking these words, there came one of the Jews in the sight of all to sacrifice on the altar which was at Modin, according to the king's commandment. Which thing when Mattathias saw, he was inflamed with zeal, and his reins trembled, neither could he forbear to show his anger according to judgment: wherefore he ran, and slew him upon the altar. Also the king's commissioner, who compelled men to sacrifice, he killed at that time, and the altar he pulled down. Thus dealt he zealously for the law of God, like as Phinees did unto Zambri the son of Salom. And Mattathias cried throughout the city with a loud voice, saying,

"Whosoever is zealous of the law, and maintaineth the covenant, let him follow me."

So he and his sons fled into the mountains, and left all that ever they had in the city. Then many that sought after justice and judgment went down into the wilderness, to dwell there: both they, and their children, and their wives, and their cattle; because afflictions increased sore upon them.

Now when it was told the king's servants, and the host that was at Jerusalem, in the city of David, that certain men, who had broken the king's commandment, were gone down into the secret places in the wilderness, they pursued after them a great number, and having overtaken them, they camped against them, and made war against them on the sabbath day. And they said unto them,

"Let that which ye have done hitherto suffice; come forth, and do according to the commandment of the king, and ye shall live."

But they said,

THE FIRST BOOK OF THE MACCABEES

"We will not come forth, neither will we do the king's commandment, to profane the sabbath day."

So then they gave them the battle with all speed. Howbeit they answered them not, neither cast they a stone at them, nor stopped the places where they lay hid, but said,

"Let us die all in our innocency: heaven and earth shall testify for us, that ye put us to death wrongfully."

So they rose up against them in battle on the sabbath, and they slew them, with their wives and children, and their cattle, to the number of a thousand people. Now when Mattathias and his friends understood hereof, they mourned for them right sore. And one of them said to another,

"If we all do as our brethren have done, and fight not for our lives and laws against the heathen, they will now quickly root us out of the earth."

At that time therefore they decreed, saying,

"Whosoever shall come to make battle with us on the sabbath day, we will fight against him; neither will we die all, as our brethren that were murdered in the secret places."

Then came there unto him a company of Assideans, who were mighty men of Israel, even all such as were voluntarily devoted unto the law. Also all they that fled for persecution joined themselves unto them, and were a stay unto them. So they joined their forces, and smote sinful men in their anger, and wicked men in their wrath: but the rest fled to the heathen for succour. Then Mattathias and his friends went round about, and pulled down the altars, and what children soever they found within the coast of Israel uncircumcised, those they circumcised valiantly. They pursued also after the proud men, and the work prospered in their hand. So they recovered the law out of the hand of the Gentiles, and out of the hand of kings, neither suffered they the sinner to triumph.

Now when the time drew near that Mattathias should die, he said unto his sons,

"Now hath pride and rebuke gotten strength, and the time of destruction, and the wrath of indignation. Now therefore,

THE FIRST BOOK OF THE MACCABEES

my sons, be ye zealous for the law, and give your lives for the covenant of your fathers. Call to remembrance what acts our fathers did in their time; so shall ye receive great honour and an everlasting name. Wherefore, ye my sons, be valiant, and show yourselves men in the behalf of the law; for by it shall ye obtain glory. And, behold, I know that your brother Simon is a man of counsel, give ear unto him alway: he shall be a father unto you. As for Judas Maccabeus, he hath been mighty and strong, even from his youth up: let him be your captain, and fight the battle of the people. Take also unto you all those that observe the law, and avenge ye the wrong of your people. Recompense fully the heathen, and take heed to the commandments of the law."

So he blessed them, and was gathered to his fathers. And he died in the hundred forty and sixth year, and his sons buried him in the sepulchres of his fathers at Modin, and all Israel made great lamentation for him.

Then his son Judas, called Maccabeus, rose up in his stead. And all his brethren helped him, and so did all they that held with his father, and they fought with cheerfulness the battle of Israel. So he got his people great honour, and put on a breastplate as a giant, and girt his warlike harness about him, and he made battles, protecting the host with his sword. In his acts he was like a lion, and like a lion's whelp roaring for his prey. For he pursued the wicked, and sought them out, and burnt up those that vexed his people. Wherefore the wicked shrunk for fear of him, and all the workers of iniquity were troubled, because salvation prospered in his hand. He grieved also many kings, and made Jacob glad with his acts, and his memorial is blessed for ever. Moreover he went through the cities of Juda, destroying the ungodly out of them, and turning away wrath from Israel: so that he was renowned unto the utmost part of the earth, and he received unto him such as were ready to perish.

PART TWO
PROPHETICAL BOOKS

THE WORDS OF AMOS

The prophetical books of the Old Testament afford the most complete refutation to be found in any literature of the "art for art's sake" heresy. For they contain undeniably sublime poetry which is also undeniably inspired by a moral purpose. The message of all the great literary prophets is alike in its unrelenting hostility to any compromise with the lax moral customs of the surrounding paganisms, in its insistence upon the monotheistic worship of God through righteousness rather than through ceremonial, and in its constant proletarian protest against the injustice of the ruling classes. Prophecies of the approaching doom of the whole political and social order are so recurrent as to become wearisome to a modern reader, but since this doom was actually fulfilled the prophets must be acknowledged to have read the signs of the times correctly. And with all this community of purpose among them, there were still great individual differences of personality and literary style.

The characteristic of Hebrew poetry of being based upon parallelism of phrase instead of upon metre made it easy to pass back and forth from prose to verse, a liberty used by the prophets so extensively that there are many borderline cases of passages that may almost equally well be regarded as verse or as rhythmical prose.

The first of the new school, Amos the herdsman of Tekoa, writing between 765 and 750 B.C., caught from his native southern mountains their rugged grandeur and simplicity. Bursting in like a moral thunderbolt upon the merry feast at Beth-el in the Northern Kingdom, he nevertheless intuitively followed the most approved method of rhetorical persuasion in opening his discourse with a pronouncement of doom upon successive neighboring peoples and then slowly and as it were inevitably narrowing the circle to include the company before him. In spite of this tactful beginning, it is not surprising that before his message was finished there was demand that he be deported as an alien incendiary back to the Southern Kingdom, there "to eat bread and prophesy there" and to "prophesy not again any more at Beth-el."

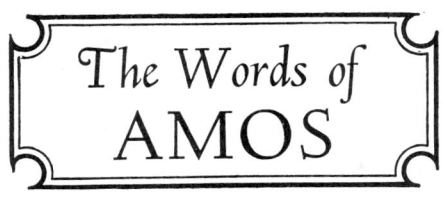

WHO WAS AMONG THE HERDSMEN OF TEKOA, WHICH HE SAW CONCERNING ISRAEL IN THE DAYS OF UZZIAH KING OF JUDAH, AND IN THE DAYS OF JEROBOAM THE SON OF JOASH KING OF ISRAEL, TWO YEARS BEFORE THE EARTHQUAKE.

"The Lord Will Roar from Zion"

The Lord will roar from Zion,
And utter his voice from Jerusalem;
And the habitations of the shepherds shall mourn,
And the top of Carmel shall wither.

Thus saith the Lord:
"For three transgressions of Damascus,
And for four,
I will not turn away the punishment thereof;
Because they have threshed Gilead with threshing instruments of iron.
But I will send a fire into the house of Hazael,
Which shall devour the palaces of Ben-hadad.
I will break also the bar of Damascus,
And cut off the inhabitant from the plain of Aven,
And him that holdeth the sceptre from the house of Eden:
And the people of Syria shall go into captivity unto Kir,"
Saith the Lord.

Thus saith the Lord:
"For three transgressions of Gaza,
And for four,
I will not turn away the punishment thereof;

THE WORDS OF AMOS

Because they carried away captive the whole captivity,
To deliver them up to Edom.
But I will send a fire on the wall of Gaza,
Which shall devour the palaces thereof:
And I will cut off the inhabitant from Ashdod,
And him that holdeth the sceptre from Ashkelon,
And I will turn mine hand against Ekron:
And the remnant of the Philistines shall perish,"
Saith the Lord God.

Thus saith the Lord:
"For three transgressions of Tyrus,
And for four,
I will not turn away the punishment thereof;
Because they delivered up the whole captivity to Edom,
And remembered not the brotherly covenant.
But I will send a fire on the wall of Tyrus,
Which shall devour the palaces thereof."

Thus saith the Lord:
"For three transgressions of Edom,
And for four,
I will not turn away the punishment thereof;
Because he did pursue his brother with the sword,
And did cast off all pity,
And his anger did tear perpetually,
And he kept his wrath for ever.
But I will send a fire upon Teman,
Which shall devour the palaces of Bozrah."

Thus saith the Lord:
"For three transgressions of the children of Ammon,
And for four,
I will not turn away the punishment thereof;
Because they have ripped up the women with child of Gilead,
That they might enlarge their border.

THE WORDS OF AMOS

But I will kindle a fire in the wall of Rabbah,
And it shall devour the palaces thereof,
With shouting in the day of battle,
With a tempest in the day of the whirlwind:
And their king shall go into captivity,
He and his princes together,"
Saith the Lord.

Thus saith the Lord:
"For three transgressions of Moab,
And for four,
I will not turn away the punishment thereof;
Because he burned the bones
Of the king of Edom into lime.
But I will send a fire upon Moab,
And it shall devour the palaces of Kirioth:
And Moab shall die with tumult,
With shouting, and with the sound of the trumpet:
And I will cut off the judge from the midst thereof,
And will slay all the princes thereof with him,"
Saith the Lord.

Thus saith the Lord:
"For three transgressions of Judah,
And for four,
I will not turn away the punishment thereof;
Because they have despised the law of the Lord,
And have not kept his commandments,
And their lies caused them to err,
After the which their fathers have walked.
But I will send a fire upon Judah,
And it shall devour the palaces of Jerusalem."

Thus saith the Lord:
"For three transgressions of Israel,
And for four,

THE WORDS OF AMOS

I will not turn away the punishment thereof;
Because they sold the righteous for silver,
And the poor for a pair of shoes;
That pant after the dust of the earth on the head of the poor,
And turn aside the way of the meek:
And a man and his father will go in unto the same maid,
To profane my holy name:
And they lay themselves down upon clothes laid to pledge to every altar,
And they drink the wine of the condemned in the house of their god.

Yet destroyed I the Amorite before them,
Whose height was like the height of the cedars,
And he was strong as the oaks;
Yet I destroyed his fruit from above,
And his roots from beneath.
Also I brought you up from the land of Egypt,
And led you forty years through the wilderness,
To possess the land of the Amorite.
And I raised up of your sons for prophets,
And of your young men for Nazarites.
Is it not even thus, O ye children of Israel?"
Saith the Lord.
"But ye gave the Nazarites wine to drink;
And commanded the prophets,
Saying, 'Prophesy not.'

Behold, I am pressed under you,
As a cart is pressed that is full of sheaves.
Therefore the flight shall perish from the swift,
And the strong shall not strengthen his force,
Neither shall the mighty deliver himself:
Neither shall he stand that handleth the bow;
And he that is swift of foot shall not deliver himself:
Neither shall he that rideth the horse deliver himself.
And he that is courageous among the mighty
Shall flee away naked in that day,"
Saith the Lord.

THE WORDS OF AMOS

"Hear This Word That the Lord Hath Spoken"

Hear this word that the Lord hath spoken against you, O children of Israel,
Against the whole family which I brought up from the land of Egypt, saying,
"You only have I known of all the families of the earth":
Therefore I will punish you for all your iniquities.

Can two walk together, except they be agreed?
Will a lion roar in the forest, when he hath no prey?
Will a young lion cry out of his den, if he have taken nothing?
Can a bird fall in a snare upon the earth, where no gin is for him?
Shall one take up a snare from the earth, and have taken nothing at all?
Shall a trumpet be blown in the city, and the people not be afraid?
Shall there be evil in a city, and the Lord hath not done it?
Surely the Lord God will do nothing, but he revealeth his secret unto his servants the prophets.
The lion hath roared, who will not fear?
The Lord God hath spoken, who can but prophesy?

Publish in the palaces at Ashdod,
And in the palaces in the land of Egypt,
And say, "Assemble yourselves upon the mountains of Samaria,
And behold the great tumults in the midst thereof,
And the oppressed in the midst thereof."
"For they know not to do right," saith the Lord,
"Who store up violence and robbery in their palaces."

Therefore thus saith the Lord God:
"An adversary there shall be even round about the land;
And he shall bring down thy strength from thee,
And thy palaces shall be spoiled."

Thus saith the Lord:
"As the shepherd taketh out of the mouth of the lion two legs, or a piece of an ear;

THE WORDS OF AMOS

So shall the children of Israel be taken out that dwell in Samaria in the
    corner of a bed,
And in Damascus in a couch.

Hear ye, and testify in the house of Jacob,"
Saith the Lord God, the God of hosts,
"That in the day that I shall visit the transgressions of Israel upon him
I will also visit the altars of Beth-el:
And the horns of the altar shall be cut off, and fall to the ground.
And I will smite the winter house with the summer house;
And the houses of ivory shall perish,
And the great houses shall have an end,"
Saith the Lord.

"Hear This Word, Ye Kine of Bashan"

Hear this word, ye kine of Bashan,
That are in the mountain of Samaria,
Which oppress the poor, which crush the needy,
Which say to their masters, "Bring, and let us drink."
The Lord God hath sworn by his holiness,
That, lo, the days shall come upon you,
That he will take you away with hooks,
And your posterity with fishhooks.
"And ye shall go out at the breaches,
Every cow at that which is before her;
And ye shall cast them into the palace,"
Saith the Lord.

"Come to Beth-el, and transgress;
At Gilgal multiply transgression;
And bring your sacrifices every morning,
And your tithes after three years:
And offer a sacrifice of thanksgiving with leaven,
And proclaim and publish the free offerings:
For this liketh you, O ye children of Israel,"
Saith the Lord God.

THE WORDS OF AMOS

"And I also have given you cleanness of teeth in all your cities,
And want of bread in all your places:
Yet have ye not returned unto me,"
Saith the Lord.

"And also I have withheld the rain from you,
When there were yet three months to the harvest:
And I caused it to rain upon one city,
And caused it not to rain upon another city:
One piece was rained upon,
And the piece whereupon it rained not withered.
So two or three cities wandered unto one city, to drink water;
But they were not satisfied:
Yet have ye not returned unto me,
Saith the Lord.

"I have smitten you with blasting and mildew:
When your gardens and your vineyards and your fig trees and your
     olive trees increased,
The palmerworm devoured them:
Yet have ye not returned unto me,"
Saith the Lord.

"I have sent among you the pestilence after the manner of Egypt:
Your young men have I slain with the sword,
And have taken away your horses;
And I have made the stink of your camps to come up unto your
     nostrils:
Yet have ye not returned unto me,"
Saith the Lord.

"I have overthrown some of you, as God overthrew Sodom and Go-
     morrah,
And ye were as a firebrand plucked out of the burning:
Yet have ye not returned unto me,"
Saith the Lord.

THE WORDS OF AMOS

"Therefore thus will I do unto thee, O Israel:
And because I will do this unto thee,
Prepare to meet thy God, O Israel."

For, lo, he that formeth the mountains, and createth the wind,
And declareth unto man what is his thought,
That maketh the morning darkness,
And treadeth upon the high places of the earth,
The Lord, the God of hosts, is his name.

"Hear Ye This Word Which I Take Up Against You"

Hear ye this word which I take up against you,
Even a lamentation, O house of Israel:
"The virgin of Israel is fallen; she shall no more rise:
She is forsaken upon her land; there is none to raise her up."
For thus saith the Lord God;
"The city that went out by a thousand shall leave a hundred,
And that which went forth by a hundred shall leave ten, to the
　　　house of Israel."

"Seek Ye Me, and Ye Shall Live"

Thus saith the Lord unto the house of Israel,
"Seek ye me, and ye shall live:
But seek not Beth-el,
Nor enter into Gilgal,
And pass not to Beer-sheba:
For Gilgal shall surely go into captivity,
And Beth-el shall come to nought."

Seek the Lord, and ye shall live;
Lest he break out like fire in the house of Joseph, and devour it,
And there be none to quench it in Beth-el. Ye who turn judgment
　　　to wormwood,
And leave off righteousness in the earth,
Seek him that maketh the seven stars and Orion,
And turneth the shadow of death into the morning,
And maketh the day dark with night:

THE WORDS OF AMOS

That calleth for the waters of the sea,
And poureth them out upon the face of the earth:
The Lord is his name.

"Wailing Shall Be in All Streets"

The Lord, the God of hosts, the Lord, saith thus:
"Wailing shall be in all streets;
And they shall say in all the highways, 'Alas! alas!'
And they shall call the husbandman to mourning,
And such as are skilful of lamentation to wailing.
And in all vineyards shall be wailing:
For I will pass through thee,"
Saith the Lord.

"Woe unto you that desire the day of the Lord!
To what end is it for you?
The day of the Lord is darkness, and not light.
As if a man did flee from a lion,
And a bear met him;
Or went into the house, and leaned his hand on the wall,
And a serpent bit him.
Shall not the day of the Lord be darkness, and not light?
Even very dark, and no brightness in it?

I hate, I despise your feast days,
And I will not smell in your solemn assemblies.
Though ye offer me burnt offerings and your meat offerings,
I will not accept them:
Neither will I regard the peace offerings of your fat beasts.
Take thou away from me the noise of thy songs;
For I will not hear the melody of thy viols.
But let judgment run down as waters,
And righteousness as a mighty stream."

"Woe to Them That Are at Ease in Zion"

Woe to them that are at ease in Zion,
And trust in the mountain of Samaria,
Which are named chief of the nations,

THE WORDS OF AMOS

To whom the house of Israel came!
Pass ye unto Calneh, and see;
And from thence go ye to Hamath the great:
Then go down to Gath of the Philistines:
Be they better than these kingdoms?
Or their border greater than your border?
Ye that put far away the evil day,
And cause the seat of violence to come near;
That lie upon beds of ivory,
And stretch themselves upon their couches,
And eat the lambs out of the flock,
And the calves out of the midst of the stall;
That chant to the sound of the viol,
And invent to themselves instruments of music, like David;
That drink wine in bowls,
And anoint themselves with the chief ointments:
But they are not grieved for the affliction of Joseph.
Therefore now shall they go captive with the first that go captive,
And the banquet of them that stretched themselves shall be removed.

The Lord God hath sworn by himself,
Saith the Lord the God of hosts,
"I abhor the excellency of Jacob, and hate his palaces:
Therefore will I deliver up the city with all that is therein."
And it shall come to pass,
If there remain ten men in one house, they shall die.
And a man's uncle shall take him up,
And he that burneth him shall say unto him that is by the sides of
    the house,
"Is there yet any with thee?"
And he shall say, "No."
Then shall he say, "Hold thy tongue":
For we may not make mention of the name of the Lord.
For, behold, the Lord commandeth,
And he will smite the great house with breaches,
And the little house with clefts.

THE WORDS OF AMOS

Symbolism of the Grasshoppers, the Fire, and the Plumbline

Thus hath the Lord God showed unto me; and, behold, he formed grasshoppers in the beginning of the shooting up of the latter growth; and, lo, it was the latter growth after the king's mowings. And it came to pass that when they had made an end of eating the grass of the land, then I said, "O Lord God, forgive, I beseech thee: by whom shall Jacob arise? for he is small." The Lord repented for this: "It shall not be," saith the Lord.

Thus hath the Lord God showed unto me: and, behold, the Lord God called to contend by fire, and it devoured the great deep, and did eat up a part. Then said I, "O Lord God, cease, I beseech thee: by whom shall Jacob arise? for he is small." The Lord repented for this: "This also shall not be," saith the Lord God.

Thus he showed me: and, behold, the Lord stood upon a wall made by a plumbline, with a plumbline in his hand. And the Lord said unto me, "Amos, what seest thou?" And I said, "A plumbline." Then said the Lord, "Behold, I will set a plumbline in the midst of my people Israel; I will not again pass by them any more; and the high places of Isaac shall be desolate, and the sanctuaries of Israel shall be laid waste; and I will rise against the house of Jeroboam with the sword."

"Amos Hath Conspired Against Thee"

Then Amaziah the priest of Beth-el sent to Jeroboam king of Israel, saying,

"*Amos hath conspired against thee in the midst of the house of Israel:*
The land is not able to bear all his words.
For thus Amos saith,
'Jeroboam shall die by the sword,
And Israel shall surely be led away captive out of their own land.'"

Also Amaziah said unto Amos,

"O thou seer, go, flee thee away into the land of Judah,
And there eat bread, and prophesy there.

THE WORDS OF AMOS

But prophesy not again any more at Beth-el:
For it is the king's chapel, and it is the king's court."

Then answered Amos, and said to Amaziah,

"I was no prophet, neither was I a prophet's son;
But I was a herdsman, and a gatherer of sycamore fruit:
And the Lord took me as I followed the flock,
And the Lord said unto me,
'Go, prophesy unto my people Israel.'
Now therefore hear thou the word of the Lord:
Thou sayest, 'Prophesy not against Israel,
And drop not thy word against the house of Isaac.'
Therefore thus saith the Lord:
'Thy wife shall be a harlot in the city,
And thy sons and thy daughters shall fall by the sword,
And thy land shall be divided by line;
And thou shalt die in a polluted land:
And Israel shall surely go into captivity forth of his land."

Symbolism of the Fruit

Thus hath the Lord God showed unto me: and behold a basket of summer fruit. And he said, "Amos, what seest thou?" And I said, "A basket of summer fruit." Then said the Lord unto me, "The end is come upon my people of Israel; I will not again pass by them any more.

"And the songs of the temple shall be howlings in that day," saith the Lord God: "there shall be many dead bodies in every place; they shall cast them forth with silence."

Hear this, O ye that swallow up the needy, even to make the poor of the land to fail, saying, "When will the new moon be gone, that we may sell corn? and the sabbath, that we may set forth wheat?" making the ephah small, and the shekel great, and falsifying the balances by deceit. "That we may buy the poor for silver, and the needy for a pair of shoes; yea, and sell the refuse of the wheat?"

The Lord hath sworn by the excellency of Jacob, "Surely I

THE WORDS OF AMOS

will never forget any of their works." Shall not the land tremble for this, and every one mourn that dwelleth therein? and it shall rise up wholly as a flood; and it shall be cast out and drowned, as by the flood of Egypt.

"And it shall come to pass in that day," saith the Lord God, "that I will cause the sun to go down at noon, and I will darken the earth in the clear day: and I will turn your feasts into mourning, and all your songs into lamentation; and I will bring up sackcloth upon all loins, and baldness upon every head; and I will make it as the mourning of an only son, and the end thereof as a bitter day.

"Behold, the days come," saith the Lord God, "that I will send a famine in the land, not a famine of bread, nor a thirst for water, but of hearing the words of the Lord: and they shall wander from sea to sea, and from the north even to the east, they shall run to and fro to seek the word of the Lord, and shall not find it. In that day shall the fair virgins and young men faint for thirst. They that swear by the sin of Samaria, and say, 'Thy god, O Dan, liveth'; and, 'The manner of Beer-sheba liveth'; even they shall fall, and never rise up again."

"Smite the Lintel"

I saw the Lord standing upon the altar: and he said,

"Smite the lintel of the door, that the posts may shake:
And cut them in the head, all of them;
And I will slay the last of them with the sword:
He that fleeth of them shall not flee away,
And he that escapeth of them shall not be delivered.
Though they dig into hell,
Thence shall mine hand take them;
Though they climb up to heaven,
Thence will I bring them down:
And though they hide themselves in the top of Carmel,
I will search and take them out thence;
And though they be hid from my sight in the bottom of the sea,

THE WORDS OF AMOS

Thence will I command the serpent, and he shall bite them:
And though they go into captivity before their enemies,
Thence will I command the sword, and it shall slay them:
And I will set mine eyes upon them for evil, and not for good."

And the Lord God of hosts is he that toucheth the land, and it shall melt,
And all that dwell therein shall mourn:
And it shall rise up wholly like a flood;
And shall be drowned, as by the flood of Egypt.
It is he that buildeth his stories in the heaven,
And hath founded his troop in the earth;
He that calleth for the waters of the sea,
And poureth them out upon the face of the earth:
The Lord is his name.

"Are ye not as children of the Ethiopians unto me,
O children of Israel?" saith the Lord.
"Have not I brought up Israel out of the land of Egypt?
And the Philistines from Caphtor,
And the Syrians from Kir?
Behold, the eyes of the Lord God are upon the sinful kingdom,
And I will destroy it from off the face of the earth;
Saving that I will not utterly destroy the house of Jacob,"
Saith the Lord.

THE WORD OF THE LORD THAT CAME UNTO HOSEA

THE DEPARTURE of Amos did not for long preserve the Northern Kingdom from hearing words of prophecy. Within ten years a follower of Amos appeared in the person of one of its own citizens, Hosea. But though in essentials his message was similar to that of Amos, the manner was much milder. Hosea preferred entreaty to denunciation, he emphasized God's love for his people, and where the imagery of Amos breathed of fire, famine, and slaughter by the sword, Hosea drew his from the peaceful life of husbandry. All of the prophets made much use of symbolism in their writings and frequently tried to make their points clear by symbolic actions, but no other carried this so far as Hosea if his words are to be taken literally that he actually married a harlot in order to symbolize the relation of God to his faithless people. Extravagant as such an action seems, it is not utterly incredible as an extreme example of the utter devotion of the prophets to their mission.

The Word of the Lord That Came unto HOSEA

THE SON OF BEERI, IN THE DAYS OF UZZIAH, JOTHAM, AHAZ, AND HEZEKIAH, KINGS OF JUDAH, AND IN THE DAYS OF JEROBOAM THE SON OF JOASH, KING OF ISRAEL.

Symbolism of Gomer

THE BEGINNING OF THE WORD of the Lord by Hosea. And the Lord said to Hosea, "Go, take unto thee a wife of whoredoms and children of whoredoms: for the land hath committed great whoredom, departing from the Lord." So he went and took Gomer the daughter of Diblaim; which conceived, and bore him a son. And the Lord said unto him, "Call his name Jezreel; for yet a little while, and I will avenge the blood of Jezreel upon the house of Jehu, and will cause to cease the kingdom of the house of Israel. And it shall come to pass at that day, that I will break the bow of Israel in the valley of Jezreel." And she conceived again, and bore a daughter. And God said unto him, "Call her name Lo-ruhamah: for I will no more have mercy upon the house of Israel; but I will utterly take them away. But I will have mercy upon the house of Judah, and will save them by the Lord their God, and will not save them by bow, nor by sword, nor by battle, by horses, nor by horsemen." Now when she had weaned Lo-ruhamah, she conceived, and bore a son. Then said God, "Call his name Lo-ammi: for ye are not my people, and I will not be your God.

"Yet the number of the children of Israel shall be as the sand of the sea, which cannot be measured nor numbered; and it shall come to pass, that in the place where it was said unto them,

THE WORD OF THE LORD UNTO HOSEA

'Ye are not my people,' there it shall be said unto them, 'Ye are the sons of the living God.' Then shall the children of Judah and the children of Israel be gathered together, and appoint themselves one head, and they shall come up out of the land: for great shall be the day of Jezreel.

"Say ye unto your brethren, 'Ammi'; and to your sisters, 'Ruhamah.' Plead with your mother, plead: for she is not my wife, neither am I her husband: let her therefore put away her whoredoms out of her sight, and her adulteries from between her breasts; lest I strip her naked, and set her as in the day that she was born, and make her as a wilderness, and set her like a dry land, and slay her with thirst. And I will not have mercy upon her children; for they be the children of whoredoms. For their mother hath played the harlot: she that conceived them hath done shamefully: for she said, 'I will go after my lovers, that give me my bread and my water, my wool and my flax, mine oil and my drink.'

"Therefore, behold, I will hedge up thy way with thorns, and make a wall, that she shall not find her paths. And she shall follow after her lovers, but she shall not overtake them; and she shall seek them, but shall not find them: then shall she say, 'I will go and return to my first husband; for then was it better with me than now.' For she did not know that I gave her corn, and wine, and oil, and multiplied her silver and gold, which they prepared for Baal.

"Therefore will I return, and take away my corn in the time thereof, and my wine in the season thereof, and will recover my wool and my flax given to cover her nakedness. And now will I discover her lewdness in the sight of her lovers, and none shall deliver her out of mine hand. I will also cause all her mirth to cease, her feast days, her new moons, and her sabbaths, and all her solemn feasts. And I will destroy her vines and her fig trees, whereof she hath said, 'These are my rewards that my lovers have given me': and I will make them a forest, and the beasts of the field shall eat them. And I will visit upon her the days of Baalim, wherein she burned incense to them, and she decked

THE WORD OF THE LORD UNTO HOSEA

herself with her earrings and her jewels, and she went after her lovers, and forgot me," saith the Lord.

"Therefore, behold, I will allure her, and bring her into the wilderness, and speak comfortably unto her. And I will give her her vineyards from thence, and the valley of Achor for a door of hope: and she shall sing there, as in the days of her youth, and as in the day when she came up out of the land of Egypt. And it shall be at that day," saith the Lord, "that thou shalt call me Ishi; and shalt call me no more Baali. For I will take away the names of Baalim out of her mouth, and they shall no more be remembered by their name. And in that day will I make a covenant for them with the beasts of the field, and with the fowls of heaven, and with the creeping things of the ground: and I will break the bow of the sword and the battle out of the earth, and will make them to lie down safely. And I will betroth thee unto me for ever; yea, I will betroth thee unto me in righteousness, and in judgment, and in lovingkindness, and in mercies. I will even betroth thee unto me in faithfulness: and thou shalt know the Lord. And it shall come to pass in that day, I will hear," saith the Lord, "I will hear the heavens, and they shall hear the earth; and the earth shall hear the corn, and the wine, and the oil; and they shall hear Jezreel, and I will sow her unto me in the earth; and I will have mercy upon her that had not obtained mercy; and I will say to them which were not my people, 'Thou art my people'; and they shall say, 'Thou art my God.'"

"When Israel Was a Child"

"When Israel was a child, then I loved him,
And called my son out of Egypt.
As they called them so they went from them:
They sacrificed unto Baalim,
And burned incense to graven images.
I taught Ephraim also to go, taking them by their arms;
But they knew not that I healed them.
I drew them with cords of a man, with bands of love:

THE WORD OF THE LORD UNTO HOSEA

And I was to them as they that take off the yoke on their jaws,
And I laid meat unto them.

He shall not return into the land of Egypt,
But the Assyrian shall be his king,
Because they refused to return.
And the sword shall abide on his cities,
And shall consume his branches, and devour them,
Because of their own counsels.
And my people are bent to backsliding from me:
Though they called them to the most High,
None at all would exalt him.

How shall I give thee up, Ephraim?
How shall I deliver thee, Israel?
How shall I make thee as Admah?
How shall I set thee as Zeboim?
Mine heart is turned within me,
My repentings are kindled together.
I will not execute the fierceness of mine anger,
I will not return to destroy Ephraim:
For I am God, and not man;
The Holy One in the midst of thee:
And I will not enter into the city.
They shall walk after the Lord:
He shall roar like a lion:
When he shall roar,
Then the children shall tremble from the west.
They shall tremble as a bird out of Egypt,
And as a dove out of the land of Assyria:
And I will place them in their houses,"
Saith the Lord.

"O Israel, Return unto the Lord"

O Israel, return unto the Lord thy God;
For thou hast fallen by thine iniquity.
Take with you words, and turn to the Lord:

THE WORD OF THE LORD UNTO HOSEA

Say unto him, "Take away all iniquity, and receive us graciously:
So will we render the calves of our lips.
Asshur shall not save us; we will not ride upon horses:
Neither will we say any more to the work of our hands, 'Ye are our
 gods':
For in thee the fatherless findeth mercy."

"I will heal their backsliding, I will love them freely:
For mine anger is turned away from him.
I will be as the dew unto Israel:
He shall grow as the lily, and cast forth his roots as Lebanon.
His branches shall spread, and his beauty shall be as the olive tree,
 and his smell as Lebanon.
They that dwell under his shadow shall return;
They shall revive as the corn, and grow as the vine:
The scent thereof shall be as the wine of Lebanon.
Ephraim shall say, 'What have I to do any more with idols?'
I have heard him, and observed him:
I am like a green fir tree.
From me is thy fruit found."

Who is wise, and he shall understand these things?
Prudent, and he shall know them?
For the ways of the Lord are right,
And the just shall walk in them:
But the transgressors shall fall therein.

THE WORD OF THE LORD THAT CAME UNTO MICAH THE MORASTHITE

THE CONQUEST of the kingdom of Samaria by the Assyrians in 722 B.C. made an end of the Northern culture and literature. While probably not all of the inhabitants were carried into captivity, the expulsion was sufficiently ruthless to break up the ten "lost tribes" so completely that they vanish from history, never to reappear save in such fanciful accounts as that in the Book of Mormon. In this stormy period when a like extermination threatened the two tribes of the Southern Kingdom, a new prophet arose there who in some measure combined the characteristics of Amos and Hosea. Micah the Morasthite was certain that God would chastise the sins of priests and princes by the overthrow of the national power, but beyond that time of punishment he foresaw an era of redemption. His was probably the first voice in the Western world to announce the dream of universal peace. Those who two thousand years later doubt that war can ever be abolished should reflect that when this vision came to Micah the chances of its fulfilment seemed almost infinitely less than they do even to-day. True, it was with him a kind of corollary of the new-found prophetic faith in God as a God of righteousness rather than a God of war, but as those who held this faith were still but voices in the wilderness, Micah's hope of peace must have seemed to his contemporaries no more wild and radical than the rest of his beliefs.

The Word of the Lord That Came unto MICAH THE MORASTHITE

IN THE DAYS OF JOTHAM, AHAZ, AND HEZE-
KIAH, KINGS OF JUDAH, WHICH HE SAW
CONCERNING SAMARIA AND JERUSALEM.

"Hear, All Ye People"

Hear, all ye people;
Hearken, O earth, and all that therein is:
And let the Lord God be witness against you,
The Lord from his holy temple

For, behold, the Lord cometh forth out of his place,
And will come down, and tread upon the high places of the earth.
And the mountains shall be molten under him,
And the valleys shall be cleft,
As wax before the fire,
As the waters poured down a steep place.

For the transgression of Jacob is all this, and for the sins of the house of
    Israel.
What is the transgression of Jacob?
Is it not Samaria?
And what are the high places of Judah?
Are they not Jerusalem?

Therefore I will make Samaria as a heap of the field,
And as plantings of a vineyard:

MICAH THE MORASTHITE

And I will pour down the stones thereof into the valley,
And I will discover the foundations thereof.

And all the graven images thereof shall be beaten to pieces,
And all the hires thereof shall be burned with the fire,
And all the idols thereof will I lay desolate:
For she gathered it of the hire of a harlot,
And they shall return to the hire of a harlot.

Therefore I will wail and howl,
I will go stripped and naked:
I will make a wailing like the dragons,
And mourning as the owls.

For her wound is incurable;
For it is come unto Judah;
He is come unto the gate of my people,
Even to Jerusalem.

"Hear, I Pray You, O Heads of Jacob"

Hear, I pray you, O heads of Jacob,
And ye princes of the house of Israel;
Is it not for you to know judgment?
Who hate the good, and love the evil;
Who pluck off their skin from off them,
And their flesh from off their bones;
Who also eat the flesh of my people,
And flay their skin from off them;
And they break their bones, and chop them in pieces,
As for the pot, and as flesh within the caldron.

Then shall they cry unto the Lord,
But he will not hear them:
He will even hide his face from them at that time.
As they have behaved themselves ill in their doings.

Thus saith the Lord
Concerning the prophets that make my people err,

MICAH THE MORASTHITE

That bite with their teeth, and cry, "Peace";
And he that putteth not into their mouths,
They even prepare war against him:

"Therefore night shall be unto you,
That ye shall not have a vision;
And it shall be dark unto you, that ye shall not divine;
And the sun shall go down over the prophets,
And the day shall be dark over them.
Then shall the seers be ashamed,
And the diviners confounded:
Yea, they shall all cover their lips;
For there is no answer of God."

But truly I am full of power
By the spirit of the Lord, and of judgment, and of might,
To declare unto Jacob his transgression,
And to Israel his sin.

Hear this, I pray you, ye heads of the house of Jacob,
And princes of the house of Israel,
That abhor judgment,
And pervert all equity.

They build up Zion with blood,
And Jerusalem with iniquity.
The heads thereof judge for reward,
And the priests thereof teach for hire,
And the prophets thereof divine for money:
Yet will they lean upon the Lord, and say,
"Is not the Lord among us?
None evil can come upon us."

Therefore shall Zion for your sake be plowed as a field,
And Jerusalem shall become heaps,
And the mountain of the house as the high places of the forest.

MICAH THE MORASTHITE

"But in the Last Days"

But in the last days it shall come to pass,
That the mountain of the house of the Lord
Shall be established in the top of the mountains,
And it shall be exalted above the hills;
And people shall flow unto it.

And many nations shall come, and say,
"Come, and let us go up to the mountain of the Lord,
And to the house of the God of Jacob;
And he will teach us of his ways,
And we will walk in his paths":
For the law shall go forth of Zion,
And the word of the Lord from Jerusalem.

And he shall judge among many people,
And rebuke strong nations afar off;
And they shall beat their swords into plowshares,
And their spears into pruninghooks:
Nation shall not lift up a sword against nation,
Neither shall they learn war any more.
But they shall sit every man under his vine
And under his fig tree;
And none shall make them afraid:
For the mouth of the Lord of hosts hath spoken it.
For all people will walk every one in the name of his god,
And we will walk in the name of the Lord our God for ever and ever.

"In that day," saith the Lord,
"Will I assemble her that halteth,
And I will gather her that is driven out,
And her that I have afflicted;
And I will make her that halted a remnant,
And her that was cast far off a strong nation":

MICAH THE MORASTHITE
And the Lord shall reign over them in Mount Zion
From henceforth, even for ever.

"Now Gather Thyself in Troops"

Now gather thyself in troops, O daughter of troops:
He hath laid siege against us:
They shall smite the judge of Israel with a rod upon the cheek.
But thou, Beth-lehem Ephratah,
Though thou be little among the thousands of Judah,
Yet out of thee shall he come forth unto me that is to be ruler of Israel;
Whose goings forth have been from of old, from everlasting.
Therefore will he give them up,
Until the time that she which travaileth hath brought forth:
Then the remnant of his brethren shall return unto the children of
    Israel.

And he shall stand and feed in the strength of the Lord,
In the majesty of the name of the Lord his God;
And they shall abide:
For now shall he be great unto the ends of the earth.
And this man shall be the peace,
When the Assyrian shall come into our land:
And when he shall tread in our palaces,
Then shall we raise against him seven shepherds,
And eight principal men.
And they shall waste the land of Assyria with the sword,
And the land of Nimrod in the entrances thereof:
Thus shall he deliver us from the Assyrian,
When he cometh into our land,
And when he treadeth within our borders.

And the remnant of Jacob
Shall be in the midst of many people
As a dew from the Lord,
As the showers upon the grass,
That tarrieth not for man,

MICAH THE MORASTHITE

Nor waiteth for the sons of men.
And the remnant of Jacob
Shall be among the Gentiles in the midst of many people
As a lion among the beasts of the forest,
As a young lion among the flocks of sheep:
Who, if he go through, both treadeth down, and teareth in pieces,
And none can deliver.
Thine hand shall be lifted up upon thine adversaries,
And all thine enemies shall be cut off.

"Hear Ye Now What the Lord Saith"

Hear ye now what the Lord saith:
"Arise, contend thou before the mountains,
And let the hills hear thy voice."

Hear ye, O mountains, the Lord's controversy,
And ye strong foundations of the earth:
For the Lord hath a controversy with his people,
And he will plead with Israel.

"O my people, what have I done unto thee?
And wherein have I wearied thee?
Testify against me.
For I brought thee up out of the land of Egypt,
And redeemed thee out of the house of servants;
And I sent before thee Moses, Aaron, and Miriam.'

Wherewith shall I come before the Lord,
And bow myself before the high God?
Shall I come before him with burnt offerings,
With calves of a year old?
Will the Lord be pleased with thousands of rams,
Or with ten thousands of rivers of oil?
Shall I give my firstborn for my transgression,
The fruit of my body for the sin of my soul?

MICAH THE MORASTHITE

He hath showed thee, O man, what is good;
And what doth the Lord require of thee,
But to do justly, and to love mercy,
And to walk humbly with thy God?

THE VISION OF ISAIAH

Isaiah, *usually considered the greatest of the prophets, differed from his predecessors in being an aristocrat and a city dweller. During his long prophetic career in Jerusalem, extending from 740 to 701 B.C., he exercised much influence upon political affairs, particularly during the critical time of the Assyrian invasion. A wise statesman, he had opposed the policy of alliance with Egypt against Assyria, perceiving that the Egyptian day was over, and had counseled the maintenance of friendly relations with Nineveh even at the cost of tribute, but when war came, in spite of his efforts, he heartened the spirit of King Hezekiah to fight to the death. The fortunate outcome of that event increased his influence which continued until the paganizing group under Manasseh came into power when, according to tradition, Isaiah suffered martyrdom through being sawn asunder.*

In spite of his aristocratic birth and breeding, Isaiah sympathized with the proletarian aspirations of the prophetic school, but deeming the complete moral regeneration of the people impossible he placed his hope in the survival of a "Saving Remnant" and the eventual appearance of some mighty leader strong enough to establish justice throughout the land. From him stemmed the Messianic ideal that was to acquire ever-increasing weight through the centuries of defeat that were to follow. And in large measure he did succeed in creating the very "Remnant" that he sought, so that the prophetic spirit was enabled to survive the fifty years of persecution under Manasseh and emerge temporarily triumphant in the reign of Josiah. Owing to his reputation and the variety of his poetic gifts which brought to an immense command of technical resources a wide range of emotional experience, many later poems came to be ascribed to him, chief among them the separate Exilic collection from Chapters XL to LXVI entitled in this text "The Rhapsody of the Unknown Prophet."

The Vision of ISAIAH

THE SON OF AMOZ, WHICH HE SAW CONCERNING JUDAH AND JERUSALEM IN THE DAYS OF UZZIAH, JOTHAM, AHAZ, AND HEZEKIAH, KINGS OF JUDAH.

The Call of the Prophet

IN THE YEAR THAT KING UZZIAH DIED I saw also the Lord sitting upon a throne, high and lifted up, and his train filled the temple. Above it stood the seraphims: each one had six wings; with twain he covered his face, and with twain he covered his feet, and with twain he did fly. And one cried unto another, and said, "Holy, holy, holy, is the Lord of hosts: the whole earth is full of his glory." And the posts of the door moved at the voice of him that cried, and the house was filled with smoke.

Then said I, "Woe is me! for I am undone; because I am a man of unclean lips, and I dwell in the midst of a people of unclean lips: for mine eyes have seen the King, the Lord of hosts."

Then flew one of the seraphims unto me, having a live coal in his hand, which he had taken with the tongs from off the altar: and he laid it upon my mouth, and said, "Lo, this hath touched thy lips; and thine iniquity is taken away, and thy sin purged."

Also I heard the voice of the Lord, saying, "Whom shall I send, and who will go for us?"

Then said I, "Here am I; send me."

And he said, "Go, and tell this people, 'Hear ye indeed, but understand not; and see ye indeed, but perceive not.' Make the heart of this people fat, and make their ears heavy, and shut their eyes; lest they see with their eyes, and hear with their ears, and understand with their heart, and convert, and be healed."

THE VISION OF ISAIAH

Then said I, "Lord, how long?"

And he answered, "Until the cities be wasted without inhabitant, and the houses without man, and the land be utterly desolate, and the Lord have removed men far away, and there be a great forsaking in the midst of the land. But yet in it shall be a tenth, and it shall return, and shall be eaten: as a teil tree, and as an oak, whose substance is in them, when they cast their leaves: so the holy seed shall be the substance thereof."

"Hear, O Heavens"

Hear, O heavens, and give ear, O earth:
For the Lord hath spoken:
"I have nourished and brought up children,
And they have rebelled against me.
The ox knoweth his owner,
And the ass his master's crib;
But Israel doth not know,
My people doth not consider."

Ah sinful nation, a people laden with iniquity,
A seed of evildoers, children that are corrupters!
They have forsaken the Lord,
They have provoked the Holy One of Israel unto anger,
They are gone away backward.

Why should ye be stricken any more? ye will revolt more and more;
The whole head is sick, and the whole heart faint.
From the sole of the foot even unto the head there is no soundness in it;
But wounds, and bruises, and putrifying sores:
They have not been closed, neither bound up, neither mollified with
    ointment.
Your country is desolate, your cities are burned with fire:
Your land, strangers devour it in your presence,
And it is desolate, as overthrown by strangers.
And the daughter of Zion is left as a cottage in a vineyard,
As a lodge in a garden of cucumbers, as a besieged city.
Except the Lord of hosts had left unto us a very small remnant,

THE VISION OF ISAIAH

We should have been as Sodom, we should have been like unto
 Gomorrah.

Hear the word of the Lord,
Ye rulers of Sodom!
Give ear unto the law of our God,
Ye people of Gomorrah!
"To what purpose is the multitude of your sacrifices unto me?"
Saith the Lord:
"I am full of the burnt offerings of rams,
And the fat of fed beasts;
And I delight not in the blood of bullocks,
Or of lambs, or of he-goats.
When ye come to appear before me,
Who hath required this at your hand,
To tread my courts?
Bring no more vain oblations;
Incense is an abomination unto me;
The new moons and sabbaths, the calling of assemblies,
I cannot away with;
It is iniquity, even the solemn meeting.
Your new moons and your appointed feasts my soul hateth:
They are a trouble unto me; I am weary to bear them.
And when ye spread forth your hands,
I will hide mine eyes from you:
Yea, when ye make many prayers,
I will not hear:
Your hands are full of blood.
Wash you, make you clean;
Put away the evil of your doings from before mine eyes;
Cease to do evil;
Learn to do well;
Seek judgment, relieve the oppressed,
Judge the fatherless, plead for the widow.

Come now, and let us reason together,"
Saith the Lord:

THE VISION OF ISAIAH

"Though your sins be as scarlet,
They shall be as white as snow;
Though they be red like crimson,
They shall be as wool.
If ye be willing and obedient,
Ye shall eat the good of the land:
But if ye refuse and rebel,
Ye shall be devoured with the sword":
For the mouth of the Lord hath spoken it.

"And It Shall Come to Pass"

And it shall come to pass in the last days,
That the mountain of the Lord's house
Shall be established in the top of the mountains,
And shall be exalted above the hills;
And all nations shall flow unto it.
And many people shall go and say,
"Come ye, and let us go up to the mountain of the Lord,
To the house of the God of Jacob;
And he will teach us of his ways,
And we will walk in his paths;
For out of Zion shall go forth the law,
And the word of the Lord from Jerusalem."
And he shall judge among the nations,
And shall rebuke many people;
And they shall beat their swords into plowshares,
And their spears into pruninghooks;
Nation shall not lift up sword against nation,
Neither shall they learn war any more.

"Therefore Thou Hast Forsaken Thy People"

Therefore thou hast forsaken thy people the house of Jacob,
Because they be replenished from the east,
And are soothsayers like the Philistines,
And they please themselves in the children of strangers.
Their land also is full of silver and gold,

THE VISION OF ISAIAH

Neither is there any end of their treasures;
Their land is also full of horses,
Neither is there any end of their chariots;
Their land also is full of idols;
They worship the work of their own hands,
That which their own fingers have made;
And the mean man boweth down,
And the great man humbleth himself:
Therefore forgive them not.

"Enter into the Rock"

Enter into the rock, and hide thee in the dust,
For fear of the Lord, and for the glory of his majesty.
The lofty looks of man shall be humbled,
And the haughtiness of men shall be bowed down,
And the Lord alone shall be exalted in that day.
For the day of the Lord of hosts
Shall be upon every one that is proud and lofty,
And upon every one that is lifted up;
And he shall be brought low;
And upon all the cedars of Lebanon, that are high and lifted up,
And upon all the oaks of Bashan,
And upon all the high mountains,
And upon all the hills that are lifted up,
And upon every high tower,
And upon every fenced wall,
And upon all the ships of Tarshish,
And upon all pleasant pictures.
And the loftiness of man shall be bowed down,
And the haughtiness of men shall be made low;
And the Lord alone shall be exalted in that day.
And the idols he shall utterly abolish.
And they shall go into the holes of the rocks,
And into the caves of the earth,
For fear of the Lord, and for the glory of his majesty,
When he ariseth to shake terribly the earth.

THE VISION OF ISAIAH

In that day a man shall cast his idols of silver, and his idols of gold,
Which they made each one for himself to worship,
To the moles and to the bats;
To go into the clefts of the rocks,
And into the tops of the ragged rocks,
For fear of the Lord, and for the glory of his majesty,
When he ariseth to shake terribly the earth.
Cease ye from man, whose breath is in his nostrils:
For wherein is he to be accounted of?

"Because the Daughters of Zion Are Haughty"

Because the daughters of Zion are haughty,
And walk with stretched forth necks and wanton eyes,
Walking and mincing as they go,
And making a tinkling with their feet:
Therefore the Lord will smite with a scab
The crown of the head of the daughters of Zion,
And the Lord will discover their secret parts.
In that day the Lord will take away
The bravery of their tinkling ornaments about their feet,
And their cauls, and their round tires like the moon,
The chains, and the bracelets, and the mufflers,
The bonnets, and the ornaments of the legs,
And the headbands, and the tablets, and the earrings,
The rings, and nose jewels,
The changeable suits of apparel,
And the mantles, and the wimples, and the crisping pins,
The glasses, and the fine linen, and the hoods, and the veils.
And it shall come to pass,
That instead of sweet smell there shall be stink;
And instead of a girdle a rent;
And instead of well-set hair baldness;
And instead of a stomacher a girding of sackcloth;
And burning instead of beauty.
Thy men shall fall by the sword,
And thy mighty in the war.

THE VISION OF ISAIAH

And her gates shall lament and mourn;
And she being desolate shall sit upon the ground.

And in that day seven women shall take hold of one man, saying, "We will eat our own bread, and wear our own apparel: only let us be called by thy name, to take away our reproach."

"Now Will I Sing to My Wellbeloved"

Now will I sing to my wellbeloved
A song of my beloved touching his vineyard.

My wellbeloved hath a vineyard
In a very fruitful hill;
And he fenced it, and gathered out the stones thereof,
And planted it with the choicest vine,
And built a tower in the midst of it,
And also made a winepress therein;
And he looked that it should bring forth grapes,
And it brought forth wild grapes.

And now, O inhabitants of Jerusalem, and men of Judah,
Judge, I pray you, betwixt me and my vineyard.
What could have been done more to my vineyard,
That I have not done in it?
Wherefore, when I looked that it should bring forth grapes,
Brought it forth wild grapes?

And now go to; I will tell you
What I will do to my vineyard:
I will take away the hedge thereof, and it shall be eaten up;
And break down the wall thereof, and it shall be trodden down;
And I will lay it waste: it shall not be pruned, nor digged;
But there shall come up briers and thorns:
I will also command the clouds
That they rain no rain upon it.

For the vineyard of the Lord of hosts is the house of Israel,
And the men of Judah his pleasant plant;

THE VISION OF ISAIAH

And he looked for judgment, but behold oppression;
For righteousness, but behold a cry.

"The People That Walked in Darkness"

The people that walked in darkness
Have seen a great light;
They that dwell in the land of the shadow of death,
Upon them hath the light shined.
Thou hast multiplied the nation, increased the joy;
They joy before thee according to the joy in harvest,
And as men rejoice when they divide the spoil.
For thou hast broken the yoke of his burden,
And the staff of his shoulder,
The rod of his oppressor,
As in the day of Midian.
For every battle of the warrior is with confused noise,
And garments rolled in blood;
But this shall be with burning and fuel of fire.
For unto us a child is born, unto us a son is given;
And the government shall be upon his shoulder;
And his name shall be called
Wonderful, Counsellor, The mighty God,
The everlasting Father, The Prince of peace.
Of the increase of his government and peace
There shall be no end,
Upon the throne of David, and upon his kingdom,
To order it, and to establish it
With judgment and with justice
From henceforth even for ever.
The zeal of the Lord of hosts will perform this.

"The Lord Sent a Word"

The Lord sent a word into Jacob,
And it hath lighted upon Israel.
And all the people shall know,
Even Ephraim and the inhabitant of Samaria,

THE VISION OF ISAIAH

That say in the pride and stoutness of heart,
"The bricks are fallen down, but we will build with hewn stones;
The sycamores are cut down, but we will change them into cedars."
Therefore the Lord shall set up the adversaries of Rezin against
 him,
And join his enemies together;
The Syrians before, and the Philistines behind;
And they shall devour Israel with open mouth.
For all this his anger is not turned away,
But his hand is stretched out still.

For the people turneth not unto him that smiteth them,
Neither do they seek the Lord of hosts.
Therefore the Lord will cut off from Israel
Head and tail, branch and rush, in one day.
The ancient and honourable, he is the head;
And the prophet that teacheth lies, he is the tail.
For the leaders of this people cause them to err;
And they that are led of them are destroyed.
Therefore the Lord shall have no joy in their young men,
Neither shall have mercy on their fatherless and widows:
For every one is a hypocrite and an evildoer,
And every mouth speaketh folly.
For all this his anger is not turned away,
But his hand is stretched out still.

For wickedness burneth as the fire:
It shall devour the briers and thorns,
And shall kindle in the thickets of the forest,
And they shall mount up like the lifting up of smoke.
Through the wrath of the Lord of hosts is the land darkened,
And the people shall be as the fuel of the fire:
No man shall spare his brother.
And he shall snatch on the right hand, and be hungry;
And he shall eat on the left hand, and they shall not be satisfied:
They shall eat every man the flesh of his own arm:
Manasseh, Ephraim; and Ephraim, Manasseh:

THE VISION OF ISAIAH

And they together shall be against Judah.
For all this his anger is not turned away,
But his hand is stretched out still.

Woe unto them that decree unrighteous decrees,
And that write grievousness which they have prescribed;
To turn aside the needy from judgment,
And to take away the right from the poor of my people,
That widows may be their prey,
And that they may rob the fatherless!
And what will ye do in the day of visitation,
And in the desolation which shall come from far?
To whom will ye flee for help?
And where will ye leave your glory?
Without me they shall bow down under the prisoners,
And they shall fall under the slain.
For all this his anger is not turned away,
But his hand is stretched out still.

"O Assyrian, the Rod of Mine Anger"

O Assyrian, the rod of mine anger,
And the staff in their hand is mine indignation.
I will send him against a hypocritical nation,
And against the people of my wrath will I give him a charge,
To take the spoil, and to take the prey,
And to tread them down like the mire of the streets.
Howbeit he meaneth not so,
Neither doth his heart think so;
But it is in his heart to destroy
And cut off nations not a few.

For he saith, "Are not my princes altogether kings?
Is not Calno as Carchemish?
Is not Hamath as Arpad?
Is not Samaria as Damascus?
As my hand hath found the kingdoms of the idols,

THE VISION OF ISAIAH

And whose graven images did excel them of Jerusalem and of
    Samaria;
Shall I not, as I have done unto Samaria and her idols,
So do to Jerusalem and her idols?"
Wherefore it shall come to pass,
That when the Lord hath performed his whole work upon Mount
    Zion and on Jerusalem,
I will punish the fruit of the stout heart of the king of Assyria,
And the glory of his high looks.

For he saith, "By the strength of my hand I have done it,
And by my wisdom: for I am prudent;
And I have removed the bounds of the people,
And I have robbed their treasures,
And I have put down the inhabitants like a valiant man;
And my hand hath found as a nest
The riches of the people;
And as one gathereth eggs that are left,
Have I gathered all the earth;
And there was none that moved the wind,
Or opened the mouth, or peeped."
Shall the ax boast itself against him that heweth therewith?
Or shall the saw magnify itself against him that shaketh it?
As if the rod should shake itself against them that lift it up,
Or as if the staff should lift up itself, as if it were no wood.

Therefore shall the Lord, the Lord of hosts,
Send among his fat ones leanness;
And under his glory he shall kindle a burning
Like the burning of a fire.
And the Light of Israel shall be for a fire,
And His Holy One for a flame;
And it shall burn and devour his thorns
And his briers in one day;
And shall consume the glory of his forest, and of his fruitful field,
    both soul and body;
And they shall be as when a standardbearer fainteth.

THE VISION OF ISAIAH

And the rest of the trees of his forest shall be few,
That a child may write them.

And it shall come to pass in that day,
That the remnant of Israel,
And such as are escaped of the house of Jacob,
Shall no more again stay upon him that smote them;
But shall stay upon the Lord, the Holy One of Israel.
The remnant shall return, even the remnant of Jacob,
Unto the mighty God.
For though thy people Israel be as the sand of the sea,
Yet a remnant of them shall return:
The consumption decreed shall overflow with righteousness.
For the Lord God of hosts shall make a consumption,
Even determined, in the midst of all the land.

Therefore thus saith the Lord God of hosts,
"O my people that dwellest in Zion,
Be not afraid of the Assyrian:
He shall smite thee with a rod,
And shall lift up his staff against thee, after the manner of Egypt;
Yet a very little while, and the indignation shall cease,
And mine anger in their destruction."
And the Lord of hosts shall stir up a scourge for him
According to the slaughter of Midian at the rock of Oreb;
And as his rod was upon the sea,
So shall he lift it up after the manner of Egypt.
And it shall come to pass in that day,
That his burden shall be taken away from off thy shoulder,
And his yoke from off thy neck,
And the yoke shall be destroyed because of the anointing.

He is come to Aiath, he is passed to Migron;
At Michmash he hath laid up his carriages;
They are gone over the passage;
They have taken up their lodging at Geba;
Ramah is afraid; Gibeah of Saul is fled.

THE VISION OF ISAIAH

Lift up thy voice, O daughter of Gallim;
Cause it to be heard unto Laish, O poor Anathoth.
Madmenah is removed;
The inhabitants of Gebim gather themselves to flee.
As yet shall he remain at Nob that day;
He shall shake his hand against the mount of the daughter of Zion,
The hill of Jerusalem.

Behold, the Lord, the Lord of hosts,
Shall lop the bough with terror;
And the high ones of stature shall be hewn down,
And the haughty shall be humbled.
And he shall cut down the thickets of the forest with iron,
And Lebanon shall fall by a mighty one.

"And There Shall Come Forth a Rod"

And there shall come forth a rod out of the stem of Jesse,
And a Branch shall grow out of his roots.
And the spirit of the Lord shall rest upon him,
The spirit of wisdom and understanding,
The spirit of counsel and might,
The spirit of knowledge and of the fear of the Lord;
And shall make him of quick understanding in the fear of the Lord:
And he shall not judge after the sight of his eyes,
Neither reprove after the hearing of his ears;
But with righteousness shall he judge the poor,
And reprove with equity for the meek of the earth;
And he shall smite the earth with the rod of his mouth,
And with the breath of his lips shall he slay the wicked.
And righteousness shall be the girdle of his loins,
And faithfulness the girdle of his reins.
The wolf also shall dwell with the lamb,
And the leopard shall lie down with the kid;
And the calf and the young lion and the fatling together;
And a little child shall lead them.
And the cow and the bear shall feed;

THE VISION OF ISAIAH

Their young ones shall lie down together:
And the lion shall eat straw like the ox.
And the sucking child shall play on the hole of the asp,
And the weaned child shall put his hand on the cockatrice's den.
They shall not hurt nor destroy
In all my holy mountain:
For the earth shall be full of the knowledge of the Lord,
As the waters cover the sea.

"Behold, I Will Stir Up the Medes"

Behold, I will stir up the Medes against them, which shall not regard silver;

And as for gold, they shall not delight in it.
Their bows also shall dash the young men to pieces;
And they shall have no pity on the fruit of the womb;
Their eye shall not spare children.
And Babylon, the glory of kingdoms,
The beauty of the Chaldees's excellency,
Shall be as when God overthrew Sodom and Gomorrah.
It shall never be inhabited,
Neither shall it be dwelt in from generation to generation:
Neither shall the Arabian pitch tent there;
Neither shall the shepherds make their fold there.
But wild beasts of the desert shall lie there;
And their houses shall be full of doleful creatures;
And owls shall dwell there,
And satyrs shall dance there.
And the wild beasts of the islands shall cry in their desolate houses,
And dragons in their pleasant palaces:
And her time is near to come,
And her days shall not be prolonged.

For the Lord will have mercy on Jacob, and will yet choose Israel, and set them in their own land: and the strangers shall be joined with them, and they shall cleave to the house of Jacob. And the people shall take them, and bring them to their place:

THE VISION OF ISAIAH

and the house of Israel shall possess them in the land of the Lord for servants and handmaids: and they shall take them captives, whose captives they were; and they shall rule over their oppressors. And it shall come to pass in the day that the Lord shall give thee rest from thy sorrow, and from thy fear, and from the hard bondage wherein thou wast made to serve, that thou shalt take up this proverb against the king of Babylon, and say,

"How hath the oppressor ceased!
The golden city ceased!
The Lord hath broken the staff of the wicked,
And the sceptre of the rulers.
He who smote the people in wrath with a continual stroke,
He that ruled the nations in anger,
Is persecuted, and none hindereth.
The whole earth is at rest, and is quiet:
They break forth into singing.
Yea, the fir trees rejoice at thee,
And the cedars of Lebanon, saying,
'Since thou art laid down,
No feller is come up against us.'
Hell from beneath is moved for thee
To meet thee at thy coming:
It stirreth up the dead for thee,
Even all the chief ones of the earth;
It hath raised up from their thrones all the kings of the nations.
All they shall speak and say unto thee,
'Art thou also become weak as we?
Art thou become like unto us?'
Thy pomp is brought down to the grave,
And the noise of thy viols:
The worm is spread under thee,
And the worms cover thee.
How art thou fallen from heaven,
O Lucifer, son of the morning!

THE VISION OF ISAIAH

How art thou cut down to the ground,
Which didst weaken the nations!
For thou hast said in thine heart, 'I will ascend into heaven,
I will exalt my throne above the stars of God:
I will sit also upon the mount of the congregation,
In the sides of the north:
I will ascend above the heights of the clouds;
I will be like the most High.'
Yet thou shalt be brought down to hell,
To the sides of the pit.
They that see thee shall narrowly look upon thee,
And consider thee, saying,
'Is this the man that made the earth to tremble,
That did shake kingdoms;
That made the world as a wilderness, and destroyed the cities thereof;
That opened not the house of his prisoners?'
All the kings of the nations, even all of them, lie in glory,
Every one in his own house.
But thou art cast out of thy grave
Like an abominable branch,
And as the raiment of those that are slain,
Thrust through with a sword,
That go down to the stones of the pit;
As a carcase trodden under feet."

"Rejoice Not Thou, Whole Palestina"

Rejoice not thou, whole Palestina,
Because the rod of him that smote thee is broken:
For out of the serpent's root shall come forth a cockatrice,
And his fruit shall be a fiery flying serpent.
And the firstborn of the poor shall feed,
And the needy shall lie down in safety:
And I will kill thy root with famine,
And he shall slay thy remnant.
Howl, O gate; cry, O city;

THE VISION OF ISAIAH

Thou, whole Palestina, art dissolved:
For there shall come from the north a smoke,
And none shall be alone in his appointed times.

"Because in the Night Ar of Moab"

Because in the night Ar of Moab is laid waste, and brought to silence;
Because in the night Kir of Moab is laid waste, and brought to silence;
He is gone up to Bajith, and to Dibon, the high places, to weep:
Moab shall howl over Nebo, and over Medeba:
On all their heads shall be baldness, and every beard cut off.
In their streets they shall gird themselves with sackcloth:
On the tops of their houses, and in their streets, every one shall howl,
Weeping abundantly.

And Heshbon shall cry, and Elealeh:
Their voice shall be heard even unto Jahaz:
Therefore the armed soldiers of Moab shall cry out;
His life shall be grievous unto him.
My heart shall cry out for Moab;
His fugitives shall flee unto Zoar, a heifer of three years old:
For by the mounting up of Luhith with weeping shall they go it up;
For in the way of Horonaim they shall raise up a cry of destruction.

For the waters of Nimrim shall be desolate:
For the hay is withered away,
The grass faileth,
There is no green thing.
Therefore the abundance they have gotten,
And that which they have laid up,
Shall they carry away to the brook of the willows.

For the cry is gone round about the borders of Moab;
The howling thereof unto Eglaim,
And the howling thereof unto Beer-elim.
For the waters of Dimon shall be full of blood:
For I will bring more upon Dimon,
Lions upon him that escapeth of Moab,
And upon the remnant of the land.

THE VISION OF ISAIAH

For it shall be that, as a wandering bird cast out of the nest,
So the daughters of Moab shall be at the fords of Arnon.

We have heard of the pride of Moab;
He is very proud:
Even of his haughtiness, and his pride, and his wrath:
But his lies shall not be so.
Therefore shall Moab howl for Moab, every one shall howl:
For the foundations of Kir-hareseth shall ye mourn; surely they
    are stricken.

For the fields of Heshbon languish, and the vine of Sibmah:
The lords of the heathen have broken down the principal plants
    thereof,
They are come even unto Jazer, they wandered through the wilder-
    ness:
Her branches are stretched out, they are gone over the sea.
Therefore I will bewail with the weeping of Jazer the vine of Sibmah:
I will water thee with my tears, O Heshbon, and Elealeh:
For the shouting for thy summer fruits and for thy harvest is fallen.

And gladness is taken away, and joy out of the plentiful field;
And in the vineyards there shall be no singing, neither shall there be
    shouting:
The treaders shall tread out no wine in their presses; I have made
    their vintage shouting to cease.
Wherefore my bowels shall sound like a harp for Moab,
And mine inward parts for Kir-haresh.

"Behold, Damascus Is Taken Away"

"Behold, Damascus is taken away from being a city,
And it shall be a ruinous heap.
The cities of Aroer are forsaken:
They shall be for flocks, which shall lie down,
And none shall make them afraid.
The fortress also shall cease from Ephraim,
And the kingdom from Damascus, and the remnant of Syria:

THE VISION OF ISAIAH

"They shall be as the glory of the children of Israel,"
Saith the Lord of hosts.
"And in that day it shall come to pass,
That the glory of Jacob shall be made thin,
And the fatness of his flesh shall wax lean.
And it shall be as when the harvestman gathereth the corn,
And reapeth the ears with his arm;
And it shall be as he that gathereth ears
In the valley of Rephaim.

Yet gleaning grapes shall be left in it,
As the shaking of an olive tree,
Two or three berries in the top of the uppermost bough,
Four or five in the outmost fruitful branches thereof,"
Saith the Lord God of Israel.
At that day shall a man look to his Maker,
And his eyes shall have respect to the Holy One of Israel.
And he shall not look to the altars, the work of his hands,
Neither shall respect that which his fingers have made,
Either the groves, or the images.

In that day shall his strong cities be as a forsaken bough, and an up-
     permost branch,
Which they left because of the children of Israel:
And there shall be desolation.
Because thou hast forgotten the God of thy salvation,
And hast not been mindful of the rock of thy strength,
Therefore shalt thou plant pleasant plants,
And shalt set it with strange slips:
In the day shalt thou make thy plant to grow,
And in the morning shalt thou make thy seed to flourish:
But the harvest shall be a heap
In the day of grief and of desperate sorrow.

Woe to the multitude of many people,
Which make a noise like the noise of the seas;
And to the rushing of nations,

THE VISION OF ISAIAH

That make a rushing like the rushing of mighty waters!
The nations shall rush like the rushing of many waters:
But God shall rebuke them, and they shall flee far off,
And shall be chased as the chaff of the mountains before the wind,
And like a rolling thing before the whirlwind.
And behold at eveningtide trouble;
And before the morning he is not.
This is the portion of them that spoil us,
And the lot of them that rob us.

"Woe to the Land Shadowing with Wings"

Woe to the land shadowing with wings,
Which is beyond the rivers of Ethiopia:
That sendeth ambassadors by the sea,
Even in vessels of bulrushes upon the waters,
Saying, "Go, ye swift messengers, to a nation scattered and peeled,
To a people terrible from their beginning hitherto;
A nation meted out and trodden down,
Whose land the rivers have spoiled!"

All ye inhabitants of the world, and dwellers on the earth, see ye, when he lifteth up an ensign on the mountains; and when be bloweth a trumpet, hear ye. For so the Lord said unto me, "I will take my rest, and I will consider in my dwelling place like a clear heat upon herbs, and like a cloud of dew in the heat of harvest." For afore the harvest, when the bud is perfect, and the sour grape is ripening in the flower, he shall both cut off the sprigs with pruninghooks, and take away and cut down the branches. They shall be left together unto the fowls of the mountains, and to the beasts of the earth: and the fowls shall summer upon them, and all the beasts of the earth shall winter upon them. In that time shall the present be brought unto the Lord of hosts

> *Of a people scattered and peeled,*
> *And from a people terrible from their beginning hitherto;*

THE VISION OF ISAIAH

*A nation meted out and trodden under foot,
Whose land the rivers have spoiled.*

The Burden of Egypt

Behold, the Lord rideth upon a swift cloud, and shall come into Egypt: and the idols of Egypt shall be moved at his presence, and the heart of Egypt shall melt in the midst of it. "And I will set the Egyptians against the Egyptians: and they shall fight every one against his brother, and every one against his neighbour; city against city, and kingdom against kingdom. And the spirit of Egypt shall fail in the midst thereof; and I will destroy the counsel thereof: and they shall seek to the idols, and to the charmers, and to them that have familiar spirits, and to the wizards. And the Egyptians will I give over into the hand of a cruel lord; and a fierce king shall rule over them," saith the Lord, the Lord of hosts. And the waters shall fail from the sea, and the river shall be wasted and dried up. And they shall turn the rivers far away; and the brooks of defence shall be emptied and dried up: the reeds and flags shall wither. The paper reeds by the brooks, by the mouth of the brooks, and every thing sown by the brooks, shall wither, be driven away, and be no more. The fishers also shall mourn, and all they that cast angle into the brooks shall lament, and they that spread nets upon the waters shall languish. Moreover they that work in fine flax, and they that weave networks, shall be confounded. And they shall be broken in the purposes thereof, all that make sluices and ponds for fish.

Surely the princes of Zoan are fools, the counsel of the wise counsellors of Pharaoh is become brutish: how say ye unto Pharaoh, "I am the son of the wise, the son of ancient kings"? Where are they? where are thy wise men? and let them tell thee now, and let them know what the Lord of hosts hath purposed upon Egypt. The princes of Zoan are become fools, the princes of Noph are deceived; they have also seduced Egypt, even they that are the stay of the tribes thereof. The Lord hath mingled a perverse spirit in the midst thereof: and they have caused Egypt

THE VISION OF ISAIAH

to err in every work thereof, as a drunken man staggereth in his vomit. Neither shall there be any work for Egypt, which the head or tail, branch or rush, may do.

In that day shall Egypt be like unto women: and it shall be afraid and fear because of the shaking of the hand of the Lord of hosts, which he shaketh over it. And the land of Judah shall be a terror unto Egypt, every one that maketh mention thereof shall be afraid in himself, because of the counsel of the Lord of hosts, which he hath determined against it.

In that day shall five cities in the land of Egypt speak the language of Canaan, and swear to the Lord of hosts; one shall be called "the city of destruction."

In that day shall there be an altar to the Lord in the midst of the land of Egypt, and a pillar at the border thereof to the Lord. And it shall be for a sign and for a witness unto the Lord of hosts in the land of Egypt: for they shall cry unto the Lord because of the oppressors, and he shall send them a saviour, and a great one, and he shall deliver them.

And the Lord shall be known to Egypt, and the Egyptians shall know the Lord in that day, and shall do sacrifice and oblation; yea, they shall vow a vow unto the Lord, and perform it.

And the Lord shall smite Egypt: he shall smite and heal it: and they shall return even to the Lord, and he shall be intreated of them, and shall heal them.

In that day shall there be a highway out of Egypt to Assyria, and the Assyrian shall come into Egypt, and the Egyptian into Assyria, and the Egyptians shall serve with the Assyrians.

In that day shall Israel be the third with Egypt and with Assyria, even a blessing in the midst of the land: whom the Lord of hosts shall bless, saying, "Blessed be Egypt my people, and Assyria the work of my hands, and Israel mine inheritance."

"As Whirlwinds in the South Pass Through"

As whirlwinds in the south pass through;
So it cometh from the desert,
From a terrible land.

THE VISION OF ISAIAH

A grievous vision is declared unto me;
The treacherous dealer dealeth treacherously,
And the spoiler spoileth.
"Go up, O Elam:
Besiege, O Media;
All the sighing thereof have I made to cease."
Therefore are my loins filled with pain:
Pangs have taken hold upon me,
As the pangs of a woman that travaileth:
I was bowed down at the hearing of it;
I was dismayed at the seeing of it.
My heart panted, fearfulness affrighted me:
The night of my pleasure hath he turned into fear unto me.
Prepare the table, watch in the watchtower, eat, drink:
"Arise, ye princes, and anoint the shield."
For thus hath the Lord said unto me,
"Go, set a watchman, let him declare what he seeth."
And he saw a chariot with a couple of horsemen,
A chariot of asses, and a chariot of camels;
And he hearkened diligently with much heed:
And he cried, "My lord,
I stand continually upon the watchtower in the daytime,
And I am set in my ward whole nights":
And, behold, here cometh a chariot of men, with a couple of horse-
    men.
And he answered and said,
"Babylon is fallen, is fallen;
And all the graven images of her gods he hath broken unto the
    ground."

"He Calleth to Me Out of Seir"

He calleth to me out of Seir,
"Watchman, what of the night?
Watchman, what of the night?"
The watchman said, "The morning cometh,

[436]

THE VISION OF ISAIAH

And also the night:
If ye will enquire, enquire ye:
Return, come."

"In the Forest in Arabia"

In the forest in Arabia shall ye lodge,
O ye travelling companies of Dedanim.
The inhabitants of the land of Tema
Brought water to him that was thirsty,
They prevented with their bread him that fled.
For they fled from the swords,
From the drawn sword, and from the bent bow,
And from the grievousness of war.

For thus hath the Lord said unto me,
"Within a year, according to the years of a hireling,
And all the glory of Kedar shall fail."

"Howl, Ye Ships of Tarshish"

Howl, ye ships of Tarshish;
For it is laid waste,
So that there is no house,
No entering in:
From the land of Chittim it is revealed to them.
Be still, ye inhabitants of the isle;
Thou whom the merchants of Sidon, that pass over the sea, have
  replenished.
And by great waters the seed of Sihor,
The harvest of the river, is her revenue;
And she is a mart of nations.
Be thou ashamed, O Sidon:
For the sea hath spoken, even the strength of the sea,
Saying, "I travail not, nor bring forth children,
Neither do I nourish up young men, nor bring up virgins."
As at the report concerning Egypt, so shall they be sorely pained at
  the report of Tyre.

THE VISION OF ISAIAH

Pass ye over to Tarshish;
Howl, ye inhabitants of the isle.
Is this your joyous city,
Whose antiquity is of ancient days?
Her own feet shall carry her afar off to sojourn.
Who hath taken this counsel against Tyre, the crowning city,
Whose merchants are princes,
Whose traffickers are the honourable of the earth?
The Lord of hosts hath purposed it,
To stain the pride of all glory,
And to bring into contempt all the honourable of the earth.

Pass through thy land as a river, O daughter of Tarshish:
There is no more strength.
He stretched out his hand over the sea,
He shook the kingdoms:
The Lord hath given a commandment against the merchant city,
To destroy the strong holds thereof.
And he said, "Thou shalt no more rejoice,
O thou oppressed virgin, daughter of Sidon:
Arise, pass over to Chittim;
There also shalt thou have no rest."
Behold the land of the Chaldeans;
This people was not, till the Assyrian founded it for them that
    dwell in the wilderness:
They set up the towers thereof, they raised up the palaces thereof;
And he brought it to ruin.

Howl, ye ships of Tarshish:
For your strength is laid waste.

And it shall come to pass in that day, that Tyre shall be forgotten seventy years, according to the days of one king: after the end of seventy years shall Tyre sing as a harlot,

"Take a harp,
    Go about the city,

THE VISION OF ISAIAH

Thou harlot that hast been forgotten;
Make sweet melody,

Sing many songs,
That thou mayest be remembered."

And it shall come to pass after the end of seventy years, that the Lord will visit Tyre, and she shall turn to her hire, and shall commit fornication with all the kingdoms of the world upon the face of the earth. And her merchandise and her hire shall be holiness to the Lord: it shall not be treasured nor laid up; for her merchandise shall be for them that dwell before the Lord, to eat sufficiently, and for durable clothing.

"Behold, the Lord Maketh the Earth Empty"

Behold, the Lord maketh the earth empty,
And maketh it waste,
And turneth it upside down,
And scattereth abroad the inhabitants thereof.

And it shall be,
As with the people, so with the priest;
As with the servant, so with his master;
As with the maid, so with her mistress;
As with the buyer, so with the seller;
As with the lender, so with the borrower;
As with the taker of usury, so with the giver of usury to him.
The land shall be utterly emptied, and utterly spoiled:
For the Lord hath spoken this word.

The earth mourneth and fadeth away,
The world languisheth and fadeth away,
The haughty people of the earth do languish.
The earth also is defiled under the inhabitants thereof;
Because they have transgressed the laws,
Changed the ordinance,
Broken the everlasting covenant.
Therefore hath the curse devoured the earth,

THE VISION OF ISAIAH

And they that dwell therein are desolate:
Therefore the inhabitants of the earth are burned,
And few men left.

The new wine mourneth,
The vine languisheth,
All the merryhearted do sigh.
The mirth of tabrets ceaseth,
The noise of them that rejoice endeth,
The joy of the harp ceaseth.
They shall not drink wine with a song;
Strong drink shall be bitter to them that drink it.
The city of confusion is broken down:
Every house is shut up, that no man may come in.
There is a crying for wine in the streets;
All joy is darkened,
The mirth of the land is gone.
In the city is left desolation,
And the gate is smitten with destruction.

When thus it shall be in the midst of the land among the people,
There shall be as the shaking of an olive tree,
And as the gleaning grapes when the vintage is done.
They shall lift up their voice,
They shall sing for the majesty of the Lord,
They shall cry aloud from the sea:
"Wherefore glorify ye the Lord in the fires,
Even the name of the Lord God of Israel
In the isles of the sea."

From the uttermost part of the earth have we heard songs,
Even glory to the righteous.
But I said, "My leanness, my leanness, woe unto me!
The treacherous dealers have dealt treacherously;
Yea, the treacherous dealers have dealt very treacherously."
Fear, and the pit, and the snare, are upon thee,
O inhabitant of the earth.

THE VISION OF ISAIAH

And it shall come to pass,
That he who fleeth from the noise of the fear shall fall into the pit;
And he that cometh up out of the midst of the pit shall be taken in
    the snare:
For the windows from on high are open,
And the foundations of the earth do shake.
The earth is utterly broken down,
The earth is clean dissolved,
The earth is moved exceedingly.
The earth shall reel to and fro like a drunkard,
And shall be removed like a cottage;
And the transgression thereof shall be heavy upon it;
And it shall fall, and not rise again.

And it shall come to pass in that day,
That the Lord shall punish the host of the high ones that are on high,
And the kings of the earth upon the earth.
And they shall be gathered together,
As prisoners are gathered in the pit,
And shall be shut up in the prison,
And after many days shall they be visited.
Then the moon shall be confounded, and the sun ashamed,
When the Lord of hosts shall reign in Mount Zion, and in Jeru-
    salem,
And before his ancients gloriously.

"O Lord, Thou Art My God"

O Lord, thou art my God; I will exalt thee;
I will praise thy name;
For thou hast done wonderful things;
Thy counsels of old are faithfulness and truth.
For thou hast made of a city a heap;
Of a defenced city a ruin:
A palace of strangers to be no city;
It shall never be built.
Therefore shall the strong people glorify thee,

THE VISION OF ISAIAH

The city of the terrible nations shall fear thee.
For thou hast been a strength to the poor,
A strength to the needy in his distress,
A refuge from the storm,
A shadow from the heat,
When the blast of the terrible ones
Is as a storm against the wall.
Thou shalt bring down the noise of strangers,
As the heat in a dry place;
Even the heat with the shadow of a cloud:
The branch of the terrible ones shall be brought low.

Lo, this is our God;
We have waited for him,
And he will save us:
This is the Lord;
We have waited for him,
We will be glad and rejoice in his salvation.

"In That Day Shall This Song Be Sung"

In that day shall this song be sung in the land of Judah:

"We have a strong city;
Salvation will God appoint for walls and bulwarks.
Open ye the gates,
That the righteous nation which keepeth the truth may enter in.
Thou wilt keep him in perfect peace,
Whose mind is stayed on thee:
Because he trusteth in thee.
Trust ye in the Lord for ever:
For in the Lord JEHOVAH is everlasting strength:

For he bringeth down them that dwell on high;
The lofty city, he layeth it low;
He layeth it low, even to the ground;
He bringeth it even to the dust.

THE VISION OF ISAIAH

The foot shall tread it down,
Even the feet of the poor,
And the steps of the needy."
The way of the just is uprightness:
Thou, most upright, dost weigh the path of the just.
Yea, in the way of thy judgments, O Lord,
Have we waited for thee;
The desire of our soul is to thy name,
And to the remembrance of thee.
With my soul have I desired thee in the night;
Yea, with my spirit within me will I seek thee early:
For when thy judgments are in the earth,
The inhabitants of the world learn righteousness.
Let favour be showed to the wicked,
Yet will he not learn righteousness:
In the land of uprightness will he deal unjustly,
And will not behold the majesty of the Lord.

"Lord, Thou Wilt Ordain Peace"

Lord, thou wilt ordain peace for us:
For thou also hast wrought all our works in us.
O Lord our God, other lords beside thee have had dominion over us
But by thee only will we make mention of thy name.
They are dead, they shall not live;
They are deceased, they shall not rise:
Therefore hast thou visited and destroyed them,
And made all their memory to perish.
Thou hast increased the nation, O Lord,
Thou hast increased the nation: thou art glorified:
Thou hadst removed it far unto all the ends of the earth.

Thy dead men shall live,
Together with my dead body shall they arise.
Awake and sing, ye that dwell in dust:
For thy dew is as the dew of herbs,
And the earth shall cast out the dead.

THE VISION OF ISAIAH

"In That Day the Lord"

In that day the Lord with his sore and great and strong sword shall punish Leviathan the piercing serpent, even Leviathan that crooked serpent; and he shall slay the dragon that is in the sea.

> In that day sing ye unto her, "A vineyard of red wine.
> I the Lord do keep it; I will water it every moment:
> Lest any hurt it, I will keep it night and day.
> Fury is not in me:
> Who would set the briers and thorns against me in battle?
> I would go through them, I would burn them together.
> Or let him take hold of my strength,
> That he may make peace with me;
> And he shall make peace with me."
> He shall cause them that come of Jacob to take root:
> Israel shall blossom and bud,
> And fill the face of the world with fruit.

The Covenant with Death

Woe to the crown of pride, to the drunkards of Ephraim, whose glorious beauty is a fading flower, which are on the head of the fat valleys of them that are overcome with wine! Behold, the Lord hath a mighty and strong one, which as a tempest of hail and a destroying storm, as a flood of mighty waters overflowing, shall cast down to the earth with the hand. The crown of pride, the drunkards of Ephraim, shall be trodden under feet: and the glorious beauty, which is on the head of the fat valley, shall be a fading flower, and as the hasty fruit before the summer; which when he that looketh upon it seeth, while it is yet in his hand he eateth it up.

In that day shall the Lord of hosts be for a crown of glory, and for a diadem of beauty, unto the residue of his people, and for a spirit of judgment to him that sitteth in judgment, and for strength to them that turn the battle to the gate.

But they also have erred through wine, and through strong

THE VISION OF ISAIAH

drink are out of the way; the priest and the prophet have erred through strong drink, they are swallowed up of wine, they are out of the way through strong drink; they err in vision, they stumble in judgment. For all tables are full of vomit and filthiness, so that there is no place clean. Whom shall he teach knowledge? and whom shall he make to understand doctrine? them that are weaned from the milk, and drawn from the breasts. For precept must be upon precept, precept upon precept; line upon line, line upon line; here a little, and there a little: for with stammering lips and another tongue will he speak to this people. To whom he said, "This is the rest wherewith ye may cause the weary to rest; and this is the refreshing": yet they would not hear. But the word of the Lord was unto them precept upon precept, precept upon precept; line upon line, line upon line; here a little, and there a little; that they might go, and fall backward, and be broken, and snared, and taken.

Wherefore hear the word of the Lord, ye scornful men, that rule this people which is in Jerusalem. Because ye have said, "We have made a covenant with death, and with hell are we at agreement; when the overflowing scourge shall pass through, it shall not come unto us: for we have made lies our refuge, and under falsehood have we hid ourselves": therefore thus saith the Lord God, "Behold, I lay in Zion for a foundation a stone, a tried stone, a precious corner stone, a sure foundation: he that believeth shall not make haste. Judgment also will I lay to the line, and righteousness to the plummet": and the hail shall sweep away the refuge of lies, and the waters shall overflow the hiding place. And your covenant with death shall be disannulled, and your agreement with hell shall not stand; when the overflowing scourge shall pass through, then ye shall be trodden down by it. From the time that it goeth forth it shall take you: for morning by morning shall it pass over, by day and by night: and it shall be a vexation only to understand the report. For the bed is shorter than that a man can stretch himself on it: and the covering narrower than that he can wrap himself in it.

For the Lord shall rise up as in Mount Perazim, he shall be

THE VISION OF ISAIAH

wroth as in the valley of Gibeon, that he may do his work, his strange work; and bring to pass his act, his strange act. Now therefore be ye not mockers, lest your bands be made strong: for I have heard from the Lord God of hosts a consumption, even determined upon the whole earth.

Give ye ear, and hear my voice; hearken, and hear my speech. Doth the plowman plow all day to sow? doth he open and break the colds of his ground? When he hath made plain the face thereof, doth he not cast abroad the fitches, and scatter the cummin, and cast in the principal wheat and the appointed barley and the rye in their place? For his God doth instruct him to discretion, and doth teach him. For the fitches are not threshed with a threshing instrument, neither is a cart wheel turned about upon the cummin; but the fitches are beaten out with a staff, and the cummin with a rod. Bread corn is bruised; because he will not ever be threshing it, nor break it with the wheel of his cart, nor bruise it with his horsemen. This also cometh forth from the Lord of hosts, which is wonderful in counsel, and excellent in working.

"Woe to Them That Go Down to Egypt"

Woe to them that go down to Egypt for help;
And stay on horses, and trust in chariots, because they are many;
And in horsemen, because they are very strong;
But they look not unto the Holy One of Israel,
Neither seek the Lord!
Yet he also is wise, and will bring evil,
And will not call back his words:
But will arise against the house of the evildoers,
And against the help of them that work iniquity.
Now the Egyptians are men, and not God;
And their horses flesh, and not spirit.
When the Lord shall stretch out his hand,
Both he that helpeth shall fall,
And he that is helped shall fall down,
And they all shall fail together.

THE VISION OF ISAIAH

For thus hath the Lord spoken unto me,
"Like as the lion and the young lion roaring on his prey,
When a multitude of shepherds is called forth against him,
He will not be afraid of their voice,
Nor abase himself for the noise of them":
So shall the Lord of hosts come down to fight for Mount Zion,
And for the hill thereof.
As birds flying,
So will the Lord of hosts defend Jerusalem;
Defending also he will deliver it;
And passing over he will preserve it.
Turn ye unto him from whom the children of Israel have deeply revolted.
For in that day every man shall cast away his idols of silver, and his idols of gold,
Which your own hands have made unto you for a sin.
Then shall the Assyrian fall with the sword, not of a mighty man;
And the sword, not of a mean man, shall devour him:
"But he shall flee from the sword,
And his young men shall be discomfited.
And he shall pass over to his strong hold for fear,
And his princes shall be afraid of the ensign,"
Saith the Lord, whose fire is in Zion,
And his furnace in Jerusalem.

The Character of the Liberal

Behold, a king shall reign in righteousness, and princes shall rule in judgment. And a man shall be as a hiding place from the wind, and a covert from the tempest; as rivers of water in a dry place, as the shadow of a great rock in a weary land. And the eyes of them that see shall not be dim, and the ears of them that hear shall hearken. The heart also of the rash shall understand knowledge, and the tongue of the stammerers shall be ready to speak plainly. The vile person shall be no more called liberal, nor the churl said to be bountiful. For the vile person will speak villainy, and his heart will work iniquity, to practise hypocrisy,

THE VISION OF ISAIAH

and to utter error against the Lord, to make empty the soul of the hungry, and he will cause the drink of the thirsty to fail. The instruments also of the churl are evil: he deviseth wicked devices to destroy the poor with lying words, even when the needy speaketh right. But the liberal deviseth liberal things; and by liberal things shall he stand.

The Women That Are at Ease

Rise up, ye women that are at ease; hear my voice, ye careless daughters; give ear unto my speech. Many days and years shall ye be troubled, ye careless women: for the vintage shall fail, the gathering shall not come. Tremble, ye women that are at ease; be troubled, ye careless ones: strip you, and make you bare, and gird sackcloth upon your loins. They shall lament for the teats, for the pleasant fields, for the fruitful vine. Upon the land of my people shall come up thorns and briers; yea, upon all the houses of joy in the joyous city: because the palaces shall be forsaken; the multitude of the city shall be left; the forts and towers shall be for dens for ever, a joy of wild asses, a pasture of flocks; until the spirit be poured upon us from on high, and the wilderness be a fruitful field, and the fruitful field be counted for a forest. Then judgment shall dwell in the wilderness, and righteousness remain in the fruitful field. And the work of righteousness shall be peace; and the effect of righteousness quietness and assurance for ever. And my people shall dwell in a peaceable habitation, and in sure dwellings, and in quiet resting places; when it shall hail, coming down on the forest; and the city shall be low in a low place. Blessed are ye that sow beside all waters, that send forth thither the feet of the ox and the ass.

"Come Near, Ye Nations, to Hear"

Come near, ye nations, to hear;
And hearken, ye people:
Let the earth hear, and all that is therein;
The world, and all things that come forth of it.
For the indignation of the Lord is upon all nations,

THE VISION OF ISAIAH

And his fury upon all their armies:
He hath utterly destroyed them,
He hath delivered them to the slaughter.
Their slain also shall be cast out,
And their stink shall come up out of their carcases,
And the mountains shall be melted with their blood.
And all the host of heaven shall be dissolved,
And the heavens shall be rolled together as a scroll:
And all their host shall fall down,
As the leaf falleth off from the vine,
And as a falling fig from the fig tree.
For my sword shall be bathed in heaven:
Behold, it shall come down upon Idumea,
And upon the people of my curse, to judgment.
The sword of the Lord is filled with blood,
It is made fat with fatness, with the blood of lambs and goats,
With the fat of the kidneys of rams:
For the Lord hath a sacrifice in Bozrah,
And a great slaughter in the land of Idumea.
And the unicorns shall come down with them,
And the bullocks with the bulls;
And their land shall be soaked with blood,
And their dust made fat with fatness.
For it is the day of the Lord's vengeance,
And the year of recompenses for the controversy of Zion.
And the streams thereof shall be turned into pitch,
And the dust thereof into brimstone,
And the land thereof shall become burning pitch.
It shall not be quenched night nor day;
The smoke thereof shall go up for ever:
From generation to generation it shall lie waste;
None shall pass through it for ever and ever.
But the cormorant and the bittern shall possess it;
The owl also and the raven shall dwell in it:
And he shall stretch out upon it the line of confusion, and the stones
    of emptiness.

THE VISION OF ISAIAH

They shall call the nobles thereof to the kingdom,
But none shall be there,
And all her princes shall be nothing.
And thorns shall come up in her palaces,
Nettles and brambles in the fortresses thereof:
And it shall be a habitation of dragons,
And a court for owls.
The wild beasts of the desert shall also meet with the wild beasts of
    the island,
And the satyr shall cry to his fellow;
The screech owl also shall rest there,
And find for herself a place of rest.
There shall the great owl make her nest,
And lay, and hatch, and gather under her shadow:
There shall the vultures also be gathered,
Every one with her mate.

"Seek Ye Out of the Book of the Lord"

Seek ye out of the book of the Lord, and read:
No one of these shall fail,
None shall want her mate:
For my mouth it hath commanded,
And his spirit it hath gathered them.
And he hath cast the lot for them,
And his hand hath divided it unto them by line:
They shall possess it for ever,
From generation to generation shall they dwell therein.
The wilderness and the solitary place shall be glad for them;
And the desert shall rejoice, and blossom as the rose.
It shall blossom abundantly, and rejoice even with joy and singing:
The glory of Lebanon shall be given unto it, the excellency of Carmel
    and Sharon,
They shall see the glory of the Lord, and the excellency of our God.
Strengthen ye the weak hands,
And confirm the feeble knees.
Say to them that are of a fearful heart, "Be strong, fear not:

THE VISION OF ISAIAH

Behold, your God will come with vengeance,
Even God with a recompense; he will come and save you."
Then the eyes of the blind shall be opened,
And the ears of the deaf shall be unstopped.
Then shall the lame man leap as a hart,
And the tongue of the dumb sing:
For in the wilderness shall waters break out,
And streams in the desert.
And the parched ground shall become a pool,
And the thirsty land springs of water:
In the habitation of dragons, where each lay,
Shall be grass with reeds and rushes.
And a highway shall be there, and a way,
And it shall be called "the way of holiness";
The unclean shall not pass over it; but it shall be for those:
The wayfaring men, though fools, shall not err therein.
No lion shall be there, nor any ravenous beast shall go up thereon,
It shall not be found there;
But the redeemed shall walk there:
And the ransomed of the Lord shall return,
And come to Zion with songs and everlasting joy upon their heads:
They shall obtain joy and gladness,
And sorrow and sighing shall flee away.

The Song of Hezekiah

The writing of Hezekiah king of Judah, when he had been sick, and was recovered of his sickness:

"I said in the cutting off of my days, 'I shall go to the gates of the grave:
I am deprived of the residue of my years.'
I said, 'I shall not see the Lord, even the Lord, in the land of the
    living:
I shall behold man no more with the inhabitants of the world.'
Mine age is departed,
And is removed from me as a shepherd's tent:
I have cut off like a weaver my life:

THE VISION OF ISAIAH

He will cut me off with pining sickness:
From day even to night wilt thou make an end of me.
I reckoned till morning, that, as a lion, so will he break all my bones:
From day even to night wilt thou make an end of me.
Like a crane or a swallow, so did I chatter:
I did mourn as a dove:
Mine eyes fail with looking upward:
O Lord, I am oppressed; undertake for me.
What shall I say?
He hath both spoken unto me,
And himself hath done it:
I shall go softly all my years in the bitterness of my soul.
O Lord, by these things men live,
And in all these things is the life of my spirit:
So wilt thou recover me, and make me to live.
Behold, for peace I had great bitterness:
But thou hast in love to my soul delivered it from the pit of corrup-
 tion:
For thou hast cast all my sins behind thy back.
For the grave cannot praise thee,
Death cannot celebrate thee:
They that go down into the pit cannot hope for thy truth.
The living, the living, he shall praise thee,
As I do this day:
The father to the children shall make known thy truth.
The Lord was ready to save me:
Therefore we will sing my songs to the stringed instruments
All the days of our life in the house of the Lord."

THE WORD OF THE LORD WHICH CAME UNTO ZEPHANIAH

A TEMPORARY *incursion of Scythians into southwestern Asia in the year 627 B.C. led the grim prophet Zephaniah to imagine that the day of doom for all nations was at hand. He had nothing constructive to offer, and his dire expectations were unfulfilled, but they gave rise to some effective poetry in which much use was made of that device of cumulative iteration which is one of the outstanding features of Hebraic verse.*

The Word of the Lord Which Came unto ZEPHANIAH

THE SON OF CUSHI, THE SON OF GEDALIAH, THE SON OF AMARIAH, THE SON OF HIZKIAH, IN THE DAYS OF JOSIAH THE SON OF AMON, KING OF JUDAH.

"I Will Utterly Consume All Things"

"I will utterly consume all things
From off the land," saith the Lord.
"I will consume man and beast;
I will consume the fowls of the heaven, and the fishes of the sea,
And the stumblingblocks with the wicked;
And I will cut off man from off the land,"
Saith the Lord.
"I will also stretch out mine hand upon Judah,
And upon all the inhabitants of Jerusalem;
And I will cut off the remnant of Baal from this place,
And the name of the Chemarims with the priests;
And them that worship the host of heaven upon the housetops;
And them that worship and that swear by the Lord,
And that swear by Malcham;
And them that are turned back from the Lord;
And those that have not sought the Lord,
Nor enquired for him."

Hold thy peace at the presence of the Lord God,
For the day of the Lord is at hand!
For the Lord hath prepared a sacrifice,
He hath bid his guests.

THE WORD UNTO ZEPHANIAH

And it shall come to pass in the day of the Lord's sacrifice,
That I will punish the princes, and the king's children,
And all such as are clothed with strange apparel.
In the same day also will I punish all those that leap on the threshold,
Which fill their masters' houses with violence and deceit.

"And it shall come to pass in that day," saith the Lord,
"That there shall be the noise of a cry from the Fish Gate,
And a howling from the second,
And a great crashing from the hills.
Howl, ye inhabitants of Maktesh,
For all the merchant people are cut down;
All they that bear silver are cut off.

And it shall come to pass at that time, that I will search Jerusalem
    with candles,
And punish the men that are settled on their lees,
That say in their heart,
'The Lord will not do good, neither will he do evil.'
Therefore their goods shall become a booty,
And their houses a desolation:
They shall also build houses, but not inhabit them;
And they shall plant vineyards, but not drink the wine thereof."

The great day of the Lord is near,
It is near, and hasteth greatly,
The voice of the day of the Lord:
The mighty man shall cry there bitterly.
That day is a day of wrath,
A day of trouble and distress,
A day of wasteness and desolation,
A day of darkness and gloominess,
A day of clouds and thick darkness,
A day of the trumpet and alarm against the fenced cities,
And against the high towers.

THE WORD UNTO ZEPHANIAH

"And I will bring distress upon men, that they shall walk like blind men,"
Because they have sinned against the Lord:
And their blood shall be poured out as dust,
And their flesh as the dung.
Neither their silver nor their gold
Shall be able to deliver them in the day of the Lord's wrath;
But the whole land shall be devoured by the fire of his jealousy:
For he shall make even a speedy riddance of all them that dwell in the land.

"Gather Yourselves Together"

Gather yourselves together,
Yea, gather together, O nation not desired;
Before the decree bring forth,
Before the day pass as the chaff,
Before the fierce anger of the Lord come upon you,
Before the day of the Lord's anger come upon you.
Seek ye the Lord, all ye meek of the earth,
Which have wrought his judgment;
Seek righteousness, seek meekness:
It may be ye shall be hid in the day of the Lord's anger.

For Gaza shall be forsaken,
And Ashkelon a desolation:
They shall drive out Ashdod at the noon day,
And Ekron shall be rooted up.
Woe unto the inhabitants of the sea coast,
The nation of the Cherethites!
The word of the Lord is against you;
O Canaan, the land of the Philistines,
I will even destroy thee, that there shall be no inhabitant.
And the sea coast shall be dwellings and cottages for shepherds,
And folds for flocks.
And the coast shall be for the remnant of the house of Judah;
They shall feed thereupon:

THE WORD UNTO ZEPHANIAH
In the houses of Ashkelon shall they lie down in the evening:
For the Lord their God shall visit them,
And turn away their captivity.

"I have heard the reproach of Moab,
And the revilings of the children of Ammon,
Whereby they have reproached my people,
And magnified themselves against their border.
Therefore as I live,"
Saith the Lord of hosts, the God of Israel,
"Surely Moab shall be as Sodom,
And the children of Ammon as Gomorrah,
Even the breeding of nettles, and saltpits,
And a perpetual desolation:
The residue of my people shall spoil them,
And the remnant of my people shall possess them."
This shall they have for their pride,
Because they have reproached and magnified themselves
Against the people of the Lord of hosts.
The Lord will be terrible unto them:
For he will famish all the gods of the earth;
And men shall worship him, every one from his place,
Even all the isles of the heathen.

"Ye Ethiopians also,
Ye shall be slain by my sword."
And he will stretch out his hand against the north,
And destroy Assyria;
And will make Nineveh a desolation,
And dry like a wilderness.
And flocks shall lie down in the midst of her,
All the beasts of the nations:
Both the cormorant and the bittern
Shall lodge in the upper lintels of it;
Their voice shall sing in the windows;
Desolation shall be in the thresholds:
For he shall uncover the cedar work.

THE WORD UNTO ZEPHANIAH

This is the rejoicing city
That dwelt carelessly,
That said in her heart,
"I am, and there is none beside me":
How is she become a desolation,
A place for beasts to lie down in!
Every one that passeth by her shall hiss,
And wag his hand.

THE VISION OF NAHUM THE ELKOHITE

THE DECLINE of Assyria toward the end of the seventh century was watched from a distance by the Jews with very natural feelings of gratified revenge intermingled with nobler emotions of exultation at the approaching overthrow of a savagely militaristic nation. Thus at the moment of its disappearance Assyria, incapable of producing great literature itself, was at least the cause of a piece of great literature from one of its enemies—the poem of the prophet Nahum on the fall of hated Nineveh (612 B.C.), a superb union of rhapsodic passion and powerfully vivid realism.

The Vision of NAHUM THE ELKOHITE

"He That Dasheth in Pieces"

He that dasheth in pieces is come up before thy face:
Keep the munition,
Watch the way, make thy loins strong,
Fortify thy power mightily.

The shield of his mighty men is made red,
The valiant men are in scarlet:
The chariots shall be with flaming torches
In the day of his preparation,
And the fir trees shall be terribly shaken.
The chariots shall rage in the streets,
They shall jostle one against another in the broad ways:
They shall seem like torches,
They shall run like the lightnings.
He shall recount his worthies:
They shall stumble in their walk;
They shall make haste to the wall thereof,
And the defence shall be prepared.

The gates of the rivers shall be opened,
And the palace shall be dissolved.
And Huzzab shall be led away captive,
She shall be brought up,
And her maids shall lead her as with the voice of doves,
Taboring upon their breasts.
But Nineveh is of old like a pool of water:
Yet they shall flee away.

NAHUM THE ELKOHITE

"Stand, stand," shall they cry;
But none shall look back.
Take ye the spoil of silver,
Take the spoil of gold:
For there is none end of the store
And glory out of all the pleasant furniture.

She is empty, and void, and waste:
And the heart melteth, and the knees smite together,
And much pain is in all loins,
And the faces of them all gather blackness.
Where is the dwelling of the lions,
And the feeding place of the young lions,
Where the lion, even the old lion, walked,
And the lion's whelp, and none made them afraid?
The lion did tear in pieces enough for his whelps,
And strangled for his lionesses,
And filled his holes with prey,
And his dens with ravin.

"Behold, I am against thee," saith the Lord of hosts,
"And I will burn her chariots in the smoke,
And the sword shall devour thy young lions:
And I will cut off thy prey from the earth,
And the voice of thy messengers shall no more be heard."

Woe to the bloody city!
It is all full of lies and robbery;
The prey departeth not;
The noise of a whip, and the noise of the rattling of the wheels,
And of the prancing horses, and of the jumping chariots.
The horseman lifteth up both the bright sword and the glittering
    spear:
And there is a multitude of slain, and a great number of carcases;
And there is none end of their corpses;
They stumble upon their corpses:

NAHUM THE ELKOHITE

Because of the multitude of the whoredoms of the wellfavoured
    harlot,
The mistress of witchcrafts, that selleth nations through her
    whoredoms,
And families through her witchcrafts.

"Behold, I am against thee," saith the Lord of hosts;
"And I will discover thy skirts upon thy face,
And I will show the nations thy nakedness,
And the kingdoms thy shame.
And I will cast abominable filth upon thee,
And make thee vile, and will set thee as a gazingstock.
And it shall come to pass, that all they that look upon thee shall
    flee from thee,
And say, 'Nineveh is laid waste:
Who will bemoan her?'
Whence shall I seek comforters for thee?

Art thou better than populous No,
That was situate among the rivers,
That had the waters round about it,
Whose rampart was the sea,
And her wall was from the sea?
Ethiopia and Egypt were her strength,
And it was infinite;
Put and Lubim were thy helpers.
Yet was she carried away;
She went into captivity.
Her young children also were dashed in pieces at the top of all the
    streets;
And they cast lots for her honourable men,
And her great men were bound in chains.

Thou also shalt be drunken;
Thou shalt be hid, thou also shalt seek strength because of the
    enemy.
All thy strong holds shall be like fig trees with the firstripe figs:

NAHUM THE ELKOHITE

*If they be shaken, they shall even fall into the mouth of the eater.
Behold, thy people in the midst of thee are women;
The gates of thy land shall be set wide open unto thine enemies;
The fire shall devour thy bars.*

*Draw thee waters for the siege, fortify thy strong holds;
Go into clay, and tread the mortar,
Make strong the brickkiln.
There shall the fire devour thee;
The sword shall cut thee off,
It shall eat thee up like the cankerworm:
Make thyself many as the cankerworm,
Make thyself many as the locusts.*

*Thou hast multiplied thy merchants above the stars of heaven:
The cankerworm spoileth, and fleeth away.
Thy crowned are as the locusts,
And thy captains as the great grasshoppers,
Which camp in the hedges in the cold day,
But when the sun ariseth they flee away,
And their place is not known where they are.*

*Thy shepherds slumber, O king of Assyria;
Thy nobles shall dwell in the dust!
Thy people is scattered upon the mountains,
And no man gathereth them.
There is no healing of thy bruise;
Thy wound is grievous:
All that hear the bruit of thee shall clap the hands over thee:
For upon whom hath not thy wickedness passed continually?"*

THE BURDEN OF HABAKKUK

HABAKKUK, a more reflective and philosophical poet only a few years after Nahum, could take no pleasure in the fall of Assyria, as he perceived that it would be followed by the tyranny of Babylon. This led him to raise, for the first time in the Bible, the question: is it true that the wicked are punished and the righteous prosper?—the same problem that was to concern Jeremiah and the author of the Book of Job. But though Habakkuk raised it, he quickly put it by with the comfortable assurance that the traditional dogma was correct, if not immediately, then in the long run. With less fire than the older prophets but with equal moral earnestness he renewed their protest against avarice, intemperance, and idolatry.

The Burden of HABAKKUK

"O Lord, How Long?"

O Lord, how long shall I cry,
And thou wilt not hear!
Even cry out unto thee of violence,
And thou wilt not save!
Why dost thou show me iniquity,
And cause me to behold grievance?
For spoiling and violence are before me:
And there are that raise up strife and contention.
Therefore the law is slacked,
And judgment doth never go forth:
For the wicked doth compass about the righteous;
Therefore wrong judgment proceedeth.

"Behold ye among the heathen,
And regard, and wonder marvellously:
For I will work a work in your days,
Which ye will not believe, though it be told you.
For, lo, I raise up the Chaldeans,
That bitter and hasty nation,
Which shall march through the breadth of the land,
To possess the dwelling places that are not theirs.

They are terrible and dreadful:
Their judgment and their dignity shall proceed of themselves.
Their horses also are swifter than the leopards,
And are more fierce than the evening wolves:

THE BURDEN OF HABAKKUK

And their horsemen shall spread themselves,
And their horsemen shall come from far;
They shall fly as the eagle that hasteth to eat.

They shall come all for violence:
Their faces shall sup up as the east wind,
And they shall gather the captivity as the sand.
And they shall scoff at the kings,
And the princes shall be a scorn unto them:
They shall deride every strong hold;
For they shall heap dust, and take it.
Then shall his mind change, and he shall pass over,
And offend, imputing this his power unto his god."

Art thou not from everlasting,
O Lord my God, mine Holy One?
O Lord, thou hast ordained them for judgment;
And, O mighty God, thou hast established them for correction.
Thou art of purer eyes than to behold evil,
And canst not look on iniquity:
Wherefore lookest thou upon them that deal treacherously,
And holdest thy tongue when the wicked devoureth
The man that is more righteous than he?
And makest men as the fishes of the sea,
As the creeping things, that have no ruler over them?

They take up all of them with the angle,
They catch them in their net,
And gather them in their drag:
Therefore they rejoice and are glad.
Therefore they sacrifice unto their net,
And burn incense unto their drag;
Because by them their portion is fat,
And their meat plenteous.
Shall they therefore empty their net,
And not spare continually to slay the nations?

I will stand upon my watch,

THE BURDEN OF HABAKKUK

And set me upon the tower,
And will watch to see what he will say unto me,
And what I shall answer when I am reproved.

And the Lord answered me, and said,
"Write the vision, and make it plain upon tables,
That he may run that readeth it.
For the vision is yet for an appointed time,
But at the end it shall speak, and not lie:
Though it tarry, wait for it;
Because it will surely come, it will not tarry.

Behold, his soul which is lifted up is not upright in him:
But the just shall live by his faith.
Yea also, because he transgresseth by wine,
He is a proud man, neither keepeth at home,
Who enlargeth his desire as hell,
And is as death, and cannot be satisfied,
But gathereth unto him all nations,
And heapeth unto him all people.

Shall not all these take up a parable against him,
And a taunting proverb against him, and say,
'Woe to him that increaseth that which is not his!
How long? and to him that ladeth himself with thick clay!'
Shall they not rise up suddenly that shall bite thee,
And awake that shall vex thee,
And thou shalt be for booties unto them?
Because thou hast spoiled many nations,
All the remnant of the people shall spoil thee;
Because of men's blood, and for the violence of the land,
Of the city, and of all that dwell therein."

Woe to him that coveteth an evil covetousness to his house,
That he may set his nest on high,
That he may be delivered from the power of evil!
Thou hast consulted shame to thy house by cutting off many people,
And hast sinned against thy soul.

THE BURDEN OF HABAKKUK

For the stone shall cry out of the wall,
And the beam out of the timber shall answer it.

Woe to him that buildeth a town with blood,
And establisheth a city by iniquity!
Behold, is it not of the Lord of hosts
That the people shall labour in the very fire,
And the people shall weary themselves for very vanity?
For the earth shall be filled with the knowledge of the glory of the
    Lord,
As the waters cover the sea.

Woe unto him that giveth his neighbour drink,
That puttest thy bottle to him, and makest him drunken also,
That thou mayest look on their nakedness!
Thou art filled with shame for glory:
Drink thou also, and let thy foreskin be uncovered:
The cup of the Lord's right hand shall be turned unto thee,
And shameful spewing shall be on thy glory.
For the violence of Lebanon shall cover thee,
And the spoil of beasts, which made them afraid,
Because of men's blood, and for the violence of the land,
Of the city, and of all that dwell therein.

What profiteth the graven image that the maker thereof hath graven
    it;
The molten image, and a teacher of lies,
That the maker of his work trusteth therein,
To make dumb idols?

Woe unto him that saith to the wood, "Awake";
To the dumb stone, "Arise, it shall teach!"
Behold, it is laid over with gold and silver,
And there is no breath at all in the midst of it.
But the Lord is in his holy temple:
Let all the earth keep silence before him.

THE WORDS OF JEREMIAH

IN THE WORK OF JEREMIAH *the personal note is stressed more than in that of any of the others. He was essentially one born out of his due time to set the crooked straight—when there was no longer any hope of straightening it. Descended from a family of priests and vowed from birth to the worship of Jehovah, he watched the decline of monarchy and priesthood—and mortally offended both through his prophecies of national destruction—during the melancholy years that followed the death of Josiah at the battle of Megiddo in 608 B.C. Under Josiah's weak and vacillating successors the Deuteronomic reforms were abandoned, and the rulers drifted from one political intrigue into another ending in the capture of Jerusalem by Nebuchadrezzar, king of Babylon, in 597 B.C. and the carrying off of Josiah's grandson, Jehoiachin, into captivity. Then, a few years later, Zedekiah, the subject ruler appointed by Nebuchadrezzar, engaged in a futile rebellion with the result that the Babylonians returned and destroyed Jerusalem in 586 B.C.*

Owing to Jeremiah's opposition to these suicidal policies, he was denounced by court and people as unpatriotic and spent a long time in prison. The ending of his life was as bitter as the rest of it. After resisting a proposal of Jewish refugees to fly to Egypt, he was carried off by them by force, a victim of the old tradition that it was well to have a prophet about to read the will of God, even though his advice was rarely followed.

What made his life the harder was that he lacked the manifest joy in conflict of many of the other prophets. Tender and sensitive by nature, he shrank from the very obloquy which his relentless conscience obliged him to invoke. His own deepest experience was expressed in his gospel of inner integrity as the ultimate reliance, the final covenant with God, when throne and temple are destroyed.

The Words of JEREMIAH

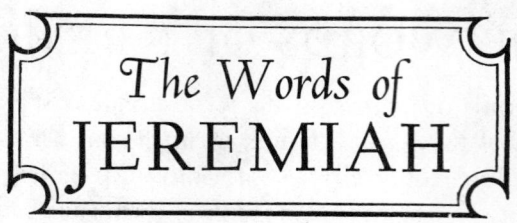

THE SON OF HILKIAH, OF THE PRIESTS THAT WERE IN ANATHOTH IN THE LAND OF BENJAMIN: TO WHOM THE WORD OF THE LORD CAME IN THE DAYS OF JOSIAH THE SON OF AMON KING OF JUDAH, IN THE THIRTEENTH YEAR OF HIS REIGN. IT CAME ALSO IN THE DAYS OF JEHOIAKIM THE SON OF JOSIAH KING OF JUDAH, UNTO THE END OF THE ELEVENTH YEAR OF ZEDEKIAH THE SON OF JOSIAH KING OF JUDAH, UNTO THE CARRYING AWAY OF JERUSALEM CAPTIVE IN THE FIFTH MONTH.

The Call of Jeremiah

THE WORD OF THE LORD came unto me, saying, "Before I formed thee in the belly I knew thee; and before thou camest forth out of the womb I sanctified thee, and I ordained thee a prophet unto the nations."

Then said I, "Ah, Lord God! behold, I cannot speak; for I am a child."

But the Lord said unto me, "Say not, 'I am a child': for thou shalt go to all that I shall send thee, and whatsoever I command thee thou shalt speak. Be not afraid of their faces: for I am with thee to deliver thee," saith the Lord.

Then the Lord put forth his hand, and touched my mouth. And the Lord said unto me, "Behold, I have put my words in thy mouth. See, I have this day set thee over the nations and over the kingdoms, to root out, and to pull down, and to destroy, and to throw down, to build, and to plant."

Moreover the word of the Lord came unto me, saying, "Jeremiah, what seest thou?"

And I said, "I see a rod of an almond tree."

THE WORDS OF JEREMIAH

Then said the Lord unto me, "Thou hast well seen: for I will hasten my word to perform it."

And the word of the Lord came unto me the second time, saying, "What seest thou?"

And I said, "I see a seething pot; and the face thereof is toward the north."

Then the Lord said unto me, "Out of the north an evil shall break forth upon all the inhabitants of the land. For, lo, I will call all the families of the kingdoms of the north," saith the Lord; "and they shall come, and they shall set every one his throne at the entering of the gates of Jerusalem, and against all the walls thereof round about, and against all the cities of Judah. And I will utter my judgments against them touching all their wickedness, who have forsaken me, and have burned incense unto other gods, and worshipped the works of their own hands. Thou therefore gird up thy loins, and arise, and speak unto them all that I command thee: be not dismayed at their faces, lest I confound thee before them. For, behold, I have made thee this day a defenced city, and an iron pillar, and brazen walls against the whole land, against the kings of Judah, against the princes thereof, against the priests thereof, and against the people of the land. And they shall fight against thee; but they shall not prevail against thee; for I am with thee," saith the Lord, "to deliver thee."

Jeremiah's Manifesto

Moreover the word of the Lord came to me, saying, "Go and cry in the ears of Jerusalem, saying, 'Thus saith the Lord: "I remember thee, the kindness of thy youth, the love of thine espousals, when thou wentest after me in the wilderness, in a land that was not sown. Israel was holiness unto the Lord, and the firstfruits of his increase: all that devour him shall offend; evil shall come upon them," saith the Lord.'"

Hear ye the word of the Lord, O house of Jacob, and all the families of the house of Israel: thus saith the Lord, "What iniq-

THE WORDS OF JEREMIAH

uity have your fathers found in me, that they are gone far from me, and have walked after vanity, and are become vain? Neither said they, 'Where is the Lord that brought us up out of the land of Egypt, that led us through the wilderness, through a land of deserts and of pits, through a land of drought, and of the shadow of death, through a land that no man passed through, and where no man dwelt?' And I brought you into a plentiful country, to eat the fruit thereof and the goodness thereof; but when ye entered, ye defiled my land, and made mine heritage an abomination. The priests said not, 'Where is the Lord?' and they that handle the law knew me not: the pastors also transgressed against me, and the prophets prophesied by Baal, and walked after things that do not profit.

"Wherefore I will yet plead with you," saith the Lord, "and with your children's children will I plead. For pass over the isles of Chittim, and see; and send unto Kedar, and consider diligently, and see if there be such a thing. Hath a nation changed their gods, which are yet no gods? but my people have changed their glory for that which doth not profit. Be astonished, O ye heavens, at this, and be horribly afraid, be ye very desolate," saith the Lord. "For my people have committed two evils; they have forsaken me the fountain of living waters, and hewed them out cisterns, broken cisterns, that can hold no water.

"Is Israel a servant? is he a homeborn slave? why is he spoiled? The young lions roared upon him, and yelled, and they made his land waste: his cities are burned without inhabitant. Also the children of Noph and Tahpanhes have broken the crown of thy head. Hast thou not procured this unto thyself, in that thou hast forsaken the Lord thy God, when he led thee by the way? And now what hast thou to do in the way of Egypt, to drink the waters of Sihor? or what hast thou to do in the way of Assyria, to drink the waters of the river? Thine own wickedness shall correct thee, and thy backslidings shall reprove thee: know therefore and see that it is an evil thing and bitter, that thou hast forsaken the Lord thy God, and that my fear is not in thee," saith the Lord God of hosts.

THE WORDS OF JEREMIAH

"For of old time I have broken thy yoke, and burst thy bands; and thou saidst, 'I will not transgress'; when upon every high hill and under every green tree thou wanderest, playing the harlot. Yet I had planted thee a noble vine, wholly a right seed: how then art thou turned into the degenerate plant of a strange vine unto me? For though thou wash thee with nitre, and take thee much soap, yet thine iniquity is marked before me," saith the Lord God. "How canst thou say, 'I am not polluted, I have not gone after Baalim'? see thy way in the valley, know what thou hast done: thou art a swift dromedary traversing her ways; a wild ass used to the wilderness, that snuffeth up the wind at her pleasure; in her occasion who can turn her away? all they that seek her will not weary themselves; in her month they shall find her. Withhold thy foot from being unshod, and thy throat from thirst: but thou saidst, 'There is no hope: no; for I have loved strangers, and after them will I go.' As the thief is ashamed when he is found, so is the house of Israel ashamed; they, their kings, their princes, and their priests, and their prophets, saying to a stock, 'Thou art my father'; and to a stone, 'Thou hast brought me forth'; for they have turned their back unto me, and not their face: but in the time of their trouble they will say, 'Arise, and save us.' But where are thy gods that thou hast made thee? let them arise, if they can save thee in the time of thy trouble: for according to the number of thy cities are thy gods, O Judah. Wherefore will ye plead with me? ye all have transgressed against me," saith the Lord. "In vain have I smitten your children; they received no correction: your own sword hath devoured your prophets, like a destroying lion."

O generation, see ye the word of the Lord: "Have I been a wilderness unto Israel? a land of darkness? wherefore say my people, 'We are lords; we will come no more unto thee'? Can a maid forget her ornaments, or a bride her attire? yet my people have forgotten me days without number. Why trimmest thou thy way to seek love? therefore hast thou also taught the wicked ones thy ways. Also in thy skirts is found the blood of the souls of the poor innocents: I have not found it by secret search, but

THE WORDS OF JEREMIAH

upon all these. Yet thou sayest, 'Because I am innocent, surely his anger shall turn from me.' Behold, I will plead with thee, because thou sayest, 'I have not sinned.' Why gaddest thou about so much to change thy way? thou also shalt be ashamed of Egypt, as thou wast ashamed of Assyria. Yea, thou shalt go forth from him, and thine hands upon thine head: for the Lord hath rejected thy confidences, and thou shalt not prosper in them."

"Declare Ye in Judah"

Declare ye in Judah, and publish in Jerusalem;
And say, "Blow ye the trumpet in the land:
Cry, gather together, and say,
'Assemble yourselves, and let us go into the defenced cities.'
Set up the standard toward Zion:
Retire, stay not:
For I will bring evil from the north,
And a great destruction.
The lion is come up from his thicket,
And the destroyer of the Gentiles is on his way;
He is gone forth from his place to make thy land desolate;
And thy cities shall be laid waste, without an inhabitant.
For this gird you with sackcloth, lament and howl:
For the fierce anger of the Lord is not turned back from us."

"And it shall come to pass at that day," saith the Lord,
"That the heart of the king shall perish,
And the heart of the princes;
And the priests shall be astonished,
And the prophets shall wonder."

Then said I, "Ah, Lord God!
Surely thou hast greatly deceived this people and Jerusalem,
Saying, 'Ye shall have peace';
Whereas the sword reacheth unto the soul."

THE WORDS OF JEREMIAH

At that time shall it be said to this people and to Jerusalem,
"A dry wind of the high places in the wilderness toward the daughter
    of my people,
Not to fan, nor to cleanse,
Even a full wind from those places shall come unto me:
Now also will I give sentence against them."

Behold, he shall come up as clouds,
And his chariots shall be as a whirlwind:
His horses are swifter than eagles.
Woe unto us! for we are spoiled.
O Jerusalem, wash thine heart from wickedness,
That thou mayest be saved.
How long shall thy vain thoughts lodge within thee?
For a voice declareth from Dan,
And publisheth affliction from Mount Ephraim.
Make ye mention to the nations;
Behold, publish against Jerusalem,
That watchers come from a far country,
And give out their voice against the cities of Judah.
As keepers of a field, are they against her round about;
"Because she hath been rebellious against me," saith the Lord.
"Thy way and thy doings have procured these things unto thee;
That is thy wickedness, because it is bitter,
Because it reacheth unto thine heart."

My bowels, my bowels! I am pained at my very heart;
My heart maketh a noise in me;
I cannot hold my peace,
Because thou hast heard, O my soul,
The sound of the trumpet,
The alarm of war.
Destruction upon destruction is cried;
For the whole land is spoiled:
Suddenly are my tents spoiled,
And my curtains in a moment.

THE WORDS OF JEREMIAH

How long shall I see the standard,
And hear the sound of the trumpet?

"For my people is foolish, they have not known me;
They are sottish children, and they have none understanding:
They are wise to do evil, but to do good they have no knowledge."

I beheld the earth, and, lo, it was without form, and void;
And the heavens, and they had no light.
I beheld the mountains, and, lo, they trembled,
And all the hills moved lightly.
I beheld, and, lo, there was no man,
And all the birds of the heavens were fled.
I beheld, and, lo, the fruitful place was a wilderness,
And all the cities thereof were broken down at the presence of the
    Lord, and by his fierce anger.

For thus hath the Lord said,
"The whole land shall be desolate;
Yet will I not make a full end.
For this shall the earth mourn,
And the heavens above be black:
Because I have spoken it,
I have purposed it, and will not repent,
Neither will I turn back from it."

The whole city shall flee
For the noise of the horsemen and bowmen;
They shall go into thickets, and climb up upon the rocks:
Every city shall be forsaken, and not a man dwell therein.

And when thou art spoiled, what wilt thou do?
Though thou clothest thyself with crimson,
Though thou deckest thee with ornaments of gold,
Though thou rentest thy face with painting,
In vain shalt thou make thyself fair;
Thy lovers will despise thee, they will seek thy life.
For I have heard a voice as of a woman in travail,

THE WORDS OF JEREMIAH

And the anguish as of her that bringeth forth her first child,
The voice of the daughter of Zion,
That bewaileth herself, that spreadeth her hands,
Saying, "Woe is me now!
For my soul is wearied because of murderers."

"O Ye Children of Benjamin"

O ye children of Benjamin,
Gather yourselves to flee out of the midst of Jerusalem,
And blow the trumpet in Tekoa,
And set up a sign of fire in Beth-haccerem:
For evil appeareth out of the north,
And great destruction.

I have likened the daughter of Zion to a comely and delicate woman.
The shepherds with their flocks shall come unto her;
They shall pitch their tents against her round about;
They shall feed every one in his place.

Prepare ye war against her;
Arise, and let us go up at noon.

Woe unto us! for the day goeth away,
For the shadows of the evening are stretched out.

Arise, and let us go by night,
And let us destroy her palaces.

For thus hath the Lord of hosts said,
"Hew ye down trees, and cast a mount against Jerusalem:
This is the city to be visited;
She is wholly oppression in the midst of her.
As a fountain casteth out her waters,
So she casteth out her wickedness:
Violence and spoil is heard in her;
Before me continually is grief and wounds.
Be thou instructed, O Jerusalem,
Lest my soul depart from thee;

THE WORDS OF JEREMIAH

Lest I make thee desolate,
A land not inhabited."

Thus saith the Lord of hosts,
"They shall thoroughly glean the remnant of Israel as a vine:
Turn back thine hand as a grapegatherer into the baskets."

To whom shall I speak, and give warning, that they may hear?
Behold, their ear is uncircumcised, and they cannot hearken:
Behold, the word of the Lord is unto them a reproach;
They have no delight in it.
Therefore I am full of the fury of the Lord;
I am weary with holding in:
I will pour it out upon the children abroad,
And upon the assembly of young men together:
For even the husband with the wife shall be taken,
The aged with him that is full of days.
And their houses shall be turned unto others,
With their fields and wives together:
"For I will stretch out my hand
Upon the inhabitants of the land," saith the Lord.
"For the least of them even unto the greatest of them.
Every one is given to covetousness;
And from the prophet even unto the priest every one dealeth falsely.
They have healed also the hurt of the daughter of my people slightly,
Saying, 'Peace, peace'; when there is no peace.

Were they ashamed when they had committed abomination?
Nay, they were not at all ashamed,
Neither could they blush:
Therefore they shall fall among them that fall:
At the time that I visit them they shall be cast down," saith the
    Lord.

Thus saith the Lord,
"Stand ye in the ways, and see,
And ask for the old paths, where is the good way,
And walk therein, and ye shall find rest for your souls.

THE WORDS OF JEREMIAH

But they said, 'We will not walk therein.'
Also I set watchmen over you, saying,
'Hearken to the sound of the trumpet.'
But they said, 'We will not hearken.'

Therefore hear, ye nations,
And know, O congregation, what is among them.
Hear, O earth:
Behold, I will bring evil upon this people,
Even the fruit of their thoughts,
Because they have not hearkened unto my words,
Nor to my law, but rejected it.
To what purpose cometh there to me incense from Sheba,
And the sweet cane from a far country?
Your burnt offerings are not acceptable,
Nor your sacrifices sweet unto me."

Therefore thus saith the Lord,
"Behold, I will lay stumblingblocks before this people,
And the fathers and the sons together shall fall upon them;
The neighbour and his friend shall perish."

Thus saith the Lord,
"Behold, a people cometh from the north country,
And a great nation shall be raised from the sides of the earth.
They shall lay hold on bow and spear;
They are cruel, and have no mercy;
Their voice roareth like the sea;
And they ride upon horses,
Set in array as men for war against thee,
O daughter of Zion."
We have heard the fame thereof:
Our hands wax feeble:
Anguish hath taken hold of us,
And pain, as of a woman in travail.
Go not forth into the field,
Nor walk by the way;

THE WORDS OF JEREMIAH

For the sword of the enemy
And fear is on every side.
O daughter of my people,
Gird thee with sackcloth, and wallow thyself in ashes:
Make thee mourning, as for an only son,
Most bitter lamentation:
For the spoiler shall suddenly come upon us.

"*I have set thee for a tower and a fortress among my people,*
That thou mayest know and try their way."

They are all grievous revolters, walking with slanders:
They are brass and iron;
They are all corrupters.
The bellows are burned, the lead is consumed of the fire;
The founder melteth in vain:
For the wicked are not plucked away.
"*Reprobate silver*" *shall men call them,*
Because the Lord hath rejected them.

The Judgment Because of Tophet

Cut off thine hair, O Jerusalem, and cast it away, and take up a lamentation on high places; for the Lord hath rejected and forsaken the generation of his wrath.

"For the children of Judah have done evil in my sight," saith the Lord: "they have set their abominations in the house which is called by my name, to pollute it. And they have built the high places of Tophet, which is in the valley of the son of Hinnom, to burn their sons and their daughters in the fire; which I commanded them not, neither came it into my heart.

"Therefore, behold, the days come," saith the Lord, "that it shall no more be called Tophet, nor the valley of the son of Hinnom, but the valley of slaughter: for they shall bury in Tophet, till there be no place. And the carcases of this people shall be meat for the fowls of the heaven, and for the beasts of the earth; and none shall fray them away. Then will I cause to cease from the cities of Judah, and from the streets of Jerusalem,

THE WORDS OF JEREMIAH

the voice of mirth, and the voice of gladness, the voice of the bridegroom, and the voice of the bride: for the land shall be desolate.

"At that time," saith the Lord, "they shall bring out the bones of the kings of Judah, and the bones of his princes, and the bones of the priests, and the bones of the prophets, and the bones of the inhabitants of Jerusalem, out of their graves: and they shall spread them before the sun, and the moon, and all the host of heaven, whom they have loved, and whom they have served, and after whom they have walked, and whom they have sought, and whom they have worshipped: they shall not be gathered, nor be buried; they shall be for dung upon the face of the earth. And death shall be chosen rather than life by all the residue of them that remain of this evil family, which remain in all the places whither I have driven them," saith the Lord of hosts.

"The Way of the Heathen"

Hear ye the word which the Lord speaketh unto you, O house of Israel: Thus saith the Lord,

"Learn not the way of the heathen,
  And be not dismayed at the signs of heaven;
For the heathen are dismayed at them.
For the customs of the people are vain:
For one cutteth a tree out of the forest,
The work of the hands of the workman, with the ax.
They deck it with silver and with gold;
They fasten it with nails and with hammers, that it move not.
They are upright as the palm tree, but speak not:
They must needs be borne, because they cannot go.
Be not afraid of them;
For they cannot do evil,
Neither also is it in them to do good."

Forasmuch as there is none like unto thee, O Lord;
Thou art great, and thy name is great in might.
Who would not fear thee, O King of nations?

THE WORDS OF JEREMIAH

For to thee doth it appertain:
Forasmuch as among all the wise men of the nations,
And in all their kingdoms,
There is none like unto thee.

But they are altogether brutish and foolish:
The stock is a doctrine of vanities.
Silver spread into plates is brought from Tarshish,
And gold from Uphaz,
The work of the workman, and of the hands of the founder:
Blue and purple is their clothing:
They are all the work of cunning men.

But the Lord is the true God,
He is the living God, and an everlasting king:
At his wrath the earth shall tremble,
And the nations shall not be able to abide his indignation.
He hath made the earth by his power,
He hath established the world by his wisdom,
And hath stretched out the heavens by his discretion.
When he uttereth his voice, there is a multitude of waters in the
    heavens,
And he causeth the vapours to ascend from the ends of the earth;
He maketh lightnings with rain,
And bringeth forth the wind out of his treasures.
Every man is brutish in his knowledge:
Every founder is confounded by the graven image:
For his molten image is falsehood,
And there is no breath in them.
They are vanity, and the work of errors:
In the time of their visitation they shall perish.

The portion of Jacob is not like them:
For he is the former of all things;
And Israel is the rod of his inheritance:
The Lord of hosts is his name.

THE WORDS OF JEREMIAH

"Wherefore Doth the Way of the Wicked Prosper?"

Righteous art thou, O Lord, when I plead with thee:
Yet let me talk with thee of thy judgments.
Wherefore doth the way of the wicked prosper?
Wherefore are all they happy that deal very treacherously?
Thou hast planted them, yea, they have taken root:
They grow, yea, they bring forth fruit:
Thou art near in their mouth,
And far from their reins.
But thou, O Lord, knowest me:
Thou hast seen me, and tried mine heart toward thee:
Pull them out like sheep for the slaughter,
And prepare them for the day of slaughter.
How long shall the land mourn,
And the herbs of every field wither,
For the wickedness of them that dwell therein?
The beasts are consumed, and the birds;
Because they said, "He shall not see our last end."

"If thou hast run with the footmen, and they have wearied thee,
Then how canst thou contend with horses?
And if in the land of peace, wherein thou trustedst, they wearied thee,
Then how wilt thou do in the swelling of Jordan?"

Symbolism of the Girdle

Thus saith the Lord unto me, "Go and get thee a linen girdle, and put it upon thy loins, and put it not in water."

So I got a girdle according to the word of the Lord, and put it on my loins.

And the word of the Lord came unto me the second time, saying, "Take the girdle that thou hast got, which is upon thy loins, and arise, go to Euphrates, and hide it there in a hole of the rock."

So I went, and hid it by Euphrates, as the Lord commanded me.

THE WORDS OF JEREMIAH

And it came to pass after many days, that the Lord said unto me, "Arise, go to Euphrates, and take the girdle from thence, which I commanded thee to hide there."

Then I went to Euphrates, and digged, and took the girdle from the place where I had hid it: and, behold, the girdle was marred, it was profitable for nothing.

Then the word of the Lord came unto me, saying, "Thus saith the Lord: after this manner will I mar the pride of Judah, and the great pride of Jerusalem. This evil people, which refuse to hear my words, which walk in the imagination of their heart, and walk after other gods, to serve them, and to worship them, shall even be as this girdle, which is good for nothing. For as the girdle cleaveth to the loins of a man, so have I caused to cleave unto me the whole house of Israel and the whole house of Judah," saith the Lord; "that they might be unto me for a people, and for a name, and for a praise, and for a glory: but they would not hear."

Speech to the King and Queen

Say unto the king and to the queen, "Humble yourselves, sit down: for your principalities shall come down, even the crown of your glory." The cities of the south shall be shut up, and none shall open them: Judah shall be carried away captive all of it, it shall be wholly carried away captive. "Lift up your eyes, and behold them that come from the north: where is the flock that was given thee, thy beautiful flock? What wilt thou say when he shall punish thee? for thou hast taught them to be captains, and as chief over thee: shall not sorrows take thee, as a woman in travail?

"And if thou say in thine heart, 'Wherefore come these things upon me?' for the greatness of thine iniquity are thy skirts discovered, and thy heels made bare. Can the Ethiopian change his skin, or the leopard his spots? then may ye also do good, that are accustomed to do evil. Therefore will I scatter them as the stubble that passeth away by the wind of the wilderness. This is thy lot, the portion of thy measures from me," saith the

THE WORDS OF JEREMIAH

Lord; "because thou hast forgotten me, and trusted in falsehood. Therefore will I discover thy skirts upon thy face, that thy shame may appear. I have seen thine adulteries, and thy neighings, the lewdness of thy whoredom, and thine abominations on the hills in the fields. Woe unto thee, O Jerusalem! wilt thou not be made clean? when shall it once be?"

"Judah Mourneth"

Judah mourneth, and the gates thereof languish;
They are black unto the ground;
And the cry of Jerusalem is gone up.
And their nobles have sent their little ones to the waters:
They came to the pits, and found no water;
They returned with their vessels empty;
They were ashamed and confounded, and covered their heads.
Because the ground is chapt,
For there was no rain in the earth,
The plowmen were ashamed,
They covered their heads.
Yea, the hind also calved in the field, and forsook it,
Because there was no grass.
And the wild asses did stand in the high places,
They snuffed up the wind like dragons;
Their eyes did fail, because there was no grass.

Sentences

The sin of Judah is written with a pen of iron, and with the point of a diamond: it is graven upon the table of their heart, and upon the horns of your altars; whilst their children remember their altars and their groves by the green trees upon the high hills.

"O my mountain in the field, I will give thy substance and all thy treasures to the spoil, and thy high places for sin, throughout all thy borders. And thou, even thyself, shalt discontinue from thine heritage that I gave thee; and I will cause thee to

THE WORDS OF JEREMIAH

serve thine enemies in the land which thou knowest not: for ye have kindled a fire in mine anger, which shall burn for ever."

Thus saith the Lord: "Cursed be the man that trusteth in man, and maketh flesh his arm, and whose heart departeth from the Lord. For he shall be like the heath in the desert, and shall not see when good cometh; but shall inhabit the parched places in the wilderness, in a salt land and not inhabited.

"Blessed is the man that trusteth in the Lord, and whose hope the Lord is. For he shall be as a tree planted by the waters, and that spreadeth out her roots by the river, and shall not see when heat cometh, but her leaf shall be green; and shall not be careful in the year of drought, neither shall cease from yielding fruit."

The heart is deceitful above all things, and desperately wicked: who can know it?

"I the Lord search the heart, I try the reins, even to give every man according to his ways, and according to the fruit of his doings."

As the partridge sitteth on eggs, and hatcheth them not; so he that getteth riches, and not by right, shall leave them in the midst of his days, and at his end shall be a fool.

A glorious high throne from the beginning is the place of our sanctuary, O Lord, the hope of Israel, all that forsake thee shall be ashamed, and they that depart from me shall be written in the earth, because they have forsaken the Lord, the fountain of living waters.

Sermon on the Sabbath

Thus said the Lord unto me: "Go and stand in the gate of the children of the people, whereby the kings of Judah come in, and by the gates which they go out, and in all the gates of Jerusalem; and say unto them, 'Hear ye the word of the Lord, ye kings of Judah, and all Judah, and all the inhabitants of Jerusalem, that

THE WORDS OF JEREMIAH

enter in by these gates.' Thus saith the Lord: 'Take heed to yourselves, and bear no burden on the sabbath day, nor bring it in by the gates of Jerusalem; neither carry forth a burden out of your houses on the sabbath day, neither do ye any work, but hallow ye the sabbath day, as I commanded your fathers. But they obeyed not, neither inclined their ear, but made their neck stiff, that they might not hear, nor receive instruction. And it shall come to pass, if ye diligently hearken unto me,' saith the Lord, 'to bring in no burden through the gates of this city on the sabbath day, but hallow the sabbath day, to do no work therein; then shall there enter into the gates of this city kings and princes sitting upon the throne of David, riding in chariots and on horses, they, and their princes, the men of Judah, and the inhabitants of Jerusalem: and this city shall remain for ever. And they shall come from the cities of Judah, and from the places about Jerusalem, and from the land of Benjamin, and from the plain, and from the mountains, and from the south, bringing burnt offerings, and sacrifices, and meat offerings, and incense, and bringing sacrifices of praise, unto the house of the Lord. But if ye will not hearken unto me to hallow the sabbath day, and not to bear a burden, even entering in at the gates of Jerusalem, on the sabbath day; then will I kindle a fire in the gates thereof, and it shall devour the palaces of Jerusalem, and it shall not be quenched.'"

Parable of the Potter

The word which came to Jeremiah from the Lord, saying, "Arise, and go down to the potter's house, and there I will cause thee to hear my words."

Then I went down to the potter's house, and, behold, he wrought a work on the wheels. And the vessel that he made of clay was marred in the hand of the potter: so he made it again another vessel, as seemed good to the potter to make it.

Then the word of the Lord came to me, saying, "O house of Israel, cannot I do with you as this potter?" saith the Lord. "Behold, as the clay is in the potter's hand, so are ye in mine hand, O house of Israel. At what instant I shall speak concerning a

THE WORDS OF JEREMIAH

nation, and concerning a kingdom, to pluck up, and to pull down, and to destroy it; if that nation, against whom I have pronounced, turn from their evil, I will repent of the evil that I thought to do unto them. And at what instant I shall speak concerning a nation, and concerning a kingdom, to build and to plant it; if it do evil in my sight, that it obey not my voice, then I will repent of the good wherewith I said I would benefit them."

Jeremiah's Discourse in Tophet

Thus saith the Lord, "Go and get a potter's earthen bottle, and take of the ancients of the people, and of the ancients of the priests; and go forth unto the valley of the son of Hinnom, which is by the entry of the east gate, and proclaim there the words that I shall tell thee, and say, 'Hear ye the word of the Lord, O kings of Judah, and inhabitants of Jerusalem; thus saith the Lord of hosts, the God of Israel: behold, I will bring evil upon this place, the which whosoever heareth, his ears shall tingle. Because they have forsaken me, and have estranged this place, and have burned incense in it unto other gods, whom neither they nor their fathers have known, nor the kings of Judah, and have filled this place with the blood of innocents; they have built also the high places of Baal, to burn their sons with fire for burnt offerings unto Baal, which I commanded not, nor spake it, neither came it into my mind: therefore, behold, the days come,' saith the Lord, 'that this place shall no more be called Tophet, nor the valley of the son of Hinnom, but the valley of slaughter. And I will make void the counsel of Judah and Jerusalem in this place; and I will cause them to fall by the sword before their enemies, and by the hands of them that seek their lives: and their carcases will I give to be meat for the fowls of the heaven, and for the beasts of the earth. And I will make this city desolate, and a hissing; every one that passeth thereby shall be astonished and hiss because of all the plagues thereof. And I will cause them to eat the flesh of their sons and the flesh of their daughters, and they shall eat every one the flesh of his friend in

THE WORDS OF JEREMIAH

the siege and straitness, wherewith their enemies, and they that seek their lives, shall straiten them.'

"Then shalt thou break the bottle in the sight of the men that go with thee, and shalt say unto them, 'Thus saith the Lord of hosts: even so will I break this people and this city, as one breaketh a potter's vessel, that cannot be made whole again: and they shall bury them in Tophet, till there be no place to bury. Thus will I do unto this place,' saith the Lord, 'and to the inhabitants thereof, and even make this city as Tophet: and the houses of Jerusalem, and the houses of the kings of Judah, shall be defiled as the place of Tophet, because of all the houses upon whose roofs they have burned incense unto all the host of heaven, and have poured out drink offerings unto other gods.'"

Jeremiah in the Stocks

Then came Jeremiah from Tophet, whither the Lord had sent him to prophesy; and he stood in the court of the Lord's house; and said to all the people, "Thus saith the Lord of hosts, the God of Israel: 'Behold, I will bring upon this city and upon all her towns all the evil that I have pronounced against it, because they have hardened their necks, that they might not hear my words.'"

Now Pashur the son of Immer the priest, who was also chief governor in the house of the Lord, heard that Jeremiah prophesied these things. Then Pashur smote Jeremiah the prophet, and put him in the stocks that were in the high gate of Benjamin, which was by the house of the Lord. And it came to pass on the morrow, that Pashur brought forth Jeremiah out of the stocks. Then said Jeremiah unto him, "The Lord hath not called thy name Pashur, but Magor-missabib. For thus saith the Lord, 'Behold, I will make thee a terror to thyself, and to all thy friends: and they shall fall by the sword of their enemies, and thine eyes shall behold it: and I will give all Judah into the hand of the king of Babylon, and he shall carry them captive into Babylon, and shall slay them with the sword. Moreover I will deliver all the strength of this city, and all the labours thereof, and all the

THE WORDS OF JEREMIAH

precious things thereof, and all the treasures of the kings of Judah will I give into the hand of their enemies, which shall spoil them, and take them, and carry them to Babylon. And thou, Pashur, and all that dwell in thine house shall go into captivity: and thou shalt come to Babylon, and there thou shalt die, and shalt be buried there, thou, and all thy friends, to whom thou hast prophesied lies.'"

"O Lord Thou Hast Deceived Me"

O Lord, thou hast deceived me, and I was deceived:
Thou art stronger than I, and hast prevailed:
I am in derision daily, every one mocketh me.
For since I spoke, I cried out,
I cried violence and spoil;
Because the word of the Lord was made a reproach unto me,
And a derision, daily.
Then I said, "I will not make mention of him,
Nor speak any more in his name."

But his word was in mine heart as a burning fire shut up in my bones,
And I was weary with forbearing,
And I could not stay.
For I heard the defaming of many,
Fear on every side.
"Report," say they,
"And we will report it."
All my familiars watched for my halting,
Saying, "Peradventure he will be enticed, and we shall prevail against him,
And we shall take our revenge on him."

But the Lord is with me as a mighty terrible one:
Therefore my persecutors shall stumble, and they shall not prevail:
They shall be greatly ashamed;
For they shall not prosper:
Their everlasting confusion shall never be forgotten.

THE WORDS OF JEREMIAH

But, O Lord of hosts, that triest the righteous,
And seest the reins and the heart,
Let me see thy vengeance on them:
For unto thee have I opened my cause.

Cursed be the day wherein I was born:
Let not the day wherein my mother bore me be blessed.
Cursed be the man who brought tidings to my father,
Saying, "A man child is born unto thee";
Making him very glad.
And let that man be as the cities which the Lord overthrew, and repented not:
And let him hear the cry in the morning, and the shouting at noontide;
Because he slew me not from the womb;
Or that my mother might have been my grave,
And her womb to be always great with me.
Wherefore came I forth out of the womb to see labour and sorrow,
That my days should be consumed with shame?

Parable of the Figs

The Lord showed me, and, behold, two baskets of figs were set before the temple of the Lord, after that Nebuchadrezzar king of Babylon had carried away captive Jeconiah the son of Jehoiakim king of Judah, and the princes of Judah, with the carpenters and smiths, from Jerusalem, and had brought them to Babylon. One basket had very good figs, even like the figs that are first ripe: and the other basket had very naughty figs, which could not be eaten, they were so bad.

Then said the Lord unto me, "What seest thou, Jeremiah?"

And I said, "Figs; the good figs, very good; and the evil, very evil, that cannot be eaten, they are so evil."

Again the word of the Lord came unto me, saying, "Thus saith the Lord, the God of Israel: 'Like these good figs, so will I acknowledge them that are carried away captive of Judah, whom I have sent out of this place into the land of the Chaldeans for

THE WORDS OF JEREMIAH

their good. For I will set mine eyes upon them for good, and I will bring them again to this land: and I will build them, and not pull them down; and I will plant them, and not pluck them up. And I will give them a heart to know me, that I am the Lord: and they shall be my people, and I will be their God: for they shall return unto me with their whole heart.'

"And as the evil figs, which cannot be eaten, they are so evil," surely thus saith the Lord, "so will I give Zedekiah the king of Judah, and his princes, and the residue of Jerusalem, that remain in this land, and them that dwell in the land of Egypt: and I will deliver them to be removed into all the kingdoms of the earth for their hurt, to be a reproach and a proverb, a taunt and a curse, in all places whither I shall drive them. And I will send the sword, the famine, and the pestilence, among them, till they be consumed from off the land that I gave unto them and to their fathers."

The Cup of the Lord's Fury

The word that came to Jeremiah concerning all the people of Judah in the fourth year of Jehoiakim the son of Josiah king of Judah, that was the first year of Nebuchadrezzar king of Babylon: the which Jeremiah the prophet spoke unto all the people of Judah, and to all the inhabitants of Jerusalem, saying,

"From the thirteenth year of Josiah the son of Amon king of Judah, even unto this day, that is the three and twentieth year, the word of the Lord hath come unto me, and I have spoken unto you, rising early and speaking; but ye have not hearkened. And the Lord hath sent unto you all his servants the prophets, rising early and sending them; but ye have not hearkened, nor inclined your ear to hear.

"They said, 'Turn ye again now every one from his evil way, and from the evil of your doings, and dwell in the land that the Lord hath given unto you and to your fathers for ever and ever: and go not after other gods to serve them, and to worship them, and provoke me not to anger with the works of your hands; and I will do you no hurt.'

THE WORDS OF JEREMIAH

"'Yet ye have not hearkened unto me,' saith the Lord; 'that ye might provoke me to anger with the works of your hands to your own hurt.'

"Therefore thus saith the Lord of hosts: 'Because ye have not heard my words, behold, I will send and take all the families of the north,' saith the Lord, 'and Nebuchadrezzar the king of Babylon, my servant, and will bring them against this land, and against the inhabitants thereof, and against all these nations round about, and will utterly destroy them, and make them an astonishment, and a hissing, and perpetual desolations. Moreover I will take from them the voice of mirth, and the voice of gladness, the voice of the bridegroom, and the voice of the bride, the sound of the millstones, and the light of the candle. And this whole land shall be a desolation, and an astonishment; and these nations shall serve the king of Babylon seventy years. And it shall come to pass, when seventy years are accomplished, that I will punish the king of Babylon, and that nation,' saith the Lord, 'for their iniquity, and the land of the Chaldeans, and will make it perpetual desolations. And I will bring upon that land all my words which I have pronounced against it, even all that is written in this book, which Jeremiah hath prophesied against all the nations. For many nations and great kings shall serve themselves of them also: and I will recompense them according to their deeds, and according to the works of their own hands.'

"For thus saith the Lord God of Israel unto me: 'Take the wine cup of this fury at my hand, and cause all the nations, to whom I send thee, to drink it. And they shall drink, and be moved, and be mad, because of the sword that I will send among them.'"

Jeremiah's Sermon in the Temple

In the beginning of the reign of Jehoiakim the son of Josiah king of Judah came this word from the Lord, saying, "Thus saith the Lord: stand in the court of the Lord's house, and speak unto all the cities of Judah, which come to worship in the Lord's house, all the words that I command thee to speak unto them;

THE WORDS OF JEREMIAH

diminish not a word, if so be they will hearken, and turn every man from his evil way, that I may repent me of the evil, which I purpose to do unto them because of the evil of their doings. And thou shalt say unto them, 'Thus saith the Lord: "If ye will not hearken to me, to walk in my law, which I have set before you, to hearken to the words of my servants the prophets, whom I sent unto you, both rising up early, and sending them, but ye have not hearkened; then will I make this house like Shiloh, and will make this city a curse to all the nations of the earth."'"

Now it came to pass, when Jeremiah had made an end of speaking all that the Lord had commanded him to speak unto all the people, that the priests and the prophets and all the people took him, saying, "Thou shalt surely die. Why hast thou prophesied in the name of the Lord, saying, 'This house shall be like Shiloh, and this city shall be desolate without an inhabitant'?" And all the people were gathered against Jeremiah in the house of the Lord.

When the princes of Judah heard these things, then they came up from the king's house unto the house of the Lord, and sat down in the entry of the new gate of the Lord's house. Then spoke the priests and the prophets unto the princes and to all the people, saying, "This man is worthy to die; for he hath prophesied against this city, as ye have heard with your ears."

Then spoke Jeremiah unto all the princes and to all the people, saying, "The Lord sent me to prophesy against this house and against this city all the words that ye have heard. Therefore now amend your ways and your doings, and obey the voice of the Lord your God; and the Lord will repent him of the evil that he hath pronounced against you. As for me, behold, I am in your hand: do with me as seemeth good and meet unto you. But know ye for certain, that if ye put me to death, ye shall surely bring innocent blood upon yourselves, and upon this city, and upon the inhabitants thereof: for of a truth the Lord hath sent me unto you to speak all these words in your ears."

Then said the princes and all the people unto the priests and

THE WORDS OF JEREMIAH

to the prophets; "This man is not worthy to die: for he hath spoken to us in the name of the Lord our God."

Then rose up certain of the elders of the land, and spoke to all the assembly of the people, saying, "Micah the Morasthite prophesied in the days of Hezekiah king of Judah, and spoke to all the people of Judah, saying, 'Thus saith the Lord of hosts: "Zion shall be plowed like a field, and Jerusalem shall become heaps, and the mountain of the house as the high places of a forest."' Did Hezekiah king of Judah and all Judah put him at all to death? did he not fear the Lord, and besought the Lord, and the Lord repented him of the evil which he had pronounced against them? Thus might we procure great evil against our souls."

Jeremiah's Letter to the Captives in Babylon

Now these are the words of the letter that Jeremiah the prophet sent from Jerusalem unto the residue of the elders which were carried away captives, and to the priests, and to the prophets, and to all the people whom Nebuchadrezzar had carried away captive from Jerusalem to Babylon (after that Jeconiah the king, and the queen, and the eunuchs, the princes of Judah and Jerusalem, and the carpenters, and the smiths, were departed from Jerusalem), by the hand of Elasah the son of Shaphan, and Gemariah the son of Hilkiah (whom Zedekiah king of Judah sent unto Babylon to Nebuchadrezzar king of Babylon), saying,

"Thus saith the Lord of hosts, the God of Israel, unto all that are carried away captives, whom I have caused to be carried away from Jerusalem unto Babylon: 'Build ye houses, and dwell in them; and plant gardens, and eat the fruit of them; take ye wives, and beget sons and daughters; and take wives for your sons, and give your daughters to husbands, that they may bear sons and daughters; that ye may be increased there, and not diminished. And seek the peace of the city whither I have caused you to be carried away captives, and pray unto the Lord for it: for in the peace thereof shall ye have peace.'

"For thus saith the Lord of hosts, the God of Israel: 'Let not

THE WORDS OF JEREMIAH

your prophets and your diviners, that be in the midst of you, deceive you, neither hearken to your dreams which ye cause to be dreamed. For they prophesy falsely unto you in my name: I have not sent them,' saith the Lord.

"For thus saith the Lord, 'After seventy years be accomplished at Babylon I will visit you, and perform my good word toward you, in causing you to return to this place. For I know the thoughts that I think toward you,' saith the Lord, 'thoughts of peace, and not of evil, to give you an expected end. Then shall ye call upon me, and ye shall go and pray unto me, and I will hearken unto you. And ye shall seek me, and find me, when ye shall search for me with all your heart. And I will be found of you,' saith the Lord: 'and I will turn away your captivity, and I will gather you from all the nations, and from all the places whither I have driven you,' saith the Lord: 'and I will bring you again into the place whence I caused you to be carried away captive.'

"Because ye have said, 'The Lord hath raised us up prophets in Babylon'; know that thus saith the Lord of the king that sitteth upon the throne of David, and of all the people that dwelleth in this city, and of your brethren that are not gone forth with you into captivity: 'Behold, I will send upon them the sword, the famine, and the pestilence, and will make them like vile figs, that cannot be eaten, they are so evil. And I will persecute them with the sword, with the famine, and with the pestilence, and will deliver them to be removed to all the kingdoms of the earth, to be a curse, and an astonishment, and a hissing, and a reproach, among all the nations whither I have driven them: because they have not hearkened to my words,' saith the Lord, 'which I sent unto them by my servants the prophets, rising up early and sending them; but ye would not hear,' saith the Lord.

"'Hear ye therefore the word of the Lord, all ye of the captivity, whom I have sent from Jerusalem to Babylon,' thus saith the Lord of hosts, the God of Israel, of Ahab the son of Kolaiah, and of Zedekiah the son of Maaseiah, which prophesy a lie unto you in my name: 'Behold, I will deliver them into the hand of

THE WORDS OF JEREMIAH

Nebuchadrezzar king of Babylon; and he shall slay them before your eyes; and of them shall be taken up a curse by all the captivity of Judah which are in Babylon, saying, "The Lord make thee like Zedekiah and like Ahab, whom the king of Babylon roasted in the fire"; because they have committed villainy in Israel, and have committed adultery with their neighbours' wives, and have spoken lying words in my name, which I have not commanded them; even I know, and am a witness,' saith the Lord."

Thus shalt thou also speak to Shemaiah the Nehelamite, saying, "Thus speaketh the Lord of hosts, the God of Israel, 'Because thou hast sent letters in thy name unto all the people that are at Jerusalem, and to Zephaniah the son of Maaseiah the priest, and to all the priests, saying,

" ' "The Lord hath made thee priest in the stead of Jehoiada the priest, that ye should be officers in the house of the Lord, for every man that is mad, and maketh himself a prophet, that thou shouldest put him in prison, and in the stocks. Now therefore why hast thou not reproved Jeremiah of Anathoth, which maketh himself a prophet to you? For therefore he sent unto us in Babylon, saying, "This captivity is long: build ye houses, and dwell in them; and plant gardens, and eat the fruit of them' " ' " (And Zephaniah the priest read this letter in the ears of Jeremiah the prophet.)

Then came the word of the Lord unto Jeremiah, saying, "Send to all them of the captivity, saying, 'Thus saith the Lord concerning Shemaiah the Nehelamite: because that Shemaiah hath prophesied unto you, and I sent him not, and he caused you to trust in a lie: therefore thus saith the Lord: "Behold, I will punish Shemaiah the Nehelamite, and his seed: he shall not have a man to dwell among this people; neither shall he behold the good that I will do for my people," saith the Lord; "because he hath taught rebellion against the Lord." ' "

Prophecy of the Return

Thus saith the Lord: "Behold, I will bring again the captivity of Jacob's tents, and have mercy on his dwellingplaces; and the

THE WORDS OF JEREMIAH

city shall be builded upon her own heap, and the palace shall remain after the manner thereof. And out of them shall proceed thanksgiving and the voice of them that make merry: and I will multiply them, and they shall not be few; I will also glorify them, and they shall not be small. Their children also shall be as aforetime, and their congregation shall be established before me, and I will punish all that oppress them. And their nobles shall be of themselves, and their governor shall proceed from the midst of them; and I will cause him to draw near, and he shall approach unto me: for who is this that engaged his heart to approach unto me?" saith the Lord. "And ye shall be my people, and I will be your God."

Behold, the whirlwind of the Lord goeth forth with fury, a continuing whirlwind: it shall fall with pain upon the head of the wicked. The fierce anger of the Lord shall not return, until he have done it, and until he have performed the intents of his heart: in the latter days ye shall consider it.

"At the same time," saith the Lord, "will I be the God of all the families of Israel, and they shall be my people." Thus saith the Lord, "The people which were left of the sword found grace in the wilderness; even Israel, when I went to cause him to rest."

The Lord hath appeared of old unto me, saying, "Yea, I have loved thee with an everlasting love: therefore with lovingkindness have I drawn thee. Again I will build thee, and thou shalt be built, O virgin of Israel: thou shalt again be adorned with thy tabrets, and shalt go forth in the dances of them that make merry. Thou shalt yet plant vines upon the mountains of Samaria: the planters shall plant, and shall eat them as common things. For there shall be a day, that the watchmen upon the Mount Ephraim shall cry, 'Arise ye, and let us go up to Zion unto the Lord our God.'"

For thus saith the Lord: "Sing with gladness for Jacob, and shout among the chief of the nations: publish ye, praise ye, and say, 'O Lord, save thy people, the remnant of Israel.' Behold, I will bring them from the north country, and gather them from the coasts of the earth, and with them the blind and the lame,

THE WORDS OF JEREMIAH

the woman with child and her that travaileth with child together: a great company shall return thither. They shall come with weeping, and with supplications will I lead them: I will cause them to walk by the rivers of waters in a straight way, wherein they shall not stumble: for I am a father to Israel, and Ephraim is my firstborn."

Hear the word of the Lord, O ye nations, and declare it in the isles afar off, and say, "He that scattered Israel will gather him, and keep him, as a shepherd doth his flock. For the Lord hath redeemed Jacob, and ransomed him from the hand of him that was stronger than he. Therefore they shall come and sing in the height of Zion, and shall flow together to the goodness of the Lord, for wheat, and for wine, and for oil, and for the young of the flock and of the herd: and their soul shall be as a watered garden; and they shall not sorrow any more at all. Then shall the virgin rejoice in the dance, both young men and old together: for I will turn their mourning into joy, and will comfort them, and make them rejoice from their sorrow. And I will satiate the soul of the priests with fatness, and my people shall be satisfied with my goodness," saith the Lord.

Thus saith the Lord: "A voice was heard in Ramah, lamentation, and bitter weeping; Rachel weeping for her children refused to be comforted for her children, because they were not."

Thus saith the Lord: "Refrain thy voice from weeping, and thine eyes from tears: for thy work shall be rewarded," saith the Lord; "and they shall come again from the land of the enemy. And there is hope in thine end," saith the Lord, "that thy children shall come again to their own border. I have surely heard Ephraim bemoaning himself thus: 'Thou hast chastised me, and I was chastised, as a bullock unaccustomed to the yoke: turn thou me, and I shall be turned; for thou art the Lord my God. Surely after that I was turned, I repented; and after that I was instructed. I smote upon my thigh: I was ashamed, yea, even confounded, because I did bear the reproach of my youth.' Is Ephraim my dear son? is he a pleasant child? for since I spoke against him, I do earnestly remember him still: therefore my

THE WORDS OF JEREMIAH

bowels are troubled for him; I will surely have mercy upon him," saith the Lord.

"Set thee up waymarks, make thee high heaps: set thine heart toward the highway, even the way which thou wentest: turn again, O virgin of Israel, turn again to these thy cities."

The New Covenant

"Behold, the days come," saith the Lord, "that I will sow the house of Israel and the house of Judah with the seed of man, and with the seed of beast. And it shall come to pass, that like as I have watched over them, to pluck up, and to break down, and to throw down, and to destroy, and to afflict; so will I watch over them, to build, and to plant," saith the Lord.

"In those days they shall say no more, 'The fathers have eaten a sour grape, and the children's teeth are set on edge.' But every one shall die for his own iniquity: every man that eateth the sour grape, his teeth shall be set on edge.

"Behold, the days come," saith the Lord, "that I will make a new covenant with the house of Israel, and with the house of Judah: not according to the covenant that I made with their fathers in the day that I took them by the hand to bring them out of the land of Egypt; which my covenant they broke, although I was a husband unto them," saith the Lord: "but this shall be the covenant that I will make with the house of Israel. After those days," saith the Lord, "I will put my law in their inward parts, and write it in their hearts; and will be their God, and they shall be my people. And they shall teach no more every man his neighbour, and every man his brother, saying, 'Know the Lord': for they shall all know me, from the least of them unto the greatest of them," saith the Lord: "for I will forgive their iniquity, and I will remember their sin no more."

The Writing of Jeremiah's Prophecies

And it came to pass in the fourth year of Jehoiakim the son of Josiah king of Judah, that this word came unto Jeremiah from the Lord, saying, "Take thee a roll of a book, and write therein

THE WORDS OF JEREMIAH

all the words that I have spoken unto thee against Israel, and against Judah, and against all the nations, from the day I spoke unto thee, from the days of Josiah, even unto this day. It may be that the house of Judah will hear all the evil which I purpose to do unto them; that they may return every man from his evil way; that I may forgive their iniquity and their sin." Then Jeremiah called Baruch the son of Neriah: and Baruch wrote from the mouth of Jeremiah all the words of the Lord, which he had spoken unto him, upon a roll of a book.

And Jeremiah commanded Baruch, saying, "I am shut up; I cannot go into the house of the Lord: therefore go thou, and read in the roll, which thou hast written from my mouth, the words of the Lord in the ears of the people in the Lord's house upon the fasting day: and also thou shalt read them in the ears of all Judah that come out of their cities. It may be they will present their supplication before the Lord, and will return every one from his evil way: for great is the anger and the fury that the Lord hath pronounced against this people." And Baruch the son of Neriah did according to all that Jeremiah the prophet commanded him, reading in the book the words of the Lord in the Lord's house.

And it came to pass in the fifth year of Jehoiakim the son of Josiah king of Judah, in the ninth month, that they proclaimed a fast before the Lord to all the people in Jerusalem, and to all the people that came from the cities of Judah unto Jerusalem. Then read Baruch in the book the words of Jeremiah in the house of the Lord, in the chamber of Gemariah the son of Shaphan the scribe, in the higher court, at the entry of the new gate of the Lord's house, in the ears of all the people.

When Michaiah the son of Gemariah, the son of Shaphan, had heard out of the book all the words of the Lord, then he went down into the king's house, into the scribe's chamber: and, lo, all the princes sat there, even Elishama the scribe, and Delaiah the son of Shemaiah, and Elnathan the son of Achbor, and Gemariah the son of Shaphan, and Zedekiah the son of Hananiah, and all the princes. Then Michaiah declared unto

THE WORDS OF JEREMIAH

them all the words that he had heard, when Baruch read the book in the ears of the people.

Therefore all the princes sent Jehudi the son of Nethaniah, the son of Shelemiah, the son of Cushi, unto Baruch, saying, "Take in thine hand the roll wherein thou hast read in the ears of the people, and come." So Baruch the son of Neriah took the roll in his hand, and came unto them.

And they said unto him, "Sit down now, and read it in our ears." So Baruch read it in their ears.

Now it came to pass, when they had heard all the words, they were afraid both one and other, and said unto Baruch, "We will surely tell the king of all these words."

And they asked Baruch, saying, "Tell us now: how didst thou write all these words at his mouth?"

Then Baruch answered them, "He pronounced all these words unto me with his mouth, and I wrote them with ink in the book."

Then said the princes unto Baruch, "Go, hide thee, thou and Jeremiah; and let no man know where ye be."

And they went in to the king into the court, but they laid up the roll in the chamber of Elishama the scribe, and told all the words in the ears of the king. So the king sent Jehudi to fetch the roll: and he took it out of Elishama the scribe's chamber. And Jehudi read it in the ears of the king, and in the ears of all the princes which stood beside the king.

Now the king sat in the winterhouse in the ninth month: and there was a fire on the hearth burning before him. And it came to pass that when Jehudi had read three or four leaves, he cut it with the penknife, and cast it into the fire that was on the hearth, until all the roll was consumed in the fire that was on the hearth. Yet they were not afraid, nor rent their garments, neither the king nor any of his servants that heard all these words. Nevertheless Elnathan and Delaiah and Gemariah had made intercession to the king that he would not burn the roll: but he would not hear them. But the king commanded Jerahmeel the son of Hammelech, and Seraiah the son of Azriel, and Shel-

THE WORDS OF JEREMIAH

emiah the son of Abdeel, to take Baruch the scribe and Jeremiah the prophet: but the Lord hid them.

Then the word of the Lord came to Jeremiah, after that the king had burned the roll, and the words which Baruch wrote at the mouth of Jeremiah, saying, "Take thee again another roll, and write in it all the former words that were in the first roll, which Jehoiakim the king of Judah hath burned."

Then took Jeremiah another roll, and gave it to Baruch the scribe, the son of Neriah; who wrote therein from the mouth of Jeremiah all the words of the book which Jehoiakim king of Judah had burned in the fire: and there were added besides unto them many like words.

The Imprisonment of Jeremiah

And King Zedekiah the son of Josiah reigned instead of Coniah the son of Jehoiakim, whom Nebuchadrezzar king of Babylon made king in the land of Judah. But neither he, nor his servants, nor the people of the land, did hearken unto the words of the Lord, which he spoke by the prophet Jeremiah. And Zedekiah the king sent Jehucal the son of Shelemiah and Zephaniah the son of Maaseiah the priest to the prophet Jeremiah, saying, "Pray now unto the Lord our God for us."

Then Pharaoh's army was come forth out of Egypt: and when the Chaldeans that besieged Jerusalem heard tidings of them, they departed from Jerusalem. Then came the word of the Lord unto the prophet Jeremiah, saying, "Thus saith the Lord, the God of Israel: 'Thus shall ye say to the king of Judah, that sent you unto me to enquire of me: "Behold, Pharaoh's army, which is come forth to help you, shall return to Egypt into their own land. And the Chaldeans shall come again, and fight against this city, and take it, and burn it with fire."' Thus saith the Lord: 'Deceive not yourselves, saying, "The Chaldeans shall surely depart from us": for they shall not depart. For though ye had smitten the whole army of the Chaldeans that fight against you, and there remained but wounded men among them, yet should they rise up every man in his tent, and burn this city with fire.'"

THE WORDS OF JEREMIAH

And it came to pass that when the army of the Chaldeans was broken up from Jerusalem for fear of Pharaoh's army, then Jeremiah went forth out of Jerusalem to go into the land of Benjamin, to separate himself thence in the midst of the people. And when he was in the gate of Benjamin, a captain of the ward was there, whose name was Irijah, the son of Shelemiah, the son of Hananiah; and he took Jeremiah the prophet, saying, "Thou fallest away to the Chaldeans."

Then said Jeremiah, "It is false; I fall not away to the Chaldeans." But he hearkened not to him: so Irijah took Jeremiah, and brought him to the princes. Wherefore the princes were wroth with Jeremiah, and smote him, and put him in prison in the house of Jonathan the scribe: for they had made that the prison.

When Jeremiah was entered into the dungeon, and into the cabins, and Jeremiah had remained there many days; then Zedekiah the king sent, and took him out: and the king asked him secretly in his house, and said, "Is there any word from the Lord?"

And Jeremiah said, "There is: for," said he, "thou shalt be delivered into the hand of the king of Babylon." Moreover Jeremiah said unto King Zedekiah, "What have I offended against thee, or against thy servants, or against this people, that ye have put me in prison? Where are now your prophets which prophesied unto you, saying, 'The king of Babylon shall not come against you, nor against this land'? Therefore hear now, I pray thee, O my lord the king: let my supplication, I pray thee, be accepted before thee; that thou cause me not to return to the house of Jonathan the scribe, lest I die there."

Then Zedekiah the king commanded that they should commit Jeremiah into the court of the prison, and that they should give him daily a piece of bread out of the bakers' street, until all the bread in the city were spent. Thus Jeremiah remained in the court of the prison.

Then Shephatiah the son of Mattan, and Gedaliah the son of Pashur, and Jucal the son of Shelemiah, and Pashur the son of

THE WORDS OF JEREMIAH

Malchiah, heard the words that Jeremiah had spoken unto all the people, saying, "Thus saith the Lord, 'He that remaineth in this city shall die by the sword, by the famine, and by the pestilence: but he that goeth forth to the Chaldeans shall live; for he shall have his life for a prey, and shall live.' Thus saith the Lord, 'This city shall surely be given into the hand of the king of Babylon's army, which shall take it.'"

Therefore the princes said unto the king, "We beseech thee, let this man be put to death: for thus he weakeneth the hands of the men of war that remain in this city, and the hands of all the people, in speaking such words unto them: for this man seeketh not the welfare of this people, but the hurt."

Then Zedekiah the king said, "Behold, he is in your hand: for the king is not he that can do any thing against you."

Then took they Jeremiah, and cast him into the dungeon of Malchiah the son of Hammelech, that was in the court of the prison: and they let down Jeremiah with cords. And in the dungeon there was no water, but mire: so Jeremiah sunk in the mire.

Now when Ebed-melech the Ethiopian, one of the eunuchs which was in the king's house, heard that they had put Jeremiah in the dungeon—the king then sitting in the gate of Benjamin—Ebed-melech went forth out of the king's house, and spoke to the king, saying, "My lord the king, these men have done evil in all that they have done to Jeremiah the prophet, whom they have cast into the dungeon; and he is like to die for hunger in the place where he is: for there is no more bread in the city."

Then the king commanded Ebed-melech the Ethiopian, saying, "Take from hence thirty men with thee, and take up Jeremiah the prophet out of the dungeon, before he die."

So Ebed-melech took the men with him, and went into the house of the king under the treasury, and took thence old cast clouts and old rotten rags, and let them down by cords into the dungeon to Jeremiah. And Ebed-melech the Ethiopian said unto Jeremiah, "Put now these old cast clouts and rotten rags under thine armholes under the cords." And Jeremiah did so. So they

THE WORDS OF JEREMIAH

drew up Jeremiah with cords, and took him up out of the dungeon: and Jeremiah remained in the court of the prison.

Then Zedekiah the king sent, and took Jeremiah the prophet unto him into the third entry that is in the house of the Lord: and the king said unto Jeremiah, "I will ask thee a thing; hide nothing from me."

Then Jeremiah said unto Zedekiah, "If I declare it unto thee, wilt thou not surely put me to death? and if I give thee counsel, wilt thou not hearken unto me?"

So Zedekiah the king swore secretly unto Jeremiah, saying, "As the Lord liveth, that made us this soul, I will not put thee to death, neither will I give thee into the hand of these men that seek thy life."

Then said Jeremiah unto Zedekiah, "Thus saith the Lord, the God of hosts, the God of Israel: 'If thou wilt assuredly go forth unto the king of Babylon's princes, then thy soul shall live, and this city shall not be burned with fire, and thou shalt live, and thine house: but if thou wilt not go forth to the king of Babylon's princes, then shall this city be given into the hand of the Chaldeans, and they shall burn it with fire, and thou shalt not escape out of their hand.'"

And Zedekiah the king said unto Jeremiah, "I am afraid of the Jews that are fallen to the Chaldeans, lest they deliver me into their hand, and they mock me."

But Jeremiah said, "They shall not deliver thee. Obey, I beseech thee, the voice of the Lord, which I speak unto thee: so it shall be well unto thee, and thy soul shall live. But if thou refuse to go forth, this is the word that the Lord hath showed me: behold, all the women that are left in the king of Judah's house shall be brought forth to the king of Babylon's princes, and those women shall say, 'Thy friends have set thee on, and have prevailed against thee: thy feet are sunk in the mire, and they are turned away back.' So they shall bring out all thy wives and thy children to the Chaldeans: and thou shalt not escape out of their hand, but shalt be taken by the hand of the king of Babylon: and thou shalt cause this city to be burned with fire."

THE WORDS OF JEREMIAH

Then said Zedekiah unto Jeremiah, "Let no man know of these words, and thou shalt not die. But if the princes hear that I have talked with thee, and they come unto thee, and say unto thee, 'Declare unto us now what thou hast said unto the king, hide it not from us, and we will not put thee to death; also what the king said unto thee': then thou shalt say unto them, 'I presented my supplication before the king, that he would not cause me to return to Jonathan's house, to die there.'"

Then came all the princes unto Jeremiah, and asked him: and he told them according to all these words that the king had commanded. So they left off speaking with him; for the matter was not perceived. So Jeremiah abode in the court of the prison until the day that Jerusalem was taken: and he was there when Jerusalem was taken.

In the ninth year of Zedekiah king of Judah, in the tenth month, came Nebuchadrezzar king of Babylon and all his army against Jerusalem, and they besieged it. And in the eleventh year of Zedekiah, in the fourth month, the ninth day of the month, the city was broken up. And all the princes of the king of Babylon came in, and sat in the middle gate, even Nergal-sharezer, Samgar-nebo, Sarsechim, Rab-saris, Nergal-sharezer, Rab-mag, with all the residue of the princes of the king of Babylon.

And it came to pass, that when Zedekiah the king of Judah saw them, and all the men of war, then they fled, and went forth out of the city by night, by the way of the king's garden, by the gate betwixt the two walls: and he went out the way of the plain. But the Chaldeans' army pursued after them, and overtook Zedekiah in the plains of Jericho: and when they had taken him, they brought him up to Nebuchadrezzar king of Babylon to Riblah in the land of Hamath, where he gave judgment upon him. Then the king of Babylon slew the sons of Zedekiah in Riblah before his eyes: also the king of Babylon slew all the nobles of Judah. Moreover he put out Zedekiah's eyes, and bound him with chains, to carry him to Babylon.

And the Chaldeans burned the king's house, and the houses

THE WORDS OF JEREMIAH

of the people, with fire, and broke down the walls of Jerusalem. Then Nebuzar-adan the captain of the guard carried away captive into Babylon the remnant of the people that remained in the city, and those that fell away, that fell to him, with the rest of the people that remained. But Nebuzar-adan the captain of the guard left of the poor of the people, which had nothing, in the land of Judah, and gave them vineyards and fields at the same time.

Now Nebuchadrezzar king of Babylon gave charge concerning Jeremiah to Nebuzar-adan the captain of the guard, saying, "Take him, and look well to him, and do him no harm; but do unto him even as he shall say unto thee."

So Nebuzar-adan the captain of the guard sent, and Nebushasban, Rab-saris, and Nergal-sharezer, Rab-mag, and all the king of Babylon's princes, even they sent, and took Jeremiah out of the court of the prison, and committed him unto Gedaliah the son of Ahikam the son of Shaphan, that he should carry him home: so he dwelt among the people.

Now the word of the Lord came unto Jeremiah, while he was shut up in the court of the prison, saying, "Go and speak to Ebed-melech the Ethiopian, saying, 'Thus saith the Lord of hosts, the God of Israel: "Behold, I will bring my words upon this city for evil, and not for good; and they shall be accomplished in that day before thee. But I will deliver thee in that day," saith the Lord: "and thou shalt not be given into the hand of the men of whom thou art afraid. For I will surely deliver thee, and thou shalt not fall by the sword, but thy life shall be for a prey unto thee: because thou hast put thy trust in me," saith the Lord.'"

The word that came to Jeremiah from the Lord, after that Nebuzar-adan the captain of the guard had let him go from Ramah, when he had taken him being bound in chains among all that were carried away captive of Jerusalem and Judah, which were carried away captive unto Babylon.

And the captain of the guard took Jeremiah, and said unto

THE WORDS OF JEREMIAH

him, "The Lord thy God hath pronounced this evil upon this place. Now the Lord hath brought it, and done according as he hath said: because ye have sinned against the Lord, and have not obeyed his voice, therefore this thing is come upon you. And now, behold, I loose thee this day from the chains which were upon thine hand. If it seem good unto thee to come with me into Babylon, come; and I will look well unto thee: but if it seem ill unto thee to come with me into Babylon, forbear: behold, all the land is before thee: whither it seemeth good and convenient for thee to go, thither go." Now while he was not yet gone back, he said, "Go back also to Gedaliah the son of Ahikam the son of Shaphan, whom the king of Babylon hath made governor over the cities of Judah, and dwell with him among the people: or go wheresoever it seemeth convenient unto thee to go." So the captain of the guard gave him victuals and a reward, and let him go.

Then went Jeremiah unto Gedaliah the son of Ahikam to Mizpah; and dwelt with him among the people that were left in the land.

Jeremiah Taken to Egypt

Then all the captains of the forces, and Johanan the son of Kareah, and Jezaniah the son of Hoshaiah, and all the people from the least even unto the greatest, came near, and said unto Jeremiah the prophet, "Let, we beseech thee, our supplication be accepted before thee, and pray for us unto the Lord thy God, even for all this remnant (for we are left but a few of many, as thine eyes do behold us): that the Lord thy God may show us the way wherein we may walk, and the thing that we may do."

Then Jeremiah the prophet said unto them, "I have heard you; behold, I will pray unto the Lord your God according to your words; and it shall come to pass that whatsoever thing the Lord shall answer you, I will declare it unto you; I will keep nothing back from you."

Then they said to Jeremiah, "The Lord be a true and faithful

THE WORDS OF JEREMIAH

witness between us, if we do not even according to all things for the which the Lord thy God shall send thee to us. Whether it be good, or whether it be evil, we will obey the voice of the Lord our God, to whom we send thee; that it may be well with us, when we obey the voice of the Lord our God."

And it came to pass after ten days that the word of the Lord came unto Jeremiah. Then called he Johanan the son of Kareah, and all the captains of the forces which were with him, and all the people from the least even to the greatest, and said unto them,

"Thus saith the Lord, the God of Israel, unto whom ye sent me to present your supplication before him: 'If ye will still abide in this land, then will I build you, and not pull you down, and I will plant you, and not pluck you up: for I repent me of the evil that I have done unto you. Be not afraid of the king of Babylon, of whom ye are afraid; be not afraid of him,' saith the Lord: 'for I am with you to save you, and to deliver you from his hand. And I will show mercies unto you, that he may have mercy upon you, and cause you to return to your own land.

" 'But if ye say, "We will not dwell in this land, neither obey the voice of the Lord your God," saying, "No; but we will go into the land of Egypt, where we shall see no war, nor hear the sound of the trumpet, nor have hunger of bread; and there will we dwell," now therefore hear the word of the Lord, ye remnant of Judah': Thus saith the Lord of hosts, the God of Israel: 'If ye wholly set your faces to enter into Egypt, and go to sojourn there: then it shall come to pass that the sword, which ye feared, shall overtake you there in the land of Egypt, and the famine, whereof ye were afraid, shall follow close after you there in Egypt; and there ye shall die. So shall it be with all the men that set their faces to go into Egypt to sojourn there; they shall die by the sword, by the famine, and by the pestilence: and none of them shall remain or escape from the evil that I will bring upon them.' For thus saith the Lord of hosts, the God of Israel: 'As mine anger and my fury hath been poured forth upon the inhabitants of Jerusalem; so shall my fury be poured forth

THE WORDS OF JEREMIAH

upon you, when ye shall enter into Egypt: and ye shall be an execration, and an astonishment, and a curse, and a reproach; and ye shall see this place no more.'

"The Lord hath said concerning you, O ye remnant of Judah: 'Go ye not into Egypt': know certainly that I have admonished you this day. For ye dissembled in your hearts, when ye sent me unto the Lord your God, saying, 'Pray for us unto the Lord our God; and according unto all that the Lord our God shall say, so declare unto us, and we will do it.' And now I have this day declared it to you; but ye have not obeyed the voice of the Lord your God, nor any thing for the which he hath sent me unto you. Now therefore know certainly that ye shall die by the sword, by the famine, and by the pestilence, in the place whither ye desire to go and to sojourn."

And it came to pass that when Jeremiah had made an end of speaking unto all the people all the words of the Lord their God, for which the Lord their God had sent him to them, even all these words, then spoke Azariah the son of Hoshaiah, and Johanan the son of Kareah, and all the proud men, saying unto Jeremiah,

"Thou speakest falsely: the Lord our God hath not sent thee to say, 'Go not into Egypt to sojourn there': but Baruch the son of Neriah setteth thee on against us, for to deliver us into the hand of the Chaldeans, that they might put us to death, and carry us away captives into Babylon."

So Johanan the son of Kareah, and all the captains of the forces, and all the people, obeyed not the voice of the Lord, to dwell in the land of Judah. But Johanan the son of Kareah, and all the captains of the forces, took all the remnant of Judah, that were returned from all nations, whither they had been driven, to dwell in the land of Judah: even men, and women, and children, and the king's daughters, and every person that Nebuzar-adan the captain of the guard had left with Gedaliah the son of Ahikam the son of Shaphan, and Jeremiah the prophet and Baruch the son of Neriah.

THE WORDS OF JEREMIAH

So they came into the land of Egypt: for they obeyed not the voice of the Lord: thus came they even to Tahpanhes.

Jeremiah's Book on Babylon

The word which Jeremiah the prophet commanded Seraiah the son of Neriah, the son of Maaseiah, when he went with Zedekiah the king of Judah into Babylon in the fourth year of his reign. And this Seraiah was a quiet prince. So Jeremiah wrote in a book all the evil that should come upon Babylon, even all these words that are written against Babylon. And Jeremiah said to Seraiah, "When thou comest to Babylon, and shalt see, and shalt read all these words; then shalt thou say, 'O Lord, thou hast spoken against this place to cut it off, that none shall remain in it, neither man nor beast, but that it shall be desolate for ever.' And it shall be, when thou hast made an end of reading this book, that thou shalt bind a stone to it, and cast it into the midst of Euphrates: and thou shalt say, 'Thus shall Babylon sink, and shall not rise from the evil that I will bring upon her: and they shall be weary.'" Thus far are the words of Jeremiah.

LAMENTATIONS

THE ANONYMOUS BOOK OF LAMENTATIONS—*attributed to Jeremiah mainly because of its subject, the Fall of Jerusalem—carries something of the prophetic spirit but is essentially a highly artificial literary product in the form of an elaborate dirge adapted for professional mourners. In the original, the poem is an acrostic, each line beginning with a different letter of the alphabet, and the lines are arranged in regular triplets or couplets, the whole carefully divided to form a series of dirges within a dirge. Unfortunately, little idea of this complicated structure is conveyed by the King James translation. On the other hand, the sincerity of the mournful emotions aroused by the most tragic event in Jewish history is extremely well conveyed. The poem is a good illustration of the truth to which such modern forms as the sonnet bear witness: that strictness of pattern is not necessarily any impediment to the expression of emotional sincerity.*

LAMENTATIONS

I

How doth the city sit solitary, that was full of people!
How is she become as a widow! she that was great among the nations,
And princess among the provinces, how is she become tributary!

She weepeth sore in the night, and her tears are on her cheeks;
Among all her lovers she hath none to comfort her;
All her friends have dealt treacherously with her, they are become her enemies.

Judah is gone into captivity because of affliction, and because of great servitude;
She dwelleth among the heathen, she findeth no rest:
All her persecutors overtook her between the straits.

The ways of Zion do mourn, because none come to the solemn feasts:
All her gates are desolate: her priests sigh,
Her virgins are afflicted, and she is in bitterness.

Her adversaries are the chief, her enemies prosper;
For the Lord hath afflicted her for the multitude of her transgressions:
Her children are gone into captivity before the enemy.

And from the daughter of Zion all her beauty is departed:
Her princes are become like harts that find no pasture,
And they are gone without strength before the pursuer.

Jerusalem remembered in the days of her affliction and of her miseries all her pleasant things that she had in the days of old;
When her people fell into the hand of the enemy, and none did help her,
The adversaries saw her, and did mock at her sabbaths.

LAMENTATIONS

Jerusalem hath grievously sinned: therefore she is removed.
All that honoured her despise her, because they have seen her nakedness:
Yea, she sigheth, and turneth backward.

Her filthiness is in her skirts; she remembereth not her last end;
Therefore she came down wonderfully: she had no comforter.
"O Lord, behold my affliction: for the enemy hath magnified himself."

The adversary hath spread out his hand upon all her pleasant things:
For she hath seen that the heathen entered into her sanctuary,
Whom thou didst command that they should not enter into thy congregation.

All her people sigh, they seek bread;
They have given their pleasant things for meat to relieve the soul:
"See, O Lord, and consider; for I am become vile.

Is it nothing to you, all ye that pass by?
Behold, and see if there be any sorrow like unto my sorrow,
    which is done unto me,
Wherewith the Lord hath afflicted me in the day of his fierce anger.

From above hath he sent fire into my bones, and it prevaileth against
    them:
He hath spread a net for my feet, he hath turned me back:
He hath made me desolate and faint all the day.

The yoke of my transgressions is bound by his hand: they are
    wreathed,
And come up upon my neck: he hath made my strength to fall;
The Lord hath delivered me into their hands, from whom I am not
    able to rise up.

The Lord hath trodden under foot all my mighty men in the midst
    of me:
He hath called an assembly against me to crush my young men:
The Lord hath trodden the virgin, the daughter of Judah, as in a
    winepress.

LAMENTATIONS

For these things I weep; mine eye, mine eye runneth down with water,
Because the comforter that should relieve my soul is far from me:
My children are desolate, because the enemy prevailed."

Zion spreadeth forth her hands, and there is none to comfort her:
The Lord hath commanded concerning Jacob, that his adversaries
    should be round about him:
Jerusalem is as a menstruous woman among them.

"The Lord is righteous; for I have rebelled against his commandment:
Hear, I pray you, all people, and behold my sorrow:
My virgins and my young men are gone into captivity.

I called for my lovers, but they deceived me:
My priests and mine elders gave up the ghost in the city,
While they sought their meat to relieve their souls.

Behold, O Lord; for I am in distress: my bowels are troubled;
Mine heart is turned within me; for I have grievously rebelled:
Abroad the sword bereaveth, at home there is as death.

They have heard that I sigh: there is none to comfort me:
All mine enemies have heard of my trouble; they are glad that thou
    hast done it:
Thou wilt bring the day that thou hast called, and they shall be like
    unto me.

Let all their wickedness come before thee;
And do unto them, as thou hast done unto me for all my transgressions:
For my sighs are many, and my heart is faint."

II

How hath the Lord covered the daughter of Zion with a cloud in
    his anger,
And cast down from heaven unto the earth the beauty of Israel,
And remembered not his footstool in the day of his anger!

The Lord hath swallowed up all the habitations of Jacob, and hath
    not pitied:

LAMENTATIONS

He hath thrown down in his wrath the strong holds of the daughter
of Judah;
He hath brought them down to the ground: he hath polluted the
kingdom and the princes thereof.

He hath cut off in his fierce anger all the horn of Israel:
He hath drawn back his right hand from before the enemy,
And he burned against Jacob like a flaming fire, which devoureth
round about.

He hath bent his bow like an enemy: he stood with his right hand as
an adversary,
And slew all that were pleasant to the eye in the tabernacle of the
daughter of Zion:
He poured out his fury like fire.

The Lord was as an enemy: he hath swallowed up Israel,
He hath swallowed up all her palaces: he hath destroyed his strong
holds,
And hath increased in the daughter of Judah mourning and lamentation.

And he hath violently taken away his tabernacle, as if it were of a
garden:
He hath destroyed his places of the assembly: the Lord hath caused
the solemn feasts and sabbaths to be forgotten in Zion,
And hath despised in the indignation of his anger the king and the
priest.

The Lord hath cast off his altar, he hath abhorred his sanctuary,
He hath given up into the hand of the enemy the walls of her
palaces;
They have made a noise in the house of the Lord, as in the day of a
solemn feast.

The Lord hath purposed to destroy the wall of the daughter of
Zion:
He hath stretched out a line, he hath not withdrawn his hand from
destroying:

LAMENTATIONS

Therefore he made the rampart and the wall to lament; they languished together.

Her gates are sunk into the ground; he hath destroyed and broken her bars:
Her king and her princes are among the Gentiles: the law is no more;
Her prophets also find no vision from the Lord.

The elders of the daughter of Zion sit upon the ground, and keep silence:
They have cast up dust upon their heads; they have girded themselves with sackcloth:
The virgins of Jerusalem hang down their heads to the ground.

Mine eyes do fail with tears, my bowels are troubled,
My liver is poured upon the earth, for the destruction of the daughter of my people;
Because the children and the sucklings swoon in the streets of the city.

They say to their mothers, "Where is corn and wine?"
When they swooned as the wounded in the streets of the city,
When their soul was poured out into their mothers' bosom.

What thing shall I take to witness for thee? what thing shall I liken to thee, O daughter of Jerusalem?
What shall I equal to thee, that I may comfort thee, O virgin daughter of Zion?
For thy breach is great like the sea: who can heal thee?

Thy prophets have seen vain and foolish things for thee:
And they have not discovered thine iniquity, to turn away thy captivity;
But have seen for thee false burdens and causes of banishment.

All that pass by clap their hands at thee;
They hiss and wag their head at the daughter of Jerusalem,
Saying, "Is this the city that men call the perfection of beauty,
The joy of the whole earth?"

LAMENTATIONS

All thine enemies have opened their mouth against thee:
They hiss and gnash the teeth: they say, "We have swallowed her
    up:
Certainly this is the day that we looked for;
We have found, we have seen it."

The Lord hath done that which he had devised;
He hath fulfilled his word that he had commanded in the days of
    old:
He hath thrown down, and hath not pitied:
And he hath caused thine enemy to rejoice over thee,
He hath set up the horn of thine adversaries.

Their heart cried unto the Lord, O wall of the daughter of Zion,
Let tears run down like a river day and night:
Give thyself no rest; let not the apple of thine eye cease.

Arise, cry out in the night, in the beginning of the watches;
Pour out thine heart like water before the face of the Lord: lift up
    thy hands toward him
For the life of thy young children, that faint for hunger in the top of
    every street.

Behold, O Lord, and consider to whom thou hast done this.
Shall the women eat their fruit, and children of a span long?
Shall the priest and the prophet be slain in the sanctuary of the Lord?

The young and the old lie on the ground in the streets:
My virgins and my young men are fallen by the sword;
Thou hast slain them in the day of thine anger; thou hast killed,
    and not pitied.

Thou hast called as in a solemn day my terrors round about,
So that in the day of the Lord's anger none escaped nor remained:
Those that I have swaddled and brought up hath mine enemy con‑
    sumed.

III

I am the man that hath seen affliction by the rod of his wrath.
He hath led me, and brought me into darkness, but not into light.

LAMENTATIONS

Surely against me is he turned; he turneth his hand against me all the day.

My flesh and my skin hath he made old; he hath broken my bones.
He hath builded against me, and compassed me with gall and travail.
He hath set me in dark places, as they that be dead of old.

He hath hedged me about, that I cannot get out: he hath made my chain heavy.
Also when I cry and shout, he shutteth out my prayer.
He hath inclosed my ways with hewn stone, he hath made my paths crooked.

He was unto me as a bear lying in wait, and as a lion in secret places
He hath turned aside my ways, and pulled me in pieces: he hath made me desolate.
He hath bent his bow, and set me as a mark for the arrow.

He hath caused the arrows of his quiver to enter into my reins.
I was a derision to all my people; and their song all the day.
He hath filled me with bitterness, he hath made me drunken with wormwood.

He hath also broken my teeth with gravel stones, he hath covered me with ashes.
And thou hast removed my soul far off from peace: I forgot prosperity.
And I said, "My strength and my hope is perished from the Lord":

Remembering mine affliction and my misery, the wormwood and the gall.
My soul hath them still in remembrance, and is humbled in me.
This I recall to my mind, therefore have I hope.

It is of the Lord's mercies that we are not consumed, because his compassions fail not.
They are new every morning: great is thy faithfulness.
"The Lord is my portion," saith my soul; "therefore will I hope in him."

LAMENTATIONS

The Lord is good unto them that wait for him, to the soul that seeketh him.
It is good that a man should both hope and quietly wait for the salvation of the Lord.
It is good for a man that he bear the yoke in his youth.

He sitteth alone and keepeth silence, because he hath borne it upon him.
He putteth his mouth in the dust; if so be there may be hope.
He giveth his cheek to him that smiteth him: he is filled full with reproach.

For the Lord will not cast off for ever:
But though he cause grief, yet will he have compassion according to the multitude of his mercies.
For he doth not afflict willingly nor grieve the children of men.

To crush under his feet all the prisoners of the earth,
To turn aside the right of a man before the face of the most High,
To subvert a man in his cause, the Lord approveth not.

Who is he that saith, and it cometh to pass, when the Lord commandeth it not?
Out of the mouth of the most High proceedeth not evil and good?
Wherefore doth a living man complain, a man for the punishment of his sins?

Let us search and try our ways, and turn again to the Lord.
Let us lift up our heart with our hands unto God in the heavens.
We have transgressed and have rebelled: thou hast not pardoned.

Thou hast covered with anger, and persecuted us: thou hast slain, thou hast not pitied.
Thou hast covered thyself with a cloud, that our prayer should not pass through.
Thou hast made us as the off-scouring and refuse in the midst of the people.

LAMENTATIONS

All our enemies have opened their mouths against us.
Fear and a snare is come upon us, desolation and destruction.
Mine eye runneth down with rivers of water for the destruction of the daughter of my people.

Mine eye trickleth down, and ceaseth not, without any intermission,
Till the Lord look down, and behold from heaven.
Mine eye affecteth mine heart because of all the daughters of my city.

Mine enemies chased me sore, like a bird, without cause.
They have cut off my life in the dungeon, and cast a stone upon me.
Waters flowed over mine head; then I said, "I am cut off."

I called upon thy name, O Lord, out of the low dungeon.
Thou hast heard my voice: "Hide not thine ear at my breathing, at my cry."
Thou drewest near in the day that I called upon thee: thou saidst, "Fear not."

O Lord, thou hast pleaded the causes of my soul; thou hast redeemed my life.
O Lord, thou hast seen my wrong: judge thou my cause.
Thou hast seen all their vengeance and all their imaginations against me.

Thou hast heard their reproach, **O Lord**, and all their imaginations against me;
The lips of those that rose up against me, and their device against me all the day.
Behold their sitting down, and their rising up; I am their music.

Render unto them a recompense, O Lord, according to the work of their hands.
Give them sorrow of heart, thy curse unto them.
Persecute and destroy them in anger from under the heavens of the Lord.

LAMENTATIONS

IV

How is the gold become dim! how is the most fine gold changed!
The stones of the sanctuary are poured out in the top of every street.

The precious sons of Zion, comparable to fine gold,
How are they esteemed as earthen pitchers, the work of the hands of the potter!

Even the sea monsters draw out the breast, they give suck to their young ones:
The daughter of my people is become cruel, like the ostriches in the wilderness.

The tongue of the sucking child cleaveth to the roof of his mouth for thirst:
The young children ask bread, and no man breaketh it unto them.

They that did feed delicately are desolate in the streets:
They that were brought up in scarlet embrace dunghills.

For the punishment of the iniquity of the daughter of my people is greater than the punishment of the sin of Sodom,
That was overthrown as in a moment, and no hands stayed on her.

Her Nazarites were purer than snow, they were whiter than milk,
They were more ruddy in body than rubies, their polishing was of sapphire:

Their visage is blacker than a coal; they are not known in the streets:
Their skin cleaveth to their bones; it is withered, it is become like a stick.

They that be slain with the sword are better than they that be slain with hunger:
For these pine away, stricken through for want of the fruits of the field.

The hands of the pitiful women have sodden their own children:
They were their meat in the destruction of the daughter of my people.

LAMENTATIONS

The Lord hath accomplished his fury; he hath poured out his fierce anger,
And hath kindled a fire in Zion, and it hath devoured the foundations thereof.

The kings of the earth, and all the inhabitants of the world,
Would not have believed that the adversary and the enemy should have entered into the gates of Jerusalem.

For the sins of her prophets, and the iniquities of her priests,
That have shed the blood of the just in the midst of her,

They have wandered as blind men in the streets,
They have polluted themselves with blood, so that men could not touch their garments.

They cried unto them,
"Depart ye; it is unclean; depart, depart, touch not":
When they fled away and wandered, they said among the heathen,
"They shall no more sojourn there."

The anger of the Lord hath divided them; he will no more regard them:
They respected not the persons of the priests, they favoured not the elders.

As for us, our eyes as yet failed for our vain help:
In our watching we have watched for a nation that could not save us.

They hunt our steps, that we cannot go in our streets:
Our end is near, our days are fulfilled; for our end is come.

Our persecutors are swifter than the eagles of the heaven:
They pursued us upon the mountains, they laid wait for us in the wilderness.

The breath of our nostrils, the anointed of the Lord, was taken in their pits,
Of whom we said, "Under his shadow we shall live among the heathen."

LAMENTATIONS

Rejoice and be glad, O daughter of Edom, that dwellest in the land
   of Uz;
The cup also shall pass through unto thee: thou shalt be drunken,
   and shalt make thyself naked.

The punishment of thine iniquity is accomplished, O daughter of
   Zion; he will no more carry thee away into captivity:
He will visit thine iniquity, O daughter of Edom; he will discover
   thy sins.

v

Remember, O Lord, what is come upon us:
Consider, and behold our reproach.

Our inheritance is turned to strangers,
Our houses to aliens.

We are orphans and fatherless,
Our mothers are as widows.

We have drunken our water for money;
Our wood is sold unto us.

Our necks are under persecution:
We labour, and have no rest.

We have given the hand to the Egyptians,
And to the Assyrians, to be satisfied with bread.

Our fathers have sinned, and are not;
And we have borne their iniquities.

Servants have ruled over us:
There is none that doth deliver us out of their hand.

We got our bread with the peril of our lives
Because of the sword of the wilderness.

Our skin was black like an oven
Because of the terrible famine.

LAMENTATIONS

They ravished the women in Zion,
And the maids in the cities of Judah.

Princes are hanged up by their hand:
The faces of elders were not honoured.

They took the young men to grind,
And the children fell under the wood.

The elders have ceased from the gate,
The young men from their music.

The joy of our heart is ceased;
Our dance is turned into mourning.

The crown is fallen from our head:
Woe unto us, that we have sinned!

For this our heart is faint;
For these things our eyes are dim.

Because of the mountain of Zion, which is desolate,
The foxes walk upon it.

Thou, O Lord, remainest for ever;
Thy throne from generation to generation.

Wherefore dost thou forget us for ever,
And forsake us so long time?

Turn thou us unto thee, O Lord, and we shall be turned;
Renew our days as of old.

But thou hast utterly rejected us;
Thou art very wroth against us.

THE BOOK OF THE PROPHET EZEKIEL

OF THE THREE GREAT PROPHETS, *Isaiah was primarily the poet, Jeremiah the preacher, and Ezekiel the mystic. The work of the third offers peculiar difficulties to comprehension or appreciation, yet is in some ways the most fascinating of all. Ezekiel's excessive devotion to symbolism and dumb show seems at times puerile and at times repellent, but out of it came the beautiful literary form of the parable; his fantastic visions are often so obscure as to be almost meaningless but they exercised a direct and powerful influence on such later works as the Book of Daniel, the Book of Revelation, Dante's "Paradiso," Milton's "Paradise Lost," and the Prophetical Books of William Blake; his style is often utterly prosaic but is capable of such deep pathos as that of his dirge over Egypt or of rising to such splendor of poetic expression as is seen in his Lamentation for Tyre; his emphasis upon personal responsibility was so great as to lead him to reject the favorite Jewish doctrine of vicarious righteousness, but on the other hand he elaborated the system of ritual and ceremony that became the very basis of formal Judaism.*

Of all his contradictory achievements, it was this last on which Ezekiel, literally a priest and spiritually half-priest, half-prophet, himself laid the greatest stress. Among the first of those carried into Babylonia, he passed his life among the exiles, and it was his special mission to maintain their morale by the use of every possible way of approach, this singleness of purpose supplying an underlying unity to the exercise of his diversified talents. And of all the means that he employed, it was the development of ritual that finally proved the most effective. The ceremonial chapters of his book, however, though of immense historical importance, have practically no literary value for us to-day; they are therefore omitted from this text.

The Book of the Prophet
EZEKIEL

The Vision of God

Now it came to pass in the thirtieth year, in the fourth month, in the fifth day of the month, as I was among the captives by the river of Chebar, that the heavens were opened, and I saw visions of God. In the fifth day of the month, which was the fifth year of King Jehoiachin's captivity, the word of the Lord came expressly unto Ezekiel the priest, the son of Buzi, in the land of the Chaldeans by the river Chebar; and the hand of the Lord was there upon him.

And I looked, and, behold, a whirlwind came out of the north, a great cloud, and a fire infolding itself, and a brightness was about it, and out of the midst thereof as the colour of amber, out of the midst of the fire. Also out of the midst thereof came the likeness of four living creatures. And this was their appearance; they had the likeness of a man. And every one had four faces, and every one had four wings. And their feet were straight feet; and the sole of their feet was like the sole of a calf's foot: and they sparkled like the colour of burnished brass. And they had the hands of a man under their wings on their four sides; and they four had their faces and their wings. Their wings were joined one to another; they turned not when they went; they went every one straight forward. As for the likeness of their faces, they four had the face of a man, and the face of a lion, on the right side: and they four had the face of an ox on the left side; they four also had the face of an eagle. Thus were their faces: and their wings were stretched upward; two wings of every one were joined one to another, and two covered their

THE BOOK OF THE PROPHET EZEKIEL

bodies. And they went every one straight forward: whither the spirit was to go, they went; and they turned not when they went. As for the likeness of the living creatures, their appearance was like burning coals of fire, and like the appearance of lamps; it went up and down among the living creatures; and the fire was bright, and out of the fire went forth lightning. And the living creatures ran and returned as the appearance of a flash of lightning.

Now as I beheld the living creatures, behold one wheel upon the earth by the living creatures, with his four faces. The appearance of the wheels and their work was like unto the colour of a beryl: and they four had one likeness: and their appearance and their work was as it were a wheel in the middle of a wheel. When they went, they went upon their four sides: and they turned not when they went. As for their rings, they were so high that they were dreadful; and their rings were full of eyes round about them four. And when the living creatures went, the wheels went by them: and when the living creatures were lifted up from the earth, the wheels were lifted up. Whithersoever the spirit was to go, they went, thither was their spirit to go; and the wheels were lifted up over against them: for the spirit of the living creature was in the wheels. When those went, these went; and when those stood, these stood; and when those were lifted up from the earth, the wheels were lifted up over against them: for the spirit of the living creature was in the wheels. And the likeness of the firmament upon the heads of the living creature was as the colour of the terrible crystal, stretched forth over their heads above. And under the firmament were their wings straight, the one toward the other: every one had two, which covered on this side, and every one had two, which covered on that side, their bodies. And when they went, I heard the noise of their wings, like the noise of great waters, as the voice of the Almighty, the voice of speech, as the noise of a host: when they stood, they let down their wings. And there was a voice from the firmament that was over their heads, when they stood, and had let down their wings.

THE BOOK OF THE PROPHET EZEKIEL

And above the firmament that was over their heads was the likeness of a throne, as the appearance of a sapphire stone: and upon the likeness of the throne was the likeness as the appearance of a man above upon it. And I saw as the colour of amber, as the appearance of fire round about within it, from the appearance of his loins even upward, and from the appearance of his loins even downward, I saw as it were the appearance of fire, and it had brightness round about. As the appearance of the bow that is in the cloud in the day of rain, so was the appearance of the brightness round about. This was the appearance of the likeness of the glory of the Lord. And when I saw it, I fell upon my face, and I heard a voice of one that spoke. And he said unto me,

"Son of Man, stand upon thy feet, and I will speak unto thee."

And the spirit entered into me when he spoke unto me, and set me upon my feet, that I heard him that spoke unto me. And he said unto me,

"Son of Man, I send thee to the children of Israel, to a rebellious nation that hath rebelled against me: they and their fathers have transgressed against me, even unto this very day. For they are impudent children and stiffhearted. I do send thee unto them; and thou shalt say unto them, 'Thus saith the Lord God.' And they, whether they will hear or whether they will forbear (for they are a rebellious house), yet shall know that there hath been a prophet among them.

"And thou, Son of Man, be not afraid of them, neither be afraid of their words, though briers and thorns be with thee, and thou dost dwell among scorpions: be not afraid of their words, nor be dismayed at their looks, though they be a rebellious house. And thou shalt speak my words unto them, whether they will hear, or whether they will forbear: for they are most rebellious. But thou, Son of Man, hear what I say unto thee: be not thou rebellious like that rebellious house: open thy mouth, and eat that I give thee."

And when I looked, behold, a hand was sent unto me; and, lo, a roll of a book was therein; and he spread it before me; and

THE BOOK OF THE PROPHET EZEKIEL

it was written within and without: and there was written therein lamentations, and mourning, and woe.

Moreover he said unto me, "Son of Man, eat that thou findest; eat this roll, and go speak unto the house of Israel."

So I opened my mouth, and he caused me to eat that roll. And he said unto me,

"Son of Man, cause thy belly to eat, and fill thy bowels with this roll that I give thee."

Then did I eat it; and it was in my mouth as honey for sweetness. And he said unto me,

"Son of Man, go, get thee unto the house of Israel, and speak with my words unto them. For thou art not sent to a people of a strange speech and of a hard language, but to the house of Israel; not to many people of a strange speech and of a hard language, whose words thou canst not understand. Surely, had I sent thee to them, they would have hearkened unto thee. But the house of Israel will not hearken unto thee; for they will not hearken unto me: for all the house of Israel are impudent and hardhearted. Behold, I have made thy face strong against their faces, and thy forehead strong against their foreheads. As an adamant harder than flint have I made thy forehead: fear them not, neither be dismayed at their looks, though they be a rebellious house."

Moreover he said unto me,

"Son of Man, all my words that I shall speak unto thee receive in thine heart, and hear with thine ears. And go, get thee to them of the captivity, unto the children of thy people, and speak unto them, and tell them, 'Thus saith the Lord God'; whether they will hear, or whether they will forbear."

Then the spirit took me up, and I heard behind me a voice of a great rushing, saying, "Blessed be the glory of the Lord from his place." I heard also the noise of the wings of the living creatures that touched one another, and the noise of the wheels over against them, and a noise of a great rushing. So the spirit lifted me up, and took me away, and I went in bitterness, in the heat of my spirit; but the hand of the Lord was strong upon me.

THE BOOK OF THE PROPHET EZEKIEL

Then I came to them of the captivity at Tel-abib, that dwelt by the river of Chebar, and I sat where they sat, and remained there astonished among them seven days.

The Symbolic Siege of Jerusalem

"Thou also, Son of Man, take thee a tile, and lay it before thee, and portray upon it the city, even Jerusalem: and lay siege against it, and build a fort against it, and cast a mount against it; set the camp also against it, and set battering rams against it round about. Moreover take thou unto thee an iron pan, and set it for a wall of iron between thee and the city: and set thy face against it, and it shall be besieged, and thou shalt lay siege against it. This shall be a sign to the house of Israel.

"Lie thou also upon thy left side, and lay the iniquity of the house of Israel upon it: according to the number of the days that thou shalt lie upon it thou shalt bear their iniquity. For I have laid upon thee the years of their iniquity, according to the number of the days, three hundred and ninety days: so shalt thou bear the iniquity of the house of Israel. And when thou hast accomplished them, lie again on thy right side, and thou shalt bear the iniquity of the house of Judah forty days: I have appointed thee each day for a year. Therefore thou shalt set thy face toward the siege of Jerusalem, and thine arm shall be uncovered, and thou shalt prophesy against it. And, behold, I will lay bands upon thee, and thou shalt not turn thee from one side to another, till thou hast ended the days of thy siege. Take thou also unto thee wheat, and barley, and beans, and lentils, and millet, and fitches, and put them in one vessel, and make thee bread thereof, according to the number of the days that thou shalt lie upon thy side, three hundred and ninety days shalt thou eat thereof. And thy meat which thou shalt eat shall be by weight, twenty shekels a day: from time to time shalt thou eat it. Thou shalt drink also water by measure, the sixth part of a hin: from time to time shalt thou drink. And thou shalt eat it as barley cakes, and thou shalt bake it with dung that cometh out of man, in their sight." And the Lord said, "Even thus shall the

THE BOOK OF THE PROPHET EZEKIEL

children of Israel eat their defiled bread among the Gentiles, whither I will drive them."

Then said I, "Ah Lord God! behold, my soul hath not been polluted: for from my youth up even till now have I not eaten of that which dieth of itself, or is torn in pieces; neither came there abominable flesh into my mouth."

Then he said unto me, "Lo, I have given thee cow's dung for man's dung, and thou shalt prepare thy bread therewith." Moreover he said unto me, "Son of Man, behold, I will break the staff of bread in Jerusalem: and they shall eat bread by weight, and with care, and they shall drink water by measure, and with astonishment, that they may want bread and water, and be astonished one with another, and consume away for their iniquity.

"And thou, Son of Man, take thee a sharp knife, take thee a barber's razor, and cause it to pass upon thine head and upon thy beard: then take thee balances to weigh, and divide the hair. Thou shalt burn with fire a third part in the midst of the city, when the days of the siege are fulfilled: and thou shalt take a third part, and smite about it with a knife: and a third part thou shalt scatter in the wind; and I will draw out a sword after them. Thou shalt also take thereof a few in number, and bind them in thy skirts. Then take of them again, and cast them into the midst of the fire, and burn them in the fire; for thereof shall a fire come forth into all the house of Israel."

Thus saith the Lord God: "This is Jerusalem: I have set it in the midst of the nations and countries that are round about her. And she hath changed my judgments into wickedness more than the nations, and my statutes more than the countries that are round about her: for they have refused my judgments and my statutes, they have not walked in them."

Therefore thus saith the Lord God: "Because ye multiplied more than the nations that are round about you, and have not walked in my statutes, neither have kept my judgments, neither have done according to the judgments of the nations that are round about you, behold, I, even I, am against thee, and will

THE BOOK OF THE PROPHET EZEKIEL

execute judgments in the midst of thee in the sight of the nations. And I will do in thee that which I have not done, and whereunto I will not do any more the like, because of all thine abominations. Therefore the fathers shall eat the sons in the midst of thee, and the sons shall eat their fathers; and I will execute judgments in thee, and the whole remnant of thee will I scatter into all the winds.

"Wherefore, as I live," saith the Lord God, "surely, because thou hast defiled my sanctuary with all thy detestable things, and with thine abominations, therefore will I also diminish thee; neither shall mine eye spare, neither will I have any pity. A third part of thee shall die with the pestilence, and with famine shall they be consumed in the midst of thee: and a third part shall fall by the sword round about thee; and I will scatter a third part into all the winds, and I will draw out a sword after them. Thus shall mine anger be accomplished, and I will cause my fury to rest upon them, and I will be comforted: and they shall know that I the Lord have spoken it in my zeal, when I have accomplished my fury in them. Moreover I will make thee waste, and a reproach among the nations that are round about thee, in the sight of all that pass by. So it shall be a reproach and a taunt, an instruction and an astonishment unto the nations that are round about thee, when I shall execute judgments in thee in anger and in fury and in furious rebukes. I the Lord have spoken it."

Jerusalem the Harlot

Again the word of the Lord came unto me, saying, "Son of Man, cause Jerusalem to know her abominations, and say, 'Thus saith the Lord God unto Jerusalem: "Thy birth and thy nativity is of the land of Canaan; thy father was an Amorite, and thy mother a Hittite. And as for thy nativity, in the day thou wast born thy navel was not cut, neither wast thou washed in water to supple thee; thou wast not salted at all, nor swaddled at all. None eye pitied thee, to do any of these unto thee, to have com-

THE BOOK OF THE PROPHET EZEKIEL

passion upon thee; but thou wast cast out in the open field, to the loathing of thy person, in the day that thou wast born.

"'"And when I passed by thee, and saw thee polluted in thine own blood, I said unto thee when thou wast in thy blood, 'Live'; yea, I said unto thee when thou wast in thy blood, 'Live.' I have caused thee to multiply as the bud of the field, and thou hast increased and waxed great, and thou art come to excellent ornaments: thy breasts are fashioned, and thine hair is grown, whereas thou wast naked and bare. Now when I passed by thee, and looked upon thee, behold, thy time was the time of love; and I spread my skirt over thee, and covered thy nakedness: yea, I swore unto thee, and entered into a covenant with thee," saith the Lord God, "and thou becamest mine. Then washed I thee with water; yea, I thoroughly washed away thy blood from thee, and I anointed thee with oil. I clothed thee also with broidered work, and shod thee with badgers' skin, and I girded thee about with fine linen, and I covered thee with silk. I decked thee also with ornaments, and I put bracelets upon thy hands, and a chain on thy neck. And I put a jewel on thy forehead, and earrings in thine ears, and a beautiful crown upon thine head. Thus wast thou decked with gold and silver; and thy raiment was of fine linen, and silk, and broidered work; thou didst eat fine flour, and honey, and oil: and thou wast exceedingly beautiful, and thou didst prosper into a kingdom. And thy renown went forth among the heathen for thy beauty: for it was perfect through my comeliness, which I had put upon thee," saith the Lord God.

"'"But thou didst trust in thine own beauty, and playedst the harlot because of thy renown, and pouredst out thy fornications on every one that passed by; his it was. And of thy garments thou didst take, and deckedst thy high places with divers colours, and playedst the harlot thereupon: the like things shall not come, neither shall it be so. Thou hast also taken thy fair jewels of my gold and of my silver, which I had given thee, and madest to thyself images of men, and didst commit whoredom

THE BOOK OF THE PROPHET EZEKIEL

with them, and tookest thy broidered garments, and coveredst them: and thou hast set mine oil and mine incense before them. My meat also which I gave thee, fine flour, and oil, and honey, wherewith I fed thee, thou hast even set it before them for a sweet savour: and thus it was," saith the Lord God. "Moreover thou hast taken thy sons and thy daughters, whom thou hast borne unto me, and these hast thou sacrificed unto them to be devoured. Is this of thy whoredoms a small matter, that thou hast slain my children, and delivered them to cause them to pass through the fire for them? And in all thine abominations and thy whoredoms thou hast not remembered the days of thy youth, when thou wast naked and bare, and wast polluted in thy blood. And it came to pass after all thy wickedness—woe, woe unto thee!" saith the Lord God, "that thou hast also built unto thee an eminent place, and hast made thee a high place in every street. Thou hast built thy high place at every head of the way, and hast made thy beauty to be abhorred, and hast opened thy feet to every one that passed by, and multiplied thy whoredoms. Thou hast also committed fornication with the Egyptians thy neighbours, great of flesh; and hast increased thy whoredoms, to provoke me to anger. Behold, therefore I have stretched out my hand over thee, and have diminished thine ordinary food, and delivered thee unto the will of them that hate thee, the daughters of the Philistines, which are ashamed of thy lewd way. Thou hast played the whore also with the Assyrians, because thou wast unsatiable; yea, thou hast played the harlot with them, and yet couldest not be satisfied. Thou hast moreover multiplied thy fornication in the land of Canaan unto Chaldea; and yet thou wast not satisfied herewith. How weak is thine heart," saith the Lord God, "seeing thou doest all these things, the work of an imperious whorish woman; in that thou buildest thine eminent place in the head of every way, and makest thine high place in every street; and hast not been as a harlot, in that thou scornest hire; but as a wife that committeth adultery, which taketh strangers instead of her husband! They give gifts to all whores: but thou givest thy gifts to all thy

THE BOOK OF THE PROPHET EZEKIEL

lovers, and hirest them, that they may come unto thee on every side for thy whoredom. And the contrary is in thee from other women in thy whoredoms, whereas none followed thee to commit whoredoms: and in that thou givest a reward, and no reward is given unto thee, therefore thou art contrary."'

"Wherefore, O harlot, hear the word of the Lord: 'Thus saith the Lord God: "Because thy filthiness was poured out, and thy nakedness discovered through thy whoredoms with thy lovers, and with all the idols of thy abominations, and by the blood of thy children, which thou didst give unto them, behold, therefore I will gather all thy lovers, with whom thou hast taken pleasure, and all them that thou hast loved, with all them that thou hast hated; I will even gather them round about against thee, and will discover thy nakedness unto them, that they may see all thy nakedness. And I will judge thee, as women that break wedlock and shed blood are judged; and I will give thee blood in fury and jealousy. And I will also give thee into their hand, and they shall throw down thine eminent place, and shall break down thy high places: they shall strip thee also of thy clothes, and shall take thy fair jewels, and leave thee naked and bare. They shall also bring up a company against thee, and they shall stone thee with stones, and thrust thee through with their swords. And they shall burn thine houses with fire, and execute judgments upon thee in the sight of many women: and I will cause thee to cease from playing the harlot, and thou also shall give no hire any more. So will I make my fury toward thee to rest, and my jealousy shall depart from thee, and I will be quiet, and will be no more angry. Because thou hast not remembered the days of thy youth, but hast fretted me in all these things; behold, therefore I also will recompense thy way upon thine head," saith the Lord God: "and thou shalt not commit this lewdness above all thine abominations."'"

The Parable of the Two Eagles

And the word of the Lord came unto me, saying, "Son of Man, put forth a riddle, and speak a parable unto the house of

THE BOOK OF THE PROPHET EZEKIEL

Israel, and say, 'Thus saith the Lord God: "A great eagle with great wings, longwinged, full of feathers, which had divers colours, came unto Lebanon, and took the highest branch of the cedar: he cropped off the top of his young twigs, and carried it into a land of traffic; he set it in a city of merchants. He took also of the seed of the land, and planted it in a fruitful field; he placed it by great waters, and set it as a willow tree. And it grew, and became a spreading vine of low stature, whose branches turned toward him, and the roots thereof were under him: so it became a vine, and brought forth branches, and shot forth sprigs. There was also another great eagle with great wings and many feathers: and, behold, this vine did bend her roots toward him, and shot forth her branches toward him, that he might water it by the furrows of her plantation. It was planted in a good soil by great waters, that it might bring forth branches, and that it might bear fruit, that it might be a goodly vine,"' Say thou, 'Thus saith the Lord God: "Shall it prosper? shall he not pull up the roots thereof, and cut off the fruit thereof, that it wither? it shall wither in all the leaves of her spring, even without great power or many people to pluck it up by the roots thereof. Yea, behold, being planted, shall it prosper? shall it not utterly wither, when the east wind toucheth it? it shall wither in the furrows where it grew."'"

Moreover the word of the Lord came unto me, saying, "Say now to the rebellious house, 'Know ye not what these things mean?' Tell them, 'Behold, the king of Babylon is come to Jerusalem, and hath taken the king thereof, and the princes thereof, and led them with him to Babylon; and hath taken of the king's seed, and made a covenant with him, and hath taken an oath of him: he hath also taken the mighty of the land: that the kingdom might be base, that it might not lift itself up, but that by keeping of his covenant it might stand. But he rebelled against him in sending his ambassadors into Egypt, that they might give him horses and much people. Shall he prosper? shall he escape that doeth such things? or shall he break the covenant, and be delivered? As I live,' saith the Lord God, 'surely in the place

THE BOOK OF THE PROPHET EZEKIEL

where the king dwelleth that made him king, whose oath he despised, and whose covenant he broke, even with him in the midst of Babylon he shall die. Neither shall Pharaoh with his mighty army and great company make for him in the war, by casting up mounts, and building forts, to cut off many persons: seeing he despised the oath by breaking the covenant, when, lo, he had given his hand, and hath done all these things, he shall not escape.' Therefore thus saith the Lord God: 'As I live, surely mine oath that he hath despised, and my covenant that he hath broken, even it will I recompense upon his own head. And I will spread my net upon him, and he shall be taken in my snare, and I will bring him to Babylon, and will plead with him there for his trespass that he hath trespassed against me. And all his fugitives with all his bands shall fall by the sword, and they that remain shall be scattered toward all winds: and ye shall know that I the Lord have spoken it.'

"Thus saith the Lord God: 'I will also take of the highest branch of the high cedar, and will set it; I will crop off from the top of his young twigs a tender one, and will plant it upon a high mountain and eminent. In the mountain of the height of Israel will I plant it: and it shall bring forth boughs, and bear fruit, and be a goodly cedar: and under it shall dwell all fowl of every wing; in the shadow of the branches thereof shall they dwell. And all the trees of the field shall know that I the Lord have brought down the high tree, have exalted the low tree, have dried up the green tree, and have made the dry tree to flourish: I the Lord have spoken and have done it.'"

The Principle of Personal Responsibility

The word of the Lord came unto me again, saying, "What mean ye, that ye use this proverb concerning the land of Israel, saying,

> *'The fathers have eaten sour grapes,*
> *And the children's teeth are set on edge'?*

"As I live," saith the Lord God, "ye shall not have occasion

THE BOOK OF THE PROPHET EZEKIEL

any more to use this proverb in Israel. Behold, all souls are mine; as the soul of the father, so also the soul of the son is mine: the soul that sinneth, it shall die.

"But if a man be just, and do that which is lawful and right, and hath not eaten upon the mountains, neither hath lifted up his eyes to the idols of the house of Israel, neither hath defiled his neighbour's wife, neither hath come near to a menstruous woman, and hath not oppressed any, but hath restored to the debtor his pledge, hath spoiled none by violence, hath given his bread to the hungry, and hath covered the naked with a garment; he that hath not given forth upon usury, neither hath taken any increase, that hath withdrawn his hand from iniquity, hath executed true judgment between man and man, hath walked in my statutes, and hath kept my judgments, to deal truly; he is just, he shall surely live," saith the Lord God.

"If he beget a son that is a robber, a shedder of blood, and that doeth the like to any one of these things, and that doeth not any of those duties, but even hath eaten upon the mountains, and defiled his neighbour's wife, hath oppressed the poor and needy, hath spoiled by violence, hath not restored the pledge, and hath lifted up his eyes to the idols, hath committed abomination, hath given forth upon usury, and hath taken increase: shall he then live? he shall not live: he hath done all these abominations; he shall surely die; his blood shall be upon him.

"Now, lo, if he beget a son, that seeth all his father's sins which he hath done, and considereth, and doeth not such like, that hath not eaten upon the mountains, neither hath lifted up his eyes to the idols of the house of Israel, hath not defiled his neighbour's wife, neither hath oppressed any, hath not withheld the pledge, neither hath spoiled by violence, but hath given his bread to the hungry, and hath covered the naked with a garment, that hath taken off his hand from the poor, that hath not received usury nor increase, hath executed my judgments, hath walked in my statutes; he shall not die for the iniquity of his father, he shall surely live.

"As for his father, because he cruelly oppressed, spoiled his

THE BOOK OF THE PROPHET EZEKIEL

brother by violence, and did that which is not good among his people, lo, even he shall die in his iniquity.

"Yet say ye, 'Why? doth not the son bear the iniquity of the father?' When the son hath done that which is lawful and right, and hath kept all my statutes, and hath done them, he shall surely live. The soul that sinneth, it shall die. The son shall not bear the iniquity of the father, neither shall the father bear the iniquity of the son: the righteousness of the righteous shall be upon him, and the wickedness of the wicked shall be upon him. But if the wicked will turn from all his sins that he hath committed, and keep all my statutes, and do that which is lawful and right, he shall surely live, he shall not die. All his transgressions that he hath committed, they shall not be mentioned unto him: in his righteousness that he hath done he shall live. Have I any pleasure at all that the wicked should die?" saith the Lord God: "and not that he should return from his ways, and live?

"But when the righteous turneth away from his righteousness, and committeth iniquity, and doeth according to all the abominations that the wicked man doeth, shall he live? All his righteousness that he hath done shall not be mentioned: in his trespass that he hath trespassed, and in his sin that he hath sinned, in them shall he die.

"Yet ye say, 'The way of the Lord is not equal.' Hear now, O house of Israel: is not my way equal? are not your ways unequal? When a righteous man turneth away from his righteousness, and committeth iniquity, and dieth in them; for his iniquity that he hath done shall he die. Again, when the wicked man turneth away from his wickedness that he hath committed, and doeth that which is lawful and right, he shall save his soul alive. Because he considereth, and turneth away from all his transgressions that he hath committed, he shall surely live, he shall not die. Yet saith the house of Israel, 'The way of the Lord is not equal.' O house of Israel, are not my ways equal? are not your ways unequal? Therefore I will judge you, O house of Israel, every one according to his ways," saith the Lord God. "Repent,

THE BOOK OF THE PROPHET EZEKIEL

and turn yourselves from all your transgressions; so iniquity shall not be your ruin.

"Cast away from you all your transgressions, whereby ye have transgressed; and make you a new heart and a new spirit: for why will ye die, O house of Israel? For I have no pleasure in the death of him that dieth," saith the Lord God: "wherefore turn yourselves, and live ye."

Aholah and Aholibah

The word of the Lord came again unto me, saying, "Son of Man, there were two women, the daughters of one mother: and they committed whoredoms in Egypt; they committed whoredoms in their youth: there were their breasts pressed, and there they bruised the teats of their virginity. And the names of them were Aholah the elder, and Aholibah her sister: and they were mine, and they bore sons and daughters. Thus were their names; Samaria is Aholah, and Jerusalem Aholibah.

"And Aholah played the harlot when she was mine; and she doted on her lovers, on the Assyrians her neighbours, which were clothed with blue, captains and rulers, all of them desirable young men, horsemen riding upon horses. Thus she committed her whoredoms with them, with all them that were the chosen men of Assyria, and with all on whom she doted: with all their idols she defiled herself. Neither left she her whoredoms brought from Egypt: for in her youth they lay with her, and they bruised the breasts of her virginity, and poured their whoredom upon her. Wherefore I have delivered her into the hand of her lovers, into the hand of the Assyrians, upon whom she doted. These discovered her nakedness: they took her sons and her daughters, and slew her with the sword: and she became famous among women; for they had executed judgment upon her.

"And when her sister Aholibah saw this, she was more corrupt in her inordinate love than she, and in her whoredoms more than her sister in her whoredoms. She doted upon the Assyrians her neighbours, captains and rulers clothed most gorgeously,

THE BOOK OF THE PROPHET EZEKIEL

horsemen riding upon horses, all of them desirable young men. Then I saw that she was defiled, that they took both one way, and that she increased her whoredoms: for when she saw men portrayed upon the wall, the images of the Chaldeans portrayed with vermilion, girded with girdles upon their loins, exceeding in dyed attire upon their heads, all of them princes to look to, after the manner of the Babylonians of Chaldea, the land of their nativity: and as soon as she saw them with her eyes, she doted upon them, and sent messengers unto them into Chaldea. And the Babylonians came to her into the bed of love, and they defiled her with their whoredom, and she was polluted with them, and her mind was alienated from them. So she discovered her whoredoms, and discovered her nakedness: then my mind was alienated from her, like as my mind was alienated from her sister. Yet she multiplied her whoredoms, in calling to remembrance the days of her youth, wherein she had played the harlot in the land of Egypt. For she doted upon their paramours, whose flesh is as the flesh of asses, and whose issue is like the issues of horses. Thus thou calledst to remembrance the lewdness of thy youth, in bruising thy teats by the Egyptians for the paps of thy youth.

"Therefore, O Aholibah," thus saith the Lord God, "behold, I will raise up thy lovers against thee, from whom thy mind is alienated, and I will bring them against thee on every side: the Babylonians, and all the Chaldeans, Pekod, and Shoa, and Koa, and all the Assyrians with them: all of them desirable young men, captains and rulers, great lords and renowned, all of them riding upon horses. And they shall come against thee with chariots, wagons, and wheels, and with an assembly of people, which shall set against thee buckler and shield and helmet round about: and I will set judgment before them, and they shall judge thee according to their judgments. And I will set my jealousy against thee, and they shall deal furiously with thee: they shall take away thy nose and thine ears; and thy remnant shall fall by the sword: they shall take thy sons and thy daughters; and thy residue shall be devoured by the fire. They shall also

THE BOOK OF THE PROPHET EZEKIEL

strip thee out of thy clothes, and take away thy fair jewels. Thus will I make thy lewdness to cease from thee, and thy whoredom brought from the land of Egypt: so that thou shalt not lift up thine eyes unto them, nor remember Egypt any more."

The Lamentation for Tyre

The word of the Lord came again unto me, saying, "Now, thou Son of Man, take up a lamentation for Tyrus; and say unto Tyrus, 'O thou that art situate at the entry of the sea, which art a merchant of the people for many isles, thus saith the Lord God: "O Tyrus, thou hast said, 'I am of perfect beauty.' Thy borders are in the midst of the seas, thy builders have perfected thy beauty. They have made all thy ship boards of fir trees of Senir: they have taken cedars from Lebanon to make masts for thee. Of the oaks of Bashan have they made thine oars; the company of the Ashurites have made thy benches of ivory, brought out of the isles of Chittim. Fine linen with broidered work from Egypt was that which thou spreadest forth to be thy sail; blue and purple from the isles of Elishah was that which covered thee. The inhabitants of Sidon and Arvad were thy mariners: thy wise men, O Tyrus, that were in thee, were thy pilots. The ancients of Gebal and the wise men thereof were in thee thy calkers: all the ships of the sea with their mariners were in thee to occupy thy merchandise. They of Persia and of Lud and of Phut were in thine army, thy men of war: they hanged the shield and helmet in thee; they set forth thy comeliness. The men of Arvad with thine army were upon thy walls round about, and the Gammadims were in thy towers: they hanged their shields upon thy walls round about; they have made thy beauty perfect. Tarshish was thy merchant by reason of the multitude of all kind of riches; with silver, iron, tin, and lead, they traded in thy fairs. Javan, Tubal, and Meshech, they were thy merchants: they traded the persons of men and vessels of brass in thy market. They of the house of Togarmah traded in thy fairs with horses and horsemen and mules. The men of Dedan were thy merchants; many isles were the merchandise of

THE BOOK OF THE PROPHET EZEKIEL

thine hand: they brought thee for a present horns of ivory and ebony. Syria was thy merchant by reason of the multitude of the wares of thy making: they occupied in thy fairs with emeralds, purple, and broidered work, and fine linen, and coral, and agate. Judah, and the land of Israel, they were thy merchants: they traded in thy market wheat of Minnith, and Pannag, and honey, and oil, and balm. Damascus was thy merchant in the multitude of the wares of thy making, for the multitude of all riches; in the wine of Helbon, and white wool. Dan also and Javan going to and fro occupied in thy fairs: bright iron, cassia, and calamus, were in thy market. Dedan was thy merchant in precious clothes for chariots. Arabia, and all the princes of Kedar, they occupied with thee in lambs, and rams, and goats: in these were they thy merchants. The merchants of Sheba and Raamah, they were thy merchants: they occupied in thy fairs with chief of all spices, and with all precious stones, and gold. Haran, and Canneh, and Eden, the merchants of Sheba, Asshur, and Chilmad, were thy merchants. These were thy merchants in all sorts of things, in blue clothes, and broidered work, and in chests of rich apparel, bound with cords, and made of cedar, among thy merchandise. The ships of Tarshish did sing of thee in thy market: and thou wast replenished, and made very glorious in the midst of the seas.

"' "Thy rowers have brought thee into great waters: the east wind hath broken thee in the midst of the seas. Thy riches, and thy fairs, thy merchandise, thy mariners, and thy pilots, thy calkers, and the occupiers of thy merchandise, and all thy men of war, that are in thee, and in all thy company which is in the midst of thee, shall fall into the midst of the seas in the day of thy ruin. The suburbs shall shake at the sound of the cry of thy pilots. And all that handle the oar, the mariners, and all the pilots of the sea, shall come down from their ships, they shall stand upon the land; and shall cause their voice to be heard against thee, and shall cry bitterly, and shall cast up dust upon their heads, they shall wallow themselves in the ashes: and they shall make themselves utterly bald for thee, and gird them with

THE BOOK OF THE PROPHET EZEKIEL

sackcloth, and they shall weep for thee with bitterness of heart and bitter wailing. And in their wailing they shall take up a lamentation for thee, and lament over thee, saying, 'What city is like Tyrus, like the destroyed in the midst of the sea?' When thy wares went forth out of the seas, thou filledst many people; thou didst enrich the kings of the earth with the multitude of thy riches and of thy merchandise. In the time when thou shalt be broken by the seas in the depths of the waters thy merchandise and all thy company in the midst of thee shall fall. All the inhabitants of the isles shall be astonished at thee, and their kings shall be sore afraid, they shall be troubled in their countenance. The merchants among the people shall hiss at thee; thou shalt be a terror, and never shalt be any more."'"

The Dragon of the Sea

And it came to pass in the twelfth year, in the twelfth month, in the first day of the month, that the word of the Lord came unto me, saying, "Son of Man, take up a lamentation for Pharaoh king of Egypt, and say unto him, 'Thou art like a young lion of the nations, and thou art as a whale in the seas: and thou camest forth with thy rivers, and troubledst the waters with thy feet, and fouledst their rivers.'

"Thus saith the Lord God: 'I will therefore spread out my net over thee with a company of many people; and they shall bring thee up in my net. Then will I leave thee upon the land, I will cast thee forth upon the open field, and will cause all the fowls of the heaven to remain upon thee, and I will fill the beasts of the whole earth with thee. And I will lay thy flesh upon the mountains, and fill the valleys with thy height. I will also water with thy blood the land wherein thou swimmest, even to the mountains; and the rivers shall be full of thee. And when I shall put thee out, I will cover the heaven, and make the stars thereof dark; I will cover the sun with a cloud, and the moon shall not give her light. All the bright lights of heaven will I make dark over thee, and set darkness upon thy land,' saith the Lord God.

"I will also vex the hearts of many people, when I shall bring

THE BOOK OF THE PROPHET EZEKIEL

thy destruction among the nations, into the countries which thou hast not known. Yea, I will make many people amazed at thee, and their kings shall be horribly afraid for thee, when I shall brandish my sword before them; and they shall tremble at every moment, every man for his own life, in the day of thy fall. For thus saith the Lord God: 'The sword of the king of Babylon shall come upon thee. By the swords of the mighty will I cause thy multitude to fall, the terrible of the nations, all of them: and they shall spoil the pomp of Egypt, and all the multitude thereof shall be destroyed. I will destroy also all the beasts thereof from beside the great waters; neither shall the foot of man trouble them any more, nor the hoofs of beasts trouble them. Then will I make their waters deep, and cause their rivers to run like oil,' saith the Lord God. 'When I shall make the land of Egypt desolate, and the country shall be destitute of that whereof it was full, when I shall smite all them that dwell therein, then shall they know that I am the Lord. This is the lamentation wherewith they shall lament her: the daughters of the nations shall lament her: they shall lament for her, even for Egypt, and for all her multitude,' saith the Lord God."

"Wail for the Multitude of Egypt"

It came to pass also in the twelfth year, in the fifteenth day of the month, that the word of the Lord came unto me, saying,

> *"Son of Man, wail for the multitude of Egypt, and cast them down,*
> *Even her, and the daughters of the famous nations,*
> *Unto the nether parts of the earth,*
> *With them that go down into the pit:*
>
> *'Whom dost thou pass in beauty?*
> *Go down, and be thou laid with the uncircumcised.*
>
> *They shall fall in the midst of them that are slain by the sword:*
> *She is delivered to the sword:*
> *Draw her and all her multitudes.'*

THE BOOK OF THE PROPHET EZEKIEL

The strong among the mighty shall speak to him
Out of the midst of hell with them that help him:
'They are gone down, they lie uncircumcised, slain by the sword.'

Asshur is there and all her company: his graves are about him:
All of them slain, fallen by the sword:

Whose graves are set in the sides of the pit,
And her company is round about her grave:
All of them slain, fallen by the sword,
Which caused terror in the land of the living.

There is Elam and all her multitude round about her grave,
All of them slain, fallen by the sword,
Which are gone down uncircumcised into the nether parts of the
    earth,
Which caused their terror in the land of the living;
Yet have they borne their shame with them that go down to the pit.

They have set her a bed in the midst of the slain with all her multi-
    tude:
Her graves are round about him:
All of them uncircumcised, slain by the sword:
Though their terror was caused in the land of the living,
Yet have they borne their shame with them that go down to the pit:
He is put in the midst of them that be slain.

There is Meshech, Tubal, and all her multitude:
Her graves are round about him:
All of them uncircumcised, slain by the sword,
Though they caused their terror in the land of the living.

And they shall not lie with the mighty that are fallen of the uncir-
    cumcised,
Which are gone down to hell with their weapons of war:
And they have laid their swords under their heads,
But their iniquities shall be upon their bones,
Though they were the terror of the mighty in the land of the living.

THE BOOK OF THE PROPHET EZEKIEL

Yea, thou shalt be broken in the midst of the uncircumcised,
And shalt lie with them that are slain with the sword.

There is Edom, her kings, and all her princes,
Which with their might are laid by them that were slain by the sword:
They shall lie with the uncircumcised,
And with them that go down to the pit.

There be the princes of the north,
All of them, and all the Sidonians,
Which are gone down with the slain;
With their terror they are ashamed of their might;
And they lie uncircumcised with them that be slain by the sword,
And bear their shame with them that go down to the pit.

Pharaoh shall see them, and shall be comforted over all his multitude,
Even Pharaoh and all his army slain by the sword," saith the Lord God.

"*For I have caused my terror in the land of the living:*
And he shall be laid in the midst of the uncircumcised with them that are slain with the sword,
Even Pharaoh and all his multitude," saith the Lord God.

The Shepherds of Israel

And the word of the Lord came unto me, saying, "Son of Man, prophesy against the shepherds of Israel, prophesy, and say unto them, 'Thus saith the Lord God unto the shepherds: "Woe be to the shepherds of Israel that do feed themselves! should not the shepherds feed the flocks? Ye eat the fat, and ye clothe you with the wool, ye kill them that are fed: but ye feed not the flock. The diseased have ye not strengthened, neither have ye healed that which was sick, neither have ye bound up that which was broken, neither have ye brought again that which was driven away, neither have ye sought that which was lost; but with force and with cruelty have ye ruled them. And they were scattered, because there is no shepherd: and they became

THE BOOK OF THE PROPHET EZEKIEL

meat to all the beasts of the field, when they were scattered. My sheep wandered through all the mountains, and upon every high hill: yea, my flock was scattered upon all the face of the earth, and none did search or seek after them."

" 'Therefore, ye shepherds, hear the word of the Lord: "As I live," saith the Lord God, "surely because my flock became a prey, and my flock became meat to every beast of the field, because there was no shepherd, neither did my shepherds search for my flock, but the shepherds fed themselves, and fed not my flock": therefore, O ye shepherds, hear the word of the Lord: "Behold, I am against the shepherds; and I will require my flock at their hand, and cause them to cease from feeding the flock; neither shall the shepherds feed themselves any more; for I will deliver my flock from their mouth, that they may not be meat for them."

" 'For thus saith the Lord God "Behold, I, even I, will both search my sheep, and seek them out. As a shepherd seeketh out his flock in the day that he is among his sheep that are scattered; so will I seek out my sheep, and will deliver them out of all places where they have been scattered in the cloudy and dark day. And I will bring them out from the people, and gather them from the countries, and will bring them to their own land, and feed them upon the mountains of Israel by the rivers, and in all the inhabited places of the country. I will feed them in a good pasture, and upon the high mountains of Israel shall their fold be: there shall they lie in a good fold, and in a fat pasture shall they feed upon the mountains of Israel. I will feed my flock, and I will cause them to lie down," saith the Lord God. "I will seek that which was lost, and bring again that which was driven away, and will bind up that which was broken, and will strengthen that which was sick: but I will destroy the fat and the strong; I will feed them with judgment.

" ' "And as for you, O my flock," thus saith the Lord God: "Behold, I judge between cattle and cattle, between the rams and the he-goats. Seemeth it a small thing unto you to have eaten up the good pasture, but ye must tread down with your feet the

THE BOOK OF THE PROPHET EZEKIEL

residue of your pastures? and to have drunk of the deep waters, but ye must foul the residue with your feet? And as for my flock, they eat that which ye have trodden with your feet; and they drink that which ye have fouled with your feet."

"'Therefore thus saith the Lord God unto them: "Behold, I, even I, will judge between the fat cattle and between the lean cattle. Because ye have thrust with side and with shoulder, and pushed all the diseased with your horns, till ye have scattered them abroad; therefore will I save my flock, and they shall no more be a prey; and I will judge between cattle and cattle. And I will set up one shepherd over them, and he shall feed them, even my servant David; he shall feed them, and he shall be their shepherd. And I the Lord will be their God, and my servant David a prince among them; I the Lord have spoken it. And I will make with them a covenant of peace, and will cause the evil beasts to cease out of the land: and they shall dwell safely in the wilderness, and sleep in the woods. And I will make them and the places round about my hill a blessing; and I will cause the shower to come down in his season; there shall be showers of blessing. And the tree of the field shall yield her fruit, and the earth shall yield her increase, and they shall be safe in their land, and shall know that I am the Lord, when I have broken the bands of their yoke, and delivered them out of the hand of those that served themselves of them. And they shall no more be a prey to the heathen, neither shall the beast of the land devour them; but they shall dwell safely, and none shall make them afraid. And I will raise up for them a plant of renown, and they shall be no more consumed with hunger in the land, neither bear the shame of the heathen any more. Thus shall they know that I the Lord their God am with them, and that they, even the house of Israel, are my people," saith the Lord God. "And ye my flock, the flock of my pasture, are men, and I am your God," saith the Lord God.'"

The Valley of Dry Bones

The hand of the Lord was upon me, and carried me out in the spirit of the Lord, and set me down in the midst of the valley

THE BOOK OF THE PROPHET EZEKIEL

which was full of bones, and caused me to pass by them round about: and, behold, there were very many in the open valley; and, lo, they were very dry.

And he said unto me, "Son of Man, can these bones live?"

And I answered, "O Lord God, thou knowest."

Again he said unto me, "Prophesy upon these bones, and say unto them, 'O ye dry bones, hear the word of the Lord. Thus saith the Lord God unto these bones: "Behold, I will cause breath to enter into you, and ye shall live: and I will lay sinews upon you, and will bring up flesh upon you, and cover you with skin, and put breath in you, and ye shall live; and ye shall know that I am the Lord."'"

So I prophesied as I was commanded: and as I prophesied, there was a noise, and behold a shaking, and the bones came together, bone to his bone. And when I beheld, lo, the sinews and the flesh came up upon them, and the skin covered them above: but there was no breath in them.

Then said he unto me, "Prophesy unto the wind, prophesy, Son of Man, and say to the wind, 'Thus saith the Lord God: "Come from the four winds, O breath, and breathe upon these slain, that they may live."'"

So I prophesied as he commanded me, and the breath came into them, and they lived, and stood up upon their feet, an exceeding great army.

Then he said unto me, "Son of Man, these bones are the whole house of Israel: behold, they say, 'Our bones are dried, and our hope is lost: we are cut off for our parts.' Therefore prophesy and say unto them, 'Thus saith the Lord God: "Behold, O my people, I will open your graves, and cause you to come up out of your graves, and bring you into the land of Israel. And ye shall know that I am the Lord, when I have opened your graves, O my people, and brought you up out of your graves, and shall put my spirit in you, and ye shall live, and I shall place you in your own land: then shall ye know that I the Lord have spoken it, and performed it," saith the Lord.'"

THE BOOK OF THE PROPHET EZEKIEL

Symbolism of the Two Sticks

The word of the Lord came again unto me, saying, "Moreover, thou Son of Man, take thee one stick, and write upon it, 'For Judah, and for the children of Israel his companions'; then take another stick, and write upon it, 'For Joseph, the stick of Ephraim, and for all the house of Israel his companions'; and join them one to another into one stick; and they shall become one in thine hand. And when the children of thy people shall speak unto thee, saying, 'Wilt thou not show us what thou meanest by these?' say unto them, 'Thus saith the Lord God: "Behold, I will take the stick of Joseph, which is in the hand of Ephraim, and the tribes of Israel his fellows, and will put them with him, even with the stick of Judah, and make them one stick, and they shall be one in mine hand."'

"And the sticks whereon thou writest shall be in thine hand before their eyes. And say unto them, 'Thus saith the Lord God: "Behold, I will take the children of Israel from among the heathen, whither they be gone, and will gather them on every side, and bring them into their own land: and I will make them one nation in the land upon the mountains of Israel; and one king shall be king to them all: and they shall be no more two nations, neither shall they be divided into two kingdoms any more at all: neither shall they defile themselves any more with their idols, nor with their detestable things, nor with any of their transgressions: but I will save them out of all their dwelling places, wherein they have sinned, and will cleanse them: so shall they be my people, and I will be their God. And David my servant shall be king over them; and they all shall have one shepherd: they shall also walk in my judgments, and observe my statutes, and do them. And they shall dwell in the land that I have given unto Jacob my servant, wherein your fathers have dwelt; and they shall dwell therein, even they, and their children, and their children's children for ever: and my servant David shall be their prince for ever."'"

THE BOOK OF THE PROPHET EZEKIEL

The Invasion of Gog

And the word of the Lord came unto me, saying, "Son of Man, set thy face against Gog, the land of Magog, the chief prince of Meshech and Tubal, and prophesy against him, and say, 'Thus saith the Lord God: "Behold, I am against thee, O Gog, the chief prince of Meshech and Tubal: and I will turn thee back, and put hooks into thy jaws, and I will bring thee forth, and all thine army, horses and horsemen, all of them clothed with all sorts of armour, even a great company with bucklers and shields, all of them handling swords: Persia, Ethiopia, and Libya with them; all of them with shield and helmet: Gomer, and all his bands; the house of Togarmah of the north quarters, and all his bands: and many people with thee. Be thou prepared, and prepare for thyself, thou, and all thy company that are assembled unto thee, and be thou a guard unto them.

" ' "After many days thou shalt be visited: in the latter years thou shalt come into the land that is brought back from the sword, and is gathered out of many people, against the mountains of Israel, which have been always waste: but it is brought forth out of the nations, and they shall dwell safely all of them. Thou shalt ascend and come like a storm, thou shalt be like a cloud to cover the land, thou, and all thy bands, and many people with thee."

" 'Thus saith the Lord God: "It shall also come to pass, that at the same time shall things come into thy mind, and thou shalt think an evil thought: and thou shalt say, 'I will go up to the land of unwalled villages; I will go to them that are at rest, that dwell safely, all of them dwelling without walls, and having neither bars nor gates,' to take a spoil, and to take a prey; to turn thine hand upon the desolate places that are now inhabited, and upon the people that are gathered out of the nations, which have gotten cattle and goods, that dwell in the midst of the land. Sheba, and Dedan, and the merchants of Tarshish, with all the young lions thereof, shall say unto thee, 'Art thou come

THE BOOK OF THE PROPHET EZEKIEL

to take a spoil? hast thou gathered thy company to take a prey? to carry away silver and gold, to take away cattle and goods, to take a great spoil?'"'

"Therefore, Son of Man, prophesy and say unto Gog, 'Thus saith the Lord God: "In that day when my people of Israel dwelleth safely, shalt thou not know it? And thou shalt come from thy place out of the north parts, thou, and many people with thee, all of them riding upon horses, a great company, and a mighty army: and thou shalt come up against my people of Israel, as a cloud to cover the land; it shall be in the latter days, and I will bring thee against my land, that the heathen may know me, when I shall be sanctified in thee, O Gog, before their eyes."

"'Thus saith the Lord God: "Art thou he of whom I have spoken in old time by my servants the prophets of Israel, which prophesied in those days many years that I would bring thee against them? And it shall come to pass at the same time when Agog shall come against the land of Israel," saith the Lord God, "that my fury shall come up in my face. For in my jealousy and in the fire of my wrath have I spoken: surely in that day there shall be a great shaking in the land of Israel: so that the fishes of the sea, and the fowls of the heaven, and the beasts of the field, and all creeping things that creep upon the earth, and all the men that are upon the face of the earth, shall shake at my presence, and the mountains shall be thrown down, and the steep places shall fall, and every wall shall fall to the ground. And I will call for a sword against him throughout all my mountains," saith the Lord God: "every man's sword shall be against his brother. And I will plead against him with pestilence and with blood; and I will rain upon him, and upon his bands, and upon the many people that are with him, an overflowing rain, and great hailstones, fire, and brimstone. Thus will I magnify myself, and sanctify myself; and I will be known in the eyes of many nations, and they shall know that I am the Lord."'

"Therefore, thou Son of Man, prophesy against Gog, and say, 'Thus saith the Lord God: "Behold, I am against thee, O

THE BOOK OF THE PROPHET EZEKIEL

Gog, the chief prince of Meshech and Tubal: and I will turn thee back, and leave but the sixth part of thee, and will cause thee to come up from the north parts, and will bring thee upon the mountains of Israel: and I will smite thy bow out of thy left hand, and will cause thine arrows to fall out of thy right hand. Thou shalt fall upon the mountains of Israel, thou, and all thy bands, and the people that is with thee: I will give thee unto the ravenous birds of every sort, and to the beasts of the field to be devoured. Thou shalt fall upon the open field: for I have spoken it," saith the Lord God. "And I will send a fire on Magog, and among them that dwell carelessly in the isles: and they shall know that I am the Lord. So will I make my holy name known in the midst of my people Israel; and I will not let them pollute my holy name any more: and the heathen shall know that I am the Lord, the Holy One in Israel.

"' "Behold, it is come, and it is done," saith the Lord God; "this is the day whereof I have spoken. And they that dwell in the cities of Israel shall go forth, and shall set on fire and burn the weapons, both the shields and the bucklers, the bows and the arrows, and the handstaves, and the spears, and they shall burn them with fire seven years: so that they shall take no wood out of the field, neither cut down any out of the forests; for they shall burn the weapons with fire: and they shall spoil those that spoiled them, and rob those that robbed them," saith the Lord God.'

"And it shall come to pass in that day, that I will give unto Gog a place there of graves in Israel, the valley of the passengers on the east of the sea: and it shall stop the noses of the passengers: and there shall they bury Gog and all his multitude: and they shall call it the valley of Hamon-gog. And seven months shall the house of Israel be burying of them, that they may cleanse the land. Yea, all the people of the land shall bury them; and it shall be to them a renown the day that I shall be glorified," saith the Lord God. "And they shall sever out men of continual employment, passing through the land to bury with the passengers those that remain upon the face of the earth, to cleanse it:

THE BOOK OF THE PROPHET EZEKIEL

after the end of seven months shall they search. And the passengers that pass through the land, when any seeth a man's bone, then shall he set up a sign by it, till the buriers have buried it in the valley of Hamon-gog. And also the name of the city shall be Hamonah. Thus shall they cleanse the land.

"And, thou Son of Man, thus saith the Lord God: 'Speak unto every feathered fowl, and to every beast of the field, "Assemble yourselves, and come; gather yourselves on every side to my sacrifice that I do sacrifice for you, even a great sacrifice upon the mountains of Israel, that ye may eat flesh, and drink blood. Ye shall eat the flesh of the mighty, and drink the blood of the princes of the earth, of rams, of lambs, and of goats, of bullocks, all of them fatlings of Bashan. And ye shall eat fat till ye be full, and drink blood till ye be drunken, of my sacrifice which I have sacrificed for you. Thus ye shall be filled at my table with horses and chariots, with mighty men, and with all men of war," ' saith the Lord God.

"And I will set my glory among the heathen, and all the heathen shall see my judgment that I have executed, and my hand that I have laid upon them. So the house of Israel shall know that I am the Lord their God from that day and forward.

"And the heathen shall know that the house of Israel went into captivity for their iniquity: because they trespassed against me, therefore hid I my face from them, and gave them into the hand of their enemies: so fell they all by the sword. According to their uncleanness and according to their transgressions have I done unto them, and hid my face from them. Therefore thus saith the Lord God: 'Now will I bring again the captivity of Jacob, and have mercy upon the whole house of Israel, and will be jealous for my holy name; after that they have borne their shame, and all their trespasses whereby they have trespassed against me, when they dwelt safely in their land, and none made them afraid. When I have brought them again from the people, and gathered them out of their enemies' lands, and am sanctified in them in the sight of many nations; then shall they know that

THE BOOK OF THE PROPHET EZEKIEL

I am the Lord their God, which caused them to be led into captivity among the heathen: but I have gathered them unto their own land, and have left none of them any more there. Neither will I hide my face any more from them: for I have poured out my spirit upon the house of Israel,' saith the Lord God."

THE RHAPSODIES OF THE UNKNOWN PROPHET

The exilic author of the latter part of the Book of Isaiah would certainly be ranked with the three Great Prophets if even his name were known. There is in his poetry a sustained ecstasy, a kind of ultimate of lyric rapture, unequaled elsewhere in the Bible. And its source was an original intuition which afforded an entirely new interpretation of Jewish history. Hitherto, the misfortunes of the race had been regarded by the prophets as a divine chastisement for its sins. The Second Isaiah, or Deutero-Isaiah, as he is sometimes called for lack of a better name, boldly discarded this traditional explanation and substituted for it a profoundly philosophical enrichment of that idea of vicarious righteousness which Ezekiel summarily rejected. It was precisely the function of the innocent to suffer for the guilty, the Unknown Prophet maintained; the good are those who give their lives for others and through their sacrifice the basest are benefited in spite of their own unworthiness; and what is true of the individual is true of the race; so Israel bore the sins of others and her redemption would mean the redemption of mankind. From the pure air of these lofty heights far above the welter of individual happiness the poet derived his serene ecstasy. And he was led on to embody his conception in the figure of a suffering Messiah as its crowning realization, to which he devoted all the combined suggestions of sublimity and pathos that a powerful imagination could supply. Possibly some dim influence of the sacrificial god of Adonis and Attis worship was present here, but if so the Unknown Prophet spiritualized it beyond recognition. It would not be untrue to say that he was the first Christian, five centuries before Christ. Indeed, his conception of vicarious atonement was taken over by many forms of orthodox Christianity, in which, however, it was usually narrowed rather than broadened.

The Rhapsodies of the UNKNOWN PROPHET

"Comfort Ye, Comfort Ye My People"

"Comfort ye, comfort ye my people,"
Saith your God.
"Speak ye comfortably to Jerusalem,
And cry unto her,
That her warfare is accomplished,
That her iniquity is pardoned:
For she hath received of the Lord's hand
Double for all her sins."

The voice of him that crieth in the wilderness,
"Prepare ye the way of the Lord,
Make straight in the desert a highway for our God.
Every valley shall be exalted,
And every mountain and hill shall be made low:
And the crooked shall be made straight,
And the rough places plain:
And the glory of the Lord shall be revealed,
And all flesh shall see it together:
For the mouth of the Lord hath spoken it."

The voice said, "Cry."
And he said, "What shall I cry?"
"All flesh is grass,
And all the goodliness thereof is as the flower of the field:
The grass withereth, the flower fadeth:
Because the spirit of the Lord bloweth upon it:
Surely the people is grass.

THE UNKNOWN PROPHET

The grass withereth, the flower fadeth:
But the word of our God shall stand for ever."

O Zion, that bringest good tidings,
Get thee up into the high mountain;
O Jerusalem, that bringest good tidings,
Lift up thy voice with strength;
Lift it up,
Be not afraid;
Say unto the cities of Judah,
"Behold your God!"

Behold, the Lord God will come with strong hand,
And his arm shall rule for him:
Behold, his reward is with him,
And his work before him.
He shall feed his flock like a shepherd:
He shall gather the lambs with his arm,
And carry them in his bosom,
And shall gently lead those that are with young.

Who hath measured the waters in the hollow of his hand,
And meted out heaven with the span,
And comprehended the dust of the earth in a measure,
And weighed the mountains in scales,
And the hills in a balance?

Who hath directed the Spirit of the Lord,
Or being his counsellor hath taught him?
With whom took he counsel,
And who instructed him,
And taught him in the path of judgment,
And taught him knowledge,
And showed to him the way of understanding?

Behold, the nations are as a drop of a bucket,
And are counted as the small dust of the balance:
Behold, he taketh up the isles as a very little thing.

THE UNKNOWN PROPHET

And Lebanon is not sufficient to burn,
Nor the beasts thereof sufficient for a burnt offering.
All nations before him are as nothing;
And they are counted to him less than nothing, and vanity.

To whom then will ye liken God?
Or what likeness will ye compare unto him?
Have ye not known? have ye not heard?
Hath it not been told you from the beginning?
Have ye not understood from the foundations of the earth?
It is he that sitteth upon the circle of the earth,
And the inhabitants thereof are as grasshoppers;
That stretcheth out the heavens as a curtain,
And spreadeth them out as a tent to dwell in;
That bringeth the princes to nothing;
He maketh the judges of the earth as vanity.
Yea, they shall not be planted;
Yea, they shall not be sown;
Yea, their stock shall not take root in the earth;
And he shall also blow upon them, and they shall wither,
And the whirlwind shall take them away as stubble.

"To whom then will ye liken me,
Or shall I be equal?" saith the Holy One.
Lift up your eyes on high,
And behold who hath created these things,
That bringeth out their host by number:
He calleth them all by names
By the greatness of his might, for that he is strong in power;
Not one faileth.

Why sayest thou, O Jacob,
And speakest, O Israel,
"My way is hid from the Lord,
And my judgment is passed over from my God?"
Hast thou not known?
Hast thou not heard,

THE UNKNOWN PROPHET

That the everlasting God,
The Lord, the Creator of the ends of the earth,
Fainteth not, neither is weary?
There is no searching of his understanding.

He giveth power to the faint;
And to them that have no might he increaseth strength.
Even the youths shall faint and be weary,
And the young men shall utterly fall:
But they that wait upon the Lord shall renew their strength;
They shall mount up with wings as eagles;
They shall run, and not be weary;
And they shall walk, and not faint.

"Behold My Servant"

Behold my servant, whom I uphold;
Mine elect, in whom my soul delighteth;
I have put my spirit upon him:
He shall bring forth judgment to the Gentiles.
He shall not cry, nor lift up,
Nor cause his voice to be heard in the street.
A bruised reed shall he not break,
And the smoking flax shall he not quench:
He shall bring forth judgment unto truth.
He shall not fail nor be discouraged,
Till he have set judgment in the earth:
And the isles shall wait for his law.

"Remember These, O Jacob and Israel"

Remember these, O Jacob and Israel:
For thou art my servant:
I have formed thee;
Thou art my servant:
O Israel, thou shalt not be forgotten of me.
I have blotted out, as a thick cloud, thy transgressions,
And, as a cloud, thy sins:
Return unto me; for I have redeemed thee.

THE UNKNOWN PROPHET

Sing, O ye heavens;
For the Lord hath done it:
Shout, ye lower parts of the earth:
Break forth into singing, ye mountains,
O forest, and every tree therein:
For the Lord hath redeemed Jacob,
And glorified himself in Israel.

Thus saith the Lord, thy redeemer,
And he that formed thee from the womb,
"I am the Lord that maketh all things;
That stretcheth forth the heavens alone;
That spreadeth abroad the earth by myself;
That frustrateth the tokens of the liars,
And maketh diviners mad;
That turneth wise men backward,
And maketh their knowledge foolish;
That confirmeth the word of his servant,
And performeth the counsel of his messengers;
That saith to Jerusalem, 'Thou shalt be inhabited';
And to the cities of Judah, 'Ye shall be built,
And I will raise up the decayed places thereof';
That saith to the deep, 'Be dry,
And I will dry up thy rivers';
That saith of Cyrus, 'He is my shepherd,
And shall perform all my pleasure';
Even saying to Jerusalem, 'Thou shalt be built';
And to the temple, 'Thy foundation shall be laid.'"

Thus saith the Lord to his anointed,
To Cyrus, whose right hand I have held,
To subdue nations before him;
And I will loose the loins of kings,
To open before him the two-leaved gates;
And the gates shall not be shut:
"I will go before thee,
And make the crooked places straight:

THE UNKNOWN PROPHET

I will break in pieces the gates of brass,
And cut in sunder the bars of iron;
And I will give thee the treasures of darkness,
And hidden riches of secret places,
That thou mayest know that I, the Lord,
Which call thee by thy name, am the God of Israel.
For Jacob my servant's sake,
And Israel mine elect,
I have even called thee by thy name;
I have surnamed thee, though thou hast not known me.
I am the Lord, and there is none else,
There is no God beside me;
I girded thee, though thou hast not known me:
That they may know from the rising of the sun,
And from the west, that there is none beside me.
I am the Lord,
And there is none else.
I form the light, and create darkness:
I make peace, and create evil:
I the Lord do all these things.

Drop down, ye heavens, from above, and let the skies pour down
    righteousness;
Let the earth open, and let them bring forth salvation,
And let righteousness spring up together;
I the Lord have created it.
Woe unto him that striveth with his Maker!
Let the potsherd strive with the potsherds of the earth.
Shall the clay say to him that fashioneth it, 'What makest thou?'
Or thy work, 'He hath no hands?'
Woe unto him that saith unto his father, 'What begettest thou?'
Or to the woman, 'What hast thou brought forth?'"

Thus saith the Lord, the Holy One of Israel, and his Maker,
"Ask me of things to come concerning my sons,
And concerning the work of my hands command ye me.
I have made the earth, and created man upon it;

THE UNKNOWN PROPHET

I, even my hands, have stretched out the heavens,
And all their host have I commanded.
I have raised him up in righteousness, and I will direct all his ways;
He shall build my city, and he shall let go my captives,
Not for price nor reward," saith the Lord of hosts.

"Come Down, and Sit in the Dust"

Come down, and sit in the dust, O virgin daughter of Babylon,
Sit on the ground;
There is no throne, O daughter of the Chaldeans;
For thou shalt no more be called tender and delicate.
Take the millstones, and grind meal;
Uncover thy locks, make bare the leg, uncover the thigh, pass over the rivers.
Thy nakedness shall be uncovered, yea, thy shame shall be seen;
I will take vengeance, and I will not meet thee as a man.
As for our redeemer, the Lord of hosts is his name,
The Holy One of Israel.
Sit thou silent, and get thee into darkness, O daughter of the Chaldeans;
For thou shalt no more be called the Lady of Kingdoms.

"Listen, O Isles, Unto Me"

Listen, O isles, unto me;
And hearken, ye people, from far;
The Lord hath called me from the womb;
From the bowels of my mother hath he made mention of my name.
And he hath made my mouth like a sharp sword;
In the shadow of his hand hath he hid me,
And made me a polished shaft;
In his quiver hath he hid me;
And said unto me, "Thou art my servant,
O Israel, in whom I will be glorified."
Then I said, "I have laboured in vain,
I have spent my strength for nought, and in vain:

THE UNKNOWN PROPHET

Yet surely my judgment is with the Lord,
And my work with my God."

And now, saith the Lord
That formed me from the womb to be his servant,
To bring Jacob again to him,
Though Israel be not gathered,
Yet shall I be glorious in the eyes of the Lord,
And my God shall be my strength.
And he said, "It is a light thing
That thou shouldest be my servant
To raise up the tribes of Jacob,
And to restore the preserved of Israel:
I will also give thee for a light to the Gentiles,
That thou mayest be my salvation unto the end of the earth."

"Awake! Awake! Put on Strength"

Awake! awake! put on strength,
O arm of the Lord!
Awake, as in the ancient days,
In the generations of old!
Art thou not it that hath cut Rahab,
And wounded the dragon?
Art thou not it which hath dried the sea,
The waters of the great deep;
That hath made the depths of the sea a way
For the ransomed to pass over?
Therefore the redeemed of the Lord shall return,
And come with singing unto Zion;
And everlasting joy shall be upon their head;
They shall obtain gladness and joy;
And sorrow and mourning shall flee away.

Awake, awake; put on
Thy strength, O Zion;
Put on thy beautiful garments,

THE UNKNOWN PROPHET

O Jerusalem, the holy city!
For henceforth there shall no more come into thee
The uncircumcised and the unclean.
Shake thyself from the dust;
Arise, and sit down, O Jerusalem;
Loose thyself from the bands of thy neck,
O captive daughter of Zion.
For thus saith the Lord,
"Ye have sold yourselves for nought;
And ye shall be redeemed without money."

How beautiful upon the mountains
Are the feet of him that bringeth good tidings,
That publisheth peace;
That bringeth good tidings of good,
That publisheth salvation;
That saith unto Zion, "Thy God reigneth!"
Thy watchmen shall lift up the voice;
With the voice together shall they sing:
For they shall see eye to eye,
When the Lord shall bring again Zion.

Break forth into joy,
Sing together, ye waste places of Jerusalem:
For the Lord hath comforted his people,
He hath redeemed Jerusalem.
The Lord hath made bare his holy arm
In the eyes of all the nations;
And all the ends of the earth
Shall see the salvation of our God.

"Behold, My Servant Shall Deal Prudently"

Behold, my servant shall deal prudently,
He shall be exalted and extolled, and be very high.
As many were astonished at thee;
His visage was so marred more than any man,
And his form more than the sons of men:

THE UNKNOWN PROPHET

So shall he sprinkle many nations;
The kings shall shut their mouths at him:
For that which had not been told them shall they see;
And that which they had not heard shall they consider.

Who hath believed our report?
And to whom is the arm of the Lord revealed?
For he shall grow up before him as a tender plant,
And as a root out of a dry ground:
He hath no form nor comeliness;
And when we shall see him, there is no beauty that we should
    desire him.
He is despised and rejected of men;
A man of sorrows, and acquainted with grief:
And we hid as it were our faces from him;
He was despised, and we esteemed him not.

Surely he hath borne our griefs,
And carried our sorrows:
Yet we did esteem him stricken,
Smitten of God, and afflicted.
But he was wounded for our transgressions,
He was bruised for our iniquities:
The chastisement of our peace was upon him;
And with his stripes we are healed.
All we like sheep have gone astray;
We have turned every one to his own way;
And the Lord hath laid on him
The iniquity of us all.

He was oppressed, and he was afflicted,
Yet he opened not his mouth:
He is brought as a lamb to the slaughter,
And as a sheep before her shearers is dumb,
So he openeth not his mouth.
He was taken from prison and from judgment:
And who shall declare his generation?

THE UNKNOWN PROPHET

For he was cut off out of the land of the living:
For the transgression of my people was he stricken.
And he made his grave with the wicked,
And with the rich in his death;
Because he had done no violence,
Neither was any deceit in his mouth.

Yet it pleased the Lord to bruise him;
He hath put him to grief:
When thou shalt make his soul an offering for sin,
The pleasure of the Lord shall prosper in his hand.
He shall see of the travail of his soul, and shall be satisfied:
By his knowledge shall my righteous servant justify many;
For he shall bear their iniquities.
Therefore will I divide him a portion with the great,
And he shall divide the spoil with the strong;
Because he hath poured out his soul unto death:
And he was numbered with the transgressors;
And he bore the sin of many,
And made intercession for the transgressors.

"Sing, O Barren"

"Sing, O barren,
Thou that didst not bear;
Break forth into singing, and cry aloud,
Thou that didst not travail with child:
For more are the children of the desolate
Than the children of the married wife,"
Saith the Lord.
"Enlarge the place of thy tent,
And let them stretch forth the curtains of thine habitations:
Spare not, lengthen thy cords,
And strengthen thy stakes;
For thou shalt break forth on the right hand and on the left;
And thy seed shall inherit the Gentiles,

THE UNKNOWN PROPHET

And make the desolate cities to be inhabited.
Fear not; for thou shalt not be ashamed:
Neither be thou confounded; for thou shalt not be put to shame:
For thou shalt forget the shame of thy youth,
And shalt not remember the reproach of thy widowhood any more.
For thy Maker is thine husband;
The Lord of hosts is his name;
And thy Redeemer the Holy One of Israel;
The God of the whole earth shall he be called.

For a small moment have I forsaken thee;
But with great mercies will I gather thee.
In a little wrath I hid my face from thee for a moment;
But with everlasting kindness will I have mercy on thee,"
Saith the Lord thy Redeemer.
"For this is as the waters of Noah unto me:
For as I have sworn that the waters of Noah should no more go over
    the earth;
So have I sworn that I would not be wroth with thee, nor rebuke
    thee.
For the mountains shall depart,
And the hills be removed;
But my kindness shall not depart from thee,
Neither shall the covenant of my peace be removed,"
Saith the Lord that hath mercy on thee.

"O thou afflicted,
Tossed with tempest, and not comforted,
Behold, I will lay thy stones with fair colours,
And lay thy foundations with sapphires.
And I will make thy windows of agates,
And thy gates of carbuncles,
And all thy borders of pleasant stones.
And all thy children shall be taught of the Lord;
And great shall be the peace of thy children."

THE UNKNOWN PROPHET

"Ho, Every One That Thirsteth"

"Ho, every one that thirsteth, come ye to the waters,
And he that hath no money; come ye, buy, and eat;
Yea, come, buy wine and milk
Without money and without price.
Wherefore do ye spend money for that which is not bread?
And your labour for that which satisfieth not?
Hearken diligently unto me, and eat ye that which is good,
And let your soul delight itself in fatness.

Incline your ear, and come unto me;
Hear, and your soul shall live;
And I will make an everlasting covenant with you,
Even the sure mercies of David.
Behold, I have given him for a witness to the people,
A leader and commander to the people.
Behold, thou shalt call a nation that thou knowest not,
And nations that knew not thee shall run unto thee
Because of the Lord thy God,
And for the Holy One of Israel; for he hath glorified thee.

Seek ye the Lord while he may be found,
Call ye upon him while he is near:
Let the wicked forsake his way,
And the unrighteous man his thoughts:
And let him return unto the Lord,
And he will have mercy upon him;
And to our God,
For he will abundantly pardon.
For my thoughts are not your thoughts,
Neither are your ways my ways," saith the Lord.
"For as the heavens
Are higher than the earth,
So are my ways higher than your ways,
And my thoughts than your thoughts.

THE UNKNOWN PROPHET

For as the rain cometh down, and the snow from heaven,
And returneth not thither, but watereth the earth,
And maketh it bring forth and bud,
That it may give seed to the sower, and bread to the eater:
So shall my word be that goeth forth out of my mouth:
It shall not return unto me void,
But it shall accomplish that which I please,
And it shall prosper in the thing whereto I sent it.

For ye shall go out with joy,
And be led forth with peace:
The mountains and the hills shall break forth before you into singing,
And all the trees of the field shall clap their hands.
Instead of the thorn shall come up the fir tree,
And instead of the brier shall come up the myrtle tree:
And it shall be to the Lord for a name,
For an everlasting sign that shall not be cut off."

"Arise, Shine!"

Arise, shine! for thy light is come,
And the glory of the Lord is risen upon thee.
For, behold, the darkness shall cover the earth,
And gross darkness the people:
But the Lord shall arise upon thee,
And his glory shall be seen upon thee.
And the Gentiles shall come to thy light,
And kings to the brightness of thy rising.

Lift up thine eyes round about, and see!
All they gather themselves together, they come to thee:
Thy sons shall come from far,
And thy daughters shall be nursed at thy side.
Then thou shalt see, and flow together,
And thine heart shall fear, and be enlarged;
Because the abundance of the sea shall be converted unto thee,
The forces of the Gentiles shall come unto thee.

THE UNKNOWN PROPHET

The multitude of camels shall cover thee,
The dromedaries of Midian and Ephah;
All they from Sheba shall come:
They shall bring gold and incense,
And they shall show forth the praises of the Lord.
All the flocks of Kedar shall be gathered together unto thee,
The rams of Nebaioth shall minister unto thee:
They shall come up with acceptance on mine altar,
And I will glorify the house of my glory.

Who are these that fly as a cloud,
And as the doves to their windows?
Surely the isles shall wait for me,
And the ships of Tarshish first,
To bring thy sons from far,
Their silver and their gold with them,
Unto the name of the Lord thy God,
And to the Holy One of Israel, because he hath glorified thee.

And the sons of strangers shall build up thy walls,
And their kings shall minister unto thee:
For in my wrath I smote thee,
But in my favour have I had mercy on thee.
Therefore thy gates shall be open continually,
They shall not be shut day nor night,
That men may bring unto thee the forces of the Gentiles,
And that their kings may be brought.
For the nation and kingdom that will not serve thee shall perish;
Yea, those nations shall be utterly wasted.

The glory of Lebanon shall come unto thee,
The fir tree, the pine tree, and the box together,
To beautify the place of my sanctuary;
And I will make the place of my feet glorious.
The sons also of them that afflicted thee shall come bending unto thee,
And all they that despised thee shall bow themselves down at the
    soles of thy feet;

THE UNKNOWN PROPHET

And they shall call thee "the city of the Lord,
The Zion of the Holy One of Israel."

Whereas thou hast been forsaken and hated,
So that no man went through thee,
I will make thee an eternal excellency,
A joy of many generations.
Thou shalt also suck the milk of the Gentiles,
And shalt suck the breast of kings:
And thou shalt know that I the Lord am thy Saviour
And thy Redeemer, the mighty One of Jacob.

For brass I will bring gold,
And for iron I will bring silver,
And for wood brass,
And for stones iron;
I will also make thy officers peace,
And thine exactors righteousness.
Violence shall no more be heard in thy land,
Wasting nor destruction within thy borders;
But thou shalt call thy walls Salvation,
And thy gates Praise.

The sun shall be no more thy light by day,
Neither for brightness shall the moon give light unto thee:
But the Lord shall be unto thee an everlasting light,
And thy God thy glory.
Thy sun shall no more go down,
Neither shall thy moon withdraw itself:
For the Lord shall be thine everlasting light,
And the days of thy mourning shall be ended.

Thy people also shall be all righteous:
They shall inherit the land for ever,
The branch of my planting, the work of my hands,
That I may be glorified.
A little one shall become a thousand,
And a small one a strong nation:

THE UNKNOWN PROPHET
I the Lord will hasten it
In his time.

"The Spirit of the Lord God Is Upon Me"

The Spirit of the Lord God is upon me;
Because the Lord hath anointed me
To preach good tidings unto the meek;
He hath sent me to bind up the brokenhearted,
To proclaim liberty to the captives,
And the opening of the prison to them that are bound;
To proclaim the acceptable year of the Lord,
And the day of vengeance of our God;
To comfort all that mourn;
To appoint unto them that mourn in Zion,
To give unto them beauty for ashes,
The oil of joy for mourning,
The garment of praise for the spirit of heaviness,
That they might be called trees of righteousness,
The planting of the Lord, that he might be glorified.

And they shall build the old wastes,
They shall raise up the former desolations,
And they shall repair the waste cities,
The desolations of many generations.
And strangers shall stand and feed your flocks,
And the sons of the alien shall be your plowmen and your vine-
    dressers.
But ye shall be named the Priests of the Lord:
Men shall call you the Ministers of our God:
Ye shall eat the riches of the Gentiles,
And in their glory shall ye boast yourselves.

For your shame ye shall have double;
And for confusion they shall rejoice in their portion:
Therefore in their land they shall possess the double:
Everlasting joy shall be unto them.
For I the Lord love judgment,

THE UNKNOWN PROPHET

I hate robbery for burnt offering;
And I will direct their work in truth,
And I will make an everlasting covenant with them.
And their seed shall be known among the Gentiles,
And their offspring among the people:
All that see them shall acknowledge them,
That they are the seed which the Lord hath blessed.

I will greatly rejoice in the Lord,
My soul shall be joyful in my God;
For he hath clothed me with the garments of salvation,
He hath covered me with the robe of righteousness,
As a bridegroom decketh himself with ornaments,
And as a bride adorneth herself with her jewels.
For as the earth bringeth forth her bud,
And as the garden causeth the things that are sown in it to spring
    forth;
So the Lord God will cause righteousness and praise
To spring forth before all the nations.

"For Zion's Sake"

For Zion's sake will I not hold my peace,
And for Jerusalem's sake I will not rest,
Until the righteousness thereof go forth as brightness,
And the salvation thereof as a lamp that burneth.

And the Gentiles shall see thy righteousness,
And all kings thy glory:
And thou shalt be called by a new name,
Which the mouth of the Lord shall name.

Thou shalt also be a crown of glory in the hand of the Lord,
And a royal diadem in the hand of thy God.

Thou shalt no more be termed Forsaken;
Neither shall thy land any more be termed Desolate:
But thou shalt be called Hephzi-bah,
And thy land Beulah:

THE UNKNOWN PROPHET

For the Lord delighteth in thee,
And thy land shall be married.

For as a young man marrieth a virgin,
So shall thy sons marry thee:
And as the bridegroom rejoiceth over the bride,
So shall thy God rejoice over thee.

I have set watchmen upon thy walls, O Jerusalem,
Which shall never hold their peace day nor night:
Ye that make mention of the Lord,
Keep not silence,
And give him no rest, till he establish,
And till he make Jerusalem a praise in the earth.

The Lord hath sworn by his right hand,
And by the arm of his strength,
"Surely I will no more give thy corn
To be meat for thine enemies;
And the sons of the stranger shall not drink thy wine,
For the which thou hast laboured:
But they that have gathered it shall eat it,
And praise the Lord;
And they that have brought it together shall drink it
In the courts of my holiness."

Go through, go through the gates!
Prepare ye the way of the people!
Cast up, cast up the highway!
Gather out the stones!
Lift up a standard for the people!

Behold, the Lord hath proclaimed unto the end of the world,
"Say ye to the daughter of Zion,
'Behold, thy salvation cometh;
Behold, his reward is with him,
And his work before him.'
And they shall call them, 'Thy holy people,

THE UNKNOWN PROPHET

    The redeemed of the Lord:
    And thou shalt be called, 'Sought out,
    A city not forsaken.'"

"Who Is This That Cometh from Edom?"

"Who is this that cometh from Edom?
  With dyed garments from Bozrah?
  This that is glorious in his apparel,
  Travelling in the greatness of his strength?"

"I that speak in righteousness,
  Mighty to save."

"Wherefore art thou red in thine apparel,
  And thy garments like him that treadeth in the winefat?"

"I have trodden the winepress alone;
  And of the people there was none with me:
  For I will tread them in mine anger,
  And trample them in my fury;
  And their blood shall be sprinkled upon my garments,
  And I will stain all my raiment.
  For the day of vengeance is in mine heart,
  And the year of my redeemed is come.

And I looked, and there was none to help;
  And I wondered that there was none to uphold:
  Therefore mine own arm brought salvation unto me;
  And my fury, it upheld me.
  And I will tread down the people in mine anger,
  And make them drunk in my fury,
  And I will bring down their strength to the earth."

"I Will Mention the Lovingkindnesses of the Lord"

  I will mention the lovingkindnesses of the Lord,
  And the praises of the Lord,
  According to all that the Lord hath bestowed on us,
  And the great goodness toward the house of Israel,

THE UNKNOWN PROPHET

Which he hath bestowed on them according to his mercies,
And according to the multitude of his lovingkindnesses.
For he said, "Surely they are my people,
Children that will not lie":
So he was their Saviour.
In all their affliction he was afflicted,
And the angel of his presence saved them:
In his love and in his pity he redeemed them;
And he bore them, and carried them all the days of old.

But they rebelled, and vexed his holy Spirit:
Therefore he was turned to be their enemy,
And he fought against them.
Then he remembered the days of old,
Moses, and his people, saying,
"Where is he that brought them up out of the sea with the shepherd
    of his flock?
Where is he that put his holy Spirit within him?
That led them by the right hand of Moses
With his glorious arm,
Dividing the water before them,
To make himself an everlasting name?
That led them through the deep,
As a horse in the wilderness,
That they should not stumble?
As a beast goeth down into the valley,
The Spirit of the Lord caused him to rest":
So didst thou lead thy people,
To make thyself a glorious name.

Look down from heaven,
And behold from the habitation of thy holiness and of thy glory:
Where is thy zeal and thy strength,
The sounding of thy bowels and of thy mercies toward me?
Are they restrained?
Doubtless thou art our father,
Though Abraham be ignorant of us,

THE UNKNOWN PROPHET

And Israel acknowledge us not:
Thou, O Lord, art our father, our redeemer;
Thy name is from everlasting.

O Lord, why hast thou made us to err from thy ways,
And hardened our hearts from thy fear?
Return for thy servants' sake,
The tribes of thine inheritance.
The people of thy holiness have possessed it but a little while:
Our adversaries have trodden down thy sanctuary.
We are thine:
Thou never barest rule over them;
They were not called by thy name.

THE VISION OF OBADIAH

IN THE WORK OF OBADIAH, *the shortest book in the Old Testament, we are definitely among the Minor Prophets, not merely in the sense of brevity, but in the scale of importance. The short poems of such older writers as Nahum and Habakkuk dealt with major issues and in the grand manner. Obadiah, though actually writing shortly after the beginning of the Exile, is symptomatic of approaching decline in the weakness of both his style and content. His poem was simply a plaintive reproach addressed to the neighboring nation of Edom for not having allied itself with the Jews in their last struggle with Babylon.*

The Vision of OBADIAH

"We Have Heard a Rumour from the Lord"
Thus saith the Lord God concerning Edom:
"We have heard a rumour from the Lord,
And an ambassador is sent among the heathen:
'Arise ye, and let us rise up against her in battle.'
Behold, I have made thee small among the heathen:
Thou art greatly despised.
The pride of thine heart hath deceived thee,
Thou that dwellest in the clefts of the rock,
Whose habitation is high;
That saith in his heart, 'Who shall bring me down to the ground?'
Though thou exalt thyself as the eagle,
And though thou set thy nest among the stars,
Thence will I bring thee down," saith the Lord.

"If thieves came to thee,
If robbers by night
(How art thou cut off!),
Would they not have stolen till they had enough?
If the grapegatherers came to thee,
Would they not leave some grapes?
How are the things of Esau searched out!
How are his hidden things sought up!
All the men of thy confederacy have brought thee even to the border:
The men that were at peace with thee have deceived thee, and prevailed against thee;
They that eat thy bread have laid a wound under thee":
There is none understanding in him.

THE VISION OF OBADIAH

"Shall I not in that day," saith the Lord,
"Even destroy the wise men out of Edom,
And understanding out of the mount of Esau?
And thy mighty men, O Teman, shall be dismayed,
To the end that every one of the mount of Esau may be cut off by slaughter."

For thy violence against thy brother Jacob shame shall cover thee,
And thou shalt be cut off for ever.
In the day that thou stoodest on the other side,
In the day that the strangers carried away captive his forces,
And foreigners entered into his gates, and cast lots upon Jerusalem,
Even thou wast as one of them.
But thou shouldest not have looked on the day of thy brother
In the day that he became a stranger;
Neither shouldest thou have rejoiced over the children of Judah
In the day of their destruction;
Neither shouldest thou have spoken proudly in the day of distress.

THE MESSAGE OF HAGGAI

THE PROPHET HAGGAI *performed a meritorious and useful task in arousing the people of Jerusalem to rebuild the Temple in 520 B.C. But in his work there is no trace of the ancient splendor of prophecy, now lost forever. His writings were simply good sermons in an excellent cause.*

The Message of HAGGAI

The Rebuilding of the Temple

IN THE SECOND YEAR OF DARIUS the king, in the sixth month, in the first day of the month, came the word of the Lord by Haggai the prophet unto Zerubbabel the son of Shealtiel, governor of Judah, and to Joshua the son of Josedech, the high priest, saying,

"Thus speaketh the Lord of hosts, saying, 'This people say, "The time is not come, the time that the Lord's house should be built."'

"Now therefore," thus saith the Lord of hosts:
"Consider your ways.
  Ye have sown much, and bring in little;
  Ye eat, but ye have not enough;
  Ye drink, but ye are not filled with drink;
  Ye clothe you, but there is none warm;
  And he that earneth wages earneth wages to put it into a bag with holes."
Thus saith the Lord of hosts:
"Consider your ways.
  Go up to the mountain, and bring wood, and build the house;
  And I will take pleasure in it, and I will be glorified," saith the Lord.
"Ye looked for much, and, lo, it came to little;
  And when ye brought it home, I did blow upon it.
Why?" saith the Lord of hosts.
"Because of mine house that is waste,
  And ye run every man unto his own house.

THE MESSAGE OF HAGGAI

Therefore the heaven over you is stayed from dew,
And the earth is stayed from her fruit.
And I called for a drought upon the land,
And upon the mountains, and upon the corn,
And upon the new wine, and upon the oil,
And upon that which the ground bringeth forth,
And upon men, and upon cattle,
And upon all the labour of the hands."

Then Zerubbabel the son of Shealtiel, and Joshua the son of Josedech, the high priest, with all the remnant of the people, obeyed the voice of the Lord their God, and the words of Haggai the prophet, as the Lord their God had sent him, and the people did fear before the Lord. Then spoke Haggai the Lord's messenger in the Lord's message unto the people, saying,

" 'I am with you,' saith the Lord."

And the Lord stirred up the spirit of Zerubbabel the son of Shealtiel, governor of Judah, and the spirit of Joshua the son of Josedech, the high priest, and the spirit of all the remnant of the people; and they came and did work in the house of the Lord of hosts, their God, in the four and twentieth day of the sixth month, in the second year of Darius the king.

THE VISION OF ZECHARIAH

In the work of zechariah, *a contemporary of Haggai who assisted him in urging on the rebuilding of the Temple, the influence of Ezekiel is seen in the emphasis upon symbolism but without the wealth of suggestion that Ezekiel put behind it.*

The Angel in the Myrtle Trees

UPON THE FOUR AND TWENTIETH DAY of the eleventh month, which is the month Sebat, in the second year of Darius, came the word of the Lord unto Zechariah, the son of Berechiah, the son of Iddo the prophet, saying,

"I saw by night, and beheld a man riding upon a red horse, and he stood among the myrtle trees that were in the bottom; and behind him were there red horses, speckled, and white. Then said I, 'O my lord, what are these?' And the angel that talked with me said unto me, 'I will show thee what these be.'

"And the man that stood among the myrtle trees answered and said, 'These are they whom the Lord hath sent to walk to and fro through the earth.' And they answered the angel of the Lord that stood among the myrtle trees, and said, 'We have walked to and fro through the earth, and, behold, all the earth sitteth still, and is at rest.'

"Then the angel of the Lord answered and said, 'O Lord of hosts, how long wilt thou not have mercy on Jerusalem and on the cities of Judah, against which thou hast had indignation these threescore and ten years?' And the Lord answered the angel that talked with me with good words and comfortable words. So the angel that communed with me said unto me, 'Cry thou, saying, "Thus saith the Lord of hosts: 'I am jealous for Jerusalem and for Zion with a great jealousy. And I am very sore displeased with the heathen that are at ease: for I was but a little displeased, and they helped forward the affliction. Therefore,' thus saith the Lord; 'I am returned to Jerusalem

THE VISION OF ZECHARIAH

with mercies: my house shall be built in it,' saith the Lord of hosts, 'and a line shall be stretched forth upon Jerusalem.'" Cry yet, saying, "Thus saith the Lord of hosts: 'My cities through prosperity shall yet be spread abroad; and the Lord shall yet comfort Zion, and shall yet choose Jerusalem.'"'

"Then lifted I up mine eyes, and saw, and beheld four horns. And I said unto the angel that talked with me, 'What be these?' And he answered me, 'These are the horns which have scattered Judah, Israel, and Jerusalem.'

"And the Lord showed me four carpenters. Then said I, 'What come these to do?' And he spoke, saying, 'These are the horns which have scattered Judah, so that no man did lift up his head: but these are come to fray them, to cast out the horns of the Gentiles, which lifted up their horn over the land of Judah to scatter it.'

"I lifted up mine eyes again, and looked, and beheld a man with a measuring line in his hand. Then said I, 'Whither goest thou?' And he said unto me, 'To measure Jerusalem, to see what is the breadth thereof, and what is the length thereof.' And, behold, the angel that talked with me went forth, and another angel went out to meet him, and said unto him, 'Run, speak to this young man, saying, "Jerusalem shall be inhabited as towns without walls for the multitude of men and cattle therein"': 'For I,' saith the Lord, 'will be unto her a wall of fire round about, and will be the glory in the midst of her.'"

THE WORD OF THE LORD
THAT CAME TO JOEL

WITH JOEL, *writing in the fifth century B.C., there was a momentary return to verse and an attempt to recapture the manner of the older prophets, but he was betrayed by the slightness of his theme, which was merely a plague of locusts. Granted that such a misfortune was a very genuine calamity, it did not justify the use of language that had been appropriate enough in describing the destruction of Nineveh or the approaching doom of the whole world.*

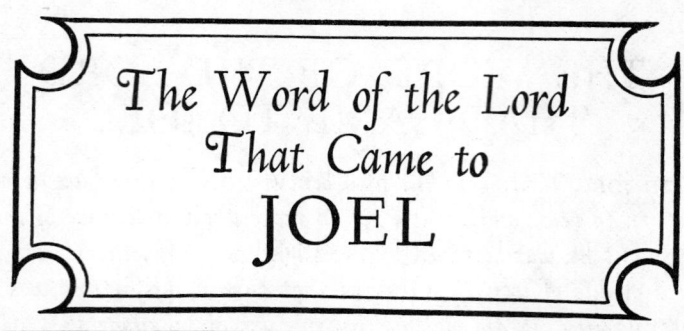

The Word of the Lord That Came to JOEL

"Alas for the Day!"

SANCTIFY YE A FAST, call a solemn assembly, gather the elders and all the inhabitants of the land into the house of the Lord your God, and cry unto the Lord,

"Alas for the day! for the day of the Lord is at hand,
And as a destruction from the Almighty shall it come.
Is not the meat cut off before our eyes,
Yea, joy and gladness from the house of our God?
The seed is rotten under their clods,
The garners are laid desolate,
The barns are broken down;
For the corn is withered.
How do the beasts groan!
The herds of cattle are perplexed,
Because they have no pasture;
Yea, the flocks of sheep are made desolate.

O Lord, to thee will I cry:
For the fire hath devoured the pastures of the wilderness,
And the flame hath burned all the trees of the field.
The beasts of the field cry also unto thee:
For the rivers of waters are dried up,
And the fire hath devoured the pastures of the wilderness.

Blow ye the trumpet in Zion,
And sound an alarm in my holy mountain:

THE WORD OF THE LORD UNTO JOEL

Let all the inhabitants of the land tremble:
For the day of the Lord cometh,
For it is nigh at hand;
A day of darkness and of gloominess,
A day of clouds and of thick darkness,
As the morning spread upon the mountains;
A great people and a strong;
There hath not been ever the like,
Neither shall be any more after it,
Even to the years of many generations

A fire devoureth before them;
And behind them a flame burneth:
The land is as the garden of Eden before them,
And behind them a desolate wilderness;
Yea, and nothing shall escape them.
The appearance of them is as the appearance of horses;
And as horsemen, so shall they run.
Like the noise of chariots on the tops of mountains shall they leap,
Like the noise of a flame of fire that devoureth the stubble,
As a strong people set in battle array.
Before their face the people shall be much pained:
All faces shall gather blackness.
They shall run like mighty men;
They shall climb the wall like men of war;
And they shall march every one on his ways,
And they shall not break their ranks:
Neither shall one thrust another;
They shall walk every one in his path:
And when they fall upon the sword, they shall not be wounded.
They shall run to and fro in the city;
They shall run upon the wall,
They shall climb up upon the houses;
They shall enter in at the windows like a thief.
The earth shall quake before them;
The heavens shall tremble:

THE WORD OF THE LORD UNTO JOEL
The sun and the moon shall be dark,
And the stars shall withdraw their shining":

And the Lord shall utter his voice before his army: for his camp is very great: for he is strong that executeth his word: for the day of the Lord is great and very terrible; and who can abide it?

MALACHI, MY MESSENGER

The short book which brings the Old Testament to a close in the traditional arrangement was not, as most readers of the Bible suppose, written by a prophet named Malachi; the word Malachi meaning messenger—in this case the anticipated "messenger of the covenant" or Messiah—refers to the subject, not the author, of the brief series of discourses that make up the book. In them is followed the rabbinical method of question and answer which appears so prominently in the writings of the Apostle Paul. The intuitive inspiration of the genuine prophets has been finally replaced in the Book of Malachi by the rationalizing attitude characteristic of later times so that, though the theme is still derived from prophecy, the manner of presentation is now that of a wholly different school.

MALACHI, My Messenger

The Messenger of the Covenant

"BEHOLD, I WILL SEND MY MESSENGER, and he shall prepare the way before me: and the Lord, whom ye seek, shall suddenly come to his temple, even the messenger of the covenant, whom ye delight in: behold, he shall come," saith the Lord of hosts.

But who may abide the day of his coming? and who shall stand when he appeareth? For he is like a refiner's fire, and like fuller's soap: and he shall sit as a refiner and purifier of silver: and he shall purify the sons of Levi, and purge them as gold and silver, that they may offer unto the Lord an offering in righteousness. Then shall the offering of Judah and Jerusalem be pleasant unto the Lord, as in the days of old, and as in former years.

"And I will come near to you to judgment; and I will be a swift witness against the sorcerers, and against the adulterers, and against false swearers, and against those that oppress the hireling in his wages, the widow, and the fatherless, and that turn aside the stranger from his right, and fear not me," saith the Lord of hosts. "For I am the Lord, I change not; therefore ye sons of Jacob are not consumed.

"Even from the days of your fathers ye are gone away from mine ordinances, and have not kept them. Return unto me, and I will return unto you," saith the Lord of hosts. "But ye said, 'Wherein shall we return?'

"Will a man rob God? Yet ye have robbed me. But ye say, 'Wherein have we robbed thee?' In tithes and offerings. Ye are

MALACHI, MY MESSENGER

cursed with a curse: for ye have robbed me, even this whole nation. Bring ye all the tithes into the storehouse, that there may be meat in mine house, and prove me now herewith," saith the Lord of hosts, "if I will not open you the windows of heaven, and pour you out a blessing, that there shall not be room enough to receive it. And I will rebuke the devourer for your sakes, and he shall not destroy the fruits of your ground; neither shall your vine cast her fruit before the time in the field," saith the Lord of hosts. "And all nations shall call you blessed: for ye shall be a delightsome land," saith the Lord of hosts.

"Your words have been stout against me," saith the Lord. "Yet ye say, 'What have we spoken so much against thee?' Ye have said, 'It is vain to serve God: and what profit is it that we have kept his ordinance, and that we have walked mournfully before the Lord of hosts? And now we call the proud happy; yea, they that work wickedness are set up; yea, they that tempt God are even delivered.'"

Then they that feared the Lord spoke often one to another: and the Lord hearkened, and heard it, and a book of remembrance was written before him for them that feared the Lord, and that thought upon his name.

"And they shall be mine," saith the Lord of hosts, "in that day when I make up my jewels; and I will spare them, as a man spareth his own son that serveth him. Then shall ye return, and discern between the righteous and the wicked, between him that serveth God and him that serveth him not. For, behold, the day cometh that shall burn as an oven; and all the proud, yea, and all that do wickedly, shall be stubble: and the day that cometh shall burn them up," saith the Lord of hosts, "that it shall leave them neither root nor branch. But unto you that fear my name shall the Sun of righteousness arise with healing in his wings; and ye shall go forth, and grow up as calves of the stall. And ye shall tread down the wicked; for they shall be ashes under the soles of your feet in the day that I shall do this," saith the Lord of hosts.

MALACHI, MY MESSENGER

"Remember ye the law of Moses my servant, which I commanded unto him in Horeb for all Israel, with the statutes and judgments.

"Behold, I will send you Elijah the prophet before the coming of the great and dreadful day of the Lord: and he shall turn the heart of the fathers to the children, and the heart of the children to their fathers, lest I come and smite the earth with a curse."

PART THREE

POETRY, DRAMA, FICTION, AND PHILOSOPHY

THE BOOK OF PSALMS

AN ANTHOLOGY OF SACRED POETRY

THE PSALMS are the Jewish hymnbook, a tremendous anthology of sacred poetry stretching over a thousand years. The earliest poems go back to the time of David (1065-1015 B.C.) and were possibly the product of his hand; many were written during the Kingdom and the Exile; the majority are post-Exilic. The collection assumed its present form probably as late as 150 B.C.

Owing to the inclusion of numerous earlier anthologies in the final compilation, several psalms appear more than once, XIV being the same as LIII, a part of XL being repeated as LXX, and parts of LVII and LX being combined as CVIII. Many of the poems express a vindictive spirit of personal revenge which is repellent to the modern reader, but by far the greater number are as enlightened in their ethics as they are lofty in their religious spirit. Certainly no other western hymnbook even distantly approaches the collection of the Psalms in literary value.

The Book of PSALMS

AN ANTHOLOGY OF SACRED POETRY

PSALM ONE

Blessed is the man that walketh not in the counsel of the ungodly,
Nor standeth in the way of sinners,
Nor sitteth in the seat of the scornful.
But his delight is in the law of the Lord;
And in his law doth he meditate day and night.
And he shall be like a tree planted by the rivers of water,
That bringeth forth his fruit in his season;
His leaf also shall not wither;
And whatsoever he doeth shall prosper.
The ungodly are not so;
But are like the chaff which the wind driveth away.
Therefore the ungodly shall not stand in the judgment,
Nor sinners in the congregation of the righteous.
For the Lord knoweth the way of the righteous;
But the way of the ungodly shall perish.

PSALM TWO

Why do the heathen rage,
And the people imagine a vain thing?
The kings of the earth set themselves,
And the rulers take counsel together,
Against the Lord, and against his anointed, saying,
"Let us break their bands asunder,
And cast away their cords from us."
He that sitteth in the heavens shall laugh;

THE BOOK OF PSALMS

The Lord shall have them in derision.
Then shall he speak unto them in his wrath,
And vex them in his sore displeasure.
"Yet have I set my king
Upon my holy hill of Zion."
I will declare the decree:
The Lord hath said unto me, "Thou art my Son;
This day have I begotten thee.
Ask of me, and I shall give thee the heathen for thine inheritance,
And the uttermost parts of the earth for thy possession.
Thou shalt break them with a rod of iron;
Thou shalt dash them in pieces like a potter's vessel."
Be wise now therefore, O ye kings;
Be instructed, ye judges of the earth.
Serve the Lord with fear,
And rejoice with trembling.
Kiss the Son, lest he be angry, and ye perish from the way,
When his wrath is kindled but a little.
Blessed are all they that put their trust in him.

PSALM FOUR

Hear me when I call, O God of my righteousness;
Thou hast enlarged me when I was in distress:
Have mercy upon me, and hear my prayer.
O ye sons of men, how long will ye turn my glory into shame?
How long will ye love vanity, and seek after leasing?
But know that the Lord hath set apart him that is godly for himself:
The Lord will hear when I call unto him.
Stand in awe, and sin not:
Commune with your own heart upon your bed, and be still.
Offer the sacrifices of righteousness,
And put your trust in the Lord.
There be many that say, "Who will show us any good?"
Lord, lift thou up the light of thy countenance upon us.
Thou hast put gladness in my heart,
More than in the time that their corn and their wine increased.

THE BOOK OF PSALMS

I will both lay me down in peace, and sleep,
For thou, Lord, only makest me dwell in safety.

PSALM SIX

O Lord, rebuke me not in thine anger,
Neither chasten me in thy hot displeasure.
Have mercy upon me, O Lord; for I am weak;
O Lord, heal me; for my bones are vexed.
My soul is also sore vexed:
But thou, O Lord, how long?
Return, O Lord, deliver my soul:
O save me for thy mercies' sake.
For in death there is no remembrance of thee:
In the grave who shall give thee thanks?
I am weary with my groaning;
All the night make I my bed to swim;
I water my couch with my tears.
Mine eye is consumed because of grief;
It waxeth old because of all mine enemies.
Depart from me, all ye workers of iniquity;
For the Lord hath heard the voice of my weeping.
The Lord hath heard my supplication;
The Lord will receive my prayer.
Let all mine enemies be ashamed and sore vexed:
Let them return and be ashamed suddenly.

PSALM EIGHT

O Lord our Lord,
How excellent is thy name in all the earth!
Who hast set thy glory above the heavens.
Out of the mouth of babes and sucklings hast thou ordained strength
Because of thine enemies,
That thou mightest still the enemy and the avenger.
When I consider thy heavens, the work of thy fingers,
The moon and the stars, which thou hast ordained;
What is man, that thou art mindful of him?

THE BOOK OF PSALMS

And the son of man, that thou visitest him?
For thou hast made him a little lower than the angels,
And hast crowned him with glory and honour.
Thou madest him to have dominion over the works of thy hands;
Thou hast put all things under his feet:
All sheep and oxen,
Yea, and the beasts of the field;
The fowl of the air, and the fish of the sea,
And whatsoever passeth through the paths of the seas.
O Lord our Lord,
How excellent is thy name in all the earth!

PSALM NINE

I will praise thee, O Lord, with my whole heart;
I will show forth all thy marvellous works.
I will be glad and rejoice in thee;
I will sing praise to thy name, O thou most High.
When mine enemies are turned back,
They shall fall and perish at thy presence.
For thou hast maintained my right and my cause;
Thou sattest in the throne judging right.
Thou hast rebuked the heathen, thou hast destroyed the wicked,
Thou hast put out their name for ever and ever.
O thou enemy, destructions are come to a perpetual end;
And thou hast destroyed cities;
Their memorial is perished with them.
But the Lord shall endure for ever;
He hath prepared his throne for judgment.
And he shall judge the world in righteousness,
He shall minister judgment to the people in uprightness.
The Lord also will be a refuge for the oppressed,
A refuge in times of trouble.
And they that know thy name will put their trust in thee,
For thou, Lord, hast not forsaken them that seek thee.
Sing praises to the Lord, which dwelleth in Zion:
Declare among the people his doings.

THE BOOK OF PSALMS

When he maketh inquisition for blood, he remembereth them;
He forgetteth not the cry of the humble.
Have mercy upon me, O Lord;
Consider my trouble which I suffer of them that hate me,
Thou that liftest me up from the gates of death:
That I may show forth all thy praise
In the gates of the daughter of Zion:
I will rejoice in thy salvation.
The heathen are sunk down in the pit that they made;
In the net which they hid is their own foot taken.
The Lord is known by the judgment which he executeth;
The wicked is snared in the work of his own hands.
The wicked shall be turned into hell,
And all the nations that forget God.
For the needy shall not alway be forgotten,
The expectation of the poor shall not perish for ever.
Arise, O Lord; let not man prevail:
Let the heathen be judged in thy sight.
Put them in fear, O Lord:
That the nations may know themselves to be but men.

PSALM FOURTEEN

The fool hath said in his heart, "There is no God."
They are corrupt, they have done abominable works,
There is none that doeth good.
The Lord looked down from heaven upon the children of men,
To see if there were any that did understand, and seek God.
They are all gone aside, they are all together become filthy:
There is none that doeth good, no, not one.
Have all the workers of iniquity no knowledge?
Who eat up my people as they eat bread,
And call not upon the Lord.
There were they in great fear:
For God is in the generation of the righteous.
Ye have shamed the counsel of the poor,
Because the Lord is his refuge.

THE BOOK OF PSALMS

Oh that the salvation of Israel were come out of Zion!
When the Lord bringeth back the captivity of his people,
Jacob shall rejoice, and Israel shall be glad.

PSALM FIFTEEN

Lord, who shall abide in thy tabernacle?
Who shall dwell in thy holy hill?
"He that walketh uprightly, and worketh righteousness,
And speaketh the truth in his heart.
He that backbiteth not with his tongue,
Nor doeth evil to his neighbour,
Nor taketh up a reproach against his neighbour.
In whose eyes a vile person is contemned;
But he honoureth them that fear the Lord.
He that sweareth to his own hurt, and changeth not.
He that putteth not out his money to usury,
Nor taketh reward against the innocent.
He that doeth these things shall never be moved."

PSALM SIXTEEN

Preserve me, O God:
For in thee do I put my trust.
O my soul, thou hast said unto the Lord,
"Thou art my Lord: my goodness extendeth not to thee";
But to the saints that are in the earth,
And to the excellent, in whom is all my delight.
Their sorrows shall be multiplied that hasten after another god:
Their drink offerings of blood will I not offer,
Nor take up their names into my lips.
The Lord is the portion of mine inheritance and of my cup:
Thou maintainest my lot.
The lines are fallen unto me in pleasant places;
Yea, I have a goodly heritage.
I will bless the Lord, who hath given me counsel;
My reins also instruct me in the night seasons.
I have set the Lord always before me:

THE BOOK OF PSALMS

Because he is at my right hand, I shall not be moved.
Therefore my heart is glad, and my glory rejoiceth;
My flesh also shall rest in hope.
For thou wilt not leave my soul in hell;
Neither wilt thou suffer thine Holy One to see corruption
Thou wilt show me the path of life:
In thy presence is fulness of joy;
At thy right hand there are pleasures for evermore.

PSALM NINETEEN

The heavens declare the glory of God;
And the firmament showeth his handiwork.
Day unto day uttereth speech,
And night unto night showeth knowledge.
There is no speech nor language,
Where their voice is not heard.
Their line is gone out through all the earth,
And their words to the end of the world.
In them hath he set a tabernacle for the sun,
Which is as a bridegroom coming out of his chamber,
And rejoiceth as a strong man to run a race.
His going forth is from the end of the heaven,
And his circuit unto the ends of it:
And there is nothing hid from the heat thereof.
The law of the Lord is perfect, converting the soul:
The testimony of the Lord is sure, making wise the simple.
The statutes of the Lord are right, rejoicing the heart:
The commandment of the Lord is pure, enlightening the eyes.
The fear of the Lord is clean, enduring for ever:
The judgments of the Lord are true and righteous altogether.
More to be desired are they than gold, yea, than much fine gold;
Sweeter also than honey and the honeycomb.
Moreover by them is thy servant warned;
In keeping of them there is great reward.
Who can understand his errors?
Cleanse thou me from secret faults.

THE BOOK OF PSALMS

Keep back thy servant also from presumptuous sins;
Let them not have dominion over me: then shall I be upright,
And I shall be innocent from the great transgression.
Let the words of my mouth, and the meditation of my heart, be
    acceptable in thy sight,
O Lord, my strength, and my redeemer.

PSALM TWENTY

The Lord hear thee in the day of trouble;
The name of the God of Jacob defend thee;
Send thee help from the sanctuary,
And strengthen thee out of Zion;
Remember all thy offerings,
And accept thy burnt sacrifice;
Grant thee according to thine own heart,
And fulfil all thy counsel.
We will rejoice in thy salvation,
And in the name of our God we will set up our banners:
The Lord fulfil all thy petitions.
Now know I that the Lord saveth his anointed;
He will hear him from his holy heaven
With the saving strength of his right hand.
Some trust in chariots, and some in horses:
But we will remember the name of the Lord our God.
They are brought down and fallen:
But we are risen, and stand upright.
Save, Lord:
Let the king hear us when we call.

PSALM TWENTY-ONE

The king shall joy in thy strength, O Lord;
And in thy salvation how greatly shall he rejoice!
Thou hast given him his heart's desire,
And hast not withheld the request of his lips.
For thou preventest him with the blessings of goodness;
Thou settest a crown of pure gold on his head.

THE BOOK OF PSALMS

He asked life of thee, and thou gavest it him,
Even length of days for ever and ever.
His glory is great in thy salvation;
Honour and majesty hast thou laid upon him.
For thou hast made him most blessed for ever;
Thou hast made him exceeding glad with thy countenance.
For the king trusteth in the Lord,
And through the mercy of the most High he shall not be moved.
Thine hand shall find out all thine enemies;
Thy right hand shall find out those that hate thee.
Thou shalt make them as a fiery oven in the time of thine anger:
The Lord shall swallow them up in his wrath,
And the fire shall devour them.
Their fruit shalt thou destroy from the earth,
And their seed from among the children of men.
For they intended evil against thee:
They imagined a mischievous device, which they are not able to perform.
Therefore shalt thou make them turn their back,
When thou shalt make ready thine arrows upon thy strings against the face of them.
Be thou exalted, Lord, in thine own strength:
So will we sing and praise thy power.

PSALM TWENTY-TWO

My God, my God, why hast thou forsaken me?
Why art thou so far from helping me, and from the words of my
    roaring?
O my God, I cry in the daytime, but thou hearest not;
And in the night season, and am not silent.
But thou art holy,
O thou that inhabitest the praises of Israel.
Our fathers trusted in thee;
They trusted, and thou didst deliver them.
They cried unto thee, and were delivered;
They trusted in thee, and were not confounded.

THE BOOK OF PSALMS

But I am a worm, and no man;
A reproach of men, and despised of the people.
All they that see me laugh me to scorn;
They shoot out the lip, they shake the head, saying,
"He trusted on the Lord that he would deliver him:
Let him deliver him, seeing he delighted in him."
But thou art he that took me out of the womb:
Thou didst make me hope when I was upon my mother's breasts.
I was cast upon thee from the womb:
Thou art my God from my mother's belly.
Be not far from me; for trouble is near;
For there is none to help.
Many bulls have compassed me;
Strong bulls of Bashan have beset me round.
They gaped upon me with their mouths,
As a ravening and a roaring lion.
I am poured out like water,
And all my bones are out of joint:
My heart is like wax;
It is melted in the midst of my bowels.
My strength is dried up like a potsherd;
And my tongue cleaveth to my jaws;
And thou hast brought me into the dust of death.
For dogs have compassed me:
The assembly of the wicked have inclosed me;
They pierced my hands and my feet.
I may tell all my bones:
They look and stare upon me.
They part my garments among them,
And cast lots upon my vesture.
But be not thou far from me, O Lord:
O my strength, haste thee to help me.
Deliver my soul from the sword,
My darling from the power of the dog.
Save me from the lion's mouth;
For thou hast heard me from the horns of the unicorns.

THE BOOK OF PSALMS

I will declare thy name unto my brethren;
In the midst of the congregation will I praise thee.
Ye that fear the Lord, praise him;
All ye the seed of Jacob, glorify him;
And fear him, all ye the seed of Israel.
For he hath not despised nor abhorred the affliction of the afflicted;
Neither hath he hid his face from him;
But when he cried unto him, he heard.
My praise shall be of thee in the great congregation:
I will pay my vows before them that fear him.
The meek shall eat and be satisfied;
They shall praise the Lord that seek him;
Your heart shall live for ever.
All the ends of the world shall remember and turn unto the Lord,
And all the kindreds of the nations shall worship before thee.
For the kingdom is the Lord's;
And he is the governor among the nations.
All they that be fat upon earth shall eat and worship;
All they that go down to the dust shall bow before him,
And none can keep alive his own soul.
A seed shall serve him;
It shall be accounted to the Lord for a generation.
They shall come, and shall declare his righteousness
Unto a people that shall be born, that he hath done this.

PSALM TWENTY-THREE

The Lord is my shepherd; I shall not want.
He maketh me to lie down in green pastures;
He leadeth me beside the still waters.
He restoreth my soul;
He leadeth me in the paths of righteousness for his name's sake.
Yea, though I walk through the valley of the shadow of death,
I will fear no evil: for thou art with me;
Thy rod and thy staff they comfort me.
Thou preparest a table before me in the presence of mine enemies:
Thou anointest my head with oil; my cup runneth over.

THE BOOK OF PSALMS

Surely goodness and mercy shall follow me all the days of my life,
And I will dwell in the house of the Lord for ever.

PSALM TWENTY-FOUR

The earth is the Lord's, and the fulness thereof;
The world, and they that dwell therein.
For he hath founded it upon the seas,
And established it upon the floods.
Who shall ascend into the hill of the Lord?
Or who shall stand in his holy place?
He that hath clean hands, and a pure heart;
Who hath not lifted up his soul unto vanity, nor sworn deceitfully.
He shall receive the blessing from the Lord,
And righteousness from the God of his salvation.
This is the generation of them that seek him,
That seek thy face, O Jacob.
Lift up your heads, O ye gates;
And be ye lift up, ye everlasting doors;
And the King of glory shall come in.
Who is this King of glory?
The Lord strong and mighty,
The Lord mighty in battle.
Lift up your heads, O ye gates;
Even lift them up, ye everlasting doors;
And the King of glory shall come in.
Who is this King of glory?
The Lord of hosts,
He is the King of glory.

PSALM TWENTY-SEVEN

The Lord is my light and my salvation; whom shall I fear?
The Lord is the strength of my life; of whom shall I be afraid?
When the wicked, even mine enemies and my foes,
Came upon me to eat up my flesh, they stumbled and fell.
Though a host should encamp against me,
My heart shall not fear:

THE BOOK OF PSALMS

Though war should rise against me,
In this will I be confident.
One thing have I desired of the Lord, that will I seek after;
That I may dwell in the house of the Lord all the days of my life,
To behold the beauty of the Lord, and to enquire in his temple.
For in the time of trouble he shall hide me in his pavilion;
In the secret of his tabernacle shall he hide me;
He shall set me up upon a rock.
And now shall mine head be lifted up above mine enemies round
    about me:
Therefore will I offer in his tabernacle sacrifices of joy;
I will sing, yea, I will sing praises unto the Lord.
Hear, O Lord, when I cry with my voice:
Have mercy also upon me, and answer me.
When thou saidst, "Seek ye my face," my heart said unto thee,
"Thy face, Lord, will I seek."
Hide not thy face far from me;
Put not thy servant away in anger:
Thou hast been my help;
Leave me not, neither forsake me, O God of my salvation.
When my father and my mother forsake me,
Then the Lord will take me up.
Teach me thy way, O Lord,
And lead me in a plain path,
Because of mine enemies.
Deliver me not over unto the will of mine enemies:
For false witnesses are risen up against me, and such as breathe out
    cruelty.
I had fainted, unless I had believed to see the goodness of the Lord
In the land of the living. Wait on the Lord;
Be of good courage, and he shall strengthen thine heart;
Wait, I say, on the Lord.

PSALM TWENTY-NINE

Give unto the Lord, O ye mighty,
Give unto the Lord glory and strength.

THE BOOK OF PSALMS

Give unto the Lord the glory due unto his name;
Worship the Lord in the beauty of holiness.
The voice of the Lord is upon the waters:
The God of glory thundereth,
The Lord is upon many waters.
The voice of the Lord is powerful;
The voice of the Lord is full of majesty.
The voice of the Lord breaketh the cedars;
Yea, the Lord breaketh the cedars of Lebanon.
He maketh them also to skip like a calf;
Lebanon and Sirion like a young unicorn.
The voice of the Lord divideth the flames of fire.
The voice of the Lord shaketh the wilderness;
The Lord shaketh the wilderness of Kadesh.
The voice of the Lord maketh the hinds to calve,
And discovereth the forests:
And in his temple doth every one speak of his glory.
The Lord sitteth upon the flood;
Yea, the Lord sitteth King for ever.
The Lord will give strength unto his people;
The Lord will bless his people with peace.

PSALM THIRTY

I will extol thee, O Lord; for thou hast lifted me up,
And hast not made my foes to rejoice over me.
O Lord my God,
I cried unto thee, and thou hast healed me.
O Lord, thou hast brought up my soul from the grave;
Thou hast kept me alive, that I should not go down to the pit.
Sing unto the Lord, O ye saints of his,
And give thanks at the remembrance of his holiness.
For his anger endureth but a moment;
In his favour is life:
Weeping may endure for a night,
But joy cometh in the morning.

THE BOOK OF PSALMS

And in my prosperity I said,
"I shall never be moved."
Lord, by thy favour thou hast made my mountain to stand strong:
Thou didst hide thy face, and I was troubled.
I cried to thee, O Lord;
And unto the Lord I made supplication:
"What profit is there in my blood, when I go down to the pit?
Shall the dust praise thee? shall it declare thy truth?
Hear, O Lord, and have mercy upon me:
Lord, be thou my helper."
Thou hast turned for me my mourning into dancing;
Thou hast put off my sackcloth, and girded me with gladness;
To the end that my glory may sing praise to thee, and not be silent.
O Lord my God, I will give thanks unto thee for ever.

PSALM THIRTY-SEVEN

Fret not thyself because of evildoers,
Neither be thou envious against the workers of iniquity.
For they shall soon be cut down like the grass,
And wither as the green herb.
Trust in the Lord, and do good;
So shalt thou dwell in the land, and verily thou shalt be fed.
Delight thyself also in the Lord;
And he shall give thee the desires of thine heart.
Commit thy way unto the Lord;
Trust also in him, and he shall bring it to pass.
And he shall bring forth thy righteousness as the light,
And thy judgment as the noonday.
Rest in the Lord, and wait patiently for him:
Fret not thyself because of him who prospereth in his way,
Because of the man who bringeth wicked devices to pass.
Cease from anger, and forsake wrath:
Fret not thyself in any wise to do evil.
For evildoers shall be cut off:
But those that wait upon the Lord, they shall inherit the earth.

THE BOOK OF PSALMS

For yet a little while, and the wicked shall not be:
Yea, thou shalt diligently consider his place, and it shall not be.
But the meek shall inherit the earth;
And shall delight themselves in the abundance of peace.
The wicked plotteth against the just,
And gnasheth upon him with his teeth.
The Lord shall laugh at him:
For he seeth that his day is coming.
The wicked have drawn out the sword, and have bent their bow,
To cast down the poor and needy, and to slay such as be of upright conversation.
Their sword shall enter into their own heart,
And their bows shall be broken.
A little that a righteous man hath
Is better than the riches of many wicked.
For the arms of the wicked shall be broken:
But the Lord upholdeth the righteous.
The Lord knoweth the days of the upright:
And their inheritance shall be for ever.
They shall not be ashamed in the evil time:
And in the days of famine they shall be satisfied.
But the wicked shall perish,
And the enemies of the Lord shall be as the fat of lambs:
They shall consume;
Into smoke shall they consume away.
The wicked borroweth, and payeth not again:
But the righteous showeth mercy, and giveth.
For such as be blessed of him shall inherit the earth;
And they that be cursed of him shall be cut off.
The steps of a good man are ordered by the Lord,
And he delighteth in his way.
Though he fall, he shall not be utterly cast down,
For the Lord upholdeth him with his hand.
I have been young, and now am old;
Yet have I not seen the righteous forsaken,

THE BOOK OF PSALMS
Nor his seed begging bread.
He is ever merciful, and lendeth;
And his seed is blessed.
Depart from evil, and do good;
And dwell for evermore.
For the Lord loveth judgment,
And forsaketh not his saints;
They are preserved for ever:
But the seed of the wicked shall be cut off.
The righteous shall inherit the land,
And dwell therein for ever.
The mouth of the righteous speaketh wisdom,
And his tongue talketh of judgment.
The law of his God is in his heart;
None of his steps shall slide.
The wicked watcheth the righteous,
And seeketh to slay him.
The Lord will not leave him in his hand,
Nor condemn him when he is judged.
Wait on the Lord, and keep his way,
And he shall exalt thee to inherit the land:
When the wicked are cut off, thou shalt see it.
I have seen the wicked in great power,
And spreading himself like a green bay tree.
Yet he passed away, and, lo, he was not;
Yea, I sought him, but he could not be found.
Mark the perfect man, and behold the upright:
For the end of that man is peace.
But the transgressors shall be destroyed together:
The end of the wicked shall be cut off.
But the salvation of the righteous is of the Lord: he is
 their strength in the time of trouble.
And the Lord shall help them, and deliver them:
He shall deliver them from the wicked, and save them,
Because they trust in him.

THE BOOK OF PSALMS

PSALM THIRTY-NINE

I said, "I will take heed to my ways,
That I sin not with my tongue:
I will keep my mouth with a bridle,
While the wicked is before me."
I was dumb with silence, I held my peace, even from good;
And my sorrow was stirred.
My heart was hot within me,
While I was musing the fire burned:
Then spoke I with my tongue.
"Lord, make me to know mine end,
And the measure of my days, what it is;
That I may know how frail I am.
Behold, thou hast made my days as a handbreadth;
And mine age is as nothing before thee:
Verily every man at his best state is altogether vanity.
Surely every man walketh in a vain show;
Surely they are disquieted in vain:
He heapeth up riches, and knoweth not who shall gather them.
And now, Lord, what wait I for?
My hope is in thee.
Deliver me from all my transgressions;
Make me not the reproach of the foolish.
I was dumb, I opened not my mouth;
Because thou didst it.
Remove thy stroke away from me:
I am consumed by the blow of thine hand.
When thou with rebukes dost correct man for inquity,
Thou makest his beauty to consume away like a moth:
Surely every man is vanity.
Hear my prayer, O Lord, and give ear unto my cry:
Hold not thy peace at my tears:
For I am a stranger with thee,
And a sojourner, as all my fathers were.

THE BOOK OF PSALMS

O spare me, that I may recover strength,
Before I go hence, and be no more."

PSALM FORTY-TWO

As the hart panteth after the water brooks,
So panteth my soul after thee, O God.
My soul thirsteth for God, for the living God:
When shall I come and appear before God?
My tears have been my meat day and night,
While they continually say unto me, "Where is thy God?"
When I remember these things, I pour out my soul in me:
For I had gone with the multitude, I went with them to the
    house of God,
With the voice of joy and praise, with a multitude that kept
    holy-day.
Why art thou cast down, O my soul?
And why art thou disquieted in me?
Hope thou in God: for I shall yet praise him
For the help of his countenance.
O my God, my soul is cast down within me:
Therefore will I remember thee from the land of Jordan,
And of the Hermonites, from the hill Mizar.
Deep calleth unto deep at the noise of thy waterspouts;
All thy waves and thy billows are gone over me.
Yet the Lord will command his lovingkindness in the daytime,
And in the night his song shall be with me,
And my prayer unto the God of my life.
I will say unto God my rock, "Why hast thou forgotten me?
Why go I mourning because of the oppression of the enemy?"
As with a sword in my bones, mine enemies reproach me,
While they say daily unto me, "Where is thy God?"
Why art thou cast down, O my soul?
And why art thou disquieted within me?
Hope thou in God: for I shall yet praise him,
Who is the health of my countenance, and my God.

THE BOOK OF PSALMS

PSALM FORTY-THREE

Judge me, O God, and plead my cause against an ungodly nation;
O deliver me from the deceitful and unjust man.
For thou art the God of my strength;
Why dost thou cast me off?
Why go I mourning because of the oppression of the enemy?
O send out thy light and thy truth:
Let them lead me;
Let them bring me unto thy holy hill, and to thy tabernacles.
Then will I go unto the altar of God, unto God my exceeding joy:
Yea, upon the harp will I praise thee, O God my God.
Why art thou cast down, O my soul?
And why art thou disquieted within me?
Hope in God: for I shall yet praise him,
Who is the health of my countenance, and my God.

PSALM FORTY-FIVE

My heart is inditing a good matter;
I speak of the things which I have made touching the king;
My tongue is the pen of a ready writer.
Thou art fairer than the children of men;
Grace is poured into thy lips:
Therefore God hath blessed thee for ever.
Gird thy sword upon thy thigh, O most mighty,
With thy glory and thy majesty.
And in thy majesty ride prosperously
Because of truth and meekness and righteousness;
And thy right hand shall teach thee terrible things.
Thine arrows are sharp
In the heart of the king's enemies;
Whereby the people fall under thee.
Thy throne, O God, is for ever and ever;
The sceptre of thy kingdom is a right sceptre.
Thou lovest righteousness, and hatest wickedness:

THE BOOK OF PSALMS

Therefore God, thy God, hath anointed thee
With the oil of gladness above thy fellows.
All thy garments smell of myrrh, and aloes, and cassia,
Out of the ivory palaces, whereby they have made thee glad.
Kings' daughters were among thy honourable women;
Upon thy right hand did stand the queen in gold of Ophir.
Hearken, O daughter, and consider, and incline thine ear;
Forget also thine own people, and thy father's house;
So shall the king greatly desire thy beauty:
For he is thy Lord; and worship thou him.
And the daughter of Tyre shall be there with a gift;
Even the rich among the people shall intreat thy favour.
The king's daughter is all glorious within;
Her clothing is of wrought gold.
She shall be brought unto the king in raiment of needlework;
The virgins her companions that follow her shall be brought unto thee.
With gladness and rejoicing shall they be brought;
They shall enter into the king's palace.
Instead of thy fathers shall be thy children,
Whom thou mayest make princes in all the earth.
I will make thy name to be remembered in all generations:
Therefore shall the people praise thee for ever and ever.

PSALM FORTY-SIX

God is our refuge and strength,
A very present help in trouble.
Therefore will not we fear, though the earth be removed,
And though the mountains be carried into the midst of the sea;
Though the waters thereof roar and be troubled,
Though the mountains shake with the swelling thereof.
There is a river, the streams whereof shall make glad the city of God,
The holy place of the tabernacles of the most High.
God is in the midst of her; she shall not be moved:

THE BOOK OF PSALMS

God shall help her, and that right early.
The heathen raged, the kingdoms were moved;
He uttered his voice, the earth melted.
The Lord of hosts is with us;
The God of Jacob is our refuge.
Come, behold the works of the Lord,
What desolations he hath made in the earth.
He maketh wars to cease unto the end of the earth;
He breaketh the bow, and cutteth the spear in sunder;
He burneth the chariot in the fire.
"Be still, and know that I am God:
I will be exalted among the heathen,
I will be exalted in the earth."
The Lord of hosts is with us;
The God of Jacob is our refuge.

PSALM FORTY-SEVEN

O clap your hands, all ye people;
Shout unto God with the voice of triumph.
For the Lord most high is terrible;
He is a great King over all the earth.
He shall subdue the people under us,
And the nations under our feet.
He shall choose our inheritance for us,
The excellency of Jacob whom he loved.
God is gone up with a shout,
The Lord with the sound of a trumpet.
Sing praises to God, sing praises:
Sing praises unto our King, sing praises.
For God is the King of all the earth:
Sing ye praises with understanding.
God reigneth over the heathen;
God sitteth upon the throne of his holiness.
The princes of the people are gathered together,
Even the people of the God of Abraham:

THE BOOK OF PSALMS

For the shields of the earth belong unto God;
He is greatly exalted.

PSALM FORTY-EIGHT

Great is the Lord, and greatly to be praised
In the city of our God, in the mountain of his holiness.
Beautiful for situation, the joy of the whole earth,
Is Mount Zion, on the sides of the north,
The city of the great King.
God is known in her palaces for a refuge.
For, lo, the kings were assembled,
They passed by together.
They saw it, and so they marvelled;
They were troubled, and hastened away.
Fear took hold upon them there,
And pain, as of a woman in travail.
Thou breakest the ships of Tarshish with an east wind.
As we have heard, so have we seen
In the city of the Lord of hosts, in the city of our God:
God will establish it for ever.
We have thought of thy lovingkindness, O God,
In the midst of thy temple.
According to thy name, O God,
So is thy praise unto the ends of the earth:
Thy right hand is full of righteousness.
Let Mount Zion rejoice,
Let the daughters of Judah be glad,
Because of thy judgments.
Walk about Zion, and go round about her;
Tell the towers thereof.
Mark ye well her bulwarks,
Consider her palaces;
That ye may tell it to the generation following.
For this God is our God for ever and ever;
He will be our guide even unto death.

THE BOOK OF PSALMS

PSALM FORTY-NINE

Hear this, all ye people;
Give ear, all ye inhabitants of the world,
Both low and high,
Rich and poor, together.
My mouth shall speak of wisdom,
And the meditation of my heart shall be of understanding.
I will incline mine ear to a parable;
I will open my dark saying upon the harp.
Wherefore should I fear in the days of evil,
When the iniquity of my heels shall compass me about?
They that trust in their wealth,
And boast themselves in the multitude of their riches,
None of them can by any means redeem his brother,
Nor give to God a ransom for him (for the redemption of their
    soul is precious,
And it ceaseth for ever) that he should still live for ever,
And not see corruption.
For he seeth that wise men die,
Likewise the fool and the brutish person perish,
And leave their wealth to others.
Their inward thought is that their houses shall continue for ever,
And their dwelling places to all generations;
They call their lands after their own names.
Nevertheless man being in honour abideth not;
He is like the beasts that perish.
This their way is their folly:
Yet their posterity approve their sayings.
Like sheep they are laid in the grave;
Death shall feed on them;
And the upright shall have dominion over them in the morning;
And their beauty shall consume in the grave from their dwelling.
But God will redeem my soul from the power of the grave:
For he shall receive me.
Be not thou afraid when one is made rich,

THE BOOK OF PSALMS

When the glory of his house is increased;
For when he dieth he shall carry nothing away;
His glory shall not descend after him.
Though while he lived he blessed his soul,
And men will praise thee, when thou doest well to thyself,
He shall go to the generation of his fathers;
They shall never see light. Man that is in honour, and understand-
 eth not,
Is like the beasts that perish.

PSALM FIFTY-ONE

Have mercy upon me, O God, according to thy lovingkindness:
According unto the multitude of thy tender mercies blot out my
 transgressions.
Wash me thoroughly from mine iniquity,
And cleanse me from my sin.
For I acknowledge my transgressions,
And my sin is ever before me.
Against thee, thee only, have I sinned,
And done this evil in thy sight:
That thou mightest be justified when thou speakest,
And be clear when thou judgest.
Behold, I was shaped in iniquity;
And in sin did my mother conceive me.
Behold, thou desirest truth in the inward parts,
And in the hidden part thou shalt make me to know wisdom.
Purge me with hyssop, and I shall be clean:
Wash me, and I shall be whiter than snow.
Make me to hear joy and gladness;
That the bones which thou hast broken may rejoice.
Hide thy face from my sins,
And blot out all mine iniquities.
Create in me a clean heart, O God;
And renew a right spirit within me.
Cast me not away from thy presence;
And take not thy holy spirit from me.

THE BOOK OF PSALMS

Restore unto me the joy of thy salvation;
And uphold me with thy free spirit.
Then will I teach transgressors thy ways;
And sinners shall be converted unto thee.
Deliver me from bloodguiltiness, O God, thou God of my salvation:
And my tongue shall sing aloud of thy righteousness.
O Lord, open thou my lips;
And my mouth shall show forth thy praise.
For thou desirest not sacrifice; else would I give it:
Thou delightest not in burnt offering.
The sacrifices of God are a broken spirit;
A broken and a contrite heart, O God, thou wilt not despise.
Do good in thy good pleasure unto Zion;
Build thou the walls of Jerusalem.
Then shalt thou be pleased with the sacrifices of righteousness, with
    burnt offering and whole burnt offering:
Then shall they offer bullocks upon thine altar.

PSALM SIXTY-TWO

Truly my soul waiteth upon God:
From him cometh my salvation.
He only is my rock and my salvation;
He is my defence; I shall not be greatly moved.
How long will ye imagine mischief against a man?
Ye shall be slain all of you:
As a bowing wall shall ye be, and as a tottering fence.
They only consult to cast him down from his excellency;
They delight in lies;
They bless with their mouth, but they curse inwardly.
My soul, wait thou only upon God;
For my expectation is from him.
He only is my rock and my salvation:
He is my defence; I shall not be moved.
In God is my salvation and my glory;
The rock of my strength, and my refuge, is in God.
Trust in him at all times, ye people;

THE BOOK OF PSALMS

Pour out your heart before him:
God is a refuge for us.
Surely men of low degree are vanity, and men of high degree are a lie:
To be laid in the balance, they are altogether lighter than vanity.
Trust not in oppression,
And become not vain in robbery;
If riches increase, set not your heart upon them.
God hath spoken once;
Twice have I heard this;
That power belongeth unto God.
Also unto thee, O Lord, belongeth mercy:
For thou renderest to every man according to his work.

PSALM SIXTY-THREE

O God, thou art my God; early will I seek thee:
My soul thirsteth for thee, my flesh longeth for thee
In a dry and thirsty land, where no water is;
To see thy power and thy glory,
So as I have seen thee in the sanctuary.
Because thy lovingkindness is better than life,
My lips shall praise thee.
Thus will I bless thee while I live;
I will lift up my hands in thy name.
My soul shall be satisfied as with marrow and fatness;
And my mouth shall praise thee with joyful lips,
When I remember thee upon my bed,
And meditate on thee in the night watches.
Because thou hast been my help,
Therefore in the shadow of thy wings will I rejoice.
My soul followeth hard after thee:
Thy right hand upholdeth me.
But those that seek my soul, to destroy it,
Shall go into the lower parts of the earth.
They shall fall by the sword;
They shall be a portion for foxes.
But the king shall rejoice in God;

THE BOOK OF PSALMS
Every one that sweareth by him shall glory:
But the mouth of them that speak lies shall be stopped.

PSALM SIXTY-FIVE

Praise waiteth for thee, O God, in Zion,
And unto thee shall the vow be performed.
O thou that hearest prayer,
Unto thee shall all flesh come.
Iniquities prevail against me:
As for our transgressions, thou shalt purge them away.
Blessed is the man whom thou choosest, and causest to approach
    unto thee,
That he may dwell in thy courts:
We shall be satisfied with the goodness of thy house,
Even of thy holy temple.
By terrible things in righteousness wilt thou answer us,
O God of our salvation;
Who art the confidence of all the ends of the earth,
And of them that are afar off upon the sea:
Which by his strength setteth fast the mountains;
Being girded with power:
Which stilleth the noise of the seas, the noise of their waves,
And the tumult of the people.
They also that dwell in the uttermost parts are afraid at thy tokens:
Thou makest the outgoings of the morning and evening to rejoice.
Thou visitest the earth, and waterest it,
Thou greatly enrichest it
With the river of God, which is full of water:
Thou preparest them corn, when thou hast so provided for it.
Thou waterest the ridges thereof abundantly;
Thou settlest the furrows thereof:
Thou makest it soft with showers;
Thou blessest the springing thereof.
Thou crownest the year with thy goodness,
And thy paths drop fatness.

THE BOOK OF PSALMS

They drop upon the pastures of the wilderness,
And the little hills rejoice on every side.
The pastures are clothed with flocks;
The valleys also are covered over with corn;
They shout for joy, they also sing.

PSALM SIXTY-SEVEN

God be merciful unto us, and bless us,
And cause his face to shine upon us;
That thy way may be known upon earth,
Thy saving health among all nations.
Let the people praise thee, O God;
Let all the people praise thee.
O let the nations be glad and sing for joy:
For thou shalt judge the people righteously,
And govern the nations upon earth.
Let the people praise thee, O God;
Let all the people praise thee.
Then shall the earth yield her increase;
And God, even our own God, shall bless us.
God shall bless us;
And all the ends of the earth shall fear him.

PSALM SIXTY-EIGHT

Let God arise, let his enemies be scattered;
Let them also that hate him flee before him.
As smoke is driven away, so drive them away;
As wax melteth before the fire,
So let the wicked perish at the presence of God.
But let the righteous be glad; let them rejoice before God;
Yea, let them exceedingly rejoice.
Sing unto God, sing praises to his name:
Extol him that rideth upon the heavens
By his name JAH, and rejoice before him.
A father of the fatherless, and a judge of the widows,

THE BOOK OF PSALMS

Is God in his holy habitation.
God setteth the solitary in families;
He bringeth out those which are bound with chains:
But the rebellious dwell in a dry land.
O God, when thou wentest forth before thy people,
When thou didst march through the wilderness,
The earth shook,
The heavens also dropped at the presence of God;
Even Sinai itself was moved at the presence of God, the God of
　　Israel.
Thou, O God, didst send a plentiful rain,
Whereby thou didst confirm thine inheritance, when it was weary.
Thy congregation hath dwelt therein:
Thou, O God, hast prepared of thy goodness for the poor.
The Lord gave the word:
Great was the company of those that published it.
Kings of armies did flee apace;
And she that tarried at home divided the spoil.
Though ye have lain among the pots,
Yet shall ye be as the wings of a dove covered with silver,
And her feathers with yellow gold.
When the Almighty scattered kings in it,
It was as snow in Zalmon.
The hill of God is as the hill of Bashan;
A high hill as the hill of Bashan.
Why leap ye, ye high hills?
This is the hill which God desireth to dwell in;
Yea, the Lord will dwell in it for ever.
The chariots of God are twenty thousand, even thousands of angels:
The Lord is among them, as in Sinai, in the holy place.
Thou hast ascended on high, thou hast led captivity captive;
Thou hast received gifts for men;
Yea, for the rebellious also, that the Lord God might dwell among
　　them.
Blessed be the Lord, who daily loadeth us with benefits,

THE BOOK OF PSALMS

Even the God of our salvation.
He that is our God is the God of salvation;
And unto God the Lord belong the issues from death.
But God shall wound the head of his enemies,
And the hairy scalp of such a one as goeth on still in his trespasses.
The Lord said, "I will bring again from Bashan,
I will bring my people again from the depths of the sea;
That thy foot may be dipped in the blood of thine enemies,
And the tongue of thy dogs in the same."
They have seen thy goings, O God;
Even the goings of my God, my King, in the sanctuary.
The singers went before, the players on instruments followed after;
Among them were the damsels playing with timbrels.
Bless ye God in the congregations,
Even the Lord, from the fountain of Israel.
There is little Benjamin with their ruler,
The princes of Judah and their council,
The princes of Zebulun, and the princes of Naphtali.
Thy God hath commanded thy strength:
Strengthen, O God, that which thou hast wrought for us.
Because of thy temple at Jerusalem
Shall kings bring presents unto thee.
Rebuke the company of spearmen,
The multitude of the bulls, with the calves of the people,
Till every one submit himself with pieces of silver;
Scatter thou the people that delight in war.
Princes shall come out of Egypt;
Ethiopia shall soon stretch out her hands unto God.
Sing unto God, ye kingdoms of the earth;
O sing praises unto the Lord,
To him that rideth upon the heavens of heavens, which were of old;
Lo, he doth send out his voice, and that a mighty voice.
Ascribe ye strength unto God;
His excellency is over Israel,
And his strength is in the clouds.

THE BOOK OF PSALMS

O God, thou art terrible out of thy holy places.
The God of Israel is he that giveth strength and power unto his
    people.
Blessed be God.

PSALM SEVENTY-TWO

Give the king thy judgments, O God,
And thy righteousness unto the king's son.
He shall judge thy people with righteousness,
And thy poor with judgment.
The mountains shall bring peace to the people,
And the little hills, by righteousness.
He shall judge the poor of the people,
He shall save the children of the needy,
And shall break in pieces the oppressor.
They shall fear thee as long as the sun and moon endure,
Throughout all generations.
He shall come down like rain upon the mown grass,
As showers that water the earth.
In his days shall the righteous flourish;
And abundance of peace so long as the moon endureth.
He shall have dominion also from sea to sea,
And from the river unto the ends of the earth.
They that dwell in the wilderness shall bow before him;
And his enemies shall lick the dust.
The kings of Tarshish and of the isles shall bring presents;
The kings of Sheba and Seba shall offer gifts.
Yea, all kings shall fall down before him;
All nations shall serve him.
For he shall deliver the needy when he crieth;
The poor also, and him that hath no helper.
He shall spare the poor and needy,
And shall save the souls of the needy.
He shall redeem their soul from deceit and violence,
And precious shall their blood be in his sight.
And he shall live, and to him shall be given of the gold of Sheba:

THE BOOK OF PSALMS

Prayer also shall be made for him continually;
And daily shall he be praised.
There shall be a handful of corn in the earth upon the top of the mountains;
The fruit thereof shall shake like Lebanon:
And they of the city shall flourish like grass of the earth.
His name shall endure for ever;
His name shall be continued as long as the sun,
And men shall be blessed in him;
All nations shall call him blessed.
Blessed be the Lord God, the God of Israel,
Who only doeth wondrous things.
And blessed be his glorious name for ever;
And let the whole earth be filled with his glory.
Amen, and Amen.

PSALM EIGHTY-FOUR

How amiable are thy tabernacles,
O Lord of hosts!
My soul longeth, yea, even fainteth for the courts of the Lord;
My heart and my flesh crieth out for the living God.
Yea, the sparrow hath found a house,
And the swallow a nest for herself, where she may lay her young,
Even thine altars, O Lord of hosts,
My King, and my God.
Blessed are they that dwell in thy house:
They will be still praising thee.
Blessed is the man whose strength is in thee;
In whose heart are the ways of them.
Who passing through the valley of Baca make it a well;
The rain also filleth the pools.
They go from strength to strength,
Every one of them in Zion appeareth before God.
O Lord God of hosts, hear my prayer:
Give ear, O God of Jacob.
Behold, O God our shield,

THE BOOK OF PSALMS

And look upon the face of thine anointed.
For a day in thy courts is better than a thousand.
I had rather be a doorkeeper in the house of my God,
Than to dwell in the tents of wickedness.
For the Lord God is a sun and shield:
The Lord will give grace and glory:
No good thing will he withhold from them that walk uprightly.
O Lord of hosts,
Blessed is the man that trusteth in thee.

PSALM EIGHTY-FIVE

Lord, thou hast been favourable unto thy land;
Thou hast brought back the captivity of Jacob.
Thou hast forgiven the iniquity of thy people,
Thou hast covered all their sin.
Thou hast taken away all thy wrath;
Thou hast turned thyself from the fierceness of thine anger.
Turn us, O God of our salvation,
And cause thine anger toward us to cease.
Wilt thou be angry with us for ever?
Wilt thou draw out thine anger to all generations?
Wilt thou not revive us again,
That thy people may rejoice in thee?
Show us thy mercy, O Lord,
And grant us thy salvation.
I will hear what God the Lord will speak,
For he will speak peace unto his people, and to his saints:
But let them not turn again to folly.
Surely his salvation is nigh them that fear him,
That glory may dwell in our land.
Mercy and truth are met together;
Righteousness and peace have kissed each other.
Truth shall spring out of the earth;
And righteousness shall look down from heaven.
Yea, the Lord shall give that which is good;
And our land shall yield her increase.

THE BOOK OF PSALMS

Righteousness shall go before him
And shall set us in the way of his steps.

PSALM EIGHTY-SEVEN

His foundation is in the holy mountains.
The Lord loveth the gates of Zion
More than all the dwellings of Jacob.
Glorious things are spoken of thee,
O city of God.
I will make mention of Rahab and Babylon to them that know me:
Behold Philistia, and Tyre, with Ethiopia:
"This man was born there."
And of Zion it shall be said, "This man was born in her":
And the highest himself shall establish her.
The Lord shall count, when he writeth up the people,
That this man was born there.
As well the singers as the players on instruments shall be there:
All my springs are in thee.

PSALM EIGHTY-EIGHT

O Lord God of my salvation,
I have cried day and night before thee:
Let my prayer come before thee;
Incline thine ear unto my cry;
For my soul is full of troubles,
And my life draweth nigh unto the grave.
I am counted with them that go down into the pit;
I am as a man that hath no strength,
Free among the dead,
Like the slain that lie in the grave,
Whom thou rememberest no more,
And they are cut off from thy hand.
Thou hast laid me in the lowest pit,
In darkness, in the deeps.
Thy wrath lieth hard upon me,
And thou hast afflicted me with all thy waves.

THE BOOK OF PSALMS

Thou hast put away mine acquaintance far from me;
Thou hast made me an abomination unto them;
I am shut up, and I cannot come forth.
Mine eye mourneth by reason of affliction;
Lord, I have called daily upon thee,
I have stretched out my hands unto thee.
Wilt thou show wonders to the dead?
Shall the dead arise and praise thee?
Shall thy lovingkindness be declared in the grave?
Or thy faithfulness in destruction?
Shall thy wonders be known in the dark?
And thy righteousness in the land of forgetfulness?
But unto thee have I cried, O Lord;
And in the morning shall my prayer prevent thee.
Lord, why castest thou off my soul?
Why hidest thou thy face from me?
I am afflicted and ready to die from my youth up;
While I suffer thy terrors I am distracted.
Thy fierce wrath goeth over me;
Thy terrors have cut me off.
They came round about me daily like water;
They compassed me about together.
Lover and friend hast thou put far from me,
And mine acquaintance into darkness.

PSALM NINETY

Lord, thou hast been our dwelling place
In all generations.
Before the mountains were brought forth,
Or ever thou hadst formed the earth and the world,
Even from everlasting to everlasting, thou art God.
Thou turnest man to destruction;
And sayest, "Return, ye children of men."
For a thousand years in thy sight
Are but as yesterday when it is past,
And as a watch in the night.

THE BOOK OF PSALMS

Thou carriest them away as with a flood, they are as a sleep:
In the morning they are like grass which groweth up.
In the morning it flourisheth, and groweth up;
In the evening it is cut down, and withereth.
For we are consumed by thine anger,
And by thy wrath are we troubled.
Thou hast set our iniquities before thee,
Our secret sins in the light of thy countenance.
For all our days are passed away in thy wrath:
We spend our years as a tale that is told.
The days of our years are threescore years and ten;
And if by reason of strength they be fourscore years,
Yet is their strength labour and sorrow;
For it is soon cut off, and we fly away.
Who knoweth the power of thine anger?
Even according to thy fear, so is thy wrath.
So teach us to number our days,
That we may apply our hearts unto wisdom.
Return, O Lord, how long?
And let it repent thee concerning thy servants.
O satisfy us early with thy mercy;
That we may rejoice and be glad all our days.
Make us glad according to the days wherein thou hast afflicted us,
And the years wherein we have seen evil.
Let thy work appear unto thy servants,
And thy glory unto their children.
And let the beauty of the Lord our God be upon us:
And establish thou the work of our hands upon us;
Yea, the work of our hands establish thou it.

PSALM NINETY-ONE

He that dwelleth in the secret place of the most High
Shall abide under the shadow of the Almighty.
I will say of the Lord, "He is my refuge and my fortress;
My God, in him will I trust."
Surely he shall deliver thee from the snare of the fowler,

THE BOOK OF PSALMS

And from the noisome pestilence.
He shall cover thee with his feathers,
And under his wings shalt thou trust;
His truth shall be thy shield and buckler.
Thou shalt not be afraid for the terror by night;
Nor for the arrow that flieth by day;
Nor for the pestilence that walketh in darkness;
Nor for the destruction that wasteth at noonday.
A thousand shall fall at thy side,
And ten thousand at thy right hand;
But it shall not come nigh thee.
Only with thine eyes shalt thou behold
And see the reward of the wicked.
Because thou hast made the Lord, which is my refuge,
Even the most High, thy habitation;
There shall no evil befall thee,
Neither shall any plague come nigh thy dwelling.
For he shall give his angels charge over thee,
To keep thee in all thy ways.
They shall bear thee up in their hands,
Lest thou dash thy foot against a stone.
Thou shalt tread upon the lion and adder;
The young lion and the dragon shalt thou trample under feet.
Because he hath set his love upon me, therefore will I deliver him:
I will set him on high, because he hath known my name.
He shall call upon me, and I will answer him;
I will be with him in trouble;
I will deliver him, and honour him.
With long life will I satisfy him,
And show him my salvation.

PSALM NINETY-TWO

It is a good thing to give thanks unto the Lord,
And to sing praises unto thy name, O most High:
To show forth thy lovingkindness in the morning,

THE BOOK OF PSALMS

And thy faithfulness every night,
Upon an instrument of ten strings, and upon the psaltery;
Upon the harp with a solemn sound.
For thou, Lord, hast made me glad through thy work;
I will triumph in the works of thy hands.
O Lord, how great are thy works!
And thy thoughts are very deep.
A brutish man knoweth not;
Neither doth a fool understand this.
When the wicked spring as the grass,
And when all the workers of iniquity do flourish;
It is that they shall be destroyed for ever:
But thou, Lord, art most high for evermore.
For, lo, thine enemies, O Lord, for, lo, thine enemies shall perish;
All the workers of iniquity shall be scattered.
But my horn shalt thou exalt like the horn of a unicorn:
I shall be anointed with fresh oil.
Mine eye also shall see my desire on mine enemies,
And mine ears shall hear my desire of the wicked that rise up
    against me.
The righteous shall flourish like the palm tree:
He shall grow like a cedar in Lebanon.
Those that be planted in the house of the Lord
Shall flourish in the courts of our God.
They shall still bring forth fruit in old age;
They shall be fat and flourishing;
To show that the Lord is upright;
He is my rock, and there is no unrighteousness in him.

PSALM NINETY-THREE

The Lord reigneth, he is clothed with majesty;
The Lord is clothed with strength, wherewith he hath girded himself:
The world also is established, that it cannot be moved.
Thy throne is established of old;

THE BOOK OF PSALMS

Thou art from everlasting.
The floods have lifted up, O Lord,
The floods have lifted up their voice;
The floods lift up their waves.
The Lord on high is mightier
Than the noise of many waters,
Yea, than the mighty waves of the sea.
Thy testimonies are very sure:
Holiness becometh thine house,
O Lord, for ever.

PSALM NINETY-FIVE

O come, let us sing unto the Lord;
Let us make a joyful noise to the rock of our salvation.
Let us come before his presence with thanksgiving,
And make a joyful noise unto him with psalms.
For the Lord is a great God,
And a great King above all gods.
In his hand are the deep places of the earth;
The strength of the hills is his also.
The sea is his, and he made it,
And his hands formed the dry land.
O come, let us worship and bow down:
Let us kneel before the Lord our maker.
For he is our God;
And we are the people of his pasture, and the sheep of his hand.
To-day if ye will hear his voice,
Harden not your heart, as in the provocation,
And as in the day of temptation in the wilderness:
When your fathers tempted me,
Proved me, and saw my work.
Forty years long was I grieved with this generation,
And said, "It is a people that do err in their heart,
And they have not known my ways":
Unto whom I swore in my wrath
That they should not enter into my rest.

THE BOOK OF PSALMS

PSALM NINETY-EIGHT

O sing unto the Lord a new song,
For he hath done marvellous things:
His right hand, and his holy arm, hath gotten him the victory.
The Lord hath made known his salvation;
His righteousness hath he openly showed in the sight of the heathen.
He hath remembered his mercy and his truth toward the house of
    Israel:
All the ends of the earth have seen the salvation of our God.
Make a joyful noise unto the Lord, all the earth:
Make a loud noise and rejoice, and sing praise.
Sing unto the Lord with the harp,
With the harp, and the voice of a psalm.
With trumpets and sound of cornet
Make a joyful noise before the Lord, the King.
Let the sea roar, and the fulness thereof;
The world, and they that dwell therein.
Let the floods clap their hands;
Let the hills be joyful together
Before the Lord; for he cometh to judge the earth,
With righteousness shall he judge the world,
And the people with equity.

PSALM ONE HUNDRED

Make a joyful noise unto the Lord, all ye lands.
Serve the Lord with gladness:
Come before his presence with singing.
Know ye that the Lord he is God:
It is he that hath made us, and not we ourselves;
We are his people, and the sheep of his pasture.
Enter into his gates with thanksgiving,
And into his courts with praise:
Be thankful unto him, and bless his name.
For the Lord is good; his mercy is everlasting;
And his truth endureth to all generations.

THE BOOK OF PSALMS

PSALM ONE HUNDRED TWO

Hear my prayer, O Lord,
And let my cry come unto thee.
Hide not thy face from me in the day when I am in trouble;
Incline thine ear unto me;
In the day when I call answer me speedily.
For my days are consumed like smoke,
And my bones are burned as a hearth.
My heart is smitten, and withered like grass;
So that I forget to eat my bread.
By reason of the voice of my groaning
My bones cleave to my skin.
I am like a pelican of the wilderness;
I am like an owl of the desert.
I watch, and am as a sparrow
Alone upon the house top.
Mine enemies reproach me all the day;
And they that are mad against me are sworn against me.
For I have eaten ashes like bread,
And mingled my drink with weeping,
Because of thine indignation and thy wrath:
For thou hast lifted me up, and cast me down.
My days are like a shadow that declineth;
And I am withered like grass.
But thou, O Lord, shalt endure for ever;
And thy remembrance unto all generations.
Thou shalt arise, and have mercy upon Zion:
For the time to favour her, yea, the set time, is come.
For thy servants take pleasure in her stones,
And favour the dust thereof.
So the heathen shall fear the name of the Lord,
And all the kings of the earth thy glory.
When the Lord shall build up Zion,
He shall appear in his glory.
He will regard the prayer of the destitute,

THE BOOK OF PSALMS

And not despise their prayer.
This shall be written for the generation to come;
And the people which shall be created shall praise the Lord.
For he hath looked down from the height of his sanctuary;
From heaven did the Lord behold the earth;
To hear the groaning of the prisoner;
To loose those that are appointed to death;
To declare the name of the Lord in Zion,
And his praise in Jerusalem;
When the people are gathered together,
And the kingdoms, to serve the Lord.
He weakened my strength in the way;
He shortened my days.
I said, "O my God, take me not away in the midst of my days:
Thy years are throughout all generations.
Of old hast thou laid the foundation of the earth,
And the heavens are the work of thy hands.
They shall perish, but thou shalt endure;
Yea, all of them shall wax old like a garment;
As a vesture shalt thou change them, and they shall be changed:
But thou art the same,
And thy years shall have no end.
The children of thy servants shall continue,
And their seed shall be established before thee."

PSALM ONE HUNDRED THREE

Bless the Lord, O my soul,
And all that is within me, bless his holy name.
Bless the Lord, O my soul,
And forget not all his benefits:
Who forgiveth all thine iniquities;
Who healeth all thy diseases;
Who redeemeth thy life from destruction;
Who crowneth thee with lovingkindness and tender mercies;
Who satisfieth thy mouth with good things;
So that thy youth is renewed like the eagle's.

THE BOOK OF PSALMS

The Lord executeth righteousness
And judgment for all that are oppressed.
He made known his ways unto Moses,
His acts unto the children of Israel.
The Lord is merciful and gracious,
Slow to anger, and plenteous in mercy.
He will not always chide,
Neither will he keep his anger for ever.
He hath not dealt with us after our sins,
Nor rewarded us according to our iniquities.
For as the heaven is high above the earth,
So great is his mercy toward them that fear him.
As far as the east is from the west,
So far hath he removed our transgressions from us.
Like as a father pitieth his children,
So the Lord pitieth them that fear him.
For he knoweth our frame;
He remembereth that we are dust.
As for man, his days are as grass;
As a flower of the field, so he flourisheth.
For the wind passeth over it, and it is gone;
And the place thereof shall know it no more.
But the mercy of the Lord is from everlasting to everlasting upon
    them that fear him,
And his righteousness unto children's children;
To such as keep his covenant,
And to those that remember his commandments to do them.
The Lord hath prepared his throne in the heavens;
And his kingdom ruleth over all.
Bless the Lord, ye his angels,
That excel in strength, that do his commandments,
Hearkening unto the voice of his word.
Bless ye the Lord, all ye his hosts;
Ye ministers of his, that do his pleasure.
Bless the Lord, all his works

THE BOOK OF PSALMS
In all places of his dominion:
Bless the Lord, O my soul.

PSALM ONE HUNDRED FOUR

Bless the Lord, O my soul.
O Lord my God, thou art very great;
Thou art clothed with honour and majesty.
Who coverest thyself with light as with a garment;
Who stretchest out the heavens like a curtain;
Who layeth the beams of his chambers in the waters;
Who maketh the clouds his chariot;
Who walketh upon the wings of the wind;
Who maketh his angels spirits,
His ministers a flaming fire;
Who laid the foundations of the earth,
That it should not be removed for ever.
Thou coveredst it with the deep as with a garment;
The waters stood above the mountains.
At thy rebuke they fled;
At the voice of thy thunder they hastened away.
They go up by the mountains, they go down by the valleys
Unto the place which thou hast founded for them.
Thou hast set a bound that they may not pass over,
That they turn not again to cover the earth.
He sendeth the springs into the valleys,
Which run among the hills.
They give drink to every beast of the field;
The wild asses quench their thirst.
By them shall the fowls of the heaven have their habitation,
Which sing among the branches.
He watereth the hills from his chambers:
The earth is satisfied with the fruit of thy works.
He causeth the grass to grow for the cattle,
And herb for the service of man:
That he may bring forth food out of the earth;

THE BOOK OF PSALMS

And wine that maketh glad the heart of man,
And oil to make his face to shine,
And bread which strengtheneth man's heart.
The trees of the Lord are full of sap,
The cedars of Lebanon, which he hath planted,
Where the birds make their nests;
As for the stork, the fir trees are her house.
The high hills are a refuge for the wild goats,
And the rocks for the conies.
He appointed the moon for seasons;
The sun knoweth his going down.
Thou makest darkness, and it is night,
Wherein all the beasts of the forest do creep forth.
The young lions roar after their prey,
And seek their meat from God.
The sun ariseth, they gather themselves together,
And lay them down in their dens.
Man goeth forth unto his work
And to his labour until the evening.
O Lord, how manifold are thy works!
In wisdom hast thou made them all;
The earth is full of thy riches.
So is this great and wide sea,
Wherein are things creeping innumerable,
Both small and great beasts.
There go the ships;
There is that leviathan, whom thou hast made to play therein.
These wait all upon thee,
That thou mayest give them their meat in due season.
That thou givest them they gather;
Thou openest thine hand, they are filled with good.
Thou hidest thy face, they are troubled;
Thou takest away their breath, they die,
And return to their dust.
Thou sendest forth thy spirit, they are created,
And thou renewest the face of the earth.

THE BOOK OF PSALMS

The glory of the Lord shall endure for ever;
The Lord shall rejoice in his works.
He looketh on the earth, and it trembleth;
He toucheth the hills, and they smoke.
I will sing unto the Lord as long as I live;
I will sing praise to my God while I have my being.
My meditation of him shall be sweet;
I will be glad in the Lord.
Let the sinners be consumed out of the earth,
And let the wicked be no more.
Bless thou the Lord, O my soul.
Praise ye the Lord.

PSALM ONE HUNDRED EIGHT

O God, my heart is fixed;
I will sing and give praise, even with my glory.
Awake, psaltery and harp:
I myself will awake early.
I will praise thee, O Lord, among the people,
And I will sing praises unto thee among the nations.
For thy mercy is great above the heavens,
And thy truth reacheth unto the clouds.
Be thou exalted, O God, above the heavens,
And thy glory above all the earth,
That thy beloved may be delivered;
Save with thy right hand, and answer me.
God hath spoken in his holiness: "I will rejoice,
I will divide Shechem, and mete out the valley of Succoth.
Gilead is mine; Manasseh is mine;
Ephraim also is the strength of mine head; Judah is my lawgiver;
Moab is my washpot; over Edom will I cast out my shoe;
Over Philistia will I triumph.
Who will bring me into the strong city?
Who will lead me into Edom?"
Wilt not thou, O God, who hast cast us off?
And wilt not thou, O God, go forth with our hosts?

THE BOOK OF PSALMS

Give us help from trouble:
For vain is the help of man.
Through God we shall do valiantly:
For he it is that shall tread down our enemies.

PSALM ONE HUNDRED TEN

The Lord said unto my lord, "Sit thou at my right hand,
Until I make thine enemies thy footstool."
The Lord shall send the rod of thy strength out of Zion:
Rule thou in the midst of thine enemies.
Thy people shall be willing in the day of thy power,
In the beauties of holiness from the womb of the morning:
Thou hast the dew of thy youth.
The Lord hath sworn, and will not repent:
"Thou art a priest for ever
After the order of Melchizedek."
The Lord at thy right hand
Shall strike through kings in the day of his wrath.
He shall judge among the heathen,
He shall fill the places with the dead bodies;
He shall wound the heads over many countries.
He shall drink of the brook in the way:
Therefore shall he lift up the head.

PSALM ONE HUNDRED FOURTEEN

When Israel went out of Egypt,
The house of Jacob from a people of strange language,
Judah was his sanctuary,
And Israel his dominion.
The sea saw it, and fled;
Jordan was driven back;
The mountains skipped like rams,
And the little hills like lambs.
What ailed thee, O thou sea, that thou fleddest?
Thou Jordan, that thou wast driven back?
Ye mountains, that ye skipped like rams;

THE BOOK OF PSALMS

And ye little hills, like lambs?
Tremble, thou earth, at the presence of the Lord,
At the presence of the God of Jacob;
Which turned the rock into a standing water,
The flint into a fountain of waters.

PSALM ONE HUNDRED FIFTEEN

Not unto us, O Lord, not unto us,
But unto thy name give glory,
For thy mercy, and for thy truth's sake.
Wherefore should the heathen say,
"Where is now their God?"
But our God is in the heavens;
He hath done whatsoever he hath pleased.
Their idols are silver and gold,
The work of men's hands.
They have mouths, but they speak not;
Eyes have they, but they see not;
They have ears, but they hear not;
Noses have they, but they smell not;
They have hands, but they handle not;
Feet have they, but they walk not;
Neither speak they through their throat.
They that make them are like unto them;
So is every one that trusteth in them.
O Israel, trust thou in the Lord:
He is their help and their shield.
O house of Aaron, trust in the Lord:
He is their help and their shield.
Ye that fear the Lord, trust in the Lord:
He is their help and their shield.
The Lord hath been mindful of us: he will bless us;
He will bless the house of Israel;
He will bless the house of Aaron.
He will bless them that fear the Lord,
Both small and great.

THE BOOK OF PSALMS

The Lord shall increase you more and more,
You and your children.
Ye are blessed of the Lord
Which made heaven and earth.
The heaven, even the heavens, are the Lord's:
But the earth hath he given to the children of men.
The dead praise not the Lord,
Neither any that go down into silence.
But we will bless the Lord
From this time forth and for evermore.
Praise the Lord.

PSALM ONE HUNDRED SIXTEEN

I love the Lord, because he hath heard
My voice and my supplications.
Because he hath inclined his ear unto me,
Therefore will I call upon him as long as I live.
The sorrows of death compassed me,
And the pains of hell got hold upon me;
I found trouble and sorrow.
Then called I upon the name of the Lord:
"O Lord, I beseech thee, deliver my soul."
Gracious is the Lord, and righteous;
Yea, our God is merciful.
The Lord preserveth the simple;
I was brought low, and he helped me.
Return unto thy rest, O my soul;
For the Lord hath dealt bountifully with thee.
For thou hast delivered my soul from death,
Mine eyes from tears,
And my feet from falling.
I will walk before the Lord
In the land of the living.
I believed, therefore have I spoken:
I was greatly afflicted;
I said in my haste,

THE BOOK OF PSALMS

"All men are liars."
What shall I render unto the Lord
For all his benefits toward me?
I will take the cup of salvation,
And call upon the name of the Lord.
I will pay my vows unto the Lord
Now in the presence of all his people.
Precious in the sight of the Lord
Is the death of his saints.
O Lord, truly I am thy servant;
I am thy servant, and the son of thine handmaid;
Thou hast loosed my bonds.
I will offer to thee the sacrifice of thanksgiving,
And will call upon the name of the Lord.
I will pay my vows unto the Lord
Now in the presence of all his people,
In the courts of the Lord's house,
In the midst of thee, O Jerusalem.
Praise ye the Lord.

PSALM ONE HUNDRED TWENTY

In my distress I cried unto the Lord,
And he heard me.
Deliver my soul, O Lord, from lying lips,
And from a deceitful tongue.
What shall be given unto thee? or what shall be done unto thee,
Thou false tongue?
Sharp arrows of the mighty,
With coals of juniper.
Woe is me, that I sojourn in Mesech,
That I dwell in the tents of Kedar!
My soul hath long dwelt
With him that hateth peace.
I am for peace:
But when I speak, they are for war.

THE BOOK OF PSALMS

PSALM ONE HUNDRED TWENTY-ONE

I will lift up mine eyes unto the hills,
From whence cometh my help.
My help cometh from the Lord,
Which made heaven and earth.
He will not suffer thy foot to be moved;
He that keepeth thee will not slumber.
Behold, he that keepeth Israel
Shall neither slumber nor sleep.
The Lord is thy keeper;
The Lord is thy shade upon thy right hand.
The sun shall not smite thee by day,
Nor the moon by night.
The Lord shall preserve thee from all evil;
He shall preserve thy soul.
The Lord shall preserve thy going out and thy coming in
From this time forth, and even for evermore.

PSALM ONE HUNDRED TWENTY-TWO

I was glad when they said unto me,
"Let us go into the house of the Lord."
Our feet shall stand
Within thy gates, O Jerusalem.
Jerusalem is builded
As a city that is compact together:
Whither the tribes go up, the tribes of the Lord,
Unto the testimony of Israel,
To give thanks unto the name of the Lord.
For there are set thrones of judgment,
The thrones of the house of David.
Pray for the peace of Jerusalem:
They shall prosper that love thee.
Peace be within thy walls,
And prosperity within thy palaces.

THE BOOK OF PSALMS

For my brethren and companions' sakes,
I will now say, "Peace be within thee."
Because of the house of the Lord our God
I will seek thy good.

PSALM ONE HUNDRED TWENTY-THREE

Unto thee lift I up mine eyes,
O thou that dwellest in the heavens.
Behold, as the eyes of servants look unto the hand of their masters,
And as the eyes of a maiden unto the hand of her mistress,
So our eyes wait upon the Lord our God,
Until that he have mercy upon us.
Have mercy upon us, O Lord, have mercy upon us:
For we are exceedingly filled with contempt.
Our soul is exceedingly filled
With the scorning of those that are at ease,
And with the contempt of the proud.

PSALM ONE HUNDRED TWENTY-FOUR

"If it had not been the Lord who was on our side,"
Now may Israel say,
"If it had not been the Lord who was on our side,
 When men rose up against us;
 Then they had swallowed us up quick,
 When their wrath was kindled against us;
 Then the waters had overwhelmed us,
 The stream had gone over our soul:
 Then the proud waters had gone over our soul.
Blessed be the Lord,
Who hath not given us as a prey to their teeth.
Our soul is escaped as a bird out of the snare of the fowlers;
The snare is broken, and we are escaped.
Our help is in the name of the Lord,
Who made heaven and earth."

THE BOOK OF PSALMS

PSALM ONE HUNDRED TWENTY-FIVE

They that trust in the Lord
Shall be as Mount Zion, which cannot be removed,
    but abideth for ever.
As the mountains are round about Jerusalem,
So the Lord is round about his people
From henceforth even for ever.
For the rod of the wicked shall not rest upon the lot of the righteous,
Lest the righteous put forth their hands unto iniquity.
Do good, O Lord, unto those that be good,
And to them that are upright in their hearts.
As for such as turn aside unto their crooked ways,
The Lord shall lead them forth with the workers of iniquity:
But peace shall be upon Israel.

PSALM ONE HUNDRED TWENTY-SIX

When the Lord turned again the captivity of Zion,
We were like them that dream.
Then was our mouth filled with laughter,
And our tongue with singing:
Then said they among the heathen,
"The Lord hath done great things for them."
The Lord hath done great things for us;
Whereof we are glad.
Turn again our captivity, O Lord,
As the streams in the south.
They that sow in tears shall reap in joy.
He that goeth forth and weepeth, bearing precious seed,
Shall doubtless come again with rejoicing,
    bringing his sheaves with him.

PSALM ONE HUNDRED TWENTY-SEVEN

Except the Lord build the house,
They labour in vain that build it;
Except the Lord keep the city,

THE BOOK OF PSALMS

The watchman waketh but in vain.
It is vain for you to rise up early, to sit up late,
To eat the bread of sorrows:
For so he giveth his beloved sleep.
Lo, children are a heritage of the Lord,
And the fruit of the womb is his reward.
As arrows are in the hand of a mighty man,
So are children of youth.
Happy is the man that hath his quiver full of them;
They shall not be ashamed,
But they shall speak with the enemies in the gate.

PSALM ONE HUNDRED TWENTY-EIGHT

Blessed is every one that feareth the Lord,
That walketh in his ways.
For thou shalt eat the labour of thine hands;
Happy shalt thou be, and it shall be well with thee.
Thy wife shall be as a fruitful vine by the sides of thine house;
Thy children like olive plants round about thy table.
Behold, that thus shall the man be blessed
That feareth the Lord.
The Lord shall bless thee out of Zion,
And thou shalt see the good of Jerusalem all the days of thy life.
Yea, thou shalt see thy children's children,
And peace upon Israel.

PSALM ONE HUNDRED TWENTY-NINE

"Many a time have they afflicted me from my youth,"
 May Israel now say:
"Many a time have they afflicted me from my youth;
 Yet they have not prevailed against me.
 The plowers plowed upon my back:
 They made long their furrows."
The Lord is righteous:
He hath cut asunder the cords of the wicked.
Let them all be confounded

THE BOOK OF PSALMS
And turned back that hate Zion.
Let them be as the grass upon the housetops,
Which withereth afore it groweth up:
Wherewith the mower filleth not his hand;
Nor he that bindeth sheaves his bosom.
Neither do they which go by say,
"The blessing of the Lord be upon you;
We bless you in the name of the Lord."

PSALM ONE HUNDRED THIRTY

Out of the depths have I cried unto thee, O Lord.
Lord, hear my voice:
Let thine ears be attentive to the voice of my supplications.
If thou, Lord, shouldest mark iniquities,
O Lord, who shall stand?
But there is forgiveness with thee,
That thou mayest be feared.
I wait for the Lord, my soul doth wait,
And in his word do I hope.
My soul waiteth for the Lord
More than they that watch for the morning,
I say, more than they that watch for the morning.
Let Israel hope in the Lord,
For with the Lord there is mercy,
And with him is plenteous redemption.
And he shall redeem Israel
From all his iniquities.

PSALM ONE HUNDRED THIRTY-ONE

Lord, my heart is not haughty, nor mine eyes lofty;
Neither do I exercise myself in great matters,
Or in things too high for me.
Surely I have behaved and quieted myself,
As a child that is weaned of his mother;

THE BOOK OF PSALMS

My soul is even as a weaned child.
Let Israel hope in the Lord
From henceforth and for ever.

PSALM ONE HUNDRED THIRTY-THREE

Behold, how good and how pleasant it is
For brethren to dwell together in unity!
It is like the precious ointment upon the head,
That ran down upon the beard,
Even Aaron's beard:
That went down to the skirts of his garments;
As the dew of Hermon,
That descended upon the mountains of Zion:
For there the Lord commanded the blessing,
Even life for evermore.

PSALM ONE HUNDRED THIRTY-SIX

O give thanks unto the Lord, for he is good:
For his mercy endureth for ever.
O give thanks unto the God of gods:
For his mercy endureth for ever.
O give thanks to the Lord of lords:
For his mercy endureth for ever.
To him who alone doeth great wonders:
For his mercy endureth for ever.
To him that by wisdom made the heavens:
For his mercy endureth for ever.
To him that stretched out the earth above the waters:
For his mercy endureth for ever.
To him that made great lights
(For his mercy endureth for ever):
The sun to rule by day
(For his mercy endureth for ever):
The moon and stars to rule by night

THE BOOK OF PSALMS

(For his mercy endureth for ever).
To him that smote Egypt in their firstborn
(For his mercy endureth for ever):
And brought out Israel from among them
(For his mercy endureth for ever):
With a strong hand, and a stretched-out arm
(For his mercy endureth for ever).
To him which divided the Red Sea into parts
(For his mercy endureth for ever):
And made Israel to pass through the midst of it
(For his mercy endureth for ever):
But overthrew Pharaoh and his host in the Red Sea
(For his mercy endureth for ever).
To him which led his people through the wilderness:
For his mercy endureth for ever.
To him which smote great kings
(For his mercy endureth for ever):
And slew famous kings
(For his mercy endureth for ever):
Sihon king of the Amorites
(For his mercy endureth for ever):
And Og the king of Bashan
(For his mercy endureth for ever):
And gave their land for a heritage
(For his mercy endureth for ever):
Even a heritage unto Israel his servant
(For his mercy endureth for ever).
Who remembered us in our low estate
(For his mercy endureth for ever):
And hath redeemed us from our enemies
(For his mercy endureth for ever).
Who giveth food to all flesh:
For his mercy endureth for ever.
O give thanks unto the God of heaven:
For his mercy endureth for ever.

THE BOOK OF PSALMS

PSALM ONE HUNDRED THIRTY-SEVEN

By the rivers of Babylon,
There we sat down, yea, we wept,
When we remembered Zion.
We hanged our harps
Upon the willows in the midst thereof.
For there they that carried us away captive required of us a song,
And they that wasted us required of us mirth, saying,
"Sing us one of the songs of Zion."
How shall we sing the Lord's song
In a strange land?
If I forget thee, O Jerusalem,
Let my right hand forget her cunning.
If I do not remember thee,
Let my tongue cleave to the roof of my mouth;
If I prefer not Jerusalem above my chief joy.
Remember, O Lord, the children of Edom in the day of Jerusalem;
Who said, "Raze it, raze it, even to the foundation thereof."
O daughter of Babylon, who art to be destroyed;
Happy shall he be that rewardeth thee as thou hast served us.
Happy shall he be that taketh and dasheth thy little ones against
    the stones.

PSALM ONE HUNDRED THIRTY-NINE

O Lord, thou hast searched me, and known me.
Thou knowest my downsitting and mine uprising,
Thou understandest my thought afar off.
Thou compassest my path and my lying down,
And art acquainted with all my ways.
For there is not a word in my tongue,
But lo, O Lord, thou knowest it altogether.
Thou hast beset me behind and before,
And laid thine hand upon me.
Such knowledge is too wonderful for me;

THE BOOK OF PSALMS

It is high, I cannot attain unto it.
Whither shall I go from thy spirit?
Or whither shall I flee from thy presence?
If I ascend up into heaven, thou art there;
If I make my bed in hell, behold, thou art there.
If I take the wings of the morning,
And dwell in the uttermost parts of the sea,
Even there shall thy hand lead me,
And thy right hand shall hold me.
If I say, "Surely the darkness shall cover me,"
Even the night shall be light about me;
Yea, the darkness hideth not from thee,
But the night shineth as the day:
The darkness and the light are both alike to thee.
For thou hast possessed my reins;
Thou hast covered me in my mother's womb.
I will praise thee; for I am fearfully and wonderfully made:
Marvellous are thy works;
And that my soul knoweth right well.
My substance was not hid from thee,
When I was made in secret,
And curiously wrought in the lowest parts of the earth.
Thine eyes did see my substance, yet being unperfect;
And in thy book all my members were written,
Which in continuance were fashioned,
When as yet there was none of them.
How precious also are thy thoughts unto me, O God!
How great is the sum of them!

PSALM ONE HUNDRED FORTY-FIVE

I will extol thee, my God, O king;
And I will bless thy name for ever and ever.
Every day will I bless thee;
And I will praise thy name for ever and ever.
Great is the Lord, and greatly to be praised;
And his greatness is unsearchable.

THE BOOK OF PSALMS

One generation shall praise thy works to another,
And shall declare thy mighty acts.
I will speak of the glorious honour of thy majesty,
And of thy wondrous works.
And men shall speak of the might of thy terrible acts;
And I will declare thy greatness.
They shall abundantly utter the memory of thy great goodness,
And shall sing of thy righteousness.
The Lord is gracious, and full of compassion;
Slow to anger, and of great mercy.
The Lord is good to all,
And his tender mercies are over all his works.
All thy works shall praise thee, O Lord,
And thy saints shall bless thee.
They shall speak of the glory of thy kingdom,
And talk of thy power;
To make known to the sons of men his mighty acts,
And the glorious majesty of his kingdom.
Thy kingdom is an everlasting kingdom,
And thy dominion endureth throughout all generations.
The Lord upholdeth all that fall,
And raiseth up all those that be bowed down.
The eyes of all wait upon thee,
And thou givest them their meat in due season.
Thou openest thine hand,
And satisfiest the desire of every living thing.
The Lord is righteous in all his ways,
And holy in all his works.
The Lord is nigh unto all them that call upon him,
To all that call upon him in truth.
He will fulfil the desire of them that fear him;
He also will hear their cry, and will save them.
The Lord preserveth all them that love him;
But all the wicked will he destroy.
My mouth shall speak the praise of the Lord;
And let all flesh bless his holy name for ever and ever.

THE BOOK OF PSALMS

PSALM ONE HUNDRED FORTY-SEVEN

Praise ye the Lord:
For it is good to sing praises unto our God;
For it is pleasant, and praise is comely.
The Lord doth build up Jerusalem;
He gathereth together the outcasts of Israel.
He healeth the broken in heart,
And bindeth up their wounds.
He telleth the number of the stars;
He calleth them all by their names.
Great is our Lord, and of great power;
His understanding is infinite.
The Lord lifteth up the meek:
He casteth the wicked down to the ground.
Sing unto the Lord with thanksgiving;
Sing praise upon the harp unto our God,
Who covereth the heaven with clouds,
Who prepareth rain for the earth,
Who maketh grass to grow upon the mountains.
He giveth to the beast his food,
And to the young ravens which cry.
He delighteth not in the strength of the horse;
He taketh not pleasure in the legs of a man.
The Lord taketh pleasure in them that fear him,
In those that hope in his mercy.
Praise the Lord, O Jerusalem;
Praise thy God, O Zion.
For he hath strengthened the bars of thy gates;
He hath blessed thy children within thee.
He maketh peace in thy borders,
And filleth thee with the finest of the wheat.
He sendeth forth his commandment upon earth;
His word runneth very swiftly.
He giveth snow like wool;
He scattereth the hoarfrost like ashes.

THE BOOK OF PSALMS

He casteth forth his ice like morsels:
Who can stand before his cold?
He sendeth out his word, and melteth them;
He causeth his wind to blow, and the waters flow.
He showeth his word unto Jacob,
His statutes and his judgments unto Israel.
He hath not dealt so with any nation,
And as for his judgments, they have not known them.
Praise ye the Lord.

PSALM ONE HUNDRED FORTY-EIGHT

Praise ye the Lord.
Praise ye the Lord from the heavens:
Praise him in the heights.
Praise ye him, all his angels:
Praise ye him, all his hosts.
Praise ye him, sun and moon:
Praise him, all ye stars of light.
Praise him, ye heavens of heavens,
And ye waters that be above the heavens.
Let them praise the name of the Lord:
For he commanded, and they were created.
He hath also established them for ever and ever;
He hath made a decree which shall not pass.
Praise the Lord from the earth,
Ye dragons, and all deeps,
Fire and hail, snow and vapours,
Stormy wind fulfilling his word,
Mountains and all hills,
Fruitful trees and all cedars,
Beasts and all cattle,
Creeping things and flying fowl,
Kings of the earth and all people,
Princes and all judges of the earth:
Both young men and maidens,
Old men and children,

THE BOOK OF PSALMS

Let them praise the name of the Lord;
For his name alone is excellent;
His glory is above the earth and heaven.
He also exalteth the horn of his people,
The praise of all his saints;
Even of the children of Israel, a people near unto him.
Praise ye the Lord.

PSALM ONE HUNDRED FORTY-NINE

Praise ye the Lord.
Sing unto the Lord a new song,
And his praise in the congregation of saints.
Let Israel rejoice in him that made him:
Let the children of Zion be joyful in their King.
Let them praise his name in the dance:
Let them sing praises unto him with the timbrel and harp.
For the Lord taketh pleasure in his people:
He will beautify the meek with salvation.
Let the saints be joyful in glory:
Let them sing aloud upon their beds.
Let the high praises of God be in their mouth,
And a two-edged sword in their hand;
To execute vengeance upon the heathen,
And punishments upon the people;
To bind their kings with chains,
And their nobles with fetters of iron;
To execute upon them the judgment written:
This honour have all his saints.
Praise ye the Lord.

PSALM ONE HUNDRED FIFTY

Praise ye the Lord.
Praise God in his sanctuary:
Praise him in the firmament of his power.
Praise him for his mighty acts:
Praise him according to his excellent greatness.

THE BOOK OF PSALMS

Praise him with the sound of the trumpet:
Praise him with the psaltery and harp.
Praise him with the timbrel and dance:
Praise him with stringed instruments and organs.
Praise him upon the loud cymbals:
Praise him upon the high-sounding cymbals.
Let every thing that hath breath praise the Lord.
Praise ye the Lord.

THE BOOK OF PROVERBS
AN ANTHOLOGY OF GNOMIC POETRY

PROVERBS—*prudential social maxims*—*are indigenous in every people. Among the Jews the writing of them became a conscious art pursued extensively in the post-Exilic period. Many collections were made, the earliest based directly upon an Egyptian work, "The Wisdom of Amenenope"; the final collection of collections was put together about 300 B.C.*

Just as it was customary to ascribe most of the Psalms, in the absence of other known authors, to the poetical King David, so King Solomon received the credit for most of the Proverbs on the strength of his reputation for wisdom.

But the term "Wisdom" came in the later period to include much more than mere knowledge of the world and the laws of conduct. Since the structure of the world and the laws of conduct alike revealed the ways of God, the wisdom of the Sages resembled, in its humbler degree, the Divine Wisdom itself; hence the term was frequently used as synonymous with the Divine Plan according to which all things were created, and in this sense was similar to "The Word" in the first chapter of the Gospel according to John.

"Wisdom Literature" was the Jewish equivalent of Greek philosophy in so far as the latter had a religious cast, but it always kept closer to its popular origin and always emphasized practice above theory. Similarly, it was, of course, devoid of the scientific spirit so prominent in Greek philosophy.

The Book of PROVERBS

AN ANTHOLOGY OF GNOMIC POETRY

To know wisdom and instruction;
To discern the words of understanding;
To receive instruction in wise dealing,
In righteousness and judgment and equity;
To give subtilty to the simple,
To the young man knowledge and discretion:
That the wise man may hear, and increase in learning;
And that the man of understanding may attain unto sound counsels:
To understand a proverb, and a figure;
The words of the wise, and their dark sayings.

The fear of the Lord is the beginning of knowledge:
But the foolish despise wisdom and instruction.

"Hear, My Sons, the Instruction of a Father"

Hear, my sons, the instruction of a father,
And to attend to know understanding:
For I give you good doctrine;
Forsake ye not my law.
For I was a son unto my father,
Tender and only beloved in the sight of my mother.
And he taught me, and said unto me,

"Let thine heart retain my words;
Keep my commandments, and live:
Get wisdom, get understanding;
Forget it not, neither decline from the words of my mouth:

THE BOOK OF PROVERBS

Forsake her not, and she shall preserve thee;
Love her, and she shall keep thee.
Wisdom is the principal thing; therefore get wisdom:
Yea, with all thou hast gotten get understanding.
Exalt her, and she shall promote thee:
She shall bring thee to honour, when thou dost embrace her.
She shall give to thine head a chaplet of grace:
A crown of beauty shall she deliver to thee."

"The Lips of a Strange Woman Drop Honey"

The lips of a strange woman drop honey,
And her mouth is smoother than oil:
But her latter end is bitter as wormwood,
Sharp as a two-edged sword.
Her feet go down to death;
Her steps take hold on Sheol;
So that she findeth not the level path of life:
Her ways are unstable and she knoweth it not.
Now therefore, my sons, hearken unto me,
And depart not from the words of my mouth.
Remove thy way far from her,
And come not nigh the door of her house:
Lest thou give thine honour unto others,
And thy years unto the cruel:
Lest strangers be filled with thy strength;
And thy labours be in the house of an alien;
And thou mourn at thy latter end,
When thy flesh and thy body are consumed,
And say, "How have I hated instruction,
And my heart despised reproof;
Neither have I obeyed the voice of my teachers,
Nor inclined mine ear to them that instructed me!
I was well nigh in all evil
In the midst of the congregation and assembly."

Drink waters out of thine own cistern,
And running waters out of thine own well.

THE BOOK OF PROVERBS

Should thy springs be dispersed abroad,
And the rivers of water in the streets?
Let them be for thyself alone,
And not for strangers with thee.
Let thy fountain be blessed;
And rejoice in the wife of thy youth.
As a loving hind and a pleasant doe,
Let her breasts satisfy thee at all times;
And be thou ravished always with her love.
For why shouldest thou, my son, be ravished with a strange woman,
And embrace the bosom of a stranger?

"Go to the Ant, Thou Sluggard"

Go to the ant, thou sluggard;
Consider her ways, and be wise:
Which having no chief,
Overseer, or ruler,
Provideth her meat in the summer,
And gathereth her food in the harvest.

How long wilt thou sleep, O sluggard?
When wilt thou arise out of thy sleep?
Yet a little sleep, a little slumber,
A little folding of the hands to sleep:
So shall thy poverty come as a robber,
And thy want as an armed man.

"There Be Six Things Which the Lord Hateth"

There be six things which the Lord hateth;
Yea, seven which are an abomination unto him:
Haughty eyes, a lying tongue,
And hands that shed innocent blood;
A heart that deviseth wicked imaginations,
Feet that be swift in running to mischief;
A false witness that uttereth lies,
And he that soweth discord among brethren.

THE BOOK OF PROVERBS
"My Son, Keep the Commandment of Thy Father"

My son, keep the commandment of thy father,
And forsake not the law of thy mother:
Bind them continually upon thine heart,
Tie them about thy neck.

When thou walkest, it shall lead thee;
When thou sleepest, it shall watch over thee;
And when thou awakest, it shall talk with thee.

For the commandment is a lamp;
And the law is light;
And reproofs of instruction are the way of life:

To keep thee from the evil woman,
From the flattery of the stranger's tongue.
Lust not after her beauty in thine heart;
Neither let her take thee with her eyelids.

For on account of a whorish woman a man is brought to a piece of bread:
And the adulteress hunteth for the precious life.

Can a man take fire in his bosom,
And his clothes not be burned?
Or can one walk upon hot coals,
And his feet not be scorched?

So he that goeth in to his neighbour's wife;
Whosoever toucheth her shall not be unpunished.

Men do not despise a thief, if he steal
To satisfy his soul when he is hungry:
But if he be found, he shall restore sevenfold;
He shall give all the substance of his house.

He that committeth adultery with a woman is void of understanding:
He doeth it that would destroy his own soul.
Wounds and dishonour shall he get;
And his reproach shall not be wiped away,

THE BOOK OF PROVERBS

For jealousy is the rage of a man;
And he will not spare in the day of vengeance.
He will not regard any ransom;
Neither will he rest content, though thou givest many gifts.

"At the Window of My House"

At the window of my house
I looked forth through my lattice;
And I beheld among the simple ones,
I discerned among the youths,
A young man void of understanding,
Passing through the street near her corner,
And he went the way to her house;
In the twilight, in the evening of the day,
In the blackness of night and the darkness.

And, behold, there met him a woman
With the attire of a harlot, and wily of heart.
She is clamorous and wilful;
Her feet abide not in her house:
Now she is in the streets, now in the broad places,
And lieth in wait at every corner.
So she caught him, and kissed him,
And with an impudent face she said unto him:

"Sacrifices of peace offerings are with me;
This day have I paid my vows.
Therefore came I forth to meet thee,
Diligently to seek thy face, and I have found thee.
I have spread my couch with carpets of tapestry,
With striped cloths of the yarn of Egypt.
I have perfumed my bed
With myrrh, aloes, and cinnamon.
Come, let us take our fill of love until the morning;
Let us solace ourselves with loves.
For the goodman is not at home,
He is gone a long journey:

THE BOOK OF PROVERBS

He hath taken a bag of money with him;
He will come home at the full moon."

With her much fair speech she causeth him to yield,
With the flattering of her lips she forceth him away.
He goeth after her straightway,
As an ox goeth to the slaughter,
Or as fetters to the correction of the fool;
Till an arrow strike through his liver;
As a bird hasteth to the snare,
And knoweth not that it is for his life.

Now therefore, my sons, hearken unto me,
And attend to the words of my mouth.
Let not thine heart decline to her ways,
Go not astray in her paths.
For she hath cast down many wounded:
Yea, all her slain are a mighty host.
Her house is the way to Sheol,
Going down to the chambers of death.

"Doth Not Wisdom Cry"

Doth not wisdom cry,
And understanding put forth her voice?
In the top of high places by the way,
Where the paths meet, she standeth;
Beside the gates, at the entry of the city,
At the coming in at the doors, she crieth aloud:

"Unto you, O men, I call;
And my voice is to the sons of men.
O ye simple, understand subtilty;
And, ye fools, be ye of an understanding heart.
Hear, for I will speak excellent things;
And the opening of my lips shall be right things.
For my mouth shall utter truth;
And wickedness is an abomination to my lips.

THE BOOK OF PROVERBS

*All the words of my mouth are in righteousness;
There is nothing crooked or perverse in them.
They are all plain to him that understandeth,
And right to them that find knowledge.
Receive my instruction, and not silver;
And knowledge rather than choice gold.
For wisdom is better than rubies;
And all the things that may be desired are not to be compared unto her.*

*I wisdom have made subtilty my dwelling,
And find out knowledge and discretion.
The fear of the Lord is to hate evil:
Pride, and arrogancy, and the evil way,
And the froward mouth, do I hate.
Counsel is mine, and sound knowledge:
I am understanding; I have might.
By me kings reign,
And princes decree justice.
By me princes rule,
And nobles, even all the judges of the earth.
I love them that love me;
And those that seek me diligently shall find me.
Riches and honour are with me;
Yea, durable riches and righteousness.
My fruit is better than gold, yea, than fine gold;
And my revenue than choice silver.
I walk in the way of righteousness,
In the midst of the paths of judgment:
That I may cause those that love me to inherit substance,
And that I may fill their treasuries.*

*The Lord possessed me in the beginning of his way,
Before his works of old.
I was set up from everlasting, from the beginning,
Or ever the earth was.
When there were no depths, I was brought forth;
When there were no fountains abounding with water.*

THE BOOK OF PROVERBS

Before the mountains were settled,
Before the hills was I brought forth:
While as yet he had not made the earth, nor the fields,
Nor the beginning of the dust of the world.
When he established the heavens, I was there:
When he set a circle upon the face of the deep:
When he made firm the skies above:
When the fountain of the deep became strong:
When he gave to the sea its bound,
That the waters should not transgress his commandment:
When he marked out the foundations of the earth:
Then I was by him, as a master workman:
And I was daily his delight,
Rejoicing always before him;
Rejoicing in his habitable earth;
And my delight was with the sons of men.

Now therefore, my sons, hearken unto me:
For blessed are they that keep my ways.
Hear instruction, and be wise,
And refuse it not.
Blessed is the man that heareth me,
Watching daily at my gates,
Waiting at the posts of my doors.
For whoso findeth me findeth life,
And shall obtain favour of the Lord.
But he that sinneth against me wrongeth his own soul:
All they that hate me love death."

"Wisdom Hath Builded Her House"

Wisdom hath builded her house,
She hath hewn out her seven pillars:
She hath killed her beasts; she hath mingled her wine;
She hath also furnished her table.
She hath sent forth her maidens, she crieth
Upon the highest places of the city,

THE BOOK OF PROVERBS

"Whoso is simple, let him turn in hither":
As for him that is void of understanding, she saith to him,
"Come, eat ye of my bread,
And drink of the wine which I have mingled.
Leave off, ye simple ones, and live;
And walk in the way of understanding."

"He That Correcteth a Scorner"

He that correcteth a scorner getteth to himself shame:
And he that reproveth a wicked man getteth himself a blot.
Reprove not a scorner, lest he hate thee:
Reprove a wise man, and he will love thee.
Give instruction to a wise man, and he will be yet wiser:
Teach a righteous man, and he will increase in learning.

"The Fear of the Lord Is the Beginning of Wisdom"

The fear of the Lord is the beginning of wisdom:
And the knowledge of the Holy One is understanding.
For by me thy days shall be multiplied,
And the years of thy life shall be increased.
If thou art wise, thou art wise for thyself:
And if thou scornest, thou alone shalt bear it.

"The Foolish Woman Is Clamorous"

The foolish woman is clamorous;
She is simple, and knoweth nothing.
And she sitteth at the door of her house,
On a seat in the high places of the city,
To call to them that pass by,
Who go right on their ways,
Whoso is simple, let him turn in hither:
And as for him that is void of understanding, she saith to him,
"Stolen waters are sweet,
And bread eaten in secret is pleasant."
But he knoweth not that the dead are there;
That her guests are in the depths of Sheol.

THE BOOK OF PROVERBS

The Proverbs of Solomon

A wise son maketh a glad father:
But a foolish son is the heaviness of his mother.

Treasures of wickedness profit nothing:
But righteousness delivereth from death.

He becometh poor that dealeth with a slack hand:
But the hand of the diligent maketh rich.

He that gathereth in summer is a wise son:
But he that sleepeth in harvest is a son that causeth shame.

The memory of the just is blessed:
But the name of the wicked shall rot.

The wise in heart will receive commandments:
But a prating fool shall fall.

He that walketh uprightly walketh surely:
But he that perverteth his ways shall be known.

He that winketh with the eye causeth sorrow:
But a prating fool shall fall.

Hatred stirreth up strifes:
But love covereth all transgressions.

The rich man's wealth is his strong city:
The destruction of the poor is their poverty.

The labour of the righteous tendeth to life;
The increase of the wicked to sin.

He is in the way of life that heedeth correction:
But he that forsaketh reproof erreth.

He that hideth hatred is of lying lips;
And he that uttereth a slander is a fool.

In the multitude of words there wanteth not transgression:
But he that refraineth his lips doeth wisely.

THE BOOK OF PROVERBS

The tongue of the righteous is as choice silver:
The heart of the wicked is little worth.

The lips of the righteous feed many:
But the foolish die for lack of understanding.

It is as sport to a fool to do wickedness:
And so is wisdom to a man of understanding.

The fear of the wicked, it shall come upon him:
And the desire of the righteous shall be granted.

When the whirlwind passeth, the wicked is no more:
But the righteous is an everlasting foundation.

As vinegar to the teeth, and as smoke to the eyes,
So is the sluggard to them that send him.

The fear of the Lord prolongeth days:
But the years of the wicked shall be shortened.

A false balance is an abomination to the Lord
But a just weight is his delight.

When pride cometh, then cometh shame:
But with the lowly is wisdom.

He that goeth about as a talebearer revealeth secrets:
But he that is of a faithful spirit concealeth the matter.

Where no wise guidance is, the people falleth:
But in the multitude of counsellors there is safety.

As a jewel of gold in a swine's snout,
So is a fair woman which is without discretion.

The liberal soul shall be made fat:
And he that watereth shall be watered also himself.

He that withholdeth corn, the people shall curse him:
But blessing shall be upon the head of him that selleth it.

He that trusteth in his riches shall fall:
But the righteous shall flourish as the green leaf.

THE BOOK OF PROVERBS

He that troubleth his own house shall inherit the wind:
And the foolish shall be servant to the wise of heart.

The fruit of the righteous is a tree of life;
And he that is wise winneth souls.

Behold, the righteous shall be recompensed in the earth:
How much more the wicked and the sinner!

Whoso loveth correction loveth knowledge:
But he that hateth reproof is brutish.

A virtuous woman is a crown to her husband:
But she that maketh ashamed is as rottenness in his bones.

Better is he that is lightly esteemed, and hath a servant,
Than he that honoureth himself, and lacketh bread.

A righteous man regardeth the life of his beast:
But the tender mercies of the wicked are cruel.

He that tilleth his land shall have plenty of bread:
But he that followeth after vain persons is void of understanding.

The way of the foolish is right in his own eyes:
But he that is wise hearkeneth unto counsel.

A fool's vexation is presently known:
But a prudent man concealeth shame.

He that uttereth truth showeth forth righteousness,
But a false witness deceit.

There is that speaketh rashly like the piercings of a sword:
But the tongue of the wise is health.

The lip of truth shall be established for ever:
But a lying tongue is but for a moment.

Deceit is in the heart of them that devise evil:
But to the counsellors of peace is joy.

Lying lips are an abomination to the Lord:
But they that deal truly are his delight.

THE BOOK OF PROVERBS

A prudent man concealeth knowledge:
But the heart of fools proclaimeth foolishness.

The hand of the diligent shall bear rule:
But the slothful shall be put under taskwork.

The soul of the sluggard desireth, and hath nothing:
But the soul of the diligent shall be made fat.

There is that maketh himself rich, yet hath nothing:
There is that maketh himself poor, yet hath great wealth.

The ransom of a man's life is his riches:
But the poor heareth no threatening.

By pride cometh only contention:
But with the well-advised is wisdom.

Wealth gotten by vanity shall be diminished:
But he that gathereth by labour shall have increase.

Hope deferred maketh the heart sick:
But when the desire cometh, it is a tree of life.

A wicked messenger falleth into evil:
But a faithful ambassador is health.

Poverty and shame shall be to him that refuseth correction:
But he that regardeth reproof shall be honoured.

The desire accomplished is sweet to the soul:
But it is an abomination to fools to depart from evil.

A good man leaveth an inheritance to his children's children;
And the wealth of the sinner is laid up for the righteous.

Much food is in the tillage of the poor:
But there is that is destroyed by reason of injustice.

He that spareth his rod hateth his son:
But he that loveth him chasteneth him betimes.

The righteous eateth to the satisfying of his soul:
But the belly of the wicked shall want.

THE BOOK OF PROVERBS

*Every wise woman buildeth her house:
But the foolish plucketh it down with her own hands.*

*Where no oxen are, the crib is clean:
But much increase is by the strength of the ox.*

*The heart knoweth its own bitterness;
And a stranger doth not intermeddle with its joy.*

*There is a way which seemeth right unto a man,
But the end thereof are the ways of death.*

*Even in laughter the heart is sorrowful;
And the end of mirth is heaviness.*

*The backslider in heart shall be filled with his own ways:
And a good man shall be satisfied from himself.*

*The simple believeth every word:
But the prudent man looketh well to his going.*

*The poor is hated even of his own neighbour:
But the rich hath many friends.*

*He that despiseth his neighbour sinneth:
But he that hath pity on the poor, happy is he.*

*In the multitude of people is the king's glory:
But in the want of people is the destruction of the prince.*

*He that is slow to anger is of great understanding:
But he that is hasty of spirit exalteth folly.*

*A sound heart is the life of the flesh:
But envy is the rottenness of the bones.*

*He that oppresseth the poor reproacheth his Maker:
But he that hath mercy on the needy honoureth him.*

*A soft answer turneth away wrath:
But a grievous word stirreth up anger.*

*In the house of the righteous is much treasure:
But in the revenues of the wicked is trouble.*

THE BOOK OF PROVERBS

A merry heart maketh a cheerful countenance:
But by sorrow of heart the spirit is broken.

All the days of the afflicted are evil:
But he that is of cheerful heart hath a continual feast.

Better is little with the fear of the Lord,
Than great treasure and trouble therewith.

Better is a dinner of herbs where love is,
Than a stalled ox and hatred therewith.

A wise son maketh a glad father:
But a foolish man despiseth his mother.

A man hath joy in the answer of his mouth:
And a word in due season, how good is it!

To the wise the way of life goeth upward,
That he may depart from Sheol beneath.

He that is greedy of gain troubleth his own house:
But he that hateth gifts shall live.

A just balance and scales are the Lord's:
All the weights of the bag are his work.

It is an abomination to kings to commit wickedness:
For the throne is established by righteousness.

Righteous lips are the delight of kings;
And they love him that speaketh right.

The wrath of a king is as messengers of death:
But a wise man will pacify it.

In the light of the king's countenance is life;
And his favour is as a cloud of the latter rain.

How much better is it to get wisdom than gold!
Yea, to get understanding is rather to be chosen than silver.

The high way of the upright is to depart from evil:
He that keepeth his way preserveth his soul.

THE BOOK OF PROVERBS

Pride goeth before destruction,
And a haughty spirit before a fall.

Pleasant words are as a honeycomb,
Sweet to the soul, and health to the bones.

The hoary head is a crown of glory.
It shall be found in the way of righteousness.

He that is slow to anger is better than the mighty;
And he that ruleth his spirit than he that taketh a city.

The lot is cast into the lap;
But the whole disposing thereof is of the Lord.

Better is a dry morsel and quietness therewith,
Than a house full of feasting with strife.

A servant that dealeth wisely shall have rule over a son that
    causeth shame,
And shall have part in the inheritance among the brethren.

The fining pot is for silver, and the furnace for gold:
But the Lord trieth the hearts.

An evildoer giveth heed to wicked lips;
And a liar giveth ear to a mischievous tongue.

Whoso mocketh the poor reproacheth his Maker:
And he that is glad at calamity shall not be unpunished.

Children's children are the crown of old men;
And the glory of children are their fathers.

Excellent speech becometh not a fool:
Much less do lying lips a prince.

A rebuke entereth deeper into one that hath understanding
Than a hundred stripes into a fool.

Let a bear robbed of her whelps meet a man,
Rather than a fool in his folly.

THE BOOK OF PROVERBS

Whoso rewardeth evil for good,
Evil shall not depart from his house.

The beginning of strife is as when one letteth out water:
Therefore leave off contention, before there be quarrelling.

He that justifieth the wicked, and he that condemneth the righteous,
Both of them alike are an abomination to the Lord.

Wherefore is there a price in the hand of a fool to buy wisdom,
Seeing he hath no understanding?

A friend loveth at all times,
And a brother is born for adversity.

A man void of understanding striketh hands,
And becometh surety in the presence of his neighbour.

He that begetteth a fool doeth it to his sorrow:
And the father of a fool hath no joy.

A merry heart is a good medicine:
But a broken spirit drieth up the bones.

Wisdom is before the face of him that hath understanding:
But the eyes of a fool are in the ends of the earth.

A foolish son is a grief to his father,
And bitterness to her that bore him.

He that spareth his words hath knowledge:
And he that is of a cool spirit is a man of understanding.

Even a fool, when he holdeth his peace, is counted wise:
When he shutteth his lips, he is esteemed as prudent.

The words of a man's mouth are as deep waters;
The wellspring of wisdom is as a flowing brook.

A fool's lips enter into contention,
And his mouth calleth for stripes.

THE BOOK OF PROVERBS

A fool's mouth is his destruction,
And his lips are the snare of his soul.

The words of a whisperer are as dainty morsels,
And they go down into the innermost parts of the belly.

He also that is slack in his work
Is brother to him that is a destroyer.

The name of the Lord is a strong tower:
The righteous runneth into it, and is safe.

The rich man's wealth is his strong city,
And as a high wall in his own imagination.

Before destruction the heart of man is haughty,
And before honour goeth humility.

He that giveth answer before he heareth,
It is folly and shame unto him.

A brother offended is harder to be won than a strong city:
And such contentions are like the bars of a castle.

Death and life are in the power of the tongue;
And they that love it shall eat the fruit thereof.

Whoso findeth a wife findeth a good thing,
And obtaineth favour of the Lord.

The poor useth entreaties:
But the rich answereth roughly.

He that maketh many friends doeth it to his own destruction:
But there is a friend that sticketh closer than a brother.

Better is the poor that walketh in his integrity
Than he that is perverse in his lips and is a fool.

Also, that the soul be without knowledge is not good;
And he that hasteth with his feet sinneth.

Wealth addeth many friends:
But the poor is separated from his friend.

THE BOOK OF PROVERBS

Many will intreat the favour of the liberal man:
And every man is a friend to him that giveth gifts.

All the brethren of the poor do hate him:
How much more do his friends go far from him!

Delicate living is not seemly for a fool;
Much less for a servant to have rule over princes.

House and riches are an inheritance from fathers:
But a prudent wife is from the Lord.

Divers weights, and divers measures.
Both of them alike are an abomination to the Lord.

Even a child maketh himself known by his doings,
Whether his work be pure, and whether it be right.

The hearing ear, and the seeing eye,
The Lord hath made even both of them.

Love not sleep, lest thou come to poverty;
Open thine eyes, and thou shalt be satisfied with bread.

"It is naught, it is naught," saith the buyer:
But when he is gone his way, then he boasteth.

There is gold, and abundance of rubies:
But the lips of knowledge are a precious jewel.

The horse is prepared against the day of battle:
But victory is of the Lord.

A good name is rather to be chosen than great riches,
And loving favour rather than silver and gold.

The rich and the poor meet together:
The Lord is the maker of them all.

Train up a child in the way he should go,
And even when he is old he will not depart from it.

The mouth of strange women is a deep pit:
He that is abhorred of the Lord shall fall therein.

THE BOOK OF PROVERBS

Foolishness is bound up in the heart of a child;
But the rod of correction shall drive it far from him.

He that oppresseth the poor to increase his gain,
And he that giveth to the rich, cometh only to want.

Remove not the ancient landmark,
Which thy fathers have set.

Seest thou a man diligent in his business? he shall stand before
    kings;
He shall not stand before mean men.

Withhold not correction from the child:
For if thou beat him with the rod, he shall not die.
Thou shalt beat him with the rod,
And shalt deliver his soul from Sheol.

"Who Hath Woe?"

Who hath woe? who hath sorrow? who hath contentions?
Who hath complaining? who hath wounds without cause?
Who hath redness of eyes?
They that tarry long at the wine;
They that go to seek out mixed wine.

Look not thou upon the wine when it is red,
When it giveth its colour in the cup,
When it goeth down smoothly:
At the last it biteth like a serpent,
And stingeth like an adder.
Thine eyes shall behold strange things,
And thine heart shall utter froward things.
Yea, thou shalt be as he that lieth down in the midst of the sea,
Or as he that lieth upon the top of a mast.
"They have stricken me," shalt thou say, "and I was not hurt;
They have beaten me, and I felt it not:
When shall I awake? I will seek it yet again."

THE BOOK OF PROVERBS

The Hezekiah Collection

These also are proverbs of Solomon, which the men of Hezekiah king of Judah copied out.

It is the glory of God to conceal a thing:
But the glory of kings is to search out a matter.
The heaven for height, and the earth for depth,
And the heart of kings is unsearchable.
Take away the dross from the silver,
And there cometh forth a vessel for the finer:
Take away the wicked from before the king,
And his throne shall be established in righteousness.
Put not thyself forward in the presence of the king,
And stand not in the place of great men:
For better is it that it be said unto thee, "Come up hither!"
Than that thou shouldest be put lower in the presence of the prince,
Whom thine eyes have seen.

A word fitly spoken
Is like apples of gold in baskets of silver.

As an earring of gold, and an ornament of fine gold,
So is a wise reprover upon an obedient ear.

As the cold of snow in the time of harvest,
So is a faithful messenger to them that send him;
For he refresheth the soul of his masters.

As clouds and wind without rain,
So is he that boasteth himself of his gifts falsely.

By long forbearing is a ruler persuaded,
And a soft tongue breaketh the bone.

Hast thou found honey? eat so much as is sufficient for thee;
Lest thou be filled therewith, and vomit it.

Let thy foot be seldom in thy neighbour's house;
Lest he be weary of thee, and hate thee.

THE BOOK OF PROVERBS

A man that beareth false witness against his neighbour
Is a maul, and a sword, and a sharp arrow.

Confidence in an unfaithful man in time of trouble
Is like a broken tooth, and a foot out of joint.

As one that taketh off a garment in cold weather, and as vinegar
    upon nitre,
So is he that singeth songs to a heavy heart.

If thine enemy be hungry, give him bread to eat;
And if he be thirsty, give him water to drink:
For thou shalt heap coals of fire upon his head,
And the Lord shall reward thee.

The north wind bringeth forth rain:
So doth a backbiting tongue an angry countenance.

It is better to dwell in the corner of the housetop,
Than with a contentious woman in a wide house.

As cold waters to a thirsty soul,
So is good news from a far country.

As a troubled fountain, and a corrupted spring,
So is a righteous man that giveth way before the wicked.

It is not good to eat much honey:
So for men to search out their own glory is not glory.

He whose spirit is without restraint
Is like a city that is broken down and hath no wall.

As snow in summer, and as rain in harvest,
So honour is not seemly for a fool.

As the sparrow in her wandering, as the swallow in her flying,
So the curse that is causeless lighteth not.

A whip for the horse, a bridle for the ass,
And a rod for the back of fools.
Answer not a fool according to his folly,

THE BOOK OF PROVERBS

Lest thou also be like unto him.
Answer a fool according to his folly,
Lest he be wise in his own conceit.
He that sendeth a message by the hand of a fool
Cutteth off his own feet, and drinketh in damage.
The legs of the lame hang loose:
So is a parable in the mouth of fools.
As a bag of gems in a heap of stones,
So is he that giveth honour to a fool.
As a thorn that goeth up into the hand of a drunkard,
So is a parable in the mouth of fools.
As an archer that woundeth all,
So is he that hireth the fool and he that hireth them that pass by.
As a dog that returneth to his vomit,
So is a fool that repeateth his folly.
Seest thou a man wise in his own conceit?
There is more hope of a fool than of him.

The sluggard saith, "There is a lion in the way!
A lion is in the streets!"
As the door turneth upon its hinges,
So doth the sluggard upon his bed.
The sluggard burieth his hand in the dish;
It wearieth him to bring it again to his mouth.
The sluggard is wiser in his own conceit
Than seven men that can render a reason.

He that passeth by, and vexeth himself with strife belonging not to
 him,
Is like one that taketh a dog by the ears.

As a madman who casteth firebrands,
Arrows, and death;
So is the man that deceiveth his neighbour,
And saith, "Am not I in sport?"

For lack of wood the fire goeth out:
And where there is no whisperer, contention ceaseth.

THE BOOK OF PROVERBS

As coals are to hot embers, and wood to fire;
So is a contentious man to inflame strife.

The words of a whisperer are as dainty morsels,
And they go down into the innermost parts of the belly.

Fervent lips and a wicked heart
Are like an earthen vessel overlaid with silver dross.

He that hateth dissembleth with his lips,
But he layeth up deceit within him:
When he speaketh fair, believe him not;
For there are seven abominations in his heart:
Though his hatred cover itself with guile,
His wickedness shall be openly showed before the congregation.

A lying tongue hateth those whom it hath wounded;
And a flattering mouth worketh ruin.

Boast not thyself of to-morrow;
For thou knowest not what a day may bring forth.

Let another man praise thee, and not thine own mouth;
A stranger, and not thine own lips.

A stone is heavy, and the sand weighty;
But a fool's vexation is heavier than them both.

Wrath is cruel, and anger is outrageous;
But who is able to stand before jealousy?

Better is open rebuke
Than love that is hidden.

Faithful are the wounds of a friend:
But the kisses of an enemy are profuse.

The full soul loatheth a honeycomb:
But to the hungry soul every bitter thing is sweet.

As a bird that wandereth from her nest,
So is a man that wandereth from his place.

THE BOOK OF PROVERBS

Ointment and perfume rejoice the heart:
So doth the sweetness of a man's friend that cometh of hearty counsel.

Thine own friend, and thy father's friend, forsake not;
And go not to thy brother's house in the day of thy calamity:
Better is a neighbour that is near than a brother far off.

He that blesseth his friend with a loud voice, rising early in the
    morning,
It shall be counted a curse to him.

A continual dropping in a very rainy day
And a contentious woman are alike:
He that would restrain her restraineth the wind,
And his right hand encountereth oil.

Iron sharpeneth iron;
So a man sharpeneth the countenance of his friend.

As in water face answereth to face,
So the heart of man to man.

Sheol and Abaddon are never satisfied;
And the eyes of man are never satisfied.

Though thou shouldest bray a fool in a mortar with a pestle among
    bruised corn,
Yet will not his foolishness depart from him.

The wicked flee when no man pursueth:
But the righteous are bold as a lion.

A needy man that oppresseth the poor
Is like a sweeping rain which leaveth no food.

He that augmenteth his substance by usury and increase,
Gathereth it for him that hath pity on the poor.

The rich man is wise in his own conceit;
But the poor that hath understanding searcheth him out.

As a roaring lion, and a ranging bear;
So is a wicked ruler over a poor people.

THE BOOK OF PROVERBS

The prince that lacketh understanding is also a great oppressor:
But he that hateth covetousness shall prolong his days.

He that tilleth his land shall have plenty of bread:
But he that followeth after vain persons shall have poverty enough.

The bloodthirsty hate him that is perfect:
And as for the upright, they seek his life.

If a ruler hearkeneth to falsehood,
All his servants are wicked.

The poor man and the oppressor meet together:
The Lord lighteneth the eyes of them both.

The king that faithfully judgeth the poor,
His throne shall be established for ever.

The rod and reproof give wisdom:
But a child left to himself causeth shame to his mother.

Correct thy son, and he shall give thee rest;
Yea, he shall give delight unto thy soul.

Where there is no vision, the people cast off restraint:
But he that keepeth the law, happy is he.

Seest thou a man that is hasty in his words?
There is more hope of a fool than of him.

He that delicately bringeth up his servant from a child
Shall have him become a son at the last.
An angry man stirreth up strife,
And a wrathful man aboundeth in transgression.
A man's pride shall bring him low:
But he that is of a lowly spirit shall obtain honour.
Whoso is partner with a thief hateth his own soul:
He heareth the adjuration and uttereth nothing.
The fear of man bringeth a snare:
But whoso putteth his trust in the Lord shall be safe.
Many seek the ruler's favour:

THE BOOK OF PROVERBS

But a man's judgment cometh from the Lord.
An unjust man is an abomination to the righteous:
And he that is upright in the way is an abomination to the wicked.

The Words of Agur

The words of Agur the son of Jakeh: the oracle.

The man saith unto Ithiel, unto Ithiel and Ucal:
"Surely I am more brutish than any man,
And have not the understanding of a man:
And I have not learned wisdom,
Neither have I the knowledge of the Holy One.
Who hath ascended up into heaven, and descended?
Who hath gathered the wind in his fists?
Who hath bound the waters in his garment?
Who hath established all the ends of the earth?
What is his name, and what is his son's name, if thou knowest?"

Every word of God is tried:
He is a shield unto them that trust in him.
Add thou not unto his words,
Lest he reprove thee, and thou be found a liar.

Two things have I asked of thee;
Deny me them not before I die:
Remove far from me vanity and lies:
Give me neither poverty nor riches;
Feed me with the food that is needful for me:
Lest I be full, and deny thee, and say, "Who is the Lord?"
Or lest I be poor, and steal,
And use profanely the name of my God.

Slander not a servant unto his master,
Lest he curse thee, and thou be held guilty.

There is a generation that curseth their father,
And doth not bless their mother.
There is a generation that are pure in their own eyes,
And yet are not washed from their filthiness.

THE BOOK OF PROVERBS

There is a generation, oh how lofty are their eyes!
And their eyelids are lifted up.
There is a generation whose teeth are as swords, and their jaw teeth
  as knives,
To devour the poor from off the earth, and the needy from among
  men.

The horseleach hath two daughters, crying, "Give, give."
There are three things that are never satisfied,
Yea, four that say not, "Enough":
The grave; and the barren womb;
The earth that is not satisfied with water;
And the fire that saith not, "Enough."
The eye that mocketh at his father,
And despiseth to obey his mother,
The ravens of the valley shall pick it out,
And the young eagles shall eat it.

There be three things which are too wonderful for me,
Yea, four which I know not:
The way of an eagle in the air;
The way of a serpent upon a rock;
The way of a ship in the midst of the sea;
And the way of a man with a maid.
So is the way of an adulterous woman;
She eateth, and wipeth her mouth,
And saith, "I have done no wickedness."

For three things the earth doth tremble,
And for four, which it cannot bear:
For a servant when he is king;
And a fool when he is filled with meat;
For an odious woman when she is married;
And a handmaid that is heir to her mistress.

There be four things which are little upon the earth,
But they are exceeding wise:
The ants are a people not strong,

THE BOOK OF PROVERBS

Yet they provide their meat in the summer;
The conies are but a feeble folk,
Yet make they their houses in the rocks;
The locusts have no king,
Yet go they forth all of them by bands;
The lizard taketh hold with her hands,
Yet is she in kings' palaces.

There be three things which are stately in their march,
Yea, four which are stately in going:
The lion, which is mightiest among beasts,
And turneth not away for any;
The greyhound; the he-goat also;
And the king, against whom there is no rising up.

If thou hast done foolishly in lifting up thyself,
Or if thou hast thought evil,
Lay thine hand upon thy mouth.
For the churning of milk bringeth forth butter,
And the wringing of the nose bringeth forth blood:
So the forcing of wrath bringeth forth strife.

The Words of King Lemuel

The words of King Lemuel: the oracle which his mother taught him.

What, my son? and what, O son of my womb?
And what, O son of my vows?
Give not thy strength unto women,
Nor thy ways to that which destroyeth kings.
It is not for kings, O Lemuel, it is not for kings to drink wine;
Nor for princes to say, "Where is strong drink?"
Lest they drink, and forget the law,
And pervert the judgment of any that is afflicted.
Give strong drink unto him that is ready to perish,
And wine unto the bitter in soul:
Let him drink, and forget his poverty,

THE BOOK OF PROVERBS

And remember his misery no more.
Open thy mouth for the dumb,
In the cause of all such as are left desolate.
Open thy mouth, judge righteously,
And minister judgment to the poor and needy.

"A Virtuous Woman Who Can Find?"

A virtuous woman who can find?
For her price is far above rubies.
The heart of her husband trusteth in her,
And he shall have no lack of gain.
She doeth him good and not evil
All the days of her life.
She seeketh wool and flax,
And worketh willingly with her hands.
She is like the merchant-ships;
She bringeth her food from afar.
She riseth also while it is yet night,
And giveth meat to her household,
And their task to her maidens.
She considereth a field, and buyeth it:
With the fruit of her hands she planteth a vineyard.
She girdeth her loins with strength,
And maketh strong her arms.
She perceiveth that her merchandise is profitable:
Her lamp goeth not out by night.
She layeth her hands to the distaff,
And her hands hold the spindle.
She spreadeth out her hand to the poor;
Yea, she reacheth forth her hands to the needy.
She is not afraid of the snow for her household;
For all her household are clothed with scarlet.
She maketh for herself carpets of tapestry;
Her clothing is fine linen and purple.
Her husband is known in the gates,
When he sitteth among the elders of the land.

THE BOOK OF PROVERBS

*She maketh linen garments and selleth them;
And delivereth girdles unto the merchant.
Strength and dignity are her clothing;
And she laugheth at the time to come.
She openeth her mouth with wisdom;
And the law of kindness is on her tongue.
She looketh well to the ways of her household,
And eateth not the bread of idleness.
Her children rise up, and call her blessed;
Her husband also, and he praiseth her, saying:
"Many daughters have done virtuously,
But thou excellest them all."
Favour is deceitful, and beauty is vain:
But a woman that feareth the Lord, she shall be praised.
Give her of the fruit of her hands;
And let her works praise her in the gates.*

THE BOOK OF JOB

A PHILOSOPHICAL DRAMA

The book of job is the nearest approach to formal drama in the Bible. Into the framework of an old pre-Deuteronomic folk tale, retained in the Prologue and Epilogue, one of the greatest of the world's poets inserted, in the fourth century, a series of impassioned dialogues culminating in the speech of the Lord out of the whirlwind. The folk tale itself already had a spacious setting in the golden age of the Patriarchs when the Sons of God walked with men, but in essence it was a simple story of piety rewarded after suffering, such as is common in most religious literature; its underlying idea is still reflected in the current phrases, now however often used with a shade of disparagement—"he has the patience of Job" or "he is as patient as Job."

In the dramatic section of the book, Job is shown as anything but patient. With increasing anger, scorn, and despair he answers the traditional insistence of his three friends that his sufferings are a punishment for sin, until the argument is ended by the voice of the Lord, and Job, overwhelmed by the Divine Majesty, admits that the problem of evil is too deep for the human mind to solve.

A stupid interpolator inserted just before the whirlwind an insufferably long and tedious speech by a fourth friend of Job; since it contributes nothing of importance to the discussion and interrupts the dramatic flow of the poem, it is omitted in this text.

In one section, where there is an obviously incorrect sequence of speeches, a slight rearrangement also seemed necessary, following the order adopted by Moulton in "The Modern Reader's Bible."

The Book of JOB

A PHILOSOPHICAL DRAMA

Characters in the Prologue and Epilogue

THE LORD	SECOND MESSENGER
SATAN	THIRD MESSENGER
THE SONS OF GOD	JOB'S WIFE
JOB	ELIPHAZ THE TEMANITE
FIRST MESSENGER	BILDAD THE SHUHITE
ZOPHAR THE NAAMATHITE	

Characters in the Drama

JOB	BILDAD THE SHUHITE
ELIPHAZ THE TEMANITE	ZOPHAR THE NAAMATHITE
VOICE OUT OF THE WHIRLWIND	

Prologue

THERE WAS A MAN in the land of Uz, whose name was Job; and that man was perfect and upright, and one that feared God, and eschewed evil. And there were born unto him seven sons and three daughters. His substance also was seven thousand sheep, and three thousand camels, and five hundred yoke of oxen, and five hundred she-asses, and a very great household; so that this man was the greatest of all the children of the east. And his sons went and held a feast in the house of each one upon his day; and they sent and called for their three sisters to eat and to drink with them. And it was so, when the days of their feasting were gone about, that Job sent and sanctified them, and rose up early

THE BOOK OF JOB

in the morning, and offered burnt offerings according to the number of them all: for Job said,

> *"It may be that my sons have sinned,*
> *And renounced God in their hearts."*

Thus did Job continually.

Now there was a day when the sons of God came to present themselves before the Lord, and Satan came also among them. And the Lord said unto Satan,
"Whence comest thou?"
Then Satan answered the Lord, and said,

> *"From going to and fro in the earth,*
> *And from walking up and down in it."*

And the Lord said unto Satan,

> *"Hast thou considered my servant Job?*
> *For there is none like him in the earth,*
> *A perfect and an upright man,*
> *One that feareth God, and escheweth evil."*

Then Satan answered the Lord, and said,

> *"Doth Job fear God for nought?*
> *Hast not thou made a hedge about him,*
> *And about his house, and about all that he hath, on every side?*
> *Thou hast blessed the work of his hands,*
> *And his substance is increased in the land.*
> *But put forth thine hand now,*
> *And touch all that he hath,*
> *And he will renounce thee to thy face."*

And the Lord said unto Satan,

> *"Behold, all that he hath is in thy power;*
> *Only upon himself put not forth thine hand."*

So Satan went forth from the presence of the Lord.
And it fell on a day when his sons and his daughters were eat-

THE BOOK OF JOB

ing and drinking wine in their eldest brother's house, that there came a messenger unto Job, and said,

> "The oxen were plowing,
> And the asses feeding beside them:
> And the Sabeans fell upon them, and took them away;
> Yea, they have slain the servants with the edge of the sword;
> And I only am escaped alone to tell thee."

While he was yet speaking, there came also another, and said,

> "The fire of God is fallen from heaven,
> And hath burned up the sheep, and the servants, and consumed them;
> And I only am escaped alone to tell thee."

While he was yet speaking, there came also another, and said,

> "The Chaldeans made three bands,
> And fell upon the camels, and have taken them away,
> Yea, and slain the servants with the edge of the sword;
> And I only am escaped alone to tell thee."

While he was yet speaking, there came also another, and said,

> "Thy sons and thy daughters were eating
> And drinking wine in their eldest brother's house:
> And, behold, there came a great wind from the wilderness,
> And smote the four corners of the house,
> And it fell upon the young men, and they are dead;
> And I only am escaped alone to tell thee."

Then Job arose, and rent his mantle, and shaved his head, and fell down upon the ground, and worshipped; and he said,

> "Naked came I out of my mother's womb,
> And naked shall I return thither:
> The Lord gave, and the Lord hath taken away;
> Blessed be the name of the Lord."

In all this Job sinned not, nor charged God with foolishness. Again there was a day when the sons of God came to present

THE BOOK OF JOB

themselves before the Lord, and Satan came also among them to present himself before the Lord. And the Lord said unto Satan, "From whence comest thou?"

And Satan answered the Lord, and said,

> "From going to and fro in the earth,
> And from walking up and down in it."

And the Lord said unto Satan,

"Hast thou considered my servant Job?
For there is none like him in the earth,
A perfect and an upright man,
One that feareth God, and escheweth evil:
And he still holdeth fast his integrity,
Although thou movedst me against him, to destroy him without cause."

And Satan answered the Lord, and said,

> "Skin for skin!
> Yea, all that a man hath will he give for his life.
> But put forth thine hand now,
> And touch his bone and his flesh,
> And he will renounce thee to thy face."

And the Lord said unto Satan, "Behold, he is in thine hand; only spare his life."

So Satan went forth from the presence of the Lord, and smote Job with sore boils from the sole of his foot unto his crown. And he took him a potsherd to scrape himself withal; and he sat among the ashes. Then said his wife unto him,

> "Dost thou still hold fast thine integrity?
> Renounce God, and die."

But he said unto her,

> "Thou speakest as one of the foolish women speaketh.
> What? shall we receive good at the hand of God,
> And shall we not receive evil?"

THE BOOK OF JOB

In all this did not Job sin with his lips.

Now when Job's three friends heard of all this evil that was come upon him, they came every one from his own place; Eliphaz the Temanite, and Bildad the Shuhite, and Zophar the Naamathite: and they made an appointment together to come to bemoan him and to comfort him. And when they lifted up their eyes afar off, and knew him not, they lifted up their voice, and wept; and they rent every one his mantle, and sprinkled dust upon their heads toward heaven. So they sat down with him upon the ground seven days and seven nights, and none spoke a word unto him: for they saw that his grief was very great.

Part I

JOB. *Let the day perish wherein I was born,*
And the night which said, "There is a man child conceived."
Let that day be darkness;
Let not God regard it from above,
Neither let the light shine upon it.
Let darkness and the shadow of death claim it for their own;
Let a cloud dwell upon it;
Let all that maketh black the day terrify it.
As for that night, let thick darkness seize upon it:
Let it not rejoice among the days of the year;
Let it not come into the number of the months.
Lo, let that night be barren;
Let no joyful voice come therein.
Let them curse it that curse the day,
Who are ready to rouse up Leviathan.
Let the stars of the twilight thereof be dark:
Let it look for light, but have none;
Neither let it behold the eyelids of the morning:
Because it shut not up the doors of my mother's womb,
Nor hid trouble from mine eyes.
Why died I not from the womb?
Why did I not give up the ghost when I came out of the belly?
Why did the knees receive me?

THE BOOK OF JOB

Or why the breasts, that I should suck?
For now should I have lain down and been quiet;
I should have slept; then had I been at rest:
With kings and counsellors of the earth,
Which built up waste places for themselves;
Or with princes that had gold,
Who filled their houses with silver:
Or as a hidden untimely birth I had not been;
As infants which never saw light.
There the wicked cease from troubling;
And there the weary be at rest.
There the prisoners are at ease together;
They hear not the voice of the taskmaster.
The small and great are there;
And the servant is free from his master.
Wherefore is light given to him that is in misery,
And life unto the bitter in soul;
Which long for death, but it cometh not;
And dig for it more than for hid treasures;
Which rejoice exceedingly,
And are glad, when they can find the grave?
Why is light given to a man whose way is hid,
And whom God hath hedged in?
For my sighing cometh before I eat,
And my roarings are poured out like water.
For the thing which I fear cometh upon me,
And that which I am afraid of cometh unto me.
I am not at ease, neither am I quiet, neither have I rest;
But trouble cometh.

ELIPHAZ THE TEMANITE. If one essay to commune with thee,
    wilt thou be grieved?
But who can withhold himself from speaking?
Behold, thou hast instructed many,
And thou hast strengthened the weak hands.
Thy words have upheld him that was falling,
And thou hast confirmed the feeble knees.

THE BOOK OF JOB

But now it is come unto thee, and thou faintest;
It toucheth thee, and thou art troubled.
Is not thy fear of God thy confidence,
And thy hope the integrity of thy ways?
Remember, I pray thee, who ever perished, being innocent?
Or where were the upright cut off?
According as I have seen, they that plow iniquity,
And sow trouble, reap the same.
By the breath of God they perish,
And by the blast of his anger are they consumed.
The roaring of the lion, and the voice of the fierce lion,
And the teeth of the young lions, are broken.
The old lion perisheth for lack of prey,
And the whelps of the lioness are scattered abroad.
Now a thing was secretly brought to me,
And mine ear received a whisper thereof.
In thoughts from the visions of the night,
When deep sleep falleth on men,
Fear came upon me, and trembling,
Which made all my bones to shake.
Then a spirit passed before my face;
The hair of my flesh stood up.
It stood still, but I could not discern the appearance thereof;
A form was before mine eyes:
There was silence, and I heard a voice, saying,
"Shall mortal man be more just than God?
Shall a man be more pure than his Maker?
Behold, he putteth no trust in his servants;
And his angels he chargeth with folly:
How much more them that dwell in houses of clay,
Whose foundation is in the dust,
Which are crushed before the moth!
Betwixt morning and evening they are destroyed:
They perish for ever without any regarding it.
Is not their tent-cord plucked within them?
They die, and that without wisdom."

THE BOOK OF JOB

Call now; is there any that will answer thee?
And to which of the holy ones wilt thou turn?
For vexation killeth the foolish man,
And jealousy slayeth the silly one.
I have seen the foolish taking root:
But suddenly I cursed his habitation.
His children are far from safety,
And they are crushed in the gate,
Neither is there any to deliver them.
Whose harvest the hungry eateth up,
And taketh it even out of the thorns,
And the snare gapeth for their substance.
For affliction cometh not forth of the dust,
Neither doth trouble spring out of the ground;
But man is born unto trouble,
As the sparks fly upward.
But as for me, I would seek unto God,
And unto God would I commit my cause:
Which doeth great things and unsearchable;
Marvellous things without number:
Who giveth rain upon the earth,
And sendeth waters upon the fields:
So that he setteth up on high those that be low;
And those which mourn are exalted to safety.
He frustrateth the devices of the crafty,
So that their hands cannot perform their enterprise.
He taketh the wise in their own craftiness:
And the counsel of the froward is carried headlong.
They meet with darkness in the daytime,
And grope at noonday as in the night.
But he saveth from the sword of their mouth,
Even the needy from the hand of the mighty.
So the poor hath hope,
And iniquity stoppeth her mouth.
Behold, happy is the man whom God correcteth:
Therefore despise not thou the chastening of the Almighty.

THE BOOK OF JOB

For he maketh sore, and bindeth up;
He woundeth, and his hands make whole.
He shall deliver thee in six troubles;
Yea, in seven there shall no evil touch thee.
In famine he shall redeem thee from death;
And in war from the power of the sword.
Thou shalt be hid from the scourge of the tongue;
Neither shalt thou be afraid of destruction when it cometh.
At destruction and dearth thou shalt laugh;
Neither shalt thou be afraid of the beasts of the earth.
For thou shalt be in league with the stones of the field;
And the beasts of the field shall be at peace with thee.
And thou shalt know that thy tent is in peace;
And thou shalt visit thy fold, and shalt miss nothing.
Thou shalt know also that thy seed shall be great,
And thine offspring as the grass of the earth.
Thou shalt come to thy grave in a full age,
Like as a shock of corn cometh in in its season.
Lo this, we have searched it, so it is;
Hear it, and know thou it for thy good.
JOB. Oh that my vexation were but weighed,
And my calamity laid in the balances together!
For now it would be heavier than the sand of the seas:
Therefore have my words been rash.
For the arrows of the Almighty are within me,
The poison whereof my spirit drinketh up:
The terrors of God do set themselves in array against me.
Doth the wild ass bray when he hath grass?
Or loweth the ox over his fodder?
Can that which hath no savour be eaten without salt?
Or is there any taste in the white of an egg?
My soul refuseth to touch them;
They are as loathsome meat to me.
Oh that I might have my request;
And that God would grant me the thing that I long for!
Even that it would please God to crush me;

THE BOOK OF JOB

That he would let loose his hand, and cut me off!
Then should I yet have comfort;
Yea, I would exult in pain that spareth not:
For I have not denied the words of the Holy One.
What is my strength, that I should wait?
And what is mine end, that I should be patient?
Is my strength the strength of stones?
Or is my flesh of brass?
Is it not that I have no help in me,
And that effectual working is driven quite from me?
To him that is ready to faint kindness should be showed from his **friend**;
Even to him that forsaketh the fear of the Almighty.
My brethren have dealt deceitfully as a brook,
As the channel of brooks that pass away;
Which are black by reason of the ice,
And wherein the snow hideth itself:
What time they wax warm, they vanish:
When it is hot, they are consumed out of their place.
The caravans that travel by the way of them turn aside;
They go up into the waste, and perish.
The caravans of Tema looked,
The companies of Sheba waited for them.
They were ashamed because they had hoped;
They came thither, and were confounded.
For now ye are nothing;
Ye see a terror, and are afraid.
Did I say, "Give unto me?"
Or, "Offer a present for me of your substance?"
Or, "Deliver me from the adversary's hand?"
Or, "Redeem me from the hand of the oppressors?"
Teach me, and I will hold my peace:
And cause me to understand wherein I have erred.
How forcible are words of uprightness!
But what doth your arguing reprove?
Do ye imagine to reprove words?
Seeing that the speeches of one that is desperate are as wind.

THE BOOK OF JOB

Yea, ye would cast lots upon the fatherless,
And make merchandise of your friend.
Now therefore be pleased to look upon me;
For surely I shall not lie to your face.
Return, I pray you, let there be no injustice;
Yea, return again, my cause is righteous.
Is there injustice on my tongue?
Cannot my taste discern mischievous things?

Is there not a warfare to man upon earth?
And are not his days like the days of a hireling?
As a servant that earnestly desireth the shadow,
And as a hireling that looketh for his wages:
So am I made to possess months of vanity,
And wearisome nights are appointed to me.
When I lie down, I say,
"When shall I arise?" but the night is long;
And I am full of tossings to and fro unto the dawning of the day.
My flesh is clothed with worms and clods of dust;
My skin closeth up and breaketh out afresh.
My days are swifter than a weaver's shuttle,
And are spent without hope.
Oh remember that my life is wind:
Mine eyes shall no more see good.
The eye of him that seeth me shall behold me no more:
Thine eyes shall be upon me, but I shall not be.
As the cloud is consumed and vanisheth away,
So he that goeth down to Sheol shall come up no more.
He shall return no more to his house,
Neither shall his place know him any more.
Therefore I will not refrain my mouth;
I will speak in the anguish of my spirit;
I will complain in the bitterness of my soul.
Am I a sea, or a sea-monster,
That thou settest a watch over me?
When I say, "My bed shall comfort me.

THE BOOK OF JOB

My couch shall ease my complaint";
Then thou scarest me with dreams,
And terrifiest me through visions:
So that my soul chooseth strangling,
And death rather than these my bones.
I loathe my life; I would not live always:
Let me alone; for my days are vanity.
What is man, that thou shouldest magnify him,
And that thou shouldest set thine heart upon him,
And that thou shouldest visit him every morning,
And try him every moment?
How long wilt thou not look away from me,
Nor let me alone till I swallow down my spittle?
If I have sinned, what do I unto thee, O thou watcher of men?
Why hast thou set me as a mark for thee,
So that I am a burden to myself?
And why dost thou not pardon my transgression, and take away mine
    iniquity?
For now shall I lie down in the dust;
And thou shalt seek me diligently, but I shall not be.
BILDAD THE SHUHITE. How long wilt thou speak these things?
And how long shall the words of thy mouth be like a mighty wind?
Doth God pervert judgment?
Or doth the Almighty pervert justice?
If thy children have sinned against him,
And he have delivered them into the hand of their transgression:
If thou wouldest seek diligently unto God,
And make thy supplication to the Almighty;
If thou wert pure and upright;
Surely now he would awake for thee,
And make the habitation of thy righteousness prosperous.
And though thy beginning was small,
Yet thy latter end should greatly increase.
For inquire, I pray thee, of the former age,
And apply thyself to that which their fathers have searched out
(For we are but of yesterday, and know nothing,

THE BOOK OF JOB

Because our days upon earth are a shadow) :
Shall not they teach thee, and tell thee,
And utter words out of their heart?
Can the rush grow up without mire?
Can the flag grow without water?
Whilst it is yet in its greenness, and not cut down,
It withereth before any other herb.
So are the paths of all that forget God;
And the hope of the godless man shall perish:
Whose confidence shall break in sunder,
And whose trust is a spider's web.
He shall lean upon his house, but it shall not stand:
He shall hold fast thereby, but it shall not endure.
He is green before the sun,
And his shoots go forth over his garden.
His roots are wrapped about the heap,
He beholdeth the place of stones.
If he be destroyed from his place,
Then it shall deny him, saying, "I have not seen thee."
Behold, this is the joy of his way,
And out of the earth shall others spring.
Behold, God will not cast away a perfect man,
Neither will he uphold the evildoers.
He will yet fill thy mouth with laughter,
And thy lips with shouting.
They that hate thee shall be clothed with shame;
And the tent of the wicked shall be no more.

JOB. Of a truth I know that it is so:
But how can man be just with God?
If he be pleased to contend with him,
He cannot answer him one of a thousand.
He is wise in heart, and mighty in strength:
Who hath hardened himself against him, and prospered?
Which removeth the mountains, and they know it not,
When he overturneth them in his anger.

THE BOOK OF JOB

Which shaketh the earth out of her place,
And the pillars thereof tremble.
Which commandeth the sun, and it riseth not;
And sealeth up the stars.
Which alone stretcheth out the heavens,
And treadeth upon the waves of the sea.
Which maketh the Bear, Orion, and the Pleiades,
And the chambers of the south.
Which doeth great things past finding out;
Yea, marvellous things without number.
Lo, he goeth by me, and I see him not:
He passeth on also, but I perceive him not.
Behold, he seizeth the prey, who can hinder him?
Who will say unto him, "What doest thou?"
God will not withdraw his anger;
The helpers of Rahab do stoop under him.
How much less shall I answer him,
And choose out my words to reason with him?
Whom, though I were righteous, yet would I not answer;
I would make supplication to mine adversary.
If I had called, and he had answered me;
Yet would I not believe that he hearkened unto my voice.
For he breaketh me with a tempest,
And multiplieth my wounds without cause.
He will not suffer me to take my breath,
But filleth me with bitterness.
If we speak of the strength of the mighty, lo, he is there!
And if of judgment, who will appoint me a time?
Though I be righteous, mine own mouth shall condemn me:
Though I be perfect, it shall prove me perverse.
I am perfect; I regard not myself;
I despise my life.
It is all one; therefore I say,
He destroyeth the perfect and the wicked.
If the scourge slay suddenly,
He will mock at the trial of the innocent.

THE BOOK OF JOB

The earth is given into the hand of the wicked:
He covereth the faces of the judges thereof;
If it be not he, who then is it?
Now my days are swifter than a post:
They flee away, they see no good.
They are passed away as the swift ships:
As the eagle that swoopeth on the prey.
If I say, "I will forget my complaint,
I will put off my sad countenance, and be of good cheer":
I am afraid of all my sorrows,
I know that thou wilt not hold me innocent.
I shall be condemned;
Why then do I labour in vain?
If I wash myself with snow water,
And make my hands never so clean;
Yet wilt thou plunge me in the ditch,
And mine own clothes shall abhor me.
For he is not a man, as I am, that I should answer him,
That we should come together in judgment.
There is no daysman betwixt us,
That might lay his hand upon us both.
Let him take his rod away from me,
And let not his terror make me afraid:
Then would I speak, and not fear him;
For I am not so in myself.

My soul is weary of my life;
I will give free course to my complaint;
I will speak in the bitterness of my soul.
I will say unto God, "Do not condemn me;
Show me wherefore thou contendest with me.
Is it good unto thee that thou shouldest oppress,
That thou shouldest despise the work of thine hands,
And shine upon the counsel of the wicked?
Hast thou eyes of flesh,
Or seest thou as man seeth?

THE BOOK OF JOB

Are thy days as the days of man,
Or thy years as man's days,
That thou inquirest after mine iniquity,
And searchest after my sin,
Although thou knowest that I am not wicked;
And there is none that can deliver out of thine hand?
Thine hands have framed me and fashioned me
Together round about; yet thou dost destroy me.
Remember, I beseech thee, that thou hast fashioned me as clay;
And wilt thou bring me into dust again?
Hast thou not poured me out as milk,
And curdled me like cheese?
Thou hast clothed me with skin and flesh,
And knit me together with bones and sinews.
Thou hast granted me life and favour,
And thy visitation hath preserved my spirit.
Yet these things thou didst hide in thine heart;
I know that this is with thee:
If I sin, then thou markest me,
And thou wilt not acquit me from mine iniquity.
If I be wicked, woe unto me;
And if I be righteous, yet shall I not lift up my head;
Being filled with ignominy
And looking upon mine affliction.
And if my head exalt itself, thou huntest me as a lion:
And again thou showest thyself marvellous upon me.
Thou renewest thy witnesses against me,
And increasest thine indignation upon me;
Changes and warfare are with me.
Wherefore then hast thou brought me forth out of the womb?
I had given up the ghost, and no eye had seen me.
I should have been as though I had not been;
I should have been carried from the womb to the grave.
Are not my days few? cease then,
And let me alone, that I may take comfort a little,
Before I go whence I shall not return,

THE BOOK OF JOB

Even to the land of darkness and of the shadow of death;
A land of thick darkness, as darkness itself;
A land of the shadow of death, without any order,
And where the light is as darkness."
ZOPHAR THE NAAMATHITE. Should not the multitude of words
    be answered?
And should a man full of talk be justified?
Should thy boastings make men hold their peace?
And when thou mockest, shall no man make thee ashamed?
For thou sayest, "My doctrine is pure,
And I am clean in thine eyes."
But oh that God would speak,
And open his lips against thee;
And that he would show thee the secrets of wisdom,
That it is manifold in effectual working!
Know therefore that God exacteth of thee less than thine iniquity
    deserveth.
Canst thou by searching find out God?
Canst thou find out the Almighty unto perfection?
It is high as heaven; what canst thou do?
Deeper than Sheol; what canst thou know?
The measure thereof is longer than the earth,
And broader than the sea,
If he pass through, and shut up,
And call unto judgment, then who can hinder him?
For he knoweth vain men:
He seeth iniquity also, even though he consider it not.
But vain man is void of understanding,
Yea, man is born as a wild ass's colt.
If thou set thine heart aright,
And stretch out thine hands toward him;
If iniquity be in thine hand, put it far away,
And let not unrighteousness dwell in thy tents;
Surely then shalt thou lift up thy face without spot;
Yea, thou shalt be steadfast, and shalt not fear:
For thou shalt forget thy misery;

THE BOOK OF JOB

Thou shalt remember it as waters that are passed away:
And thy life shall be clearer than the noonday;
Though there be darkness, it shall be as the morning.
And thou shalt be secure, because there is hope;
Yea, thou shalt search about thee, and shalt take thy rest in safety.
Also thou shalt lie down, and none shall make thee afraid;
Yea, many shall make suit unto thee.
But the eyes of the wicked shall fail,
And they shall have no way to flee,
And their hope shall be the giving up of the ghost.
JOB. No doubt but ye are the people,
And wisdom shall die with you.
But I have understanding as well as you;
I am not inferior to you:
Yea, who knoweth not such things as these?
I am as one that is a laughing-stock to his neighbour,
A man that called upon God, and he answered him:
The just, the perfect man is a laughing-stock.
In the thought of him that is at ease there is contempt for misfortune;
It is ready for them whose foot slippeth.
The tents of robbers prosper,
And they that provoke God are secure;
Into whose hand God bringeth abundantly.
But ask now the beasts, and they shall teach thee;
And the fowls of the air and they shall tell thee:
Or speak to the earth, and it shall teach thee;
And the fishes of the sea shall declare unto thee.
Who knoweth not in all these,
That the hand of the Lord hath wrought this?
In whose hand is the soul of every living thing,
And the breath of all mankind.
Doth not the ear try words,
Even as the palate tasteth its meat?
With aged men is wisdom,
And in length of days understanding
With him is wisdom and might;

THE BOOK OF JOB

He hath counsel and understanding.
Behold, he breaketh down, and it cannot be built again;
He shutteth up a man, and there can be no opening.
Behold, he withholdeth the waters, and they dry up;
Again, he sendeth them out, and they overturn the earth.
With him is strength and effectual working;
The deceived and the deceiver are his.
He leadeth counsellors away spoiled,
And judges maketh he fools.
He looseth the bonds of kings,
And bindeth their loins with a girdle.
He leadeth priests away spoiled,
And overthroweth the mighty.
He removeth the speech of the trusty,
And taketh away the understanding of the elders.
He poureth contempt upon princes,
And looseth the belt of the strong.
He discovereth deep things out of darkness,
And bringeth out to light the shadow of death.
He increaseth the nations, and destroyeth them:
He spreadeth the nations abroad, and bringeth them in.
He taketh away the heart of the chiefs of the people of the earth,
And causeth them to wander in a wilderness where there is no way.
They grope in the dark without light,
And he maketh them to stagger like a drunken man.

JOB. Lo, mine eye hath seen all this,
Mine ear hath heard and understood it.
What ye know, the same do I know also:
I am not inferior unto you.
Surely I would speak to the Almighty,
And I desire to reason with God.
But ye are forgers of lies,
Ye are all physicians of no value.
Oh that ye would altogether hold your peace!
And it should be your wisdom.

THE BOOK OF JOB

Hear now my reasoning,
And hearken to the pleadings of my lips.
Will ye speak unrighteously for God,
And talk deceitfully for him?
Will ye respect his person?
Will ye contend for God?
Is it good that he should search you out?
Or as one deceiveth a man, will ye deceive him?
He will surely reprove you,
If ye do secretly respect persons.
Shall not his excellency make you afraid,
And his dread fall upon you?
Your memorable sayings are proverbs of ashes,
Your defences are defences of clay.
Hold your peace, let me alone, that I may speak,
And let come on me what will.
Wherefore should I take my flesh in my teeth,
And put my life in mine hand?
Though he slay me, yet will I wait for him:
Nevertheless I will maintain my ways before him.
This also shall be my salvation;
For a godless man shall not come before him.
Hear diligently my speech,
And let my declaration be in your ears.
Behold now, I have ordered my cause;
I know that I am righteous.
Who is he that will contend with me?
For now shall I hold my peace and give up the ghost.
Only do not two things unto me,
Then will I not hide myself from thy face:
Withdraw thine hand far from me;
And let not thy terror make me afraid.
Then call thou, and I will answer;
Or let me speak, and answer thou me.
How many are mine iniquities and sins?
Make me to know my transgression and my sin.

THE BOOK OF JOB

Wherefore hidest thou thy face,
And holdest me for thine enemy?
Wilt thou harass a driven leaf?
And wilt thou pursue the dry stubble?
For thou writest bitter things against me,
And makest me to inherit the iniquities of my youth:
Thou puttest my feet also in the stocks, and markest all my paths;
Thou drawest thee a line about the soles of my feet:
Though I am like a rotten thing that consumeth,
Like a garment that is moth-eaten.

Man that is born of a woman
Is of few days, and full of trouble.
He cometh forth like a flower, and is cut down:
He fleeth also as a shadow, and continueth not.
And dost thou open thine eyes upon such a one,
And bringest me into judgment with thee?
Who can bring a clean thing out of an unclean? not one.
Seeing his days are determined, the number of his months is with thee,
And thou hast appointed his bounds that he cannot pass;
Look away from him, that he may rest,
Till he shall accomplish, as a hireling, his day.
For there is hope of a tree, if it be cut down, that it will sprout again,
And that the tender branch thereof will not cease.
Though the root thereof wax old in the earth,
And the stock thereof die in the ground;
Yet through the scent of water it will bud,
And put forth boughs like a plant.
But man dieth, and wasteth away:
Yea, man giveth up the ghost, and where is he?
As the waters fail from the sea,
And the river decayeth and drieth up;
So man lieth down and riseth not:
Till the heavens be no more, they shall not awake,
Nor be roused out of their sleep.
Oh that thou wouldest hide me in Sheol,

THE BOOK OF JOB

That thou wouldest keep me secret, until thy wrath be past,
That thou wouldest appoint me a set time, and remember me!
If a man die, shall he live again?
All the days of my warfare would I wait,
Till my release should come.
Thou shouldest call, and I would answer thee:
Thou wouldest have a desire to the work of thine hands.
But now thou numberest my steps:
Dost thou not watch over my sin?
My transgression is sealed up in a bag,
And thou fastenest up mine iniquity.
And surely the mountain falling cometh to nought,
And the rock is removed out of its place;
The waters wear the stones;
The overflowings thereof wash away the dust of the earth:
And thou destroyest the hope of man.
Thou prevailest for ever against him, and he passeth;
Thou changest his countenance, and sendest him away.
His sons come to honour, and he knoweth it not;
And they are brought low, but he perceiveth it not of them.
But his flesh upon him hath pain,
And his soul within him mourneth.

Part II

ELIPHAZ THE TEMANITE. Should a wise man make answer with vain knowledge,
And fill his belly with the east wind?
Should he reason with unprofitable talk,
Or with speeches wherewith he can do no good?
Yea, thou doest away with fear,
And restrainest devotion before God.
For thine iniquity teacheth thy mouth,
And thou choosest the tongue of the crafty.
Thine own mouth condemneth thee, and not I;
Yea, thine own lips testify against thee.

THE BOOK OF JOB

Art thou the first man that was born?
Or wast thou brought forth before the hills?
Hast thou heard the secret counsel of God?
And dost thou restrain wisdom to thyself?
What knowest thou, that we know not?
What understandest thou, which is not in us?
With us are both the grayheaded and the very aged men,
Much elder than thy father.
Are the consolations of God too small for thee,
And the word that dealeth gently with thee?
Why doth thine heart carry thee away?
And why do thine eyes wink?
That thou turnest thy spirit against God,
And lettest such words go out of thy mouth.
What is man, that he should be clean?
And he which is born of a woman, that he should be righteous?
Behold, he putteth no trust in his holy ones;
Yea, the heavens are not clean in his sight.
How much less one that is abominable and corrupt,
A man that drinketh iniquity like water!
I will show thee, hear thou me;
And that which I have seen I will declare
(Which wise men have told
From their fathers, and have not hid it;
Unto whom alone the land was given,
And no stranger passed among them):
The wicked man travaileth with pain all his days,
Even the number of years that are laid up for the oppressor.
A sound of terrors is in his ears;
In prosperity the spoiler shall come upon him:
He believeth not that he shall return out of darkness,
And he is waited for of the sword:
He wandereth abroad for bread, saying, "Where is it?"
He knoweth that the day of darkness is ready at his hand:
Distress and anguish make him afraid;

THE BOOK OF JOB

They prevail against him, as a king ready to the battle:
Because he hath stretched out his hand against God,
And behaveth himself proudly against the Almighty;
He runneth upon him with a stiff neck,
With the thick bosses of his bucklers:
Because he hath covered his face with his fatness,
And made collops of fat on his flanks;
And he hath dwelt in desolate cities,
In houses which no man inhabited,
Which were ready to become heaps.
He shall not be rich, neither shall his substance continue,
Neither shall their produce bend to the earth.
He shall not depart out of darkness;
The flame shall dry up his branches,
And by the breath of his mouth shall he go away.
Let him not trust in vanity, deceiving himself:
For vanity shall be his recompense.
It shall be accomplished before his time,
And his branch shall not be green.
He shall shake off his unripe grape as the vine,
And shall cast off his flower as the olive.
For the company of the godless shall be barren,
And fire shall consume the tents of bribery.
They conceive mischief, and bring forth iniquity,
And their belly prepareth deceit.
JOB. I have heard many such things:
Miserable comforters are ye all.
Shall vain words have an end?
Or what provoketh thee that thou answerest?
I also could speak as ye do;
If your soul were in my soul's stead,
I could join words together against you,
And shake mine head at you.
But I would strengthen you with my mouth,
And the solace of my lips should assuage your grief.

THE BOOK OF JOB

Though I speak, my grief is not assuaged:
And though I forbear, what am I eased?
But now he hath made me weary:
Thou hast made desolate all my company.
And thou hast laid fast hold on me, which is a witness against me:
And my leanness riseth up against me, it testifieth to my face.
He hath torn me in his wrath, and persecuted me;
He hath gnashed upon me with his teeth:
Mine adversary sharpeneth his eyes upon me.
They have gaped upon me with their mouth;
They have smitten me upon the cheek reproachfully:
They gather themselves together against me.
God delivereth me to the ungodly,
And casteth me into the hands of the wicked.
I was at ease, and he broke me asunder;
Yea, he hath taken me by the neck, and dashed me to pieces:
He hath also set me up for his mark.
His archers compass me round about,
He cleaveth my reins asunder, and doth not spare;
He poureth out my gall upon the ground.
He breaketh me with breach upon breach;
He runneth upon me like a giant.
I have sewed sackcloth upon my skin,
And have laid my horn in the dust.
My face is foul with weeping,
And on my eyelids is the shadow of death;
Although there is no violence in mine hands,
And my prayer is pure.
O earth, cover not thou my blood,
And let my cry have no resting place.
Even now, behold, my witness is in heaven,
And he that voucheth for me is on high.
My friends scorn me:
But mine eye poureth out tears unto God;
That he would maintain the right of a man with God,

THE BOOK OF JOB

And of a son of man with his neighbour!
For when a few years are come,
I shall go the way whence I shall not return.

My spirit is consumed, my days are extinct,
The grave is ready for me.
Surely there are mockers with me,
And mine eye abideth in their provocation.
Give now a pledge, be surety for me with thyself;
Who is there that will strike hands with me?
For thou hast hid their heart from understanding:
Therefore shalt thou not exalt them.
He that denounceth his friends for a prey,
Even the eyes of his children shall fail.
He hath made me also a byword of the people;
And I am become an open abhorring.
Mine eye also is dim by reason of sorrow,
And all my members are as a shadow.
Upright men shall be astonished at this,
And the innocent shall stir up himself against the godless.
Yet shall the righteous hold on his way,
And he that hath clean hands shall wax stronger and stronger.
But return ye, all of you, and come now:
And I shall not find a wise man among you.
My days are past, my purposes are broken off,
Even the thoughts of my heart.
They change the night into day:
"The light," say they, "is near unto the darkness."
If I look for Sheol as mine house;
If I have spread my couch in the darkness;
If I have said to corruption, "Thou art my father!"
To the worm, "Thou art my mother, and my sister!"
Where then is my hope?
And as for my hope, who shall see it?
It shall go down to the bars of Sheol,
When once there is rest in the dust.

THE BOOK OF JOB

BILDAD THE SHUHITE. *How long will ye lay snares for words?*
Consider, and afterwards we will speak.
Wherefore are we counted as beasts,
And are become unclean in your sight?
Thou that tearest thyself in thine anger,
Shall the earth be forsaken for thee?
Or shall the rock be removed out of its place?
Yea, the light of the wicked shall be put out,
And the spark of his fire shall not shine.
The light shall be dark in his tent,
And his lamp above him shall be put out.
The steps of his strength shall be straitened,
And his own counsel shall cast him down.
For he is cast into a net by his own feet,
And he walketh upon the toils.
A gin shall take him by the heel,
And a snare shall lay hold on him.
A noose is hid for him in the ground,
And a trap for him in the way.
Terrors shall make him afraid on every side,
And shall chase him at his heels.
His strength shall be hungerbitten,
And calamity shall be ready for his halting.
It shall devour the members of his body,
Yea, the firstborn of death shall devour his members.
He shall be rooted out of his tent wherein he trusteth;
And he shall be brought to the king of terrors.
There shall dwell in his tent that which is none of his:
Brimstone shall be scattered upon his habitation.
His roots shall be dried up beneath,
And above shall his branch be cut off.
His remembrance shall perish from the earth,
And he shall have no name in the street.
He shall be driven from light into darkness,
And chased out of the world.
He shall have neither son nor son's son among his people,

THE BOOK OF JOB

Nor any remaining where he sojourned.
They that come after shall be astonished at his day,
As they that went before were affrighted.
Surely such are the dwellings of the unrighteous,
And this is the place of him that knoweth not God.
JOB. How long will ye vex my soul,
And break me in pieces with words?
These ten times have ye reproached me:
Ye are not ashamed that ye deal hardly with me.
And be it indeed that I have erred,
Mine error remaineth with myself.
If indeed ye will magnify yourselves against me,
And plead against me my reproach:
Know now that God hath subverted me in my cause,
And hath compassed me with his net.
Behold, I cry out of wrong, but I am not heard:
I cry for help, but there is no judgment.
He hath fenced up my way that I cannot pass.
And hath set darkness in my paths.
He hath stripped me of my glory,
And taken the crown from my head.
He hath broken me down on every side, and I am gone:
And mine hope hath he plucked up like a tree.
He hath also kindled his wrath against me,
And he counteth me unto him as one of his adversaries.
His troops come on together, and cast up their way against me,
And encamp round about my tent.
He hath put my brethren far from me,
And mine acquaintance are wholly estranged from me.
My kinsfolk have failed,
And my familiar friends have forgotten me.
They that dwell in mine house, and my maids, count me for a stranger:
I am an alien in their sight.
I call unto my servant, and he giveth me no answer,
Though I intreat him with my mouth.
My breath is strange to my wife,

THE BOOK OF JOB

And my supplication to the children of my mother's womb.
Even young children despise me;
If I arise, they speak against me.
All my inward friends abhor me:
And they whom I loved are turned against me.
My bone cleaveth to my skin and to my flesh,
And I am escaped with the skin of my teeth.
Have pity upon me, have pity upon me, O ye my friends;
For the hand of God hath touched me.
Why do ye persecute me as God,
And are not satisfied with my flesh?
Oh that my words were now written!
Oh that they were inscribed in a book!
That with an iron pen and lead
They were graven in the rock for ever!
But I know that my redeemer liveth,
And that he shall stand up at the last upon the earth:
And after my skin hath been thus destroyed,
Yet from my flesh shall I see God:
Whom I shall see for myself,
And mine eyes shall behold, and not another.
My reins are consumed within me.
If ye say, "How we will persecute him!"
Seeing that the root of the matter is found in me;
Be ye afraid of the sword:
For wrath bringeth the punishments of the sword,
That ye may know there is a judgment.
ZOPHAR THE NAAMATHITE. *Therefore do my thoughts give answer to me,*
Even by reason of my haste that is in me.
I have heard the reproof which putteth me to shame,
And the spirit of my understanding answereth me.
Knowest thou not this of old time,
Since man was placed upon earth,
That the triumphing of the wicked is short,
And the joy of the godless but for a moment?
Though his excellency mount up to the heavens,

THE BOOK OF JOB

And his head reach unto the clouds;
Yet he shall perish for ever like his own dung:
They which have seen him shall say, "Where is he?"
He shall fly away as a dream, and shall not be found:
Yea, he shall be chased away as a vision of the night.
The eye which saw him shall see him no more;
Neither shall his place any more behold him.
His children shall seek the favour of the poor,
And his hands shall give back his wealth.
His bones are full of his youth,
But it shall lie down with him in the dust.
Though wickedness be sweet in his mouth,
Though he hide it under his tongue;
Though he spare it, and will not let it go,
But keep it still within his mouth;
Yet his meat in his bowels is turned,
It is the gall of asps within him.
He hath swallowed down riches, and he shall vomit them up again:
God shall cast them out of his belly.
He shall suck the poison of asps:
The viper's tongue shall slay him.
He shall not look upon the rivers,
The flowing streams of honey and butter.
That which he laboured for shall he restore, and shall not swallow it
    down;
According to the substance that he hath gotten, he shall not rejoice.
For he hath oppressed and forsaken the poor;
He hath violently taken away a house, and he shall not build it up.
Because he knew no quietness within him,
He shall not save aught of that wherein he delighteth.
There was nothing left that he devoured not;
Therefore his prosperity shall not endure.
In the fulness of his sufficiency he shall be in straits:
The hand of every one that is in misery shall come upon him.
When he is about to fill his belly,
God shall cast the fierceness of his wrath upon him,

THE BOOK OF JOB

And shall rain it upon him while he is eating.
He shall flee from the iron weapon,
And the bow of brass shall strike him through.
He draweth it forth, and it cometh out of his body:
Yea, the glittering point cometh out of his gall;
Terrors are upon him.
All darkness is laid up for his treasures:
A fire not blown by man shall devour him;
It shall consume that which is left in his tent.
The heavens shall reveal his iniquity,
And the earth shall rise up against him.
The increase of his house shall depart,
His goods shall flow away in the day of his wrath.
This is the portion of a wicked man from God,
And the heritage appointed unto him by God.
JOB. Hear diligently my speech;
And let this be your consolations.
Suffer me, and I also will speak;
And after that I have spoken, mock on.
As for me, is my complaint to man?
And why should I not be impatient?
Mark me, and be astonished,
And lay your hand upon your mouth.
Even when I remember I am troubled,
And horror taketh hold on my flesh.
Wherefore do the wicked live,
Become old, yea, wax mighty in power?
Their seed is established with them in their sight,
And their offspring before their eyes.
Their houses are safe from fear,
Neither is the rod of God upon them.
Their bull gendereth, and faileth not;
Their cow calveth, and casteth not her calf.
They send forth their little ones like a flock,
And their children dance.
They sing to the timbrel and harp,

THE BOOK OF JOB

And rejoice at the sound of the pipe.
They spend their days in prosperity,
And in a moment they go down to Sheol.
Yet they said unto God, "Depart from us!
For we desire not the knowledge of thy ways.
What is the Almighty, that we should serve him?
And what profit should we have, if we pray unto him?"
Eliphaz the Temanite. Lo, their prosperity is not in their hand:
The counsel of the wicked is far from me.
Job. How oft is it that the lamp of the wicked is put out?
That their calamity cometh upon them?
That God distributeth sorrow in his anger?
That they are as stubble before the wind,
And as chaff that the storm carrieth away?
Bildad the Shuhite. God layeth up his iniquity for his children.
Job. Let him recompense it unto himself, that he may know it.
Let his own eyes see his destruction,
And let him drink of the wrath of the Almighty.
For what pleasure hath he in his house after him,
When the number of his months is cut off in the midst?
Zophar the Naamathite. Shall any teach God knowledge?
Seeing he judgeth those that are high.
Job. One dieth in his full strength,
Being wholly at ease and quiet:
His breasts are full of milk,
And the marrow of his bones is moistened.
And another dieth in bitterness of soul,
And never tasteth of good.
They lie down alike in the dust,
And the worm covereth them.
Behold, I know your thoughts,
And the devices which ye wrongfully imagine against me.
For ye say, "Where is the house of the prince?
And where is the tent wherein the wicked dwelt?"
Have ye not asked them that go by the way?
And do ye not know their tokens?

THE BOOK OF JOB

That the evil man is reserved to the day of calamity?
That they are led forth to the day of wrath?
Who shall declare his way to his face?
And who shall repay him what he hath done?
Yet shall he be borne to the grave,
And shall keep watch over the tomb.
The clods of the valley shall be sweet unto him,
And all men shall draw after him,
As there were innumerable before him.
How then comfort ye me in vain,
Seeing in your answers there remaineth only falsehood?

Part III

ELIPHAZ THE TEMANITE. Can a man be profitable unto God?
Surely he that is wise is profitable unto himself.
Is it any pleasure to the Almighty, that thou art righteous?
Or is it gain to him, that thou makest thy ways perfect?
Is it for thy fear of him that he reproveth thee,
That he entereth with thee into judgment?
Is not thy wickedness great?
Neither is there any end to thine iniquities.
For thou hast taken pledges of thy brother for nought,
And stripped the naked of their clothing.
Thou hast not given water to the weary to drink,
And thou hast withheld bread from the hungry.
But as for the mighty man, he had the earth;
And the honourable man, he dwelt in it.
Thou hast sent widows away empty,
And the arms of the fatherless have been broken.
Therefore snares are round about thee,
And sudden fear troubleth thee,
Or darkness, that thou canst not see,
And abundance of waters cover thee.
Is not God in the height of heaven?
And behold the height of the stars, how high they are!
And thou sayest, "What doth God know?

THE BOOK OF JOB

Can he judge through the thick darkness?"
Thick clouds are a covering to him, that he seeth not;
And he walketh in the circuit of heaven.
Wilt thou keep the old way
Which wicked men have trodden?
Who were snatched away before their time,
Whose foundation was poured out as a stream:
Who said unto God, "Depart from us!"
And, "What can the Almighty do for us?"
Yet he filled their houses with good things:
But the counsel of the wicked is far from me.
The righteous see it, and are glad;
And the innocent laugh them to scorn:
Saying, "Surely they that did rise up against us are cut off,
And the remnant of them the fire hath consumed."
Acquaint now thyself with him, and be at peace:
Thereby good shall come unto thee.
Receive, I pray thee, the law from his mouth,
And lay up his words in thine heart.
If thou return to the Almighty, thou shalt be built up;
If thou put away unrighteousness far from thy tents.
And lay thou thy treasure in the dust,
And the gold of Ophir among the stones of the brooks;
And the Almighty shall be thy treasure,
And precious silver unto thee.
For then shalt thou delight thyself in the Almighty,
And shalt lift up thy face unto God.
Thou shalt make thy prayer unto him, and he shall hear thee;
And thou shalt pay thy vows.
Thou shalt also decree a thing, and it shall be established unto thee;
And light shall shine upon thy ways.
When they cast thee down, thou shalt say, "There is lifting up";
And the humble person he shall save.
He shall deliver even him that is not innocent:
Yea, he shall be delivered through the cleanness of thine hands.
JOB. Even to-day is my complaint rebellious:

THE BOOK OF JOB

My stroke is heavier than my groaning.
Oh that I knew where I might find him,
That I might come even to his seat!
I would order my cause before him,
And fill my mouth with arguments.
I would know the words which he would answer me,
And understand what he would say unto me.
Would he contend with me in the greatness of his power?
Nay; but he would give heed unto me.
There the upright might reason with him;
So should I be delivered for ever from my judge.
Behold, I go forward, but he is not there;
And backward, but I cannot perceive him;
On the left hand, when he doth work, but I cannot behold him:
He hideth himself on the right hand, that I cannot see him.
But he knoweth the way that I take;
When he hath tried me, I shall come forth as gold.
My foot hath held fast to his steps;
His way have I kept, and turned not aside.
I have not gone back from the commandment of his lips;
I have treasured up the words of his mouth more than my necessary food.
But he is in one mind, and who can turn him?
And what his soul desireth, even that he doeth.
For he performeth that which is appointed for me:
And many such things are with him.
Therefore am I troubled at his presence;
When I consider, I am afraid of him.
For God hath made my heart faint,
And the Almighty hath troubled me:
Because I was not cut off before the darkness,
Neither did he cover the thick darkness from my face.

Why are times not laid up by the Almighty?
And why do not they which know him see his days?
There are that remove the landmarks;
They violently take away flocks, and feed them.

THE BOOK OF JOB

They drive away the ass of the fatherless,
They take the widow's ox for a pledge.
They turn the needy out of the way:
The poor of the earth hide themselves together.
Behold, as wild asses in the desert
They go forth to their work, seeking diligently for meat;
The wilderness yieldeth them food for their children.
They cut their provender in the field;
And they glean the vintage of the wicked.
They lie all night naked without clothing,
And have no covering in the cold.
They are wet with the showers of the mountains,
And embrace the rock for want of a shelter.
There are that pluck the fatherless from the breast,
And take a pledge of the poor:
So that they go about naked without clothing,
And being a-hungered they carry the sheaves;
They make oil within the walls of these men;
They tread their winepresses, and suffer thirst.
From out of the populous city men groan,
And the soul of the wounded crieth out:
Yet God imputeth it not for folly.
These are of them that rebel against the light;
They know not the ways thereof,
Nor abide in the paths thereof.
The murderer riseth with the light, he killeth the poor and needy;
And in the night he is as a thief.
The eye also of the adulterer waiteth for the twilight,
Saying, "No eye shall see me":
And he disguiseth his face.
In the dark they dig through houses:
They shut themselves up in the daytime;
They know not the light.
For the morning is to all of them as the shadow of death;
For they know the terrors of the shadow of death.
He is swift upon the face of the waters;

[734]

THE BOOK OF JOB

Their portion is cursed in the earth:
He turneth not by the way of the vineyards.
Drought and heat consume the snow waters:
So doth Sheol those which have sinned.
The womb shall forget him; the worm shall feed sweetly on him;
He shall be no more remembered:
And unrighteousness shall be broken as a tree.
He devoureth the barren that beareth not;
And doeth not good to the widow.
He draweth away the mighty also by his power:
He riseth up, and no man is sure of life.
God giveth them to be in security, and they rest thereon;
And his eyes are upon their ways.
They are exalted; yet a little while, and they are gone;
Yea, they are brought low, they are taken out of the way as all other,
And are cut off as the tops of the ears of corn.
And if it be not so now, who will prove me a liar,
And make my speech nothing worth?
BILDAD THE SHUHITE. Dominion and fear are with him;
He maketh peace in his high places.
Is there any number of his armies?
And upon whom doth not his light arise?
How then can man be just with God?
Or how can he be clean that is born of a woman?
Behold, even the moon hath no brightness,
And the stars are not pure in his sight:
How much less man, that is a worm!
And the son of man, which is a worm!
Sheol is naked before him,
And Abaddon hath no covering.
He stretcheth out the north over empty space,
And hangeth the earth upon nothing.
He bindeth up the waters in his thick clouds;
And the cloud is not rent under them.
He closeth in the face of his throne,
And spreadeth his cloud upon it.

THE BOOK OF JOB

He hath described a boundary upon the face of the waters,
Unto the confines of light and darkness.
The pillars of heaven tremble
And are astonished at his rebuke.
He stirreth up the sea with his power,
And by his understanding he smiteth through Rahab.
By his spirit the heavens are garnished;
His hand hath pierced the swift serpent.
Lo, these are but the outskirts of his ways:
And how small a whisper do we hear of him!
But the thunder of his power who can understand?
JOB. How hast thou helped him that is without power!
How hast thou saved the arm that hath no strength!
How hast thou counselled him that hath no wisdom,
And plentifully declared sound knowledge!
To whom hast thou uttered words?
And whose spirit came forth from thee?
They that are deceased tremble
Beneath the waters and the inhabitants thereof.
As God liveth, who hath taken away my right;
And the Almighty, who hath vexed my soul
(For my life is yet whole in me,
And the spirit of God is in my nostrils);
Surely my lips shall not speak unrighteousness,
Neither shall my tongue utter deceit.
God forbid that I should justify you:
Till I die I will not put away mine integrity from me.
My righteousness I hold fast, and will not let it go:
My heart shall not reproach me so long as I live.
ZOPHAR THE NAAMATHITE. Let mine enemy be as the wicked,
And let him that riseth up against me be as the unrighteous.
For what is the hope of the godless, though he get him gain,
When God taketh away his soul?
Will God hear his cry,
When trouble cometh upon him?
Will he delight himself in the Almighty,

THE BOOK OF JOB

And call upon God at all times?
I will teach you concerning the hand of God;
That which is with the Almighty will I not conceal.
Behold, all ye yourselves have seen it;
Why then are ye become altogether vain?
This is the portion of a wicked man with God,
And the heritage of oppressors, which they receive from the Almighty.
If his children be multiplied, it is for the sword;
And his offspring shall not be satisfied with bread.
Those that remain of him shall be buried in death,
And his widows shall make no lamentation.
Though he heap up silver as the dust,
And prepare raiment as the clay;
He may prepare it, but the just shall put it on,
And the innocent shall divide the silver.
He buildeth his house as the moth,
And as a booth which the keeper maketh.
He lieth down rich, but he shall not be gathered;
He openeth his eyes, and he is not.
Terrors overtake him like waters;
A tempest stealeth him away in the night.
The east wind carrieth him away, and he departeth;
And it sweepeth him out of his place.
For God shall hurl at him, and not spare:
He would fain flee out of his hand.
Men shall clap their hands at him,
And shall hiss him out of his place.

Surely there is a mine for silver,
And a place for gold which they refine.
Iron is taken out of the earth,
And brass is molten out of the stone.
Man setteth an end to darkness,
And searcheth out to the furthest bound
The stones of thick darkness and of the shadow of death.
He breaketh open a shaft away from where men sojourn;

THE BOOK OF JOB

They are forgotten of the foot that passeth by;
They hang afar from men, they swing to and fro.
As for the earth, out of it cometh bread:
And underneath it is turned up as it were by fire.
The stones thereof are the place of sapphires,
And it hath dust of gold.
That path no bird of prey knoweth,
Neither hath the falcon's eye seen it:
The proud beasts have not trodden it,
Nor hath the fierce lion passed thereby.
He putteth forth his hand upon the flinty rock;
He overturneth the mountains by the roots.
He cutteth out channels among the rocks;
And his eye seeth every precious thing.
He bindeth the streams that they trickle not;
And the thing that is hid bringeth he forth to light.
But where shall wisdom be found?
And where is the place of understanding?
Man knoweth not the price thereof;
Neither is it found in the land of the living.
The deep saith, "It is not in me":
And the sea saith, "It is not with me."
It cannot be gotten for gold,
Neither shall silver be weighed for the price thereof.
It cannot be valued with the gold of Ophir,
With the precious onyx, or the sapphire.
Gold and glass cannot equal it:
Neither shall the exchange thereof be jewels of fine gold.
No mention shall be made of coral or of crystal:
Yea, the price of wisdom is above rubies.
The topaz of Ethiopia shall not equal it,
Neither shall it be valued with pure gold.
Whence then cometh wisdom?
And where is the place of understanding?
Seeing it is hid from the eyes of all living,
And kept close from the fowls of the air.

THE BOOK OF JOB

Destruction and Death say,
"We have heard a rumour thereof with our ears."
God understandeth the way thereof,
And he knoweth the place thereof.
For he looketh to the ends of the earth,
And seeth under the whole heaven;
To make a weight for the wind;
Yea, he meteth out the waters by measure.
When he made a decree for the rain,
And a way for the lightning of the thunder:
Then did he see it, and declare it;
He established it, yea, and searched it out.
And unto man he said,
"Behold, the fear of the Lord, that is wisdom;
And to depart from evil is understanding."
Job. *Oh that I were as in the months of old,*
As in the days when God watched over me;
When his lamp shined upon my head,
And by his light I walked through darkness;
As I was in the ripeness of my days,
When the secret of God was upon my tent;
When the Almighty was yet with me,
And my children were about me;
When my steps were washed with butter,
And the rock poured me out rivers of oil!
When I went forth to the gate unto the city,
When I prepared my seat in the street,
The young men saw me and hid themselves,
And the aged rose up and stood;
The princes refrained talking,
And laid their hand on their mouth;
The voice of the nobles was hushed,
And their tongue cleaved to the roof of their mouth.
For when the ear heard me, then it blessed me;
And when the eye saw me, it gave witness unto me:
Because I delivered the poor that cried,

THE BOOK OF JOB

The fatherless also, that had none to help him.
The blessing of him that was ready to perish came upon me:
And I caused the widow's heart to sing for joy.
I put on righteousness, and it clothed me:
My justice was as a robe and a diadem.
I was eyes to the blind,
And feet was I to the lame.
I was a father to the needy:
And the cause of him that I knew not I searched out.
And I broke the jaws of the unrighteous,
And plucked the prey out of his teeth.
Then I said, "I shall die in my nest,
And I shall multiply my days as the sand:
My root is spread out to the waters,
And the dew lieth all night upon my branch:
My glory is fresh in me,
And my bow is renewed in my hand."
Unto me men gave ear, and waited,
And kept silence for my counsel.
After my words they spoke not again;
And my speech dropped upon them.
And they waited for me as for the rain;
And they opened their mouth wide as for the latter rain.
If I laughed on them, they believed it not;
And the light of my countenance they cast not down.
I chose out their way, and sat as chief,
And dwelt as a king in the army,
As one that comforteth the mourners.

But now they that are younger than I have me in derision,
Whose fathers I disdained to set with the dogs of my flock.
Yea, the strength of their hands, whereto should it profit me?
Men in whom ripe age is perished.
They are gaunt with want and famine;
They gnaw the dry ground, in the gloom of wasteness and desolation.
They pluck salt-wort by the bushes;

THE BOOK OF JOB

And the roots of the broom are their meat.
They are driven forth from the midst of men;
They cry after them as after a thief.
In the clefts of the valleys must they dwell,
In holes of the earth and of the rocks.
Among the bushes they bray;
Under the nettles they are gathered together.
They are children of fools, yea, children of base men;
They were scourged out of the land.
And now I am become their song,
Yea, I am a byword unto them.
They abhor me, they stand aloof from me,
And spare not to spit in my face.
For he hath loosed his cord, and afflicted me,
And they have cast off the bridle before me.
Upon my right hand rise the rabble;
They thrust aside my feet,
And they cast up against me their ways of destruction.
They mar my path,
They set forward my calamity,
Even men that have no helper.
As through a wide breach they come:
In the midst of the ruin they roll themselves upon me.
Terrors are turned upon me,
They chase mine honour as the wind;
And my welfare is passed away as a cloud.
And now my soul is poured out within me;
Days of affliction have taken hold upon me.
In the night season my bones are pierced in me,
And the pains that gnaw me take no rest.
By the great force of my disease is my garment disfigured:
It bindeth me about as the collar of my coat.
He hath cast me into the mire,
And I am become like dust and ashes.
I cry unto thee, and thou dost not answer me:
I stand up, and thou lookest at me.

THE BOOK OF JOB

Thou art turned to be cruel to me:
With the might of thy hand thou persecutest me.
Thou liftest me up to the wind, thou causest me to ride upon it;
And thou dissolvest me in the storm.
For I know that thou wilt bring me to death,
And to the house appointed for all living.
Surely against a ruinous heap he will not put forth his hand;
Though it be in his destruction, one may utter a cry because of these
    things.
Did not I weep for him that was in trouble?
Was not my soul grieved for the needy?
When I looked for good, then evil came;
And when I waited for light, there came darkness.
My bowels boil, and rest not;
Days of affliction are come upon me.
I go mourning without the sun:
I stand up in the assembly, and cry for help.
I am a brother to jackals,
And a companion to ostriches.
My skin is black, and falleth from me,
And my bones are burned with heat.
Therefore is my harp turned to mourning,
And my pipe into the voice of them that weep.

I made a covenant with mine eyes;
How then should I look upon a maid?
For what is the portion of God from above,
And the heritage of the Almighty from on high?
Is it not calamity to the unrighteous,
And disaster to the workers of iniquity?
Doth not he see my ways,
And number all my steps?
If I have walked with vanity,
And my foot hath hastened to deceit
(Let me be weighed in an even balance,

THE BOOK OF JOB

That God may know mine integrity);
If my step hath turned out of the way,
And mine heart walked after mine eyes,
And if any spot hath cleaved to mine hands:
Then let me sow, and let another eat;
Yea, let the produce of my field be rooted out.
If mine heart have been enticed unto a woman,
And I have laid wait at my neighbour's door:
Then let my wife grind unto another,
And let others bow down upon her.
For that were a heinous crime;
Yea, it were an iniquity to be punished by the judges:
For it is a fire that consumeth unto Destruction,
And would root out all mine increase.
If I did despise the cause of my manservant or of my maidservant
When they contended with me:
What then shall I do when God riseth up?
And when he visiteth, what shall I answer him?
Did not he that made me in the womb make him?
And did not one fashion us in the womb?
If I have withheld the poor from their desire,
Or have caused the eyes of the widow to fail;
Or have eaten my morsel alone,
And the fatherless hath not eaten thereof
(Nay, from my youth he grew up with me as with a father,
And I have been her guide from my mother's womb);
If I have seen any perish for want of clothing,
Or that the needy had no covering;
If his loins have not blessed me,
And if he were not warmed with the fleece of my sheep;
If I have lifted up my hand against the fatherless,
Because I saw my help in the gate:
Then let my shoulder fall from the shoulder blade,
And mine arm be broken from the bone.
For calamity from God was a terror to me,

THE BOOK OF JOB

And by reason of his excellency I could do nothing.
If I have made gold my hope,
And have said to the fine gold, "Thou art my confidence";
If I rejoiced because my wealth was great,
And because mine hand had gotten much;
If I beheld the sun when it shined,
Or the moon walking in brightness;
And my heart hath been secretly enticed,
And my mouth hath kissed my hand:
This also were an iniquity to be punished by the judges:
For I should have lied to God that is above.
If I rejoiced at the destruction of him that hated me,
Or lifted up myself when evil found him
(Yea, I suffered not my mouth to sin
By asking his life with a curse);
If the men of my tent said not,
"Who can find one that hath not been satisfied with his flesh?"
The stranger did not lodge in the street;
But I opened my doors to the traveller;
If like Adam I covered my transgressions,
By hiding mine iniquity in my bosom;
Because I feared the great multitude,
And the contempt of families terrified me,
So that I kept silence, and went not out of the door—
Oh that I had one to hear me!
(Lo, here is my signature, let the Almighty answer me);
And that I had the indictment which mine adversary hath written!
Surely I would carry it upon my shoulder;
I would bind it unto me as a crown.
I would declare unto him the number of my steps;
As a prince would I go near unto him.
If my land cry out against me,
And the furrows thereof weep together;
If I have eaten the fruits thereof without money,
Or have caused the owners thereof to lose their life:

THE BOOK OF JOB

Let thistles grow instead of wheat,
And cockle instead of barley.

The words of Job are ended.

Part IV

Voice out of the Whirlwind. *Who is this that darkeneth counsel*
By words without knowledge?
Gird up now thy loins like a man;
For I will demand of thee, and declare thou unto me.
Where wast thou when I laid the foundations of the earth?
Declare, if thou hast understanding.
Who determined the measures thereof, if thou knowest?
Or who stretched the line upon it?
Whereupon were the foundations thereof fastened?
Or who laid the corner stone thereof;
When the morning stars sang together,
And all the sons of God shouted for joy?
Or who shut up the sea with doors,
When it broke forth, as if it had issued out of the womb;
When I made the cloud the garment thereof,
And thick darkness a swaddlingband for it,
And prescribed for it my decree,
And set bars and doors,
And said, "Hitherto shalt thou come, but no further;
And here shall thy proud waves be stayed"?
Hast thou commanded the morning since thy days began,
And caused the dayspring to know its place;
That it might take hold of the ends of the earth,
And the wicked be shaken out of it?
It is changed as clay under the seal;
And all things stand forth as a garment:
And from the wicked their light is withheld,
And the high arm is broken.
Hast thou entered into the springs of the sea?

THE BOOK OF JOB

Or hast thou walked in the recesses of the deep?
Have the gates of death been revealed unto thee?
Or hast thou seen the gates of the shadow of death?
Hast thou comprehended the breadth of the earth?
Declare, if thou knowest it all.
Where is the way to the dwelling of light,
And as for darkness, where is the place thereof;
That thou shouldest take it to the bound thereof,
And that thou shouldest discern the paths to the house thereof?
Doubtless, thou knowest, for thou wast then born,
And the number of thy days is great!
Hast thou entered the treasuries of the snow,
Or hast thou seen the treasuries of the hail,
Which I have reserved against the time of trouble,
Against the day of battle and war?
By what way is the light parted,
Or the east wind scattered upon the earth?
Who hath cleft a channel for the waterflood,
Or a way for the lightning of the thunder;
To cause it to rain on a land where no man is;
On the wilderness, wherein there is no man;
To satisfy the waste and desolate ground;
And to cause the tender grass to spring forth?
Hath the rain a father?
Or who hath begotten the drops of dew?
Out of whose womb came the ice?
And the hoary frost of heaven, who hath gendered it?
The waters are hidden as with stone,
And the face of the deep is frozen.
Canst thou bind the cluster of the Pleiades,
Or loose the bands of Orion?
Canst thou lead forth the Mazzaroth in their season?
Or canst thou guide the Bear with her train?
Knowest thou the ordinances of the heavens?
Canst thou establish the dominion thereof in the earth?
Canst thou lift up thy voice to the clouds,

THE BOOK OF JOB

That abundance of waters may cover thee?
Canst thou send forth lightnings, that they may go,
And say unto thee, "Here we are"?
Who hath put wisdom in the inward parts?
Or who hath given understanding to the mind?
Who can number the clouds by wisdom?
Or who can pour out the bottles of heaven,
When the dust runneth into a mass,
And the clods cleave fast together?
Wilt thou hunt the prey for the lioness?
Or satisfy the appetite of the young lions,
When they couch in their dens,
And abide in the covert to lie in wait?
Who provideth for the raven his food,
When his young ones cry unto God,
And wander for lack of meat?

Knowest thou the time when the wild goats of the rock bring forth?
Or canst thou mark when the hinds do calve?
Canst thou number the months that they fulfil?
Or knowest thou the time when they bring forth?
They bow themselves, they bring forth their young,
They cast out their sorrows.
Their young ones are in good liking, they grow up in the open field;
They go forth, and return not again.
Who hath sent out the wild ass free?
Or who hath loosed the bands of the wild ass?
Whose house I have made the wilderness,
And the salt land his dwelling place.
He scorneth the tumult of the city,
Neither heareth he the shoutings of the driver.
The range of the mountains is his pasture,
And he searcheth after every green thing.
Will the wild ox be content to serve thee?
Or will he abide by thy crib?
Canst thou bind the wild ox with his band in the furrow?

THE BOOK OF JOB

Or will he harrow the valleys after thee?
Wilt thou trust him, because his strength is great?
Or wilt thou leave to him thy labour?
Wilt thou confide in him, that he will bring home thy seed,
And gather the corn of thy threshing-floor?
    The wing of the ostrich rejoiceth;
But are her pinions and feathers kindly?
For she leaveth her eggs on the earth,
And warmeth them in the dust,
And forgetteth that the foot may crush them,
Or that the wild beast may trample them.
She is hardened against her young ones, as if they were not hers:
Though her labour be in vain, she is without fear;
Because God hath deprived her of wisdom,
Neither hath he imparted to her understanding.
What time she lifteth up herself on high,
She scorneth the horse and his rider.
    Hast thou given the horse his might?
Hast thou clothed his neck with the quivering mane?
Hast thou made him to leap as a locust?
The glory of his snorting is terrible.
He paweth in the valley, and rejoiceth in his strength:
He goeth out to meet the armed men.
He mocketh at fear, and is not dismayed;
Neither turneth he back from the sword.
The quiver rattleth against him,
The flashing spear and the javelin.
He swalloweth the ground with fierceness and rage;
Neither believeth he that it is the voice of the trumpet.
As oft as the trumpet soundeth he saith, "Aha!"
And he smelleth the battle afar off,
The thunder of the captains, and the shouting.
    Doth the hawk soar by thy wisdom,
And stretch her wings toward the south?
Doth the eagle mount up at thy command,
And make her nest on high?

THE BOOK OF JOB

She dwelleth on the rock, and hath her lodging there,
Upon the crag of the rock, and the strong hold.
From thence she spieth out the prey;
Her eyes behold it afar off.
Her young ones also suck up blood:
And where the slain are, there is she.

Shall he that cavilleth contend with the Almighty?
He that argueth with God, let him answer it.
JOB. Behold, I am of small account; what shall I answer thee?
I lay mine hand upon my mouth.
Once have I spoken, and I will not answer;
Yea twice, but I will proceed no further.
VOICE OUT OF THE WHIRLWIND. Gird up thy loins now like a man:
I will demand of thee, and declare thou unto me.
Wilt thou even disannul my judgment?
Wilt thou condemn me, that thou mayest be justified?
Or hast thou an arm like God?
And canst thou thunder with a voice like him?
Deck thyself now with excellency and dignity;
And array thyself with honour and majesty.
Pour forth the overflowings of thine anger:
And look upon every one that is proud, and abase him.
Look on every one that is proud, and bring him low;
And tread down the wicked where they stand.
Hide them in the dust together;
Bind their faces in the hidden place.
Then will I also confess of thee
That thine own right hand can save thee.
    Behold now Behemoth, which I made with thee;
He eateth grass as an ox.
Lo now, his strength is in his loins,
And his force is in the muscles of his belly.
He moveth his tail like a cedar:
The sinews of his thighs are knit together.
His bones are as tubes of brass;

THE BOOK OF JOB

His limbs are like bars of iron.
He is the chief of the ways of God:
He only that made him can make his sword to approach unto him.
Surely the mountains bring him forth food;
Where all the beasts of the field do play.
He lieth under the lotus trees,
In the covert of the reed, and the fen.
The lotus trees cover him with their shadow;
The willows of the brook compass him about.
Behold, if a river overflow, he trembleth not:
He is confident, though Jordan swell even to his mouth.
Shall any take him when he is on the watch,
Or pierce through his nose with a snare?

    Canst thou draw out Leviathan with a fishhook?
Or press down his tongue with a cord?
Canst thou put a rope into his nose?
Or pierce his jaw through with a hook?
Will he make many supplications unto thee?
Or will he speak soft words unto thee?
Will he make a covenant with thee,
That thou shouldest take him for a servant for ever?
Wilt thou play with him as with a bird?
Or wilt thou bind him for thy maidens?
Shall the bands of fishermen make traffic of him?
Shall they part him among the merchants?
Canst thou fill his skin with barbed irons,
Or his head with fish spears?
Lay thine hand upon him;
Remember the battle, and do so no more.
Behold, the hope of him is in vain:
Shall not one be cast down even at the sight of him?
None is so fierce that he dare stir him up:
Who then is he that can stand before me?
Who hath first given unto me, that I should repay him?
Whatsoever is under the whole heaven is mine.

THE BOOK OF JOB

*I will not keep silence concerning his limbs,
Nor his mighty strength, nor his comely proportion.
Who can strip off his outer garment?
Who shall come within his double bridle?
Who can open the doors of his face?
Round about his teeth is terror.
His strong scales are his pride,
Shut up together as with a close seal.
One is so near to another,
That no air can come between them.
They are joined one to another;
They stick together, that they cannot be sundered.
His sneezings flash forth light,
And his eyes are like the eyelids of the morning.
Out of his mouth go burning torches,
And sparks of fire leap forth.
Out of his nostrils a smoke goeth,
As of a seething pot and burning rushes.
His breath kindleth coals,
And a flame goeth forth from his mouth.
In his neck abideth strength,
And terror danceth before him.
The flakes of his flesh are joined together:
They are firm upon him; they cannot be moved.
His heart is as firm as a stone;
Yea, firm as the nether millstone.
When he raiseth himself up, the mighty are afraid:
By reason of consternation they are beside themselves.
If one lay at him with the sword, it cannot avail;
Nor the spear, the dart, nor the pointed shaft.
He counteth iron as straw,
And brass as rotten wood.
The arrow cannot make him flee:
Slingstones are turned with him into stubble.
Clubs are counted as stubble:
He laugheth at the rushing of the javelin.*

THE BOOK OF JOB

His underparts are like sharp potsherds:
He spreadeth as it were a threshing wain upon the mire.
He maketh the deep to boil like a pot:
He maketh the sea like ointment.
He maketh a path to shine after him:
One would think the deep to be hoary.
Upon earth there is not his like,
That is made without fear.
He beholdeth every thing that is high:
He is king over all the sons of pride.
JOB. *I know that thou canst do all things,*
And that no purpose of thine can be restrained.
"Who is this that hideth counsel without knowledge?"
Therefore have I uttered that which I understood not,
Things too wonderful for me, which I knew not.
Hear, I beseech thee, and I will speak;
I will demand of thee, and declare thou unto me.
I had heard of thee by the hearing of the ear;
But now mine eye seeth thee,
Wherefore I abhor myself, and repent
In dust and ashes.

Epilogue

And it was so, that after the Lord had spoken these words unto Job, the Lord said to Eliphaz the Temanite, "My wrath is kindled against thee, and against thy two friends: for ye have not spoken of me the thing that is right, as my servant Job hath. Now therefore, take unto you seven bullocks and seven rams, and go to my servant Job, and offer up for yourselves a burnt offering; and my servant Job shall pray for you; for him will I accept, that I deal not with you after your folly; for ye have not spoken of me the thing that is right, as my servant Job hath."

So Eliphaz the Temanite and Bildad the Shuhite and Zophar the Naamathite went, and did according as the Lord commanded them: and the Lord accepted Job.

And the Lord turned the captivity of Job, when he prayed for

THE BOOK OF JOB

his friends: and the Lord gave Job twice as much as he had before. Then came there unto him all his brethren, and all his sisters, and all they that had been of his acquaintance before, and did eat bread with him in his house: and they bemoaned him, and comforted him concerning all the evil that the Lord had brought upon him: every man also gave him a piece of money, and every one a ring of gold.

So the Lord blessed the latter end of Job more than his beginning: and he had fourteen thousand sheep, and six thousand camels, and a thousand yoke of oxen, and a thousand she-asses. He had also seven sons and three daughters. And he called the name of the first, Jemimah; and the name of the second, Keziah; and the name of the third, Keren-happuch. And in all the land were no women found so fair as the daughters of Job: and their father gave them inheritance among their brethren. And after this Job lived a hundred and forty years, and saw his sons, and his sons' sons, even four generations. So Job died, being old and full of days.

ECCLESIASTES; OR, THE PREACHER

THE BOOK OF ECCLESIASTES *was the work of an unknown second-century author who wrote under the pen name of Koheleth, or the Preacher. In his view of the world the doubts of Job have deepened to an all-embracing pessimism as to the value of existence. Because of this general tone, the work has always been the favorite book of the Bible among unbelievers. To offset a tendency so hostile to the main spirit of Jewish literature, later editors incorporated in the book a series of traditional proverbs and also inserted pious comments of their own. But in spite of these editorial efforts the tenor of the work remains so heretical that without its erroneous ascription to King Solomon it would hardly have found a place among the Jewish Sacred Scriptures or been included in the Christian Bible.*

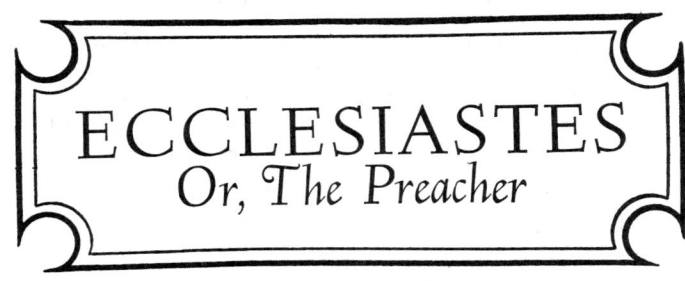

Introduction

THE WORDS OF THE PREACHER, the son of David, king in Jerusalem.

Vanity of vanities, saith the Preacher; vanity of vanities, all is vanity. What profit hath man of all his labour wherein he laboureth under the sun?

One generation goeth, and another generation cometh; and the earth abideth for ever. The sun also ariseth, and the sun goeth down, and hasteth to his place where he ariseth. The wind goeth toward the south, and turneth about unto the north; it turneth about continually in its course, and the wind returneth again to its circuits. All the rivers run into the sea, yet the sea is not full; unto the place whither the rivers go, thither they go again.

All things are full of weariness; man cannot utter it: the eye is not satisfied with seeing, nor the ear filled with hearing.

That which hath been is that which shall be; and that which hath been done is that which shall be done: and there is no new thing under the sun. Is there a thing whereof men say, "See, this is new"? It hath been already, in the ages which were before us.

There is no remembrance of the former generations; neither shall there be any remembrance of the latter generations that are to come, among those that shall come after.

Essay I

I the Preacher was king over Israel in Jerusalem. And I applied my heart to seek and to search out by wisdom concerning all

ECCLESIASTES

that is done under heaven: it is a sore travail that God hath given to the sons of men to be exercised therewith. I have seen all the works that are done under the sun; and, behold, all is vanity and a striving after wind. That which is crooked cannot be made straight: and that which is wanting cannot be numbered. I communed with mine own heart, saying, "Lo, I have gotten me great wisdom above all that were before me in Jerusalem: yea, my heart hath had great experience of wisdom and knowledge." And I applied my heart to know wisdom, and to know madness and folly: I perceived that this also was a striving after wind. For in much wisdom is much grief: and he that increaseth knowledge increaseth sorrow.

I said in mine heart, "Go to now, I will prove thee with mirth; therefore enjoy pleasure": and, behold, this also was vanity. I said of laughter, "It is mad": and of mirth, "What doeth it?" I searched in mine heart how to cheer my flesh with wine, mine heart yet guiding me with wisdom, and how to lay hold on folly, till I might see what it was good for the sons of men that they should do under the heaven all the days of their life. I made me great works; I builded me houses; I planted me vineyards; I made me gardens and parks, and I planted trees in them of all kinds of fruit: I made me pools of water, to water therefrom the forest where trees were reared. I bought menservants and maidens, and had servants born in my house; also I had great possessions of herds and flocks, above all that were before me in Jerusalem: I gathered me also silver and gold, and the peculiar treasure of kings and of the provinces. I got me men singers and women singers, and the delights of the sons of men, concubines very many. So I was great, and increased more than all that were before me in Jerusalem: also my wisdom remained with me. And whatsoever mine eyes desired I kept not from them: I withheld not my heart from any joy, for my heart rejoiced because of all my labour; and this was my portion from all my labour. Then I looked on all the works that my hands had wrought, and on the labour that I had laboured to do: and, behold, all was vanity and a striving after wind, and there was no profit under the sun.

ECCLESIASTES

And I turned myself to behold wisdom, and madness and folly: for what can the man do that cometh after the king? even that which hath been already done. Then I saw that wisdom excelleth folly, as far as light excelleth darkness. The wise man's eyes are in his head, and the fool walketh in darkness: and yet I perceived that one event happeneth to them all. Then said I in my heart, "As it happeneth to the fool, so will it happen even to me"; and why was I then more wise? Then I said in my heart, that this also was vanity. For of the wise man, even as of the fool, there is no remembrance for ever; seeing that in the days to come all will have been already forgotten. And how doth the wise man die even as the fool! So I hated life; because the work that is wrought under the sun was grievous unto me: for all is vanity and a striving after wind.

And I hated all my labour wherein I laboured under the sun: seeing that I must leave it unto the man that shall be after me. And who knoweth whether he shall be a wise man or a fool? yet shall he have rule over all my labour wherein I have laboured, and wherein I have showed wisdom under the sun. This also is vanity. Therefore I turned about to cause my heart to despair concerning all the labour wherein I had laboured under the sun. For there is a man whose labour is with wisdom, and with knowledge, and with skilfulness; yet to a man that hath not laboured therein shall he leave it for his portion. This also is vanity and a great evil. For what hath a man of all his labour, and of the striving of his heart, wherein he laboureth under the sun? For all his days are but sorrows, and his travail is grief; yea, even in the night his heart taketh no rest. This also is vanity.

There is nothing better for a man than that he should eat and drink, and make his soul enjoy good in his labour. This also I saw, that it is from the hand of God. For who can eat, or who can have enjoyment, more than I? For to the man that pleaseth him God giveth wisdom, and knowledge, and joy: but to the sinner he giveth travail, to gather and to heap up, that he may give to him that pleaseth God. This also is vanity and a striving after wind.

ECCLESIASTES

Essay II

To everything there is a season,
And a time to every purpose under the heaven:
A time to be born, and a time to die;
A time to plant, and a time to pluck up that which is planted;
A time to kill, and a time to heal;
A time to break down, and a time to build up;
A time to weep, and a time to laugh;
A time to mourn, and a time to dance;
A time to cast away stones, and a time to gather stones together;
A time to embrace, and a time to refrain from embracing;
A time to seek, and a time to lose;
A time to keep, and a time to cast away;
A time to rend, and a time to sew;
A time to keep silence, and a time to speak;
A time to love, and a time to hate;
A time for war, and a time for peace.

What profit hath he that worketh in that wherein he laboureth? I have seen the travail which God hath given to the sons of men to be exercised therewith. He hath made every thing beautiful in its time: also he hath set the world in their heart, yet so that man cannot find out the work that God hath done from the beginning even to the end.

I know that there is nothing better for them, than to rejoice, and to do good so long as they live. And also that every man should eat and drink, and enjoy good in all his labour, is the gift of God. I know that, whatsoever God doeth, it shall be for ever: nothing can be put to it, nor any thing taken from it: and God hath done it, that men should fear before him. That which is hath been already; and that which is to be hath already been: and God seeketh again that which is passed away.

And moreover I saw under the sun, in the place of judgment, that wickedness was there; and in the place of righteousness, that wickedness was there. I said in mine heart, "God shall

ECCLESIASTES

judge the righteous and the wicked: for there is a time for every purpose and for every work." I said in mine heart, "It is because of the sons of men that God may prove them, and that they may see that they themselves are but as beasts." For that which befalleth the sons of men befalleth beasts; even one thing befalleth them: as the one dieth, so dieth the other; yea, they have all one breath; and man hath no pre-eminence above the beasts: for all is vanity. All go unto one place; all are of the dust, and all turn to dust again. Who knoweth the spirit of man whether it goeth upward, and the spirit of the beast whether it goeth downward to the earth? Wherefore I saw that there is nothing better, than that a man should rejoice in his works; for that is his portion: for who shall bring him back to see what shall be after him?

Then I returned and saw all the oppressions that are done under the sun: and behold, the tears of such as were oppressed, and they had no comforter; and on the side of their oppressors there was power, but they had no comforter. Wherefore I praised the dead which are already dead more than the living which are yet alive; yea, better than them both did I esteem him which hath not yet been, who hath not seen the evil work that is done under the sun.

Then I saw all labour and every skilful work, that for this a man is envied of his neighbour. This also is vanity and a striving after wind. The fool foldeth his hands together, and eateth his own flesh. Better is a handful with quietness, than two handfuls with labour and striving after wind.

Then I returned and saw vanity under the sun. There is one that is alone, and he hath not a second; yea, he hath neither son nor brother; yet is there no end of all his labour, neither are his eyes satisfied with riches. For whom then, saith he, do I labour, and deprive my soul of good? This also is vanity, yea, it is a sore travail. Two are better than one; because they have a good reward for their labour. For if they fall, the one will lift up his fellow: but woe to him that is alone when he falleth, and hath not another to lift him up. Again, if two lie together, then they

ECCLESIASTES

have warmth: but how can one be warm alone? And if a man prevail against him that is alone, two shall withstand him; and a threefold cord is not quickly broken.

Better is a poor and wise youth than an old and foolish king, who knoweth not how to receive admonition any more. For out of prison he came forth to be king; yea, even in his kingdom he was born poor. I saw all the living which walk under the sun, that they were with the youth, the second, that stood up in his stead. There was no end of all the people, even of all them over whom he was: yet they that come after shall not rejoice in him. Surely this also is vanity and a striving after wind.

Keep thy foot when thou goest to the house of God; for to draw nigh to hear is better than to give the sacrifice of fools: for they know not that they do evil. Be not rash with thy mouth, and let not thine heart be hasty to utter any thing before God; for God is in heaven, and thou upon earth: therefore let thy words be few. For a dream cometh with a multitude of business; and a fool's voice with a multitude of words. When thou vowest a vow unto God, defer not to pay it; for he hath no pleasure in fools: pay that which thou vowest. Better is it that thou shouldest not vow than that thou shouldest vow and not pay. Suffer not thy mouth to cause thy flesh to sin; neither say thou before the angel, that it was an error: wherefore should God be angry at thy voice, and destroy the work of thine hands? For thus it cometh to pass through the multitude of dreams and vanities and many words: but fear thou God.

If thou seest the oppression of the poor, and the violent taking away of judgment and justice in a province, marvel not at the matter: for one higher than the high regardeth; and there be higher than they. Moreover the profit of the earth is for all: the king himself is served by the field.

Essay III

He that loveth silver shall not be satisfied with silver; nor he that loveth abundance with increase: this also is vanity. When goods increase, they are increased that eat them: and what ad-

ECCLESIASTES

vantage is there to the owner thereof, saving the beholding of them with his eyes? The sleep of a labouring man is sweet, whether he eat little or much: but the fulness of the rich will not suffer him to sleep.

There is a grievous evil which I have seen under the sun, namely, riches kept by the owner thereof to his hurt: and those riches perish by evil adventure; and if he hath begotten a son, there is nothing in his hand. As he came forth of his mother's womb, naked shall he go again as he came, and shall take nothing for his labour, which he may carry away in his hand. And this also is a grievous evil, that in all points as he came, so shall he go: and what profit hath he that he laboureth for the wind? All his days also he eateth in darkness, and he is sore vexed and hath sickness and wrath.

Behold, that which I have seen to be good and to be comely is for one to eat and to drink, and to enjoy good in all his labour, wherein he laboureth under the sun, all the days of his life which God hath given him: for this is his portion. Every man also to whom God hath given riches and wealth, and hath given him power to eat thereof, and to take his portion, and to rejoice in his labour; this is the gift of God. For he shall not much remember the days of his life; because God answereth him in the joy of his heart.

There is an evil which I have seen under the sun, and it is heavy upon men: a man to whom God giveth riches, wealth, and honour, so that he lacketh nothing for his soul of all that he desireth, yet God giveth him not power to eat thereof, but a stranger eateth it; this is vanity, and it is an evil disease. If a man beget a hundred children, and live many years, so that the days of his years be many, but his soul be not filled with good, and moreover he have no burial; I say that an untimely birth is better than he: for it cometh in vanity, and departeth in darkness, and the name thereof is covered with darkness; moreover it hath not seen the sun nor known it; this hath rest rather than the other: yea, though he live a thousand years twice told, and yet enjoy no good: do not all go to one place? All the labour of

ECCLESIASTES

man is for his mouth, and yet the appetite is not filled. For what advantage hath the wise more than the fool? or what hath the poor man, that knoweth to walk before the living? Better is the sight of the eyes than the wandering of the desire: this also is vanity and a striving after wind.

Whatsoever hath been, the name thereof was given long ago, and it is known that it is man: neither can he contend with him that is mightier than he. Seeing there be many things that increase vanity, what is man the better? For who knoweth what is good for man in his life, all the days of his vain life which he spendeth as a shadow? for who can tell a man what shall be after him under the sun?

A good name is better than precious ointment; and the day of death than the day of one's birth. It is better to go to the house of mourning, than to go to the house of feasting: for that is the end of all men; and the living will lay it to his heart. Sorrow is better than laughter: for by the sadness of the countenance the heart is made glad. The heart of the wise is in the house of mourning; but the heart of fools is in the house of mirth. It is better to hear the rebuke of the wise, than for a man to hear the song of fools. For as the crackling of thorns under a pot, so is the laughter of the fool: this also is vanity.

Surely extortion maketh a wise man foolish; and a gift destroyeth the understanding. Better is the end of a thing than the beginning thereof: and the patient in spirit is better than the proud in spirit. Be not hasty in thy spirit to be angry: for anger resteth in the bosom of fools. Say not thou, "What is the cause that the former days were better than these?" for thou dost not inquire wisely concerning this. Wisdom is as good as an inheritance: yea, more excellent is it for them that see the sun. For wisdom is a defence, even as money is a defence: but the excellency of knowledge is that wisdom preserveth the life of him that hath it. Consider the work of God: for who can make that straight, which he hath made crooked? In the day of prosperity be joyful, and in the day of adversity consider: God hath

ECCLESIASTES

even made the one side by side with the other, to the end that man should not find out any thing that shall be after him.

All this have I seen in the days of my vanity: there is a righteous man that perisheth in his righteousness, and there is a wicked man that prolongeth his life in his evildoing. Be not righteous over much; neither make thyself over wise: why shouldest thou destroy thyself? Be not over much wicked, neither be thou foolish: why shouldest thou die before thy time? It is good that thou shouldest take hold of this; yea, also from that withdraw not thine hand: for he that feareth God shall come forth of them all.

Essay IV

Wisdom is a strength to the wise man more than ten rulers which are in a city. Surely there is not a righteous man upon earth that doeth good, and sinneth not. Also take not heed unto all words that are spoken; lest thou hear thy servant curse thee: for oftentimes also thine own heart knoweth that thou thyself likewise hast cursed others.

All this have I proved in wisdom: I said, "I will be wise" but it was far from me. That which is is far off, and exceeding deep; who can find it out? I turned about, and my heart was set to know and to search out, and to seek wisdom and the reason of things, and to know that wickedness is folly, and that foolishness is madness: and I find a thing more bitter than death, even the woman whose heart is snares and nets, and her hands as bands: whoso pleaseth God shall escape from her; but the sinner shall be taken by her. "Behold, this have I found," saith the Preacher, laying one thing to another, to find out the account, which my soul still seeketh, but I have not found: "one man among a thousand have I found; but a woman among all those have I not found. Behold, this only have I found, that God made man upright; but they have sought out many inventions."

Who is as the wise man? and who knoweth the interpretation of a thing? A man's wisdom maketh his face to shine, and

ECCLESIASTES

the hardness of his face is changed. I counsel thee: keep the king's command, and that in regard of the oath of God. Be not hasty to go out of his presence; persist not in an evil thing: for he doeth whatsoever pleaseth him. Because the king's word hath power; and who may say unto him, "What doest thou?" Whoso keepeth the commandment shall know no evil thing; and a wise man's heart discerneth time and judgment: for to every purpose there is a time and judgment; because the misery of man is great upon him: for he knoweth not that which shall be; for who can tell him how it shall be? There is no man that hath power over the spirit to retain the spirit; neither hath he power over the day of death; and there is no discharge in that war: neither shall wickedness deliver him that is given to it. All this have I seen, and applied my heart unto every work that is done under the sun: there is a time wherein one man hath power over another to his hurt.

And withal I saw the wicked buried, and they came to the grave; and they that had done right went away from the holy place, and were forgotten in the city: this also is vanity. Because sentence against an evil work is not executed speedily, therefore the heart of the sons of men is fully set in them to do evil. Though a sinner do evil a hundred times, and prolong his days, yet surely I know that it shall be well with them that fear God, which fear before him: but it shall not be well with the wicked, neither shall he prolong his days, which are as a shadow; because he feareth not before God. There is a vanity which is done upon the earth; that there be righteous men, unto whom it happeneth according to the work of the wicked; again, there be wicked men, to whom it happeneth according to the work of the righteous: I said that this also is vanity. Then I commended mirth, because a man hath no better thing under the sun than to eat, and to drink, and to be merry: for that shall abide with him in his labour all the days of his life which God hath given him under the sun.

When I applied my heart to know wisdom, and to see the business that is done upon the earth (for also there is that nei-

ECCLESIASTES

ther day nor night seeth sleep with his eyes): then I beheld all the work of God, that man cannot find out the work that is done under the sun: because however much a man labour to seek it out, yet he shall not find it; yea moreover, though a wise man think to know it, yet shall he not be able to find it.

For all this I laid to my heart, even to explore all this; that the righteous, and the wise, and their works, are in the hand of God: whether it be love or hatred, man knoweth it not; all is before them. All things come alike to all: there is one event to the righteous and to the wicked; to the good and to the clean and to the unclean; to him that sacrificeth and to him that sacrificeth not: as is the good, so is the sinner; and he that sweareth, as he that feareth an oath. This is an evil in all that is done under the sun, that there is one event unto all: yea also, the heart of the sons of men is full of evil, and madness is in their heart while they live, and after that they go to the dead. For to him that is joined with all the living there is hope: for a living dog is better than a dead lion. For the living know that they shall die: but the dead know not any thing, neither have they any more a reward; for the memory of them is forgotten. As well their love, as their hatred and their envy, is now perished; neither have they any more a portion for ever in any thing that is done under the sun.

Go thy way, eat thy bread with joy, and drink thy wine with a merry heart; for God hath already accepted thy works. Let thy garments be always white; and let not thy head lack ointment. Live joyfully with the wife whom thou lovest all the days of the life of thy vanity, which he hath given thee under the sun, all the days of thy vanity: for that is thy portion in life, and in thy labour wherein thou labourest under the sun. Whatsoever thy hand findeth to do, do it with thy might; for there is no work, nor device, nor knowledge, nor wisdom, in the grave, whither thou goest.

I returned, and saw under the sun that the race is not to the swift, nor the battle to the strong, neither yet bread to the wise, nor yet riches to men of understanding, nor yet favour to men of

ECCLESIASTES

skill; but time and chance happeneth to them all. For man also knoweth not his time: as the fishes that are taken in an evil net, and as the birds that are caught in the snare, even so are the sons of men snared in an evil time, when it falleth suddenly upon them.

I have also seen wisdom under the sun on this wise, and it seemed great unto me: there was a little city, and few men within it; and there came a great king against it, and besieged it, and built great bulwarks against it: now there was found in it a poor wise man, and he by his wisdom delivered the city; yet no man remembered that same poor man. Then said I, "Wisdom is better than strength: nevertheless the poor man's wisdom is despised, and his words are not heard."

The words of the wise spoken in quiet
Are heard more than the cry of him that ruleth among fools.

Wisdom is better than weapons of war:
But one sinner destroyeth much good.

Dead flies cause the ointment of the perfumer to send forth a stinking savour:
So doth a little folly outweigh wisdom and honour.

A wise man's heart is at his right hand;
But a fool's heart at his left.
Yea also, when the fool walketh by the way,
His understanding faileth him,
And he saith to every one that he is a fool.

If the spirit of the ruler rise up against thee, leave not thy place;
For yielding allayeth great offences.
There is an evil which I have seen under the sun,
As it were an error which proceedeth from the ruler:
Folly is set in great dignity,
And the rich sit in low place.

ECCLESIASTES

I have seen servants upon horses,
And princes walking as servants upon the earth.

He that diggeth a pit shall fall into it;
And whoso breaketh through a fence, a serpent shall bite him.

Whoso heweth out stones shall be hurt therewith;
And he that cleaveth wood is endangered thereby.

If the iron be blunt,
And one do not whet the edge,
Then must he put to more strength:
But wisdom is profitable to direct.

If the serpent bite before it be charmed,
Then is there no advantage in the charmer.

The words of a wise man's mouth are gracious;
But the lips of a fool will swallow up himself.
The beginning of the words of his mouth is foolishness:
And the end of his talk is mischievous madness.
A fool also multiplieth words:
Yet man knoweth not what shall be;
And that which shall be after him, who can tell him?
The labour of fools wearieth every one of them,
For he knoweth not how to go to the city.

Woe to thee, O land, when thy king is a child,
And thy princes eat in the morning!
Happy art thou, O land, when thy king is the son of nobles,
And thy princes eat in due season,
For strength, and not for drunkenness!

By slothfulness the roof sinketh in;
And through idleness of the hands the house leaketh.

A feast is made for laughter,
And wine maketh glad the life:
And money answereth all things.

ECCLESIASTES

Curse not the king, no, not in thy thought;
And curse not the rich in thy bedchamber:
For a bird of the air shall carry the voice,
And that which hath wings shall tell the matter.

Cast thy bread upon the waters:
For thou shalt find it after many days.

Give a portion to seven, yea, even unto eight;
For thou knowest not what evil shall be upon the earth.

If the clouds be full of rain,
They empty themselves upon the earth:
And if a tree fall toward the south, or toward the north,
In the place where the tree falleth, there shall it be.

He that observeth the wind shall not sow;
And he that regardeth the clouds shall not reap.

As thou knowest not what is the way of the wind,
Nor how the bones do grow in the womb of her that is with child;
Even so thou knowest not the work of God who doeth all.
In the morning sow thy seed,
And in the evening withhold not thine hand:
For thou knowest not which shall prosper,
Whether this or that, or whether they both shall be alike good.

Essay V

Truly the light is sweet, and a pleasant thing it is for the eyes to behold the sun. Yea, if a man live many years, let him rejoice in them all; but let him remember the days of darkness, for they shall be many. All that cometh is vanity.

Rejoice, O young man, in thy youth; and let thy heart cheer thee in the days of thy youth, and walk in the ways of thine heart, and in the sight of thine eyes: but know thou, that for all these things God will bring thee into judgment. Therefore remove sorrow from thy heart, and put away evil from thy flesh: for youth and the prime of life are vanity.

ECCLESIASTES

Remember also thy Creator in the days of thy youth,
Or ever the evil days come,
And the years draw nigh, when thou shalt say,
"I have no pleasure in them";
Or ever the sun, and the light,
And the moon, and the stars, be darkened,
And the clouds return after the rain:
In the day when the keepers of the house shall tremble,
And the strong men shall bow themselves,
And the grinders cease because they are few,
And those that look out of the windows be darkened,
And the doors shall be shut in the street;
When the sound of the grinding is low,
And one shall rise up at the voice of a bird,
And all the daughters of music shall be brought low;
Yea, they shall be afraid of that which is high,
And terrors shall be in the way;
And the almond tree shall blossom,
And the grasshopper shall be a burden,
And the caper-berry shall fail:
Because man goeth to his long home,
And the mourners go about the streets:
Or ever the silver cord be loosed,
Or the golden bowl be broken,
Or the pitcher be broken at the fountain,
Or the wheel broken at the cistern;
And the dust return to the earth as it was,
And the spirit return unto God who gave it.

Vanity of vanities, saith the Preacher; all is vanity.

And further, because the Preacher was wise, he still taught the people knowledge; yea, he pondered, and sought out, and set in order many proverbs. The Preacher sought to find out acceptable words, and that which was written uprightly, even words of truth.

The words of the wise are as goads, and as nails well fastened

ECCLESIASTES

are the words of the masters of assemblies, which are given from one shepherd. And furthermore, my son, be admonished: of making many books there is no end; and much study is a weariness of the flesh.

This is the end of the matter; all hath been heard: fear God, and keep his commandments; for this is the whole duty of man. For God shall bring every work into judgment, with every hidden thing, whether it be good or whether it be evil.

THE SONG OF SONGS

A FRAGMENTARY WEDDING IDYLL

The venerated name of Solomon sufficed to secure the inclusion in the Jewish Canon not only of Ecclesiastes but also of another work still more secular in character—the impassioned collection of love lyrics known as the Song of Songs, which later Christian writers could justify only as a far-fetched allegory of the love of Christ for his Church. Though the work, dating from the fourth century, was certainly not by Solomon and is certainly not an allegory, its actual author is unknown and its interpretation remains somewhat baffling. The difficulties arise from the fact that the hints of consecutive narrative and dramatic speech are too insistent to permit the theory that we have here a mere anthology and, on the other hand, are not sufficiently definite to indicate actual drama. Numerous attempts to interpret it as a romantic play depicting a struggle between King Solomon and a shepherd swain for the love of a shepherdess, in which the king is defeated according to the best democratic tradition, have enjoyed considerable popularity in modern times but are, of course, hopelessly unhistorical. The best explanation seems to be suggested by the discovery of an oriental wedding custom according to which during the ceremony the bride and groom were supposed to play the parts of a king and queen surrounded by their attendants. With his sure instinct for literary form, Richard Moulton has pointed out resemblances between the Song of Songs and the pastoral idylls of Theocritus and other Sicilian poets. Putting these suggestions together, one reaches the conclusion that the poem is a semidramatic idyll written originally for some notable wedding, to be presented with music, choruses, and dance, but now in too fragmentary a state to allow more than the most hypothetical reconstruction.

Fortunately, the difficulties of the problem need not inhibit in the least the reader's enjoyment of the lyric beauty of the poem.

THE SONG OF SONGS

A FRAGMENTARY WEDDING IDYLL

CHARACTERS

KING SOLOMON
THE SHULAMITE
THE BROTHERS
CHORUS OF THE DAUGHTERS OF JERUSALEM

Scene I

THE SHULAMITE

Let him kiss me with the kisses of his mouth:
For thy love is better than wine.
Thine ointments have a goodly fragrance;
Thy name is as ointment poured forth;
Therefore do the virgins love thee.

THE DAUGHTERS OF JERUSALEM

Draw me. We will run after thee.

THE SHULAMITE

The king hath brought me into his chambers.

THE DAUGHTERS OF JERUSALEM

We will be glad and rejoice in thee,
We will make mention of thy love more than of wine:
Rightly do they love thee.

THE SONG OF SONGS

THE SHULAMITE

I am black, but comely,
O ye daughters of Jerusalem,
As the tents of Kedar,
As the curtains of Solomon.
Look not upon me, because I am swarthy,
Because the sun hath scorched me.

My mother's sons were incensed against me,
They made me keeper of the vineyards;
But mine own vineyard have I not kept.

Tell me, O thou whom my soul loveth,
Where thou feedest thy flock, where thou makest it to rest at noon:
For why should I be as one that is veiled
Beside the flocks of thy companions?

KING SOLOMON

If thou know not, O thou fairest among women,
Go thy way forth by the footsteps of the flock,
And feed thy kids beside the shepherds' tents.

I have compared thee, O my love,
To a steed in Pharaoh's chariots.
Thy cheeks are comely with plaits of hair,
Thy neck with strings of jewels.
We will make thee plaits of gold
With studs of silver.

THE SHULAMITE

While the king sat at his table,
My spikenard sent forth its fragrance.
My beloved is unto me as a bundle of myrrh,
That lieth betwixt my breasts.
My beloved is unto me as a cluster of henna-flowers
In the vineyards of En-gedi.

THE SONG OF SONGS

KING SOLOMON

Behold, thou art fair, my love; behold, thou art fair;
Thine eyes are as doves.

THE SHULAMITE

Behold, thou art fair, my beloved, yea, pleasant:
Also our couch is green.
The beams of our house are cedars,
And our rafters are firs.

I am a rose of Sharon,
A lily of the valleys.

KING SOLOMON

As a lily among thorns,
So is my love among the daughters.

THE SHULAMITE

As the apple tree among the trees of the wood,
So is my beloved among the sons.
I sat down under his shadow with great delight,
And his fruit was sweet to my taste.

He brought me to the banqueting house,
And his banner over me was love.
Stay ye me with raisins, comfort me with apples:
For I am sick of love.
His left hand is under my head,
And his right hand doth embrace me.

I adjure you, O daughters of Jerusalem,
By the roes, and by the hinds of the field,
That ye stir not up, nor awaken love,
Until it please.

THE SONG OF SONGS

Scene II

THE SHULAMITE

The voice of my beloved! behold, he cometh,
Leaping upon the mountains, skipping upon the hills.
My beloved is like a roe or a young hart:
Behold, he standeth behind our wall,
He looketh in at the windows,
He showeth himself through the lattice.
My beloved spoke, and said unto me,
"Rise up, my love, my fair one, and come away.
For, lo, the winter is past,
The rain is over and gone;
The flowers appear on the earth;
The time of the singing of birds is come,
And the voice of the turtle is heard in our land;
The fig tree ripeneth her green figs,
And the vines are in blossom,
They give forth their fragrance.
Arise, my love, my fair one, and come away.
O my dove, that art in the clefts of the rock, in the covert of the steep
    place,
Let me see thy countenance, let me hear thy voice;
For sweet is thy voice, and thy countenance is comely."

THE BROTHERS

Take us the foxes, the little foxes, that spoil the vineyards;
For our vineyards are in blossom.

THE SHULAMITE

My beloved is mine, and I am his:
He feedeth his flock among the lilies.
Until the day be cool, and the shadows flee away,
Turn, my beloved, and be thou like a roe or a young hart
Upon the mountains of Bether.

THE SONG OF SONGS

By night on my bed I sought him whom my soul loveth:
I sought him, but I found him not.
I said, "I will rise now, and go about the city,
In the streets and in the broad ways,
I will seek him whom my soul loveth":
I sought him, but I found him not.
The watchmen that go about the city found me:
To whom I said, "Saw ye him whom my soul loveth?"
It was but a little that I passed from them,
When I found him whom my soul loveth:
I held him, and would not let him go,
Until I had brought him into my mother's house,
And into the chamber of her that conceived me.

I adjure you, O daughters of Jerusalem,
By the roes, and by the hinds of the field,
That ye stir not up, nor awaken love,
Until it please.

Scene III

THE DAUGHTERS OF JERUSALEM

Who is this that cometh up out of the wilderness like pillars of smoke,
Perfumed with myrrh and frankincense,
With all powders of the merchant?

Behold, it is the litter of Solomon;
Threescore mighty men are about it,
Of the mighty men of Israel.
They all handle the sword, and are expert in war:
Every man hath his sword upon his thigh,
Because of fear in the night.

King Solomon made himself a palanquin
Of the wood of Lebanon.
He made the pillars thereof of silver,
The bottom thereof of gold. the seat of it of purple,

THE SONG OF SONGS

The midst thereof being paved with love,
From the daughters of Jerusalem.

Go forth, O ye daughters of Zion, and behold King Solomon,
With the crown wherewith his mother hath crowned him in the day of
    his espousals,
And in the day of the gladness of his heart.

KING SOLOMON

Behold thou art fair, my love; behold, thou art fair;
Thine eyes are as doves behind thy veil:
Thy hair is as a flock of goats,
That lie along the side of Mount Gilead.

Thy teeth are like a flock of ewes that are newly shorn,
Which are come up from the washing;
Whereof every one hath twins,
And none is bereaved among them.

Thy lips are like a thread of scarlet,
And thy mouth is comely:
Thy temples are like a piece of pomegranate
Behind thy veil.
Thy neck is like the tower of David builded for an armoury,
Whereon there hang a thousand bucklers,
All the shields of the mighty men.
Thy two breasts are like two fawns that are twins of a roe,
Which feed among the lilies.

Until the day be cool, and the shadows flee away,
I will get me to the mountain of myrrh,
And to the hill of frankincense.

Thou art all fair, my love;
And there is no spot in thee.
Come with me from Lebanon, my bride,
With me from Lebanon:
Look from the top of Amana,

THE SONG OF SONGS

From the top of Senir and Hermon,
From the lions' dens,
From the mountains of the leopards.

Thou hast ravished my heart, my sister, my bride;
Thou hast ravished my heart with one of thine eyes.
With one chain of thy neck.
How fair is thy love, my sister, my bride!
How much better is thy love than wine!
And the smell of thine ointments than all manner of spices!
Thy lips, O my bride, drop as the honeycomb:
Honey and milk are under thy tongue;
And the smell of thy garments is like the smell of Lebanon.

A garden shut up is my sister, my bride;
A spring shut up, a fountain sealed.
Thy shoots are an orchard of pomegranates, with precious fruits;
Henna with spikenard plants,
Spikenard and saffron,
Calamus and cinnamon, with all trees of frankincense;
Myrrh and aloes, with all the chief spices.
Thou art a fountain of gardens,
A well of living waters,
And flowing streams from Lebanon.

THE SHULAMITE

Awake, O north wind; and come, thou south;
Blow upon my garden, that the spices thereof may flow out.
Let my beloved come into his garden,
And eat his precious fruits.

KING SOLOMON

I am come into my garden, my sister, my bride:
I have gathered my myrrh with my spice;
I have eaten my honeycomb with my honey;
I have drunk my wine with my milk.

THE SONG OF SONGS

Eat, O friends;
Drink, yea, drink abundantly, O beloved.

Scene IV

THE SHULAMITE

I was asleep, but my heart waked:
It is the voice of my beloved that knocketh, saying,
"Open to me, my sister, my love, my dove, my undefiled:
For my head is filled with dew,
My locks with the drops of the night."

I have put off my coat; how shall I put it on?
I have washed my feet; how shall I defile them?
My beloved put in his hand by the hole of the door,
And my heart was moved for him.
I rose up to open to my beloved;
And my hands dropped with myrrh,
And my fingers with liquid myrrh,
Upon the handles of the bolt.

I opened to my beloved;
But my beloved had withdrawn himself, and was gone.
My soul had failed me when he spoke:
I sought him, but I could not find him;
I called him, but he gave me no answer.
The watchmen that go about the city found me,
They smote me, they wounded me;
The keepers of the walls took away my mantle from me.

I adjure you, O daughters of Jerusalem, if ye find my beloved,
That ye tell him, that I am sick of love.

THE DAUGHTERS OF JERUSALEM

What is thy beloved more than another beloved,
O thou fairest among women?
What is thy beloved more than another beloved,
That thou dost so adjure us?

THE SONG OF SONGS

THE SHULAMITE

My beloved is white and ruddy,
The chiefest among ten thousand.
His head is as the most fine gold,
His locks are bushy, and black as a raven.
His eyes are like doves beside the water brooks;
Washed with milk, and fitly set.
His cheeks are as a bed of spices, as banks of sweet herbs:

His lips are as lilies, dropping liquid myrrh.
His hands are as rings of gold set with beryl:
His body is as ivory work overlaid with sapphires.
His legs are as pillars of marble, set upon sockets of fine gold:
His aspect is like Lebanon, excellent as the cedars.
His mouth is most sweet: yea, he is altogether lovely.
This is my beloved, and this is my friend,
O daughters of Jerusalem.

THE DAUGHTERS OF JERUSALEM

Whither is thy beloved gone,
O thou fairest among women?
Whither hath thy beloved turned him,
That we may seek him with thee?

THE SHULAMITE

My beloved is gone down to his garden, to the beds of spices,
To feed in the gardens, and to gather lilies.
I am my beloved's, and my beloved is mine:
He feedeth his flock among the lilies.

Scene V

KING SOLOMON

Thou art beautiful, O my love, as Tirzah,
Comely as Jerusalem,
Terrible as an army with banners.

THE SONG OF SONGS

Turn away thine eyes from me,
For they have overcome me.
Thy hair is as a flock of goats,
That lie along the side of Gilead.

Thy teeth are like a flock of ewes,
Which are come up from the washing;
Whereof every one hath twins,
And none is bereaved among them.
Thy temples are like a piece of pomegranate
Behind thy veil.

There are threescore queens, and fourscore concubines,
And virgins without number.
My dove, my undefiled, is but one;
She is the only one of her mother;
She is the choice one of her that bore her.
The daughters saw her, and called her blessed;
Yea, the queens and the concubines, and they praised her.

THE DAUGHTERS OF JERUSALEM

Who is she that looketh forth as the morning,
Fair as the moon,
Clear as the sun,
Terrible as an army with banners?

THE SHULAMITE

I went down into the garden of nuts,
To see the green plants of the valley,
To see whether the vine budded,
And the pomegranates were in flower.
Or ever I was aware, my soul set me
Among the chariots of my princely people.

THE DAUGHTERS OF JERUSALEM

Return, return, O Shulamite;
Return, return, that we may look upon thee.

THE SONG OF SONGS

THE SHULAMITE

Why will ye look upon the Shulamite,
As upon the dance of Mahanaim?

KING SOLOMON

How beautiful are thy feet in sandals, O prince's daughter!
The joints of thy thighs are like jewels,
The work of the hands of a cunning workman.
Thy navel is like a round goblet,
Wherein no mingled wine is wanting:
Thy belly is like a heap of wheat
Set about with lilies.

Thy two breasts are like two fawns
That are twins of a roe.
Thy neck is like the tower of ivory;
Thine eyes as the pools in Heshbon, by the gate of Bath-rabbim;
Thy nose is like the tower of Lebanon
Which looketh toward Damascus.

Thine head upon thee is like Carmel,
And the hair of thine head like purple;
The king is held captive in the tresses thereof.
How fair and how pleasant art thou,
O love, for delights!
This thy stature is like to a palm tree,
And thy breasts to clusters of grapes.

I said, "I will climb up into the palm tree,
I will take hold of the branches thereof":
Let thy breasts be as clusters of the vine,
And the smell of thy breath like apples;
And thy mouth like the best wine,
That goeth down smoothly for my beloved,
Gliding through the lips of those that are asleep.

THE SONG OF SONGS

THE SHULAMITE

I am my beloved's,
And his desire is toward me.

Come, my beloved, let us go forth into the field;
Let us lodge in the villages.
Let us get up early to the vineyards;
Let us see whether the vine hath budded, and its blossom be open,
And the pomegranates be in flower:

There will I give thee my love.
The mandrakes give forth fragrance,
And at our doors are all manner of precious fruits, new and old.
Which I have laid up for thee, O my beloved.

Oh that thou wert as my brother,
That sucked the breasts of my mother!
When I should find thee without, I would kiss thee;
Yea, and none would despise me.

I would lead thee, and bring thee into my mother's house,
Who would instruct me;
I would cause thee to drink of spiced wine,
Of the juice of my pomegranate.
His left hand should be under my head,
And his right hand should embrace me.

I adjure you, O daughters of Jerusalem,
That ye stir not up, nor awaken love,
Until it please.

Scene VI

THE DAUGHTERS OF JERUSALEM

Who is this that cometh up from the wilderness,
Leaning upon her beloved?

THE SONG OF SONGS

KING SOLOMON

Under the apple tree I awakened thee:
There thy mother was in travail with thee,
There was she in travail that brought thee forth.

THE SHULAMITE

Set me as a seal upon thine heart, as a seal upon thine arm:
For love is strong as death;
Jealousy is cruel as the grave:
The flashes thereof are flashes of fire,
A very flame of the Lord.
Many waters cannot quench love,
Neither can the floods drown it:
If a man would give all the substance of his house for love,
He would utterly be contemned.

THE BROTHERS

We have a little sister,
And she hath no breasts:
What shall we do for our sister
In the day when she shall be spoken for?
If she be a wall,
We will build upon her a turret of silver:
And if she be a door,
We will inclose her with boards of cedar.

THE SHULAMITE

I am a wall, and my breasts like the towers thereof:
Then was I in his eyes as one that found peace.

Solomon had a vineyard at Baal-hamon;
He let out the vineyard unto keepers;
Every one for the fruit thereof was to bring a thousand pieces of silver.

THE SONG OF SONGS

My vineyard, which is mine, is before me:
Thou, O Solomon, shalt have the thousand,
And those that keep the fruit thereof two hundred.

KING SOLOMON

Thou that dwellest in the gardens,
The companions hearken for thy voice:
Cause me to hear it.

THE SHULAMITE

Make haste, my beloved,
And be thou like to a roe or to a young hart
Upon the mountains of spices.

RUTH

A TALE

The prophetical literature of the Old Testament was a thing in itself, not giving rise to any later literary form, except to the degree that allegory can be said to have sprung from it; the methods of the Jewish historians were also in large measure peculiar to themselves; but in the short tales that appear in the Old Testament and in the Apocrypha one meets examples of the most universal and ultimately the most popular type of all literature—prose fiction, destined at long last to develop into the modern novel.

The Book of Ruth, as already mentioned, was written in the fourth century as a protest against the harsh policy of Nehemiah and Ezra in forbidding racial intermarriage. By skilfully taking advantage of an old legend of a Moabite strain in King David, and accounting for it by the marriage of David's ancestor, Boaz, to Ruth, a woman of Moab, the author was able to reënforce his generous thesis by the appeal to tradition. Surely no other work of protest was ever written in so gentle or appealing a manner. In fact, it was done too beautifully for its own purpose, and men remembered its pastoral simplicity and its charm of individual characterization while they forgot its message of tolerance.

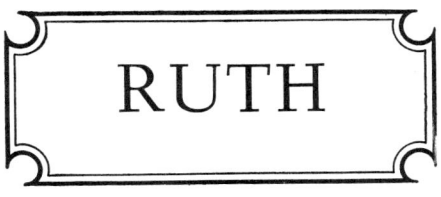

RUTH

A TALE

Now it came to pass in the days when the judges ruled, that there was a famine in the land. And a certain man of Bethlehem-judah went to sojourn in the country of Moab, he, and his wife, and his two sons. And the name of the man was Elimelech, and the name of his wife Naomi, and the name of his two sons Mahlon and Chilion, Ephrathites of Beth-lehem-judah. And they came into the country of Moab, and continued there. And Elimelech Naomi's husband died; and she was left, and her two sons. And they took them wives of the women of Moab; the name of the one was Orpah, and the name of the other Ruth: and they dwelled there about ten years. And Mahlon and Chilion died also both of them; and the woman was left of her two sons and her husband.

Then she arose with her daughters-in-law, that she might return from the country of Moab: for she had heard in the country of Moab how that the Lord had visited his people in giving them bread. Wherefore she went forth out of the place where she was, and her two daughters-in-law with her; and they went on the way to return unto the land of Judah.

And Naomi said unto her two daughters-in-law, "Go, return each to her mother's house: the Lord deal kindly with you, as ye have dealt with the dead, and with me. The Lord grant you that ye may find rest, each of you in the house of her husband."

Then she kissed them; and they lifted up their voice, and wept. And they said unto her, "Surely we will return with thee unto thy people."

RUTH

And Naomi said, "Turn again, my daughters: why will ye go with me? are there yet any more sons in my womb, that they may be your husbands? Turn again, my daughters, go your way; for I am too old to have a husband. If I should say, I have hope, if I should have a husband also to-night, and should also bear sons; would ye tarry for them till they were grown? would ye stay for them from having husbands? nay, my daughters; for it grieveth me much for your sakes that the hand of the Lord is gone out against me."

And they lifted up their voice, and wept again: and Orpah kissed her mother-in-law; but Ruth cleaved unto her. And she said, "Behold, thy sister-in-law is gone back unto her people, and unto her gods: return thou after thy sister-in-law."

And Ruth said, "Intreat me not to leave thee, or to return from following after thee: for whither thou goest, I will go; and where thou lodgest, I will lodge: thy people shall be my people, and thy God my God: where thou diest, will I die, and there will I be buried: the Lord do so to me, and more also, if ought but death part thee and me."

When she saw that she was steadfastly minded to go with her, then she left speaking unto her.

So they two went until they came to Beth-lehem. And it came to pass, when they were come to Beth-lehem, that all the city was moved about them, and they said, "Is this Naomi?"

And she said unto them, "Call me not Naomi, call me Mara: for the Almighty hath dealt very bitterly with me. I went out full, and the Lord hath brought me home again empty: why then call ye me Naomi, seeing the Lord hath testified against me, and the Almighty hath afflicted me?"

So Naomi returned, and Ruth the Moabitess, her daughter-in-law, with her, which returned out of the country of Moab: and they came to Beth-lehem in the beginning of barley harvest. And Naomi had a kinsman of her husband's, a mighty man of wealth, of the family of Elimelech; and his name was Boaz. And Ruth the Moabitess said unto Naomi, "Let me now go to the

RUTH

field, and glean ears of corn after him in whose sight I shall find grace." And she said unto her, "Go, my daughter." And she went, and came, and gleaned in the field after the reapers: and her hap was to light on a part of the field belonging unto Boaz, who was of the kindred of Elimelech.

And, behold, Boaz came from Beth-lehem, and said unto the reapers, "The Lord be with you." And they answered him, "The Lord bless thee."

Then said Boaz unto his servant that was set over the reapers, "Whose damsel is this?"

And the servant that was set over the reapers answered and said, "It is the Moabitish damsel that came back with Naomi out of the country of Moab: and she said, 'I pray you, let me glean and gather after the reapers among the sheaves': so she came, and hath continued even from the morning until now, that she tarried a little in the house."

Then said Boaz unto Ruth, "Hearest thou not, my daughter? Go not to glean in another field, neither go from hence, but abide here fast by my maidens: let thine eyes be on the field that they do reap, and go thou after them: have I not charged the young men that they shall not touch thee? and when thou art athirst, go unto the vessels, and drink of that which the young men have drawn."

Then she fell on her face, and bowed herself to the ground, and said unto him, "Why have I found grace in thine eyes, that thou shouldest take knowledge of me, seeing I am a stranger?"

And Boaz answered and said unto her, "It hath fully been showed me all that thou hast done unto thy mother-in-law since the death of thine husband: and how thou hast left thy father and thy mother, and the land of thy nativity, and art come unto a people which thou knewest not heretofore. The Lord recompense thy work, and a full reward be given thee of the Lord God of Israel, under whose wings thou art come to trust."

Then she said, "Let me find favour in thy sight, my lord; for

RUTH

that thou hast comforted me, and for that thou hast spoken friendly unto thine handmaid, though I be not like unto one of thine handmaidens."

And Boaz said unto her, "At mealtime come thou thither, and eat of the bread, and dip thy morsel in the vinegar."

And she sat beside the reapers: and he reached her parched corn, and she did eat, and was sufficed, and left. And when she was risen up to glean, Boaz commanded his young men, saying, "Let her glean even among the sheaves, and reproach her not: and let fall also some of the handfuls of purpose for her, and leave them, that she may glean them, and rebuke her not."

So she gleaned in the field until even, and beat out that she had gleaned: and it was about an ephah of barley. And she took it up, and went into the city: and her mother-in-law saw what she had gleaned: and she brought forth, and gave to her that she had reserved after she was sufficed.

And her mother-in-law said unto her, "Where hast thou gleaned to-day? and where wroughtest thou? blessed be he that did take knowledge of thee."

And she showed her mother-in-law with whom she had wrought, and said, "The man's name with whom I wrought to-day is Boaz."

And Naomi said unto her daughter-in-law, "Blessed be he of the Lord, who hath not left off his kindness to the living and to the dead." And Naomi said unto her, "The man is near of kin unto us, one of our next kinsmen."

And Ruth the Moabitess said, "He said unto me also, 'Thou shalt keep fast by my young men, until they have ended all my harvest.'"

And Naomi said unto Ruth her daughter-in-law, "It is good, my daughter, that thou go out with his maidens, that they meet thee not in any other field."

So she kept fast by the maidens of Boaz to glean unto the end of barley harvest and of wheat harvest; and dwelt with her mother-in-law.

Then Naomi her mother-in-law said unto her, "My daughter,

RUTH

shall I not seek rest for thee, that it may be well with thee? And now is not Boaz of our kindred, with whose maidens thou wast? Behold, he winnoweth barley to-night in the threshingfloor. Wash thyself therefore, and anoint thee, and put thy raiment upon thee, and get thee down to the floor: but make not thyself known unto the man, until he shall have done eating and drinking. And it shall be, when he lieth down, that thou shalt mark the place where he shall lie, and thou shalt go in, and uncover his feet, and lay thee down; and he will tell thee what thou shalt do."

And she said unto her, "All that thou sayest unto me I will do."

And she went down unto the floor, and did according to all that her mother-in-law bade her. And when Boaz had eaten and drunk, and his heart was merry, he went to lie down at the end of the heap of corn: and she came softly, and uncovered his feet, and laid her down. And it came to pass at midnight, that the man was afraid, and turned himself: and, behold, a woman lay at his feet.

And he said, "Who art thou?"

And she answered, "I am Ruth thine handmaid: spread therefore thy skirt over thine handmaid; for thou art a near kinsman."

And he said, "Blessed be thou of the Lord, my daughter: for thou hast showed more kindness in the latter end than at the beginning, inasmuch as thou followedst not young men, whether poor or rich. And now, my daughter, fear not: I will do to thee all that thou requirest: for all the city of my people doth know that thou art a virtuous woman. And now it is true that I am thy near kinsman: howbeit there is a kinsman nearer than I. Tarry this night, and it shall be in the morning, that if he will perform unto thee the part of kinsman, well; let him do the kinsman's part: but if he will not do the part of a kinsman to thee, then will I do the part of a kinsman to thee, as the Lord liveth: lie down until the morning."

And she lay at his feet until the morning: and she rose up before one could know another.

RUTH

And he said, "Let it not be known that a woman came into the floor." Also he said, "Bring the veil that thou hast upon thee, and hold it."

And when she held it, he measured six measures of barley, and laid it on her: and she went into the city. And when she came to her mother-in-law, she said, "Who art thou, my daughter?"

And she told her all that the man had done to her. And she said, "These six measures of barley gave he me; for he said to me, 'Go not empty unto thy mother-in-law.'"

Then said she, "Sit still, my daughter, until thou know how the matter will fall: for the man will not be in rest, until he have finished the thing this day."

Then went Boaz up to the gate, and sat him down there: and, behold, the kinsman of whom Boaz spoke came by; unto whom he said, "Ho, such a one! turn aside, sit down here."

And he turned aside, and sat down. And he took ten men of the elders of the city, and said, "Sit ye down here." And they sat down.

And he said unto the kinsman, "Naomi, that is come again out of the country of Moab, selleth a parcel of land, which was our brother Elimelech's: and I thought to advertise thee, saying, 'Buy it before the inhabitants, and before the elders of my people. If thou wilt redeem it, redeem it': but if thou wilt not redeem it, then tell me, that I may know: for there is none to redeem it beside thee; and I am after thee."

And he said, "I will redeem it."

Then said Boaz, "What day thou buyest the field of the hand of Naomi, thou must buy it also of Ruth the Moabitess, the wife of the dead, to raise up the name of the dead upon his inheritance."

And the kinsman said, "I cannot redeem it for myself, lest I mar mine own inheritance: redeem thou my right to thyself; for I cannot redeem it."

(Now this was the manner in former time in Israel concerning redeeming and concerning changing, for to confirm all

RUTH

things; a man plucked off his shoe, and gave it to his neighbour: and this was a testimony in Israel.) Therefore the kinsman said unto Boaz, "Buy it for thee." So he drew off his shoe.

And Boaz said unto the elders, and unto all the people, "Ye are witnesses this day, that I have bought all that was Elimelech's, and all that was Chilion's and Mahlon's, of the hand of Naomi. Moreover Ruth the Moabitess, the wife of Mahlon, have I purchased to be my wife, to raise up the name of the dead upon his inheritance, that the name of the dead be not cut off from among his brethren, and from the gate of his place: ye are witnesses this day."

And all the people that were in the gate, and the elders, said, "We are witnesses. The Lord make the woman that is come into thine house like Rachel and like Leah, which two did build the house of Israel: and do thou worthily in Ephratah, and be famous in Beth-lehem: and let thy house be like the house of Pharez, whom Tamar bore unto Judah, of the seed which the Lord shall give thee of this young woman."

So Boaz took Ruth, and she was his wife: and when he went in unto her, the Lord gave her conception, and she bore a son.

And the women said unto Naomi, "Blessed be the Lord, which hath not left thee this day without a kinsman, that his name may be famous in Israel. And he shall be unto thee a restorer of thy life, and a nourisher of thine old age: for thy daughter-in-law which loveth thee, which is better to thee than seven sons, hath borne him."

And Naomi took the child, and laid it in her bosom, and became nurse unto it. And the women her neighbours gave it a name, saying, "There is a son born to Naomi; and they called his name Obed: he is the father of Jesse, the father of David."

JONAH

A TALE

The most ridiculously misunderstood of all the works in the Bible has been the Book of Jonah. Misplaced in ancient times among the prophetical writings simply because its hero is the prophet Jonah—as if one were to ascribe the authorship of "Uncle Tom's Cabin" to Uncle Tom himself; and then in modern times becoming a cause célèbre between fundamentalists and skeptics on account of the dubious possibility of a man's being able to survive "in the belly of a fish," the one party maintaining that it would be quite possible if the fish were large enough and the man could somehow get there intact, the other denying that any such fish is to be found in all the seven seas. Amid these absurdities, the real value and beauty of the book were lost sight of equally by the pious and the impious.

Like Ruth, the Book of Jonah belongs to the realm of protest fiction. Written probably in the third century, it shows how the racial bigotry of the prophet was rebuked by the religious tolerance of God himself who still regarded as his children the inhabitants of that wickedest of cities, Nineveh. The work stands with Ruth and some passages in the work of the Unknown Prophet of the Exile as the noblest expression of the universality of religion to be found in the Old Testament.

A TALE

Now the word of the Lord came unto Jonah the son of Amittai, saying, "Arise, go to Nineveh, that great city, and cry against it; for their wickedness is come up before me."

But Jonah rose up to flee unto Tarshish from the presence of the Lord, and went down to Joppa; and he found a ship going to Tarshish: so he paid the fare thereof, and went down into it, to go with them unto Tarshish from the presence of the Lord.

But the Lord sent out a great wind into the sea, and there was a mighty tempest in the sea, so that the ship was like to be broken. Then the mariners were afraid, and cried every man unto his god, and cast forth the wares that were in the ship into the sea, to lighten it of them. But Jonah was gone down into the sides of the ship; and he lay, and was fast asleep.

So the shipmaster came to him, and said unto him, "What meanest thou, O sleeper? arise, call upon thy God, if so be that God will think upon us, that we perish not."

And they said every one to his fellow, "Come, and let us cast lots, that we may know for whose cause this evil is upon us." So they cast lots, and the lot fell upon Jonah.

Then said they unto him, "Tell us, we pray thee, for whose cause this evil is upon us; what is thine occupation? and whence comest thou? what is thy country? and of what people art thou?"

And he said unto them, "I am a Hebrew; and I fear the Lord, the God of heaven, which hath made the sea and the dry land."

Then were the men exceedingly afraid, and said unto him, "Why hast thou done this?" For the men knew that he fled from

JONAH

the presence of the Lord, because he had told them. Then said they unto him, "What shall we do unto thee, that the sea may be calm unto us?" for the sea wrought, and was tempestuous.

And he said unto them, "Take me up, and cast me forth into the sea; so shall the sea be calm unto you: for I know that for my sake this great tempest is upon you."

Nevertheless the men rowed hard to bring it to the land; but they could not: for the sea wrought, and was tempestuous against them. Wherefore they cried unto the Lord, and said, "We beseech thee, O Lord, we beseech thee, let us not perish for this man's life, and lay not upon us innocent blood: for thou, O Lord, hast done as it pleased thee."

So they took up Jonah, and cast him forth into the sea: and the sea ceased from her raging. Then the men feared the Lord exceedingly, and offered a sacrifice unto the Lord, and made vows.

Now the Lord had prepared a great fish to swallow up Jonah. And Jonah was in the belly of the fish three days and three nights. Then Jonah prayed unto the Lord his God out of the fish's belly and said,

> "I cried by reason of mine affliction unto the Lord,
> And he heard me;
> Out of the belly of hell cried I,
> And thou heardest my voice.
> For thou hadst cast me into the deep,
> In the midst of the seas;
> And the floods compassed me about:
> All thy billows and thy waves passed over me.
> Then I said, 'I am cast out of thy sight;
> Yet I will look again toward thy holy temple.'
> The waters compassed me about, even to the soul:
> The depth closed me round about,
> The weeds were wrapped about my head.
> I went down to the bottoms of the mountains;
> The earth with her bars was about me for ever:

JONAH

Yet hast thou brought up my life from corruption, O Lord my God.
When my soul fainted within me I remembered the Lord:
And my prayer came in unto thee,
Into thine holy temple.
They that observe lying vanities forsake their own mercy.
But I will sacrifice unto thee with the voice of thanksgiving;
I will pay that that I have vowed.
Salvation is of the Lord."

And the Lord spoke unto the fish, and it vomited out Jonah upon the dry land.

And the word of the Lord came unto Jonah the second time, saying, "Arise, go unto Nineveh, that great city, and preach unto it the preaching that I bid thee."

So Jonah arose, and went unto Nineveh, according to the word of the Lord. Now Nineveh was an exceedingly great city of three days' journey. And Jonah began to enter into the city a day's journey, and he cried, and said, "Yet forty days, and Nineveh shall be overthrown."

So the people of Nineveh believed God, and proclaimed a fast, and put on sackcloth, from the greatest of them even to the least of them. For word came unto the king of Nineveh, and he arose from his throne, and he laid his robe from him, and covered him with sackcloth, and sat in ashes. And he caused it to be proclaimed and published through Nineveh by the decree of the king and his nobles, saying,

"Let neither man nor beast, herd nor flock, taste any thing: let them not feed, nor drink water: but let man and beast be covered with sackcloth, and cry mightily unto God: yea, let them turn every one from his evil way, and from the violence that is in their hands. Who can tell if God will turn and repent, and turn away from his fierce anger, that we perish not?"

And God saw their works, that they turned from their evil way; and God repented of the evil that he had said that he would do unto them; and he did it not.

JONAH

But it displeased Jonah exceedingly, and he was very angry. And he prayed unto the Lord, and said,

"I pray thee, O Lord, was not this my saying, when I was yet in my country? Therefore I fled before unto Tarshish: for I knew that thou art a gracious God, and merciful, slow to anger, and of great kindness, and repentest thee of the evil. Therefore now, O Lord, take, I beseech thee, my life from me; for it is better for me to die than to live."

Then said the Lord, "Doest thou well to be angry?"

So Jonah went out of the city, and sat on the east side of the city, and there made him a booth, and sat under it in the shadow, till he might see what would become of the city.

And the Lord God prepared a gourd, and made it to come up over Jonah, that it might be a shadow over his head, to deliver him from his grief. So Jonah was exceeding glad of the gourd.

But God prepared a worm when the morning rose the next day, and it smote the gourd that it withered.

And it came to pass, when the sun did arise, that God prepared a vehement east wind; and the sun beat upon the head of Jonah, that he fainted, and wished in himself to die, and said, "It is better for me to die than to live."

And God said to Jonah, "Doest thou well to be angry for the gourd?"

And he said, "I do well to be angry, even unto death."

Then said the Lord,

"Thou hast had pity on the gourd, for the which thou hast not laboured, neither madest it grow; which came up in a night, and perished in a night. And should not I spare Nineveh, that great city, wherein are more than sixscore thousand persons, that cannot discern between their right hand and their left hand; and also much cattle?"

DANIEL

A TALE

Though parts of the book of Daniel may belong to the third century, the bulk of it was undoubtedly written during the Maccabean rebellion in the second century to encourage the Jews in their patriotic struggle. Dim stories of a legendary Exilic prophet were woven together and supplemented by an allegorical account of later history down to the contemporary period of Antiochus Epiphanes. The ending is an example of apocalyptic or "revealed" literature in which a hidden meaning is conveyed by the text to those initiated—a most useful form in times of persecution. In the case of Daniel the specific meaning was so well concealed that the origin of the work was soon forgotten, and as with Jonah its authorship was ascribed to its central character. When writings circulated only in manuscript it was, of course, the easiest thing in the world for utter confusion to arise as to the date of the original composition.

"The Song of the Three Children," which appears as a Psalm of Praise in the Prayer Book of the Church of England, is a part of the Apocryphal version of Daniel.

DANIEL

A TALE

IN THE THIRD YEAR of the reign of Jehoiakim king of Judah came Nebuchadnezzar king of Babylon unto Jerusalem, and besieged it. And the Lord gave Jehoiakim king of Judah into his hand, with part of the vessels of the house of God: which he carried into the land of Shinar to the house of his god; and he brought the vessels into the treasure house of his god.

And the king spoke unto Ashpenaz the master of his eunuchs, that he should bring certain of the children of Israel, and of the king's seed, and of the princes; children in whom was no blemish, but well favoured, and skilful in all wisdom, and cunning in knowledge, and understanding science, and such as had ability in them to stand in the king's palace, and whom they might teach the learning and the tongue of the Chaldeans.

And the king appointed them a daily provision of the king's meat, and of the wine which he drank: so nourishing them three years, that at the end thereof they might stand before the king.

Now among these were of the children of Judah, Daniel, Hananiah, Mishael, and Azariah: unto whom the prince of the eunuchs gave names: for he gave unto Daniel the name of Belteshazzar; and to Hananiah, of Shadrach; and to Mishael, of Meshach; and to Azariah, of Abed-nego.

But Daniel purposed in his heart that he would not defile himself with the portion of the king's meat, nor with the wine which he drank: therefore he requested of the prince of the eunuchs that he might not defile himself.

Now God had brought Daniel into favour and tender love

DANIEL

with the prince of the eunuchs. And the prince of the eunuchs said unto Daniel, "I fear my lord the king, who hath appointed your meat and your drink: for why should he see your faces worse liking than the children which are of your sort? then shall ye make me endanger my head to the king."

Then said Daniel to Melzar, whom the prince of the eunuchs had set over Daniel, Hananiah, Mishael, and Azariah, "Prove thy servants, I beseech thee, ten days; and let them give us pulse to eat, and water to drink. Then let our countenances be looked upon before thee, and the countenance of the children that eat of the portion of the king's meat: and as thou seest, deal with thy servants."

So he consented to them in this matter, and proved them ten days. And at the end of ten days their countenances appeared fairer and fatter in flesh than all the children which did eat the portion of the king's meat. Thus Melzar took away the portion of their meat, and the wine that they should drink; and gave them pulse.

As for these four children, God gave them knowledge and skill in all learning and wisdom: and Daniel had understanding in all visions and dreams. Now at the end of the days that the king had said he should bring them in, then the prince of the eunuchs brought them in before Nebuchadnezzar.

And the king communed with them; and among them all was found none like Daniel, Hananiah, Mishael, and Azariah: therefore stood they before the king. And in all matters of wisdom and understanding, that the king enquired of them, he found them ten times better than all the magicians and astrologers that were in all his realm. And Daniel continued even unto the first year of King Cyrus.

And in the second year of the reign of Nebuchadnezzar Nebuchadnezzar dreamed dreams, wherewith his spirit was troubled, and his sleep broke from him. Then the king commanded to call the magicians, and the astrologers, and the sorcerers, and the Chaldeans, for to show the king his dreams. So they came and stood before the king.

DANIEL

And the king said unto them, "I have dreamed a dream, and my spirit was troubled to know the dream."

Then spoke the Chaldeans to the king in Syriac, "O king, live for ever: tell thy servants the dream, and we will show the interpretation."

The king answered and said to the Chaldeans, "The thing is gone from me: if ye will not make known unto me the dream, with the interpretation thereof, ye shall be cut in pieces, and your houses shall be made a dunghill. But if ye show the dream, and the interpretation thereof, ye shall receive of me gifts and rewards and great honour: therefore show me the dream, and the interpretation thereof."

They answered again and said, "Let the king tell his servants the dream, and we will show the interpretation of it."

The king answered and said, "I know of certainty that ye would gain the time, because ye see the thing is gone from me. But if ye will not make known unto me the dream, there is but one decree for you: for ye have prepared lying and corrupt words to speak before me, till the time be changed: therefore tell me the dream, and I shall know that ye can show me the interpretation thereof."

The Chaldeans answered before the king, and said, "There is not a man upon the earth that can show the king's matter: therefore there is no king, lord, nor ruler that asked such things at any magician, or astrologer, or Chaldean. And it is a rare thing that the king requireth, and there is none other that can show it before the king, except the gods, whose dwelling is not with flesh."

For this cause the king was angry and very furious, and commanded to destroy all the wise men of Babylon. And the decree went forth that the wise men should be slain; and they sought Daniel and his fellows to be slain.

Then Daniel answered with counsel and wisdom to Arioch the captain of the king's guard, which was gone forth to slay the wise men of Babylon: he answered and said to Arioch the king's captain, "Why is the decree so hasty from the king?"

DANIEL

Then Arioch made the thing known to Daniel. Then Daniel went in, and desired of the king that he would give him time, and that he would show the king the interpretation.

Then Daniel went to his house, and made the thing known to Hananiah, Mishael, and Azariah, his companions: that they would desire mercies of the God of heaven concerning this secret; that Daniel and his fellows should not perish with the rest of the wise men of Babylon. Then was the secret revealed unto Daniel in a night vision.

Therefore Daniel went in unto Arioch, whom the king had ordained to destroy the wise men of Babylon: he went and said thus unto him: "Destroy not the wise men of Babylon: bring me in before the king, and I will show unto the king the interpretation."

Then Arioch brought in Daniel before the king in haste, and said thus unto him, "I have found a man of the captives of Judah, that will make known unto the king the interpretation." The king answered and said to Daniel, whose name was Belteshazzar, "Art thou able to make known unto me the dream which I have seen, and the interpretation thereof."

Daniel answered in the presence of the king, and said, "The secret which the king hath demanded cannot the wise men, the astrologers, the magicians, the soothsayers, show unto the king; but there is a God in heaven that revealeth secrets, and maketh known to the king Nebuchadnezzar what shall be in the latter days.

"Thou, O king, sawest, and beheld a great image. This great image, whose brightness was excellent, stood before thee; and the form thereof was terrible. This image's head was of fine gold, his breast and his arms of silver, his belly and his thighs of brass, his legs of iron, his feet part of iron and part of clay. Thou sawest till that a stone was cut out without hands, which smote the image upon his feet that were of iron and clay, and broke them to pieces. Then was the iron, the clay, the brass, the silver, and the gold, broken to pieces together, and became like the chaff of the summer threshingfloors; and the wind carried

DANIEL

them away, that no place was found for them: and the stone that smote the image became a great mountain, and filled the whole earth. This is the dream; and we will tell the interpretation thereof before the king.

"Thou, O king, art a king of kings: for the God of heaven hath given thee a kingdom, power, and strength, and glory. And wheresoever the children of men dwell, the beasts of the field and the fowls of the heaven hath he given into thine hand, and hath made thee ruler over them all. Thou art this head of gold. And after thee shall arise another kingdom inferior to thee, and another third kingdom of brass, which shall bear rule over all the earth. And the fourth kingdom shall be strong as iron: forasmuch as iron breaketh in pieces and subdueth all things: and as iron that breaketh all these, shall it break in pieces and bruise.

"And whereas thou sawest the feet and toes, part of potters' clay, and part of iron, the kingdom shall be divided; but there shall be in it of the strength of the iron, forasmuch as thou sawest the iron mixed with miry clay. And as the toes of the feet were part of iron, and part of clay, so the kingdom shall be partly strong, and partly broken. And whereas thou sawest iron mixed with miry clay, they shall mingle themselves with the seed of men: but they shall not cleave one to another, even as iron is not mixed with clay. And in the days of these kings shall the God of heaven set up a kingdom, which shall never be destroyed: and the kingdom shall not be left to other people, but it shall break in pieces and consume all these kingdoms, and it shall stand for ever. Forasmuch as thou sawest that the stone was cut out of the mountain without hands, and that it broke in pieces the iron, the brass, the clay, the silver, and the gold; the great God hath made known to the king what shall come to pass hereafter: and the dream is certain, and the interpretation thereof sure."

The king answered unto Daniel, and said, "Of a truth it is, that your God is a God of gods, and a Lord of kings, and a revealer of secrets, seeing thou couldest reveal this secret."

Then the king made Daniel a great man, and gave him many

DANIEL

great gifts, and made him ruler over the whole province of Babylon, and chief of the governors over all the wise men of Babylon. Then Daniel requested of the king, and he set Shadrach, Meshach, and Abed-nego, over the affairs of the province of Babylon: but Daniel sat in the gate of the king.

Nebuchadnezzar the king made an image of gold, whose height was threescore cubits, and the breadth thereof six cubits: he set it up in the plain of Dura, in the province of Babylon. Then Nebuchadnezzar the king sent to gather together the princes, the governors, and the captains, the judges, the treasurers, the counsellors, the sheriffs, and all the rulers of the provinces, to come to the dedication of the image which Nebuchadnezzar the king had set up. Then the princes, the governors, and captains, the judges, the treasurers, the counsellors, the sheriffs, and all the rulers of the provinces, were gathered together unto the dedication of the image that Nebuchadnezzar the king had set up; and they stood before the image that Nebuchadnezzar had set up.

Then a herald cried aloud, "To you it is commanded, O people, nations, and languages, that at what time ye hear the sound of the cornet, flute, harp, sackbut, psaltery, dulcimer, and all kinds of music, ye fall down and worship the golden image that Nebuchadnezzar the king hath set up: and whoso falleth not down and worshippeth shall the same hour be cast into the midst of a burning fiery furnace."

Therefore at that time, when all the people heard the sound of the cornet, flute, harp, sackbut, psaltery, and all kinds of music, all the people, the nations, and the languages, fell down and worshipped the golden image that Nebuchadnezzar the king had set up.

Wherefore at that time certain Chaldeans came near, and accused the Jews. They spoke and said to the king Nebuchadnezzar,

"O king, live for ever. Thou, O king, hast made a decree, that every man that shall hear the sound of the cornet, flute,

DANIEL

harp, sackbut, psaltery, and dulcimer, and all kinds of music, shall fall down and worship the golden image: and whoso falleth not down and worshippeth, that he should be cast into the midst of a burning fiery furnace. There are certain Jews whom thou hast set over the affairs of the province of Babylon, Shadrach, Meshach, and Abed-nego; these men, O king, have not regarded thee: they serve not thy gods, nor worship the golden image which thou hast set up."

Then Nebuchadnezzar in his rage and fury commanded to bring Shadrach, Meshach, and Abed-nego. Then they brought these men before the king.

Nebuchadnezzar spoke and said unto them, "Is it true, O Shadrach, Meshach, and Abed-nego, do not ye serve my gods, nor worship the golden image which I have set up? Now if ye be ready that at what time ye hear the sound of the cornet, flute, harp, sackbut, psaltery, and dulcimer, and all kinds of music, ye fall down and worship the image which I have made: well; but if ye worship not, ye shall be cast the same hour into the midst of a burning fiery furnace; and who is that God that shall deliver you out of my hands?"

Shadrach, Meshach, and Abed-nego, answered and said to the king, "O Nebuchadnezzar, we are not careful to answer thee in this matter. If it be so, our God whom we serve is able to deliver us from the burning fiery furnace, and he will deliver us out of thine hand, O king. But if not, be it known unto thee, O king, that we will not serve thy gods, nor worship the golden image which thou hast set up."

Then was Nebuchadnezzar full of fury, and the form of his visage was changed against Shadrach, Meshach, and Abed-nego: therefore he spoke, and commanded that they should heat the furnace one seven times more than it was wont to be heated. And he commanded the most mighty men that were in his army to bind Shadrach, Meshach, and Abed-nego, and to cast them into the burning fiery furnace. Then these men were bound in their coats, their hose, and their hats, and their other garments, and were cast into the midst of the burning fiery furnace. There-

DANIEL

fore because the king's commandment was urgent, and the furnace exceeding hot, the flame of the fire slew those men that took up Shadrach, Meshach, and Abed-nego. And these three men, Shadrach, Meshach, and Abed-nego, fell down bound into the midst of the burning fiery furnace.

Then the three, as out of one mouth, praised, glorified, and blessed God in the furnace, saying,

> "Blessed art thou, O Lord God of our fathers:
> And to be praised and exalted above all for ever.
>
> And blessed is thy glorious and holy name:
> And to be praised and exalted above all for ever.
>
> Blessed art thou in the temple of thine holy glory:
> And to be praised and glorified above all for ever.
>
> Blessed art thou that beholdest the depths, and sittest upon the cherubims:
> And to be praised and exalted above all for ever.
>
> Blessed art thou on the glorious throne of thy kingdom:
> And to be praised and glorified above all for ever.
>
> Blessed art thou in the firmament of heaven:
> And above all to be praised and glorified for ever.
>
> O all ye works of the Lord, bless ye the Lord:
> Praise and exalt him above all for ever.
>
> O ye heavens, bless ye the Lord:
> Praise and exalt him above all for ever.
>
> O ye angels of the Lord, bless ye the Lord:
> Praise and exalt him above all for ever.
>
> O all ye waters that be above the heaven, bless ye the Lord:
> Praise and exalt him above all for ever.
>
> O all ye powers of the Lord, bless ye the Lord:
> Praise and exalt him above all for ever.

DANIEL

O ye sun and moon, bless ye the Lord:
Praise and exalt him above all for ever.

O ye stars of heaven, bless ye the Lord:
Praise and exalt him above all for ever.

O every shower and dew, bless ye the Lord:
Praise and exalt him above all for ever.

O all ye winds, bless ye the Lord:
Praise and exalt him above all for ever.

O ye fire and heat, bless ye the Lord:
Praise and exalt him above all for ever.

O ye winter and summer, bless ye the Lord:
Praise and exalt him above all for ever.

O ye dews and storms of snow, bless ye the Lord:
Praise and exalt him above all for ever.

O ye nights and days, bless ye the Lord:
Praise and exalt him above all for ever.

O ye light and darkness, bless ye the Lord:
Praise and exalt him above all for ever.

O ye ice and cold, bless ye the Lord:
Praise and exalt him above all for ever.

O ye frost and snow, bless ye the Lord:
Praise and exalt him above all for ever.

O ye lightnings and clouds, bless ye the Lord:
Praise and exalt him above all for ever.

O let the earth bless the Lord:
Praise and exalt him above all for ever.

O ye mountains and little hills, bless ye the Lord:
Praise and exalt him above all for ever.

O all ye things that grow on the earth, bless ye the Lord:
Praise and exalt him above all for ever.

DANIEL

O ye fountains, bless ye the Lord:
Praise and exalt him above all for ever.

O ye seas and rivers, bless ye the Lord:
Praise and exalt him above all for ever.

O ye whales, and all that move in the waters, bless ye the Lord:
Praise and exalt him above all for ever.

O all ye fowls of the air, bless ye the Lord:
Praise and exalt him above all for ever.

O all ye beasts and cattle, bless ye the Lord:
Praise and exalt him above all for ever.

O ye children of men, bless ye the Lord:
Praise and exalt him above all for ever.

O Israel, bless ye the Lord:
Praise and exalt him above all for ever.

O ye priests of the Lord, bless ye the Lord:
Praise and exalt him above all for ever.

O ye servants of the Lord, bless ye the Lord:
Praise and exalt him above all for ever.

O ye spirits and souls of the righteous, bless ye the Lord:
Praise and exalt him above all for ever.

O ye holy and humble men of heart, bless ye the Lord:
Praise and exalt him above all for ever.

O give thanks unto the Lord, because he is gracious:
For his mercy endureth for ever.

O all ye that worship the Lord, bless the God of gods, praise him,
    and give him thanks:
For his mercy endureth for ever."

Then Nebuchadnezzar the king was astonished, and rose up in haste, and spoke, and said unto his counsellors, "Did not we

DANIEL

cast three men bound into the midst of the fire?" They answered and said unto the king, "True, O king."

He answered and said, "Lo, I see four men loose, walking in the midst of the fire, and they have no hurt; and the form of the fourth is like the Son of God."

Then Nebuchadnezzar came near to the mouth of the burning fiery furnace, and spoke, and said, "Shadrach, Meshach, and Abed-nego, ye servants of the most high God, come forth, and come hither."

Then Shadrach, Meshach, and Abed-nego, came forth of the midst of the fire. And the princes, governors, and captains, and the king's counsellors, being gathered together, saw these men, upon whose bodies the fire had no power, nor was a hair of their head singed, neither were their coats changed, nor the smell of fire had passed on them.

Then Nebuchadnezzar spoke, and said, "Blessed be the God of Shadrach, Meshach, and Abed-nego, who hath sent his angel, and delivered his servants that trusted in him, and have changed the king's word, and yielded their bodies, that they might not serve nor worship any god, except their own God. Therefore I make a decree, that every people, nation, and language, which speak any thing amiss against the God of Shadrach, Meshach, and Abed-nego, shall be cut in pieces, and their houses shall be made a dunghill: because there is no other God that can deliver after this sort."

Then the king promoted Shadrach, Meshach, and Abed-nego, in the province of Babylon.

Nebuchadnezzar the king, unto all people, nations, and languages, that dwell in all the earth:

Peace be multiplied unto you. I thought it good to show the signs and wonders that the high God hath wrought toward me. How great are his signs! and how mighty are his wonders! his kingdom is an everlasting kingdom, and his dominion is from generation to generation.

I Nebuchadnezzar was at rest in mine house, and flourishing in my palace. I saw a dream which made me afraid, and the thoughts upon my bed and the visions of my head troubled me. Therefore made I a decree

DANIEL

to bring in all the wise men of Babylon before me, that they might make known unto me the interpretation of the dream. Then came in the magicians, the astrologers, the Chaldeans, and the soothsayers: and I told the dream before them; but they did not make known unto me the interpretation thereof.

But at the last Daniel came in before me, whose name was Belteshazzar, according to the name of my god, and in whom is the spirit of the holy gods: and before him I told the dream, saying, "O Belteshazzar, master of the magicians, because I know that the spirit of the holy gods is in thee, and no secret troubleth thee, tell me the visions of my dream that I have seen, and the interpretation thereof. Thus were the visions of mine head in my bed: I saw, and beheld a tree in the midst of the earth, and the height thereof was great. The tree grew, and was strong, and the height thereof reached unto heaven, and the sight thereof to the end of all the earth. The leaves thereof were fair, and the fruit thereof much, and in it was meat for all: the beasts of the field had shadow under it, and the fowls of the heaven dwelt in the boughs thereof, and all flesh was fed of it. I saw in the visions of my head upon my bed, and, behold, a watcher and a holy one came down from heaven. He cried aloud, and said thus, 'Hew down the tree, and cut off his branches, shake off his leaves, and scatter his fruit: let the beasts get away from under it, and the fowls from his branches: nevertheless leave the stump of his roots in the earth, even with a band of iron and brass, in the tender grass of the field; and let it be wet with the dew of heaven, and let his portion be with the beasts in the grass of the earth: let his heart be changed from man's, and let a beast's heart be given unto him; and let seven times pass over him. This matter is by the decree of the watchers, and the demand by the word of the holy ones: to the intent that the living may know that the most High ruleth in the kingdom of men, and giveth it to whomsoever he will, and setteth up over it the basest of men.' This dream I King Nebuchadnezzar have seen. Now thou, O Belteshazzar, declare the interpretation thereof, forasmuch as all the wise men of my kingdom are not able to make known unto me the interpretation: but thou art able; for the spirit of the holy gods is in thee."

Then Daniel, whose name was Belteshazzar, was astonished for one hour, and his thoughts troubled him. The king spoke, and said, "Bel-

DANIEL

teshazzar, let not the dream, or the interpretation thereof, trouble thee." Belteshazzar answered and said, "My lord, the dream be to them that hate thee, and the interpretation thereof to thine enemies. The tree that thou sawest, which grew, and was strong, whose height reached unto the heaven, and the sight thereof to all the earth; whose leaves were fair, and the fruit thereof much, and in it was meat for all; under which the beasts of the field dwelt, and upon whose branches the fowls of the heaven had their habitation: it is thou, O king, that art grown and become strong: for thy greatness is grown, and reacheth unto heaven, and thy dominion to the end of the earth. And whereas the king saw a watcher and a holy one coming down from heaven, and saying, 'Hew the tree down, and destroy it; yet leave the stump of the roots thereof in the earth, even with a band of iron and brass, in the tender grass of the field; and let it be wet with the dew of heaven, and let his portion be with the beasts of the field, till seven times pass over him': this is the interpretation, O king, and this is the decree of the most High, which is come upon my lord the king: that they shall drive thee from men, and thy dwelling shall be with the beasts of the field, and they shall make thee to eat grass as oxen, and they shall wet thee with the dew of heaven, and seven times shall pass over thee, till thou know that the most High ruleth in the kingdom of men, and giveth it to whomsoever he will. And whereas they commanded to leave the stump of the tree roots; thy kingdom shall be sure unto thee, after that thou shalt have known that the heavens do rule. Wherefore, O king, let my counsel be acceptable unto thee, and break off thy sins by righteousness, and thine iniquities by showing mercy to the poor; if it may be a lengthening of thy tranquillity."

All this came upon the king Nebuchadnezzar. At the end of twelve months he walked in the palace of the kingdom of Babylon. The king spoke, and said, "Is not this great Babylon, that I have built for the house of the kingdom by the might of my power, and for the honour of my majesty?" While the word was in the king's mouth, there fell a voice from heaven, saying, "O King Nebuchadnezzar, to thee it is spoken: 'The kingdom is departed from thee. And they shall drive thee from men, and thy dwelling shall be with the beasts of the field: they shall make thee to eat grass as oxen, and seven times shall pass over thee,

DANIEL

until thou know that the most High ruleth in the kingdom of men, and giveth it to whomsoever he will.'"

The same hour was the thing fulfilled upon Nebuchadnezzar: and he was driven from men, and did eat grass as oxen, and his body was wet with the dew of heaven, till his hairs were grown like eagles' feathers, and his nails like birds' claws. And at the end of the days I Nebuchadnezzar lifted up mine eyes unto heaven, and mine understanding returned unto me, and I blessed the most High, and I praised and honoured him that liveth for ever, whose dominion is an everlasting dominion, and his kingdom is from generation to generation.

Belshazzar the king made a great feast to a thousand of his lords, and drank wine before the thousand.

Belshazzar, while he tasted the wine, commanded to bring the golden and silver vessels which his father Nebuchadnezzar had taken out of the temple which was in Jerusalem; that the king, and his princes, his wives, and his concubines, might drink therein.

Then they brought the golden vessels that were taken out of the temple of the house of God which was at Jerusalem; and the king, and his princes, his wives, and his concubines, drank in them.

They drank wine, and praised the gods of gold, and of silver, of brass, of iron, of wood, and of stone.

In the same hour came forth fingers of a man's hand, and wrote over against the candlestick upon the plaster of the wall of the king's palace: and the king saw the part of the hand that wrote. Then the king's countenance was changed, and his thoughts troubled him, so that the joints of his loins were loosed, and his knees smote one against another.

The king cried aloud to bring in the astrologers, the Chaldeans, and the soothsayers. And the king spoke, and said to the wise men of Babylon, "Whosoever shall read this writing, and show me the interpretation thereof, shall be clothed with scarlet, and have a chain of gold about his neck, and shall be the third ruler in the kingdom."

DANIEL

Then came in all the king's wise men: but they could not read the writing, nor make known to the king the interpretation thereof. Then was King Belshazzar greatly troubled, and his countenance was changed in him, and his lords were astonished.

Now the queen by reason of the words of the king and his lords came into the banquet house: and the queen spoke and said, "O king, live for ever: let not thy thoughts trouble thee, nor let thy countenance be changed. There is a man in thy kingdom, in whom is the spirit of the holy gods; and in the days of thy father light and understanding and wisdom, like the wisdom of the gods, was found in him; whom the king Nebuchadnezzar thy father, the king, I say, thy father, made master of the magicians, astrologers, Chaldeans, and soothsayers. Forasmuch as an excellent spirit, and knowledge, and understanding, interpreting of dreams, and showing of hard sentences, and dissolving of doubts, were found in the same Daniel, whom the king named Belteshazzar: now let Daniel be called, and he will show the interpretation."

Then was Daniel brought in before the king. And the king spoke and said unto Daniel, "Art thou that Daniel, which art of the children of the captivity of Judah, whom the king my father brought out of Jewry? I have even heard of thee, that the spirit of the gods is in thee, and that light and understanding and excellent wisdom is found in thee. And now the wise men, the astrologers, have been brought in before me, that they should read this writing, and make known unto me the interpretation thereof: but they could not show the interpretation of the thing: and I have heard of thee, that thou canst make interpretations, and dissolve doubts: now if thou canst read the writing, and make known to me the interpretation thereof, thou shalt be clothed with scarlet, and have a chain of gold about thy neck, and shalt be the third ruler in the kingdom."

Then Daniel answered and said before the king, "Let thy gifts be to thyself, and give thy rewards to another; yet I will read the writing unto the king, and make known to him the interpretation.

DANIEL

"O thou king, the most high God gave Nebuchadnezzar thy father a kingdom, and majesty, and glory, and honour: and for the majesty that he gave him, all people, nations, and languages, trembled and feared before him: whom he would he slew; and whom he would he kept alive; and whom he would he set up; and whom he would he put down. But when his heart was lifted up, and his mind hardened in pride, he was deposed from his kingly throne, and they took his glory from him: and he was driven from the sons of men; and his heart was made like the beasts, and his dwelling was with the wild asses: they fed him with grass like oxen, and his body was wet with the dew of heaven; till he knew that the most high God ruled in the kingdom of men, and that he appointeth over it whomsoever he will.

"And thou his son, O Belshazzar, hast not humbled thine heart, though thou knewest all this; but hast lifted up thyself against the Lord of heaven; and they have brought the vessels of his house before thee, and thou, and thy lords, thy wives, and thy concubines, have drunk wine in them; and thou hast praised the gods of silver, and gold, of brass, iron, wood, and stone, which see not, nor hear, nor know: and the God in whose hand thy breath is, and whose are all thy ways, hast thou not glorified:

"Then was the part of the hand sent from him; and this writing was written. And this is the writing that was written, MENE, MENE, TEKEL, UPHARSIN. This is the interpretation of the thing: MENE: God hath numbered thy kingdom, and finished it. TEKEL: thou art weighed in the balances, and art found wanting. PERES: thy kingdom is divided, and given to the Medes and Persians."

Then commanded Belshazzar, and they clothed Daniel with scarlet, and put a chain of gold about his neck, and made a proclamation concerning him, that he should be the third ruler in the kingdom.

In that night was Belshazzar the king of the Chaldeans slain. And Darius the Median took the kingdom, being about threescore and two years old.

It pleased Darius to set over the kingdom a hundred and

DANIEL

twenty princes, which should be over the whole kingdom; and over these three presidents; of whom Daniel was first: that the princes might give accounts unto them, and the king should have no damage. Then this Daniel was preferred above the presidents and princes, because an excellent spirit was in him; and the king thought to set him over the whole realm.

Then the presidents and princes sought to find occasion against Daniel concerning the kingdom; but they could find none occasion nor fault; forasmuch as he was faithful, neither was there any error or fault found in him. Then said these men, "We shall not find any occasion against this Daniel, except we find it against him concerning the law of his God."

Then these presidents and princes assembled together to the king, and said thus unto him, "King Darius, live for ever. All the presidents of the kingdom, the governors, and the princes, the counsellors, and the captains, have consulted together to establish a royal statute, and to make a firm decree, that whosoever shall ask a petition of any God or man for thirty days, save of thee, O king, he shall be cast into the den of lions. Now, O king, establish the decree, and sign the writing, that it be not changed, according to the law of the Medes and Persians, which altereth not."

Wherefore King Darius signed the writing and the decree.

Now when Daniel knew that the writing was signed, he went into his house; and his windows being open in his chamber toward Jerusalem, he kneeled upon his knees three times a day, and prayed, and gave thanks before his God, as he did aforetime.

Then these men assembled, and found Daniel praying and making supplication before his God. Then they came near, and spoke before the king concerning the king's decree: "Hast thou not signed a decree, that every man that shall ask a petition of any God or man within thirty days, save of thee, O king, shall be cast into the den of lions?"

The king answered and said, "The thing is true, according to the law of the Medes and Persians, which altereth not."

DANIEL

Then answered they and said before the king, "That Daniel, which is of the children of the captivity of Judah, regardeth not thee, O king, nor the decree that thou hast signed, but maketh his petition three times a day."

Then the king, when he heard these words, was sore displeased with himself, and set his heart on Daniel to deliver him: and he laboured till the going down of the sun to deliver him. Then these men assembled unto the king, and said unto the king, "Know, O king, that the law of the Medes and Persians is that no decree nor statute which the king establisheth may be changed."

Then the king commanded, and they brought Daniel, and cast him into the den of lions. Now the king spoke and said unto Daniel, "Thy God whom thou servest continually, he will deliver thee." And a stone was brought, and laid upon the mouth of the den; and the king sealed it with his own signet, and with the signet of his lords; that the purpose might not be changed concerning Daniel.

Then the king went to his palace, and passed the night fasting: neither were instruments of music brought before him: and his sleep went from him. Then the king arose very early in the morning, and went in haste unto the den of lions. And when he came to the den, he cried with a lamentable voice unto Daniel: and the king spoke and said to Daniel, "O Daniel, servant of the living God, is thy God, whom thou servest continually, able to deliver thee from the lions?"

Then said Daniel unto the king, "O king, live for ever. My God hath sent his angel, and hath shut the lions' mouths, that they have not hurt me: forasmuch as before him innocency was found in me; and also before thee, O king, have I done no hurt."

Then was the king exceeding glad for him, and commanded that they should take Daniel up out of the den. So Daniel was taken up out of the den, and no manner of hurt was found upon him, because he believed in his God.

And the king commanded, and they brought those men which had accused Daniel, and they cast them into the den of lions, them, their children, and their wives; and the lions had the mas-

DANIEL

tery of them, and broke all their bones in pieces or ever they came at the bottom of the den.

Then King Darius wrote unto all people, nations, and languages, that dwell in all the earth:

Peace be multiplied unto you. I make a decree: that in every dominion of my kingdom men tremble and fear before the God of Daniel: for he is the living God, and steadfast for ever, and his kingdom that which shall not be destroyed, and his dominion shall be even unto the end. He delivereth and rescueth, and he worketh signs and wonders in heaven and in earth, who hath delivered Daniel from the power of the lions.

So this Daniel prospered in the reign of Darius, and in the reign of Cyrus the Persian.

In the first year of Belshazzar king of Babylon Daniel had a dream and visions of his head upon his bed: then he wrote the dream, and told the sum of the matters.

Daniel spoke and said, "I saw in my vision by night, and, behold, the four winds of the heaven strove upon the great sea. And four great beasts came up from the sea, diverse one from another. The first was like a lion, and had eagle's wings: I beheld till the wings thereof were plucked, and it was lifted up from the earth, and made stand upon the feet as a man, and a man's heart was given to it. And behold another beast, a second, like to a bear, and it raised up itself on one side, and it had three ribs in the mouth of it between the teeth of it: and they said thus unto it, 'Arise, devour much flesh.' After this I beheld, and lo another, like a leopard, which had upon the back of it four wings of a fowl; the beast had also four heads; and dominion was given to it. After this I saw in the night visions, and behold a fourth beast, dreadful and terrible, and strong exceedingly; and it had great iron teeth: it devoured and broke in pieces, and stamped the residue with the feet of it: and it was diverse from all the beasts that were before it; and it had ten horns. I considered the horns, and, behold, there came up among them another little horn, before whom there were three of the first

DANIEL

horns plucked up by the roots: and, behold, in this horn were eyes like the eyes of man, and a mouth speaking great things.

"I beheld till the thrones were cast down, and the Ancient of days did sit, whose garment was white as snow, and the hair of his head like the pure wool: his throne was like the fiery flame, and his wheels as burning fire. A fiery stream issued and came forth from before him: thousand thousands ministered unto him, and ten thousand times ten thousand stood before him: the judgment was set, and the books were opened. I beheld them because of the voice of the great words which the horn spoke: I beheld even till the beast was slain, and his body destroyed, and given to the burning flame. As concerning the rest of the beasts, they had their dominion taken away: yet their lives were prolonged for a season and time. I saw in the night visions, and, behold, one like the Son of Man came with the clouds of heaven, and came to the Ancient of days, and they brought him near before him. And there was given him dominion, and glory, and a kingdom, that all people, nations, and languages should serve him: his dominion is an everlasting dominion, which shall not pass away, and his kingdom that which shall not be destroyed.

"I Daniel was grieved in my spirit in the midst of my body, and the visions of my head troubled me. I came near unto one of them that stood by, and asked him the truth of all this. So he told me, and made me know the interpretation of the things. 'These great beasts, which are four, are four kings, which shall arise out of the earth. But the saints of the most High shall take the kingdom, and possess the kingdom for ever, even for ever and ever.'

"Then I would know the truth of the fourth beast, which was diverse from all the others, exceedingly dreadful, whose teeth were of iron, and his nails of brass; which devoured, broke in pieces, and stamped the residue with his feet; and of the ten horns that were in his head, and of the other which came up, and before whom three fell; even of that horn that had eyes, and a mouth that spoke very great things, whose look was more stout than his fellows. I beheld, and the same horn made war with

DANIEL

the saints, and prevailed against them; until the Ancient of days came, and judgment was given to the saints of the most High; and the time came that the saints possessed the kingdom.

"Thus he said, 'The fourth beast shall be the fourth kingdom upon earth, which shall be diverse from all kingdoms, and shall devour the whole earth, and shall tread it down, and break it in pieces. And the ten horns out of this kingdom are ten kings that shall arise: and another shall rise after them; and he shall be diverse from the first, and he shall subdue three kings. And he shall speak great words against the most High, and shall wear out the saints of the most High, and think to change times and laws: and they shall be given into his hand until a time and times and the dividing of time. But the judgment shall sit, and they shall take away his dominion, to consume and to destroy it unto the end. And the kingdom and dominion, and the greatness of the kingdom under the whole heaven, shall be given to the people of the saints of the most High, whose kingdom is an everlasting kingdom, and all dominions shall serve and obey him.' Hitherto is the end of the matter. As for me Daniel, my cogitations much troubled me, and my countenance changed in me: but I kept the matter in my heart."

"In the third year of the reign of king Belshazzar a vision appeared unto me, even unto me Daniel, after that which appeared unto me at the first. And I saw in a vision; and it came to pass, when I saw, that I was at Shushan in the palace, which is in the province of Elam; and I saw in a vision, and I was by the river of Ulai. Then I lifted up mine eyes, and saw, and, behold, there stood before the river a ram which had two horns: and the two horns were high; but one was higher than the other, and the higher came up last. I saw the ram pushing westward, and northward, and southward; so that no beasts might stand before him, neither was there any that could deliver out of his hand; but he did according to his will, and became great. And as I was considering, behold, a he-goat came from the west on the face of the whole earth, and touched not the ground: and

DANIEL

the goat had a notable horn between his eyes. And he came to the ram that had two horns, which I had seen standing before the river, and ran unto him in the fury of his power. And I saw him come close unto the ram, and he was moved with choler against him, and smote the ram, and broke his two horns: and there was no power in the ram to stand before him, but he cast him down to the ground, and stamped upon him: and there was none that could deliver the ram out of his hand. Therefore the he-goat waxed very great: and when he was strong, the great horn was broken; and for it came up four notable ones toward the four winds of heaven. And out of one of them came forth a little horn, which waxed exceeding great, toward the south, and toward the east, and toward the pleasant land. And it waxed great, even to the host of heaven; and it cast down some of the host and of the stars to the ground, and stamped upon them. Yea, he magnified himself even to the prince of the host, and by him the daily sacrifice was taken away, and the place of his sanctuary was cast down. And a host was given him against the daily sacrifice by reason of transgression, and it cast down the truth to the ground; and it practised, and prospered.

"Then I heard one saint speaking, and another saint said unto that certain saint which spoke, 'How long shall be the vision concerning the daily sacrifice, and the transgression of desolation, to give both the sanctuary and the host to be trodden under foot?' And he said unto me, 'Unto two thousand and three hundred days; then shall the sanctuary be cleansed.'

"And it came to pass, when I, even I Daniel, had seen the vision, and sought for the meaning, then, behold, there stood before me as the appearance of a man. And I heard a man's voice between the banks of Ulai, which called, and said, 'Gabriel, make this man to understand the vision.'

"So he came near where I stood: and when he came, I was afraid, and fell upon my face: but he said unto me, 'Understand, O Son of Man: for at the time of the end shall be the vision.' Now as he was speaking with me, I was in a deep sleep on my face toward the ground: but he touched me, and set me upright.

DANIEL

"And he said, 'Behold, I will make thee know what shall be in the last end of the indignation: for at the time appointed the end shall be. The ram which thou sawest having two horns are the kings of Media and Persia. And the rough goat is the king of Grecia: and the great horn that is between his eyes is the first king. Now that being broken, whereas four stood up for it, four kingdoms shall stand up out of the nation, but not in his power. And in the latter time of their kingdom, when the transgressors are come to the full, a king of fierce countenance, and understanding dark sentences, shall stand up. And his power shall be mighty, but not by his own power: and he shall destroy wonderfully, and shall prosper, and practise, and shall destroy the mighty and the holy people. And through his policy also he shall cause craft to prosper in his hand; and he shall magnify himself in his heart, and by peace shall destroy many: he shall also stand up against the Prince of princes; but he shall be broken without hand. And the vision of the evening and the morning which was told is true; wherefore shut thou up the vision; for it shall be for many days.'

"And I Daniel fainted, and was sick certain days; afterward I rose up, and did the king's business; and I was astonished at the vision, but none understood it."

In the third year of Cyrus king of Persia a thing was revealed unto Daniel, whose name was called Belteshazzar; and the thing was true, but the time appointed was long: and he understood the thing, and had understanding of the vision.

"In those days I Daniel was mourning three full weeks. I ate no pleasant bread, neither came flesh nor wine in my mouth, neither did I anoint myself at all, till three whole weeks were fulfilled. And in the four and twentieth day of the first month, as I was by the side of the great river, which is Hiddekel, I lifted up mine eyes, and looked, and beheld a certain man clothed in linen, whose loins were girded with fine gold of Uphaz. His body also was like the beryl, and his face as the appearance of lightning, and his eyes as lamps of fire, and his arms and his feet

DANIEL

like in colour to polished brass, and the voice of his words like the voice of a multitude. And I Daniel alone saw the vision: for the men that were with me saw not the vision; but a great quaking fell upon them, so that they fled to hide themselves. Therefore I was left alone, and saw this great vision, and there remained no strength in me: for my comeliness was turned in me into corruption, and I retained no strength. Yet heard I the voice of his words: and when I heard the voice of his words, then was I in a deep sleep on my face, and my face toward the ground.

"And, behold, a hand touched me, which set me upon my knees and upon the palms of my hands. And he said unto me, 'O Daniel, a man greatly beloved, understand the words that I speak unto thee, and stand upright: for unto thee am I now sent.' And when he had spoken this word unto me, I stood trembling.

"Then said he unto me, 'Fear not, Daniel: for from the first day that thou didst set thine heart to understand, and to chasten thyself before thy God, thy words were heard, and I am come for thy words. But the prince of the kingdom of Persia withstood me one and twenty days: but, lo, Michael, one of the chief princes, came to help me; and I remained there with the kings of Persia. Now I am come to make thee understand what shall befall thy people in the latter days: for yet the vision is for many days.

"'And now will I show thee the truth. Behold, there shall stand up yet three kings in Persia; and the fourth shall be far richer than they all: and by his strength through his riches he shall stir up all against the realm of Grecia. And a mighty king shall stand up, that shall rule with great dominion, and do according to his will. And when he shall stand up, his kingdom shall be broken, and shall be divided toward the four winds of heaven; and not to his posterity, nor according to his dominion which he ruled: for his kingdom shall be plucked up, even for others beside those.

"'And the king of the south shall be strong, and one of his princes; and he shall be strong above him, and have dominion; his dominion shall be a great dominion. And in those times there

DANIEL

shall many stand up against the king of the south: also the robbers of thy people shall exalt themselves to establish the vision; but they shall fall. So the king of the north shall come, and cast up a mount, and take the most fenced cities: and the arms of the south shall not withstand, neither his chosen people, neither shall there be any strength to withstand. But he that cometh against him shall do according to his own will, and none shall stand before him: and he shall stand in the glorious land, which by his hand shall be consumed.

" 'He shall even return, and have intelligence with them that forsake the holy covenant. And arms shall stand on his part, and they shall pollute the sanctuary of strength, and shall take away the daily sacrifice, and they shall place the abomination that maketh desolate. And such as do wickedly against the covenant shall he corrupt by flatteries: but the people that do know their God shall be strong, and do exploits. And they that understand among the people shall instruct many: yet they shall fall by the sword, and by flame, by captivity, and by spoil, many days.

" 'And at that time shall Michael stand up, the great prince which standeth for the children of thy people: and there shall be a time of trouble, such as never was since there was a nation even to that same time: and at that time thy people shall be delivered, every one that shall be found written in the book. And many of them that sleep in the dust of the earth shall awake, some to everlasting life, and some to shame and everlasting contempt. And they that be wise shall shine as the brightness of the firmament; and they that turn many to righteousness as the stars for ever and ever. But thou, O Daniel, shut up the words, and seal the book, even to the time of the end: many shall run to and fro, and knowledge shall be increased.' "

ESTHER

A TALE

ESTHER IS *the latest of all the books in the orthodox Jewish Canon, written about 150 B.C. in honor of the recently established Feast of Purim, the origin of which it traces to imaginary events in the fifth century. As so often in Jewish literature, the immediate purpose of the work is obscured by the sheer narrative skill of the writer in creating absorbing incidents and realistic characters. Morally, the book is on a low plane in its spirit of bloodthirsty revenge, but aesthetically it remains one of the greatest of tales.*

ESTHER

A TALE

Now it came to pass in the days of Ahasuerus (this is Ahasuerus which reigned, from India even unto Ethiopia, over a hundred and seven and twenty provinces): that in those days, when the king Ahasuerus sat on the throne of his kingdom, which was in Shushan the palace, in the third year of his reign, he made a feast unto all his princes and his servants; the power of Persia and Media, the nobles and princes of the provinces, being before him: when he showed the riches of his glorious kingdom and the honour of his excellent majesty many days, even a hundred and fourscore days.

And when these days were expired, the king made a feast unto all the people that were present in Shushan the palace, both unto great and small, seven days, in the court of the garden of the king's palace; where were white, green, and blue hangings, fastened with cords of fine linen and purple to silver rings and pillars of marble: the beds were of gold and silver, upon a pavement of red, and blue, and white, and black marble. And they gave them drink in vessels of gold (the vessels being diverse one from another), and royal wine in abundance, according to the state of the king. And the drinking was according to the law; none did compel: for so the king had appointed to all the officers of his house that they should do according to every man's pleasure. Also Vashti the queen made a feast for the women in the royal house which belonged to King Ahasuerus.

On the seventh day, when the heart of the king was merry with wine, he commanded Mehuman, Biztha, Harbona, Bigtha, and Abagtha, Zethar, and Carcas, the seven chamberlains that

ESTHER

served in the presence of Ahasuerus the king, to bring Vashti the queen before the king with the crown royal, to show the people and the princes her beauty: for she was fair to look on. But the queen Vashti refused to come at the king's commandment by his chamberlains: therefore was the king very wroth, and his anger burned in him.

Then the king said to the wise men, which knew the times (for so was the king's manner toward all that knew law and judgment: and the next unto him was Carshena, Shethar, Admatha, Tarshish, Meres, Marsena, and Memucan, the seven princes of Persia and Media, which saw the king's face, and which sat the first in the kingdom): "What shall we do unto the queen Vashti according to law, because she hath not performed the commandment of the king Ahasuerus by the chamberlains?"

And Memucan answered before the king and the princes, "Vashti the queen hath not done wrong to the king only, but also to all the princes, and to all the people that are in all the provinces of the king Ahasuerus. For this deed of the queen shall come abroad unto all women, so that they shall despise their husbands in their eyes, when it shall be reported, 'The king Ahasuerus commanded Vashti the queen to be brought in before him, but she came not.' Likewise shall the ladies of Persia and Media say this day unto all the king's princes, which have heard of the deed of the queen. Thus shall there arise too much contempt and wrath. If it please the king, let there go a royal commandment from him, and let it be written among the laws of the Persians and the Medes, that it be not altered that Vashti come no more before King Ahasuerus; and let the king give her royal estate unto another that is better than she. And when the king's decree which he shall make shall be published throughout all his empire (for it is great), all the wives shall give to their husbands honour, both to great and small."

And the saying pleased the king and the princes; and the king did according to the word of Memucan: for he sent letters into all the king's provinces, into every province according to the writing thereof, and to every people after their language,

ESTHER

that every man should bear rule in his own house, and that it should be published according to the language of every people.

After these things, when the wrath of King Ahasuerus was appeased, he remembered Vashti, and what she had done, and what was decreed against her.

Then said the king's servants that ministered unto him, "Let there be fair young virgins sought for the king: and let the king appoint officers in all the provinces of his kingdom, that they may gather together all the fair young virgins unto Shushan the palace, to the house of the women, unto the custody of Hegai the king's chamberlain, keeper of the women; and let their things for purification be given them: and let the maiden which pleaseth the king be queen instead of Vashti."

And the thing pleased the king; and he did so.

Now in Shushan the palace there was a certain Jew, whose name was Mordecai, the son of Jair, the son of Shimei, the son of Kish, a Benjamite; who had been carried away from Jerusalem with the captivity which had been carried away with Jeconiah king of Judah, whom Nebuchadnezzar the king of Babylon had carried away. And he brought up Hadassah, that is, Esther, his uncle's daughter: for she had neither father nor mother, and the maid was fair and beautiful; whom Mordecai, when her father and mother were dead, took for his own daughter.

So it came to pass, when the king's commandment and his decree was heard, and when many maidens were gathered together unto Shushan the palace, to the custody of Hegai, that Esther was brought also unto the king's house, to the custody of Hegai, keeper of the women.

And the maiden pleased him, and she obtained kindness of him; and he speedily gave her her things for purification, with such things as belonged to her, and seven maidens, which were meet to be given her, out of the king's house: and he preferred her and her maids unto the best place of the house of the women. Esther had not showed her people nor her kindred: for Mordecai had charged her that she should not show it. And Mordecai

ESTHER

walked every day before the court of the women's house, to know how Esther did, and what should become of her.

Now when every maid's turn was come to go in to King Ahasuerus, after that she had been twelve months, according to the manner of the women (for so were the days of their purifications accomplished, to wit, six months with oil of myrrh, and six months with sweet odours, and with other things for the purifying of the women); then thus came every maiden unto the king; whatsoever she desired was given her to go with her out of the house of the women unto the king's house. In the evening she went, and on the morrow she returned into the second house of the women, to the custody of Shaashgaz, the king's chamberlain, which kept the concubines: she came in unto the king no more, except the king delighted in her, and that she were called by name.

Now when the turn of Esther, the daughter of Abihail the uncle of Mordecai, who had taken her for his daughter, was come to go in unto the king, she required nothing but what Hegai the king's chamberlain, the keeper of the women, appointed. And Esther obtained favour in the sight of all them that looked upon her. So Esther was taken unto King Ahasuerus into his house royal in the tenth month, which is the month Tebeth, in the seventh year of his reign.

And the king loved Esther above all the women, and she obtained grace and favour in his sight more than all the virgins; so that he set the royal crown upon her head, and made her queen instead of Vashti. Then the king made a great feast unto all his princes and his servants, even Esther's feast; and he made a release to the provinces, and gave gifts, according to the state of the king. And when the virgins were gathered together the second time, then Mordecai sat in the king's gate. Esther had not yet showed her kindred nor her people; as Mordecai had charged her: for Esther did the commandment of Mordecai, like as when she was brought up with him.

In those days, while Mordecai sat in the king's gate, two of

ESTHER

the king's chamberlains, Bigthan and Teresh, of those which kept the door, were wroth, and sought to lay hand on the king Ahasuerus. And the thing was known to Mordecai, who told it unto Esther the queen; and Esther certified the king thereof in Mordecai's name. And when inquisition was made of the matter, it was found out; therefore they were both hanged on a tree: and it was written in the book of the chronicles before the king.

After these things did King Ahasuerus promote Haman the son of Hammedatha the Agagite, and advanced him, and set his seat above all the princes that were with him. And all the king's servants, that were in the king's gate, bowed, and reverenced Haman: for the king had so commanded concerning him. But Mordecai bowed not, nor did him reverence. Then the king's servants, which were in the king's gate, said unto Mordecai, "Why transgressest thou the king's commandment?"

Now it came to pass, when they spoke daily unto him, and he hearkened not unto them, that they told Haman, to see whether Mordecai's matters would stand: for he had told them that he was a Jew. And when Haman saw that Mordecai bowed not, nor did him reverence, then was Haman full of wrath. And he thought scorn to lay hands on Mordecai alone; for they had showed him the people of Mordecai: wherefore Haman sought to destroy all the Jews that were throughout the whole kingdom of Ahasuerus, even the people of Mordecai.

And Haman said unto King Ahasuerus, "There is a certain people scattered abroad and dispersed among the people in all the provinces of thy kingdom; and their laws are diverse from all people; neither keep they the king's laws: therefore it is not for the king's profit to suffer them. If it please the king, let it be written that they may be destroyed: and I will pay ten thousand talents of silver to the hands of those that have the charge of the business, to bring it into the king's treasuries."

And the king took his ring from his hand, and gave it unto Haman the son of Hammedatha the Agagite, the Jews' enemy.

ESTHER

And the king said unto Haman, "The silver is given to thee, the people also, to do with them as it seemeth good to thee."

Then were the king's scribes called on the thirteenth day of the first month, and there was written according to all that Haman had commanded unto the king's lieutenants, and to the governors that were over every province, and to the rulers of every people of every province according to the writing thereof, and to every people after their language; in the name of King Ahasuerus was it written, and sealed with the king's ring.

And the letters were sent by posts into all the king's provinces, to destroy, to kill, and to cause to perish, all Jews, both young and old, little children and women, in one day, even upon the thirteenth day of the twelfth month, which is the month Adar, and to take the spoil of them for a prey. The copy of the writing for a commandment to be given in every province was published unto all people, that they should be ready against that day. The posts went out, being hastened by the king's commandment, and the decree was given in Shushan the palace. And the king and Haman sat down to drink; but the city Shushan was perplexed.

When Mordecai perceived all that was done, Mordecai rent his clothes, and put on sackcloth with ashes, and went out into the midst of the city, and cried with a loud and a bitter cry; and came even before the king's gate: for none might enter into the king's gate clothed with sackcloth. And in every province, whithersoever the king's commandment and his decree came, there was great mourning among the Jews, and fasting, and weeping, and wailing; and many lay in sackcloth and ashes.

So Esther's maids and her chamberlains came and told it her. Then was the queen exceedingly grieved; and she sent raiment to clothe Mordecai, and to take away his sackcloth from him: but he received it not.

Then called Esther for Hatach, one of the king's chamberlains, whom he had appointed to attend upon her, and gave him a commandment to Mordecai, to know what it was, and why it

ESTHER

was. So Hatach went forth to Mordecai unto the street of the city, which was before the king's gate. And Mordecai told him of all that had happened unto him, and of the sum of the money that Haman had promised to pay to the king's treasuries for the Jews, to destroy them. Also he gave him the copy of the writing of the decree that was given at Shushan to destroy them, to show it unto Esther, and to declare it unto her, and to charge her that she should go in unto the king, to make supplication unto him, and to make request before him for her people. And Hatach came and told Esther the words of Mordecai.

Again Esther spoke unto Hatach, and gave him commandment unto Mordecai; "All the king's servants, and the people of the king's provinces, do know that whosoever, whether man or woman, shall come unto the king into the inner court, who is not called, there is one law of his to put him to death, except such to whom the king shall hold out the golden sceptre, that he may live: but I have not been called to come in unto the king these thirty days." And they told to Mordecai Esther's words.

Then Mordecai commanded to answer Esther, "Think not with thyself that thou shalt escape in the king's house, more than all the Jews. For if thou altogether holdest thy peace at this time, then shall there enlargement and deliverance arise to the Jews from another place; but thou and thy father's house shall be destroyed: and who knoweth whether thou art come to the kingdom for such a time as this?"

Then Esther bade them return Mordecai this answer, "Go, gather together all the Jews that are present in Shushan, and fast ye for me, and neither eat nor drink three days, night or day: I also and my maidens will fast likewise; and so will I go in unto the king, which is not according to the law: and if I perish, I perish."

So Mordecai went his way, and did according to all that Esther had commanded him.

Now it came to pass on the third day, that Esther put on her

ESTHER

royal apparel, and stood in the inner court of the king's house, over against the king's house: and the king sat upon his royal throne in the royal house, over against the gate of the house. And it was so, when the king saw Esther the queen standing in the court, that she obtained favour in his sight: and the king held out to Esther the golden sceptre that was in his hand. So Esther drew near, and touched the top of the sceptre.

Then said the king unto her, "What wilt thou, Queen Esther? and what is thy request? it shall be even given thee to the half of the kingdom."

And Esther answered, "If it seem good unto the king, let the king and Haman come this day unto the banquet that I have prepared for him."

Then the king said, "Cause Haman to make haste, that he may do as Esther hath said."

So the king and Haman came to the banquet that Esther had prepared.

And the king said unto Esther at the banquet of wine, "What is thy petition? and it shall be granted thee: and what is thy request? even to the half of the kingdom it shall be performed."

Then answered Esther, and said, "My petition and my request is: if I have found favour in the sight of the king, and if it please the king to grant my petition, and to perform my request, let the king and Haman come to the banquet that I shall prepare for them, and I will do to-morrow as the king hath said."

Then went Haman forth that day joyful and with a glad heart: but when Haman saw Mordecai in the king's gate, that he stood not up, nor moved for him, he was full of indignation against Mordecai. Nevertheless Haman refrained himself: and when he came home, he sent and called for his friends, and Zeresh his wife. And Haman told them of the glory of his riches, and the multitude of his children, and all the things wherein the king had promoted him, and how he had advanced him above the princes and servants of the king.

Haman said moreover, "Yea, Esther the queen did let no man

ESTHER

come in with the king unto the banquet that she had prepared but myself; and to-morrow am I invited unto her also with the king. Yet all this availeth me nothing, so long as I see Mordecai the Jew sitting at the king's gate."

Then said Zeresh his wife and all his friends unto him, "Let a gallows be made of fifty cubits high, and to-morrow speak thou unto the king that Mordecai may be hanged thereon: then go thou in merrily with the king unto the banquet."

And the thing pleased Haman; and he caused the gallows to be made.

On that night could not the king sleep, and he commanded to bring the book of records of the chronicles; and they were read before the king. And it was found written, that Mordecai had told of Bigthan and Teresh, two of the king's chamberlains, the keepers of the door, who sought to lay hand on the king Ahasuerus.

And the king said, "What honour and dignity hath been done to Mordecai for this?"

Then said the king's servants that ministered unto him, "There is nothing done for him."

And the king said, "Who is in the court?"

Now Haman was come into the outward court of the king's house, to speak unto the king to hang Mordecai on the gallows that he had prepared for him. And the king's servants said unto him, "Behold, Haman standeth in the court."

And the king said, "Let him come in."

So Haman came in. And the king said unto him, "What shall be done unto the man whom the king delighteth to honour?"

Now Haman thought in his heart, "To whom would the king delight to do honour more than to myself?" And Haman answered the king, "For the man whom the king delighteth to honour, let the royal apparel be brought which the king useth to wear, and the horse that the king rideth upon, and the crown royal which is set upon his head: and let this apparel and horse be delivered to the hand of one of the king's most noble princes,

ESTHER

that they may array the man withal whom the king delighteth to honour, and bring him on horseback through the street of the city, and proclaim before him, thus shall it be done to the man whom the king delighteth to honour."

Then the king said to Haman, "Make haste, and take the apparel and the horse, as thou hast said, and do even so to Mordecai the Jew, that sitteth at the king's gate: let nothing fail of all that thou hast spoken."

Then took Haman the apparel and the horse, and arrayed Mordecai, and brought him on horseback through the street of the city, and proclaimed before him, "Thus shall it be done unto the man whom the king delighteth to honour."

And Mordecai came again to the king's gate. But Haman hastened to his house mourning, and having his head covered. And Haman told Zeresh his wife and all his friends every thing that had befallen him.

Then said his wise men and Zeresh his wife unto him, "If Mordecai be of the seed of the Jews, before whom thou hast begun to fall, thou shalt not prevail against him, but shalt surely fall before him."

And while they were yet talking with him, came the king's chamberlains, and hastened to bring Haman unto the banquet that Esther had prepared.

So the king and Haman came to banquet with Esther the queen. And the king said again unto Esther on the second day at the banquet of wine, "What is thy petition, Queen Esther? and it shall be granted thee: and what is thy request? and it shall be performed, even to the half of the kingdom."

Then Esther the queen answered and said, "If I have found favour in thy sight, O king, and if it please the king, let my life be given me at my petition, and my people at my request: for we are sold, I and my people, to be destroyed, to be slain, and to perish. But if we had been sold for bondmen and bondwomen, I had held my tongue, although the enemy could not countervail the king's damage."

ESTHER

Then the king Ahasuerus answered and said unto Esther the queen, "Who is he, and where is he, that durst presume in his heart to do so?"

And Esther said, "The adversary and enemy is this wicked Haman." Then Haman was afraid before the king and the queen.

And the king arising from the banquet of wine in his wrath went into the palace garden: and Haman stood up to make request for his life to Esther the queen; for he saw that there was evil determined against him by the king.

Then the king returned out of the palace garden into the place of the banquet of wine; and Haman was fallen upon the bed whereon Esther was. Then said the king, "Will he force the queen also before me in the house?"

As the word went out of the king's mouth, they covered Haman's face. And Harbona, one of the chamberlains, said before the king, "Behold also, the gallows fifty cubits high, which Haman had made for Mordecai, who had spoken good for the king, standeth in the house of Haman."

Then the king said, "Hang him thereon."

So they hanged Haman on the gallows that he had prepared for Mordecai. Then was the king's wrath pacified.

On that day did the king Ahasuerus give the house of Haman the Jew's enemy unto Esther the queen. And Mordecai came before the king; for Esther had told what he was unto her. And the king took off his ring, which he had taken from Haman, and gave it unto Mordecai. And Esther set Mordecai over the house of Haman.

And Esther spoke yet again before the king, and fell down at his feet, and besought him with tears to put away the mischief of Haman the Agagite, and his device that he had devised against the Jews. Then the king held out the golden sceptre toward Esther.

So Esther arose, and stood before the king, and said, "If it please the king, and if I have found favour in his sight, and the thing seem right before the king, and I be pleasing in his eyes, let it be written to reverse the letters devised by Haman the

ESTHER

son of Hammedatha the Agagite, which he wrote to destroy the Jews which are in all the king's provinces: for how can I endure to see the evil that shall come unto my people? or how can I endure to see the destruction of my kindred?"

Then the king Ahasuerus said unto Esther the queen and to Mordecai the Jew, "Behold, I have given Esther the house of Haman, and him they have hanged upon the gallows, because he laid his hand upon the Jews. Write ye also for the Jews, as it liketh you, in the king's name, and seal it with the king's ring: for the writing which is written in the king's name, and sealed with the king's ring, may no man reverse."

Then were the king's scribes called at that time in the third month, that is, the month Sivan, on the three and twentieth day thereof; and it was written according to all that Mordecai commanded unto the Jews, and to the lieutenants, and the deputies and rulers of the provinces which are from India unto Ethiopia, a hundred twenty and seven provinces, unto every province according to the writing thereof, and unto every people after their language, and to the Jews according to their writing, and according to their language.

And he wrote in the king Ahasuerus's name, and sealed it with the king's ring, and sent letters by posts on horseback, and riders on mules, camels, and young dromedaries: wherein the king granted the Jews which were in every city to gather themselves together, and to stand for their life, to destroy, to slay, and to cause to perish, all the power of the people and province that would assault them, both little ones and women, and to take the spoil of them for a prey, upon one day in all the provinces of King Ahasuerus, namely, upon the thirteenth day of the twelfth month, which is the month Adar.

The copy of the writing for a commandment to be given in every province was published unto all people, and that the Jews should be ready against that day to avenge themselves on their enemies. So the posts that rode upon mules and camels went out, being hastened and pressed on by the king's commandment. And the decree was given at Shushan the palace.

ESTHER

And Mordecai went out from the presence of the king in royal apparel of blue and white, and with a great crown of gold, and with a garment of fine linen and purple: and the city of Shushan rejoiced and was glad.

The Jews had light, and gladness, and joy, and honour. And in every province, and in every city, whithersoever the king's commandment and his decree came, the Jews had joy and gladness, a feast and a good day. And many of the people of the land became Jews; for the fear of the Jews fell upon them.

Now in the twelfth month, that is, the month Adar, on the thirteenth day of the same, when the king's commandment and his decree drew near to be put in execution, in the day that the enemies of the Jews hoped to have power over them (though it was turned to the contrary, that the Jews had rule over them that hated them); the Jews gathered themselves together in their cities throughout all the provinces of the king Ahasuerus, to lay hand on such as sought their hurt: and no man could withstand them; for the fear of them fell upon all people. And all the rulers of the provinces, and the lieutenants, and the deputies, and officers of the king, helped the Jews; because the fear of Mordecai fell upon them. For Mordecai was great in the king's house, and his fame went out throughout all the provinces: for this man Mordecai waxed greater and greater.

Thus the Jews smote all their enemies with the stroke of the sword, and slaughter, and destruction, and did what they would unto those that hated them. And in Shushan the palace the Jews slew and destroyed five hundred men. And Parshandatha, and Dalphon, and Aspatha, and Poratha, and Adalia, and Aridatha, and Parmashta, and Arisai, and Aridai, and Vajezatha, the ten sons of Haman the son of Hammedatha, the enemy of the Jews, slew they; but on the spoil laid they not their hand. On that day the number of those that were slain in Shushan the palace was brought before the king.

And the king said unto Esther the queen, "The Jews have slain and destroyed five hundred men in Shushan the palace, and the ten sons of Haman; what have they done in the rest of

ESTHER

the king's provinces? now what is thy petition? and it shall be granted thee: or what is thy request further? and it shall be done."

Then said Esther, "If it please the king, let it be granted to the Jews which are in Shushan to do to-morrow also according unto this day's decree, and let Haman's ten sons be hanged upon the gallows."

And the king commanded it so to be done: and the decree was given at Shushan; and they hanged Haman's ten sons. For the Jews that were in Shushan gathered themselves together on the fourteenth day also of the month Adar, and slew three hundred men at Shushan; but on the prey they laid not their hand. But the other Jews that were in the king's provinces gathered themselves together, and stood for their lives, and had rest from their enemies, and slew of their foes seventy and five thousand, but they laid not their hands on the prey.

On the thirteenth day of the month Adar; and on the fourteenth day of the same rested they, and made it a day of feasting and gladness. But the Jews that were at Shushan assembled together on the thirteenth day thereof, and on the fourteenth thereof; and on the fifteenth day of the same they rested, and made it a day of feasting and gladness. Therefore the Jews of the villages, that dwelt in the unwalled towns, made the fourteenth day of the month Adar a day of gladness and feasting, and a good day, and of sending portions one to another.

And Mordecai wrote these things, and sent letters unto all the Jews that were in all the provinces of the king Ahasuerus, both nigh and far, to establish this among them, that they should keep the fourteenth day of the month Adar, and the fifteenth day of the same, yearly, as the days wherein the Jews rested from their enemies, and the month which was turned unto them from sorrow to joy, and from mourning into a good day: that they should make them days of feasting and joy, and of sending portions one to another, and gifts to the poor.

And the Jews undertook to do as they had begun, and as Mordecai had written unto them; because Haman the son of

ESTHER

Hammedatha, the Agagite, the enemy of all the Jews, had devised against the Jews to destroy them, and had cast Pur, that is, the lot, to consume them, and to destroy them; but when Esther came before the king, he commanded by letters that his wicked device, which he devised against the Jews, should return upon his own head, and that he and his sons should be hanged on the gallows.

Wherefore they called these days Purim after the name of Pur. Therefore for all the words of this letter, and of that which they had seen concerning this matter, and which had come unto them, the Jews ordained, and took upon them, and upon their seed, and upon all such as joined themselves unto them, so as it should not fail, that they would keep these two days according to their writing, and according to their appointed time every year; and that these days should be remembered and kept throughout every generation, every family, every province, and every city; and that these days of Purim should not fail from among the Jews, nor the memorial of them perish from their seed.

Then Esther the queen, the daughter of Abihail, and Mordecai the Jew, wrote with all authority, to confirm this second letter of Purim. And he sent the letters unto all the Jews, to the hundred twenty and seven provinces of the kingdom of Ahasuerus, with words of peace and truth, to confirm these days of Purim in their times appointed, according as Mordecai the Jew and Esther the queen had enjoined them, and as they had decreed for themselves and for their seed, the matters of the fastings and their cry. And the decree of Esther confirmed these matters of Purim; and it was written in the book.

JUDITH

A TALE

The Jewish sacred canon was gradually built up between the fourth and the end of the second century B.C., by which latter time it was complete. It included originally only the Torah or Law, consisting merely of the Pentateuch; next to be regarded as sacred was the section known as the Prophets which included the historical as well as prophetical works; lastly, and always regarded as of somewhat less sanctity than the other two, was the miscellaneous collection of Hagiographa or Writings embracing all the rest of the Protestant Old Testament. The additional works known since the fifth century A.D. as the Apocrypha were rejected from the Palestinian Canon either because they were written later than 100 B.C., by which time the Canon was definitely established, or because, though written earlier, they had not yet attained sufficiently high repute. They were accepted as sacred by the more liberal Jews of Alexandria, were included in the Septuagint and Vulgate translations, and were officially placed on an equality with the rest of the Old Testament by the Roman Catholic Church at the Council of Trent (1545–63). By the Church of England, on the other hand, they were admitted into the Canon in a subordinate position for purposes of "edification" but not for "the establishment of doctrine." They appear in the King James Version as "the Bookes called Apocrypha," between the Old and New Testaments, and were usually included in Protestant Bibles until about sixty years ago. From the literary point of view, their disappearance is regrettable.

Since the purpose of the present edition is entirely "edification" and not "doctrine," it seems fitting to include at least parts of the more notable Apocryphal works. Of these none is more famous than the patriotic tale of Judith written in the second century. Though the book is slightly inferior to Esther as narrative, the central figure of Judith, celebrated in innumerable paintings and passages of literature, is both nobler and psychologically more interesting than that of the scheming concubine of the king Ahasuerus.

A TALE

IN THE EIGHTEENTH YEAR, the two and twentieth day of the first month, there was talk in the house of Nabuchodonosor king of the Assyrians, that he should, as he said, avenge himself on all the earth. So he called unto him all his officers, and all his nobles, and communicated with them his secret counsel, and concluded the afflicting of the whole earth out of his own mouth. Then they decreed to destroy all flesh, that did not obey the commandment of his mouth.

And when he had ended his counsel, Nabuchodonosor king of the Assyrians called Holofernes the chief captain of his army, which was next unto him, and said unto him, "Thus saith the great king, the lord of the whole earth: behold, thou shalt go forth from my presence, and take with thee men that trust in their own strength, of footmen a hundred and twenty thousand; and the number of horses with their riders twelve thousand.

"And thou shalt go against all the west country, because they disobeyed my commandment. And thou shalt declare unto them, that they prepare for me earth and water: for I will go forth in my wrath against them, and will cover the whole face of the earth with the feet of mine army, and I will give them for a spoil unto them: so that their slain shall fill their valleys and brooks, and the river shall be filled with their dead, till it overflow: and I will lead them captives to the utmost parts of all the earth."

Then Holofernes went forth from the presence of his lord, and called all the governors and captains, and the officers of the

JUDITH

army of Assur; and he mustered the chosen men for the battle, as his lord had commanded him, unto a hundred and twenty thousand, and twelve thousand archers on horseback; and he ranged them, as a great army is ordered for the war. And he took camels and asses for their carriages, a very great number; and sheep and oxen and goats without number for their provision: and plenty of victual for every man of the army, and very much gold and silver out of the king's house; then he went forth and all his power to go before King Nabuchodonosor in the voyage, and to cover all the face of the earth westward with their chariots, and horsemen, and their chosen footmen. A great number also of sundry countries came with them like locusts, and like the sand of the earth: for the multitude was without number.

And they went forth of Nineveh three days' journey toward the plain of Bectileth, and pitched from Bectileth near the mountain which is at the left hand of the upper Cilicia.

Then he took all his army, his footmen, and horsemen, and chariots, and went from thence into the hill country; and destroyed Phud and Lud, and spoiled all the children of Rasses, and the children of Ismael, which were toward the wilderness at the south of the land of the Chellians.

Then he went over Euphrates, and went through Mesopotamia, and destroyed all the high cities that were upon the river Arbonai, till ye come to the sea. And he took the borders of Cilicia, and killed all that resisted him, and came to the borders of Japheth, which were toward the south, over against Arabia. He compassed also all the children of Madian, and burned up their tabernacles, and spoiled their sheepcotes.

Then he went down into the plain of Damascus in the time of wheat harvest, and burnt up all their fields, and destroyed their flocks and herds, also he spoiled their cities, and utterly wasted their countries, and smote all their young men with the edge of the sword. Therefore the fear and dread of him fell upon all the inhabitants of the sea coasts, which were in Sidon and Tyrus, and them that dwelt in Sur and Ocina, and all that

JUDITH

dwelt in Jemnaan; and they that dwelt in Azotus and Ascalon feared him greatly.

Now the children of Israel, that dwelt in Judea, heard all that Holofernes the chief captain of Nabuchodonosor king of the Assyrians had done to the nations, and after what manner he had spoiled all their temples, and brought them to nought.

Therefore they were exceedingly afraid of him, and were troubled for Jerusalem, and for the temple of the Lord their God: for they were newly returned from the captivity, and all the people of Judea were lately gathered together: and the vessels, and the altar, and the house, were sanctified after the profanation.

Therefore they sent into all the coasts of Samaria, and the villages, and to Bethoron, and Belmen, and Jericho, and to Choba, and Esora, and to the valley of Salem: and possessed themselves beforehand of all the tops of the high mountains, and fortified the villages that were in them, and laid up victuals for the provision of war: for their fields were of late reaped.

Then was it declared to Holofernes, the chief captain of the army of Assur, that the children of Israel had prepared for war, and had shut up the passages of the hill country, and had fortified all the tops of the high hills, and had laid impediments in the champaign countries: wherewith he was very angry and called all the princes of Moab, and the captains of Ammon, and all the governors of the sea coast.

Then came unto him all the chief of the children of Esau, and all the governors of the people of Moab, and the captains of the sea coast, and said, "Let our lord now hear a word, that there be not an overthrow in thine army. For this people of the children of Israel do not trust in their spears, but in the height of the mountains wherein they dwell, because it is not easy to come up to the tops of their mountains.

"Now therefore, my lord, fight not against them in battle array, and there shall not so much as one man of thy people perish. Remain in thy camp, and keep all the men of thine army, and let thy servants get into their hands the fountain of water,

JUDITH

which issueth forth of the foot of the mountain: for all the inhabitants of Bethulia have their water thence; so shall thirst kill them, and they shall give up their city, and we and our people shall go up to the tops of the mountains that are near, and will camp upon them, to watch that none go out of the city. So they and their wives and their children shall be consumed with famine, and before the sword come against them, they shall be overthrown in the streets where they dwell.

"Thus shalt thou render them an evil reward; because they rebelled, and met not thy person peaceably."

And these words pleased Holofernes and all his servants, and he appointed to do as they had spoken. So the camp of the children of Ammon departed, and with them five thousand of the Assyrians, and they pitched in the valley, and took the waters, and the fountains of the waters of the children of Israel.

Then the children of Esau went up with the children of Ammon, and camped in the hill country over against Dothaim: and they sent some of them toward the south, and toward the east, over against Ekrebel, which is near unto Chusi, that is upon the brook Mochmur; and the rest of the army of the Assyrians camped in the plain, and covered the face of the whole land; and their tents and carriages were pitched to a very great multitude.

Then the children of Israel cried unto the Lord their God, because their heart failed, for all their enemies had compassed them round about, and there was no way to escape out from among them. Thus all the company of Assur remained about them, both their footmen, chariots, and horsemen, four and thirty days, so that all their vessels of water failed all the inhabitants of Bethulia. And the cisterns were emptied, and they had not water to drink their fill for one day; for they gave them drink by measure. Therefore their young children were out of heart, and their women and young men fainted for thirst, and fell down in the streets of the city, and by the passages of the gates, and there was no longer any strength in them.

Then all the people assembled to Ozias, and to the chief of the city, both young men, and women, and children, and cried

JUDITH

with a loud voice, and said before all the elders, "God be judge between us and you: for ye have done us great injury, in that ye have not required peace of the children of Assur. For now we have no helper: but God hath sold us into their hands, that we should be thrown down before them with thirst and great destruction.

"Now therefore call them unto you, and deliver the whole city for a spoil to the people of Holofernes, and to all his army. For it is better for us to be made a spoil unto them than to die for thirst: for we will be his servants, that our souls may live, and not see the death of our infants before our eyes, nor our wives nor our children to die."

Then there was great weeping with one consent in the midst of the assembly; and they cried unto the Lord God with a loud voice.

Then said Ozias to them, "Brethren, be of good courage, let us yet endure five days, in the which space the Lord our God may turn his mercy toward us; for he will not forsake us utterly. And if these days pass, and there come no help unto us, I will do according to your word."

And he dispersed the people, every one to their own charge; and they went unto the walls and towers of their city, and sent the women and children into their houses: and they were very low brought in the city.

Now at that time Judith heard thereof, which was the daughter of Merari, the son of Ox, the son of Joseph, the son of Oziel, the son of Elcia, the son of Ananias, the son of Gedeon, the son of Raphaim, the son of Acitho, the son of Eliu, the son of Eliab, the son of Nathanael, the son of Samael, the son of Salasadai, the son of Israel. And Manasses was her husband, of her tribe and kindred, who died in the barley harvest. For as he stood overseeing them that bound sheaves in the field, the heat came upon his head, and he fell on his bed, and died in the city of Bethulia: and they buried him with his fathers in the field between Dothaim and Balamo.

So Judith was a widow in her house three years and four

JUDITH

months. And she made her a tent upon the top of her house, and put on sackcloth upon her loins, and wore her widow's apparel. And she fasted all the days of her widowhood, save the eves of the sabbaths, and the sabbaths, and the eves of the new moons, and the new moons, and the feasts and solemn days of the house of Israel. She was also of a goodly countenance, and very beautiful to behold: and her husband Manasses had left her gold, and silver, and menservants, and maidservants, and cattle, and lands; and she remained upon them. And there was none that gave her an ill word; for she feared God greatly.

Now when she heard the evil words of the people against the governor, that they fainted for lack of water; for Judith had heard all the words that Ozias had spoken unto them, and that he had sworn to deliver the city unto the Assyrians after five days; then she sent her waitingwoman, that had the government of all things that she had, to call Ozias and Chabris and Charmis, the ancients of the city.

And they came unto her, and she said unto them, "Hear me now, O ye governors of the inhabitants of Bethulia: for your words that ye have spoken before the people this day are not right, touching this oath which ye made and pronounced between God and you, and have promised to deliver the city to our enemies, unless within these days the Lord turn to help you. And now who are ye that have tempted God this day, and stand instead of God among the children of men?

"And now try the Lord Almighty, but ye shall never know any thing. For ye cannot find the depth of the heart of man, neither can ye perceive the things that he thinketh: then how can ye search out God, that hath made all these things, and know his mind, or comprehend his purpose?

"Nay, my brethren, provoke not the Lord our God to anger. For if he will not help us within these five days, he hath power to defend us when he will, even every day, or to destroy us before our enemies. Do not bind the counsels of the Lord our God: for God is not as man, that he may be threatened; neither is he as the son of man, that he should be wavering. Therefore

JUDITH

let us wait for salvation of him, and call upon him to help us, and he will hear our voice, if it please him."

Then said Ozias to her, "All that thou hast spoken hast thou spoken with a good heart, and there is none that may gainsay thy words. For this is not the first day wherein thy wisdom is manifested; but from the beginning of thy days all the people have known thy understanding, because the disposition of thine heart is good. But the people were very thirsty, and compelled us to do unto them as we have spoken, and to bring an oath upon ourselves, which we will not break. Therefore now pray thou for us, because thou art a godly woman, and the Lord will send us rain to fill our cisterns, and we shall faint no more."

Then said Judith unto them, "Hear me, and I will do a thing, which shall go throughout all generations to the children of our nation. Ye shall stand this night in the gate, and I will go forth with my waitingwoman: and within the days that ye have promised to deliver the city to our enemies the Lord will visit Israel by mine hand. But enquire not ye of mine act: for I will not declare it unto you, till the things be finished that I do."

Then said Ozias and the princes unto her, "Go in peace, and the Lord God be before thee, to take vengeance on our enemies." So they returned from the tent, and went to their wards.

Then Judith fell upon her face, and put ashes upon her head, and uncovered the sackcloth wherewith she was clothed; and about the time that the incense of that evening was offered in Jerusalem in the house of the Lord Judith cried with a loud voice, and said,

"O God, O my God, hear me also a widow. Behold, the Assyrians are multiplied in their power; they are exalted with horse and man; they glory in the strength of their footmen; they trust in shield, and spear, and bow, and sling; and know not that thou art the Lord that brakest the battles: the Lord is thy name.

"Throw down their strength in thy power, and bring down their force in thy wrath: for they have purposed to defile thy sanctuary, and to pollute the tabernacle where thy glorious name resteth, and to cast down with sword the horn of thy altar.

JUDITH

"Behold their pride, and send thy wrath upon their heads: give into mine hand, which am a widow, the power that I have conceived. Smite by the deceit of my lips the servant with the prince, and the prince with the servant: break down their stateliness by the hand of a woman."

Now after that she had ceased to cry unto the God of Israel, and had made an end of all these words, she arose where she had fallen down, and called her maid, and went down into the house, in the which she abode in the sabbath days, and in her feast days, and pulled off the sackcloth which she had on, and put off the garments of her widowhood, and washed her body all over with water, and anointed herself with precious ointment, and braided the hair of her head, and put on a tire upon it, and put on her garments of gladness, wherewith she was clad during the life of Manasses her husband. And she took sandals upon her feet, and put about her her bracelets, and her chains, and her rings, and her earrings, and all her ornaments, and decked herself bravely, to allure the eyes of all men that should see her.

Then she gave her maid a bottle of wine, and a cruse of oil, and filled a bag with parched corn, and lumps of figs, and with fine bread; so she folded all these things together, and laid them upon her. Thus they went forth to the gate of the city of Bethulia, and found standing there Ozias, and the ancients of the city, Chabris and Charmis.

And when they saw her, that her countenance was altered, and her apparel was changed, they wondered at her beauty very greatly, and said unto her, "The God, the God of our fathers, give thee favour, and accomplish thine enterprises to the glory of the children of Israel, and to the exaltation of Jerusalem." Then they worshipped God.

And she said unto them, "Command the gates of the city to be opened unto me, that I may go forth to accomplish the things whereof ye have spoken with me."

So they commanded the young men to open unto her, as she had spoken. And when they had done so, Judith went out, she,

JUDITH

and her maid with her; and the men of the city looked after her, until she was gone down the mountain, and till she had passed the valley, and could see her no more.

Thus they went straight forth in the valley: and the first watch of the Assyrians met her, and took her, and asked her, "Of what people art thou? and whence comest thou? and whither goest thou?"

And she said, "I am a woman of the Hebrews, and am fled from them: for they shall be given you to be consumed: and I am coming before Holofernes the chief captain of your army, to declare words of truth; and I will show him a way, whereby he shall go, and win all the hill country, without losing the body or life of any one of his men."

Now when the men heard her words, and beheld her countenance, they wondered greatly at her beauty, and said unto her, "Thou hast saved thy life, in that thou hast hastened to come down to the presence of our lord: now therefore come to his tent, and some of us shall conduct thee, until they have delivered thee to his hands. And when thou standest before him, be not afraid in thine heart, but show unto him according to thy word; and he will entreat thee well."

Then they chose out of them a hundred men to accompany her and her maid; and they brought her to the tent of Holofernes.

Then was there a concourse throughout all the camp: for her coming was noised among the tents, and they came about her, as she stood without the tent of Holofernes, till they told him of her. And they wondered at her beauty, and admired the children of Israel because of her, and every one said to his neighbour, "Who would despise this people, that have among them such women? surely it is not good that one man of them be left, who being let go might deceive the whole earth." And they that lay near Holofernes went out, and all his servants, and they brought her into the tent.

Now Holofernes rested upon his bed under a canopy, which was woven with purple, and gold, and emeralds, and precious

JUDITH

stones. So they showed him of her; and he came out before his tent with silver lamps going before him. And when Judith was come before him and his servants, they all marvelled at the beauty of her countenance; and she fell down upon her face, and did reverence unto him: and his servants took her up.

Then said Holofernes unto her, "Woman, be of good comfort, fear not in thine heart: for I never hurt any that was willing to serve Nabuchodonosor, the king of all the earth. Now therefore, if thy people that dwelleth in the mountains had not set light by me, I would not have lifted up my spear against them: but they have done these things to themselves. But now tell me wherefore thou art fled from them, and art come unto us: for thou art come for safeguard; be of good comfort, thou shalt live this night, and hereafter: for none shall hurt thee, but entreat thee well, as they do the servants of King Nabuchodonosor my lord."

Then Judith said unto him, "Receive the words of thy servant, and suffer thine handmaid to speak in thy presence, and I will declare no lie to my lord this night. And if thou wilt follow the words of thine handmaid, God will bring the thing perfectly to pass by thee; and my lord shall not fail of his purposes. As Nabuchodonosor king of all the earth liveth, and as his power liveth, who hath sent thee for the upholding of every living thing: for not only men shall serve him by thee, but also the beasts of the field, and the cattle, and the fowls of the air, shall live by thy power under Nabuchodonosor and all his house. For we have heard of thy wisdom and thy policies, and it is reported in all the earth, that thou only art excellent in all the kingdom, and mighty in knowledge, and wonderful in feats of war. Our nation shall not be punished, neither can the sword prevail against them, except they sin against their God. And now, that my lord be not defeated and frustrate of his purpose, even death is now fallen upon them, and their sin hath overtaken them, wherewith they will provoke their God to anger, whensoever they shall do that which is not fit to be done: for their victuals fail them, and all their water is scant, and they

JUDITH

have determined to lay hands upon their cattle, and purposed to consume all those things, that God hath forbidden them to eat by his laws, and are resolved to spend the firstfruits of the corn, and the tenths of wine and oil, which they had sanctified, and reserved for the priests that serve in Jerusalem before the face of our God; the which things it is not lawful for any of the people so much as to touch with their hands.

"For they have sent some to Jerusalem, because they also that dwell there have done the like, to bring them a license from the senate. Now when they shall bring them word, they will forthwith do it, and they shall be given thee to be destroyed the same day. Wherefore I thine handmaid, knowing all this, am fled from their presence; and God hath sent me to work things with thee, whereat all the earth shall be astonished, and whosoever shall hear it.

"For thy servant is religious, and serveth the God of heaven day and night: now therefore, my lord, I will remain with thee, and thy servant will go out by night into the valley, and I will pray unto God, and he will tell me when they have committed their sins: and I will come and show it unto thee: then thou shalt go forth with all thine army, and there shall be none of them that shall resist thee. And I will lead thee through the midst of Judea, until thou come before Jerusalem; and I will set thy throne in the midst thereof; and thou shalt drive them as sheep that have no shepherd, and a dog shall not so much as open his mouth at thee: for these things were told me according to my foreknowledge, and they were declared unto me, and I am sent to tell thee."

Then her words pleased Holofernes and all his servants; and they marvelled at her wisdom, and said, "There is not such a woman from one end of the earth to the other, both for beauty of face, and wisdom of words."

Likewise Holofernes said unto her, "God hath done well to send thee before the people, that strength might be in our hands, and destruction upon them that lightly regard my lord. And now thou art both beautiful in thy countenance, and witty

JUDITH

in thy words: surely if thou do as thou hast spoken, thy God shall be my God, and thou shalt dwell in the house of King Nabuchodonosor, and shalt be renowned through the whole earth."

Then he commanded to bring her in where his plate was set; and bade that they should prepare for her of his own meats, and that she should drink of his own wine. And Judith said, "I will not eat thereof, lest there be an offence: but provision shall be made for me of the things that I have brought."

Then Holofernes said unto her, "If thy provision should fail, how should we give thee the like? for there be none with us of thy nation."

Then said Judith unto him, "As thy soul liveth, my lord, thine handmaid shall not spend those things that I have, before the Lord work by mine hand the things that he hath determined."

Then the servants of Holofernes brought her into the tent, and she slept till midnight, and she arose when it was toward the morning watch, and sent to Holofernes, saying, "Let my lord now command that thine handmaid may go forth unto prayer."

Then Holofernes commanded his guard that they should not stay her: thus she abode in the camp three days, and went out in the night into the valley of Bethulia, and washed herself in a fountain of water by the camp. And when she came out, she besought the Lord God of Israel to direct her way to the raising up of the children of her people. So she came in clean, and remained in the tent, until she did eat her meat at evening.

And in the fourth day Holofernes made a feast to his own servants only, and called none of the officers to the banquet. Then said he to Bagoas the eunuch, who had charge over all that he had, "Go now, and persuade this Hebrew woman which is with thee, that she come unto us, and eat and drink with us. For, lo, it will be a shame for our person, if we shall let such a woman go, not having had her company; for if we draw her not unto us, she will laugh us to scorn."

Then went Bagoas from the presence of Holofernes, and came

JUDITH

to her, and he said, "Let not this fair damsel fear to come to my lord, and to be honoured in his presence, and drink wine, and be merry with us, and be made this day as one of the daughters of the Assyrians, which serve in the house of Nabuchodonosor."

Then said Judith unto him, "Who am I now, that I should gainsay my lord? surely whatsoever pleaseth him I will do speedily, and it shall be my joy unto the day of my death."

So she arose, and decked herself with her apparel and all her woman's attire, and her maid went and laid soft skins on the ground for her over against Holofernes, which she had received of Bagoas for her daily use, that she might sit and eat upon them.

Now when Judith came in and sat down, Holofernes his heart was ravished with her, and his mind was moved, and he desired greatly her company; for he waited a time to deceive her, from the day that he had seen her.

Then said Holofernes unto her, "Drink now, and be merry with us." So Judith said, "I will drink now, my lord, because my life is magnified in me this day more than all the days since I was born."

Then she took and ate and drank before him what her maid had prepared. And Holofernes took great delight in her, and drank much more wine than he had drunk at any time in one day since he was born.

Now when the evening was come, his servants made haste to depart, and Bagoas shut his tent without, and dismissed the waiters from the presence of his lord; and they went to their beds: for they were all weary, because the feast had been long. And Judith was left alone in the tent, and Holofernes lying along upon his bed: for he was filled with wine. Now Judith had commanded her maid to stand without her bedchamber, and to wait for her coming forth, as she did daily: for she said she would go forth to her prayers, and she spoke to Bagoas according to the same purpose. So all went forth, and none was left in the bedchamber, neither little nor great. Then Judith standing by his bed, said in her heart, "O Lord God of all

JUDITH

power, look at this present upon the works of mine hands for the exaltation of Jerusalem. For now is the time to help thine inheritance, and to execute mine enterprises to the destruction of the enemies which are risen against us."

Then she came to the pillar of the bed, which was at Holofernes's head, and took down his falchion from thence, and approached to his bed, and took hold of the hair of his head, and said, "Strengthen me, O Lord God of Israel, this day." And she smote twice upon his neck with all her might, and she took away his head from him, and tumbled his body down from the bed, and pulled down the canopy from the pillars; and anon after she went forth, and gave Holofernes his head to her maid. And she put it in her bag of meat: so they twain went together according to their custom unto prayer: and when they passed the camp, they compassed the valley, and went up the mountain of Bethulia, and came to the gates thereof.

Then said Judith afar off to the watchmen at the gate, "Open, open now the gate: God, even our God, is with us, to show his power yet in Jerusalem, and his forces against the enemy, as he hath even done this day."

Now when the men of her city heard her voice, they made haste to go down to the gate of their city, and they called the elders of the city. And then they ran all together, both small and great, for it was strange unto them that she was come: so they opened the gate, and received them, and made a fire for a light, and stood round about them.

Then she said to them with a loud voice, "Praise, praise God, praise God, I say, for he hath not taken away his mercy from the house of Israel, but hath destroyed our enemies by mine hands this night."

So she took the head out of the bag, and showed it, and said unto them, "Behold the head of Holofernes, the chief captain of the army of Assur, and behold the canopy, wherein he did lie in his drunkenness; and the Lord hath smitten him by the hand of a woman. As the Lord liveth, who hath kept me in my way

JUDITH

that I went, my countenance hath deceived him to his destruction, and yet hath he not committed sin with me, to defile and shame me."

Then all the people were wonderfully astonished, and bowed themselves, and worshipped God, and said with one accord, "Blessed be thou, O our God, which hast this day brought to nought the enemies of thy people."

Then said Ozias unto her, "O daughter, blessed art thou of the most high God above all the women upon the earth; and blessed be the Lord God, which hath created the heavens and the earth, which hath directed thee to the cutting off of the head of the chief of our enemies. For this thy confidence shall not depart from the heart of men, which remember the power of God for ever. And God turn these things to thee for a perpetual praise, to visit thee in good things, because thou hast not spared thy life for the affliction of our nation, but hast revenged our ruin, walking a straight way before our God." And all the people said, "So be it, so be it."

SUSANNA AND THE ELDERS

A TALE

The perfect little tale of *Susanna and the Elders* has supplied another favorite theme for painters and poets. It was written about 130 B.C., and first appeared as an addition to the Apocryphal version of Daniel.

SUSANNA
and the Elders

A TALE

THERE DWELT a man in Babylon, called Joacim: and he took a wife, whose name was Susanna, the daughter of Chelcias, a very fair woman, and one that feared the Lord. Her parents also were righteous, and taught their daughter according to the law of Moses.

Now Joacim was a great rich man, and had a fair garden joining unto his house: and to him resorted the Jews; because he was more honourable than all others.

The same year were appointed two of the ancients of the people to be judges, such as the Lord spoke of, that wickedness came from Babylon from ancient judges, who seemed to govern the people. These kept much at Joacim's house: and all that had any suits in law came unto them.

Now when the people departed away at noon, Susanna went into her husband's garden to walk. And the two elders saw her going in every day, and walking; so that their lust was inflamed toward her. And they perverted their own mind, and turned away their eyes, that they might not look unto heaven, nor remember just judgments.

And albeit they both were wounded with her love, yet durst not one show another his grief. For they were ashamed to declare their lust, that they desired to have to do with her. Yet they watched diligently from day to day to see her. And the one said to the other, "Let us now go home: for it is dinner time."

So when they were gone out, they parted the one from the other, and turning back again they came to the same place; and after that they had asked one another the cause, they acknowl-

[858]

SUSANNA AND THE ELDERS

edged their lust: then appointed they a time both together, when they might find her alone.

And it fell out, as they watched a fit time, she went in as before with two maids only, and she was desirous to wash herself in the garden: for it was hot. And there was nobody there save the two elders, that had hid themselves, and watched her.

Then she said to her maids, "Bring me oil and washing balls, and shut the garden doors, that I may wash me."

And they did as she bade them, and shut the garden doors, and went out themselves at privy doors to fetch the things that she had commanded them: but they saw not the elders, because they were hid.

Now when the maids were gone forth, the two elders rose up, and ran unto her, saying, "Behold, the garden doors are shut, that no man can see us, and we are in love with thee; therefore consent unto us, and lie with us. If thou wilt not, we will bear witness against thee, that a young man was with thee: and therefore thou didst send away thy maids from thee."

Then Susanna sighed, and said, "I am straitened on every side: for if I do this thing, it is death unto me: and if I do it not, I cannot escape your hands. It is better for me to fall into your hands, and not do it, than to sin in the sight of the Lord."

With that Susanna cried with a loud voice: and the two elders cried out against her. Then ran the one, and opened the garden door.

So when the servants of the house heard the cry in the garden, they rushed in at a privy door, to see what was done unto her. But when the elders had declared their matter, the servants were greatly ashamed: for there was never such a report made of Susanna.

And it came to pass the next day, when the people were assembled to her husband Joacim, the two elders came also full of mischievous imagination against Susanna to put her to death; and said before the people, "Send for Susanna, the daughter of Chelcias, Joacim's wife."

And so they sent. So she came with her father and mother,

SUSANNA AND THE ELDERS

her children, and all her kindred. Now Susanna was a very delicate woman, and beauteous to behold. And these wicked men commanded to uncover her face (for she was covered), that they might be filled with her beauty. Therefore her friends and all that saw her wept.

Then the two elders stood up in the midst of the people, and laid their hands upon her head. And she weeping looked up toward heaven: for her heart trusted in the Lord. And the elders said, "As we walked in the garden alone, this woman came in with two maids, and shut the garden doors, and sent the maids away. Then a young man, who there was hid, came unto her, and lay with her. Then we that stood in a corner of the garden, seeing this wickedness, ran unto them. And when we saw them together, the man we could not hold: for he was stronger than we, and opened the door, and leaped out. But having taken this woman, we asked who the young man was, but she would not tell us: these things do we testify."

Then the assembly believed them, as those that were the elders and judges of the people: so they condemned her to death.

Then Susanna cried out with a loud voice, and said, "O everlasting God, that knowest the secrets, and knowest all things before they be: thou knowest that they have borne false witness against me, and, behold, I must die; whereas I never did such things as these men have maliciously invented against me."

And the Lord heard her voice.

Therefore when she was led to be put to death, the Lord raised up the holy spirit of a young youth, whose name was Daniel: who cried with a loud voice, "I am clear from the blood of this woman."

Then all the people turned them toward him, and said, "What mean these words that thou hast spoken?"

So he standing in the midst of them said, "Are ye such fools, ye sons of Israel, that without examination or knowledge of the truth ye have condemned a daughter of Israel? Return again to

SUSANNA AND THE ELDERS

the place of judgment: for they have borne false witness against her."

Wherefore all the people turned again in haste, and the elders said unto him, "Come, sit down among us, and show it us, seeing God hath given thee the honour of an elder."

Then said Daniel unto them, "Put these two aside one far from another, and I will examine them."

So when they were put asunder one from another, he called one of them, and said unto him, "O thou that art waxed old in wickedness, now thy sins which thou hast committed aforetime are come to light: for thou hast pronounced false judgment, and hast condemned the innocent, and hast let the guilty go free; albeit the Lord saith, 'The innocent and righteous shalt thou not slay.' Now then, if thou hast seen her, tell me under what tree sawest thou them companying together?"

Who answered, "Under the mastic tree."

And Daniel said, "Very well; thou hast lied against thine own head; for even now the angel of God hath received the sentence of God to cut thee in two."

So he put him aside, and commanded to bring the other, and said unto him, "O thou seed of Chanaan, and not of Juda, beauty hath deceived thee, and lust hath perverted thine heart. Thus have ye dealt with the daughters of Israel, and they for fear companied with you: but the daughter of Juda would not abide your wickedness. Now therefore tell me under what tree didst thou take them companying together?"

Who answered, "Under a holm tree."

Then said Daniel unto him, "Well; thou hast also lied against thine own head: for the angel of God waiteth with the sword to cut thee in two, that he may destroy you."

With that all the assembly cried out with a loud voice, and praised God, who saveth them that trust in him. And they arose against the two elders, for Daniel had convicted them of false witness by their own mouth: and according to the law of Moses they did unto them in such sort as they maliciously intended to

SUSANNA AND THE ELDERS

do to their neighbour: and they put them to death. Thus the innocent blood was saved the same day.

Therefore Chelcias and his wife praised God for their daughter Susanna, with Joacim her husband, and all the kindred, because there was no dishonesty found in her.

TOBIT

A TALE

Tobit *is a delightful idyllic story of mingled realism and fantasy, in which conjugal quarrels, debts, dead men, a faithful dog, a maiden possessed by a demon, and the angel Raphael all function happily together. It has been placed as early as 350 B.C. and as late as A.D. 75. The reader is charmed by the simplicity of the style while the scholar finds an additional interest in the Persian and Egyptian influences which went into its making.*

TOBIT

THE BOOK OF THE WORDS OF TOBIT, SON OF TOBIEL, THE SON OF ANANIEL, THE SON OF ADUEL, THE SON OF GABAEL, OF THE SEED OF ASAEL, OF THE TRIBE OF NEPHTHALI; WHO IN THE TIME OF ENEMESSAR KING OF THE ASSYRIANS WAS LED CAPTIVE OUT OF THISBE, WHICH IS AT THE RIGHT HAND OF THAT CITY, WHICH IS CALLED PROPERLY NEPHTHALI IN GALILEE ABOVE ASER.

I TOBIT HAVE WALKED all the days of my life in the way of truth and justice, and I did many almsdeeds to my brethren, and my nation, who came with me to Nineveh, into the land of the Assyrians. And when I was in mine own country, in the land of Israel, being but young, all the tribe of Nephthali my father fell from the house of Jerusalem, which was chosen out of all the tribes of Israel, that all the tribes should sacrifice there, where the temple of the habitation of the most High was consecrated and built for all ages. Now all the tribes which together revolted, and the house of my father Nephthali, sacrificed unto the heifer Baal. But I alone went often to Jerusalem at the feasts, as it was ordained unto all the people of Israel by an everlasting decree, having the firstfruits and tenths of increase, with that which was first shorn, and them gave I at the altar to the priests, the children of Aaron. The first tenth part of all increase I gave to the sons of Aaron, who ministered at Jerusalem: another tenth part I sold away, and went, and spent it every year at Jerusalem: and the third I gave unto them to whom it was meet, as Debora my father's mother had commanded me, because I was left an orphan by my father. Furthermore, when I was come to the age of a man, I married Anna of mine own kindred, and of her I begot Tobias. And when we were carried away captives to Nineveh, all my brethren and those that were of my kindred did eat of

TOBIT

the bread of the Gentiles. But I kept myself from eating; because I remembered God with all my heart.

And the most High gave me grace and favour before Enemessar, so that I was his purveyor. And I went into Media, and left in trust with Gabael, the brother of Gabrias, at Rages a city of Media ten talents of silver. Now when Enemessar was dead, Sennacherib his son reigned in his stead; whose estate was troubled, that I could not go into Media. And in the time of Enemessar I gave many alms to my brethren, and gave my bread to the hungry, and my clothes to the naked: and if I saw any of my nation dead, or cast about the walls of Nineveh, I buried him. And if the king Sennacherib had slain any, when he was come, and fled from Judea, I buried them privily; for in his wrath he killed many; but the bodies were not found, when they were sought for of the king. And when one of the Ninevites went and complained of me to the king, that I buried them, and hid myself; understanding that I was sought for to be put to death, I withdrew myself for fear. Then all my goods were forcibly taken away, neither was there any thing left me, beside my wife Anna and my son Tobias. And there passed not five and fifty days, before two of his sons killed him, and they fled into the mountains of Ararath; and Sarchedonus his son reigned in his stead; who appointed over his father's accounts, and over all his affairs, Achiacharus my brother Anael's son. And Achiacharus intreating for me, I returned to Nineveh. Now Achiacharus was cupbearer, and keeper of the signet, and steward, and overseer of the accounts: and Sarchedonus appointed him next unto him: and he was my brother's son.

Now when I was come home again, and my wife Anna was restored unto me, with my son Tobias, in the feast of Pentecost, which is the holy feast of the seven weeks, there was a good dinner prepared me, in the which I sat down to eat. And when I saw abundance of meat, I said to my son, "Go and bring what poor man soever thou shalt find out of our brethren, who is mindful of the Lord; and, lo, I tarry for thee."

TOBIT

But he came again, and said, "Father, one of our nation is strangled, and is cast out in the marketplace."

Then before I had tasted of any meat, I started up, and took him up into a room until the going down of the sun. Then I returned, and washed myself, and ate my meat in heaviness, remembering that prophecy of Amos, as he said,

> "*Your feasts shall be turned into mourning,*
> *And all your mirth into lamentation.*"

Therefore I wept: and after the going down of the sun I went and made a grave, and buried him. But my neighbours mocked me, and said, "This man is not yet afraid to be put to death for this matter: who fled away; and yet, lo, he burieth the dead again."

The same night also I returned from the burial, and slept by the wall of my courtyard, being polluted, and my face was uncovered: and I knew not that there were sparrows in the wall, and mine eyes being open, the sparrows muted warm dung into mine eyes, and a whiteness came in mine eyes; and I went to the physicians, but they helped me not: moreover Achiacharus did nourish me, until I went into Elymais.

And my wife Anna did take women's works to do. And when she had sent them home to the owners, they paid her wages, and gave her also besides a kid. And when it was in my house, and began to cry, I said unto her, "From whence is this kid? is it not stolen? render it to the owners; for it is not lawful to eat any thing that is stolen."

But she replied upon me, "It was given for a gift more than the wages."

Howbeit I did not believe her, but bade her render it to the owners: and I was abashed at her. But she replied upon me, "Where are thine alms and thy righteous deeds? behold, thou and all thy works are known."

Then I being grieved did weep, and in my sorrow prayed, saying, "O Lord, thou art just, and all thy works and all thy ways are mercy and truth, and thou judgest truly and justly for

TOBIT

ever. Remember me, and look on me, punish me not for my sins and ignorances, and the sins of my fathers, who have sinned before thee: for they obeyed not thy commandments: wherefore thou hast delivered us for a spoil, and unto captivity, and unto death, and for a proverb of reproach to all the nations among whom we are dispersed. And now thy judgments are many and true: deal with me according to my sins and my fathers': because we have not kept thy commandments, neither have walked in truth before thee. Now therefore deal with me as seemeth best unto thee, and command my spirit to be taken from me, that I may be dissolved, and become earth: for it is profitable for me to die rather than to live, because I have heard false reproaches, and have much sorrow: command therefore that I may now be delivered out of this distress, and go into the everlasting place: turn not thy face away from me."

It came to pass the same day, that in Ecbatana, a city of Media, Sara the daughter of Raguel was also reproached by her father's maids; because that she had been married to seven husbands, whom Asmodeus the evil spirit had killed, before they had lain with her.

"Dost thou not know," said they, "that thou hast strangled thine husbands? thou hast had already seven husbands, neither wast thou named after any of them. Wherefore dost thou beat us for them? if they be dead, go thy ways after them, let us never see of thee either son or daughter."

When she heard these things, she was very sorrowful, so that she thought to have strangled herself; and she said, "I am the only daughter of my father, and if I do this, it shall be a reproach unto him, and I shall bring his old age with sorrow unto the grave."

Then she prayed toward the window, and said, "Blessed art thou, O Lord my God, and thine holy and glorious name is blessed and honourable for ever: let all thy works praise thee for ever. And now, O Lord, I set mine eyes and my face toward thee, and say, 'Take me out of the earth, that I may hear no more

TOBIT

the reproach. Thou knowest, Lord, that I am pure from all sin with man, and that I never polluted my name, nor the name of my father, in the land of my captivity: I am the only daughter of my father, neither had he any child to be his heir, neither any near kinsman, nor any son of his alive, to whom I may keep myself for a wife: my seven husbands are already dead; and why should I live? but if it please not thee that I should die, command some regard to be had of me, and pity taken of me, that I hear no more reproach.'"

So the prayers of them both were heard before the majesty of the great God. And Raphael was sent to heal them both, that is, to scale away the whiteness of Tobit's eyes, and to give Sara the daughter of Raguel for a wife to Tobias the son of Tobit; and to bind Asmodeus the evil spirit; because she belonged to Tobias by right of inheritance. The selfsame time came Tobit home, and entered into his house, and Sara the daughter of Raguel came down from her upper chamber.

In that day Tobit remembered the money which he had committed to Gabael in Rages of Media, and said with himself, "I have wished for death; wherefore do I not call for my son Tobias, that I may signify to him of the money before I die?" And when he had called him, he said,

My son, when I am dead, bury me; and despise not thy mother, but honour her all the days of thy life, and do that which shall please her, and grieve her not. Remember, my son, that she saw many dangers for thee, when thou wast in her womb; and when she is dead, bury her by me in one grave. My son, be mindful of the Lord our God all thy days, and let not thy will be set to sin, or to transgress his commandments: do uprightly all thy life long, and follow not the ways of unrighteousness. For if thou deal truly, thy doings shall prosperously succeed to thee, and to all them that live justly.

"Give alms of thy substance; and when thou givest alms, let

TOBIT

not thine eye be envious, neither turn thy face from any poor, and the face of God shall not be turned away from thee. If thou hast abundance, give alms accordingly: if thou have but a little, be not afraid to give according to that little: for thou layest up a good treasure for thyself against the day of necessity. Because that alms do deliver from death, and suffereth not to come into darkness. For alms is a good gift unto all that give it in the sight of the most High.

"Beware of all whoredom, my son, and chiefly take a wife of the seed of thy fathers, and take not a strange woman to wife, which is not of thy father's tribe: for we are the children of the prophets, Noe, Abraham, Isaac, and Jacob: remember, my son, that our fathers from the beginning, even that they all married wives of their own kindred, and were blessed in their children, and their seed shall inherit the land. Now therefore, my son, love thy brethren, and despise not in thy heart thy brethren, the sons and daughters of thy people, in not taking a wife of them: for in pride is destruction and much trouble, and in lewdness is decay and great want: for lewdness is the mother of famine.

"Let not the wages of any man, which hath wrought for thee, tarry with thee, but give him it out of hand: for if thou serve God, he will also repay thee. Be circumspect, my son, in all things thou doest, and be wise in all thy conversation. Do that to no man which thou hatest. Drink not wine to make thee drunken: neither let drunkenness go with thee in thy journey. Give of thy bread to the hungry, and of thy garments to them that are naked; and according to thine abundance give alms, and let not thine eye be envious, when thou givest alms. Pour out thy bread on the burial of the just, but give nothing to the wicked. Ask counsel of all that are wise, and despise not any counsel that is profitable.

"Bless the Lord thy God alway, and desire of him that thy ways may be directed, and that all thy paths and counsels may prosper: for every nation hath not counsel; but the Lord himself

TOBIT

giveth all good things, and he humbleth whom he will, as he will; now therefore, my son, remember my commandments, neither let them be put out of thy mind.

"And now I signify this to thee, that I committed ten talents to Gabael the son of Gabrias at Rages in Media. And fear not, my son, that we are made poor: for thou hast much wealth, if thou fear God, and depart from all sin, and do that which is pleasing in his sight."

Tobias then answered and said, "Father, I will do all things which thou hast commanded me: but how can I receive the money, seeing I know him not?"

Then he gave him the handwriting, and said unto him, "Seek thee a man which may go with thee, while I yet live, and I will give him wages: and go and receive the money."

Therefore when he went to seek a man, he found Raphael that was an angel. But he knew not; and he said unto him, "Canst thou go with me to Rages? and knowest thou those places well?"

To whom the angel said, "I will go with thee, and I know the way well: for I have lodged with our brother Gabael."

Then Tobias said unto him, "Tarry for me, till I tell my father."

Then he said unto him, "Go, and tarry not."

So he went in and said to his father, "Behold, I have found one which will go with me."

Then he said, "Call him unto me, that I may know of what tribe he is, and whether he be a trusty man to go with thee."

So he called him, and he came in, and they saluted one another. Then Tobit said unto him, "Brother, show me of what tribe and family thou art."

To whom he said, "Dost thou seek for a tribe or family, or a hired man to go with thy son?"

Then Tobit said unto him, "I would know, brother, thy kindred and name."

Then he said, "I am Azarias, the son of Ananias the great, and of thy brethren."

Then Tobit said, "Thou art welcome, brother; be not now

angry with me, because I have enquired to know thy tribe and thy family; for thou art my brother, of an honest and good stock: for I know Ananias and Jonathas, sons of that great Samaias, as we went together to Jerusalem to worship, and offered the firstborn, and the tenths of the fruits; and they were not seduced with the error of our brethren: my brother, thou art of a good stock. But tell me, what wages shall I give thee? wilt thou a drachm a day, and things necessary, as to mine own son? Yea, moreover, if ye return safe, I will add something to thy wages."

So they were well pleased. Then said he to Tobias, "Prepare thyself for the journey, and God send you a good journey."

And when his son had prepared all things for the journey, his father said, "Go thou with this man, and God, which dwelleth in heaven, prosper your journey, and the angel of God keep you company." So they went forth both, and the young man's dog with them.

But Anna his mother wept, and said to Tobit, "Why hast thou sent away our son? is he not the staff of our hand, in going in and out before us? Be not greedy to add money to money: but let it be as refuse in respect of our child. For that which the Lord hath given us to live with doth suffice us."

Then said Tobit to her, "Take no care, my sister; he shall return in safety, and thine eyes shall see him. For the good angel will keep him company, and his journey shall be prosperous, and he shall return safe."

Then she made an end of weeping.

And as they went on their journey, they came in the evening to the river Tigris, and they lodged there. And when the young man went down to wash himself, a fish leaped out of the river, and would have devoured him.

Then the angel said unto him, "Take the fish." And the young man laid hold of the fish, and drew it to land.

To whom the angel said, "Open the fish, and take the heart and the liver and the gall, and put them up safely."

So the young man did as the angel commanded him; and when

TOBIT

they had roasted the fish, they did eat it: then they both went on their way, till they drew near to Ecbatana. Then the young man said to the angel, "Brother Azarias, to what use is the heart and the liver and the gall of the fish?"

And he said unto him, "Touching the heart and the liver, if a devil or an evil spirit trouble any, we must make a smoke thereof before the man or the woman, and the party shall be no more vexed. As for the gall, it is good to anoint a man that hath whiteness in his eyes, and he shall be healed."

And when they were come near to Rages, the angel said to the young man, "Brother, to-day we shall lodge with Raguel, who is thy cousin; he also hath one only daughter, named Sara; I will speak for her, that she may be given thee for a wife. For to thee doth the right of her appertain, seeing thou only art of her kindred. And the maid is fair and wise: now therefore hear me, and I will speak to her father; and when we return from Rages we will celebrate the marriage: for I know that Raguel cannot marry her to another according to the law of Moses, but he shall be guilty of death, because the right of inheritance doth rather appertain to thee than to any other."

Then the young man answered the angel, "I have heard, brother Azarias, that this maid hath been given to seven men, who all died in the marriage chamber. And now I am the only son of my father, and I am afraid, lest, if I go in unto her, I die, as the other before: for a wicked spirit loveth her, which hurteth no body, but those which come unto her: wherefore I also fear lest I die, and bring my father's and my mother's life because of me to the grave with sorrow: for they have no other son to bury them."

Then the angel said unto him, "Dost thou not remember the precepts which thy father gave thee, that thou shouldest marry a wife of thine own kindred? wherefore hear me, O my brother; for she shall be given thee to wife; and make thou no reckoning of the evil spirit; for this same night shall she be given thee in marriage. And when thou shalt come into the marriage chamber, thou shalt take the ashes of perfume, and shalt lay upon

TOBIT

them some of the heart and liver of the fish, and shalt make a smoke with it: and the devil shall smell it, and flee away, and never come again any more: but when thou shalt come to her, rise up both of you, and pray to God which is merciful, who will have pity on you, and save you: fear not, for she is appointed unto thee from the beginning; and thou shalt preserve her, and she shall go with thee. Moreover I suppose that she shall bear thee children."

Now when Tobias had heard these things, he loved her, and his heart was effectually joined to her.

And when they were come to Ecbatana, they came to the house of Raguel, and Sara met them: and after they had saluted one another, she brought them into the house. Then said Raguel to Edna his wife, "How like is this young man to Tobit my cousin!" And Raguel asked them, "From whence are ye, brethren?" To whom they said, "We are of the sons of Nephthalim, which are captives in Nineveh." Then he said to them, "Do ye know Tobit our kinsman?" And they said, "We know him." Then said he, "Is he in good health?" And they said, "He is both alive, and in good health": and Tobias said, "He is my father."

Then Raguel leaped up, and kissed him, and wept, and blessed him, and said unto him, "Thou art the son of an honest and good man." But when he had heard that Tobit was blind, he was sorrowful, and wept. And likewise Edna his wife and Sara his daughter wept. Moreover they entertained them cheerfully; and after that they had killed a ram of the flock, they set store of meat on the table.

Then said Tobias to Raphael, "Brother Azarias, speak of those things of which thou didst talk in the way, and let this business be dispatched."

So he communicated the matter with Raguel: and Raguel said to Tobias, "Eat and drink, and make merry: for it is meet that thou shouldest marry my daughter: nevertheless I will declare unto thee the truth. I have given my daughter in marriage

TOBIT

to seven men, who died that night they came in unto her: nevertheless for the present be merry."

But Tobias said, "I will eat nothing here, till we agree and swear one to another."

Raguel said, "Then take her from henceforth according to the manner, for thou art her cousin, and she is thine, and the merciful God give you good success in all things."

Then he called his daughter Sara, and she came to her father, and he took her by the hand, and gave her to be wife to Tobias, saying, "Behold, take her after the law of Moses, and lead her away to thy father." And he blessed them; and called Edna his wife, and took paper, and did write an instrument of covenants, and sealed it. Then they began to eat.

After Raguel called his wife Edna, and said unto her, "Sister, prepare another chamber, and bring her in thither." Which when she had done as he had bidden her, she brought her thither: and she wept, and she received the tears of her daughter, and said unto her, "Be of good comfort, my daughter; the Lord of heaven and earth give thee joy for this thy sorrow: be of good comfort, my daughter."

And when they had supped, they brought Tobias in unto her. And as he went, he remembered the words of Raphael, and took the ashes of the perfumes, and put the heart and the liver of the fish thereupon, and made a smoke therewith. The which smell when the evil spirit had smelled, he fled into the utmost parts of Egypt, and the angel bound him.

And after that they were both shut in together, Tobias rose out of the bed, and said, "Sister, arise, and let us pray that God would have pity on us."

Then began Tobias to say, "Blessed art thou, O God of our fathers, and blessed is thy holy and glorious name for ever; let the heavens bless thee, and all thy creatures. Thou madest Adam, and gavest him Eve his wife for a helper and stay: of them came mankind: thou hast said, 'It is not good that man should be alone; let us make unto him an aid like unto himself.' And now, O Lord,

TOBIT

I take not this my sister for lust, but uprightly: therefore mercifully ordain that we may become aged together." And she said with him, "Amen." So they slept both that night.

And Raguel arose, and went and made a grave, saying, "I fear lest he also be dead." But when Raguel was come into his house, he said unto his wife Edna, "Send one of the maids, and let her see whether he be alive: if he be not, that we may bury him, and no man know it."

So the maid opened the door, and went in, and found them both asleep, and came forth, and told them that he was alive.

Then Raguel praised God, and said, "O God, thou art worthy to be praised with all pure and holy praise; therefore let thy saints praise thee with all thy creatures; and let all thine angels and thine elect praise thee for ever. Thou art to be praised, for thou hast made me joyful; and that is not come to me which I suspected; but thou hast dealt with us according to thy great mercy. Thou art to be praised, because thou hast had mercy of two that were the only begotten children of their fathers: grant them mercy, O Lord, and finish their life in health with joy and mercy."

Then Raguel bade his servants to fill the grave. And he kept the wedding feast fourteen days. For before the days of the marriage were finished, Raguel had said unto him by an oath, that he should not depart till the fourteen days of the marriage were expired; and then he should take the half of his goods, and go in safety to his father; and should have the rest when I and my wife be dead.

Then Tobias called Raphael, and said unto him, "Brother Azarias, take with thee a servant, and two camels, and go to Rages of Media to Gabael, and bring me the money, and bring him to the wedding. For Raguel hath sworn that I shall not depart. But my father counteth the days; and if I tarry long, he will be very sorry."

So Raphael went out, and lodged with Gabael, and gave him the handwriting: who brought forth bags which were sealed up, and gave them to him. And early in the morning they went

TOBIT

forth both together, and came to the wedding: and Tobias blessed his wife.

Now Tobit his father counted every day: and when the days of the journey were expired, and they came not, then Tobit said, "Are they detained? or is Gabael dead, and there is no man to give him the money?" Therefore he was very sorry.

Then his wife said unto him, "My son is dead, seeing he stayeth long"; and she began to bewail him, and said, "Now I care for nothing, my son, since I have let thee go, the light of mine eyes."

To whom Tobit said, "Hold thy peace, take no care, for he is safe."

But she said, "Hold thy peace, and deceive me not; my son is dead." And she went out every day into the way which they went, and did eat no meat on the daytime, and ceased not whole nights to bewail her son Tobias, until the fourteen days of the wedding were expired, which Raguel had sworn that he should spend there.

Then Tobias said to Raguel, "Let me go, for my father and my mother look no more to see me."

But his father-in-law said unto him, "Tarry with me, and I will send to thy father, and they shall declare unto him how things go with thee."

But Tobias said, "No; but let me go to my father."

Then Raguel arose, and gave him Sara his wife, and half his goods, servants, and cattle, and money. And he blessed them, and sent them away, saying, "The God of heaven give you a prosperous journey, my children." And he said to his daughter, "Honour thy father and thy mother-in-law, which are now thy parents, that I may hear good report of thee." And he kissed her. Edna also said to Tobias, "The Lord of heaven restore thee, my dear brother, and grant that I may see thy children of my daughter Sara before I die, that I may rejoice before the Lord: behold,

TOBIT

I commit my daughter unto thee of special trust; wherefore do not entreat her evil."

After these things Tobias went his way, praising God that he had given him a prosperous journey, and blessed Raguel and Edna his wife, and went on his way till they drew near unto Nineveh.

Then Raphael said to Tobias, "Thou knowest, brother, how thou didst leave thy father: let us haste before thy wife, and prepare the house. And take in thine hand the gall of the fish." So they went their way, and the dog went after them.

Now Anna sat looking about toward the way for her son. And when she espied him coming, she said to his father, "Behold, thy son cometh, and the man that went with him."

Then said Raphael, "I know, Tobias, that thy father will open his eyes. Therefore anoint thou his eyes with the gall, and being pricked therewith, he shall rub, and the whiteness shall fall away, and he shall see thee."

Then Anna ran forth, and fell upon the neck of her son, and said unto him, "Seeing I have seen thee, my son, from henceforth I am content to die." And they wept both.

Tobit also went forth toward the door, and stumbled: but his son ran unto him, and took hold of his father: and he stroked of the gall on his father's eyes, saying, "Be of good hope, my father."

And when his eyes began to smart, he rubbed them; and the whiteness peeled away from the corners of his eyes: and when he saw his son, he fell upon his neck. And he wept, and said, "Blessed art thou, O God, and blessed is thy name for ever; and blessed are all thine holy angels: for thou hast scourged, and hast taken pity on me: for, behold, I see my son Tobias." And his son went in rejoicing, and told his father the great things that had happened to him in Media.

Then Tobit went out to meet his daughter-in-law at the gate of Nineveh, rejoicing, and praising God: and they which saw him go marvelled, because he had received his sight. But Tobit gave thanks before them, because God had mercy on him. And

TOBIT

when he came near to Sara his daughter-in-law, he blessed her, saying, "Thou art welcome, daughter: God be blessed, which hath brought thee unto us, and blessed be thy father and thy mother." And there was joy among all his brethren which were at Nineveh. And Achiacharus and Nasbas his brother's son, came: and Tobias's wedding was kept seven days with great joy.

Then Tobit called his son Tobias, and said unto him, "My son, see that the man have his wages, which went with thee, and thou must give him more."

And Tobias said unto him, "O father, it is no harm to me to give him half of those things which I have brought: for he hath brought me again to thee in safety, and made whole my wife, and brought me the money, and likewise healed thee."

Then the old man said, "It is due unto him."

So he called the angel, and he said unto him, "Take half of all that ye have brought, and go away in safety."

Then he took them both apart, and said unto them, "Bless God, praise him, and magnify him, and praise him for the things which he hath done unto you in the sight of all that live. It is good to praise God, and exalt his name, and honourably to show forth the works of God; therefore be not slack to praise him. It is good to keep close the secret of a king, but it is honourable to reveal the works of God. Do that which is good, and no evil shall touch you. Prayer is good with fasting and alms and righteousness. A little with righteousness is better than much with unrighteousness. It is better to give alms than to lay up gold: for alms doth deliver from death, and shall purge away all sin. Those that exercise alms and righteousness shall be filled with life: but they that sin are enemies to their own life. Surely I will keep close nothing from you. For I said, 'It was good to keep close the secret of a king, but that it was honourable to reveal the works of God.'

"Now therefore, when thou didst pray, and Sara thy daughter-in-law, I did bring the remembrance of your prayers before the Holy One: and when thou didst bury the dead, I was with thee likewise. And when thou didst not delay to rise up, and

TOBIT

leave thy dinner, to go and cover the dead, thy good deed was not hid from me: but I was with thee. And now God hath sent me to heal thee and Sara thy daughter-in-law. I am Raphael, one of the seven holy angels, which present the prayers of the saints, and which go in and out before the glory of the Holy One."

Then they were both troubled, and fell upon their faces: for they feared. But he said unto them, "Fear not, for it shall go well with you; praise God therefore. For not of any favour of mine, but by the will of our God I came; wherefore praise him for ever. All these days I did appear unto you; but I did neither eat nor drink, but ye did see a vision. Now therefore give God thanks: for I go up to him that sent me; but write all things which are done in a book."

And when they arose, they saw him no more. Then they confessed the great and wonderful works of God, and how the angel of the Lord had appeared unto them.

THE WISDOM OF JESUS, THE SON OF SIRACH; OR, ECCLESIASTICUS

The book of ecclesiasticus *is really the crown of Hebrew "Wisdom Literature" and by all the rules of reason should have been included in the Canon, even its second-century date being early enough to have permitted it. But it lacked the prestige of a great name, which saved Daniel, Ecclesiastes, and the Song of Songs, and this one defect was fatal to its claims.*

THE WISDOM OF JESUS, THE SON OF SIRACH; OR, ECCLESIASTICUS

A Prologue Made by an Uncertain Author

THIS JESUS was the son of Sirach, and grandchild to Jesus of the same name with him: this man therefore lived in the latter times, after the people had been led away captive, and called home again, and almost after all the prophets. Now his grandfather Jesus, as he himself witnesseth, was a man of great diligence and wisdom among the Hebrews, who did not only gather the grave and short sentences of wise men, that had been before him, but himself also uttered some of his own, full of much understanding and wisdom. When as therefore the first Jesus died, leaving this book almost perfected, Sirach his son receiving it after him left it to his own son Jesus, who, having gotten it into his hands, compiled it all orderly into one volume, and called it Wisdom, entitling it both by his own name, his father's name, and his grandfather's; alluring the hearer by the very name of Wisdom to have a greater love to the study of this book. It containeth therefore wise sayings, dark sentences, and parables, and certain particular ancient godly stories of men that pleased God; also his prayer and song; moreover, what benefits God had vouchsafed his people, and what plagues he had heaped upon their enemies. This Jesus did imitate Solomon, and was no less famous for wisdom and learning, both being indeed a man of great learning, and so reputed also.

"All Wisdom Cometh from the Lord"

All wisdom cometh from the Lord,
And is with him for ever.

ECCLESIASTICUS

Who can number the sand of the sea,
And the drops of rain,
And the days of eternity?
Who can find out the height of heaven,
And the breadth of the earth,
And the deep, and wisdom?
Wisdom hath been created before all things,
And the understanding of prudence from everlasting.
The word of God most high is the fountain of wisdom;
And her ways are everlasting commandments.

To whom hath the root of wisdom been revealed?
Or who hath known her wise counsels?
(Unto whom hath the knowledge of wisdom been made manifest?
And who hath understood her great experience?)

There is one wise and greatly to be feared,
The Lord sitting upon his throne.
He created her, and saw her, and numbered her,
And poured her out upon all his works.
She is with all flesh according to his gift,
And he hath given her to them that love him.

The fear of the Lord
Is honour, and glory, and gladness,
And a crown of rejoicing.
The fear of the Lord
Maketh a merry heart,
And giveth joy, and gladness, and a long life.
Whoso feareth the Lord,
It shall go well with him at the last,
And he shall find favour in the day of his death.
To fear the Lord
Is the beginning of wisdom:
And it was created with the faithful in the womb.
She hath built an everlasting foundation with men,
And she shall continue with their seed.

ECCLESIASTICUS

To fear the Lord
Is fulness of wisdom,
And filleth men with her fruits.
She filleth all their house with things desirable,
And the garners with her increase.
The fear of the Lord is a crown of wisdom,
Making peace and perfect health to flourish;
Both which are the gifts of God:
And it enlargeth their rejoicing that love him.
Wisdom raineth down skill and knowledge of understanding,
And exalteth them to honour that hold her fast.
The root of wisdom is to fear the Lord,
And the branches thereof are long life.

"Honour a Physician"

Honour a physician with the honour due unto him for the uses
    which ye may have of him:
For the Lord hath created him.
For of the most High cometh healing,
And he shall receive honour of the king.
The skill of the physician shall lift up his head:
And in the sight of great men he shall be in admiration.
The Lord hath created medicines out of the earth;
And he that is wise will not abhor them.
Was not the water made sweet with wood,
That the virtue thereof might be known?
And he hath given men skill,
That he might be honoured in his marvellous works.
With such doth he heal (men),
And taketh away their pains.
Of such doth the apothecary make a confection;
And of his works there is no end;
And from him is peace over all the earth.
My son, in thy sickness be not negligent:
But pray unto the Lord, and he will make thee whole.
Leave off from sin, and order thine hands aright,

ECCLESIASTICUS

And cleanse thy heart from all wickedness.
Give a sweet savour, and a memorial of fine flour;
And make a fat offering, as not being.
Then give place to the physician,
For the Lord hath created him:
Let him not go from thee,
For thou hast need of him.
There is a time when in their hands there is good success.
For they shall also pray unto the Lord, that he would prosper that,
Which they give for ease and remedy to prolong life.
He that sinneth before his Maker,
Let him fall into the hand of the physician.

"The Pride of the Height"

The pride of the height,
The clear firmament,
The beauty of heaven, with his glorious show;

The sun when it appeareth,
Declaring at his rising a marvellous instrument,
The work of the most High:
At noon it parcheth the country,
And who can abide the burning heat thereof?
A man blowing a furnace is in works of heat,
But the sun burneth the mountains three times more;
Breathing out fiery vapours,
And sending forth bright beams,
It dimmeth the eyes.
Great is the Lord that made it;
And at his commandment it runneth hastily.

He made the moon also to serve in her season
For a declaration of times, and a sign of the world.
From the moon is the sign of feasts,
A light decreaseth in her perfection.
The month is called after her name,
Increasing wonderfully in her changing,

ECCLESIASTICUS

Being an instrument of the armies above,
Shining in the firmament of heaven;

The beauty of heaven, the glory of the stars,
An ornament giving light in the highest places of the Lord.
At the commandment of the Holy One they will stand in their order,
And never faint in their watches.

Look upon the rainbow, and praise him that made it;
Very beautiful it is in the brightness thereof.
It compasseth the heaven about with a glorious circle,
And the hands of the most High have bended it.

By his commandment he maketh the snow to fall apace,
And sendeth swiftly the lightnings of his judgment.
Through this the treasures are opened:
And clouds fly forth as fowls.
By his great power he maketh the clouds firm,
And the hailstones are broken small.
At his sight the mountains are shaken,
And at his will the south wind bloweth.
The noise of the thunder maketh the earth to tremble:
So doth the northern storm and the whirlwind:
As birds flying he scattereth the snow,
And the falling down thereof is as the lighting of grasshoppers.
The eye marvelleth at the beauty of the whiteness thereof,
And the heart is astonished at the raining of it.
The hoarfrost also as salt he poureth on the earth,
And being congealed, it lieth on the top of sharp stakes.
When the cold north wind bloweth,
And the water is congealed into ice,
It abideth upon every gathering together of water,
And clotheth the water as with a breastplate.
It devoureth the mountains,
And burneth the wilderness,
And consumeth the grass as fire.
A present remedy of all is a mist coming speedily:
A dew coming after heat refresheth.

ECCLESIASTICUS

By his counsel he appeaseth the deep,
And planteth islands therein.
They that sail on the sea tell of the danger thereof;
And when we hear it with our ears, we marvel thereat.
For therein be strange and wondrous works,
Variety of all kinds of beasts and whales created.
By him the end of them hath prosperous success,
And by his word all things consist.

We may speak much, and yet come short:
Wherefore in sum, he is all.
How shall we be able to magnify him?
For he is great above all his works.
The Lord is terrible and very great,
And marvellous is his power.
When ye glorify the Lord, exalt him as much as ye can;
For even yet will he far exceed:
And when ye exalt him, put forth all your strength, and be not weary;
For ye can never go far enough.
Who hath seen him, that he might tell us?
And who can magnify him as he is?
There are yet hid greater things than these be,
For we have seen but a few of his works.
For the Lord hath made all things;
And to the godly hath he given wisdom.

"Let Us Now Praise Famous Men"

Let us now praise famous men,
And our fathers that begot us.
The Lord hath wrought great glory by them
Through his great power from the beginning.
Such as did bear rule in their kingdoms,
Men renowned for their power,
Giving counsel by their understanding,
And declaring prophecies:
Leaders of the people by their counsels,

ECCLESIASTICUS

And by their knowledge of learning meet for the people,
Wise and eloquent in their instructions:
Such as found out musical tunes,
And recited verses in writing:
Rich men furnished with ability,
Living peaceably in their habitations:
All these were honoured in their generations,
And were the glory of their times.
There be of them, that have left a name behind them,
That their praises might be reported.
And some there be, which have no memorial;
Who are perished, as though they had never been;
And are become as though they had never been born;
And their children after them.
But these were merciful men,
Whose righteousness hath not been forgotten.
With their seed shall continually remain a good inheritance,
And their children are within the covenant.
Their seed standeth fast,
And their children for their sakes.
Their seed shall remain for ever,
And their glory shall not be blotted out.
Their bodies are buried in peace;
But their name liveth for evermore.
The people will tell of their wisdom,
And the congregation will show forth their praise.

Enoch pleased the Lord, and was translated,
Being an example of repentance to all generations.
Noah was found perfect and righteous;
In the time of wrath he was taken in exchange (for the world);
Therefore was he left as a remnant unto the earth, when the flood
    came.
An everlasting covenant was made with him,
That all flesh should perish no more by the flood.
Abraham was a great father of many people:

ECCLESIASTICUS

In glory was there none like unto him;
Who kept the law of the most High, and was in covenant with him.
He established the covenant in his flesh;
And when he was proved, he was found faithful.
Therefore he assured him by an oath,
That he would bless the nations in his seed,
And that he would multiply him as the dust of the earth,
And exalt his seed as the stars,
And cause them to inherit from sea to sea,
And from the river unto the utmost part of the land.

And he brought out of him a merciful man,
Which found favour in the sight of all flesh,
Even Moses, beloved of God and men,
Whose memorial is blessed.
He made him like to the glorious saints,
And magnified him, so that his enemies stood in fear of him.
By his words he caused the wonders to cease,
And he made him glorious in the sight of kings,
And gave him a commandment for his people,
And showed him part of his glory.

He exalted Aaron, a holy man like unto him,
Even his brother, of the tribe of Levi.
An everlasting covenant he made with him,
And gave him the priesthood among the people;
He beautified him with comely ornaments,
And clothed him with a robe of glory.
He put upon him perfect glory;
And strengthened him with rich garments,
With breeches, with a long robe, and the ephod.
And he compassed him with pomegranates,
And with many golden bells round about,
That as he went there might be a sound,
And a noise made that might be heard in the temple,
For a memorial to the children of his people;
With a holy garment,

ECCLESIASTICUS

With gold, and blue silk, and purple,
The work of the embroiderer,
With a breastplate of judgment,
And with Urim and Thummim;
With twisted scarlet, the work of the cunning workman,
With precious stones graven like seals,
And set in gold, the work of the jeweller,
With a writing engraved for a memorial,
After the number of the tribes of Israel.
He set a crown of gold upon the mitre,
Wherein was engraved Holiness, an ornament of honour,
A costly work, the desires of the eyes, goodly and beautiful.
Before him there were none such,
Neither did ever any stranger put them on,
But only his children and his children's children perpetually.

As is the fat taken away from the peace offering,
So was David chosen out of the children of Israel.
He played with lions as with kids,
And with bears as with lambs.
Slew he not a giant, when he was yet but young?
And did he not take away reproach from the people,
When he lifted up his hand with the stone in the sling,
And beat down the boasting of Goliath?

Solomon reigned in a peaceable time, and was honoured;
For God made all quiet round about him,
That he might build a house in his name,
And prepare his sanctuary for ever.
How wise wast thou in thy youth,
And, as a flood, filled with understanding!
Thy soul covered the whole earth,
And thou filledst it with dark parables.
Thy name went far unto the islands;
And for thy peace thou wast beloved.
Ezekias fortified his city,
And brought in water into the midst thereof:

ECCLESIASTICUS

He digged the hard rock with iron,
And made wells for waters.
In his time Sennacherib came up,
And sent Rabsaces, and lifted up his hand against Zion,
And boasted proudly.
Then trembled their hearts and hands,
And they were in pain, as women in travail.
But they called upon the Lord which is merciful,
And stretched out their hands toward him:
And immediately the Holy One heard them out of heaven,
And delivered them by the ministry of Esay.
He smote the host of the Assyrians,
And his angel destroyed them.
For Ezekias had done the thing that pleased the Lord,
And was strong in the ways of David his father.

The remembrance of Josias
Is like the composition of the perfume that is made by the art of the
    apothecary:
It is sweet as honey in all mouths,
And as music at a banquet of wine.
He behaved himself uprightly in the conversion of the people,
And took away the abominations of iniquity.
He directed his heart unto the Lord,
And in the time of the ungodly he established the worship of God.

All, except David and Ezekias and Josias, were defective:
For they forsook the law of the most High,
Even the kings of Juda failed.
Therefore he gave their power unto others,
And their glory to a strange nation.
They burnt the chosen city of the sanctuary,
And made the streets desolate, according to the prophecy of Jeremias.

How shall we magnify Zorobabel?
Even he was as a signet on the right hand:
So was Jesus the son of Josedec:

ECCLESIASTICUS

Who in their time builded the house,
And set up a holy temple to the Lord,
Which was prepared for everlasting glory.
And among the elect was Neemias,
Whose renown is great,
Who raised up for us the walls that were fallen,
And set up the gates and the bars,
And raised up our ruins again.

But upon the earth was no man created like Enoch;
For he was taken from the earth.
Neither was there a man born like unto Joseph,
A governor of his brethren, a stay of the people,
Whose bones were regarded of the Lord.
Sem and Seth were in great honour among men,
And so was Adam above every living thing in the creation.

"Simon, the High Priest"

Simon the high priest, the son of Onias,
Who in his life repaired the house again,
And in his days fortified the temple:
And by him was built from the foundation the double height,
The high fortress of the wall about the temple:
In his days the cistern to receive water,
Being in compass as the sea,
Was covered with plates of brass:
He took care of the temple that it should not fall,
And fortified the city against besieging:
How was he honoured in the midst of the people
In his coming out of the sanctuary!

He was as the morning star in the midst of a cloud,
And as the moon at the full:
As the sun shining upon the temple of the most High,
And as the rainbow giving light in the bright clouds:
And as the flower of roses in the spring of the year,
As lilies by the rivers of waters,

ECCLESIASTICUS

And as the branches of the frankincense tree in the time of summer:
As fire and incense in the censer,
And as a vessel of beaten gold set with all manner of precious stones:
And as a fair olive tree budding forth fruit,
And as a cypress tree which groweth up to the clouds.

When he put on the robe of honour,
And was clothed with the perfection of glory,
When he went up to the holy altar,
He made the garment of holiness honourable.
When he took the portions out of the priests' hands,
He himself stood by the hearth of the altar,
Compassed with his brethren round about, as a young cedar in Libanus;
And as palm trees compassed they him round about.
So were all the sons of Aaron in their glory,
And the oblations of the Lord in their hands,
Before all the congregation of Israel.
And finishing the service at the altar,
That he might adorn the offering of the most high Almighty,
He stretched out his hand to the cup,
And poured of the blood of the grape,
He poured out at the foot of the altar
A sweetsmelling savour unto the most high King of all.
Then shouted the sons of Aaron,
And sounded the silver trumpets,
And made a great noise to be heard,
For a remembrance before the most High.

Then all the people together hastened,
And fell down to the earth upon their faces
To worship their Lord God Almighty, the most High.
The singers also sang praises with their voices,
With great variety of sounds was there made sweet melody.
And the people besought the Lord, the most High,
By prayer before him that is merciful,
Till the solemnity of the Lord was ended,
And they had finished his service.

ECCLESIASTICUS

Then he went down, and lifted up his hands over the whole congregation
    of the children of Israel,
To give the blessing of the Lord with his lips,
And to rejoice in his name.
And they bowed themselves down to worship the second time,
That they might receive a blessing from the most High.

Now therefore bless ye the God of all,
Which only doeth wondrous things every where,
Which exalteth our days from the womb,
And dealeth with us according to his mercy.

THE WISDOM OF SOLOMON

THE WISDOM OF SOLOMON *was produced about 50 B.C. in Alexandria. Jewish and Greek ideas are intermingled in it, and some of them come rather close to Christian thought. Thus, while well worthy of inclusion for its own sake, it also forms a convenient transition to the New Testament.* +

The Wisdom of SOLOMON

The Immortality of the Righteous

THE SOULS OF THE RIGHTEOUS are in the hand of God, and there shall no torment touch them. In the sight of the unwise they seemed to die: and their departure is taken for misery, and their going from us to be utter destruction: but they are in peace. For though they be punished in the sight of men, yet is their hope full of immortality. And having been a little chastised, they shall be greatly rewarded: for God proved them, and found them worthy for himself. As gold in the furnace hath he tried them, and received them as a burnt offering. And in the time of their visitation they shall shine, and run to and fro like sparks among the stubble. They shall judge the nations, and have dominion over the people, and their Lord shall reign for ever. They that put their trust in him shall understand the truth: and such as be faithful in love shall abide with him: for grace and mercy is to his saints, and he hath care for his elect.

The Reward of the Righteous

Then shall the righteous man stand in great boldness before the face of such as have afflicted him, and made no account of his labours.

When they see it, they shall be troubled with terrible fear, and shall be amazed at the strangeness of his salvation, so far beyond all that they looked for. And they repenting and groaning for anguish of spirit shall say within themselves,

"This was he, whom we had sometimes in derision, and a proverb of reproach. We fools accounted his life madness, and

THE WISDOM OF SOLOMON

his end to be without honour. How is he numbered among the children of God, and his lot is among the saints! Therefore have we erred from the way of truth, and the light of righteousness hath not shined unto us, and the sun of righteousness rose not upon us. We wearied ourselves in the way of wickedness and destruction: yea, we have gone through deserts, where there lay no way: but as for the way of the Lord, we have not known it. What hath pride profited us? or what good hath riches with our vaunting brought us? All those things are passed away like a shadow, and as a post that hastened by; and as a ship that passeth over the waves of the water, which when it is gone by, the trace thereof cannot be found, neither the pathway of the keel in the waves; or as when a bird hath flown through the air, there is no token of her way to be found, but the light air being beaten with the stroke of her wings, and parted with the violent noise and motion of them, is passed through, and therein afterwards no sign where she went is to be found; or like as when an arrow is shot at a mark, it parteth the air, which immediately cometh together again, so that a man cannot know where it went through: even so we in like manner, as soon as we were born, began to draw to our end, and had no sign of virtue to show; but were consumed in our own wickedness."

For the hope of the ungodly is like dust that is blown away with the wind; like a thin froth that is driven away with the storm; like as the smoke which is dispersed here and there with a tempest, and passeth away as the remembrance of a guest that tarrieth but a day.

But the righteous live for evermore; their reward also is with the Lord, and the care of them is with the most High. Therefore shall they receive a glorious kingdom, and a beautiful crown from the Lord's hand: for with his right hand shall he cover them, and with his arm shall he protect them.

In Praise of Wisdom

Wisdom, which is the worker of all things, taught me: for in her is an understanding spirit, holy, one only, manifold, subtil,

THE WISDOM OF SOLOMON

lively, clear, undefiled, plain, not subject to hurt, loving the thing that is good, quick, which cannot be letted, ready to do good, kind to man, steadfast, sure, free from care, having all power, overseeing all things, and going through all understanding, pure, and most subtil, spirits.

For wisdom is more moving than any motion: she passeth and goeth through all things by reason of her pureness. For she is the breath of the power of God, and a pure influence flowing from the glory of the Almighty: therefore can no defiled thing fall into her. For she is the brightness of the everlasting light, the unspotted mirror of the power of God, and the image of his goodness. And being but one, she can do all things: and remaining in herself, she maketh all things new: and in all ages entering into holy souls, she maketh them friends of God, and prophets. For God loveth none but him that dwelleth with wisdom. For she is more beautiful than the sun, and above all the order of stars: being compared with the light, she is found before it. For after this cometh night: but vice shall not prevail against wisdom. Wisdom reacheth from one end to another mightily: and sweetly doth she order all things.

The God of Love

Thou canst show thy great strength at all times when thou wilt; and who may withstand the power of thine arm? For the whole world before thee is as a little grain of the balance, yea, as a drop of the morning dew that falleth down upon the earth. But thou hast mercy upon all; for thou canst do all things, and winkest at the sins of men, because they should amend. For thou lovest all the things that are, and abhorrest nothing which thou hast made: for never wouldest thou have made any thing, if thou hadst hated it. And how could any thing have endured, if it had not been thy will? or been preserved, if not called by thee? But thou sparest all: for they are thine, O Lord, thou lover of souls.

THE NEW TESTAMENT

THE GOSPEL ACCORDING TO MARK

A BIOGRAPHY OF JESUS OF NAZARETH

There is *no more vexed problem in the range of Biblical literature than that of the dates of the four Gospels. The question turns mainly on whether the strange Greek in which they are written is simply the work of Jews thinking in Aramaic though writing in Greek, or whether it represents rather an effort to translate literally into Greek original Aramaic Gospels now lost—a view recently urged with very strong arguments by Professor Torrey of Yale. Should his contentions be established, it will mean the throwing back of the dates of the Gospels a full generation to a pre-Pauline period, substituting the years A.D. 40–70 as the time of their composition, instead of A.D. 70–100 as has hitherto been usually assumed.*

In any case, however, there is no reason to suppose that there will be any change in the accepted order of the Gospels. The narrative of the events of Jesus' life, attributed to Mark, the companion of Peter in Rome, was unquestionably used by the authors of Matthew and Luke and was thus the earliest of the four. Almost exclusively a story of action, with very little emphasis on Jesus' teachings, and written in the popular style of the day in its delighted acceptance of demonology and marvels, the Gospel according to Mark was esteemed somewhat less than the others by the early church. But from the modern point of view it is particularly valuable as the most nearly authentic of all the accounts, supplying us with the little that we actually know about the life of Jesus and, in spite of its brevity, giving a clear picture of him as the great revolutionary humanitarian. Swift and vigorous in its narration, it rises without effort to supreme heights of tragedy in the closing scenes.

The passage printed as an Appendix is generally admitted to be a later addition to the original Gospel.

The Gospel According to MARK

A BIOGRAPHY OF JESUS OF NAZARETH

Part I

Ministry in Galilee

THE BEGINNING OF THE GOSPEL of Jesus Christ, the Son of God: as it is written in the prophets,

> "Behold, I send my messenger before thy face,
> Which shall prepare thy way before thee.
> The voice of one crying in the wilderness,
> 'Prepare ye the way of the Lord,
> Make his paths straight.'"

John did baptize in the wilderness, and preach the baptism of repentance for the remission of sins. And there went out unto him all the land of Judæa, and they of Jerusalem, and were all baptized of him in the river of Jordan, confessing their sins. And John was clothed with camel's hair, and with a girdle of a skin about his loins; and he did eat locusts and wild honey; and preached, saying,

"There cometh one mightier than I after me, the latchet of whose shoes I am not worthy to stoop down and unloose. I indeed have baptized you with water: but he shall baptize you with the Holy Ghost."

And it came to pass in those days, that Jesus came from Nazareth of Galilee, and was baptized of John in Jordan. And straightway coming up out of the water, he saw the heavens opened, and the Spirit like a dove descending upon him: and there came a voice from heaven, saying, "Thou art my beloved Son, in whom I am well pleased."

And immediately the Spirit driveth him into the wilderness. And he was there in the wilderness forty days, tempted of Satan; and was with the wild beasts; and the angels ministered unto him.

Now after that John was put in prison, Jesus came into Galilee, preaching the gospel of the kingdom of God, and saying, "The time is fulfilled, and the kingdom of God is at hand: repent ye, and believe the gospel."

Now as he walked by the sea of Galilee, he saw Simon and Andrew his brother casting a net into the sea: for they were fishers. And Jesus said unto them,

"Come ye after me, and I will make you to become fishers of men."

And straightway they forsook their nets, and followed him.

And when he had gone a little farther thence, he saw James the son of Zebedee, and John his brother, who also were in the ship mending their nets. And straightway he called them: and they left their father Zebedee in the ship with the hired servants, and went after him.

And they went into Capernaum; and straightway on the sabbath day he entered into the synagogue, and taught. And they were astonished at his doctrine: for he taught them as one that had authority, and not as the scribes. And there was in their synagogue a man with an unclean spirit; and he cried out, saying, "Let us alone; what have we to do with thee, thou Jesus of Nazareth? art thou come to destroy us? I know thee who thou art, the Holy One of God." And Jesus rebuked him, saying,

"Hold thy peace, and come out of him."

And when the unclean spirit had torn him, and cried with a loud voice, he came out of him. And they were all amazed, inso-

THE GOSPEL ACCORDING TO MARK

much that they questioned among themselves, saying, "What thing is this? what new doctrine is this? for with authority commandeth he even the unclean spirits, and they do obey him." And immediately his fame spread abroad throughout all the region round about Galilee.

And forthwith, when they were come out of the synagogue, they entered into the house of Simon and Andrew, with James and John. But Simon's wife's mother lay sick of a fever, and anon they tell him of her. And he came and took her by the hand, and lifted her up; and immediately the fever left her, and she ministered unto them. And at even, when the sun did set, they brought unto him all that were diseased, and them that were possessed with devils. And all the city was gathered together at the door. And he healed many that were sick of divers diseases, and cast out many devils; and suffered not the devils to speak, because they knew him.

And in the morning, rising up a great while before day, he went out, and departed into a solitary place, and there prayed. And Simon and they that were with him followed after him. And when they had found him, they said unto him, "All men seek for thee." And he said unto them,

"Let us go into the next towns, that I may preach there also: for therefore came I forth."

And he preached in their synagogues throughout all Galilee, and cast out devils.

And there came a leper to him, beseeching him, and kneeling down to him, and saying unto him, "If thou wilt, thou canst make me clean."

And Jesus, moved with compassion, put forth his hand, and touched him, and saith unto him, "I will; be thou clean."

And as soon as he had spoken, immediately the leprosy departed from him, and he was cleansed. And he straitly charged him, and forthwith sent him away; and saith unto him, "See thou say nothing to any man: but go thy way, show thyself to

THE GOSPEL ACCORDING TO MARK

the priest, and offer for thy cleansing those things which Moses commanded, for a testimony unto them."

But he went out, and began to publish it much, and to blaze abroad the matter, insomuch that Jesus could no more openly enter into the city, but was without in desert places: and they came to him from every quarter.

And again he entered into Capernaum after some days; and it was noised that he was in the house. And straightway many were gathered together, insomuch that there was no room to receive them, no, not so much as about the door: and he preached the word unto them. And they come unto him, bringing one sick of the palsy, which was borne of four. And when they could not come nigh unto him for the press, they uncovered the roof where he was: and when they had broken it up, they let down the bed wherein the sick of the palsy lay.

When Jesus saw their faith, he said unto the sick of the palsy, "Son, thy sins be forgiven thee."

But there were certain of the scribes sitting there, and reasoning in their hearts, "Why doth this man thus speak blasphemies? who can forgive sins but God only?" And immediately when Jesus perceived in his spirit that they so reasoned within themselves, he said unto him,

"Why reason ye these things in your hearts? Whether is it easier to say to the sick of the palsy, 'Thy sins be forgiven thee'; or to say, 'Arise, and take up thy bed, and walk'? But that ye may know that the Son of Man hath power on earth to forgive sins (he saith to the sick of the palsy), I say unto thee, 'Arise, and take up thy bed, and go thy way into thine house.'"

And immediately he arose, took up the bed, and went forth before them all; insomuch that they were all amazed, and glorified God, saying, "We never saw it on this fashion."

And he went forth again by the sea side; and all the multitude resorted unto him, and he taught them.

And as he passed by, he saw Levi the son of Alphæus sitting

THE GOSPEL ACCORDING TO MARK

at the receipt of custom, and said unto him, "Follow me." And he arose and followed him.

And it came to pass, that, as Jesus sat at meat in his house, many publicans and sinners sat also together with Jesus and his disciples: for there were many, and they followed him. And when the scribes and Pharisees saw him eat with publicans and sinners, they said unto his disciples, "How is it that he eateth and drinketh with publicans and sinners?" When Jesus heard it, he saith unto them,

"They that are whole have no need of the physician, but they that are sick: I came not to call the righteous, but sinners to repentance."

And the disciples of John and of the Pharisees used to fast: and they come and say unto him, "Why do the disciples of John and of the Pharisees fast, but thy disciples fast not?"

And Jesus said unto them,

"Can the children of the bridechamber fast, while the bridegroom is with them? as long as they have the bridegroom with them, they cannot fast. But the days will come, when the bridegroom shall be taken away from them, and then shall they fast in those days. No man also seweth a piece of new cloth on an old garment: else the new piece that filled it up taketh away from the old, and the rent is made worse. And no man putteth new wine into old bottles: else the new wine doth burst the bottles, and the wine is spilled, and the bottles will be marred: but new wine must be put into new bottles."

And it came to pass that he went through the corn fields on the sabbath day; and his disciples began, as they went, to pluck the ears of corn. And the Pharisees said unto him, "Behold, why do they on the sabbath day that which is not lawful?"

And he said unto them,

"Have ye never read what David did, when he had need, and was an hungred, he, and they that were with him? How he went into the house of God in the days of Abiathar the high priest, and did eat the showbread, which is not lawful to eat but for the priests, and gave also to them which were with him?"

And he said unto them,

"The sabbath was made for man, and not man for the sabbath: Therefore the Son of Man is Lord also of the sabbath."

And he entered again into the synagogue; and there was a man there which had a withered hand. And they watched him, whether he would heal him on the sabbath day; that they might accuse him.

And he saith unto the man which had the withered hand, "Stand forth." And he saith unto them, "Is it lawful to do good on the sabbath days, or to do evil? to save life, or to kill?" But they held their peace.

And when he had looked round about on them with anger, being grieved for the hardness of their hearts, he saith unto the man, "Stretch forth thine hand."

And he stretched it out: and his hand was restored whole as the other. And the Pharisees went forth, and straightway took counsel with the Herodians against him, how they might destroy him.

But Jesus withdrew himself with his disciples to the sea: and a great multitude from Galilee followed him, and from Judæa, and from Jerusalem, and from Idumæa, and from beyond Jordan; and they about Tyre and Sidon, a great multitude, when they had heard what great things he did, came unto him. And he spoke to his disciples, that a small ship should wait on him because of the multitude, lest they should throng him. For he had healed many; insomuch that they pressed upon him for to touch him, as many as had plagues. And unclean spirits, when they saw him, fell down before him, and cried, saying, "Thou art the Son of God." And he straitly charged them that they should not make him known.

And he goeth up into a mountain, and calleth unto him whom he would: and they came unto him. And he ordained twelve, that they should be with him, and that he might send them

THE GOSPEL ACCORDING TO MARK

forth to preach, and to have power to heal sicknesses, and to cast out devils: and Simon he surnamed Peter; and James the son of Zebedee, and John the brother of James; and he surnamed them Boanerges, which is, the sons of thunder: and Andrew, and Philip, and Bartholomew, and Matthew, and Thomas, and James the son of Alphæus, and Thaddæus, and Simon the Canaanite, and Judas Iscariot, which also betrayed him.

And they went into a house. And the multitude cometh together again, so that they could not so much as eat bread. And when his friends heard of it, they went out to lay hold on him: for they said, "He is beside himself."

There came then his brethren and his mother, and, standing without, sent unto him, calling him. And the multitude sat about him, and they said unto him, "Behold, thy mother and thy brethren without seek for thee." And he answered them, saying,

"Who is my mother, or my brethren?"

And he looked round about on them which sat about him, and said,

"Behold my mother and my brethren! For whosoever shall do the will of God, the same is my brother, and my sister, and mother."

And the same day, when the even was come, he saith unto them, "Let us pass over unto the other side."

And when they had sent away the multitude, they took him even as he was in the ship. And there were also with him other little ships. And there arose a great storm of wind, and the waves beat into the ship, so that it was now full. And he was in the hinder part of the ship, asleep on a pillow: and they awake him, and say unto him, "Master, carest thou not that we perish?"

And he arose, and rebuked the wind, and said unto the sea, "Peace, be still." And the wind ceased, and there was great calm.

And he said unto them, "Why are ye so fearful? how is it that ye have no faith?"

THE GOSPEL ACCORDING TO MARK

And they feared exceedingly, and said one to another, "What manner of man is this, that even the wind and the sea obey him?"

And they came over unto the other side of the sea, into the country of the Gadarenes. And when he was come out of the ship, immediately there met him out of the tombs a man with an unclean spirit, who had his dwelling among the tombs; and no man could bind him, no, not with chains: because that he had been often bound with fetters and chains, and the chains had been plucked asunder by him, and the fetters broken in pieces: neither could any man tame him. And always, night and day, he was in the mountains, and in the tombs, crying, and cutting himself with stones. But when he saw Jesus afar off, he ran and worshipped him, and cried with a loud voice, and said, "What have I to do with thee, Jesus, thou Son of the most high God? I adjure thee by God, that thou torment me not."

For he said unto him, "Come out of the man, thou unclean spirit."

And he asked him, "What is thy name?"

And he answered, saying, "My name is Legion: for we are many."

And he besought him much that he would not send them away out of the country.

Now there was there nigh unto the mountains a great herd of swine feeding. And all the devils besought him, saying, "Send us into the swine, that we may enter into them." And forthwith Jesus gave them leave. And the unclean spirits went out, and entered into the swine: and the herd ran violently down a steep place into the sea (they were about two thousand); and were choked in the sea.

And they that fed the swine fled, and told it in the city, and in the country. And they went out to see what it was that was done. And they come to Jesus, and see him that was possessed with the devil, and had the legion, sitting, and clothed, and in his right mind: and they were afraid.

And they that saw it told them how it befell to him that was possessed with the devil, and also concerning the swine. And

THE GOSPEL ACCORDING TO MARK

they began to pray him to depart out of their coasts. And when he was come into the ship, he that had been possessed with the devil prayed him that he might be with him.

Howbeit Jesus suffered him not, but saith unto him, "Go home to thy friends, and tell them how great things the Lord hath done for thee, and hath had compassion on thee."

And he departed, and began to publish in Decapolis how great things Jesus had done for him: and all men did marvel. And when Jesus was passed over again by ship unto the other side, much people gathered unto him: and he was nigh unto the sea.

And, behold, there cometh one of the rulers of the synagogue, Jairus by name; and when he saw him, he fell at his feet, and besought him greatly, saying, "My little daughter lieth at the point of death: I pray thee, come and lay thy hands on her, that she may be healed; and she shall live."

And Jesus went with him; and much people followed him, and thronged him. And a certain woman, which had an issue of blood twelve years, and had suffered many things of many physicians, and had spent all that she had, and was nothing bettered but rather grew worse, when she had heard of Jesus, came in the press behind, and touched his garment. For she said, "If I may touch but his clothes, I shall be whole." And straightway the fountain of her blood was dried up; and she felt in her body that she was healed of that plague.

And Jesus, immediately knowing in himself that virtue had gone out of him, turned him about in the press, and said, "Who touched my clothes?"

And his disciples said unto him, "Thou seest the multitude thronging thee, and sayest thou, 'Who touched me?'"

And he looked round about to see her that had done this thing. But the woman fearing and trembling, knowing what was done in her, came and fell down before him, and told him all the truth.

And he said unto her, "Daughter, thy faith hath made thee whole; go in peace, and be whole of thy plague."

THE GOSPEL ACCORDING TO MARK

While he yet spoke, there came from the ruler of the synagogue's house certain which said, "Thy daughter is dead: why troublest thou the Master any further?"

As soon as Jesus heard the word that was spoken, he saith unto the ruler of the synagogue, "Be not afraid, only believe."

And he suffered no man to follow him, save Peter, and James, and John the brother of James. And he cometh to the house of the ruler of the synagogue, and seeth the tumult, and them that wept and wailed greatly.

And when he was come in, he saith unto them, "Why make ye this ado, and weep? the damsel is not dead, but sleepeth."

And they laughed him to scorn. But when he had put them all out, he taketh the father and the mother of the damsel, and them that were with him, and entereth in where the damsel was lying. And he took the damsel by the hand, and said unto her, "Talitha cumi"; which is, being interpreted, "Damsel, I say unto thee, arise."

And straightway the damsel arose, and walked; for she was of the age of twelve years. And they were astonished with a great astonishment. And he charged them straitly that no man should know it; and commanded that something should be given her to eat.

And he went out from thence, and came into his own country; and his disciples follow him. And when the sabbath day was come, he began to teach in the synagogue: and many hearing him were astonished, saying, "From whence hath this man these things? and what wisdom is this which is given unto him, that even such mighty works are wrought by his hands? Is not this the carpenter, the son of Mary, the brother of James, and Joses, and of Juda, and Simon? and are not his sisters here with us?" And they were offended at him.

But Jesus said unto them, "A prophet is not without honour, but in his own country, and among his own kin, and in his own house."

And he could there do no mighty work, save that he laid his

THE GOSPEL ACCORDING TO MARK

hands upon a few sick folk, and healed them. And he marvelled because of their unbelief.

And he went round about the villages, teaching.

And he called unto him the twelve, and began to send them forth by two and two; and gave them power over unclean spirits; and commanded them that they should take nothing for their journey, save a staff only; no scrip, no bread, no money in their purse: but be shod with sandals; and not put on two coats. And he said unto them, "In what place soever ye enter into a house, there abide till ye depart from that place. And whosoever shall not receive you, nor hear you, when ye depart thence, shake off the dust under your feet for a testimony against them. Verily I say unto you, 'It shall be more tolerable for Sodom and Gomorrah in the day of judgment, than for that city.'"

And they went out, and preached that men should repent. And they cast out many devils, and anointed with oil many that were sick, and healed them.

And King Herod heard of him (for his name was spread abroad): and he said, "John the Baptist is risen from the dead, and therefore mighty works do show forth themselves in him." Others said, "It is Elias." And others said, "It is a prophet, or as one of the prophets."

But when Herod heard thereof, he said, "It is John, whom I beheaded: he is risen from the dead."

For Herod himself had sent forth and laid hold upon John, and bound him in prison for Herodias's sake, his brother Philip's wife: for he had married her. For John had said unto Herod, "It is not lawful for thee to have thy brother's wife."

Therefore Herodias had a quarrel against him, and would have killed him; but she could not: for Herod feared John, knowing that he was a just man and a holy, and observed him; and when he heard him, he did many things, and heard him gladly.

And when a convenient day was come, that Herod on his

THE GOSPEL ACCORDING TO MARK

birthday made a supper to his lords, high captains, and chief estates of Galilee; and when the daughter of the said Herodias came in, and danced, and pleased Herod and them that sat with him, the king said unto the damsel, "Ask of me whatsoever thou wilt, and I will give it thee." And he swore unto her, "Whatsoever thou shalt ask of me, I will give it thee, unto the half of my kingdom."

And she went forth, and said unto her mother, "What shall I ask?"

And she said, "The head of John the Baptist."

And she came in straightway with haste unto the king, and asked, saying, "I will that thou give me by and by in a charger the head of John the Baptist."

And the king was exceeding sorry; yet for his oath's sake, and for their sakes which sat with him, he would not reject her. And immediately the king sent an executioner, and commanded his head to be brought: and he went and beheaded him in the prison, and brought his head in a charger, and gave it to the damsel: and the damsel gave it to her mother. And when his disciples heard of it, they came and took up his corpse, and laid it in a tomb.

And the apostles gathered themselves together unto Jesus, and told him all things, both what they had done, and what they had taught. And he said unto them, "Come ye yourselves apart into a desert place, and rest a while": for there were many coming and going, and they had no leisure so much as to eat.

And they departed into a desert place by ship privately. And the people saw them departing, and many knew him, and ran afoot thither out of all cities, and outwent them, and came together unto him. And Jesus, when he came out, saw much people, and was moved with compassion toward them, because they were as sheep not having a shepherd: and he began to teach them many things.

And when the day was now far spent, his disciples came unto him, and said, "This is a desert place, and now the time is

THE GOSPEL ACCORDING TO MARK

far passed. Send them away, that they may go into the country round about, and into the villages, and buy themselves bread: for they have nothing to eat."

He answered and said unto them, "Give ye them to eat."

And they say unto him, "Shall we go and buy two hundred pennyworth of bread, and give them to eat?"

He saith unto them, "How many loaves have ye? go and see."

And when they knew, they say, "Five, and two fishes."

And he commanded them to make all sit down by companies upon the green grass. And they sat down in ranks, by hundreds, and by fifties. And when he had taken the five loaves and the two fishes, he looked up to heaven, and blessed, and broke the loaves, and gave them to his disciples to set before them; and the two fishes divided he among them all. And they did all eat, and were filled. And they took up twelve baskets full of the fragments, and of the fishes. And they that did eat of the loaves were about five thousand men.

And straightway he constrained his disciples to get into the ship, and to go to the other side before unto Bethsaida, while he sent away the people. And when he had sent them away, he departed into a mountain to pray. And when even was come, the ship was in the midst of the sea, and he alone on the land.

And he saw them toiling in rowing; for the wind was contrary unto them: and about the fourth watch of the night he cometh unto them, walking upon the sea, and would have passed by them. But when they saw him walking upon the sea, they supposed it had been a spirit, and cried out: for they all saw him, and were troubled. And immediately he talked with them, and saith unto them, "Be of good cheer: it is I; be not afraid."

And he went up unto them into the ship; and the wind ceased: and they were sore amazed in themselves beyond measure, and wondered. For they considered not the miracle of the loaves: for their heart was hardened.

And when they had passed over, they came into the land of

THE GOSPEL ACCORDING TO MARK

Gennesaret, and drew to the shore. And when they were come out of the ship, straightway they knew him, and ran through that whole region round about, and began to carry about in beds those that were sick, where they heard he was. And whithersoever he entered, into villages, or cities, or country, they laid the sick in the streets, and besought him that they might touch if it were but the border of his garment: and as many as touched him were made whole.

Then came together unto him the Pharisees, and certain of the scribes, which came from Jerusalem. And when they saw some of his disciples eat bread with defiled, that is to say, with unwashed, hands, they found fault. For the Pharisees, and all the Jews, except they wash their hands oft, eat not, holding the tradition of the elders. And when they come from the market, except they wash, they eat not. And many other things there be, which they have received to hold, as the washing of cups, and pots, brazen vessels, and of tables.

Then the Pharisees and scribes asked him, "Why walk not thy disciples according to the tradition of the elders, but eat bread with unwashed hands?"

He answered and said unto them,

"Well hath Esaias prophesied of you hypocrites, as it is written,

> "'This people honoureth me with their lips,
> But their heart is far from me;
> Howbeit in vain do they worship me,
> Teaching for doctrines the commandments of men.'

"For laying aside the commandment of God, ye hold the tradition of men, as the washing of pots and cups: and many other such like things ye do."

And he said unto them,

"Full well ye reject the commandment of God, that ye may keep your own tradition. For Moses said, 'Honour thy father

THE GOSPEL ACCORDING TO MARK

and thy mother'; and, 'Whoso curseth father or mother, let him die the death': but ye say, 'If a man shall say to his father or mother, "It is Corban, that is to say, a gift, by whatsoever thou mightest be profited by me; he shall be free."' And ye suffer him no more to do ought for his father or his mother; making the word of God of none effect through your tradition, which ye have delivered: and many such like things do ye."

And when he had called all the people unto him, he said unto them,

"Hearken unto me every one of you, and understand: there is nothing from without a man, that entering into him can defile him: but the things which come out of him, those are they that defile the man. If any man have ears to hear, let him hear."

And when he was entered into the house from the people, his disciples asked him concerning the parable. And he saith unto them,

"Are ye so without understanding also? Do ye not perceive, that whatsoever thing from without entereth into the man, it cannot defile him; because it entereth not into his heart, but into the belly, and goeth out into the draught, purging all meats?"

And he said,

"That which cometh out of the man, that defileth the man. For from within, out of the heart of men, proceed evil thoughts, adulteries, fornications, murders, thefts, covetousness, wickedness, deceit, lasciviousness, an evil eye, blasphemy, pride, foolishness. All these evil things come from within, and defile the man."

And from thence he arose, and went into the borders of Tyre and Sidon, and entered into a house, and would have no man know it: but he could not be hid. For a certain woman, whose young daughter had an unclean spirit, heard of him, and came and fell at his feet. The woman was a Greek, a Syrophenician by nation; and she besought him that he would cast forth the devil out of her daughter.

THE GOSPEL ACCORDING TO MARK

But Jesus said unto her, "Let the children first be filled: for it is not meet to take the children's bread, and to cast it unto the dogs."

And she answered and said unto him, "Yes, Lord: yet the dogs under the table eat of the children's crumbs."

And he said unto her, "For this saying go thy way; the devil is gone out of thy daughter."

And when she was come to her house, she found the devil gone out, and her daughter laid upon the bed.

And again, departing from the coasts of Tyre and Sidon, he came unto the sea of Galilee, through the midst of the coasts of Decapolis. And they bring unto him one that was deaf, and had an impediment in his speech; and they beseech him to put his hand upon him. And he took him aside from the multitude, and put his fingers into his ears, and he spit, and touched his tongue; and looking up to heaven, he sighed, and saith unto him, "Ephphatha," that is, "Be opened." And straightway his ears were opened, and the string of his tongue was loosed, and he spoke plain.

And he charged them that they should tell no man: but the more he charged them, so much the more a great deal they published it; and were beyond measure astonished, saying, "He hath done all things well: he maketh both the deaf to hear, and the dumb to speak."

In those days the multitude being very great, and having nothing to eat, Jesus called his disciples unto him, and saith unto them,

"I have compassion on the multitude, because they have now been with me three days, and have nothing to eat: and if I send them away fasting to their own houses, they will faint by the way: for divers of them came from far."

And his disciples answered him, "From whence can a man satisfy these men with bread here in the wilderness?"

And he asked them, "How many loaves have ye?"

THE GOSPEL ACCORDING TO MARK

And they said, "Seven."

And he commanded the people to sit down on the ground: and he took the seven loaves, and gave thanks, and broke, and gave to his disciples to set before them; and they did set them before the people. And they had a few small fishes: and he blessed, and commanded to set them also before them. So they did eat, and were filled: and they took up of the broken meat that was left seven baskets. And they that had eaten were about four thousand: and he sent them away.

And straightway he entered into a ship with his disciples, and came into the parts of Dalmanutha. And the Pharisees came forth, and began to question with him, seeking of him a sign from heaven, tempting him. And he sighed deeply in his spirit, and saith,

"Why doth this generation seek after a sign? verily I say unto you, 'There shall no sign be given unto this generation.'"

And he left them, and entering into the ship again departed to the other side.

Now the disciples had forgotten to take bread, neither had they in the ship with them more than one loaf. And he charged them, saying,

"Take heed, beware of the leaven of the Pharisees, and of the leaven of Herod."

And they reasoned among themselves, saying, "It is because we have no bread."

And when Jesus knew it, he saith unto them,

"Why reason ye, because ye have no bread? perceive ye not yet, neither understand? have ye your heart yet hardened? Having eyes, see ye not? and having ears, hear ye not? and do ye not remember? When I broke the five loaves among five thousand, how many baskets full of fragments took ye up?" They say unto him, "Twelve."

"And when the seven among four thousand, how many baskets full of fragments took ye up?" And they said, "Seven."

And he said unto them,

THE GOSPEL ACCORDING TO MARK
"How is it that ye do not understand?"

And he cometh to Bethsaida; and they bring a blind man unto him, and besought him to touch him. And he took the blind man by the hand, and led him out of the town; and when he had spit on his eyes, and put his hands upon him, he asked him if he saw ought. And he looked up, and said, "I see men as trees walking."

After that he put his hands again upon his eyes, and made him look up: and he was restored, and saw every man clearly. And he sent him away to his house, saying, "Neither go into the town, nor tell it to any in the town."

And Jesus went out, and his disciples, into the towns of Cæsarea Philippi: and by the way he asked his disciples, saying unto them, "Whom do men say that I am?"

And they answered, "John the Baptist: but some say, 'Elias'; and others, 'One of the prophets.'"

And he saith unto them, "But whom say ye that I am?"

And Peter answereth and saith unto him, "Thou art the Christ."

And he charged them that they should tell no man of him. And he began to teach them, that the Son of Man must suffer many things, and be rejected of the elders, and of the chief priests, and scribes, and be killed, and after three days rise again. And he spoke that saying openly. And Peter took him, and began to rebuke him. But when he had turned about and looked on his disciples, he rebuked Peter, saying,

"Get thee behind me, Satan: for thou savourest not the things that be of God, but the things that be of men."

And when he had called the people unto him with his disciples also, he said unto them,

"Whosoever will come after me, let him deny himself, and take up his cross, and follow me. For whosoever will save his life shall lose it; but whosoever shall lose his life for my sake

THE GOSPEL ACCORDING TO MARK

and the gospel's, the same shall save it. For what shall it profit a man, if he shall gain the whole world, and lose his own soul? Or what shall a man give in exchange for his soul? Whosoever therefore shall be ashamed of me and of my words in this adulterous and sinful generation; of him also shall the Son of Man be ashamed, when he cometh in the glory of his Father with the holy angels."

And he said unto them,

"Verily I say unto you that there be some of them that stand here, which shall not taste of death, till they have seen the kingdom of God come with power."

And after six days Jesus taketh with him Peter, and James, and John, and leadeth them up into a high mountain apart by themselves: and he was transfigured before them. And his raiment became shining, exceeding white as snow; so as no fuller on earth can white them. And there appeared unto them Elias with Moses: and they were talking with Jesus. And Peter answered and said to Jesus,

"Master, it is good for us to be here: and let us make three tabernacles; one for thee, and one for Moses, and one for Elias."

For he wist not what to say; for they were sore afraid.

And there was a cloud that overshadowed them: and a voice came out of the cloud, saying, "This is my beloved Son: hear him."

And suddenly, when they had looked round about, they saw no man any more, save Jesus only with themselves.

And as they came down from the mountain, he charged them that they should tell no man what things they had seen, till the Son of Man were risen from the dead. And they kept that saying with themselves, questioning one with another what the rising from the dead should mean.

And they asked him, saying, "Why say the scribes that Elias must first come?"

And he answered and told them,

"Elias verily cometh first, and restoreth all things; and how it is written of the Son of Man, that he must suffer many things,

THE GOSPEL ACCORDING TO MARK

and be set at nought. But I say unto you that Elias is indeed come, and they have done unto him whatsoever they listed, as it is written of him."

And when he came to his disciples, he saw a great multitude about them, and the scribes questioning with them. And straightway all the people, when they beheld him, were greatly amazed, and running to him saluted him. And he asked the scribes, "What question ye with them?"

And one of the multitude answered and said, "Master, I have brought unto thee my son, which hath a dumb spirit; and wheresoever he taketh him, he teareth him: and he foameth, and gnasheth with his teeth, and pineth away: and I spoke to thy disciples that they should cast him out; and they could not."

He answereth him, and saith,

"O faithless generation, how long shall I be with you? how long shall I suffer you? bring him unto me."

And they brought him unto him: and when he saw him, straightway the spirit tore him; and he fell on the ground, and wallowed foaming. And he asked his father, "How long is it ago since this came unto him?"

And he said, "Of a child. And ofttimes it hath cast him into the fire, and into the waters, to destroy him: but if thou canst do any thing, have compassion on us, and help us."

Jesus said unto him, "If thou canst believe, all things are possible to him that believeth."

And straightway the father of the child cried out, and said with tears,

"Lord, I believe; help thou mine unbelief."

When Jesus saw that the people came running together, he rebuked the foul spirit, saying unto him,

"Thou dumb and deaf spirit, I charge thee, come out of him, and enter no more into him."

And the spirit cried, and rent him sore, and came out of him: and he was as one dead; insomuch that many said, "He is dead." But Jesus took him by the hand, and lifted him up; and he arose.

THE GOSPEL ACCORDING TO MARK

And when he was come into the house, his disciples asked him privately, "Why could not we cast him out?"

And he said unto them, "This kind can come forth by nothing, but by prayer and fasting."

And they departed thence, and passed through Galilee; and he would not that any man should know it. For he taught his disciples, and said unto them, "The Son of Man is delivered into the hands of men, and they shall kill him; and after that he is killed, he shall rise the third day." But they understood not that saying, and were afraid to ask him.

And he came to Capernaum: and being in the house he asked them, "What was it that ye disputed among yourselves by the way?"

But they held their peace: for by the way they had disputed among themselves, who should be the greatest.

And he sat down, and called the twelve, and saith unto them, "If any man desire to be first, the same shall be last of all, and servant of all."

And he took a child, and set him in the midst of them: and when he had taken him in his arms, he said unto them,

"Whosoever shall receive one of such children in my name, receiveth me: and whosoever shall receive me, receiveth not me, but him that sent me."

And John answered him, saying, "Master, we saw one casting out devils in thy name, and he followeth not us: and we forbad him, because he followeth not us."

But Jesus said, "Forbid him not: for there is no man which shall do a miracle in my name, that can lightly speak evil of me. For he that is not against us is on our part. For whosoever shall give you a cup of water to drink in my name, because ye belong to Christ, verily I say unto you, he shall not lose his reward. And whosoever shall offend one of these little ones that believe in me, it is better for him that a millstone were hanged about his neck, and he were cast into the sea."

THE GOSPEL ACCORDING TO MARK

Part II

Ministry in Judaea

And he arose from thence, and cometh into the coasts of Judæa by the farther side of Jordan: and the people resort unto him again; and, as he was wont, he taught them again.

And they were in the way going up to Jerusalem; and Jesus went before them: and they were amazed; and as they followed, they were afraid. And he took again the twelve, and began to tell them what things should happen unto him, saying,

"Behold, we go up to Jerusalem; and the Son of Man shall be delivered unto the chief priests, and unto the scribes; and they shall condemn him to death, and shall deliver him to the Gentiles: and they shall mock him, and shall scourge him, and shall spit upon him, and shall kill him: and the third day he shall rise again."

And James and John, the sons of Zebedee, come unto him, saying, "Master, we would that thou shouldest do for us whatsoever we shall desire."

And he said unto them, "What would ye that I should do for you?"

They said unto him, "Grant unto us that we may sit, one on thy right hand, and the other on thy left hand, in thy glory."

But Jesus said unto them, "Ye know not what ye ask: can ye drink of the cup that I drink of? and be baptized with the baptism that I am baptized with?"

And they said unto him, "We can."

And Jesus said unto them, "Ye shall indeed drink of the cup that I drink of; and with the baptism that I am baptized withal shall ye be baptized: but to sit on my right hand and on my left hand is not mine to give; but it shall be given to them for whom it is prepared."

And when the ten heard it, they began to be much displeased

THE GOSPEL ACCORDING TO MARK

with James and John. But Jesus called them to him, and saith unto them,

"Ye know that they which are accounted to rule over the Gentiles exercise lordship over them; and their great ones exercise authority upon them. But so shall it not be among you: but whosoever will be great among you, shall be your minister: and whosoever of you will be the chiefest, shall be servant of all. For even the Son of Man came not to be ministered unto, but to minister, and to give his life a ransom for many."

And they came to Jericho: and as he went out of Jericho with his disciples and a great number of people, blind Bartimæus, the son of Timæus, sat by the highway side begging. And when he heard that it was Jesus of Nazareth, he began to cry out, and say, "Jesus, thou son of David, have mercy on me." And many charged him that he should hold his peace: but he cried the more a great deal, "Thou son of David, have mercy on me."

And Jesus stood still, and commanded him to be called. And they call the blind man, saying unto him, "Be of good comfort, rise; he calleth thee."

And he, casting away his garment, rose, and came to Jesus.

And Jesus answered and said unto him, "What wilt thou that I should do unto thee?"

The blind man said unto him, "Lord, that I might receive my sight."

And Jesus said unto him, "Go thy way; thy faith hath made thee whole."

And immediately he received his sight, and followed Jesus in the way.

And when they came nigh to Jerusalem, unto Bethphage and Bethany, at the Mount of Olives, he sendeth forth two of his disciples, and saith unto them, "Go your way into the village over against you: and as soon as ye be entered into it, ye shall find a colt tied, whereon never man sat; loose him, and bring

THE GOSPEL ACCORDING TO MARK

him. And if any man say unto you, 'Why do ye this?' say ye that the Lord hath need of him; and straightway he will send him hither."

And they went their way, and found the colt tied by the door without in a place where two ways met; and they loose him. And certain of them that stood there said unto them, "What do ye, loosing the colt?" And they said unto them even as Jesus had commanded: and they let them go.

And they brought the colt to Jesus, and cast their garments on him; and he sat upon him. And many spread their garments in the way: and others cut down branches off the trees, and strewed them in the way. And they that went before, and they that followed, cried, saying, "Hosanna! Blessed is he that cometh in the name of the Lord! Blessed be the kingdom of our father David, that cometh in the name of the Lord! Hosanna in the highest."

And Jesus entered into Jerusalem, and into the temple: and when he had looked round about upon all things, and now the eventide was come, he went out unto Bethany with the twelve.

And on the morrow, when they were come from Bethany, he was hungry: and seeing a fig tree afar off having leaves, he came, if haply he might find any thing thereon: and when he came to it, he found nothing but leaves; for the time of figs was not yet. And Jesus answered and said unto it, "No man eat fruit of thee hereafter for ever." And his disciples heard it.

And they come to Jerusalem: and Jesus went into the temple, and began to cast out them that sold and bought in the temple, and overthrew the tables of the moneychangers and the seats of them that sold doves, and would not suffer that any man should carry any vessel through the temple. And he taught, saying unto them,

"Is it not written, 'My house shall be called of all nations the house of prayer'? but ye have made it a den of thieves."

And the scribes and chief priests heard it, and sought how

THE GOSPEL ACCORDING TO MARK

they might destroy him: for they feared him, because all the people was astonished at his doctrine. And when even was come, he went out of the city.

And in the morning, as they passed by, they saw the fig tree dried up from the roots. And Peter calling to remembrance saith unto him, "Master, behold, the fig tree which thou cursedst is withered away." And Jesus answering saith unto them,

"Have faith in God. For verily I say unto you, whosoever shall say unto this mountain, 'Be thou removed, and be thou cast into the sea'; and shall not doubt in his heart, but shall believe that those things which he saith shall come to pass; he shall have whatsoever he saith. Therefore I say unto you, what things soever ye desire, when ye pray, believe that ye receive them, and ye shall have them. And when ye stand praying, forgive, if ye have ought against any: that your Father also which is in heaven may forgive you your trespasses. But if ye do not forgive, neither will your Father which is in heaven forgive your trespasses."

After two days was the feast of the passover, and of unleavened bread: and the chief priests and the scribes sought how they might take him by craft, and put him to death. But they said, "Not on the feast day, lest there be an uproar of the people."

And being in Bethany in the house of Simon the leper, as he sat at meat, there came a woman having an alabaster box of ointment of spikenard very precious; and she broke the box, and poured it on his head. And there were some that had indignation within themselves, and said, "Why was this waste of the ointment made? For it might have been sold for more than three hundred pence, and have been given to the poor."

And they murmured against her. And Jesus said,

"Let her alone; why trouble ye her? she hath wrought a good work on me. For ye have the poor with you always, and whensoever ye will ye may do them good: but me ye have not always. She hath done what she could: she is come aforehand to anoint

THE GOSPEL ACCORDING TO MARK

my body to the burying. Verily I say unto you, wheresoever this gospel shall be preached throughout the whole world, this also that she hath done shall be spoken of for a memorial of her."

And Judas Iscariot, one of the twelve, went unto the chief priests, to betray him unto them. And when they heard it, they were glad, and promised to give him money. And he sought how he might conveniently betray him.

And the first day of unleavened bread, when they killed the passover, his disciples said unto him, "Where wilt thou that we go and prepare that thou mayest eat the passover?"

And he sendeth forth two of his disciples, and saith unto them, "Go ye into the city, and there shall meet you a man bearing a pitcher of water: follow him. And wheresoever he shall go in, say ye to the goodman of the house, 'The Master saith, "Where is the guestchamber, where I shall eat the passover with my disciples?"' And he will show you a large upper room furnished and prepared: there make ready for us."

And his disciples went forth, and came into the city, and found as he had said unto them: and they made ready the passover. And in the evening he cometh with the twelve. And as they sat and did eat, Jesus said, "Verily I say unto you, 'One of you which eateth with me shall betray me.'"

And they began to be sorrowful, and to say unto him one by one, "Is it I?" and another said, "Is it I?"

And he answered and said unto them, "It is one of the twelve, that dippeth with me in the dish. The Son of Man indeed goeth, as it is written of him: but woe to that man by whom the Son of Man is betrayed! good were it for that man if he had never been born."

And as they did eat, Jesus took bread, and blessed, and broke it, and gave to them, and said, "Take, eat: this is my body."

And he took the cup, and when he had given thanks, he gave it to them: and they all drank of it. And he said unto them, "This is my blood of the new testament, which is shed for many.

THE GOSPEL ACCORDING TO MARK

Verily I say unto you, 'I will drink no more of the fruit of the vine, until that day that I drink it new in the kingdom of God.' "

And when they had sung a hymn, they went out into the Mount of Olives. And Jesus saith unto them, "All ye shall be offended because of me this night: for it is written, 'I will smite the shepherd, and the sheep shall be scattered.' But that after I am risen, I will go before you into Galilee."

But Peter said unto him, "Although all shall be offended, yet will not I."

And Jesus saith unto him, "Verily I say unto thee, 'This day, even in this night, before the cock crow twice, thou shalt deny me thrice.'"

But he spoke the more vehemently, "If I should die with thee, I will not deny thee in any wise." Likewise also said they all.

And they came to a place which was named Gethsemane: and he saith to his disciples, "Sit ye here, while I shall pray."

And he taketh with him Peter and James and John, and began to be sore amazed, and to be very heavy; and saith unto them, "My soul is exceeding sorrowful unto death: tarry ye here, and watch."

And he went forward a little, and fell on the ground, and prayed that, if it were possible, the hour might pass from him. And he said, "Abba, Father, all things are possible unto thee; take away this cup from me: nevertheless not what I will, but what thou wilt."

And he cometh, and findeth them sleeping, and saith unto Peter,

"Simon, sleepest thou? couldest not thou watch one hour? Watch ye and pray, lest ye enter into temptation. The spirit truly is ready, but the flesh is weak."

And again he went away, and prayed, and spoke the same words. And when he returned, he found them asleep again (for their eyes were heavy), neither wist they what to answer him. And he cometh the third time, and saith unto them,

"Sleep on now, and take your rest: it is enough, the hour is

THE GOSPEL ACCORDING TO MARK

come; behold, the Son of Man is betrayed into the hands of sinners. Rise up, let us go; lo, he that betrayed me is at hand."

And immediately, while he yet spoke, cometh Judas, one of the twelve, and with him a great multitude with swords and staves, from the chief priests and the scribes and the elders. And he that betrayed him had given them a token, saying, "Whomsoever I shall kiss, that same is he; take him, and lead him away safely."

And as soon as he was come, he goeth straightway to him, and saith, "Master, master"; and kissed him.

And they laid their hands on him, and took him. And one of them that stood by drew a sword, and smote a servant of the high priest, and cut off his ear. And Jesus answered and said unto them, "Are ye come out, as against a thief, with swords and with staves to take me? I was daily with you in the temple teaching, and ye took me not: but the scriptures must be fulfilled."

And they all forsook him, and fled. And there followed him a certain young man, having a linen cloth cast about his naked body; and the young men laid hold on him: and he left the linen cloth, and fled from them naked.

And they led Jesus away to the high priest: and with him were assembled all the chief priests and the elders and the scribes. And Peter followed him afar off, even into the palace of the high priest: and he sat with the servants, and warmed himself at the fire.

And the chief priests and all the council sought for witness against Jesus to put him to death; and found none. For many bore false witness against him, but their witness agreed not together. And there arose certain, and bore false witness against him, saying, "We heard him say, 'I will destroy this temple that is made with hands, and within three days I will build another made without hands.'"

But neither so did their witness agree together.

And the high priest stood up in the midst, and asked Jesus, saying, "Answerest thou nothing? what is it which these witness against thee?"

But he held his peace, and answered nothing.

THE GOSPEL ACCORDING TO MARK

Again the high priest asked him, and said unto him, "Art thou the Christ, the Son of the Blessed?"

And Jesus said, "I am: and ye shall see the Son of Man sitting on the right hand of power, and coming in the clouds of heaven."

Then the high priest rent his clothes, and saith, "What need we any further witnesses? Ye have heard the blasphemy: what think ye?"

And they all condemned him to be guilty of death. And some began to spit on him, and to cover his face, and to buffet him, and to say unto him, "Prophesy": and the servants did strike him with the palms of their hands.

And as Peter was beneath in the palace, there cometh one of the maids of the high priest: and when she saw Peter warming himself, she looked upon him, and said, "And thou also wast with Jesus of Nazareth."

But he denied, saying, "I know not, neither understand I what thou sayest." And he went out into the porch; and the cock crew.

And a maid saw him again, and began to say to them that stood by, "This is one of them." And he denied it again. And a little after, they that stood by said again to Peter, "Surely thou art one of them: for thou art a Galilæan, and thy speech agreeth thereto." But he began to curse and to swear, saying, "I know not this man of whom ye speak." And the second time the cock crew. And Peter called to mind the word that Jesus said unto him, "Before the cock crow twice, thou shalt deny me thrice." And when he thought thereon, he wept.

And straightway in the morning the chief priests held a consultation with the elders and scribes and the whole council, and bound Jesus, and carried him away, and delivered him to Pilate.

And Pilate asked him, "Art thou the King of the Jews?"

And he answering said unto him, "Thou sayest it."

And the chief priests accused him of many things: but he answered nothing.

And Pilate asked him again, saying, "Answerest thou nothing? behold how many things they witness against thee."

THE GOSPEL ACCORDING TO MARK

But Jesus yet answered nothing; so that Pilate marvelled.

Now at that feast he released unto them one prisoner, whomsoever they desired. And there was one named Barabbas, which lay bound with them that had made insurrection with him, who had committed murder in the insurrection. And the multitude crying aloud began to desire him to do as he had ever done unto them.

But Pilate answered them, saying, "Will ye that I release unto you the King of the Jews?" (For he knew that the chief priests had delivered him for envy.)

But the chief priests moved the people, that he should rather release Barabbas unto them.

And Pilate answered and said again unto them, "What will ye then that I shall do unto him whom ye call the King of the Jews?" And they cried out again, "Crucify him!"

Then Pilate said unto them, "Why, what evil hath he done?" And they cried out the more exceedingly, "Crucify him!"

And so Pilate, willing to content the people, released Barabbas unto them, and delivered Jesus, when he had scourged him, to be crucified. And the soldiers led him away into the hall, called "Prætorium"; and they call together the whole band. And they clothed him with purple, and plaited a crown of thorns, and put it about his head, and began to salute him, "Hail, King of the Jews!" And they smote him on the head with a reed, and did spit upon him, and bowing their knees worshipped him. And when they had mocked him, they took off the purple from him, and put his own clothes on him, and led him out to crucify him.

And they compel one Simon a Cyrenian, who passed by, coming out of the country, the father of Alexander and Rufus, to bear his cross. And they bring him unto the place Golgotha, which is, being interpreted, "The place of a skull." And they gave him to drink wine mingled with myrrh: but he received it not. And when they had crucified him, they parted his garments, casting lots upon them, what every man should take.

THE GOSPEL ACCORDING TO MARK

And it was the third hour, and they crucified him. And the superscription of his accusation was written over:

THE KING OF THE JEWS.

And with him they crucify two thieves; the one on his right hand, and the other on his left. And the scripture was fulfilled, which saith, "And he was numbered with the transgressors."

And they that passed by railed on him, wagging their heads, and saying, "Ah, thou that destroyest the temple, and buildest it in three days, save thyself, and come down from the cross."

Likewise also the chief priests mocking said among themselves with the scribes, "He saved others; himself he cannot save. Let Christ the King of Israel descend now from the cross that we may see and believe."

And they that were crucified with him reviled him.

And when the sixth hour was come, there was darkness over the whole land until the ninth hour.

And at the ninth hour Jesus cried with a loud voice, saying, "Eloi, Eloi, lama sabachthani?" which is, being interpreted,

"My God, my God, why hast thou forsaken me?"

And some of them that stood by, when they heard it, said, "Behold, he calleth Elias." And one ran and filled a sponge full of vinegar, and put it on a reed, and gave him to drink, saying, "Let alone; let us see whether Elias will come to take him down."

And Jesus cried with a loud voice, and gave up the ghost.

And the veil of the temple was rent in twain from the top to the bottom. And when the centurion, which stood over against him, saw that he so cried out, and gave up the ghost, he said, "Truly this man was the Son of God."

There were also women looking on afar off: among whom was Mary Magdalene, and Mary the mother of James the less and of Joses, and Salome (who also, when he was in Galilee, followed him, and ministered unto him); and many other women which came up with him unto Jerusalem.

And now when the even was come, because it was the prep

THE GOSPEL ACCORDING TO MARK

aration, that is, the day before the sabbath, Joseph of Arimathæa, an honourable counsellor, which also waited for the kingdom of God, came, and went in boldly unto Pilate, and craved the body of Jesus. And Pilate marvelled if he were already dead: and calling unto him the centurion, he asked him whether he had been any while dead. And when he knew it of the centurion, he gave the body to Joseph. And he bought fine linen, and took him down, and wrapped him in the linen, and laid him in a sepulchre which was hewn out of a rock, and rolled a stone unto the door of the sepulchre. And Mary Magdalene and Mary the mother of Joses beheld where he was laid.

And when the sabbath was past, Mary Magdalene, and Mary the mother of James, and Salome, had bought sweet spices, that they might come and anoint him. And very early in the morning the first day of the week, they came unto the sepulchre at the rising of the sun. And they said among themselves, "Who shall roll us away the stone from the door of the sepulchre?"

And when they looked, they saw that the stone was rolled away: for it was very great. And entering into the sepulchre, they saw a young man sitting on the right side, clothed in a long white garment; and they were affrighted.

And he saith unto them, "Be not affrighted: ye seek Jesus of Nazareth, which was crucified: he is risen; he is not here: behold the place where they laid him. But go your way, tell his disciples and Peter that he goeth before you into Galilee: there shall ye see him, as he said unto you."

And they went out quickly, and fled from the sepulchre; for they trembled and were amazed: neither said they any thing to any man; for they were afraid.

Appendix

Now when Jesus was risen early the first day of the week, he appeared first to Mary Magdalene, out of whom he had cast seven devils. And she went and told them that had been with him, as they mourned and wept. And they, when they had heard that he was alive, and had been seen of her, believed not.

THE GOSPEL ACCORDING TO MARK

After that he appeared in another form unto two of them, as they walked, and went into the country. And they went and told it unto the residue: neither believed they them.

Afterward he appeared unto the eleven as they sat at meat, and upbraided them with their unbelief and hardness of heart, because they believed not them which had seen him after he was risen. And he said unto them, "Go ye into all the world, and preach the gospel to every creature. He that believeth and is baptized shall be saved; but he that believeth not shall be damned. And these signs shall follow them that believe: in my name shall they cast out devils; they shall speak with new tongues; they shall take up serpents; and if they drink any deadly thing, it shall not hurt them; they shall lay hands on the sick, and they shall recover."

So then after the Lord had spoken unto them, he was received up into heaven, and sat on the right hand of God. And they went forth, and preached every where, the Lord working with them, and confirming the word with signs following. Amen.

THE GOSPEL ACCORDING TO MATTHEW

SELECTIONS

From the gospel according to Matthew we derive our main knowledge of the teachings of Jesus. An early tradition attributed to the disciple Matthew a collection of "Precepts of Our Lord," which if it really existed may well have been the basis of the collection incorporated in the Gospel. The profundity of thought and the distinctive literary style of the Sermon on the Mount and the parables are in such striking contrast to the surrounding portions of the Gospel that one feels certain they must have come from Jesus himself. If one is ever justified in inferring from speech the personality of the speaker, this is surely an instance of it.

The Gospel according to Matthew was especially addressed to the Jews in an effort to prove that Jesus was the Messiah whom they had expected; hence the stress upon the fulfilment in his career of Old Testament prophecies and also upon his descent from David (in the genealogical table omitted in this text).

As the value of the Gospel according to Matthew lies for us in the reported utterances of Jesus, there seemed no reason for reprinting here the narrative sections taken from Mark, except that, with regard to the Trial, Crucifixion, and Resurrection, even slight differences among the Gospels possess such interest that it seemed well to include all four accounts.

The Gospel According to MATTHEW

The Birth of Jesus

Now the birth of Jesus Christ was on this wise: when as his mother Mary was espoused to Joseph, before they came together, she was found with child of the Holy Ghost. Then Joseph her husband, being a just man, and not willing to make her a public example, was minded to put her away privily. But while he thought on these things, behold, the angel of the Lord appeared unto him in a dream, saying,

"Joseph, thou son of David, fear not to take unto thee Mary thy wife: for that which is conceived in her is of the Holy Ghost. And she shall bring forth a son, and thou shalt call his name JESUS: for he shall save his people from their sins."

Now all this was done, that it might be fulfilled which was spoken of the Lord by the prophet, saying,

"*Behold, a virgin shall be with child,*
And shall bring forth a son,
And they shall call his name Emmanuel,
Which being interpreted is, 'God with us.'"

Then Joseph being raised from sleep did as the angel of the Lord had bidden him, and took unto him his wife: and knew her not till she had brought forth her firstborn son: and he called his name JESUS.

Now when Jesus was born in Bethlehem of Judæa in the days of Herod the king, behold, there came wise men from the east to Jerusalem, saying,

THE GOSPEL ACCORDING TO MATTHEW

"Where is he that is born King of the Jews? for we have seen his star in the east, and are come to worship him."

When Herod the king had heard these things, he was troubled, and all Jerusalem with him. And when he had gathered all the chief priests and scribes of the people together, he demanded of them where Christ should be born. And they said unto him, "In Bethlehem of Judæa: for thus it is written by the prophet,

> "'And thou Bethlehem, in the land of Juda,
> Art not the least among the princes of Juda:
> For out of thee shall come a Governor,
> That shall rule my people Israel.'"

Then Herod, when he had privily called the wise men, enquired of them diligently what time the star appeared. And he sent them to Bethlehem, and said, "Go and search diligently for the young child; and when ye have found him, bring me word again, that I may come and worship him also."

When they had heard the king, they departed; and, lo, the star, which they saw in the east, went before them, till it came and stood over where the young child was. When they saw the star, they rejoiced with exceeding great joy. And when they were come into the house, they saw the young child with Mary his mother, and fell down, and worshipped him: and when they had opened their treasures, they presented unto him gifts; gold, and frankincense, and myrrh. And being warned of God in a dream that they should not return to Herod, they departed into their own country another way.

And when they were departed, behold, the angel of the Lord appeareth to Joseph in a dream, saying, "Arise, and take the young child and his mother, and flee into Egypt, and be thou there until I bring thee word: for Herod will seek the young child to destroy him."

When he arose, he took the young child and his mother by night, and departed into Egypt: and was there until the death of Herod: that it might be fulfilled which was spoken of the Lord by the prophet, saying, "Out of Egypt have I called my son."

THE GOSPEL ACCORDING TO MATTHEW

Then Herod, when he saw that he was mocked of the wise men, was exceedingly wroth, and sent forth, and slew all the children that were in Bethlehem, and in all the coasts thereof, from two years old and under, according to the time which he had diligently enquired of the wise men. Then was fulfilled that which was spoken by Jeremy the prophet, saying,

> "In Rama was there a voice heard,
> Lamentation, and weeping, and great mourning,
> Rachel weeping for her children,
> And would not be comforted,
> Because they are not."

But when Herod was dead, behold, an angel of the Lord appeareth in a dream to Joseph in Egypt, saying, "Arise, and take the young child and his mother, and go into the land of Israel: for they are dead which sought the young child's life."

And he arose, and took the young child and his mother, and came into the land of Israel. But when he heard that Archelaus did reign in Judæa in the room of his father Herod, he was afraid to go thither: notwithstanding, being warned of God in a dream, he turned aside into the parts of Galilee. And he came and dwelt in a city called Nazareth: that it might be fulfilled which was spoken by the prophets, "He shall be called a Nazarene."

The Temptation

Then was Jesus led up of the spirit into the wilderness to be tempted of the devil. And when he had fasted forty days and forty nights, he was afterward a-hungered. And when the tempter came to him, he said, "If thou be the Son of God, command that these stones be made bread." But he answered and said, "It is written, 'Man shall not live by bread alone, but by every word that proceedeth out of the mouth of God.'"

Then the devil taketh him up into the holy city, and setteth him on a pinnacle of the temple. And saith unto him, "If thou be the Son of God, cast thyself down: for it is written,

THE GOSPEL ACCORDING TO MATTHEW

"'He shall give his angels charge concerning thee:
And in their hands they shall bear thee up,
Lest at any time thou dash thy foot against a stone.'"

Jesus said unto him, "It is written again, 'Thou shalt not tempt the Lord thy God.'"

Again, the devil taketh him up into an exceeding high mountain, and showeth him all the kingdoms of the world, and the glory of them; and saith unto him, "All these things will I give thee, if thou wilt fall down and worship me." Then saith Jesus unto him, "Get thee hence, Satan: for it is written, 'Thou shalt worship the Lord thy God, and him only shalt thou serve.'"

Then the devil leaveth him, and behold, angels came and ministered unto him.

Now when Jesus had heard that John was cast into prison, he departed into Galilee; and leaving Nazareth, he came and dwelt in Capernaum, which is upon the sea coast, in the borders of Zabulon and Nephthalim: that it might be fulfilled which was spoken by Esaias the prophet, saying,

"The land of Zabulon, and the land of Nephthalim,
By the way of the sea, beyond Jordan,
Galilee of the Gentiles;
The people which sat in darkness
Saw great light;
And to them which sat in the region and shadow of death
Light is sprung up."

From that time Jesus began to preach, and to say, "Repent: for the kingdom of heaven is at hand."

The Sermon on the Mount

And seeing the multitudes, he went up into a mountain: and when he was set, his disciples came unto him: and he opened his mouth, and taught them, saying,

"Blessed are the poor in spirit:
For theirs is the kingdom of heaven.

THE GOSPEL ACCORDING TO MATTHEW

Blessed are they that mourn:
For they shall be comforted.

Blessed are the meek:
For they shall inherit the earth.

Blessed are they which do hunger and thirst after righteousness:
For they shall be filled.

Blessed are the merciful:
For they shall obtain mercy.

Blessed are the pure in heart:
For they shall see God.

Blessed are the peacemakers:
For they shall be called the children of God.

Blessed are they which are persecuted for righteousness' sake:
For theirs is the kingdom of heaven.

Blessed are ye, when men shall revile you, and persecute you, and
shall say all manner of evil against you falsely, for my sake.
Rejoice, and be exceeding glad: for great is your reward in heaven: for
so persecuted they the prophets which were before you.

"Ye are the salt of the earth: but if the salt have lost his savour, wherewith shall it be salted? it is thenceforth good for nothing, but to be cast out, and to be trodden under foot of men.

"Ye are the light of the world. A city that is set on a hill cannot be hid. Neither do men light a candle, and put it under a bushel, but on a candlestick; and it giveth light unto all that are in the house. Let your light so shine before men, that they may see your good works, and glorify your Father which is in heaven.

"Think not that I am come to destroy the law, or the prophets: I am not come to destroy, but to fulfil. For verily I say unto you, 'Till heaven and earth pass, one jot or one tittle shall in no wise pass from the law, till all be fulfilled.' Whosoever therefore shall break one of these least commandments, and shall teach

THE GOSPEL ACCORDING TO MATTHEW

men so, he shall be called the least in the kingdom of heaven: but whosoever shall do and teach them, the same shall be called great in the kingdom of heaven. For I say unto you, 'Except your righteousness shall exceed the righteousness of the scribes and Pharisees, ye shall in no case enter into the kingdom of heaven.'

"Ye have heard that it was said by them of old time, 'Thou shalt not kill'; and whosoever shall kill shall be in danger of the judgment. But I say unto you, 'Whosoever is angry with his brother without a cause shall be in danger of the judgment: and whosoever shall say to his brother, "Raca," shall be in danger of the council: but whosoever shall say, "Thou fool," shall be in danger of hell fire.' Therefore if thou bring thy gift to the altar, and there rememberest that thy brother hath ought against thee; leave there thy gift before the altar, and go thy way; first be reconciled to thy brother, and then come and offer thy gift. Agree with thine adversary quickly, while thou art in the way with him; lest at any time the adversary deliver thee to the judge, and the judge deliver thee to the officer, and thou be cast into prison. Verily I say unto thee, 'Thou shalt by no means come out thence, till thou hast paid the uttermost farthing.'

"Ye have heard that it was said by them of old time, 'Thou shalt not commit adultery.' But I say unto you, 'Whosoever looketh on a woman to lust after her hath committed adultery with her already in his heart. And if thy right eye offend thee, pluck it out, and cast it from thee: for it is profitable for thee that one of thy members should perish, and not that thy whole body should be cast into hell. And if thy right hand offend thee, cut it off, and cast it from thee: for it is profitable for thee that one of thy members should perish, and not that thy whole body should be cast into hell.' It hath been said, 'Whosoever shall put away his wife, let him give her a writing of divorcement.' But I say unto you, 'Whosoever shall put away his wife, saving for the cause of fornication, causeth her to commit adultery: and whosoever shall marry her that is divorced committeth adultery.'

THE GOSPEL ACCORDING TO MATTHEW

"Again, ye have heard that it hath been said by them of old time, 'Thou shalt not forswear thyself, but shalt perform unto the Lord thine oaths.' But I say unto you, 'Swear not at all; neither by heaven; for it is God's throne: nor by the earth; for it is his footstool: neither by Jerusalem; for it is the city of the great King. Neither shalt thou swear by thy head, because thou canst not make one hair white or black. But let your communication be, "Yea, yea"; "Nay, nay": for whatsoever is more than these cometh of evil.'

"Ye have heard that it hath been said, 'An eye for an eye, and a tooth for a tooth.' But I say unto you, 'Resist not evil: but whosoever shall smite thee on thy right cheek, turn to him the other also. And if any man will sue thee at the law, and take away thy coat, let him have thy cloak also. And whosoever shall compel thee to go a mile, go with him twain. Give to him that asketh thee, and from him that would borrow of thee turn not thou away.'

"Ye have heard that it hath been said, 'Thou shalt love thy neighbour, and hate thine enemy.' But I say unto you, 'Love your enemies, bless them that curse you, do good to them that hate you, and pray for them which despitefully use you, and persecute you; that ye may be the children of your Father which is in heaven: for he maketh his sun to rise on the evil and on the good, and sendeth rain on the just and on the unjust.' For if ye love them which love you, what reward have ye? do not even the publicans the same? And if ye salute your brethren only, what do ye more than others? do not even the publicans so? Be ye therefore perfect, even as your Father which is in heaven is perfect.

"Take heed that ye do not your alms before men, to be seen of them: otherwise ye have no reward of your Father which is in heaven. Therefore when thou doest thine alms, do not sound a trumpet before thee, as the hypocrites do in the synagogues and in the streets, that they may have glory of men. Verily I say unto you, 'They have their reward.' But when thou doest alms, let not thy left hand know what thy right hand doeth: that

THE GOSPEL ACCORDING TO MATTHEW

thine alms may be in secret: and thy Father which seeth in secret himself shall reward thee openly.

"And when thou prayest, thou shalt not be as the hypocrites are: for they love to pray standing in the synagogues and in the corners of the streets, that they may be seen of men. Verily I say unto you, 'They have their reward.' But thou, when thou prayest, enter into thy closet, and when thou hast shut thy door, pray to thy Father which is in secret; and thy Father which seeth in secret shall reward thee openly. But when ye pray, use not vain repetitions, as the heathen do: for they think that they shall be heard for their much speaking. Be not ye therefore like unto them: for your Father knoweth what things ye have need of, before ye ask him. After this manner therefore pray ye:

> " 'Our Father which art in heaven,
> Hallowed be thy name.
> Thy kingdom come.
> Thy will be done
> In earth, as it is in heaven.
>
> Give us this day
> Our daily bread.
> And forgive us our debts,
> As we forgive our debtors.
> And lead us not into temptation,
> But deliver us from evil:
>
> For thine is the kingdom,
> And the power,
> And the glory,
> For ever. Amen.'

"For if ye forgive men their trespasses, your heavenly Father will also forgive you: but if ye forgive not men their trespasses, neither will your Father forgive your trespasses.

"Moreover when ye fast, be not, as the hypocrites, of a sad countenance: for they disfigure their faces, that they may appear unto men to fast. Verily I say unto you, 'They have their re-

THE GOSPEL ACCORDING TO MATTHEW

ward.' But thou, when thou fastest, anoint thine head, and wash thy face; that thou appear not unto men to fast, but unto thy Father which is in secret: and thy Father, which seeth in secret shall reward thee openly.

> "Lay not up for yourselves treasures upon earth,
> Where moth and rust doth corrupt,
> And where thieves break through and steal:
>
> But lay up for yourselves treasures in heaven,
> Where neither moth nor rust doth corrupt,
> And where thieves do not break through nor steal.

For where your treasure is, there will your heart be also.

"The light of the body is the eye: if therefore thine eye be single, thy whole body shall be full of light. But if thine eye be evil, thy whole body shall be full of darkness. If therefore the light that is in thee be darkness, how great is that darkness!

"No man can serve two masters: for either he will hate the one, and love the other; or else he will hold to the one, and despise the other. Ye cannot serve God and Mammon.

"Therefore I say unto you, 'Take no thought for your life, what ye shall eat, or what ye shall drink; nor yet for your body, what ye shall put on.' Is not the life more than meat, and the body than raiment? Behold the fowls of the air: for they sow not, neither do they reap, nor gather into barns; yet your heavenly Father feedeth them. Are ye not much better than they? Which of you by taking thought can add one cubit unto his stature? And why take ye thought for raiment? Consider the lilies of the field, how they grow; they toil not, neither do they spin: and yet I say unto you that even Solomon in all his glory was not arrayed like one of these.

"Wherefore, if God so clothe the grass of the field, which to-day is, and to-morrow is cast into the oven, shall he not much more clothe you, O ye of little faith? Therefore take no thought, saying, 'What shall we eat?' or, 'What shall we drink?' or, 'Wherewithal shall we be clothed?' (For after all these things

THE GOSPEL ACCORDING TO MATTHEW

do the Gentiles seek): for your heavenly Father knoweth that ye have need of all these things. But seek ye first the kingdom of God, and his righteousness; and all these things shall be added unto you. Take therefore no thought for the morrow: for the morrow shall take thought for the things of itself. Sufficient unto the day is the evil thereof.

"Judge not, that ye be not judged. For with what judgment ye judge, ye shall be judged: and with what measure ye mete, it shall be measured to you again. And why beholdest thou the mote that is in thy brother's eye, but considerest not the beam that is in thine own eye? Or how wilt thou say to thy brother, 'Let me pull out the mote out of thine eye'; and, behold, a beam is in thine own eye? Thou hypocrite, first cast out the beam out of thine own eye; and then shalt thou see clearly to cast out the mote out of thy brother's eye.

>"Give not that which is holy unto the dogs,
>Neither cast ye your pearls before swine,
>Lest they trample them under their feet,
>And turn again and rend you.
>
>Ask, and it shall be given you;
>Seek, and ye shall find;
>Knock, and it shall be opened unto you:
>
>For every one that asketh receiveth;
>And he that seeketh findeth;
>And to him that knocketh it shall be opened.

Or what man is there of you, whom if his son ask bread, will he give him a stone? Or if he ask a fish, will he give him a serpent? If ye then, being evil, know how to give good gifts unto your children, how much more shall your Father which is in heaven give good things to them that ask him? Therefore all things whatsoever ye would that men should do to you, do ye even so to them: for this is the law and the prophets.

"Enter ye in at the strait gate: for wide is the gate, and broad is the way, that leadeth to destruction, and many there be

THE GOSPEL ACCORDING TO MATTHEW

which go in thereat: because strait is the gate, and narrow is the way, which leadeth unto life, and few there be that find it.

"Beware of false prophets, which come to you in sheep's clothing, but inwardly they are ravening wolves. Ye shall know them by their fruits. Do men gather grapes of thorns, or figs of thistles? Even so every good tree bringeth forth good fruit; but a corrupt tree bringeth forth evil fruit. A good tree cannot bring forth evil fruit, neither can a corrupt tree bring forth good fruit. Every tree that bringeth not forth good fruit is hewn down, and cast into the fire. Wherefore by their fruits ye shall know them.

"Not every one that saith unto me, 'Lord, Lord,' shall enter into the kingdom of heaven; but he that doeth the will of my Father which is in heaven. Many will say to me in that day, 'Lord, Lord, have we not prophesied in thy name? and in thy name have cast out devils? and in thy name done many wonderful works?' And then will I profess unto them, 'I never knew you: depart from me, ye that work iniquity.'

"Therefore whosoever heareth these sayings of mine, and doeth them, I will liken him unto a wise man, which built his house upon a rock: and the rain descended, and the floods came and the winds blew, and beat upon that house; and it fell not: for it was founded upon a rock. And every one that heareth these sayings of mine, and doeth them not, shall be likened unto a foolish man, which built his house upon the sand: and the rain descended, and the floods came, and the winds blew, and beat upon that house; and it fell: and great was the fall of it."

And it came to pass, when Jesus had ended these sayings, the people were astonished at his doctrine: for he taught them as one having authority, and not as the scribes.

Jesus and John the Baptist

And it came to pass, when Jesus had made an end of commanding his twelve disciples, he departed thence to teach and to preach in their cities. Now when John had heard in the prison the works of Christ, he sent two of his disciples, and

THE GOSPEL ACCORDING TO MATTHEW

said unto him, "Art thou he that should come, or do we look for another?"

Jesus answered and said unto them,

"Go and show John again those things which ye do hear and see: the blind receive their sight, and the lame walk, the lepers are cleansed, and the deaf hear, the dead are raised up, and the poor have the gospel preached to them. And blessed is he, whosoever shall not be offended in me."

And as they departed, Jesus began to say unto the multitudes concerning John,

"What went ye out into the wilderness to see? A reed shaken with the wind? But what went ye out for to see? A man clothed in soft raiment? behold, they that wear soft clothing are in kings' houses. But what went ye out for to see? A prophet? yea, I say unto you, and more than a prophet.

"For this is he, of whom it is written, 'Behold, I send my messenger before thy face, which shall prepare thy way before thee.' Verily I say unto you, 'Among them that are born of women there hath not risen a greater than John the Baptist: notwithstanding he that is least in the kingdom of heaven is greater than he. And from the days of John the Baptist until now the kingdom of heaven suffereth violence, and the violent take it by force. For all the prophets and the law prophesied until John. And if ye will receive it, this is Elias, which was for to come. He that hath ears to hear, let him hear.'

"But whereunto shall I liken this generation? It is like unto children sitting in the markets, and calling unto their fellows, and saying, 'We have piped unto you, and ye have not danced; we have mourned unto you, and ye have not lamented.' For John came neither eating nor drinking, and they say, 'He hath a devil.' The Son of Man came eating and drinking, and they say, 'Behold a man gluttonous, and a winebibber, a friend of publicans and sinners.' But wisdom is justified of her children."

Then began he to upbraid the cities wherein most of his mighty works were done, because they repented not:

"Woe unto thee, Chorazin! woe unto thee, Bethsaida! for if

THE GOSPEL ACCORDING TO MATTHEW

the mighty works, which were done in you, had been done in Tyre and Sidon, they would have repented long ago in sackcloth and ashes. But I say unto you, 'It shall be more tolerable for Tyre and Sidon at the day of judgment, than for you.' And thou, Capernaum, which art exalted unto heaven, shalt be brought down to hell: for if the mighty works, which have been done in thee, had been done in Sodom, it would have remained until this day. But I say unto you that it shall be more tolerable for the land of Sodom in the day of judgment, than for thee."

At that time Jesus answered and said,

"I thank thee, O Father, Lord of heaven and earth, because thou hast hid these things from the wise and prudent, and hast revealed them unto babes. Even so, Father: for so it seemed good in thy sight. All things are delivered unto me of my Father: and no man knoweth the Son, but the Father; neither knoweth any man the Father, save the Son, and he to whomsoever the Son will reveal him.

"Come unto me, all ye that labour and are heavy laden, and I will give you rest. Take my yoke upon you, and learn of me; for I am meek and lowly in heart: and ye shall find rest unto your souls. For my yoke is easy, and my burden is light."

Parables of the Kingdom

The same day went Jesus out of the house, and sat by the sea side. And great multitudes were gathered together unto him, so that he went into a ship, and sat; and the whole multitude stood on the shore. And he spoke many things unto them in parables, saying,

"Behold, a sower went forth to sow. And when he sowed, some seeds fell by the way side, and the fowls came and devoured them up. Some fell upon stony places, where they had not much earth: and forthwith they sprung up, because they had no deepness of earth: and when the sun was up, they were scorched; and because they had no root, they withered away. And some fell among thorns; and the thorns sprung up, and choked them. But other fell into good ground, and brought

THE GOSPEL ACCORDING TO MATTHEW

forth fruit, some a hundredfold, some sixtyfold, some thirtyfold. Who hath ears to hear, let him hear."

And the disciples came, and said unto him, "Why speakest thou unto them in parables?"

He answered and said unto them, "Because it is given unto you to know the mysteries of the kingdom of heaven, but to them it is not given. For whosoever hath, to him shall be given, and he shall have more abundance: but whosoever hath not, from him shall be taken away even that he hath. Therefore speak I to them in parables: because they seeing see not; and hearing they hear not, neither do they understand. And in them is fulfilled the prophecy of Esaias, which saith, 'By hearing ye shall hear, and shall not understand; and seeing ye shall see, and shall not perceive': for this people's heart is waxed gross, and their ears are dull of hearing, and their eyes they have closed; lest at any time they should see with their eyes, and hear with their ears, and should understand with their heart, and should be converted, and I should heal them. But blessed are your eyes, for they see: and your ears, for they hear. For verily I say unto you that many prophets and righteous men have desired to see those things which ye see, and have not seen them; and to hear those things which ye hear, and have not heard them.

"Hear ye therefore the parable of the sower. When any one heareth the word of the kingdom, and understandeth it not, then cometh the wicked one, and catcheth away that which was sown in his heart. This is he which received seed by the way side. But he that received the seed into stony places, the same is he that heareth the word, and anon with joy receiveth it; yet hath he not root in himself, but endureth for a while: for when tribulation or persecution ariseth because of the word, by and by he is offended. He also that received seed among the thorns is he that heareth the word; and the care of this world, and the deceitfulness of riches, choke the word, and he becometh unfruitful. But he that received seed into the good ground is he that heareth the word, and understandeth it; which also beareth

THE GOSPEL ACCORDING TO MATTHEW

fruit, and bringeth forth, some a hundredfold, some sixty, some thirty."

Another parable put he forth unto them, saying,

"The kingdom of heaven is likened unto a man which sowed good seed in his field. But while men slept, his enemy came and sowed tares among the wheat, and went his way. But when the blade was sprung up, and brought forth fruit, then appeared the tares also. So the servants of the householder came and said unto him, 'Sir, didst not thou sow good seed in thy field? from whence then hath it tares?' He said unto them, 'An enemy hath done this.' The servants said unto him, 'Wilt thou then that we go and gather them up?' But he said, 'Nay; lest while ye gather up the tares, ye root up also the wheat with them. Let both grow together until the harvest: and in the time of harvest I will say to the reapers, "Gather ye together first the tares, and bind them in bundles to burn them: but gather the wheat into my barn."'"

Another parable put he forth unto them, saying,

"The kingdom of heaven is like to a grain of mustard seed, which a man took, and sowed in his field: which indeed is the least of all seeds: but when it is grown, it is the greatest among herbs, and becometh a tree, so that the birds of the air come and lodge in the branches thereof."

Another parable spoke he unto them:

"The kingdom of heaven is like unto leaven, which a woman took, and hid in three measures of meal, till the whole was leavened." All these things spoke Jesus unto the multitude in parables; and without a parable spoke he not unto them: that it might be fulfilled which was spoken by the prophet, saying,

"*I will open my mouth in parables;*
I will utter things which have been kept secret from the foundation of the world."

Then Jesus sent the multitude away, and went into the house:

THE GOSPEL ACCORDING TO MATTHEW

and his disciples came unto him, saying, "Declare unto us the parable of the tares of the field."

He answered and said unto them, "He that soweth the good seed is the Son of Man; the field is the world; the good seed are the children of the kingdom; but the tares are the children of the wicked one; the enemy that sowed them is the devil; the harvest is the end of the world; and the reapers are the angels. As therefore the tares are gathered and burned in the fire; so shall it be in the end of this world. The Son of Man shall send forth his angels, and they shall gather out of his kingdom all things that offend, and them which do iniquity; and shall cast them into a furnace of fire: there shall be wailing and gnashing of teeth. Then shall the righteous shine forth as the sun in the kingdom of their Father. Who hath ears to hear, let him hear.

"Again, the kingdom of heaven is like unto treasure hid in a field; the which when a man hath found, he hideth, and for joy thereof goeth and selleth all that he hath, and buyeth that field.

"Again, the kingdom of heaven is like unto a merchant man, seeking goodly pearls, who, when he had found one pearl of great price, went and sold all that he had, and bought it.

"Again, the kingdom of heaven is like unto a net, that was cast into the sea, and gathered of every kind: which, when it was full, they drew to shore, and sat down, and gathered the good into vessels, but cast the bad away. So shall it be at the end of the world: the angels shall come forth, and sever the wicked from among the just, and shall cast them into the furnace of fire: there shall be wailing and gnashing of teeth."

Jesus saith unto them, "Have ye understood all these things?"

They say unto him, "Yea, Lord."

Then said he unto them,

"Therefore every scribe which is instructed unto the kingdom of heaven is like unto a man that is a householder, which bringeth forth out of his treasure things new and old."

And it came to pass, that when Jesus had finished these parables, he departed thence.

THE GOSPEL ACCORDING TO MATTHEW

Then came Peter to him, and said, "Lord, how oft shall my brother sin against me, and I forgive him? till seven times?"

Jesus saith unto him, "I say not unto thee, 'Until seven times': but, 'Until seventy times seven.'

"Therefore is the kingdom of heaven likened unto a certain king, which would take account of his servants. And when he had begun to reckon, one was brought unto him, which owed him ten thousand talents. But forasmuch as he had not to pay, his lord commanded him to be sold, and his wife, and children, and all that he had, and payment to be made. The servant therefore fell down, and worshipped him, saying, 'Lord, have patience with me, and I will pay thee all.' Then the lord of that servant was moved with compassion, and loosed him, and forgave him the debt.

"But the same servant went out, and found one of his fellowservants, which owed him a hundred pence: and he laid hands on him, and took him by the throat, saying, 'Pay me that thou owest.' And his fellowservant fell down at his feet, and besought him, saying, 'Have patience with me, and I will pay thee all.' And he would not: but went and cast him into prison, till he should pay the debt. So when his fellowservants saw what was done, they were very sorry, and came and told unto their lord all that was done. Then his lord, after that he had called him, said unto him, 'O thou wicked servant, I forgave thee all that debt, because thou desiredst me. Shouldest not thou also have had compassion on thy fellowservant, even as I had pity on thee?' And his lord was wroth, and delivered him to the tormentors, till he should pay all that was due unto him. So likewise shall my heavenly Father do also unto you, if ye from your hearts forgive not every one his brother their trespasses."

And it came to pass, that when Jesus had finished these sayings, he departed from Galilee, and came into the coasts of Judæa beyond Jordan; and great multitudes followed him; and he healed them there.

The Pharisees also came unto him, tempting him, and saying

THE GOSPEL ACCORDING TO MATTHEW

unto him, "Is it lawful for a man to put away his wife for every cause?"

And he answered and said unto them, "Have ye not read that he which made them at the beginning made them male and female, and said, 'For this cause shall a man leave father and mother, and shall cleave to his wife: and they twain shall be one flesh'? Wherefore they are no more twain, but one flesh. What therefore God hath joined together, let not man put asunder."

They say unto him, "Why did Moses then command to give a writing of divorcement, and to put her away?"

He saith unto them,

"Moses because of the hardness of your hearts suffered you to put away your wives: but from the beginning it was not so. And I say unto you, 'Whosoever shall put away his wife, except it be for fornication, and shall marry another, committeth adultery: and whoso marrieth her which is put away doth commit adultery.'"

His disciples say unto him, "If the case of the man be so with his wife, it is not good to marry."

But he said unto them,

"All men cannot receive this saying, save they to whom it is given. For there are some eunuchs, which were so born from their mother's womb: and there are some eunuchs, which were made eunuchs of men: and there be eunuchs, which have made themselves eunuchs for the kingdom of heaven's sake. He that is able to receive it, let him receive it."

Then were there brought unto him little children, that he should put his hands on them, and pray: and the disciples rebuked them. But Jesus said,

"Suffer little children, and forbid them not, to come unto me: for of such is the kingdom of heaven."

And he laid his hands on them, and departed thence.

And, behold, one came and said unto him, "Good Master, what good thing shall I do, that I may have eternal life?"

THE GOSPEL ACCORDING TO MATTHEW

And he said unto him,

"Why callest thou me good? there is none good but one, that is, God: but if thou wilt enter into life, keep the commandments."

He saith unto him, "Which?"

Jesus said, "Thou shalt do no murder, thou shalt not commit adultery, thou shalt not steal, thou shalt not bear false witness; honour thy father and thy mother: and, thou shalt love thy neighbour as thyself."

The young man saith unto him, "All these things have I kept from my youth up: what lack I yet?"

Jesus said unto him,

"If thou wilt be perfect, go and sell that thou hast, and give to the poor, and thou shalt have treasure in heaven: and come and follow me."

But when the young man heard that saying, he went away sorrowful: for he had great possessions.

Then said Jesus unto his disciples,

"Verily I say unto you that a rich man shall hardly enter into the kingdom of heaven. And again I say unto you, 'It is easier for a camel to go through the eye of a needle, than for a rich man to enter into the kingdom of God.'"

When his disciples heard it, they were exceedingly amazed, saying, "Who then can be saved?"

But Jesus beheld them, and said unto them,

"With men this is impossible; but with God all things are possible."

Then answered Peter and said unto him, "Behold, we have forsaken all, and followed thee; what shall we have therefore?"

And Jesus said unto them,

"Verily I say unto you that ye which have followed me, in the regeneration when the Son of Man shall sit in the throne of his glory, ye also shall sit upon twelve thrones, judging the twelve tribes of Israel. And every one that hath forsaken houses, or brethren, or sisters, or father, or mother, or wife, or children, or lands, for my name's sake, shall receive a hundredfold, and shall inherit everlasting life. But many that are first shall be last; and the last shall be first.

"For the kingdom of heaven is like unto a man that is a householder, which went out early in the morning to hire labourers into his vineyard. And when he had agreed with the labourers for a penny a day, he sent them into his vineyard. And he went out about the third hour, and saw others standing idle in the marketplace, and said unto them, 'Go ye also into the vineyard, and whatsoever is right I will give you.' And they went their way. Again he went out about the sixth and ninth hour, and did likewise. And about the eleventh hour he went out, and found others standing idle, and saith unto them, 'Why stand ye here all the day idle?' They say unto him, 'Because no man hath hired us.' He saith unto them, 'Go ye also into the vineyard; and whatsoever is right, that shall ye receive.'

"So when even was come, the lord of the vineyard saith unto his steward, 'Call the labourers, and give them their hire, beginning from the last unto the first.' And when they came that were hired about the eleventh hour, they received every man a penny. But when the first came, they supposed that they should have received more; and they likewise received every man a penny. And when they had received it, they murmured against the goodman of the house, saying, 'These last have wrought but one hour, and thou hast made them equal unto us, which have borne the burden and heat of the day.' But he answered one of them, and said, 'Friend, I do thee no wrong: didst not thou agree with me for a penny? Take that thine is, and go thy way: I will give unto this last, even as unto thee. Is it not lawful for me to do what I will with mine own? Is thine eye evil, because I am good?' So the last shall be first, and the first last: for many be called, but few chosen."

On the Priests, Scribes, and Pharisees

And when he was come into the temple, the chief priests and the elders of the people came unto him as he was teaching,

THE GOSPEL ACCORDING TO MATTHEW

and said, "By what authority doest thou these things? and who gave thee this authority?"

And Jesus answered and said unto them,

"I also will ask you one thing, which if ye tell me, I in like wise will tell you by what authority I do these things. The baptism of John, whence was it? from heaven, or of men?"

And they reasoned with themselves, saying, "If we shall say, 'From heaven'; he will say unto us, 'Why did ye not then believe him?' But if we shall say, 'Of men'; we fear the people; for all hold John as a prophet." And they answered Jesus, and said, "We cannot tell."

And he said unto them, "Neither tell I you by what authority I do these things.

"But what think ye? A certain man had two sons; and he came to the first, and said, 'Son, go work to-day in my vineyard.' He answered and said, 'I will not': but afterward he repented, and went. And he came to the second, and said likewise. And he answered and said, 'I go, sir': and went not. Whether of them twain did the will of his father?"

They say unto him, "The first."

Jesus saith unto them,

"Verily I say unto you that the publicans and the harlots go into the kingdom of God before you. For John came unto you in the way of righteousness, and ye believed him not: but the publicans and the harlots believed him: and ye, when ye had seen it, repented not afterward, that ye might believe him.

"Hear another parable: there was a certain householder, which planted a vineyard, and hedged it round about, and digged a winepress in it, and built a tower, and let it out to husbandmen, and went into a far country: and when the time of the fruit drew near, he sent his servants to the husbandmen, that they might receive the fruits of it. And the husbandmen took his servants, and beat one, and killed another, and stoned another. Again, he sent other servants more than the first: and they did unto them likewise. But last of all he sent unto them his son, saying, 'They will reverence my son.' But when the husband-

THE GOSPEL ACCORDING TO MATTHEW

men saw the son, they said among themselves, 'This is the heir; come, let us kill him, and let us seize on his inheritance.' And they caught him, and cast him out of the vineyard, and slew him. When the lord therefore of the vineyard cometh, what will he do unto those husbandmen?"

They say unto him, "He will miserably destroy those wicked men, and will let out his vineyard unto other husbandmen, which shall render him the fruits in their seasons."

Jesus saith unto them, "Did ye never read in the scriptures,

> "'The stone which the builders rejected,
> The same is become the head of the corner:
> This is the Lord's doing,
> And it is marvellous in our eyes'?

Therefore say I unto you, 'The kingdom of God shall be taken from you, and given to a nation bringing forth the fruits thereof. And whosoever shall fall on this stone shall be broken: but on whomsoever it shall fall, it will grind him to powder.'"

And when the chief priests and Pharisees had heard his parables, they perceived that he spoke of them. But when they sought to lay hands on him, they feared the multitude, because they took him for a prophet.

Then went the Pharisees, and took counsel how they might entangle him in his talk. And they sent out unto him their disciples with the Herodians, saying, "Master, we know that thou art true, and teachest the way of God in truth, neither carest thou for any man: for thou regardest not the person of men. Tell us therefore, what thinkest thou? Is it lawful to give tribute unto Cæsar, or not?"

But Jesus perceived their wickedness, and said, "Why tempt ye me, ye hypocrites? Show me the tribute money."

And they brought unto him a penny.

And he saith unto them, "Whose is this image and superscription?"

They say unto him, "Cæsar's."

Then saith he unto them,

THE GOSPEL ACCORDING TO MATTHEW

"Render therefore unto Cæsar the things which are Cæsar's; and unto God the things that are God's."

When they had heard these words, they marvelled, and left him, and went their way.

The same day came to him the Sadducees, which say that there is no resurrection, and asked him, saying, "Master, Moses said, 'If a man die, having no children, his brother shall marry his wife, and raise up seed unto his brother.' Now there were with us seven brethren: and the first, when he had married a wife, deceased, and, having no issue, left his wife unto his brother: likewise the second also, and the third, unto the seventh. And last of all the woman died also. Therefore in the resurrection whose wife shall she be of the seven? for they all had her."

Jesus answered and said unto them,

"Ye do err, not knowing the scriptures, nor the power of God. For in the resurrection they neither marry, nor are given in marriage, but are as the angels of God in heaven. But as touching the resurrection of the dead, have ye not read that which was spoken unto you by God, saying, 'I am the God of Abraham, and the God of Isaac, and the God of Jacob'? God is not the God of the dead, but of the living."

And when the multitude heard this, they were astonished at his doctrine. But when the Pharisees had heard that he had put the Sadducees to silence, they were gathered together. Then one of them, which was a lawyer, asked him a question, tempting him, and saying, "Master, which is the great commandment in the law?"

Jesus said unto him,

"Thou shalt love the Lord thy God with all thy heart, and with all thy soul, and with all thy mind. This is the first and great commandment. And the second is like unto it, 'Thou shalt love thy neighbour as thyself.' On these two commandments hang all the law and the prophets."

While the Pharisees were gathered together, Jesus asked them, saying, "What think ye of Christ? whose son is he?"

They say unto him, "The son of David."

THE GOSPEL ACCORDING TO MATTHEW

He saith unto them, "How then doth David in spirit call him Lord, saying,

> "'The Lord said unto my Lord,
> "Sit thou on my right hand,
> Till I make thine enemies thy footstool"'?

If David then call him Lord, how is he his son?"

And no man was able to answer him a word, neither durst any man from that day forth ask him any more questions.

Then spoke Jesus to the multitude, and to his disciples, saying, "The scribes and the Pharisees sit in Moses's seat. All therefore whatsoever they bid you observe, that observe and do; but do not ye after their works: for they say, and do not. For they bind heavy burdens and grievous to be borne, and lay them on men's shoulders; but they themselves will not move them with one of their fingers. But all their works they do for to be seen of men: they make broad their phylacteries, and enlarge the borders of their garments, and love the uppermost rooms at feasts, and the chief seats in the synagogues, and greetings in the markets, and to be called of men, 'Rabbi, Rabbi.' But be not ye called 'Rabbi': for one is your Master, even Christ; and all ye are brethren. And call no man your father upon the earth; for one is your Father, which is in heaven. Neither be ye called masters: for one is your Master, even Christ. But he that is greatest among you shall be your servant. And whosoever shall exalt himself shall be abased; and he that shall humble himself shall be exalted.

"But woe unto you, scribes and Pharisees, hypocrites! for ye shut up the kingdom of heaven against men: for ye neither go in yourselves, neither suffer ye them that are entering to go in. Woe unto you, scribes and Pharisees, hypocrites! for ye devour widows' houses, and for a pretence make long prayer: therefore ye shall receive the greater damnation. Woe unto you, scribes and Pharisees, hypocrites! for ye compass sea and land to make one proselyte, and when he is made, ye make him twofold more the child of hell than yourselves. Woe unto you, ye blind guides, which say, 'Whosoever shall swear by the temple, it is nothing;

THE GOSPEL ACCORDING TO MATTHEW

but whosoever shall swear by the gold of the temple, he is a debtor!' Ye fools and blind: for whether is greater, the gold, or the temple that sanctifieth the gold? And, 'Whosoever shall swear by the altar, it is nothing; but whosoever sweareth by the gift that is upon it, he is guilty.' Ye fools and blind: for whether is greater, the gift, or the altar that sanctifieth the gift? Whoso therefore shall swear by the altar, sweareth by it, and by all things thereof. And whoso shall swear by the temple, sweareth by it, and by him that dwelleth therein. And he that shall swear by heaven, sweareth by the throne of God, and by him that sitteth thereon.

"Woe unto you, scribes and Pharisees, hypocrites! for ye pay tithe of mint and anise and cummin, and have omitted the weightier matters of the law, judgment, mercy, and faith: these ought ye to have done, and not to leave the other undone. Ye blind guides, which strain at a gnat, and swallow a camel. Woe unto you, scribes and Pharisees, hypocrites! for ye make clean the outside of the cup and of the platter, but within they are full of extortion and excess. Thou blind Pharisee, cleanse first that which is within the cup and platter, that the outside of them may be clean also. Woe unto you, scribes and Pharisees, hypocrites! for ye are like unto whited sepulchres, which indeed appear beautiful outward, but are within full of dead men's bones, and of all uncleanness. Even so ye also outwardly appear righteous unto men, but within ye are full of hypocrisy and iniquity. Woe unto you, scribes and Pharisees, hypocrites! because ye build the tombs of the prophets, and garnish the sepulchres of the righteous, and say, 'If we had been in the days of our fathers, we would not have been partakers with them in the blood of the prophets.' Wherefore ye be witnesses unto yourselves, that ye are the children of them which killed the prophets. Fill ye up then the measure of your fathers. Ye serpents, ye generation of vipers, how can ye escape the damnation of hell?

"Wherefore, behold, I send unto you prophets, and wise men and scribes: and some of them ye shall kill and crucify; and some of them shall ye scourge in your synagogues, and persecute them

THE GOSPEL ACCORDING TO MATTHEW

from city to city: that upon you may come all the righteous blood shed upon the earth, from the blood of righteous Abel unto the blood of Zacharias son of Barachias, whom ye slew between the temple and the altar. Verily I say unto you, 'All these things shall come upon this generation.'

"O Jerusalem, Jerusalem, thou that killest the prophets, and stonest them which are sent unto thee, how often would I have gathered thy children together, even as a hen gathereth her chickens under her wings, and ye would not! Behold, your house is left unto you desolate. For I say unto you, 'Ye shall not see me henceforth, till ye shall say, "Blessed is he that cometh in the name of the Lord."'"

The Last Judgment

And Jesus went out, and departed from the temple: and his disciples came to him for to show him the buildings of the temple. And Jesus said unto them,

"See ye not all these things? verily I say unto you, 'There shall not be left here one stone upon another, that shall not be thrown down.'"

And as he sat upon the Mount of Olives, the disciples came unto him privately, saying, "Tell us, when shall these things be? and what shall be the sign of thy coming, and of the end of the world?"

And Jesus answered and said unto them,

"Take heed that no man deceive you. For many shall come in my name, saying, 'I am Christ'; and shall deceive many. And ye shall hear of wars and rumours of wars: see that ye be not troubled: for all these things must come to pass, but the end is not yet. For nation shall rise against nation, and kingdom against kingdom: and there shall be famines, and pestilences, and earthquakes, in divers places. All these are the beginning of sorrows. Then shall they deliver you up to be afflicted, and shall kill you: and ye shall be hated of all nations for my name's sake. And then shall many be offended, and shall betray one another, and shall hate one another. And many false prophets shall rise, and

THE GOSPEL ACCORDING TO MATTHEW

shall deceive many. And because iniquity shall abound, the love of many shall wax cold. But he that shall endure unto the end, the same shall be saved. And this gospel of the kingdom shall be preached in all the world for a witness unto all nations; and then shall the end come.

"When ye therefore shall see the abomination of desolation, spoken of by Daniel the prophet, stand in the holy place (whoso readeth, let him understand), then let them which be in Judæa flee into the mountains: let him which is on the housetop not come down to take any thing out of his house: neither let him which is in the field return back to take his clothes. And woe unto them that are with child, and to them that give suck in those days! But pray ye that your flight be not in the winter, neither on the sabbath day: for then shall be great tribulation, such as was not since the beginning of the world to this time, no, nor ever shall be. And except those days should be shortened, there should no flesh be saved: but for the elect's sake those days shall be shortened. Then if any man shall say unto you, 'Lo, here is Christ,' or, 'There,' believe it not. For there shall arise false Christs, and false prophets, and shall show great signs and wonders; insomuch that, if it were possible, they shall deceive the very elect. Behold, I have told you before. Wherefore if they shall say unto you, 'Behold, he is in the desert'; go not forth: 'Behold, he is in the secret chambers'; believe it not. For as the lightning cometh out of the east, and shineth even unto the west; so shall also the coming of the Son of Man be. For wheresoever the carcase is, there will the eagles be gathered together.

"Immediately after the tribulation of those days shall the sun be darkened, and the moon shall not give her light, and the stars shall fall from heaven, and the powers of the heavens shall be shaken. And then shall appear the sign of the Son of Man in heaven: and then shall all the tribes of the earth mourn, and they shall see the Son of Man coming in the clouds of heaven with power and great glory. And he shall send his angels with a great sound of a trumpet, and they shall gather together his elect from

THE GOSPEL ACCORDING TO MATTHEW

the four winds, from one end of heaven to the other. Now learn a parable of the fig tree; when his branch is yet tender, and putteth forth leaves, ye know that summer is nigh: so likewise ye, when ye shall see all these things, know that it is near, even at the doors. Verily I say unto you, 'This generation shall not pass, till all these things be fulfilled.' Heaven and earth shall pass away, but my words shall not pass away.

"But of that day and hour knoweth no man, no, not the angels of heaven, but my Father only. But as the days of Noe were, so shall also the coming of the Son of Man be. For as in the days that were before the flood they were eating and drinking, marrying and giving in marriage, until the day that Noe entered into the ark, and knew not until the flood came, and took them all away; so shall also the coming of the Son of Man be. Then shall two be in the field; the one shall be taken, and the other left. Two women shall be grinding at the mill; the one shall be taken, and the other left.

"Watch therefore: for ye know not what hour your Lord doth come. But know this, that if the goodman of the house had known in what watch the thief would come, he would have watched, and would not have suffered his house to be broken up. Therefore be ye also ready: for in such an hour as ye think not the Son of Man cometh. Who then is a faithful and wise servant, whom his lord hath made ruler over his household, to give them meat in due season? Blessed is that servant, whom his lord when he cometh shall find so doing. Verily I say unto you that he shall make him ruler over all his goods. But and if that evil servant shall say in his heart, 'My lord delayeth his coming,' and shall begin to smite his fellowservants, and to eat and drink with the drunken, the lord of that servant shall come in a day when he looketh not for him, and in an hour that he is not aware of, and shall cut him asunder, and appoint him his portion with the hypocrites: there shall be weeping and gnashing of teeth.

"Then shall the kingdom of heaven be likened unto ten virgins, which took their lamps, and went forth to meet the bride-

THE GOSPEL ACCORDING TO MATTHEW

groom. And five of them were wise, and five were foolish. They that were foolish took their lamps, and took no oil with them: but the wise took oil in their vessels with their lamps. While the bridegroom tarried, they all slumbered and slept. And at midnight there was a cry made, 'Behold, the bridegroom cometh; go ye out to meet him.' Then all those virgins arose, and trimmed their lamps. And the foolish said unto the wise, 'Give us of your oil; for our lamps are gone out.' But the wise answered, saying, 'Not so; lest there be not enough for us and you: but go ye rather to them that sell, and buy for yourselves.' And while they went to buy, the bridegroom came; and they that were ready went in with him to the marriage: and the door was shut. Afterward came also the other virgins, saying, 'Lord, Lord, open to us!' But he answered and said, 'Verily I say unto you, "I know you not."' Watch therefore, for ye know neither the day nor the hour wherein the Son of Man cometh.

"For the kingdom of heaven is as a man travelling into a far country, who called his own servants, and delivered unto them his goods. And unto one he gave five talents, to another two, and to another one; to every man according to his several ability; and straightway took his journey. Then he that had received the five talents went and traded with the same, and made them other five talents. And likewise he that had received two, he also gained other two. But he that had received one went and digged in the earth, and hid his lord's money. After a long time the lord of those servants cometh, and reckoneth with them.

"And so he that had received five talents came and brought other five talents, saying, 'Lord, thou deliveredst unto me five talents: behold, I have gained beside them five talents more.' His lord said unto him, 'Well done, thou good and faithful servant: thou hast been faithful over a few things, I will make thee ruler over many things: enter thou into the joy of thy lord.'

"He also that had received two talents came and said, 'Lord, thou deliveredst unto me two talents: behold, I have gained two other talents beside them.' His lord said unto him, 'Well

THE GOSPEL ACCORDING TO MATTHEW

done, good and faithful servant; thou hast been faithful over a few things, I will make thee ruler over many things: enter thou into the joy of thy lord.'

"Then he which had received the one talent came and said, 'Lord, I knew thee that thou art a hard man, reaping where thou hast not sown, and gathering where thou hast not strewed: and I was afraid, and went and hid thy talent in the earth: lo, there thou hast that is thine.'

"His lord answered and said unto him, 'Thou wicked and slothful servant, thou knewest that I reap where I sowed not, and gather where I have not strewed. Thou oughtest therefore to have put my money to the exchangers, and then at my coming I should have received mine own with usury. Take therefore the talent from him, and give it unto him which hath ten talents. For unto every one that hath shall be given, and he shall have abundance: but from him that hath not shall be taken away even that which he hath. And cast ye the unprofitable servant into outer darkness: there shall be weeping and gnashing of teeth.'

"When the Son of Man shall come in his glory, and all the holy angels with him, then shall he sit upon the throne of his glory. And before him shall be gathered all nations: and he shall separate them one from another, as a shepherd divideth his sheep from the goats: and he shall set the sheep on his right hand, but the goats on the left.

"Then shall the King say unto them on his right hand, 'Come, ye blessed of my Father, inherit the kingdom prepared for you from the foundation of the world! For I was a-hungered, and ye gave me meat: I was thirsty, and ye gave me drink: I was a stranger, and ye took me in: naked, and ye clothed me: I was sick, and ye visited me: I was in prison, and ye came unto me.' Then shall the righteous answer him, saying, 'Lord, when saw we thee a-hungered, and fed thee? or thirsty, and gave thee drink? When saw we thee a stranger, and took thee in? or naked, and clothed thee? Or when saw we thee sick, or in prison, and came unto thee?' And the King shall answer and say unto them,

THE GOSPEL ACCORDING TO MATTHEW

'Verily I say unto you, "Inasmuch as ye have done it unto one of the least of these my brethren, ye have done it unto me."'

"Then shall he say also unto them on the left hand, 'Depart from me, ye cursed, into everlasting fire, prepared for the devil and his angels. For I was a-hungered, and ye gave me no meat: I was thirsty, and ye gave me no drink: I was a stranger, and ye took me not in: naked, and ye clothed me not: sick, and in prison, and ye visited me not.' Then shall they also answer him, saying, 'Lord, when saw we thee a-hungered, or athirst, or a stranger, or naked, or sick, or in prison, and did not minister unto thee?' Then shall he answer them, saying, 'Verily I say unto you, "Inasmuch as ye did it not to one of the least of these, ye did it not to me."' And these shall go away into everlasting punishment: but the righteous into life eternal."

The Trial of Jesus

When the morning was come, all the chief priests and elders of the people took counsel against Jesus to put him to death: and when they had bound him, they led him away, and delivered him to Pontius Pilate the governor.

Then Judas, which had betrayed him, when he saw that he was condemned, repented himself, and brought again the thirty pieces of silver to the chief priests and elders, saying, "I have sinned in that I have betrayed the innocent blood." And they said, "What is that to us? see thou to that." And he cast down the pieces of silver in the temple, and departed, and went and hanged himself. And the chief priests took the silver pieces, and said, "It is not lawful for to put them into the treasury, because it is the price of blood." And they took counsel, and bought with them the potter's field, to bury strangers in. Wherefore that field was called the Field of Blood, unto this day. Then was fulfilled that which was spoken by Jeremy the prophet, saying, "And they took the thirty pieces of silver, the price of him that was valued, whom they of the children of Israel did value; and gave them for the potter's field, as the Lord appointed me."

THE GOSPEL ACCORDING TO MATTHEW

And Jesus stood before the governor: and the governor asked him, saying, "Art thou the King of the Jews?"

And Jesus said unto him, "Thou sayest."

And when he was accused of the chief priests and elders, he answered nothing.

Then said Pilate unto him, "Hearest thou not how many things they witness against thee?"

And he answered him too never a word; insomuch that the governor marvelled greatly.

Now at that feast the governor was wont to release unto the people a prisoner, whom they would. And they had then a notable prisoner, called Barabbas.

Therefore when they were gathered together, Pilate said unto them, "Whom will ye that I release unto you? Barabbas, or Jesus which is called Christ?" For he knew that for envy they had delivered him.

When he was set down on the judgment seat, his wife sent unto him, saying, "Have thou nothing to do with that just man: for I have suffered many things this day in a dream because of him."

But the chief priests and elders persuaded the multitude that they should ask Barabbas, and destroy Jesus. The governor answered and said unto them, "Whether of the twain will ye that I release unto you?" They said, "Barabbas."

Pilate saith unto them, "What shall I do then with Jesus which is called Christ?" They all say unto him, "Let him be crucified."

And the governor said, "Why, what evil hath he done?" But they cried out the more, saying, "Let him be crucified."

When Pilate saw that he could prevail nothing, but that rather a tumult was made, he took water, and washed his hands before the multitude, saying, "I am innocent of the blood of this just person: see ye to it." Then answered all the people, and said, "His blood be on us, and on our children."

The Crucifixion of Jesus

Then released he Barabbas unto them: and when he had scourged Jesus, he delivered him to be crucified. Then the sol-

THE GOSPEL ACCORDING TO MATTHEW

diers of the governor took Jesus into the common hall, and gathered unto him the whole band of soldiers. And they stripped him, and put on him a scarlet robe. And when they had plaited a crown of thorns, they put it upon his head, and a reed in his right hand: and they bowed the knee before him, and mocked him, saying, "Hail, King of the Jews!" And they spit upon him, and took the reed, and smote him on the head. And after that they had mocked him, they took the robe off from him, and put his own raiment on him, and led him away to crucify him.

And as they came out, they found a man of Cyrene, Simon by name: him they compelled to bear his cross. And when they were come unto a place called Golgotha, that is to say, "A place of a skull," they gave him vinegar to drink mingled with gall: and when he had tasted thereof, he would not drink. And they crucified him, and parted his garments, casting lots: that it might be fulfilled which was spoken by the prophet, "They parted my garments among them, and upon my vesture did they cast lots."

And sitting down they watched him there; and set up over his head his accusation written: THIS IS JESUS THE KING OF THE JEWS.

Then were there two thieves crucified with him, one on the right hand, and another on the left.

And they that passed by reviled him, wagging their heads, and saying, "Thou that destroyest the temple, and buildest it in three days, save thyself. If thou be the Son of God, come down from the cross."

Likewise also the chief priests mocking him, with the scribes and elders, said, "He saved others; himself he cannot save. If he be the King of Israel, let him now come down from the cross, and we will believe him. He trusted in God; let him deliver him now, if he will have him: for he said, 'I am the Son of God.'"

The thieves also, which were crucified with him, cast the same in his teeth.

Now from the sixth hour there was darkness over all the land unto the ninth hour.

THE GOSPEL ACCORDING TO MATTHEW

And about the ninth hour Jesus cried with a loud voice, saying, "Eli, Eli, lama sabachthani?" that is to say, "My God, my God, why hast thou forsaken me?"

Some of them that stood there, when they heard that, said, "This man calleth for Elias." And straightway one of them ran, and took a sponge, and filled it with vinegar, and put it on a reed, and gave him to drink. The rest said, "Let be, let us see whether Elias will come to save him."

Jesus, when he had cried again with a loud voice, yielded up the ghost. And, behold, the veil of the temple was rent in twain from the top to the bottom; and the earth did quake, and the rocks rent; and the graves were opened; and many bodies of the saints which slept arose, and came out of the graves after his resurrection, and went into the holy city, and appeared unto many. Now when the centurion, and they that were with him, watching Jesus, saw the earthquake, and those things that were done, they feared greatly, saying, "Truly this was the Son of God."

And many women were there beholding afar off, which followed Jesus from Galilee, ministering unto him: among which was Mary Magdalene, and Mary the mother of James and Joses, and the mother of Zebedee's children.

When the even was come, there came a rich man of Arimathæa, named Joseph, who also himself was Jesus's disciple. He went to Pilate, and begged the body of Jesus. Then Pilate commanded the body to be delivered. And when Joseph had taken the body, he wrapped it in a clean linen cloth, and laid it in his own new tomb, which he had hewn out in the rock: and he rolled a great stone to the door of the sepulchre, and departed. And there was Mary Magdalene, and the other Mary, sitting over against the sepulchre.

Now the next day, that followed the day of the preparation, the chief priests and Pharisees came together unto Pilate, saying, "Sir, we remember that that deceiver said, while he was yet alive, 'After three days I will rise again.' Command therefore

THE GOSPEL ACCORDING TO MATTHEW

that the sepulchre be made sure until the third day, lest his disciples come by night, and steal him away, and say unto the people, 'He is risen from the dead': so the last error shall be worse than the first." Pilate said unto them, "Ye have a watch: go your way, make it as sure as ye can." So they went, and made the sepulchre sure, sealing the stone, and setting a watch.

The Resurrection of Jesus

In the end of the sabbath, as it began to dawn toward the first day of the week, came Mary Magdalene and the other Mary to see the sepulchre.

And, behold, there was a great earthquake: for the angel of the Lord descended from heaven, and came and rolled back the stone from the door, and sat upon it. His countenance was like lightning, and his raiment white as snow: and for fear of him the keepers did shake, and became as dead men.

And the angel answered and said unto the women, "Fear not ye: for I know that ye seek Jesus, which was crucified. He is not here: for he is risen, as he said. Come, see the place where the Lord lay. And go quickly, and tell his disciples that he is risen from the dead; and, behold, he goeth before you into Galilee; there shall ye see him: lo, I have told you."

And they departed quickly from the sepulchre with fear and great joy; and did run to bring his disciples word.

And as they went to tell his disciples, behold, Jesus met them, saying, "All hail!" And they came and held him by the feet, and worshipped him. Then said Jesus unto them, "Be not afraid: go tell my brethren that they go into Galilee, and there shall they see me."

Now when they were going, behold, some of the watch came into the city, and showed unto the chief priests all the things that were done. And when they were assembled with the elders, and had taken counsel, they gave large money unto the soldiers, saying, "Say ye, His disciples came by night, and stole him away while we slept. And if this come to the governor's ears, we will

THE GOSPEL ACCORDING TO MATTHEW

persuade him, and secure you." So they took the money, and did as they were taught: and this saying is commonly reported among the Jews until this day.

Then the eleven disciples went away into Galilee, into a mountain where Jesus had appointed them. And when they saw him, they worshipped him: but some doubted.

And Jesus came and spoke unto them, saying, "All power is given unto me in heaven and in earth. Go ye therefore, and teach all nations, baptizing them in the name of the Father, and of the Son, and of the Holy Ghost: teaching them to observe all things whatsoever I have commanded you: and, lo, I am with you alway, even unto the end of the world." Amen.

THE GOSPEL ACCORDING TO LUKE

SELECTIONS

With the gospel according to Luke we are in the presence of a known author, Luke the physician, companion of Paul, who wrote in self-conscious fashion to correct the numerous unauthentic stories about the life of Jesus that were already in circulation. In addition to making use of Mark and Matthew, he drew upon original sources of his own, especially in his account of the missionary work of Jesus in Samaria, which he is thought to have derived perhaps from the Apostle Philip who labored in that region.

His book was as clearly intended for the Greeks and Romans as the Gospel according to Matthew was plainly meant primarily for the Jews. Throughout, his work breathes a cosmopolitan and humanitarian spirit; the tone is gentler than that of Mark or Matthew; women play a greater part in the narrative; and the author's fondness for poetry is seen in his preservation of religious songs.

The Gospel According to
LUKE

Preface

FORASMUCH as many have taken in hand to set forth in order a declaration of those things which are most surely believed among us, even as they delivered them unto us, which from the beginning were eyewitnesses, and ministers of the word; it seemed good to me also, having had perfect understanding of all things from the very first, to write unto thee in order, most excellent Theophilus, that thou mightest know the certainty of those things, wherein thou hast been instructed.

The Birth of John the Baptist

There was in the days of Herod, the king of Judæa, a certain priest named Zacharias, of the course of Abia: and his wife was of the daughters of Aaron, and her name was Elisabeth. And they were both righteous before God, walking in all the commandments and ordinances of the Lord blameless. And they had no child, because that Elisabeth was barren, and they both were now well stricken in years. And it came to pass that while he executed the priest's office before God in the order of his course, according to the custom of the priest's office, his lot was to burn incense when he went into the temple of the Lord. And the whole multitude of the people were praying without at the time of incense. And there appeared unto him an angel of the Lord standing on the right side of the altar of incense. And when Zacharias saw him, he was troubled, and fear fell upon him. But the angel said unto him,

"Fear not, Zacharias: for thy prayer is heard; and thy wife

THE GOSPEL ACCORDING TO LUKE

Elisabeth shall bear thee a son, and thou shalt call his name John. And thou shalt have joy and gladness; and many shall rejoice at his birth. For he shall be great in the sight of the Lord, and shall drink neither wine nor strong drink; and he shall be filled with the Holy Ghost, even from his mother's womb. And many of the children of Israel shall he turn to the Lord their God. And he shall go before him in the spirit and power of Elias, to turn the hearts of the fathers to the children, and the disobedient to the wisdom of the just; to make ready a people prepared for the Lord."

And Zacharias said unto the angel,

"Whereby shall I know this? for I am an old man, and my wife well stricken in years."

And the angel answering said unto him,

"I am Gabriel, that stand in the presence of God; and am sent to speak unto thee, and to show thee these glad tidings. And, behold, thou shalt be dumb, and not able to speak, until the day that these things shall be performed, because thou believest not my words, which shall be fulfilled in their season."

And the people waited for Zacharias, and marvelled that he tarried so long in the temple. And when he came out, he could not speak unto them: and they perceived that he had seen a vision in the temple: for he beckoned unto them, and remained speechless. And it came to pass, that, as soon as the days of his ministration were accomplished, he departed to his own house. And after those days his wife Elisabeth conceived, and hid herself five months, saying,

"Thus hath the Lord dealt with me in the days wherein he looked on me, to take away my reproach among men."

And in the sixth month the angel Gabriel was sent from God unto a city of Galilee, named Nazareth, to a virgin espoused to a man whose name was Joseph, of the house of David; and the virgin's name was Mary. And the angel came in unto her, and said,

"Hail, thou that art highly favoured, the Lord is with thee: blessed art thou among women."

THE GOSPEL ACCORDING TO LUKE

And when she saw him, she was troubled at his saying, and cast in her mind what manner of salutation this should be. And the angel said unto her,

"Fear not, Mary: for thou hast found favour with God. And, behold, thou shalt conceive in thy womb, and bring forth a son, and shalt call his name JESUS. He shall be great, and shall be called the Son of the Highest: and the Lord God shall give unto him the throne of his father David: and he shall reign over the house of Jacob for ever; and of his kingdom there shall be no end."

Then said Mary unto the angel,

"How shall this be, seeing I know not a man?"

And the angel answered and said unto her,

"The Holy Ghost shall come upon thee, and the power of the Highest shall overshadow thee: therefore also that holy thing which shall be born of thee shall be called the Son of God. And, behold, thy cousin Elisabeth, she hath also conceived a son in her old age: and this is the sixth month with her, who was called barren. For with God nothing shall be impossible."

And Mary said,

"Behold the handmaid of the Lord; be it unto me according to thy word."

And the angel departed from her. And Mary arose in those days, and went into the hill country with haste, into a city of Juda; and entered into the house of Zacharias, and saluted Elisabeth. And it came to pass that, when Elisabeth heard the salutation of Mary, the babe leaped in her womb; and Elisabeth was filled with the Holy Ghost: and she spoke out with a loud voice, and said,

"Blessed art thou among women, and blessed is the fruit of thy womb. And whence is this to me, that the mother of my Lord should come to me? For, lo, as soon as the voice of thy salutation sounded in mine ears, the babe leaped in my womb for joy. And blessed is she that believed: for there shall be a performance of those things which were told her from the Lord."

And Mary said,

THE GOSPEL ACCORDING TO LUKE

"My soul doth magnify the Lord,
And my spirit hath rejoiced in God my Saviour.
For he hath regarded the low estate of his handmaiden:
For, behold, from henceforth all generations shall call me blessed.
For he that is mighty hath done to me great things;
And holy is his name.
And his mercy is on them that fear him
From generation to generation.
He hath showed strength with his arm;
He hath scattered the proud in the imagination of their hearts.
He hath put down the mighty from their seats,
And exalted them of low degree.
He hath filled the hungry with good things;
And the rich he hath sent empty away.
He hath helped his servant Israel,
In remembrance of his mercy;
And he spoke to our fathers,
To Abraham, and to his seed for ever."

And Mary abode with her about three months, and returned to her own house.

Now Elisabeth's full time came that she should be delivered; and she brought forth a son. And her neighbours and her cousins heard how the Lord had showed great mercy upon her; and they rejoiced with her. And it came to pass that on the eighth day they came to circumcise the child; and they called him Zacharias, after the name of his father. And his mother answered and said, "Not so; but he shall be called John."

And they said unto her, "There is none of thy kindred that is called by this name."

And they made signs to his father, how he would have him called. And he asked for a writing table, and wrote, saying, "His name is John." And they marvelled all. And his mouth was opened immediately, and his tongue loosed, and he spoke, and praised God. And fear came on all that dwelt round about them: and all these sayings were noised abroad throughout all the hill

THE GOSPEL ACCORDING TO LUKE

country of Judæa. And all they that heard them laid them up in their hearts, saying, "What manner of child shall this be!" And the hand of the Lord was with him.

And his father Zacharias was filled with the Holy Ghost, and prophesied, saying,

> "Blessed be the Lord God of Israel;
> For he hath visited and redeemed his people,
> And hath raised up a horn of salvation for us
> In the house of his servant David;
> As he spoke by the mouth of his holy prophets,
> Which have been since the world began:
> That we should be saved from our enemies,
> And from the hand of all that hate us;
> To perform the mercy promised to our fathers,
> And to remember his holy covenant;
> The oath which he swore to our father Abraham,
> That he would grant unto us,
> That we being delivered out of the hand of our enemies
> Might serve him without fear,
> In holiness and righteousness before him,
> All the days of our life.
> And thou, child, shalt be called the prophet of the Highest:
> For thou shalt go before the face of the Lord to prepare his ways;
> To give knowledge of salvation unto his people
> By the remission of their sins,
> Through the tender mercy of our God;
> Whereby the dayspring from on high hath visited us,
> To give light to them that sit in darkness and in the shadow of death,
> To guide our feet into the way of peace."

And the child grew, and waxed strong in spirit, and was in the deserts till the day of his showing unto Israel.

The Birth and Youth of Jesus

And it came to pass in those days that there went out a decree from Cæsar Augustus, that all the world should be taxed.

THE GOSPEL ACCORDING TO LUKE

(And this taxing was first made when Cyrenius was governor of Syria.) And all went to be taxed, every one into his own city. And Joseph also went up from Galilee, out of the city of Nazareth, into Judæa, unto the city of David, which is called Bethlehem (because he was of the house and lineage of David): to be taxed with Mary his espoused wife, being great with child. And so it was, that, while they were there, the days were accomplished that she should be delivered. And she brought forth her firstborn son, and wrapped him in swaddling clothes, and laid him in a manger; because there was no room for them in the inn.

And there were in the same country shepherds abiding in the field, keeping watch over their flock by night. And, lo, the angel of the Lord came upon them, and the glory of the Lord shone round about them: and they were sore afraid. And the angel said unto them,

"Fear not: for, behold, I bring you good tidings of great joy, which shall be to all people. For unto you is born this day in the city of David a Saviour, which is Christ the Lord. And this shall be a sign unto you; ye shall find the babe wrapped in swaddling clothes, lying in a manger."

And suddenly there was with the angel a multitude of the heavenly host praising God, and saying,

"Glory to God in the highest, and on earth peace, good will toward men."

And it came to pass, as the angels were gone away from them into heaven, the shepherds said one to another,

"Let us now go even unto Bethlehem, and see this thing which is come to pass, which the Lord hath made known unto us."

And they came with haste, and found Mary, and Joseph, and the babe lying in a manger. And when they had seen it, they made known abroad the saying which was told them concerning this child. And all they that heard it wondered at those things which were told them by the shepherds. But Mary kept all these things, and pondered them in her heart. And the shepherds returned, glorifying and praising God for all the things that they had heard and seen, as it was told unto them.

THE GOSPEL ACCORDING TO LUKE

And when eight days were accomplished for the circumcising of the child, his name was called JESUS, which was so named of the angel before he was conceived in the womb. And when the days of her purification according to the law of Moses were accomplished, they brought him to Jerusalem, to present him to the Lord (as it is written in the law of the Lord, "Every male that openeth the womb shall be called holy to the Lord") and to offer a sacrifice according to that which is said in the law of the Lord, "A pair of turtledoves, or two young pigeons." And, behold, there was a man in Jerusalem, whose name was Simeon; and the same man was just and devout, waiting for the consolation of Israel: and the Holy Ghost was upon him. And it was revealed unto him by the Holy Ghost, that he should not see death, before he had seen the Lord's Christ. And he came by the Spirit into the temple: and when the parents brought in the child Jesus, to do for him after the custom of the law, then took he him up in his arms, and blessed God, and said,

> "*Lord, now lettest thou thy servant depart in peace,*
> *According to thy word:*
> *For mine eyes have seen thy salvation,*
> *Which thou hast prepared before the face of all people;*
> *A light to lighten the Gentiles,*
> *And the glory of thy people Israel.*"

And Joseph and his mother marvelled at those things which were spoken of him. And Simeon blessed them, and said unto Mary his mother, "Behold, this child is set for the fall and rising again of many in Israel; and for a sign which shall be spoken against (yea, a sword shall pierce through thy own soul also), that the thoughts of many hearts may be revealed."

And there was one Anna, a prophetess, the daughter of Phanuel, of the tribe of Aser: she was of a great age, and had lived with a husband seven years from her virginity; and she was a widow of about fourscore and four years, which departed not from the temple, but served God with fastings and prayers night and day. And she coming in that instant gave thanks likewise

THE GOSPEL ACCORDING TO LUKE

unto the Lord, and spoke of him to all them that looked for redemption in Jerusalem.

And when they had performed all things according to the law of the Lord, they returned into Galilee, to their own city Nazareth. And the child grew, and waxed strong in spirit, filled with wisdom: and the grace of God was upon him.

Now his parents went to Jerusalem every year at the feast of the passover. And when he was twelve years old, they went up to Jerusalem after the custom of the feast. And when they had fulfilled the days, as they returned, the child Jesus tarried behind in Jerusalem; and Joseph and his mother knew not of it. But they, supposing him to have been in the company, went a day's journey; and they sought him among their kinsfolk and acquaintance. And when they found him not, they turned back again to Jerusalem, seeking him. And it came to pass that after three days they found him in the temple, sitting in the midst of the doctors, both hearing them, and asking them questions. And all that heard him were astonished at his understanding and answers.

And when they saw him, they were amazed: and his mother said unto him,

"Son, why hast thou thus dealt with us? behold, thy father and I have sought thee sorrowing."

And he said unto them,

"How is it that ye sought me? wist ye not that I must be about my Father's business?"

And they understood not the saying which he spoke unto them. And he went down with them, and came to Nazareth, and was subject unto them: but his mother kept all these sayings in her heart. And Jesus increased in wisdom and stature, and in favour with God and man.

Jesus and John the Baptist

Now in the fifteenth year of the reign of Tiberius Cæsar, Pontius Pilate being governor of Judæa, and Herod being tetrarch of Galilee, and his brother Philip tetrarch of Ituræa and

THE GOSPEL ACCORDING TO LUKE

of the region of Trachonitis, and Lysanias the tetrarch of Abilene, Annas and Caiaphas being the high priests, the word of God came unto John the son of Zacharias in the wilderness. And he came into all the country about Jordan, preaching the baptism of repentance for the remission of sins; as it is written in the book of the words of Isaias the prophet, saying,

> "The voice of one crying in the wilderness,
> Prepare ye the way of the Lord,
> Make his paths straight.
> Every valley shall be filled,
> And every mountain and hill shall be brought low;
> And the crooked shall be made straight,
> And the rough ways shall be made smooth;
> And all flesh shall see the salvation of God."

Then said he to the multitude that came forth to be baptized of him,

"O generation of vipers, who hath warned you to flee from the wrath to come? Bring forth therefore fruits worthy of repentance, and begin not to say within yourselves, 'We have Abraham to our father': for I say unto you that God is able of these stones to raise up children unto Abraham. And now also the axe is laid unto the root of the trees: every tree therefore which bringeth not forth good fruit is hewn down, and cast into the fire."

And the people asked him, saying,

"What shall we do then?"

He answereth and saith unto them,

"He that hath two coats, let him impart to him that hath none; and he that hath meat, let him do likewise."

Then came also publicans to be baptized, and said unto him,

"Master, what shall we do?"

And he said unto them,

"Exact no more than that which is appointed you."

And the soldiers likewise demanded of him, saying,

"And what shall we do?"

THE GOSPEL ACCORDING TO LUKE

And he said unto them,

"Do violence to no man, neither accuse any falsely; and be content with your wages."

And as the people were in expectation, and all men mused in their hearts of John, whether he were the Christ, or not, John answered, saying unto them all,

"I indeed baptize you with water; but one mightier than I cometh, the latchet of whose shoes I am not worthy to unloose: he shall baptize you with the Holy Ghost and with fire: whose fan is in his hand, and he will thoroughly purge his floor, and will gather the wheat into his garner; but the chaff he will burn with fire unquenchable."

And many other things in his exhortation preached he unto the people.

But Herod the tetrarch, being reproved by him for Herodias his brother Philip's wife, and for all the evils which Herod had done, added yet this above all, that he shut up John in prison.

Now when all the people were baptized, it came to pass, that Jesus also being baptized, and praying, the heaven was opened, and the Holy Ghost descended in a bodily shape like a dove upon him, and a voice came from heaven, which said,

"Thou art my beloved Son; in thee I am well pleased."

And Jesus himself began to be about thirty years of age, being (as was supposed) the son of Joseph, which was the son of Heli.

Incidents of the Ministry of Jesus

And it came to pass, when the time was come that he should be received up, he steadfastly set his face to go to Jerusalem, and sent messengers before his face: and they went, and entered into a village of the Samaritans, to make ready for him. And they did not receive him, because his face was as though he would go to Jerusalem. And when his disciples James and John saw this, they said, "Lord, wilt thou that we command fire to come down from heaven, and consume them, even as Elias did?"

But he turned, and rebuked them, and said, "Ye know not

THE GOSPEL ACCORDING TO LUKE

what manner of spirit ye are of. For the Son of Man is not come to destroy men's lives, but to save them." And they went to another village.

And it came to pass that, as they went in the way, a certain man said unto him, "Lord, I will follow thee whithersoever thou goest."

And Jesus said unto him, "Foxes have holes, and birds of the air have nests; but the Son of Man hath not where to lay his head."

And he said unto another, "Follow me!"

But he said, "Lord, suffer me first to go and bury my father."

Jesus said unto him, "Let the dead bury their dead: but go thou and preach the kingdom of God."

And another also said, "Lord, I will follow thee; but let me first go bid them farewell, which are at home at my house."

And Jesus said unto him, "No man, having put his hand to the plow, and looking back, is fit for the kingdom of God."

After these things the Lord appointed other seventy also, and sent them two and two before his face into every city and place, whither he himself would come. Therefore said he unto them,

"The harvest truly is great, but the labourers are few: pray ye therefore the Lord of the harvest, that he would send forth labourers into his harvest. Go your ways: behold, I send you forth as lambs among wolves. Carry neither purse, nor scrip, nor shoes: and salute no man by the way. And into whatsoever house ye enter, first say, 'Peace be to this house.' And if the son of peace be there, your peace shall rest upon it: if not, it shall turn to you again. And in the same house remain, eating and drinking such things as they give: for the labourer is worthy of his hire. Go not from house to house. And into whatsoever city ye enter, and they receive you, eat such things as are set before you: and heal the sick that are therein, and say unto them, 'The kingdom of God is come nigh unto you.' But into whatsoever city ye enter, and they receive you not, go your ways out into the streets of the same, and say, 'Even the very dust of your city, which cleaveth on us, we do wipe off against you: notwith-

THE GOSPEL ACCORDING TO LUKE

standing be ye sure of this, that the kingdom of God is come nigh unto you.' But I say unto you, that it shall be more tolerable in that day for Sodom than for that city. Woe unto thee, Chorazin! woe unto thee, Bethsaida! for if the mighty works had been done in Tyre and Sidon, which have been done in you, they had a great while ago repented, sitting in sackcloth and ashes. But it shall be more tolerable for Tyre and Sidon at the judgment than for you. And thou, Capernaum, which art exalted to heaven, shalt be thrust down to hell. He that heareth you heareth me; and he that despiseth you despiseth me; and he that despiseth me despiseth him that sent me."

And the seventy returned again with joy, saying, "Lord, even the devils are subject unto us through thy name."

And he said unto them,

"I beheld Satan as lightning fall from heaven. Behold, I give unto you power to tread on serpents and scorpions, and over all the power of the enemy: and nothing shall by any means hurt you. Notwithstanding in this rejoice not, that the spirits are subject unto you; but rather rejoice, because your names are written in heaven."

In that hour Jesus rejoiced in spirit, and said,

"I thank thee, O Father, Lord of heaven and earth, that thou hast hid these things from the wise and prudent, and hast revealed them unto babes: even so, Father; for so it seemed good in thy sight. All things are delivered to me of my Father: and no man knoweth who the Son is, but the Father; and who the Father is, but the Son, and he to whom the Son will reveal him."

And he turned him unto his disciples, and said privately,

"Blessed are the eyes which see the things that ye see: for I tell you, that many prophets and kings have desired to see those things which ye see, and have not seen them; and to hear those things which ye hear, and have not heard them."

And, behold, a certain lawyer stood up, and tempted him, saying, "Master, what shall I do to inherit eternal life?"

He said unto him, "What is written in the law? how readest thou?"

THE GOSPEL ACCORDING TO LUKE

And he answering said, "Thou shalt love the Lord thy God with all thy heart, and with all thy soul, and with all thy strength, and with all thy mind; and thy neighbour as thyself."

And he said unto him, "Thou hast answered right: this do, and thou shalt live."

But he, willing to justify himself, said unto Jesus, "And who is my neighbour?"

And Jesus answering said,

"A certain man went down from Jerusalem to Jericho, and fell among thieves, which stripped him of his raiment, and wounded him, and departed, leaving him half dead. And by chance there came down a certain priest that way: and when he saw him, he passed by on the other side. And likewise a Levite, when he was at the place, came and looked on him, and passed by on the other side. But a certain Samaritan, as he journeyed, came where he was: and when he saw him, he had compassion on him, and went to him, and bound up his wounds, pouring in oil and wine, and set him on his own beast, and brought him to an inn, and took care of him. And on the morrow when he departed, he took out two pence, and gave them to the host, and said unto him, 'Take care of him; and whatsoever thou spendest more, when I come again, I will repay thee.' Which now of these three, thinkest thou, was neighbour unto him that fell among the thieves?"

And he said, "He that showed mercy on him."

Then said Jesus unto him, "Go, and do thou likewise."

Now it came to pass, as they went, that he entered into a certain village: and a certain woman named Martha received him into her house. And she had a sister called Mary, which also sat at Jesus' feet, and heard his word. But Martha was cumbered about much serving, and came to him, and said, "Lord, dost thou not care that my sister hath left me to serve alone? bid her therefore that she help me."

And Jesus answered and said unto her, "Martha, Martha, thou art careful and troubled about many things. But one thing is

THE GOSPEL ACCORDING TO LUKE

needful: and Mary hath chosen that good part, which shall not be taken away from her."

And he was casting out a devil, and it was dumb. And it came to pass, when the devil was gone out, the dumb spoke; and the people wondered. But some of them said, "He casteth out devils through Beelzebub the chief of the devils." And others, tempting him, sought of him a sign from heaven.

But he, knowing their thoughts, said unto them,

"Every kingdom divided against itself is brought to desolation; and a house divided against a house falleth. If Satan also be divided against himself, how shall his kingdom stand? because ye say that I cast out devils through Beelzebub. And if I by Beelzebub cast out devils, by whom do your sons cast them out? therefore shall they be your judges. But if I with the finger of God cast out devils, no doubt the kingdom of God is come upon you. When a strong man armed keepeth his palace, his goods are in peace: but when a stronger than he shall come upon him, and overcome him, he taketh from him all his armour wherein he trusted, and divideth his spoils. He that is not with me is against me: and he that gathereth not with me scattereth. When the unclean spirit is gone out of a man, he walketh through dry places, seeking rest; and finding none, he saith, 'I will return unto my house whence I came out.' And when he cometh, he findeth it swept and garnished. Then goeth he, and taketh to him seven other spirits more wicked than himself; and they enter in, and dwell there: and the last state of that man is worse than the first."

And it came to pass, as he spoke these things, a certain woman of the company lifted up her voice, and said unto him, "Blessed is the womb that bore thee, and the paps which thou hast sucked."

But he said, "Yea rather, blessed are they that hear the word of God, and keep it."

And when the people were gathered thick together, he began to say,

THE GOSPEL ACCORDING TO LUKE

"This is an evil generation: they seek a sign; and there shall no sign be given it, but the sign of Jonas the prophet. For as Jonas was a sign unto the Ninevites, so shall also the Son of Man be to this generation. The queen of the south shall rise up in the judgment with the men of this generation, and condemn them: for she came from the utmost parts of the earth to hear the wisdom of Solomon; and, behold, a greater than Solomon is here. The men of Nineveh shall rise up in the judgment with this generation, and shall condemn it: for they repented at the preaching of Jonas; and, behold, a greater than Jonas is here."

And as he spoke, a certain Pharisee besought him to dine with him: and he went in, and sat down to meat. And when the Pharisee saw it, he marvelled that he had not first washed before dinner. And the Lord said unto him,

"Now do ye Pharisees make clean the outside of the cup and the platter; but your inward part is full of ravening and wickedness. Ye fools, did not he that made that which is without make that which is within also? But rather give alms of such things as ye have; and, behold, all things are clean unto you. Woe unto you, Pharisees! for ye love the uppermost seats in the synagogues, and greetings in the markets. Woe unto you, scribes and Pharisees, hypocrites! for ye are as graves which appear not, and the men that walk over them are not aware of them."

Then answered one of the lawyers, and said unto him, "Master, thus saying thou reproachest us also."

And he said, "Woe unto you also, ye lawyers! for ye lade men with burdens grievous to be borne, and ye yourselves touch not the burdens with one of your fingers. Woe unto you, lawyers! for ye have taken away the key of knowledge: ye entered not in yourselves, and them that were entering in ye hindered."

And as he said these things unto them, the scribes and the Pharisees began to urge him vehemently, and to provoke him to speak of many things: laying wait for him, and seeking to catch something out of his mouth, that they might accuse him.

In the mean time, when there were gathered together an in-

THE GOSPEL ACCORDING TO LUKE

numerable multitude of people, insomuch that they trod one upon another, he began to say unto his disciples first of all,

"Beware ye of the leaven of the Pharisees, which is hypocrisy. For there is nothing covered, that shall not be revealed; neither hid, that shall not be known. Therefore whatsoever ye have spoken in darkness shall be heard in the light; and that which ye have spoken in the ear in closets shall be proclaimed upon the housetops.

"And I say unto you my friends, 'Be not afraid of them that kill the body, and after that have no more that they can do.' But I will forewarn you whom ye shall fear: 'Fear him, which after he hath killed hath power to cast into hell'; yea, I say unto you, 'Fear him.' Are not five sparrows sold for two farthings, and not one of them is forgotten before God? But even the very hairs of your head are all numbered. Fear not therefore: ye are of more value than many sparrows.

"Also I say unto you, 'Whosoever shall confess me before men, him shall the Son of Man also confess before the angels of God: but he that denieth me before men shall be denied before the angels of God. And whosoever shall speak a word against the Son of Man, it shall be forgiven him: but unto him that blasphemeth against the Holy Ghost it shall not be forgiven. And when they bring you unto the synagogues, and unto magistrates, and powers, take ye no thought how or what thing ye shall answer, or what ye shall say: for the Holy Ghost shall teach you in the same hour what ye ought to say.'"

And one of the company said unto him, "Master, speak to my brother, that he divide the inheritance with me."

And he said unto him, "Man, who made me a judge or a divider over you?"

And he said unto them, "Take heed, and beware of covetousness: for a man's life consisteth not in the abundance of the things which he possesseth."

And he spoke a parable unto them, saying,

"The ground of a certain rich man brought forth plentifully:

THE GOSPEL ACCORDING TO LUKE

And he thought within himself, saying, 'What shall I do, because I have no room where to bestow my fruits?' And he said, 'This will I do: I will pull down my barns, and build greater; and there will I bestow all my fruits and my goods. And I will say to my soul, "Soul, thou hast much goods laid up for many years; take thine ease, eat, drink, and be merry."' But God said unto him, 'Thou fool, this night thy soul shall be required of thee: then whose shall those things be, which thou hast provided?' So is he that layeth up treasure for himself, and is not rich toward God.

"Blessed are those servants, whom the lord when he cometh shall find watching: verily I say unto you, that he shall gird himself, and make them to sit down to meat, and will come forth and serve them. And if he shall come in the second watch, or come in the third watch, and find them so, blessed are those servants. And this know, that if the goodman of the house had known what hour the thief would come, he would have watched, and not have suffered his house to be broken through. Be ye therefore ready also: for the Son of Man cometh at an hour when ye think not."

Then Peter said unto him, "Lord, speakest thou this parable unto us, or even to all?"

And the Lord said,

"Who then is that faithful and wise steward, whom his lord shall make ruler over his household, to give them their portion of meat in due season? Blessed is that servant, whom his lord when he cometh shall find so doing. Of a truth I say unto you that he will make him ruler over all that he hath. But and if that servant say in his heart, 'My lord delayeth his coming,' and shall begin to beat the menservants and maidens, and to eat and drink, and to be drunken, the lord of that servant will come in a day when he looketh not for him, and at an hour when he is not aware, and will cut him in sunder, and will appoint him his portion with the unbelievers. And that servant, which knew his lord's will, and prepared not himself, neither did according to his will, shall be beaten with many stripes. But he that knew

THE GOSPEL ACCORDING TO LUKE

not, and did commit things worthy of stripes, shall be beaten with few stripes. For unto whomsoever much is given, of him shall be much required: and to whom men have committed much, of him they will ask the more.

"I am come to send fire on the earth; and what will I, if it be already kindled? But I have a baptism to be baptized with; and how am I straitened till it be accomplished! Suppose ye that I am come to give peace on earth? I tell you, 'Nay; but rather division': for from henceforth there shall be five in one house divided, three against two, and two against three. The father shall be divided against the son, and the son against the father; the mother against the daughter, and the daughter against the mother; the mother-in-law against her daughter-in-law, and the daughter-in-law against her mother-in-law."

And he said also to the people,

"When ye see a cloud rise out of the west, straightway ye say, 'There cometh a shower'; and so it is. And when ye see the south wind blow, ye say, 'There will be heat'; and it cometh to pass. Ye hypocrites, ye can discern the face of the sky and of the earth; but how is it that ye do not discern this time? Yea, and why even of yourselves judge ye not what is right?

"When thou goest with thine adversary to the magistrate, as thou art in the way, give diligence that thou mayest be delivered from him; lest he hale thee to the judge, and the judge deliver thee to the officer, and the officer cast thee into prison. I tell thee, thou shalt not depart thence, till thou hast paid the very last mite."

And he was teaching in one of the synagogues on the sabbath. And, behold, there was a woman which had a spirit of infirmity eighteen years, and was bowed together, and could in no wise lift up herself. And when Jesus saw her, he called her to him, and said unto her, "Woman, thou art loosed from thine infirmity." And he laid his hands on her: and immediately she was made straight, and glorified God.

And the ruler of the synagogue answered with indignation, because that Jesus had healed on the sabbath day, and said unto

THE GOSPEL ACCORDING TO LUKE

the people, "There are six days in which men ought to work: in them therefore come and be healed, and not on the sabbath day."

The Lord then answered him, and said, "Thou hypocrite, doth not each one of you on the sabbath loose his ox or his ass from the stall, and lead him away to watering? And ought not this woman, being a daughter of Abraham, whom Satan hath bound, lo, these eighteen years, be loosed from this bond on the sabbath day?"

And when he had said these things, all his adversaries were ashamed: and all the people rejoiced for all the glorious things that were done by him. And he went through the cities and villages, teaching, and journeying toward Jerusalem.

Then said one unto him, "Lord, are there few that be saved?"

And he said unto them,

"Strive to enter in at the strait gate: 'For many,' I say unto you, 'will seek to enter in, and shall not be able.' When once the master of the house is risen up, and hath shut to the door, and ye begin to stand without, and to knock at the door, saying, 'Lord, Lord, open unto us'; and he shall answer and say unto you, 'I know you not whence ye are': then shall ye begin to say, 'We have eaten and drunk in thy presence, and thou hast taught in our streets.' But he shall say, 'I tell you, I know you not whence ye are; depart from me, all ye workers of iniquity.' There shall be weeping and gnashing of teeth, when ye shall see Abraham, and Isaac, and Jacob, and all the prophets, in the kingdom of God, and you yourselves thrust out. And they shall come from the east, and from the west, and from the north, and from the south, and shall sit down in the kingdom of God. And, behold, there are last which shall be first and there are first which shall be last."

The same day there came certain of the Pharisees, saying unto him, "Get thee out, and depart hence: for Herod will kill thee."

And he said unto them, "Go ye, and tell that fox, 'Behold, I cast out devils, and I do cures to-day and to-morrow, and the

THE GOSPEL ACCORDING TO LUKE

third day I shall be perfected.' Nevertheless I must walk to-day, and to-morrow, and the day following: for it cannot be that a prophet perish out of Jerusalem."

And it came to pass, as he went into the house of one of the chief Pharisees to eat bread on the sabbath day, that they watched him. And, behold, there was a certain man before him which had the dropsy. And Jesus answering spoke unto the lawyers and Pharisees, saying, "Is it lawful to heal on the sabbath day?"

And they held their peace. And he took him, and healed him, and let him go; and answered them, saying, "Which of you shall have an ass or an ox fallen into a pit, and will not straightway pull him out on the sabbath day?"

And they could not answer him again to these things.

And he put forth a parable to those which were bidden, when he marked how they chose out the chief rooms: saying unto them,

"When thou art bidden of any man to a wedding, sit not down in the highest room; lest a more honourable man than thou be bidden of him; and he that bade thee and him come and say to thee, 'Give this man place'; and thou begin with shame to take the lowest room. But when thou art bidden, go and sit down in the lowest room; that when he that bade thee cometh, he may say unto thee, 'Friend, go up higher': then shalt thou have worship in the presence of them that sit at meat with thee. For whosoever exalteth himself shall be abased; and he that humbleth himself shall be exalted."

Then said he also to him that bade him,

"When thou makest a dinner or a supper, call not thy friends, nor thy brethren, neither thy kinsmen, nor thy rich neighbours; lest they also bid thee again, and a recompence be made thee. But when thou makest a feast, call the poor, the maimed, the lame, the blind: and thou shalt be blessed; for they cannot recompense thee: for thou shalt be recompensed at the resurrection of the just."

And when one of them that sat at meat with him heard these

things, he said unto him, "Blessed is he that shall eat bread in the kingdom of God."

Then said he unto him,

"A certain man made a great supper, and bade many: and sent his servant at supper time to say to them that were bidden, 'Come; for all things are now ready.' And they all with one consent began to make excuse. The first said unto him, 'I have bought a piece of ground, and I must needs go and see it: I pray thee have me excused.' And another said, 'I have bought five yoke of oxen, and I go to prove them: I pray thee have me excused.' And another said, 'I have married a wife, and therefore I cannot come.' So that servant came, and showed his lord these things. Then the master of the house being angry said to his servant, 'Go out quickly into the streets and lanes of the city, and bring in hither the poor, and the maimed, and the halt, and the blind.' And the servant said, 'Lord, it is done as thou hast commanded, and yet there is room.' And the lord said unto the servant, 'Go out into the highways and hedges, and compel them to come in, that my house may be filled. For I say unto you that none of those men which were bidden shall taste of my supper.'"

And there went great multitudes with him: and he turned, and said unto them,

"If any man come to me, and hate not his father, and mother, and wife, and children, and brethren, and sisters, yea, and his own life also, he cannot be my disciple. And whosoever doth not bear his cross, and come after me, cannot be my disciple. For which of you, intending to build a tower, sitteth not down first, and counteth the cost, whether he have sufficient to finish it? Lest haply, after he hath laid the foundation, and is not able to finish it, all that behold it begin to mock him, saying, 'This man began to build, and was not able to finish.' Or what king, going to make war against another king, sitteth not down first, and consulteth whether he be able with ten thousand to meet him that cometh against him with twenty thousand? Or else, while the other is yet a great way off, he sendeth an embassage,

THE GOSPEL ACCORDING TO LUKE

and desireth conditions of peace. So likewise, whosoever he be of you that forsaketh not all that he hath, he cannot be my disciple."

Then drew near unto him all the publicans and sinners for to hear him. And the Pharisees and scribes murmured, saying, "This man receiveth sinners, and eateth with them."

And he spoke this parable unto them, saying,

"What man of you, having a hundred sheep, if he lose one of them, doth not leave the ninety and nine in the wilderness, and go after that which is lost, until he find it? And when he hath found it, he layeth it on his shoulders, rejoicing. And when he cometh home, he calleth together his friends and neighbours, saying unto them, 'Rejoice with me; for I have found my sheep which was lost.' I say unto you that likewise joy shall be in heaven over one sinner that repenteth, more than over ninety and nine just persons, which need no repentance.

"Either what woman having ten pieces of silver, if she lose one piece, doth not light a candle, and sweep the house, and seek diligently till she find it? And when she hath found it, she calleth her friends and her neighbours together, saying, 'Rejoice with me; for I have found the piece which I had lost.' Likewise, I say unto you, there is joy in the presence of the angels of God over one sinner that repenteth."

And he said,

"A certain man had two sons: and the younger of them said to his father, 'Father, give me the portion of goods that falleth to me.' And he divided unto them his living. And not many days after the younger son gathered all together, and took his journey into a far country, and there wasted his substance with riotous living. And when he had spent all, there arose a mighty famine in that land; and he began to be in want. And he went and joined himself to a citizen of that country; and he sent him into his fields to feed swine. And he would fain have filled his belly with the husks that the swine did eat: and no man gave unto him.

"And when he came to himself, he said, 'How many hired

THE GOSPEL ACCORDING TO LUKE

servants of my father's have bread enough and to spare, and I perish with hunger! I will arise and go to my father, and will say unto him, "Father, I have sinned against heaven, and before thee, and am no more worthy to be called thy son: make me as one of thy hired servants."'

"And he arose, and came to his father. But when he was yet a great way off, his father saw him, and had compassion, and ran, and fell on his neck, and kissed him. And the son said unto him, 'Father, I have sinned against heaven, and in thy sight, and am no more worthy to be called thy son.' But the father said to his servants, 'Bring forth the best robe, and put it on him; and put a ring on his hand, and shoes on his feet: and bring hither the fatted calf, and kill it; and let us eat, and be merry: for this my son was dead, and is alive again; he was lost, and is found.' And they began to be merry.

"Now his elder son was in the field: and as he came and drew nigh to the house, he heard music and dancing. And he called one of the servants, and asked what these things meant. And he said unto him, 'Thy brother is come; and thy father hath killed the fatted calf, because he hath received him safe and sound.' And he was angry, and would not go in: therefore came his father out, and intreated him. And he answering said to his father, 'Lo, these many years do I serve thee, neither transgressed I at any time thy commandment: and yet thou never gavest me a kid, that I might make merry with my friends: but as soon as this thy son was come, which hath devoured thy living with harlots, thou hast killed for him the fatted calf.' And he said unto him, 'Son, thou art ever with me, and all that I have is thine. It was meet that we should make merry, and be glad: for this thy brother was dead, and is alive again; and was lost, and is found.'"

And he said also unto his disciples,

"There was a certain rich man, which had a steward; and the same was accused unto him that he had wasted his goods. And he called him, and said unto him, 'How is it that I hear this of thee? give an account of thy stewardship; for thou mayest be no

THE GOSPEL ACCORDING TO LUKE

longer steward.' Then the steward said within himself, 'What shall I do? for my lord taketh away from me the stewardship: I cannot dig; to beg I am ashamed. I am resolved what to do, that, when I am put out of the stewardship, they may receive me into their houses.' So he called every one of his lord's debtors unto him, and said unto the first, 'How much owest thou unto my lord?' And he said, 'A hundred measures of oil.' And he said unto him, 'Take thy bill, and sit down quickly, and write fifty.' Then said he to another, 'And how much owest thou?' And he said, 'A hundred measures of wheat.' And he said unto him, 'Take thy bill, and write fourscore.' And the lord commended the unjust steward, because he had done wisely: for the children of this world are in their generation wiser than the children of light. And I say unto you, 'Make to yourselves friends of the mammon of unrighteousness'; that, when ye fail, they may receive you into everlasting habitations. He that is faithful in that which is least is faithful also in much: and he that is unjust in the least is unjust also in much. If therefore ye have not been faithful in the unrighteous mammon, who will commit to your trust the true riches? And if ye have not been faithful in that which is another man's, who shall give you that which is your own?

"No servant can serve two masters: for either he will hate the one, and love the other; or else he will hold to the one, and despise the other. Ye cannot serve God and mammon."

And the Pharisees also, who were covetous, heard all these things: and they derided him. And he said unto them,

"Ye are they which justify yourselves before men; but God knoweth your hearts: for that which is highly esteemed among men is abomination in the sight of God. The law and the prophets were until John: since that time the kingdom of God is preached, and every man presseth into it. And it is easier for heaven and earth to pass, than one tittle of the law to fail.

"There was a certain rich man, which was clothed in purple and fine linen, and fared sumptuously every day: and there was a certain beggar named Lazarus, which was laid at his gate, full

THE GOSPEL ACCORDING TO LUKE

of sores, and desiring to be fed with the crumbs which fell from the rich man's table: moreover the dogs came and licked his sores. And it came to pass, that the beggar died, and was carried by the angels into Abraham's bosom: the rich man also died, and was buried; and in hell he lift up his eyes, being in torments, and seeth Abraham afar off, and Lazarus in his bosom.

"And he cried and said, 'Father Abraham, have mercy on me, and send Lazarus, that he may dip the tip of his finger in water, and cool my tongue; for I am tormented in this flame.' But Abraham said, 'Son, remember that thou in thy lifetime receivedst thy good things, and likewise Lazarus evil things: but now he is comforted, and thou art tormented. And beside all this, between us and you there is a great gulf fixed: so that they which would pass from hence to you cannot; neither can they pass to us, that would come from thence.'

"Then he said, 'I pray thee therefore, father, that thou wouldest send him to my father's house: for I have five brethren; that he may testify unto them, lest they also come into this place of torment.' Abraham saith unto him, 'They have Moses and the prophets; let them hear them.'

"And he said, 'Nay, Father Abraham: but if one went unto them from the dead, they will repent.' And he said unto him, 'If they hear not Moses and the prophets, neither will they be persuaded, though one rose from the dead.'"

Then said he unto the disciples,

"It is impossible but that offences will come: but woe unto him through whom they come! It were better for him that a millstone were hanged about his neck, and he cast into the sea, than that he should offend one of these little ones. Take heed to yourselves: if thy brother trespass against thee, rebuke him; and if he repent, forgive him. And if he trespass against thee seven times in a day, and seven times in a day turn again to thee, saying, 'I repent'; thou shalt forgive him."

And the apostles said unto the Lord, "Increase our faith."

THE GOSPEL ACCORDING TO LUKE

And the Lord said,

"If ye had faith as a grain of mustard seed, ye might say unto this sycamine tree, 'Be thou plucked up by the root, and be thou planted in the sea'; and it should obey you. But which of you, having a servant plowing or feeding cattle, will say unto him by and by, when he is come from the field, 'Go and sit down to meat'? And will not rather say unto him, 'Make ready wherewith I may sup, and gird thyself, and serve me, till I have eaten and drunken; and afterward thou shalt eat and drink'? Doth he thank that servant because he did the things that were commanded him? I trow not. So likewise ye, when ye shall have done all those things which are commanded you, say, 'We are unprofitable servants: we have done that which was our duty to do.'"

And it came to pass, as he went to Jerusalem, that he passed through the midst of Samaria and Galilee. And as he entered into a certain village, there met him ten men that were lepers, which stood afar off: and they lifted up their voices, and said, "Jesus, Master, have mercy on us."

And when he saw them, he said unto them, "Go show yourselves unto the priests." And it came to pass, that, as they went, they were cleansed. And one of them, when he saw that he was healed, turned back, and with a loud voice glorified God, and fell down on his face at his feet, giving him thanks: and he was a Samaritan.

And Jesus answering said, "Were there not ten cleansed? but where are the nine? There are not found that returned to give glory to God, save this stranger." And he said unto him, "Arise, go thy way: thy faith hath made thee whole."

And he spoke a parable unto them to this end, that men ought always to pray, and not to faint, saying,

"There was in a city a judge, which feared not God, neither regarded man: and there was a widow in that city; and she came unto him, saying, 'Avenge me of mine adversary.' And he would not for a while: but afterward he said within himself,

THE GOSPEL ACCORDING TO LUKE

Though I fear not God, nor regard man; yet because this widow troubleth me, I will avenge her, lest by her continual coming she weary me.'"

And the Lord said, "Hear what the unjust judge saith. And shall not God avenge his own elect, which cry day and night unto him, though he bear long with them? I tell you that he will avenge them speedily. Nevertheless when the Son of Man cometh, shall he find faith on the earth?"

And he spoke this parable unto certain which trusted in themselves that they were righteous, and despised others:

"Two men went up into the temple to pray; the one a Pharisee, and the other a publican. The Pharisee stood and prayed thus with himself, 'God, I thank thee, that I am not as other men are, extortioners, unjust, adulterers, or even as this publican. I fast twice in the week, I give tithes of all that I possess.' And the publican, standing afar off, would not lift up so much as his eyes unto heaven, but smote upon his breast, saying, 'God be merciful to me a sinner.' I tell you, this man went down to his house justified rather than the other: for every one that exalteth himself shall be abased; and he that humbleth himself shall be exalted."

And Jesus entered and passed through Jericho. And, behold, there was a man named Zacchæus, which was the chief among the publicans, and he was rich. And he sought to see Jesus who he was; and could not for the press, because he was little of stature. And he ran before, and climbed up into a sycamore tree to see him: for he was to pass that way.

And when Jesus came to the place, he looked up, and saw him, and said unto him, "Zacchæus, make haste, and come down; for to-day I must abide at thy house." And he made haste, and came down, and received him joyfully. And when they saw it, they all murmured, saying that he was gone to be guest with a man that is a sinner.

And Zacchæus stood, and said unto the Lord: "Behold, Lord, the half of my goods I give to the poor; and if I have taken any thing from any man by false accusation, I restore him fourfold."

THE GOSPEL ACCORDING TO LUKE

And Jesus said unto him, "This day is salvation come to this house, forsomuch as he also is a son of Abraham."

The Trial of Jesus

And as soon as it was day, the elders of the people and the chief priests and the scribes came together, and led him into their council, saying, "Art thou the Christ? tell us."

And he said unto them, "If I tell you, ye will not believe: and if I also ask you, ye will not answer me, nor let me go. Hereafter shall the Son of Man sit on the right hand of the power of God."

Then said they all, "Art thou then the Son of God?"

And he said unto them, "Ye say that I am."

And they said, "What need we any further witness? for we ourselves have heard of his own mouth."

And the whole multitude of them arose, and led him unto Pilate. And they began to accuse him, saying, "We found this fellow perverting the nation, and forbidding to give tribute to Cæsar, saying that he himself is Christ a King."

And Pilate asked him, saying, "Art thou the King of the Jews?"

And he answered him and said, "Thou sayest it."

Then said Pilate to the chief priests and to the people, "I find no fault in this man."

And they were the more fierce, saying, "He stirreth up the people, teaching throughout all Jewry, beginning from Galilee to this place."

When Pilate heard of Galilee, he asked whether the man were a Galilæan. And as soon as he knew that he belonged unto Herod's jurisdiction, he sent him to Herod, who himself also was at Jerusalem at that time. And when Herod saw Jesus, he was exceeding glad: for he was desirous to see him of a long season, because he had heard many things of him; and he hoped to have seen some miracle done by him. Then he questioned with him in many words; but he answered him nothing. And the chief priests and scribes stood and vehemently accused him. And Herod with his men of war set him at nought, and mocked

THE GOSPEL ACCORDING TO LUKE

him, and arrayed him in a gorgeous robe, and sent him again to Pilate. And the same day Pilate and Herod were made friends together: for before they were at enmity between themselves.

And Pilate, when he had called together the chief priests and the rulers and the people, said unto them, "Ye have brought this man unto me, as one that perverteth the people: and, behold, I, having examined him before you, have found no fault in this man touching those things whereof ye accuse him: no, nor yet Herod: for I sent you to him; and, lo, nothing worthy of death is done unto him. I will therefore chastise him, and release him." (For of necessity he must release one unto them at the feast.)

And they cried out all at once, saying, "Away with this man, and release unto us Barabbas" (who for a certain sedition made in the city, and for murder, was cast into prison).

Pilate therefore, willing to release Jesus, spoke again to them.

But they cried, saying, "Crucify him, crucify him!"

And he said unto them the third time, "Why, what evil hath he done? I have found no cause of death in him: I will therefore chastise him, and let him go."

And they were instant with loud voices, requiring that he might be crucified. And the voices of them and of the chief priests prevailed.

The Crucifixion of Jesus

And Pilate gave sentence that it should be as they required. And he released unto them him that for sedition and murder was cast into prison, whom they had desired; but he delivered Jesus to their will.

And as they led him away, they laid hold upon one Simon, a Cyrenian, coming out of the country, and on him they laid the cross, that he might bear it after Jesus. And there followed him a great company of people, and of women, which also bewailed and lamented him. But Jesus turning unto them said,

THE GOSPEL ACCORDING TO LUKE

"Daughters of Jerusalem, weep not for me, but weep for yourselves, and for your children. For, behold, the days are coming, in the which they shall say, 'Blessed are the barren, and the wombs that never bore, and the paps which never gave suck.' Then shall they begin to say to the mountains, 'Fall on us!' and to the hills, 'Cover us!' For if they do these things in a green tree, what shall be done in the dry?"

And there were also two other, malefactors, led with him to be put to death. And when they were come to the place, which is called Calvary, there they crucified him, and the malefactors, one on the right hand, and the other on the left.

Then said Jesus, "Father, forgive them; for they know not what they do."

And they parted his raiment, and cast lots. And the people stood beholding. And the rulers also with them derided him, saying, "He saved others; let him save himself, if he be Christ, the chosen of God."

And the soldiers also mocked him, coming to him, and offering him vinegar, and saying, "If thou be the King of the Jews, save thyself."

And a superscription also was written over him in letters of Greek, and Latin, and Hebrew: THIS IS THE KING OF THE JEWS.

And one of the malefactors which were hanged railed on him, saying, "If thou be Christ, save thyself and us." But the other answering rebuked him, saying, "Dost not thou fear God, seeing thou art in the same condemnation? And we indeed justly; for we receive the due reward of our deeds: but this man hath done nothing amiss."

And he said unto Jesus, "Lord, remember me when thou comest into thy kingdom."

And Jesus said unto him, "Verily I say unto thee, 'To-day shalt thou be with me in paradise.'"

And it was about the sixth hour, and there was a darkness over all the earth until the ninth hour. And the sun was darkened, and the veil of the temple was rent in the midst.

THE GOSPEL ACCORDING TO LUKE

And when Jesus had cried with a loud voice, he said, "Father, into thy hands, I commend my spirit": and having said thus, he gave up the ghost.

Now when the centurion saw what was done, he glorified God, saying, "Certainly this was a righteous man." And all the people that came together to that sight, beholding the things which were done, smote their breasts, and returned.

And all his acquaintance, and the women that followed him from Galilee, stood afar off, beholding these things.

And, behold, there was a man named Joseph, a counsellor; and he was a good man, and a just (the same had not consented to the counsel and deed of them): he was of Arimathæa, a city of the Jews: who also himself waited for the kingdom of God. This man went unto Pilate, and begged the body of Jesus. And he took it down, and wrapped it in linen, and laid it in a sepulchre that was hewn in stone, wherein never man before was laid. And that day was the preparation, and the sabbath drew on. And the women also, which came with him from Galilee, followed after, and beheld the sepulchre, and how his body was laid. And they returned, and prepared spices and ointments; and rested the sabbath day according to the commandment.

The Resurrection of Jesus

Now upon the first day of the week, very early in the morning, they came unto the sepulchre, bringing the spices which they had prepared, and certain others with them.

And they found the stone rolled away from the sepulchre. And they entered in, and found not the body of the Lord Jesus.

And it came to pass, as they were much perplexed thereabout, behold, two men stood by them in shining garments: and as they were afraid, and bowed down their faces to the earth, he said unto them, "Why seek ye the living among the dead? He is not here, but is risen: remember how he spoke unto you when he was yet in Galilee, saying, 'The Son of Man must be delivered into the hands of sinful men, and be crucified, and the third day rise again.'"

THE GOSPEL ACCORDING TO LUKE

And they remembered his words, and returned from the sepulchre, and told all these things unto the eleven, and to all the rest. It was Mary Magdalene, and Joanna, and Mary the mother of James, and other women that were with them, which told these things unto the apostles. And their words seemed to them as idle tales, and they believed them not.

Then arose Peter, and ran unto the sepulchre; and stooping down, he beheld the linen clothes laid by themselves, and departed, wondering in himself at that which was to come to pass.

And, behold, two of them went that same day to a village called Emmaus, which was from Jerusalem about threescore furlongs. And they talked together of all these things which had happened. And it came to pass, that, while they communed together and reasoned, Jesus himself drew near, and went with them. But their eyes were held that they should not know him.

And he said unto them, "What manner of communications are these that ye have one to another, as ye walk, and are sad?"

And the one of them, whose name was Cleopas, answering said unto him, "Art thou only a stranger in Jerusalem, and hast not known the things which are come to pass there in these days?"

And he said unto them, "What things?"

And they said unto him, "Concerning Jesus of Nazareth, which was a prophet mighty in deed and word before God and all the people: and how the chief priests and our rulers delivered him to be condemned to death, and have crucified him. But we trusted that it had been he which should have redeemed Israel: and beside all this, to-day is the third day since these things were done. Yea, and certain women also of our company made us astonished, which were early at the sepulchre; and when they found not his body, they came, saying that they had also seen a vision of angels, which said that he was alive. And certain of them which were with us went to the sepulchre, and found it even so as the women had said: but him they saw not."

Then he said unto them, "O fools, and slow of heart to be-

THE GOSPEL ACCORDING TO LUKE

lieve all that the prophets have spoken! Ought not Christ to have suffered these things, and to enter into his glory?"

And beginning at Moses and all the prophets, he expounded unto them in all the scriptures the things concerning himself. And they drew nigh unto the village, whither they went: and he made as though he would have gone further. But they constrained him, saying, "Abide with us: for it is toward evening, and the day is far spent." And he went in to tarry with them.

And it came to pass, as he sat at meat with them, he took bread, and blessed it, and broke, and gave to them. And their eyes were opened, and they knew him; and he vanished out of their sight.

And they said one to another, "Did not our heart burn within us, while he talked with us by the way, and while he opened to us the scriptures?"

And they rose up the same hour, and returned to Jerusalem, and found the eleven gathered together, and them that were with them, saying, "The Lord is risen indeed, and hath appeared to Simon." And they told what things were done in the way, and how he was known of them in breaking of bread.

And as they thus spoke, Jesus himself stood in the midst of them, and saith unto them, "Peace be unto you!" But they were terrified and affrighted, and supposed that they had seen a spirit.

And he said unto them, "Why are ye troubled? and why do thoughts arise in your hearts? Behold my hands and my feet, that it is I myself: handle me, and see; for a spirit hath not flesh and bones, as ye see me have."

And when he had thus spoken, he showed them his hands and his feet. And while they yet believed not for joy, and wondered, he said unto them, "Have ye here any meat?" And they gave him a piece of a broiled fish, and of a honeycomb. And he took it, and did eat before them. And he said unto them, "These are the words which I spoke unto you, while I was yet with you, that all things must be fulfilled, which were written in the law

THE GOSPEL ACCORDING TO LUKE

of Moses, and in the prophets, and in the psalms, concerning me."

Then opened he their understanding, that they might understand the scriptures, and said unto them, "Thus it is written, and thus it behoved Christ to suffer, and to rise from the dead the third day: and that repentance and remission of sins should be preached in his name among all nations, beginning at Jerusalem. And ye are witnesses of these things. And, behold, I send the promise of my Father upon you: but tarry ye in the city of Jerusalem, until ye be endued with power from on high."

And he led them out as far as to Bethany, and he lifted up his hands, and blessed them. And it came to pass, while he blessed them, he was parted from them, and carried up into heaven. And they worshipped him, and returned to Jerusalem with great joy: and were continually in the temple, praising and blessing God. Amen.

THE GOSPEL ACCORDING TO JOHN

THE GOSPEL according to John is unquestionably the latest of the four. It stands apart from the three Synoptic Gospels in purpose, method, and spirit. Written about the thesis that Jesus was not merely the human Messiah expected by the Jews but was also in very truth the divine Son of God, it presents a rearrangement and reinterpretation of the events of his life to prove its argument, while also the influence of Alexandrian and Greek philosophy is evident in the doctrine of the Logos or "Word" set forth in the Prologue. The author was less a biographer than a religious mystic for whom the inner life was all-important. The shift in emphasis from works to faith, from conduct to mystic union, which is also evident in the writings of Paul, is here carried very much further. The love of man which the book preaches rests upon, is inspired by, and is often only a symbol of the love for God; the love of man for God and the love of God for man are marvelously intertwined as the central theme of the work. A further contrast to the Synoptic Gospels is furnished by the fact that in the Gospel according to John there is no difference between the style of the speeches attributed to Jesus and that of the rest of the book. Whoever may have been the author, he was most certainly not the Apostle John, but someone who much later reworked the Gospel story with the utmost freedom to make it express what he considered ultimate religious truth.

The Gospel According to JOHN

Prologue

IN THE BEGINNING was the Word, and the Word was with God, and the Word was God. The same was in the beginning with God. All things were made by him; and without him was not any thing made that was made. In him was life; and the life was the light of men. And the light shineth in darkness; and the darkness comprehended it not.

John the Baptist and Jesus

There was a man sent from God, whose name was John. The same came for a witness, to bear witness of the Light, that all men through him might believe. He was not that Light, but was sent to bear witness of that Light. That was the true Light, which lighteth every man that cometh into the world. He was in the world, and the world was made by him, and the world knew him not. He came unto his own, and his own received him not. But as many as received him, to them gave he power to become the sons of God, even to them that believe on his name: which were born, not of blood, nor of the will of the flesh, nor of the will of man, but of God. And the Word was made flesh, and dwelt among us (and we beheld his glory, the glory as of the only begotten of the Father), full of grace and truth.

John bore witness of him, and cried, saying, "This was he of whom I spoke, 'He that cometh after me is preferred before me: for he was before me.'" And of his fulness have all we received, and grace for grace. For the law was given by Moses, but grace and truth came by Jesus Christ. No man hath seen God at any

[1007]

THE GOSPEL ACCORDING TO JOHN

time; the only begotten Son, which is in the bosom of the Father, he hath declared him. And this is the record of John, when the Jews sent priests and Levites from Jerusalem to ask him, "Who art thou?" And he confessed, and denied not; but confessed, "I am not the Christ."

And they asked him, "What then? Art thou Elias?"

And he saith, "I am not."

"Art thou that prophet?"

And he answered, "No."

Then said they unto him, "Who art thou? that we may give an answer to them that sent us. What sayest thou of thyself?"

He said, "I am the voice of one crying in the wilderness, 'Make straight the way of the Lord,' as said the prophet Esaias."

And they which were sent were of the Pharisees. And they asked him, and said unto him, "Why baptizest thou then, if thou be not that Christ, nor Elias, neither that prophet?"

John answered them, saying, "I baptize with water: but there standeth one among you, whom ye know not; he it is, who coming after me is preferred before me, whose shoe's latchet I am not worthy to unloose."

These things were done in Bethabara beyond Jordan, where John was baptizing.

The next day John seeth Jesus coming unto him, and saith, "Behold the Lamb of God, which taketh away the sin of the world. This is he of whom I said, 'After me cometh a man which is preferred before me: for he was before me.' And I knew him not: but that he should be made manifest to Israel, therefore am I come baptizing with water."

And John bore record, saying, "I saw the Spirit descending from heaven like a dove, and it abode upon him. And I knew him not: but he that sent me to baptize with water, the same said unto me, 'Upon whom thou shalt see the Spirit descending, and remaining on him, the same is he which baptizeth with the Holy Ghost.' And I saw, and bore record that this is the Son of God."

THE GOSPEL ACCORDING TO JOHN

The Gathering of the Disciples

Again the next day after, John stood, and two of his disciples, and looking upon Jesus as he walked, he saith, "Behold the Lamb of God!"

And the two disciples heard him speak, and they followed Jesus. Then Jesus turned, and saw them following, and saith unto them, "What seek ye?"

They said unto him, "Rabbi" (which is to say, being interpreted, "Master"), "where dwellest thou?"

He saith unto them, "Come and see."

They came and saw where he dwelt, and abode with him that day: for it was about the tenth hour.

One of the two which heard John speak, and followed him, was Andrew, Simon Peter's brother. He first findeth his own brother Simon, and saith unto him, "We have found the Messias, which is, being interpreted, the Christ." And he brought him to Jesus. And when Jesus beheld him, he said, "Thou art Simon the son of Jona: thou shalt be called Cephas," which is by interpretation "a stone."

The day following Jesus would go forth into Galilee, and findeth Philip, and saith unto him, "Follow me." (Now Philip was of Bethsaida, the city of Andrew and Peter.) Philip findeth Nathanael, and saith unto him, "We have found him, of whom Moses in the law, and the prophets, did write, Jesus of Nazareth, the son of Joseph." And Nathanael said unto him, "Can there any good thing come out of Nazareth?" Philip saith unto him, "Come and see!"

Jesus saw Nathanael coming to him, and saith of him, "Behold an Israelite indeed, in whom is no guile!"

Nathanael saith unto him, "Whence knowest thou me?"

Jesus answered and said unto him, "Before that Philip called thee, when thou wast under the fig tree, I saw thee."

Nathanael answered and saith unto him, "Rabbi, thou art the Son of God; thou art the King of Israel."

THE GOSPEL ACCORDING TO JOHN

Jesus answered and said unto him, "Because I said unto thee, 'I saw thee under the fig tree,' believest thou? thou shalt see greater things than these." And he saith unto him, "Verily, verily, I say unto you, 'Hereafter ye shall see heaven open, and the angels of God ascending and descending upon the Son of Man.'"

The Marriage in Cana

And the third day there was a marriage in Cana of Galilee; and the mother of Jesus was there: and both Jesus was called, and his disciples, to the marriage. And when they wanted wine, the mother of Jesus saith unto him, "They have no wine."

Jesus saith unto her, "Woman, what have I to do with thee? mine hour is not yet come."

His mother saith unto the servants, "Whatsoever he saith unto you, do it."

And there were set there six waterpots of stone, after the manner of the purifying of the Jews, containing two or three firkins apiece. Jesus saith unto them, "Fill the waterpots with water." And they filled them up to the brim. And he saith unto them, "Draw out now, and bear unto the governor of the feast." And they bore it. When the ruler of the feast had tasted the water that was made wine, and knew not whence it was (but the servants which drew the water knew), the governor of the feast called the bridegroom, and saith unto him, "Every man at the beginning doth set forth good wine; and when men have well drunk, then that which is worse: but thou hast kept the good wine until now."

This beginning of miracles did Jesus in Cana of Galilee, and manifested forth his glory; and his disciples believed on him.

The Visit of Nicodemus by Night

There was a man of the Pharisees, named Nicodemus, a ruler of the Jews. The same came to Jesus by night, and said unto him, "Rabbi, we know that thou art a teacher come from God: for no

THE GOSPEL ACCORDING TO JOHN

man can do these miracles that thou doest, except God be with him."

Jesus answered and said unto him, "Verily, verily, I say unto thee, 'Except a man be born again, he cannot see the kingdom of God.'"

Nicodemus saith unto him, "How can a man be born when he is old? can he enter the second time into his mother's womb, and be born?"

Jesus answered, "Verily, verily, I say unto thee, 'Except a man be born of water and of the Spirit, he cannot enter into the kingdom of God.' That which is born of the flesh is flesh; and that which is born of the Spirit is spirit. Marvel not that I said unto thee, 'Ye must be born again.' The wind bloweth where it listeth, and thou hearest the sound thereof, but canst not tell whence it cometh, and whither it goeth: so is every one that is born of the Spirit."

Nicodemus answered and said unto him, "How can these things be?"

Jesus answered and said unto him, "Art thou a master of Israel, and knowest not these things? Verily, verily, I say unto thee, 'We speak that we do know, and testify that we have seen; and ye receive not our witness.' If I have told you earthly things, and ye believe not, how shall ye believe, if I tell you of heavenly things? And no man hath ascended up to heaven, but he that came down from heaven, even the Son of Man which is in heaven. And as Moses lifted up the serpent in the wilderness, even so must the Son of Man be lifted up: that whosoever believeth in him should not perish, but have eternal life. For God so loved the world, that he gave his only begotten Son, that whosoever believeth in him should not perish, but have everlasting life. For God sent not his Son into the world to condemn the world; but that the world through him might be saved. He that believeth on him is not condemned: but he that believeth not is condemned already, because he hath not believed in the name of the only begotten Son of God. And this is

THE GOSPEL ACCORDING TO JOHN

the condemnation, that light is come into the world, and men loved darkness rather than light, because their deeds were evil. For every one that doeth evil hateth the light, neither cometh to the light, lest his deeds should be reproved. But he that doeth truth cometh to the light, that his deeds may be made manifest, that they are wrought in God."

The Woman of Samaria

When therefore the Lord knew how the Pharisees had heard that Jesus made and baptized more disciples than John (though Jesus himself baptized not, but his disciples), he left Judæa, and departed again into Galilee. And he must needs go through Samaria. Then cometh he to a city of Samaria, which is called Sychar, near to the parcel of ground that Jacob gave to his son Joseph. Now Jacob's well was there. Jesus therefore, being wearied with his journey, sat thus on the well: and it was about the sixth hour. There cometh a woman of Samaria to draw water: Jesus saith unto her, "Give me to drink." (For his disciples were gone away unto the city to buy meat.)

Then saith the woman of Samaria unto him, "How is it that thou, being a Jew, askest drink of me, which am a woman of Samaria? for the Jews have no dealings with the Samaritans."

Jesus answered and said unto her, "If thou knewest the gift of God, and who it is that saith to thee, 'Give me to drink'; thou wouldest have asked of him, and he would have given thee living water."

The woman saith unto him, "Sir, thou hast nothing to draw with, and the well is deep: from whence then hast thou that living water? Art thou greater than our father Jacob, which gave us the well, and drank thereof himself, and his children, and his cattle?"

Jesus answered and said unto her, "Whosoever drinketh of this water shall thirst again: but whosoever drinketh of the water that I shall give him shall never thirst; but the water that I shall give him shall be in him a well of water springing up into everlasting life."

THE GOSPEL ACCORDING TO JOHN

The woman saith unto him, "Sir, give me this water, that I thirst not, neither come hither to draw."

Jesus saith unto her, "Go, call thy husband, and come hither."

The woman answered and said, "I have no husband."

Jesus said unto her, "Thou hast well said, 'I have no husband': for thou hast had five husbands; and he whom thou now hast is not thy husband: in that saidst thou truly."

The woman saith unto him, "Sir, I perceive that thou art a prophet. Our fathers worshipped in this mountain; and ye say that in Jerusalem is the place where men ought to worship."

Jesus saith unto her, "Woman, believe me, the hour cometh, when ye shall neither in this mountain, nor yet at Jerusalem, worship the Father. Ye worship ye know not what: we know what we worship: for salvation is of the Jews. But the hour cometh, and now is, when the true worshippers shall worship the Father in spirit and in truth: for the Father seeketh such to worship him. God is a Spirit: and they that worship him must worship him in spirit and in truth."

The woman saith unto him, "I know that Messias cometh, which is called Christ: when he is come, he will tell us all things."

Jesus saith unto her, "I that speak unto thee am he."

And upon this came his disciples, and marvelled that he talked with the woman: yet no man said, "What seekest thou?" or, "Why talkest thou with her?" The woman then left her waterpot, and went her way into the city, and saith to the men, "Come, see a man, which told me all things that ever I did: is not this the Christ?" Then they went out of the city, and came unto him.

In the meanwhile his disciples prayed him, saying, "Master, eat."

But he said unto them, "I have meat to eat that ye know not of."

Therefore said the disciples one to another, "Hath any man brought him ought to eat?"

Jesus saith unto them, "My meat is to do the will of him that

THE GOSPEL ACCORDING TO JOHN

sent me, and to finish his work. Say not ye, 'There are yet four months, and then cometh harvest'? behold, I say unto you, 'Lift up your eyes, and look on the fields; for they are white already to harvest.' And he that reapeth receiveth wages, and gathereth fruit unto life eternal: that both he that soweth and he that reapeth may rejoice together. And herein is that saying true, 'One soweth, and another reapeth.' I sent you to reap that whereon ye bestowed no labour: other men laboured, and ye are entered into their labours."

And many of the Samaritans of that city believed on him for the saying of the woman, which testified, "He told me all that ever I did." So when the Samaritans were come unto him, they besought him that he would tarry with them: and he abode there two days. And many more believed because of his own word.

The Pool of Bethesda

After this there was a feast of the Jews; and Jesus went up to Jerusalem. Now there is at Jerusalem by the sheep market a pool, which is called in the Hebrew tongue Bethesda, having five porches. In these lay a great multitude of impotent folk, of blind, halt, withered, waiting for the moving of the water. For an angel went down at a certain season into the pool, and troubled the water; whosoever then first after the troubling of the water stepped in was made whole of whatsoever disease he had. And a certain man was there, which had an infirmity thirty and eight years.

When Jesus saw him lie, and knew that he had been now a long time in that case, he saith unto him, "Wilt thou be made whole?"

The impotent man answered him, "Sir, I have no man, when the water is troubled, to put me into the pool: but while I am coming, another steppeth down before me."

Jesus saith unto him, "Rise, take up thy bed, and walk."

And immediately the man was made whole, and took up his bed, and walked: and on the same day was the sabbath. The

THE GOSPEL ACCORDING TO JOHN

Jews therefore said unto him that was cured, "It is the sabbath day: it is not lawful for thee to carry thy bed." He answered them, "He that made me whole, the same said unto me, 'Take up thy bed, and walk.'" Then asked they him, "What man is that which said unto thee, 'Take up thy bed, and walk'?" And he that was healed wist not who it was: for Jesus had conveyed himself away, a multitude being in that place. Afterward Jesus findeth him in the temple, and said unto him, "Behold, thou art made whole: sin no more, lest a worse thing come unto thee." The man departed, and told the Jews that it was Jesus, which had made him whole. And therefore did the Jews persecute Jesus, and sought to slay him, because he had done these things on the sabbath day.

But Jesus answered them, "My Father worketh hitherto, and I work." Therefore the Jews sought the more to kill him, because he not only had broken the sabbath, but said also that God was his Father, making himself equal with God.

The Woman Taken in Adultery

Jesus went unto the Mount of Olives. And early in the morning he came again into the temple, and all the people came unto him; and he sat down, and taught them. And the scribes and Pharisees brought unto him a woman taken in adultery; and when they had set her in the midst, they say unto him,

"Master, this woman was taken in adultery, in the very act. Now Moses in the law commanded us that such should be stoned: but what sayest thou?"

This they said, tempting him, that they might have to accuse him. But Jesus stooped down, and with his finger wrote on the ground, as though he heard them not. So when they continued asking him, he lifted up himself, and said unto them,

"He that is without sin among you, let him first cast a stone at her." And again he stooped down, and wrote on the ground. And they which heard it, being convicted by their own conscience, went out one by one, beginning at the eldest, even unto the last: and Jesus was left alone, and the woman standing in the

THE GOSPEL ACCORDING TO JOHN

midst. When Jesus had lifted up himself, and saw none but the woman, he said unto her,

"Woman, where are those thine accusers? hath no man condemned thee?"

She said, "No man, Lord." And Jesus said unto her,

"Neither do I condemn thee: go, and sin no more."

The Pool of Siloam

And as Jesus passed by, he saw a man which was blind from his birth. And his disciples asked him, saying, "Master, who did sin, this man, or his parents, that he was born blind?"

Jesus answered, "Neither hath this man sinned, nor his parents: but that the works of God should be made manifest in him. I must work the works of him that sent me, while it is day: the night cometh, when no man can work. As long as I am in the world, I am the light of the world."

When he had thus spoken, he spat on the ground, and made clay of the spittle, and he anointed the eyes of the blind man with the clay, and said unto him, "Go, wash in the pool of Siloam" (which is by interpretation "sent").

He went his way therefore, and washed, and came seeing. The neighbours therefore, and they which before had seen him that he was blind, said, "Is not this he that sat and begged?"

Some said, "This is he": others said, "He is like him": but he said, "I am he."

Therefore said they unto him, "How were thine eyes opened?"

He answered and said, "A man that is called Jesus made clay, and anointed mine eyes, and said unto me, 'Go to the pool of Siloam, and wash': and I went and washed, and I received sight."

Then said they unto him, "Where is he?"

He said, "I know not."

They brought to the Pharisees him that aforetime was blind. And it was the sabbath day when Jesus made the clay, and opened his eyes.

Then again the Pharisees also asked him how he had received

THE GOSPEL ACCORDING TO JOHN

his sight. He said unto them, "He put clay upon mine eyes, and I washed, and do see."

Therefore said some of the Pharisees, "This man is not of God, because he keepeth not the sabbath day."

Others said, "How can a man that is a sinner do such miracles?"

And there was a division among them. They say unto the blind man again, "What sayest thou of him, that he hath opened thine eyes?"

He said, "He is a prophet."

But the Jews did not believe concerning him, that he had been blind, and received his sight, until they called the parents of him that had received his sight. And they asked them, saying, "Is this your son, who ye say was born blind? how then doth he now see?"

His parents answered them and said, "We know that this is our son, and that he was born blind: but by what means he now seeth, we know not; or who hath opened his eyes, we know not: he is of age; ask him: he shall speak for himself."

These words spoke his parents, because they feared the Jews: for the Jews had agreed already, that if any man did confess that he was Christ, he should be put out of the synagogue. Therefore said his parents, "He is of age; ask him."

Then again called they the man that was blind, and said unto him, "Give God the praise: we know that this man is a sinner."

He answered and said, "Whether he be a sinner or no, I know not: one thing I know, that, whereas I was blind, now I see."

Then said they to him again, "What did he to thee? how opened he thine eyes?"

He answered them, "I have told you already, and ye did not hear: wherefore would ye hear it again? will ye also be his disciples?"

Then they reviled him, and said, "Thou art his disciple; but we are Moses' disciples. We know that God spoke unto Moses: as for this fellow, we know not from whence he is."

THE GOSPEL ACCORDING TO JOHN

The man answered and said unto them, "Why herein is a marvellous thing, that ye know not from whence he is, and yet he hath opened mine eyes. Now we know that God heareth not sinners: but if any man be a worshipper of God, and doeth his will, him he heareth. Since the world began was it not heard that any man opened the eyes of one that was born blind. If this man were not of God, he could do nothing."

They answered and said unto him, "Thou wast altogether born in sins, and dost thou teach us?" And they cast him out.

Jesus heard that they had cast him out; and when he had found him, he said unto him, "Dost thou believe on the Son of God?"

He answered and said, "Who is he, Lord, that I might believe on him?"

And Jesus said unto him, "Thou hast both seen him, and it is he that talketh with thee."

And he said, "Lord, I believe." And he worshipped him.

And Jesus said, "For judgment I am come into this world, that they which see not might see; and that they which see might be made blind."

And some of the Pharisees which were with him heard these words, and said unto him, "Are we blind also?"

Jesus said unto them, "If ye were blind, ye should have no sin: but now ye say, 'We see'; therefore your sin remaineth.

"Verily, verily, I say unto you, 'He that entereth not by the door into the sheepfold, but climbeth up some other way, the same is a thief and a robber. But he that entereth in by the door is the shepherd of the sheep. To him the porter openeth; and the sheep hear his voice: and he calleth his own sheep by name, and leadeth them out. And when he putteth forth his own sheep, he goeth before them, and the sheep follow him: for they know his voice. And a stranger will they not follow, but will flee from him: for they know not the voice of strangers.'"

This parable spoke Jesus unto them: but they understood not what things they were which he spoke unto them. Then said Jesus unto them again,

THE GOSPEL ACCORDING TO JOHN

"Verily, verily, I say unto you, 'I am the door of the sheep.' All that ever came before me are thieves and robbers: but the sheep did not hear them.

"I am the door: by me if any man enter in, he shall be saved, and shall go in and out, and find pasture. The thief cometh not, but for to steal, and to kill, and to destroy: I am come that they might have life, and that they might have it more abundantly.

"I am the good shepherd: the good shepherd giveth his life for the sheep. But he that is a hireling, and not the shepherd, whose own the sheep are not, seeth the wolf coming, and leaveth the sheep, and fleeth: and the wolf catcheth them, and scattereth the sheep. The hireling fleeth, because he is a hireling, and careth not for the sheep.

"I am the good shepherd, and know my sheep, and am known of mine. As the Father knoweth me, even so know I the Father: and I lay down my life for the sheep. And other sheep I have, which are not of this fold: them also I must bring, and they shall hear my voice; and there shall be one fold, and one shepherd. Therefore doth my Father love me, because I lay down my life, that I might take it again. No man taketh it from me, but I lay it down of myself. I have power to lay it down, and I have power to take it again. This commandment have I received of my Father."

There was a division therefore again among the Jews for these sayings, and many of them said, "He hath a devil, and is mad; why hear ye him?" Others said, "These are not the words of him that hath a devil. Can a devil open the eyes of the blind?"

In Solomon's Porch

And it was at Jerusalem the feast of the dedication, and it was winter. And Jesus walked in the temple in Solomon's porch. Then came the Jews round about him, and said unto him, "How long dost thou make us to doubt? If thou be the Christ, tell us plainly."

Jesus answered them, "I told you, and ye believed not: the works that I do in my Father's name, they bear witness of me.

THE GOSPEL ACCORDING TO JOHN

But ye believe not, because ye are not of my sheep, as I said unto you. My sheep hear my voice, and I know them, and they follow me: and I give unto them eternal life; and they shall never perish, neither shall any man pluck them out of my hand. My Father, which gave them me, is greater than all; and no man is able to pluck them out of my Father's hand. I and my Father are one."

Then the Jews took up stones again to stone him.

Jesus answered them, "Many good works have I showed you from my Father; for which of those works do ye stone me?"

The Jews answered him, saying, "For a good work we stone thee not; but for blasphemy; and because that thou, being a man, makest thyself God."

Jesus answered them, "Is it not written in your law, I said, 'Ye are gods'? If he called them gods, unto whom the word of God came, and the scripture cannot be broken; say ye of him, whom the Father hath sanctified, and sent into the world, 'Thou blasphemest'; because I said, 'I am the Son of God'? If I do not the works of my Father, believe me not. But if I do, though ye believe not me, believe the works: that ye may know, and believe, that the Father is in me, and I in him."

Therefore they sought again to take him: but he escaped out of their hand, and went away again beyond Jordan into the place where John at first baptized; and there he abode. And many resorted unto him, and said, "John did no miracle: but all things that John spoke of this man were true." And many believed on him there.

The Raising of Lazarus

Now a certain man was sick, named Lazarus, of Bethany, the town of Mary and her sister Martha. (It was that Mary which anointed the Lord with ointment, and wiped his feet with her hair, whose brother Lazarus was sick.) Therefore his sisters sent unto him, saying, "Lord, behold, he whom thou lovest is sick." When Jesus heard that, he said, "This sickness is not unto death, but for the glory of God, that the Son of God might be glorified

THE GOSPEL ACCORDING TO JOHN

thereby." Now Jesus loved Martha, and her sister, and Lazarus. When he had heard therefore that he was sick, he abode two days still in the same place where he was. Then after that saith he to his disciples, "Let us go into Judæa again." His disciples say unto him, "Master, the Jews of late sought to stone thee; and goest thou thither again?" Jesus answered, "Are there not twelve hours in the day? If any man walk in the day, he stumbleth not, because he seeth the light of this world. But if a man walk in the night, he stumbleth, because there is no light in him."

These things said he: and after that he saith unto them, "Our friend Lazarus sleepeth; but I go, that I may awake him out of sleep." Then said his disciples, "Lord, if he sleep, he shall do well." Howbeit Jesus spoke of his death: but they thought that he had spoken of taking of rest in sleep. Then said Jesus unto them plainly, "Lazarus is dead. And I am glad for your sakes that I was not there, to the intent ye may believe; nevertheless let us go unto him." Then said Thomas, which is called Didymus, unto his fellow disciples, "Let us also go, that we may die with him." Then when Jesus came, he found that he had lain in the grave four days already. Now Bethany was nigh unto Jerusalem, about fifteen furlongs off: and many of the Jews came to Martha and Mary, to comfort them concerning their brother. Then Martha, as soon as she heard that Jesus was coming, went and met him: but Mary sat still in the house. Then said Martha unto Jesus, "Lord, if thou hadst been here, my brother had not died. But I know that even now, whatsoever thou wilt ask of God, God will give it thee." Jesus saith unto her, "Thy brother shall rise again." Martha saith unto him. "I know that he shall rise again in the resurrection at the last day." Jesus said unto her, "I am the resurrection, and the life: he that believeth in me, though he were dead, yet shall he live: and whosoever liveth and believeth in me shall never die. Believest thou this?" She saith unto him, "Yea, Lord: I believe that thou art the Christ, the Son of God, which should come into the world." And when

THE GOSPEL ACCORDING TO JOHN

she had so said, she went her way, and called Mary her sister secretly, saying, "The Master is come, and calleth for thee." As soon as she heard that, she arose quickly, and came unto him.

Now Jesus was not yet come into the town, but was in that place where Martha met him. The Jews then which were with her in the house, and comforted her, when they saw Mary, that she rose up hastily, and went out, followed her, saying, "She goeth unto the grave to weep there." Then when Mary was come where Jesus was, and saw him, she fell down at his feet, saying unto him, "Lord, if thou hadst been here, my brother had not died." When Jesus therefore saw her weeping, and the Jews also weeping which came with her, he groaned in the spirit, and was troubled, and said, "Where have ye laid him?" They said unto him, "Lord, come and see." Jesus wept. Then said the Jews, "Behold how he loved him!" And some of them said, "Could not this man, which opened the eyes of the blind, have caused that even this man should not have died?" Jesus therefore again groaning in himself cometh to the grave. It was a cave, and a stone lay upon it. Jesus said, "Take ye away the stone." Martha, the sister of him that was dead, saith unto him, "Lord, by this time he stinketh: for he hath been dead four days." Jesus saith unto her, "Said I not unto thee that, if thou wouldest believe, thou shouldest see the glory of God?" Then they took away the stone from the place where the dead was laid. And Jesus lifted up his eyes, and said, "Father, I thank thee that thou hast heard me. And I knew that thou hearest me always: but because of the people which stand by I said it, that they may believe that thou hast sent me." And when he thus had spoken, he cried with a loud voice, "Lazarus, come forth!" And he that was dead came forth, bound hand and foot with graveclothes: and his face was bound about with a napkin. Jesus saith unto them, "Loose him, and let him go!" Then many of the Jews which came to Mary, and had seen the things which Jesus did, believed on him. But some of them went their ways to the Pharisees, and told them what things Jesus had done.

Then gathered the chief priests and the Pharisees a council,

THE GOSPEL ACCORDING TO JOHN

and said, "What do we? for this man doeth many miracles. If we let him thus alone, all men will believe on him: and the Romans shall come and take away both our place and nation." And one of them, named Caiaphas, being the high priest that same year, said unto them, "Ye know nothing at all, nor consider that it is expedient for us, that one man should die for the people, and that the whole nation perish not." And this spoke he not of himself: but being high priest that year, he prophesied that Jesus should die for that nation; and not for that nation only, but that also he should gather together in one the children of God that were scattered abroad. Then from that day forth they took counsel together for to put him to death. Jesus therefore walked no more openly among the Jews; but went thence unto a country near to the wilderness, into a city called Ephraim, and there continued with his disciples. And the Jews' passover was nigh at hand: and many went out of the country up to Jerusalem before the passover, to purify themselves. Then sought they for Jesus, and spoke among themselves, as they stood in the temple. "What think ye, that he will not come to the feast?" Now both the chief priests and the Pharisees had given a commandment that, if any man knew where he were, he should show it, that they might take him.

Thus Jesus six days before the passover came to Bethany, where Lazarus was which had been dead, whom he raised from the dead. There they made him a supper; and Martha served: but Lazarus was one of them that sat at the table with him. Then took Mary a pound of ointment of spikenard, very costly, and anointed the feet of Jesus, and wiped his feet with her hair: and the house was filled with the odour of the ointment. Then saith one of his disciples, Judas Iscariot, Simon's son, which should betray him, "Why was not this ointment sold for three hundred pence, and given to the poor?" This he said, not that he cared for the poor; but because he was a thief, and had the bag, and bore what was put therein. Then said Jesus, "Let her alone: against the day of my burying hath she kept this. For the poor always ye have with you; but me ye have not always."

THE GOSPEL ACCORDING TO JOHN

Much people of the Jews therefore knew that he was there: and they came not for Jesus' sake only, but that they might see Lazarus also, whom he had raised from the dead. But the chief priests consulted that they might put Lazarus also to death; because that by reason of him many of the Jews went away, and believed on Jesus.

On the next day much people that were come to the feast, when they heard that Jesus was coming to Jerusalem, took branches of palm trees, and went forth to meet him, and cried, "Hosanna! Blessed is the King of Israel that cometh in the name of the Lord!"

The Last Supper

Now before the feast of the passover, when Jesus knew that his hour was come that he should depart out of this world unto the Father, having loved his own which were in the world, he loved them unto the end. And supper being ended, the devil having now put into the heart of Judas Iscariot, Simon's son, to betray him, Jesus, knowing that the Father had given all things into his hands, and that he was come from God, and went to God, riseth from supper, and laid aside his garments; and took a towel, and girded himself. After that, he poureth water into a basin, and began to wash the disciples' feet, and to wipe them with the towel wherewith he was girded. Then cometh he to Simon Peter: and Peter saith unto him, "Lord, dost thou wash my feet?" Jesus answered and said unto him, "What I do thou knowest not now; but thou shalt know hereafter." Peter saith unto him, "Thou shalt never wash my feet." Jesus answered him, "If I wash thee not, thou hast no part with me." Simon Peter saith unto him, "Lord, not my feet only, but also my hands and my head." Jesus saith to him, "He that is washed needeth not save to wash his feet, but is clean every whit: and ye are clean, but not all." For he knew who should betray him; therefore said he, "Ye are not all clean." So after he had washed their feet, and had taken his garments, and was set down again, he said unto them, "Know ye what I have done to you? Ye call me Master

THE GOSPEL ACCORDING TO JOHN

and Lord: and ye say well; for so I am. If I then, your Lord and Master, have washed your feet; ye also ought to wash one another's feet. For I have given you an example, that ye should do as I have done to you. Verily, verily, I say unto you, 'The servant is not greater than his lord; neither he that is sent greater than he that sent him.' If ye know these things, happy are ye if ye do them. I speak not of you all: I know whom I have chosen: but that the scripture may be fulfilled, 'He that eateth bread with me hath lifted up his heel against me.' Now I tell you before it come, that, when it is come to pass, ye may believe that I am he. Verily, verily, I say unto you, 'He that receiveth whomsoever I send receiveth me; and he that receiveth me receiveth him that sent me.'"

When Jesus had thus said, he was troubled in spirit, and testified, and said, "Verily, verily, I say unto you that one of you shall betray me."

Then the disciples looked one on another, doubting of whom he spoke. Now there was leaning on Jesus' bosom one of his disciples, whom Jesus loved. Simon Peter therefore beckoned to him, that he should ask who it should be of whom he spoke. He then lying on Jesus' breast saith unto him, "Lord, who is it?"

Jesus answered, "He it is, to whom I shall give a sop, when I have dipped it." And when he had dipped the sop, he gave it to Judas Iscariot, the son of Simon. And after the sop Satan entered into him. Then said Jesus unto him, "That thou doest, do quickly." Now no man at the table knew for what intent he spoke this unto him. For some of them thought, because Judas had the bag, that Jesus had said unto him, "Buy those things that we have need of against the feast"; or, that he should give something to the poor. He then having received the sop went immediately out: and it was night.

Therefore, when he was gone out, Jesus said, "Now is the Son of Man glorified, and God is glorified in him. If God be glorified in him, God shall also glorify him in himself, and shall straightway glorify him. Little children, yet a little while I am with you. Ye shall seek me: and as I said unto the Jews, 'Whither

THE GOSPEL ACCORDING TO JOHN

I go, ye cannot come'; so now I say to you. A new commandment I give unto you: that ye love one another; as I have loved you, that ye also love one another. By this shall all men know that ye are my disciples, if ye have love one to another."

Simon Peter said unto him, "Lord, whither goest thou?"

Jesus answered him, "Whither I go, thou canst not follow me now; but thou shalt follow me afterwards."

Peter said unto him, "Lord, why cannot I follow thee now? I will lay down my life for thy sake."

Jesus answered him, "Wilt thou lay down thy life for my sake? Verily, verily, I say unto thee, 'The cock shall not crow, till thou hast denied me thrice.'

"Let not your heart be troubled: ye believe in God, believe also in me. In my Father's house are many mansions: if it were not so, I would have told you. I go to prepare a place for you. And if I go and prepare a place for you, I will come again, and receive you unto myself; that where I am, there ye may be also. And whither I go ye know, and the way ye know."

Thomas saith unto him,

"Lord, we know not whither thou goest; and how can we know the way?"

Jesus saith unto him,

"I am the way, the truth, and the life: no man cometh unto the Father, but by me. If ye had known me, ye should have known my Father also: and from henceforth ye know him, and have seen him."

Philip saith unto him,

"Lord, show us the Father, and it sufficeth us."

Jesus saith unto him,

"Have I been so long time with you, and yet hast thou not known me, Philip? he that hath seen me hath seen the Father; and how sayest thou then, 'Show us the Father'? Believest thou not that I am in the Father, and the Father in me? the words that I speak unto you I speak not of myself: but the Father that dwelleth in me, he doeth the works. Believe me that I am in the Father, and the Father in me: or else believe me for the very works'

THE GOSPEL ACCORDING TO JOHN

sake Verily, verily, I say unto you, 'He that believeth on me, the works that I do shall he do also; and greater works than these shall he do; because I go unto my Father.' And whatsoever ye shall ask in my name, that will I do, that the Father may be glorified in the Son. If ye shall ask any thing in my name, I will do it.

"If ye love me, keep my commandments. And I will pray the Father, and he shall give you another Comforter, that he may abide with you for ever; even the Spirit of truth; whom the world cannot receive, because it seeth him not, neither knoweth him: but ye know him; for he dwelleth with you, and shall be in you. I will not leave you comfortless: I will come to you. Yet a little while, and the world seeth me no more; but ye see me: because I live, ye shall live also. At that day ye shall know that I am in my Father, and ye in me, and I in you. He that hath my commandments, and keepeth them, he it is that loveth me: and he that loveth me shall be loved of my Father, and I will love him, and will manifest myself to him."

Judas (not Iscariot) saith unto him,

"Lord, how is it that thou wilt manifest thyself unto us, and not unto the world?"

Jesus answered and said unto him,

"If a man love me, he will keep my words: and my Father will love him, and we will come unto him, and make our abode with him. He that loveth me not keepeth not my sayings: and the word which ye hear is not mine, but the Father's which sent me.

"These things have I spoken unto you, being yet present with you. But the Comforter, which is the Holy Ghost, whom the Father will send in my name, he shall teach you all things, and bring all things to your remembrance, whatsoever I have said unto you. Peace I leave with you, my peace I give unto you: not as the world giveth, give I unto you. Let not your heart be troubled, neither let it be afraid. Ye have heard how I said unto you, 'I go away, and come again unto you.' If ye loved me, ye would rejoice because I said, 'I go unto the Father': for my Father is

THE GOSPEL ACCORDING TO JOHN

greater than I. And now I have told you before it come to pass that, when it is come to pass, ye might believe. Hereafter I will not talk much with you: for the prince of this world cometh, and hath nothing in me. But that the world may know that I love the Father; and as the Father gave me commandment, even so I do.

"I am the true vine, and my Father is the husbandman. Every branch in me that beareth not fruit he taketh away: and every branch that beareth fruit, he purgeth it, that it may bring forth more fruit. Now ye are clean through the word which I have spoken unto you. Abide in me, and I in you. As the branch cannot bear fruit of itself, except it abide in the vine; no more can ye, except ye abide in me. I am the vine, ye are the branches: he that abideth in me, and I in him, the same bringeth forth much fruit: for without me ye can do nothing. If a man abide not in me, he is cast forth as a branch, and is withered; and men gather them, and cast them into the fire, and they are burned. If ye abide in me, and my words abide in you, ye shall ask what ye will, and it shall be done unto you. Herein is my Father glorified, that ye bear much fruit; so shall ye be my disciples. As the Father hath loved me, so have I loved you: continue ye in my love. If ye keep my commandments, ye shall abide in my love; even as I have kept my Father's commandments, and abide in his love. These things have I spoken unto you, that my joy might remain in you, and that your joy might be full. This is my commandment: that ye love one another, as I have loved you. Greater love hath no man than this, that a man lay down his life for his friends. Ye are my friends, if ye do whatsoever I command you. Henceforth I call you not servants; for the servant knoweth not what his lord doeth: but I have called you friends; for all things that I have heard of my Father I have made known unto you. Ye have not chosen me, but I have chosen you, and ordained you, that ye should go and bring forth fruit, and that your fruit should remain: that whatsoever ye shall ask of the Father in my name he may give it you.

"These things I command you, that ye love one another. If the

THE GOSPEL ACCORDING TO JOHN

world hate you, ye know that it hated me before it hated you. If ye were of the world, the world would love his own: but because ye are not of the world, but I have chosen you out of the world, therefore the world hateth you. Remember the word that I said unto you, 'The servant is not greater than his lord.' If they have persecuted me, they will also persecute you; if they have kept my saying, they will keep yours also. But all these things will they do unto you for my name's sake, because they know not him that sent me. If I had not come and spoken unto them, they had not had sin: but now they have no cloak for their sin. He that hateth me hateth my Father also. If I had not done among them the works which none other man did, they had not had sin: but now have they both seen and hated both me and my Father: But this cometh to pass that the word might be fulfilled that is written in their law, 'They hated me without a cause.' But when the Comforter is come, whom I will send unto you from the Father, even the Spirit of truth, which proceedeth from the Father, he shall testify of me: and ye also shall bear witness, because ye have been with me from the beginning.

"These things have I spoken unto you, that ye should not be offended. They shall put you out of the synagogues: yea, the time cometh that whosoever killeth you will think that he doeth God service. And these things will they do unto you, because they have not known the Father, nor me. But these things have I told you, that when the time shall come, ye may remember that I told you of them. And these things I said not unto you at the beginning, because I was with you. But now I go my way to him that sent me; and none of you asketh me, 'Whither goest thou?' But because I have said these things unto you, sorrow hath filled your heart. Nevertheless I tell you the truth: 'It is expedient for you that I go away: for if I go not away, the Comforter will not come unto you; but if I depart, I will send him unto you. And when he is come, he will reprove the world of sin, and of righteousness, and of judgment: of sin, because they believe not on me; of righteousness, because I go to my Father, and ye see me no more; of judgment, because the prince of this world is

THE GOSPEL ACCORDING TO JOHN

judged.' I have yet many things to say unto you, but ye cannot bear them now. Howbeit when he, the Spirit of truth, is come, he will guide you into all truth: for he shall not speak of himself; but whatsoever he shall hear, that shall he speak: and he will show you things to come. He shall glorify me: for he shall receive of mine, and shall show it unto you. All things that the Father hath are mine: therefore said I, that he shall take of mine, and shall show it unto you. A little while, and ye shall not see me: and again, a little while, and ye shall see me, because I go to the Father."

Then said some of his disciples among themselves, "What is this that he saith unto us, 'A little while, and ye shall not see me': and again, 'A little while, and ye shall see me': and, 'Because I go to the Father'?" They said therefore, "What is this that he saith, 'A little while'? We cannot tell what he saith."

Now Jesus knew that they were desirous to ask him, and said unto them, "Do ye enquire among yourselves of that I said, 'A little while, and ye shall not see me': and again, 'A little while, and ye shall see me'? Verily, verily, I say unto you that ye shall weep and lament, but the world shall rejoice: and ye shall be sorrowful, but your sorrow shall be turned into joy. A woman when she is in travail hath sorrow, because her hour is come: but as soon as she is delivered of the child, she remembereth no more the anguish, for joy that a man is born into the world. And ye now therefore have sorrow: but I will see you again, and your heart shall rejoice, and your joy no man taketh from you. And in that day ye shall ask me nothing. Verily, verily, I say unto you, 'Whatsoever ye shall ask the Father in my name, he will give it you.' Hitherto have ye asked nothing in my name: ask, and ye shall receive, that your joy may be full. These things have I spoken unto you in proverbs: but the time cometh, when I shall no more speak unto you in proverbs, but I shall show you plainly of the Father. At that day ye shall ask in my name: and I say not unto you that I will pray the Father for you: for the Father himself loveth you, because ye have loved me, and have believed that I came out from God. I came forth from the Fa-

THE GOSPEL ACCORDING TO JOHN

ther, and am come into the world: again, I leave the world, and go to the Father."

His disciples said unto him, "Lo, now speakest thou plainly, and speakest no proverb. Now are we sure that thou knowest all things, and needest not that any man should ask thee: by this we believe that thou camest forth from God."

Jesus answered them,

"Do ye now believe? Behold, the hour cometh, yea, is now come, that ye shall be scattered, every man to his own, and shall leave me alone: and yet I am not alone, because the Father is with me. These things I have spoken unto you, that in me ye might have peace. In the world ye shall have tribulation: but be of good cheer; I have overcome the world."

These words spoke Jesus, and lifted up his eyes to heaven, and said,

"Father, the hour is come; glorify thy Son, that thy Son also may glorify thee: as thou hast given him power over all flesh, that he should give eternal life to as many as thou hast given him. And this is life eternal, that they might know thee the only true God, and Jesus Christ, whom thou hast sent. I have glorified thee on the earth: I have finished the work which thou gavest me to do. And now, O Father, glorify thou me with thine own self with the glory which I had with thee before the world was.

"I have manifested thy name unto the men which thou gavest me out of the world: thine they were, and thou gavest them me; and they have kept thy word. Now they have known that all things whatsoever thou hast given me are of thee. For I have given unto them the words which thou gavest me; and they have received them, and have known surely that I came out from thee, and they have believed that thou didst send me. I pray for them: I pray not for the world, but for them which thou hast given me; for they are thine. And all mine are thine, and thine are mine; and I am glorified in them. And now I am no more in the world, but these are in the world, and I come to thee. Holy Father, keep through thine own name those whom thou hast

THE GOSPEL ACCORDING TO JOHN

given me, that they may be one, as we are. While I was with them in the world, I kept them in thy name: those that thou gavest me I have kept, and none of them is lost, but the son of perdition; that the scripture might be fulfilled. And now come I to thee; and these things I speak in the world, that they might have my joy fulfilled in themselves. I have given them thy word; and the world hath hated them, because they are not of the world, even as I am not of the world. I pray not that thou shouldest take them out of the world, but that thou shouldest keep them from the evil. They are not of the world, even as I am not of the world. Sanctify them through thy truth: thy word is truth. As thou hast sent me into the world, even so have I also sent them into the world. And for their sakes I sanctify myself, that they also might be sanctified through the truth.

"Neither pray I for these alone, but for them also which shall believe on me through their word, that they all may be one; as thou, Father, art in me, and I in thee, that they also may be one in us: that the world may believe that thou hast sent me. And the glory which thou gavest me I have given them; that they may be one, even as we are one: I in them, and thou in me, that they may be made perfect in one; and that the world may know that thou hast sent me, and hast loved them, as thou hast loved me. Father, I will that they also, whom thou hast given me, be with me where I am; that they may behold my glory, which thou hast given me: for thou lovedst me before the foundation of the world. O righteous Father, the world hath not known thee: but I have known thee, and these have known that thou hast sent me. And I have declared unto them thy name, and will declare it: that the love wherewith thou hast loved me may be in them, and I in them."

The Betrayal of Jesus

When Jesus had spoken these words, he went forth with his disciples over the brook Cedron, where was a garden, into the which he entered, and his disciples. And Judas also, which betrayed him, knew the place: for Jesus ofttimes resorted thither

THE GOSPEL ACCORDING TO JOHN

with his disciples. Judas then, having received a band of men and officers from the chief priests and Pharisees, cometh thither with lanterns and torches and weapons. Jesus therefore, knowing all things that should come upon him, went forth, and said unto them,

"Whom seek ye?"

They answered him, "Jesus of Nazareth."

Jesus saith unto them, "I am he."

And Judas also, which betrayed him, stood with them. As soon then as he had said unto them, "I am he," they went backward, and fell to the ground. Then asked he them again,

"Whom seek ye?"

And they said, "Jesus of Nazareth."

Jesus answered,

"I have told you that I am he: if therefore ye seek me, let these go their way" (that the saying might be fulfilled, which he spoke, "Of them which thou gavest me have I lost none").

Then Simon Peter having a sword drew it, and smote the high priest's servant, and cut off his right ear. The servant's name was Malchus. Then said Jesus unto Peter,

"Put up thy sword into the sheath: the cup which my Father hath given me, shall I not drink it?"

Then the band and the captain and officers of the Jews took Jesus, and bound him, and led him away to Annas first; for he was father-in-law to Caiaphas, which was the high priest that same year. Now Caiaphas was he, which gave counsel to the Jews, that it was expedient that one man should die for the people.

And Simon Peter followed Jesus, and so did another disciple: that disciple was known unto the high priest, and went in with Jesus into the palace of the high priest. But Peter stood at the door without. Then went out that other disciple, which was known unto the high priest, and spoke unto her that kept the door, and brought in Peter. Then saith the damsel that kept the door unto Peter, "Art not thou also one of this man's disciples?" He saith, "I am not." And the servants and officers stood there,

THE GOSPEL ACCORDING TO JOHN

who had made a fire of coals; for it was cold: and they warmed themselves: and Peter stood with them, and warmed himself.

The high priest then asked Jesus of his disciples, and of his doctrine. Jesus answered him,

"I spoke openly to the world; I ever taught in the synagogue, and in the temple, whither the Jews always resort; and in secret have I said nothing. Why askest thou me? ask them which heard me, what I have said unto them: behold, they know what I said."

And when he had thus spoken, one of the officers which stood by struck Jesus with the palm of his hand, saying, "Answerest thou the high priest so?"

Jesus answered him,

"If I have spoken evil, bear witness of the evil: but if well, why smitest thou me?" Now Annas had sent him bound unto Caiaphas the high priest. And Simon Peter stood and warmed himself. They said therefore unto him, "Art not thou also one of his disciples?" He denied it, and said, "I am not." One of the servants of the high priest, being his kinsman whose ear Peter cut off, saith, "Did not I see thee in the garden with him?" Peter then denied again: and immediately the cock crew.

The Trial of Jesus

Then led they Jesus from Caiaphas unto the hall of judgment: and it was early; and they themselves went not into the judgment hall, lest they should be defiled; but that they might eat the passover.

Pilate then went out unto them, and said, "What accusation bring ye against this man?"

They answered and said unto him, "If he were not a malefactor, we would not have delivered him up unto thee."

Then said Pilate unto them, "Take ye him, and judge him according to your law."

The Jews therefore said unto him, "It is not lawful for us to put any man to death" (that the saying of Jesus might be fulfilled, which he spoke, signifying what death he should die).

THE GOSPEL ACCORDING TO JOHN

Then Pilate entered into the judgment hall again, and called Jesus, and said unto him, "Art thou the King of the Jews?"

Jesus answered him,

"Sayest thou this thing of thyself, or did others tell it thee of me?"

Pilate answered,

"Am I a Jew? Thine own nation and the chief priests have delivered thee unto me: what hast thou done?"

Jesus answered,

"My kingdom is not of this world: if my kingdom were of this world, then would my servants fight, that I should not be delivered to the Jews: but now is my kingdom not from hence."

Pilate therefore said unto him,

"Art thou a king then?"

Jesus answered,

"Thou sayest that I am a king. To this end was I born, and for this cause came I into the world, that I should bear witness unto the truth. Every one that is of the truth heareth my voice."

Pilate saith unto him, "What is truth?"

And when he had said this, he went out again unto the Jews, and saith unto them, "I find in him no fault at all. But ye have a custom, that I should release unto you one at the passover: will ye therefore that I release unto you the King of the Jews?"

Then cried they all again, saying, "Not this man, but Barabbas." Now Barabbas was a robber.

The Crucifixion of Jesus

Then Pilate therefore took Jesus, and scourged him. And the soldiers plaited a crown of thorns, and put it on his head, and they put on him a purple robe, and said, "Hail, King of the Jews!" and they smote him with their hands.

Pilate therefore went forth again, and saith unto them, "Behold, I bring him forth to you, that ye may know that I find no fault in him." Then came Jesus forth, wearing the crown of thorns, and the purple robe. And Pilate saith unto them, "Behold the

THE GOSPEL ACCORDING TO JOHN

man!" When the chief priests therefore and officers saw him, they cried out, saying, "Crucify him, crucify him." Pilate saith unto them, "Take ye him, and crucify him: for I find no fault in him." The Jews answered him, "We have a law, and by our law he ought to die, because he made himself the Son of God."

When Pilate therefore heard that saying, he was the more afraid, and went again into the judgment hall, and saith unto Jesus, "Whence art thou?" But Jesus gave him no answer.

Then saith Pilate unto him, "Speakest thou not unto me? knowest thou not that I have power to crucify thee, and have power to release thee?"

Jesus answered, "Thou couldest have no power at all against me, except it were given thee from above: therefore he that delivered me unto thee hath the greater sin."

And from thenceforth Pilate sought to release him: but the Jews cried out, saying, "If thou let this man go, thou art not Cæsar's friend: whosoever maketh himself a king speaketh against Cæsar."

When Pilate therefore heard that saying, he brought Jesus forth, and sat down in the judgment seat in a place that is called the Pavement, but, in Hebrew, Gabbatha. And it was the preparation of the passover, and about the sixth hour: and he saith unto the Jews, "Behold your King!"

But they cried out, "Away with him, away with him, crucify him!"

Pilate saith unto them, "Shall I crucify your King?"

The chief priests answered, "We have no king but Cæsar."

Then delivered he him therefore unto them to be crucified. And they took Jesus, and led him away. And he bearing his cross went forth into a place called the place of a skull, which is called, in the Hebrew, Golgotha, where they crucified him, and two others with him, on either side one, and Jesus in the midst. And Pilate wrote a title, and put it on the cross. And the writing was JESUS OF NAZARETH, THE KING OF THE JEWS. This title then read many of the Jews: for the place where Jesus was

THE GOSPEL ACCORDING TO JOHN

crucified was nigh to the city: and it was written in Hebrew, and Greek, and Latin.

Then said the chief priests of the Jews to Pilate, "Write not, 'The King of the Jews'; but that he said, 'I am King of the Jews.'"

Pilate answered, "What I have written I have written."

Then the soldiers, when they had crucified Jesus, took his garments, and made four parts, to every soldier a part; and also his coat: now the coat was without seam, woven from the top throughout. They said therefore among themselves, "Let us not rend it, but cast lots for it, whose it shall be": that the scripture might be fulfilled, which saith,

> "They parted my raiment among them,
> And for my vesture they did cast lots."

These things therefore the soldiers did.

Now there stood by the cross of Jesus his mother, and his mother's sister, Mary the wife of Cleophas, and Mary Magdalene. When Jesus therefore saw his mother, and the disciple standing by, whom he loved, he saith unto his mother, "Woman, behold thy son!" Then saith he to the disciple, "Behold thy mother!" And from that hour that disciple took her unto his own home.

After this, Jesus knowing that all things were now accomplished, that the scripture might be fulfilled, saith, "I thirst." Now there was set a vessel full of vinegar: and they filled a sponge with vinegar, and put it upon hyssop, and put it to his mouth. When Jesus therefore had received the vinegar, he said, "It is finished": and he bowed his head, and gave up the ghost.

The Jews therefore, because it was the preparation, that the bodies should not remain upon the cross on the sabbath day (for that sabbath day was a high day), besought Pilate that their legs might be broken, and that they might be taken away. Then came the soldiers, and broke the legs of the first, and of the other which was crucified with him. But when they came to Jesus, and saw that he was dead already, they broke not his legs:

THE GOSPEL ACCORDING TO JOHN

but one of the soldiers with a spear pierced his side, and forthwith came there out blood and water. And he that saw it bore record, and his record is true: and he knoweth that he saith true, that ye might believe. For these things were done, that the scripture should be fulfilled, "A bone of him shall not be broken." And again another scripture saith, "They shall look on him whom they pierced."

And after this Joseph of Arimathæa, being a disciple of Jesus, but secretly for fear of the Jews, besought Pilate that he might take away the body of Jesus: and Pilate gave him leave. He came therefore, and took the body of Jesus. And there came also Nicodemus, which at the first came to Jesus by night, and brought a mixture of myrrh and aloes, about a hundred pound weight. Then took they the body of Jesus, and wound it in linen clothes with the spices, as the manner of the Jews is to bury. Now in the place where he was crucified there was a garden; and in the garden a new sepulchre, wherein was never man yet laid. There laid they Jesus therefore because of the Jews' preparation day; for the sepulchre was nigh at hand.

The Resurrection of Jesus

The first day of the week cometh Mary Magdalene early, when it was yet dark, unto the sepulchre, and seeth the stone taken away from the sepulchre. Then she runneth, and cometh to Simon Peter, and to the other disciple, whom Jesus loved, and saith unto them, "They have taken away the Lord out of the sepulchre, and we know not where they have laid him."

Peter therefore went forth, and that other disciple, and came to the sepulchre. So they ran both together: and the other disciple did outrun Peter, and came first to the sepulchre. And he stooping down, and looking in, saw the linen clothes lying; yet went he not in. Then cometh Simon Peter following him, and went into the sepulchre, and seeth the linen clothes lie, and the napkin, that was about his head, not lying with the linen clothes, but wrapped together in a place by itself. Then went in also that other disciple, which came first to the sepulchre, and he

THE GOSPEL ACCORDING TO JOHN

saw, and believed. For as yet they knew not the scripture, that he must rise again from the dead. Then the disciples went away again unto their own home.

But Mary stood without at the sepulchre weeping: and as she wept, she stooped down, and looked into the sepulchre, and seeth two angels in white sitting, the one at the head, and the other at the feet, where the body of Jesus had lain. And they say unto her, "Woman, why weepest thou?" She saith unto them, "Because they have taken away my Lord, and I know not where they have laid him." And when she had thus said, she turned herself back, and saw Jesus standing, and knew not that it was Jesus. Jesus saith unto her, "Woman, why weepest thou? whom seekest thou?" She, supposing him to be the gardener, saith unto him, "Sir, if thou have borne him hence, tell me where thou hast laid him, and I will take him away." Jesus saith unto her, "Mary!" She turned herself, and saith unto him, "Rabboni"; which is to say, "Master." Jesus saith unto her, "Touch me not; for I am not yet ascended to my Father: but go to my brethren, and say unto them, 'I ascend unto my Father, and your Father; and to my God, and your God.'" Mary Magdalene came and told the disciples that she had seen the Lord, and that he had spoken these things unto her.

Then the same day at evening, being the first day of the week, when the doors were shut where the disciples were assembled for fear of the Jews, came Jesus and stood in the midst, and saith unto them, "Peace be unto you!" And when he had so said, he showed unto them his hands and his side. Then were the disciples glad, when they saw the Lord. Then said Jesus to them again, "Peace be unto you: as my Father hath sent me, even so send I you." And when he had said this, he breathed on them, and saith unto them, "Receive ye the Holy Ghost! Whosoever sins ye remit, they are remitted unto them; and whosoever sins ye retain, they are retained."

But Thomas, one of the twelve, called Didymus, was not with them when Jesus came. The other disciples therefore said unto him, "We have seen the Lord." But he said unto them, "Except

THE GOSPEL ACCORDING TO JOHN

I shall see in his hands the print of the nails, and put my finger into the print of the nails, and thrust my hand into his side, I will not believe."

And after eight days again his disciples were within, and Thomas with them: then came Jesus, the doors being shut, and stood in the midst, and said, "Peace be unto you!" Then saith he to Thomas, "Reach hither thy finger, and behold my hands; and reach hither thy hand, and thrust it into my side: and be not faithless, but believing." And Thomas answered and said unto him, "My Lord and my God." Jesus saith unto him, "Thomas, because thou hast seen me, thou hast believed: blessed are they that have not seen, and yet have believed."

And many other signs truly did Jesus in the presence of his disciples, which are not written in this book: but these are written, that ye might believe that Jesus is the Christ, the Son of God; and that believing ye might have life through his name.

After these things Jesus showed himself again to the disciples at the Sea of Tiberias; and on this wise showed he himself. There were together Simon Peter, and Thomas called Didymus, and Nathanael of Cana in Galilee, and the sons of Zebedee, and two other of his disciples. Simon Peter saith unto them, "I go a-fishing." They say unto him, "We also go with thee." They went forth, and entered into a ship immediately; and that night they caught nothing. But when the morning was now come, Jesus stood on the shore: but the disciples knew not that it was Jesus. Then Jesus saith unto them, "Children, have ye any meat?" They answered him, "No." And he said unto them, "Cast the net on the right side of the ship, and ye shall find." They cast therefore, and now they were not able to draw it for the multitude of fishes. Therefore that disciple whom Jesus loved saith unto Peter, "It is the Lord." Now when Simon Peter heard that it was the Lord, he girt his fisher's coat unto him (for he was naked), and did cast himself into the sea. And the other disciples came in a little ship (for they were not far from land, but as it were two hundred cubits), dragging the net with fishes. As soon then as

THE GOSPEL ACCORDING TO JOHN

they were come to land, they saw a fire of coals there, and fish laid thereon, and bread. Jesus saith unto them, "Bring of the fish which ye have now caught." Simon Peter went up, and drew the net to land full of great fishes, a hundred and fifty and three: and for all there were so many, yet was not the net broken. Jesus saith unto them, "Come and dine." And none of the disciples durst ask him, "Who art thou?" knowing that it was the Lord. Jesus then cometh, and taketh bread, and giveth them, and fish likewise. This is now the third time that Jesus showed himself to his disciples, after that he was risen from the dead.

So when they had dined, Jesus saith to Simon Peter, "Simon, son of Jonas, lovest thou me more than these?" He saith unto him, "Yea, Lord; thou knowest that I love thee." He saith unto him, "Feed my lambs." He saith to him again the second time, "Simon, son of Jonas, lovest thou me?" He saith unto him, "Yea, Lord; thou knowest that I love thee." He saith unto him, "Feed my sheep." He saith unto him the third time, "Simon, son of Jonas, lovest thou me?" Peter was grieved because he said unto him the third time, "Lovest thou me?" And he said unto him, "Lord, thou knowest all things; thou knowest that I love thee." Jesus saith unto him, "Feed my sheep. Verily, verily, I say unto thee, 'When thou wast young, thou girdedst thyself, and walkedst whither thou wouldest: but when thou shalt be old, thou shalt stretch forth thy hands, and another shall gird thee, and carry thee whither thou wouldest not.'" This spoke he, signifying by what death he should glorify God. And when he had spoken this, he saith unto him, "Follow me." Then Peter, turning about, seeth the disciple whom Jesus loved following; which also leaned on his breast at supper, and said, "Lord, which is he that betrayeth thee?" Peter seeing him saith to Jesus, "Lord, and what shall this man do?" Jesus saith unto him, "If I will that he tarry till I come, what is that to thee? follow thou me." Then went this saying abroad among the brethren, that that disciple should not die: yet Jesus said not unto him, "He shall not die"; but, "If I will that he tarry till I come, what is that to thee?"

THE GOSPEL ACCORDING TO JOHN

This is the disciple which testifieth of these things, and wrote these things: and we know that his testimony is true. And there are also many other things which Jesus did, the which, if they should be written every one, I suppose that even the world itself could not contain the books that should be written. Amen.

THE ACTS OF THE APOSTLES

A HISTORY OF THE EARLY CHURCH

THE ACTS OF THE APOSTLES *is a continuation of the Gospel according to Luke by the same author. It is the chief source for our knowledge of early Christianity. Through its vivid narrative we are enabled to follow the spread of Christianity from Judea through Asia Minor and Greece and finally to Rome, the capital of the world. In its spacious atmosphere the famous ancient cities rise before us—Jerusalem, Antioch, Ephesus, Athens, Corinth, Rome—invaded and most of them conquered by the dauntless Christian missionaries. The reader will note how the story gains in credibility when it reaches events with which Luke was personally familiar. Though no more skeptical of marvelous happenings than were others of his generation, he seems to have been scrupulously accurate within the limits of his own knowledge. Dominating the later chapters is the great figure of Paul, through whom Christianity became a world religion. Thus the Acts of the Apostles is the best possible introduction to the letters of Paul himself.*

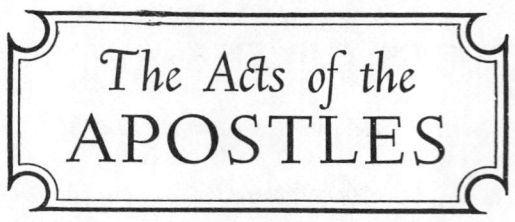

The Acts of the APOSTLES

A HISTORY OF THE EARLY CHURCH

The Ascension

THE FORMER TREATISE have I made, O Theophilus, of all that Jesus began both to do and teach, until the day in which he was taken up, after that he through the Holy Ghost had given commandments unto the apostles whom he had chosen: to whom also he showed himself alive after his passion by many infallible proofs, being seen of them forty days, and speaking of the things pertaining to the kingdom of God: and, being assembled together with them, commanded them that they should not depart from Jerusalem, but wait for the promise of the Father, which, saith he, "Ye have heard of me. For John truly baptized with water; but ye shall be baptized with the Holy Ghost not many days hence."

When they therefore were come together, they asked of him, saying, "Lord, wilt thou at this time restore again the kingdom to Israel?" And he said unto them, "It is not for you to know the times or the seasons, which the Father hath put in his own power. But ye shall receive power, after that the Holy Ghost is come upon you: and ye shall be witnesses unto me both in Jerusalem, and in all Judæa, and in Samaria, and unto the uttermost part of the earth."

And when he had spoken these things, while they beheld, he was taken up; and a cloud received him out of their sight. And while they looked steadfastly toward heaven as he went up, behold, two men stood by them in white apparel; which also said,

THE ACTS OF THE APOSTLES

"Ye men of Galilee, why stand ye gazing up into heaven? this same Jesus, which is taken up from you into heaven, shall so come in like manner as ye have seen him go into heaven."

Then returned they unto Jerusalem from the mount called Olivet, which is from Jerusalem a sabbath day's journey.

And when they were come in, they went up into an upper room, where abode both Peter, and James, and John, and Andrew, Philip, and Thomas, Bartholomew, and Matthew, James the son of Alphæus, and Simon Zelotes, and Judas the brother of James. These all continued with one accord in prayer and supplication, with the women, and Mary the mother of Jesus, and with his brethren.

And in those days Peter stood up in the midst of the disciples, and said—the number of names together were about a hundred and twenty—"Men and brethren, this scripture must needs have been fulfilled, which the Holy Ghost by the mouth of David spoke before concerning Judas, which was guide to them that took Jesus. For he was numbered with us, and had obtained part of this ministry." (Now this man purchased a field with the reward of iniquity; and falling headlong, he burst asunder in the midst, and all his bowels gushed out. And it was known unto all the dwellers at Jerusalem; insomuch as that field is called in their proper tongue Aceldama, that is to say, the Field of Blood.) "For it is written in the Book of Psalms,

> "'Let his habitation be desolate,
> And let no man dwell therein':

and

> "'His bishopric let another take.'

"Wherefore of these men which have companied with us all the time that the Lord Jesus went in and out among us, beginning from the baptism of John, unto that same day that he was taken up from us, must one be ordained to be a witness with us of his resurrection."

And they appointed two, Joseph called Barsabas, who was surnamed Justus, and Matthias. And they prayed, and said,

THE ACTS OF THE APOSTLES

"Thou, Lord, which knowest the hearts of all men, show whether of these two thou hast chosen, that he may take part of this ministry and apostleship, from which Judas by transgression fell, that he might go to his own place." And they gave forth their lots; and the lot fell upon Matthias; and he was numbered with the eleven apostles.

Pentecost

And when the day of Pentecost was fully come, they were all with one accord in one place. And suddenly there came a sound from heaven as of a rushing mighty wind, and it filled all the house where they were sitting. And there appeared unto them cloven tongues like as of fire, and it sat upon each of them. And they were all filled with the Holy Ghost, and began to speak with other tongues, as the Spirit gave them utterance.

And there were dwelling at Jerusalem Jews, devout men, out of every nation under heaven. Now when this was noised abroad, the multitude came together, and were confounded, because that every man heard them speak in his own language. And they were all amazed and marvelled, saying one to another, "Behold, are not all these which speak Galilæans? And how hear we every man in our own tongue, wherein we were born? Parthians, and Medes, and Elamites, and the dwellers in Mesopotamia, and in Judæa, and Cappadocia, in Pontus, and Asia, Phrygia, and Pamphylia, in Egypt, and in the parts of Libya about Cyrene, and strangers of Rome, Jews and proselytes, Cretans and Arabians, we do hear them speak in our tongues the wonderful works of God." And they were all amazed, and were in doubt, saying one to another, "What meaneth this?" Others mocking said, "These men are full of new wine."

But Peter, standing up with the eleven, lifted up his voice, and said unto them, "Ye men of Judæa, and all ye that dwell at Jerusalem, be this known unto you, and hearken to my words: for these are not drunken, as ye suppose, seeing it is but the third hour of the day. But this is that which was spoken by the prophet Joel:

THE ACTS OF THE APOSTLES

" ' "And it shall come to pass in the last days," saith God,
"I will pour out of my Spirit upon all flesh:
And your sons and your daughters shall prophesy,
And your young men shall see visions,
And your old men shall dream dreams:
And on my servants and on my handmaidens
I will pour out in those days of my Spirit;
And they shall prophesy:
And I will show wonders in heaven above,
And signs in the earth beneath;
Blood, and fire, and vapour of smoke:
The sun shall be turned into darkness,
And the moon into blood,
Before that great and notable day of the Lord come:
And it shall come to pass,
That whosoever shall call on the name of the Lord shall be saved." '

"Ye men of Israel, hear these words: Jesus of Nazareth, a man approved of God among you by miracles and wonders and signs, which God did by him in the midst of you, as ye yourselves also know: him, being delivered by the determinate counsel and foreknowledge of God, ye have taken, and by wicked hands have crucified and slain: whom God hath raised up, having loosed the pains of death: because it was not possible that he should be held of it. For David speaketh concerning him,

" 'I foresaw the Lord always before my face,
For he is on my right hand, that I should not be moved:
Therefore did my heart rejoice, and my tongue was glad;
Moreover also my flesh shall rest in hope:
Because thou wilt not leave my soul in hell,
Neither wilt thou suffer thine Holy One to see corruption.
Thou hast made known to me the ways of life;
Thou shalt make me full of joy with thy countenance.'

"Men and brethren, let me freely speak unto you of the patriarch David, that he is both dead and buried, and his sepulchre

THE ACTS OF THE APOSTLES

is with us unto this day. Therefore being a prophet, and knowing that God had sworn with an oath to him, that of the fruit of his loins, according to the flesh, he would raise up Christ to sit on his throne; he seeing this before spoke of the resurrection of Christ, that his soul was not left in hell, neither his flesh did see corruption. This Jesus hath God raised up, whereof we all are witnesses. Therefore being by the right hand of God exalted, and having received of the Father the promise of the Holy Ghost, he hath shed forth this, which ye now see and hear. For David is not ascended into the heavens: but he saith himself,

" 'The Lord said unto my Lord,
"Sit thou on my right hand,
Until I make thy foes thy footstool." '

"Therefore let all the house of Israel know assuredly that God hath made that same Jesus, whom ye have crucified, both Lord and Christ."

Now when they heard this, they were pricked in their heart, and said unto Peter and to the rest of the apostles, "Men and brethren, what shall we do?" Then Peter said unto them, "Repent, and be baptized every one of you in the name of Jesus Christ for the remission of sins, and ye shall receive the gift of the Holy Ghost. For the promise is unto you, and to your children, and to all that are afar off, even as many as the Lord our God shall call." And with many other words did he testify and exhort, saying, "Save yourselves from this untoward generation."

Then they that gladly received his word were baptized: and the same day there were added unto them about three thousand souls. And they continued steadfastly in the apostles' doctrine and fellowship, and in breaking of bread, and in prayers. And fear came upon every soul: and many wonders and signs were done by the apostles. And all that believed were together, and had all things common; and sold their possessions and goods, and parted them to all men, as every man had need. And they, continuing daily with one accord in the temple, and breaking bread from house to house, did eat their meat with gladness and

THE ACTS OF THE APOSTLES

singleness of heart, praising God, and having favour with all the people. And the Lord added to the church daily such as should be saved.

The Ministry of Peter and John

Now Peter and John went up together into the temple at the hour of prayer, being the ninth hour. And a certain man lame from his mother's womb was carried, whom they laid daily at the gate of the temple which is called Beautiful, to ask alms of them that entered into the temple; who seeing Peter and John about to go into the temple asked an alms. And Peter, fastening his eyes upon him with John, said, "Look on us."

And he gave heed unto them, expecting to receive something of them. Then Peter said, "Silver and gold have I none; but such as I have give I thee: in the name of Jesus Christ of Nazareth rise up and walk."

And he took him by the right hand, and lifted him up: and immediately his feet and ankle bones received strength. And he leaping up stood, and walked, and entered with them into the temple, walking, and leaping, and praising God.

And all the people saw him walking and praising God: and they knew that it was he which sat for alms at the Beautiful Gate of the temple: and they were filled with wonder and amazement at that which had happened unto him.

And as the lame man which was healed held Peter and John, all the people ran together unto them in the porch that is called Solomon's, greatly wondering.

And as they spoke unto the people, the priests, and the captain of the temple, and the Sadducees, came upon them, being grieved that they taught the people, and preached through Jesus the resurrection from the dead. And they laid hands on them, and put them in hold unto the next day: for it was now eventide. Howbeit many of them which heard the word believed; and the number of the men was about five thousand.

And it came to pass on the morrow, that their rulers, and elders, and scribes, and Annas the high priest, and Caiaphas, and

THE ACTS OF THE APOSTLES

John, and Alexander, and as many as were of the kindred of the high priest, were gathered together at Jerusalem. And when they had set them in the midst, they asked, "By what power, or by what name, have ye done this?"

Then Peter, filled with the Holy Ghost, said unto them, "Ye rulers of the people, and elders of Israel, if we this day be examined of the good deed done to the impotent man, by what means he is made whole; be it known unto you all, and to all the people of Israel, that by the name of Jesus Christ of Nazareth, whom ye crucified, whom God raised from the dead, even by him doth this man stand here before you whole. This is the stone which was set at nought of you builders, which is become the head of the corner. Neither is there salvation in any other: for there is none other name under heaven given among men, whereby we must be saved."

Now when they saw the boldness of Peter and John, and perceived that they were unlearned and ignorant men, they marvelled; and they took knowledge of them, that they had been with Jesus. And beholding the man which was healed standing with them, they could say nothing against it.

But when they had commanded them to go aside out of the council, they conferred among themselves, saying, "What shall we do to these men? for that indeed a notable miracle hath been done by them is manifest to all them that dwell in Jerusalem; and we cannot deny it. But that it spread no further among the people, let us straitly threaten them, that they speak henceforth to no man in this name."

And they called them, and commanded them not to speak at all nor teach in the name of Jesus.

But Peter and John answered and said unto them, "Whether it be right in the sight of God to hearken unto you more than unto God, judge ye. For we cannot but speak the things which we have seen and heard." So when they had further threatened them, they let them go, finding nothing how they might punish them, because of the people: for all men glorified God for that

THE ACTS OF THE APOSTLES

which was done. For the man was above forty years old, on whom this miracle of healing was showed.

And being let go, they went to their own company, and reported all that the chief priests and elders had said unto them. And when they heard that, they lifted up their voice to God with one accord, and said, "Lord, thou art God, which hast made heaven, and earth, and the sea, and all that in them is: who by the mouth of thy servant David hast said,

"'Why did the heathen rage,
And the people imagine vain things?
The kings of the earth stood up, and the rulers were
    gathered together
Against the Lord, and against his Christ.'

"For a truth against thy holy child Jesus, whom thou hast anointed, both Herod, and Pontius Pilate, with the Gentiles, and the people of Israel, were gathered together, for to do whatsoever thy hand and thy counsel determined before to be done. And now, Lord, behold their threatenings: and grant unto thy servants, that with all boldness they may speak thy word, by stretching forth thine hand to heal; and that signs and wonders may be done by the name of thy holy child Jesus."

And when they had prayed, the place was shaken where they were assembled together; and they were all filled with the Holy Ghost, and they spoke the word of God with boldness.

And the multitude of them that believed were of one heart and of one soul: neither said any of them that ought of the things which he possessed was his own; but they had all things common. And with great power gave the apostles witness of the resurrection of the Lord Jesus: and great grace was upon them all. Neither was there any among them that lacked: for as many as were possessors of lands or houses sold them, and brought the prices of the things that were sold, and laid them down at the apostles' feet: and distribution was made unto every man according as he had need. And Joses, who by the apostles was

THE ACTS OF THE APOSTLES

surnamed Barnabas (which is, being interpreted, "the son of consolation"), a Levite, and of the country of Cyprus, having land, sold it, and brought the money, and laid it at the apostles' feet.

But a certain man named Ananias, with Sapphira his wife, sold a possession, and kept back part of the price, his wife also being privy to it, and brought a certain part, and laid it at the apostles' feet.

But Peter said, "Ananias, why hath Satan filled thine heart to lie to the Holy Ghost, and to keep back part of the price of the land? While it remained, was it not thine own? and after it was sold, was it not in thine own power? why hast thou conceived this thing in thine heart? thou hast not lied unto men, but unto God."

And Ananias hearing these words fell down, and gave up the ghost: and great fear came on all them that heard these things. And the young men arose, wound him up, and carried him out, and buried him.

And it was about the space of three hours after, when his wife, not knowing what was done, came in. And Peter answered unto her, "Tell me whether ye sold the land for so much?"

And she said, "Yea, for so much."

Then Peter said unto her, "How is it that ye have agreed together to tempt the Spirit of the Lord? behold, the feet of them which have buried thy husband are at the door, and shall carry thee out."

Then fell she down straightway at his feet, and yielded up the ghost: and the young men came in, and found her dead, and, carrying her forth, buried her by her husband. And great fear came upon all the church, and upon as many as heard these things.

And by the hands of the apostles were many signs and wonders wrought among the people (and they were all with one accord in Solomon's porch. And of the rest durst no man join himself to them: but the people magnified them. And believers were the more added to the Lord, multitudes both of men and women); insomuch that they brought forth the sick into the streets, and laid them on beds and couches, that at the least the

THE ACTS OF THE APOSTLES

shadow of Peter passing by might overshadow some of them. There came also a multitude out of the cities round about unto Jerusalem, bringing sick folks, and them which were vexed with unclean spirits: and they were healed every one.

Then the high priest rose up, and all they that were with him (which is the sect of the Sadducees), and were filled with indignation, and laid their hands on the apostles, and put them in the common prison.

But the angel of the Lord by night opened the prison doors, and brought them forth, and said, "Go, stand and speak in the temple to the people all the words of this life."

And when they heard that, they entered into the temple early in the morning, and taught. But the high priest came, and they that were with him, and called the council together, and all the senate of the children of Israel, and sent to the prison to have them brought.

But when the officers came, and found them not in the prison, they returned, and told, saying, "The prison truly found we shut with all safety, and the keepers standing without before the doors: but when we had opened, we found no man within."

Now when the high priest and the captain of the temple and the chief priests heard these things, they doubted of them whereunto this would grow.

Then came one and told them, saying, "Behold, the men whom ye put in prison are standing in the temple, and teaching the people."

Then went the captain with the officers, and brought them without violence: for they feared the people, lest they should have been stoned. And when they had brought them, they set them before the council: and the high priest asked them, saying, "Did not we straitly command you that ye should not teach in this name? and, behold, ye have filled Jerusalem with your doctrine, and intend to bring this man's blood upon us."

Then Peter and the other apostles answered and said, "We ought to obey God rather than men. The God of our fathers raised up Jesus, whom ye slew and hanged on a tree. Him hath

THE ACTS OF THE APOSTLES

God exalted with his right hand to be a Prince and a Saviour, for to give repentance to Israel, and forgiveness of sins. And we are his witnesses of these things; and so is also the Holy Ghost, whom God hath given to them that obey him."

When they heard that, they were cut to the heart, and took counsel to slay them. Then stood there up one in the council, a Pharisee, named Gamaliel, a doctor of the law, had in reputation among all the people, and commanded to put the apostles forth a little space and said unto them, "Ye men of Israel, take heed to yourselves what ye intend to do as touching these men. For before these days rose up Theudas, boasting himself to be somebody; to whom a number of men, about four hundred, joined themselves: who was slain; and all, as many as obeyed him, were scattered, and brought to nought. After this man rose up Judas of Galilee in the days of the taxing, and drew away much people after him; he also perished; and all, even as many as obeyed him, were dispersed. And now I say unto you, 'Refrain from these men, and let them alone': for if this counsel or this work be of men, it will come to nought: but if it be of God, ye cannot overthrow it; lest haply ye be found even to fight against God."

And to him they agreed: and when they had called the apostles, and beaten them, they commanded that they should not speak in the name of Jesus, and let them go.

And they departed from the presence of the council, rejoicing that they were counted worthy to suffer shame for his name. And daily in the temple, and in every house, they ceased not to teach and preach Jesus Christ.

The Martyrdom of Stephen

And in those days, when the number of the disciples was multiplied, there arose a murmuring of the Grecians against the Hebrews, because their widows were neglected in the daily ministration. Then the twelve called the multitude of the disciples unto them, and said,

"It is not reason that we should leave the word of God, and serve tables. Wherefore, brethren, look ye out among you seven

THE ACTS OF THE APOSTLES

men of honest report, full of the Holy Ghost and wisdom, whom we may appoint over this business. But we will give ourselves continually to prayer, and to the ministry of the word."

And the saying pleased the whole multitude: and they chose Stephen, a man full of faith and of the Holy Ghost, and Philip, and Prochorus, and Nicanor, and Timon, and Parmenas, and Nicolas a proselyte of Antioch: whom they set before the apostles: and when they had prayed, they laid their hands on them. And the word of God increased; and the number of the disciples multiplied in Jerusalem greatly; and a great company of the priests were obedient to the faith. And Stephen, full of faith and power, did great wonders and miracles among the people.

Then there arose certain of the synagogue, which is called the synagogue of the Libertines, and Cyrenians, and Alexandrians, and of them of Cilicia and of Asia, disputing with Stephen. And they were not able to resist the wisdom and the spirit by which he spoke. Then they suborned men, which said, "We have heard him speak blasphemous words against Moses, and against God."

And they stirred up the people, and the elders, and the scribes, and came upon him, and caught him, and brought him to the council, and set up false witnesses, which said, "This man ceaseth not to speak blasphemous words against this holy place, and the law: for we have heard him say that this Jesus of Nazareth shall destroy this place, and shall change the customs which Moses delivered us."

And all that sat in the council, looking steadfastly on him, saw his face as it had been the face of an angel.

Then said the high priest, "Are these things so?"

And he said, "Men, brethren, and fathers, hearken:

"Our fathers had the tabernacle of witness in the wilderness, as he had appointed, speaking unto Moses, that he should make it according to the fashion that he had seen. Which also our fathers that came after brought in with Jesus into the possession of the Gentiles, whom God drove out before the face of our fathers, unto the days of David; who found favour before God, and desired to find a tabernacle for the God of Jacob. But Solomon built him a house. Howbeit the most High dwelleth not in temples made with hands; as saith the prophet,

" ' "Heaven is my throne, and earth is my footstool:
What house will ye build me?" saith the Lord:
"Or what is the place of my rest?
Hath not my hand made all these things?" '

"Ye stiffnecked and uncircumcised in heart and ears, ye do always resist the Holy Ghost: as your fathers did, so do ye. Which of the prophets have not your fathers persecuted? and they have slain them which showed before of the coming of the Just One; of whom ye have been now the betrayers and murderers: who have received the law by the disposition of angels, and have not kept it."

When they heard these things, they were cut to the heart, and they gnashed on him with their teeth.

But he, being full of the Holy Ghost, looked up steadfastly into heaven, and saw the glory of God, and Jesus standing on the right hand of God, and said, "Behold, I see the heavens opened, and the Son of Man standing on the right hand of God."

Then they cried out with a loud voice, and stopped their ears, and ran upon him with one accord, and cast him out of the city, and stoned him: and the witnesses laid down their clothes at a young man's feet, whose name was Saul.

And they stoned Stephen, calling upon God, and saying, "Lord Jesus, receive my spirit." And he kneeled down, and cried with a loud voice, "Lord, lay not this sin to their charge." And when he had said this, he fell asleep. And Saul was consenting unto his death.

And at that time there was a great persecution against the church which was at Jerusalem; and they were all scattered abroad throughout the regions of Judæa and Samaria, except the apostles. And devout men carried Stephen to his burial, and made great lamentation over him. As for Saul, he made havoc of the church, entering into every house, and haling men and

THE ACTS OF THE APOSTLES

women committed them to prison. Therefore they that were scattered abroad went everywhere preaching the word.

The Ministry of Philip

Then Philip went down to the city of Samaria, and preached Christ unto them. And the people with one accord gave heed unto those things which Philip spoke, hearing and seeing the miracles which he did. For unclean spirits, crying with loud voice, came out of many that were possessed with them: and many taken with palsies, and that were lame, were healed. And there was great joy in that city.

But there was a certain man, called Simon, which beforetime in the same city used sorcery, and bewitched the people of Samaria, giving out that himself was some great one: to whom they all gave heed, from the least to the greatest, saying, "This man is the great power of God." And to him they had regard, because that of long time he had bewitched them with sorceries. But when they believed Philip preaching the things concerning the kingdom of God, and the name of Jesus Christ, they were baptized, both men and women. Then Simon himself believed also: and when he was baptized, he continued with Philip, and wondered, beholding the miracles and signs which were done.

Now when the apostles which were at Jerusalem heard that Samaria had received the word of God, they sent unto them Peter and John, who, when they were come down, prayed for them, that they might receive the Holy Ghost (for as yet he was fallen upon none of them: only they were baptized in the name of the Lord Jesus). Then laid they their hands on them, and they received the Holy Ghost. And when Simon saw that through laying on of the apostles' hands the Holy Ghost was given, he offered them money, saying, "Give me also this power, that on whomsoever I lay hands, he may receive the Holy Ghost."

But Peter said unto him, "Thy money perish with thee, because thou hast thought that the gift of God may be purchased with money. Thou hast neither part nor lot in this matter: for thy heart is not right in the sight of God. Repent therefore of this thy wickedness, and pray God, if perhaps the thought of thine heart may be forgiven thee. For I perceive that thou art in the gall of bitterness, and in the bond of iniquity."

Then answered Simon, and said, "Pray ye to the Lord for me, that none of these things which ye have spoken come upon me."

And they, when they had testified and preached the word of the Lord, returned to Jerusalem, and preached the gospel in many villages of the Samaritans.

And the angel of the Lord spoke unto Philip, saying, "Arise, and go toward the south unto the way that goeth down from Jerusalem unto Gaza, which is desert."

And he arose and went: and, behold, a man of Ethiopia, a eunuch of great authority under Candace queen of the Ethiopians, who had the charge of all her treasure, and had come to Jerusalem for to worship, was returning, and sitting in his chariot read Esaias the prophet.

Then the Spirit said unto Philip, "Go near, and join thyself to this chariot."

And Philip ran thither to him, and heard him read the prophet Esaias, and said, "Understandest thou what thou readest?"

And he said, "How can I, except some man should guide me?" And he desired Philip that he would come up and sit with him.

The place of the scripture which he read was this,

> "He was led as a sheep to the slaughter;
> And like a lamb dumb before his shearer,
> So opened he not his mouth:
> In his humiliation his judgment was taken away:
> And who shall declare his generation?
> For his life is taken from the earth."

And the eunuch answered Philip, and said, "I pray thee, of whom speaketh the prophet this? of himself, or of some other man?"

Then Philip opened his mouth, and began at the same scripture, and preached unto him Jesus. And as they went on their

THE ACTS OF THE APOSTLES

way, they came unto a certain water: and the eunuch said, "See, here is water; what doth hinder me to be baptized?"

And Philip said, "If thou believest with all thine heart, thou mayest." And he answered and said, "I believe that Jesus Christ is the Son of God."

And he commanded the chariot to stand still: and they went down both into the water, both Philip and the eunuch; and he baptized him. And when they were come up out of the water, the Spirit of the Lord caught away Philip, that the eunuch saw him no more: and he went on his way rejoicing. But Philip was found at Azotus: and passing through he preached in all the cities, till he came to Cæsarea.

The Conversion of Saul

And Saul, yet breathing out threatenings and slaughter against the disciples of the Lord, went unto the high priest, and desired of him letters to Damascus to the synagogues, that if he found any of this way, whether they were men or women, he might bring them bound unto Jerusalem.

And as he journeyed, he came near Damascus: and suddenly there shone round about him a light from heaven, and he fell to the earth, and heard a voice saying unto him,

"Saul, Saul, why persecutest thou me?"

And he said, "Who art thou, Lord?"

And the Lord said,

"I am Jesus whom thou persecutest: it is hard for thee to kick against the pricks."

And he trembling and astonished said,

"Lord, what wilt thou have me to do?"

And the Lord said unto him, "Arise, and go into the city, and it shall be told thee what thou must do."

And the men which journeyed with him stood speechless, hearing a voice, but seeing no man. And Saul arose from the earth; and when his eyes were opened, he saw no man: but they led him by the hand, and brought him into Damascus. And he was three days without sight, and neither did eat nor drink.

THE ACTS OF THE APOSTLES

And there was a certain disciple at Damascus, named Ananias; and to him said the Lord in a vision, "Ananias!" And he said, "Behold, I am here, Lord."

And the Lord said unto him, "Arise, and go into the street which is called Straight, and enquire in the house of Judas for one called Saul, of Tarsus: for, behold, he prayeth, and hath seen in a vision a man named Ananias coming in, and putting his hand on him, that he might receive his sight."

Then Ananias answered, "Lord, I have heard by many of this man, how much evil he hath done to thy saints at Jerusalem: and here he hath authority from the chief priests to bind all that call on thy name."

But the Lord said unto him, "Go thy way: for he is a chosen vessel unto me, to bear my name before the Gentiles, and kings, and the children of Israel: for I will show him how great things he must suffer for my name's sake."

And Ananias went his way, and entered into the house; and putting his hands on him said, "Brother Saul, the Lord, even Jesus, that appeared unto thee in the way as thou camest, hath sent me, that thou mightest receive thy sight, and be filled with the Holy Ghost."

And immediately there fell from his eyes as it had been scales: and he received sight forthwith, and arose, and was baptized. And when he had received meat, he was strengthened.

Then was Saul certain days with the disciples which were at Damascus. And straightway he preached Christ in the synagogues, that he is the Son of God. But all that heard him were amazed, and said: "Is not this he that destroyed them which called on this name in Jerusalem, and came hither for that intent, that he might bring them bound unto the chief priests?"

But Saul increased the more in strength, and confounded the Jews which dwelt at Damascus, proving that this is very Christ. And after that many days were fulfilled, the Jews took counsel to kill him: but their laying await was known of Saul. And they watched the gates day and night to kill him. Then the disciples took him by night, and let him down by the wall in a basket.

THE ACTS OF THE APOSTLES

And when Saul was come to Jerusalem, he essayed to join himself to the disciples: but they were all afraid of him, and believed not that he was a disciple. But Barnabas took him, and brought him to the apostles, and declared unto them how he had seen the Lord in the way, and that he had spoken to him, and how he had preached boldly at Damascus in the name of Jesus. And he was with them coming in and going out at Jerusalem. And he spoke boldly in the name of the Lord Jesus, and disputed against the Grecians: but they went about to slay him. Which when the brethren knew, they brought him down to Cæsarea, and sent him forth to Tarsus.

The Spread of the Gospel

Then had the churches rest throughout all Judæa and Galilee and Samaria, and were edified; and walking in the fear of the Lord, and in the comfort of the Holy Ghost, were multiplied. And it came to pass, as Peter passed throughout all quarters, he came down also to the saints which dwelt at Lydda. And there he found a certain man named Æneas, which had kept his bed eight years, and was sick of the palsy. And Peter said unto him, "Æneas, Jesus Christ maketh thee whole: arise, and make thy bed." And he arose immediately. And all that dwelt at Lydda and Saron saw him, and turned to the Lord.

Now there was at Joppa a certain disciple named Tabitha, which by interpretation is called Dorcas: this woman was full of good works and almsdeeds which she did. And it came to pass in those days, that she was sick, and died: whom when they had washed, they laid her in an upper chamber. And forasmuch as Lydda was nigh to Joppa, and the disciples had heard that Peter was there, they sent unto him two men, desiring him that he would not delay to come to them. Then Peter arose and went with them. When he was come, they brought him into the upper chamber: and all the widows stood by him weeping, and showing the coats and garments which Dorcas made, while she was with them. But Peter put them all forth, and kneeled down, and prayed; and turning him to the body said,

THE ACTS OF THE APOSTLES

"Tabitha, arise!"

And she opened her eyes: and when she saw Peter, she sat up. And he gave her his hand, and lifted her up, and when he had called the saints and widows, presented her alive. And it was known throughout all Joppa; and many believed in the Lord. And it came to pass that he tarried many days in Joppa with one Simon a tanner.

There was a certain man in Cæsarea called Cornelius, a centurion of the band called the Italian band, a devout man, and one that feared God with all his house, which gave much alms to the people, and prayed to God always. He saw in a vision, evidently about the ninth hour of the day, an angel of God coming in to him, and saying unto him, "Cornelius!"

And when he looked on him, he was afraid, and said, "What is it, Lord?"

And he said unto him, "Thy prayers and thine alms are come up for a memorial before God. And now send men to Joppa, and call for one Simon, whose surname is Peter. He lodgeth with one Simon a tanner, whose house is by the sea side: he shall tell thee what thou oughtest to do."

And when the angel which spoke unto Cornelius was departed, he called two of his household servants, and a devout soldier of them that waited on him continually; and when he had declared all these things unto them, he sent them to Joppa.

On the morrow, as they went on their journey, and drew nigh unto the city, Peter went up upon the housetop to pray about the sixth hour: and he became very hungry, and would have eaten: but while they made ready, he fell into a trance, and saw heaven opened, and a certain vessel descending unto him, as it had been a great sheet knit at the four corners, and let down to the earth: wherein were all manner of fourfooted beasts of the earth, and wild beasts, and creeping things, and fowls of the air. And there came a voice to him,

"Rise, Peter; kill, and eat."

But Peter said, "Not so, Lord; for I have never eaten any thing that is common or unclean."

THE ACTS OF THE APOSTLES

And the voice spoke unto him again the second time, "What God hath cleansed, that call not thou common."

This was done thrice: and the vessel was received up again into heaven.

Now while Peter doubted in himself what this vision which he had seen should mean, behold, the men which were sent from Cornelius had made enquiry for Simon's house, and stood before the gate, and called, and asked whether Simon, which was surnamed Peter, were lodged there. Then called he them in, and lodged them. And on the morrow Peter went away with them, and certain brethren from Joppa accompanied him. And the morrow after they entered into Cæsarea. And Cornelius waited for them, and had called together his kinsmen and near friends. And as Peter was coming in, Cornelius met him, and fell down at his feet, and worshipped him. But Peter took him up, saying, "Stand up; I myself also am a man."

And as he talked with him, he went in, and found many that were come together. And he said unto them, "Ye know how that it is an unlawful thing for a man that is a Jew to keep company, or come unto one of another nation; but God hath showed me that I should not call any man common or unclean. Therefore came I unto you without gainsaying, as soon as I was sent for: I ask therefore for what intent ye have sent for me?"

And Cornelius said, "Four days ago I was fasting until this hour; and at the ninth hour I prayed in my house, and, behold, a man stood before me in bright clothing, and said, 'Cornelius, thy prayer is heard, and thine alms are had in remembrance in the sight of God. Send therefore to Joppa, and call hither Simon, whose surname is Peter; he is lodged in the house of one Simon a tanner by the sea side: who, when he cometh, shall speak unto thee.' Immediately therefore I sent to thee; and thou hast well done that thou art come. Now therefore are we all here present before God, to hear all things that are commanded thee of God."

Then Peter opened his mouth, and said, "Of a truth I perceive that God is no respecter of persons:

THE ACTS OF THE APOSTLES

but in every nation he that feareth him, and worketh righteousness, is accepted with him. The word which God sent unto the children of Israel, preaching peace by Jesus Christ (he is Lord of all), that word, I say, ye know, which was published throughout all Judæa, and began from Galilee, after the baptism which John preached: how God anointed Jesus of Nazareth with the Holy Ghost and with power: who went about doing good, and healing all that were oppressed of the devil; for God was with him. And we are witnesses of all things which he did both in the land of the Jews, and in Jerusalem; whom they slew and hanged on a tree. Him God raised up the third day, and showed him openly: not to all the people, but unto witnesses chosen before of God, even to us, who did eat and drink with him after he rose from the dead. And he commanded us to preach unto the people, and to testify that it is he which was ordained of God to be the Judge of quick and dead. To him give all the prophets witness, that through his name whosoever believeth in him shall receive remission of sins."

While Peter yet spoke these words, the Holy Ghost fell on all them which heard the word. And they of the circumcision which believed were astonished, as many as came with Peter, because that on the Gentiles also was poured out the gift of the Holy Ghost. For they heard them speak with tongues, and magnify God. Then answered Peter,

"Can any man forbid water, that these should not be baptized, which have received the Holy Ghost as well as we?"

And he commanded them to be baptized in the name of the Lord. Then prayed they him to tarry certain days.

And the apostles and brethren that were in Judæa heard that the Gentiles had also received the word of God. And when Peter was come up to Jerusalem, they that were of the circumcision contended with him, saying, "Thou wentest in to men uncircumcised, and didst eat with them."

But Peter rehearsed the matter from the beginning, and expounded it by order unto them, saying, "The Spirit bade me go

THE ACTS OF THE APOSTLES

with them, nothing doubting. And as I began to speak, the Holy Ghost fell on them, as on us at the beginning. Then remembered I the word of the Lord, how that he said, 'John indeed baptized with water; but ye shall be baptized with the Holy Ghost.' Forasmuch then as God gave them the like gift as he did unto us, who believed on the Lord Jesus Christ; what was I, that I could withstand God?"

When they heard these things, they held their peace, and glorified God, saying, "Then hath God also to the Gentiles granted repentance unto life."

Now they which were scattered abroad upon the persecution that arose about Stephen travelled as far as Phenice, and Cyprus, and Antioch, preaching the word to none but unto the Jews only. And some of them were men of Cyprus and Cyrene, which, when they were come to Antioch, spoke unto the Grecians, preaching the Lord Jesus. And the hand of the Lord was with them: and a great number believed, and turned unto the Lord.

Then tidings of these things came unto the ears of the church which was in Jerusalem: and they sent forth Barnabas, that he should go as far as Antioch, who, when he came, and had seen the grace of God, was glad, and exhorted them all, that with purpose of heart they would cleave unto the Lord. For he was a good man, and full of the Holy Ghost and of faith: and much people was added unto the Lord.

Then departed Barnabas to Tarsus, for to seek Saul: and when he had found him, he brought him unto Antioch. And it came to pass, that a whole year they assembled themselves with the church, and taught much people. And the disciples were called Christians first in Antioch.

And in these days came prophets from Jerusalem unto Antioch. And there stood up one of them named Agabus, and signified by the Spirit that there should be great dearth throughout all the world: which came to pass in the days of Claudius Cæsar. Then the disciples, every man according to his ability, determined to send relief unto the brethren which dwelt in Judæa: which also they did, and sent it to the elders by the hands of Barnabas and Saul.

Now about that time Herod the king stretched forth his hands to vex certain of the church. And he killed James the brother of John with the sword. And because he saw it pleased the Jews, he proceeded further to take Peter also. (Then were the days of unleavened bread.) And when he had apprehended him, he put him in prison, and delivered him to four quaternions of soldiers to keep him; intending after Easter to bring him forth to the people. Peter therefore was kept in prison: but prayer was made without ceasing of the church unto God for him.

And when Herod would have brought him forth, the same night Peter was sleeping between two soldiers, bound with two chains: and the keepers before the door kept the prison. And, behold, the angel of the Lord came upon him, and a light shone in the prison: and he smote Peter on the side, and raised him up, saying, "Arise up quickly." And his chains fell off from his hands.

And the angel said unto him, "Gird thyself, and bind on thy sandals." And so he did. And he saith unto him, "Cast thy garment about thee, and follow me." And he went out, and followed him; and wist not that it was true which was done by the angel; but thought he saw a vision.

When they were past the first and the second ward, they came unto the iron gate that leadeth unto the city; which opened to them of his own accord: and they went out, and passed on through one street; and forthwith the angel departed from him. And when Peter was come to himself, he said, "Now I know of a surety that the Lord hath sent his angel, and hath delivered me out of the hand of Herod, and from all the expectation of the people of the Jews."

And when he had considered the thing, he came to the house of Mary the mother of John, whose surname was Mark; where many were gathered together praying. And as Peter knocked at

THE ACTS OF THE APOSTLES

the door of the gate, a damsel came to hearken, named Rhoda. And when she knew Peter's voice, she opened not the gate for gladness, but ran in, and told how Peter stood before the gate. And they said unto her, "Thou art mad." But she constantly affirmed that it was even so. Then said they, "It is his angel."

But Peter continued knocking: and when they had opened the door, and saw him, they were astonished. But he, beckoning unto them with the hand to hold their peace, declared unto them how the Lord had brought him out of the prison. And he said, "Go show these things unto James, and to the brethren." And he departed, and went into another place.

Now as soon as it was day, there was no small stir among the soldiers, what was become of Peter. And when Herod had sought for him, and found him not, he examined the keepers, and commanded that they should be put to death. And he went down from Judæa to Cæsarea, and there abode.

And Herod was highly displeased with them of Tyre and Sidon: but they came with one accord to him, and, having made Blastus the king's chamberlain their friend, desired peace; because their country was nourished by the king's country. And upon a set day Herod, arrayed in royal apparel, sat upon his throne, and made an oration unto them. And the people gave a shout, saying, "It is the voice of a god, and not of a man." And immediately the angel of the Lord smote him, because he gave not God the glory: and he was eaten of worms, and gave up the ghost.

But the word of God grew and multiplied. And Barnabas and Saul returned from Jerusalem, when they had fulfilled their ministry, and took with them John, whose surname was Mark.

Paul's First Missionary Journey

Now there were in the church that was at Antioch certain prophets and teachers; as Barnabas, and Simeon that was called Niger, and Lucius of Cyrene, and Manaen, which had been brought up with Herod the tetrarch, and Saul. As they ministered to the Lord, and fasted, the Holy Ghost said, "Separate me Barnabas and Saul for the work whereunto I have called them." And when they had fasted and prayed, and laid their hands on them, they sent them away.

So they, being sent forth by the Holy Ghost, departed unto Seleucia; and from thence they sailed to Cyprus. And when they were at Salamis, they preached the word of God in the synagogues of the Jews: and they had also John to their minister. And when they had gone through the isle unto Paphos, they found a certain sorcerer, a false prophet, a Jew, whose name was Barjesus: which was with the deputy of the country, Sergius Paulus, a prudent man; who called for Barnabas and Saul, and desired to hear the word of God. But Elymas the sorcerer (for so is his name by interpretation) withstood them, seeking to turn away the deputy from the faith.

Then Saul (who also is called Paul), filled with the Holy Ghost, set his eyes on him, and said, "O full of all subtilty and all mischief, thou child of the devil, thou enemy of all righteousness, wilt thou not cease to pervert the right ways of the Lord? And now, behold, the hand of the Lord is upon thee, and thou shalt be blind, not seeing the sun for a season." And immediately there fell on him a mist and a darkness; and he went about seeking some to lead him by the hand. Then the deputy, when he saw what was done, believed, being astonished at the doctrine of the Lord.

Now when Paul and his company loosed from Paphos, they came to Perga in Pamphylia: and John departing from them returned to Jerusalem. But when they departed from Perga, they came to Antioch in Pisidia, and went into the synagogue on the sabbath day, and sat down. And after the reading of the law and the prophets the rulers of the synagogue sent unto them, saying, "Ye men and brethren, if ye have any word of exhortation for the people, say on."

Then Paul stood up, and beckoning with his hand said, "Men of Israel, and ye that fear God, give audience. God according to his promise hath raised unto Israel a Saviour, Jesus. Men and brethren, children of the stock of Abraham, and who-

THE ACTS OF THE APOSTLES

soever among you feareth God, to you is the word of this salvation sent. For they that dwell at Jerusalem, and their rulers, because they knew him not, nor yet the voices of the prophets which are read every sabbath day, they have fulfilled them in condemning him. And though they found no cause of death in him, yet desired they Pilate that he should be slain. And when they had fulfilled all that was written of him, they took him down from the tree, and laid him in a sepulchre. But God raised him from the dead: and he was seen many days of them which came up with him from Galilee to Jerusalem, who are his witnesses unto the people. And we declare unto you glad tidings, how that the promise which was made unto the fathers, God hath fulfilled the same unto us their children, in that he hath raised up Jesus again; as it is also written in the second psalm, 'Thou art my Son, this day have I begotten thee.'"

And when the Jews were gone out of the synagogue, the Gentiles besought that these words might be preached to them next sabbath. Now when the congregation was broken up, many of the Jews and religious proselytes followed Paul and Barnabas: who, speaking to them, persuaded them to continue in the grace of God. And the next sabbath day came almost the whole city together to hear the word of God.

But when the Jews saw the multitudes, they were filled with envy, and spoke against those things which were spoken by Paul, contradicting and blaspheming. Then Paul and Barnabas waxed bold, and said, "It was necessary that the word of God should first have been spoken to you: but seeing ye put it from you, and judge yourselves unworthy of everlasting life, lo, we turn to the Gentiles. For so hath the Lord commanded us, saying, 'I have set thee to be a light of the Gentiles, that thou shouldest be for salvation unto the ends of the earth.'"

And when the Gentiles heard this, they were glad, and glorified the word of the Lord: and as many as were ordained to eternal life believed. And the word of the Lord was published throughout all the region. But the Jews stirred up the devout and honourable women, and the chief men of the city, and raised persecution against Paul and Barnabas, and expelled them out of their coasts. But they shook off the dust of their feet against them, and came unto Iconium. And the disciples were filled with joy, and with the Holy Ghost.

And it came to pass in Iconium, that they went both together into the synagogue of the Jews, and so spoke that a great multitude both of the Jews and also of the Greeks believed. But the unbelieving Jews stirred up the Gentiles, and made their minds evil affected against the brethren. Long time therefore abode they speaking boldly in the Lord, which gave testimony unto the word of his grace, and granted signs and wonders to be done by their hands. But the multitude of the city was divided: and part held with the Jews, and part with the apostles. And when there was an assault made both of the Gentiles, and also of the Jews with their rulers, to use them despitefully, and to stone them, they were aware of it, and fled unto Lystra and Derbe, cities of Lycaonia, and unto the region that lieth round about: and there they preached the gospel.

And there sat a certain man at Lystra, impotent in his feet, being a cripple from his mother's womb, who never had walked: the same heard Paul speak: who steadfastly beholding him, and perceiving that he had faith to be healed, said with a loud voice, "Stand upright on thy feet." And he leaped and walked. And when the people saw what Paul had done, they lifted up their voices, saying in the speech of Lycaonia, "The gods are come down to us in the likeness of men." And they called Barnabas, Jupiter; and Paul, Mercurius, because he was the chief speaker. Then the priest of Jupiter, which was before their city, brought oxen and garlands unto the gates, and would have done sacrifice with the people. Which when the apostles, Barnabas and Paul, heard of, they rent their clothes, and ran in among the people, crying out, and saying, "Sirs, why do ye these things? We also are men of like passions with you, and preach unto you that ye should turn from these vanities unto the living God, which made heaven, and earth, and the sea, and

THE ACTS OF THE APOSTLES

all things that are therein: who in times past suffered all nations to walk in their own ways. Nevertheless he left not himself without witness, in that he did good, and gave us rain from heaven, and fruitful seasons, filling our hearts with food and gladness." And with these sayings scarce restrained they the people, that they had not done sacrifice unto them.

And there came thither certain Jews from Antioch and Iconium, who persuaded the people, and, having stoned Paul, drew him out of the city, supposing he had been dead. Howbeit, as the disciples stood round about him, he rose up, and came into the city: and the next day he departed with Barnabas to Derbe. And when they had preached the gospel to that city, and had taught many, they returned again to Lystra, and to Iconium, and Antioch, confirming the souls of the disciples, and exhorting them to continue in the faith, and that we must through much tribulation enter into the kingdom of God. And when they had ordained them elders in every church, and had prayed with fasting, they commended them to the Lord, on whom they believed. And after they had passed throughout Pisidia, they came to Pamphylia. And when they had preached the word in Perga, they went down into Attalia: and thence sailed to Antioch, from whence they had been recommended to the grace of God for the work which they fulfilled. And when they were come, and had gathered the church together, they rehearsed all that God had done with them, and how he had opened the door of faith unto the Gentiles. And there they abode long time with the disciples.

And certain men which came down from Judæa taught the brethren, and said, "Except ye be circumcised after the manner of Moses, ye cannot be saved."

When therefore Paul and Barnabas had no small dissension and disputation with them, they determined that Paul and Barnabas, and certain other of them, should go up to Jerusalem unto the apostles and elders about this question. And being brought on their way by the church, they passed through

THE ACTS OF THE APOSTLES

Phenice and Samaria, declaring the conversion of the Gentiles: and they caused great joy unto all the brethren. And when they were come to Jerusalem, they were received of the church, and of the apostles and elders, and they declared all things that God had done with them. But there rose up certain of the sect of the Pharisees which believed, saying that it was needful to circumcise them, and to command them to keep the law of Moses.

And the apostles and elders came together for to consider of this matter. And when there had been much disputing, Peter rose up, and said unto them,

"Men and brethren, ye know how that a good while ago God made choice among us, that the Gentiles by my mouth should hear the word of the gospel, and believe. And God, which knoweth the hearts, bore them witness, giving them the Holy Ghost, even as he did unto us; and put no difference between us and them, purifying their hearts by faith. Now therefore why tempt ye God, to put a yoke upon the neck of the disciples, which neither our fathers nor we were able to bear? But we believe that through the grace of the Lord Jesus Christ we shall be saved, even as they."

Then all the multitude kept silence, and gave audience to Barnabas and Paul, declaring what miracles and wonders God had wrought among the Gentiles by them. And after they had held their peace, James answered, saying,

"Men and brethren, hearken unto me: Simeon hath declared how God at the first did visit the Gentiles, to take out of them a people for his name. And to this agree the words of the prophets. Wherefore my sentence is, that we trouble not them, which from among the Gentiles are turned to God: but that we write unto them, that they abstain from pollutions of idols, and from fornication, and from things strangled, and from blood."

Then pleased it the apostles and elders, with the whole church, to send chosen men of their own company to Antioch with Paul and Barnabas; namely, Judas surnamed Barsabas, and

THE ACTS OF THE APOSTLES

Silas, chief men among the brethren: and they wrote letters by them after this manner:

The apostles and elders and brethren send greeting unto the brethren which are of the Gentiles in Antioch and Syria and Cilicia:

Forasmuch as we have heard, that certain which went out from us have troubled you with words, subverting your souls, saying, "Ye must be circumcised, and keep the law": to whom we gave no such commandment: it seemed good unto us, being assembled with one accord, to send chosen men unto you with our beloved Barnabas and Paul, men that have hazarded their lives for the name of our Lord Jesus Christ. We have sent therefore Judas and Silas, who shall also tell you the same things by mouth. For it seemed good to the Holy Ghost, and to us, to lay upon you no greater burden than these necessary things; that ye abstain from meats offered to idols, and from blood, and from things strangled, and from fornication: from which if ye keep yourselves, ye shall do well. Fare ye well.

So when they were dismissed, they came to Antioch: and when they had gathered the multitude together, they delivered the epistle: which when they had read, they rejoiced for the consolation. And Judas and Silas, being prophets also themselves, exhorted the brethren with many words, and confirmed them. And after they had tarried there a space, they were let go in peace from the brethren unto the apostles. Notwithstanding it pleased Silas to abide there still. Paul also and Barnabas continued in Antioch, teaching and preaching the word of the Lord, with many others also.

Paul's Second Missionary Journey

And some days after Paul said unto Barnabas, "Let us go again and visit our brethren in every city where we have preached the word of the Lord, and see how they do." And Barnabas determined to take with them John, whose surname was Mark. But Paul thought not good to take him with them, who departed from them from Pamphylia, and went not with them to the work. And the contention was so sharp between them that they departed asunder one from the other: and so Barnabas took Mark, and sailed unto Cyprus; and Paul chose Silas, and departed, being recommended by the brethren unto the grace of God. And he went through Syria and Cilicia, confirming the churches.

Then came he to Derbe and Lystra: and, behold, a certain disciple was there, named Timotheus, the son of a certain woman, which was a Jewess, and believed; but his father was a Greek, which was well reported of by the brethren that were at Lystra and Iconium. Him would Paul have to go forth with him; and took and circumcised him because of the Jews which were in those quarters: for they knew all that his father was a Greek. And as they went through the cities, they delivered them the decrees for to keep, that were ordained of the apostles and elders which were at Jerusalem. And so were the churches established in the faith, and increased in number daily. Now when they had gone throughout Phrygia and the region of Galatia, and were forbidden of the Holy Ghost to preach the word in Asia, after they were come to Mysia, they essayed to go into Bithynia: but the Spirit suffered them not. And they passing by Mysia came down to Troas.

And a vision appeared to Paul in the night: there stood a man of Macedonia, and prayed him, saying, "Come over into Macedonia, and help us."

And after he had seen the vision, immediately we endeavoured to go into Macedonia, assuredly gathering that the Lord had called us for to preach the gospel unto them. Therefore loosing from Troas, we came with a straight course to Samothrace, and the next day to Neapolis; and from thence to Philippi, which is the chief city of that part of Macedonia, and a colony: and we were in that city abiding certain days.

And on the sabbath we went out of the city by a river side, where prayer was wont to be made; and we sat down, and spoke unto the women which resorted thither. And a certain

THE ACTS OF THE APOSTLES

woman named Lydia, a seller of purple, of the city of Thyatira, which worshipped God, heard us: whose heart the Lord opened, that she attended unto the things which were spoken of Paul. And when she was baptized, and her household, she besought us, saying, "If ye have judged me to be faithful to the Lord, come into my house, and abide there." And she constrained us.

And it came to pass, as we went to prayer, a certain damsel possessed with a spirit of divination met us, which brought her masters much gain by soothsaying: the same followed Paul and us, and cried, saying, "These men are the servants of the most high God, which show unto us the way of salvation." And this did she many days. But Paul, being grieved, turned and said to the spirit, "I command thee in the name of Jesus Christ to come out of her." And he came out the same hour.

And when her masters saw that the hope of their gains was gone, they caught Paul and Silas, and drew them into the marketplace unto the rulers, and brought them to the magistrates, saying, "These men, being Jews, do exceedingly trouble our city, and teach customs, which are not lawful for us to receive, neither to observe, being Romans."

And the multitude rose up together against them: and the magistrates rent off their clothes, and commanded to beat them. And when they had laid many stripes upon them, they cast them into prison, charging the jailor to keep them safely: who, having received such a charge, thrust them into the inner prison, and made their feet fast in the stocks.

And at midnight Paul and Silas prayed, and sang praises unto God: and the prisoners heard them. And suddenly there was a great earthquake, so that the foundations of the prison were shaken: and immediately all the doors were opened, and every one's bands were loosed. And the keeper of the prison awaking out of his sleep, and seeing the prison doors open, he drew out his sword, and would have killed himself, supposing that the prisoners had been fled. But Paul cried with a loud voice, saying, "Do thyself no harm: for we are all here."

THE ACTS OF THE APOSTLES

Then he called for a light, and sprang in, and came trembling, and fell down before Paul and Silas, and brought them out, and said, "Sirs, what must I do to be saved?"

And they said, "Believe on the Lord Jesus Christ, and thou shalt be saved, and thy house."

And they spoke unto him the word of the Lord, and to all that were in his house. And he took them the same hour of the night, and washed their stripes; and was baptized, he and all his, straightway. And when he had brought them into his house, he set meat before them, and rejoiced, believing in God with all his house.

And when it was day, the magistrates sent the serjeants, saying, "Let those men go." And the keeper of the prison told this saying to Paul, "The magistrates have sent to let you go: now therefore depart, and go in peace."

But Paul said unto them, "They have beaten us openly uncondemned, being Romans, and have cast us into prison; and now do they thrust us out privily? nay verily; but let them come themselves and fetch us out."

And the serjeants told these words unto the magistrates: and they feared, when they heard that they were Romans. And they came and besought them, and brought them out, and desired them to depart out of the city. And they went out of the prison, and entered into the house of Lydia: and when they had seen the brethren, they comforted them, and departed.

Now when they had passed through Amphipolis and Apollonia, they came to Thessalonica, where was a synagogue of the Jews: and Paul, as his manner was, went in unto them, and three sabbath days reasoned with them out of the scriptures, opening and alleging that Christ must needs have suffered, and risen again from the dead; and that "this Jesus, whom I preach unto you, is Christ." And some of them believed, and consorted with Paul and Silas; and of the devout Greeks a great multitude, and of the chief women not a few.

But the Jews which believed not, moved with envy, took unto them certain lewd fellows of the baser sort, and gathered a company, and set all the city on an uproar, and assaulted the house of Jason, and sought to bring them out to the people. And when they found them not, they drew Jason and certain brethren unto the rulers of the city, crying, "These that have turned the world upside down are come hither also; whom Jason hath received: and these all do contrary to the decrees of Cæsar, saying that there is another king, one Jesus."

And they troubled the people and the rulers of the city, when they heard these things. And when they had taken security of Jason, and of the other, they let them go.

And the brethren immediately sent away Paul and Silas by night unto Berea: who coming thither went into the synagogue of the Jews. These were more noble than those in Thessalonica, in that they received the word with all readiness of mind, and searched the scriptures daily, whether those things were so. Therefore many of them believed; also of honourable women which were Greeks, and of men, not a few. But when the Jews of Thessalonica had knowledge that the word of God was preached of Paul at Berea, they came thither also, and stirred up the people. And then immediately the brethren sent away Paul to go as it were to the sea: but Silas and Timotheus abode there still.

And they that conducted Paul brought him unto Athens: and receiving a commandment unto Silas and Timotheus for to come to him with all speed, they departed.

Now while Paul waited for them at Athens, his spirit was stirred in him, when he saw the city wholly given to idolatry. Therefore disputed he in the synagogue with the Jews, and with the devout persons, and in the market daily with them that met with him. Then certain philosophers of the Epicureans, and of the Stoics, encountered him. And some said, "What will this babbler say?" other some, "He seemeth to be a setter forth of strange gods": because he preached unto them Jesus, and the resurrection. And they took him, and brought him unto Areopagus, saying, "May we know what this new doctrine, whereof thou speakest, is? For thou bringest certain strange things to

THE ACTS OF THE APOSTLES

our ears: we would know therefore what these things mean." (For all the Athenians and strangers which were there spent their time in nothing else, but either to tell, or to hear some new thing.)

Then Paul stood in the midst of Mars' Hill, and said, "Ye men of Athens, I perceive that in all things ye are too superstitious. For as I passed by, and beheld your devotions, I found an altar with this inscription: TO THE UNKNOWN GOD. Whom therefore ye ignorantly worship, him declare I unto you. God that made the world and all things therein, seeing that he is Lord of heaven and earth, dwelleth not in temples made with hands; neither is worshipped with men's hands, as though he needed any thing, seeing he giveth to all life, and breath, and all things; and hath made of one blood all nations of men for to dwell on all the face of the earth, and hath determined the times before appointed, and the bounds of their habitation; that they should seek the Lord, if haply they might feel after him, and find him, though he be not far from every one of us: for in him we live, and move, and have our being; as certain also of your own poets have said, 'For we are also his offspring.' Forasmuch then as we are the offspring of God, we ought not to think that the Godhead is like unto gold, or silver, or stone, graven by art and man's device. And the times of this ignorance God winked at; but now commandeth all men everywhere to repent: because he hath appointed a day, in the which he will judge the world in righteousness by that man whom he hath ordained; whereof he hath given assurance unto all men, in that he hath raised him from the dead."

And when they heard of the resurrection of the dead, some mocked: and others said, "We will hear thee again of this matter."

So Paul departed from among them. Howbeit certain men cleaved unto him, and believed: among the which was Dionysius the Areopagite, and a woman named Damaris, and others with them.

After these things Paul departed from Athens, and came to

THE ACTS OF THE APOSTLES

Corinth; and found a certain Jew named Aquila, born in Pontus, lately come from Italy, with his wife Priscilla (because that Claudius had commanded all Jews to depart from Rome); and came unto them. And because he was of the same craft, he abode with them, and wrought: for by their occupation they were tentmakers. And he reasoned in the synagogue every sabbath, and persuaded the Jews and the Greeks. And when Silas and Timotheus were come from Macedonia, Paul was pressed in the spirit, and testified to the Jews that Jesus was Christ. And when they opposed themselves, and blasphemed, he shook his raiment, and said unto them, "Your blood be upon your own heads; I am clean: from henceforth I will go unto the Gentiles."

And he departed thence, and entered into a certain man's house, named Justus, one that worshipped God, whose house joined hard to the synagogue. And Crispus, the chief ruler of the synagogue, believed on the Lord with all his house; and many of the Corinthians hearing believed, and were baptized. Then spoke the Lord to Paul in the night by a vision,

"Be not afraid, but speak, and hold not thy peace: for I am with thee, and no man shall set on thee to hurt thee: for I have much people in this city." And he continued there a year and six months, teaching the word of God among them.

And when Gallio was the deputy of Achaia, the Jews made insurrection with one accord against Paul, and brought him to the judgment seat, saying, "This fellow persuadeth men to worship God contrary to the law."

And when Paul was now about to open his mouth, Gallio said unto the Jews, "If it were a matter of wrong or wicked lewdness, O ye Jews, reason would that I should bear with you: but if it be a question of words and names, and of your law, look ye to it; for I will be no judge of such matters." And he drove them from the judgment seat. Then all the Greeks took Sosthenes, the chief ruler of the synagogue, and beat him before the judgment seat. And Gallio cared for none of those things.

And Paul after this tarried there yet a good while, and then took his leave of the brethren, and sailed thence into Syria, and with him Priscilla and Aquila; having shorn his head in Cenchrea: for he had a vow. And he came to Ephesus, and left them there: but he himself entered into the synagogue, and reasoned with the Jews. When they desired him to tarry longer time with them, he consented not; but bade them farewell, saying, "I must by all means keep this feast that cometh in Jerusalem: but I will return again unto you, if God will." And he sailed from Ephesus.

And when he had landed at Cæsarea, and gone up, and saluted the church, he went down to Antioch. And after he had spent some time there, he departed, and went over all the country of Galatia and Phrygia in order, strengthening all the disciples.

And a certain Jew named Apollos, born at Alexandria, an eloquent man, and mighty in the scriptures, came to Ephesus. This man was instructed in the way of the Lord; and being fervent in the spirit, he spoke and taught diligently the things of the Lord, knowing only the baptism of John. And he began to speak boldly in the synagogue: whom when Aquila and Priscilla had heard, they took him unto them, and expounded unto him the way of God more perfectly. And when he was disposed to pass into Achaia, the brethren wrote, exhorting the disciples to receive him: who, when he was come, helped them much which had believed through grace: for he mightily convinced the Jews, and that publicly, showing by the scriptures that Jesus was Christ.

Paul's Third Missionary Journey

And it came to pass, that, while Apollos was at Corinth, Paul having passed through the upper coasts came to Ephesus, and finding certain disciples, he said unto them, "Have ye received the Holy Ghost since ye believed?"

And they said unto him, "We have not so much as heard whether there be any Holy Ghost."

And he said unto them, "Unto what then were ye baptized?"

And they said, "Unto John's baptism."

THE ACTS OF THE APOSTLES

Then said Paul, "John verily baptized with the baptism of repentance, saying unto the people that they should believe on him which should come after him, that is, on Christ Jesus."

When they heard this, they were baptized in the name of the Lord Jesus. And when Paul had laid his hands upon them, the Holy Ghost came on them; and they spoke with tongues, and prophesied. And all the men were about twelve.

And he went into the synagogue, and spoke boldly for the space of three months, disputing and persuading the things concerning the kingdom of God. But when divers were hardened, and believed not, but spoke evil of that way before the multitude, he departed from them, and separated the disciples, disputing daily in the school of one Tyrannus. And this continued by the space of two years; so that all they which dwelt in Asia heard the word of the Lord Jesus, both Jews and Greeks. And God wrought special miracles by the hands of Paul: so that from his body were brought unto the sick handkerchiefs or aprons, and the diseases departed from them, and the evil spirits went out of them. Then certain of the vagabond Jews, exorcists, took upon them to call over them which had evil spirits the name of the Lord Jesus, saying, "We adjure you by Jesus whom Paul preacheth." And there were seven sons of one Sceva, a Jew, and chief of the priests, which did so. And the evil spirit answered and said, "Jesus I know, and Paul I know; but who are ye?" And the man in whom the evil spirit was leaped on them, and overcame them, and prevailed against them, so that they fled out of that house naked and wounded. And this was known to all the Jews and Greeks also dwelling at Ephesus; and fear fell on them all, and the name of the Lord Jesus was magnified. And many that believed came, and confessed, and showed their deeds. Many of them also which used curious arts brought their books together, and burned them before all men: and they counted the price of them, and found it fifty thousand pieces of silver. So mightily grew the word of God and prevailed.

After these things were ended, Paul purposed in the spirit,

THE ACTS OF THE APOSTLES

when he had passed through Macedonia and Achaia, to go to Jerusalem, saying, "After I have been there, I must also see Rome." So he sent into Macedonia two of them that ministered unto him, Timotheus and Erastus; but he himself stayed in Asia for a season.

And the same time there arose no small stir about that way. For a certain man named Demetrius, a silversmith, which made silver shrines for Diana, brought no small gain unto the craftsmen; whom he called together with the workmen of like occupation, and said,

"Sirs, ye know that by this craft we have our wealth. Moreover ye see and hear, that not alone at Ephesus, but almost throughout all Asia, this Paul hath persuaded and turned away much people, saying that they be no gods, which are made with hands: so that not only this our craft is in danger to be set at nought; but also that the temple of the great goddess Diana should be despised, and her magnificence should be destroyed, whom all Asia and the world worshippeth."

And when they heard these sayings, they were full of wrath, and cried out, saying,

"Great is Diana of the Ephesians!" And the whole city was filled with confusion: and having caught Gaius and Aristarchus, men of Macedonia, Paul's companions in travel, they rushed with one accord into the theatre. And when Paul would have entered in unto the people, the disciples suffered him not. And certain of the chief of Asia, which were his friends, sent unto him, desiring him that he would not adventure himself into the theatre. Some therefore cried one thing, and some another: for the assembly was confused; and the more part knew not wherefore they were come together. And they drew Alexander out of the multitude, the Jews putting him forward. And Alexander beckoned with the hand, and would have made his defence unto the people. But when they knew that he was a Jew, all with one voice about the space of two hours cried out,

"Great is Diana of the Ephesians!"

And when the town clerk had appeased the people, he said,

THE ACTS OF THE APOSTLES

"Ye men of Ephesus, what man is there that knoweth not how that the city of the Ephesians is a worshipper of the great goddess Diana, and of the image which fell down from Jupiter? Seeing then that these things cannot be spoken against, ye ought to be quiet, and to do nothing rashly. For ye have brought hither these men, which are neither robbers of churches, nor yet blasphemers of your goddess. Wherefore if Demetrius, and the craftsmen which are with him, have a matter against any man, the law is open, and there are deputies: let them implead one another. But if ye enquire any thing concerning other matters, it shall be determined in a lawful assembly. For we are in danger to be called in question for this day's uproar, there being no cause whereby we may give an account of this concourse."

And when he had thus spoken, he dismissed the assembly.

And after the uproar was ceased, Paul called unto him the disciples, and embraced them, and departed for to go into Macedonia. And when he had gone over those parts, and had given them much exhortation, he came into Greece, and there abode three months. And when the Jews laid wait for him, as he was about to sail into Syria, he purposed to return through Macedonia. And there accompanied him into Asia Sopater of Berea; and of the Thessalonians, Aristarchus and Secundus; and Gaius of Derbe, and Timotheus; and of Asia, Tychicus and Trophimus. These going before tarried for us at Troas.

And we sailed away from Philippi after the days of unleavened bread, and came unto them to Troas in five days; where we abode seven days. And upon the first day of the week, when the disciples came together to break bread, Paul preached unto them, ready to depart on the morrow; and continued his speech until midnight. And there were many lights in the upper chamber, where they were gathered together. And there sat in a window a certain young man named Eutychus, being fallen into a deep sleep: and as Paul was long preaching, he sunk down with sleep, and fell down from the third loft, and was taken up dead. And Paul went down, and fell on him, and embracing him said, "Trouble not yourselves; for his life is in him."

THE ACTS OF THE APOSTLES

When he therefore was come up again, and had broken bread, and eaten, and talked a long while, even till break of day, so he departed. And they brought the young man alive, and were not a little comforted.

And we went before to ship, and sailed unto Assos, there intending to take in Paul: for so had he appointed, minding himself to go afoot. And when he met with us at Assos, we took him in, and came to Mitylene. And we sailed thence, and came the next day over against Chios; and the next day we arrived at Samos, and tarried at Trogyllium; and the next day we came to Miletus. For Paul had determined to sail by Ephesus, because he would not spend the time in Asia: for he hastened, if it were possible for him, to be at Jerusalem the day of Pentecost.

And from Miletus he sent to Ephesus, and called the elders of the church. And when they were come to him, he said unto them,

"Ye know, from the first day that I came into Asia, after what manner I have been with you at all seasons, serving the Lord with all humility of mind, and with many tears, and temptations, which befell me by the lying in wait of the Jews: and how I kept back nothing that was profitable unto you, but have showed you, and have taught you publicly, and from house to house, testifying both to the Jews, and also to the Greeks, repentance toward God, and faith toward our Lord Jesus Christ.

"And now, behold, I go bound in the spirit unto Jerusalem, not knowing the things that shall befall me there: save that the Holy Ghost witnesseth in every city, saying that bonds and afflictions abide me. But none of these things move me, neither count I my life dear unto myself, so that I might finish my course with joy, and the ministry, which I have received of the Lord Jesus, to testify the gospel of the grace of God. And now, behold, I know that ye all, among whom I have gone preaching the kingdom of God, shall see my face no more. Wherefore I take you to record this day, that I am pure from the blood of all men. For I have not shunned to declare unto you all the counsel of God.

THE ACTS OF THE APOSTLES

"Take heed therefore unto yourselves, and to all the flock, over the which the Holy Ghost hath made you overseers, to feed the church of God, which he hath purchased with his own blood. For I know this, that after my departing shall grievous wolves enter in among you, not sparing the flock. Also of your own selves shall men arise, speaking perverse things, to draw away disciples after them. Therefore watch, and remember, that by the space of three years I ceased not to warn every one night and day with tears.

"And now, brethren, I commend you to God, and to the word of his grace, which is able to build you up, and to give you an inheritance among all them which are sanctified. I have coveted no man's silver, or gold, or apparel. Yea, ye yourselves know, that these hands have ministered unto my necessities, and to them that were with me. I have showed you all things, how that so labouring ye ought to support the weak, and to remember the words of the Lord Jesus, how he said, 'T is more blessed to give than to receive.'"

And when he had thus spoken, he kneeled down, and prayed with them all. And they all wept sore, and fell on Paul's neck, and kissed him, sorrowing most of all for the words which he spoke, that they should see his face no more. And they accompanied him unto the ship.

And it came to pass that after we were gotten from them, and had launched, we came with a straight course unto Cos, and the day following unto Rhodes, and from thence unto Patara; and finding a ship sailing over unto Phenicia, we went aboard, and set forth. Now when we had discovered Cyprus, we left it on the left hand, and sailed into Syria, and landed at Tyre: for there the ship was to unlade her burden. And finding disciples, we tarried there seven days: who said to Paul through the Spirit, that he should not go up to Jerusalem. And when we had accomplished those days, we departed and went our way; and they all brought us on our way, with wives and children, till we were out of the city: and we kneeled down on the shore, and prayed. And when we had taken our leave one of another, we took ship; and they returned home again. And when we had finished our course from Tyre, we came to Ptolemais, and saluted the brethren, and abode with them one day.

And the next day we that were of Paul's company departed, and came unto Cæsarea: and we entered into the house of Philip the evangelist, which was one of the seven; and abode with him. And the same man had four daughters, virgins, which did prophesy. And as we tarried there many days, there came down from Judæa a certain prophet, named Agabus. And when he was come unto us, he took Paul's girdle, and bound his own hands and feet, and said, "Thus saith the Holy Ghost, 'So shall the Jews at Jerusalem bind the man that owneth this girdle, and shall deliver him into the hands of the Gentiles.'"

And when we heard these things, both we, and they of that place, besought him not to go up to Jerusalem.

Then Paul answered, "What mean ye to weep and to break mine heart? for I am ready not to be bound only, but also to die at Jerusalem for the name of the Lord Jesus."

And when he would not be persuaded, we ceased, saying, "The will of the Lord be done."

Paul Seized and Imprisoned

And after those days we took up our carriages, and went up to Jerusalem. There went with us also certain of the disciples of Cæsarea, and brought with them one Mnason of Cyprus, an old disciple, with whom we should lodge. And when we were come to Jerusalem, the brethren received us gladly. And the day following Paul went in with us unto James; and all the elders were present. And when he had saluted them, he declared particularly what things God had wrought among the Gentiles by his ministry. And when they heard it, they glorified the Lord, and said unto him,

"Thou seest, brother, how many thousands of Jews there are which believe; and they are all zealous of the law: and they are informed of thee, that thou teachest all the Jews which are among the Gentiles to forsake Moses, saying that they ought

THE ACTS OF THE APOSTLES

not to circumcise their children, neither to walk after the customs. What is it therefore? the multitude must needs come together: for they will hear that thou art come. Do therefore this that we say to thee: we have four men which have a vow on them; them take, and purify thyself with them, and be at charges with them, that they may shave their heads: and all may know that those things, whereof they were informed concerning thee, are nothing; but that thou thyself also walkest orderly, and keepest the law. As touching the Gentiles which believe, we have written and concluded that they observe no such thing, save only that they keep themselves from things offered to idols, and from blood, and from strangled, and from fornication."

Then Paul took the men, and the next day purifying himself with them entered into the temple, to signify the accomplishment of the days of purification, until that an offering should be offered for every one of them. And when the seven days were almost ended, the Jews which were of Asia, when they saw him in the temple, stirred up all the people, and laid hands on him, crying out, "Men of Israel, help! This is the man that teacheth all men everywhere against the people, and the law, and this place: and further brought Greeks also into the temple, and hath polluted this holy place." (For they had seen before with him in the city Trophimus an Ephesian, whom they supposed that Paul had brought into the temple.)

And all the city was moved, and the people ran together: and they took Paul, and drew him out of the temple: and forthwith the doors were shut. And as they went about to kill him, tidings came unto the chief captain of the band that all Jerusalem was in an uproar. Who immediately took soldiers and centurions, and ran down unto them: and when they saw the chief captain and the soldiers, they left beating of Paul. Then the chief captain came near, and took him, and commanded him to be bound with two chains; and demanded who he was, and what he had done. And some cried one thing, some another, among the multitude: and when he could not know the certainty for the tumult, he commanded him to be carried into the castle. And when he came upon the stairs, so it was, that he was borne of the soldiers for the violence of the people. For the multitude of the people followed after, crying, "Away with him!"

And as Paul was to be led into the castle, he said unto the chief captain, "May I speak unto thee?" Who said, "Canst thou speak Greek? Art not thou that Egyptian which before these days madest an uproar, and leddest out into the wilderness four thousand men that were murderers?"

But Paul said, "I am a man which am a Jew of Tarsus, a city in Cilicia, a citizen of no mean city: and, I beseech thee, suffer me to speak unto the people."

And when he had given him licence, Paul stood on the stairs, and beckoned with the hand unto the people. And when there was made a great silence, he spoke unto them in the Hebrew tongue, saying,

"Men, brethren, and fathers, hear ye my defence which I make now unto you. I am verily a man which am a Jew, born in Tarsus, a city in Cilicia, yet brought up in this city at the feet of Gamaliel, and taught according to the perfect manner of the law of the fathers, and was zealous toward God, as ye all are this day. And I persecuted this way unto the death, binding and delivering into prisons both men and women. As also the high priest doth bear me witness, and all the estate of the elders: from whom also I received letters unto the brethren, and went to Damascus, to bring them which were there bound unto Jerusalem, for to be punished. And it came to pass that, as I made my journey, and was come nigh unto Damascus about noon, suddenly there shone from heaven a great light round about me. And I fell unto the ground, and heard a voice saying unto me, 'Saul, Saul, why persecutest thou me?' And I answered, 'Who art thou, Lord?' And he said unto me, 'I am Jesus of Nazareth, whom thou persecutest.' And they that were with me saw indeed the light, and were afraid; but they heard not the voice of him that spoke to me. And I said, 'What shall I do, Lord?' And the Lord said unto me, 'Arise, and go into Damascus; and there it shall be told thee of all things which are appointed for thee

THE ACTS OF THE APOSTLES

to do.' And when I could not see for the glory of that light, being led by the hand of them that were with me, I came into Damascus.

"And one Ananias, a devout man according to the law, having a good report of all the Jews which dwelt there, came unto me, and stood, and said unto me, 'Brother Saul, receive thy sight.' And the same hour I looked up upon him. And he said, 'The God of our fathers hath chosen thee, that thou shouldest know his will, and see that Just One, and shouldest hear the voice of his mouth. For thou shalt be his witness unto all men of what thou hast seen and heard. And now why tarriest thou? arise, and be baptized, and wash away thy sins, calling on the name of the Lord.'

"And it came to pass that, when I was come again to Jerusalem, even while I prayed in the temple, I was in a trance; and saw him saying unto me, 'Make haste, and get thee quickly out of Jerusalem: for they will not receive thy testimony concerning me.' And I said, 'Lord, they know that I imprisoned and beat in every synagogue them that believed on thee: and when the blood of thy martyr Stephen was shed, I also was standing by, and consenting unto his death, and kept the raiment of them that slew him.' And he said unto me, 'Depart: for I will send thee far hence unto the Gentiles.'"

And they gave him audience unto this word, and then lifted up their voices, and said, "Away with such a fellow from the earth: for it is not fit that he should live!"

And as they cried out, and cast off their clothes, and threw dust into the air, the chief captain commanded him to be brought into the castle, and bade that he should be examined by scourging; that he might know wherefore they cried so against him. And as they bound him with thongs, Paul said unto the centurion that stood by, "Is it lawful for you to scourge a man that is a Roman, and uncondemned?"

When the centurion heard that, he went and told the chief captain, saying, "Take heed what thou doest: for this man is a Roman."

THE ACTS OF THE APOSTLES

Then the chief captain came, and said unto him, "Tell me, art thou a Roman?" He said, "Yea."

And the chief captain answered, "With a great sum obtained I this freedom." And Paul said, "But I was free born."

Then straightway they departed from him which should have examined him: and the chief captain also was afraid, after he knew that he was a Roman, and because he had bound him. On the morrow, because he would have known the certainty wherefore he was accused of the Jews, he loosed him from his bands, and commanded the chief priests and all their council to appear, and brought Paul down, and set him before them. And Paul, earnestly beholding the council, said,

"Men and brethren, I have lived in all good conscience before God until this day."

And the high priest Ananias commanded them that stood by him to smite him on the mouth.

Then said Paul unto him, "God shall smite thee, thou whited wall: for sittest thou to judge me after the law, and commandest me to be smitten contrary to the law?"

And they that stood by said, "Revilest thou God's high priest?"

Then said Paul, "I wist not, brethren, that he was the high priest: for it is written, 'Thou shalt not speak evil of the ruler of thy people.'"

But when Paul perceived that the one part were Sadducees, and the other Pharisees, he cried out in the council, "Men and brethren, I am a Pharisee, the son of a Pharisee: of the hope and resurrection of the dead I am called in question."

And when he had so said, there arose a dissension between the Pharisees and the Sadducees: and the multitude was divided. For the Sadducees say that there is no resurrection, neither angel, nor spirit: but the Pharisees confess both. And there arose a great cry: and the scribes that were of the Pharisees' part arose, and strove, saying, "We find no evil in this man: but if a spirit or an angel hath spoken to him, let us not fight against God."

THE ACTS OF THE APOSTLES

And when there arose a great dissension, the chief captain, fearing lest Paul should have been pulled in pieces of them, commanded the soldiers to go down, and to take him by force from among them, and to bring him into the castle. And the night following the Lord stood by him, and said, "Be of good cheer, Paul: for as thou hast testified of me in Jerusalem, so must thou bear witness also at Rome."

And when it was day, certain of the Jews banded together, and bound themselves under a curse, saying that they would neither eat nor drink till they had killed Paul. And they were more than forty which had made this conspiracy. And they came to the chief priests and elders, and said, "We have bound ourselves under a great curse, that we will eat nothing until we have slain Paul. Now therefore ye with the council signify to the chief captain that he bring him down unto you to-morrow, as though ye would enquire something more perfectly concerning him: and we, or ever he come near, are ready to kill him."

And when Paul's sister's son heard of their lying in wait, he went and entered into the castle, and told Paul. Then Paul called one of the centurions unto him, and said, "Bring this young man unto the chief captain: for he hath a certain thing to tell him."

So he took him, and brought him to the chief captain, and said, "Paul the prisoner called me unto him, and prayed me to bring this young man unto thee, who hath something to say unto thee."

Then the chief captain took him by the hand, and went with him aside privately, and asked him, "What is that thou hast to tell me?"

And he said, "The Jews have agreed to desire thee that thou wouldest bring down Paul to-morrow into the council, as though they would enquire somewhat of him more perfectly. But do not thou yield unto them: for there lie in wait for him of them more than forty men, which have bound themselves with an oath, that they will neither eat nor drink till they have killed him: and now are they ready, looking for a promise from thee."

THE ACTS OF THE APOSTLES

So the chief captain then let the young man depart, and charged him, "See thou tell no man that thou hast showed these things to me."

And he called unto him two centurions, saying, "Make ready two hundred soldiers to go to Cæsarea, and horsemen threescore and ten, and spearmen two hundred, at the third hour of the night; and provide them beasts, that they may set Paul on, and bring him safe unto Felix the governor."

And he wrote a letter after this manner:

Claudius Lysias unto the most excellent governor Felix sendeth greeting:

This man was taken of the Jews, and should have been killed of them: then came I with an army, and rescued him, having understood that he was a Roman. And when I would have known the cause wherefore they accused him, I brought him forth into their council: whom I perceived to be accused of questions of their law, but to have nothing laid to his charge worthy of death or of bonds. And when it was told me how that the Jews laid wait for the man, I sent straightway to thee, and gave commandment to his accusers also to say before thee what they had against him. Farewell.

Then the soldiers, as it was commanded them, took Paul, and brought him by night to Antipatris. On the morrow they left the horsemen to go with him, and returned to the castle: who, when they came to Cæsarea, and delivered the epistle to the governor, presented Paul also before him. And when the governor had read the letter, he asked of what province he was. And when he understood that he was of Cilicia, "I will hear thee," said he, "when thine accusers are also come." And he commanded him to be kept in Herod's judgment hall.

And after five days Ananias the high priest descended with the elders, and with a certain orator named Tertullus, who informed the governor against Paul. And when he was called forth, Tertullus began to accuse him, saying, "Seeing that by thee we enjoy great quietness, and that very worthy deeds are done unto this nation by thy providence, we accept it always,

THE ACTS OF THE APOSTLES

and in all places, most noble Felix, with all thankfulness. Notwithstanding, that I be not further tedious unto thee, I pray thee that thou wouldest hear us of thy clemency a few words. For we have found this man a pestilent fellow, and a mover of sedition among all the Jews throughout the world, and a ringleader of the sect of the Nazarenes: who also hath gone about to profane the temple: whom we took, and would have judged according to our law. But the chief captain Lysias came upon us, and with great violence took him away out of our hands, commanding his accusers to come unto thee: by examining of whom thyself mayest take knowledge of all these things, whereof we accuse him." And the Jews also assented, saying that these things were so.

Then Paul, after that the governor had beckoned unto him to speak, answered, "Forasmuch as I know that thou hast been of many years a judge unto this nation, I do the more cheerfully answer for myself: because that thou mayest understand that there are yet but twelve days since I went up to Jerusalem for to worship. And they neither found me in the temple disputing with any man, neither raising up the people, neither in the synagogues, nor in the city: neither can they prove the things whereof they now accuse me. But this I confess unto thee, that after the way which they call heresy, so worship I the God of my fathers, believing all things which are written in the law and in the prophets; and have hope toward God, which they themselves also allow, that there shall be a resurrection of the dead, both of the just and unjust. And herein do I exercise myself, to have always a conscience void of offence toward God, and toward men.

"Now after many years I came to bring alms to my nation, and offerings. Whereupon certain Jews from Asia found me purified in the temple, neither with multitude, nor with tumult. Who ought to have been here before thee, and object, if they had ought against me. Or else let these same here say, if they have found any evil doing in me, while I stood before the council, except it be for this one voice that I cried standing among them, 'Touching the resurrection of the dead I am called in question by you this day.'"

And when Felix heard these things, having more perfect knowledge of that way, he deferred them, and said, "When Lysias the chief captain shall come down, I will know the uttermost of your matter."

And he commanded a centurion to keep Paul, and to let him have liberty, and that he should forbid none of his acquaintance to minister or come unto him. And after certain days, when Felix came with his wife Drusilla, which was a Jewess, he sent for Paul, and heard him concerning the faith in Christ. And as he reasoned of righteousness, temperance, and judgment to come, Felix trembled, and answered, "Go thy way for this time; when I have a convenient season, I will call for thee."

He hoped also that money should have been given him of Paul, that he might loose him: wherefore he sent for him the oftener, and communed with him. But after two years Porcius Festus came into Felix' room: and Felix, willing to show the Jews a pleasure, left Paul bound.

Now when Festus was come into the province, after three days he ascended from Cæsarea to Jerusalem. Then the high priest and the chief of the Jews informed him against Paul, and besought him, and desired favour against him, that he would send for him to Jerusalem, laying wait in the way to kill him. But Festus answered that Paul should be kept at Cæsarea, and that he himself would depart shortly thither. "Let them therefore," said he, "which among you are able, go down with me, and accuse this man, if there be any wickedness in him."

And when he had tarried among them more than ten days, he went down unto Cæsarea; and the next day sitting on the judgment seat commanded Paul to be brought. And when he was come, the Jews which came down from Jerusalem stood round about, and laid many and grievous complaints against Paul, which they could not prove. While he answered for himself, "Neither against the law of the Jews, neither against the temple, nor yet against Cæsar, have I offended anything at all."

THE ACTS OF THE APOSTLES

But Festus, willing to do the Jews a pleasure, answered Paul, and said, "Wilt thou go up to Jerusalem, and there be judged of these things before me?"

Then said Paul,

"I stand at Cæsar's judgment seat, where I ought to be judged: to the Jews have I done no wrong, as thou very well knowest. For if I be an offender, or have committed any thing worthy of death, I refuse not to die: but if there be none of these things whereof these accuse me, no man may deliver me unto them. I appeal unto Cæsar."

Then Festus, when he had conferred with the council, answered,

"Hast thou appealed unto Cæsar? unto Cæsar shalt thou go!"

Paul's Defence before Agrippa

And after certain days King Agrippa and Bernice came unto Cæsarea to salute Festus. And when they had been there many days, Festus declared Paul's cause unto the king, saying,

"There is a certain man left in bonds by Felix: about whom, when I was at Jerusalem, the chief priests and the elders of the Jews informed me, desiring to have judgment against him. To whom I answered, 'It is not the manner of the Romans to deliver any man to die, before that he which is accused have the accusers face to face, and have licence to answer for himself concerning the crime laid against him.' Therefore, when they were come hither, without any delay on the morrow I sat on the judgment seat, and commanded the man to be brought forth. Against whom when the accusers stood up, they brought none accusation of such things as I supposed: but had certain questions against him of their own superstition, and of one Jesus, which was dead, whom Paul affirmed to be alive. And because I doubted of such manner of questions, I asked him whether he would go to Jerusalem, and there be judged of these matters. But when Paul had appealed to be reserved unto the hearing of Augustus, I commanded him to be kept till I might send him to Cæsar."

THE ACTS OF THE APOSTLES

Then Agrippa said unto Festus, "I would also hear the man myself."

"To-morrow," said he, "thou shalt hear him."

And on the morrow, when Agrippa was come, and Bernice, with great pomp, and was entered into the place of hearing, with the chief captains, and principal men of the city, at Festus' commandment Paul was brought forth.

And Festus said, "King Agrippa, and all men which are here present with us, ye see this man, about whom all the multitude of the Jews have dealt with me, both at Jerusalem, and also here, crying that he ought not to live any longer.

"But when I found that he had committed nothing worthy of death, and that he himself hath appealed to Augustus, I have determined to send him, of whom I have no certain thing to write unto my lord. Wherefore I have brought him forth before you, and specially before thee, O King Agrippa, that, after examination had, I might have somewhat to write. For it seemeth to me unreasonable to send a prisoner, and not withal to signify the crimes laid against him."

Then Agrippa said unto Paul, "Thou art permitted to speak for thyself."

Then Paul stretched forth the hand, and answered for himself: "I think myself happy, King Agrippa, because I shall answer for myself this day before thee touching all the things whereof I am accused of the Jews: especially because I know thee to be expert in all customs and questions which are among the Jews: wherefore I beseech thee to hear me patiently.

"My manner of life from my youth, which was at the first among mine own nation at Jerusalem, know all the Jews; which knew me from the beginning, if they would testify, that after the most straitest sect of our religion I lived a Pharisee. And now I stand and am judged for the hope of the promise made of God unto our fathers: unto which promise our twelve tribes, instantly serving God day and night, hope to come. For which hope's sake, King Agrippa, I am accused of the Jews.

"Why should it be thought a thing incredible with you that

THE ACTS OF THE APOSTLES

God should raise the dead? I verily thought with myself that I ought to do many things contrary to the name of Jesus of Nazareth. Which thing I also did in Jerusalem: and many of the saints did I shut up in prison, having received authority from the chief priests; and when they were put to death, I gave my voice against them. And I punished them oft in every synagogue, and compelled them to blaspheme; and being exceedingly mad against them, I persecuted them even unto strange cities.

"Whereupon as I went to Damascus with authority and commission from the chief priests, at midday, O king, I saw in the way a light from heaven, above the brightness of the sun, shining round about me and them which journeyed with me. And when we were all fallen to the earth, I heard a voice speaking unto me, and saying in the Hebrew tongue, 'Saul, Saul, why persecutest thou me? it is hard for thee to kick against the pricks.'

"And I said, 'Who art thou, Lord?'

"And he said, 'I am Jesus whom thou persecutest. But rise, and stand upon thy feet: for I have appeared unto thee for this purpose, to make thee a minister and a witness both of these things which thou hast seen, and of those things in the which I will appear unto thee; delivering thee from the people, and from the Gentiles, unto whom now I send thee, to open their eyes, and to turn them from darkness to light, and from the power of Satan unto God, that they may receive forgiveness of sins, and inheritance among them which are sanctified by faith that is in me.'

"Whereupon, O King Agrippa, I was not disobedient unto the heavenly vision: but showed first unto them of Damascus, and at Jerusalem, and throughout all the coasts of Judæa, and then to the Gentiles, that they should repent and turn to God, and do works meet for repentance.

"For these causes the Jews caught me in the temple, and went about to kill me. Having therefore obtained help of God, I continue unto this day, witnessing both to small and great, saying none other things than those which the prophets and Moses did

THE ACTS OF THE APOSTLES

say should come: that Christ should suffer, and that he should be the first that should rise from the dead, and should show light unto the people, and to the Gentiles."

And as he thus spoke for himself, Festus said with a loud voice, "Paul, thou art beside thyself; much learning doth make thee mad."

But he said, "I am not mad, most noble Festus; but speak forth the words of truth and soberness. For the king knoweth of these things, before whom also I speak freely: for I am persuaded that none of these things are hidden from him; for this thing was not done in a corner.

"King Agrippa, believest thou the prophets? I know that thou believest."

Then Agrippa said unto Paul, "Almost thou persuadest me to be a Christian."

And Paul said, "I would to God that not only thou, but also all that hear me this day, were both almost, and altogether such as I am, except these bonds."

And when he had thus spoken, the king rose up, and the governor, and Bernice, and they that sat with them: and when they were gone aside, they talked between themselves, saying, "This man doeth nothing worthy of death or of bonds."

Then said Agrippa unto Festus, "This man might have been set at liberty, if he had not appealed unto Cæsar."

Paul Taken to Rome

And when it was determined that we should sail into Italy, they delivered Paul and certain other prisoners unto one named Julius, a centurion of Augustus' band. And entering into a ship of Adramyttium, we launched, meaning to sail by the coasts of Asia; one Aristarchus, a Macedonian of Thessalonica, being with us. And the next day we touched at Sidon. And Julius courteously entreated Paul, and gave him liberty to go unto his friends to refresh himself.

And when we had launched from thence, we sailed under Cyprus, because the winds were contrary. And when we had sailed over the sea of Cilicia and Pamphylia, we came to Myra, a city of Lycia. And there the centurion found a ship of Alexandria sailing into Italy; and he put us therein. And when we had sailed slowly many days, and scarce were come over against Cnidus, the wind not suffering us, we sailed under Crete, over against Salmone; and, hardly passing it, came unto a place which is called the Fair Havens; nigh whereunto was the city of Lasea.

Now when much time was spent, and when sailing was now dangerous, because the fast was now already past, Paul admonished them, and said unto them, "Sirs, I perceive that this voyage will be with hurt and much damage, not only of the lading and ship, but also of our lives."

Nevertheless the centurion believed the master and the owner of the ship more than those things which were spoken by Paul. And because the haven was not commodious to winter in, the more part advised to depart thence also, if by any means they might attain to Phenice, and there to winter; which is a haven of Crete, and lieth toward the southwest and northwest. And when the south wind blew softly, supposing that they had obtained their purpose, loosing thence, they sailed close by Crete.

But not long after there arose against it a tempestuous wind, called Euroclydon. And when the ship was caught, and could not bear up into the wind, we let her drive. And running under a certain island which is called Clauda, we had much work to come by the boat: which when they had taken up, they used helps, undergirding the ship; and, fearing lest they should fall into the quicksands, struck sail, and so were driven. And we being exceedingly tossed with a tempest, the next day they lightened the ship; and the third day we cast out with our own hands the tackling of the ship. And when neither sun nor stars in many days appeared, and no small tempest lay on us, all hope that we should be saved was then taken away.

But after long abstinence Paul stood forth in the midst of them, and said, "Sirs, ye should have hearkened unto me, and not have loosed from Crete, and to have gained this harm and loss. And now I exhort you to be of good cheer: for there shall

THE ACTS OF THE APOSTLES

be no loss of any man's life among you, but of the ship. For there stood by me this night the angel of God, whose I am, and whom I serve, saying, 'Fear not, Paul; thou must be brought before Cæsar: and, lo, God hath given thee all them that sail with thee.'

"Wherefore, sirs, be of good cheer: for I believe God, that it shall be even as it was told me. Howbeit we must be cast upon a certain island."

But when the fourteenth night was come, as we were driven up and down in Adria, about midnight the shipmen deemed that they drew near to some country; and sounded, and found it twenty fathoms: and when they had gone a little further, they sounded again, and found it fifteen fathoms. Then fearing lest we should have fallen upon rocks, they cast four anchors out of the stern, and wished for the day.

And as the shipmen were about to flee out of the ship, when they had let down the boat into the sea, under colour as though they would have cast anchors out of the foreship, Paul said to the centurion and to the soldiers, "Except these abide in the ship, ye cannot be saved."

Then the soldiers cut off the ropes of the boat, and let her fall off. And while the day was coming on, Paul besought them all to take meat, saying, "This day is the fourteenth day that ye have tarried and continued fasting, having taken nothing. Wherefore I pray you to take some meat: for this is for your health: for there shall not a hair fall from the head of any of you."

And when he had thus spoken, he took bread, and gave thanks to God in presence of them all: and when he had broken it, he began to eat. Then were they all of good cheer, and they also took some meat. And we were in all in the ship two hundred threescore and sixteen souls.

And when they had eaten enough, they lightened the ship, and cast out the wheat into the sea. And when it was day, they knew not the land: but they discovered a certain creek with a shore, into the which they were minded, if it were possible, to thrust in the ship. And when they had taken up the anchors, they

THE ACTS OF THE APOSTLES

committed themselves unto the sea, and loosed the rudder bands, and hoisted up the mainsail to the wind, and made toward shore. And falling into a place where two seas met, they ran the ship aground; and the forepart stuck fast, and remained unmoveable, but the hinder part was broken with the violence of the waves. And the soldiers' counsel was to kill the prisoners, lest any of them should swim out, and escape. But the centurion, willing to save Paul, kept them from their purpose; and commanded that they which could swim should cast themselves first into the sea, and get to land: and the rest, some on boards, and some on broken pieces of the ship. And so it came to pass, that they escaped all safe to land.

And when they were escaped, then they knew that the island was called Melita. And the barbarous people showed us no little kindness: for they kindled a fire, and received us every one, because of the present rain, and because of the cold. And when Paul had gathered a bundle of sticks, and laid them on the fire, there came a viper out of the heat, and fastened on his hand. And when the barbarians saw the venomous beast hang on his hand, they said among themselves, "No doubt this man is a murderer, whom, though he hath escaped the sea, yet vengeance suffereth not to live." And he shook off the beast into the fire, and felt no harm. Howbeit they looked when he should have swollen, or fallen down dead suddenly: but after they had looked a great while, and saw no harm come to him, they changed their minds, and said that he was a god.

In the same quarters were possessions of the chief man of the island, whose name was Publius; who received us, and lodged us three days courteously. And it came to pass that the father of Publius lay sick of a fever and of a bloody flux: to whom Paul entered in, and prayed, and laid his hands on him, and healed him. So when this was done, others also, which had diseases in the island, came, and were healed: who also honoured us with many honours; and when we departed, they laded us with such things as were necessary.

And after three months we departed in a ship of Alexandria,

THE ACTS OF THE APOSTLES

which had wintered in the isle, whose sign was Castor and Pollux. And landing at Syracuse, we tarried there three days. And from thence we fetched a compass, and came to Rhegium: and after one day the south wind blew, and we came the next day to Puteoli: where we found brethren, and were desired to tarry with them seven days: and so we went toward Rome. And from thence, when the brethren heard of us, they came to meet us as far as Forum Appii, and the Three Taverns: whom when Paul saw, he thanked God, and took courage.

And when we came to Rome, the centurion delivered the prisoners to the captain of the guard: but Paul was suffered to dwell by himself with a soldier that kept him. And Paul dwelt two whole years in his own hired house, and received all that came in unto him, preaching the kingdom of God, and teaching those things which concern the Lord Jesus Christ, with all confidence, no man forbidding him.

THE LETTERS OF PAUL: TO THE THESSALONIANS. I

No OTHER LETTERS *ever written have begun to have the influence of those produced by Paul of Tarsus as an adjunct of his missionary labors; composed to meet the specific needs of particular congregations established by him, occasional in their utterance, adapted to local times and places, they nevertheless often touched upon themes of such universal religious influence and treated them in so profound a manner—yet always with the special organization of the church in mind—that they became the prime factor in the development of both the inner and outer aspects of Christianity as at once a subjective attitude of spirit and an objective institution. In spite of being rather labored, Paul's literary style was equal to the expression of a great variety of moods, ranging through emotional tenderness, passionate invective, eloquent persuasion, and cool logical reasoning. His rabbinical training is evident in his Scriptural learning and in the argumentative form of his discourses with their frequent use of rhetorical questions, striking antitheses, and legal illustrations.*

The letters were written between A.D. 50 and A.D. 70 when Paul could speak with authority as the foremost Christian missionary. In the earliest of them, written to the members of the church which he had founded in Thessalonica, he reveals the importance that the idea of the second coming of Christ had for him as for all the Christians of his era, expecting as they did that this great event would occur within their own lifetime. Gradually, however, as the years passed, it came to have a less prominent place in Paul's teaching, as the hope of the second coming became more and more transmuted into the almost equally consolatory doctrine of personal immortality.

The Letters of PAUL

TO THE THESSALONIANS. I

Unto the church of the Thessalonians which is in God the Father and in the Lord Jesus Christ:

Grace be unto you, and peace, from God our Father, and the Lord Jesus Christ.

WE GIVE THANKS to God always for you all, making mention of you in our prayers; remembering without ceasing your work of faith, and labour of love, and patience of hope in our Lord Jesus Christ, in the sight of God and our Father; knowing, brethren beloved, your election of God. For our gospel came not unto you in word only, but also in power, and in the Holy Ghost, and in much assurance; as ye know what manner of men we were among you for your sake. And ye became followers of us, and of the Lord, having received the word in much affliction, with joy of the Holy Ghost: so that ye were examples to all that believe in Macedonia and Achaia. For from you sounded out the word of the Lord not only in Macedonia and Achaia, but also in every place your faith to God-ward is spread abroad; so that we need not to speak any thing. For they themselves show of us what manner of entering in we had unto you, and how ye turned to God from idols to serve the living and true God; and to wait for his Son from heaven, whom he raised from the dead, even Jesus, which delivered us from the wrath to come.

For yourselves, brethren, know our entrance in unto you, that it was not in vain: but even after that we had suffered before, and were shamefully entreated, as ye know, at Philippi, we

THE LETTERS OF PAUL

were bold in our God to speak unto you the gospel of God with much contention. For our exhortation was not of deceit, nor of uncleanness, nor in guile: but as we were allowed of God to be put in trust with the gospel, even so we speak; not as pleasing men, but God, which trieth our hearts. For neither at any time used we flattering words, as ye know, nor a cloak of covetousness; God is witness: nor of men sought we glory, neither of you, nor yet of others, when we might have been burdensome, as the apostles of Christ. But we were gentle among you, even as a nurse cherisheth her children: so being affectionately desirous of you, we were willing to have imparted unto you, not the gospel of God only, but also our own souls, because ye were dear unto us. For ye remember, brethren, our labour and travail: for labouring night and day, because we would not be chargeable unto any of you, we preached unto you the gospel of God. Ye are witnesses, and God also, how holily and justly and unblameably we behaved ourselves among you that believe: as ye know how we exhorted and comforted and charged every one of you, as a father doth his children, that ye would walk worthy of God, who hath called you unto his kingdom and glory. For this cause also thank we God without ceasing, because, when ye received the word of God which ye heard of us, ye received it not as the word of men, but as it is in truth, the word of God, which effectually worketh also in you that believe. For ye, brethren, became followers of the churches of God which in Judæa are in Christ Jesus: for ye also have suffered like things of your own countrymen, even as they have of the Jews: who both killed the Lord Jesus, and their own prophets, and have persecuted us; and they please not God, and are contrary to all men, forbidding us to speak to the Gentiles that they might be saved, to fill up their sins always: for the wrath is come upon them to the uttermost.

But we, brethren, being taken from you for a short time in presence, not in heart, endeavoured the more abundantly to see your face with great desire. Wherefore we would have come unto you, even I Paul, once and again; but Satan hindered us.

THE LETTERS OF PAUL

For what is our hope, or joy, or crown of rejoicing? Are not even ye in the presence of our Lord Jesus Christ at his coming? For ye are our glory and joy.

Wherefore when we could no longer forbear, we thought it good to be left at Athens alone; and sent Timotheus, our brother, and minister of God, and our fellowlabourer in the gospel of Christ, to establish you, and to comfort you concerning your faith: that no man should be moved by these afflictions: for yourselves know that we are appointed thereunto. For verily, when we were with you, we told you before that we should suffer tribulation; even as it came to pass, and ye know. For this cause, when I could no longer forbear, I sent to know your faith, lest by some means the tempter have tempted you, and our labour be in vain. But now when Timotheus came from you unto us, and brought us good tidings of your faith and charity, and that ye have good remembrance of us always, desiring greatly to see us, as we also to see you: therefore, brethren, we were comforted over you in all our affliction and distress by your faith: for now we live, if ye stand fast in the Lord. For what thanks can we render to God again for you, for all the joy wherewith we joy for your sakes before our God, night and day praying exceedingly that we might see your face, and might perfect that which is lacking in your faith?

Now God himself and our Father, and our Lord Jesus Christ, direct our way unto you. And the Lord make you to increase and abound in love one toward another, and toward all men, even as we do toward you, to the end he may establish your hearts unblamable in holiness before God, even our Father, at the coming of our Lord Jesus Christ with all his saints. Furthermore then we beseech you, brethren, and exhort you by the Lord Jesus, that as ye have received of us how ye ought to walk and to please God, so ye would abound more and more. For ye know what commandments we gave you by the Lord Jesus. For this is the will of God, even your sanctification, that ye should abstain from fornication; that every one of you should know how to possess his vessel in sanctification and honour, not in the lust of concupiscence, even as the Gentiles which know not God; that no man go beyond and defraud his brother in any matter: because that the Lord is the avenger of all such, as we also have forewarned you and testified. For God hath not called us unto uncleanness, but unto holiness. He therefore that despiseth, despiseth not man, but God, who hath also given unto us his holy Spirit.

But as touching brotherly love ye need not that I write unto you: for ye yourselves are taught of God to love one another. And indeed ye do it toward all the brethren which are in all Macedonia: but we beseech you, brethren, that ye increase more and more, and that ye study to be quiet, and to do your own business, and to work with your own hands, as we commanded you; that ye may walk honestly toward them that are without, and that ye may have lack of nothing.

But I would not have you to be ignorant, brethren, concerning them which are asleep, that ye sorrow not, even as others which have no hope. For if we believe that Jesus died and rose again, even so them also which sleep in Jesus will God bring with him. For this we say unto you by the word of the Lord, that we which are alive and remain unto the coming of the Lord shall not prevent them which are asleep. For the Lord himself shall descend from heaven with a shout, with the voice of the archangel, and with the trump of God: and the dead in Christ shall rise first. Then we which are alive and remain shall be caught up together with them in the clouds, to meet the Lord in the air: and so shall we ever be with the Lord. Wherefore comfort one another with these words.

But of the times and the seasons, brethren, ye have no need that I write unto you. For yourselves know perfectly that the day of the Lord so cometh as a thief in the night. For when they shall say, "Peace and safety"; then sudden destruction cometh upon them, as travail upon a woman with child; and they shall not escape. But ye, brethren, are not in darkness, that that day should overtake you as a thief. Ye are all the children of light, and the children of the day: we are not of the night, nor of dark-

THE LETTERS OF PAUL

ness. Therefore let us not sleep, as do others; but let us watch and be sober. For they that sleep sleep in the night; and they that be drunken are drunken in the night. But let us, who are of the day, be sober, putting on the breastplate of faith and love; and for a helmet, the hope of salvation. For God hath not appointed us to wrath, but to obtain salvation by our Lord Jesus Christ, who died for us, that, whether we wake or sleep, we should live together with him. Wherefore comfort yourselves together, and edify one another, even as also ye do.

And we beseech you, brethren, to know them which labour among you, and are over you in the Lord, and admonish you; and to esteem them very highly in love for their work's sake. And be at peace among yourselves. Now we exhort you, brethren, warn them that are unruly, comfort the feebleminded, support the weak, be patient toward all men. See that none render evil for evil unto any man; but ever follow that which is good, both among yourselves, and to all men. Rejoice evermore. Pray without ceasing. In every thing give thanks: for this is the will of God in Christ Jesus concerning you. Quench not the Spirit. Despise not prophesyings. Prove all things; hold fast that which is good. Abstain from all appearance of evil. And the very God of peace sanctify you wholly; and I pray God your whole spirit and soul and body be preserved blameless unto the coming of our Lord Jesus Christ. Faithful is he that calleth you, who also will do it. Brethren, pray for us. Greet all the brethren with a holy kiss. I charge you by the Lord that this epistle be read unto all the holy brethren. The grace of our Lord Jesus Christ be with you. Amen.

PAUL, AND SILVANUS, AND TIMOTHEUS

ATHENS

THE LETTERS OF PAUL: TO THE THESSALONIANS. II

IN HIS SECOND LETTER to the Thessalonians, Paul went further into the question of the second coming and showed that it could not already have occurred, as some contended, because according to the teachings of Jesus, as these were traditionally understood, it must be preceded by the reign of Antichrist who had not yet appeared. The discussion is interesting as a revelation of the dogmatic and doctrinal character intrinsic in Paul's Christianity tending somewhat to neutralize its strong ethical bent and liberal spirit.

The Letters of PAUL

TO THE THESSALONIANS. II

Unto the church of the Thessalonians in God our Father and the Lord Jesus Christ:

Grace unto you, and peace, from God our Father and the Lord Jesus Christ.

WE ARE BOUND to thank God always for you, brethren, as it is meet, because that your faith groweth exceedingly, and the charity of every one of you all toward each other aboundeth, so that we ourselves glory in you in the churches of God for your patience and faith in all your persecutions and tribulations that ye endure: which is a manifest token of the righteous judgment of God, that ye may be counted worthy of the kingdom of God, for which ye also suffer: seeing it is a righteous thing with God to recompense tribulation to them that trouble you, and to you who are troubled rest with us, when the Lord Jesus shall be revealed from heaven with his mighty angels, in flaming fire taking vengeance on them that know not God, and that obey not the gospel of our Lord Jesus Christ: who shall be punished with everlasting destruction from the presence of the Lord, and from the glory of his power, when he shall come to be glorified in his saints, and to be admired in all them that believe (because our testimony among you was believed) in that day. Wherefore also we pray always for you, that our God would count you worthy of this calling, and fulfil all the good pleasure of his goodness, and the work of faith with power, that the name of our Lord Jesus Christ may be glorified in you, and ye in

THE LETTERS OF PAUL

him, according to the grace of our God and the Lord Jesus Christ.

Now we beseech you, brethren, by the coming of our Lord Jesus Christ, and by our gathering together unto him, that ye be not soon shaken in mind, or be troubled, neither by spirit, nor by word, nor by letter as from us, as that the day of Christ is at hand. Let no man deceive you by any means: for that day shall not come, except there come a falling away first, and that man of sin be revealed, the son of perdition, who opposeth and exalteth himself above all that is called God, or that is worshipped; so that he as God sitteth in the temple of God, showing himself that he is God. Remember ye not that, when I was yet with you, I told you these things? And now ye know what withholdeth that he might be revealed in his time. For the mystery of iniquity doth already work: only he who now letteth will let, until he be taken out of the way. And then shall that Wicked be revealed, whom the Lord shall consume with the spirit of his mouth, and shall destroy with the brightness of his coming: even him, whose coming is after the working of Satan with all power and signs and lying wonders, and with all deceivableness of unrighteousness in them that perish; because they received not the love of the truth, that they might be saved. And for this cause God shall send them strong delusion, that they should believe a lie: that they all might be damned who believed not the truth, but had pleasure in unrighteousness.

But we are bound to give thanks alway to God for you, brethren beloved of the Lord, because God hath from the beginning chosen you to salvation through sanctification of the Spirit and belief of the truth: whereunto he called you by our gospel, to the obtaining of the glory of our Lord Jesus Christ. Therefore, brethren, stand fast, and hold the traditions which ye have been taught, whether by word, or our epistle. Now our Lord Jesus Christ himself, and God, even our Father, which hath loved us, and hath given us everlasting consolation and good hope through grace, comfort your hearts, and establish you in every good word and work.

THE LETTERS OF PAUL

The salutation of Paul with mine own hand, which is the token in every epistle: so I write. The grace of our Lord Jesus Christ be with you all. Amen.

PAUL, AND SILVANUS, AND TIMOTHEUS

ATHENS

THE LETTERS OF PAUL: TO THE GALATIANS

PAUL'S LIBERALISM *appears at its best in his letter to the Galatians, termed by Professor Edgar J. Goodspeed "a charter of religious freedom." Its immediate occasion was the backsliding of the churches founded by him in the cities of Galatia which under the influence of other teachers had reverted to a narrow Judaizing insistence upon the ceremonial side of the Mosaic law. Paul realized clearly that this tendency, if allowed to develop, would make Christianity into a local Jewish heresy instead of the world religion which he conceived it to be. Hence the energy of his denunciation, rivaling the utterance of the Old Testament prophets in its contempt for empty forms and ritual.*

TO THE GALATIANS

Paul, an apostle (not of men, neither by man, but by Jesus Christ, and God the Father, who raised him from the dead); and all the brethren which are with me,

Unto the churches of Galatia:

Grace be to you and peace from God the Father, and from our Lord Jesus Christ, who gave himself for our sins, that he might deliver us from this present evil world, according to the will of God and our Father: to whom be glory for ever and ever. Amen.

I MARVEL THAT YE ARE SO soon removed from him that called you into the grace of Christ unto another gospel: which is not another; but there be some that trouble you, and would pervert the gospel of Christ. But though we, or an angel from heaven, preach any other gospel unto you than that which we have preached unto you, let him be accursed. As we said before, so say I now again, "If any man preach any other gospel unto you than that ye have received, let him be accursed." For do I now persuade men, or God? or do I seek to please men? for if I yet pleased men, I should not be the servant of Christ. But I certify you, brethren, that the gospel which was preached of me is not after man. For I neither received it of man, neither was I taught it, but by the revelation of Jesus Christ.

For ye have heard of my conversation in time past in the Jews' religion, how that beyond measure I persecuted the church of God, and wasted it: and profited in the Jews' religion above many my equals in mine own nation, being more exceedingly zealous of the traditions of my fathers. But when it pleased God, who separated me from my mother's womb, and called me by his grace, to reveal his Son in me, that I might preach him among the heathen; immediately I conferred not with flesh and blood: neither went I up to Jerusalem to them which were apostles before me; but I went into Arabia, and returned again unto Damascus. Then after three years I went up to Jerusalem to see Peter, and abode with him fifteen days. But other of the apostles saw I none, save James the Lord's brother. Now the things which I write unto you, behold, before God, I lie not. Afterwards I came into the regions of Syria and Cilicia; and was unknown by face unto the churches of Judæa which were in Christ: but they had heard only that he which persecuted us in times past now preacheth the faith which once he destroyed. And they glorified God in me.

Then fourteen years after I went up again to Jerusalem with Barnabas, and took Titus with me also. And I went up by revelation, and communicated unto them that gospel which I preach among the Gentiles, but privately to them which were of reputation, lest by any means I should run, or had run, in vain. But neither Titus, who was with me, being a Greek, was compelled to be circumcised: and that because of false brethren unawares brought in, who came in privily to spy out our liberty which we have in Christ Jesus, that they might bring us into bondage: to whom we gave place by subjection, no, not for an hour; that the truth of the gospel might continue with you. But of these who seemed to be somewhat (whatsoever they were, it maketh no matter to me: God accepteth no man's person): for they who seemed to be somewhat in conference added nothing to me: but contrariwise, when they saw that the gospel of the uncircumcision was committed unto me, as the gospel of the circumcision was unto Peter (for he that wrought effectually in Peter to the apostleship of the circumcision, the same was mighty in me toward the Gentiles): and when James, Cephas, and John, who seemed to be pillars, perceived the grace that was given unto me, they gave to me and Barnabas the right hands of fellowship; that we should go unto the heathen, and they unto the circumcision. Only they would that we should remember the poor; the same which I also was forward to do.

But when Peter was come to Antioch, I withstood him to the face, because he was to be blamed. For before that certain came from James, he did eat with the Gentiles: but when they were come, he withdrew and separated himself, fearing them which were of the circumcision. And the other Jews dissembled likewise with him; insomuch that Barnabas also was carried away with their dissimulation. But when I saw that they walked not uprightly according to the truth of the gospel, I said unto Peter before them all, "If thou, being a Jew, livest after the manner of Gentiles, and not as do the Jews, why compellest thou the Gentiles to live as do the Jews?"

We who are Jews by nature, and not sinners of the Gentiles, knowing that a man is not justified by the works of the law, but by the faith of Jesus Christ, even we have believed in Jesus Christ, that we might be justified by the faith of Christ, and not by the works of the law: for by the works of the law shall no flesh be justified. But if, while we seek to be justified by Christ, we ourselves also are found sinners, is therefore Christ the minister of sin? God forbid. For if I build again the things which I destroyed, I make myself a transgressor. For I through the law am dead to the law, that I might live unto God. I am crucified with Christ: nevertheless I live; yet not I, but Christ liveth in me: and the life which I now live in the flesh I live by the faith of the Son of God, who loved me, and gave himself for me. I do not frustrate the grace of God: for if righteousness come by the law, then Christ is dead in vain.

O foolish Galatians, who hath bewitched you, that ye should not obey the truth, before whose eyes Jesus Christ hath been evidently set forth, crucified among you? This only would I learn of you: received ye the Spirit by the works of the law, or by

THE LETTERS OF PAUL

the hearing of faith? Are ye so foolish? having begun in the Spirit, are ye now made perfect by the flesh? Have ye suffered so many things in vain? if it be yet in vain. He therefore that ministereth to you the Spirit, and worketh miracles among you, doeth he it by the works of the law, or by the hearing of faith?

Even as Abraham believed God, and it was accounted to him for righteousness. Know ye therefore that they which are of faith, the same are the children of Abraham. And the scripture, foreseeing that God would justify the heathen through faith, preached before the gospel unto Abraham, saying, "In thee shall all nations be blessed." So then they which be of faith are blessed with faithful Abraham. Now to Abraham and his seed were the promises made. He saith not, "And to seeds," as of many; but as of one, "And to thy seed," which is Christ. And this I say, that the covenant, that was confirmed before of God in Christ, the law, which was four hundred and thirty years after, cannot disannul, that it should make the promise of none effect. For if the inheritance be of the law, it is no more of promise: but God gave it to Abraham by promise.

But before faith came, we were kept under the law, shut up unto the faith which should afterwards be revealed. Wherefore the law was our schoolmaster to bring us unto Christ, that we might be justified by faith. But after that faith is come, we are no longer under a schoolmaster.

For ye are all the children of God by faith in Christ Jesus. For as many of you as have been baptized into Christ have put on Christ. There is neither "Jew" nor "Greek," there is neither "bond" nor "free," there is neither "male" nor "female": for ye are all one in Christ Jesus. And if ye be Christ's, then are ye Abraham's seed, and heirs according to the promise.

For it is written that Abraham had two sons, the one by a bondmaid, the other by a freewoman. But he who was of the bondwoman was born after the flesh; but he of the freewoman was by promise. Which things are an allegory: for these are the two covenants; the one from the Mount Sinai, which gendereth

THE LETTERS OF PAUL

to bondage, which is Agar. For this Agar is Mount Sinai in Arabia, and answereth to Jerusalem which now is, and is in bondage with her children. But Jerusalem which is above is free, which is the mother of us all. For it is written,

> "Rejoice, thou barren that bearest not;
> Break forth and cry, thou that travailest not:
> For the desolate hath many more children than she
> which hath a husband."

Now we, brethren, as Isaac was, are the children of promise. But as then he that was born after the flesh persecuted him that was born after the Spirit, even so it is now. Nevertheless what saith the scripture? Cast out the bondwoman and her son: for the son of the bondwoman shall not be heir with the son of the freewoman. So then, brethren, we are not children of the bondwoman, but of the free.

For, brethren, ye have been called unto liberty; only use not liberty for an occasion to the flesh, but by love serve one another. For all the law is fulfilled in one word, even in this: "Thou shalt love thy neighbour as thyself." But if ye bite and devour one another, take heed that ye be not consumed one of another.

This I say then: walk in the Spirit, and ye shall not fulfil the lust of the flesh. For the flesh lusteth against the Spirit, and the Spirit against the flesh: and these are contrary the one to the other: so that ye cannot do the things that ye would. But if ye be led of the Spirit, ye are not under the law.

Now the works of the flesh are manifest, which are these: adultery, fornication, uncleanness, lasciviousness, idolatry, witchcraft, hatred, variance, emulations, wrath, strife, seditions, heresies, envyings, murders, drunkenness, revellings, and such like: of the which I tell you before, as I have also told you in time past, that they which do such things shall not inherit the kingdom of God.

THE LETTERS OF PAUL

But the fruit of the Spirit is love, joy, peace, longsuffering, gentleness, goodness, faith, meekness, temperance: against such there is no law. And they that are Christ's have crucified the flesh with the affections and lusts. If we live in the Spirit, let us also walk in the Spirit. Let us not be desirous of vain glory, provoking one another, envying one another.

Brethren, if a man be overtaken in a fault, ye which are spiritual, restore such a one in the spirit of meekness; considering thyself, lest thou also be tempted. Bear ye one another's burdens, and so fulfil the law of Christ. For if a man think himself to be something, when he is nothing, he deceiveth himself. But let every man prove his own work, and then shall he have rejoicing in himself alone, and not in another. For every man shall bear his own burden. Let him that is taught in the word communicate unto him that teacheth in all good things. Be not deceived; God is not mocked: for whatsoever a man soweth, that shall he also reap. For he that soweth to his flesh shall of the flesh reap corruption; but he that soweth to the Spirit shall of the Spirit reap life everlasting. And let us not be weary in well doing: for in due season we shall reap, if we faint not. As we have therefore opportunity, let us do good unto all men, especially unto them who are of the household of faith.

Ye see how large a letter I have written unto you with mine own hand. As many as desire to make a fair show in the flesh, they constrain you to be circumcised; only lest they should suffer persecution for the cross of Christ. For neither they themselves who are circumcised keep the law; but desire to have you circumcised, that they may glory in your flesh. But God forbid that I should glory, save in the cross of our Lord Jesus Christ, by whom the world is crucified unto me, and I unto the world. For in Christ Jesus neither circumcision availeth any thing, nor uncircumcision, but a new creature. And as many as walk according to this rule, peace be on them, and mercy, and upon the Israel of God. From henceforth let no man trouble me: for I bear in my body the marks of the Lord Jesus.

THE LETTERS OF PAUL

Brethren, the grace of our Lord Jesus Christ be with your spirit. Amen.

P AUL, AN APOSTLE (NOT OF MEN, NEITHER BY MAN, BUT BY JESUS CHRIST; AND GOD THE FATHER, WHO RAISED HIM FROM THE DEAD), AND ALL THE BRETHREN WHO ARE WITH ME

ROME

THE LETTERS OF PAUL: TO THE CORINTHIANS. I

First corinthians, *probably preceded by an earlier letter, contains the best formulation and noblest expression of Paul's ethics. It was written in answer to a detailed list of questions sent to him by the perplexed members of the Church in Corinth. Besides meeting the specific problems raised, Paul set forth the general nature of the social obligations involved and the pragmatic character of all conduct. Only in his treatment of women did the ascetic strain inseparable from the mystic element in him interfere seriously with the rationality of his outlook.*

The Letters of PAUL

TO THE CORINTHIANS. I

Unto the Church of God which is at Corinth, to them that are sanctified in Christ Jesus, called to be saints, with all that in every place call upon the name of Jesus Christ our Lord, both theirs and ours:

Grace be unto you, and peace, from God our Father, and from the Lord Jesus Christ. I thank my God always on your behalf, for the grace of God which is given you by Jesus Christ; that in every thing ye are enriched by him, in all utterance, and in all knowledge; even as the testimony of Christ was confirmed in you: so that ye come behind in no gift; waiting for the coming of our Lord Jesus Christ: who shall also confirm you unto the end, that ye may be blameless in the day of our Lord Jesus Christ. God is faithful, by whom ye were called unto the fellowship of his Son Jesus Christ our Lord.

Now I beseech you, brethren, by the name of our Lord Jesus Christ, that ye all speak the same thing, and that there be no divisions among you; but that ye be perfectly joined together in the same mind and in the same judgment. For it hath been declared unto me of you, my brethren, by them which are of the house of Chloe, that there are contentions among you. Now this I say, that every one of you saith, "I am of Paul"; and "I of Apollos"; and "I of Cephas"; and "I of Christ." Is Christ divided? was Paul crucified for you? or were ye baptized in the name of Paul? I thank God that I baptized none of you, but Crispus and Gaius; lest any should say that I had baptized in mine own name. And I baptized also the household of Stephanas: besides,

THE LETTERS OF PAUL

I know not whether I baptized any other. For Christ sent me not to baptize, but to preach the gospel: not with wisdom of words, lest the cross of Christ should be made of none effect.

For the preaching of the cross is to them that perish foolishness; but unto us which are saved it is the power of God. For it is written,

> "I will destroy the wisdom of the wise,
> And will bring to nothing the understanding of the prudent."

Where is the wise? where is the scribe? where is the disputer of this world? hath not God made foolish the wisdom of this world? For after that in the wisdom of God the world by wisdom knew not God, it pleased God by the foolishness of preaching to save them that believe. For the Jews require a sign, and the Greeks seek after wisdom: but we preach Christ crucified, unto the Jews a stumblingblock, and unto the Greeks foolishness; but unto them which are called, both Jews and Greeks, Christ the power of God, and the wisdom of God. Because the foolishness of God is wiser than men; and the weakness of God is stronger than men.

For ye see your calling, brethren, how that not many wise men after the flesh, not many mighty, not many noble, are called: but God hath chosen the foolish things of the world to confound the wise; and God hath chosen the weak things of the world to confound the things which are mighty. And base things of the world, and things which are despised, hath God chosen, yea, and things which are not, to bring to nought things that are: that no flesh should glory in his presence. But of him are ye in Christ Jesus, who of God is made unto us wisdom, and righteousness, and sanctification, and redemption: that, according as it is written, "He that glorieth, let him glory in the Lord."

And I, brethren, when I came to you, came not with excellency of speech or of wisdom, declaring unto you the testimony of God. For I determined not to know any thing among you, save Jesus Christ, and him crucified. And I was with you in weakness, and in fear, and in much trembling. And my speech

THE LETTERS OF PAUL

and my preaching was not with enticing words of man's wisdom, but in demonstration of the Spirit and of power: that your faith should not stand in the wisdom of men, but in the power of God.

Howbeit we speak wisdom among them that are perfect: yet not the wisdom of this world, nor of the princes of this world, that come to nought: but we speak the wisdom of God in a mystery, even the hidden wisdom, which God ordained before the world unto our glory, which none of the princes of this world knew: for had they known it, they would not have crucified the Lord of glory. But as it is written,

> "*Eye hath not seen, nor ear heard,*
> *Neither have entered into the heart of man,*
> *The things which God hath prepared for them that love him.*"

But God hath revealed them unto us by his Spirit: for the Spirit searcheth all things, yea, the deep things of God. For what man knoweth the things of a man, save the spirit of man which is in him? even so the things of God knoweth no man, but the Spirit of God. Now we have received, not the spirit of the world, but the spirit which is of God; that we might know the things that are freely given to us of God. Which things also we speak, not in the words which man's wisdom teacheth, but which the Holy Ghost teacheth; comparing spiritual things with spiritual. But the natural man receiveth not the things of the Spirit of God: for they are foolishness unto him: neither can he know them, because they are spiritually discerned. But he that is spiritual judgeth all things, yet he himself is judged of no man. For who hath known the mind of the Lord, that he may instruct him? But we have the mind of Christ.

And I, brethren, could not speak unto you as unto spiritual, but as unto carnal, even as unto babes in Christ. I have fed you with milk, and not with meat: for hitherto ye were not able to bear it, neither yet now are ye able. For ye are yet carnal: for whereas there is among you envying, and strife, and divisions, are ye not carnal, and walk as men? For while one saith, "I am of

Paul"; and another, "I am of Apollos"; are ye not carnal? Who then is Paul, and who is Apollos, but ministers by whom ye believed, even as the Lord gave to every man? I have planted, Apollos watered; but God gave the increase. So then neither is he that planteth any thing, neither he that watereth; but God that giveth the increase. Now he that planteth and he that watereth are one: and every man shall receive his own reward according to his own labour.

For we are labourers together with God: ye are God's husbandry, ye are God's building. According to the grace of God which is given unto me, as a wise masterbuilder, I have laid the foundation, and another buildeth thereon. But let every man take heed how he buildeth thereupon. For other foundation can no man lay than that is laid, which is Jesus Christ. Now if any man build upon this foundation gold, silver, precious stones, wood, hay, stubble; every man's work shall be made manifest: for the day shall declare it, because it shall be revealed by fire; and the fire shall try every man's work of what sort it is. If any man's work abide which he hath built thereupon, he shall receive a reward. If any man's work shall be burned, he shall suffer loss: but he himself shall be saved; yet so as by fire.

Know ye not that ye are the temple of God, and that the Spirit of God dwelleth in you? If any man defile the temple of God, him shall God destroy; for the temple of God is holy, which temple ye are.

Let no man deceive himself. If any man among you seemeth to be wise in this world, let him become a fool, that he may be wise. For the wisdom of this world is foolishness with God. For it is written, "He taketh the wise in their own craftiness." And again, "The Lord knoweth the thoughts of the wise, that they are vain."

Therefore let no man glory in men. For all things are yours; whether Paul, or Apollos, or Cephas, or the world, or life, or death, or things present, or things to come; all are yours; and ye are Christ's; and Christ is God's.

Now concerning the things whereof ye wrote unto me: it is

good for a man not to touch a woman. Nevertheless, to avoid fornication, let every man have his own wife, and let every woman have her own husband. Let the husband render unto the wife due benevolence: and likewise also the wife unto the husband. The wife hath not power of her own body, but the husband: and likewise also the husband hath not power of his own body, but the wife. Defraud ye not one the other, except it be with consent for a time, that ye may give yourselves to fasting and prayer; and come together again, that Satan tempt you not for your incontinency.

But I speak this by permission, and not of commandment. For I would that all men were even as I myself. But every man hath his proper gift of God, one after this manner, and another after that.

I say therefore to the unmarried and widows, it is good for them if they abide even as I. But if they cannot contain, let them marry: for it is better to marry than to burn.

And unto the married I command, yet not I, but the Lord, let not the wife depart from her husband: but and if she depart, let her remain unmarried, or be reconciled to her husband: and let not the husband put away his wife.

But to the rest speak I, not the Lord: if any brother hath a wife that believeth not, and she be pleased to dwell with him, let him not put her away. And the woman which hath a husband that believeth not, and if he be pleased to dwell with her, let her not leave him. For the unbelieving husband is sanctified by the wife, and the unbelieving wife is sanctified by the husband: else were your children unclean; but now are they holy. But if the unbelieving depart, let him depart. A brother or a sister is not under bondage in such cases: but God hath called us to peace. For what knowest thou, O wife, whether thou shalt save thy husband? or how knowest thou, O man, whether thou shalt save thy wife?

But as God hath distributed to every man, as the Lord hath called every one, so let him walk. And so ordain I in all churches. Is any man called being circumcised? let him not become uncircumcised. Is any called in uncircumcision? let him not be circumcised. Circumcision is nothing, and uncircumcision is nothing, but the keeping of the commandments of God. Let every man abide in the same calling wherein he was called. Art thou called being a servant? care not for it: but if thou mayest be made free, use it rather. For he that is called in the Lord, being a servant, is the Lord's freeman: likewise also he that is called, being free, is Christ's servant. Ye are bought with a price; be not ye the servants of men. Brethren, let every man, wherein he is called, therein abide with God.

Now concerning virgins I have no commandment of the Lord: yet I give my judgment, as one that hath obtained mercy of the Lord to be faithful. I suppose therefore that this is good for the present distress, I say, that it is good for a man so to be. Art thou bound unto a wife? seek not to be loosed. Art thou loosed from a wife? seek not a wife. But and if thou marry, thou hast not sinned; and if a virgin marry, she hath not sinned. Nevertheless such shall have trouble in the flesh: but I spare you.

But this I say, brethren, the time is short: it remaineth, that both they that have wives be as though they had none; and they that weep, as though they wept not; and they that rejoice, as though they rejoiced not; and they that buy, as though they possessed not; and they that use this world, as not abusing it: for the fashion of this world passeth away.

But I would have you without carefulness. He that is unmarried careth for the things that belong to the Lord, how he may please the Lord: but he that is married careth for the things that are of the world, how he may please his wife. There is difference also between a wife and a virgin. The unmarried woman careth for the things of the Lord, that she may be holy both in body and in spirit: but she that is married careth for the things of the world, how she may please her husband. And this I speak for your own profit; not that I may cast a snare upon you, but for that which is comely, and that ye may attend upon the Lord without distraction. But if any man think that he behaveth himself uncomely toward his virgin, if she pass the flower of her age, and need so require, let him do what he will, he sinneth not: let them marry. Nevertheless he that standeth steadfast in his heart, having no necessity, but hath power over his own will, and hath so decreed in his heart that he will keep his virgin, doeth well. So then he that giveth her in marriage doeth well; but he that giveth her not in marriage doeth better. The wife is bound by the law as long as her husband liveth; but if her husband be dead, she is at liberty to be married to whom she will; only in the Lord. But she is happier if she so abide, after my judgment: and I think also that I have the Spirit of God.

Now as touching things offered unto idols, we know that we all have knowledge. Knowledge puffeth up, but charity edifieth. And if any man think that he knoweth any thing, he knoweth nothing yet as he ought to know. But if any man love God, the same is known of him. As concerning therefore the eating of those things that are offered in sacrifice unto idols, we know that an idol is nothing in the world, and that there is none other God but one. For though there be that are called gods, whether in heaven or in earth (as there be gods many, and lords many), but to us there is but one God, the Father, of whom are all things, and we in him; and one Lord Jesus Christ, by whom are all things, and we by him. Howbeit there is not in every man that knowledge: for some with conscience of the idol unto this hour eat it as a thing offered unto an idol; and their conscience being weak is defiled. But meat commendeth us not to God: for neither, if we eat, are we the better; neither, if we eat not, are we the worse. But take heed lest by any means this liberty of yours become a stumblingblock to them that are weak. For if any man see thee which hast knowledge sit at meat in the idol's temple, shall not the conscience of him which is weak be emboldened to eat those things which are offered to idols; and through thy knowledge shall the weak brother perish, for whom Christ died? But when ye sin so against the brethren, and wound their weak conscience, ye sin against Christ. Wherefore, if meat make my brother to offend, I will eat no flesh while the world standeth, lest I make my brother to offend.

Though I preach the gospel, I have nothing to glory of: for necessity is laid upon me; yea, woe is unto me, if I preach not the gospel! For if I do this thing willingly, I have a reward: but if against my will, a dispensation of the gospel is committed unto me. What is my reward then? Verily that, when I preach the gospel, I may make the gospel of Christ without charge, that I abuse not my power in the gospel. For though I be free from all men, yet have I made myself servant unto all, that I might gain the more. And unto the Jews I became as a Jew, that I might gain the Jews; to them that are under the law, as under the law, that I might gain them that are under the law; to them that are without law, as without law (being not without law to God, but under the law to Christ), that I might gain them that are without law. To the weak became I as weak, that I might gain the weak: I am made all things to all men, that I might by all means save some. And this I do for the gospel's sake, that I might be partaker thereof with you.

Know ye not that they which run in a race run all, but one receiveth the prize? So run, that ye may obtain. And every man that striveth for the mastery is temperate in all things. Now they do it to obtain a corruptible crown; but we an incorruptible. I therefore so run, not as uncertainly; so fight I, not as one that beateth the air: but I keep under my body, and bring it into subjection: lest that by any means, when I have preached to others, I myself should be a castaway.

But I would have you know, that the head of every man is Christ; and the head of the woman is the man; and the head of Christ is God. Every man praying or prophesying, having his head covered, dishonoureth his head. But every woman that prayeth or prophesieth with her head uncovered dishonoureth her head: for that is even all one as if she were shaven. For if the woman be not covered, let her also be shorn: but if it be a shame for a woman to be shorn or shaven, let her be covered. For a man indeed ought not to cover his head, forasmuch as he is the image and glory of God: but the woman is the glory of the man. For the man is not of the woman; but the woman of the man. Neither was the man created for the woman; but the woman for the man. For this cause ought the woman to have power on her head because of the angels. Nevertheless neither is the man without the woman, neither the woman without the man, in the Lord. For as the woman is of the man, even so is the man also by the woman; but all things of God. Judge in yourselves: is it comely that a woman pray unto God uncovered? Doth not even nature itself teach you, that, if a man have long hair, it is a shame unto him? But if a woman have long hair, it is a glory to her: for her hair is given her for a covering.

Now in this that I declare unto you I praise you not, that ye come together not for the better, but for the worse. For first of all, when ye come together in the church, I hear that there be divisions among you; and I partly believe it. For there must be also heresies among you, that they which are approved may be made manifest among you.

When ye come together therefore into one place, this is not to eat the Lord's supper. For in eating every one taketh before other his own supper: and one is hungry, and another is drunken. What? have ye not houses to eat and to drink in? or despise ye the church of God, and shame them that have not? What shall I say to you? shall I praise you in this? I praise you not.

For I have received of the Lord that which also I delivered unto you, that the Lord Jesus the same night in which he was betrayed took bread: and when he had given thanks, he broke it and said, "Take, eat: this is my body, which is broken for you: this do in remembrance of me." After the same manner also he took the cup, when he had supped, saying, "This cup is the new testament in my blood: this do ye, as oft as ye drink it, in remembrance of me." For as often as ye eat this bread, and drink this

THE LETTERS OF PAUL

cup, ye do show the Lord's death till he come. Wherefore whosoever shall eat this bread, and drink this cup of the Lord, unworthily, shall be guilty of the body and blood of the Lord. But let a man examine himself, and so let him eat of that bread, and drink of that cup.

Now concerning spiritual gifts, brethren, I would not have you ignorant. Ye know that ye were Gentiles, carried away unto these dumb idols, even as ye were led. Wherefore I give you to understand, that no man speaking by the Spirit of God calleth Jesus accursed: and that no man can say that Jesus is the Lord, but by the Holy Ghost.

Now there are diversities of gifts, but the same Spirit. And there are differences of administrations, but the same Lord. And there are diversities of operations, but it is the same God which worketh all in all. But the manifestation of the Spirit is given to every man to profit withal. For to one is given by the Spirit the word of wisdom; to another the word of knowledge by the same Spirit; to another faith by the same Spirit; to another the gifts of healing by the same Spirit; to another the working of miracles; to another prophecy; to another discerning of spirits; to another divers kinds of tongues; to another the interpretation of tongues: but all these worketh that one and the selfsame Spirit, dividing to every man severally as he will.

For as the body is one, and hath many members, and all the members of that one body, being many, are one body: so also is Christ. For by one Spirit are we all baptized into one body, whether we be Jews or Gentiles, whether we be bond or free; and have been all made to drink into one Spirit. For the body is not one member, but many.

Now ye are the body of Christ, and members in particular. And God hath set some in the church, first apostles, secondarily prophets, thirdly teachers, after that miracles, then gifts of healings, helps, governments, diversities of tongues. Are all apostles? are all prophets? are all teachers? are all workers of miracles? have all the gifts of healing? do all speak with

THE LETTERS OF PAUL

tongues? do all interpret? But covet earnestly the best gifts: and yet show I unto you a more excellent way.

Though I speak with the tongues of men and of angels, and have not charity, I am become as sounding brass, or a tinkling cymbal. And though I have the gift of prophecy, and understand all mysteries, and all knowledge; and though I have all faith, so that I could remove mountains, and have not charity, I am nothing. And though I bestow all my goods to feed the poor, and though I give my body to be burned, and have not charity, it profiteth me nothing. Charity suffereth long, and is kind; charity envieth not; charity vaunteth not itself, is not puffed up, doth not behave itself unseemly, seeketh not her own, is not easily provoked, thinketh no evil; rejoiceth not in iniquity, but rejoiceth in the truth; beareth all things, believeth all things, hopeth all things, endureth all things. Charity never faileth: but whether there be prophecies, they shall fail; whether there be tongues, they shall cease; whether there be knowledge, it shall vanish away. For we know in part, and we prophesy in part. But when that which is perfect is come, then that which is in part shall be done away. When I was a child, I spoke as a child, I understood as a child, I thought as a child: but when I became a man, I put away childish things. For now we see through a glass, darkly; but then face to face: now I know in part; but then shall I know even as also I am known. And now abideth faith, hope, charity, these three; but the greatest of these is charity.

Moreover, brethren, I declare unto you the gospel which I preached unto you, which also ye have received, and wherein ye stand; by which also ye are saved, if ye keep in memory what I preached unto you, unless ye have believed in vain. For I delivered unto you first of all that which I also received, how that Christ died for our sins according to the scriptures; and that he was buried, and that he rose again the third day according to the scriptures: and that he was seen of Cephas, then of the twelve: after that, he was seen of above five hundred brethren

THE LETTERS OF PAUL

at once; of whom the greater part remain unto this present, but some are fallen asleep. After that, he was seen of James; then of all the apostles. And last of all he was seen of me also, as of one born out of due time. For I am the least of the apostles, that am not meet to be called an apostle, because I persecuted the church of God. But by the grace of God I am what I am: and his grace which was bestowed upon me was not in vain; but I laboured more abundantly than they all: yet not I, but the grace of God which was with me. Therefore whether it were I or they, so we preach, and so ye believed.

Now if Christ be preached that he rose from the dead, how say some among you that there is no resurrection of the dead? But if there be no resurrection of the dead, then is Christ not risen: and if Christ be not risen, then is our preaching vain, and your faith is also vain. Yea, and we are found false witnesses of God; because we have testified of God that he raised up Christ: whom he raised not up, if so be that the dead rise not. For if the dead rise not, then is not Christ raised: and if Christ be not raised, your faith is vain; ye are yet in your sins. Then they also which are fallen asleep in Christ are perished. If in this life only we have hope in Christ, we are of all men most miserable.

But now is Christ risen from the dead, and become the firstfruits of them that slept. For since by man came death, by man came also the resurrection of the dead. For as in Adam all die, even so in Christ shall all be made alive. But every man in his own order: Christ the firstfruits; afterward they that are Christ's at his coming. Then cometh the end, when he shall have delivered up the kingdom to God, even the Father; when he shall have put down all rule and all authority and power. For he must reign, till he hath put all enemies under his feet. The last enemy that shall be destroyed is death. For he hath put all things under his feet. But when he saith all things are put under him, it is manifest that he is excepted, which did put all things under him. And when all things shall be subdued unto him, then shall the Son also himself be subject unto him that put all things under him, that God may be all in all.

THE LETTERS OF PAUL

Else what shall they do which are baptized for the dead, if the dead rise not at all? why are they then baptized for the dead? and why stand we in jeopardy every hour? I protest by your rejoicing which I have in Christ Jesus our Lord, I die daily. If after the manner of men I have fought with beasts at Ephesus, what advantageth it me, if the dead rise not? let us eat and drink; for to-morrow we die. Be not deceived: evil communications corrupt good manners. Awake to righteousness, and sin not; for some have not the knowledge of God: I speak this to your shame.

But some man will say, "How are the dead raised up? and with what body do they come?" Thou fool, that which thou sowest is not quickened, except it die: and that which thou sowest, thou sowest not that body that shall be, but bare grain, it may chance of wheat, or of some other grain: but God giveth it a body as it hath pleased him, and to every seed his own body. All flesh is not the same flesh: but there is one kind of flesh of men, another flesh of beasts, another of fishes, and another of birds. There are also celestial bodies, and bodies terrestrial: but the glory of the celestial is one, and the glory of the terrestrial is another. There is one glory of the sun, and another glory of the moon, and another glory of the stars: for one star differeth from another star in glory. So also is the resurrection of the dead. It is sown in corruption; it is raised in incorruption; it is sown in dishonour; it is raised in glory; it is sown in weakness; it is raised in power: it is sown a natural body: it is raised a spiritual body. There is a natural body, and there is a spiritual body. And so it is written, "The first man Adam was made a living soul"; the last Adam was made a quickening spirit. Howbeit that was not first which is spiritual, but that which is natural; and afterward that which is spiritual. The first man is of the earth, earthy: the second man is the Lord from heaven. As is the earthy, such are they also that are earthy: and as is the heavenly, such are they also that are heavenly. And as we have borne the image of the earthy, we shall also bear the image of the heavenly.

Now this I say, brethren, that flesh and blood cannot inherit the kingdom of God; neither doth corruption inherit incorruption. Behold, I show you a mystery; we shall not all sleep, but we shall all be changed, in a moment, in the twinkling of an eye, at the last trump: for the trumpet shall sound, and the dead shall be raised incorruptible, and we shall be changed. For this corruptible must put on incorruption, and this mortal must put on immortality. So when this corruptible shall have put on incorruption, and this mortal shall have put on immortality, then shall be brought to pass the saying that is written, "Death is swallowed up in victory. O death, where is thy sting? O grave, where is thy victory?" The sting of death is sin; and the strength of sin is the law. But thanks be to God, which giveth us the victory through our Lord Jesus Christ. Therefore, my beloved brethren, be ye steadfast, unmovable, always abounding in the work of the Lord, forasmuch as ye know that your labour is not in vain in the Lord.

Now concerning the collection for the saints, as I have given order to the churches of Galatia, even so do ye. Upon the first day of the week let every one of you lay by him in store, as God hath prospered him, that there be no gatherings when I come. And when I come, whomsoever ye shall approve by your letters, them will I send to bring your liberality unto Jerusalem. And if it be meet that I go also, they shall go with me.

Now I will come unto you, when I shall pass through Macedonia: for I do pass through Macedonia. And it may be that I will abide, yea, and winter with you, that ye may bring me on my journey whithersoever I go. For I will not see you now by the way; but I trust to tarry a while with you, if the Lord permit. But I will tarry at Ephesus until Pentecost. For a great door and effectual is opened unto me, and there are many adversaries.

Now if Timotheus come, see that he may be with you without fear: for he worketh the work of the Lord, as I also do. Let no man therefore despise him: but conduct him forth in peace, that he may come unto me: for I look for him with the brethren.

As touching our brother Apollos, I greatly desired him to come unto you with the brethren: but his will was not at all to come at this time; but he will come when he shall have convenient time.

Watch ye, stand fast in the faith, quit you like men, be strong. Let all your things be done with charity.

I beseech you, brethren (ye know the house of Stephanas, that it is the firstfruits of Achaia, and that they have addicted themselves to the ministry of the saints), that ye submit yourselves unto such, and to every one that helpeth with us, and laboureth. I am glad of the coming of Stephanas and Fortunatus and Achaicus: for that which was lacking on your part they have supplied. For they have refreshed my spirit and yours: therefore acknowledge ye them that are such.

The churches of Asia salute you. Aquila and Priscilla salute you much in the Lord, with the church that is in their house. All the brethren greet you. Greet ye one another with a holy kiss.

The salutation of me Paul with mine own hand. If any man love not the Lord Jesus Christ, let him be Anathema Maran-atha. The grace of our Lord Jesus Christ be with you. My love be with you all in Christ Jesus. Amen.

> PAUL, CALLED TO BE AN APOSTLE OF JESUS CHRIST THROUGH THE WILL OF GOD, AND SOSTHENES OUR BROTHER

PHILIPPI

THE LETTERS OF PAUL: TO THE CORINTHIANS. II

In second corinthians two letters are probably combined, both written subsequently to the ethical discourse in First Corinthians. Paul's efforts to rationalize and spiritualize the conduct of his disciples in one of the most corrupt of Greek cities had been quite unsuccessful, resulting merely in the temporary triumph of a group opposed to him. In much bitterness of spirit he composed the personal apologia of chapters 10–13, apparently sent as a separate letter which proved effective in recalling the Corinthians to their allegiance. Later, after receiving this good news, he sent a final letter represented by the earlier chapters of the book.

The turbulent side of Paul's character and its latent fanaticism appear plainly in the letter of self-defense which shows how foreign to his real nature was the attitude of Christian humility which only the sternest discipline enabled him usually to maintain. Its revelation of inner warfare affords the key to his continual emphasis upon the conflict between the spiritual man and the carnal man as the very basis of religious experience.

The Letters of PAUL

TO THE CORINTHIANS. II

Unto the church of God which is at Corinth, with all the saints which are in all Achaia:

Grace be to you and peace from God our Father, and from the Lord Jesus Christ.

Blessed be god, even the Father of our Lord Jesus Christ, the Father of mercies, and the God of all comfort; who comforteth us in all our tribulation, that we may be able to comfort them which are in any trouble, by the comfort wherewith we ourselves are comforted of God. For as the sufferings of Christ abound in us, so our consolation also aboundeth by Christ. And whether we be afflicted, it is for your consolation and salvation, which is effectual in the enduring of the same sufferings which we also suffer: or whether we be comforted, it is for your consolation and salvation. And our hope of you is steadfast, knowing, that as ye are partakers of the sufferings, so shall ye be also of the consolation.

For we would not, brethren, have you ignorant of our trouble which came to us in Asia, that we were pressed out of measure, above strength, insomuch that we despaired even of life: but we had the sentence of death in ourselves, that we should not trust in ourselves, but in God which raiseth the dead, who delivered us from so great a death, and doth deliver: in whom we trust that he will yet deliver us; ye also helping together by prayer for us, that for the gift bestowed upon us by the means of many persons thanks may be given by many on our behalf.

THE LETTERS OF PAUL

For our rejoicing is this, the testimony of our conscience, that in simplicity and godly sincerity, not with fleshly wisdom, but by the grace of God, we have had our conversation in the world, and more abundantly to you-ward. For we write none other things unto you than what ye read or acknowledge; and I trust ye shall acknowledge even to the end; as also ye have acknowledged us in part, that we are your rejoicing, even as ye also are ours in the day of the Lord Jesus.

Now where the Spirit of the Lord is, there is liberty. But we all, with open face beholding as in a glass the glory of the Lord, are changed into the same image from glory to glory, even as by the Spirit of the Lord.

Therefore seeing we have this ministry, as we have received mercy, we faint not; but have renounced the hidden things of dishonesty, not walking in craftiness, nor handling the word of God deceitfully; but by manifestation of the truth commending ourselves to every man's conscience in the sight of God. But if our gospel be hid, it is hid to them that are lost: in whom the god of this world hath blinded the minds of them which believe not, lest the light of the glorious gospel of Christ, who is the image of God, should shine unto them. For we preach not ourselves, but Christ Jesus the Lord; and ourselves your servants for Jesus' sake. For God, who commanded the light to shine out of darkness, hath shined in our hearts, to give the light of the knowledge of the glory of God in the face of Jesus Christ.

But we have this treasure in earthen vessels, that the excellency of the power may be of God, and not of us. We are troubled on every side, yet not distressed; we are perplexed, but not in despair; persecuted, but not forsaken; cast down, but not destroyed; always bearing about in the body the dying of the Lord Jesus, that the life also of Jesus might be made manifest in our body. For we which live are alway delivered unto death for Jesus' sake, that the life also of Jesus might be made manifest in our mortal flesh. So then death worketh in us, but life in you. We having the same spirit of faith, according as it is written,

THE LETTERS OF PAUL

"I believed, and therefore have I spoken"; we also believe, and therefore speak; knowing that he which raised up the Lord Jesus shall raise up us also by Jesus, and shall present us with you. For all things are for your sakes, that the abundant grace might through the thanksgiving of many redound to the glory of God.

For which cause we faint not; but though our outward man perish, yet the inward man is renewed day by day. For our light affliction, which is but for a moment, worketh for us a far more exceeding and eternal weight of glory; while we look not at the things which are seen, but at the things which are not seen: for the things which are seen are temporal; but the things which are not seen are eternal.

Now I Paul myself beseech you by the meekness and gentleness of Christ, who in presence am base among you, but being absent am bold toward you: but I beseech you, that I may not be bold when I am present with that confidence, wherewith I think to be bold against some, which think of us as if we walked according to the flesh. For though we walk in the flesh, we do not war after the flesh (for the weapons of our warfare are not carnal, but mighty through God to the pulling down of strong holds); casting down imaginations, and every high thing that exalteth itself against the knowledge of God, and bringing into captivity every thought to the obedience of Christ; and having in a readiness to revenge all disobedience, when your obedience is fulfilled.

Do ye look on things after the outward appearance? If any man trust to himself that he is Christ's, let him of himself think this again, that, as he is Christ's, even so are we Christ's. For though I should boast somewhat more of our authority, which the Lord hath given us for edification, and not for your destruction, I should not be ashamed: that I may not seem as if I would terrify you by letters. "For his letters," say they, "are weighty and powerful; but his bodily presence is weak, and his speech contemptible." Let such a one think this, that, such as we are in

THE LETTERS OF PAUL

word by letters when we are absent, such will we be also in deed when we are present. For we dare not make ourselves of the number, or compare ourselves with some that commend themselves: but they measuring themselves by themselves, and comparing themselves among themselves, are not wise. But we will not boast of things without our measure, but according to the measure of the rule which God hath distributed to us, a measure to reach even unto you. For we stretch not ourselves beyond our measure, as though we reached not unto you: for we are come as far as to you also in preaching the gospel of Christ: not boasting of things without our measure, that is, of other men's labours; but having hope, when your faith is increased, that we shall be enlarged by you according to our rule abundantly, to preach the gospel in the regions beyond you, and not to boast in another man's line of things made ready to our hand. But he that glorieth, let him glory in the Lord. For not he that commendeth himself is approved, but whom the Lord commendeth.

Would to God ye could bear with me a little in my folly: and indeed bear with me. For I am jealous over you with godly jealousy: for I have espoused you to one husband, that I may present you as a chaste virgin to Christ. But I fear, lest by any means, as the serpent beguiled Eve through his subtilty, so your minds should be corrupted from the simplicity that is in Christ. For if he that cometh preacheth another Jesus, whom we have not preached, or if ye receive another spirit, which ye have not received, or another gospel, which ye have not accepted, ye might well bear with him. For I suppose I was not a whit behind the very chiefest apostles. But though I be rude in speech, yet not in knowledge; but we have been thoroughly made manifest among you in all things. Have I committed an offence in abasing myself that ye might be exalted, because I have preached to you the gospel of God freely? I robbed other churches, taking wages of them, to do you service. And when I was present with you, and wanted, I was chargeable to no man:

for that which was lacking to me the brethren which came from Macedonia supplied: and in all things I have kept myself from being burdensome unto you, and so will I keep myself.

As the truth of Christ is in me, no man shall stop me of this boasting in the regions of Achaia. Wherefore? because I love you not? God knoweth. But what I do, that I will do, that I may cut off occasion from them which desire occasion; that wherein they glory, they may be found even as we. For such are false apostles, deceitful workers, transforming themselves into the apostles of Christ. And no marvel; for Satan himself is transformed into an angel of light. Therefore it is no great thing if his ministers also be transformed as the ministers of righteousness; whose end shall be according to their works.

I say again, let no man think me a fool; if otherwise, yet as a fool receive me, that I may boast myself a little. That which I speak, I speak it not after the Lord, but as it were foolishly, in this confidence of boasting. Seeing that many glory after the flesh, I will glory also. For ye suffer fools gladly, seeing ye yourselves are wise. For ye suffer, if a man bring you into bondage, if a man devour you, if a man take of you, if a man exalt himself, if a man smite you on the face.

I speak as concerning reproach, as though we had been weak. Howbeit whereinsoever any is bold (I speak foolishly), I am bold also. Are they Hebrews? so am I. Are they Israelites? so am I. Are they the seed of Abraham? so am I. Are they ministers of Christ (I speak as a fool)? I am more; in labours more abundant, in stripes above measure, in prisons more frequent, in deaths oft. Of the Jews five times received I forty stripes save one. Thrice was I beaten with rods, once was I stoned, thrice I suffered shipwreck, a night and a day I have been in the deep; in journeyings often, in perils of waters, in perils of robbers, in perils by mine own countrymen, in perils by the heathen, in perils in the city, in perils in the wilderness, in perils in the sea, in perils among false brethren; in weariness and painfulness, in watchings often, in hunger and thirst, in fastings often, in cold and nakedness. Beside those things that are without, that

THE LETTERS OF PAUL

which cometh upon me daily, the care of all the churches. Who is weak, and I am not weak? who is offended, and I burn not? If I must needs glory, I will glory of the things which concern mine infirmities. The God and Father of our Lord Jesus Christ, which is blessed for evermore, knoweth that I lie not. In Damascus the governor under Aretas the king kept the city of the Damascenes with a garrison, desirous to apprehend me: and through a window in a basket was I let down by the wall, and escaped his hands.

It is not expedient for me doubtless to glory. I will come to visions and revelations of the Lord. I knew a man in Christ above fourteen years ago (whether in the body, I cannot tell; or whether out of the body, I cannot tell: God knoweth); such a one caught up to the third heaven. And I knew such a man (whether in the body, or out of the body, I cannot tell: God knoweth); how that he was caught up into paradise, and heard unspeakable words, which it is not lawful for a man to utter. Of such a one will I glory: yet of myself I will not glory, but in mine infirmities. For though I would desire to glory, I shall not be a fool; for I will say the truth: but now I forbear, lest any man should think of me above that which he seeth me to be, or that he heareth of me. And lest I should be exalted above measure through the abundance of the revelations, there was given to me a thorn in the flesh, the messenger of Satan to buffet me, lest I should be exalted above measure. For this thing I besought the Lord thrice, that it might depart from me. And he said unto me, "My grace is sufficient for thee: for my strength is made perfect in weakness." Most gladly therefore will I rather glory in my infirmities, that the power of Christ may rest upon me. Therefore I take pleasure in infirmities, in reproaches, in necessities, in persecutions, in distresses for Christ's sake: for when I am weak, then am I strong.

I am become a fool in glorying; ye have compelled me: for I ought to have been commended of you: for in nothing am I behind the very chiefest apostles, though I be nothing. Truly the signs of an apostle were wrought among you in all patience, in

THE LETTERS OF PAUL

signs, and wonders, and mighty deeds. For what is it wherein ye were inferior to other churches, except it be that I myself was not burdensome to you? forgive me this wrong.

Behold, the third time I am ready to come to you; and I will not be burdensome to you: for I seek not yours, but you: for the children ought not to lay up for the parents, but the parents for the children. And I will very gladly spend and be spent for you; though the more abundantly I love you, the less I be loved. But be it so, I did not burden you: nevertheless, being crafty, I caught you with guile. Did I make a gain of you by any of them whom I sent unto you? I desired Titus, and with him I sent a brother. Did Titus make a gain of you? walked we not in the same spirit? walked we not in the same steps? Again, think ye that we excuse ourselves unto you? we speak before God in Christ: but we do all things, dearly beloved, for your edifying. For I fear, lest, when I come, I shall not find you such as I would, and that I shall be found unto you such as ye would not: lest there be debates, envyings, wraths, strifes, backbitings, whisperings, swellings, tumults: and lest, when I come again, my God will humble me among you, and that I shall bewail many which have sinned already, and have not repented of the uncleanness and fornication and lasciviousness which they have committed.

This is the third time I am coming to you. In the mouth of two or three witnesses shall every word be established. I told you before, and foretell you, as if I were present, the second time; and being absent now I write to them which heretofore have sinned, and to all other, that, if I come again, I will not spare: since ye seek a proof of Christ speaking in me, which to you-ward is not weak, but is mighty in you. For though he was crucified through weakness, yet he liveth by the power of God. For we also are weak in him, but we shall live with him by the power of God toward you.

Examine yourselves, whether ye be in the faith; prove your own selves. Know ye not your own selves, how that Jesus

THE LETTERS OF PAUL

Christ is in you, except ye be reprobates? But I trust that ye shall know that we are not reprobates.

Now I pray to God that ye do no evil; not that we should appear approved, but that ye should do that which is honest, though we be as reprobates. For we can do nothing against the truth, but for the truth. For we are glad, when we are weak, and ye are strong: and this also we wish, even your perfection.

Therefore I write these things being absent, lest being present I should use sharpness, according to the power which the Lord hath given me to edification, and not to destruction.

Finally, brethren, farewell. Be perfect, be of good comfort, be of one mind, live in peace; and the God of love and peace shall be with you. Greet one another with a holy kiss. All the saints salute you. The grace of the Lord Jesus Christ, and the love of God, and the communion of the Holy Ghost, be with you all. Amen.

> PAUL, AN APOSTLE OF JESUS CHRIST BY THE WILL OF GOD, AND TIMOTHY OUR BROTHER

PHILIPPI

THE LETTERS OF PAUL: TO THE ROMANS

PAUL'S LETTER to the Romans, written at a time when he felt uncertain of ever being able to carry out his cherished wish to preach the gospel in the imperial city, is the longest and most theoretical of his discourses, the especial delight of theologians and doctrinal Christians. In it he expounds with the utmost skill and subtlety that dogma of salvation by faith rather than by works which was destined to turn Christianity from an objective ethics into a subjective religion of the inner spirit—a development strictly analogous to that seen in the prophet Jeremiah. First Corinthians and Romans taken separately are almost in complete contradiction; taken together, they illustrate the extraordinary range of Paul's experience and the complex attitude of one who was equally a mystic and a man of action.

The Letters of PAUL

TO THE ROMANS

To all that be in Rome, beloved of God, called to be saints:
Grace to you and peace from God our Father, and the Lord Jesus Christ.

FIRST, I THANK MY GOD through Jesus Christ for you all, that your faith is spoken of throughout the whole world. For God is my witness, whom I serve with my spirit in the gospel of his Son, that without ceasing I make mention of you always in my prayers; making request, if by any means now at length I might have a prosperous journey by the will of God to come unto you. For I long to see you, that I may impart unto you some spiritual gift, to the end ye may be established; that is, that I may be comforted together with you by the mutual faith both of you and me.

Now I would not have you ignorant, brethren, that oftentimes I purposed to come unto you (but was let hitherto), that I might have some fruit among you also, even as among other Gentiles. I am debtor both to the Greeks, and to the Barbarians; both to the wise, and to the unwise. So, as much as in me is, I am ready to preach the gospel to you that are at Rome also. For I am not ashamed of the gospel of Christ: for it is the power of God unto salvation to every one that believeth; to the Jew first, and also to the Greek. For therein is the righteousness of God revealed from faith to faith: as it is written, "The just shall live by faith."

For the wrath of God is revealed from heaven against all ungodliness and unrighteousness of men, who hold the truth in unrighteousness; because that which may be known of God is manifest in them; for God hath showed it unto them. For the invisible things of him from the creation of the world are clearly seen, being understood by the things that are made, even his eternal power and Godhead; so that they are without excuse: because that, when they knew God, they glorified him not as God, neither were thankful; but became vain in their imaginations, and their foolish heart was darkened. Professing themselves to be wise, they became fools, and changed the glory of the uncorruptible God into an image made like to corruptible man, and to birds, and fourfooted beasts, and creeping things. Wherefore God also gave them up to uncleanness through the lusts of their own hearts, to dishonour their own bodies between themselves: who changed the truth of God into a lie, and worshipped and served the creature more than the Creator, who is blessed for ever. Amen.

For this cause God gave them up unto vile affections: for even their women did change the natural use into that which is against nature: and likewise also the men, leaving the natural use of the woman, burned in their lust one toward another; men with men working that which is unseemly, and receiving in themselves that recompense of their error which was meet. And even as they did not like to retain God in their knowledge, God gave them over to a reprobate mind, to do those things which are not convenient; being filled with all unrighteousness, fornication, wickedness, covetousness, maliciousness; full of envy, murder, debate, deceit, malignity; whisperers, backbiters, haters of God, despiteful, proud, boasters, inventors of evil things, disobedient to parents, without understanding, covenantbreakers, without natural affection, implacable, unmerciful: who knowing the judgment of God, that they which commit such things are worthy of death, not only do the same, but have pleasure in them that do them.

For not the hearers of the law are just before God, but the doers of the law shall be justified. For when the Gentiles, which have not the law, do by nature the things contained in the law, these, having not the law, are a law unto themselves: which show the work of the law written in their hearts, their conscience also bearing witness, and their thoughts the meanwhile accusing or else excusing one another, in the day when God shall judge the secrets of men by Jesus Christ according to my gospel.

Behold, thou art called a Jew, and restest in the law, and makest thy boast of God, and knowest his will, and approvest the things that are more excellent, being instructed out of the law; and art confident that thou thyself art a guide of the blind, a light of them which are in darkness, an instructor of the foolish, a teacher of babes, which hast the form of knowledge and of the truth in the law. Thou therefore which teachest another, teachest thou not thyself? thou that preachest a man should not steal, dost thou steal? Thou that sayest a man should not commit adultery, dost thou commit adultery? thou that abhorrest idols, dost thou commit sacrilege? Thou that makest thy boast of the law, through breaking the law dishonourest thou God? For the name of God is blasphemed among the Gentiles through you, as it is written. For circumcision verily profiteth, if thou keep the law: but if thou be a breaker of the law, thy circumcision is made uncircumcision. Therefore if the uncircumcision keep the righteousness of the law, shall not his uncircumcision be counted for circumcision? And shall not uncircumcision which is by nature, if it fulfil the law, judge thee, who by the letter and circumcision dost transgress the law? For he is not a Jew, which is one outwardly; neither is that circumcision, which is outward in the flesh: but he is a Jew, which is one inwardly; and circumcision is that of the heart, in the spirit, and not in the letter; whose praise is not of men, but of God.

What advantage then hath the Jew? or what profit is there of circumcision? Much every way: chiefly, because that unto them were committed the oracles of God. For what if some did not believe? shall their unbelief make the faith of God without effect? God forbid: yea, let God be true, but every man a liar; as it is written,

THE LETTERS OF PAUL

"That thou mightest be justified in thy sayings,
And mightest overcome when thou art judged."

But if our unrighteousness commend the righteousness of God, what shall we say? Is God unrighteous who taketh vengeance (I speak as a man)? God forbid: for then how shall God judge the world? For if the truth of God hath more abounded through my lie unto his glory; why yet am I also judged as a sinner? And not rather (as we be slanderously reported, and as some affirm that we say), "Let us do evil, that good may come"? whose damnation is just.

What then? are we better than they? No, in no wise: for we have before proved both Jews and Gentiles, that they are all under sin; as it is written,

"There is none righteous, no, not one:
There is none that understandeth,
There is none that seeketh after God.
They are all gone out of the way, they are together become unprofitable;
There is none that doeth good, no, not one.
Their throat is an open sepulchre;
With their tongues they have used deceit;
The poison of asps is under their lips:
Whose mouth is full of cursing and bitterness:
Their feet are swift to shed blood
Destruction and misery are in their ways:
And the way of peace have they not known:
There is no fear of God before their eyes."

Now we know that what things soever the law saith, it saith to them who are under the law: that every mouth may be stopped, and all the world may become guilty before God. Therefore by the deeds of the law there shall no flesh be justified in his sight: for by the law is the knowledge of sin.

But now the righteousness of God without the law is manifested, being witnessed by the law and the prophets; even the righteousness of God which is by faith of Jesus Christ unto all and upon all them that believe: for there is no difference: for all have sinned, and come short of the glory of God, being justified freely by his grace through the redemption that is in Christ Jesus, whom God hath set forth to be a propitiation through faith in his blood, to declare his righteousness for the remission of sins that are past, through the forbearance of God; to declare, I say, at this time his righteousness: that he might be just, and the justifier of him which believeth in Jesus.

Where is boasting then? It is excluded. By what law? of works? Nay: but by the law of faith. Therefore we conclude that a man is justified by faith without the deeds of the law. Is he the God of the Jews only? is he not also of the Gentiles? Yes, of the Gentiles also: seeing it is one God, which shall justify the circumcision by faith, and uncircumcision through faith. Do we then make void the law through faith? God forbid: yea, we establish the law.

Therefore being justified by faith, we have peace with God through our Lord Jesus Christ: by whom also we have access by faith into his grace wherein we stand, and rejoice in hope of the glory of God. And not only so, but we glory in tribulations also: knowing that tribulation worketh patience; and patience, experience; and experience, hope: and hope maketh not ashamed; because the love of God is shed abroad in our hearts by the Holy Ghost which is given unto us.

For when we were yet without strength, in due time Christ died for the ungodly. For scarcely for a righteous man will one die: yet peradventure for a good man some would even dare to die. But God commendeth his love toward us, in that, while we were yet sinners, Christ died for us. Much more then, being now justified by his blood, we shall be saved from wrath through him. For if, when we were enemies, we were reconciled to God by the death of his Son, much more, being reconciled, we shall be saved by his life. And not only so, but we also joy in God through our Lord Jesus Christ, by whom we have now received the atonement.

THE LETTERS OF PAUL

Wherefore, as by one man sin entered into the world, and death by sin; and so death passed upon all men, for that all have sinned: therefore as by the offence of one judgment came upon all men to condemnation; even so by the righteousness of one the free gift came upon all men unto justification of life. For as by one man's disobedience many were made sinners, so by the obedience of one shall many be made righteous. Moreover the law entered, that the offence might abound. But where sin abounded, grace did much more abound: that as sin hath reigned unto death, even so might grace reign through righteousness unto eternal life by Jesus Christ our Lord.

What shall we say then? Shall we continue in sin, that grace may abound? God forbid. How shall we, that are dead to sin, live any longer therein? Know ye not that so many of us as were baptized into Jesus Christ were baptized into his death? Therefore we are buried with him by baptism into death: that like as Christ was raised up from the dead by the glory of the Father, even so we also should walk in newness of life. For if we have been planted together in the likeness of his death, we shall be also in the likeness of his resurrection: knowing this, that our old man is crucified with him, that the body of sin might be destroyed, that henceforth we should not serve sin. For he that is dead is freed from sin. Now if we be dead with Christ, we believe that we shall also live with him: knowing that Christ being raised from the dead dieth no more; death hath no more dominion over him. For in that he died, he died unto sin once: but in that he liveth, he liveth unto God. Likewise reckon ye also yourselves to be dead indeed unto sin, but alive unto God through Jesus Christ our Lord.

Know ye not, brethren (for I speak to them that know the law), how that the law hath dominion over a man as long as he liveth? For the woman which hath a husband is bound by the law to her husband so long as he liveth; but if the husband be dead, she is loosed from the law of her husband. So then if, while her husband liveth, she be married to another man, she shall be called an adulteress: but if her husband be dead, she is free from that law; so that she is no adulteress, though she be married to another man. Wherefore, my brethren, ye also are become dead to the law by the body of Christ; that ye should be married to another, even to him who is raised from the dead, that we should bring forth fruit unto God. For when we were in the flesh, the motions of sins, which were by the law, did work in our members to bring forth fruit unto death. But now we are delivered from the law, that being dead wherein we were held; that we should serve in newness of spirit, and not in the oldness of the letter. What shall we say then? Is the law sin? God forbid. Nay, I had not known sin, but by the law: for I had not known lust, except the law had said, "Thou shalt not covet."

But sin, taking occasion by the commandment, wrought in me all manner of concupiscence. For without the law sin was dead. For I was alive without the law once: but when the commandment came, sin revived, and I died. And the commandment, which was ordained to life, I found to be unto death. For sin, taking occasion by the commandment, deceived me, and by it slew me. Wherefore the law is holy, and the commandment holy, and just, and good.

Was then that which is good made death unto me? God forbid. But sin, that it might appear sin, working death in me by that which is good; that sin by the commandment might become exceeding sinful. For we know that the law is spiritual: but I am carnal, sold under sin. For that which I do I allow not: for what I would, that do I not; but what I hate, that do I. If then I do that which I would not, I consent unto the law that it is good. Now then it is no more I that do it, but sin that dwelleth in me. For I know that in me (that is, in my flesh) dwelleth no good thing: for to will is present with me; but how to perform that which is good I find not. For the good that I would I do not: but the evil which I would not, that I do. Now if I do that I would not, it is no more I that do it, but sin that dwelleth in me. I find then a law, that, when I would do good, evil is present with me. For I delight in the law of God after the inward man:

but I see another law in my members, warring against the law of my mind, and bringing me into captivity to the law of sin which is in my members.

O wretched man that I am! who shall deliver me from the body of this death? I thank God through Jesus Christ our Lord. So then with the mind I myself serve the law of God; but with the flesh the law of sin.

There is therefore now no condemnation to them which are in Christ Jesus, who walk not after the flesh, but after the Spirit. For the law of the Spirit of life in Christ Jesus hath made me free from the law of sin and death. For what the law could not do, in that it was weak through the flesh, God sending his own Son in the likeness of sinful flesh, and for sin, condemned sin in the flesh: that the righteousness of the law might be fulfilled in us, who walk not after the flesh, but after the Spirit. For they that are after the flesh do mind the things of the flesh; but they that are after the Spirit the things of the Spirit. For to be carnally minded is death; but to be spiritually minded is life and peace.

The Spirit itself beareth witness with our spirit, that we are the children of God: and if children, then heirs; heirs of God, and joint heirs with Christ; if so be that we suffer with him, that we may be also glorified together. For I reckon that the sufferings of this present time are not worthy to be compared with the glory which shall be revealed in us. For the earnest expectation of the creature waiteth for the manifestation of the sons of God. For the creature was made subject to vanity, not willingly, but by reason of him who hath subjected the same in hope, because the creature itself also shall be delivered from the bondage of corruption into the glorious liberty of the children of God. For we know that the whole creation groaneth and travaileth in pain together until now. And not only they, but ourselves also, which have the firstfruits of the Spirit, even we ourselves groan within ourselves, waiting for

THE LETTERS OF PAUL

the adoption, to wit, the redemption of our body. For we are saved by hope: but hope that is seen is not hope: for what a man seeth, why doth he yet hope for? But if we hope for that we see not, then do we with patience wait for it.

Likewise the Spirit also helpeth our infirmities: for we know not what we should pray for as we ought: but the Spirit itself maketh intercession for us with groanings which cannot be uttered. And he that searcheth the hearts knoweth what is the mind of the Spirit, because he maketh intercession for the saints according to the will of God. And we know that all things work together for good to them that love God, to them who are the called according to his purpose. For whom he did foreknow, he also did predestinate to be conformed to the image of his Son, that he might be the firstborn among many brethren. Moreover whom he did predestinate, them he also called: and whom he called, them he also justified: and whom he justified, them he also glorified.

What shall we then say to these things? If God be for us, who can be against us? He that spared not his own Son, but delivered him up for us all, how shall he not with him also freely give us all things? Who shall lay any thing to the charge of God's elect? It is God that justifieth. Who is he that condemneth? It is Christ that died, yea rather, that is risen again, who is even at the right hand of God, who also maketh intercession for us.

Who shall separate us from the love of Christ? shall tribulation, or distress, or persecution, or famine, or nakedness, or peril, or sword? As it is written,

> "For thy sake we are killed all the day long;
> We are accounted as sheep for the slaughter."

Nay, in all these things we are more than conquerors through him that loved us. For I am persuaded, that neither death, nor life, nor angels, nor principalities, nor powers, nor things present, nor things to come, nor height, nor depth, nor any other creature, shall be able to separate us from the love of God, which is in Christ Jesus our Lord.

I say the truth in Christ, I lie not, my conscience also bearing me witness in the Holy Ghost, that I have great heaviness and continual sorrow in my heart. For I could wish that myself were accursed from Christ for my brethren, my kinsmen according to the flesh: who are Israelites; to whom pertaineth the adoption, and the glory, and the covenants, and the giving of the law, and the service of God, and the promises; whose are the fathers, and of whom as concerning the flesh Christ came, who is over all, God blessed for ever. Amen.
They are not all Israel, which are of Israel: neither, because they are the seed of Abraham, are they all children: but, "In Isaac shall thy seed be called." That is, they which are the children of the flesh, these are not the children of God: but the children of the promise are counted for the seed. For this is the word of promise, "At this time will I come, and Sarah shall have a son." And not only this; but when Rebecca also had conceived by one, even by our father Isaac (for the children being not yet born, neither having done any good or evil, that the purpose of God according to election might stand, not of works, but of him that calleth), it was said unto her, "The elder shall serve the younger." As it is written, "Jacob have I loved, but Esau have I hated."
What shall we say then? Is there unrighteousness with God? God forbid. For he saith to Moses, "I will have mercy on whom I will have mercy, and I will have compassion on whom I will have compassion." So then it is not of him that willeth, nor of him that runneth, but of God that showeth mercy. For the scripture saith unto Pharaoh, "Even for this same purpose have I raised thee up, that I might show my power in thee, and that my name might be declared throughout all the earth." Therefore hath he mercy on whom he will have mercy, and whom he will he hardeneth.

THE LETTERS OF PAUL

Thou wilt say then unto me, "Why doth he yet find fault? For who hath resisted his will?"

Nay but, O man, who art thou that repliest against God? Shall the thing formed say to him that formed it, "Why hast thou made me thus?" Hath not the potter power over the clay, of the same lump to make one vessel unto honour, and another unto dishonour? What if God, willing to show his wrath, and to make his power known, endured with much longsuffering the vessels of wrath fitted to destruction: and that he might make known the riches of his glory on the vessels of mercy, which he had afore prepared unto glory.

What shall we say then? That the Gentiles, which followed not after righteousness, have attained to righteousness, even the righteousness which is of faith. But Israel, which followed after the law of righteousness, hath not attained to the law of righteousness. Wherefore? Because they sought it not by faith, but as it were by the works of the law. For they stumbled at that stumblingstone; as it is written, "Behold, I lay in Zion a stumblingstone and rock of offence: and whosoever believeth on him shall not be ashamed."

Brethren, my heart's desire and prayer to God for Israel is, that they might be saved. For I bear them record that they have a zeal of God, but not according to knowledge. For they being ignorant of God's righteousness, and going about to establish their own righteousness, have not submitted themselves unto the righteousness of God. For Christ is the end of the law for righteousness to every one that believeth. For Moses describeth the righteousness which is of the law, that "the man which doeth those things shall live by them." But the righteousness which is of faith speaketh on this wise, "Say not in thine heart, 'Who shall ascend into heaven?'" (that is, to bring Christ down from above) or, "'Who shall descend into the deep?'" (that is, to bring up Christ again from the dead). But what saith it? "The word is nigh thee, even in thy mouth, and in thy heart": that is, the word of faith, which we preach; that if thou shalt confess with thy mouth the Lord Jesus, and shalt believe in thine heart that God hath raised him from the dead, thou shalt be saved.

I beseech you therefore, brethren, by the mercies of God, that ye present your bodies a living sacrifice, holy, acceptable unto God, which is your reasonable service. And be not conformed to this world: but be ye transformed by the renewing of your mind, that ye may prove what is that good, and acceptable, and perfect, will of God.

Let love be without dissimulation. Abhor that which is evil; cleave to that which is good. Be kindly affectioned one to another with brotherly love; in honour preferring one another; not slothful in business; fervent in spirit; serving the Lord; rejoicing in hope; patient in tribulation; continuing instant in prayer; distributing to the necessity of saints; given to hospitality. Bless them which persecute you: bless, and curse not. Rejoice with them that do rejoice, and weep with them that weep. Be of the same mind one toward another. Mind not high things, but condescend to men of low estate. Be not wise in your own conceits. Recompense to no man evil for evil. Provide things honest in the sight of all men. If it be possible, as much as lieth in you, live peaceably with all men. Dearly beloved, avenge not yourselves, but rather give place unto wrath: for it is written, "'Vengeance is mine: I will repay,' saith the Lord." Therefore if thine enemy hunger, feed him; if he thirst, give him drink: for in so doing thou shalt heap coals of fire on his head. Be not overcome of evil, but overcome evil with good.

Let every soul be subject unto the higher powers. For there is no power but of God: the powers that be are ordained of God. Whosoever therefore resisteth the power, resisteth the ordinance of God: and they that resist shall receive to themselves damnation. For rulers are not a terror to good works, but to the evil. Wilt thou then not be afraid of the power? do that which is good, and thou shalt have praise of the same: for he is the minister of God to thee for good. But if thou do that which is evil, be afraid; for he beareth not the sword in vain: for he is the minister of God, a revenger to execute wrath upon him that doeth evil. Wherefore ye must needs be subject, not only for wrath, but also for conscience' sake. For for this cause pay ye tribute also: for they are God's ministers, attending continually upon this very thing. Render therefore to all their dues: tribute to whom tribute is due; custom to whom custom; fear to whom fear; honour to whom honour.

Him that is weak in the faith receive ye, but not to doubtful disputations. For one believeth that he may eat all things: another, who is weak, eateth herbs. Let not him that eateth despise him that eateth not; and let not him which eateth not judge him that eateth: for God hath received him. Who art thou that judgest another man's servant? to his own master he standeth or falleth. Yea, he shall be held up: for God is able to make him stand. One man esteemeth one day above another: another esteemeth every day alike. Let every man be fully persuaded in his own mind. He that regardeth the day, regardeth it unto the Lord; and he that regardeth not the day, to the Lord he doth not regard it. He that eateth, eateth to the Lord, for he giveth God thanks; and he that eateth not, to the Lord he eateth not, and giveth God thanks. For none of us liveth to himself, and no man dieth to himself. For whether we live, we live unto the Lord; and whether we die, we die unto the Lord: whether we live therefore, or die, we are the Lord's. For to this end Christ both died, and rose, and revived, that he might be Lord both of the dead and living. But why dost thou judge thy brother? or why dost thou set at nought thy brother? for we shall all stand before the judgment seat of Christ. For it is written,

"'As I live,' saith the Lord, 'every knee shall bow to me,
And every tongue shall confess to God.'"

So then every one of us shall give account of himself to God.

THE LETTERS OF PAUL

Now to him that is of power to establish you according to my gospel, and the preaching of Jesus Christ, according to the revelation of the mystery, which was kept secret since the world began, but now is made manifest, and by the scriptures of the prophets, according to the commandment of the everlasting God, made known to all nations for the obedience of faith: to God only wise, be glory through Jesus Christ for ever. Amen.

> PAUL, A SERVANT OF JESUS CHRIST, CALLED TO BE AN APOSTLE, SEPARATED UNTO THE GOSPEL OF GOD

CORINTH

THE LETTERS OF PAUL: TO THE PHILIPPIANS

When paul at last reached Rome, he came not as a triumphant missionary but as a prisoner with martyrdom in store for him. The weary years of captivity and suffering had not broken his spirit; he was still tireless as ever in preaching to all who would hear; but his letters from Rome to his Asiatic disciples reveal a new attitude of chastened resignation, vast tolerance, and universal kindliness, the final fruition of his life of struggle, showing that in the end he succeeded in incorporating into his very self the originally foreign ideals that he had striven for. From this point of view, his last letters, though much slighter than the earlier ones, are the most moving and poignant of all. The spirit of his letter to the Philippians, especially, seems close to that of the finest passages in the Gospels.

The Letters of PAUL

TO THE PHILIPPIANS

To all the saints in Christ Jesus which are at Philippi, with the bishops and deacons:

Grace be unto you, and peace, from God our Father, and from the Lord Jesus Christ.

I THANK MY GOD upon every remembrance of you, always in every prayer of mine for you all making request with joy, for your fellowship in the gospel from the first day until now, being confident of this very thing, that he which hath begun a good work in you will perform it until the day of Jesus Christ: even as it is meet for me to think this of you all, because I have you in my heart; inasmuch as both in my bonds, and in the defence and confirmation of the gospel, ye all are partakers of my grace. For God is my record, how greatly I long after you all in the bowels of Jesus Christ.

But I would ye should understand, brethren, that the things which happened unto me have fallen out rather unto the furtherance of the gospel, so that my bonds in Christ are manifest in all the palace, and in all other places, and many of the brethren in the Lord, waxing confident by my bonds, are much more bold to speak the word without fear. Some indeed preach Christ even of envy and strife, and some also of good will: the one preach Christ of contention, not sincerely, supposing to add affliction to my bonds: but the other of love, knowing that I am set for the defence of the gospel. What then? notwithstanding, every way, whether in pretence, or in truth, Christ is preached; and I therein do rejoice, yea, and will rejoice. For I know that this shall turn to my salvation through your prayer, and the supply of the Spirit of Jesus Christ, according to my earnest expectation and my hope, that in nothing I shall be ashamed, but that with all boldness, as always, so now also Christ shall be magnified in my body, whether it be by life, or by death.

For to me to live is Christ, and to die is gain. But if I live in the flesh, this is the fruit of my labour: yet what I shall choose I wot not. For I am in a strait betwixt two, having a desire to depart, and to be with Christ (which is far better); nevertheless to abide in the flesh is more needful for you. And having this confidence, I know that I shall abide and continue with you all for your furtherance and joy of faith, that your rejoicing may be more abundant in Jesus Christ for me by my coming to you again.

Only let your conversation be as it becometh the gospel of Christ: that whether I come and see you, or else be absent, I may hear of your affairs, that ye stand fast in one spirit, with one mind striving together for the faith of the gospel, and in nothing terrified by your adversaries: which is to them an evident token of perdition, but to you of salvation, and that of God. For unto you it is given in the behalf of Christ, not only to believe on him, but also to suffer for his sake, having the same conflict which ye saw in me, and now hear to be in me.

If there be therefore any consolation in Christ, if any comfort of love, if any fellowship of the Spirit, if any bowels and mercies, fulfil ye my joy, that ye be likeminded, having the same love, being of one accord, of one mind. Let nothing be done through strife or vainglory; but in lowliness of mind let each esteem other better than themselves. Look not every man on his own things, but every man also on the things of others.

Let this mind be in you, which was also in Christ Jesus: who, being in the form of God, thought it not robbery to be equal with God, but made himself of no reputation, and took upon him the form of a servant, and was made in the likeness of men; and being found in fashion as a man, he humbled himself, and became obedient unto death, even the death of the cross. Wherefore God also hath highly exalted him, and given him a name which is above every name, that at the name of Jesus every knee should bow, of things in heaven, and things in earth, and things under the earth, and that every tongue should confess that Jesus Christ is Lord, to the glory of God the Father.

Wherefore, my beloved, as ye have always obeyed, not as in my presence only, but now much more in my absence, work out your own salvation with fear and trembling. For it is God which worketh in you both to will and to do of his good pleasure.

Do all things without murmurings and disputings, that ye may be blameless and harmless, the sons of God, without rebuke, in the midst of a crooked and perverse nation, among whom ye shine as lights in the world, holding forth the word of life; that I may rejoice in the day of Christ, that I have not run in vain, neither laboured in vain.

Yea, and if I be offered upon the sacrifice and service of your faith, I joy, and rejoice with you all. For the same cause also do ye joy, and rejoice with me.

But I trust in the Lord Jesus to send Timotheus shortly unto you, that I also may be of good comfort, when I know your state. For I have no man likeminded, who will naturally care for your state. For all seek their own, not the things which are Jesus Christ's. But ye know the proof of him, that, as a son with the father, he hath served with me in the gospel. Him therefore I hope to send presently, so soon as I shall see how it will go with me. But I trust in the Lord that I also myself shall come shortly.

Yet I supposed it necessary to send to you Epaphroditus, my brother, and companion in labour, and fellowsoldier, but your messenger, and he that ministered to my wants. For he longed after you all, and was full of heaviness, because that ye had heard that he had been sick. For indeed he was sick nigh unto death: but God had mercy on him; and not on him only, but on me also, lest I should have sorrow upon sorrow. I sent him therefore the more carefully, that, when ye see him again, ye may rejoice, and that I may be the less sorrowful. Receive him therefore in the Lord with all gladness; and hold such in reputation: because for the work of Christ he was nigh unto death, not regarding his life, to supply your lack of service toward me.

Therefore, my brethren dearly beloved and longed for, my joy and crown, so stand fast in the Lord, my dearly beloved. I beseech Euodias, and beseech Syntyche, that they be of the same mind in the Lord. And I intreat thee also, true yokefellow, help those women which laboured with me in the gospel, with Clement also, and with other my fellowlabourers, whose names are in the book of life.

Rejoice in the Lord always: and again I say, "Rejoice." Let your moderation be known unto all men. The Lord is at hand. Be careful for nothing; but in every thing by prayer and supplication with thanksgiving let your requests be made known unto God. And the peace of God, which passeth all understanding, shall keep your hearts and minds through Christ Jesus.

Finally, brethren, whatsoever things are true, whatsoever things are honest, whatsoever things are just, whatsoever things are pure, whatsoever things are lovely, whatsoever things are of good report; if there be any virtue, and if there be any praise, think on these things. Those things, which ye have both learned, and received, and heard, and seen in me, do: and the God of peace shall be with you.

But I rejoiced in the Lord greatly, that now at the last your care of me hath flourished again; wherein ye were also careful, but ye lacked opportunity. Not that I speak in respect of want: for I have learned, in whatsoever state I am, therewith to be content. I know both how to be abased, and I know how to abound: everywhere and in all things I am instructed both to be full and to be hungry, both to abound and to suffer need. I can do all things through Christ which strengtheneth me. Notwithstanding ye have well done, that ye did communicate with my affliction. Now ye Philippians know also, that in the beginning of the gospel, when I departed from Macedonia, no church communicated with me as concerning giving and receiving, but ye only. For even in Thessalonica ye sent once and again unto my necessity. Not because I desire a gift: but I desire fruit that may abound to your account. But I have all, and abound: I am full, having received of Epaphroditus the things which were sent from you, an odour of a sweet smell, a sacrifice acceptable, well-pleasing to God. But my God shall supply all your need according to his riches in glory by Christ Jesus. Now unto God and our Father be glory for ever and ever. Amen.

Salute every saint in Christ Jesus. The brethren which are with me greet you. All the saints salute you, chiefly they that are of Cæsar's household. The grace of our Lord Jesus Christ be with you all. Amen.

PAUL AND TIMOTHEUS, THE SERVANTS OF JESUS CHRIST

ROME

THE LETTERS OF PAUL: TO THE COLOSSIANS

EVEN IN HIS ROMAN PRISON *Paul remained the head of the churches that he had founded in Asia, the trusted counselor to whom they sent for advice on matters of theory and conduct. His letter to the church at Colossæ is a later parallel of that to the Galatians, emphasizing like it the importance of the spirit of religion and decrying the reliance on ceremonial, but couched in the milder and more tolerant language of all of the epistles written after his captivity. His rejection of the ascetic practices popular in the East is expressive of the final harmony attained by him in the disciplining of his many-sided nature in which the ascetic tendency was held in check by a clear realization of its dangers.*

TO THE COLOSSIANS

To the saints and faithful brethren in Christ which are at Colossæ: Grace be unto you, and peace, from God our Father and the Lord Jesus Christ.

WE GIVE THANKS TO GOD and the Father of our Lord Jesus Christ, praying always for you, since we heard of your faith in Christ Jesus, and of the love which ye have to all the saints, for the hope which is laid up for you in heaven, whereof ye heard before in the word of the truth of the gospel, which is come unto you, as it is in all the world, and bringeth forth fruit, as it doth also in you, since the day ye heard of it, and knew the grace of God in truth.

I would that ye knew what great conflict I have for you, and for them at Laodicea, and for as many as have not seen my face in the flesh, that their hearts might be comforted, being knit together in love, and unto all riches of the full assurance of understanding, to the acknowledgment of the mystery of God, and of the Father, and of Christ, in whom are hid all the treasures of wisdom and knowledge.

And this I say, lest any man should beguile you with enticing words. For though I be absent in the flesh, yet I am with you in the spirit, joying and beholding your order, and the steadfastness of your faith in Christ. As ye have therefore received Christ Jesus the Lord, so walk ye in him: rooted and built up in him, and established in the faith, as ye have been taught, abounding therein with thanksgiving.

THE LETTERS OF PAUL

Beware lest any man spoil you through philosophy and vain deceit, after the tradition of men, after the rudiments of the world, and not after Christ. For in him dwelleth all the fulness of the Godhead bodily. And ye are complete in him, which is the head of all principality and power.

Let no man therefore judge you in meat, or in drink, or in respect of a holyday, or of the new moon, or of the sabbath days: which are a shadow of things to come; but the body is of Christ.

Let no man beguile you of your reward in a voluntary humility and worshipping of angels, intruding into those things which he hath not seen, vainly puffed up by his fleshly mind, and not holding the Head, from which all the body by joints and bands having nourishment ministered, and knit together, increaseth with the increase of God. Wherefore if ye be dead with Christ from the rudiments of the world, why, as though living in the world, are ye subject to ordinances—"Touch not!" "Taste not!" "Handle not!"—which all are to perish with the using, after the commandments and doctrines of men? Which things have indeed a show of wisdom in will worship, and humility, and neglecting of the body; not in any honour to the satisfying of the flesh.

If ye then be risen with Christ, seek those things which are above, where Christ sitteth on the right hand of God. Set your affection on things above, not on things on the earth. For ye are dead, and your life is hid with Christ in God. When Christ, who is our life, shall appear, then shall ye also appear with him in glory.

Lie not one to another, seeing that ye have put off the old man with his deeds, and have put on the new man, which is renewed in knowledge after the image of him that created him: where there is neither Greek nor Jew, circumcision nor uncircumcision, Barbarian, Scythian, bond nor free: but Christ is all, and in all. Put on therefore, as the elect of God, holy and beloved, bowels of mercies, kindness, humbleness of mind, meekness, longsuffering; forbearing one another, and forgiving one another, if any man have a quarrel against any: even as Christ forgave you, so also do ye. And above all these things put on charity, which is the bond of perfectness. And let the peace of God rule in your hearts, to the which also ye are called in one body; and be ye thankful.

Let the word of Christ dwell in you richly in all wisdom; teaching and admonishing one another in psalms and hymns and spiritual songs, singing with grace in your hearts to the Lord. And whatsoever ye do in word or deed, do all in the name of the Lord Jesus, giving thanks to God and the Father by him.

Wives, submit yourselves unto your own husbands, as it is fit in the Lord.

Husbands, love your wives, and be not bitter against them.

Children, obey your parents in all things: for this is well pleasing unto the Lord.

Fathers, provoke not your children to anger, lest they be discouraged.

Servants, obey in all things your masters according to the flesh; not with eyeservice, as men-pleasers; but in singleness of heart, fearing God; and whatsoever ye do, do it heartily, as to the Lord, and not unto men, knowing that of the Lord ye shall receive the reward of the inheritance: for ye serve the Lord Christ. But he that doeth wrong shall receive for the wrong which he hath done: and there is no respect of persons.

Masters, give unto your servants that which is just and equal; knowing that ye also have a Master in heaven.

Continue in prayer, and watch in the same with thanksgiving, withal praying also for us, that God would open unto us a door of utterance, to speak the mystery of Christ, for which I am also in bonds: that I may make it manifest, as I ought to speak. Walk in wisdom toward them that are without, redeeming the time. Let your speech be always with grace, seasoned with salt, that ye may know how ye ought to answer every man.

All my state shall Tychicus declare unto you, who is a beloved brother, and a faithful minister and fellowservant in the

THE LETTERS OF PAUL

Lord: whom I have sent unto you for the same purpose, that he might know your estate, and comfort your hearts.

And when this epistle is read among you, cause that it be read also in the church of the Laodiceans; and that ye likewise read the epistle from Laodicea. The salutation by the hand of me Paul. Remember my bonds. Grace be with you. Amen.

>PAUL, AN APOSTLE OF JESUS CHRIST BY THE WILL OF GOD, AND TIMOTHEUS OUR BROTHER

ROME

THE LETTERS OF PAUL: TO PHILEMON

DEEPLY VERSED though he was in the literature of the Old Testament, Paul was nearer to Saint Augustine than he was to the Prophets or the Jesus of the Synoptic Gospels. Their protests against the injustice of the social order and their hopes of establishing a kingdom of righteousness on earth are altered in his teaching into a stress on private morality within the institution of the Church, so that personal salvation and the establishment of the Church as the means thereto replace the revolutionary aim to reorganize society on the basis of love and justice. Thus, so far as a change of human conditions on earth is concerned, Pauline Christianity represents a retrenchment and loss of hope, though to his own mind this meant merely a neglect of the unessential in concentrating upon ultimate and purely spiritual considerations. Paul took no interest in questions of politics or in questions of social organization, advising submission to earthly rulers in order to avoid entanglement in what to him were unimportant issues.

His social conservatism is shown in the events connected with the writing of his last letter, sent to a Christian landowner of Laodicea named Philemon asking pardon for Philemon's escaped slave Onesimus who had come to Rome where he had been converted by Paul. In accordance with his conception of duty, Paul sent the slave back to his master who under Roman law had powers almost of life and death in such a case; but lest Philemon should be tempted to exercise these powers, Paul gave Onesimus this letter, asking that he be received as a fellow Christian, and provided also that the letter should be read publicly in the powerful church of Colossæ, near Laodicea, so that the pressure of social opinion might be brought to bear upon the master if necessary. It would be interesting to know whether Philemon proved himself enough of a Christian to respond to Paul's request or on the contrary acted like most Roman masters and put Onesimus to the torture on his return.

The Letters of PAUL

TO PHILEMON

Unto Philemon our dearly beloved, and fellowlabourer, and to our beloved Apphia, and Archippus our fellowsoldier, and to the church in thy house:

Grace to you, and peace, from God our Father and the Lord Jesus Christ.

I THANK MY GOD, making mention of thee always in my prayers, hearing of thy love and faith, which thou hast toward the Lord Jesus, and toward all saints; that the communication of thy faith may become effectual by the acknowledging of every good thing which is in you in Christ Jesus. For we have great joy and consolation in thy love, because the bowels of the saints are refreshed by thee, brother. Wherefore, though I might be much bold in Christ to enjoin thee that which is convenient, yet for love's sake I rather beseech thee, being such a one as Paul the aged, and now also a prisoner of Jesus Christ. I beseech thee for my son Onesimus, whom I have begotten in my bonds; which in time past was to thee unprofitable, but now profitable to thee and to me: whom I have sent again: thou therefore receive him, that is, mine own bowels: whom I would have retained with me, that in thy stead he might have ministered unto me in the bonds of the gospel: but without thy mind would I do nothing; that thy benefit should not be as it were of necessity, but willingly.

For perhaps he therefore departed for a season, that thou shouldest receive him for ever; not now as a servant, but above

THE LETTERS OF PAUL

a servant, a brother beloved, specially to me, but how much more unto thee, both in the flesh, and in the Lord?

If thou count me therefore a partner, receive him as myself. If he hath wronged thee, or oweth thee ought, put that on mine account; I Paul have written it with mine own hand, I will repay it: albeit I do not say to thee how thou owest unto me even thine own self besides. Yea, brother, let me have joy of thee in the Lord: refresh my bowels in the Lord.

Having confidence in thy obedience I wrote unto thee, knowing that thou wilt also do more than I say. But withal prepare me also a lodging: for I trust that through your prayers I shall be given unto you.

There salute thee Epaphras, my fellowprisoner in Christ Jesus; Marcus, Aristarchus, Demas, Lucas, my fellowlabourers.

The grace of our Lord Jesus Christ be with your spirit. Amen.

PAUL, A PRISONER OF JESUS CHRIST, AND TIMOTHEUS OUR BROTHER

ROME

A LETTER TO THE HEBREWS

The letter to the hebrews, accredited to Paul by later tradition, was written under the influence of his ideas but in a very different style, smooth, flowing, and much less intense, without any of the sudden breaks and transitions and personal thrusts by which Paul held the attention of his readers and drove his message home. In contrast to Paul's authoritative speech, the language of Hebrews is that of a much softer pleading. The work is less a letter than a deliberate literary oration or sermon, addressed not to any particular congregation as Paul's always were, but to Christianized Jews in general, its aim being to remind them that Judaism, while needful as a preparation for Christianity, was now definitely superseded by a higher form of religion. The special type of Christianity expounded is based upon Paul's doctrine of justification by faith to the neglect of other aspects of his teaching. While inferior in interest to Paul's own writings, the oration contains passages of great eloquence.

A Letter to the HEBREWS

God, who at sundry times and in divers manners spoke in time past unto the fathers by the prophets, hath in these last days spoken unto us by his Son, whom he hath appointed heir of all things, by whom also he made the worlds; who, being the brightness of his glory, and the express image of his person, and upholding all things by the word of his power, when he had by himself purged our sins, sat down on the right hand of the Majesty on high, being made so much better than the angels, as he hath by inheritance obtained a more excellent name than they.

Therefore we ought to give the more earnest heed to the things which we have heard, lest at any time we should let them slip. For if the word spoken by angels was steadfast, and every transgression and disobedience received a just recompense of reward, how shall we escape, if we neglect so great salvation?

For unto the angels hath he not put in subjection the world to come, whereof we speak. But one in a certain place testified, saying,

> "What is man, that thou art mindful of him?
> Or the Son of Man, that thou visitest him?
> Thou madest him a little lower than the angels;
> Thou crownedst him with glory and honour,
> And didst set him over the works of thy hands:
> Thou hast put all things in subjection under his feet."

For in that he put all in subjection under him, he left nothing that is not put under him. But now we see not yet all things put

A LETTER TO THE HEBREWS

under him. But we see Jesus, who was made a little lower than the angels for the suffering of death, crowned with glory and honour; that he by the grace of God should taste death for every man. For it became him, for whom are all things, and by whom are all things, in bringing many sons unto glory, to make the captain of their salvation perfect through sufferings. For verily he took not on him the nature of angels; but he took on him the seed of Abraham. Wherefore in all things it behooved him to be made like unto his brethren, that he might be a merciful and faithful high priest in things pertaining to God, to make reconciliation for the sins of the people. For in that he himself hath suffered being tempted, he is able to succour them that are tempted. Wherefore, holy brethren, partakers of the heavenly calling, consider the Apostle and High Priest of our profession, Christ Jesus.

For we have not a high priest which cannot be touched with the feeling of our infirmities; but was in all points tempted like as we are, yet without sin. Let us therefore come boldly unto the throne of grace, that we may obtain mercy, and find grace to help in time of need. For every high priest taken from among men is ordained for men in things pertaining to God, that he may offer both gifts and sacrifices for sins: who can have compassion on the ignorant, and on them that are out of the way; for that he himself also is compassed with infirmity. And by reason hereof he ought, as for the people, so also for himself, to offer for sins. And no man taketh this honour unto himself, but he that is called of God, as was Aaron. So also Christ glorified not himself to be made a high priest; but he that said unto him,

"*Thou art my Son, to-day have I begotten thee.*"

As he saith also in another place,

"*Thou art a priest for ever*
After the order of Melchizedec."

Who in the days of his flesh, when he had offered up prayers and supplications with strong crying and tears unto him that

A LETTER TO THE HEBREWS

was able to save him from death, and was heard in that he feared, though he were a Son, yet learned he obedience by the things which he suffered; and being made perfect, he became the author of eternal salvation unto all them that obey him; called of God a high priest after the order of Melchizedec.

For this Melchizedec, king of Salem, priest of the most high God, who met Abraham returning from the slaughter of the kings, and blessed him (first being by interpretation "king of righteousness," and after that also king of Salem, which is "king of peace"; without father, without mother, without descent, having neither beginning of days, nor end of life; but made like unto the Son of God) abideth a priest continually.

Now consider how great this man was, unto whom even the patriarch Abraham gave the tenth of the spoils. And verily they that are of the sons of Levi, who receive the office of the priesthood, have a commandment to take tithes of the people according to the law, that is, of their brethren, though they come out of the loins of Abraham: but he whose descent is not counted from them received tithes of Abraham, and blessed him that had the promises. And without all contradiction the less is blessed of the better. And here men that die receive tithes; but there he receiveth them, of whom it is witnessed that he liveth. And as I may so say, Levi also, who receiveth tithes, payed tithes in Abraham. For he was yet in the loins of his father, when Melchizedec met him.

If therefore perfection were by the Levitical priesthood (for under it the people received the law), what further need was there that another priest should rise after the order of Melchizedec, and not be called after the order of Aaron? For the priesthood being changed, there is made of necessity a change also of the law. For he of whom these things are spoken pertaineth to another tribe, of which no man gave attendance at the altar. For it is evident that our Lord sprang out of Juda; of which tribe Moses spoke nothing concerning priesthood.

And it is yet far more evident: for that after the similitude of Melchizedec there ariseth another priest, who is made, not

A LETTER TO THE HEBREWS

after the law of a carnal commandment, but after the power of an endless life. For he testifieth,

> *"Thou art a priest for ever*
> *After the order of Melchizedec."*

For there is verily a disannulling of the commandment going before for the weakness and unprofitableness thereof. For the law made nothing perfect, but the bringing in of a better hope did; by the which we draw nigh unto God. And inasmuch as not without an oath he was made priest (for those priests were made without an oath; but this with an oath by him that said unto him, "The Lord swore and will not repent. 'Thou art a priest for ever after the order of Melchizedec'"): by so much was Jesus made a surety of a better testament. And they truly were many priests, because they were not suffered to continue by reason of death: but this man, because he continueth ever, hath an unchangeable priesthood.

Wherefore he is able also to save them to the uttermost that come unto God by him, seeing he ever liveth to make intercession for them. For such a high priest became us, who is holy, harmless, undefiled, separate from sinners, and made higher than the heavens; who needeth not daily, as those high priests, to offer up sacrifice, first for his own sins, and then for the people's: for this he did once, when he offered up himself. For the law maketh men high priests which have infirmity; but the word of the oath, which was since the law, maketh the Son, who is consecrated for evermore.

Now faith is the substance of things hoped for, the evidence of things not seen. For by it the elders obtained a good report. Through faith we understand that the worlds were framed by the word of God, so that things which are seen were not made of things which do appear.

By faith Abel offered unto God a more excellent sacrifice than Cain, by which he obtained witness that he was righteous, God testifying of his gifts: and by it he being dead yet speaketh.

A LETTER TO THE HEBREWS

By faith Enoch was translated that he should not see death; and was not found, because God had translated him: for before his translation he had this testimony, that he pleased God. But without faith it is impossible to please him: for he that cometh to God must believe that he is, and that he is a rewarder of them that diligently seek him.

By faith Noah, being warned of God of things not seen as yet, moved with fear, prepared an ark to the saving of his house; by the which he condemned the world, and became heir of the righteousness which is by faith.

By faith Abraham, when he was called to go out into a place which he should after receive for an inheritance, obeyed; and he went out, not knowing whither he went. By faith he sojourned in the land of promise, as in a strange country, dwelling in tabernacles with Isaac and Jacob, the heirs with him of the same promise: for he looked for a city which hath foundations, whose builder and maker is God.

Through faith also Sara herself received strength to conceive seed, and was delivered of a child when she was past age, because she judged him faithful who had promised. Therefore sprang there even of one, and him as good as dead, so many as the stars of the sky in multitude, and as the sand which is by the sea shore innumerable.

These all died in faith, not having received the promises, but having seen them afar off, and were persuaded of them, and embraced them, and confessed that they were strangers and pilgrims on the earth. For they that say such things declare plainly that they seek a country. And truly, if they had been mindful of that country from whence they came out, they might have had opportunity to have returned. But now they desire a better country, that is, a heavenly: wherefore God is not ashamed to be called their God: for he hath prepared for them a city.

By faith Abraham, when he was tried, offered up Isaac: and he that had received the promises offered up his only begotten son, of whom it was said that "in Isaac shall thy seed be called":

A LETTER TO THE HEBREWS

accounting that God was able to raise him up, even from the dead; from whence also he received him in a figure.

By faith Isaac blessed Jacob and Esau concerning things to come.

By faith Jacob, when he was a-dying, blessed both the sons of Joseph; and worshipped, leaning upon the top of his staff.

By faith Joseph, when he died, made mention of the departing of the children of Israel; and gave commandment concerning his bones.

By faith Moses, when he was born, was hid three months of his parents, because they saw he was a proper child; and they were not afraid of the king's commandment.

By faith Moses, when he was come to years, refused to be called the son of Pharaoh's daughter, choosing rather to suffer affliction with the people of God, than to enjoy the pleasures of sin for a season, esteeming the reproach of Christ greater riches than the treasures in Egypt: for he had respect unto the recompense of the reward.

By faith he forsook Egypt, not fearing the wrath of the king: for he endured, as seeing him who is invisible.

Through faith he kept the passover, and the sprinkling of blood, lest he that destroyed the firstborn should touch them.

By faith they passed through the Red Sea as by dry land: which the Egyptians essaying to do were drowned.

By faith the walls of Jericho fell down, after they were compassed about seven days.

By faith the harlot Rahab perished not with them that believed not, when she had received the spies with peace.

And what shall I more say? for the time would fail me to tell of Gideon, and of Barak, and of Samson, and of Jephthah; of David also, and Samuel, and of the prophets: who through faith subdued kingdoms, wrought righteousness, obtained promises, stopped the mouths of lions, quenched the violence of fire, escaped the edge of the sword, out of weakness were made strong, waxed valiant in fight, turned to flight the armies of the aliens.

A LETTER TO THE HEBREWS

Women received their dead raised to life again: and others were tortured, not accepting deliverance, that they might obtain a better resurrection; and others had trial of cruel mockings and scourgings, yea, moreover of bonds and imprisonment. They were stoned, they were sawn asunder, were tempted, were slain with the sword: they wandered about in sheepskins and goatskins; being destitute, afflicted, tormented (of whom the world was not worthy); they wandered in deserts, and in mountains, and in dens and caves of the earth. And these all, having obtained a good report through faith, received not the promise, God having provided some better thing for us, that they without us should not be made perfect.

Wherefore seeing we also are compassed about with so great a cloud of witnesses, let us lay aside every weight, and the sin which doth so easily beset us, and let us run with patience the race that is set before us, looking unto Jesus the author and finisher of our faith; who for the joy that was set before him endured the cross, despising the shame, and is set down at the right hand of the throne of God.

Let brotherly love continue. Be not forgetful to entertain strangers: for thereby some have entertained angels unawares. Remember them that are in bonds, as bound with them; and them which suffer adversity, as being yourselves also in the body. Marriage is honourable in all, and the bed undefiled: but whoremongers and adulterers God will judge. Let your conversation be without covetousness; and be content with such things as ye have: for he hath said, "I will never leave thee, nor forsake thee." So that we may boldly say,

"*The Lord is my helper; I will not fear*
What man shall do unto me."

Remember them which have the rule over you, who have spoken unto you the word of God: whose faith follow, considering the end of their conversation. Jesus Christ the same yesterday, and to-day, and for ever.

A LETTER TO THE HEBREWS

Now the God of peace, that brought again from the dead our Lord Jesus, that great shepherd of the sheep, through the blood of the everlasting covenant, make you perfect in every good work to do his will, working in you that which is wellpleasing in his sight, through Jesus Christ; to whom be glory for ever and ever. Amen.

ITALY

A LETTER OF JAMES

Whether the canonical epistle of James was written by the brother of Jesus or by a later writer of the same name cannot be regarded as conclusively settled, though the latter was most probably the case. Like Hebrews, it is a sermon rather than a letter, but it is much more direct, practical, and familiar in tone, and it is inspired by greater moral earnestness. Its spirit is similar to that of the Synoptic Gospels, and its passionate protest against social injustice, together with its stout affirmation of the doctrine of salvation by works, seems to represent a conscious reaction against the subjective tendency of Paul's teachings. Almost rejected from the Canon because of its anti-Pauline character and denounced by Martin Luther for the same reason, it is yet the most modern work in the Bible in its impassioned social-mindedness and in its style of mingled tenderness and satire.

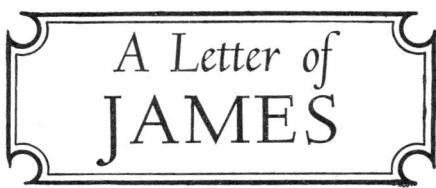

A Letter of JAMES

James, a servant of God and of the Lord Jesus Christ, to the twelve tribes which are scattered abroad, greeting.

My brethren, count it all joy when ye fall into divers temptations; knowing this, that the trying of your faith worketh patience. But let patience have her perfect work, that ye may be perfect and entire, wanting nothing.

If any of you lack wisdom, let him ask of God, that giveth to all men liberally, and upbraideth not; and it shall be given him. But let him ask in faith, nothing wavering. For he that wavereth is like a wave of the sea driven with the wind and tossed. For let not that man think that he shall receive any thing of the Lord. A double-minded man is unstable in all his ways.

Let the brother of low degree rejoice in that he is exalted: but the rich, in that he is made low: because as the flower of the grass he shall pass away. For the sun is no sooner risen with a burning heat, but it withereth the grass, and the flower thereof falleth, and the grace of the fashion of it perisheth: so also shall the rich man fade away in his ways.

Blessed is the man that endureth temptation: for when he is tried, he shall receive the crown of life, which the Lord hath promised to them that love him. Let no man say when he is tempted, "I am tempted of God": for God cannot be tempted with evil, neither tempteth he any man: but every man is tempted, when he is drawn away of his own lust, and enticed. Then when lust hath conceived, it bringeth forth sin: and sin, when it is finished, bringeth forth death. Do not err, my beloved brethren. Every good gift and every perfect gift is from above, and cometh down from the Father of lights, with whom is no variableness, neither shadow of turning. Of his own will begot he us with the word of truth, that we should be a kind of first-fruits of his creatures.

Whereof, my beloved brethren, let every man be swift to hear, slow to speak, slow to wrath: for the wrath of man worketh not the righteousness of God. Wherefore lay apart all filthiness and superfluity of naughtiness, and receive with meekness the engrafted word, which is able to save your souls. But be ye doers of the word, and not hearers only, deceiving your own selves. For if any be a hearer of the word, and not a doer, he is like unto a man beholding his natural face in a glass: for he beholdeth himself, and goeth his way, and straightway forgetteth what manner of man he was. But whoso looketh into the perfect law of liberty, and continueth therein, he being not a forgetful hearer, but a doer of the work, this man shall be blessed in his deed. If any man among you seem to be religious, and bridleth not his tongue, but deceiveth his own heart, this man's religion is vain. Pure religion and undefiled before God and the Father is this: to visit the fatherless and widows in their affliction, and to keep himself unspotted from the world.

My brethren, have not the faith of our Lord Jesus Christ, the Lord of glory, with respect of persons. For if there come unto your assembly a man with a gold ring, in goodly apparel, and there come in also a poor man in vile raiment; and ye have respect to him that weareth the gay clothing, and say unto him, "Sit thou here in a good place"; and say to the poor, "Stand thou there, or sit here under my footstool": are ye not then partial in your selves, and are become judges of evil thoughts?

Hearken, my beloved brethren, hath not God chosen the poor of this world rich in faith, and heirs of the kingdom which he hath promised to them that love him? but ye have despised the poor. Do not rich men oppress you, and draw you before the judgment seats? Do not they blaspheme that worthy name by

A LETTER OF JAMES

the which ye are called? If ye fulfil the royal law according to the scripture, "Thou shalt love thy neighbour as thyself," ye do well. But if ye have respect to persons, ye commit sin, and are convinced of the law as transgressors. For whosoever shall keep the whole law, and yet offend in one point, he is guilty of all. For he that said, "Do not commit adultery," said also, "Do not kill." Now if thou commit no adultery, yet if thou kill, thou art become a transgressor of the law. So speak ye, and so do, as they that shall be judged by the law of liberty. For he shall have judgment without mercy, that hath showed no mercy; and mercy rejoiceth against judgment.

What doth it profit, my brethren, though a man say he hath faith, and have not works? can faith save him? If a brother or sister be naked, and destitute of daily food, and one of you say unto them, "Depart in peace, be ye warmed and filled"; notwithstanding ye give them not those things which are needful to the body; what doth it profit? Even so faith, if it hath not works, is dead, being alone.

Yea, a man may say, "Thou hast faith, and I have works": show me thy faith without thy works, and I will show thee my faith by my works. Thou believest that there is one God; thou doest well: the devils also believe, and tremble. But wilt thou know, O vain man, that faith without works is dead?

Was not Abraham our father justified by works, when he had offered Isaac his son upon the altar? Seest thou how faith wrought with his works, and by works was faith made perfect? And the scripture was fulfilled which saith, "Abraham believed God, and it was imputed unto him for righteousness: and he was called the Friend of God." Ye see then how that by works a man is justified, and not by faith only.

Likewise also was not Rahab the harlot justified by works, when she had received the messengers, and had sent them out another way? For as the body without the spirit is dead, so faith without works is dead also.

My brethren, be not many masters, knowing that we shall

receive the greater condemnation. For in many things we offend all. If any man offend not in word, the same is a perfect man, and able also to bridle the whole body. Behold, we put bits in the horses' mouths, that they may obey us; and we turn about their whole body. Behold also the ships, which though they be so great, and are driven of fierce winds, yet are they turned about with a very small helm, whithersoever the governor listeth. Even so the tongue is a little member, and boasteth great things. Behold, how great a matter a little fire kindleth! And the tongue is a fire, a world of iniquity: so is the tongue among our members that it defileth the whole body, and setteth on fire the course of nature; and it is set on fire of hell. For every kind of beasts, and of birds, and of serpents, and of things in the sea, is tamed, and hath been tamed of mankind: but the tongue can no man tame; it is an unruly evil, full of deadly poison. Therewith bless we God, even the Father; and therewith curse we men, which are made after the similitude of God. Out of the same mouth proceedeth blessing and cursing. My brethren, these things ought not so to be. Doth a fountain send forth at the same place sweet water and bitter? Can the fig tree, my brethren, bear olive berries? either a vine, figs? so can no fountain both yield salt water and fresh.

Who is a wise man and endued with knowledge among you? let him show out of a good conversation his works with meekness of wisdom. But if ye have bitter envying and strife in your hearts, glory not, and lie not against the truth. This wisdom descendeth not from above, but is earthly, sensual, devilish. For where envying and strife is, there is confusion and every evil work. But the wisdom that is from above is first pure, then peaceable, gentle, and easy to be intreated, full of mercy and good fruits, without partiality, and without hypocrisy. And the fruit of righteousness is sown in peace of them that make peace.

From whence come wars and fightings among you? come they

A LETTER OF JAMES

not hence, even of your lusts that war in your members? Ye lust, and have not: ye kill, and desire to have, and cannot obtain: ye fight and war, yet ye have not, because ye ask not. Ye ask, and receive not, because ye ask amiss, that ye may consume it upon your lusts. Ye adulterers and adulteresses, know ye not that the friendship of the world is enmity with God? whosoever therefore will be a friend of the world is the enemy of God. Do ye think that the scripture saith in vain, "The spirit that dwelleth in us lusteth to envy"? But he giveth more grace. Wherefore he saith, "God resisteth the proud, but giveth grace unto the humble." Submit your selves therefore to God. Resist the devil, and he will flee from you. Draw nigh to God, and he will draw nigh to you. Cleanse your hands, ye sinners; and purify your hearts, ye double-minded. Be afflicted, and mourn, and weep: let your laughter be turned to mourning, and your joy to heaviness. Humble yourselves in the sight of the Lord, and he shall lift you up. Speak not evil one of another, brethren. He that speaketh evil of his brother, and judgeth his brother, speaketh evil of the law, and judgeth the law: but if thou judge the law, thou art not a doer of the law, but a judge. There is one lawgiver, who is able to save and to destroy: who art thou that judgest another? Go to now, ye that say, "To-day or to-morrow we will go into such a city, and continue there a year, and buy and sell, and get gain": whereas ye know not what shall be on the morrow. For what is your life? It is even a vapour, that appeareth for a little time, and then vanisheth away. For that ye ought to say, "If the Lord will, we shall live, and do this, or that." But now ye rejoice in your boastings: all such rejoicing is evil. Therefore to him that knoweth to do good, and doeth it not, to him it is sin.

Go to now, ye rich men, weep and howl for your miseries that shall come upon you. Your riches are corrupted, and your garments are motheaten. Your gold and silver is cankered; and the rust of them shall be a witness against you, and shall eat your flesh as it were fire. Ye have heaped treasure together for the last days. Behold, the hire of the labourers who have reaped down your fields, which is of you kept back by fraud, crieth: and the cries of them which have reaped are entered into the ears of the Lord of Sabaoth. Ye have lived in pleasure on the earth, and been wanton; ye have nourished your hearts, as in a day of slaughter. Ye have condemned and killed the just; and he doth not resist you.

Be patient therefore, brethren, unto the coming of the Lord. Behold, the husbandman waiteth for the precious fruit of the earth, and hath long patience for it, until he receive the early and latter rain. Be ye also patient; establish your hearts: for the coming of the Lord draweth nigh. Grudge not one against another, brethren, lest ye be condemned: behold, the judge standeth before the door. Take, my brethren, the prophets, who have spoken in the name of the Lord, for an example of suffering affliction, and of patience. Behold, we count them happy which endure. Ye have heard of the patience of Job, and have seen the end of the Lord; that the Lord is very pitiful, and of tender mercy.

But above all things, my brethren, swear not, neither by heaven, neither by the earth, neither by any other oath: but let your yea be yea; and your nay, nay; lest ye fall into condemnation.

Is any among you afflicted? let him pray. Is any merry? let him sing psalms. Is any sick among you? let him call for the elders of the church; and let them pray over him, anointing him with oil in the name of the Lord: and the prayer of faith shall save the sick, and the Lord shall raise him up; and if he have committed sins, they shall be forgiven him. Confess your faults one to another, and pray one for another, that ye may be healed. The effectual fervent prayer of a righteous man availeth much. Elias was a man subject to like passions as we are, and he prayed earnestly that it might not rain: and it rained not on the earth by the space of three years and six months. And he prayed

A LETTER OF JAMES

again, and the heaven gave rain, and the earth brought forth her fruit. Brethren, if any of you do err from the truth, and one convert him; let him know, that he which converteth the sinner from the error of his way shall save a soul from death, and shall hide a multitude of sins.

A LETTER OF JOHN

The first of the three canonical epistles of John, much superior to the other two which were nearly rejected from the Canon because of their obvious inferiority, was probably written by the author of the Gospel according to John. Its theme is the same mystical commingling of divine and human love celebrated in the larger work, and its message is delivered in the same well-modulated tone of gentle sweetness. It is supposed to have been written in answer to the Gnostic heresies which were losing themselves in endless intellectual disquisitions upon the dual nature of Christ—a problem which raises no difficulty for the writer with his mystical intuition of the unity of the human and divine.

A Letter of JOHN

THAT WHICH WAS FROM THE BEGINNING, which we have heard, which we have seen with our eyes, which we have looked upon, and our hands have handled, of the Word of life (for the life was manifested, and we have seen it, and bear witness, and show unto you that eternal life, which was with the Father, and was manifested unto us); that which we have seen and heard declare we unto you, that ye also may have fellowship with us: and truly our fellowship is with the Father, and with his Son Jesus Christ. And these things write we unto you, that your joy may be full.

This then is the message which we have heard of him, and declare unto you, that God is light, and in him is no darkness at all. If we say that we have fellowship with him, and walk in darkness, we lie, and do not the truth: but if we walk in the light, as he is in the light, we have fellowship one with another, and the blood of Jesus Christ his Son cleanseth us from all sin. If we say that we have no sin, we deceive ourselves, and the truth is not in us. If we confess our sins, he is faithful and just to forgive us our sins, and to cleanse us from all unrighteousness. If we say that we have not sinned, we make him a liar, and his word is not in us. My little children, these things write I unto you, that ye sin not. And if any man sin, we have an advocate with the Father, Jesus Christ the righteous: and he is the propitiation for our sins: and not for ours only, but also for the sins of the whole world. And hereby we do know that we know him, if we keep his commandments. He that saith, "I know him," and keepeth not his commandments, is a liar, and the truth is not

A LETTER OF JOHN

in him. But whoso keepeth his word, in him verily is the love of God perfected: hereby know we that we are in him. He that saith he abideth in him ought himself also so to walk, even as he walked.

Brethren, I write no new commandment unto you, but an old commandment which ye had from the beginning. The old commandment is the word which ye have heard from the beginning. Again, a new commandment I write unto you, which thing is true in him and in you: because the darkness is past, and the true light now shineth. He that saith he is in the light, and hateth his brother, is in darkness even until now. He that loveth his brother abideth in the light, and there is none occasion of stumbling in him. But he that hateth his brother is in darkness, and walketh in darkness, and knoweth not whither he goeth, because that darkness hath blinded his eyes.

I write unto you, little children, because your sins are forgiven you for his name's sake. I write unto you, fathers, because ye have known him that is from the beginning. I write unto you, young men, because ye have overcome the wicked one. I write unto you, little children, because ye have known the Father. I have written unto you, fathers, because ye have known him that is from the beginning. I have written unto you, young men, because ye are strong, and the word of God abideth in you, and ye have overcome the wicked one. Love not the world, neither the things that are in the world. If any man love the world, the love of the Father is not in him. For all that is in the world, the lust of the flesh, and the lust of the eyes, and the pride of life, is not of the Father, but is of the world. And the world passeth away, and the lust thereof: but he that doeth the will of God abideth for ever.

Little children, it is the last time: and as ye have heard that Antichrist shall come, even now are there many Antichrists; whereby we know that it is the last time. They went out from us, but they were not of us; for if they had been of us, they would no doubt have continued with us: but they went out, that they might be made manifest that they were not all of us. But ye have

A LETTER OF JOHN

an unction from the Holy One, and ye know all things. I have not written unto you because ye know not the truth, but because ye know it, and that no lie is of the truth. Who is a liar but he that denieth that Jesus is the Christ? He is Antichrist, that denieth the Father and the Son. Whosoever denieth the Son, the same hath not the Father (but) he that acknowledgeth the Son hath the Father also.

Behold, what manner of love the Father hath bestowed upon us, that we should be called the sons of God: therefore the world knoweth us not, because it knew him not. Beloved, now are we the sons of God, and it doth not yet appear what we shall be: but we know that, when he shall appear, we shall be like him; for we shall see him as he is. And every man that hath this hope in him purifieth himself, even as he is pure. Whosoever committeth sin transgresseth also the law: for sin is the transgression of the law. And ye know that he was manifested to take away our sins; and in him is no sin. Whosoever abideth in him sinneth not: whosoever sinneth hath not seen him, neither known him. Little children, let no man deceive you: he that doeth righteousness is righteous, even as he is righteous. He that committeth sin is of the devil; for the devil sinneth from the beginning. For this purpose the Son of God was manifested, that he might destroy the works of the devil. Whosoever is born of God doth not commit sin; for his seed remaineth in him: and he cannot sin, because he is born of God. In this the children of God are manifest, and the children of the devil: whosoever doeth not righteousness is not of God, neither he that loveth not his brother. For this is the message that ye heard from the beginning, that we should love one another.

We know that we have passed from death unto life, because we love the brethren. He that loveth not his brother abideth in death. Whosoever hateth his brother is a murderer: and ye know that no murderer hath eternal life abiding in him. Hereby perceive we the love of God, because he laid down his life for us: and we ought to lay down our lives for the brethren. But whoso hath this world's good, and seeth his brother have need,

A LETTER OF JOHN

and shutteth up his bowels of compassion from him, how dwelleth the love of God in him? My little children, let us not love in word, neither in tongue; but in deed and in truth. And hereby we know that we are of the truth, and shall assure our hearts before him. For if our heart condemn us, God is greater than our heart, and knoweth all things. Beloved, if our heart condemn us not, then have we confidence toward God. And whatsoever we ask, we receive of him, because we keep his commandments, and do those things that are pleasing in his sight. And this is his commandment, That we should believe on the name of his Son Jesus Christ, and love one another, as he gave us commandment. And he that keepeth his commandments dwelleth in him, and he in him. And hereby we know that he abideth in us, by the Spirit which he hath given us.

Beloved, believe not every spirit, but try the spirits whether they are of God: because many false prophets are gone out into the world. Hereby know ye the Spirit of God: every spirit that confesseth that Jesus Christ is come in the flesh is of God: and every spirit that confesseth not that Jesus Christ is come in the flesh is not of God: and this is that spirit of Antichrist, whereof ye have heard that it should come; and even now already is it in the world. Ye are of God, little children, and have overcome them: because greater is he that is in you than he that is in the world. They are of the world: therefore speak they of the world, and the world heareth them. We are of God: he that knoweth God heareth us; he that is not of God heareth not us. Hereby know we the spirit of truth, and the spirit of error.

Beloved, let us love one another: for love is of God; and every one that loveth is born of God, and knoweth God. He that loveth not knoweth not God; for God is love. In this was manifested the love of God toward us, because that God sent his only begotten Son into the world, that we might live through him. Herein is love, not that we loved God, but that he loved us, and sent his Son to be the propitiation for our sins. Beloved, if God so loved us, we ought also to love one another.

No man hath seen God at any time. If we love one another,

A LETTER OF JOHN

God dwelleth in us, and his love is perfected in us. Hereby know we that we dwell in him, and he in us, because he hath given us of his Spirit. And we have seen and do testify that the Father sent the Son to be the Saviour of the world. Whosoever shall confess that Jesus is the Son of God, God dwelleth in him, and he in God. And we have known and believed the love that God hath to us. God is love; and he that dwelleth in love dwelleth in God, and God in him. Herein is our love made perfect, that we may have boldness in the day of judgment: because as he is, so are we in this world.

There is no fear in love; but perfect love casteth out fear: because fear hath torment. He that feareth is not made perfect in love. We love him, because he first loved us. If a man say, "I love God," and hateth his brother, he is a liar: for he that loveth not his brother whom he hath seen, how can he love God whom he hath not seen? And this commandment have we from him, that he who loveth God love his brother also.

THE REVELATION OF JESUS CHRIST

The inevitable conflict between Christianity and the Roman Empire was long postponed through the imperial policy of religious toleration and the political quietism of the Christians under the leadership of Paul, but this period of forbearance came to an end with the official proclamation of emperor worship by Domitian. Persecution, hitherto confined to individuals such as Paul and Peter, now overtook all Christians who were unwilling to purchase safety at the price of conforming to the Roman religion. In this dark hour of suppression and threatened extinction, the Book of Revelation was written by John, a prophet of Ephesus, in circumstances similar to those in which the Book of Daniel had been composed two centuries earlier. Steeped in the apocalyptic literature of Ezekiel, Zechariah, and Daniel, the author constructed a grandiose symbolic epic of the approaching overthrow of Rome as the veritable kingdom of Antichrist foretold by the prophets. Though the influence of Paul is evident in the epistolary form of the prologue, the spirit of the work is essentially Hebraic rather than Christian.

Dominated by conceptions of war and revenge, the work is ethically on a lower plane than the rest of the New Testament, but from the strictly literary point of view it is the most magnificent of the later books of the Bible. Carefully composed upon a symbolic pattern furnished by the sacred number seven, it presents a cumulative series of astounding visions in which color, form, the sounds of musical instruments, and the tumultuous noises of storm and earthquake all unite to create an overwhelming impression of the final struggle between the embattled hosts of good and evil. Deliberately obscure in its allegory that it might not be understood of the pagans, the drama is enacted in an unearthly metallic atmosphere, at times grimly lurid and then again blinding in its splendor; and always to the accompaniment of piercing choruses of despair or victory. It is fitting that the Bible should close with this culminating example of the apocalyptic form, so deeply infused with the prophetic spirit, a kind of resurrection of the Old Testament in Christian guise.

The Revelation of JESUS CHRIST

WHICH GOD GAVE UNTO HIM, TO SHOW UNTO HIS SERVANTS THINGS WHICH MUST SHORTLY COME TO PASS; AND HE SENT AND SIGNIFIED IT BY HIS ANGEL UNTO HIS SERVANT JOHN, WHO BORE RECORD OF THE WORD OF GOD, AND OF THE TESTIMONY OF JESUS CHRIST, AND OF ALL THINGS THAT HE SAW.

BLESSED IS HE THAT READETH, AND THEY THAT HEAR THE WORDS OF THIS PROPHECY, AND KEEP THOSE THINGS WHICH ARE WRITTEN THEREIN: FOR THE TIME IS AT HAND.

Prologue

John to the seven churches which are in Asia: grace be unto you, and peace, from him which is, and which was, and which is to come; and from the seven Spirits which are before his throne; and from Jesus Christ, who is the faithful witness, and the first begotten of the dead, and the prince of the kings of the earth. Unto him that loved us, and washed us from our sins in his own blood, and hath made us kings and priests unto God and his Father; to him be glory and dominion for ever and ever. Amen.

Behold, he cometh with clouds; and every eye shall see him, and they also which pierced him: and all kindreds of the earth shall wail because of him. Even so: amen.

"I am Alpha and Omega, the beginning and the ending," saith the Lord, which is, and which was, and which is to come, the Almighty.

I John, who also am your brother, and companion in tribulation, and in the kingdom and patience of Jesus Christ, was in

THE REVELATION OF JESUS CHRIST

the isle that is called Patmos, for the word of God, and for the testimony of Jesus Christ. I was in the Spirit on the Lord's day, and heard behind me a great voice, as of a trumpet, saying, "I am Alpha and Omega, the first and the last," and, "What thou seest, write in a book, and send it unto the seven churches which are in Asia; unto Ephesus, and unto Smyrna, and unto Pergamos, and unto Thyatira, and unto Sardis, and unto Philadelphia, and unto Laodicea."

And I turned to see the voice that spoke with me. And being turned, I saw seven golden candlesticks; and in the midst of the seven candlesticks one like unto the Son of Man, clothed with a garment down to the foot, and girt about the paps with a golden girdle. His head and his hairs were white like wool, as white as snow; and his eyes were as a flame of fire; and his feet like unto fine brass, as if they burned in a furnace; and his voice as the sound of many waters. And he had in his right hand seven stars: and out of his mouth went a sharp two-edged sword: and his countenance was as the sun shineth in his strength. And when I saw him, I fell at his feet as dead. And he laid his right hand upon me, saying unto me,

"Fear not; I am the first and the last: I am he that liveth, and was dead; and, behold, I am alive for evermore, Amen; and have the keys of hell and of death. Write the things which thou hast seen, and the things which are, and the things which shall be hereafter; the mystery of the seven stars which thou sawest in my right hand, and the seven golden candlesticks. The seven stars are the angels of the seven churches: and the seven candlesticks which thou sawest are the seven churches.

"Unto the angel of the church of Ephesus write: 'These things saith he that holdeth the seven stars in his right hand, who walketh in the midst of the seven golden candlesticks: I know thy works, and thy labour, and thy patience, and how thou canst not bear them which are evil: and thou hast tried them which say they are apostles, and are not, and hast found them liars, and hast borne, and hast patience, and for my name's sake

THE REVELATION OF JESUS CHRIST

hast laboured, and hast not fainted. Nevertheless I have somewhat against thee, because thou hast left thy first love. Remember therefore from whence thou art fallen, and repent, and do the first works; or else I will come unto thee quickly, and will remove thy candlestick out of his place, except thou repent. But this thou hast, that thou hatest the deeds of the Nicolaitanes, which I also hate. He that hath an ear, let him hear what the Spirit saith unto the churches: "To him that overcometh will I give to eat of the tree of life, which is in the midst of the paradise of God."'

"And unto the angel of the church in Smyrna write: 'These things saith the first and the last, which was dead, and is alive: I know thy works, and tribulation, and poverty (but thou art rich), and I know the blasphemy of them which say they are Jews, and are not, but are the synagogue of Satan. Fear none of those things which thou shalt suffer: behold, the devil shall cast some of you into prison, that ye may be tried; and ye shall have tribulation ten days: be thou faithful unto death, and I will give thee a crown of life. He that hath an ear, let him hear what the Spirit saith unto the churches: "He that overcometh shall not be hurt of the second death."'

"And to the angel of the church in Pergamos write: 'These things saith he which hath the sharp sword with two edges: I know thy works, and where thou dwellest, even where Satan's seat is: and thou holdest fast my name, and hast not denied my faith, even in those days wherein Antipas was my faithful martyr, who was slain among you, where Satan dwelleth. But I have a few things against thee, because thou hast there them that hold the doctrine of Balaam, who taught Balak to cast a stumblingblock before the children of Israel, to eat things sacrificed unto idols, and to commit fornication. So hast thou also them that hold the doctrine of the Nicolaitanes, which thing I hate. Repent; or else I will come unto thee quickly, and will fight against them with the sword of my mouth. He that hath an ear, let him hear what the Spirit saith unto the churches:

THE REVELATION OF JESUS CHRIST

"To him that overcometh will I give to eat of the hidden manna, and will give him a white stone, and in the stone a new name written, which no man knoweth saving he that receiveth it."'

"And unto the angel of the church in Thyatira write: 'These things saith the Son of God, who hath his eyes like unto a flame of fire, and his feet are like fine brass: I know thy works, and charity, and service, and faith, and thy patience, and thy works; and the last to be more than the first. Notwithstanding I have a few things against thee, because thou sufferest that woman Jezebel, which calleth herself a prophetess, to teach and to seduce my servants to commit fornication, and to eat things sacrificed unto idols. And I gave her space to repent of her fornication; and she repented not. Behold, I will cast her into a bed, and them that commit adultery with her into great tribulation, except they repent of their deeds. And I will kill her children with death; and all the churches shall know that I am he which searcheth the reins and hearts: and I will give unto every one of you according to your works. But unto you I say, and unto the rest in Thyatira, as many as have not this doctrine, and which have not known the depths of Satan, as they speak; I will put upon you none other burden. But that which ye have already hold fast till I come. And he that overcometh, and keepeth my works unto the end, to him will I give power over the nations, and he shall rule them with a rod of iron; as the vessels of a potter shall they be broken to shivers: even as I received of my Father. And I will give him the morning star. He that hath an ear, let him hear what the Spirit saith unto the churches.'

"And unto the angel of the church in Sardis write: 'These things saith he that hath the seven Spirits of God, and the seven stars: I know thy works, that thou hast a name that thou livest, and art dead. Be watchful, and strengthen the things which remain, that are ready to die: for I have not found thy works perfect before God. Remember therefore how thou hast received and heard, and hold fast, and repent. If therefore thou shalt not watch, I will come on thee as a thief, and thou shalt not know what hour I will come upon thee. Thou hast a few

THE REVELATION OF JESUS CHRIST

names even in Sardis which have not defiled their garments; and they shall walk with me in white: for they are worthy. He that overcometh, the same shall be clothed in white raiment; and I will not blot out his name out of the book of life, but I will confess his name before my Father, and before his angels. He that hath an ear, let him hear what the Spirit saith unto the churches.'

"And to the angel of the church in Philadelphia write: 'These things saith he that is holy, he that is true, he that hath the key of David, he that openeth, and no man shutteth; and shutteth, and no man openeth: I know thy works: behold, I have set before thee an open door, and no man can shut it: for thou hast a little strength, and hast kept my word, and hast not denied my name. Behold, I will make them of the synagogue of Satan, which say they are Jews, and are not, but do lie; behold, I will make them to come and worship before thy feet, and to know that I have loved thee. Because thou hast kept the word of my patience, I also will keep thee from the hour of temptation, which shall come upon all the world, to try them that dwell upon the earth. Behold, I come quickly: hold that fast which thou hast, that no man take thy crown. Him that overcometh will I make a pillar in the temple of my God, and he shall go no more out: and I will write upon him the name of my God, and the name of the city of my God, which is new Jerusalem, which cometh down out of heaven from my God: and I will write upon him my new name. He that hath an ear, let him hear what the Spirit saith unto the churches.'

"And unto the angel of the church of the Laodiceans write: 'These things saith the Amen, the faithful and true witness, the beginning of the creation of God: I know thy works, that thou art neither cold nor hot: I would thou wert cold or hot. So then because thou art lukewarm, and neither cold nor hot, I will spew thee out of my mouth. Because thou sayest, "I am rich, and increased with goods, and have need of nothing"; and knowest not that thou art wretched, and miserable, and poor, and blind, and naked: I counsel thee to buy of me gold tried in the fire, that thou mayest be rich; and white raiment, that thou mayest be

THE REVELATION OF JESUS CHRIST

clothed, and that the shame of thy nakedness do not appear; and anoint thine eyes with eyesalve, that thou mayest see. As many as I love, I rebuke and chasten: be zealous therefore, and repent. Behold, I stand at the door, and knock: if any man hear my voice, and open the door, I will come in to him, and will sup with him, and he with me. To him that overcometh will I grant to sit with me in my throne, even as I also overcame, and am set down with my Father in his throne. He that hath an ear, let him hear what the Spirit saith unto the churches.'"

I. *The Book Sealed with Seven Seals*

After this I looked, and, behold, a door was opened in heaven: and the first voice which I heard was as it were of a trumpet talking with me; which said,

"Come up hither, and I will show thee things which must be hereafter."

And immediately I was in the spirit: and, behold, a throne was set in heaven, and one sat on the throne. And he that sat was to look upon like a jasper and a sardine stone: and there was a rainbow round about the throne, in sight like unto an emerald. And round about the throne were four and twenty seats: and upon the seats I saw four and twenty elders sitting, clothed in white raiment; and they had on their heads crowns of gold. And out of the throne proceeded lightnings and thunderings and voices: and there were seven lamps of fire burning before the throne, which are the seven Spirits of God. And before the throne there was a sea of glass like unto crystal: and in the midst of the throne, and round about the throne, were four beasts full of eyes before and behind. And the first beast was like a lion, and the second beast like a calf, and the third beast had a face as a man, and the fourth beast was like a flying eagle. And the four beasts had each of them six wings about him; and they were full of eyes within: and they rest not day and night, saying,

"Holy, holy, holy, Lord God Almighty, which was, and is, and is to come."

THE REVELATION OF JESUS CHRIST

And when those beasts give glory and honour and thanks to him that sat on the throne, who liveth for ever and ever, the four and twenty elders fall down before him that sat on the throne, and worship him that liveth for ever and ever, and cast their crowns before the throne, saying,

"Thou art worthy, O Lord, to receive glory and honour and power: for thou hast created all things, and for thy pleasure they are and were created."

And I saw in the right hand of him that sat on the throne a book written within and on the backside, sealed with seven seals. And I saw a strong angel proclaiming with a loud voice,

"Who is worthy to open the book, and to loose the seals thereof?"

And no man in heaven, nor in earth, neither under the earth, was able to open the book, neither to look thereon. And I wept much, because no man was found worthy to open and to read the book, neither to look thereon. And one of the elders saith unto me,

"Weep not: behold, the Lion of the tribe of Judah, the Root of David, hath prevailed to open the book, and to loose the seven seals thereof."

And I beheld, and, lo, in the midst of the throne and of the four beasts, and in the midst of the elders, stood a Lamb as it had been slain, having seven horns and seven eyes, which are the seven Spirits of God sent forth into all the earth. And he came and took the book out of the right hand of him that sat upon the throne. And when he had taken the book, the four beasts and four and twenty elders fell down before the Lamb, having every one of them harps, and golden vials full of odours, which are the prayers of saints. And they sung a new song, saying,

"Thou art worthy to take the book, and to open the seals thereof: for thou wast slain, and hast redeemed us to God by thy blood out of every kindred, and tongue, and people, and nation; and hast made us unto our God kings and priests: and we shall reign on the earth."

And I beheld, and I heard the voice of many angels round

THE REVELATION OF JESUS CHRIST

about the throne and the beasts and the elders: and the number of them was ten thousand times ten thousand, and thousands of thousands, saying with a loud voice,

"Worthy is the Lamb that was slain to receive power, and riches, and wisdom, and strength, and honour, and glory, and blessing."

And every creature which is in heaven, and on the earth, and under the earth, and such as are in the sea, and all that are in them, heard I saying,

"Blessing, and honour, and glory, and power, be unto him that sitteth upon the throne, and unto the Lamb for ever and ever."

And the four beasts said,
"Amen!"

And the four and twenty elders fell down and worshipped him that liveth for ever and ever.

II. *The Opening of the Seals*

And I saw when the Lamb opened one of the seals, and I heard, as it were the noise of thunder, one of the four beasts saying,

"Come and see."

And I saw, and beheld a white horse: and he that sat on him had a bow; and a crown was given unto him: and he went forth conquering, and to conquer. And when he had opened the second seal, I heard the second beast say,

"Come and see."

And there went out another horse that was red: and power was given to him that sat thereon to take peace from the earth, and that they should kill one another: and there was given unto him a great sword. And when he had opened the third seal, I heard the third beast say,

"Come and see."

And I beheld, and lo a black horse; and he that sat on him had a pair of balances in his hand. And I heard a voice in the midst of the four beasts say, "A measure of wheat for a penny,

THE REVELATION OF JESUS CHRIST

and three measures of barley for a penny; and see thou hurt not the oil and the wine." And when he had opened the fourth seal, I heard the voice of the fourth beast say,

"Come and see."

And I looked, and beheld a pale horse: and his name that sat on him was Death, and Hell followed with him. And power was given unto them over the fourth part of the earth, to kill with sword, and with hunger, and with death, and with the beasts of the earth. And when he had opened the fifth seal, I saw under the altar the souls of them that were slain for the word of God, and for the testimony which they held. And they cried with a loud voice, saying,

"How long, O Lord, holy and true, dost thou not judge and avenge our blood on them that dwell on the earth?"

And white robes were given unto every one of them; and it was said unto them, that they should rest yet for a little season, until their fellowservants also and their brethren, that should be killed as they were, should be fulfilled.

And I beheld when he had opened the sixth seal, and, lo, there was a great earthquake; and the sun became black as sackcloth of hair, and the moon became as blood; and the stars of heaven fell unto the earth, even as a fig tree casteth her untimely figs, when she is shaken of a mighty wind. And the heaven departed as a scroll when it is rolled together; and every mountain and island were moved out of their places. And the kings of the earth, and the great men, and the rich men, and the chief captains, and the mighty men, and every bondman, and every free man, hid themselves in the dens and in the rocks of the mountains, and said to the mountains and rocks, "Fall on us, and hide us from the face of him that sitteth on the throne, and from the wrath of the Lamb: for the great day of his wrath is come; and who shall be able to stand?"

And after these things I saw four angels standing on the four corners of the earth, holding the four winds of the earth, that the wind should not blow on the earth, nor on the sea, nor on any tree. And I saw another angel ascending from the east, hav-

THE REVELATION OF JESUS CHRIST

ing the seal of the living God: and he cried with a loud voice to the four angels, to whom it was given to hurt the earth and the sea, saying, "Hurt not the earth, neither the sea, nor the trees, till we have sealed the servants of our God in their foreheads."

And I heard the number of them which were sealed: and there were sealed a hundred and forty and four thousand of all the tribes of the children of Israel.

After this I beheld, and, lo, a great multitude, which no man could number, of all nations, and kindreds, and people, and tongues, stood before the throne, and before the Lamb, clothed with white robes, and palms in their hands, and cried with a loud voice, saying, "Salvation to our God which sitteth upon the throne, and unto the Lamb."

And all the angels stood round about the throne, and about the elders and the four beasts, and fell before the throne on their faces, and worshipped God, saying,

"Amen! Blessing, and glory, and wisdom, and thanksgiving, and honour, and power, and might, be unto our God for ever and ever. Amen!"

And one of the elders answered, saying unto me,

"What are these which are arrayed in white robes? and whence came they?"

And I said unto him, "Sir, thou knowest."

And he said to me,

"These are they which came out of great tribulation, and have washed their robes, and made them white in the blood of the Lamb. Therefore are they before the throne of God, and serve him day and night in his temple: and he that sitteth on the throne shall dwell among them. They shall hunger no more, neither thirst any more; neither shall the sun light on them, nor any heat. For the Lamb which is in the midst of the throne shall feed them, and shall lead them unto living fountains of waters: and God shall wipe away all tears from their eyes."

And when he had opened the seventh seal, there was silence in heaven about the space of half an hour. And I saw the seven angels which stood before God; and to them were given seven

THE REVELATION OF JESUS CHRIST

trumpets. And another angel came and stood at the altar, having a golden censer; and there was given unto him much incense, that he should offer it with the prayers of all saints upon the golden altar which was before the throne. And the smoke of the incense, which came with the prayers of the saints, ascended up before God out of the angel's hand. And the angel took the censer, and filled it with fire of the altar, and cast it into the earth: and there were voices, and thunderings, and lightnings, and an earthquake.

III. The Seven Trumpets

And the seven angels which had the seven trumpets prepared themselves to sound.

The first angel sounded, and there followed hail and fire mingled with blood, and they were cast upon the earth: and the third part of trees was burnt up, and all green grass was burnt up.

And the second angel sounded, and as it were a great mountain burning with fire was cast into the sea: and the third part of the sea became blood; and the third part of the creatures which were in the sea, and had life, died; and the third part of the ships were destroyed.

And the third angel sounded, and there fell a great star from heaven, burning as it were a lamp, and it fell upon the third part of the rivers, and upon the fountains of waters; and the name of the star is called Wormwood: and the third part of the waters became wormwood; and many men died of the waters, because they were made bitter.

And the fourth angel sounded, and the third part of the sun was smitten, and the third part of the moon, and the third part of the stars; so as the third part of them was darkened, and the day shone not for a third part of it, and the night likewise. And I beheld, and heard an angel flying through the midst of heaven, saying with a loud voice,

"Woe, woe, woe, to the inhabiters of the earth by reason of the other voices of the trumpet of the three angels, which are yet to sound!"

THE REVELATION OF JESUS CHRIST

And the fifth angel sounded, and I saw a star fall from heaven unto the earth: and to him was given the key of the bottomless pit. And he opened the bottomless pit; and there arose a smoke out of the pit, as the smoke of a great furnace; and the sun and the air were darkened by reason of the smoke of the pit. And there came out of the smoke locusts upon the earth: and unto them was given power, as the scorpions of the earth have power. And it was commanded them that they should not hurt the grass of the earth, neither any green thing, neither any tree; but only those men which have not the seal of God in their foreheads. And to them it was given that they should not kill them, but that they should be tormented five months: and their torment was as the torment of a scorpion, when he striketh a man. And in those days shall men seek death, and shall not find it; and shall desire to die, and death shall flee from them. And the shapes of the locusts were like unto horses prepared unto battle; and on their heads were as it were crowns like gold, and their faces were as the faces of men. And they had hair as the hair of women and their teeth were as the teeth of lions. And they had breastplates, as it were breastplates of iron; and the sound of their wings was as the sound of chariots of many horses running to battle. And they had tails like unto scorpions, and there were stings in their tails: and their power was to hurt men five months. And they had a king over them, which is the angel of the bottomless pit, whose name in the Hebrew tongue is Abaddon, but in the Greek tongue hath his name Apollyon. One woe is past; and, behold, there come two woes more hereafter.

And the sixth angel sounded, and I heard a voice from the four horns of the golden altar which is before God, saying to the sixth angel which had the trumpet, "Loose the four angels which are bound in the great river Euphrates."

And the four angels were loosed, which were prepared for an hour, and a day, and a month, and a year, for to slay the third part of men. And the number of the army of the horsemen were two hundred thousand thousand: and I heard the number of them. And thus I saw the horses in the vision, and them that sat on

THE REVELATION OF JESUS CHRIST

them, having breastplates of fire, and of jacinth, and brimstone: and the heads of the horses were as the heads of lions; and out of their mouths issued fire and smoke and brimstone. By these three was the third part of men killed, by the fire, and by the smoke, and by the brimstone, which issued out of their mouths. For their power is in their mouth, and in their tails: for their tails were like unto serpents, and had heads, and with them they do hurt. And the rest of the men which were not killed by these plagues yet repented not of the works of their hands, that they should not worship devils, and idols of gold, and silver, and brass, and stone, and of wood: which neither can see, nor hear, nor walk: neither repented they of their murders, nor of their sorceries, nor of their fornication, nor of their thefts.

And I saw another mighty angel come down from heaven, clothed with a cloud: and a rainbow was upon his head, and his face was as it were the sun, and his feet as pillars of fire: and he had in his hand a little book open: and he set his right foot upon the sea, and his left foot on the earth, and cried with a loud voice, as when a lion roareth: and when he had cried, seven thunders uttered their voices. And when the seven thunders had uttered their voices, I was about to write: and I heard a voice from heaven saying unto me,

"Seal up those things which the seven thunders uttered, and write them not."

And the angel which I saw stand upon the sea and upon the earth lifted up his hand to heaven, and swore by him that liveth for ever and ever, who created heaven, and the things that therein are, and the earth, and the things that therein are, and the sea, and the things which are therein, that there should be time no longer: but in the days of the voice of the seventh angel, when he shall begin to sound, the mystery of God should be finished, as he hath declared to his servants the prophets. And the voice which I heard from heaven spoke unto me again, and said,

"Go and take the little book which is open in the hand of the angel which standeth upon the sea and upon the earth."

THE REVELATION OF JESUS CHRIST

And I went unto the angel, and said unto him,
"Give me the little book."
And he said unto me,
"Take it, and eat it up; and it shall make thy belly bitter, but it shall be in thy mouth sweet as honey."
And I took the little book out of the angel's hand, and ate it up; and it was in my mouth sweet as honey: and as soon as I had eaten it, my belly was bitter. And he said unto me,
"Thou must prophesy again before many peoples, and nations, and tongues, and kings."
And there was given me a reed like unto a rod: and the angel stood, saying, "Rise, and measure the temple of God, and the altar, and them that worship therein. But the court which is without the temple leave out, and measure it not; for it is given unto the Gentiles: and the holy city shall they tread under foot forty and two months. And I will give power unto my two witnesses, and they shall prophesy a thousand two hundred and threescore days, clothed in sackcloth. These are the two olive trees, and the two candlesticks standing before the God of the earth. And if any man will hurt them, fire proceedeth out of their mouth, and devoureth their enemies: and if any man will hurt them, he must in this manner be killed. These have power to shut heaven, that it rain not in the days of their prophecy: and have power over waters to turn them to blood, and to smite the earth with all plagues, as often as they will. And when they shall have finished their testimony, the beast that ascendeth out of the bottomless pit shall make war against them, and shall overcome them, and kill them. And their dead bodies shall lie in the street of the great city, which spiritually is called Sodom and Egypt, where also our Lord was crucified. And they of the people and kindreds and tongues and nations shall see their dead bodies three days and a half, and shall not suffer their dead bodies to be put in graves. And they that dwell upon the earth shall rejoice over them, and make merry, and shall send gifts one to another; because these two prophets tormented them that dwelt on the earth."

THE REVELATION OF JESUS CHRIST

And after three days and a half the spirit of life from God entered into them, and they stood upon their feet; and great fear fell upon them which saw them.

And they heard a great voice from heaven saying unto them, "Come up hither!" And they ascended up to heaven in a cloud; and their enemies beheld them. And the same hour was there a great earthquake, and the tenth part of the city fell, and in the earthquake were slain of men seven thousand: and the remnant were affrighted, and gave glory to the God of heaven. The second woe is past; and, behold, the third woe cometh quickly.

And the seventh angel sounded; and there were great voices in heaven, saying,

"The kingdoms of this world are become the kingdoms of our Lord, and of his Christ; and he shall reign for ever and ever."

And the four and twenty elders, which sat before God on their seats, fell upon their faces, and worshipped God, saying,

"We give thee thanks, O Lord God Almighty, which art, and wast, and art to come; because thou hast taken to thee thy great power, and hast reigned. And the nations were angry, and thy wrath is come, and the time of the dead, that they should be judged, and that thou shouldest give reward unto thy servants the prophets, and to the saints, and them that fear thy name, small and great; and shouldest destroy them which destroy the earth."

And the temple of God was opened in heaven, and there was seen in his temple the ark of his testament: and there were lightnings, and voices, and thunderings, and an earthquake, and great hail.

IV. *The Woman Clothed with the Sun*

And there appeared a great wonder in heaven: a woman clothed with the sun, and the moon under her feet, and upon her head a crown of twelve stars. And she being with child cried, travailing in birth, and pained to be delivered.

And there appeared another wonder in heaven: and behold a great red dragon, having seven heads and ten horns, and seven

THE REVELATION OF JESUS CHRIST

crowns upon his heads. And his tail drew the third part of the stars of heaven, and did cast them to the earth: and the dragon stood before the woman which was ready to be delivered, for to devour her child as soon as it was born.

And she brought forth a man child, who was to rule all nations with a rod of iron: and her child was caught up unto God, and to his throne. And the woman fled into the wilderness, where she hath a place prepared of God, that they should feed her there a thousand two hundred and threescore days.

And there was war in heaven. Michael and his angels fought against the dragon; and the dragon fought and his angels, and prevailed not; neither was their place found any more in heaven. And the great dragon was cast out, that old serpent, called the Devil, and Satan, which deceiveth the whole world: he was cast out into the earth, and his angels were cast out with him.

And I heard a loud voice saying in heaven,
"Now is come salvation, and strength, and the kingdom of our God, and the power of his Christ: for the accuser of our brethren is cast down, which accused them before our God day and night. And they overcame him by the blood of the Lamb, and by the word of their testimony; and they loved not their lives unto the death. Therefore rejoice, ye heavens, and ye that dwell in them. Woe to the inhabiters of the earth and of the sea! for the devil is come down unto you, having great wrath, because he knoweth that he hath but a short time."

And when the dragon saw that he was cast unto the earth, he persecuted the woman which brought forth the man child. And to the woman were given two wings of a great eagle, that she might fly into the wilderness, into her place, where she is nourished for a time, and times, and half a time, from the face of the serpent. And the serpent cast out of his mouth water as a flood after the woman, that he might cause her to be carried away of the flood. And the earth helped the woman, and the earth opened her mouth, and swallowed up the flood which the dragon cast out of his mouth. And the dragon was wroth with the woman, and went to make war with the remnant of her seed,

THE REVELATION OF JESUS CHRIST

which keep the commandments of God, and have the testimony of Jesus Christ.

And I stood upon the sand of the sea, and saw a beast rise up out of the sea, having seven heads and ten horns, and upon his horns ten crowns, and upon his heads the name of blasphemy. And the beast which I saw was like unto a leopard, and his feet were as the feet of a bear, and his mouth as the mouth of a lion: and the dragon gave him his power, and his seat, and great authority. And I saw one of his heads as it were wounded to death; and his deadly wound was healed: and all the world wondered after the beast. And they worshipped the dragon which gave power unto the beast: and they worshipped the beast, saying,

"Who is like unto the beast? who is able to make war with him?"

And there was given unto him a mouth speaking great things and blasphemies; and power was given unto him to continue forty and two months. And he opened his mouth in blasphemy against God, to blaspheme his name, and his tabernacle, and them that dwell in heaven. And it was given unto him to make war with the saints, and to overcome them: and power was given him over all kindreds, and tongues, and nations. And all that dwell upon the earth shall worship him, whose names are not written in the book of life of the Lamb slain from the foundation of the world.

If any man have an ear, let him hear.

> *He that leadeth into captivity*
> *Shall go into captivity:*
> *He that killeth with the sword*
> *Must be killed with the sword.*
> *Here is the patience and the faith of the saints.*

And I beheld another beast coming up out of the earth; and he had two horns like a lamb, and he spoke as a dragon. And he exerciseth all the power of the first beast before him, and causeth the earth and them which dwell therein to worship the first

THE REVELATION OF JESUS CHRIST

beast, whose deadly wound was healed. And he doeth great wonders, so that he maketh fire come down from heaven on the earth in the sight of men, and deceiveth them that dwell on the earth by the means of those miracles which he had power to do in the sight of the beast; saying to them that dwell on the earth that they should make an image to the beast, which had the wound by a sword, and did live. And he had power to give life unto the image of the beast, that the image of the beast should both speak, and cause that as many as would not worship the image of the beast should be killed. And he causeth all, both small and great, rich and poor, free and bond, to receive a mark in their right hand, or in their foreheads: and that no man might buy or sell, save he that had the mark, or the name of the beast, or the number of his name.

Here is wisdom. Let him that hath understanding count the number of the beast: for it is the number of a man; and his number is six hundred threescore and six.

And I looked, and, lo, a Lamb stood on the Mount Zion, and with him a hundred forty and four thousand, having his Father's name written in their foreheads. And I heard a voice from heaven, as the voice of many waters, and as the voice of a great thunder: and I heard the voice of harpers harping with their harps. And they sung as it were a new song before the throne, and before the four beasts, and the elders: and no man could learn that song but the hundred and forty and four thousand, which were redeemed from the earth. These are they which were not defiled with women; for they are virgins. These are they which follow the Lamb whithersoever he goeth. These were redeemed from among men, being the firstfruits unto God and to the Lamb. And in their mouth was found no guile: for they are without fault before the throne of God.

And I saw another angel fly in the midst of heaven, having the everlasting gospel to preach unto them that dwell on the earth, and to every nation, and kindred, and tongue, and people, saying with a loud voice, "Fear God, and give glory to him;

THE REVELATION OF JESUS CHRIST

for the hour of his judgment is come: and worship him that made heaven, and earth, and the sea, and the fountains of waters."

And there followed another angel, saying, "Babylon is fallen, is fallen, that great city, because she made all nations drink of the wine of the wrath of her fornication."

And the third angel followed them, saying with a loud voice,

"If any man worship the beast and his image, and receive his mark in his forehead, or in his hand, the same shall drink of the wine of the wrath of God, which is poured out without mixture into the cup of his indignation; and he shall be tormented with fire and brimstone in the presence of the holy angels, and in the presence of the Lamb: and the smoke of their torment ascendeth up for ever and ever: and they have no rest day nor night, who worship the beast and his image, and whosoever receiveth the mark of his name." Here is the patience of the saints: here are they that keep the commandments of God, and the faith of Jesus.

And I heard a voice from heaven saying unto me, "Write:

" 'Blessed are the dead which die in the Lord from henceforth: "Yea," saith the Spirit, "that they may rest from their labours; and their works do follow them." ' "

And I looked, and beheld a white cloud, and upon the cloud one sat like unto the Son of Man, having on his head a golden crown, and in his hand a sharp sickle. And another angel came out of the temple, crying with a loud voice to him that sat on the cloud,

"Thrust in thy sickle, and reap: for the time is come for thee to reap; for the harvest of the earth is ripe."

And he that sat on the cloud thrust in his sickle on the earth; and the earth was reaped.

And another angel came out of the temple which is in heaven, he also having a sharp sickle.

And another angel came out from the altar, which had power over fire; and cried with a loud cry to him that had the sharp sickle, saying,

THE REVELATION OF JESUS CHRIST

"Thrust in thy sharp sickle, and gather the clusters of the vine of the earth; for her grapes are fully ripe."

And the angel thrust in his sickle into the earth, and gathered the vine of the earth, and cast it into the great winepress of the wrath of God. And the winepress was trodden without the city, and blood came out of the winepress, even unto the horse bridles, by the space of a thousand and six hundred furlongs.

And I saw another sign in heaven, great and marvellous, seven angels having the seven last plagues; for in them is filled up the wrath of God. And I saw as it were a sea of glass mingled with fire: and them that had gotten the victory over the beast, and over his image, and over his mark, and over the number of his name, stand on the sea of glass, having the harps of God. And they sing the song of Moses the servant of God, and the song of the Lamb, saying,

> "Great and marvellous are thy works, Lord God Almighty;
> Just and true are thy ways, thou King of saints.
> Who shall not fear thee, O Lord,
> And glorify thy name?
> For thou only art holy:
> For all nations shall come and worship before thee;
> For thy judgments are made manifest."

V. *The Seven Vials*

And after that I looked, and, behold, the temple of the tabernacle of the testimony in heaven was opened: and the seven angels came out of the temple, having the seven plagues, clothed in pure and white linen, and having their breasts girded with golden girdles. And one of the four beasts gave unto the seven angels seven golden vials full of the wrath of God, who liveth for ever and ever. And the temple was filled with smoke from the glory of God, and from his power; and no man was able to enter into the temple, till the seven plagues of the seven angels were fulfilled.

THE REVELATION OF JESUS CHRIST

And I heard a great voice out of the temple saying to the seven angels,

"Go your ways, and pour out the vials of the wrath of God upon the earth."

And the first went, and poured out his vial upon the earth; and there fell a noisome and grievous sore upon the men which had the mark of the beast, and upon them which worshipped his image.

And the second angel poured out his vial upon the sea; and it became as the blood of a dead man: and every living soul died in the sea.

And the third angel poured out his vial upon the rivers and fountains of waters; and they became blood. And I heard the angel of the waters say, "Thou art righteous, O Lord, which art, and wast, and shalt be, because thou hast judged thus. For they have shed the blood of saints and prophets, and thou hast given them blood to drink; for they are worthy." And I heard another out of the altar say, "Even so, Lord God Almighty, true and righteous are thy judgments."

And the fourth angel poured out his vial upon the sun; and power was given unto him to scorch men with fire. And men were scorched with great heat, and blasphemed the name of God, which hath power over these plagues: and they repented not to give him glory.

And the fifth angel poured out his vial upon the seat of the beast; and his kingdom was full of darkness; and they gnawed their tongues for pain, and blasphemed the God of heaven because of their pains and their sores, and repented not of their deeds.

And the sixth angel poured out his vial upon the great river Euphrates; and the water thereof was dried up, that the way of the kings of the east might be prepared. And I saw three unclean spirits like frogs come out of the mouth of the dragon, and out of the mouth of the beast, and out of the mouth of the false prophet. For they are the spirits of devils, working miracles,

THE REVELATION OF JESUS CHRIST

which go forth unto the kings of the earth and of the whole world, to gather them to the battle of that great day of God Almighty.

> *Behold, I come as a thief.*
> *Blessed is he that watcheth, and keepeth his garments,*
> *Lest he walk naked, and they see his shame.*

And he gathered them together into a place called in the Hebrew tongue Armageddon.

And the seventh angel poured out his vial into the air; and there came a great voice out of the temple of heaven, from the throne, saying,

"It is done!"

And there were voices, and thunders, and lightnings; and there was a great earthquake, such as was not since men were upon the earth, so mighty an earthquake, and so great. And the great city was divided into three parts, and the cities of the nations fell: and great Babylon came in remembrance before God, to give unto her the cup of the wine of the fierceness of his wrath. And every island fled away, and the mountains were not found. And there fell upon men a great hail out of heaven, every stone about the weight of a talent: and men blasphemed God because of the plague of the hail; for the plague thereof was exceeding great.

And there came one of the seven angels which had the seven vials, and talked with me, saying unto me,

"Come hither; I will show unto thee the judgment of the great whore that sitteth upon many waters: with whom the kings of the earth have committed fornication, and the inhabitants of the earth have been made drunk with the wine of her fornication."

So he carried me away in the spirit into the wilderness: and I saw a woman sit upon a scarlet coloured beast, full of names of blasphemy, having seven heads and ten horns. And the woman

THE REVELATION OF JESUS CHRIST

was arrayed in purple and scarlet colour, and decked with gold and precious stones and pearls, having a golden cup in her hand full of abominations and filthiness of her fornication: and upon her forehead was a name written, "MYSTERY, BABYLON THE GREAT, THE MOTHER OF HARLOTS AND ABOMINATIONS OF THE EARTH." And I saw the woman drunken with the blood of the saints, and with the blood of the martyrs of Jesus: and when I saw her, I wondered with great admiration.

And the angel said unto me,

"Wherefore didst thou marvel? I will tell thee the mystery of the woman, and of the beast that carrieth her, which hath the seven heads and ten horns. The beast that thou sawest was, and is not; and shall ascend out of the bottomless pit, and go into perdition: and they that dwell on the earth shall wonder, whose names were not written in the book of life from the foundation of the world, when they behold the beast that was, and is not, and yet is. And here is the mind which hath wisdom. The seven heads are seven mountains, on which the woman sitteth. And there are seven kings: five are fallen, and one is, and the other is not yet come; and when he cometh, he must continue a short space. And the beast that was, and is not, even he is the eighth, and is of the seven, and goeth into perdition. And the ten horns which thou sawest are ten kings, which have received no kingdom as yet; but receive power as kings one hour with the beast. These have one mind, and shall give their power and strength unto the beast. These shall make war with the Lamb, and the Lamb shall overcome them: for he is Lord of lords, and King of kings: and they that are with him are called, and chosen, and faithful."

And he saith unto me,

"The waters which thou sawest, where the whore sitteth, are peoples, and multitudes, and nations, and tongues. And the ten horns which thou sawest upon the beast, these shall hate the whore, and shall make her desolate and naked, and shall eat her flesh, and burn her with fire. For God hath put in their

THE REVELATION OF JESUS CHRIST

hearts to fulfil his will, and to agree, and give their kingdom unto the beast, until the words of God shall be fulfilled. And the woman which thou sawest is that great city, which reigneth over the kings of the earth."

And after these things I saw another angel come down from heaven, having great power; and the earth was lightened with his glory. And he cried mightily with a strong voice, saying,

"Babylon the great is fallen, is fallen, and is become the habitation of devils, and the hold of every foul spirit, and a cage of every unclean and hateful bird. For all nations have drunk of the wine of the wrath of her fornication, and the kings of the earth have committed fornication with her, and the merchants of the earth are waxed rich through the abundance of her delicacies."

And I heard another voice from heaven, saying,

"Come out of her, my people, that ye be not partakers of her sins, and that ye receive not of her plagues. For her sins have reached unto heaven, and God hath remembered her iniquities. Reward her even as she rewarded you, and double unto her double according to her works: in the cup which she hath filled fill to her double. How much she hath glorified herself, and lived deliciously, so much torment and sorrow give her: for she saith in her heart, 'I sit a queen, and am no widow, and shall see no sorrow.' Therefore shall her plagues come in one day, death, and mourning, and famine; and she shall be utterly burned with fire: for strong is the Lord God who judgeth her.

"And the kings of the earth, who have committed fornication and lived deliciously with her, shall bewail her, and lament for her, when they shall see the smoke of her burning, standing afar off for the fear of her torment, saying, 'Alas, alas that great city Babylon, that mighty city! for in one hour is thy judgment come.'

"And the merchants of the earth shall weep and mourn over her; for no man buyeth their merchandise any more: the merchandise of gold, and silver, and precious stones, and of pearls, and fine linen, and purple, and silk, and scarlet, and all thyine wood, and all manner vessels of ivory, and all manner vessels of most precious wood, and of brass, and iron, and marble, and cinnamon, and odours, and ointments, and frankincense, and wine, and oil, and fine flour, and wheat, and beasts, and sheep, and horses, and chariots, and slaves, and souls of men. And the fruits that thy soul lusted after are departed from thee, and all things which were dainty and goodly are departed from thee, and thou shalt find them no more at all. The merchants of these things, which were made rich by her, shall stand afar off for the fear of her torment, weeping and wailing, and saying, 'Alas, alas that great city, that was clothed in fine linen, and purple, and scarlet, and decked with gold, and precious stones, and pearls! For in one hour so great riches is come to nought.'

"And every shipmaster, and all the company in ships, and sailors, and as many as trade by sea, stood afar off, and cried when they saw the smoke of her burning, saying, 'What city is like unto this great city!' And they cast dust on their heads, and cried, weeping and wailing, saying, 'Alas, alas that great city, wherein were made rich all that had ships in the sea by reason of her costliness! for in one hour is she made desolate.'

"Rejoice over her, thou heaven, and ye holy apostles and prophets; for God hath avenged you on her."

And a mighty angel took up a stone like a great millstone, and cast it into the sea, saying, "Thus with violence shall that great city Babylon be thrown down, and shall be found no more at all. And the voice of harpers, and musicians, and of pipers, and trumpeters, shall be heard no more at all in thee; and no craftsman, of whatsoever craft he be, shall be found any more in thee; and the sound of a millstone shall be heard no more at all in thee. And the light of a candle shall shine no more at all in thee; and the voice of the bridegroom and of the bride shall be heard no more at all in thee: for thy merchants were the great men of the earth; for by thy sorceries were all nations deceived. And in her was found the blood of prophets, and of saints, and of all that were slain upon the earth."

THE REVELATION OF JESUS CHRIST

VI. *The Last Judgment*

And after these things I heard a great voice of much people in heaven, saying,

"Alleluia; Salvation, and glory, and honour, and power, unto the Lord our God: for true and righteous are his judgments: for he hath judged the great whore, which did corrupt the earth with her fornication, and hath avenged the blood of his servants at her hand!"

And again they said, "Alleluia. And her smoke rose up for ever and ever."

And the four and twenty elders and the four beasts fell down and worshipped God that sat on the throne, saying, "Amen; Alleluia."

And a voice came out of the throne, saying, "Praise our God, all ye his servants, and ye that fear him, both small and great."

And I heard as it were the voice of a great multitude, and as the voice of many waters, and as the voice of mighty thunderings, saying, "Alleluia: for the Lord God omnipotent reigneth! Let us be glad and rejoice, and give honour to him: for the marriage of the Lamb is come, and his wife hath made herself ready. And to her was granted that she should be arrayed in fine linen, clean and white: for the fine linen is the righteousness of saints."

And he saith unto me, "Write: 'Blessed are they which are called unto the marriage supper of the Lamb.'"

And he saith unto me, "These are the true sayings of God."

And I fell at his feet to worship him. And he said unto me, "See thou do it not: I am thy fellowservant, and of thy brethren that have the testimony of Jesus: worship God: for the testimony of Jesus is the spirit of prophecy."

And I saw heaven opened, and beheld a white horse; and he that sat upon him was called Faithful and True, and in righteousness he doth judge and make war. His eyes were as a flame of fire, and on his head were many crowns; and he had a name written, that no man knew, but he himself. And he was clothed with a vesture dipped in blood: and his name is called the Word

THE REVELATION OF JESUS CHRIST

of God. And the armies which were in heaven followed him upon white horses, clothed in fine linen, white and clean. And out of his mouth goeth a sharp sword, that with it he should smite the nations: and he shall rule them with a rod of iron: and he treadeth the winepress of the fierceness and wrath of Almighty God. And he hath on his vesture and on his thigh a name written: KING OF KINGS, AND LORD OF LORDS.

And I saw an angel standing in the sun; and he cried with a loud voice, saying to all the fowls that fly in the midst of heaven,

"Come and gather yourselves together unto the supper of the great God; that ye may eat the flesh of kings, and the flesh of captains, and the flesh of mighty men, and the flesh of horses, and of them that sit on them, and the flesh of all men, both free and bond, both small and great."

And I saw the beast, and the kings of the earth, and their armies, gathered together to make war against him that sat on the horse, and against his army. And the beast was taken, and with him the false prophet that wrought miracles before him, with which he deceived them that had received the mark of the beast, and them that worshipped his image. These both were cast alive into a lake of fire burning with brimstone. And the remnant were slain with the sword of him that sat upon the horse, which sword proceeded out of his mouth: and all the fowls were filled with their flesh.

And I saw an angel come down from heaven, having the key of the bottomless pit and a great chain in his hand. And he laid hold on the dragon, that old serpent, which is the Devil, and Satan, and bound him a thousand years, and cast him into the bottomless pit, and shut him up, and set a seal upon him, that he should deceive the nations no more, till the thousand years should be fulfilled: and after that he must be loosed a little season. And I saw thrones, and they sat upon them, and judgment was given unto them: and I saw the souls of them that were beheaded for the witness of Jesus, and for the word of God, and which had not worshipped the beast, neither his image, neither had received his mark upon their foreheads, or in their hands;

THE REVELATION OF JESUS CHRIST

and they lived and reigned with Christ a thousand years. But the rest of the dead lived not again until the thousand years were finished. This is the first resurrection.

Blessed and holy is he that hath part in the first resurrection: on such the second death hath no power, but they shall be priests of God and of Christ, and shall reign with him a thousand years.

And when the thousand years are expired, Satan shall be loosed out of his prison, and shall go out to deceive the nations which are in the four quarters of the earth, Gog and Magog, to gather them together to battle: the number of whom is as the sand of the sea. And they went up on the breadth of the earth, and compassed the camp of the saints about, and the beloved city: and fire came down from God out of heaven, and devoured them. And the devil that deceived them was cast into the lake of fire and brimstone, where the beast and the false prophet are, and shall be tormented day and night for ever and ever. And I saw a great white throne, and him that sat on it, from whose face the earth and the heaven fled away; and there was found no place for them.

And I saw the dead, small and great, stand before God; and the books were opened: and another book was opened, which is the book of life: and the dead were judged out of those things which were written in the books, according to their works. And the sea gave up the dead which were in it; and death and hell delivered up the dead which were in them: and they were judged every man according to their works. And death and hell were cast into the lake of fire. This is the second death. And whosoever was not found written in the book of life was cast into the lake of fire.

VII. *The New Jerusalem*

And I saw a new heaven and a new earth: for the first heaven and the first earth were passed away; and there was no more sea. And I John saw the holy city, new Jerusalem, coming down from God out of heaven, prepared as a bride adorned for her husband. And I heard a great voice out of heaven saying,

THE REVELATION OF JESUS CHRIST

"Behold, the tabernacle of God is with men, and he will dwell with them, and they shall be his people, and God himself shall be with them, and be their God. And God shall wipe away all tears from their eyes; and there shall be no more death, neither sorrow, nor crying, neither shall there be any more pain: for the former things are passed away."

And he that sat upon the throne said,

"Behold, I make all things new." And he said unto me, "Write: for these words are true and faithful."

And he said unto me,

"It is done. I am Alpha and Omega, the beginning and the end. I will give unto him that is athirst of the fountain of the water of life freely. He that overcometh shall inherit all things; and I will be his God, and he shall be my son. But the fearful, and unbelieving, and the abominable, and murderers, and whoremongers, and sorcerers, and idolaters, and all liars, shall have their part in the lake which burneth with fire and brimstone: which is the second death."

And there came unto me one of the seven angels which had the seven vials full of the seven last plagues, and talked with me, saying,

"Come hither, I will show thee the bride, the Lamb's wife."

And he carried me away in the spirit to a great and high mountain, and showed me that great city, the holy Jerusalem, descending out of heaven from God, having the glory of God: and her light was like unto a stone most precious, even like a jasper stone, clear as crystal; and had a wall great and high, and had twelve gates, and at the gates twelve angels, and names written thereon, which are the names of the twelve tribes of the children of Israel: on the east three gates; on the north three gates; on the south three gates; and on the west three gates. And the wall of the city had twelve foundations, and in them the names of the twelve apostles of the Lamb. And he that talked with me had a golden reed to measure the city, and the gates thereof, and the wall thereof. And the city lieth foursquare, and the length is as large as the breadth: and he measured the city

THE REVELATION OF JESUS CHRIST

with the reed, twelve thousand furlongs. The length and the breadth and the height of it are equal. And he measured the wall thereof, a hundred and forty and four cubits, according to the measure of a man, that is, of the angel. And the building of the wall of it was of jasper: and the city was pure gold, like unto clear glass. And the foundations of the wall of the city were garnished with all manner of precious stones. The first foundation was jasper; the second, sapphire; the third, a chalcedony; the fourth, an emerald; the fifth, sardonyx; the sixth, sardius; the seventh, chrysolyte; the eighth, beryl; the ninth, a topaz; the tenth, a chrysoprasus; the eleventh, a jacinth; the twelfth, an amethyst. And the twelve gates were twelve pearls; every several gate was of one pearl: and the street of the city was pure gold, as it were transparent glass. And I saw no temple therein: for the Lord God Almighty and the Lamb are the temple of it. And the city had no need of the sun, neither of the moon, to shine in it: for the glory of God did lighten it, and the Lamb is the light thereof. And the nations of them which are saved shall walk in the light of it: and the kings of the earth do bring their glory and honour into it. And the gates of it shall not be shut at all by day: for there shall be no night there. And they shall bring the glory and honour of the nations into it. And there shall in no wise enter into it any thing that defileth, neither whatsoever worketh abomination, or maketh a lie: but they which are written in the Lamb's book of life.

And he showed me a pure river of water of life, clear as crystal, proceeding out of the throne of God and of the Lamb. In the midst of the street of it, and on either side of the river, was there the tree of life, which bore twelve manner of fruits, and yielded her fruit every month: and the leaves of the tree were for the healing of the nations.

And there shall be no more curse: but the throne of God and of the Lamb shall be in it; and his servants shall serve him: and they shall see his face; and his name shall be in their foreheads.

And there shall be no night there; and they need no candle,

THE REVELATION OF JESUS CHRIST

neither light of the sun; for the Lord God giveth them light: and they shall reign for ever and ever. And he said unto me,

"These sayings are faithful and true: and the Lord God of the holy prophets sent his angel to show unto his servants the things which must shortly be done. Behold, I come quickly: blessed is he that keepeth the sayings of the prophecy of this book."

Epilogue

And I John saw these things, and heard them. And when I had heard and seen, I fell down to worship before the feet of the angel which showed me these things.

Then saith he unto me,

"See thou do it not: for I am thy fellowservant, and of thy brethren the prophets, and of them which keep the sayings of this book: worship God."

And he saith unto me,

"Seal not the sayings of the prophecy of this book: for the time is at hand. He that is unjust, let him be unjust still: and he which is filthy, let him be filthy still: and he that is righteous, let him be righteous still: and he that is holy, let him be holy still. And, behold, I come quickly; and my reward is with me, to give every man according as his work shall be. I am Alpha and Omega, the beginning and the end, the first and the last. Blessed are they that do his commandments, that they may have right to the tree of life, and may enter in through the gates into the city. For without are dogs, and sorcerers, and whoremongers, and murderers, and idolaters, and whosoever loveth and maketh a lie. I Jesus have sent mine angel to testify unto you these things in the churches. I am the root and the offspring of David, and the bright and morning star. And the Spirit and the bride say, 'Come!' And let him that heareth say, 'Come!' And let him that is athirst come. And whosoever will, let him take the water of life freely."

For I testify unto every man that heareth the words of the prophecy of this book: if any man shall add unto these things,

THE REVELATION OF JESUS CHRIST

God shall add unto him the plagues that are written in this book: and if any man shall take away from the words of the book of this prophecy, God shall take away his part out of the book of life, and out of the holy city, and from the things which are written in this book.

He which testifieth these things saith, "Surely I come quickly." Amen. Even so, come, Lord Jesus.

The grace of our Lord Jesus Christ be with you all. Amen.

A NOTE ON TRANSLATIONS
DATES OF THE BOOKS
A GLOSSARY OF BIBLICAL TERMS
A CHAPTER KEY

A Note on TRANSLATIONS

THE FOURTH CENTURY A.D. saw the acceptance of Christianity as the religion of the Roman Empire, the establishment of the New Testament Canon after nearly three centuries of discussion, and the first translation of the whole Bible into Latin by the foremost scholar of the age, St. Jerome. There were by that time numerous partial translations of both the Old and New Testaments in existence: the earliest and best the Septuagint Greek translation of the Old Testament, together with Syriac, Egyptian, Ethiopic, Arabian, and Armenian translations based on it; also translations of the New Testament in these languages, together with several popular versions in Old Latin. Saint Jerome aimed to be conservative, using the work of his predecessors so far as accuracy permitted, but comparing the Latin with the original Greek texts of the New Testament, and utilizing the Septuagint and the original Hebrew for the Old Testament. He succeeded in turning out one of the three supreme Biblical translations, the other two, of course, being that by Martin Luther and the English Authorized Version. His departures from the readings currently accepted caused much resentment at the time, leading him to deplore the conservatism of mankind in words that might have been echoed by countless translators in centuries to come: "So great is the force of established usage that even acknowledged corruptions please the greater part, for they prefer to have their copies pretty rather than correct." Eventually, however, his text, known as the Vulgate, came to be universally accepted, and served as the basis for all other translations down to the time of the Reformation.

As early as the ninth and tenth centuries there were various English translations made of the Gospels, some of the Psalms, and other particular books, but the first English rendering of the whole Bible was produced by the followers of John Wycliffe in the fourteenth century. There are two forms of what is known as the Wycliffe Bible—though Wycliffe himself had nothing directly to do with either: the "Early Version" of 1382, the work of Nicholas of Hereford and others; and the "Revised Version" of 1388, a much more accurate render-

A NOTE ON TRANSLATIONS

ing by a group headed by John Purvey. Both versions were suppressed during the fifteenth century persecution of Wycliffe's followers, the Lollards; in fact, the Bible was regarded by Church and State in England as being of such a dangerous and incendiary character that long after the invention of printing no translation into the vernacular was permitted.

William Tyndale, the first after the Wycliffe groups to undertake the task, was obliged to do his work in Germany where his translation of the New Testament was published in 1526. Martin Luther was then at work upon his marvellously vigorous and powerful German rendering, and Tyndale was somewhat influenced by him. An excellent scholar, he went behind the Latin to the original sources, and so highly did his work come to be esteemed that it was used extensively in the preparation of the Authorized Version of 1611.

The first complete English printed Bible was produced in 1535 by Miles Coverdale, somewhat less of a scholar, who was content to accept the Vulgate text as corrected by Luther, Tyndale, and other reformers. Then for a few years English Bibles came thick and fast as publishers rivaled one another in striving to satisfy the popular demand: in 1537 a re-editing of Coverdale by "Thomas Matthew," supposed to have been the reformer, John Rogers; in 1539 a re-editing of Matthew by Richard Taverner; and in the same year another re-editing of Coverdale by Coverdale himself in a sumptuous folio edition known as the "Great Bible," from which the translation of the Psalms was taken into the liturgy of the Church of England as the Psalter, which is still a part of the Anglican and American Episcopal prayerbooks.

Once more the ruling classes awoke to the revolutionary implications of the Bible, and in 1543 a law was passed that "no woman (unless she be noble or gentle woman), no artificers, apprentices, servingmen under the degree of yeomen . . . husbandmen, or laborers" be allowed to peruse this radical literature. With the persecution of the reformers under Queen Mary the new translators were either executed, as was Rogers, or fled to the Continent, as did Coverdale.

Gathering in Geneva, the exiles continued their labors of which the first product was a translation of the New Testament by Coverdale and William Whittingham, followed in 1560 by a translation of the whole Bible by Whittingham, Anthony Gilby, Thomas Sampson, and others. This edition, called the Geneva Bible, made use of the latest results of Hebrew and classical scholarship but was derisively known as "the Breeches Bible" from its rendering of Genesis 3:7—"They sewed fig leaves together and made themselves breeches."

The accession of Queen Elizabeth and the re-establishment of the Church of England brought the reformers home and led to the publication in 1568 of the

A NOTE ON TRANSLATIONS

"Bishops' Bible," which was, however, little more than a revision of the Geneva Bible. It was now the turn of the Roman Catholics to seek the Continent, where one of their best scholars, Gregory Martin, made a translation of the Vulgate which was called the Douai Bible from its place of publication in 1609–10, and is the one still used by the Catholic Church. Its strongly Latinized vocabulary and literal fidelity to its source make it greatly inferior to the Authorized Version from the literary point of view.

The latter, the masterpiece of all translations in world literature, grew out of a plan presented by the scholar king, James the First, to a conference of High and Low Church parties summoned by him in 1604. "Learned men to the number of four and fifty" were appointed to accomplish the task, chief among them that Lancelot Andrewes recently celebrated by T. S. Eliot, who was familiar with fifteen languages. The Bishops' Bible was taken as the immediate basis but Tyndale's, Matthews', Coverdale's, and Whittingham's translations were also used, all with constant reference to the Greek and Hebrew sources. The translators deliberately adopted the principle of striving to reproduce the meaning and spirit of the original rather than to produce a literal word-by-word rendering, and they devoted great attention to values of euphony and rhythm; that is to say, they were not only scholars but conscious literary craftsmen.

In the words of one of them, Dr. Miles Smith, "The worke . . . cost the workemen, as light as it seemeth, the paines of twise seven times seventie two days and more." An additional period of nine months was consumed in seeing the book through the press. Thus, all told, the production took about three and a half years—a remarkably short time considering the magnitude of the work and the magnificence of the result.

For two hundred and fifty years men were entirely satisfied with the King James Version, aside from minute changes here and there which were introduced in later reprintings, but during the mid-nineteenth century such progress was made in Hebrew and classical scholarship that by 1870 a more accurate translation seemed called for. In that year the Convocation of Canterbury appointed a body of Anglican clergymen to undertake the task; in addition, other denominations were asked to assist, and American participation was invited, so that the Revised Version might stand as the Protestant Bible of the English-speaking world. Enthusiastic co-operation was given from all sides, and the work was carried on with the most painstaking thoroughness. The New Testament appeared in 1881, the Old Testament in 1884, and the Apocrypha, as a kind of supplement, in 1895.

The immediate reaction was one of disappointment, particularly with the version of the New Testament. In the case of the Old Testament, generations of

A NOTE ON TRANSLATIONS

Jewish scholars from the time of Ezra on had produced by the second century A.D. something like a generally accepted text which was further perfected by the Jewish school of Masoretic textual critics between the sixth and eighth centuries A.D.; but with the New Testament there was a great variety of available texts, and the choice between them, and between different renderings of them, being made by majority vote, was not always either consistent or judicious. Furthermore, the translators decided always to translate the same Greek word by the same English word regardless of context, which made many passages awkward or obscure. While the greater accuracy of the Revised Version, especially in the instances of Job and Ecclesiastes, has caused it to be preferred by scholars, its stylistic inferiority has prevented it from displacing the Authorized Version in the affections of most readers of the Bible.

Of recent attempts avowedly to modernize the style in the interest of still further accuracy the most important is the admirable "Short Bible" edited by Professors Edgar J. Goodspeed and J. M. Powis Smith and published by the University of Chicago Press in 1933. A scholar's edition of the whole Bible with all sections retranslated, annotated, and placed in their correct historical setting still remains to be satisfactorily achieved.

As far as literary value is concerned, however, the King James Version, produced when the language was younger and more flexible, is unlikely ever to be superseded. Its position as a world classic seems to be as secure as that of Homer, Dante, or Shakespeare, and it is the only translation in all literature of which that can be said.

Dates of the BOOKS

A REFERENCE TABLE

Before 1000 B.C.
  The Ten Commandments and Mosaic Code in *Exodus*.
  The Red Sea Song in *Numbers*.
  The Song of Deborah and Fable of Jotham in *Judges*.
Tenth Century B.C.
  Court History of King David in *Second Samuel*.
  The Blessing of Jacob in *Genesis*.
  The Blessing of Moses in *Deuteronomy*.
  The Oracles of Balaam in *Numbers*.
Ninth Century B.C.
  Earliest Draft of *First Samuel*.
  Earliest Draft of *Judges*.
  J Document in Hexateuch.
Eighth Century B.C.
  E. Document in Hexateuch.
  Amos.
  Hosea.
  Micah.
  Isaiah, chapters 1–39.
Seventh Century B.C.
  Combination of J and E Documents in Hexateuch.
  Deuteronomy.
  First and *Second Kings,* except ending.
  Zephaniah.
  Nahum.
  Habbakuk.
  Jeremiah.
Sixth Century B.C.
  Lamentations.

DATES OF THE BOOKS

    Second Kings, ending.
    Deuteronomic *Judges*.
    Deuteronomic *First* and *Second Samuel*.
    Obadiah.
    Ezekiel.
    Isaiah, chapters 40–66. The Unknown Prophet.
    Haggai.
    Zechariah.

FIFTH CENTURY B.C.
    Joel.
    Malachi.
    Nehemiah.

FOURTH CENTURY B.C.
    Leviticus.
    Chronicles.
    Ezra.
    Proverbs.
    Job.
    Song of Songs.
    Ruth.
    Tobit.

THIRD CENTURY B.C.
    Jonah.

SECOND CENTURY B.C.
    Psalms.
    Ecclesiastes.
    Daniel.
    Esther.
    First and *Second Maccabees*.
    Judith.
    Susanna and the Elders.
    Ecclesiasticus.

FIRST CENTURY B.C.
    Wisdom of Solomon.

A.D. 50–65. Letters of Paul.
A.D. 70. *Gospel of Mark* (possibly a generation earlier in first form).
A.D. 80. *Gospel of Matthew* (possibly a generation earlier in first form).
A.D. 90. *Gospel of Luke* (possibly a generation earlier in first form).
A.D. 40–90. Letter of James.

DATES OF THE BOOKS

A.D. 60–90. *Acts of the Apostles.*
A.D. 70–80. *Letter of the Hebrews.*
A.D. 90. *Revelation.*
A.D. 100–125. *Gospel of John* (possibly much earlier in first form).
A.D. 100–125. *Letter of John* (possibly much earlier in first form).

A Glossary of
BIBLICAL TERMS
WITH PAGE REFERENCES

Needless to say, this is a selective glossary, and only the most important items, in the compiler's judgment, have been included.

In using the list of personages, it is well to remember that very often only one representative of a name has been admitted, for frequently more than one character bears the same name.

The list of places must be used with caution. Despite the voluminous labors of generations of historical geographers, the identities of certain places in the Holy Land and its environing nations remain doubtful.

The highly restricted list of botanical and zoological terms calls attention to another branch of Biblical study that has not yet reached complete maturity. The translators of the Authorized Version of 1611, scholars though they were, allowed themselves considerable slackness in Englishing the names of Biblical fauna and flora, and it must be admitted that the authorities responsible for the Revised Version did not fully sustain their obligations in this respect.

The list of words is based frankly on Skeat's standard glossary. It is, perhaps, rather more restricted even than the other lists, but the compiler has assumed that native logic can go far in establishing meanings that have changed slightly since 1611. Just as the strangeness of Shakespeare is dissipated by constant reading, one learns to find his way about through further acquaintance with the Biblical text. However, the compiler ventures to caution the reader about prepositions—their strange antics since 1611 might well be the subject of a fat volume—and their metamorphoses have been too complicated to include within the scope of this glossary.

WALLACE BROCKWAY

A GLOSSARY OF BIBLICAL TERMS

Aaron, brother of Moses and first high priest of Israel. Mt. Hor, where he died, is sometimes called the Mountain of Aaron. The high priesthood descended to Aaron's third son, Eleazar, and his descendants. 84-92, 94-95, 99-104, 111-113, 115, 124-127, 130, 132-134, 144, 657, 972, 1177, 1178

Abaddon, the angel of the bottomless pit. 691

Abba, father. 927

Abed-nego, one of the three saved from the fiery furnace. His original name was Azariah, and he was apparently of the blood royal of Judah. 800, 805, 806-807, 810

Abel, son of Adam and Eve. A shepherd, he was slain by his brother Cain. Abel has seized upon the imagination of generations as the prototype of the innocent victim of all murders. But one meaning of the word—*vanity*—points the moral of the tale away from the popular conception. Another meaning *breath, transitoriness*—refers to the brevity of his life. 9, 10, 960, 1179

Abiathar, high priest of the Jews. At first much favored by David, he was disgraced for taking part in the rebellion of Adonijah. Solomon deposed him. 251, 289, 292, 297, 302, 905

Abigail, the lovely wife of the wealthy but churlish Nabal. The story of this strange marital upset, one of the high lights of the First Book of Samuel, reflects little credit either on Abigail herself or the Psalmist. 254-258, 269

Abimelech, a son of Gideon, he slew his brothers, seventy in all, only Jotham escaping. He was made king of Shechem, but was killed besieging Thebez, when a millstone shattered his skull. The story is related in the Book of Judges. 190-194, 279

Abishai, son of Zeruiah, was one of David's most faithful followers and efficient aids. He was noted for his valor and daring. 258-259, 270-271, 273, 290, 293, 294

Abner, Saul's first cousin and commander-in-chief of his army, deserted the cause of the house of Kish after Saul's death. He was largely instrumental in strengthening David's hold over Israel. Seemingly a haughty though magnanimous man, he was slain by Joab in retaliation for the death of Asahel, whom Abner had killed in self-defense. David's lament over Abner (274) is a passage of exquisite simplicity. 233, 247, 258, 259, 270-274, 300, 302

Abomination, that which excites loathing. Therefore, an idol. The word is used more often in the specific than in the general sense.

Abomination of desolation, mentioned by Jesus as a portent of the impending destruction of Jerusalem.

Abraham, patriarch and father of the Jews. Together with Sarah, his wife, he lies buried in the cave of Machpelah. The site is covered by the huge mosque of Hebron. 16-24, 26-31, 32, 33, 34, 35, 81, 86-87, 975, 976, 1117, 1177, 1178, 1180

Abram, the earlier name of Abraham. 16-21

Absalom, son of David, rebelled unsuccessfully against his father. He was accidentally caught in the branches of a tree, and in this helpless condition was slain by Joab, despite the command of David that his life be spared. David's lament for Absalom is famous, and the tragedy has inspired authors as widely separated in time and mood

A GLOSSARY OF BIBLICAL TERMS

as Dryden and William Faulkner. 281–295, 297, 300

ACELDAMA, the scene of Judas' suicide. Translated correctly as the Field of Blood, it was so called because it was purchased with the thirty pieces of silver—blood money—Judas had received for betraying Jesus. 965, 1045

ACHAIA, a Roman province which, in O. T. days, included the whole of the Peloponnesus and much of Hellas and the adjacent isles. 1079, 1080, 1082, 1104, 1136, 1138, 1142

ACHAN, a Jew stoned to death under Joshua for diverting to his own use a certain "accursed thing" from the booty taken at Jericho. The whole incident is a classic in the history of tabu, and the "accursed thing" is so because it is tabu, devoted to the use of God. 165–167

ACHISH, a Philistine king of Gath, received David kindly when he was hiding from Saul. 249, 260, 263–264, 303

ACHOR, a valley between Ai and Jericho, scene of the stoning of Achan. The word means *trouble*. 167, 402

ADAM, the first man. His story is the most familiar in the O.T. Authorities still disagree as to the meaning of the word, but *red earth* seems a likely guess, referring to the material from which his body was formed. Although Adam is the father, through his fall, of all human ills, Dante did not venture to put him in hell. According to one legend, Noah was said to have taken Adam's body with him in the ark. 5–9, 10, 744, 874, 1133, 1134

ADONIJAH, son of David. He usurped the kingdom and was pardoned, but later Solomon had him slain for an apparently trivial reason. 297–300, 301–302

AENEAS, a paralytic healed by Peter at Lydda. 1061

AGAG, a king of the Amalekites whom Saul spared in contravention of God's wishes. Saul's humanity on this occasion widened the gap between him and the priestly hierarchy led by Samuel. However, Agag did not escape, for Samuel personally hewed him to pieces. 233–235

AGUR, the traditional author of part of the Book of Proverbs, one line of which has gained unquestioned immortality: "Give me neither poverty nor riches." 693

AHAB, a wicked king of Israel. Egged on by his wife Jezebel, he seized Naboth's vineyard and systematically persecuted Elijah. He fell in battle against Ramoth in Gilead. 316–317, 319, 320, 322, 324–326, 341, 343, 353

AHAB, a lying prophet who duped the Jews captive in Babylon. Nebuchadnezzar had him burned to death. 496–497

AHASUERUS, king of Persia and husband of Esther, is identified with Xerxes. His Jewish policy is related in the Book of Esther. 826–840

AHAZ, king of Judah, favored pagan ways. Isaiah warned him of impending disaster. 352, 356

AHAZIAH, fifth king of Judah, made the tactical error of supporting the declining fortunes of the house of Ahab. He was slain by the supporters of Jehu. 342–343

AHIKAM, son of Shaphan, was one of the embassy sent by Josiah to Huldah. He protected Jeremiah during the reign of Jehoiakim. 354, 355, 508

AHIMAAZ, son of Zadok, took an important message to David during the

[1243]

A GLOSSARY OF BIBLICAL TERMS

rebellion of Absalom. 289, 292, 294–295

AHIMELECH, high priest at Nob, favored David against Saul in the final struggle between them. For this reason he was put to death, with his whole house, by Saul. His son Abiathar escaped, however, and was consecrated high priest by David. 248, 250–251

AHINOAM, one of David's wives. 258, 260, 269

AHITHOPHEL, the evil genius of Absalom's discontent. When his counsels were overcome by Hushai, he hanged himself. Ahithophel was Bath-sheba's grandfather. Under the name of Achitophel, he appears in Dryden's great tragic satire *Absalom and Achitophel* as the prototype of the first Lord Shaftesbury, the adviser of Monmouth (Absalom). The name means *brother of foolishness*. 287–289, 290–293

AHOLAH and AHOLIBAH, personifications of whoredom. The former signifies Samaria, the latter Jerusalem. They occur in Ezekiel. 542–544

AI, a town near Beth-el, taken by Joshua by means of a ruse. 165, 167–169, 272

AIJALON, halfway between Jerusalem and Jaffa, was a Levitical city and a city of refuge. 231

AJALON, a lovely valley near Aijalon, where Joshua commanded the moon to stand still. 172

ALMUG, probably sandalwood.

AMALEK, or AMALEKITES, alleged descendants of Esau, settled around Kadesh. Their encounters with the Israelites were generally disastrous to them, and their ruin was consummated by David. Probably originally Bedouins from Arabia Petraea, Amalekites eventually became a generic term for nomads in general. 103, 176, 182, 184–185, 186, 233–234, 235

AMASA, captain of Absalom's army. He was slain by Joab. 300, 302

AMIABLE, lovely.

AMMONITES or CHILDREN OF AMMON, a Semitic people east of the Jordan, were said to be the descendants of Ben-ammi, the son of Lot by his younger daughter. They were conquered by David and Joab. 27, 135, 176, 195, 228, 233, 280, 312, 313, 357

AMNON, David's eldest son, deflowered his sister Tamar and then repudiated her. Absalom killed Amnon in revenge. This incestuous triangle furnished the theme of Robinson Jeffers' *Tamar*. 281–284

AMORITES, a Syrian-Palestinian people, held the land of Canaan before its conquest by the Israelites. They retired to the mountains, and henceforth little was heard of them. 19, 82, 126, 134–136, 160, 162, 165, 170, 171–173, 388, 658

AMOS, a herdsman of Tekoa, was a minor prophet who flourished about 750 B.C. He is the reputed author of the Book of Amos. 384, 385–398

ANAK, a giant whose descendants (*Anakim*) lived in southern Canaan. They were so large that the Hebrews were mere grasshoppers compared to them. Their chief city was Hebron. They were conquered by Joshua. 126, 127

ANANIAS, a high priest, was assassinated by the Sicarii at the beginning of the last Jewish war. He appears in Acts. 1090, 1092

ANANIAS, a famous liar, was struck dead for telling Peter a falsehood. Ananias has become a generic name for a liar. 1052

ANANIAS, a Jewish disciple who be-

[1244]

A GLOSSARY OF BIBLICAL TERMS

friended Paul during his blindness and predicted his high mission. He was stoned to death. 1060, 1089

ANATHEMA, an accursed thing.

ANATHOTH, a town three miles northeast of Jerusalem, was the birthplace of Jeremiah. 302, 470

ANDREW, elder brother of Peter and one of the Apostles. Legend has it that he was martyred on an X-shaped cross. Evidently, he covered a large amount of territory in his missionary labors, for not only is he the patron saint of Scotland, but he is said to have carried the Gospel into Russia. 902, 907, 1009

ANISE, dill.

ANNA, a prophetess who was in the Temple at the time of Jesus' presentation. 978

ANNAS, high priest of the Jews under Augustus. His later career was marked with vicissitudes, and it is possible that he may have shared the high priesthood with Caiaphas, his son-in-law. He presided at Jesus' first trial, and sent him bound to Caiaphas. 980, 1033, 1034, 1049

ANTIOCH, in Pisidia, was a scene of Paul's missionary labors. 1068, 1071

ANTIOCH, in Syria, was, and still is, the seat of one of the five great patriarchates, and there the disciples of Jesus Christ were first called Christians. 1055, 1065, 1067, 1071, 1072, 1073, 1080, 1116

APOLLOS, a mighty expounder of the Scriptures. He appears in Acts and Corinthians. 1080, 1122, 1125, 1135

APOLLYON, another rendering of Abaddon. 1210

APPLE, more probably either the apricot or the orange. The climate of Palestine is not congenial to the tree, and it is, indeed, something of a rarity.

AQUILA, with his wife Priscilla, was associated with Paul's missionary work, and was generally strong for the faith. 1079, 1080, 1136

ARARAT, a lofty peak in the Caucasus on which the ark rested when the waters of the Flood were assuaged. 13

ARCHELAUS, son and successor of Herod the Great. He was deposed, because of his tyranny, in the tenth year of his reign. 937

ARIOCH, the captain of Nebuchadnezzar's bodyguard. 802–803

ARISTARCHUS, one of Paul's companions. 1082, 1083, 1098, 1174

ARMAGEDDON, the hill of Megiddo, in the plain of Jezreel. It was the scene of two great victories and of two great disasters, the latter the deaths of Saul and Josiah. Doubtless because of these associations, the author of Revelation selected it as the scene of the battle of the nations before the Last Judgment. 1220

ARTAXERXES, identified with Artaxerxes I, son of Xerxes, who reigned from 464–425 B.C. 369–370

ARVAD, a trading isle off the Phoenician coast. 544

ASA, third king of Judah, was noted for his reforms. He strengthened the realm and died, much beloved, in the forty-first year of his reign. 316

ASAHEL, son of Zeruiah. He was slain by Abner in self-defense, but his death was avenged by Joab, his brother, who slew Abner. 270–271, 273

ASHDOD, one of the five confederated cities of the Philistines, was situated midway between Gaza and Jaffa. 386, 389

[1245]

A GLOSSARY OF BIBLICAL TERMS

ASHER, eighth son of Jacob, was the ancestor of one of the Twelve Tribes. Its lands lay in the north, separated from the coast by a narrow band of Phoenician mercantile centers, and reaching the sea itself at Acco (later Ptolmais, now Acre). 44, 75, 155, 181, 185, 187

ASHTAROTH, a city east of the Jordan, in Bashan. 170

ASHTEROTH KARNAIM, a place of great antiquity, lay about twenty-five miles south of Damascus. 19

ASHTORETH, a Phoenician moon goddess identified with Venus. 313, 314

ASKELON, one of the five confederated cities of the Philistines, lay on the coast between Ashdod and Gaza. It played an important role in the Crusades. 268

ASMODEUS, an evil spirit who stole away seven successive betrothed lovers from Sara. But Tobias and Sara, when they married, prayed so fervently that Asmodeus could not touch Tobias, and at last he was carried off in fetters to the extremity of Egypt. 867

ASSHUR, the Hebrew name for Assyria. 404, 545, 548

ASSYRIA, ASSYRIANS, a great empire of antiquity, with its capital of Nineveh, on the eastern bank of the Tigris. 6, 345–346, 347–351, 352, 357, 403, 423–426, 473, 474, 525, 536, 542, 543

AWAY WITH, to endure.

AZARIAH, a name of many personages in the O.T. The most famous of these is the tenth king of Judah, better known as *Uzziah*, which see.

AZARIAH, the Hebrew name of Abednego. 800, 801, 803

AZOTUS, the N.T. name of Ashdod. 1059

BAAL, BAALIM plural, generic terms for the gods of the Syrians and Phoenicians. Baal signifies a possessor, therefore the lord of a particular place. 175, 190, 317, 320–321, 346, 356, 401, 402, 454, 472, 473

BAAL, compounded with a second word, may mean (1) an attribute of the god; (2) the place or manner of his cult; (3) something connected with the place of his worship. A list of the more important compounds follows.

BAAL-BERITH, the covenant Baal, became the god of the Israelites after the death of Gideon. 190, 191

BAAL-HAZOR, the scene of Amnon's murder. Absalom seems to have had a sheep farm here. 283

BAAL-PERAZIM, the scene of David's great victory over the Philistines, lay south of Jerusalem, on the road to Bethlehem. It is probably identical with the Mount Perazim of Isaiah 28:21. 445

BAAL-ZEPHON, a place in Egypt near where the Israelites effected the crossing of the Red Sea. It was probably on the western shore of the Gulf of Suez, a few miles below its head. 96

BAANAH, slain with his brother Rechab, for murdering Ish-bosheth, Saul's son and successor. Their mutilated bodies were exposed above the pool of Hebron. 274–275

BABEL, the site of the great tower erected to reach the skies and of the confusion of tongues visited upon the builders to prevent its completion. 15–16

BABYLON, seat of one of the great empires of antiquity whose armies sometimes appeared in the Holy Land, lay on both banks of the Euphrates. (The Babylonian Captivity refers to the

A GLOSSARY OF BIBLICAL TERMS

years the Jews were captives in Babylon. They were brought here by Nebuchadnezzar about 600 B.C. and were released by Cyrus in 536 B.C. The Avignon period of the papacy, 1309-1376, is sometimes known as the second Babylonian Captivity.) 346, 358-359, 436, 493, 512, 538-539, 566

BABYLON, as used in Revelation, signifies Rome or the Antichrist and all his works. 1217, 1220, 1221, 1222-1223

BALAAM, a prophet whom Balak, king of Moab, persuaded to curse the Israelites. On his way to the cursing place, Balaam was rebuked by his ass, which finally broke into speech. Finally, God inspired him to bless instead of curse the Israelites. 136-144, 145, 1201

BALAK, a king of Moab. See *Balaam*. 136-144

BALM OF GILEAD, probably a balsam obtained from the small evergreen tree *Commiphora meccanensis*. It was valued as an unguent and cosmetic. It was sold for its weight in silver.

BARABBAS, a robber who had committed murder during an uprising. He, instead of Jesus, was released at the Passover. 930, 1000, 1035

BARAK, the Jewish general who, inspired by Deborah, utterly routed the Canaanites in the plain of Jezreel. 177-179, 180, 1181

BAR-JESUS, a false prophet whom Paul struck with blindness. 1068

BARNABAS, Paul's companion on his first missionary voyage. A Cypriote Levite whose real name was Joseph, he is supposed to have been stoned to death in Cyprus by Jews annoyed at his success in teaching the Gospel. The epistle ascribed to him, but not included in the canon of the N.T., was probably written in the second century. 1052, 1061, 1065-1066, 1067-1074, 1115-1116

BARTHOLOMEW, one of the Twelve, whose labors were confined mainly to Asia Minor. He is supposed to have been flayed alive. 907, 1045

BARTIMAEUS, a blind beggar whom Jesus cured at Jericho. 923

BARUCH, Jeremiah's scribe and supposed author of the deuterocanonical Book of Baruch. 501-503, 511

BARZILLAI, a wealthy Gileadite who helped David to escape from Absalom. A simple man, he refused to accept a position in David's court. 300

BASHAN, a fertile section of Palestine located east of the Jordan. It extended from Gilead on the south to Mount Hermon on the north. 136, 170, 390, 418, 544, 557, 610, 629, 630, 658

BATH-SHEBA, wife of Uriah the Hittite. David committed adultery with her, and then caused the death of Uriah, after which he married Bath-sheba. Appropriately enough, she was the mother of Solomon. Dryden introduced Louise de la Kerouaille, duchess of Portsmouth, the notorious favorite of Charles II, into *Absalom and Achitophel* as Bath-sheba. 277-281, 298-299, 301

BDELLIUM, a resinous substance yielded by some tree, not yet positively identified.

BEELZEBUB, or BAAL-ZEBUB, a corruption of *Baal-zebul*, the great Syrian deity whose worship, originating in Ekron, gradually spread throughout Palestine. The Hebrew corruption of the word signifies a god of flies, and the term came to mean any false god. Milton assigns him a place next to Satan's in *Paradise Lost*. 985

A GLOSSARY OF BIBLICAL TERMS

BEER-SHEBA marked the southern limits of Palestine in O.T. days. It figures largely in the history of the patriarchs. Though still a considerable town in the time of Jerome, it is at present merely a heap of ruins. 27, 29, 40, 208, 219, 222, 272, 292, 306, 322, 356, 392, 397

BEHEMOTH, some large animal, most probably the hippopotamus.

BELIAL, a word of doubtful meaning, though general worthlessness represents its basic idea. In the N.T. Belial came to mean Satan, and Milton gave him a high place among the fallen angels. 207, 209, 215, 217, 255, 256, 290, 324, 325

BELSHAZZAR, last king of Babylon. His doom was foretold by Daniel. 813–815

BELTESHAZZAR, Daniel's Babylonian name. 800

BENAIAH, one of David's chief officers, important in suppressing the rebellion of Adonijah, whom he slew. He also killed Shimei and Joab, succeeding the latter as commander-in-chief of the army. 297–299, 302–303

BENJAMIN, Jacob's beloved youngest son and founder of one of the twelve tribes. Rachel died in giving him birth, calling him Ben-oni (*son of my sorrow*), but Jacob changed his name to Benjamin (*son of my right hand*). 56, 65, 67–68, 69, 70, 71, 72, 76

BENJAMIN (tribe), BENJAMITES, were noted for their warlike character and skill in archery. Once the entire tribe was practically destroyed for its immorality. 154, 180, 205–212, 225, 227, 249, 271, 273, 631

BENJAMIN (region) lay north of Judah and included many places of great historical interest. 223, 226, 270, 470, 477

BEN-ONI, Benjamin's name originally. 56

BEOR, Balaam's father. 136, 142, 143, 145

BERENICE, see below.

BERNICE, eldest daughter of Herod Agrippa I, was first married to her uncle Herod, king of Chalcis. After his death, she lived with her own brother, Herod II, under circumstances that gave rise to much sinister gossip. 1095, 1096, 1098

BETHANY, a village on the Jericho road, about two miles east of Jerusalem, is rich in N.T. associations. Lazarus lived there with Martha and Mary. It is intimately connected with many scenes from the life of Jesus. 923, 924, 925, 1005, 1020, 1021, 1023

BETHABARA, where Jesus was baptized by John. It lay about five miles north of the Dead Sea. 1008

BETH-EL, literally, House of God. About twelve miles north of Jerusalem it is one of the most famous places in Palestine, the scene of Jacob's ladder dream, to choose but one of the many events with which it is connected. 17, 18, 41, 47, 55-56, 165, 168, 177, 212, 221, 226, 328, 356, 390, 392, 395, 396

BETH-EL, MOUNT, a hilly section near Beth-lehem. 228

BETHESDA, a pool in Jerusalem whose waters were supposed to have curative powers. Here Jesus healed a sick man who had waited thirty-eight years to test the waters, but had always been shoved aside. Authorities are disagreed as to the site of the pool. 1014

BETH-HORON, the scene of one of Joshua's victories, lay on the road from

[1248]

A GLOSSARY OF BIBLICAL TERMS

Gideon to Azekah, on the boundary between Benjamin and Ephraim. 172

BETH-LEHEM, a town in Judea, the birthplace of Jesus. Situated about ten miles south of Jerusalem, no site is richer in Biblical lore. The story of Ruth and Boaz developed here, and here, too, Samuel anointed Saul. 236, 238, 271, 502, 787, 788, 789, 792, 935-937, 977

BETHSAIDA, where Jesus fed five thousand people on five loaves and two fishes, lay on both sides of the Jordan as it flows into the Sea of Galilee. It was the native place of Andrew, Peter, and Philip. 914, 918, 946, 983, 1009

BETHUEL, father of Rebekah. 32, 34, 35, 40

BEWRAY, to expose.

BIGTHANA, who plotted with Teresh against Ahasuerus. The conspiracy was discovered and revealed by Mordecai. 830, 834

BILDAD, a Shuhite, was the second of Job's three false friends. The Shuhites probably came from western Chaldea, near the Arabian border. 699, 703

BILHAH, one of Rachel's handmaidens, bore Dan and Naphtali to Jacob. 43, 44, 57

BITTERN is thought by some authorities to be the hedgehog, but W. Houghton dryly remarks that "it is quite probable that 'bittern' (A.V.) is right."

BOAZ, a rich citizen of Beth-lehem. For his role in the Book of Ruth, see *Ruth*. 788-793

BRAY, to crush in a mortar.

BUSH, BURNING, probably a variety of acacia.

CAESAREA, the chief town of the plain of Sharon, was the official seat of the Herods. It retained its importance even in the times of the Crusades. 1059, 1061, 1062, 1063, 1067, 1080, 1086, 1092, 1094, 1095

CAESAREA PHILIPPI, an important Roman town south of Mount Hermon. Here Peter acknowledged the divinity of Jesus, and the Transfiguration occurred on the adjacent Hermon. Caesarea Philippi marked the northern limits of Jesus' personal ministry. 918

CAIAPHAS, high priest of the Jews under Tiberius, was Annas' son-in-law. He presided at the trial of Jesus. 980, 1023, 1033, 1034, 1049

CAIN, eldest son of Adam and Eve. By killing Abel, he was the first murderer. The tragedy of Cain and Abel inspired, among others, Byron and Coleridge. 9-10, 1179

CALAMUS, SWEET, an aromatic grass of considerable value, imported into Palestine from afar.

CALEB, one of the spies Moses sent to survey the land of Canaan. As only he and Joshua reported favorably, they alone were permitted to enter the Promised Land. 127, 129, 254

CAMEL, always the Arabian, or one-humped, variety.

CANA OF GALILEE, scene of Jesus' first miracle: turning water into wine at the marriage feast. It lay about five miles south of Nazareth. 1010, 1040

CANAAN, fourth son of Ham, was the ancestor of the Phoenicians and of the various peoples who held the country west of Jordan before the Israelite conquest. 15

CANAAN corresponds roughly to the modern Palestine. The part west of Jordan was the Israelites' land of promise. 16, 17, 18, 20, 40, 47, 65, 66, 67, 70, 73, 76, 77, 86, 99, 102,

[1249]

A GLOSSARY OF BIBLICAL TERMS

125–127, 156, 159 (these last two references important, though Canaan is not mentioned by name), 177, 179, 181, 435, 456, 534, 536

CANAANITES may be either the descendants of Canaan merely or the non-Israelite inhabitants of Palestine in general. Sometimes the term is restricted to the peoples living west of the Jordan before the conquest. 18, 31, 40, 82, 162

CAPERNAUM, a town on the northwestern shore of the Sea of Galilee. Here Jesus propounded the doctrine of transubstantiation. 902, 904, 921, 938, 947, 982

CARMEL, a famous mountain in northwest Palestine, scene of the great conflict between Elijah and the prophets of Baal. It is also connected intimately with the story of Elisha. 320, 322, 330, 334, 351, 385, 397, 450, 782

CARMEL, a town in the mountainous part of Judah, was the residence of Nabal. 234, 254, 255, 257

CARRIAGE, luggage.

CAUL, a hairnet.

CEDRON, Kidron. 1032

CHALDEA, the low alluvial country around the estuaries of the Tigris and Euphrates—southern. Babylonia, in short. 438, 491, 493, 528, 536

CHALDEANS, or CHALDEES, were originally Cushites who inhabited Chaldea. As these gained dominance in Babylonia, they retained the Cushite dialect for literary purposes. Thus the Chaldeans came to mean the learned men: priests, necromancers, astronomers. 359, 427, 438, 465, 491, 493, 511, 528, 701, 800, 801–802, 803, 805, 811, 813–814, 815

CHEMOSH, the chief god of the Moabites. 136, 313, 314, 357

CHIDE, to quarrel.

CHITTIM, Cyprus or its inhabitants, supposed to be the descendants of Javan, son of Japheth. 144, 437, 472, 544

CHORAZIN, a city two miles from Capernaum, was denounced by Jesus for its evil ways. Its modern site is unknown. 946, 983

CHURL, a miser.

CILICIA, a maritime province in southeastern Asia Minor, was a scene of Paul's labors. 1055, 1074, 1088, 1092, 1099, 1115

CLEOPAS, one of the two disciples who met Jesus on the road to Emmaus. This encounter was one of the earnests of the resurrection. 1003

CLEOPHAS, the husband of Mary, the sister of the Virgin Mary, probably died before Jesus began his ministry. 1037

CLOUTS, rags.

COCKATRICE, more probably basilisk or adder.

COLOSSE, a city in Phrygia, whose inhabitants were addressed by Paul in the Epistle to the Colossians. A church existed there as early as Apostolic times. 1168

CONEY, always the rock badger, never the rabbit.

CORIANDER, an herb whose fruit is used as a carminative.

CORINTH, a luxury-loving Greek city, was a scene of Paul's labors. He addressed its citizens in two Epistles to the Corinthians. 1079, 1080, 1122, 1138

CORMORANT, an unlucky translation of the Hebrew $q\bar{a}ath$, notably in Is. xxxiv.11 and Zeph. ii.14. The pelican is probably meant in both cases. 449, 457

A GLOSSARY OF BIBLICAL TERMS

CORNELIUS, a Roman centurion baptized by Peter. 1062–1063

CRISPING PINS, curling irons used in waving the hair.

CUMMIN, a dwarf plant whose aromatic seeds are used as a condiment or medicinally.

CUSHI, the officer who brought the tidings of Absalom's death to David. 294–295

CYPRUS, a Mediterranean island, was noted in N.T. history as a scene of Paul's labors. It was Barnabas' native place. 1052, 1065, 1068, 1074, 1085, 1086, 1098

CYRUS, king of Persia, helped the Jews to return from Babylon. 564, 801, 818, 822

DAGON, a god of the Philistines, important seats of whose worship were at Gaza and Ashdod. Originally a marine deity, he later became a god of agriculture. 204

DAMASCUS, the metropolis of Syria and allegedly the oldest continuously inhabited site in the world, was noted for its luxury. Josephus said the city was founded by Uz, grandson of Shem. Its vicissitudes bulk large in O.T. history. Paul was converted at Damascus. 20, 323, 336, 340, 385, 390, 423, 431, 545, 1059–1061, 1088–1089, 1097, 1115, 1143

DAN, fifth son of Jacob, was the ancestor of one of the Twelve Tribes. Its lands lay originally along the coast, including the rich port of Jaffa, but the Amorites forced the Danites to migrate. At last they were granted a new portion in the extreme north of Palestine. 44, 75, 156, 181, 198, 475

DAN, once called Laish, or Leshem, was the most northern city in Palestine, just as Beer-sheba was the most southern. The Jordan has its source at a nearby fountain. 20, 208, 219, 272, 292, 306

DANIEL, the fourth of the major prophets, was taken captive to Babylon in the third year of the reign of Jehoiakim. He was distinguished for his purity and wisdom, and his interpretations of dreams and adventure in the lions' den are familiar stories. 800–824, 961, 1181

DANITES, the descendants of Dan. 196

DAVID, King of the Jews, is one of the most curiously attractive and repellent characters in the O.T. His friendship with Jonathan, dancing before the Lord, and making of sweet music must be set against the endless trickeries that disfigure his conduct. Even his contest with Goliath has not escaped unfriendy comment, while his death-bed savagery has few parallels in great literature. Jesus was descended from David. 237–261, 262–264, 267–295, 297–301, 302, 303, 304, 306, 307, 313, 314, 316, 346, 351–352, 394, 421, 426–427 "stem of Jesse", 487, 496, 551, 553, 572, 652, 755, 777, 905, 977, 1045, 1048, 1051, 1055, (references to Jesus Christ the Son of David not included)

DAYSMAN, an umpire, mediator.

DEBORAH, a female prophet and judge of Israel. Her incitement of Barak against Sisera, followed by her song of triumph, is a notable passage in the Book of Judges, 177–182

DELILAH, a Philistine courtesan who betrayed Samson. Their story inspired Saint-Saens' operatic cantata, *Samson et Dalila*, 202–204

DINAH, daughter of Jacob by Leah, was ravished by Shechem, a Hivite. For that reason, and with the help of a pe-

[1251]

A GLOSSARY OF BIBLICAL TERMS

culiarly low cunning, Simeon and Levi, Dinah's own brothers, revenged the insult. What Dinah thought of the whole matter is not recorded. 53–55

DISANNUL, to annul completely.

DISPENSATION, stewardship.

DIVES, the rich man of the parable of Lazarus, is not mentioned thus in the English Bible. The word—it is not a name, properly speaking—occurs only in the Latin Vulgate. 995–996

DOEG, Saul's timeserving chief herdsman. He told his master that the priests of Nob were helping David, whereupon the king ordered them and their families to be slain. When others declined to do the deed, Doeg descended upon the offenders, and slew eighty-five. 250–251

DORCAS, see *Tabitha*.

DRAGON, an interesting false rendering, sometimes for "jackal," sometimes for "sea monster." The context does not always help the reader.

DRAUGHT, a toilet drain.

EAGLE. There are plenty of eagles in the Bible, and there are at least four distinct species in Palestine. Authorities tend to agree that some member of the family Vulturidae is meant, often the vulture itself.

EAR, to plow.

EDEN, the garden of paradise where Adam and Eve dwelt until they were expelled for transgression. It was probably located somewhere between the Tigris and Euphrates, most probably in Armenia, near their sources. 5–9, 10, 593

EDIFY, to build, build up.

EDOM, the name Esau received when he sold his birthright to Jacob for a mess of pottage. 36

EDOM, the country the Lord gave to Esau after he had sold his birthright. It embraced a mountainous tract extending from the northern end of the Gulf of Akaba to the southern end of the Dead Sea. This district was also known as Mount Seir or Idumea. 50, 99, 133, 134, 143, 179, 233, 330, 331, 385, 386, 387, 579, 583–584

EDOMITES, descendants of Esau, seem to have been, like their predecessors in Edom, idolaters and cave dwellers. 248, 250, 311, 525

EGLON, king of Moab, was a man of exceeding fatness. Ehud, judge of Israel, murdered him, and so delivered his people from the Moabite incursions. 176–177

EGYPT, EGYPTIANS, one of the great empires of antiquity, was intimately connected with the Israelites through Joseph and, later, Moses. 17, 18, 58, 59, 60, 61, 62–65, 68, 69, 71–73, 77, 79, 81, 82–83, 85–98, 103, 104, 105, 110, 111, 112, 119, 123, 126, 127, 128, 132, 133, 134, 141, 142, 170, 175, 183, 208, 220, 222, 226, 233, 306, 314, 315, 388, 389, 391, 397, 398, 402, 403, 411, 425, 434–435, 437, 462, 472, 474, 492, 500, 510–512, 525, 538, 542, 543, 544, 631, 648, 658, 936–937, 1046, 1088, 1181, 1212

EHUD, a judge of Israel who slew Eglon, king of Moab. Although left-handed, he was very strong. 176–177

EKRON, one of the five confederated Philistine cities, lay about midway between Jaffa and Ashdod, though inland. 241, 386, 456

ELAH, the valley where David killed Goliath. It was situated near Ekron. 238

ELAM, ELAMITES, a district around the head of the Persian Gulf, the capital of

A GLOSSARY OF BIBLICAL TERMS

which was, in later days, Susa. It was originally peopled by the descendants of Shem. 19, 436, 548, 1046

ELEAZAR, Aaron's son and successor in the high priesthood. 133–134, 145–146

ELI, high priest of Israel, in whose care Samuel was placed. He favored the boy against his own sons, whom he cursed for their wicked ways. Eli was descended from Aaron through Ithama, the younger of his two surviving sons, and was the first of the line of Ithamar to hold the high priesthood. He died of shock at the age of ninety-eight. 214-221, 302

ELIAB, Jesse's eldest son. 236, 238

ELIAKIM, son of Hilkiah, was the majordomo of King Hezekiah. A good and trusted servant, he led the embassy to Rab-shakeh. 348, 349

ELIAKIM, the name of King Jehoiakim before it was changed by the king of Egypt. 357

ELIAS, the Greek form of Elijah, is used in the N.T. 911, 918, 919–920, 946, 973, 1008, 1190

ELIEZER, second son of Moses and Zipporah. 103–104

ELIJAH, a Tishbite, lived in the ninth century B.C. The story of his life and prophecies is told mainly in the two Books of Kings. He was fed by ravens, opposed successfully the prophets of Baal, and finally was carried up to heaven in a whirlwind. 317–326, 328–329, 331, 343, 598, 911, 918, 919–920, 946, 973, 1008, 1190 (the N.T. mentions him as Elias)

ELIPHAZ, a Temanite, was one of Job's three rather lukewarm friends. 699 *et passim* throughout Job.

ELISABETH, mother of John the Baptist. 972–975

ELISHA, the successor of Elijah, who anointed him and cast his mantle over him. He was a notable worker of miracles, and his cures of Naaman and the Shunammite's son were especially famed. He favored Jehu in his rebellion. He seems to have been a man of excessively choleric disposition, as his treatment of the mocking children shows. Even after his death he continued to work miracles, his bones being used to raise a dead man. 323, 328–341, 344

ELKANAH, Samuel's father. 214, 218

ELYMAS, the Arabic name of Bar-jesus. 1068

EMMAUS, a village north of Jerusalem, near which Jesus appeared to two disciples on the day of his resurrection. 1003

EN-DOR, a village a few miles south of Mount Tabor, was the scene of a great victory over Sisera. Here Saul consulted a witch in order to raise up the spirit of Samuel. 261–263

ENOCH, son of Jared and father of Methuselah, was one of the patriarchs. He is represented as the exemplar of perfected humanity. 1180

ENOS, son of Seth. 10

EPHESUS, an ancient Ionian city and capital of the Roman province of Asia, was the seat of one of the Seven Churches of Asia Minor. Paul addressed the Epistle to the Ephesians to its inhabitants. 1080–1083, 1084, 1134, 1200

EPHRAIM, second son of Joseph, was the ancestor of one of the Twelve Tribes. 65, 77

EPHRAIM, the part of Canaan named after Joseph's second son. It stretched from the Jordan to the coast, and lay just north of Benjamin, with Samaria

A GLOSSARY OF BIBLICAL TERMS

as its most northerly city. When Jeroboam revolted, Ephraim formed the nucleus of the new kingdom of Israel, with the first capital at Shechem. Sometimes the entire kingdom is called Ephraim. 155, 156, 180, 187, 188, 270, 293, 431, 444, 499, 553, 647

EPHRAIM, near Absalom's sheep farm, has not been identified. 283, 1023

EPHRAIM, MOUNT, was a mountainous district that extended south to the boundary of Benjamin. 177, 187, 214, 498

EPHRON, a Hittite, sold Abraham the field and cave of Machpelah. 30, 35, 76, 77

ESAIAS, the Greek name of Isaiah. 914, 938, 948, 980, 1008, 1058

ESAU, Isaac's eldest son, was Jacob's twin brother. He sold his birthright to Jacob for a mess of pottage, and Jacob received the blessing intended for Isaac, by a ruse. Eventually the brothers were reconciled, after Jacob had trembled sufficiently for his misdeeds. 36–40, 50–51, 52, 55, 56, 583, 1156

ESTHER, a noted Jewish heroine, was married to Ahasuerus (Xerxes) of Persia. She kept her nationality a secret on the advice of her cousin, Mordecai. Together they were able to circumvent the designs of Haman, the prime minister, against the Jews, and finally the schemer was hanged on the gallows he had designed for Mordecai. The feast of Purim, supposed to commemorate this deliverance, is really of far more remote antiquity than the time of Xerxes; it is possibly of Babylonian origin. 826–840

ETHIOPIA, ETHIOPIANS, also called Cush, included modern Nubia and part of Abyssinia. 5, 398, 433, 547, 462, 484, 554, 631

EUPHRATES, one of the four rivers of paradise, is the most important river in western Asia. From its source in the Armenian highlands to its mouth in the Persian Gulf, its length is 1780 miles. Babylon stood on its banks. 6, 159, 512, 1210, 1219

EUPHRATES, in Jeremiah, may have been a village. Its site is unknown. 483, 484

EVE, the first woman, "the mother of all living," and wife of Adam, from whose rib she was made. The word means *life*. 6–9, 10, 874, 1141

EZEKIEL, one of the major prophets, lived in the sixth century B.C. A member of the priestly family of Zadok, he lived in Babylonia, and is said to have been murdered in Babylon. He was excessively mystical, sometimes to the point of obscurity. 528

FAIN, gladly.

FELIX, a Roman procurator of Judea, threw Paul into prison. His rule was so cruel that he almost suffered the extreme penalty when he returned to Rome. He married the daughter of Herod Agrippa I, and was superseded by Festus. 1092, 1093–1094, 1095

FESTUS, PORCIUS, a Roman procurator of Judea, found Paul guiltless. He died in A.D. 60, having ruled the province for less than two years. 1094, 1095–1096, 1098

FISH, GREAT. The identity of the monster that swallowed the prophet Jonah remains an open question, despite the popular choice of the whale.

FITCHES, spelt. See *rye*.

FOWL may mean either any bird, a bird of prey, or a chirping bird of some sort. The A.V. translators covered three distinct Hebrew words with this vague generalization.

Fox is usually better translated jackal.

A GLOSSARY OF BIBLICAL TERMS

FRAY, to scare.

FRET, to eat away.

FROWARD, perverse.

FULLER, a bleacher or cleaner of cloth.

GAAL offered strong opposition to Abimelech. 193–194

GABRIEL, one of the archangels. He brought the good tidings to the Virgin Mary, and was also sent to Daniel to explain his visions. He is expected to sound the trumpet at the Last Judgment. 821, 972–974

GAD, Jacob's seventh son, was the ancestor of one of the Twelve Tribes. 44, 75

GAD, that part of the country occupied by the tribe of Gad, lay east of the Jordan, including the strong city of refuge, Ramoth-gilead. The mountainous character of the district was matched by the warlike, almost savage characteristics of the tribe. 155, 229

GALATIA, a province in central Asia Minor, was a scene of Paul's labors. He addressed the Epistle to the Galatians to its inhabitants. 1074, 1080, 1114, 1135

GALILEE, the northern section of Palestine west of the Sea of Galilee. 901, 902, 903, 912, 916, 927, 931, 932, 937, 938, 951, 968, 969, 970, 973, 977, 979, 997, 999, 1002, 1009, 1010, 1012, 1040, 1045, 1054, 1061, 1064, 1069

GALLIO, a Roman proconsul of Achaia, who refused to meddle with Jewish affairs. St. Jerome says that he committed suicide, but Winer thinks he was put to death by Nero. 1079

GAMALIEL, a Pharisee and famous rabbi, was the teacher of Paul. 1054, 1088

GATH, one of the five confederated Philistine cities, was the native place of Goliath. David took refuge at Gath during one of his crises. It lay almost on the boundary between Philistia and Judah, about fifteen miles from the sea. 238, 239, 241, 249, 260, 268, 288, 303, 394

GAZA, one of the five confederated cities of the Philistines, was the scene of the final tragedy in the life of Samson. It lies in southern Palestine, a few miles from the coast, and is still, under the name of Ghuzzeh, a town of some importance. 182, 202, 204, 347, 385, 456, 1058

GEDALIAH, made governor of Judah by Nebuchadnezzar, was shortly afterwards slain by Ishmael. 508, 509, 511

GEHAZI, Elisha's servant, was smitten with an incurable leprosy for his avarice. 333, 334, 335, 337–338

GENNESARET, or GENNESARETH, SEA OF, another name for the Sea of Galilee. Gennesaret was a fertile plain at the northwestern angle of the lake. 914

GERSHOM was the firstborn son of Moses and Zipporah. 81, 103

GETHSEMANE, a garden outside of Jerusalem, was the scene of Jesus' agony. It was probably at the foot of Mount Olivet. 927, 1032

GIBEAH OF BENJAMIN, a place four miles north of Jerusalem, was the scene of the tragical story of the Levite and his concubine. 206–211, 228, 230

GIBEAH OF SAUL, probably identical with Gibeah of Benjamin, was the residence of Saul until he was anointed king. 227, 235, 249, 252, 258, 425

GIBEON, one of the four cities of the Hivites, lay about seven miles north of Jerusalem. It made a pact with Joshua, and thus escaped the fate of Ai and Jericho. 169, 170, 172, 270, 271, 273, 304, 446

A GLOSSARY OF BIBLICAL TERMS

GIBEONITES, the inhabitants of Gibeon, obtained help from Joshua under false pretenses, and so were condemned to be hewers of wood and drawers of water for the congregation. Saul broke the pact and massacred many of the inhabitants, and many years later some of Saul's descendants were given up to be crucified or hung by the Gibeonites. 169–172

GIDEON, judge of Israel, was the youngest son of Joash, a wealthy Abiezrite. With but three hundred men he delivered his people from the oppressions of the Midianites. Like Saul, he owed some of his popularity to his fine bearing. 182–190, 421, 425, 1181

GIHON, one of the four rivers of Paradise, is identified with the Oxus, the modern Amu Darya. Rising in the Pamirs, it flows northwestward into the Aral Sea. 5

GILBOA, a mountain near Jezreel, where Saul was defeated and killed in a great battle with the Philistines. 261, 264–265, 267, 268

GILEAD, a district east of the Jordan, was bounded on the north by Bashan, on the south by Moab and Ammon. It was, of course, noted mainly for its balm. 58, 156, 181, 195, 208, 229, 270, 317, 385, 386, 647, 777

GILGAL probably lay somewhere between Jericho and the Jordan. Here Samuel sat as judge and Saul was made king. 170, 171–172, 176, 221, 226, 228, 229, 234–235, 390, 392

GILGAL, the place visited by Elijah and Elisha, has been identified with a place about four miles from Beth-el. 328, 335

GIN, a trap.

GOAT, WILD, probably the Syrian ibex.

GOG, chief prince of Meshech and Tubal, so appears in Ezekiel. In revelation he is identified with Antichrist. 554–556, 1226

GOLGOTHA, an elevation northwest of Jerusalem, was the scene of Jesus' crucifixion. 930, 967, 1006

GOLIATH, a giant of Gath, was slain by a stone from David's sling in a single combat to decide the battle between the Israelites and Philistines. He was over ten feet tall. 208, 239–242, 248, 250

GOMORRAH, a city on the north side of the Dead Sea, was destroyed by God for its wickedness. Its site is unknown. See *Sodom*. 18, 19, 23, 26, 152, 391, 416, 427, 457, 911

GOODMAN, a householder.

GOPHER WOOD, from which Noah made the ark, is generally identified with cypress.

GOSHEN, the part of Egypt set aside for the Israelites. It was near the eastern side of the Delta, and was a land of great plenty. It contained the treasure cities of Rameses and Pittim. The term has come to be used generically for any rich land. 72, 73, 77, 89, 91

GOURD, probably the castor-oil plant. See, especially, the passage in Jonah, 798

GRECIANS, Greek-speaking Jews. 1054, 1061, 1065

GREYHOUND, probably the domestic cock, though other interpretations have been suggested. 695

HABAKKUK, a minor prophet, probably lived in the seventh century B.C. The Book of Habakkuk is attributed to him. 465

HADASSAH, the earlier name of Esther. 828

A GLOSSARY OF BIBLICAL TERMS

HAGAR, Sarah's handmaid and mother of Ishmael by Abraham. Sarah had mother and son cast into the wilderness, and there they almost perished before an angel showed them a waterhole. 20–21, 27–28, 1117

HAGGAI, a minor prophet, flourished in the reign of Darius I, about 520 B.C. The Message of Haggai is ascribed to him. 586

HAM, one of Noah's three sons. According to legend, his descendants peopled Africa. Hence, a negro is sometimes called a Hamite. 11, 15

HAMAN, the chief minister of Ahasuerus. He conspired against the Jews, but his plots were defeated by Esther and Mordecai, and he was hanged on the gallows he had prepared for the latter. On the feast of Purim the Jews hiss whenever Haman's name is mentioned. 830–840

HAMATH, once the principal city of upper Syria, lay on the Orontes, about midway between Antioch and Damascus. It was one of Solomon's treasure cities. 126, 346, 349, 394, 423, 507

HANANIAH, the Hebrew name of Shadrach. 800, 801, 803

HANNAH, Samuel's mother. 214–218

HARAN, scene of Abraham's first settlement, lay about two hundred miles east of Antioch. 16, 17, 40, 41, 545

HAZAEL, a king of Damascus, obtained the throne through violence, though ostensibly by divine favor. The whole transaction throws an interesting light on the political activities of the prophets. Hazael often fought with the Jews. 323, 340, 342, 385

HAZEROTH, a station in the desert wanderings of the Israelites, probably lay about forty miles northeast of Sinai. 124, 125

HAZOR, a fortified place between Ramah and Kadesh, was one of the chief cities of northern Palestine. 177, 178

HEALTH, healing. Also see *Saving health*.

HEATH, the dwarf juniper.

HEAVINESS, sadness.

HEBRON, one of the oldest towns in the world, excluding now uninhabited sites, lay about twenty miles south of Jerusalem. It boasts the graves of Abraham and Sarah, Isaac, and Jacob, for the cave of Machpelah is included within its boundaries. 19, 29, 31, 56, 58, 126, 171, 173, 202, 269, 270, 271, 270, 274, 275, 287, 301

HEPHZI-BAH, mother of Manasseh, was Hezekiah's queen. 353

HEPHZI-BAH was a term applied by Isaiah to the restored Jerusalem. It means *my delight in her*. 577

HERMON, a famous mountain in northern Palestine, may have been the scene of the transfiguration of Christ. 657, 778

HEROD THE GREAT, tetrarch of Judea from 41 B.C. to 4 B.C., was responsible for the massacre of the innocents. 935–937

HEROD ANTIPAS, tetrarch of Judea from 4 B.C. to A.D. 39. He was instrumental in the death of John the Baptist. He died in exile. 911–912, 917, 979, 981, 990, 999–1000, 1051

HEROD PHILIP I was the son of Herod the Great and Mariamne. He married Herodias, and Salome was their daughter. 911, 981

HEROD PHILIP II was the son of Herod the Great and Cleopatra. He had the title of tetrarch, and died in A.D. 34. 980

[1257]

A GLOSSARY OF BIBLICAL TERMS

Herod Agrippa I, grandson of Herod the Great, received the title of king from Caligula. He was a man of great ambition, and might have gone far if he had not died prematurely. He had James the Greater put to death, and imprisoned Peter. 1066–1067

Herod Agrippa II, the last of the Herodian line, was the son of the foregoing. He was violently pro-Roman, and was said to have died in Rome about A.D. 100. Paul was tried before him. 1092

Heshbon, the chief city of the Amorites, lay some miles east of the Dead Sea. 135, 136, 170, 430, 431, 782

Heth, ancestor of the Hittites. 29, 30, 31, 40

Hezekiah, twelfth king of Judah, was noted for his decided efforts to stamp out idolatry. Sennacherib's army was destroyed in his reign. 346–353, 400, 406, 414, 451, 495, 687

Hiddekel, one of the four rivers of paradise, is identified with the Tigris. 5

Hilkiah, a famous high priest of Judah, flourished under Josiah. He found the book of the law of Moses in the Temple. He was a notable reformer. 354–355, 356

Hinnom, a valley to the south and west of Jerusalem, was the scene of the worship of Molech. As this deity is worshipped with fiery rites, the Jews later applied the name of this valley to hell itself. 480, 488

Hiram, king of Tyre, was the fast friend of David and Solomon. 306–307, 308, 311, 312

Hittites, the reputed descendants of Heth, held sway over one of the greatest empires of antiquity, extending from central Asia Minor to Syria, including portions of that land. 82, 126, 159, 162, 534

Hivites, the descendants of Canaan, lived in the northern part of western Palestine. 53, 82, 162, 170

Hophni, son of Eli, performed, with his brother Phinehas, the priestly duties of Shiloh. He lost his life in battle with the Philistines, during which the ark of the covenant was taken. 214, 220, 221

Hor, Mount, lay just north of the Gulf of Akaba. It was the scene of the death of Aaron. 133–134

Horeb, another name for Mount Sinai. 82, 103, 114, 323, 598

Horseleach. This innocent-looking word actually refers to some vampire-like monster. "Ghoul" is an acceptable translation.

Hosea, one of the minor prophets, flourished in the eighth century B.C. and gave his name to one of the Prophetical Books. 400

Hoshea, son of Nun, was Joshua's name originally. 153

Hoshea, nineteenth and last king of Israel, was also its best. He met disaster when he tried to throw off the yoke of Assyria. 345, 346–347

Huldah, a female prophet, flourished in the reign of Josiah. 355

Hur, an important lieutenant of Moses and Aaron, was, according to Jewish tradition, the husband of Miriam. 103

Hushai, David's friend, was important in quelling the revolt of Absalom. Dryden called Laurence Hyde, earl of Rochester, Hushai in *Absalom and Achitophel*. 289, 290, 291, 292

Husks, the fruit of the carob tree.

Hyssop, a plant famed for its part in the institution of the Passover. It is

[1258]

A GLOSSARY OF BIBLICAL TERMS

generally identified with a certain species of caper.

Ichabod, son of Phinehas and grandson of Eli, born just after the death of his father and grandfather. The name means *the glory has departed*. 221

Iconium, a city of Lycaonia, where Paul and Barnabas were persecuted. 1070, 1071, 1074

Idumea, another name for Edom. 449, 906

Inn, a lodging.

Instant, urgent.

Isaac, son of Abraham. To test his faith God commanded Abraham to sacrifice Isaac, but at the last moment was told to kill a ram, instead. Isaac married Rebekah and was the father of Jacob and Esau. 27, 28–29, 31, 32, 35–36, 37–40, 47, 49, 50, 56, 76, 77, 81, 82, 86, 87, 112, 113, 156, 321, 395, 396, 957, 990, 1118, 1156, 1180, 1181, 1187

Isaiah, the greatest of the Hebrew prophets. He flourished in the eighth century B.C. Jewish tradition has it that he was sawn asunder, at the age of ninety, by order of Manasseh. 349, 350, 351–353, 414

Ish-bosheth, Saul's son and successor. Baanah and Rechab, to curry favor with David, slew Ish-bosheth, but David had them put to death. 270, 272, 274–275

Ishmael, son of Abraham and Hagar, was cast out, with his mother, of his father's house. He became the ancestor of the Arabs. 20–22, 35

Israel, a name given by God to Jacob after he had wrestled with the angel, and thus his descendants were called Israelites. The word means *God fighteth*. 51

Israel, kingdom of, was the name of the northern kingdom that seceded with Jeroboam. At the height of its power it contained almost four million people. Shechem was the first capital. Jeroboam moved it to Tirzah, and Omri to Samaria. Jezreel was another royal residence. 315–346 and *passim* thereafter throughout the O.T.

Issachar, son of Jacob and Leah, founded one of the Twelve Tribes. 44, 75

Issachar, the district allotted to the ninth son of Jacob, lay in central Palestine, with Jezreel almost at its exact center. 180

Jabbok, a torrent between the Dead Sea and the Sea of Galilee. On the south bank occurred a famous interview between Jacob and Esau. 51, 135

Jacob, son of Isaac and Rebekah, whose twelve sons founded the Twelve Tribes of Israel. Jacob tricked Isaac into giving him his birthright for a mess of pottage. Through his usual trickery he accumulated much wealth in the service of Laban, two of whose daughters, Leah and Rachel, he won through service to their father. 36, 37–56, 57, 59, 67–68, 72, 73–77

Jael, wife of Heber, offered refuge to Sisera in his flight from Barak to Deborah. Then she killed him with a tent pin. 178–179, 180, 181

Jaffa, see *Joppa*.

James the Greater, one of the Twelve Apostles, was the son of Zebedee and Salome. John the Evangelist was his brother. His labors traditionally took him to Spain, and he suffered martyrdom under Herod Agrippa I. 902, 906, 910, 919, 922, 923, 927, 981, 1045, 1066

James the Less, also one of the Twelve, was the son of Alphaeus or Clopas. He is called the Lord's brother, but

[1259]

A GLOSSARY OF BIBLICAL TERMS

this probably means cousin. The General Epistle of James is attributed to him. 907, 910, 931, 968, 1003, 1045, 1067, 1072, 1086, 1115, 1116, 1133

JAPHETH, one of the three sons of Noah, was blessed by his father. He was the reputed founder of the Aryan branch of the human family, which is hence sometimes called the Japhetic. 11, 15

JASON, a Thessalonian who gave succor to Paul. 1077

JEBUS, ancient name for Jerusalem. 206

JEBUSITES were descended from Canaan's third son. 82, 126, 162, 206

JECONIAH, another name for Jehoiachin. 491, 495, 828

JEHOAHAZ, son and successor of Jehu, was tributary to Hazael, king of Damascus. He reigned over Israel for seventeen years. 344

JEHOAHAZ, son of Josiah, reigned over Judah for only a few months. He was taken captive into Egypt, where he died. 357

JEHOIACHIN, a king of Judah carried into captivity by Nebuchadnezzar. 358, 528

JEHOIAKIM, a wicked king of Judah, whose rebellion caused Nebuchadnezzar to descend on Jerusalem. He died in an engagement with the enemy, and his body was treated most ignominiously. 357-358, 470, 491, 492, 493, 500, 501-503, 800

JEHORAM, king of Israel, was the son of Ahab. He made a census of his subjects. He was killed by Jehu, and with him ended the dynasty of Omri. 330

JEHOSHAPHAT, son of Asa, succeeded his father as king of Judah. He was a devout and successful ruler, and was twice delivered from a threatened war with the peoples of Ammon, Moab, and Seir. 330-331

JEHU, the officer who led the rebellion against the house of Ahab. He dethroned Jehoram and secured the kingdom of Israel for himself. 323, 341-344

JEPHTHAH, a judge of Israel who sacrificed his only daughter because he had vowed to God the first thing that met him on his way home after his great victory over the Ammonites. 195-196

JEREMIAH, one of the greatest of the prophets, flourished at the time of Nebuchadnezzar's conquest of Jerusalem. His prophecies occur in the Book of Jeremiah and in Lamentations. He probably died in Egypt. 470, 487, 489, 491, 492-493, 494, 495, 497, 500-503, 504-507, 508-509, 510, 511, 512

JEREMY, an N.T. variant of Jeremiah. 937, 965

JERICHO, an ancient Palestinian city, was five miles west of the Jordan and seven miles northwest of the Dead Sea. Destroyed by Joshua, it was rebuilt during the reign of Ahab. It rose to great prominence under the Herods. Here Jesus cured Bartimaeus of blindness. 136, 145, 156, 160, 163, 165, 167, 169, 328, 329, 359, 371, 507, 984, 998, 1181

JEROBOAM, the first king of the divided kingdom of Israel, flourished in the tenth century B.C. He revolted against Rehoboam, and so established the Northern Kingdom, with Shechem as the capital. He was an idolater, and so his name has come to signify any wicked person. He died in the twenty-second year of his reign. 313-314, 315-316, 317, 325, 341

JERUSALEM, the most famous city in Biblical history. Though its first mention in Genesis suggests a period anterior to the year 2000 B.C., it is first referred to in Egyptian records about

A GLOSSARY OF BIBLICAL TERMS

1400 B.C. Since then its history has been uninterrupted. 171, 206, 308 and *passim* thereafter throughout the O.T. and N.T.

JESSE, the father of David. 236–237, 238, 239, 247, 249, 250, 255, 316, 426, 793

JESUS, the name of the Christ, is merely the Greek form of Joshua, which means *saviour*. Christ means *anointed*. The two words together signify Jesus' dual role as priest and king. In addition to the Gospels—900–1042, see the rest of the N.T. *passim*.

JETHRO, Moses' father-in-law, was the priest of Midian. The name, which means *his excellence*, was probably his official title. Reuel, though he is called this only once, was probably his proper name. 81, 84, 103–104

JEWRY, Judea. 814, 999

JEZEBEL, a Phoenician princess married to Ahab, king of Israel. She introduced the worship of Baal into the kingdom, and no less than eight hundred and fifty prophets of Baal and Astarte sat at her table. She persecuted Elijah and instigated the murder of Naboth. Ahab was a mere puppet in her hands. Eventually she was murdered, but not before her loose ways had made her name a byword for licentiousness. 317, 319, 320, 322, 324–325, 341, 342, 343

JEZREEL, an important city in southern Galilee, near which Saul fell in battle. Ahab made it his principal residence. 258, 264, 322, 324, 326, 341, 342, 343, 400

JOAB, the chief captain of David's army, was put to death by order of Solomon, in response to his father's deathbed suggestion. He was the son of Zeruiah, David's sister, and was a mighty man of valor. 258, 270–271, 273–274, 277–279, 284–287, 292, 293–294, 295, 298, 300, 302–303

JOASH, king of Judah, was placed on the throne by the efforts of Jehoiada, and while the great high priest lived, Joash led a good life and prospered. But when Jehoiada died, Joash revived the cult of Baal. His last years were unlucky, and finally he was slain in his bed at Millo, victim of a court conspiracy. His reign lasted forty years. 344

JOASH, a king of Israel, was on friendly terms with Elisha, who promised him three victories over the Syrians. 344

JOB, the patriarch who is the hero of the Book of Job. After being put to the most rigorous tests, he came through successfully and ended his days more prosperous than before, thus pointing the wisdom of being as "patient as Job." Some consider him a historical personage, others a religious fiction. 699–753, 1190

JOEL, a Hebrew prophet, probably flourished in the ninth century B.C., though some critics think he lived in post-Exilic times. A Book is attributed to him. 592

JOHN, one of the Twelve, was the son of Zebedee. He alone of the Apostles did not forsake Jesus in the hour of his Passion, and to his care Jesus entrusted the Virgin Mary. He was the disciple whom Jesus loved. He was vigorous in building the church of Ephesus, where he died at an advanced age, having outlived the rest of the Twelve. He wrote the Gospel bearing his name about A.D. 78, and composed Revelation while exiled at Patmos. The three Epistles, probably written from Ephesus, belong to the close of the first century. 902, 907, 1045, 1049, 1050, 1057, 1066, 1116, 1199, 1226

A GLOSSARY OF BIBLICAL TERMS

JOHN THE BAPTIST, the forerunner of the Lord, was the son of Zacharias and Elisabeth. Sanctified in his mother's womb, he had a dramatic career until his martyrdom under Herod Antipas, A.D. 29. 901, 902, 903, 905, 911–912, 945–946, 955, 972–976, 980–981, 1007–1008, 1009, 1012, 1020, 1044, 1067, 1080–1081

JONADAB, the evil genius of Amnon, whom he advised to ravish Tamar. He was the son of Shimeah, and therefore David's nephew. 281–284

JONAH, a noted prophet said to have been swallowed by a great fish, possibly a whale. Though commanded by Jehovah to fulminate against Nineveh, he went to the other way by sea. His story is supposed to be a parable of salvation which foreshadows the mission of Jesus. His stubborn nature is fully exploited in the Book of Jonah. 795–798

JONAS, the N.T. name of Jonah. 986

JONATHAN, son of Saul, was David's most beloved friend, and he tried constantly to mediate between friend and father. He was slain with Saul at Mount Gilboa. 228–232, 233, 242–248, 267, 268–269, 276, 277

JOPPA, a great seaport in southern Palestine, from which Jonah set sail. Tabitha resided at Joppa, and here Peter had his vision of tolerance. 795, 1061, 1062, 1063

JORAM, a contracted form of Jehoram. 342, 343

JORDAN, the chief stream of Palestine, in which John the Baptist baptized Jesus. It is important in both O.T. and N.T. history. 18, 50, 126, 136, 145, in Joshua 160 and *passim*, 177, 181, 187, 188, 229, 264, 271, 293, 301, 317, 328, 329, 336, 338, 483, 619, 648, 750, 902, 980, 1008

JOSEPH, a younger son of Jacob, was hated by his elder brothers for being his father's favorite. He was sold into slavery, eventually entering the household of Potiphar whose wife tried vainly to seduce him. She revenged herself by having him thrown into prison on false charges, but he interpreted the dreams of certain highly placed fellow prisoners so well that he came to Pharaoh's notice. He rose rapidly and was created food administrator of Egypt. When his brothers came to beg corn, he revealed his identity and was reconciled to them. He invited Jacob and his descendants into Egypt. After his death, his body was embalmed and carried into Palestine, and there buried at Shechem, Joseph's own patrimony. 45, 57–73, 76–77, 79, 154, 553, 1012, 1181

JOSEPH, husband of the Virgin Mary, was of the blood royal of David. He seems to have died before the crucifixion of Jesus. 935, 936, 937, 973, 977–979, 1009

JOSEPH OF ARIMATHEA, a wealthy Jew, possibly a member of the Sanhedrin, cared for the entombing of Jesus' body after the crucifixion. 932, 968, 1002, 1038

JOSEPH BARSABAS was one of two persons chosen to fill the place of Judas Iscariot. 1045

JOSHUA, the great hero of the Jews and the successor of Moses, was the son of Nun. He led the Jews into the promised land, which, as one of the spies, sent out to survey it, he too was allowed to enjoy (see *Caleb*). He was a great fighter and once commanded the sun to stand still. As a consciously epic figure, he is less lifelike than his great predecessor. 103, 112, 127, 129, 148, 159 and *passim* in Joshua

[1262]

A GLOSSARY OF BIBLICAL TERMS

JOSIAH, a king of Judah, made heroic efforts to reform his people. He was defeated by Necho of Egypt in the plain of Esdraelon and died before he could reach Jerusalem. 353–357, 454, 470, 493, 500, 503

JOTHAM, Gideon's youngest son, alone was saved when Abimelech slaughtered his brothers. He rebuked the Shechemites, in the famous parable of the trees and the bramble, for choosing the fratricide king. 191–192, 194

JUDAH, fourth son of Jacob, founded one of the Twelve Tribes. He enjoyed an ascendancy over his brethren that is emphasized in Jacob's last words. 43, 58, 67, 70, 74–75, 153

JUDAH. The tribe descended from Jacob's fourth son held lands in southern Palestine. 166, 316, 353, 1178, 1205

JUDAH, KINGDOM OF, comprised the land of the tribes of Judah and Benjamin. These acknowledged the rule of Rehoboam after the secession of Jeroboam. Judah is sometimes called the Southern Kingdom. 315–359 and *passim* thereafter throughout the O.T., especially 387, 410, 485; also 936

JUDAS, one of the Twelve, is traditionally connected with the origins of the church of Edessa.

JUDAS, a citizen of Damascus, at whose house, "in the street called Straight," Paul resided after his conversion. 1060

JUDAS OF GALILEE led a popular revolt "in the days of the taxing," A.D. 6. 1054

JUDAS ISCARIOT, one of the Apostles, betrayed Jesus for thirty pieces of silver, but later hanged himself in a fit of remorse. Dante put him at the very bottom of the Inferno. 907, 926, 1023, 1024, 1045, 1046

JUDAS MACCABAEUS, son of Mattathias, was the hero of the war against Syria. He was wholly successful and was the first of a line of priest-kings whose rule endured until the accession of Herod the Great in 40 B.C., over a century later. 378, 381

JUDE, the anglicized form of the name of the Apostle Judas.

JUDITH, a Jewish heroine whose exploits are related in the Apocryphal Book of Judith. She cut off the head of Holofernes, Nebuchadnezzar's general, and showed it to her fellow townspeople of Bethulia, and so inspired them to rush out and rout the Babylonian army. 846–856

KADESH, scene of one of the numerous defections of the children of Israel, is generally identified with the modern Ain Kades, at the northern part of the Wilderness of Paran. Miriam died here, and here, too, Moses smote the rock for water. 19, 21, 126, 132, 133, 614

KEDAR, second son of Ishmael, was the alleged father of a nomadic people bearing the same name. 437, 472, 545, 751, 773

KEDESH, a fortified place near the Sea of Merom, a widening of the upper Jordan, was the residence of Barak. 178

KEILAH, a town in the lowland of Judah, was connected with an important episode in the life of David. 251, 252

KIDRON, a torrent between Jerusalem and the Mount of Olives, is famous throughout the Bible. David fled across the Kidron, with Absalom's levies at his heels. Prophecy selected its valley as the scene of the Last Judgment. Under Josiah, the Kidron served as the common cemetery. 288, 303, 356, 357, 1032 (Cedron)

KISH, Saul's father. 223, 227, 233

KISHON, scene of the defeat of Sisera

and of Elijah's discomfiture of the prophets of Baal, was a stream that flowed into the Mediterranean several miles south of Acre. 177, 178, 181, 321

KOHATH, second of Levi's three sons, was the ancestor of an important priestly cast. 130

KORAH, a presumptuous Levite, led a rebellion against Moses, but was swallowed up by the earth, with all his followers. Dryden satirized Titus Oates under this name, though he spelled it Corah. 130–132

LABAN, son of Bethuel and brother of Rebekah, was the father of Leah and Rachel. His nephew Jacob took service under him, and so won the daughters, at the same time enriching himself in a thoroughly dishonorable fashion. Laban pursued Jacob when he left his service, but finally made a covenant with him. 33, 34, 35, 40, 41–43, 45–50

LACHISH, a stronghold of the Amorites, lay south of Jerusalem. It was destroyed by Joshua. 171, 173, 347

LAND OF PROMISE: Canaan, so called because Jehovah promised it to Abraham.

LAODICEA, seat of one of the Seven Churches of Asia Minor, lay in Phrygia. John the Divine rebuked its inhabitants for their lukewarmness, and so LAODICEANS signify people with tepid enthusiasms. 1168, 1171, 1200, 1203

LAY AT, to strike at.

LAZARUS, a citizen of Bethany, was brother of Martha and Mary. He seems to have been a man of wealth and position. Jesus raised him from the dead. 1020–1022, 1023, 1024

LAZARUS is the underdog in the parable of Dives and the beggar. 995–996

LEAH, elder daughter of Laban, was evidently an uncomely girl. Jacob was tricked into marrying her, and thereafter disliked her, though she bore him many children, including the powerful Judah. She was buried in the family vault at Machpelah. 42, 43, 44–45, 46, 47, 48, 52, 53, 793

LEAVEN, that which causes new dough to ferment and "rise."

LEBANON, a range of mountains north of Palestine, constitute a bulwark between Syria and the coast. These mountains were famous for their cedar forests. 159, 192, 307, 310, 312, 350, 404, 418, 426, 428, 450, 468, 538, 544, 562, 574, 614, 633, 639, 646, 776, 777, 778, 780, 782

LEMUEL, a wise but unidentified monarch whose sayings are recorded in Proverbs xxxi. 695

LET, to prevent.

LEVI, the original name of Matthew. 904–905

LEVI, Jacob's third son, was the father of the tribe to whom the priesthood was reserved. 43, 54–55, 74, 80

LEVIATHAN, the crocodile.

LEVI, CHILDREN OF, LEVITES, terms applied either to the descendants of Levi in general or to the priests alone. The context usually helps as to which is meant. The Levites had no lands allotted to them, but they were well taken care of by the priestly tithes. Their history varies with the periods of the Exodus, judges, and monarchy. Generally speaking, they grew in power with the years. 113, 153–154, 162, 372, 596, 1008, 1178

LIGNALOES, an aromatic wood.

LIKING, plight.

LILT may be, on W. Houghton's authority, the ranunculus, tulip, or anemone.

LOFTY, haughty.

A GLOSSARY OF BIBLICAL TERMS

Lot, son of Haran and nephew of Abraham. He escaped the destruction of Sodom, but his wife looked back and was changed into a pillar of salt. By his incestuous union with his two daughters, he was the ancestor of the Ammonites and Moabites. 16, 17, 18, 19, 20, 24–27

Lover, an intimate friend.

Lucas, Luke.

Luke, a physician and fellow worker of Paul, wrote the third Gospel and the Book of Acts. Said to have been martyred some time before A.D. 100, he was also renowned, traditionally, as an artist, and many portraits of the Virgin are ascribed to him. 1174 (Lucas)

Luz, a very ancient Canaanite town, was the scene of Jacob's dream. It is often identified, though not with absolute certainty, with Beth-el. 41, 55

Lycaonia, a region of Asia Minor, where Paul and Barnabas labored. With the shifting of the Roman provincial borders, Lycaonia was sometimes in Cappadocia, sometimes in Cilicia. 1070

Lydda, scene of one of the Pauline miracles, lay near Joppa. Destroyed by Vespasian, it was rebuilt by Hadrian, and is still a town of some importance. 1061

Lystra, a town in eastern Lycaonia, where Paul's cure of a cripple made the populace think that he and Barnabas were gods. 1070, 1071, 1074

Macedonia, scene of some of Paul's most important labors, must be visualized, of course, as the Roman province of that name rather than as the area included either in the ancient kingdom or modern region. 1074, 1078, 1082, 1083, 1104, 1107, 1135, 1142, 1166

Machpelah, a field and cave near Hebron which Abraham bought from Ephron for Sarah's tomb. He himself and many of his descendants are buried there. The spot is now covered by a mosque. 30, 35, 76, 77

Magog, probably Scythia or Armenia, was under the sway of Gog. 554, 556, 1226

Malachi, Messenger. The Book of Malachi is ascribed to an unknown Hebrew prophet who wrote about 450 B.C. 596

Mammon, a personification of riches. 943, 995

Mamre, an Amorite, upon whose lands Abraham dwelt during the interval between his Beth-el and Beersheba periods. In later chapters of Genesis it is merely a geographical term. 19, 22, 30, 31, 35, 56, 76, 77

Manasseh, eldest son of Joseph, was less favored by his grandfather than Ephraim. 65, 77

Manasseh, the tribe descended from Joseph, held lands on either side of the Jordan, with Gad between them—a sort of Polish Corridor effect. 155, 156, 183, 185, 187, 195, 422, 647

Manasseh, thirteenth king of Judah, first favored idolatry, but later recanted his errors. Despite his reformation, the Jews long held his name in abhorrence. 353, 357

Manna, the Godsent food, still remains to be identified.

Manoah, Samson's father, was of the tribe of Dan. 196–198, 205

Mansions, dwellings, not necessarily with the connotation of riches now associated with the word.

Marah, a bitter well in the wilderness of Shur, was three days distant from

A GLOSSARY OF BIBLICAL TERMS

the place where the Israelites crossed the Red Sea. Its waters were sweetened by a tree that the Lord pointed out to the complaining Israelites. 100

MARANTHA, an expression meaning, "Out Lord cometh." 1136

MARCUS, Mark. 1174

MARK, cousin of Barnabas and son of one of the Marys, was associated with Paul in certain of his labors. He wrote the second Gospel. He is said to have founded the church of Alexandria, and there he received the martyr's crown. 1066, 1067, 1073–1074

MARS' HILL, Athens, where Paul spoke for the faith, was the hill of the Areopagus. 1078

MARTHA, sister of Lazarus and Mary, was Jesus' hostess at Bethany, and is said to have attended him during the Passion. She is believed to have ended her days in Provence after spreading the Gospel throughout southern France. She was a dragon-killer. 984, 1020–1022, 1023

MARY, the Virgin Mother of Jesus, was the daughter of Joachim and Anne and cousin of Elisabeth. When Jesus was dying, he recommended her to the care of John, the author of the fourth Gospel. It is not known how long she survived her son. 907, 910, 935, 936, 937, 973–975, 977–979, 1010, 1037, 1045

MARY is the name of no less than five characters in the N.T., not including the Virgin. It is impossible, in a limited scope, to differentiate these people very conclusively. The curious reader may consult any reputable hagiology.

MARY, wife of Cleophas, was the mother of James the Less, and was closely related to the Virgin Mary—possibly she was her sister. 931, 932, 968, 969, 1003, 1037

MARY, Mark's mother, was among the earliest disciples. Traditions about her are unusually numerous and circumstantial; some say the Last Supper was held at her house. 1066

MARY, sister of Martha and Lazarus, is often identified with Mary Magdalene. 984, 985, 1020–1022, 1023

MARY MAGDALENE, the penitent sinner, is identified with Mary, sister of Martha and Lazarus, although this attribution is violently disputed by some authorities. The Magdalene, like Martha, is said to have died in southern France, though the Greek tradition takes her, in the company of the Virgin and John, to Ephesus. 931, 932, 968, 969, 1003, 1037, 1039

MATTANIAH, Zedekiah's original name. 358

MATTATHIAS, a Hebrew priest, was the head of the powerful Maccabean family seated at Modin. He devoted his sons to the cause of Jewish independence from Syria. 378–381

MATTER, fuel for a fire (James iii.5).

MATTHEW, author of the first Gospel, labored among the Parthians, Persians, and Medes. Not much is known about him, except that he was a tax gatherer before his conversion. 904–905 (Levi), 907, 1045

MAZZAROTH, the twelve signs of the zodiac. 746

MEDES, a people inhabiting Media, a region northwest of Persia proper, conquered a vast empire of singularly short duration. It was overthrown by Cyrus in 558 B.C. 345, 347, 427, 815, 816, 827

MEDIA, a wide region northwest of Persia. 436, 822, 826, 827

A GLOSSARY OF BIBLICAL TERMS

MEGIDDO, one of the great battlefields of the world from the time of Sisera to that of Allenby, lay six miles from Mount Carmel and eleven from Nazareth. 181, 343, 357

MELCHIZEDEK, a mysterious pre-Aaronic high priest, to whom Abraham paid tithes. Jesus is called a "priest after the order of Melchizedek." Jewish tradition has it that he was a survivor of the Flood: the patriarch Shem. The literature on his origins is both voluminous and curious. 648, 1177–1179

MELITA, the modern Malta, was the scene of Paul's shipwreck. 1101

MEPHIBOSHETH, son of Jonathan, was lame. He received great kindness at the hands of David. It is impossible to determine whether or not he took part in Absalom's rebellion. 276–277, 289

MESECH, MESHECH, were descended from a son of Japheth. They probably peopled the border country between Armenia and Colchia. 544, 548, 554, 556, 651

MESHA, king of Moab, rendered a tribute of sheep to Ahab, but rebelled against Joram and was defeated. The famous Moabite Stone contains an account of Mesha's wars. 330

MESHACH, one of the three companions of Daniel tested in the fiery furnace. Mishael was his name originally. 800, 805, 806–807, 810

MESOPOTAMIA, the entire country between the Tigris and the Euphrates, was important in the history of the patriarchs, 31, 1046

MESSIAS, the Anointed One, the expected king and deliverer of the Hebrews; therefore, a title of the Christ Jesus. 1009

METEYARD, measuring rod.

MICAH. a Hebrew prophet of the eighth century B.C., wrote the Book of Micah. He was called the Morasthite from his native place, Moresheth, in south Judah. 406, 495

MICHAL, the younger of Saul's two daughters, married David, but the union was not a happy one. She mocked his religious dancing, and he knew her no longer. She had once saved his life from assassins sent by Saul. 233, 243, 244–245, 258, 272, 275–276

MICHAEL, one of the archangels. 823, 824

MIDIAN, MIDIANITES, a north-Arabian tribe often in conflict with the Israelites were the reputed descendants of Midian, son of Abraham and Keturah. 58, 81, 84, 103, 136, 137, 144–146, 182–190, 192, 421, 425, 574

MILCOM, the Ammonite name for Molech. 313, 314

MILETUS, the great mart in western Asia Minor, was visited by Paul. A small Turkish village stands on the site of the once great city. 1084

MINGLED PEOPLE, the roving tribes of Asia.

MIRIAM, Moses' sister, was smitten with leprosy for murmuring against her brother's marriage with an Ethiopian, but was cured by his prayers. She died at Kadesh. 80, 100, 124–125, 411

MISHAEL, Meshach's name originally. 800, 801, 803

MIZPAH, MIZPEH, the scene of Japheth's meeting with his daughter, may be identified with Ramoth-Gilead. 49, 195, 208, 211

MIZPAH, MIZPEH was fortified by Asa against the levies of the Northern Kingdom. Here Samuel sat, on occasions, as judge. It lay less than two miles north of Jerusalem. 222, 371, 509

[1267]

A GLOSSARY OF BIBLICAL TERMS

Moab was the son of Lot's eldest daughter. He was the reputed ancestor of the Moabites. 27

Moab, Moabites, a powerful Semitic people dwelling east of the Dead Sea, were descended from Moab, the fruit of Lot's incestuous union with his own daughter. 134–144, 145, 176–177, 233, 312, 313, 314, 330–332, 344, 371, 387, 430, 457, 647, 787

Mole is really the mole rat.

Molech, a god of the Ammonites, was essentially a fire deity. 313, 356

Mordecai, Esther's counsin, saved his people from the machinations of Haman by his wise advice to the young queen. 828–840

Moses, the greatest figure in O.T. history, was the reputed author of the Pentateuch and, for that matter, even of the Book of Joshua, for the ancients evidently saw nothing strange in so mighty a magician continuing his memoirs after his death. His great work was leading the Israelites from Egypt to the Promised Land which, indeed, he was not allowed to enter. He died atop Pisgah, "but no man knoweth of his sepulchre unto this day." 80 and *passim* through 157; 580, 598, 644, 919, 958, 1007, 1011, 1181, 1218

Murrain, a deathly plague affecting cattle.

Myrrh, exuded from certain thorny shrubs native to Arabia and eastern Africa, is aromatic. It was used in preparing the holy ointment.

Naaman, a Syrian nobleman and general of Ben-hadad's army, was cured of leprosy by Elisha. 335–338

Nabal, a surly sheep owner of vast wealth who refused to pay David for "protecting" his flocks—the demand and its refusal have a curiously modern flavor. Saved from David's vengeance by his wife Abigail, he died soon after, and Abigail married David. 254–257, 260–269

Naboth, a rich Jezreelite whom Ahab murdered for his vineyard. Of course, it was a judicial murder: Naboth and his children were stoned to death. 324–325, 342, 343

Nahor, son of Terah and grandfather of Rebekah, was the father of Bethuel. 16, 31, 32, 34, 41, 49

Nahum, a prophet who flourished about 612 B.C., whose Book contains a rhapsody on the fall of the abhorred Assyrian city of Nineveh. 460

Naomi, Ruth's mother-in-law, was the widow of Elimelech. 787–793

Naphtali, Jacob's fifth son, was one of the more obscure of the Patriarch's numerous progeny. 44, 75

Naphtali, the tribe descended from Jacob's fifth son, held lands which lay west of the Sea of Galilee and extended unto Dan Kedesh, an important city of refuge, lay within its borders. 155, 156, 177, 178; 181, 185, 187, 631

Napkin, a handkerchief.

Nathan, a fiery prophet who flourished in the reigns of David and Solomon. He dared to rebuke the former for his treachery to Uriah. He anointed Solomon king. 279–280, 281, 298, 299

Nazareth, a city of Galilee, was Jesus' early home. Though unmentioned in the O.T., it seems to have been, at least in the first century, a town of nearly 20,-000 inhabitants. 901, 902, 923, 929, 932, 937, 938, 973, 977, 979, 1003, 1009, 1033, 1036, 1047, 1049, 1055, 1064, 1088, 1097

A GLOSSARY OF BIBLICAL TERMS

NEBAT, Jeroboam's father. 313, 315, 316, 317, 325, 341

NEBO, MOUNT, the highest part of the Pisgah range. From it Moses had his first and last look at the promised land. 156

NEBUCHADNEZZAR, NEBUCHADREZZAR (the first spelling is the more common, the second the more accurate), the greatest and most powerful of the Babylonian kings, carried Israel into captivity. 357, 358–359, 491, 492, 493, 495, 496, 503, 507–508, 800, 801–813, 815, 828

NEBUZAR-ADAN, the captain of Nebuchadnezzar's guard, figures importantly in the Book of Jeremiah. 359, 508–509, 511

NECHO, see *Pharaoh-Necho*.

NEHEMIAH, the courtier cupbearer of Artaxerxes, was empowered by that king to rebuild the walls of Jerusalem. 369

NEPHEW, a grandson.

NER, Saul's grandfather and father of Abner and Kish. 233, 258, 259, 270, 273, 300, 302

NERIAH, Baruch's father. 501, 503, 511

NICODEMUS, a Jewish nobleman, assisted in the burial of Jesus. 1010–1011, 1038

NINEVEH, the capital of Assyria, was the butt of many unpleasant prophecies. It lay at the junction of the Zab with the Tigris, and covered a vast amount of ground. Diodorus of Sicily said that it was fifty-five miles in circumference. 351, 457, 460, 462, 795, 797, 798, 986

NITRE, really natron, native carbonate of soda. Nitre, in the Bible, is not saltpetre.

NOAH, NOE (in Gospels), the patriarch who lived in the ark, which he had constructed according to God's specifications, during the Flood, along with his sons and their families and all varieties of animal life. His three sons were ancestors of the human family. Noah lived until the age of nine hundred and fifty years. 10–15, 962, 1180

NOD, the land where Cain lived after murdering Abel. It lay to the east of Eden. 10

NUN, Joshua's father. 124, 159

NUTS, either pistachio or walnuts.

OBADIAH, Ahab's majordomo, feared God. During the persecution of the prophets under Jezebel, Obadiah, at the peril of his life, protected more than a hundred of these holy men. 319–320

OBADIAH, author of the Book of Obadiah, was a minor prophet whose *floruit* came, probably, just after the Exile. 583

OBED, father of Jesse, was the son of Ruth and Boaz. 793

OCCUPY, to use.

OFFENCE, a cause of stumbling.

OFFEND, to cause to stumble.

OG, king of Bashan, ruled over sixty cities. A giant, he was overcome by the Israelites at Edrei. 136, 160, 170, 658

OMRI, Ahab's father, was king of Israel, having founded the third dynasty of that kingdom. He came to the throne only after overcoming strong opposition. He established his capital at Tirzah, but later moved it to the more famous city of Samaria. 316, 317

ON. Heliopolis, in Egypt, was located on the Pelusiac arm of the Nile, about twenty miles northeast of Memphis. Joseph married the daughter of a priest of On. 64, 65

ONESIMUS, the converted slave for whom Paul pled in the Epistle of Philemon,

[1269]

A GLOSSARY OF BIBLICAL TERMS

was said to have succeeded Timothy as bishop of Ephesus. 1173–1174

OPHIR, a region mentioned in the O.T. as a source of gold, was probably a seaport in southern Arabia. 311, 312, 621, 732, 738

PADAN-ARAM, a region probably near the upper water of the Euphrates, was the home of Rebekah, Leah, and Rachel. 35, 40, 47, 53, 56

PALESTINE, PALESTINA (poetical form), are renderings of the Hebrew word *Pelesheth*. Palestine is conterminous, practically, with Canaan, though Philistia is merely a part of Palestine. 99, 429, 430

PALMER WORM, a caterpillar associated with the plague of locusts.

PAMPHYLIA, a coastal region of southern Asia Minor, lay between Lycia and Cilicia. It was a scene of the missionary labors of Paul and Barnabas. 1046, 1068, 1071, 1073, 1099

PAPHOS, a town in western Cyprus where Paul confused the sorcerer Barjesus. Paphos was a center of the cult of Aphrodite, who is sometimes called the Paphian goddess. 1068

PARAN, WILDERNESS OF, an arid waste, generally 2,000 feet above sea level, corresponds roughly to the northern part of the Sinai Peninsula, just before it merges with southern Palestine. Sometimes called the Wilderness of the Wandering, here the children of Israel were tried by Godsent trials and tribulations until only the fittest survived. 28, 125, 126, 153, 254

PARTHIANS, Jews settled in Parthia, a region southeast of the Caspian Sea, and once the core of an empire rivaling Rome's. 1046

PASHUR, a priest who had Jeremiah put into the stocks. 489–490, 504

PASSOVER, an annual feast of the Jews, was instituted to commemorate God sparing the Hebrews when, passing over their houses (which were marked by the blood of a lamb), he smote the firstborn of the Egyptians. 94–95, 925–926, 979, 1023, 1024, 1034, 1035, 1036, 1066, 1181

PATMOS, where John composed Revelation, is an Aegean isle lying twenty miles south of Samos and twenty miles west of Asia Minor. The grotto where John wrote is still pointed out. 1200

PAUL, a converted Jew from Tarsus, was originally called Saul. After participating in the stoning of Stephen, he was directly challenged by God to change his ways. As the Apostle of the Gentiles, he founded many churches, to some of which he wrote Epistles. He is said to have suffered martyrdom in Rome in A.D. 67, on the same day Peter did. 1056, 1059–1061, 1065, 1067–1102; further important detail, 1115–1116, 1133, 1135, 1143, 1144

PENIEL, PENUEL, a place on the north side of the Jabbok, where Jacob wrestled with the angel. 51, 188, 189

PENTECOST, a harvest festival of the Jews celebrated fifty days after the second day of the Passover. 1046, 1084, 1135

PEOR, a mountain peak in Moab, whence Balaam was supposed to curse the host of the Israelites. Peor was near Mount Pisgah. 141, 145

PERGA, a town in Pamphylia, was a center of the cult of Diana. Here Paul and Mark parted company. 1068, 1071

PERGAMOS, seat of one of the Seven Churches of Asia Minor, was located in Mysia, a region in the western part of the peninsula. The library at Pergamos was second only to that of Alexandria. 1200, 1201

A GLOSSARY OF BIBLICAL TERMS

PERIZZITES, dwellers in the Holy Land before the Israelite conquest. The meaning of the term is not absolutely clear, but it seems to denote nomads. 18, 55, 82, 162

PERSIA, one of the great empires of antiquity, once held the Holy Land tributary. 544, 554, 822, 823

PETER, a fisherman of Galilee to whom Jesus left the conduct of his affairs on earth, was originally called Simon. He presided over the council of the Apostles at Jerusalem and wrote two Epistles. Usually held the Prince of the Apostles, *Primus inter pares*, Peter is claimed to be the founder of the papacy. Authorities agree that he was crucified at Rome in A.D. 64. Origen declares that Peter asked to be crucified head downward, for he thought himself unworthy to meet the same death as Jesus. 902–903, 907, 918, 927, 928, 929, 932, 1003, 1004, 1009, 1026, 1033–1034, 1038, 1040–1041, 1046–1053, 1057, 1061–1064, 1066, 1072, 1115–1116, 1132

PETHOR, a city on the Euphrates, was the home of Balaam. 137

PHALTI, PHALTIEL, to whom Saul gave Michal, David's wife. David got her back and lived to be very unhappy with her. 258, 272

PHARAOH, the common title of the kings of Egypt mentioned in the Bible. It is difficult, if not impossible, exactly to differentiate the various rules referred to.

PHARAOH (story of Abraham) was probably one of the Hyksos kings, possibly the founder of the fifteenth dynasty. 17–18

PHARAOH (story of Jacob) was probably a later king of the fifteenth dynasty. 59, 60–65, 66, 71, 72, 77

PHARAOH (of the oppression) is either Ahmes (eighteenth dynasty) or the mighty Rameses II (nineteenth dynasty). 79–80, 81, 82, 83

PHARAOH (of the Exodus) may have been a king almost as famous as Rameses II: Thutmosis (or Thothmes) III, who flourished about 1500 B.C. 85–98, 104, 157, 345, 658, 1156

PHARAOH (Solomon's father-in-law and ally) was probably the last sovereign of the twenty-first dynasty. 303, 310, 312

PHARAOH-NECHOH was an enterprising but unfortunate ruler. He anticipated De Lesseps in the Suez Canal idea. He defeated Josiah, but was himself defeated by Nebuchadnezzar. Through this misfortune, Egypt lost her Asiatic dominions. Nechoh flourished about 600 B.C. 357

PHARAOH'S DAUGHTER, the preserver of Moses, was probably a daughter of Rameses II. 80, 1181

PHARISEES, a party among the Jews, believed in resurrection and accepted oral traditions as well as the written law. They were punctilious in observing the rites of their religion. The Mishna is essentially a document instinct with the spirit of the Pharisees. 905, 906, 914, 917, 940, 951, 956, 957, 958–959, 968, 986, 987, 990, 991, 993, 995, 998, 1008, 1010, 1012, 1015, 1016–1017, 1018, 1022–1023, 1033, 1054 1072, 1090, 1096

PHENICE or PHENICIA refers to Phoenicia, a district along the Palestinian seacoast, including the rich seaports of Tyre and Sidon. Its inhabitants were of Semitic stock. 1065, 1072, 1085

PHILADELPHIA, seat of one of the Seven Churches of Asia Minor, was located on the border between Lydia and Caria. 1200, 1203

A GLOSSARY OF BIBLICAL TERMS

PHILEMON, a wealthy citizen of Colosse to whom Paul addressed a personal Epistle interceding for a runaway slave, the converted Onesimus. Philemon seems to have heeded the Apostle's pleas, for the Roman Catholics revere him as a saint. One tradition states that he was stoned to death. 1173

PHILIP, one of the Twelve, was a native of Bethsaida. He is rather a shadowy figure. He is said to have labored in Asia Minor and to have suffered martyrdom at Hierapolis in Phrygia, in A.D. 80. 907, 1009, 1026, 1045

PHILIP, one of the seven deacons ordained by the Apostles, converted the Samaritans and entertained Paul at Caesarea. He is said to have become bishop of Tralles, and there suffered martyrdom. His four daughters are likewise revered as saints. 1055, 1057–1059, 1086

PHILIP, see *Herod Philip I* and *Herod Philip II*.

PHILIPPI, a city of the Macedonians, to which Paul addressed an Epistle, was located twelve miles inland, northwest of the island of Thasos. In the vicinity was fought the decisive battle between the army of Brutus and Cassius and that of Anthony and Octavius Caesar. 1074, 1104, 1162

PHILISTIA, the land of the Philistines, was actually a forty-mile stretch of coast between Gerar and Joppa, though sometimes Palestine, as a whole, is meant by the term. 635, 647

PHILISTINES, a warlike race, possibly from Crete originally, occupied the coast of Palestine, often harassing the Hebrews. 196, 198, 200–205, 219–221, 225, 226, 229–233, 237–243, 244, 251, 252, 253, 260, 261, 262, 263–265, 268, 272, 275, 305, 347, 386, 394, 398, 417, 422, 456, 536

PHINEHAS, son of Eleazar, averted God's wrath from Israel by slaying both an Israelite and a Midianitish woman whom the man had brought into the community as his mistress. He succeeded Eleazar as high priest. 144, 210

PHINEHAS, son of Eli, was a man of loose morals. He was killed in the great battle in which the Philistines captured the ark of the covenant. 214, 220, 221

PHRYGIA, a district in central Asia Minor, was visited by Paul, 1046, 1074, 1080

PHUT, Put. 544

PHYLACTERIES, charms fastened on the forehead or on the left arm. They were made of small pieces of parchment inscribed with sacred or magical texts; they were protected by leathern cases.

PILATE, PONTIUS, Roman governor of Judah in the time of Jesus, played the role of a gentle skeptic throughout the trial of Jesus. He reluctantly surrendered the prisoner to the Jews, and his gentleness was fortified by his wife's intuition about Jesus. He is said to have committed suicide. 929–930, 931, 965, 966, 968–969, 979, 999–1000, 1002, 1034–1037, 1038, 1051, 1069

PISGAH, a mountain range in Moab rather than a single peak. It stretched opposite Jericho, and from it Moses and Balaam looked down on the land of Canaan. Here Moses died, but his place of burial is unknown. 135, 140, 156

POST, a messenger bearing a letter.

POTIPHAR, an Egyptian nobleman who was Joseph's master. His lascivious wife had Joseph cast into prison for not responding to her advances, and so was the indirect cause of his later greatness. 59

POTI-PHERAH, priest of On, was Joseph's

[1272]

A GLOSSARY OF BIBLICAL TERMS

father-in-law. He may be same as Potiphar. 64, 65

PRICKS, goads.

PRISCILLA, Aquila's wife, seems to have been rather more energetic than her husband. 1079, 1080, 1136

PSALTERY, a stringed instrument used for accompanying singing.

PTOLMAIS, the modern Acre, was a station in the journeys of Paul. 1086

PUBLICAN, a revenue collector, tax farmer.

PULSE (used only in Daniel i.12, 16) includes various edible seeds and grains. 801

PURIM, an annual Jewish feast, commemorated the failure of Haman's plot. It is probably much older than the story in the Book of Esther would lead us to infer. 840

PUT, an imperfectly identified region in Africa. As it was probably very near Egypt, most authorities prefer Libya or Nubia. 462, 544

QUATERNION, a foursome of soldiers.

QUICK, alive.

RABBAH, a large and strongly fortified town east of the Jordan, was the metropolis of the Ammonites. It was captured by David and Joab. 387

RABBI, a title of respect given to a teacher of the Law, "My master" is an acceptable translation. Jesus was addressed thus.

RABBONI means "My great master." Jesus is once addressed thus. 1039

RAB-SHAKEH, an Assyrian officer who persuaded Judah to rebel against Hezekiah. Rab-shakeh, signifying a cup-bearer, is probably only a title, not a name. 347-349

RACHEL, Jacob's beloved wife for whom he served Laban, her father, fourteen years. Rachel, unlike the despised Leah, was very beautiful, at least physically. The beauty of her character is more doubtful: she stole from her own father. Her tomb, two miles south of Jerusalem, is still shown. Rachel was the prototype, in some respects, of the devoted Hebrew mother, and therefore "Rachel weeping for her children" refers to the general mourning into which Israel was plunged by Herod's massacre of the innocents, when Jesus was born. 42-50, 52, 56, 226, 499, 937

RAHAB, a harlot of Jericho who hid two Israelite spies. For helping the good cause, she and her family alone were saved when Joshua captured the city. Matthew says that she abandoned her profession, and lived to become the wife of Boaz and therefore the great-grandmother of Jesse, the father of David. 160, 164, 1181, 1187

RAMA, RAMAH, the home of Elkanah, Samuel's father, was probably situated about four miles northwest of Jerusalem. 215, 222, 235, 237, 245, 246, 249, 254, 261, 425, 499, 508, 937

RAMESES, a treasure city of the Pharaohs, was built by the oppressed Israelites. It lay in the Delta, either on the Pelusiac or Tanitic branch of the Nile. 95

RAPHAEL, an archangel who watched over and helped Tobias. 868, 870-873, 875, 877-789

RAVIN, to seize upon as prey.

REARWARD, rearguard.

REBEKAH, wife of Isaac and mother of Esau and Jacob, the latter being her favorite. She assisted him in various stratagems to get the better of his brother. 31-36, 37-40, 42, 55, 76

RECEIPT, a place for receiving.

RECHAB was associated with Baanah in the killing of Ish-bosheth. 274-275

[1273]

A GLOSSARY OF BIBLICAL TERMS

Red Sea, a long, narrow body of water between Egypt and Arabia, is often mentioned in the Bible, but by far the most famous verses refer to Moses' passage of the Red Sea dryshod, the waters running to overwhelm the army of Pharaoh. In some places the Red Sea means merely the Gulf of Akaba, in other places a northern extension of the Gulf of Suez. 92, 96, 98, 100, 134, 160, 311, 658, 1181

Rehoboam, son of Solomon by an Ammonite princess, succeeded to, but did not long hold, his father's broad lands. Ten tribes rebelled and seceded to form the kingdom of Israel under the rule of Jeroboam, and Rehoboam was left with only Judah and Benjamin as his portion. The armies of Shishak of Egypt harried Judah during his reign. Rehoboam had eighteen wives and sixty concubines. 315–316

Rephaim, a pre-Israelite people of gigantic stature who lived in Palestine. 19, 275, 432

Reuben, Jacob's eldest son, was instrumental in saving Joseph's life when the other brethren wanted to kill him. His adulterous relations with Bilhah denied him his father's blessing. 43, 44, 58, 67, 74

Reuben, the tribe descended from Jacob's eldest son, held lands which lay east of the Dead Sea and just north of Gad. 130, 153, 180–181

Reuel was probably the proper name of Moses' father-in-law, whose title seems to have been Jethro. 81

Rhoda was the maid who announced Peter's arrival at Mary's house after his miraculous release from prison. 1067

Rimmon, a deity worshiped at Damascus. Elisha allowed Naaman "to bow down in the house of Rimmon" as a tactful gesture, and the phrase has come to mean conforming to an otherwise reprehensible custom to save one's face. 337

Rizpah was Saul's concubine. When the Gibeonites hanged her two sons, she protected their bodies from the birds of the air and beasts of the field. Her name has become a synonym for maternal devotion. 272

Roe, roebuck, always means the gazelle.

Rose, the narcissus or autumn crocus.

Ruth, a Moabitish woman whose devotion to Naomi, her Hebrew mother-in-law, after the death of her husband, Naomi's son, furnishes some of the most idyllic pages in the O.T. When they return to Beth-lehem, Naomi's native place, Ruth becomes a gleaner in the fields of Boaz, a near kinsman. When he discovers her identity, he treats her kindly and finally marries her. Their son Obed was the father of Jesse, who was the father of David. Ruth was thus one of the ancestresses of Christ, and is mentioned thus by Matthew. 787–793

Rye, spelt, a cereal much like common wheat.

Sabachthani, Jesus' cry from the cross: "Why hast thou forsaken me?"

Sabeans, the people of Sheba. 701

Sadducees, a Jewish party in the time of Jesus. They stuck to the letter of the Law, denying the validity of the oral tradition. 957, 1049, 1053, 1090

Salem, a place of which Melchizedek was king. It probably represents Jerusalem, according to Jewish commentators. Jerome thought otherwise. 1178

Salome, wife of Zebedee and mother of James the Greater and John the Evangelist, both members of the Twelve. Possibly the sister of the Virgin, she

[1274]

A GLOSSARY OF BIBLICAL TERMS

was one of the "three Marys," and the Church reveres her as St. Mary Salome. She was present at the crucifixion. 931, 932, 968

SAMARIA, capital of the kingdom of Israel, was founded by the ambitious Omri. It suffered much in the various wars that unsettled the Holy Land, but was finally rebuilt magnificently by Herod the Great. Today, however, a paltry hamlet is on the site of the once flourishing city. Jerome says that John the Baptist was executed at Samaria. 316, 317, 319, 324, 325, 330, 335, 339, 344, 345, 347, 389, 390, 393, 397, 406

SAMARIA, another name for the kingdom of Israel. 345, 997, 1012, 1044, 1056, 1057, 1061, 1072

SAMARITANS, properly the inhabitants of the city of Samaria, but also applied to the people of the kingdom of Israel. Also the name of a schismatic sect (not wholly Jewish in blood) whose only code was the Law: the Pentateuch. Being "a good Samaritan" is being kind to fellow beings in distress; the Samaritans were noted for their hospitality to underdogs. 981, 984, 997, 1012, 1014

SAMSON, the heroic judge of Israel whose enticement by Delilah is one of the most fascinating stories in the O.T. He lost his strength when his hair was sheared off, and he was sent to work "eyeless in Gaza at a mill with slaves." During a Philistine fete, Samson prayed that his strength be renewed, and then pulled down the temple, burying himself and his captors in its ruins. 196–205, 1181

SAMUEL, the great prophet and judge of Israel, established the monarchy in the person of Saul. He quarreled with his protége and later anointed David. 215–219, 221–227, 233, 234–237, 245, 254, 261–262, 1181

SAPPHIRA, wife of the liar Ananias, partook of his vice and suffered the same fate as he did. 1052

SARA, wife of Tobias. 867–868, 872–879

SARA, Sarah's name in the N.T. 1180

SARAH, Abraham's wife and mother of Isaac whom she bore after her normal child-bearing period was over. She was buried in the family vault at Machpelah. 21, 22–23, 27, 29, 1156

SARAI, the original name of Sarah. 16, 17, 20–21

SARDIS, the capital of Lydia, was one of the richest cities of the ancient world. Lying about fifty miles northeast of Smyrna, it was the seat of one of the Seven Churches of Asia Minor. 1200, 1202, 1203

SAUL, son of Kish and later Samuel's choice as king of the Jews. His oddly neurotic behavior makes him a peculiarly modern figure. He seems to have been alternately attracted and repelled by David, and his attitude to his own son Jonathan is sufficiently strange. His downfall began when he dared to oppose the fiats of Samuel, and he finally perished in a great battle with the Philistines on Mount Gilboa. 223–240, 242–254, 258–265

SAUL, the original name of the Apostle Saul. 1056, 1059–1061, 1065-1066, 1067–1068

SAVING HEALTH, salvation.

SEIR, LAND OF, or MOUNT, a mountainous region extending along the east side of the valley of Arabah, from the Dead Sea on the Elanitic Gulf. Sometimes the country south to the head of the Gulf of Akabah is included in the ex-

A GLOSSARY OF BIBLICAL TERMS

pression. 19, 50, 53, 143, 153, 179, 436

SENIR, the Amorite name for Mount Hermon. 544, 778

SENNACHERIB, a famous Assyrian king who flourished about 700 B.C., led his armies against Judah. During his second campaign against Hezekiah, his vast host was mysteriously destroyed. Modern rationalist critics hint that the bubonic plague was the true cause of the visitation. 347, 350, 351

SETH, third son of Adam, was the father of Enos. 10

SHADRACH, the Hebrew name of Hananiah. With Abed-nego and Meshach he was delivered unscathed from the fiery furnace. 800, 805, 806, 807, 810

SHALMANESER, an Assyrian king who flourished about 725 B.C., led two campaigns against Hosea, last king of Israel. He captured Samaria in the second of them. 345, 347

SHAMMAH, third son of Jesse and brother of David. 236, 238

SHAPHAN, the scribe of Josiah, king of Judah. He seems to have been a personage of much consequence. 354, 355, 501, 508, 511

SHARON, the coastal plain of Samaria, in western Palestine. It was a tract of great richness. 450, 774

SHEBA, a district in southern Arabia whose queen made an imposing visit to the court of Solomon. She came to trap him with difficult questions, but when he had finished, "there was no spirit in her." In the Koran she is called Balkis. 311–312, 479, 574, 632, 708

SHECHEM, an important town a few miles northeast of Samaria. It is constantly alluded to in the O.T.; it reappears as Sychar in the N.T. Jacob bought land here, and here, too, Joshua addressed the people just before his death. This was the special patrimony of Joseph, and here he was buried. 53, 55, 57, 190, 191–194, 212, 647

SHEM, the eldest son of Noah, was the alleged ancestor of the Semites. He died at the age of six hundred years. 11, 12, 15

SHEOL, the abode of the dead. It is pictured as a realm of impenetrable darkness from which return is impossible. 709, 724

SHILOH, one of the earliest and holiest of Hebrew sanctuaries. Here the ark of the covenant was kept during the period of the judges. It lay in the highlands of Ephraim, about fifteen miles to the west of the Jordan. 211, 212, 216, 220, 302, 494

SHIMEI, son of Gera, a Benjamite of the house of Saul, was noted for his enmity to David until the king seemed definitely marked for constant glory. He submitted, though David still had his doubts, and on his deathbed the old monarch made Solomon promise to keep his eye on Shimei. Finally he was killed by Benaiah for leaving Jerusalem after he had promised Solomon that he would stay within its walls. 290, 300–301, 303

SHINAR, lower Mesopotamia, the alluvial region between the Tigris and Euphrates. 15, 19, 800

SHISHAK, king of Egypt, the Sheshonk I of history. He invaded Palestine in the reign of Rehoboam and exacted tribute from that king. 314

SHITTIM WOOD, a variety of acacia.

SHUHITE, the appellation of Job's friend Bildad. The word points to a region on the lower Euphrates, near Hit. 699, 703, *passim* throughout Job.

A GLOSSARY OF BIBLICAL TERMS

SHUNEM, a village about three miles from Jezreel, was in the territory of Issachar. Here Elisha cured the Shunammite's son. 261, 333

SHUSHAN, the capital of Elam, is better known to modern readers as Susa, the capital of the Persian Empire. 369, 820, 826, 828, 832, 837, 838, 839

SIDON, a great seaport and one of the chief cities of Phoenicia, fattened on the slave trade. The prophets, quite naturally, inveighed against its luxury and evil ways. 906, 915, 916, 947, 983, 1067, 1098

SIHON, a king of the Amorites who dispossessed the Moabites of a fine territory. He attacked the Israelites next, but was defeated and slain. 135–136, 160, 170, 658

SILAS, one of the leaders of the early church at Jerusalem, was associated with Paul in his second missionary journey. He is said to have become bishop of Corinth. 1073, 1074, 1075, 1077, 1079

SILOAM, a sacred well near Jerusalem to which Jesus sent a blind man to wash. 1016–1018

SILVANUS, Silas' name in the Epistles. 1108, 1112

SIMEON, Jacob's second son by Leah, was concerned with Levi in the massacre of the Shechemites after the rape of Dinah. The tribe descended from him held lands on the southern border of Palestine. 43, 54–55, 66, 67, 69, 74

SIMEON, a devout Jew who gave thanks for Jesus in the temple. He may have been an eminent rabbi who became president of the Sanhedrin about A.D. 13. 978

SIMON, surnamed either Zelotes or the Canaanite, belonged to a faction that strongly adhered to the Mosaic ritual. He was one of the Twelve, and his labors carried him into Persia and Mesopotamia. 907, 1045

SIMON MAGUS was a Samaritan magician who tried to buy the healing gift from Peter: hence the word *simony*—traffic in spiritual offices. His later history is rather confused, but it seems that he became a lifelong enemy of Peter. He asked to be buried alive, for he was sure that he would rise on the third day. 1057–1058

SINAI, MOUNT, a peak in the Sinai Peninsula, is now usually identified with Jebel Musa (7,373 feet). Here Moses gave the Law to the children of Israel, according to a tradition that is favored by the geography of the district. 100, 105, 106, 115, 153, 180, 630, 1117–1118

SKILL, to understand, show aptness for. 307

SLIME, mud or bitumen.

SMYRNA, still the metropolis of western Asia Minor, was the seat of one of the Seven Churches. 1200, 1201

SODOM, a city supposedly located on either the northern or southern shore of the Dead Sea, was destroyed by Jehovah because of its wickedness, although Abraham had pled for its preservation. 18, 19, 23, 26, 152, 391, 416, 427, 457, 911

SOLOMON, son of David and his successor as king of the Jews. His wisdom has become proverbial. His literary ability is said to have been great, but it is impossible to know just how much remains from his pen, though Proverbs and the Song of Songs have been attributed to him, not to speak of the Apocryphal Book of the Wisdom of Solomon. All three books probably be-

A GLOSSARY OF BIBLICAL TERMS

long to a much later date. Solomon seems to have indulged his appetites with little stint, and even the queen of Sheba was as much impressed by his magnificence as by his wisdom. The fruit of their union was the ancestor, traditionally, of the royal house of Ethiopia. Solomon rebuilt the Temple on a scale the eclipsed all previous structures. 281, 297-315, 372, 772-785, 986, 1056

SPIKENARD, a costly perfume derived from the root of a kind of valerian.

STAND TO, to agree.

STEPHEN, the first of the Christian martyrs, was chief of the seven deacons appointed to mediate between the Hellenistic and Hebrew Christians in Jerusalem. Stephen is, appropriately enough, the forerunner of Paul, as the future Apostle of the Gentiles participated in the stoning, though he does not seem to have cast a missile. 1054-1056, 1065

SUCCOTH, a village to the east of the Jordan, near Shechem, was Jacob's home for a time. 53, 188, 189, 647

SUSANNA, the lovely and virtuous wife of Joachim, was accused of adultery by two elders who had vainly attempted her chastity. She was proved innocent by the youthful Daniel, and the old reprobates were put to death. The story is told in the Apocryphal Book of Susanna. 858-862

SYCAMINE TREE, the mulberry tree.

SYCAMORE, the fig mulberry.

SYCHAR, probably the N.T. name for Shechem. 1012

SYRIA, a kingdom to the north of Palestine, was frequently at war with the Jews. 323, 335, 340, 342, 344, 545, 977, 1073, 1079, 1085, 1115

SYRIANS, inhabitants of Syria. 335, 338, 340, 342, 344, 385, 398, 422

TABITHA, a female disciple who lived at Joppa. Peter happening to be in the neighboring town of Lydda when she died, he hastened to Joppa and called her back from the dead. Luke calls her Dorcas, 1061-1062

TABOR, a mountain on which Barak assembled his forces before descending on Sisera. Once identified with the Mount of the Transfiguration, it has had to cede place to Hermon. Tabor was the boundary between Issachar and Zebulum. It was the scene of the murder of the brother of Gideon. 177, 189

TAHPANHES, an important city in Lower Egypt. 472, 512

TAMAR, daughter of David and Maachah, was ravished by her half-brother Ammon, who then repudiated her. A modern version of the story is told in Robinson Jeffers' *Tamar*. 281-284

TARES, always darnel grass.

TARSHISH, identified with Tartessus, a port in southern Spain which was probably located at the mouth of the Guadalquiver. Certain passages in the Bible suggest, however, that Tarshish was merely a term used to indicate some far-off place. 418, 437, 482, 544, 545, 554, 574, 623, 632, 795, 798

TARSUS, an important town in Cilicia, was the birthplace of the Apostle Paul. Few ruins mark the site of the Roman city. The modern town is a place of some consequence, with a population of more than 20,000. 1060, 1061, 1065, 1088

TEIL TREE, the lime tree or linden.

TEKOA, TEKOAH, a village twelve miles from Jerusalem, was the birthplace of the prophet Amos. It was strongly

A GLOSSARY OF BIBLICAL TERMS

fortified by Rehoboam against invasion from the south. 284, 285, 385, 477

TERAH, Abraham's father. He lived at Ur and was an idolater. 16

TERESH, one of the two eunuchs who conspired against Ahasuerus, was hanged with his fellow conspirator after Mordecai revealed the plot. 830, 834

THARSHISH, Tarshish. 312

THEBEZ, a place memorable for the death of the villainous Abimelech, lay some distance west of the Jordan and about fifteen miles northeast of Samaria. 194, 279

THESSALONICA, the metropolis of Macedonia, was a scene of the labors of Paul and Silas, and to the members of the church there the former addressed two Epistles. As the modern Salonika, it is still a town of much importance. 1076, 1098, 1166

THOMAS, one of the Twelve Apostles, doubted the reality of the resurrection, and so was asked to inspect for himself the five wounds He had received on the cross. His missionary work carried him far, even into India, it is said, and there he is supposed to have suffered martyrdom. "Doubting Thomas" is known as the Apostle of the Indies. 907, 1021, 1026, 1039–1040, 1045

THYATIRA, seat of one of the Seven Churches of Asia Minor, lay on the boundary between Mysia and Ionia, about twenty-five miles from Sardis. 1075, 1200, 1202

THYINE WOOD, better known as the citron wood of the Greeks and Romans.

TIBERIAS, SEA OF, the Sea of Galilee, so called from a city which was a center of Jewish learning. 1040

TIMOTHEUS, the beloved disciple of the Apostle Paul, who ordained him bishop of Ephesus and addressed two Epistles to him, was stoned to death, according to a reputable tradition, about A.D. 97. It is possible that he is the "angel" of the Ephesian church addressed in Revelations ii. 1–7 (pages 1200-1201). 1074, 1077, 1082, 1083, 1106, 1108, 1112, 1135, 1164, 1166, 1171, 1174

TIMOTHY, Timotheus. 1145

TIRE, a headdress.

TISHBITE, an appellation of Elijah, referring, possibly, to the place Thisbe in the territory of Naphtali. 317, 325, 326, 343

TITUS, the faithful disciple of Paul by whom he was ordained first bishop of Crete. He died at Candia at an advanced age. 1115, 1144

TOBIAS, son of Tobit, was on his way to claim Sara as his wife, when he was attacked by a fish and saved by the archangel Raphael. Later he cured his father's blindness with the gall of the fish. He successfully wooed Sara, seven of whose previously betrothed lovers had been killed by Asmodeus, and also broke the power of the demon with his prayers. 864–867, 868–879

TOBIT, the principal character of the Book of Tobit. While sleeping in the courtyard of his home, he was blinded by sparrows "muting warm dung into his eyes." Also see *Tobias*. 864–867, 868–873, 876–879

TOPHET, TOPHETH, a place in the valley of the son of Hinnom," where human sacrifices were made to Molech. By extension the term came to mean hell itself. 356, 480, 488–489

TYRE, the chief place of Phoenicia and one of the greatest trading centers and ports in the ancient world, was the residence of Hiram, Solomon's great

A GLOSSARY OF BIBLICAL TERMS

and good friend. As if fulfilling Ezekiel's prophecy of its doom, Tyre is now the meanest kind of village, with only a few hundred inhabitants. 306, 437–439, 621, 635, 906, 915, 916, 947, 983, 1067, 1085, 1086

TYRUS, Tyre. 386, 544–546

UNICORN, a species of wild ox—the *Bos primigenius*—that is now extinct. In this case the A.V. translators copied an error from the Septuagint.

UR OF THE CHALDEES, the starting point of Abraham's journey to the land of Canaan. It lay on the Euphrates not far from the Persian Gulf. Sir Leonard Woolley's excavations at Ur have been of the first importance. 16

URIAH, a Hittite, was the captain of David's army. The king loved Bath-sheba, Uriah's wife, and therefore had him sent into the thickest part of the battle where he fell, ignorant of his wife's dishonor. David then married Bath-sheba. 277–280

Uz, where Job lived, probably corresponds to the Arabia Deserta of the classical geographers. 525, 699

UZZIAH, a king of Judah, reigned wisely and well. After inflicting a great defeat on the Philistines, he wanted to celebrate by burning incense on the altar of God. The priests objected, Uzziah insisted, and God struck him with leprosy—a sequence of events that, in the O.T., at least, has the formal beauty of a syllogism. 385, 414

VASHTI, the queen of Ahasuerus who refused to show herself to his guests. Her ensuing deposition left the room clear for Esther. 826–828, 829

ZACHARIAS, father of John the Baptist, probably lived at Hebron. John was a son of his old age, and the news was brought to Zacharias by an angel. 972–976

ZADOK, high priest at Gibeon in the time of David. His unwavering loyalty to the king through all his vicissitudes furnishes a bright chapter in a history that is shot through with treachery. He anointed Solomon king. 289, 282, 294–295, 297, 298, 299

ZALMUNNA, one of the two rulers of Midian who invaded Palestine, was defeated, along with his fellow invader Zebah, and killed by Gideon. 188–189

ZEBAH, see *Zalmunna*. 188–189

ZEBEDEE, father of the Apostles John and James the Greater, was a fisherman of Galilee. He probably lived at Bethsaida or in its vicinity, and seems to have been in easy circumstances. 902, 907, 922, 968, 1040

ZEBULUN, Jacob's tenth son, was the last borne by Leah. 45, 75

ZEBULUN, the tribe descended from Jacob's tenth son, held lands west of the Sea of Galilee. Outside of their special valor in the struggle with Sisera, this tribe enjoyed a singularly uneventful history. 177, 178, 180, 181, 185, 631

ZECHARIAH, one of the minor prophets and author of the Book of Zechariah, was a priest. He was instrumental in rebuilding the Temple. 589

ZEDEKIAH, whose name was originally Mattaniah (he was renamed by Nebuchadnezzar), was the last king of Judah. Having rebelled against the great Babylonian king, he was defeated, and his people were carried into captivity. His own sons were slain before him, and then his eyes were put out, after which he was loaded with fetters and carried to Babylon, where he died. 358–359, 470, 492, 495, 496, 503–507, 512

ZEPHANIAH, a minor prophet who flour-

A GLOSSARY OF BIBLICAL TERMS

ished about 600 B.C., wrote the Book of Zephaniah. 454

ZERUBBABEL, the chief of the tribe of Judah after the return of the Jews from the Babylonian Captivity. With the help of Haggai and Zechariah, he was largely reponsible for the rebuilding of the Temple. 586, 587

ZERUIAH, sister of David and mother of three great heroes in the Psalmist's army: Abishag, Joab, and Asabel. 258, 270, 284, 290, 293, 297, 300, 302

ZIDON, Sidon. 75, 317, 437, 438, 544

ZIKLAG, a property bestowed upon David by Achish, king of Gath. There he received the tidings of Saul's defeat and death. He afterwards exchanged Ziklag for Hebron. The situation of the place is not known. 260, 267, 274

ZILPAH, Leah's handmaid, was the mother of Gad and Asher. 43, 44, 57

ZION, Jerusalem. Zion proper was the mount of the Temple. See Isaiah, Jeremiah, Lamentations, and Psalms throughout *passim*; also, 350, 385, 393, 408, 409, 410, 589–590, 592–777

ZIPPORAH, wife of Moses, was the daughter of Jethro, priest of Midian. 81, 103

ZOPHAR, a Naamathite, was one of Job's friends. He figures in the dialogue in the Book of Job. 699, 703

A CHAPTER KEY

CORRELATING THIS EDITION OF THE BIBLE DESIGNED TO BE READ AS LIVING LITERATURE WITH THE STANDARD BIBLE TEXT, INCLUDING CHAPTER AND PAGE CITATIONS AND A SCHEDULE OF DIVISIONS

The following key relates the standard text of the Bible to The Bible Designed to Be Read As Living Literature. The first figure in each entry is the chapter number, the second the page on which that chapter begins in the present version. If the first figure is accompanied by an asterisk, it means that the chapter appears only in part. Thus, for example, in Genesis occurs the entry *33–52. This means that Chapter 33 begins on page 52, and that some of its verses are omitted. If whole books or chapters are omitted, that fact is noted in each case.

The sequence of books follows, for the convenience of students, the standard text of the Bible.

Selections from the Apocrypha have not been related to a standard edition.

THE OLD TESTAMENT

Genesis: 1–3; *2–5; 3–6; *4–9; *5–10; *6–10; *7–11; 8–12; 9–14; 10 omitted; *11–15; 12–16; 13–18; *14–19; 15 omitted; 16–20; *17–21; 18–22; 19–24; 20 omitted; *21–27; *22–28; 23–29; 24–31; *25–35; *26–36; 27–37; *28–40; 29–41; 30–43; *31–46; 32–50; *33–52; 34–53; *35–55; 36 omitted; *37–57; 38 omitted; 39–59; 40–60; 41–62; *42–65; 43–67; 44–69; *45–71; *46–73; *47–73; 48 omitted; 49–74; *50–76.

Exodus: *1–79; 2–80; *3–81; *4–83; *5–85; *6–86; *7–87; *8–88; *9–90; *10–92; 11–93; *12–94; *13–96; *14–96; *15–98; *16–100; *17–102; 18–103; *19–105; *20–106; 21–107; *22–109; 23–30 omitted; *31–111; *32–111; *33–113; *34–115; 35–40 omitted.

Leviticus: 1–18 omitted; *19–117; *20–119; 21–27 omitted.

Numbers: 1–8 omitted; *9–121; *10–122; *11–122; 12–124; *13–125; *14–127; *15–130; *16–130; 17–19 omitted; 20–132; *21–134; *22–136; 23–139; 24–142; *25–144; 26–30 omitted; *31–145; 32–36 omitted.

Deuteronomy: 1–30 omitted; *31–148; *32–149; *33–153; 34–156.

Joshua: *1–159; 2–160; *3–162;

[1282]

A CHAPTER KEY TO THE BIBLE

4–5 omitted;*6–163; 7–165;*8–167; *9–169; *10–171; 11–24 omitted.

Judges: 1 omitted; *2–175; *3–176; 4–177; *5–179; *6–182; 7–185; *8–188; *9–190; 10 omitted; *11–195; 12 omitted; 13–196; 14–198; 15–200; 16–202; 17–18 omitted; 19–205; *20–208; *21–211.

Ruth: 1–787; 2–788; 3–790; *4–792.

I Samuel: 1–214; *2–216; *3–218; *4–219; 5–6 omitted; *7–221; 8–222; 9–223; *10–226; *11–227; 12 omitted; *13–228; *14–229; 15–233; 16–236; *17–237; *18–242; 19–244; *20–246; 21–248; *22–249; *23–251; *24–253; 25–254; 26–258; *27–260; *28–261; 29–263; 30 omitted; 31–264.

II Samuel: *1–267; 2–269; *3–271; *4–274; *5–275; *6–275; 7–8 omitted; 9–276; 10 omitted; *11–277; *12–279; *13–281; *14–284; *15–287; 16–289; *17–291; *18–293; 19–24 omitted.

I Kings: *1–297; *2–300; 3–303; *4–305; 5–306; *6–308; *7–310; 8 omitted; *9–311; *10–311; *11–312; *12–315; 13–15 omitted; *16–316; 17–317; 18–318; *19–322; 20 omitted; *21–324; 22 omitted.

II Kings: 1 omitted; 2–328; *3–330; *4–332; 5–335; *6–338; 7 omitted; *8–340; *9–341; *10–344; 11–12 omitted; *13–344; 14–16 omitted; *17–345; *18–346; *19–349; 20–351; *21–353; 22–353; *23–355; *24–357; *25–358.

I Chronicles: Omitted.
II Chronicles: Omitted.
Ezra: Omitted.

Nehemiah: *1–369; *2–369; *3–371; 4–12 omitted; *13–371.

Esther: 1–826; 2–828; *3–830; 4–831; 5–832; 6–834; 7–835; 8–836; 9–838; 10 omitted.

Job: The chapters are, in each case, complete, except that the editor has substituted names of the *dramatis personae* for other speaker indications. 1–699; 2–701; 3–703; 4–704; 5–706; 6–707; 7–709; 8–710; 9–711; 10–713; 11–715; 12–716; 13–717; 14–719; 15–720; 16–722; 17–724; 18–725; 19–726; 20–727; 21–729; 22–731; 23–732; 24–733; 25–735; 26 starts on 736, though part of it is on 735; 27–736 (these last two chapters have been rearranged); 28–737; 29–739; 30–740; 31–742; 32–37 omitted; 38–745; 39–747; 40–749; 41–750; 42–752.

Psalms: See Contents, xix–xxi.

Proverbs: *1–667; 2–3 omitted; *4–667; *5–668; *6–669; *7–671; 8–672; 9–674; *10–676; *11–677; *12–678; *13–679; *14–680; *15–680; *16–681; *17–682; *18–683; *19–684; *20–685; *21–685; *22–685; *23–686; 24 omitted; *25–687; *26–688; *27–690; *28–691; *29–692; 30–693; 31–695.

Ecclesiastes: 1–755; 2–756; 3–758; 4–759; 5–760; 6–761; 7–762; 8–763; 9–765; 10–766; 11–768; 12–769.

Song of Solomon: 1–722; 2–774; 3–776; 4–777; 5–778; 6–780; 7–782; 8–783.

Isaiah: In this version the first 39 chapters comprise The Vision of Isaiah; Chapters 40 through 66 comprise The Rhapsodies of the Unknown Prophet. *1–415; *2–417; *3–419; *4–420; *5–420; 6–414 (the first 6 chapters have been rearranged); 7–8 omitted; *9–421; 10–423; *11–426; 12 omitted; *13–427; *14–427; 15–430; *16–431; 17–431; 18–433; 19–434; 20 omitted; *21–435; 22 omitted; 23–437; 24–439; *25–441; *26–442; *27–444; 28–444; 29–30 omitted; 31–446; 32–447; 33 omitted;

[1283]

A CHAPTER KEY TO THE BIBLE

34–448; 35–450; 36–37 omitted; *38–451; 39 omitted; *40–560; 41 omitted; *42–563; 43 omitted; *44–563; *45–564; 46 omitted; *47–566; 48 omitted; *49–566; 50 omitted; *51–567; *52–567; 53–569; *54–570; 55–572; 56–59 omitted; 60–573; 61–576; 62–577; 63–579; 64–66 omitted.

Jeremiah: 1–470; 2–471; 3 omitted; *4–474; 5 omitted; 6–477; *7–480; *8–481; 9 omitted; *10–481; 11 omitted; *12–483; *13–483; *14–485; 15–16 omitted; *17–485; *18–487; 19–488; *20–489; 21–23 omitted; 24–491; *25–492; *26–493; 27–28 omitted; 29–495; *30–497; *31–498; 32–35 omitted; *36–500; 37–503; 38–504; 39–507; *40–508; 41 omitted; 42–509; *43–511; 44–50 omitted; *51–512; 52 omitted.

Lamentations: 1–514; 2–516; 3–519; 4–523; 5–525.

Ezekiel: 1–528; 2–530; *3–531; 4–532; *5–533; 6–15 omitted; *16–534; 17–537; 18–539; 19–22 omitted; *23–542; 24–26 omitted; 27–544; 28–31 omitted; 32–546; 33 omitted; 34–549; 35–36 omitted; *37–551; 38–554; 39–555; 40–558.

Daniel: 1–800; *2–800; 3–805; ("The Song of the Three Children," from the Apocryphal version of Daniel, is inserted in this chapter); *4–810; 5–813; 6–815; 7–818; 8–820; 9 omitted; *10–822; *11–823; *12–824.

Hosea: 1–400; 2–401; 3–10 omitted; *11–402; 12 omitted; 14–403.

Joel: *1–592; *2–592; 3 omitted.

Amos: 1–385; 2–387; 3–389; 4–390; *5–392; *6–393; 7–395; 8–396; *9–397.

Obadiah: *1–583.

Jonah: 1–795; 2–796; 3–797; 4–798.

Micah: *1–406; 2 omitted; 3–407; *4–409; *5–410; *6–411; 7 omitted.

Nahum: 1 omitted; *2–460; 3–461.

Habakkuk: *1–465; 2–466; 3 omitted.

Zephaniah: 1–454; 2–456; 3 omitted.

Haggai: *1–586; 2 omitted.

Zechariah. *1–589; *2–590.

Malachi: 1–2 omitted; 3–596; 4–597.

THE NEW TESTAMENT

Matthew: *1–935; 2–935; 3 omitted; *4–937; 5–938; 6–941; 7–944; 8–10 omitted; 11–945; 12 omitted; *13–947; 14–17 omitted; *18–950; 19–951; *20–954; *22–956; 23–958; 24–960; 25–962; 26 omitted; 27–965; 28–969.

Mark: 1–901; 2–904; *3–906; *4–907; 5–908; 6–910; 7–914; 8–916; *9–919; *10–922; *11–923; 12–13 omitted; 14–925; 15–929; 16–932.

Luke: 1–972; 2–976; *3–979; 4–8 omitted; *9–981; 10–982; *11–985; *12–986; *13–989; *14–991; 15–993; *16–994; *17–996; *18–997; *19–998; 20–21 omitted; *22–999; 23–999; 24–1002.

John: 1–1007; *2–1010; *3–1010; *4–1012; *5–1014; 6–7 omitted; *8–1015; 9–1016; 10–1018; 11–1020; *12–1023; 13–1024; 14–1026; 15–1028; 16–1029; 17–1031; 18–1032; 19–1035; 20–1038; 21–1040.

Acts: 1–1044; 2–1046; *3–1049; 4–1049; 5–1052; 6–1054; *7–1055; 8–1056; 9–1059; *10–1062; *11–1064; 12–1066; *13–1067; 14–1070; *15–1071; 16–1074; 17–1076; 18–1078; 19–1080; 20–1083; 21–1085; *22–1088; 23–1090; 24–1092; 25–1094; 26–1096; 27–1098; 28–1101.

Romans: *1–1147; *2–1148; 3–1149; 4 omitted; *5–1151; *6–1152; 7–1152; *8–1154; *9–1156; *10–1157; 11 omitted; *12–1158; *13–1158; *14–1159; 15 omitted; *16–1160.

I Corinthians: 1–1122; 2–1123; 3–1124; 4–6 omitted; 7–1125; 8–1128; *9–1129; 10 omitted; *11–1129; *12–1131; 13–1132; 14 omitted; 15–1132; 16–1135.

II Corinthians. *1–1138; 2 omitted; *3–1139; 4–1139; 5–9 omitted; 10–1140; 11–1141; 12–1143; 13–1144.

Galatians: 1–1114; 2–1115; *3–1116; *4–1117; *5–1118; 6–1119.

Ephesians: Omitted.

Philippians: *1–1162; 2–1163; 3 omitted; 4–1165.

Colossians: *1–1168, *2–1168; *3–1169; *4–1170.

I Thessalonians: 1–1104; 2–1105; 3–1106; 4–1106; 5–1107.

II Thessalonians: 1–1110; 2–1111; *3–1112.

I Timothy: Omitted.
II Timothy: Omitted.
Titus: Omitted.
Philemon: 1173.

Hebrews: *1–1176; *2–1176; *3–1177; *4–1177; *5–1177; 6 omitted; *7–1178; 8–10 omitted; 11–1179; *12–1182; *13–1182.

James: 1–1185; 2–1186; 3–1187; 4–1188; 5–1189.

I Peter: Omitted.
II Peter: Omitted.

I John: 1–1193; *2–1193; *3–1195; 4–1196; 5 omitted.

II John: Omitted.
III John: Omitted.
Jude: Omitted.

Revelation: 1–1199; 2–1200; 3–1202; 4–1204; 5–1205; 6–1206; *7–1207; 8–1208; 9–1210; 10–1211; 11–1212; 12–1213; 13–1215; 14–1216; 15–1218; 16–1219; 17–1220; 18–1222; 19–1224; 20–1225; 21–1226; 22–1228.

A NOTE ABOUT THE DESIGN
AND PRODUCTION OF THIS BOOK

THE BIBLE DESIGNED TO BE READ AS LIVING LITERATURE *is set in* 14-point Deepdene, *a contemporary American book face designed by Frederic W. Goudy for the Lanston Monotype Company, Philadelphia, Pa. Many of the characters have been recut and refitted for the special purposes of this text.*

Of this face, Mr. Kent D. Currie has said, "The outstanding characteristic of Deepdene is its acid, 'typey' quality. The letters seem to have been cut direct rather than interpreted from drawings, and while all of Mr. Goudy's types have been singularly free of machine-like regularity, there are 'tool marks' and 'accidents' to Deepdene that contribute greatly to its character. The roman composes delightfully in an even, warm gray color. The effect as a whole is regular and well-ordered, but the variety among the individual letters speeds the eye and avoids monotony with charm. Deepdene is perhaps the most bookish face Mr. Goudy has yet created, yet it has more 'interest'—color, movement, quaintness—than any standard book face that comes to mind. He has been fortunate in securing a high degree of legibility, for Deepdene makes easy reading, whether it be a paragraph or a hundred pages. The italic is of special interest; it has more sprightliness and vigor than any italic hitherto available to every printer. It agrees admirably with the roman in color and will make a delightful page of itself.... Deepdene is brilliant and vigorous. It seems to lend spirit to the very words themselves: it inspires reading, just as we prefer lively adult penmanship to regular, schoolboy script."

The text of THE BIBLE DESIGNED TO BE READ AS LIVING LITERATURE offered a special problem in design in that it called for the setting of prose, verse, drama, letters. Typographic and production problems were naturally interwoven with many problems of editorial selection, arrangement, and presentation, as explained in the Editor's introduction. The Deepdene roman, italic, and small caps were used in various ways to meet the requirements of the text. The double title page was evolved as a means of handling the long descriptive copy; the display lines on the main title page were hand-lettered in a style that harmonizes with the text face and at the same time is in keeping with the tradition established by centuries of Bible publication.

The composition, printing, and binding of this book were done by The Haddon Craftsmen, Scranton, Pa. The general format was designed by Philip Van Doren Stern.